SELECT
DOCUMENTS IN
CANADIAN ECONOMIC
HISTORY
1783-1885

SELECT
DOCUMENTS IN
CANADIAN ECONOMIC
HISTORY
1783-1885

EDITED BY

H. A. INNIS
Associate Professor of Political Economy
University of Toronto

AND

A. R. M. LOWER
Professor of History, Wesley College
University of Manitoba

TORONTO:
THE UNIVERSITY OF TORONTO PRESS
1933

REPRINTED 2017
ISBN 978-1-4875-9191-5 (PAPER)

TABLE OF CONTENTS

PART ONE

1783–1850

PAGE

INTRODUCTION TO PART ONE - - - - - 3

SECTION I. The Colonization and Settlement of the
St. Lawrence Valley - - - - 9

Subsection A. - - - - - - - - - - 9

(a) The Course of Settlement
(b) Aspects of Pioneer Life and Problems
(c) The Opening of the Interior:—Road-making
(d) Aspects of Pioneer Agriculture
(e) Public Land Policy
(f) The Land Companies

Subsection B. Population:—Immigration and Emigration - - - - - - - 96

C. The Economic Background of Politics at
the Time of the Rebellion of 1837 125

SECTION II. The St. Lawrence System and the
Development of Communications - 133

Subsection A. The St. Lawrence as a Highway - - 135

B. Waterways, Canals, and Roads subsidiary to the Main St. Lawrence
Highway - - - - - - 150

C. The Improvement and Canalization of
the St. Lawrence - - - - - 161

D. The Initial Stages of the Railroad Era 198

E. Deep-sea Shipping out of the St. Lawrence - - - - - - - 208

F. The Telegraph - - - - - - 213

PAGE

SECTION III. TRADE AND INDUSTRY IN THE CANADAS - 217

Subsection A. The Trading System based on the St.
Lawrence - - - - - - 219

B. The Staple Trades of the Canadas - - 261

(a) The Wheat and Flour Trade
(b) Timber and Lumber
(c) Pot and Pearl Ashes

C. Prices - - - - - - - - 283

D. Industrial Growth:—The Beginnings of
Factory Industry - - - - - 290

E. Mining - - - - - - - - 306

F. Labour and Wages - - - - - 310

SECTION IV. TRADING POLICY, IMPERIAL AND LOCAL - 315

Subsection A. The Colonial Policy of Great Britain - 318

(a) Imperial Commercial Policy, 1783-1846
(b) The Commercial Revolution of the 1840's

B. The Development of Colonial Mercantilism - - - - - - - - 360

C. Economic Union:—A Colonial Zollve-
rein - - - - - - - - 366

SECTION V. MONETARY AND FINANCIAL PROBLEMS IN
THE CANADAS - - - - - - 368

Subsection A. Currency and Banking - - - - 368

B. Public Finance - - - - - - 379

SECTION VI. THE ECONOMIC LIFE OF THE MARITIME
PROVINCES - - - - - - 386

Subsection A. Colonization, Settlement, and Public
Land Policy - - - - - - 387

B. Trade and Industry in the Maritime
Provinces - - - - - - 398

(a) General Aspects of Trade
(b) The West Indian Trade

PAGE

C. The Staple Industries in Maritime Life   412

(a) The Fisheries
(b) Shipping and Ship-building
(c) Coal-mining

D. Typical Monetary and Banking Problems - - - - - - -   430
E. The Island of Cape Breton:—Its Resources and Industries - - - -   439

PART TWO

1850–1885

INTRODUCTION TO PART TWO - - - - -   447

SECTION I. THE ST. LAWRENCE DRAINAGE BASIN - -   451
Subsection A. Transport and Communication   - -   451

(a) Ocean Navigation
(b) Inland Navigation
(c) Railways

Subsection B. Lumber - - - - - - -   502
           C. Agriculture - - - - - - -   525
           D. Fishing - - - - - - - -   569
           E. Mining - - - - - - - -   570
           F. Industry - - - - - - -   588
           G. Labour - - - - - - - -   619
           H. Population - - - - - - -   629
           I. Credit and Money - - - - -   634

SECTION II. THE MARITIME PROVINCES - - - -   666
Subsection A. Transport and Communication - -   666
           B. Trade and Shipping - - - - -   675
           C. Lumber - - - - - - -   679
           D. Agriculture - - - - - - -   685
           E. Fishing - - - - - - - -   697
           F. Mining - - - - - - - -   707
           G. Industry - - - - - - -   715
           H. Credit and Money - - - - -   721

viii CONTENTS

PAGE

SECTION III. WESTERN CANADA (HUDSON BAY DRAIN-
AGE BASIN) - - - - - - - 730
Subsection A. Transport and Communication - - 730
B. Agriculture - - - - - - - 735
C. Industry - - - - - - - 760
D. Credit and Money - - - - - 769

SECTION IV. BRITISH COLUMBIA - - - - - - 771
Subsection A. Transport and Communication - - 771
B. The Gold-mining Industry - - - 780
C. Subsidiary Industries - - - - - 791
D. Money and Credit - · ·· - - 803

SECTION V. CONFEDERATION AND CREDIT - - - - 809

PART ONE

INTRODUCTION

IN 1783 a handful of English officials and soldiers, some hundreds of English merchants, a few thousand ex-New Englanders of doubtful loyalty, a scattering of other English settlers, and some eighty thousand Frenchmen encompassed the total of the British Empire in continental America. For fifteen years the British flag had floated from the Arctic to the tropics and then that vast territory had been split by revolution rather neatly along the line which divided the fur country from the fertile country. There remained but Nova Scotia, inhospitable of climate, infertile of soil, its contiguous territory, the arctic wastes of Rupert's Land, and the valley of the St. Lawrence with its furs and its Frenchmen. There was not a single English settlement left of any great importance and no one expected that there would ever be any. In bitter reality, King George now reigned in the place of King Louis, and a poor place he would have thought it to be a few years before. He had lost the fairest jewel in his crown and in its stead had to console himself with "a few acres of snow". It was as miserable an end to an empire as it was unpromising a beginning for a nation.

English opinion of the catastrophe, though divided, on the whole was dismal. England's sun was supposed to be set, a sentiment reiterated often enough to explain the lack of interest in that fragment of the empire which remained and the almost complete indifference to its fate. But there were at least a few Englishmen who did not know that they were beaten and these few had influence enough to insure that the experiment should begin over again. Despite Lord Shelburne's generosity with boundaries, enough territory was left in America to constitute colonies, and despite William Pitt's desire to leave the Americans in their commercial relationships with Britain just where they had been, Lord Sheffield and a few other die-hard mercantilists saw to it that, with the substitution of Canada and Nova Scotia for New England, the ideal of the self-contained empire should once more be set up.

Two circumstances redeemed the forlorn hope. One was to be found in the rapid extension of the fur trade from Montreal to the Pacific, by which a chain of posts and an organization was flung out across territory which, while nominally within the British boundary, could not otherwise have been held against the advancing American settlers. The other consisted in the Loyalist migration. Without this accession of English population filled with the determination to make good a lost cause, or with what served just as well in fashioning a purpose, hatred against its victors, it is unlikely that the French could have been retained indefinitely in the capacity of British subjects.

In 1850, two generations later, the handful of 1783 had increased to some two millions and a half. Each of the original settlements had become a respectable colony, and two of them, Nova Scotia and Lower Canada, were nations in embryo. But this provincial nationalism was in process of being submerged in a wider nationalism, and in one of the two groups, the St. Lawrence valley, an experiment in political welding was being attempted, an experiment which failed but the failure of which forced a larger success— Confederation. Cities had grown up, large public works had been undertaken and carried through, the forest had been pushed back almost to its logical limits, some provision in the form of schools and colleges had been made for things of the spirit, and the old paternalistic, inefficient, and corrupt governments had been replaced by the new "responsible" governments, which, while they might be just as corrupt, were very much more effective.

The colonies fell into two well-marked groups, the history of which has in large part been separate. After the original influx of Loyalist settlers which determined the identity of their racial, political, and cultural development (always excepting the French), those on the Atlantic coast ceased to have much connection with those of the St. Lawrence valley. The sea gives one type of economy to them and the river gives another to the Canadas. Our problem, in a book of this type, is to try to throw some light on the processes by which the infants left on the British door-step in 1783 became the adolescents of 1850. While underlying everything was the conditioning factor of environment, there may be distinguished various other factors in the evolution of these new British communities, British yet American without being republican.

The primary necessity in any new country in which a society, as opposed to a mere system of exploitation, is being constructed, is the actual occupation of the land by the settler. Consequently, the first and longest of the six sections into which the first part of this book is divided is given over to the question of colonization. The history of America is very largely a history of settlement, a history of the flooding of tides of humanity over new lands, of the effects of that flood on the lands and of the effects of the lands on the flood. Both are great. The continent is sub-dued and tamed. But the people who tame it are changed in the act of taming. The old civilization of Europe, its attitudes and habits of mind, is warped and twisted, and out of its clash with the new surroundings comes some-thing new, a new civilization, having much in common with the old, but still not the old.[1] Section I attempts to illustrate various aspects of this onslaught on the land.

"Laurentia", a term which might with propriety be used instead of "The Canadas", is the country of the River St. Lawrence and the Great Lakes. Topographically it is a watershed whose immediate trough is constituted by an intrusion north-eastwards of the great interior plain (in this continental plain lie four of the five Great Lakes and the river itself down to well below Quebec, in which vicinity the plain is pinched out) between the Appalachian system coming up from the south and the Laurentian Plateau to the northward. The Appalachian system covers the eastern parts of the Province of Quebec, the Laurentian Plateau includes the rest of the watershed from the gulf to Lake Superior. The St. Lawrence division of the continental plain bends up along the chief affluents and their tributaries (reaching as high as Pembroke, on the Ottawa) but is limited in area, being widest and largest in the peninsula of Ontario.

The influence of these physiographical factors is evident

---

[1]This is the well-known "frontier" thesis of F. J. Turner. See his *Frontier in American history* (New York, 1921).

in such things as the predominantly agricultural character of "old" Ontario and the lumbering and mining of "new" Ontario. Section II has as its basis the illustration of the geographical determinant afforded by the waterways of the St. Lawrence system. The life of "Laurentia" is bound up with them and the country is opened up and exploited along the lines that they dictate. They decide the orientation of its trade and hence section III, which is concerned with trade, is also built on the same geographical foundation. The relationship comes out strongly in the great staple of the period, wood, for the waterways determine the character of the industry and their drainage basin corresponds with some closeness to the range of the species of tree upon which it is chiefly built, the white pine.

But the fate of British North America has never been left to the free sweep of the forces of environment and of economics. First the French, then the British, and lastly, Canadians have tried to build up a certain type of community with activities, economic as well as political, running in predetermined channels. While in the long run mostly unsuccessful when opposed to the two fundamentals, policy has always had important effects at the moment, as, for example, in its creation of the timber trade; and when it has been in line with the fundamentals, as it was when it encouraged the trade of the western states of the Union to pass through the St. Lawrence, it has perhaps had important permanent effects. Trading policy is considered in section IV.

Even the simplest of societies soon build up rather complex methods of meeting their problems, but elaborate social and economic machinery has to be constructed if complexity is to proceed beyond a certain point. Among the pieces of mechanism of this sort that humanity has found most useful are money and credit. The advantage of studying these in a colonial *milieu* consists in the fact that we begin with a blank page and fill in as we go along. In section V, some material illustrative of these subjects will be found.

Only those phases of the life of the second area, the Maritime Provinces, which seem to be somewhat different *in esse* from the life of the Canadas are dealt with. The many activities similar to those of the upper provinces—lumbering, for example, the methods and direction of which were not very different from those of the industry elsewhere—have been passed over. But the student may be reminded that for a picture of Maritime life as a whole these things must be taken into account. The differences between the two groups consist chiefly in this, that whereas the Canadas have been dominated by a river—they might profitably be compared with the countries in the basin of the Danube— the Atlantic provinces have an economy similar to such maritime societies as Great Britain or Japan—strictly dependent upon the sea and by reason of a paucity of natural wealth (compare Great Britain and France in respect to agricultural area) compelled to turn to the wealth that the sea gives them in fish and in trade. The comparison cannot be pushed too far but the peninsular position of Nova Scotia has some features of similarity with the insular position of England in the period before the discovery of America had turned Europe's back door into its front: wealth enough for a comfortable living for a limited population but no more. New Brunswick is one remove away from the sea, a fact which shows itself in its greater degree of absorption within the Canadian nation.

Geography and climate account for much in Canadian history. As has been remarked, they account for the fur trade and thus indirectly for the present dominion in rough outline.[1] But the vicissitudes of war and those alone account for the Loyalist migration and the undeflectible trend which it gave to the country's future. Hence in reading Canadian history, account must always be taken of both sides of the shield, the one side environment, the other, what may be called, for want of a better designation, spiritual forces. While it will not do to explain everything in terms of idealism, neither can the undiluted doctrine of economic determinism be accepted, for in the course of the last century and a quarter there have been too many demonstrations of the existence of motives that are not acquisitive for it to

[1]See H. A. Innis, *The fur trade in Canada* (New Haven, 1930) for this thesis

be doubted that other factors besides the purely economic make history. It seemed impossible in 1783 that a new colony could be founded a thousand miles from the sea and, with an alien people between, retain its allegiance to the British crown, but the new colony was founded and flourished. At any given moment in the past it has always, except to the eye of faith, seemed that it would be impossible to unite the diverse communities which make up the present dominion into a national whole and to have them resist the persistent attractions of the great unity to the south, but they are being united and the likelihood of absorption was never remoter. Canadian development might approximately be characterized as the achievement of successive impossibilities. It is hoped that the material which follows will amplify and illustrate this blend of materialistic and non-materialistic factors which has determined the nature of Canadian history.

A.R.M.L.[1]

---

[1]The editor of part one of this work desires to express his gratitude to the Social Science Research Council, 230 Park Avenue, New York, for the generous grant-in-aid which enabled him to collect much of the material which appears in the pages that follow.

SECTION I

THE COLONIZATION AND SETTLEMENT OF THE ST. LAWRENCE VALLEY, 1783-1850

SUBSECTION A

(a)—THE COURSE OF SETTLEMENT

A quarter of a century after the conquest, while the French population of Canada had increased, the area of settlement still remained confined to the strip of land bordering the St. Lawrence from the gulf to the confluence of the Ottawa. With the exception of this region of the seigniories, the occupation of the valley may be said to have commenced in 1783 with the Loyalist migration. The first Loyalist settlements along the river up to the Bay of Quinte and at Niagara gradually expanded until they formed a fringe all the way from the Lower Canadian border to the western end of Lake Erie, the American Loyalists being reinforced by the Scottish settlers of Glengarry, many of whom were themselves veterans of the Revolutionary War. During Simcoe's régime and in the period before the War of 1812, other settlers came in from the United States, some British in sympathy, others republican, and took up lands along the Ottawa as far as the site of the present capital and on the edge of the older settlements in the Niagara peninsula and westward. In the same period Vermonters crossed into that part of the lower province contiguous to their state, forming the nucleus of the district at present known as the "Eastern Townships". After the war the British government assisted some unemployed artizans to emigrate and also attempted to place disbanded soldiers on the land, efforts which resulted in the occupation of a few townships well away from the main highways of the St. Lawrence and the Ottawa. With the beginning of a wave of genuine immigration in the twenties, the townships to the rear of the settlements on "the front", as the line of the St. Lawrence and the lakes used to be termed, were taken up and as this wave grew in volume (it culminated in 1834), the remaining regions of "old" Ontario south from about Arnprior to the St. Lawrence along Lake Ontario north to the Laurentian Plateau and thence westwards, south of a line from Lake Simcoe to Goderich, were occupied. In the next decade, the forties, the gaps between the older settlements, both in Lower and Upper Canada, were filled. The French had occupied all the available lands in the seigniories and now, having to go farther from the river, they began to move into the Eastern Townships and to settle among the English. In Upper Canada the settlement of the western peninsula having been completed and the Canada Company's lands on Lake Huron being in process of disposition, settlement pressed to the north of the line just referred to and the modern counties of Grey, Bruce, Dufferin, and the northern half of Simcoe—in fact all the lands south of the Laurentian Plateau were filled up. It was to be the task of the next period to assail the plateau itself.

The documents here reproduced illustrate this gradual extension of settlement and the result to which it gave rise, the growth of the community of "The Canadas".

REFERENCES: Abbé Caron, *La colonisation de la province de Québec, 1763-1791* (Quebec, 1923); W. S. Wallace, *The United Empire Loyalists* (Chronicles of Canada, Toronto, 1914); W. D. Lighthall, "English settlements in Quebec" (*Canada and its provinces*, XV, 121); A. C. Casselman, "Pioneer settlements" (*Ibid.*, XVII, 13); W. L. Smith, *The pioneers of old Ontario* (Makers of Canada, new series, Toronto, 1923); Emily P. Weaver, *The story of the counties of Ontario* (Toronto, 1913); E. A. Cruikshank, "Immigration from the United States into

Upper Canada, 1784-1812" (*Proceedings* of the Ontario Educational Association, 39th convention, 263); A. R. M. Lower, "Immigration and settlement in Canada, 1812-1820" (*Canadian Historical Review*, March, 1922); C. O. Ermatinger, *The Talbot régime* (St. Thomas, 1904).

1

The Loyalists Settle Upper Canada

(i)

From Canadian Archives, *Series Q*, XXIII, 5.

General Haldimand to Lord North

Quebec, 6th November, 1783

My Lord.

I have to express the great regret which I feel at not having received dispatches from England. There are many things of which I could wish to be informed by His Majesty's Ministers for the Rule of my conduct. I indeed know that the intention of Government is to do everything in their power to alleviate the distresses of the Royalists and to procure for them and families a comfortable subsistence; with this view I allow them provisions and have been under a necessity to provide many of them with money and cloathing. In order to exempt Government from these expences, I lose no time in preparing a settlement for them at or near Cataraqui. Since my last letters I have received a report of some intelligent persons whom I sent to examine the land on the bank of the River Ontawa &c from Carillion upwards as far as Cataraqui[1]. I inclose a copy of the report and two plans, which will give your Lordship a better idea of the country than words can, I am happy to find that there are in the gift of the crown, lands of so good a soil in a favorable climate, sufficient not only to settle the Provincial Corps when disbanded, but all such Royalists as may come from the southward with a view to find an Azylum from the tyranny and oppression of their countrymen. I foresee great advantages from this settlement, The Six Nations wish it, the Royalists settled together in numbers will form a respectable body attached to the interests of Great Britain & capable of being useful upon many occasions. Their industry will in a very few years raise in that fertile tract of country great quantities of wheat

---

[1]*Ontawa:* The St. Lawrence, presumably.

and other grains and become a granary for the lower parts of
Canada where the crops are precarious and liable to be engrossed
by a few designing and interested traders; an evil to be apprehended
this year, for wheat is at present raised to the price of two dollars
per bushel. Fisheries in Nova Scotia & the Island of Cape Breton
considered as national & commercial objects are certainly preferable to settlements where agriculture is the sole prospect, but
still, Justice and Humanity require that the Loyalists should have
a choice, and even advantages with regard to the fur trade may
result from the settlement at Cataraqui. The lands contiguous
to the fort, I have, to avoid any difficulty purchased from the
Messessaga Indians for an inconsiderable sum. . . .

Fred: Haldimand

(ii)

From Colonial office records, series 42, XVI, 70.

Extract of a letter from George Pownall Esqr secretary to the Province
of Quebec, to J.P.[1] dated Quebec 11 Novr 1784

The Loyalists and disbanded soldiers who are chiefly settled upon
the Crown Lands lately bought from the Indians on the North
side of the Lake Ontario, together with some familys at Sorel
and in the vicinage of Montreal may amount to between five and
six thousand souls including a party of Butlers Rangers who are
settled at Niagara; they are settled in fifteen townships which
I understand extend from fifty miles above Montreal to the Bay
of Quintée included. I am told that these people are very well
satisfied and are now most of them under cover; if they possess
a spirit of industry and perseverance they may possibly thrive
there, the soil is by all accounts very rich and fit for the produce
of every grain, the woods produce fine white oak and other timber,
fit for the purpose of the West India Market and the seasons are
milder and the climate better than in this lower part of the Province; but they still have difficulties to encounter, one of which
is from their being at the mercy of the savages whenever these
people may take it into their heads to quarrel with them. . . .
Another very great disadvantage these people will meet is from

---

[1]J. P.: John Pownall, the writer's father, previously secretary to the board
of trade.

their situation, which places them so far from any market for their produce, and the rapids which they have to pass in order to get down the River are both critical and dangerous untill well known, I trust however that these people will succeed from the very flattering accounts I hear of them the only doubt with me is, whether from the very great partiality they still by all accounts entertain for their old Country, if the Colonists see the policy of regaining these people and hold out the most trifling incouragement for their return, whether they will take the bait. . . .

Whether these people would not have been more useful to Great Britain, to the Province & to themselves, had they been settled below Quebec, is a question seems to me to admit of some doubt: or if they had been settled more in the center of the Province whether their example of Industry and enterprise would not have been more useful to the Province and at the same time have sooner extended amongst the old inhabitants. . . .

George Pownall

2

Proposals for a Settlement on Cape Breton of Loyalists from Quebec

From Canadian Archives, Q, XXIII, 102.

Lord Sydney, secretary of state, to General Haldimand

Whitehall, 7th June, 1784

Sir,

Mr Abraham Cuyler late Chief Magistrate of Albany has made application to me in behalf of himself and many other Families, now in the Province of Quebec, whose names are subscribed to the inclosed Memorial, and who have been driven from their habitations, on account of their loyalty and the part they have taken, praying that lands may be allotted to them in the Island of Cape Breton, whereon they propose to settle, and His Majesty being very desirous to shew every mark of attention to those unfortunate people, has been graciously pleased to comply with their desire, and has signified his Commands that the Lieutenant Governor who will be vested with the charge of the said Island of Cape Breton, shall be authorised to make the allotments of lands to them, in the same proportions as have been given to those who have taken refuge in the Province of Nova Scotia.

The season of the year advancing fast, it will be very desirable that means should be found for their removal as soon as possible, and it is His Majesty's command that you do employ any transport vessels or victuallers that may be at Quebec, not appointed for any particular service, or any small craft belonging to His Majesty, in the removal of the persons mentioned in the said Memorial, to the Rivers St Peters and St. Mary's on the said Island of Cape Breton, upon which they propose to settle, and that you do furnish them with the same proportion of Provisions as would have been bestowed upon them by Government for their subsistence had they remained within the Province of Quebec. These provisions you are to cause to be conveyed with the settlers to Cape Briton [sic], provided you have a sufficient quantity in store that can be spared from the stock which is necessary to be reserved for the consumption of the Garrison. . . .

Sydney

3

Americans Who Might be Willing to Settle in Canada

From Canadian Archives, *Q*, XXXVIII, 227.

Quebec, 4th of April, 1788

Dear Sir:—

Many are the applications to the Governor General, from people residing in the United States for lands in this Province, wishing to see themselves once more under a free government, where the laws protect the person and property of the subject.

Opinions are divided here with regard to the policy of admitting these men as settlers among us, lest they import and diffuse principles adverse to the British Constitution. I have always been of opinion that a half of the people of the Colonies, now the States, have, some from prejudices early imbibed and others from a thorough investigation of the nature of the government, been sincerely attached to the British interest during the late rebellion, tho' they did not take arms, and that they are still attached to it. Many who were but lukewarm in our cause, and some who were opposers of the King's authority are now convinced of their folly, and live to repent at leisure. . . .

If the King's ministers will receive the repentent sinners of the revolted Colonies, I conceive we might have an addition of twenty or thirty thousand souls to the number of His Majesty's subjects in this Province, in twelve months, I firmly believe that a majority of the four Eastern States sincerely desire to return to their allegiance. . . .

Hugh Finlay

Evan Nepean, Esq.

4

American Immigration:—Obstacle of Seigniorial Tenure:— Eastern Townships:—Squatters

From Canadian Archives, Q, XXXVIII, 348.

[Quebec] 30 July, 1788

Dear Sir

. . . We could absolutely get between twenty and thirty thousand people who ('tis said) are known to have been attached to the King's Government in the Colonies (now the States) in the most perilous times, to sit down as settlers in this Province immediately, but they will not accept of estates under the ancient tenure. They desire to have lands in free and common soccage, and if they cannot obtain grants in this government, they propose to cross the Allegahany and sit down in the New Country as they call it, where they hope to enjoy freedom and security under a form of government as nearly English as possible.

It is conceived by many sensible men here that settlers of the above description, men who have ever been the friends of Government would be the fittest persons of any on earth to sit down on our side of the line 45° and close to it.

I have heard from those who have been lately that way, that some families from the Vermont State have built huts and cleared away spots in our territory.

Much future mischief may perhaps be prevented, if we grant lands there to good people without loss of time, to make a strong barrier between our southern neighbours and the lower parts of this Province. Where lands are found waste, people of a certain stamp will sit down, and in some years it may be difficult to turn them of[f], and impolitic to admit them as subjects. . . .

Hugh Finlay

Evan Nepean, Esq.

5

The Progress of Upper Canada:—Religious Problems

From Canadian Archives, *Q*, LXIX, 385.

The Bishop of Quebec to Henry Dundas

Powell Place, near Quebec,
15th September, 1794

Sir,

I have the honor to inform you that I have this summer compleated the visitation of my Diocese. . . . It is not from me, Sir, that you are to learn the rapid progress of improvement in the Upper Province. The almost incredible exertions which have been made to clear the ground, the fine crops of grain which the new lands everywhere produce, & the decent & commodious farmhouse rising near the little hut in which the settler first sheltered himself & his family, exhibit a scene highly interesting & satisfactory at present, & open prospects of the future, of infinite importance & extent.

With respect to religious instruction the state of these settlers is for the most part truly deplorable. From Montreal to Kingston, a distance of 200 miles, there is not one clergyman of the Church of England; nor any house of religious worship except one small Chapel belonging to the Lutherans, & one, or perhaps two, belonging to the Presbyterians. The public worship of God is entirely suspended, or performed in a manner which can neither tend to improve the people in Religious Truth, nor to render them useful members of society. The Presbyterians and the Lutheran clergymen are, I believe, men of good character, but their influence is necessarily limited to their own little congregations. The great bulk of the people have, & can have no instruction but such as they receive occasionally from itinerant, & mendicant Methodists: a set of ignorant enthusiasts whose preaching is calculated only to perplex the understanding, & corrupt the morals; to relax the nerves of industry, & dissolve the bonds of society. . . .

In the whole progress of my visitation I found the better part of the people extremely unhappy under the privation of Religious instruction, & to the last degree earnest in their entreaties that I would use the power, which they supposed me to possess, of sending

Ministers of the Church of England among them. They represented in the strongest terms not only the uneasiness which the
more serious and reflecting persons among them feel, for themselves
and for their families; but the dreadful consequences which follow
a total want of Religious principles among some of the lowest
orders of the people whose ignorance; profligacy & barbarism, they
represent as being more shameful, & degrading, than those of the
savages, by whom they are surrounded, & whom they affect to
despise. . . .

The necessaries of life are in Upper Canada yet extremely
dear. And I believe it utterly impossible that any Clergyman
should live in a comfortable, or even decent manner, for less than
between two & three hundred pounds a year. . . .

The present moment seems precisely that which is most
favourable to the success of such a measure.[1] Of the settlers in
Upper Canada the majority is composed of Dissenters of various
descriptions: But I have the strongest reason to believe that if a
proper number of ministers of the Church of England be sent
amongst them, before each sect shall become able to provide
ministers of its own, they will to a man, conform to that church. . . .

Experience justifies the opinion that the progress of the settlements would be greatly accelerated by the erection of Churches &
establishment of ministers. Wherever this has been done the
number of settlers has always immediately increased. Sober and
thinking men are unwilling to bring their families into situations
in which they are deprived of all the benefits of religious instruction; & there are many instances of persons having rejected lands
in all other respects desirable on this account alone. . . .

Nothing, I believe, would tend more effectually to give weight
& consequence to the establishment, than a proper Church at
Quebec, exclusively appropriated to our worship. That that
worship should be performed only by the permission of the Roman
Catholic Bishop, &, with that permission, only once on the Sunday,
that the Protestant Bishop should obtain a seat in the Church by
the indulgence only of the Superiour of the Franciscans; that our
pure and reasonable service should only be performed within
walls loaded with all the pageantry & meretricious ornament of
Popish superstition, amid crucifixes, images, pictures of saints,

---

[1]That is, the supply and support of Anglican ministers by the state.

altars, tapers, & burning lamps, these, sir, are circumstances which, while they shock and disgust the enlighten'd mind, in the rational discharges of its duty, serve also strongly, & publicly, to mark a dependence of the Church of England, upon the Church of Rome, for the imperfect enjoyment of privileges, which, I trust, the Government of England will think ought to be all its own. . . .

The plan of the Committee of the Council for introducing an extensive system of education into this country, appears to have failed by attempting too much at once. We are perhaps not yet ripe for such an institution. But, as introductory to it, good Grammar Schools should be established, & encouraged in Quebec, in Montreal, & in Kingston. . . . You will see, no doubt, Sir, all the mischief that may eventually arise from the necessity of sending our youths for education to the schools of Foreign America. A necessity which certainly exists at present; & to which I know some worthy and prudent parents most reluctantly submit. . . .

J. Quebec

6

Approach of American Settlements towards the Lakes:— Plan for Town-site of Toronto

From Canadian Archives, *Q*, LXVI, 233.

Quebec, 7th October, 1793

Sir,

. . . Mr. Ogden talked highly of the Population on the South side of the Lakes Erie and Ontario; that in the Genesee country seems scarcely credible, particularly the Plantations belonging to himself & Mr Morris; that of Mr Pultney too he thought considerable. The progress of these Settlements requires much attention, and I am to request you will have the goodness to communicate to me every information you may procure of their proceedings and approach to the Lakes.

I am also to desire you will inform me of the Progress of Population and Agriculture on the North side of those Lakes, and how near they approach Toronto; the settling & cultivating the country round about that Part, must facilitate & bring forward every advantage its situation can afford, & will deserve encouragement; prior thereto every attempt must be attended with difficulty.

2—

In laying out the Town I shall advise the System of wide Streets and Squares with open Angles; but more especially that the ground which Captain Mann recommends for Public Works & Batteries be reserved; all which are marked on Mr Collins's Plan; a Copy of which I understand you have taken with you. I think it necessary to make those Reservations, tho' I cannot approve of any Fortifications being erected there at present.

Dorchester

7

Governor Simcoe's Plans for Settling Upper Canada and his Opinion of its Capabilities

From Duke de la Rochefoucault-Liancourt, *Travels in North America, in the years 1795, 1796, and 1797* (London, 1799), 231.

From the readiness which government displays in granting lands gratis, the Governor entertains not the least doubt of soon obtaining a numerous population. Many families, who at the beginning of the American war embraced the royal cause, have since the conclusion of peace settled on lands, which were bestowed on them gratis. The American soldiers, who fought under the same unfortunate banners, obtained also an indemnification in lands, on which most of them have settled. All officers, who served in that war, are likewise entitled to some hundred acres, a certain number of which are already cultivated by them. The Governor is also sanguine in his hopes of procuring many colonists from the United States; he relies on the natural fondness of these people for emigrating, and on their attachment to the English government. There arrive indeed every year a considerable number of families from different parts of the Union; they do not all settle, it is true, but some remain in the country. He also reckons upon drawing numerous settlers from New Brunswick, who cannot endure the climate of that country. And lastly, the considerable emigration from Europe, which he fancies he foresees, affords him certain hopes of obtaining thence a very numerous population. Yet, by his account, the prevailing sentiments of the people render the admission of new inhabitants, who present themselves, rather difficult; especially of those, who come from the United States. For this reason, he sends such colonists, as cannot give a satisfactory account of themselves, into the back country, and stations soldiers on the banks of the lakes, which are in front of them. He would admit every superannuated soldier of the British army, and all officers of long service, who are on half pay, to share in the distribution of such lands as the King had a right to dispose of. He would dismiss every soldier, now quartered in Canada, and give him one hundred acres of land, as soon as he should procure a young man to serve as his substitute. With his views to increase the population of the country, he blends the design of drawing young Americans into the English service, by which he will augment the number of American families, attached to the King of Great Britain. In the midst of these families of soldiers, which he intends to settle on the lakes, and on all the frontiers towards the United States, he means to place all the officers, who, as has already been observed, have any claim on the lands.

He proposes thus to form a militia, attached to the King from habit and gratitude; and this he considers as one of the most certain means for suppressing the disturbances, which might be excited by some disaffected new settlers, who inhabit the midland counties, and at the same time as one of the best measures of defence in case of an attack. By this plan of settling amidst the soldiers officers and gentlemen of respectable families, whom he hopes to attract from England, he wishes to form a class of gentry, and to promote more or less the execution of the project, clearly discernible in the new constitution, to introduce into the two Canadas an hereditary nobility.

It is asserted, that all Canada, vast as is its extent, produces not the necessary corn for the consumption of its inhabitants; the troops are supplied with flour from London, and with salt meat from Ireland. In General Simcoe's opinion Upper Canada is not only capable of satisfying the wants of all its inhabitants, but also of becoming a granary for England, and of creating a considerable trade by the exchange of this necessary of life for other commodities; nor does he entertain the least doubt, but that the activity, in agricultural pursuits, which he endeavours to excite in Upper Canada, will operate as a powerful example in regard to Lower Canada, and rouse it from its present supineness and indolence. He conceives, that the vast quantities of fish, with which the lakes abound, and especially of sturgeons in Lake Ontario, afford the means of a successful competition with Russia, which supplies England with this article to a very considerable amount.

The corn-trade is, in his judgment, far preferable to the fur-trade, which appears to him at once unprofitable for Great Britain, and a means of oppression to Canada, in as much as it throws the whole trade into the hands of a few companies, and at the same time renders them masters of the commodities, which are imported from England in return. It is his wish, that merchants may settle on Lake Ontario, in Montreal, and in Quebec; and, by the establishment of a corn-trade, destroy that monopoly which very justly excites his indignation; and he entertains hopes, that this will actually take place.

8

The Houses and Mills of the Pioneers, 1783-1800

From William Canniff, *History of the settlement of Upper Canada, with special reference to the Bay of Quinte* (Toronto, 1869), 595.

The first buildings were of logs generally put up in their natural rough state; now and then, as the Government mill at Kingston, the logs were squared. There was only one way of procuring sawed lumber, and that was by the whip-saw. But few of the settlers thought of spending the time and labor to obtain what was not strictly necessary. Houses, barns, saw-mills, flouring-mills, even breweries and still-houses were all alike constructed of logs. . . . When, however, sawing mills began to spring up here and there, sawed lumber became a more common article, and after several years, individuals, better off than others, began to put up framed buildings, both houses and barns and so forth. Sawing-mills were introduced originally into America by the Dutch, and it was their descendants who introduced them into Canada. But it was slowly done. It required no little capital to procure even the small amount of machinery which was then used and to have it brought so long a distance. Then, millwrights were not plentiful and often inferior in skill. Indeed there was nothing at hand with which to erect sawing-mills until after many years. In the meantime, the whipsaw enabled them to construct something like a door for the house and log barn; and rough sort of furniture was made for the house. But toward the close of the last century, saw-mills became somewhat numerous. The demand for lumber was forseen, and those who had a water privilege set about to get up a mill. Following the saw-mill came the grist-mill, which, though more needed than the former, because of its greater expense, was not built until a later period. It was about the first of 1800, that frame buildings began to appear in the first, second, and third townships particularly, to take the place of the log hut.

9

Making a "Location" in the Wilderness

From *Lower Canada, Journals of assembly*, 1824, appendix *R*, Philemon Wright's narrative of his founding of Hull, 1799.

We had ascended the Ottawa or Grand River one hundred and twenty miles from Montreal; the first forty-five miles we found some settlers who appeared rather inactive as far as related to their farms, but little done to what apparently might be done towards making themselves independent farmers, we however ascended the Ottawa or Grand River up the rapids fifteen miles farther to the head of the Long Sault continuing our course sixty-four miles farther up the river. From the head of the Long Sault to Hull the river is remarkably smooth and the water still and sufficiently deep to float a sloop of war. At the last mentioned place, we proposed to explore the township back of the river. Accordingly we spent twenty days, say from the 1st to the 20th of October, 1799. I should think that we climbed to the top of one hundred or more trees to view the situation of the country. . . By this means we were enabled to view the country and also the timber, and by the timber we were enabled to judge the nature of the soil, which we found to answer our expectations. And after having examined well the local situation of the township of Hull, we descended the river and arrived, after much fatigue, at Montreal, where we gave a general description of our discoveries, and returned home to Massachusetts, where after a report was made public about the situation of this part of the country, I was enabled to obtain and hire as many men as I wanted, in order to commence the new settlement. . . .

10

The Settlement of the Ottawa Valley

From J. L. Gourlay, *History of the Ottawa valley* (Ottawa, 1896), 51, 87, 158, 185.

(i)

Rice Honeywell had fought on the American side, but after the war he was attracted by a young lady, the daughter of a U.E.L. Tory at Prescott, whom he married and took to the Mohawk valley where Ira was born. The new country and land easily procured, and the prospects every new country opens up, together with the wish of his wife to be near her people, led him to come to Prescott where they both drew land. If a person disliked the place of his location ticket he could sell it, take the money and go where he chose. When Ira Honeywell was grown up his father offered him tickets for 1,000 acres in Nepean, if he would go and make good his claims, which he did, and exchanged the Mohawk and St. Lawrence for the Ottawa Valley. He was the first white settler on the Ottawa in Nepean. He selected his place and built a shanty, and chopped four acres in 1810. He came down the Rideau and must have borrowed help from Hull to build his shanty.

(ii)

The township of Goulborn was like some others very rich in lumber at the first. This made a market for produce, especially oats and hay, which were raised in the richest abundance on the fertile portions of the soil. These were disposed of at the doors where raised or within a few miles. But afterwards the farmers had to seek a market up the Ottawa, Madawaska, Bonnechère and elsewhere, and drive with teams in winter requiring from one to three weeks for the go and return, but it paid them as prices were good.

(iii)

Lumberers were the first settlers, others followed as the way opened and they could secure their lands. Lumber was the chief source of wealth all over the land. Potash followed from the land clearing, the labour in both cases being very well rewarded. The Rideau formed one boundary of the township. The survey of Marlboro made by de Pensier twenty-five years before [*1795*], fixed its southern limit. The settlements were made from different points at first and it is said the pioneers lived for years on their new lands before the people of one settlement became acquainted with those of another, from isolation and the dense woods between. Those making timber within hearing of the great pines they cut, made their first acquaintance in the Quebec market selling their lumber, or at their meeting on the river sailing down to market. Shanty roads, those cut for lumbering, were their only roads for years, except the rivers for canoes and boats in summer.

(iv)

Aylmer had a large number of French in its population, but they did not take to farming the beautiful lands lying between it and the mountain. As you go past Radmers and Simmonds to the mountains, nothing can be more inviting to the lover of agriculture than such a soil. In all that fine belt of country from below Lochaber to Portage du Fort, the farmers became rich while lumbering lasted. Their hay brought them from $15 to $20 a ton more or less, their oats 40 to 50 cents a bushel. Teams drew in the shanty at $1.50 and their keep, and men drove their oats and hay to the shanties, covering three or four dollars a day and upwards when they furnished their own provisions.

11

Origins of the Talbot and Glengarry Settlements

From Canadian Archives, Q, CCXCIV, 37, 41.

Lord Hobart to General Hunter

(i)

Downing Street, 15th Feb^y, 1803

Sir,

Several proposals having [*sic*] lately been submitted to the Consideration of Government from persons who with different Objects in view are desirous of employing their resources and exertions in the Settlement and cultivation of Lands in Canada.

Among the Individuals who have addressed themselves to me upon this Subject Mr Talbot, who acted as private Secretary to Lieutenant General Simcoe in Upper Canada, appears not only from his Character and Military Services, but from his accurate knowledge of the province which during a long residence there he had personally acquired, as well as from the nature of his Plans to merit particular attention.

This Gentleman having already made some successful attempts in the Culture of Hemp proposes to direct his attention to the growth and preparation of that valuable plant, and by his Influence and example to promote and extend it's cultivation particularly among those Settlers he conceives he may be able to introduce into the Colony and to establish in his Neighbourhood.

He has therefore applied for a Grant of Land in the distant Township of Yarmouth in the County of Norfolk on Lake Erie as being from the nature of the soil favorable to his design of raising Hemp for Exportation and also affording scope for the Establishment of such a number of families as may be induced to follow him into the Province.

In consequence of the assurances which have been received that Mr Talbot is in every respect qualified to prosecute the undertaking, I am commanded by His Majesty to authorize you without delay to take the proper steps for passing according to the usual form and Subject to the customary reservations a Grant of Five Thousand Acres in his favor in the Township above mentioned or if the same shall have been already appropriated in any other which he may select. You are at the same time to give directions that a proportion of the said Township immediately contiguous to Mr Talbot's Grant, may for the present be reserved for the purpose of hereafter appropriating to him according to circumstances a further quantity at the rate of Two hundred Acres for every family he may induce to settle there either from the Continent of Europe or America provided he shall have surrendered fifty Acres of his Original Grant to each family for which he may claim and that such family shall at the time be established in the actual possession of the said fifty Acres. . . .

Hobart

(ii)

Downing Street, 1st March, 1803

Sir,

A Body of Highlanders mostly Macdonnel's and partly disbanded Soldiers of the late Glengarry Fencible Regiment with their

Families and connexions are upon the point of quitting their present place of abode with the design of following into Upper Canada some of their relations who have already established themselves in the Province.

The merit and Service of the regiment in which a proportion of these people have served give them strong claims to any mark of favor and consideration which can Consistently be extended to them and with the encouragement usually afforded in the Province they would no doubt prove as valuable Settlers as their Connexions now residing in the District of Glengarry of whose Industry and general good conduct very favorable representations have been received here.

Government has been apprized of the Situation and disposition of the Families before described by M^r McDonnell One of the Ministers of their Church and formerly Chaplain to the Glengarry regiment who possessed considerable Influence with the whole body. He has undertaken in the event of their absolute determination to carry into execution their plan of departure to embark with them and direct their course to Canada.

In Case of their Arrival within Your Government I am commanded by His Majesty to authorize you to grant in the usual manner a Tract of the unappropriated Crown Lands in any part of the Province where they may fix in the proportion of Twelve hundred Acres to Mr Macdonnel and Two hundred Acres to every family he may introduce into the Colony.

Hobart

12

Contented Settlers in Township of London

From Montreal Gazette, July 2, 1819.

To the Emigrants who arrived at Quebec in the summer of 1818, and who came in the *Jane* of Greenock, and the *Carlow* of London, from the Parishes of Comera, Balyhidder, Weems, and Killine, in Perthshire, North Britain.

When we parted from you at Montreal for this part of the Country, we promised to inform you of the advantages, which we might find it to possess. You are probably so scattered about now, that we cannot inform you in any other way than by addressing you a letter in a newspaper; and we earnestly hope, that the

Editors of other papers, will be kind enough to give our letter one insertion, that you may all have the opportunity of hearing from us.

We have been of the party of Colonel Burwell, and assisted him to Survey about seventy thousand acres of land, in the Township of London which we have just completed, and Colonel Talbot has located us upon one hundred acres each. The Township of London is bounded in front by the river Thames, and is well watered by the north branch of it, and a great many smaller branches which intersect every concession in the Township; some of which are very excellent for Mill seats. The land is of the finest quality we ever saw. The soil is generally very black and deep; and at the same time, intermixed with a small portion of white sand. The timber is Sugar Maple, Elm, White Oak, Butternut, Cherry and Basswood. . . .

When we left Scotland, the minister of our parishes begged us to settle near each other, which we sincerely wish and hope, that such of you as are not settled to your satisfaction, will come to this part of the province. You will certainly like the country when you see it. We have had no trouble in getting our lands. When we made choice of them, we applied to Colonel Talbot, and we have two years to perform the Settlement duties in, which is all to our advantage. Several of our friends are now here, and every new Settler who has money, or is industrious, can buy provisions from our neighbours on Talbot Road, and in Westminster, on the opposite side of the River Thames, to last until they can grow them from their farms. We remain your friends,

JAMES McFARLANE
ARCHIBALD McFARLANE
JAMES CAMPBELL
JOHN CARMICHAELL

13

Niagara in 1820

From John Howison, *Sketches of Upper Canada* (3rd edition, Edinburgh, 1825), 74.

The population of Niagara amounts to seven or eight hundred souls, and it is one of the most thriving villages in Upper Canada. It contains a great many merchants' shops, and has a regular market, as the farmers who occupy the country around frequent it weekly, that they may sell their produce, or dispose of it to the merchants in exchange for goods. The mouth of the river forms an excellent harbour. Some time ago a considerable number of schooners and small craft plied between Kingston, York, and Niagara, which were employed in transporting goods, produce, and lumber; but the steam-boat now monopolizes almost all the carrying business, to the great detriment and annoyance of the owners of the vessels.

14

The Talbot Settlement

From *Ibid.*, 183.

The Talbot Settlement lies parallel to the shore of Lake Erie, and consists of two great roads, which extend seventy or eighty miles, besides back settlements. The object in giving it such a longitudinal form was, that a road might be opened to the head of Lake Erie; and this has consequently been effected, much to the advantage of the Province in general.

15

Speculation in Land:—Town Sites

From *Ibid.*, 212.

About twelve miles above the mouth of the Thames I passed a spot called the town of Chatham. It contains only one house and a sort of church; but a portion of the land there has been surveyed into building-lots, and these being now offered for sale, have given the place a claim to the appellation of a town. There are many towns like Chatham in Upper Canada, and almost all of them have originated from the speculations of scheming individuals. When a man wishes to dispose of a piece of land, or to render one part of his property valuable by bringing settlers upon the other, he surveys a few acres into building-lots. These he advertises for sale at a high price, and people immediately feel anxious to purchase them, conceiving that their situation must be very eligible indeed, otherwise they would not have been selected for the site of a town. The extravagant hopes and expectations that often fill the minds of speculators such as I allude to, would make the most enthusiastic castle-builder smile.   Often, while surveying these *embryo* towns, have I been shown particular spots of ground that were to be reserved for universities, hospitals, churches, &c. although not even a hovel had yet been erected within the precincts of the anticipated city.

16

The Destiny of Upper Canada

From *Upper Canada Herald,* quoted in *Montreal Gazette,* September 13, 1823.

The Great Canadian Empire will assuredly be to the westward of the present limits of Lower Canada, the cultivatable parts of which form a mere valley, (a grand one to be sure, since it is watered by such a river as the *St. Lawrence,*) compared with the large and rich extent of this Province.   Our out ports and, perhaps, our *grand bazaar* will be there; but, the great business of agriculture must be carried on here, and it is here and to the westward, that our population is to spread.   We are already gaining fast upon the Lower Province in respect of the number of our souls, and it is preposterous in the extreme, that we should suffer ourselves to be bamboozled in the way we have been, for want of making our just claims more clear.

17

Rapid Progress of Upper Canada

From *Quebec Mercury,* November 1, 1831.

UPPER CANADA.—It is pleasing to observe the rapid improvements which are making and in contemplation in that richly endowed portion of the British North American possessions.   In looking into a late number of the Upper Canada Gazette, we observe numerous notices of Applications intended to be made to the Legislature at its ensuing session for acts of incorporation— grants and aids to carry various important schemes of improvement into effect.   Some of these we shall notice under the heads to which they belong.

Improvement of Navigation and Harbours.—The first in point of importance is the "Act of Incorporation to authorise the improvement of the St. Lawrence for steamboat and sloop navigation".—

The advantages which would be derived from this undertaking to the commerce of the two Provinces, are too obvious to require comment. It is true much has been effected by the opening of the Rideau Canal, but that is to be looked at as a work constructed for military defence rather than as a channel of commercial intercourse. But after all, the difficulties to be overcome in the navigation of the St. Lawrence are not so formidable as to render the success of the undertaking, now proposed, at all a matter of doubt, and it may perhaps hereafter be a subject of regret, that the cheaper expedient of a Rail Road had not been substituted for that splendid monument of national liberality, the Rideau Canal, and a portion of the surplus funds, which would have been found had such a change been made, applied to the completion of that work which is now about to be undertaken by private enterprise if the required Legislative authority is given.

We find also applications for "An act to authorise a Joint Stock Company to improve the navigation of the Grand River".— For a "Grant of Money" for making a harbour at Port Dover, (Patterson's Creek)—and another "at Port Burwell, (Otter Creek)" both on Lake Erie, and another for a similar grant "for the improvement of the Harbour of the Village of Hallowell in the Bay of Quinte". These are matters of minor consequence, but they shew the general march of improvement now going on in that young country. Two rail roads are also proposed. . . .

The first application is for "An Act of Incorporation to authorise the construction of a Rail Road between Cornwall and Prescott."—In this distance is comprised the chain of dangerous rapids by which the navigation of the St. Lawrence in Upper Canada, is obstructed; if therefore the first plan goes into operation and these waters are rendered navigable for steam boats and sloops—to form a rail road along side of the canal would be a waste of means.—If the plan for rendering the rapids navigable is abandoned then the rail road would become a work of the first importance and deserving the strenuous support of both provinces.

The second Rail Road is from the River Chippawa, about one mile above the falls of Niagara, and where the navigation of Lake Erie terminates, to Queenston, which is the head of the navigation of Lake Ontario in that direction. . . .

Now that the Welland Canal is in operation the chance of a profitable return for any outlay made in such a speculation must necessarily be greatly diminished, and as its success would abstract a part of the tolls by which the Canal must be supported, it appears, a matter of doubt whether any privilege ought to be granted in any way militating against the grand water communication now opened in that section of the U[*pper*] Province.

18

A Description of the Canada Company's Lands

From Montreal Gazette, May 7, 1832.

LANDS FOR SALE IN UPPER CANADA.—The CANADA COMPANY have for sale 2,233,000 Acres of LAND of the following description;—

1st. Crown Reserves.

These are FARMS generally of 200 Acres, which were reserved when the Land was originally surveyed, and have been sold by the Crown to the Canada Company, who are now selling them out to individuals wishing to settle on them; they are scattered in almost every Township throughout the Province, which gives Emigrants who have friends or relations already settled in the Colony the means of choosing a situation in their vicinity. For the benefit of Emigrants who cannot afford to purchase a whole Lot, the Company divide their 200 Acre Lots into two and sell a half Lot, that is, a Farm of about 100 Acres, to suit the convenience of purchasers.

2d. Blocks of Land.

When the Colony was first settled several Townships were surveyed without reserving one-seventh for the Crown; but when that arrangement was determined on, the Crown's proportion of Land was reserved in *Blocks* in the unsurveyed, or partially surveyed Townships; these Blocks are situated chiefly in the Gore and Western Districts—the principal of these in Guelph, situated about 21 miles from the Head of the *Lake* Ontario; it consists of about 42,000 acres, of which about 15,000 are still for sale; it contains nearly 1,200 inhabitants, and a village, in which are a good Grist and SawMill, Stores, Taverns, a school, and all kinds of Mechanics and Tradesmen; a Presbyterian and Episcopal Church are in progress, and a Catholic Church has been built; a Minister of the kirk of Scotland resides there, and a Catholic Priest and Church of England Clergyman occasionally visit it. From the class of Emigrants that have lately gone there, and from the conveniences afforded in a settlement of some standing, it will be found a desirable residence for persons of moderate capital. Persons desirous of purchasing partially cleared Farms, can generally procure them in the Township.

The other Blocks are all excellent Land, and would be desirable purchases for communities of settlers.

3d. *The Huron Tract.*

After the experience of five years, and after every part of it having been thoroughly explored, the Commissioners can with confidence recommend the Land of the Tract as superior to any body of Land of equal magnitude, either in the Province of Upper Canada, or the States of New York, Pennsylvania, Ohio, or the Territory of Michigan. The soil is a rich loam; the Trees, the Sugar Maple, Basswood, Elm, Beech, and Cherry—Timber which is known in this country to indicate the very best land. It is a Table Land, being from 150 to 250 feet above the level of Lake Huron, but its summit is diversified and rolling; it is watered by numerous streams, and possesses every quality which ensures a good settlement.

The Town of Goderich is the Capital of the Tract; it is situated at the mouth of the River Maitland, the Basin of which forms an excellent Harbor; it contains several Stores, and there is a good Grist and Saw Mill in its immediate vicinity. Another Saw Mill on a large scale, is erecting on the River Sable, and three Grist and as many Saw Mills will be commenced in the course of this season.

One great advantage which the Huron Tract possesses over other wild Lands is, its roads; these have been cut, at an immense expense, in the very best manner that Roads are constructed in this Country. The Harbor at Goderich gives a facility of shipping produce at the one end of the Tract, while the Grand River will this summer be rendered navigable to Brantford; and it is then proposed to render the Nith also navigable, thus giving a water communication to each end of the Tract. Depots of Provisions and Tools are forming along the main Road, and Taverns are established at convenient distances from each other.

To encourage the settlement of their Lands the Canada Company have, for the present season, resolved to give settlers who purchase from them in the scattered Crown Reserves, not less than 200 Acres, or in the Township of Guelph and the Huron Tract, 100 acres.   A Passage free of expense to the Head of Lake Ontario, in the following manner:—the Emigrant deposits with the Company's agent at Quebec a sum of money equal to the price of his conveyance to the Head of the Lake, and takes a receipt for it, getting at the same time a Pass Ticket to the Company's Forwarders on the route; when he has fixed upon his land, he shews this Receipt to the Agent, or presents it at the Company's Office in York, and it is taken in part payment of his second Instalment. Stage Waggons from Hamilton to Goderich, or any intermediate part of the Settlement in the Huron Tract, have been established, which will reduce the expense of travelling to nearly one-third of what it formerly was.

The instructions of the Court of Directors to the Commissioners of the Canada Company being to sell their Lands as quickly as possible, the prices are moderate and the terms advantageous— the Purchaser is allowed to pay for his Lot by six Instalments, in five years; on paying the first of which, one-fifth, he receives a letter acknowledging the receipt of the money paid, and giving him a right to occupy the Lot.   And, on the whole, the Commissioners have used every means in their power to give the settler the best information, the cheapest modes of conveyance, and done everything they possibly could to assist and facilitate all his undertakings to render himself comfortable and independent.

Canada Company's Office,
  York, May 1, 1832

19

Stagnation of the Eastern Townships through Lack of Capital

From Montreal Gazette, March 19, 1833.

From a correspondent of the St. Francis Courier

. . . Settlements were commenced upon these lands about forty years since, and they now contain a population of forty thousand souls, but few if any more than one township, would with proper culture support.—Owing to the great expense of getting produce to market, very little more is raised than is sufficient for home consumption. Pot and Pearl ashes, which have been our principal articles for remittance, are hardly worth manufacturing, and as to a circulating medium, there is none—capital is out of the question with us—trade is consequently declining—business of every description is in a languishing state.

It must certainly be evident to every person residing in this section of the country, that some change in our circumstances is absolutely necessary to prevent ruin. Instead of having a total population of forty thousand, we ought to have an annual increase to that amount—instead of our wild lands laying [*sic*] waste and useless, they should be made productive we ought to be able to turn off immense quantities of horses, cattle, pork, butter, cheese, &c.—instead of our finest streams of water being permitted to run in a great degree, to waste, they should be brought to our aid in working mills and machinery, and made to increase our wealth. In fine, instead of being poor and almost pennyless, this should be a highly cultivated, rich, and prosperous country; nature has done her part, let man do his, and we should have nothing of which to complain. This change may be considered very desirable, but the question will probably be asked, how can all these great objects be effected. I answer, by British industry, by British capital. By British industry, I of course include our own, as I trust we all claim to be British subjects. By British capital, I mean a portion of that wealth which is now locked up in England, at present yielding little or nothing to its possessors, but which if expended here, in aid of industry, would not only effect the objects so important to us, but be rendered productive. . . .

A British Subject

20

Cash Sales of Clergy Reserves Lands

From *Montreal Gazette*, August 29, 1833.

CLERGY RESERVES.—At a public auction of Clergy Reserves, held in the Court house of this town, on Tuesday last, 1800 acres, lying in the Townships of Puslinch and Beverly, were sold at 15s. to 15s. 6d. per acre, to emigrants who tendered the purchase money at the sale, and intend to become actual settlers with as little delay as possible.

21

The Eastern Townships, their Settlement and Progress

From *Quebec Gazette*, quoted in *Montreal Gazette*, October 16, 1834.

The country of fine land extends east from the mountains west of Lake Memphramagog, about sixty miles along the United States boundary, and to the north (Kingsey included) about sixty-five miles where it is from forty to fifty miles in width. The two main branches of the St. Francis, and their united streams and tributaries, run through this tract, northward to the St. Lawrence, watering the whole country in abundance for every useful purpose.

The soil generally is a deep black loam on a dark grey slate bottom, with occasional tracts of lime-stone country. The surface is undulating rising sometimes into considerable eminences, but without any mountains which are uncultivable, except the Bald Mountain and its unextensive range in Shipton.

The settlement of these Townships began with activity, about thirty years ago [*1804*]. The first inhabitants were chiefly from the New England States, and were principally located at Stanstead and the neighbouring Townships. A settlement was made at Shipton, by natives of the United States from Montreal, subsequently some settlers from Lower Canada went up the St. Francis to Simpson, Drummondville, Wendover, Kingsey and Durham. Others penetrated from the Yamaska to Upton and the adjoining Townships; but the bulk of the population is still towards the United States frontier. It was not till within about fifteen years [*1819*], that the roads to the St. Lawrence at Labaye and Sorel, became in some degree practicable. Craig's road, to come out near the mouth of the Chaudière, made in 1810, was never completely finished, and was ill laid out over mountainous tracts; and from Kingsey to Ireland there are no settlers—a distance of nearly twenty miles—although they are numerous from Ireland to Quebec. For a long period, it could hardly be said that there was in these Townships any legal authorities or administration of justice. The inhabitants were left to themselves, and managed matters in the best way they could, sometimes on the plan followed in the United States;[1] but this was no easy matter in a population

---

[1] Thereby proving themselves true frontiersmen and doubtless exemplifying once more, as it has continuously been exemplified in the march of the frontier, the spirit of the "*Mayflower* compact" of 1620.

collected from different parts, several of whom had retired into Canada to escape the operations of law in their own country, or from misfortune, arising, no doubt, sometimes from their own irregularities. Their markets and intercourse were chiefly in the adjoining States, with the exception of some cattle and horses, which they drove through the woods for sale in Canada, or a few articles they floated down the St. Francis when the waters were high, making portages at the rapids. The settlement suffered also from some jealousy against the American settlers, but which was partly done away with by the general good conduct of the people during the war of 1812. Since 1829, when these Townships were permitted to have Representatives in the Provincial Assembly, great improvements have been made in their communications by legislative aid, and means have been taken to give security to the titles of lands and greater facilities of operation for the rising generation have been afforded them. They are evidently thriving, notwithstanding some unfavorable seasons and other causes which have led to a partial emigration to the west. The villages of Stanstead, Hatley, Compton, Lennoxville and Shipton and some others have assumed the neat and comfortable appearance of New England villages. Numerous stores are established, and manufactories, workshops, academies, places of worship and even printing offices, have made their appearance. It almost requires a traveller from New England to be informed that he is in the British dominion to perceive it. The farm-houses and out-houses are however, inferior both in respect of neatness and size, and the land although much superior, does not appear to be so well managed. The live stock is, however excellent and numerous. The price of land at present varies from half a dollar to ten, per acre, according to the situation, quality and improvement. The people evidently want the legal power of regulating their township concerns and raising money for their roads and local improvements; they want better communications with the St. Lawrence, and some means of forcing holders of wild lands to settle them or give them up to those that will. This is a great and fertile source of complaint here, as in many other parts of the Province, and must be remedied. They are anxious that men of capital should come among them and make improvements but dislike speculators on wild lands, holding them merely to profit by their enhanced value from the labour and capital of others.

22

Comparative Merits of the Eastern Townships and Upper Canada

From *Montreal Daily Advertiser*, quoted in *Montreal Gazette*, October 16, 1834.

To the Editor of the *Daily Advertiser*.

Sir,—Having lately seen an article in the *Daily Advertiser*, in which it is stated that the Eastern Townships of Lower Canada are farther for all practical purposes than the shores of Lake Ontario, or, perhaps, those of Erie, I have taken the liberty of stating those circumstances which induce me to differ from you. The average distance of the Eastern Townships from Montreal is about eighty miles or two days' journey for two horses with a sleigh, loaded with forty bushels of wheat; the expences of which and returning will be about 20s. or 6d. per bushel; the expense of bringing the same quantity from the shores of Lake Ontario, above Toronto, would be about 125 per cent. more, or 13½d. per bushel, exclusive of waste, which is considerable when there are two or three transhipments. It may be urged that I have reckoned nothing for the hire of the man and horses, but neither have I reckoned any thing for the hire of the same, necessary to the Upper Canada farmer to convey his produce to the shipping port on the Lake, through the worst roads in the world. But there are many other advantages which the farmer in Lower Canada possesses; instead of carrying his wheat many miles through a bad road, to a storekeeper, and selling it to him for 3s. per bushel, perhaps half in store pay, at an advance of from fifty to one hundred per cent. upon the Montreal prices—he comes himself to Montreal, sells his wheat at from 5s. to 5s. 6d. to the merchant for cash, or a short bill, buys his salt and other necessaries at prime cost, that is, less than the cost of conveyance, and two or three profits, or he may carry out goods for the neighbouring storekeepers at about 2s. per cwt. which will more than pay all his expenses. Again, he can get labourers at five dollars a month and their board; the Upper Canada farmer must pay double that price. His other advantages are cheap land, averaging at 6s. per acre, and a healthy climate; his brethren of the Upper Province have to pay 15s. on the average, (I have known 30s. given for wild land,) and are ravaged by fever, ague and cholera, disorders unknown in the Eastern Townships. Fortunately for Upper Canada, every little village finds some newspaper to blazon forth its beauties to the world, but the picturesque mountains, the salubrious climate, the noble streams, fertile interval lands, and rich flats of the Eastern Townships are hardly heard of out of their immediate vicinity. . . .

W.

23

Grumbling in Lower Canada:—Progress in United States

From *Montreal Gazette*, September 17, 1835.

Though we are not at all disposed to copy the AMERICANS in all their actions, we should be extremely happy if our good people of LOWER CANADA would give up the trade of grievance-mongering, and devote more of their energies to the improvement of the country, like their neighbours to the South. We are much in want of a portion of their enterprise, and our Province would be greatly benefitted, if they infect us with a little of their public spirit. We cite the following cases as worthy of imitation and as a proof of what their enterprise is achieving for that country.[1]

24

High Price of Land in Upper Canada as Deterrent to Settlement

From *Brantford Sentinel*, quoted in *Montreal Gazette*, October 13, 1835.

EMIGRATION.—In all probability not less than two hundred teams have passed through our town this season, laden with the furniture and families of emigrants who are bound for Michigan or Illinois. They are principally from the U.S. more particularly the State of New York. The cheapness of land in Michigan is the principal inducement for emigrating to that territory. It is obvious that land in the western parts of our Province is held at too high a value to encourage much American emigration to our shores— for instance a tract of a hundred acres of good land in Upper Canada can hardly be bought for £100, whereas in Michigan the same quantity and quality of land can be obtained for as many dollars. The Canada Company would do well to look to this.

---

[1]Accounts follow of the building of railroads in various parts of the United States.

25

The Progress of Toronto, 1817-35

From *Toronto Albion*, quoted in *Montreal Gazette*, October 31, 1835.

CITY OF TORONTO.—In Mr. Gourlay's statistical account of Upper Canada, published in 1817, he writes of what was then Little York, as follows:—"I suppose its population to be 1200 souls; for five miles round the capital of Upper Canada scarcely one improved farm can be seen in contact with another. The only connected settlement is about five miles to the north of Yonge street; in other directions, as far as the district goes, you might travel to its utmost limits, and not find more than one farm house for every three miles."

Such was the state of things in Upper Canada in 1817. In 1835 we find the town of Little York metamorphosed into the city of Toronto, and a population of from 12 to 14,000 souls. Supposing that on the average six persons lived in each house, there were then two hundred houses; upon the same calculation now, there must be, taking the large amount of the estimated population, 2333 houses, and supposing the average value of the houses in 1817 to be £200 each, the building property was then worth £40,000, and suppose their average value now to be £400 each, and considering the number of large and valuable houses lately built, it will be greatly too low, the building property of the city is worth £933,200, showing an outlay of £893,200 since 1817: this applies to dwelling houses alone, and when the large stores and other improvements are taken into account, the least sum that can be supposed is a million. Look again at the difference in the three principal outlets; instead of the four miles Mr. Gourlay talks of, on which there is scarcely one improved farm, there is now scarcely a lot not improved. With what propriety then can it be said that Upper Canada has not prospered, and be it recollected too, that these buildings have not been paid for by loans of a fictitious paper currency—no such thing, they have been reared by the real property of the individuals who have built them, or from real bona fide property borrowed from those who possessed a superfluity. It is not unusual to hear people croaking that there is a check to business and buildings in Toronto; every place is subject to such checks—a year or two ago Rochester was universally thought to be on the decline, it is now all activity. The truth was that the folks of Rochester had done as those of Toronto did last year, they went too fast, and a little time must be taken to recover it. It will be said that Rochester possesses water privileges almost beyond the possibility of full employment whilst Toronto is destitute of them; Toronto may have water privileges too if she pleases, and sooner or later she will have them, but Toronto has other advantages, it is the seat of Government, and a regular and steady addition to the amount of her returns arises to her from that source. But she has a far greater advantage in her relative position with her back country and Lake Ontario, and if the inhabitants of Toronto have enterprise and public spirit enough to make the most of those advantages, nothing can prevent that city from becoming important exactly as Buffalo has done. Buffalo is situated at the extremity of the Erie Canal as Toronto is of Lake Ontario. Buffalo is situated on the high road to the Western States, and supplies in a great degree the most of its inhabitants. Toronto is on the high road to Lake Simcoe, and a vast tract of fertile land between that and Lake Huron, and is also on the direct line of communication with the far West, the Michigan, and an immense territory beyond, whose produce will inevitably pass through Toronto, if the necessary facilities are created. At any expense a substantial good road must be made for the common purposes of the country from Lake Simcoe to Toronto, and a railroad having for its object the rapid and cheap transit of the persons and produce of the distant countries, avoiding the delay and uncertainty of the circuitous route of Lake Huron, the St. Clair, Erie and the Welland Canal. Let the inhabitants of Toronto but do their duty to themselves, and Toronto will successfully compete with any city on the continent of America but if they allow their rational advantages to elude their grasp because they have not energy to keep them, they have none but themselves to blame.

26

The Rival Attractions of Canada and the Western States

From *Montreal Transcript*, August 31, 1844.

The terms which the [*British American Land*] Company offer to settlers are so liberal that it is of the utmost importance to the

Colony that they should be generally known. The difficulty which the emigrant generally has to encounter in the struggle to maintain himself for the first few years, is in great part removed by the not requiring any payment at entry, and making the rent the interest of the purchase money for the first ten years. . . .

The life of a farmer is generally anything but a bed of roses in Canada, and also [there are] many instances before our eyes of signal failures even in the neighbourhood of the Townships themselves. But we are also justified in believing that . . . the agriculturist . . . has seen the gloomiest days he ever will see in Canada. The reasons for this belief are to be found in the greater facilities which are every day opening for communication with the principal markets the Province affords, and in the protection which the Legislature has at last extended to the farmer, and which protection—notwithstanding all the grumbling of the free-trade men—will not, we are quite satisfied, be withdrawn. . . . Without some such advantages as the Canada Company holds out, it is more than doubtful whether a large class of those who emigrate to this country could be induced to forego their dreams of fortune-making in that *el dorado*, the far West. The fear of sinking their capital in a country where the climate seems to battle against them, and which besides does not offer externally those signs of prosperity which are to be observed on the other side of the line, deters them from settling down amongst their own countrymen in Canada, and sends them on a wild-goose-chase to the swamps of Arkansas or Illinois. We were surprised to find on talking to numbers of the Emigrants from the Southern counties of England who arrived in Montreal early in the season, how strongly these notions possessed them. Although almost entirely ignorant of the geography and resources of both countries, they were quite satisfied that the "west" was the "place for their money," because, according to them, land could be got for next to nothing, and they were quite sure of soon becoming "their own masters."

Now the advantages offered by the Canada Company just meet the notions of this class of settlers, who from long experience of servitude at home, are naturally anxious to become "their own masters." It is the idea of independence natural to every Briton, and which we should always like to see gratified. . . .

27

Lumbering and Farming in the Ottawa District

From *Canadian Economist*, June 6, 1846.

This section is the country lying on both sides of the Ottawa River. View it in what way you please, it is valuable. The Timber Trade (independent of protection duties) is likely to prove of permanent importance, from the inherent good qualities of the article produced; and it gives a market at the door of the farmer for a good portion of the more bulky part of his produce,—for his horses, cattle, hay, oats, beans, peas, potatoes, and a portion of his wheat. Should the supply exceed the demand on the spot, he has rapid and easy communication with Montreal, at a cheaper rate than even many parishes in the immediate neighbourhood of this city. He has there a market ever open for all the articles he can raise, including the excellent pork and butter produced on his shores.

28

The Settlement of the Northern Part of "Old Ontario"

From Canadian Archives, *Correspondence of the governor-general's secretary*, no. 4638.

Crown Land Department
Montreal, 30th March, 1847

Memorandum on the Owen Sound Settlement

. . . A road was opened and constructed at public expense in 1841 from the North West angle of the Township of Garafraxa thro' an entire Wilderness, to the Owen Sound on Lake Huron, a distance of about 58 Miles—free grants of 50 Acres were made all along and on each side of the road, leaving in some cases intervening reserves of 50 acres for the future purchase of the adjoining locatees. The principal condition of these grants was, that, the grantees should clear and place once under crop one-third of the 50 acres within 4 Years, after which they are entitled to their Patents free of expenses.

Agents were appointed at each extremity of the road, now called the Owen Sound road, at Salaries of 10/- each to superintend the locations.

All the lots on that road offered as free Grants that were fit for cultivation have been disposed of, some of the reserves have been purchased and the settlement is now in a considerable state of advancement.

By the statistical returns received of the Southern division of the road now under the management of Mr Young, early in the spring of last Year, it appears that 280 Lots of land had then been located in that section of the road—of which 3162 acres had been cleared or chopped.

The number of buildings of every description, Houses, Shanties, Barns, Stables &^{c} is stated at 435.

Horses 16. Oxen, Cows and other Cattle 1130. Sheep 277. Pigs 393: Total of Live Stock, 1816 Head.
Population 1070 Souls as follows viz—

Natives of England	-	-	-	-	167
Ireland	-	-	-	-	539
Scotch	-	-	-	-	212
French Canadians	-	-	-	-	86
English ditto	-	-	-	-	57
other countries	-	-	-	-	9
					1070.

The returns from Mr Telfer for the Northern Section of the road are defective, but there appears to be about 300 lots located on that part of the road and 3051 Acres improved. . . .

T. Bouthillier

29

The Secondary Towns of Upper Canada

From W. H. Smith, *Canada, past, present and future* (Toronto, 1851), 32.

Dresden, (near Chatham), is a thriving settlement of late origin; the situation is well chosen, being at the head of navigation of the East branch of the Sydenham river, with water sufficiently deep to allow vessels of three hundred tons to load at the banks. There is a steam saw mill in the village, and during last year (1849), two merchants alone exported three hundred thousand pipe and West India staves, and thirty thousand feet of sawed walnut lumber. Being the shipping port for what will ere long be a fine agricultural country, besides being the heart of a large supply of fine white oak, there is no doubt that the village will eventually become a place of considerable local importance.

(b)—ASPECTS OF PIONEER LIFE AND PROBLEMS

The most pressing of problems in a new country is that of getting the settler on the land and in a position to support himself. Consequently interest is attached to the process by which the pioneer farm was made. As the area of settlement extends, the fabric of colonial life becomes more complex. Urban nuclei appear and something which could be called a civilization comes into existence. The documents give some idea of the problems which the pioneer had to face, and the habits to which his mode of life gave rise, such as the relief of the monotony of the wilderness by drink and by that other intoxicant, emotional religion. The type of society which was developing in the towns is also noticed.

REFERENCES: Isabel Skelton, *The backwoodswoman* (Toronto, 1924); W. S. Herrington, *Pioneer life among the Loyalists in Upper Canada* (Toronto, 1915); Adam Shortt, *Life of the settler in western Canada before the War of 1812* (Queen's University bulletins of history, no. 12); [M. G. Scherk], *Pen pictures of early pioneer life in Upper Canada*, by A Canuck (Toronto, 1905); Anna Jameson, *Winter studies and summer rambles in Canada* (reprint, Toronto, 1923); Susannah Moodie, *Roughing it in the bush* (new ed., Toronto, 1913), C. P. Traill, *Backwoods of Canada* (Toronto, 1929).

1

Steps in the Making of a Pioneer Farm

From Howison, *Sketches of Upper Canada*, 258-279, 248-251.

The chief objects to be considered in making a selection [*of a grant*] are the goodness of the land, its dryness, the existence of a spring of running water upon it, its vicinity to a road, a navigable river, a mill, a running stream, a market, and an extensive and increasing neighborhood. . . .

[First steps]

Some people choose to clear a few acres and crop them before they build a house, or go to reside upon their lots. Others erect a habitation first of all, and move into it at once with their families. The first plan is most congenial to the feelings of British emigrants; for the partial cultivation that has been effected diminishes the wildness of the surrounding forests and things are usually more comfortable and orderly within doors than they can be when the settler takes up his residence on his land before any trees have been cut down. But the expense of supporting a family, while clearing operations are going forward, is great, unless the idle

members engage themselves as servants; and the work, particularly
if hired persons are employed, does not proceed as fast as it would
do, were the principal residing upon his lot and superintending
the business himself. Therefore, all settlers who have a little
money ought to set themselves down in the woods at once, and
boldly commence chopping.   This plan may subject them to a few
hardships but it will assuredly be for their advantage in the end. . .

[Building the house]

[The Emigrant's] first object then is to get a house built.   If
his lot lies in a settlement, his neighbours will assist him in doing
this without being paid; but if far back in the woods, he must
hire people to work for him.   The usual dimensions of a house
are eighteen feet by sixteen.   The roof is covered with bark or
shingles, and the floor with rough-hewn planks, the interstices
between the logs that compose the walls being filled up with
pieces of wood and clay.   Stones are used for the back of the
fire-place, and a hollow cone of coarse basket-work does the office
of a chimney.   The whole cost of a habitation of this kind will not
exceed £12, supposing the labourers had been paid for erecting it;
but as almost every person can have much of the work done gratis,
the expense will not perhaps amount to more than £5 or £6. . . .

[Pioneer food]

Flour and pork are the only articles of subsistence which can
be conveniently transported into the woods.   The price of a barrel
of flour, containing 186 lbs., is £1, 10s.; and of a barrel of pork
holding 200 lbs., about £5.

[Methods and cost of clearing]

The clearing of land overgrown with timber is an operation
so tedious and laborious, that different plans have been devised
for abridging it, and for obtaining a crop from the ground before
it is completed.   The easiest and most economical system is that
named girdling.   The land is first cleared of brushwood and small
timber, and then a ring of bark is cut from the lower part of every
tree; and if .this is done in the autumn, the trees will be dead and
destitute of foliage the ensuing spring,[1] at which time the land is

---

[1]They will leaf out the following spring but probably die in the course of the
summer.

sown, without receiving any culture whatever except a little harrowing. This plan evidently possesses no advantage except that of enabling the settler to supply his immediate wants, at the expense of comparatively little time and labour. The crops obtained in this way are of course scanty, and of inferior quality. The dead trees must be cut down and removed at last; and being liable to fall during high winds, the lives of both labourers and cattle are endangered.

After the trees have been felled, the most suitable kinds are split into rails for fences,[1] and the remainder, being cut into logs twelve feet long, are hauled together into large piles, and burnt.[2] The land cleared in this manner is sown with wheat, and harrowed two or three times, and in general an abundant crop rewards the toils of the owner.

After the felling, dividing, and burning of the timber have been accomplished, the stumps still remain, disfiguring the fields, and impeding the effectual operation of the plough and harrow. The immediate removal of the roots of the trees is impracticable and they are therefore always allowed to fall into decay, to which state they are generally reduced in the space of eight or nine years. Pine stumps however seem scarcely susceptible of decomposition, as they frequently show no symptoms of it after half a century has elapsed. . . .[3]

The clearing, fencing, sowing, harrowing, and harvesting an acre of waste land will cost about £5, 5s. The produce is usually about twenty-five bushels of wheat, which on an average are worth £6. After the land has been in crop, its cultivation becomes much less expensive. The cost of putting in a second crop (ploughing being then necessary) will not exceed £2 per acre, while the produce will amount to perhaps thirty-five or forty bushels; thus affording a clear profit of from £4. 15s. to £6. 10s. after £1. 10s. has been deducted for harvesting and threshing.[4]

---

[1]Cedar, as a rule, was used for fence rails.

[2]See the account of the log-burning "bee" in Ralph Connor's *Man from Glengarry* (Toronto, 1901).

[3]Despite this well-known fact, settlers were frequently put into pine-covered land, and when they had destroyed the valuable timber all they had left were acres of pine stumps. Pineries, as a rule, too, were on the lighter, sandy soil. "Settlement" frequently meant the conversion of a fine pinery into a sand-blown waste. See E. A. Owens, *Pioneer sketches of the Long Point settlement* (Toronto, 1898).

[4]This is theory, of course.

[Barns]

In Upper Canada grain is always put under cover instead of being made into stacks; and therefore the farmer must build a barn, which at first is usually formed of logs, in the same way as a dwelling-house; however, it does not cost nearly so much, no inside work being necessary. But when he becomes wealthier, and is more at leisure, he may erect a frame-barn, so called because it is constructed of joiner work, and covered with boards. Such buildings are commonly made fifty feet long and forty wide, and cost about £60. . . .

[Taking grain to the mill]

A new settlement is sometimes twenty or thirty miles distant from a mill, and the roads are generally so bad, that the person who carries grain to it waits till it is ground, although he should be detained several days. When this is the case, each individual, by turns, conveys to the mill the grain of three or four of his neighbours, and thus the great waste of labour, which would be occasioned were every one to take his own produce there separately, is avoided. . . .

[Disposing of the crop]

When the farmer is able to raise a larger quantity of produce than is required for the support of his family, there are several ways in which he may dispose of the surplus. In many new settlements the influx of emigrants is so great as to produce a demand for grain more than equal to the supply. In Talbot Road, the average price of wheat has of late years, been 4s. 6d. per bushel, while in most other parts of the country it was selling for 3s. and 3s. 6d.; showing evidently, that the farmer will sometimes find the best market at his own door. But should there be no demand of this kind, he may carry his produce to the merchants. They will give him in exchange, broad-cloth, implements of husbandry, groceries, and every sort of article that is necessary for his family, and, perhaps, even money, at particular times. He will likewise often have it in his power to barter wheat for live stock of different kinds, and can hardly fail to increase his means, although without a regular market for his surplus produce, if he gets initiated into the system of traffic prevalent in the country. . . .

[*Subsisting the stock*]

As there is no grass in the woods, and as new settlers cannot raise fodder for their cattle immediately, they are obliged to buy either hay or straw, or pumpkins, to feed them, or to cut down trees for them to browze upon.   Oxen and young cows thrive well enough on the tender shoots of the birch, maple, &c.; but sheep must have hay or turnips, and ought to be secured from the wolves every night. . . .

[*Domestic service and the conditions of a new country*]

Emigrants sometimes bring servants from Britain; but such seldom remain long with them after their arrival in Canada, their ideas and prospects being directed into new channels by the system of independence and equality which prevails in the country.   The women are soon married, and the men become landholders. Some people bind their domestics by indentures, to continue with them for a certain time; but this plan seldom answers well, as persons so articled are apt to grow insolent and troublesome, whenever their bondage becomes disagreeable to them. . . .

[*Social tone of Upper Canada*]

Another circumstance tends to make Europeans partial to Upper Canada. They find themselves of much more importance there than they would at home; for the circle of society is so limited, and the number of respectable people in the Province so small, that almost every person is able to obtain some notice and attention.   There is likewise no aristocracy and consequently no man can assume a higher station in society than another, except upon the score of superior intellect or greater wealth; the latter of which is of course, rather oftener recognised as a ground of distinction than the former.   A person of respectability at once finds a place in the best company the Province affords. . . . This state of things is favourable to the existence of general harmony and good-will, but rather hostile to the cultivation and advancement of manners. . . .

[*Prices of land and commodities*]

In Upper Canada, waste land varies in value according to its situation. Near villages, and populous parts of the country, its price is from £4 to £8 an acre; however, when it lies remote from any settlement, and has no particular local advantages, it may sometimes be purchased in tracts at the rate of two or three shillings an acre. Cultivated land sells much higher, particularly when bought in small quantities, its price being then sometimes £20 or £30 per acre. A farm containing two hundred acres, thirty of which are under cultivation, and a log-house and barn, may be purchased for £250 in the Talbot Settlement, where the majority of British emigrants now take up their residence. A farm of similar extent, situated any where upon the frontier, between Niagara village and Fort Erie, could not be bought for less than eight or nine hundred pounds. In the back settlements, farms are always for sale at prices much lower than any I have mentioned; but the disadvantages incidental to their situation render them not very desirable for any person. In many of the villages of Upper Canada, lots containing half an acre sell for £50 or £60; and the lands in their immediate vicinity often bear a proportionably high value.

Waste land may be completely cleared and fenced at the rate of £4 per acre; however, if the quantity is large, and the work contracted for, the cost will not be so great. Farm-labourers, if hired by the day, receive from three shillings to four and sixpence, exclusive of board. A man's wages are £3 per month, besides board; but if he is hired by the year, he receives less in proportion. Women servants can hardly be procured, and they generally receive eighteen shillings or a guinea a month. A moderately good horse costs £20 or £25; a yoke of oxen the same sum; a good cow from £5 to £7; a sheep 4s. 6d.; a large sow £2; and other domestic animals in proportion. Wheat averages 4s. 6d. a bushel; rye 4s.; oats 1s. 10d.; buck-wheat 3s.; Indian corn 3s.; potatoes 2s.; apples 2s. 6d.; hay, per ton, £2.

[Taxation and statute labour]

In Upper Canada, the taxes are so trifling that they scarcely deserve notice. All rateable property, such as live-stock, houses, &c. is subject to a tax of one penny upon the pound, ad valorem. Cultivated lands pay one penny an acre, and waste land one farthing. Every male is obliged to work three days annually upon the public roads, or employ a substitute, or pay the sum of thirteen shillings and sixpence to the path-master, being the wages of a labouring man for three days. Heads of families, and persons who keep teams, are liable to a greater proportion of statute labour. However, notwithstanding these regulations, the roads throughout the Province in general are in very bad repair, the path-masters not being sufficiently strict in exacting the apportioned quantity of labour from each individual.

[Wages and barter]

From what I have stated, it will be seen that the necessaries of life can be obtained at a small expense in Upper Canada; but that labour is very high, and quite out of proportion to most other things. This circumstance arises from the scarcity of labourers, and from their wages being in a great measure nominal. Money is so difficult to procure, that almost all the farmers are obliged to pay those they hire with grain of some kind, which being unsaleable those who receive it are obliged to barter it away with loss for any thing else they may require. He who has a little money at command in Upper Canada will possess many advantages. He will get his work done at a cheaper rate than other people who have none; and, in making purchases, will often obtain a large discount from the seller. A third cause of the high wages of labourers is the exorbitant rate at which all merchandize of British manufacture is sold in Upper Canada, the retail prices of such being, on an average, one hundred and fifty per cent. higher than they are in Britain. The different articles of wearing apparel cost nearly twice as much as they do on the other side of the Atlantic, and are of very inferior quality.

2

Pioneer Inns and Boarding Houses

From *A few plain directions for persons intending to proceed as settlers to his majesty's province of Upper Canada. . . . By an English* farmer settled in Upper Canada (London, 1820), 44.

Boarding-houses are numerous in the cities and towns of America. Those of the first class are respectable; and at them the accommodation is good and agreeable, particularly in those where each of the company has a separate bed-room. The charges are a dollar, or four shillings a day. At inferior boarding-houses the accommodations are not comfortable, or convenient, or good. The company consists of all classes, from the man of independent property to the mechanic. The beds are indifferent, and from four to ten are crowded in one room, destitute of curtains, &c. and swarming with fleas and bugs. In such houses there is no such thing as comfort or privacy. Inns of the second class bear a great resemblance to the latter kind of boarding-houses. A person may either board at them for so much a week, or pay for each meal separately; in that case the charges are extremely high: 2s. or 2s. 6d. for breakfast; 2s. 6d. for dinner, and 2s. or 2s. 6d. for supper, without beer or liquor; besides sixpence or a shilling a night for a bed in a room where are half a dozen others. It must, however, be acknowledged, that the tables here are far more plentifully furnished with provisions than in England, and of as good a quality. The innkeepers in this country are too independent in their principles to pay the least attention to the comfort or convenience of their guests .... The chief aim of the host is to get the stranger's money; generosity and benevolence are not ingredients in his composition.

3

Pioneer Diet in Nova Scotia and in Lower Canada

From *Report of the committee on emigration from the United Kingdom, Imperial parliamentary papers*, 1826 (404), IV.

Richard John Uniack, Esqr. of Nova Scotia.

Does Nova Scotia export corn to Newfoundland?—Wheat it does, but not oats; oats have become an article of great demand, for, by a great deal of pains taken in the country, we have diverted the people to the use of oaten bread instead of flour—bread which will enable the country people to sell their flour, and to substitute oaten bread. We gave large bounties for erecting oat mills and mills for the dressing of oats and which will increase in a very little time the surplus of bread-grain in the island very much.

William Bowman Felton Esq. of Lower Canada.

Of what increase do you think the population of Lower Canada would be capable?—I think the unoccupied cultivable acres in Lower Canada do not exceed nine millions.

Do you think that the province would sustain six millions, judiciously introduced?—I think the province would sustain six millions of wheat consumers, and fortunately, to the present time, the Canadian population have not been driven to consume any inferior grain. It has been an object with all the land proprietors, and all the men of influence in the township, to prevent the people having recourse to an inferior grain. I have done all in my power to prevent the people using oats and oatmeal, and I have succeeded; not by the erection of mills, but by destroying the oat-kiln myself; the consequence has been, that they have cultivated wheat with more assiduity, and the common people live infinitely more comfortable than in this country; and speaking of the part of the country in which I reside, I may say that no man consumes in his family less than three times the quantity of any decent family in England.

4

The Rate of Progress in Social Complexity

From *Montreal Gazette*, February 2, 1832.

As after the rising of our Provincial Legislature, the session being now within a few days of its close, we shall probably experience some difficulty in filling three papers a week to advantage, we have determined, for a short time, to resume our semi-weekly publication. When the active season for business returns, we propose again to adopt the plan of issuing our paper three times a week. In the meantime, we shall publish supplementary sheets, as often as an accumulation of matter renders it expedient.

5

The Habits of Our Ancestors

(i)

From John J. Bigsby, *The shoe and canoe, or pictures of travel in the Canadas* (2 volumes, London, 1850), I, 262.

Strong drink is the bane of Canada West, especially on outlying farms, and still more especially, I fear, among half-pay officers.

(ii)

From J. S. Springer, *Forest life and forest trees* (New York, 1856), 151.

Some twenty years since [*i.e., about 1825*], these arrivals, and also those of the river-drivers, were characterized by a free indulgence in spirituous liquors and many drunken carousals. Grog shops were numerous and the dominion of King Alcohol undisputed by the masses. Liquor flowed as freely as the waters which bore their logs to the mills. Hogsheads of rum were drunk or wasted in the course of a few hours on some occasions, and excessive indulgence was the almost daily practice of the majority, even from the time of their arrival in the Spring until the commencement of another winter's campaign. . . . "In 1832, in a population not exceeding four hundred and fifty or five hundred, on the St. Croix, three thousand five hundred gallons of ardent spirits were consumed." A distinguished lumberman whose opinion is above quoted, remarks further, "So strong was the conviction that men could not work in the water without 'spirits', that I had great difficulty in employing the first crew of men to drive on the river on temperance principles. When I had made known my purpose to employ such a gang of men the answer almost invariably was, 'You may try, but depend on it, the drive will never come down!' " . . . "More prominence was given to rum as a necessary part of the supplies than to almost any other article", says Mr. Todd of St. Stephen's N.B., "in all our movements, from the stump in the swamp to the ship's hold, it was *Rum!* Rum!"

(iii)

From Alexander Sutherland, *Methodism in Canada* (London, 1903), 50.

Hezekiah Calvin Wooster was received on trial in 1793, and Daniel Coote in 1794. These two offered their services for Canada and were accepted. . . . Their journey to Canada was slow and tedious. Twenty one nights were spent in the rude cabins of dwellers in the New York wilderness before they reached their destination. . . . The way in which divine power often manifested itself under Wooster's preaching was very remarkable. Once at a quarterly meeting on the Bay of Quinte circuit, just as Wooster began his sermon, a man in the front of the gallery began to swear profanely, and otherwise to disturb the congregation. The preacher appeared to take no notice until he was in the midst of his sermon, when suddenly fixing his eyes on the profane man, he pointed his finger at him, and stamping with his foot, cried with great energy, "My God, smite him!" Instantly the man fell as if shot through the heart, and such a sense of God's presence and power came down upon the congregation that on every hand sinners cried for mercy, while the saints shouted for joy.

6

The Social Atmosphere of Toronto about 1837

From Mrs. Jameson, *Winter studies and summer rambles in Canada* (New York, 1839), I, 98.

I did not expect to find here in the capital of a new country, with the boundless forests within half a mile of us on almost every side, concentrated as it were, the worst evils of our old and most artificial social system at home, with none of its *agrémens*, and none of its advantages. Toronto is like a fourth or fifth rate provincial town with the pretensions of a capital city.

7

Social Classes in New Brunswick

From Abraham Gesner, *New Brunswick, with notes for emigrants* (London, 1847), 328.

The elements of the best society in St. John, Fredericton, and the smaller towns are very respectable: the principal officers of the Government mix freely, but unanimously, in the same circles. In the best classes, there is a due regard to politeness, courtesy and decorum. Persons of rank and some degree of eminence, are however, looked upon as forming a kind of aristocracy, which always maintains its superiority above the inferior orders, who eagerly aspire to the society they condemn as being unjustly exclusive. The medium ranks are generally stiff and ceremonious: yet their kindness is unalloyed by ostentation, and their hospitality, when bestowed, is extravagant.

There is a constant struggle between the aristocratic principle and the spirit of freedom and equality characteristic of the Americans. Persons who have risen from the lower ranks, and have arrived at affluence, are apt to overrate their importance; and such as have the advantages of birth and education are frequently supercilious. It is to be regretted that, from these causes, endless bickerings and jealousies arise, and society is divided into small circles and parties . . . .

From the declarations of a New Sporting writer it might be inferred that the ladies of St. John amuse themselves in winter by "riding down hill upon hand-sleds with the gentlemen". There might have been one or two of the above writer's acquaintances who would engage in that rustic sport: but during a residence of five years in that city, I never witnessed an instance of the kind and can affirm that the ladies of New Brunswick have as high a sense of decorum as those of the most refined societies in England.

(c)—THE OPENING OF THE INTERIOR:—ROAD-MAKING

Once the lands fringing the St. Lawrence and its chief tributaries had been taken up, the problem of getting into the interior presented itself. Heavy timber and copious rainfall made a combination very effective in preserving the inaccessibility of all districts not on some navigable water. Lower Canada had early worked out a system of road-making which served tolerably for the few miles of depth which the seigniories possessed and in the previous century had paralleled the St. Lawrence with a road from Quebec to Montreal, opened in 1736. But the wide expanse of Upper Canada was another matter. At an early period two arteries were driven through its longest stretches by General Simcoe, the great trunk roads, Dundas Street and Yonge Street and a little later the Talbot Road afforded another. For the smaller roads, one chain, sixty-six feet, was reserved in front of each location and the settler was supposed to clear half of this on securing his grant. Then the system of "statute labour" was established, by which each grantee had to spend a given number of days on road-work: he might commute his services for money. But the easy-going habits of pioneer communities as often as not turned the statute labour days into a kind of picnic and not very much was accomplished through them. One of the greatest obstacles presented itself in the clergy reserves. How could roads be made when a portion of every roadside was flanked by lots which probably would not be cleared for years?

In addition to local efforts, government undertook colonization roads to open up new tracts, a lifeless proceeding as long as the paternalism of pre-rebellion days existed. But even then the Canada Company did something for the north centre of the western district and after the Act of Union, self-government contributed much more. Unfortunately just as the making of these roads was well under way, the good land came to an end.

REFERENCES: See document 28, page 41; and A. R. M. Lower, "The assault on the Laurentian barrier" (*Canadian Historical Review*, December, 1929).

1

Pioneer Roads in the Niagara District

From La Rochefoucauld-Liancourt, *Travels in North America*, 224.

The roads from Fort Erie to Newark are tolerably open, and lie for the most part over a sandy ground, which renders it more easy to keep them in repair. The frequent passage to and fro, in this part of the country, does not destroy them.

2

Road-Making and the Clergy Reserves

From Canadian Archives, *Q*, CCCXII, 347.

Gore to Castlereagh

York, Upper Canada,
23rd December, 1809

My Lord,

. . . The utility of opening Communications in a Country so thinly peopled, and so widely extended as Upper Canada, has induced its Legislature, from time to time, out of its slender Revenue, to allot sums of money for that purpose, but the means have been found inadequate to the end: other measures were therefore thought of and adopted. Two great Roads have been made (or rather communications opened) vizt. Young and Dundas Streets, by means of granting Lots of Land, on each side of these Roads to Settlers, on condition that the Grantees of such Lots, should make and maintain the Road opposite to their respective settlements.

A plan similar to that of Young and Dundas Street, has been suggested by the Inhabitants, recommended by the Executive Council, and approved of by me for the Western District, and nothing prevents the commencement of that plan but an alteration of that Diagram mentioned in the accompanying Report, of the Crown and Clergy Reserves, for without an alteration of that Diagram by removing these Reserves from the Road, it is self-evident that no continued Line of communication can take place, for in a new Colony where Lands in Fee simple can so easily be obtained, it cannot be expected that Settlers on Lands in which they have only a Leasehold interest (as in the case of the Crown and Clergy Reserves) would be induced to open, and maintain a Road, opposite to their respective settlements:—On this account those Reserves were removed from Young and Dundas Streets. . . .

But there is a circumstance . . . to which I must take the liberty to request Your Lordships attention. This proposed Road is to pass through a very large Tract of Land, set apart by His Majesty's Commands as a fund for the erection and maintenance of Public Schools in Upper Canada.—That Tract at present, for want of communication with any other parts of the Province, is unfit for that or for any other purpose, and must remain in its present unproductive state without such communication for a period to which it is impossible to fix any limitation.

Your Lordship will allow me also to state that the Crown and Clergy Reserves will be highly benefitted by the plan proposed, for altho' they will not be in contact they will be in the vicinity of the Road, this will render them of considerable value—at present they are of none.

Francis Gore

3

The Manner of Providing for Roads in New Brunswick

From *Montreal Gazette*, October 27, 1828.

In New Brunswick the road system is under the superintendance of a board of 12 supervisors, resident in different portions of the Province. These supervisors lay before the Legislature their annual reports and accounts, and it is pleasant to observe the recommendations of the board cheerfully acquiesced in by the Legislature. Before a grant is made for a road, great care and attention seems to be given to the exploration of the routes in order that the best line, may be ascertained and definitely fixed. All roads upon which public money has been expended are by law declared public highways, and no warrants issued for the improvement of bye-roads, until it is certified by the Clerk of the Peace of the county where such roads are situated, that they have been actually laid by the Commissioners of highways, or legally recognised and used as such for three years. From all the sources of which we are in possession, we may fairly admit that roads of New Brunswick are, by a judicious management on the part of its legislature, little inferior to those of the Mother country.[1]

4

Construction of a Main Highway:—Yonge Street

From *Quebec Mercury*, November 1, 1831.

A Turnpike Road [*is projected*] on Yonge Street, on the following plan:

---

[1]The editor's wish was doubtless father to his thought.

"A Company to be chartered for the purpose of raising the necessary funds and constructing a permanently good road; the company to be repaid by tolls, and to be either limited in the amount of its profit, or be obliged to deliver up the road in thorough good repair at the end of a certain period, the road then becoming public property. The statute labour on this road to be commuted, and the money thus raised to be laid out on the side lines."

Yonge Street is the great northern road from York to Lake Simcoe, and is the direct communication with Lake Huron. The length of Yonge Street is about forty miles, and numerous new and flourishing townships have been laid out on each side of it, which are rapidly filling with emigrant settlers. The roads from these run into it.—To the inhabitants of these lands the advantage will be great, but when the importance of Yonge Street as a leading line of communication with the country and lakes above mentioned is considered, it does appear to us a rail road, might have been adventured.

5

Road-Making in Lower Canada:—Winter Roads

From T. C. Keefer, "Travel and transportation", in H. Y. Hind *et al* (eds.), *Eighty years' progress of British North America* (Toronto, 1863), 104.

The roads of the province of Quebec and of Lower Canada, until 1832, were placed under an officer appointed by the crown called a *grand voyer*, a sort of surveyor-general, who had deputies (*sousvoyers*) and surveyors under him. The roads were divided into three classes.

1. *Chemins royaux*—Post roads or "front" roads, the soil of which belonged to the crown; these generally traversed the "front" of the seigneuries.

2. *Chemins de ceinture et de traverse*—or back roads, the soil of which belonged to the seigneurs; these ran in the rear and parallel with the royal roads.

3. *Chemins de sortie et de communications*—called also "*routes*" and by-roads. These were cross-roads, connecting those in front and rear. Also banal roads, which were those leading to the seigneury mill.

All proprietors and holders (*seigneurs* and *censitaires*) were obliged to open, make, maintain and repair, as well in winter as in summer, their "front" roads across the land held by them. All bridges under four (or six) feet span were to be made by the occupant; but larger ones by the joint labor of the parties interested,— the timber being demanded from the nearest property. By joint labor, also, the cross or by-roads and mill-roads were made. In the case of the front roads, ownership or occupancy was considered a sufficient reason for making the unlucky holder construct and maintain the road; but in the case of side roads and others made by joint labor, this proprietorship exempted him from all other contributions, because he furnished the right of way. The *grand-voyer* made semi-annual inspections, and by *procès verbal*, if confirmed by the quarter-sessions, determined the dimensions, ditches, etc., and the *repartition* or appointment of labor on bridges and *routes*. . . . Winter roads in the climate of Lower Canada require special provisions, some of which are demanded by the absurd tenacity with which the *habitant* clings to a vicious system. Instead of profiting by the example of the township people beside him, he attaches the shafts of his *cariole*, *berline*, or *traineau*, the running gear of which is a low sledge, by a chain in such a manner that when the draught slackens the shafts fall on the snow. The runner likewise does not follow the horses' feet, so that the road is not beaten for two horses abreast,—and thus must forever remain an inferior or "one-horse" affair. The action of the loose shaft is similar to a horse-rake, and the snow is rolled into "winrows", giving the road a corrugated profile, forming what are called *cahots* by the French, and "cowholes" by the English; the crater between the opposite peaks being large enough to contain one of those animals. As a penance for thus destroying the roads, the law required the *habitant* to carry shovel, pick, and hoe, and to level the track behind him. It is also obligatory to have the track over ice or open country marked out by evergreen bushes called *balises*, so that the traveller may not lose his way. Besides the ordinary provisions for "breaking" the winter roads, it is required that on the 1st of December all fences along and abutting the roadside within twenty-five feet, be taken down within two feet of the ground, and kept down till the 1st of April, the posts only left standing; and, when required, *balises* are to be planted every thirty-six feet.

(d)—ASPECTS OF PIONEER AGRICULTURE

After settlement had been effected, the next task was to find some means by which the pioneer could transmute his labour not merely into a livelihood but into profit. In some countries, the exploitation of a readily marketable staple results in the rapid improvement of the technical methods of production. In the valley of the St. Lawrence no such agricultural staple was available and recourse had to be had to the invariable first crop of the pioneer in the north temperate zone, wheat. But the machinery for the cheap transport of wheat to Europe had yet to be built up, and, in any case, European demand was small. Consequently, improvement in technical methods was slow. The documents reflect this and also show the groping out for other staples such as hemp and tobacco, and towards other sources of income, animals and fruits. Perhaps their net effect is to illustrate the saying that in a new country, "the only good agriculture is bad agriculture", that is, that the only common-sense way of proceeding is by exploitation of the means of livelihood most ready to hand.

REFERENCES: R. F. Gourlay, *Statistical account of Upper Canada* (London, 1822); W. A. Langton, *Early days in Upper Canada* (Toronto, 1926); M. A. Garland, "Some frontier and American influences in Upper Canada prior to 1837" (*Transactions* of the London and Middlesex Historical Society, part XIII, 1929, 5).

1

Wasteful Methods of Pioneer Agriculture

From La Rochefoucault-Liancourt, *Travels in North America*, 281.

Although the number of cultivators is here greater than in the district of Niagara, yet the vast quantity of land under cultivation is not better managed than theirs. The difficulty of procuring labourers obstructs agricultural improvements, and encourages them to insist on enormous wages.

2

Primitive Ploughs of Loyalist Times

From H. Y. Hind, in *Eighty years' progress*, 40.

We find among the donations of George III to the U.E. Loyalists the old English plow. It consisted of a small piece of iron fixed to the colter, having the shape of the letter L, the shank of which went through the wooden beam, the foot forming the point which was sharpened for use. One handle and a plank split from a curved piece of timber, which did the duty of a mold board, completed the rude implement. At that time the traces and leading lines were made of the bark of the elm or bass-wood, which was manufactured by the early settlers into a strong rope. About the year 1808, the "hog-plow" was imported from the United States; and in 1815 a plow with a cast iron share and mold-board, all in one piece, was one of the first implements requiring more than ordinary degree of mechanical skill, which was manufactured in the province.

3

Frontier Agricultural Practices

From Howison, *Sketches of Upper Canada*, 37, 248.

Two fields were pointed out to me which had been cropped twenty one years in succession without receiving any manure whatever. . . . Indeed, were it not for the uncommon richness of the soil, which yields profusely almost without cultivation, the settlers could not obtain a subsistence from their farms until after many years occupation. In sowing wheat they use the small proportion of one bushel, and one bushel and a half, to the acre. In England, three are required. . . .

The Canadian farmers have no system in their agricultural operations, or in the management of their lands, and they prepare the soil for the reception of the seed very imperfectly. These circumstances are generally the result of ignorance but often arise from a want of capital.

4

Crops and Yields

From *Ibid.*, 246.

The soil of Upper Canada is in general excellent, and likewise of easy cultivation. Wheat is the grain that is raised in greatest quantity. A bushel and a half of seed are generally allowed for an acre, and the return averages from twenty-five to thirty-five bushels. Buck-wheat is also cultivated to a considerable extent, and an acre yields about fifteen bushels. Rye succeeds well, the crop being generally twenty bushels an acre. Oats are very indifferent and much inferior to those raised in Europe, being small and light in the grain, and comparatively not nutritious. An acre yields on an average from thirty to forty bushels. Barley is but little known in Upper Canada; however, it would appear that the seasons are rather too warm and dry to be favourable to its growth. Indian corn is much cultivated in the western parts of the Province, and yields largely, if it is not injured or destroyed by late frosts. Potatoes succeed well in most soils, but are much inferior in quality to those produced in Britain. Turnips also form a profitable crop, and are used to feed live stock during winter; but the vegetable best adapted for this purpose is the squash or gourd, which affords an abundant crop, is much liked by the cattle, and never communicates any unpleasant flavour to the milk of the cows, as turnips invariably do.

5

Making of Maple Sugar

From *Utica Almanac*, 1819, quoted in *A few plain directions*, 85.

To make Maple Sugar:—Make an incision in a number of maple trees, at the same time, in the months of February and March, and receive the juice of them in earthen or wooden vessels. Strain the juice (after it is drawn from its sediment) and boil it. Place the kettle directly over the fire in such a manner that the flames shall not play around its sides. When it is reduced to a thick syrup, and cooled, strain it again, and let it settle for two or three days; in which time it will be prepared for granulating. This operation is performed by filling the kettle half full of syrup, and boiling it a second time. To prevent its rising too suddenly, and boiling over, add to it a piece of fresh butter or fat, of the size of a walnut. You may easily determine whether it is sufficiently boiled to granulate, by cooling a little of it. It must then be put into bags, or baskets, through which the water will drain, so as to leave it in a solid form. This sugar, if refined by the usual process, may be made into as good single or double refined loaves, as ever were made of the sugar obtained from the juice of the West India cane.

Maple Molasses.—This may be made in three ways: First, from the thick syrup obtained by boiling it after it is strained for granulation: Secondly, from the drainings of the sugar: Thirdly, from the last drainings of the tree (which will not granulate) reduced by evaporating to the consistence of molasses.

6

Animals and their Products

From *Ibid.*, 64.

Most farmers feed from ten to thirty hogs every year, each weighing from twelve to eighteen stone, of fourteen pounds to the stone. The pork, which is equal to any fed in England, is packed in barrels (with salt), containing 200 pounds each, and in general sells for 4*d*. or 4½*d*. per pound. Salt here is bought for 4*s*. 6*d*. sterling a bushel. . . . Good milch cows are sold for from 5*l*. to 7*l*. sterling each. Oxen are in general used for draught. A yoke of good oxen (two) may be bought for 16*l*. sterling. Beef sells for 4*d*. a pound.

The sheep resemble the Norfolk breed in England, being rather tall, and frequently horned, with *darkish* legs and faces. A flock will average each about five pounds of wool, of a *fineish* quality; and it is commonly sold for 2*s*. 6*d*. sterling a pound. Almost every farmer keeps from 20 to 100 sheep; and as families here manufacture their own wearing apparel, blankets, &c. in a manner which does infinite credit to their ingenuity and industry, the wool is mostly consumed for those purposes. Mutton sells at 4*d*. and 5*d*. a pound.

The horses here are small, but spirited and extremely hardy. During the winter they are very much used in drawing sleighs; and, when on a journey, will travel with ease fifty miles a day. . . . A good horse will fetch from 16*l*. to 24*l*. sterling.

7

Fruit Growing in Upper Canada

From *Ibid.*, 90, 91.

The apple-tree thrives as well in this province as in any part of the world. The orchards seldom fail of producing an abundant crop, and the fruit is of an excellent quality. Great quantities of cyder are made; the price last year (1819) in the market at Kingston, by the barrel, was 9*d*. a gallon, including the cask.

Peaches are very plentiful on the borders of Lake Erie; they are sent from those districts to the lower parts of the province, and were sold last year at Kingston for 3*d*. a dozen.

[*Domestic molasses*]

Molasses of a very good quality are made by boiling the pumpkins; and this useful article of domestic consumption is manufactured at no expense, and with so little trouble or difficulty, that there are but few families who do not make considerable quantities of it every year.   Beer and a good preserve are also made from pumpkins.

8

Good Qualities of Upper Canadian Wheat

From *Montreal Gazette*, April 15, 1830.

Upper Canada Wheat, which was in demand the 1st of October last at 6*s*. 3*d*., gradually advanced until it reached 7*s*. 3*d*. the 60 lbs. and at these prices it was shipped to England, and, as we learn, paid very well, and it cannot but be gratifying to the Upper Canada farmers to know the high opinion formed of their Wheat in the English Market, as exemplified in the extract of a letter just received by us from Liverpool, of the 1st February, 1830:—"The Upper Canada Wheat that has come here by the late ships is beautiful, and sales of it have been made as high as 10*s*. 6*d*. Sterling 70 lbs. which is higher by much than any other description of Wheat will bring in our Market."—Horatio Gates and Co., Commercial Circular.

9

Canadian Dependence on the United States for Pork

From *Kingston Herald*, quoted in *Montreal Gazette*, June 4, 1830.

Among the anomalies of trade this season may be mentioned, the transportation last week of pork from Kingston to Port Hope and Niagara.   In the last mentioned place the merchants were entirely destitute of the article, until they were supplied from Kingston.   This state of things, when the richest farming districts of Upper Canada derive a large part of their supplies of pork and beef from the States, gives another proof of the infatuation of our Assembly when they voted to tax American produce imported into this country.   Had they confined their measure to the imposition of a duty on American wheat and flour, when imported into Upper Canada for *home consumption*, the plan would have received but little opposition; for only few persons would have been unwilling to pay a little extra for those two articles, in order to protect our farmers in those things with which they do supply the country. But when the proposed duty was extended to beef, pork and mutton of which Canada does not raise half enough to supply its own wants, and was also made to include all articles which were only passing through the Province for exportation, thus giving the carrying trade entirely to the Americans, every principle of patriotism and sound policy dictated the rejection of such an absurd measure.

10

The Search for a Staple for Upper Canada:—Hemp and Tobacco

From *Montreal Gazette*, July 6, 1832.

Hemp is an article for which the climate and soil of the Canadas are quite congenial: it used to be cultivated a good deal in Upper Canada; and for some years a Captain Mills, of Amherstburgh was in the habit of purchasing it from the farmers, thereby encouraging its culture. At that period our craft on the lakes were supplied with it. A sample was sent to England, and we understand was declared equal to any from Russia. . . .

Hemp may be grown in either Province; but there is another article namely, *Tobacco*, for which Upper Canada is very well suited, and which if carefully attended to, would be of great consequence. A gentleman is now in this town, and has for sale a considerable quantity of tobacco grown in the Western District. . . . The quality of the tobacco grown in that part of Canada has been pronounced to be already nearly equal to the American, and it may fairly be expected that when the culture becomes more general and from its profitable returns, more carefully attended to, it will equal the Virginia. That whole tract of country between Lakes Erie and Huron, is from soil and climate perfectly adapted for the best kind of this article; and a more profitable to the farmer could not be grown. Well attended to, one thousand pounds weight of clean tobacco would be the produce of an acre, which at a price even somewhat less than that of the Virginia, would net at Montreal about £18.

11

Whisky as an Asset to the Canadian Farmer

From *Montreal Gazette*, July 29, 1834.

To the Editor of the Montreal Gazette:

Sir.—Being much interested in the agriculture of the Canadas, particularly of the Lower Provinces. . . . I have observed with pleasure the desire some of my fellow countrymen have manifested of promoting, extending and improving agriculture by pointing out the best method by which the soil may be treated, so as to produce large crops without exhaustion. . . . Much has been said on these subjects . . . but there is one point all appear to have overlooked, viz. the finding a home consumption for our surplus production, particularly the coarser kinds of grain. We are entirely an agriculture country, and our prosperity depends thereon, as is strongly exemplified at the present moment from the depressed state of trade, caused . . . from the bad crops of the three past years, and affected also by the low prices for grain in England during the past and current years . . . making it desirable, if possible, that we should be less dependent upon foreign aid, and try . . . by a rotation of cropping to increase our production and create a home demand. . . .

It is not more than ten or twelve years since the quantity of barley grown, as also oats, compared with what is now produced in the Province, was not one half; and in place of these articles having declined in price from increased production, they have advanced, as previous to the above stated time barley never was higher than 1*s*. 8*d*. to 2*s*. per minot and since then for an average of years, not less than 2*s*. 9*d*. to 3*s*. Oats have also experienced the same advance, and are seldom now below 1*s*. 3*d*. to 1*s*. 6*d*. and frequently higher, when, formerly, they were often at 7½*d*. and never above 1*s*. This alone has been caused by the great increased demand from the Distilleries; therefore, why not give greater encouragement to these manufactories? Did our agricultural population, mechanics and labourers consume whiskey of home manufacture, in place of rum and other imported spirits, the great sum of money now sent out of the country to pay for foreign spirits would be kept in it, and would result in an actual saving to the amount so paid. It may be replied that for the rums and other West India produce consumed in the country, there is an equivalent taken out in provisions and lumber; this I admit to a certain extent, but far from the full value and besides, does little or no good to the Lower Provinces where the greater proportion of the rum is consumed. . . .

It is therefore high time that the population of Lower Canada should look to their own interest, and give encouragement to the use of a home manufactured spirit, in preference to an imported one. The quality of the whiskey manufactured in the Province is generally excellent, exceeding in quality that usually made in Great Britain. . . .

12

The Mechanization of Agriculture:—The "Harvesting Machine"

From *Christian Guardian*, quoted in *Montreal Gazette*, October 13, 1835.

We understand that a Mr. S. Williams in the Township of Whitby, has invented what he calls "a harvesting machine, which gathers, threshes and rough-cleans wheat, barley, &c. at the rate of a bushel in three minutes." The machine may be worked by horse or steam power.

13

French-Canadian Agricultural Practices

From H. Y. Hind in, *Eighty years' progress*, 34.

We do not require to go far back into the history of that part of the province to find husbandry in all its branches in a very primitive condition. Thirty years ago [*1839*], rotation of crops was wholly unknown, and no rules of art were practiced by the happy, light-hearted French Canadian, who with rigid steps pursued the systems handed down to him by his ancestors, and strictly adhered to usages which generations had sanctioned. In addition to the entire absence of rotation of crops, the practice of carting manure on to the ice of a neighboring river, in order that it might be washed away in the spring, was generally practiced, and even now prevails to a considerable extent. Barns were removed when the accumulations before the door impeded entrance or exit, and the old primitive forms of plows, harrows and all other farming implements and vehicles, were retained, with a wholesome horror of innovation in form or material. Nor need we travel far to find them still flourishing in all their original imperfections and want of adaptation to the end in view.

14

"Wheat Mining" in the Canadas

From *Ibid*, 53.

Until recently, with few exceptions, wheat has been cultivated without regard to rotation of crops, both in Upper and Lower Canada. Several reasons have led to this very improvident system of farming practice, independently of a general want of knowledge regarding the first principles of husbandry. For a long time wheat was the only product of the farm upon which reliance could be placed as a means of obtaining ready money. Wheat has always been a cash article; other farm products have often sought a market in vain, and were consequently given by the farmer in barter or exchange for many of the necessaries he required. Since the construction of railways, things have changed; a market has been found for almost every production of the farm, and with a more general spread of agricultural knowledge, a better farming practice has been established, and the value of rotation of crops acknowledged. Both in Upper and Lower Canada, vast areas of most fertile land have been rendered absolutely unproductive by continual wheat cropping. Portions of the valley of the Richelieu in Lower Canada and of the Thames in Upper Canada afford striking proofs of this deterioration in the fruitfulness of the soil. Forty bushels to the acre was by no means an uncommon yield when the land was first cleared of its forest, as it now is in the valley of the Saugeen and Maitland. Rest for a few years, or deep plowing, restores the soil nearly to its original fertility, and where the last artifice is adopted, even on what are called worn-out farms, it is found that fair and sometimes excellent crops can be obtained. This is particularly the case in Lower Canada, where for centuries the soil has been merely skimmed, and the cultivation of wheat abandoned on account of the wretched yield obtained. By deep plowing these "worn-out lands" have been restored and there is no doubt that the same artifice, if thoroughly carried out would bring many a wheat field of by-gone celebrity back to its original productiveness, if a judicious rotation of crops were adopted.

(e)—PUBLIC LAND POLICY

In all unoccupied countries the land has been considered a potential source of public revenue. It was not until the second half of the nineteenth century with the adoption of the homestead system that this view gave way completely to the objective of settlement. Few countries have had a clear-cut and consistent policy in the alienation of their public lands (the United States being a partial exception) but most have allowed them to be seized by those who have had the opportunity. In the Canadas, while the revenue from land was looked upon by the provincial oligarchies as a means of escaping from the control of democratic assemblies, yet the most reckless alienation took place in favour of those who had the *entrée* to the right circles. Poor individuals, it is true, could obtain free grants of small amounts, it being expected that the loss of revenue would be more than made up by the unearned increment of the crown and clergy reserves, but these were cluttered up with the red tape of officialdom and in the result nothing so impeded the progress of the Canadas as the uncertainties of title to land. Here again, as in the case of the colonization roads, it was not until nearly all the land was gone that self-government brought an approach to an orderly system out of the previous confusion. There is no sadder or more hopeless story than the utter confusion, lack of policy, and dishonesty characterizing the granting of the lands of the Canadas in the period before the rebellions.

REFERENCES: G. C. Paterson, *Land settlement in Upper Canada, 1783-1840* (Ontario Archives report for 1920); Sir C. P. Lucas, *Lord Durham's report on the affairs of British North America* (3 volumes, Oxford, 1912); Edward Gibbon Wakefield, *A view of the art of colonization* (London, 1849, reprinted Oxford, 1914); Camille Bertrand, "Concessions des terres du Bas-Canada, 1796-1840" (Canadian Historical Society, *Annual report*, 1928, 73); A. H. G. Macdonald, "Clergy reserves in Canada to 1828" (M.A. thesis, University of Toronto, 1925).

1

The Seigniorial System of Granting Land

(i)

The absurdities of feudal subdivision

From H. Y. Hind, in *Eighty years' progress*, 33.

There can be no doubt that the wretched mode of subdividing land and laying out farms which formerly prevailed in Lower Canada, has been instrumental in retarding the progress of husbandry in that part of the province. Very generally the farms in the old settled parts originally consisted of narrow strips whose lengths and breadths were in the ratio of ten to one; three arpents wide by thirty arpents in depth being the form of the long rectangle exhibited by a French Canadian farm when first surveyed. This is the same as if the farms were 200 yards broad by 2,000 yards long. . . . With the increase of population, and the love for the paternal roof, which distinguishes the *habitans* of Lower Canada, their farms have been again subdivided longitudinally, sometimes into three parts, or one arpent in breadth by thirty in depth, or in the proportion of 66⅔ yards broad to 2,000 long; and in the older seigneuries the ratio of breadth to length is not unfrequently as one is to sixty or 33⅓ yards broad to 2,000 yards long. These are some of the heirlooms of the old feudal system which sat like a huge incubus on Lower Canada, and whose depressing influence will long leave its mark on the energies and character of its people.

(ii)

Sources of revenue in a seigniory

From Bigsby, *The shoe and the canoe*, I, 49.

The revenues of a Canadian seigniory are derived from several sources. There is a rent of a dollar a-year from every tenement having a fire-place; a considerable fine upon every transfer of the numerous small tenancies, or rather properties; and the profits of the seigniorial flour mill—the law compelling all the habitans to grind their corn there. There are other dues of less importance. A satisfactory interest is derived from the usual amount of purchase-money laid out upon an estate of this kind.

2

Method of Apportioning and Laying out the Clergy Reserves

From Canadian Archives, *Q*, LX, 214.

Grenville to Clarke

Whitehall 8th November, 1792

Upon examination of the inclosures contained in your Letter N° 42. I am clearly of opinion that the plan for the Allocation of the Lands to be reserved for the Crown and the Clergy, as stated in the Report of the Surveyor General, adopted by the Land Committee, is contrary to the tenor and intent of the late Act, and to your Instructions grounded thereon. Such an Allottment as is there proposed for those reserves (especially in Townships bordering on the Water) would be highly unfavorable to the Crown, and the Clergy, and would place the Shares so to be reserved and allotted in a situation of less relative benefit than the Lands of equal extent granted to individuals.[1]

With respect to what is said of the expence of separate allottments in respect of each grant, this expence would certainly be considerable if the Surveyor was obliged in the several Townships actually to survey and mark out each Lot and each reservation of two-seventh parts in respect thereof, as supposed by the above Report.

I apprehend that such future increase of value as may be in some degree proportionate to the increasing value of the Lots granted to Individuals can not otherwise be effectually provided for except by their being as much as possible contiguous to and interspersed with all the different allotments of Individual property. . . .

But there appears no necessity for deviating on this occasion from what is understood to be the practice now with respect to private Lots, and if the Geometrical situation and extent of the reserve is ascertained on the Map in the same manner as those of the Grant, in respect whereof it is made, the Grantee knowing both the quantum and situation of such reservation, as well as of his Grant, incloses the residue at his own risque and expence, as at present, but with as much certainty as if there was no reservation at all. The size of the Lots may be determined with this particular view—each containing two seventh parts (the amount of the reservation) more than it otherwise would.

The question then to be determined would be in what part of every Lot the reservation should be made? Whether according to one uniform System, by adopting in all cases the rule of drawing the Boundaries of the reserve by Parallellograms of which the lines which run from North to South shall be the longest, or by any other similar fixed rule, or by occasional variations in this

---

[1]The Constitutional Act provided that the clergy reserves must be of like quality to the lands granted to individuals.

respect, guided however by an uniform principle operating according to known differences of circumstances and situation.

The decision of this question must at least in the first instance be left for local consideration, but I have the King's Commands to instruct you not to consent to any System even provisionally, which does not carefully keep in view the general idea of rendering the reserves as beneficial as was intended by the Act.

And particularly you are expressly enjoined to take care that in such Townships as border upon the Water, the reserved Lands shall be so situated as to enjoy their full proportion of that advantage according to the relative quantities of the private Grants, and the reserves established by the Act.

Grenville

3

The System of Township Leaders

From Canadian Archives, *Q*, LXV, 319.

Henry Dundas to Dorchester

Whitehall, 2, Oct. 1793

My Lord..
... The first [*point*] is what may be the quantity of Crown Land which His Majesty's Governor is authorized to grant under his Instructions in that behalf. ...

The exertions of a single & unassisted individual are unequal to the cultivation of more than 200 acres or even so much, but His Majesty's Governor for the time being will always exercise his discretion for the interest of His Sovereign and of the Province, and will of course extend the Grant in favour of a more substantial or of a meritorious Person.

I agree with the report of the Council of the 17th of March, in opinion that it must be principally by leaders and their associates that the vacant Lands of the Crown are to be settled. The Application of the Instructions must be governed by the Circumstances of the Cases which present themselves, in doing which some general Principle will of course be attended to as much as possible.

It is clear that not more than 1200 acres can be granted to any Individual. The Leader of an associated Company must certainly receive out of the Shares of his Associates, such a quantity of Land as may be a reasonable Compensation for the Money he advances to put them in possession. This is a matter of agreement between the Parties but the question for the Consideration of His Majesty's Government in the Province is this. To a Leader or principal with how many associates shall a township (excepting the reservations for the Crown and Church) be granted? and so, in less proportion than a Township? to answer this, is only duly to consider what number of acres in the particular Township petitioned for, would be an adequate compensation to the Leader for the expence of the Fees of the Grant and of superintending and fixing his Associates, because that number (including 1200 to be granted to himself) is precisely what the Associates would be enabled to make up to him out of their several Shares leaving themselves 200 each. The greater the number of Associates required, so as to leave all reasonable encouragement to the principal or Leader, the better it will be for the Province. . . .

Henry Dundas

4

Confusion in the Land Office:—Loss of Good Settlers from the United States

From Canadian Archives, Q, LXXIX, part 1, 154.

Prescott to Portland

Quebec 24th June 1797

My Lord

. . . Previously to my taking upon me this government, more than a Thousand Petitions had been recommended by the Committee of Council (called the Land Committee) and but *one* grant had been completed.

The vast accumulation of Petitions that has been suffered to take place without any final decision being made upon them, has given rise to Difficulties which appear to me almost insurmountable. The number of Petitions is from Twelve to Thirteen hundred; but they comprehend Applications from upwards of Ten thousand Persons, a great Majority of whom, it may be remarked, are to the lower orders of the People.

Great numbers have persevered from the first issuing of the Proclamation by General Clarke in the year 1792, & some of them have expended large sums in making improvements under the expectation of obtaining regular grants; Many have sold Lands under the Warrants of Survey which were then issued, but which were not followed up by Patents; and many, I am sorry to add, after having sold their property in the United States, with a view of settling on the Waste Lands in this Province have returned back, disgusted and ruined by the delay which they met in the course of their Applications. This class of people are represented as being chiefly Men of Property, good Farmers, and of tried loyal Principles; it is supposed the Numbers of them would return on a certain prospect of succeeding in their object.

Robt Prescott

5

Failure of the System of Township Leaders in Upper Canada

From Canadian Archives, _Q_, CCXCV, 144.

Percy, 1st July 1799

The Board took into consideration, the Reports made by Mr Jones, on the State of the Townships of Hope, Haldimand, Hamilton, Cramahe and Percy, together with the Counter Reports of Mr Rogers, Mr Greeley &c. In perusing these Reports, & Counter Reports, the Board meets with hardly anything but additional proofs of the fraud, duplicity, & unprincipled selfishness of the original Nominees of those Townships, who undertook to settle them with new Inhabitants, but appear to have brought into them, persons already settled in the Province; and in many instances have only borrowed their names. The Board therefore earnestly Recommends, that the Order of the President and Council, by which the Returns of the persons said to be settled in those Townships are confirmed, be suspended, and that no Warrants issue for any of those Lots until the 1st July 1800, at which time if an improvement of a House and five Acres be made, a Warrant shall issue to the person equitably entitled thereto, which warrant must be taken out within three Months from that date, or the Lot will be declared open. Those who have already exceeded that quantity, and are settled on the Lots may have their Warrants immediately.

Confirmed. P.R^I

---

[1]_Peter Russell_, president and administrator of Upper Canada, 1796-99.

6

Frauds by United Empire Loyalists in Securing Grants

From Canadian Archives, *Q*, CCXCV, 213.

29 October 1799

The Board having reason to believe that very frequent frauds have been committed by persons who are entitled to Land free of expence having asked for, and received the same two or three times over. Ordered, that hereafter no Petition be received from any person claiming as a U:E: or child of U:E: unless the same be signed by the Petitioner in the presence of a Magistrate and be accompanied by an affidavit by the Petitioner, stating that he, or she, is of the age of twenty-one years, or upwards, or married, if a female, and that he, or she, has never received any Lands from the Crown, and also by a Certificate from the same Magistrate, that the Petitioner is the person, he or she, describes himself, or herself, to be, and that he, or she, never has to the knowledge and belief of the Magistrate ever received Lands, or any Order for Lands from the Crown.

7

Governor Hunter's Efforts to Hasten Officialdom in Preparing Deeds

From Canadian Archives, *Q*, CCXCVI, 106.

The Lieutenant Governor's Office,
York 6th June 1801

Orders for the Land Granting Department.

It being highly essential, that the Deeds for Land should issue without further delay, every exertion possible must be made in, and every aid given by those concerned in passing the Patents to the Secretary's Office.

It is therefore the Lieutenant Governor's Orders, that the Clerks which are paid by Government in the Surveyor General's Office, and in the Council Office, be employed for this purpose, so as not to prevent their assistance to their respective principals. The Secretary will therefore send to each of the said Offices early in every Monday morning, for each of the four Clerks therein, eighteen Descriptions with the necessary Parchment, which Deeds are to be carefully engrossed, and sent to the Attorney General every Saturday Evening, with the necessary Papers, in the usual way, for Examination. With this Assistance added to what the Lieutenant Governor expects, will be going on at the same time, in the Secretary's Office, much is expected, for much can be done—And the Lieut. Governor means it to be understood, that the opening given him by His Grace The Duke of Portland, in regard to the Application for encreasing the Clerks Salarys, will be attended to in proportion to the diligence and correctness with which they discharge this part of their duty, in the Land granting Department for it is declared and expected that the Clerks paid by Government, in all cases do give the whole of their time to their respective Offices, and attend to their duty in the afternoon as well as in the forenoon. The present Arrear of business in the Land Granting Department requires a steady compliance to this Order, and the principals in the Office of the Surveyor General, and of the Clerk of the Council, will be responsible that the duty of the Clerks be faithfully and carefully discharged. . . .

The Magnitude of the object intended to be effected by these Orders, superceding every other consideration. The Lieutenant Governor expects that the Heads of Departments, as well as their Deputies or Clerks, will pay the most chearful obedience in the execution thereof, as he is determined that all private convenience shall give way to the Public Service, and that the duty of the Land granting Officers shall be rigidly discharged under the present shamefull arrear of Business.

By Order of the Lieutenant Governor
James Green, Sec^y

8

Rules for Free Grants of Land in Upper Canada

From *Upper Canada Gazette*, quoted in *Montreal Gazette*, July 14, 1819.

Lieutenant-Governor's Office [York],
April 26, 1819

D. M'Gregor Rogers, Esquire,
Chairman of the Land Board, Newcastle District.
Sir:—

In the first place,—With regard to such other persons besides emigrants, as the Board may be authorised to grant locations to, I am to explain to you, that by such "other persons," are to be understood such able settlers as resided in the District before the war, and produce due certificates of having done their duty in its defence.

Secondly,—With regard to military claimants. No military claimant, as such, is referred to the Board—being to receive their lands gratuitously in the military settlement, any dispensation of that sort must be approved on application to the Lieutenant Governor in Council.

Thirdly,—The sons and daughters of U. E. Loyalists being entitled to gratuitous grants of 200 acres, must apply to the Lieutenant Governor in Council.

Fourthly,—Persons arriving from the United States, and bringing due certificates of their being British born subjects are admissable by the Board.

Fifthly,—A form of Ticket of Location, will be transmitted to the Chairman of the Board, in which will be specified the conditions of settlement. . . .

Seventhly,—The settler should be thoroughly instructed that in the event of his finding any improvement on the Lot to which he may be located, he is immediately to return with his Ticket of Location to the Board, and report the circumstance for the information of the Government. Should he fail in this particular, he can expect no confirmation of the Grant to him. In this case the Board will appoint him another Location.

Eighthly,—With regard to the difficulty that may be experienced by the settler in finding his particular Lot, his Excellency bids me observe, that in order to remunerate the person who might be employed to point it out to him, the settler must be burthened with another fee; and as in the case of persons located by the Surveyor General's Office no such precaution is practised, his Excellency does not perceive the necessity of the regulation. I am, &c.

G. Hillier

Form of Location Ticket.

Land Board,   District.—A. B. born
at (*place*) in (*county*) of the age of   years
having arrived in this Province (*date*) and petitioned to become a

settler therein, has been examined by us, and we being satisfied with his character, and of the propriety of admitting him to become a settler, and having administered to him the oath of allegiance, do assign to him one hundred acres of land, being the

half of Lot No.   in the   Concession of (*Township*) in (*District*) for which, upon due proof of having cleared and cropped five acres, and cleared half the road in front of his land, of having erected and inhabited a house thereon for one year, he shall be entitled to receive a grant to him and his heirs, he paying the Patent Fee of £5. 14. 1 sterling.

N.B. If the settlement duty is not performed within two years, this Location to be of no value, but assigned to another settler.

9

Obstacles to Settlement Imposed by the Crown and Clergy Reserves

From *Montreal Gazette*, January 10, 1824.

House of Assembly, 30th December, 1823

The Honble. Mr. Papineau, after the second reading of the Bill from the Legislative Council providing for the making of roads on the Crown and Clergy Reserves, observed that if this House had lost all hopes of ever seeing a remedy for the evils resulting from the interspersion of these Reserves among the lots granted for actual settlement it would perhaps be well to adopt the provisions of the bill, as affording some palliative for these evils. For his part he was of opinion that while this evil continued, it was needless to talk about a settlement of the Country. These reserves offered an insuperable obstacle. Those who chose that plan had no idea of the difficulties of a first settlement where the utmost efforts of every one were not more than sufficient to do the share of labour upon the land in his own occupation.

He felt no objection to the free and Common Soccage Tenure; but with these reserves it was incomparably more unfavourable to the actual settler than the seigneurial tenure. . . . Hitherto the vacant seigneurial lands have been sufficient for the new settlements indispensable to our own increasing population. Seigneurial

land in situations fit for cultivation is now nearly all taken up,—
He trusted that the immense tracts of cultivable lands still unsettled in this Province would not always continue to be made
unfit for settlement by Legislative provision. It could not continue—all ought to unite in obtaining as speedy a remedy as
possible, and the repeal of the Clause of the Act Thirty-first
George Third was the only effectual one. It shewed lamentable
ignorance of the country, to have imagined that a Revenue would
ever be derived from the Reserves. While the immense Continent
of North America was, comparatively speaking, still a wilderness,
calling only for the labour of man to make it productive, it was
impossible that any labourer could be found, or indeed would be
able to pay rent, for unimproved land. . . .

10

Failure of the Tax on Wild Lands in Upper Canada

From "A Correspondent" in the *Quebec Mercury*, quoted in *Montreal Gazette*,
March 19, 1833.

The Report of the Upper Canada Assembly on the Tax on
Wild Lands, which you publish in your last paper, seems to shew
that the Legislature of that Province is inclined to adopt an
opinion which has gained ground there during the last two years,
that the tax in question is working very different, and indeed
opposite, effects to what it was intended to produce; as a means
of raising a fund for roads it is absolutely insignificant;—a sum
little more than £12,000 has been raised in nine districts of that
extensive territory, by the sacrifice of 500,000 acres of land, giving
a proportion of about £1220 only for each district, for a period of
eight years; for though those sales may be repeated from year to
year, they must be (for obvious reasons) to a much more limited
extent in future, and decrease in amount every year. Proprietors
will either now pay up their arrears or allow only the refuse lots
to be sold for non-payment. And as the lands cannot be sold
until they are eight years in arrear, the owners will save themselves
by keeping always a year or two within that period. . . .

It is alleged, however, in Upper Canada, and the fact is pretty
well sustantiated by the returns laid before the Legislature, that
this tax, besides being inefficient, has in another way produced
unexpected mischief. It was looked to as a means of compelling

land monopolists to cultivate their lands or dispose of them. Its operation has been to take them from one set of monopolists and throw them into the hands of another; and this by process of law which there is no checking or alleviating. In almost all the districts the lands thus sold have been purchased up by speculators and capitalists, whose names appear in the returns and must be well known to those who are at all acquainted with men and things in that province. In one district alone I find the name of one gentleman set down for 20,000 acres, another for 11,000, another for 2000, and so on. In all the others the same thing may be perceived to have occurred in different degrees. The speculator who purchases at these sales knows that he may keep them for eight years without paying any tax, before they can be forfeited and sold for the arrears, and he cannot employ his spare capital in any more profitable way than in buying for 4d. per acre land which he may hold up the next day at 5s. an acre, and for which in the course of eight years he has every chance of getting 10s., if that Province advances in population and prosperity as it has done of late.

The operation of the measure in question is a subject of considerable interest and importance in this Province at the present moment, when some of the good people in our Townships, misled in many instances by exaggerated notions of the utility of the measure in the Sister Province and adopting the ideas of persons who are ready to grasp at the gains that land speculators have made there by such forced sales, are recommending a similar measure to our Provincial Legislature, under the flattering idea, that it will supply an inexhaustible fund for roads and bridges, and compel large landholders to settle their lands.

11

Remaining Opportunities for Settlement in Lower Canada: —Merits of Feudal Tenure and of Freehold

From "A Correspondent" in the *Quebec Gazette*, quoted in *Montreal Gazette*, October 10, 1833.

The quantity of unoccupied land in Lower Canada is still very great. The best lands, lying along the St. Lawrence and its tributaries, are, however, occupied or held in second hands in a state of wilderness. The only very extensive tracts of wild land, fit for immediate settlement, still held by the Crown, are 1. North of the St. Lawrence, between the St. Maurice and the Ottawa; 2. South of the St. Lawrence towards the head waters of the St. Francis, the Nicolet, and the Chaudière; 3. On the Peninsula formed by the Ristigouche and the St. Lawrence. The Saguenay waters an extent of cultivable land; but that part of the country is still held under lease as hunting ground. Generally, the wild lands nearest to the settlements are monopolized, as grants *en seigneurie* under the French Government, or as grants in free and common soccage under the British Crown. In both descriptions of grants, the conditions are, in many instances, avoided by the holders: by the Seigneurs, in refusing to grant for actual settlement, or exacting unwarrantable dues and conditions; and by the holders in soccage, by neglect of settlement on each lot of two hundred acres.

The neglect of the Government and the Legislature to enforce the fulfilment of the conditions of the grants under which these lands are held in a state of wilderness, is the principal source of the discontents which prevail on the subject of unoccupied wild lands. It enables the holders to impose a monopoly price and conditions on the persons wishing to settle on them. Much of the outcry proceeds from those who have no intention to settle on the land, but wish to get more of the waste lands still held by the Crown into their own hands with a view of profiting at the expense of the actual settler, by the species of monopoly of wild lands which prevails. Experience shews that both the French and English grants can be subservient to these views and the abuses connected with them. . . .

With the fulfilment of the condition of settlement and cultivation it matters very little whether land is held *à titre de fief*, as by the French grants, or in free and common soccage; whether it is granted or sold, provided the sale is only resorted to in order to determine the preference among the competitors. If the holder of the grant *en fief* put settlers on every cultivable lot of it, and does not retard the settlement by demands or conditions exceeding those understood at the time the grant was made and accepted; or if the holder in soccage has a settler on every lot of 200 acres in a reasonable time, the result must be similar. Every person willing to settle on and cultivate these lands, will have every reasonable facility of occupying and holding suitable proportions of land, with the guarantee of the public authority that he will not be disturbed by others, but enjoy the fruit of his labour in safety. The introduction of a new tenure of land in this Province was an unnecessary innovation on what had been established during a century and a half. It was still worse to introduce a new system of laws affecting landed property, and making these laws a consequence of the tenure. The attempt to establish, as a consequence of free and common soccage, the *feudal* right of primogeniture, which has been banished by the strongest of all laws,—the results of the natural state of things in America,—can only be accounted for by the usual aberrations of ignorance and prejudice. These innovations are not, and ought not to be, a necessary consequence of either tenure.

The settlement of between four and five thousand old country people on seignorial lands north of Quebec, is sufficient proof that no innovation was necessary to induce them to settle on wild lands in Lower Canada; while these innovations are certainly of a nature to deter the descendants of the early settler from occupying free and common soccage lands.

12

Corruption in Granting Land:—The Case of Hon. W. B. Felton[1]

(i)

The case against Mr. Felton

From *Montreal Gazette*, January 23, 1836.

We shall endeavour at present to redeem our promise of giving such portions of the correspondence and documents sent down to the Assembly by Lord Gosford, respecting the lands granted to the Hon. W. B. Felton and his family, as seem to have any relation to the charges now brought against him (by the Assembly) for having improperly obtained grants much beyond the gracious intentions of His Majesty's Government.

Lord Bathurst, in 1815, authorised Sir Gordon Drummond to grant to Mr. Felton 2000 acres and to some other portions of

---

[1]The portions of this document omitted are extracts from the despatches which merely expand the synopsis given by the editor of the *Gazette*.

his family, other 2000 acres, upon the assurance that it was their intention to employ a capital of £2000 upon its improvement. . . .

Mr. Felton and his associates arrived in August, 1815, and do not appear to have been fully satisfied with the grant thus authorised, having been led to expect one somewhat more extensive, and reference was had to the Colonial Government respecting the terms on which they directed their attention to Canada. Lord Bathurst in reply, states that he cannot sanction any further grant until that already made shall be so far advanced in cultivation as to authorise such an addition.

In December, 1816, Lord Bathurst in addressing Sir John Sherbrooke, stated that he had received assurances that the conditions of the prior grant had been fulfilled by Mr. Felton and his associates, and directing His Excellency, if the land—"Should be in the advanced state of cultivation represented in the enclosed letter, that you will make them a further allotment of land, as nearly adjoining their present location as circumstances will admit, to the amount of *three thousand* acres to Mr. Felton and *seven hundred* acres to each of his associates, and that you will also assign to such of their labourers as may be desirous of becoming settlers on their own account, one hundred acres to each, in the same neighbourhood, under the usual conditions of residence and cultivation".

Lord Dalhousie, in September, 1822, forwarded to Lord Bathurst another application from Mr. Felton, for an additional grant, (of 5000 acres). . . . Lord Dalhousie, in forwarding the petition, recommended a grant of 5000 acres, which was approved of by Lord Bathurst, in his despatch of the 29th November, 1822. In April 1826, Mr. Felton again addressed Lord Bathurst, praying for a still further grant. . . . To this application, Lord Bathurst acquaints the Earl of Dalhousie—"That under the circumstances stated by Mr. Felton, and as the extensive improvements which he has made give him strong claims to my favourable consideration, I have to authorise your Lordship to make an additional grant not exceeding five thousand acres, with the usual reservations for his children and labourers."

On the 8th May, 1829, Mr. Felton applied for patents for 5000 acres of land for himself, and, 1,200 for each of his children, and enclosed a schedule of the particulars of the required grant, and subsequently to the foregoing, furnished a statement of between thirty and forty precedents, showing that the usual extent of grants to children, had been 1,200 acres each.

On the 2d. March, 1829, the Executive Council reported in favour of the grant of 5,013 acres to Mr. Felton, and on the 9th March, reference was made to the Attorney General to prepare a draft of patents for 5,013 acres according to the tenor of the Report, but no authority appears to have been given to include the grants to Mr. Felton's children, in consequence, it is presumed, of Sir James Kempt having determined upon communicating with Sir George Murray for future instructions on the subject.

Sir James Kempt appears to have been somewhat startled at a demand for 1,200 acres to each of Mr. Felton's children, then nine in number, for in addressing Sir George Murray on this subject, he says in reference to Lord Bathurst's despatch of the 3d, July, 1826. . . .

"I conceive that the despatch above alluded to sufficiently authorises the grant of 5,000 acres to Mr. Felton, but as it can scarcely be inferred from the terms "with the usual reservations for children and labourers", that it was the intention to confer a grant to such an extent upon his children, I have informed him that I could not give it without a special authority from you.

"The usual allowance to an ordinary settler, when lands were granted, has been 100 or at most 200 acres, and 1,200 is the utmost extent which the Governor is authorized, by his instructions, to grant to any one individual. Mr. Felton states that his object in settling in this country was to obtain lands and form an estate for his family, and that to accomplish this, he has already expended a very large sum of money, but as besides this grant of 5,000 acres he has already on two former occasions received altogether land to the extent of 5,541 acres, and as the present application for his children amounts to 10,800 more, I feel that I could not, without the express sanction of His Majesty's government, grant so large a quantity of land to any one family, and I therefore request that you will be pleased to inform whether you will authorise me to comply with his request."

Sir George Murray confirmed the opinions of Sir James Kempt by stating.—"I am well aware that Mr. Felton has expended a large capital in improving the grants of land which he has received, but, taking also into my consideration the extent of those grants, I do not feel myself justified in authorising an addition of more than 200 acres to Mr. Felton's grants for each of his children".

Notwithstanding this strongly expressed opinion of the Colonial Secretary, it appears that on the 24th May, 1831, patents issued granting to eight of the children 9,400 acres. This circumstance seems to have remained unnoticed until the receipt at the Colonial office of a return of lands granted to Members of the Legislative Council of Lower Canada and their families, by which it appeared that Mr. Felton had obtained grants amounting to 14,141 acres and his children 9,400, while the despatches of previous Colonial Secretaries had authorised Mr. Felton to receive 15,000 and his children only 1600, making a difference between the authority of the Secretary of State and the actual grants, of 6911 acres. Mr. Stanley's attention was directed to this discrepancy, and in April 1834 he thus addressed Lord Aylmer:—

"The point which I consider to require immediate notice . . . is the quantity of land which is stated to have been granted to Mr. Felton, the Commissioner of Crown Lands, and to his family, and which would appear, by the above mentioned return, to amount to upwards of 23,000 acres. . . . How it has happened that 1200 acres have been granted to each child, after so express a denial of what could not but be considered as a most unreasonable application on the part of Mr. Felton, considering the quantity of land which he had already received, I am at a loss to explain. I must, therefore, desire that your Lordship will call upon Mr. Felton for the necessary explanation on this point and that if the grants have not actually issued, you will take care that they are withheld; for so large a deviation from the instructions of the Secretary of State cannot possibly be sanctioned. . . .

(ii)

A defense of Mr. Felton:—Political implications

From *Montreal Gazette*, February 4, 1836.

To the Editor of the *Montreal Gazette.*

Sir,—In the documents recently published in your paper relating to the conduct of the Hon. Mr. Felton. . . . It is evident that the House wish to arrogate to themselves the right of appointment to, and removing from office all those who have either by "word" or "deed" militated against their views and designs and as Mr. Felton has most grievously offended both, it is but natural that they should unite in overthrowing one of their greatest enemies in the Eastern Townships—one who has done more to counteract the principles which have for a series of years actuated the majority, than perhaps any other individual in the British Colonies. Why, therefore, should they not pour out the phials of their wrath upon his devoted head? Did he not some twenty years ago, penetrate into the heart of the wilderness in the Township of Ascot, and lay out a large amount of capital in removing that wilderness—in erecting mills—opening roads—and promoting and encouraging the settlement of "strangers" therein? Has he not cleared 2,500 acres of forest land, which, otherwise would have been flourishing in all the luxuriance of its primeval beauty? Has he not imported cattle to *deteriorate* the breed of those possessed by the *enfans du sol?* Has he not been mainly instrumental in enabling others throughout the Townships, by the monies he disbursed in those hated and "baneful" occupations, to extend their operations in clearing land, improving the condition of their cattle, and adding to their means of destroying the dense forests which have so long adorned the land of the East? Was it not owing, in a great measure, to his exertions and perseverance, and the capital that he expended that the thriving village of Sherbrooke has emerged from its former dilapidated state, into a large and prosperous business place? . . .

Idem

Montreal, Feb. 1, 1836

13

The System of Granting Land as it stood in 1836:—Lands Available

From Canadian Archives, *Upper Canada sundries.*

A. B. Hawke to John Joseph[1]

Emigrant Office, Toronto,
20th July, 1836

Sir:

. . . In this province all crown lands and clergy reserves are sold by public auction, the first on a credit of three years, the second on a credit of nine years with interest.

---

[1]A. B. Hawke was chief emigrant agent in 1836; John Joseph was civil secretary to the lieutenant-governor.

The sales for the present year are advertised to take place monthly, in the different districts where there are lands for sale, commencing in June and ending in November. But no sales take place after that period, until May or June following, . . .

The upset price in the unsettled townships may be stated at 12/6 currency per acre, and in the new townships at 5/: a trifling advance is generally obtained above the upset price at the auction.

I do not apprehend any danger at present from the system of selling land on credit but it is a subject worthy of consideration how far it can be extended with safety. . . . The government have already thought it expedient to relinquish claims for advances made to settlers in the Bathurst district, to whom lots of one hundred acres each were given, amounting to upwards of £25,000, and I am of opinion that a similar course must ultimately be pursued in other settlements. In 1832 a considerable number of indigent immigrants were settled in the townships of Adelaide and Warwick, who were permitted to occupy their lands upon the condition that the first instalment should be paid three years after the date of the location; but there is not a single instance of which I am aware wherein any part of the interest or principal has been paid to the government, except in two or three cases where the parties sold their claims to wealthier settlers and were furnished by them with funds to fulfil their engagements with the government. . . .

It is also a subject of complaint that the system of selling lands by public auction on long credits places the actual settler at the mercy of the speculator;—that after having inspected the lands advertised at a great sacrifice of time and money, and selected lots, they are often prevented from purchasing by speculators who bid a higher price than they think it prudent to give. . . . I am aware that this evil has been checked since the purchaser has been obliged to pay the first instalment at the time of the sale. . . .

The quantity of good land at the disposal of the government and convenient for settlement will be found on examination to be very limited. The only blocks where dense settlements can be formed are in the Newcastle, Home and London districts. . . .

The finest and largest block of land fit for settlement in Upper Canada belongs to the Indians. It is situated north of the Canada Company's tract and is marked on the map "Indian Territory". This territory contains one million, five hundred thousand acres and is adjoining a triangular block which belongs to the government, estimated to contain upwards of half a million of acres, upon which there is not a single settler.

There are also several millions of acres belonging to the government in the London, Home, Newcastle and Eastern districts besides the blocks of land already mentioned, but the lots are scattered or if forming extensive tracts, the land is generally broken and difficult of access. . . .

A. B. Hawke

14

Mismanagement of the Public Lands in Upper Canada

From Canadian Archives, *Upper Canada sundries.*

William Hamilton Merritt to Sir George Arthur

St. Catherines, Feby 16th, 1839

. . . Compare this method with our management in Upper Canada—With us one seventh of the land is dormant—and although the purpose for which it was reserved is no doubt a laudable one— it has as yet proved only a fruitful source of agitation—Another seventh composing the Crown Reserves has been sold to the Canada Company— The remainder has been sold to create a fund called the Territorial Revenue, not one farthing of which has ever been appropriated in aid of the general revenue— Even the proceeds of all those Lands are vested in Great Britain when the Province is literally beggared for want of capital. . . .

Wm Hamilton Merritt

15

Specific Examples of Speculative Ownership

From Canadian Archives, *Correspondence of the governor-general's office*, no. 3412.

J. S. Currie to Sir Charles Metcalfe

Dundas, C.W., April 8th, 1844

. . . On my first arrival in Canada last year, having observed a fine tract of land in the Western District, on the border of Lake Erie, I expressed my surprise to the Government agent at Chatham that it had not been settled. He stated that 2000 acres belonged

to D. in Scotland, 600 to G. in Montreal, 1000 to Col. B., so many
to one in the States, &c, &c, that none of these parties had ever
thought of selling until the wild lands were taxed but that they
asked too high a price and so I found that nearly all [the wild
lands on the border of Lake Erie belonged to non-residents, many
of whom had purchased on speculation. The only remedy now
appears to be, in order to reach such individuals, to abolish all
taxation on stock and to fix an equal rate on wild and improved
lands: so as to compel the proprietors of these fine wild lands to
bring them into the market. . . .

J. S. Currie

[Pencil note]: Thank Mr. Currie for his communication and
keep this subject in mind for consideration. C.T.M.

(f)—THE LAND COMPANIES

By 1825 the imperial government had had quite enough of the perennial
problem of the clergy reserves and it therefore welcomed the offer of a land
company to buy half of those in Upper Canada. As bad luck would have it,
this expedient failed and the Canada Company instead got the Huron Tract, along
with the crown reserves already granted to it. It energetically began the work
of settling and is responsible for the opening up of the tract of country tributary
to Goderich on Lake Huron. The British American Land Company was a
similar undertaking in the lower province. French-Canadian sentiment was
hostile from the start, since it was believed to be a shallow imperialistic device
for robbing the *enfans du sol* of their patrimony and for "anglification". Para-
doxically, it was not successful until A. T. Galt, its presiding genius and son of
John Galt, who had acted in a similar capacity to the Canada Company, succeeded, in the late forties in coaxing the French away from the seigniories to
settle on its lands. It came to be, therefore, one of the chief instruments in
turning the Eastern Townships from an English district into a French.

REFERENCES: R. and K. Lizars, *In the days of the Canada Company* (Toronto,
1896); O. D. Skelton, *Life and times of Sir A. T. Galt* (Toronto, 1920).

1

The Policy of the Canada Company

From *Blackwood's Magazine*, September, 1826, quoted in *Montreal Gazette*,
October 5, 1826.

The Canada Company . . . will now enter into contracts with
individuals or with societies, disposed to settle in that healthy and
fertile country. . . .

The Company does not intend to send out settlers, nor to
give direct encouragement to emigrants destitute of property,
because undertakings of that kind may be done to greater advantage

by individuals possessed of capital purchasing either detached lots or larger tracts, or by families uniting their means for co-operation and society.

The Company, when required, will partially clear lots, and build such houses as may be necessary for the reception of settlers. Their lands will probably be disposed of according to the following classes.

1. Lots prepared for settlement by clearing five acres, and building a cottage. Such lots to be disposed of at an annual payment of probably little more than 1s. per acre. If the house and clearing cost £50, that sum to be redeemed within a certain number of years by annual instalments.

2. Lots similarly prepared to be disposed of at a rent supposed of 2s. per acre on lease; but the purchaser to be allowed the option at any time within the first fifteen years to purchase the lot at 20 years value of the rental.

3. Lots to be sold for ready money, without improvements.

4. Lots to be sold payable by instalments in ten years, seven years and five years, as may be agreed on.

5. Lots to be sold, with improvements, for ready money.

6. Lots to be sold, with improvements, payable by instalments.

7. Lots to be sold, with or without improvements, purchasers paying down a certain fee or gross sum; the land remaining subject to a small quit-rent or feu-duty.

A man, bred to agriculture, who arrives in Upper Canada with £100 may, in the course of a very few years, look forward to the enjoyment of comfort and independence as a proprietor of land, on which according to the terms of his bargain, he may have but little or no rent to pay, assuredly few taxes, and neither tithes nor poor rates. With persons of this description the Company will treat on the most accommodating principles.

At the office, and from the agents of the Company, either by personal application, or by letter (post paid), information will at all times be afforded regarding vessels bound for Canada, the rates of freight and passage, stores requisite for the voyage, and assistance will be given to parties when embarking, to protect them from unnecessary trouble and expense. A map of the province is ready for publication, compiled from actual survey, in which the districts, counties, and townships, are all exhibited; and those in which the Company have lands are particularly distinguished.

At the office of the Company, and of the agents, separate plans of each township, with the Company's lots therein specially marked will be open for public inspection; so that emigrants may, before their departure, select any particular neighbourhood in the country of which they may have acquired information, or where they may have friends already settled. . . .

2

Lands granted to the Canada Company:—Disposition of Proceeds

From Canadian Archives, G, *LXII*, 381.

Wilmot Horton to Secretary Herries of the treasury.

Downing Street, 20 Nov. 1826

Sir

I am directed by Lord Bathurst to state for the information of the Right Honourable the Lords Commissioners of his Majesty's Treasury, that this Department entered into arrangements with the Canada Land Company, by which it was agreed to convey to the said Company the Crown Reserves in Upper Canada not already occupied & disposed of, and one-half of the lands which have been reserved for the support of a Protestant Clergy in that Province. In consequence of this agreement a Bill was brought into Parliament during the last Session to enable his Majesty to convey to the Company the portion of the Clergy Reserves stipulated in the arrangement, & it became a law.

Commissioners were then appointed, two on the part of his Majesty's Government, & two on the part of the Company, who chose a fifth to proceed to Upper Canada to ascertain the quantity & value of the lands disposed of. These Gentlemen after remaining some months in the Colony returned to England, and presented their report; stating that the Crown Reserves contained 1,384,413 acres & one-half the Clergy Reserves 829,430 acres and that they had unanimously agreed on the average value of 3/6 (three shillings & 6 pence) per acre, current money of Upper Canada, as the price to be paid by the Company to his Majesty's Government, . . .

On examining this Report in detail it appears that in some respects the commissioners had misunderstood their instructions; & that there were still some difficulties as respected the actual conveyance of the Clergy Reserves. It was therefore deemed inexpedient to proceed with their sale; and the Company were induced to accept of a continued tract at a distance from any Settlement of one million of acres in lieu of the 829,430 acres of Clergy Reserves scattered through the settled divisions of the Colony; paying however for this tract the sum stipulated for the number of acres contained in the Reserves as returned by the Commissioners. It was further agreed that in consideration of the distance of this tract of one Million of acres the Company should be permitted to expend on its improvement one-third of the purchase money, paying the other two-thirds to his Majesty's Government. . . .

After deducting 1/3^d of the estimated value of the Clergy Reserves, which was to be laid out on the improvement of the substituted million of acres, amounting to the sum of £43,007 Sterling; the sum which the Canada Land Company is actually bound to pay in 16 years is £301,367. . . . Lord Bathurst recommends to their Lordships' consideration the following appropriations.

1st	For the Civil Establishment of Upper Canada	£8500 — —
	N.B. This sum has hitherto formed an item in the estimate voted by Parliament.	
2nd	Toward the erection of a College for Upper Canada yearly	1000 — —
3^d	For a Salary to the Roman Catholic Bishop the annual sum of	400. — —
4th	For a Provision for the Roman Catholic Priests the annual sum of	750. — —
5th	For a provision for the Presbyterian Ministers the annual sum of	750. — —
6th	As a pension to Col. Talbot in reward for the exertions of that Officer & the sacrifice which he has made of his fortune & profession in directing & superintending the settlement of the London & Western District, which are now exceedingly flourishing yearly	400. — —
7th	As a compensation to those officers of the Land Granting Department who by the adoption in Upper Canada of the regulations which govern the granting of the waste lands of the	

Crown in New South Wales & Van Dieman's Lands are deprived of their emoluments arising from fees on land patents, although their services in preparing them will still be required—for a period of seven years the annual sum of............................ 2566. 3. 8

£14366. 3. 8

3

The Canada Company's Terms to Settlers

From *Montreal Gazette*, August 28, 1828.

Canada Company—To emigrants arriving from the United Kingdom.—Notice is hereby given that the Canada Company having completed their arrangements for the Settlement of that extensive Tract of Country which lies between the Districts of Gore and London, and the shore of Lake Huron; a road is being opened from the Township of Wilmot to the mouth of the Red River, hereafter to be called the Maitland.

This road is the continuation of the one leading through Waterloo from Guelph, and Government is now opening another from Dundas to Guelph; by which route the journey from the head of Lake Ontario to Lake Huron may be performed in four or five days.

At the mouth of the Maitland, a town to be called Goderich, will be founded in the course of the summer as soon as the necessary surveys can be completed.

Along the road from Wilmot to Goderich, the Land, which is all of the best quality, will be sold in Lots of One Hundred Acres each, for which, at the option of the Purchasers, payment, at the rate of 7s. 6d. per acre, will be taken in Cash, provisions, or Labour on the roads from the first two hundred Heads of Families who offer themselves as Settlers, and supplies of provisions and Medical assistance will be provided by the Company. Saw and Grist Mills are building near the proposed site of Goderich.

Emigrants or other persons, desirous to embrace this advantageous opportunity of locating themselves, will please apply to the Agents of the Company . . ., by whom they will be furnished with Tickets addressed to the Company's Office at Guelph, where the applications will be registered according to the date of the presentation of the Tickets.

John Galt, Superintendent

Canada Company's Office
Guelph, May 28, 1828

4

How the Land Companies Ruin the Settler

From letter to *Montreal Courant*, quoted in *Montreal Gazette*, March 19, 1833.

... Your Correspondent who signs himself "A Farmer", appears not to be so well acquainted with the policy of land speculators as we are in the Townships, or he would not have supposed it necessary for the Land Company to improve land before they could sell it at very high prices, especially after monopolizing a large quantity; or that they would be so simple as to insist on the several payments as they became due.—No, The true policy of land speculators, who have the means of doing it, is to sell at very high prices, which they are enabled to do by giving what they term, a liberal credit. They commonly exact something down, say one-tenth of the purchase money, and the residue in, say, eight or ten annual payments, or interest.—Knowing full well, that as long as the purchaser is clearing and improving the land their debt is safe, they will not insist on payments being made punctually as they become due, but will appear disposed to show every indulgence, till the last when the purchaser of a wild lot of land has expended his little capital in converting it into fields, erecting buildings, &c. and when the debt and interest has mounted to a sum, utterly out of his power to meet, he is required to make payment and, after parting with everything he can possibly spare for that purpose the scene is generally closed by the surrender of his farm to the vendor.

It may be said, that the Land Company, being so respectable a body would never, or seldom ever, press the purchaser for payment, when not in his power to make it, to such a degree as to compel him to surrender to them his farm and valuable improvements. Well, be it so.—One of the greatest evils I anticipate from a British American Land Company's going into operation is— *An exorbitant price for wild lands, and a constant drain of money from the country for interest and rent, perpetuated to the end of time.* . . . If Government desire the good of the country, why not sell their lands as cheap, or nearly as cheap to the actual settler, as to any individual or Company, who may wish to purchase a quantity on speculation; would they do so, there would be no occasion for a Land Company to improve and settle the country. . . .

A Backwoodsman

5

The Canada Company:—Financial Condition:—Price of Lands

From *Montreal Gazette*, May 8, 1834.

CANADA COMPANY.—On the 27th of March, the annual meeting of this Company took place, C. Bosanquet, Esq. the Governor, in the chair. The report stated that the sale of land in the last year in the Crown Reserves had amounted to 53,019 acres at an average of 13s. per acre; in the Huron Tract, 30,900 acres, at an average of 7s. 6d. per acre; besides town lots in Guelph and Goderich to the value of about £480. The total amount realised by these sales was about £46,400, independently of town lots. The profit arising out of the Company's transactions last year was £28,000. The liabilities were reduced last year to £5000. The reports from Company's Commissioners in Canada, says a London paper, were most satisfactory. A steamboat, for the speedy conveyance of emigrants to their lands, was nearly ready; and a bill was before the Colonial Legislature for the construction of an improved harbour at Goderich. The land purchased from Government amounted to 2,484,000 acres of which 1,497,000 were unpaid for. The land sold by the Company amounted to 450,000 acres, and they had 550,000 acres on hand which had been paid for. . . .

6

Benefits of the British American Land Company to the Eastern Townships

From *Montreal Gazette*, December 13, 1835.

The formation of the BRITISH AMERICAN Land Company, the very existence of which has been proscribed by our revolutionists, continues to be regarded by the people of the Townships, as the most important event that has occurred in their history. Under its auspices, they have seen their population increase, their resources developed, their communications by land and water improved, the character of their society completely altered. From the wilderness, they have sprung into the active and stirring scenes of town and village life, and a general feeling of prosperity and happiness reigns among them. . . .

POPULATION:—IMMIGRATION AND EMIGRATION

Immigration as opposed to true pioneer movements such as those of the Loyalists can hardly be said to have commenced until the 1820's. Feeble efforts had been made from time to time to send out unemployed or distressed persons from Great Britain but it was not until about 1826 that a genuine swarming movement began. From that year until 1834, the colonies received many thousands of new inhabitants from the mother country, of every class and condition, good, bad, and indifferent. The movement ceased completely on the outbreak of the political troubles of the period of rebellion but was renewed again in the forties and went on until the exhaustion of good land rendered the attractions of the Canadas less obvious. Of the second wave, Irish paupers formed an even larger constituent than of the first; other paupers, plentiful during the first, had, owing to changing conditions in England and Scotland, pretty well disappeared. From the years 1825-1840 dates the origin of most of the present English-speaking population of Ontario and Quebec of non-Loyalist or non-American descent.

The documents suggest certain aspects of the problems presented by this rush of population; the type of person that may be expected to succeed, the hostility of the French to English immigration, the horrors of the sea-voyage and the character of the ships used (after 1850, with steam, this problem disappears), the disposition of the immigrants within the country, and the loss of many of them to the United States.

REFERENCES: George Bryce, *A short history of the Canadian people* (London, 1887), chapter VII *ff.*; H. I. Cowan, *British emigration to British North America* (Toronto, 1928); S. C. Johnson, *A history of emigration from the United Kingdom to North America, 1763-1912* (London, 1913); W. A. Carrothers, *Emigration from the British Isles* (London, 1929); E. M. Wrong, *Charles Buller and responsible government* (Oxford, 1926); F. H. Hitchens, *The colonial land and emigration commission* (Philadelphia, 1931); A. R. M. Lower, "Immigration and settlement in Canada, 1812-1820" (*Canadian Historical Review*, March, 1922) and "Canada—a motherland" (*Dalhousie Review*, January 1928); Gilbert Tucker, "The famine immigration to Canada, 1847" (*American Historical Review*, April, 1931); Frances Morehouse, "Canadian migration in the forties" (*Canadian Historical Review*, December, 1928).

1

A *Vademecum* for Intending Emigrants

From *A few plain directions*, 6, 14, 11-13.

[*The ocean voyage*]

This [*Liverpool*] is undoubtedly the best port to embark from, as vessels may there be met with at any time during the spring and summer months; and the expense of travelling to that town, even from places at a considerable distance, is not great. . . . In the winter, and very early in the spring, there are also vessels constantly going to New York; from whence there are steam-boats to Albany, and a stage to Montreal, or to Sackett's harbour opposite Kingston, by Utica. This would be the best route for persons without families, or who had but little baggage, and who were desirous of leaving England in February or March. A considerable duty or per centage (as much, I believe, as thirty per cent) on the value of their baggage, is paid at New York by persons not intending to settle in the United States, but who were only passing through them in order to proceed to the British colonies. Persons with families, and a considerable quantity of baggage, had therefore better embark for Quebec; and the commencement of April would be soon enough to leave Liverpool, as vessels cannot proceed up the river St. Lawrence to Quebec before the middle of May, on account of the ice. . . .

Persons who are strangers to the sea will find it inconvenient to *cook* for themselves. It is very probable that the ship's cook may be fond of grog; and he would perform that necessary business for a wine-glass full of rum every night, and double allowances on Saturday nights: if, however, he should possess such *a failing* as not to be fond of grog, then one of the seamen might be procured. . . .

[*What the emigrant should take with him*]

Coarse warm clothing with flannel shirts, thick worsted or yarn stockings, and strong shoes or half-boots nailed, are most suitable for the climate of Canada in winter; and duck slops, duck trowsers, and calico or homespun linen shirts, for summer wear. Fur caps may also be brought out, as they are expensive here. Any old clothes will serve during the passage out, and in travelling through the country. Beds may be taken out (*without bedsteads*). Curtains and curtain-rings, cords, blankets, sheets, warm rugs or coverlets, and several spare bed-ticks. All these latter articles are extremely dear in Canada. Scarcely any thing else need be provided, as all articles of hardware, axes suitable for the country, plough-irons, harrow-teeth, Dutch and tin ovens, tea-kettles, kettles for cooking meat in, &c., &c., &c. may be purchased at Montreal at nearly the same prices as in England.

Every thing should be well packed in strong boxes, cases, or trunks, the more portable they are the better, each not exceeding three feet in length, eighteen inches in breadth, and one foot in

7

depth, made water-tight if possible, or in barrels about the size of flour barrels, also water-tight; and all to be well lashed up or corded. Beds, bedding, curtains, &c., &c., may be sewed up in a wool-sack or very coarse harden, with a strong cord round them; this is the most convenient and best method of taking out beds. China or other earthenware, may be packed in tow or the refuse of flax.

All things being in readiness, and the vessel on the point of sailing, the emigrant will have to attend at the custom-house, with his baggage for examination; with respect to which business, the captain of the ship he goes out in will give him the necessary directions how to proceed, and assist him through it. He will also have to take an affidavit at the custom-house. He may take his sea-stores of provisions, &c., on board his vessel at any time, placing them under the charge of the mate; as they are never examined by the custom-house officers. . . . .

All spare money must be brought out in guineas or Spanish dollars, which may be purchased for good bills at any bullion office in Liverpool. Dollars are bought for about 4s. 4d. or 4s. 6d. each.

2

Immigrants' Unnecessary Impedimenta

From Howison, *Sketches of Upper Canada*, 61.

I frequently amused myself with strolling to the wharfs [*of Kingston*] and watching the arrival of the bateaux, several brigades of which came in every day, full of emigrants, and loaded with their baggage. The majority of these people seemed to have no idea that the necessaries of life could be obtained in Upper Canada; for they brought from their native country, tables, chairs, chests of drawers and great quantities of other lumber, the carriage of which must have cost infinitely more than the articles did themselves.

3

Prospects for the Settler in British North America

From John MacGregor, *Observations on emigration to British America* (London, 1829), 24-42.

Should Emigration be conducted at the public expense, it is recommended to provide the Emigrant with a year's or eighteen months' provisions, axes, and a few other implements. From my own inquiries, and all that I have observed respecting the settlers in each of our American Colonies, I am of opinion, that if each family received an axe, two hoes, an auger, a saw, a plane, a cow, seed, and provisions for one year, it is fully as much as Government should grant. It is doubtful, if more assistance were given, but that it would lead to abuse; and with such aid, the man who does not become independent of others for the means of subsistence, deserves, (according to an observation made to me by an affluent and worthy old farmer, who settled forty years ago in America, not worth a shilling,) "to be hanged as a public defaulter". . . .

It may safely be laid down as a general rule, formed on the success of the present inhabitants in the Colonies, that an industrious settler would be able, at the expiration of five, or, at the most, six years, particularly if received in agricultural produce, to repay the money expended on his account by Government. As a security for such money,—and as settlers, especially those of a *pauper* character would not, it is believed, be inclined to repay what they received from the public funds,—it would be proper to make the liquidation of this debt one of the conditions by which they should hold their lands. This would be preferable to an annual rent, which, be it ever so small, is always considered obnoxious and grievous in America:[1] . . . . .

The Emigrant who directs his course to Upper Canada, a country which has for some years afforded an asylum for some thousands of poor settlers, need not apprehend the want of fertile land, nor, after two or three years, the necessaries and many of the conveniences of life. Yet, notwithstanding the vast tracts of unoccupied land, he will, in order to secure a desirable farm, have to proceed a great distance into the back country, apart from society, and without the conveniences to be found only in a populous neighbourhood. He must not, however, be discouraged if he suffers much more, from the time he lands at Quebec or Montreal, until he plants himself and family in the woods, than he experienced in removing to America from the land of his forefathers. Every succeeding year will open more cheering prospects to him; the Emigrants who arrive after him will settle beyond him in the wilderness, and he will soon observe houses, villages, and cornfields occupying the place of gloomy and boundless forests. . . .

[1]See document no. 13, page 85.

As to the classes to which British America offers inducements to emigrate, much will depend upon individual character; but it may, however, be observed, that in consequence of the high price of labour, gentlemen farmers do not succeed, and the condition of new countries do not admit of extensive establishments. The settlers who thrive soonest, are men of steady habits, accustomed to labour.

Practical farmers possessing from £200 to £600, may purchase, in any of the Colonies, farms with from twenty to thirty acres cleared, which may be cultivated agreeably to the system of husbandry practised in the United Kingdom. The embarrassed circumstances of many of the old settlers, brought on by improvidence, or by having engaged in the timber business, will compel them to sell their farms, and commence again on woodlands.

Joiners, stonemasons, saddlers, shoemakers, tailors, blacksmiths, cart, mill, and wheelwrights, and (in the seaports), coopers may always find employment. Brewers may succeed, but in a few years there will be more encouragement for them. Butchers generally do well. For spinners, weavers, or those engaged in manufactures, there is not the smallest encouragement.

Active labouring men and women may always secure employment, kind treatment, and good wages.

To gentlemen educated for the professions of law, divinity, or physic, British America offers no flattering prospects. . . .

Young men of education, clerks in mercantile houses, or shopmen, need not expect the least encouragement, unless previously engaged by the merchants or shopkeepers in America. Many young men, however, of persevering minds, and industrious habits, have baffled every obstacle, and finally succeeded in establishing themselves in trade. Many of the richest merchants in the Colonies were of this description. . . .

Men of broken fortunes, or unprincipled adventurers, were generally the persons who have been engaged in the traffic long known by the emphatic cognomen of the "white slave trade," of transporting Emigrants to America. They travelled over the country among the labouring classes, allured them by flattering, and commonly false, accounts of the New World, to decide on emigrating, and to pay half of the passage-money in advance. A ship of the worst class, ill-found with materials, and most uncomfortably accommodated, was chartered to a certain port, where the passengers embarked: crowded closely in the hold, the provisions and water indifferent, and often unwholesome and scanty; inhaling the foul air generated by filth and dirt,—typhus fever was almost inevitably produced, and, as is too well known, many of the passengers usually became its victims. . . .

There are various ways in which men may always employ themselves, after they land in America. The heads of families cannot do better than by devoting all the time they possibly can to the clearing and preparing their new farms, for cultivation. It is often, however, necessary for them to work for provisions, or other assistance, among the old settlers; but prudent men never do so after the first year, except compelled by necessity.

Women, and children above ten years of age, can find employment, particularly during spring and autumn. Young unmarried labouring men ought to save, at least, half their wages. Food, except in the towns and at public works, is usually provided for labourers by their employers.

Children, whose parents are unable to support them, may be provided for by binding them until they become of age, as apprentices to farmers, with whom they are generally brought up as one of the family; and a cow, a sheep, and some seed, is usually given to them when they leave, to begin with on a farm. In this manner, orphans are generally taken care of. It rarely happens, that a man who has a family finds it necessary to bind any of his children to others; and he who has the most numerous offspring, is considered to have the best opportunity of prospering, in a country where land is abundant, and in which the price of labour is high.

A common plan with those who own cleared farms that they do not occupy, is to let these farms on the halves; that is, to stock the farm with horses, horned cattle, sheep, and hogs, provide half the necessary seed, and then give possession to a practical farmer, who will cultivate it, and find the labour. After harvest, the produce, even to that of the dairy, is equally divided between the proprietor and the farmer. Many farmers, who dislike commencing at once in the woods, have, by industry and frugality, supported their families very comfortably in this manner, for two or three years, besides accumulating sufficient stock and seed to commence on a new farm. Farmers from the inland counties of England, and from Dumfriesshire and Perthshire, have succeeded best in this way. . . .

In remarking generally on the condition of the inhabitants of our American Colonies, as respects their means, no class, except those engaged immediately or indirectly in commerce, has accumulated fortunes. The majority of the whole population possess considerable property in land and cattle; among the remainder, many are poor; but beggars are scarcely ever seen, unless it be in the towns, where some accidental calamity or natural infirmity brings occasionally a destitute individual to solicit charity. The Irish Emigrants are, but only for a short time after landing, frequently observed begging. . . . .

There are scarcely any taxes, and very few public burdens,— duties on articles of luxury are trifling, and on necessary articles there are rarely any, consequently all that is required for supporting a family may be purchased at low rates, fine clothing excepted.

I have particularly to advise new settlers against running in debt to the shopkeepers; doing so, has prevented many hard labouring men from prospering. The low price of spirituous liquors is also a great bane to the success of Emigrants, and the facility with which rum can be procured, is the most prolific source of domestic misery and personal depravity that exists in America.

Wherever a settlement is formed, and some progress is made in the clearing and cultivation of the soil, it begins gradually to develop the usual features of an American village. First, a saw mill, a grist mill, and a blacksmith's shop appear; then a school-house and a place of worship; and in a little time the village doctor, and pedlar with his wares, introduce themselves.

Few habitations can be more rude than those of the first settlers, which are built of logs, and covered with bark or boards, but many in the United Kingdom are far less comfortable. The most that an Emigrant can do the first year is to erect his habitation, and cut down the trees on as much ground as will be sufficient to plant ten to twelve bushels of potatoes, and to sow three or four bushels of grain. . . . .

In the course of five years an industrious man may expect, and should have, twelve acres under cultivation, one horse, two or three cows, a few sheep and pigs, and sufficient food for himself and family. In ten years the same man, with perseverance and frugality, ought to have from twenty-five to thirty acres under improvement, to possess a pair of horses, a waggon or cart, a sledge and cabriole, five or six cows, a yoke of oxen, sheep, hogs, poultry, &c. a comfortable house, a good barn, and plenty of food for himself and family. This is no extravagant calculation—I could name hundreds who began in a state of abject poverty, who, in the same period, accumulated, by steady industry, fully as much as I have stated.

4

Substantial Character of the Season's Immigrants

From *Montreal Gazette*, June 11, 1829.

Among the Emigrants who have arrived this season, we observe a more respectable class of farmers than in former years. Most of them possess considerable property. The majority of them proceed to Upper Canada, to join their friends and relations, and particularly to the Newcastle district where arrangements, we are informed, have been made for their reception. Out of 150 persons from Yorkshire, arrived in one vessel, two families from a predilection in favour of Prairie land, have gone to the Illinois Territory, and one to Wheeling, Ohio, to join their friends. Those who may not be prepared to go immediately upon lands, will find employment as work is plentiful. At the King's works on the cape and the Rideau Canal labourers are wanted, at the latter place 1000 labourers are advertised for. This is certainly the time when settlements in Lower Canada may be more conveniently carried into effect, than at any former period. We understand that arrangements are making to examine the township of Inverness, Leeds, and the adjoining settlements, on Craig's road, for the purpose of determining Emigrants to proper situations.

5

Unwillingness of Immigrant Labourers to Go on the Land

From *York Observer*, quoted in *Montreal Gazette*, August 15, 1830.

Immigrants invariably overestimate the possibilities of the new country: hence the constant recurrence down to the present of such complaints as the following:

We have been in some of the back Townships, and have to regret, that the scarcity of hands will occasion very great destruction to the wheat. Hundreds of emigrants have recently arrived, and although unemployed about the town, they refuse to enter the bush! Farmers came in from the back Townships and offered 3s. 9d. a day, and board, to labourers, and they could not induce those applied to, to proceed with them!

6

Numbers of Immigrants Arriving and Numbers Remaining, 1828, '29, '30

From *Quebec Official Gazette*, quoted in *Montreal Gazette*, December 13, 1830.

At the close of the season of 1830, it is most gratifying to find, that the result has been such as to verify the most sanguine expectations both as regards the number of Emigrants arriving in this port, the ultimate settlement of the majority in these Provinces, their present means, and their prospects for the future. In our notice of the result of the former year, 1829, we calculated the expected emigration into Quebec for 1830, in round numbers, at 30,000 souls. . . . Several facts and calculations . . . will prove that the views of those who looked to the influx of British population and capital into these Provinces, as conducive to the best interests of the country, have not been visionary: while they lead us to expect further good effects from the same cause. . . .

The total number of Emigrants from the United Kingdom in
1830, amounts to.......................... 28,100
Viz:—From Ireland....................... 17,596
    do. England...................... 6,895
    do. Scotland..................... 2,700
    do. Wales....................... 204
Irish and Scotch from Nova Scotia and New-
    foundland............................ 280
Reported at Montreal.................... 500

Total Emigrants in 1830.......................... 28,075
The amount of Emigrants in 1828 was............... 12,000
    do.   1829.................. 15,945

Total during the last three years.................... 56,020.

. . . In the year 1828, about one-twelfth part of the Emigrants, landing in Quebec, remained in Lower Canada.

In 1829, more than one-fifth part remained.

In 1830, considerably exceeding one-third part have taken up their habitation in this Province, and are now in active progress of settlement.

So much for the real increase of British Settlers in Lower Canada. Again in the year 1828, fully one-half of all the Emigrants who arrived in Quebec proceeded to some part of the United States. The proportion of persons of the latter description in 1829 was considerably smaller, while in the present year, 1830, out of an emigration exceeding 28,000 it is pretty nearly ascertained that not more than 6,500 passed through the Canadas, and finally settled in the United States. Upon information derived from Upper Canada and other places, it is fair to presume that a reflux of British settlers from the United States has entered these Provinces, amounting to but few short of the number admitted to have passed through the Canadas, on their way to settle among our Republican neighbours.

A very considerable number of Emigrants who arrived this season at New York, are known to have found their way into the Canadas, by way of Oswego; and a large portion of valuable settlers from the United Kingdom came to Montreal, thro' St. John's. Among these latter were many Highlanders and farmers from Sutherlandshire, now principally located, as the phrase is, in Chateauguay and its vicinity. In addition we have great pleasure in mentioning, that several respectable Scottish families from Perthshire who landed last June in the port of New York, are actually at this moment settled in the rising Township of Leeds. . . .

The number of unemployed poor has in former years been a great annoyance to the inhabitants, both of town and country. Humanity has been grievously put to the proof, and public sympathy was generally and successfully excited. In 1827 and 1828, when Emigration to Quebec amounted to 12,000 souls, not one-half of that of the present year, the number of unemployed, and therefore distressed strangers, was very considerable. . . . In 1829, when Emigration had advanced to near 16,000, the number of unemployed poor at the close of the season was much reduced, in proportion to that of the preceding year; and at the present time, the 9th December, 1830, at the close of an emigration on our shores amounting to 28,000 . . . it is a fact, that the number of unemployed poor strangers, in this city was never known to be so trifling, and, consequently, so little burthensome on the inhabitants.

These are facts that speak loudly in favor of the general state of the Province, as regards Emigration.

7

Exploitation of Immigrants by Inland Transport Companies

From *Montreal Gazette*, June 25, 1831.

To the Editor of the *Montreal Gazette*.

Sir,—Why is it that our poor fellow subjects, who are coming out in thousands to enrich the Province, should pay more for their transport on the waters of Canada, though proceeding to settle among us, than if they came from New York to Canada, either by way of Sackett's Harbour, Buffalo or other points? Let us look at the contrast. From New York to Albany, 150 miles, under an awning, and amply supplied with means of cooking and water, adults pay $1, children half price, infants nothing. On the Erie Canal they pay one cent a mile, where they are covered under deck, and possessed of every accommodation, and half price for children, with a liberal allowance of baggage, yet these very Canal boats pay a heavy tax to the State. Sir, when I look at the accommodation afforded the poor Emigrants seeking a place to lay their head in the adjoining State of New York, and see how the poor people, on our River, are huddled together exposed to the night dews and damps, without any accommodation, save a drink of water out of the River or Lake, I do deplore the cessation of competition among our Steamboat proprietors. I know individually they are honorable, and many of them truly generous and humane. I pray them to have compassion on these poor people, and reduce the fare to every man having a wife and family. Did they suffer the wives and children of the poor to pass free, the present rate payable by the men would amply repay them. I have heard that the charge up the Ottawa is not only very high, but is the same on the poor emigrant as on the ordinary traveller. This is not politic, nor is it humane. The vast numbers coming out has lessened our sympathy, as if the increase of misery and want should lead us to regard the objects of it less. Do, Mr. Editor, urge the proprietors to carry the pauper women and children free, or at least on as favorable terms as these can pass through the State of New York. . . .

I am, Sir,

"One who lately was an immigrant"

8

Relief of Destitute and Sick Immigrants:—Unemployables

From *Montreal Gazette*, June 30, 1831.

A Society has been set on foot in Montreal, for the Relief of Destitute Emigrants; the following is the third of a series of Resolutions, adopted at the meeting, and really, after all, with temporary shelter, except in cases of sickness, (and that is otherwise provided for,) it is the only relief which emigrants require:—

"That it be an instruction to this Committee, to confine their labours chiefly to the object of forwarding destitute emigrants to those parts of Upper and Lower Canada, in which they may be most likely to obtain labour and lands."

For the relief of the sick, some medical gentlemen, with a benevolence which does them credit, came forward: Doctors Demers, Vallee, and Stephenson offered to dispense medicines and give advice gratuitously, in an apartment of the sheds to be erected, to such pauper emigrants as may require medical assistance, and are not sufficiently indisposed to require admission into the General Hospital, and they have announced their intention in a way we shall be happy to see followed in Quebec. . . .

There is certainly much distress amongst those who remain in the cities, but there is as certainly not a small portion of the emigrants who, so long as they can subsist by exciting sympathy and extracting alms from the more wealthy, will not make an exertion to gain a livelihood by a more active, but certain operation. From circumstances which have recently come to our knowledge, we are inclined to think that much of this distress arises from an unwillingness on the part of the emigrants to open their eyes to their actual situation, to be convinced that they must submit to the consequences of the temporary glut of labour the arrival of such unexampled numbers has occasioned and take such wages as are going. Two instances have been mentioned to us, from sources every way entitled to credit, where emigrants have refused employment, not because the wages tendered to them were insufficient for their support, but because they were not such as they *expected* to obtain. The first was at Berthier, Montreal District, where a number of Irishmen were offered six dollars a month and their food, and to be employed for three months on the roads making in the rear of that settlement.   The offer was refused for reason already given; we have this from an Irishman, so that national prejudice can have no share in the information. The other was of several of the same description of persons returning to Quebec from St. Giles, where they had been offered 2s. 6d. per diem, for road work, and to be increased after the first fourteen days to 2s. 9d., and, if employed for more than a month, to 3s. at the expiration of the latter period.   This did not realize their hopes, and they returned to this city.   It is to be regretted that such characters cannot be identified, as they certainly have forfeited every claim to relief as "destitute emigrants."

But although there is a redundance of labour in the immediate neighbourhood of the cities and along the banks of the St. Lawrence, the rate of wages we have above given, in Upper Canada, shews that labour is not there a superabundant commodity, and there is a demand for it in the Eastern Townships of this Province, which may be reached from Three Rivers.   A gentleman who arrived in town from the District of St. Francis, a few days ago, reported that 300 labourers would find ready employment in that part of the Townships, so that the Resolution of the Montreal Society before quoted seems to have been the result of sound judgment and good information.

9

Horrors of the First Period of Irish Immigration

From Bigsby, The shoe and canoe, I, 23.

I hope there are few towns in Christendom where such an amount of disease and destitution exists as in Quebec. . . . This misery does not touch the native poor, but the fever-stricken, naked, and friendless Irish—a people truly "scattered and peeled" —who year after year are thrown in shoals upon the wharfs of Quebec from ships which ought to be called "itinerant pest-houses."

These unwelcome outcasts are crowded, without proper provision, into vessels fitted up almost slave-ship fashion, by the agents of impoverished and unprincipled landlords, who rely on the public and private commiseration of the western world; and it has been taxed beyond endurance.   Much of the guilt, certainly, lies upon the Irish Government, who do little or nothing to prevent so frightful a state of things. Thus matters continue to the present hour, I believe; worse rather than better.

These poor creatures, on landing, creep into any hovel they can, with all their foul things about them. When they are so numerous as to figure in the streets, they are put, I believe by the Colonial Government, into dilapidated houses, with something like rations, of which latter the worthier portion of the emigrants are apt to see but little: they are clutched by the clamorous.

The filthy and crowded state of the houses, the disgusting scenes going on in them, can only be guessed by a very bold imagination. I have trod the floor of one of such houses, almost over shoes in churned and sodden garbage, animal and vegetable. It required dissecting-room nerves to bear it.

After starving about Quebec for months, the helpless Irishman and his family begin to creep up the country on charity or government aid, and thus strew the colony with beggary and disease. A Quebec winter does not allow of lazzaronism. Some perish, some are absorbed into the general population, and many more go into the United States.

For six winter months I was medical officer to the emigrants at Quebec, whether in hospital or in forlorn lodgings; until, in fact, I nearly lost my life by typhus and dysentery.

10

Inauguration of Quarantine in Canada

From *Neilson's Quebec Gazette,* quoted in *Montreal Gazette,* February 20, 1832.

In the summer of this year the quarantine here provided for received its baptism of fire: the great outbreak of cholera which spread across the Atlantic on the immigrant ships, on which mortality became even higher than usual, was communicated to the inhabitants, first at Quebec and then up the river, to York and beyond. This scourge re-enforced French hatred of English immigration. See document no. 20, page 118.

The Assembly, on Friday morning, placed £10,000 at the disposal of His Excellency Lord Aylmer, to provide for the enforcement of quarantine regulations next summer. The site chosen for that purpose is understood to be *Grosse Isle,* an island about thirty-five miles below the port, where there is a good harbor for ships. The island will be placed entirely under the military, and all the regulations will be enforced by them. Communications by telegraph[1] can be received in two or three minutes; the telegraphs erected during the last war are still standing it being only requisite to erect one on the island.

11

Contrast between Upper and Lower Canada in Opportunities for Immigrants and the Attitude toward them

From *Kingston Chronicle*, August 18, 1832.

The *Old Quebec Gazette* states that many emigrants, disappointed at the want of employment at Quebec and Montreal, have returned home; and that many more, did they possess the means, would follow the example. Residing as we are in the centre of the Upper Province, where many public and private works are at present in operation, it is our duty to apprise those who may be disappointed at not immediately obtaining employment in the Lower Provinces that in this, every respectable mechanic and industrious labourer will meet with an encouragement far beyond his expectation; or, as the *Quebec Mercury* very justly observes, that in this "Province at least agricultural labourers and operatives in those handicraft trades most generally practised, are sought for and encouraged." The fact is so. In Kingston alone, the demand for labourers and mechanics is greater than we ever remember, and the public buildings which have been commenced this season, and which will require many more seasons to complete will be the means of insuring such characters, a constant and lucrative source of employment. The whole of the Western district, within the last two years, has been the reservoir of emigration; and there also demand exists for that class of people, who should not argue from the want of employment in Montreal or Quebec, that such is the case universally through the Colony. Let such only visit the Upper Province, and we can assure them that they will be handsomely rewarded for their trouble, and will meet a description of people who, far from throwing obstacles in the way of employment, will cherish and respect every honest mechanic and tradesman who can benefit the country. There are various societies formed for the purpose of facilitating the views

---

[1]The reference is to the old mechanical telegraph which preceded the electric telegraph.

of the emigrants, according to their respective objects, and an application to any of these, along the route from Montreal to York, will meet with immediate attention. There appears a most unaccountable prejudice in the Lower Province against the admission of any population into this country but such as is calculated to suit the views of a political faction; and when the execrable poll tax[1] has been insufficient to stem the tide of emigration, we are scarcely surprised to find other stratagems employed to aggravate a malady as alarming to some as the cholera or any other imported pestilence. The people should not be debarred from settling amongst us, only let them apply to the official sources of information, and they will there be furnished with evidence sufficient to convince them, that no reliance can be placed in the self-interested advice of alarmists or political demagogues.

12

Upper Canada's Objections to the Capitation Tax

From Report of committee, Assembly of Upper Canada, January 3, 1833, printed in *Montreal Gazette*, January 22, 1833.

The capitation tax was imposed by Lower Canada, out of hatred, possibly, of English immigration but for very good reasons: to provide a fund to meet the appalling amount of destitution and disease among immigrants, a burden heretofore largely left to the charity of the people of Quebec.

To the Honorable the House of Assembly

The Committee . . . on the subject of the tax imposed by the Legislature of Lower Canada, on emigrants and passengers from the United Kingdom, respectfully report:

That the subject referred to them involves consideration of vital importance to the rights and interests of the people of Upper Canada and demands from the House, and the Government of the Province, the most serious and prompt attention.

The Legislature of a sister Colony has assumed the power of dictating the terms on which British subjects shall be permitted to pass from the sea to this part of His Majesty's dominions; a pretention, which if allowed to be well founded, carries with it this further consequence that we thereby admit, that we may be entirely excluded from the ports of the Empire, situated in the

---

[1]The reference is to the "capitation tax" of five shillings imposed on immigrants by the legislature of Lower Canada.

Colony referred to; that our right of access to these ports, even for the purpose of shipping our exports or carrying on our commerce with other parts of the world, is dependent on the will and pleasure of her Legislature.

As Upper Canada has no other means by which to guard against the evils which may immediately flow from a measure so destructive of her rights, but by claiming the interference and protection of the Sovereign, an address to His Majesty is herewith reported, containing the arguments and views of the Committee on this most important matter, which they respectfully recommend to your Honorable House for concurrence and adoption.

Chr. A. Hagerman, Chairman

13

Immigration and Colonial Preference

From *Montreal Gazette*, February 12, 1833.

George Auldjo, chairman, Montreal committee of trade, to Nathaniel Gould, chairman, North American Colonial Association, London

Since the publication of Brougham's celebrated work, the value of the British American Provinces to Great Britain has been variously exemplified in war and in peace, but has lately been displayed in the most important light, as affording room for the surplus population of the Mother Country. The transfer of this population to a situation where it can be useful instead of burthensome, is steadily and economically effected by the present system of foreign duties, protecting the timber trade of the British American Provinces, which is capable of affording cheap conveyance to a hundred thousand emigrants annually.[1]

14

The Rival Attractions of the Midland and Western Districts of Upper Canada

From *Kingston Spectator*, quoted in *Montreal Gazette*, July 13, 1833.

Emigration to Canada has been evidently on the increase since the last mention we made of it. Nearly ten thousand souls

---

[1]One of the stock arguments in favour of the differential duties on timber. See document 13, page 273.

have landed at Quebec, and some hundreds have likewise found their way hither via New York. This number is small in comparison to what it was last year at the same time, but the superior wealth of this year's emigrants, makes some amends for their inferiority in number. The *Great Britain* when she touched here on Wednesday last, must have had nearly five hundred passengers on board, all bound for the head of the Lake, and most of them appearing tolerably provided with the good things of this life. From some strange infatuation, these strangers who leave their native homes in search of agricultural employment, shun the eastern parts of the Province as they would shun a pestilence, and flock in crowds to the more westerly districts, because the lands are there said to be more fertile. Allowing this assertion to be true, although many well informed persons contend that land as productive is to be met with in the Midland District as in any other part of the Province, still the advantages arising from settling in it fully make up for any inferiority in the nature of the soil. In the first place, produce of every kind fetches a higher price than in the far west, and the readiness in which that produce is brought to market increases the value materially; moreover cash can always be procured at the wish of the seller, a circumstance much in favour of the eastern settlers. These advantages arise from the vicinity of the Midland District to the great market of Montreal. 2dly. Every article which the farmer wants for his household, can be had at one-half the price it can be produced west of Hamilton, a circumstance which should make another important consideration on the side of this portion of the Province. 3dly. The price of good land is not so high as the same quality more to the westward, as may be ascertained by comparison with the Government sales at Belleville and those in the Western Districts. 4thly. The readiness with which religious worship of all denominations can be attended, and the establishment of schools for the education of children are considerations much in favor of the Midland District, and ought not to be overlooked by fathers of families wishing to live in the fear of God, and desirous of seeing their children brought up in the same. These are a few of the advantages arising from emigrants landing at Kingston and striking for the interior, but owing to the efforts making in all parts of Great Britain by the Canada Company to sell their lands by depreciating all others, (although they have themselves some land for sale in this District,) every person who leaves home is impressed with the idea that it is only in the Huron tract that he can expect to grow rich, and finds too late that he might have laid out his money to greater advantage, in a more settled and more healthy part of the Province. . . .

15
Scarcity of Labour in the Vicinity of Montreal
From *Montreal Gazette*, August 29, 1833.

Emigration.—Since we last noticed this subject emigrants have continued to land regularly at this port, though not in great numbers but of a very respectable description, some of whom purchased lands in the adjoining neighbourhood, but the greater part moved off to Guelph, the Huron Tract and the Western district, where they are daily making extensive purchases. So few of the labouring classes have landed at this port, that the want of them is much felt in this town and its neighbourhood, and applications have been made here in vain for servants and labourers by persons who reside twenty, thirty, and fifty miles off. . . .

16
The Number of Immigrants into Upper Canada in 1833
From *York Courier*, October 10, 1833, quoted in *Montreal Gazette*, October 29, 1833.

The number of emigrants arrived at Quebec up to the 10th October, as stated on the Exchange books, was 21,930. Several of the Fall trading vessels from London and other English ports are yet to arrive, but it is not likely they will bring out many emigrants. The total number therefore for this season, at Quebec, will probably scarcely reach 23,000 or about 28,000 less than the previous year.

The total number of emigrants who have come up to York and the Upper ports this season we understand is about 14,000, or nearly two-thirds of the whole that have landed at Quebec. This is exclusive of those that have come into the Province by way of New York, and who constitute a very important portion of this year's emigration in point of respectability and property, as well as in point of numbers. The latter we have no means of ascertaining with any degree of accuracy. We all know, however, that the number of emigrants who have come to this town direct from New York is very considerable—besides those who have proceeded to the Western Districts across the Niagara frontier, and up Lake Erie and those who have come into the Province from the States, across the Western frontier. . . .

The whole number of British Emigrants arrived at New York is 14,000 of whom we may perhaps assume that one fourth have come to this Province by the routes above described. If to these are added the emigrants who have disembarked at the different Upper Canada ports below this town, and those who have proceeded up the Ottawa: *and if we superadd the citizens of the United States who have emigrated from their native republic to this Colony during this year,* and whose numbers are by no means inconsiderable,—we think we may fairly assume that the addition to the population of Upper Canada, from emigration alone, has been at least *Twenty Thousand.*

17

Frequency of Wrecks among Immigrant Ships

From *Montreal Gazette,* June 5, 1834.

The ship which carried the poorer class of immigrant was, as a rule, of the oldest and least seaworthy character, a type commonly engaged in the timber trade and seizing the opportunity for an outward bound cargo by running up rough bunks in the hold, into which immigrants were stuffed regardless of light, ventilation, and sanitation.

The melancholy catalogue of disasters at sea, which this day we lay before our readers, accompanied as they have generally been with a most fearful loss of human life, must tend to call the attention of the British Government to the necessity of directing a proper enquiry into the character and condition of passenger ships leaving the Mother Country. From Ireland, in particular, the vessels employed in the conveyance of emigrants are miserably fitted up for that purpose, tending more to spread disease and mortality among the passengers than for their comfort and accommodation. Their character for sea-worthiness is also in many instances very dubious and the accidents which have lately occurred would seem to betray an almost criminal indifference, as to the safety of the hundreds that are crowded on board in these passenger-ships.

The Government have latterly appointed Emigrant agents at several of the principal sea-ports in Britain, and other places are expected to come into the regulation. At Liverpool, Bristol, Dublin, Belfast, Cork, Limerick and Greenock, half-pay Lieutenants of the Navy have been nominated, with salaries of about £200 each. The duty of this officer, as explained by Mr. Secretary Stanley, when he lately moved an estimate for this meritorious object, was to receive applications from persons either about to emigrate, or to send out emigrants, to give them his gratuitous advice and every information in his power, to effectually prevent the commission of frauds, and to see that the provisions of the law were carried into effect. The consequence, Mr. Stanley remarked, was that the officers, wherever appointed, had succeeded in putting an end to a great train of abuses—that in Liverpool, particularly, the comfort of the inhabitants had been a good deal promoted, and the condition of emigrants previously to their leaving Britain, greatly ameliorated. The comfort of the emigrant, as far as it relates to his being protected against fraud, or being deceived by erroneous information, has thus been attended to by the Government. There only remains now to be effected a strict and severe examination of the vessels employed in emigration, and a careful supervision of them, ere they leave the shores of Britain.

The following is a summary of the melancholy disasters of this year among the vessels bound to Quebec. . . .[1]

18

Character of the Immigrants arriving in 1834

(i)

From *Quebec Mercury*, June 3, 1834, quoted in *Montreal Gazette*, June 5, 1834.

The number of Emigrants arrived this season, as recorded at the Office of His Majesty's Chief Agent, to this date, amounts to,

From England.....................................	2,884
Ireland.....................................	6,595
Scotland.....................................	1,348
Lower Ports.............................	19
Total.............................	10,846
Same period last year,..........................	3,175

[1]Follow accounts of eighteen inbound ships lost during the months of April and May, several with all hands.

We are glad to learn that a very large portion of the Emigrants of this year have brought with them considerable property in specie and bills of exchange, whilst it is a further favourable feature of their general condition that the number dependent on immediate employment bears a small proportion to the total of arrivals. Very few indeed appear to require the charitable assistance of a benevolent public, which is particularly gratifying when the large influx of strangers is considered that within the last ten or fifteen days have arrived in Quebec, and that many of them have suffered shipwreck on St. Paul's Island and other parts of the Gulph.

(ii)

From *Cobourg Star*, quoted in *Montreal Gazette*, July 18, 1834.

The increased emigration of this year is a most pleasing proof that the Canadas continue to maintain their character among the people of the United Kingdom, as the most eligible country for the emigrant and holding out to him the fairest hopes of success. We at least are sure, that no individual of moderate fortune, and possessed of common industry and prudence, can fail to do well, and find himself in a few years in a state of independence and content; to the man of poverty we need say nothing, for Canada is emphatically the poor man's country, where he is sure to receive a ready welcome, and a helping hand. The increase of emigration this year as compared with the last is very decided, and we have no doubt that, if it were possible to institute the comparison, the wealth introduced into Canada by this year's emigration bears a still more marked advantage over that of last year's. We learn by the *Toronto Courier*, that at least 8000 emigrants have reached Toronto. Indeed emigration continues to flow almost entirely westward. We should be well pleased to receive a larger proportion of this year's emigration than we have been yet favored with; but we cannot in reason complain, knowing how particularly fortunate the District of Newcastle has been in former seasons. Our settlers of this summer are generally persons of capital, who have emigrated to Canada to join friends already settled here. Most of these will locate in well cleared and populous Townships. There is a tide in emigration, as in the affairs of men, but we trust the present ebb in this District does not arise from misinformation as to the price of lands in the back Townships. In the vicinity of the lakes which affords so many natural advantages, there are thousands of acres of beautiful and heavily-timbered wild land to be sold as cheap as any in the Province. New Townships are about being surveyed to the North of Verulam and Fenelon, of which report speaks very highly.

(iii)

From *Montreal Gazette*, August 26, 1834.

The tide of emigration begins to set towards the Eastern Townships;—Sorel, and every place below, on the south bank of the St. Lawrence is crowded with emigrants, and of a most respectable description. Many have brought with them implements of various kinds, as also some beautiful specimens of the English breeds of cattle and sheep. One person in particular, who Farmer by name, as well as by vocation has arrived at Sorel, has imported some of the largest and finest draught horses which, probably, have ever been seen on this side the Atlantic; he has both horses and mares, also bulls, and cows of the most approved breeds, and boars, sows, rams, sheep &c. He has carpenters, bricklayers, black-smiths, farming servants; and many useful artisans attached to his suite—and proposes establishing a new settlement, if he meets with that encouragement which no doubt will be accorded to him. Mr. Farmer is from the neighbourhood of Shrewsbury.

19

The First Recourse of Immigrants

From *Parliamentary papers of Great Britain*, Report, 1835, upon the timber duties; evidence of Samuel Neilson of Quebec.

The first employment of those that have nothing but their arms is to go to work in the lumbering yards.

20

French Opposition to English Immigration

From *Quebec Gazette*, quoted in *Montreal Gazette*, February 14, 1835.

Those who wish to be acquainted with the genuine sentiments of the leaders of the French party in the House of Assembly, in respect to emigrants, should read the *Minerve*, the *Echo du Pays* and *Le Canadien*, by which party the *Vindicator* is hired to delude those speaking the English language. The following is translated from the Montreal *Minerve* of the 5th instant, and is not one of the strongest expressions of the sentiments of the party: "If emigration is a benefit, and if it is for the greatest advantage of humanity that the Land Company should transport to our soil, the heaps of beggars of the Mother Country, it is to be hoped that the apostles of beneficence will rid Canada of those lepers this year. A new and fitter channel for those miserable creatures is now opened. The law for emancipating the negroes has totally disorganized the English Colonies; the negroes have fancied that the benefit of freedom consists in the indulgence of the most complete laziness; they accordingly refuse to work, and had rather be killed than change this opinion. In Jamaica, there have been revolts and horrible executions. The House of Assembly seeing the evil, and wishing to remove it, have determined to replace the black slaves who refuse to perform their apprenticeships, by white emigrants, to work for the planters. A premium of £15 is offered to the importers of European labourers. There is no doubt but that channel is better for the emigrants, than to come and cultivate the lands of the English Company in our Provinces; they will find there, at once, fruitful employment. With respect to us we wish for nothing better; because there is no doubt but what it would save us the afflicting spectacle of again seeing our fellow-citizens visited with the cholera."

21

Public Works as Unemployment Relief for Immigrants

From Canadian Archives, *Upper Canada sundries*, 1840.

Government House,
24 July, 1840

Sir,

I have the honor, by Command of the Lieutenant Governor to inform you, that the present unfinished state of the various public works in this Province having lately engaged much of the attention of the Government, in connection with the necessity of affording employment to the numerous Immigrants who are now arriving and may still be expected to arrive, His Excellency in Council has resolved to make an advance of public money towards the completion of such of these works as are likely to be productive of most immediate advantage, both with a view to the accommodation of the public and to the employment of Immigrants.

It has accordingly been resolved that the sum of £40,000 should be borrowed from the Bank of Upper Canada. . . .

S. B. Harrison

To the Provincial Secretary

MEMORANDUM

As to the appropriation of money for public works.—

There will be at the disposal of the Gov^t the following sums at the following periods viz:

July	£10,000	September	£10,000
August	10,000	October	10,000
			£40,000

From these are to be paid

Welland Canal	£13,000	
Kingston & Napanee Road	5,000	
North Toronto Road	7,000	
Hamilton & Brantford Road	570	
Dundas & Waterloo Road	5,000	
Commissioners for the Improv^t of the navigation of the Inland waters of the New Castle District	4,000	
Trent navigation	1,000	35,570
Surplus		£ 4,430

22

Emigration of Assisted Immigrants to the United States

From Canadian Archives, *Upper Canada sundries*, 1840.

The seriousness of the situation described in this document lay in the fact that most of the immigrants *viâ* the St. Lawrence at this time (and, indeed, for many years afterwards) were forwarded up country at the expense of the government, in whole or in part.

(i)

Emigrant Office,
Toronto August 27th 1840

Sir,

I have lately been much importuned by Emigrants for free passages to Niagara and Queenston. I always look upon such applications, with suspicion, knowing that the demand for labour at these places, is extremely limited.

I am satisfied that the object which most of the applicants for free passages have in view is to get to the Frontier, in order to cross over to the United States.—

The accompanying letter from M^r McDonell, the Crown Lands Agent for the Newcastle District shews that the disposition to leave the Province is not confined to the Emigrants who land at Toronto.

During the past week I am assured, that many persons have been discharged by the Yonge Street Road Commissioners—and as the Harvest is drawing to a close, I feel it my duty to call His Excellency's attention to this subject, for I cannot conceal my apprehension, that the state of things which was anticipated before I left Toronto for Montreal in May last, is fast approaching. —His Excellency will I have no doubt recollect that fears were then entertained, that as soon as any temporary stoppage in the demand for Harvest or Road labour should take place, that many Emigrants would leave the Province. . . .

Since writing the above I have received Mr Roy's return of Emigrants landed at Kingston to the 21st Instant—Mr Roy says in his letter to Mr Chief Secretary Murdoch—a copy of which is annexed to the report—"that I believe two thousand (Emigrants) have gone to the United States as permanent settlers"—being about one-fourth of the total number who landed at that port since the commencement of the season,—If we add to this fourth the numbers who followed them from the Upper ports viz Cobourg, Port Hope, and Toronto, the matter assumes a very serious aspect.—

The expenses incurred, in forwarding these people will amount to a very large sum, as many of them are so poor, as to require immediate assistance on their reaching Quebec. More than one-half who leave Montreal receive free passages—and by the time they reach Bytown, or Kingston three-fourths of the whole number have exhausted their means and require assistance.

A. B. Hawke

(ii)

Letter enclosed with preceding

· Toronto, August 24th, 1840

My dear Sir

I have every reason to believe that many persons have left and will continue to leave this Province for the United States.

On Wednesday last, I saw and conversed, with upwards of twenty persons at Cobourg who left that Port for Rochester.—They offered to work on the public works, going on at Peterboro', if we would give them 5/- per day.—I offered them 3/6 which they refused, as they assured me they could get 5/- per day in the United States. . . .

A. McDonell

A. B. Hawke

23

German and American Immigrants into Upper Canada

From *Montreal Transcript*, July 27, 1844.

CANADA LAND COMPANY.—The half-yearly meeting of the Canada Land Company took place June 28, when a dividend of six per cent. per annum was declared for the half year, payable on the 10th July. The Governor gave a general sketch of the progress they had made during the past half year, which appears to be highly satisfactory. The system of letting land on lease instead of sale, by which the emigrants require to make no immediate payments, is working well. Up to the 25th May this year, the land so disposed of by the company amounted to 36,056 acres. The new corn bill was answering well for the colony, and was giving a considerable additional stimulus to cultivation. The emigration from the mother country has hitherto not been so extensive this season, but there had been a considerable addition to the German settlers, and a much greater proportion from the United States.

24

Construction of Railroads as Employment for Immigrants

From *Montreal Transcript*, May 18, 1847.

We see from the *British Colonist* that the President and Directors of the City of Toronto and Lake Huron Railroad Company have presented a memorial to His Excellency the Governor General, praying that His Excellency would take into consideration the benefits which would devolve upon the Province by the active forwarding of their projected work, and recommend that substantial and efficient assistance be afforded them by Government for the completion of their design. The advantages which this railroad would afford to the Province in general and especially to the particular district in question are obvious, and need no comment; but what now would render the co-operation of the Government more especially desirable, would be the means that would be afforded by its active progress, of providing employment for the abundance of emigrants who will this year overrun the Colony—and that employment would be lasting, suited to their habits, and likely to keep them after its completion in that part of the country where they had acquired a knowledge of the locality, and where their location would be most desirable to the interests of the Province. In our opinion it is the only feasible method hitherto started of providing for an immense emigration such as may be this year expected.

25

Horrors of the Irish Immigration of 1847-48[1]

From William Weir, *Sixty years in Canada* (Montreal, 1903), 26.

The year 1847 was the year of the fatal ship fever. I was then in Montreal and shall never forget the sights daily witnessed.

---

[1]See Gilbert Tucker, "The famine immigration to Canada, 1847" (*American Historical Review*, April, 1931, p. 533).

. . . Large sheds were erected in a field at Point St. Charles, where the emigrants were conveyed from the ships, the saddest sight being to see the nuns, at the risk of their own lives, carrying the sick women and children in their arms from the ships to the ambulances to be taken to the sheds, the majority to be laid in the trenches in rough deal coffins. I visited the sheds one Sunday afternoon. They formed a large square with a court in the centre, where the coffins were piled. . . . On another occasion I saw the Mayor (John E. Mills) and Lord Elgin visiting the ships on horseback and afterwards riding toward the sheds. Later in the season the mayor fell a victim to the fatal disease, as did many nuns, clergymen and others whose duties brought them in contact with the afflicted sufferers. . . .

THE ECONOMIC BACKGROUND OF POLITICS AT THE TIME OF THE REBELLION OF 1837

From Canadian Archives, *Q*, CDXXX, 23, April 23, 1840, Memorandum by Sir Richard Bonnycastle.

[" Peaceful penetration" by the Americans]

. . . I had been long impressed with the idea that to re-unite the Canadas would be virtually, to separate them from the Mother Country and this was founded on the knowledge I possessed of the great exertions made and making by American Agents amongst that class of the Inhabitants which forms the body electing the Representatives of the People.

No pains have been, neither will they be, spared by American Agents dispersed throughout Upper Canada to imbue the people with the idea of the superior advantages of American Democracy and as the Yeomen of that Province have not, from their isolation, much opportunity of judging for themselves or of improvement from the facilities afforded by education in other more advanced Countries, they are consequently, the more easily at the mercy of those whose business it is to supply them, in the lonely farms of the back Townships with all the exaggerated statements and false reasoning of the American Anti-British Press.

It is notorious that almost everywhere excepting in the larger Towns, the schools for Infant instruction are supplied with political catechisms, the very essence of which is to instil hatred towards the Mother Country and to draw the most invidious parallels between the constitutions of Britain and of the United States.

The Schoolmasters in the woods are very nearly all Americans whose religious faith is of the vilest of the many wild forms of worship into which Christianity has been split in the Western Republic[1] & thus the rising generation of cultivators of the soil in Upper Canada has its reasoning faculties cramped and confined within Channels, which cannot but be prejudicial to its future growth. These Preachers and teachers of youth are assisted in their ultimate views by another set of Agents who move constantly

---

[1]Probably one of the more fervent varieties of Methodism.

throughout the Province ostensibly with a purpose of selling wooden clocks and Tin ware but really with the intention of revolutionizing the Country by lectures and the distribution of political and religious tracts. These Persons known as the Tin Pedlars were exceedingly active, as well as the schoolmasters, previous to the disturbances in 1837 and during the years 1837, 38 and 39.

To forward the views of their employers there is also another and a more powerful class of revolutionists resident in the Country, who have either purchased farms, stores or stock—One of these, a man of considerable wealth and some science applied to Government a short time before the actual outbreak for permission to settle in the Township of Madoc for the purpose of working some valuable ores which had been discovered there. The neighbourhood of this Township was inhabited by the most determined enemies of British connexion but at that time in Upper Canada, there were no signs of any intended attempt at forcible separation. Finding that he was really a person of property in the State of New York, and that he understood Geology, Mineralogy and the extraction of metals, I gave him what assistance I could and having analysed his specimens and ascertained that Madoc really contained very rich ores in a remote and uncultivated portion of it, I was in some measure the means of procuring him the privilege of washing them. He set to work in earnest, founded a mining station, named it after the Lt. Governor, erected a village, every street of which was similarly named, declared that he should from conviction, become a British Subject and held forth most loyally at an Election.

Soon after there appeared some symptoms of immediate difficulties in Lower Canada and being then in charge of the principal fortress and Depot of Stores in the Upper Province I took the necessary precautions against the introduction thereto of Spies or Agents.

This person whose name was Prendergast came to me, full of zeal and as his Iron Foundry was in full operation he offered to cast cannon balls or do anything he could for the Government.

His object was to obtain information of the state of the Fortress at Kingston and of the Ordnance Stores there and having detected some French Agents in the same game, I became immediately suspicious of the fervid loyalty of Mr. Prendergast & without raising his suspicions contrived to get rid of him.

This man had all along been one of the principal Agents from the New York borderers, had raised men, obtained vast quantities of Arms, and had in fact carried matters so far that to avoid hanging he was obliged to fly, after having sold his interest in the mines— The injury he did was incalculable.

I have mentioned his case as an example of the many similar ones we had to deal with in 1837, 8 and 9.

It was such men, and it is such men, that swayed and move the minds of the good and innocent settlers in the back Countries.

[The iniquities of the Family Compact:—Officials as land-grabbers]

No one, who has not lived amongst those excellent people, can imagine the extent to which their delusion is fostered and carried, and as from the operation of the credit system in the United States, that country appears flourishing beyond conception, farmers in British America who suffer themselves to be thus misled, get discontented and imagine that it is only the form of Government that renders their native or adopted country, less of an Eldorado than that of their neighbours. . . .

One of the greatest of their grievances, although it was really a mere bugbear, was the family compact, as it was called and that it did extensive mischief and was actually the cause of Mackenzie being able to show a head or a bold front and of disgusting the respectable persons who latterly emigrated from Britain, I have no manner of doubt.

The absurd meddling of the present Bishop (otherwise a very excellent man) in politics, the political character of the Chief Justice, his abandonment of his high Duties and long absence in England during the reign of difficulties; the idea which the people had imbibed, that his mission was to secure the old order of things and if possible to procure for himself high honours and the Governorship, and the fact of the Public offices having been held, as it were, for life by the relations or dependents of these persons, created great disgust, a disgust felt by all classes of the community not within their family pale, and by none more than by the educated gentlemen who had latterly chosen Canada as their home from England, Scotland & Ireland.

The difficulties thrown in the way of obtaining eligible lands for these settlers, the mode in which the Land Offices were conducted, and the vast tracts owned by themselves and lying idle and unproductive as the germs of fortune to their children, has been and still is, a source of great evil and of difficulty to the country, retarding its advancement quite as much and perhaps more, than the waste state of the Clergy Reserves:

In fact the Land officers, instead of being the mere Servants and Agents of the Crown, were themselves the distributors of the Provincial Territories, and if the quantities possessed by some of these officers were ascertained, wonder at the difficulties and disgusts of expectant settlers would vanish and it would only become a matter of surprise that a great many more did not relinquish all hopes of benefit in Upper Canada, and rush into the United States, where they had at least a reasonable Land Market and the liberty of choice.

Many, very many did so, and others from disappointment and sheer vexation took a prominent part in the opposition to Government in 1837. I knew one Gentleman amongst several, belonging to good families in England, who openly expressed his feelings, who had at vast expence brought out a fine stock of thorough bred cattle and sheep, and who suffering his youthful ire to get the better of his reason, joined the rebels and ruined himself entirely.

I was employed in the sale of some public land, and thus became intimately acquainted with the mode of managing things in the Land Offices. That has, however, I believe, been somewhat remedied since, but it would be a very wise measure to make an unalterable order that no person in the Commissioner of Crown Lands Office or in the Surveyor Generals, should, either of himself or by proxy deal in the purchase or sale of the Government Lands or Reserves for his own benefit or for the benefit of any connexion of his whatever— The Diagrams of the Townships are dotted and disfigured with the names of Clerks, Surveyors & others belonging to these offices, the amalgamation of which will only make the matter worse, as heretofore the Crown Lands and Surveyor General's Departments were some little check upon each other and it is almost impracticable for a Governor to detect the practices I have alluded to, whilst public officers can still impoverish the Country by a system of attending sales of wild Land for the Taxes, and as nobody can compete with them there, grasping to themselves for almost nothing the most valuable lands in the

Country I have reason to know that this was carried on to a very great extent and that officers and others who for their services had obtained small grants but had been subsequently removed from the Province, have in their absence and without any reference whatever to them, lost their properties which have passed into the possession of these people.

There should be a fixed low price per acre for all wild Public Land in Canada and in the purchase Emigrants should have the preference, and Government Land or Revenue Officers, or large wild Landholders be excluded.

It is as I have already said impossible or nearly so for the Governors to become acquainted with many of the evils of the system of Colonial rule and it is only persons in a more humble rank of public life and perhaps few had better opportunities than I had to discover practises which time has sanctioned and which have grown with the growth and strengthened with the strength of the Colony. The late brother of the Chief Justice [*Peter Robinson*] who was Commissioner of Crown Lands held a large and very valuable share of wild Land as well as of cultivated property and yet it is believed from his habitual carelessness and from suffering his clerks to have too much sway in his department, he died a Defaulter to a large amount whilst some of his underlings whose incomes were very moderate had acquired considerable influence and wealth in the community.

The check which has been lately given to the permanent continuance in office of Servants of the Crown in the colonies[1] will operate most beneficially in Upper Canada, as it will prove useful in many ways. The subordinates will never be so well shielded by the assumed power of their superiors: their superiors will be extremely careful in their own conduct and the Country hails with gratitude the removal of a dead weight which has hitherto pressed down all her energies, for it mattered not what the office was, whether it required skill in accounts, in policy, in science, or in any particular whatever, the merits of the Candidate were only considered in reference to his belonging: or assistance to, the family dominion. Thus the Commissioner of Crown Lands was a person of neither talent nor reputation.[2] The Surveyor General's Department was managed by persons unacquainted with

---

[1]By Lord John Russell's despatches of October, 1839.
[2]Peter Robinson, the brother of the chief-justice.

scientific acquirements.   The Inspectorship of Public accounts, was held by a gentleman of very low origin and possessed of none of the essentials for such an office.

These persons have it is true either removed themselves by their conduct, or have been removed, but it was not until the order in question was issued that the Public in Upper Canada had any reason to suppose that the occupants of Public offices would be one whit better.   A Surveyor General acquainted with ten [*sic?*] astronomical and Geodesic operations is much wanted there. At present the office is held by an eminent lawyer who is also Commissioner of Crown lands and as it is stated in the Newspapers that this gentleman is to be otherwise provided for on account of his services, now is perhaps the best time for remedying the gross evils which have crept into that valuable branch of the Public Service.   Some of the papers state that Sir A. McNabb the Speaker of the Provincial House of Assembly is likely to succeed to the offices of Commissioner of Crown Lands and Sur-veyor General—with every respect for that person I should conceive he would be the least fitted of any for such important offices from the fact of his having been notoriously the largest private land jobber in the Province. . . .

These defects in the Land Agencies are I am well assured not yet entirely remedied, and as long as Michigan & Ohio can compete with Upper Canada in the land market by the favourable prices and entire liberty of selection it will be useless to direct emigration on any large scale there as the emigrants will, notwithstanding the agues and fevers of the above-mentioned States, fevers too of rapid operation, unknown in Canada, and notwithstanding the difference of political and personal feeling, emigrants, I maintain, will find their way to those western regions. . . .

Since the breaking out of the disturbances there has arisen another although a minor grievance respecting the Militia and should a war take place, or it becomes necessary to assume a war-like attitude this should be attended to.

I held a large command in the Militia and am thus able to speak with certainty on the present complaint.

It had always been customary in calling out the Militia, to call it out by Regiments, or portions of Regiments, of the different Counties, and thus the officers and men were well acquainted with each other.

Latterly, there has crept in a practice of embodying certain

Regiments for one, two, three or four years and of officering them under the immediate patronage of the Government, or rather that of the Adjutant General of Militia—A Captain obtained that Rank with the pay of a Captain in the Line, which in Canada is a very good provision, on condition that he recruited a certain number of men. Officers thus crept in with whom the people were wholly unacquainted and who were wholly unacquainted with the military profession. The result was that the very worst class of recruits were obtained and deserters from the American Army and other vagabonds swelled the ranks, whilst subordination was very difficult to be attained.

[Best means of ensuring the success of the Union]

I shall not touch upon the extremely difficult question of the Clergy Reserves, one of the great grievances. It is undergoing its ordeal and although a Member by education and inclination of the Church of England, I cannot, neither do I conceive that any sensible man who has resided in Canada can, shut my eyes to the fact that the Church does not embrace the majority of the inhabitants of the Upper Province, that it never can & never will, and that therefore it is only just and reasonable that it should not be endowed with such a vast portion of the surface of that Territory. The projected measure may at least have the benefit of a trial, for it is utterly impracticable to continue the present one. Remedying as far as possible the defects which have existed or do exist; attending to the important subject of public Instruction and if possible to the construction of a Ship Navigation from Montreal to Erie, are the means of quieting the minds of the loyal or of the wavering in Upper Canada and their mind once quieted, there can be but little question that the French in the Lower Province will soon effectually open their eyes, as they were beginning to do before I left the Country in the Autumn of 1839 to the advantages of remaining a portion of the Dominions of the Queen and to the disadvantages likely to occur to them on the day when the bald-headed eagle replaces the British Lion for although it may appear trite to say so, from that day their nationality, their cherished language and the Catholic religion succumbs to the aspiring American, to that Anglo-Saxon and mixed race burning to possess Canada and Mexico.

It would be presumptuous in me to deliver at large hasty opinions upon the probable working of the Union. At first it will work well. The people of Upper Canada to a man would have preferred that their Country should have been wholly separated from Lower Canada: there is no sympathy between the races & the cruelties committed by the infuriated peasantry of French origin in '37 and '38 weaned whatever of that feeling, had not already departed.

They would have preferred the annexation of Montreal as a sea port, and the natural boundary of the Ottawa River; they would have desired a Governor of their own and a separate Legislature without any Governor General or other interference than that of the Home Authorities.

But of course to accede to such a very natural wish, would have been to have thrown overboard all consideration of Justice and of honour towards the French-Canadians and there is therefore no other course to steer than that of Union.

At first the natural preponderacy of British character and influence will prevent coalition between the discontented French Leaders and those from Upper Canada of American origin and principles, but it cannot be hidden that this will ultimately occur and that it will require the utmost vigilance and judgment to counteract. To throw as many British settlers as possible into both Sections of the Union, to promote the great canal above alluded to, so as to render Montreal the Sea port of the Upper Division, as well as the great mart for flour, timber and peltries and gradually yet imperceptibly to weaken the national prejudices and language of the French will be of course the most obvious policy. . . .

I should however venture to think that the Governor of Canada should still be the Governor General of the British North American Provinces, in order to give weight, importance and efficiency to the measure of the Union and to carry weight also with his appointment in the eyes of the neighbouring Republic, the people of which however much they may outwardly inveigh against rank are very much led by it, as I have had, with many other English travellers, plenty of opportunities of observing and amongst others the well known instance that out of the hundreds of tourists from the States to Canada during the summer scarcely any go to Toronto, although not at all out of their way, to see the Lt. Governor and capital but almost all bend their steps to the vice regal Court of the Castle of St. Lewis. . . .

April 23d, 1840

THE ST. LAWRENCE SYSTEM AND THE DEVELOPMENT OF COMMUNICATIONS, 1783-1850

INTRODUCTORY

WITHIN the period under discussion, Canada was confined to the St. Lawrence watershed and it was not until the construction of railroads.that the control of the river over colonial existence was somewhat loosened. The natural highway determined everything—the direction of colonization, the methods of exploitation, the channels of trade, political relationships with the United States. Every major Canadian activity in succession has been shaped by the great route into the interior, or at least by the combination of it and the neighbouring southerly boundary of the Laurentian plateau. First the fur trade built itself up by drawing the original staple product of the plateau eastward along its edge to Montreal, then settlement advanced up the highway, occupying its borders. Next the lumberman exploited the plateau and, like the fur trader before him, used the river and its affluents to bring his product down to the sea. The settler trod on the heels of the fur-trader in the American west and the old route exercised its domination over him so that for a generation the opening states were but the hinterland of the route's outlet, Montreal. When the Americans built the Erie Canal the supremacy of the St. Lawrence seemed to have gone, and for another generation Montreal struggled to hold its own. But when the advantages were once more approximately equalized, when the Erie Canal had been matched by the St. Lawrence Canals, the New York Central Railway by the Grand Trunk, New York harbour by the deep channel below Montreal, the river tended to regain its former key position. Its commanding place in the economy of the continent is as apparent to-day as ever (for furs, wheat has been substituted), as the agitation for a still deeper waterway indicates. The only factors which

prevent its assuming a dominant rôle are the natural factor
of climate and the political factor of the international boundary.

REFERENCES: Department of the interior, *Atlas of Canada* (Ottawa, 1915);
H. M. Ami (ed.), *North America II, Canada and Newfoundland* (Stanford's *Compendium of geography and travel*, 2nd edition, London, 1915); S. E. Dawson,
The St. Lawrence, its basin and borderlands (Toronto, 1905); W. Smith, *History of
the post office in British North America, 1639-1870* (Cambridge, 1920); H. A.
Innis, *The fur trade in Canada: an introduction to Canadian economic history* (New
Haven, 1930) and "Transportation as a factor in Canadian economic history"
(*Proceedings* of the Canadian Political Science Association, 1931); R. W. Brock,
"Physical basis of Canada" (*Canada and its provinces*, IX, 9); W. A. Mackintosh,
"The Laurentian plateau in Canadian economic development" (*Economic
Geography,* October, 1926); volume I of this work.

THE ST. LAWRENCE AS A HIGHWAY

There were about four stages in the development of transportation prior to 1850. To begin with, the natural waterways were used just as they were. Then, in the first decade of the nineteenth century, steamers were introduced on the lower river and in the second on the lakes, bringing with them demands for improvements to the river system, with resulting efforts taking such elementary forms as blasting conspicuous rocks out of rapids. Thirdly, by 1820, projects for canals were afoot but realization was slow and before many were built, the railroad was already displacing the canal in popular imagination and in utility. Consequently from the 1830's the projects for railroads, the fourth stage, become even more numerous than had previously been those for canals. Like them, the "lag" between project and accomplishment (caused by poverty) was great and it was not until the railway system of the United States had been greatly developed that Canada got its systems. The characteristic Canadian feature of the whole development is this matter of "lag", which threw the accomplishment of each stage into the period when in other countries that stage was already being superseded by the next.

Not only was much energy devoted to improving the highway, much also went into bettering the vehicle. Thus the canoe gave way to the York boat, the York boat to the Durham boat and the lake schooner, these latter in their turn to the steamer. In the next period, the railroad as it encircles the smaller lakes or parallels the rivers, will, except on the main routes, more and more displace the steamer.

REFERENCES: George A. Cuthbertson, *Freshwater* (Toronto, 1931); William Wood, *All afloat* (Chronicles of Canada, Toronto, 1914); M. J. Patton, "Shipping and canals" (*Canada and its provinces*, X, 475 *ff.*).

1

Canoe Travelling:—A Camp *en route*

From Bigsby, *The shoe and the canoe*, I, 136.

The gentlemen occupied one small square tent of thin canvass, pitched by their own hands, as the custom is. . . .

My bed, a blanket folded four times, was near the entrance of the tent. . . .

The voyageurs were asleep in their blankets round the fire; one alone was up and about, on watch, and cooking their next day's soup. Baggage lay strewn in all directions. . . .

2

The Niagara Portage:—Rates for Cartage

Memorandum for Captain Phyn from the merchants and traders interested in the trade to Detroit

The carrying place of Niagara, over which Mr Stedman has had an exclusive right of transporting, as well the Merchants goods as the Stores, Provisions &c for Government, has not for these two years last past been supplied either with Cattle or Carriages in any degree equal to the necessary demand of the Traders, and therefore Quantities of Goods have been in the Carrying Place for a very long time where they have been embezzled & even what has been rode over, in general very badly taken care of.

The rate which Mr Stedman was allowed by his Contract is £7. 10/ York[1] for 13 Barrells of 35 Gallons each equal to 4/6 for 112^{lb} & yet he has charged & obliged people to pay 6/ p. Cw^t or refused to carry their Goods over, altho he last summer agreed verbally with three Houses here namely Alexr Ellice & C°, Felix Graham & Todd & McGill, to transport at the rate of 4/6 p^r 112^{lb} or £7. 10/ for 13 Barrells of 35 Gallons each.

Now as Mr Stedman we understand, is at Quebec applying for a renewal of his Contract from his Excell^y Genl Haldimand— We would request that he may be obliged to the following or some similar regulations so far as they relate to the Traders Effects.

1   To keep in good order & repair a sufficient number of Cattle & Carriages with Drivers, so that no Traders Effects may meet with unnecessary delay from a want of them—*Alowed*

2   That without any partiality he may transport them in Rotation as they arrive—*Alowed*

3   That he shall be liable to any loss or damage happening to the Goods after they are safely on his Carriages till delivered at the proper discharging place on either side of the Carrying Place—*Alowed*

4   That he be allowed 4/6 p^r gross Hundred for all Goods taken at the lower Landing & delivered safely at the other side— and for furrs 6/ both Yk Currency, for every Pack of 120^{lb} w^t —*Alowed*

Should Mr Stedman accede to these proposals the Merchants will be perfectly satisfied; but they would wish that such contract might not be granted for more than three years—if he should persist in the prices charged for two years past, they cannot help themselves for this season; but would request in that case the term to be limited to one year & that they may have the liberty of establishing for themselves the means of transporting their goods over that important Carrying place after the month of March next. . . . [1778]

---

[1]*York:* New York currency, eight shillings to the dollar.

3

The Great Lakes Portages and Lake St. Clair

From Canadian Archives, *Q*, XLVII, 105, 112, 125.

Quebec, 6th Dec., 1788

From Niagara to the Landing place below the Falls is about seven miles and a quarter, there is a tolerable good Road, but merchandize, stores etc are carried up the River in Batteaux or in Vessels, there being sufficient depth of water all the way up, and also to lay alongside the wharf to unload: beyond this place the current becomes too strong to proceed any further without great difficulty; Boats indeed, but not vessels, can go about half a mile higher but no advantage can be obtained from it as the shore there becomes unpracticable, being a precipice of loose Rock about three times as high as where the present Landing is. From the wharf at the Landing Goods are drawn up the side of the bank about Fifty feet high upon ways upon an easy slope by a Capstan fixed at the top. From this place there is a waggon Road of seven miles to Fort Schlosser, which is one mile and a half above the Falls, where the Goods are again put into Boats and carried up Eighteen miles to Fort Erie, From whence they are conveyed in vessels across Lake Erie to Detroit etc. . . .

If they are meant to pass into Lake Huron, they should not exceed fifty Tons, on account of the shoalness of the water over the bar at the Entrance of the River from Lake St. Clair.

What is called the falls of St. Mary on the Communication between Lake Superior and Huron is a strong Rapid of near a mile in length, and about half a mile across, but above and below the Rapid it is about three quarters of a mile across from shore to shore. Canoes pass the Rapid by *going up* quite light, and by taking out part only of their loading *to come down.*

There is a Portage on the south shore of about half a league in length, partly over wet ground, and partly rock, but there is no Hill, it is a Cart Road. . . .The Channel for Canoes is near the shore, it is narrow and somewhat crooked, but has everywhere about three feet depth of water. There is a deeper channel but not safe for canoes near the middle of the Rapid, or a little towards the North Shore, by which vessels have frequently passed; but the Rebusca, the vessel at present employed on Lake Superior between the Grand Portage and this place does not come any lower than the Landing at the head of the Falls.

4

Introduction of the Durham Boat:—Its Advantages over the Batteau

From Canadian Archives, Upper Canada sundries.

R. Hamilton to Gov. Hunter

Jan. 10, 1800

. . . The transporting of our Produce to the Sea Coast naturally draws our attention to the improvement of the water communication between Montreal and Kingston. Your Excellency has already been inform'd of a new plan of transport which has been lately introduced between the Chippewa & Fort Erie, by Substituting large boats carrying one Hundred Barrels, for the Canadian Battoes, which carry only from Twenty to Twenty four. I am much gratified in being able to say that we find them answer our Expectations.—One of these boats with only Six Men and a Guide, has completely done the Bussiness of transporting all the Merchandize up, and the Peltrys down of this Season, & they have not had constant employ. In the same bussiness Five boats & Twenty five Canadians were last season engaged almost without intromission.—We have to lament that an Accident which happened to this Boat while laden with Peltry, may discourage their introduction in other places, Overtaken by a most violent thunder Storm, she filled with Water, and some of the Packs were unavoidably lost.—From the concurring testimony of nearly Twenty persons who were in the boat at the time, & who were all providentially saved, we have every reason to beleive, that no boat of any construction, could have possibly Withstood the Violence of the Storm;—That in any other Boat the people, as well as the Peltry would in all human probability have been lost.—We hope this misfortune which may never happen again, may soon be forgotten, and that these Boats will be introduced in the transport between Montreal and Kingston, where we cannot doubt but they will be found to Answer.—The Constructors of these Boats, a Mr Herling & Son, from the Ohio, went this summer to Montreal, for the purpose of inspecting the Rout from thence to Kingston, and have reported the River perfectly favourable for the Navigation of these Boats.—They say that at a certain expence, which they estimate at Fifteen hundred Dollars, they would undertake to clear the River of every impediment, to their going loaded up, and down, and this without having any benefit from the present Canals or locks, which are on too small a plan to be of any use to them. This completed, they have said to the Montreal Merchants, that they will engage to carry freight up, at a third less than the present Charge, And take down Flour and Pottash at the rate of half a Dollar pr Barrel. The sum they require is such a triffle, compared with the benefit to be expected, that the Advance could never be a Question, whether done by Government, or by the trade. Whether these men could be so far depended on, as to Warrant a Contract, I will not pretend to say, But it might be well to employ them again next summer to resurvey the River, accompanied by such confidential Person as your Excellency might direct, When the practability of the plan, & the probable expence might be more Exactly Ascertained. . . . .

R. Hamilton

5

Up the St. Lawrence by Batteau

From Howison, Sketches of Upper Canada, 23, 43, 44.

[The first portage, Lachine]

There is a portage between the two places, for the rapids of the St. Lawrence interrupt the navigation, and consequently all stores and goods, intended for the upper country, are conveyed from Montreal to La Chine by land. At the latter place, they are put into flat-bottomed boats, called *batteaux*, which are rowed up the river, with incredible labour, by Canadians, whom the forwarders engage at a certain sum during the season.   La Chine is thus rendered a place of some importance, which otherwise it would not be; but still it merely consists of a few dwelling-houses, and several large stores for the reception of the goods . . . .

[Batteau navigation]

There were five batteaux, and this number constitutes a brigade. The crew of each boat consisted of five rowers, and a man with a paddle to steer; and the whole equipment was under the command and superintendence of an individual who was styled the *conductor*. . . .

[The voyageurs' fare]

They take a meal regularly every four hours during the four and twenty, and it is to be supposed that the great labour they undergo must create a proportionable appetite; but it does seem astonishing that they should be contented with the quality of the provisions they subsist upon. Pork, pease-soup, and biscuit, compose their daily fare; and though they give their meals the appellations of breakfast, dinner, &c. this distinction is founded upon the time at which they are taken, not upon the difference of the articles presented at each.

6

First Trip of First Steamer in Canada

From *Quebec Mercury*, November 6, 1809.

On Saturday morning, at eight o'clock, arrived here [*Quebec*], from Montreal, being her first trip, the Steam boat *Accommodation*, with ten passengers. This is the first vessel of the kind that ever appeared in this harbour. She is continually crowded by visitants. She left Montreal on Wednesday, at two o'clock, so that her passage was sixty six hours; thirty of which she was at anchor. She arrived at Three Rivers in twenty four hours. She has, at present, berths for twenty passengers; which, next year, will be considerably augmented.—No wind or tide can stop her. She has 75 feet keel, and 85 feet on deck. The price for a passage up is nine dollars, and eight down, the vessel supplying provisions. The great advantage attending a vessel so constructed is, that a passage may be calculated on to a degree of certainty, in point of time; which cannot be the case with any vessel propelled by sails only. The steam boat receives her impulse from an open, double-spoked, perpendicular wheel, on each side, without any circular band or rim. To the end of each double spoke is fixed a square board, which enters the water, and by the rotatory motion of the wheel acts like a paddle. The wheels are put and kept in motion by steam, operating within the vessel. A mast is to be fixed in her, for the purpose of using a sail when the wind is favorable, which will occasionally accelerate her head way.

7

Introduction of Steamers on Upper St. Lawrence

From *Montreal Gazette*, November 13, 1815.

The great utility of Steam Boats on the St. Lawrence, between this City and Quebec, has discovered itself to our friends in Upper Canada; and we are extremely happy to hear that several Gentlemen of Kingston, have formed the plan of establishing one on a large scale, to ply between that place and Prescott. We understand the shares are already filled up. When we consider the intimate connexion subsisting between these sister provinces, and the rapidly increasing trade of Upper Canada, and the immense country bordering on the Lakes, we rejoice at the introduction of any improvement that can tend to facilitate the communication between that vast region, and this City, destined, under proper management, to become the emporium of the inland commerce of North America. We sincerely hope, that the approaching Session of both Legislatures, will be marked by mutual applications for the immediate removal of local obstructions, and ameliorating the navigation between this City and Prescott, thereby securing mutual advantages, which will, very soon compensate any expenditure, that can possibly be incured.

8

A Journey up the St. Lawrence from Quebec to York, 1819

From *A few plain directions*, 41, 42, 46, 53.

Montreal is 180 miles south-west of Quebec; seven steam-packets, provided with every accommodation which passengers can require, run between the two cities: one of them leaving Quebec every other day. The largest are of 700 tons burden; and there are no vessels of the kind in the world superior to them. Cabin passengers pay each about 2*l*. 10*s*. sterling; besides a very reasonable charge for their baggage, if it exceed a certain weight or quantity. For that sum they are furnished with provisions and beds, paying exclusively for porter, liquor, or lemonade. . . .

Steerage passengers pay 15s. sterling, and are allowed to take a moderate quantity of baggage gratis. They find their own provisions and beds; the remainder of their stock of provisions brought from England will serve. . . .

Should the steam-vessel in which the emigrant came from Quebec, continue at Montreal twenty or twenty-four hours, he can, to avoid expenses on shore, remain on board the night following his arrival; and in the morning, hire a cart in the old market-place (which is close to the wharf) to convey his baggage to La Chine, distant nine miles. There is no conveyance by water to that village on account of the rapids, and a cart may be hired for five, or at most six shillings. . . .

The emigrant has now the most difficult part of the journey before him, viz., that between La Chine and Prescott, a distance of 120 or 130 miles. There is, however, a good road (the great west road), and farm-houses at every half mile or mile, the whole way, with inns at a convenient distance from each other.

There are three modes of travelling. The most expeditious, and most expensive, is by the stage which conveys the mail: it passes through La Chine twice a week during the summer. The fare is thirteen dollars, or about 3l. sterling, from La Chine to Prescott, and the passenger is allowed the carriage of a small trunk gratis. The fare and provisions on the journey will make the whole expense amount to 3l. 12s. sterling. No money is given to the driver. When the coach arrives at Prescott, passengers can proceed to Kingston, sixty miles further, in a steam-vessel up the river St. Lawrence, or on foot.

The second method of travelling from La Chine to Kingston is by the Batteaux or Durham boats. . . . These boats do not arrive at Kingston in less than ten or twelve days. The passengers suffer many inconveniences, and some hardships: yet for women and children this is, perhaps, the least expensive mode of travelling as well as the most convenient. Provisions such as biscuit, or bread and meat, should be taken from La Chine. Passengers sleep on shore at nights, either at a house, if there happen to be one near, or under a tree. They also have to land and walk where there are rapids. . . .

The third way of travelling from La Chine to Prescott and Kingston during the summer months, is on foot. For single men it is eligible, easy, and cheap. There are farm-houses and inns on the great west road for the whole distance. By subsisting principally on bread and cheese and milk, or Sepaune and milk, the expense of each person will not be more than three shillings sterling a day; and he may walk with ease thirty miles a day, . . . Nine miles from La Chine, the road passes through the town of Point Claire; and nine miles further, is the ferry over the River Ottawa (four Miles) which is passed in a batteau. There is then a good road through a populous country to Glengary, a considerable Scotch settlement, about sixty miles from La Chine. Or after proceeding fifteen miles from the ferry over the River Ottawa, the traveller can hire a batteau (at a house by the side of the lake) to take him to Glengary down the Lake St. Francis, twenty-four miles. . . .

From Glengary to the town of Cornwall, (the next stage) the distance is twelve or fourteen miles, and the road good. From Cornwall to Prescott the River St. Lawrence is mostly seen from the road, and between those two towns the country is thickly settled; and there are several villages. When the emigrant has arrived at Prescott, he may proceed, at a small expense, to Kingston in a steam-packet (up the River St. Lawrence), or continue his journey on foot. From Prescott to Kingston the distance is sixty or sixty-five miles; the country is also well settled and the roads good. . . .

A steam-packet goes twice a week during the summer, from Kingston to the carrying-place at the head of the bay of Quinte, a distance of seventy-five miles. The fare for steerage passengers is trifling, they finding their own provisions. At the carrying-place are two inns. . . . A steam-packet proceeds from Kingston to York once a week. The fare for steerage passengers is fifteen shillings; (they furnishing themselves with provisions,) &c.; the distance 180 miles; and the length of the passage about thirty-six hours. There are also small vessels, which take passengers and goods on very moderate terms, continually going in the summer from Kingston to Hamilton and York. . . .

9

Stage and Steamer Connections with Upper Canada in 1832 and 1833

(i)

From *Montreal Gazette*, May 3, 1832.

THE UPPER CANADA COACHES leave MONTREAL EVERY DAY except Saturday and Sunday, at FOUR o'clock, A.M.

LAKE ONTARIO: The splendid new Steamboat GREAT BRITAIN. Captain Jos. Whitney.

Propelled by two low pressure Engines, of 90 horse power each.

The Public are respectfully informed that the following arrangements have been made for the months of April, May and June.

Will leave PRESCOTT every *Wednesday Morning.* Touching at BROCKVILLE, KINGSTON, COBURG, PORT HOPE, YORK, and arrive at NIAGARA early on Friday morning.

Will leave NIAGARA every Saturday afternoon, at FIVE o'clock, Calling at Oswego every Sunday morning after 5th May next; also Kingston, Brockville, and arrive at PRESCOTT on Sunday evening.

The Ladies and Gentlemen's Cabins on Board the Great Britain are finished in the same manner as the New York and Liverpool Packet ships, with State Rooms; and no expense has been spared in finishing and furnishing the boat in the most comfortable manner; every endeavour will be used to accommodate Passengers, and ensure the greatest regularity.

N.B. Notice will be given of the arrangements for the months of July, August and September.

Prescott, U.C. April 9, 1832.

AN OFFICE has been established at Prescott, U.C. for the LAKE ONTARIO STEAMBOATS, GREAT BRITAIN and QUEENS-TON. Mr. Meneilley, the agent, will at all times attend to the shipping of Articles to go by the above Boats; and every information will be given by him to Emigrants proceeding upwards. [*Advt.*]

(ii)

Travelling to and in Upper Canada

From *Montreal Gazette*, June 18, 1833.

The new arrangement of the UPPER CANADA Line of Stages and Steam Boats has now been some weeks in operation, and the additional convenience which is thereby afforded to the man of business and the traveller, is the theme of general remark. The stages now leave MONTREAL every day, at half-past ten in the forenoon, instead of the former inconveniently early hour of four in the morning. They arrive at Prescott the following day, (with the exception of Saturday's stage, which remains over at Cornwall on Sunday,) in time for passengers to join the Lake Boats. In the arrangements in descending, a great saving of the time usually occupied in travelling is effected—allowing, as it does, of travellers leaving Prescott in the morning, and yet reaching Montreal between eight or nine the same evening. Indeed, the regularity and punctuality in the arrival of the stages in this city, are deserving of high commendation. Much of the increased expedition is, doubtless, due to the placing on the line of the Iroquois, the steamer which runs between Dickinson's Landing, above Cornwall, to Prescott, (superseding the use of stages on thirty-eight miles of what used to be the very worst of roads,) but not less is it owing, certainly, to the high state of efficiency in which the Messrs Bigelow have placed their other arrangements. Of the Iroquois, we have heard many travellers lately speak in terms of high praise: —we have before described this extraordinary boat, but the following notice from the *Prescott Gazette*, is perhaps more complete than any former account.

"This convenient and ingeniously-constructed boat will be commanded for the season by Captain Barber, an experienced and skilful mariner. She has commenced her regular trips from Prescott to the head of the Long Sault, and is found to exceed the most sanguine expectations of her enterprising proprietors. She stems the rapids with the greatest ease. Her cabins are elegantly and amply furnished with every necessary convenience—her engine, machinery and apparatus, are differently constructed and arranged to any we have hitherto seen—her wheel propellers are

10

placed in the stern, and seem to answer the navigation of the rapids much better than was expected. On account of her extraordinary and daring route, against the most powerful rapids in North America as well as on account of her safe conveyance, convenient and pleasant apartments, we must pronounce this effort of her proprietors to accommodate the public, one of the most useful and ingenious enterprises ever attempted in North America." . . .

The following is, we believe, a correct table of the departures of the different boats from Prescott.

Sunday—Queenston.	Wednesday—Great Britain, Sir
Monday—United States, Perse-	James Kempt.
verance.	Thursday—Perseverance, Caro-
Tuesday—United Kingdom,	line.
Britannia, Caroline.	Friday—William IV., Britannia.

Saturday—Sir James Kempt, Caroline.

. . . To those who have business to transact on both sides of *Lake Ontario* there will be found plying between Kingston and Sacket's Harbour and Oswego, a superior class of schooners, fitted up as packets, and making, wind and weather permitting, two trips regularly each week.

To those who from business or occupation may wish to avail themselves of a route by land, stages will be found running regularly from the CARRYING PLACE, at the head of the Bay of Quinte, to York and from that town by the Shores of *Lake Ontario* to Hamilton, whence by other arrangements, they may also journey through the fine villages and beautiful country of the Gore and NIAGARA Districts to FORT GEORGE. FROM DUNDAS, which is but a few miles from Hamilton, stages will be found running to GUELPH and other portions of the lands of the Canada Company. From HAMILTON a line of stages start to SANDWICH, in the Western District passing through London and other towns in the country bordering on *Lake Erie*. From PORT STANLEY a stage is now running to St. Thomas, at which place also, a stage leaves three times a week for London, and another line for Port Talbot. At London passengers can intersect the regular mail stage running between HAMILTON and SANDWICH.

10

The "Forwarding" System, Lower to Upper Canada

(i)

Protests against rates charged

From *Montreal Gazette*, April 15, 1837.

At a meeting of the Merchants of Brockville, to take into consideration the "TARIFF" of Freight from Montreal upwards, for the ensuing Season;—the following Resolutions were proposed and carried.

Resolved, 1.—That from the advance in wages and price of provisions we think the Forwarders are entitled to *an advance on the rates of last season of Twenty-Five per cent.*

Resolved, 2.—That the present "TARIFF" now published, from the following statements, so far exceeds what we consider a *fair* advance on the rates of last season, that we feel it imperative on us, to call the attention of the Commercial Community, and the public generally to the subject. . . .

Recapitulation	Old Tariff	New Tariff
Hhd. Earthen ware ..	£0.12.4.	£2.10. 8.
Crate do...........	6.0.	1.17. 8.
Hhd. Sugar.........	1. 8.9.	4.19. 0.
Chest Tea..........	0. 2.5.	0. 7.10.
Case straw Hats.....	0. 1.5.	0.11. 4.
Bale Flannel........	0. 8.6.	2. 6. 8.
Cotton Wadding.....	0. 3.5.	3. 5. 6.
Tierce Cod-fish......	0.11.3.	1.14. 9.
	3.14.1.	17.13. 5.

Difference—£13.19.4.

. . . .

Resolved, 5th. That the advertised Tariff of the Forwarders exhibits marks of decided combination, ruinous to the trade and interests of both Provinces, and should call forth the lawful exertions of the public to counteract the evil.

Billa Flint, *Chairman*

TO THE EDITOR OF THE MONTREAL GAZETTE.

Sir.—I am induced to notice the document sent forth to the world by the Merchants of Brockville, giving a glaring and exaggerated picture of the probable effects and changes to be produced by the Tariff lately published by the Forwarders. . . .

They have made an unfair statement. They have carefully selected extreme cases which if shewn in their proper light, tell against them. They know that if Forwarders undertook to do a business entirely made up of light goods, even at the rates of the tariff, they would soon ruin themselves. They know that each boat's cargo must necessarily be an assortment of various kinds of goods. They know that taking such an assortment into consideration, their statements of percentage advances are notorious *mis*-statements, and that they cannot, for a moment be applied to the general business.

The absurdity of carrying light and bulky packages on the same principle as bars of Iron and Steel, was too gross to be continued. . . .

The assertion that boats generally go up partially filled, is unfounded. When there is lack of hardware or heavy goods, they are frequently laden so bulkily, ere they get anything like a hold of the water, that serious danger is incurred in ascending the Rapids.

A FORWARDER

(ii)

Protest against monopoly

From Canadian Archives, *Private secretary's office, Upper Canada, Registers 1840-41*, enclosure in file no. 2787.

Copy of the Resolutions passed at the Agricultural Meeting which was held at Richmond Hill in the Home District on the 9th December, 1840:— . . .

4—That the people of Upper Canada hitherto, considered the construction of the Rideau Canal, at the expense of the British Government, as a most valuable boon conferred upon them, and a mark of the deep interest their Sovereign took in their welfare, and they cannot repress their indignation that the beneficent design of this national work should so long have been frustrated by a baneful coalition of the forwarding merchants. That four private companies, acting in union, have engrossed the whole carrying trade between Kingston and Montreal while they themselves are controlled by another Company who have entire monopoly of the navigation. That when in all other countries the facility of transmission afforded by Canal navigation has diminished the charge for freight, in this instance it has produced the contrary effect, and increased the rates of transportation, to the manifest injury of our agriculture and commerce. . . .

WATERWAYS, CANALS, AND ROADS, SUBSIDIARY TO THE MAIN ST. LAWRENCE HIGHWAY

Of the tributaries of the St. Lawrence, the Saguenay, the Richelieu, and the Ottawa are the largest. The Saguenay reaches back into a fur country which was dominated by that staple until William Price, about 1825, began to exploit its resources in lumber. The firm he founded still maintains its control of the district. The Richelieu, as an important link in the highway between Canada and New York, became one of the first objects of canalization. After the Revolution, Vermont pressed for this outlet and until the Lake Champlain Canal was built in the late twenties, the Richelieu dominated the economic life of the northern part of that state. While the forest lasted, the valley was an important contributor of timber to the Quebec market. The Ottawa, as the largest of the affluents and as affording the shortest way to the upper lakes, was the natural route for the fur canoe until the amalgamation of the companies in 1821 sent that traffic to Hudson Bay. But by that date the Ottawa had become the highway for the square-timber raft and it has continued to be the greatest lumber river in Canada. Its handicap has been its *cul-de-sac* formation, since it leads nowhere, except to the forest; hence the efforts, beginning about 1838, to construct a route by canal to Lake Huron.

Once settlement began to move away from navigable rivers, a demand for canals arose. This in Upper Canada synchronized with the mania for canals in such states as Ohio and Michigan, but thanks to provincial poverty the more extreme forms of the frenzy were not in evidence. The imperial government had already built one interior route, the Rideau Canal, which was also an alternative "through highway", a "back-door" to the St. Lawrence, avoiding the American frontier, and now the local government embarked on such projects as the Trent Canal, projects which, owing to the supersession of the canal by the railway, it has never been under the necessity of completing.

REFERENCE: *Canada and its provinces*, X.

1

Road between Vermont and Montreal

From Canadian Archives, *Q*, XXIV-XXXII, 288.

To the Honorable Henry Hamilton, Esq., . . .

The memorial of Ira Allen, Esq of the State of Vermont represents:

That notwithstanding his mission to this place does not mention anything respecting opening a road by land from Vermont to St. John's; yet he beggs leave to observe that such a road would be of much consequence, as the Lake is in the spring and fall impassible and some whole winters badd ice. To remedy this the legislature of Vermont have authorized and directed the surveyor

General to cut and make a road to the Province line, which will be compleated next summer, provided any measure could be concerted to cut and make the road from thence to St. John's.

Ira Allen

Quebec, March 29th, 1785

2

Vermont and a St. Lawrence Outlet

From Canadian Archives, *Q*, LXXVII, 247.

Ira Allen to the Duke of Portland

Suffolk Street, N 38 Charing Cross
March 19th, 1796

My Lord:—

I had the honour of addressing to your Grace two memorials proposing to open a canal and praying in behalf of the State of Vermont, a sanction to navigate from Lake Champlain through the River St. Lawrence to the Atlantic Ocean, on which I feel the most anxious hopes for your Grace's favourable decision. . . . I take leave, therefore, to subjoin, to the reasons already submitted in my said memorials to your Grace the following: From the solid establishment of a wisely regulated commercial intercourse between Great Britain and Vermont, naturally productive of reciprocal benefits, the blessings of an immutable peace will be assertained between the two Countries, under these happy circumstances, Vermont tenacious and true to its own interests rather than hazzard its essential and most valued enjoyments by any concurrence whatever in designs of hostile nature, must in all possible events feel insuperable impulse to stand or fall in the faithful support of her commerce with Great Britain, and in the result, the commerce of Vermont instead of being carried on by way of New York and Boston must naturally take its course through the hands of British merchants, who also may avail themselves of the very peculiar and important advantages, in time of war, of shipping their goods to and from Canada secure from capture, in the neutral vessels of Vermont; and Government will be free to employ the ships of war, otherwise necessary for convoy, therein, or any other urgent service.

As to the apprehensions which I understand from Mr. King may possibly be suggested in opposition to the salutary measure proposed viz: "That the laying open the canal and navigation in question might tend to disseminate Republican principles among his Majesty's Canadian subjects." I have only to remark that so far from there being any ground for such apprehension, it will, nay I am warranted to assert must prove the most efficacious remedy of any that may possibly be concerted for obviating all attempts of such dissemination as well as wholly to frustrate their operation and effect. . . .

Ira Allen

3

Perils of Travelling on the Ice

From Howison, Sketches of Upper Canada, 226.

It is highly perilous for inexperienced persons to travel upon the ice, even during the most intense frost.   Besides the cracks and flaws that are to be avoided, there are places called *air-holes*, which give way the moment a cariole is driven upon them; and when this takes place, the passengers often find great difficulty in saving their own lives, much more those of the horses.   People who are in the habit of travelling much upon the ice, usually carry halters with them, for the purpose of choking the horses, should an accident of this kind happen.   The tightness of the rope closes the windpipe, and prevents the water from rushing into the lungs of the animal, while the air they contain renders its body so buoyant, that it floats upon the surface, and is easily dragged out.   However, considerable judgment is required to ensure the successful execution of this plan, as people sometimes pull the noose so tight, that they literally hang the animal they expected to save from drowning.

4

A Proposal for a Canal Across the Isthmus of Chignecto

From Ships, colonies and commerce, an appeal to the Right Hon. Wm. Huskisson
. . . on the present condition of the maritime and internal interests of the
Province of New Brunswick, by "A Colonist" (St. John, 1828).

. . . The meditated improvement in this province of opening a canal from the Bay of Fundy to the St. Lawrence is an object of national interest and peculiarly worthy of the attention of governments; and which, by affording facilities of intercourse will create an extensive business with our Canadian neighbours, which is at present very limited. . . .

5

New York to Montreal in Less than Three Days

From *Montreal Gazette*, July 27, 1829.

An instance of unprecedented despatch in travelling between New York and this place, came to our knowledge yesterday, which we consider deserving of public notice. SAMUEL GERRARD and WILLIAM EDMONSTONE, Esqrs., of this city, who came passengers in the Britannia, the 1st June packet ship from LIVERPOOL, left New York on Friday morning, and arrived here yesterday (*Sunday*) about noon, being little more than two days on their way.

6

Completion of the Rideau Canal

From *Quebec Mercury*, September 20, 1831.

. . . The expectation that the Canal would be completed early this fall will, no doubt, be realized. The whole line of locks from the summit level at the Rideau Lake to those at Bytown, had the water let into them a few days ago, and the result, we are happy to learn, proved completely satisfactory both to Colonel Durnford and Lieutenant Colonel By. . . .

7

"Forwarding" Rates on the Ottawa

From *Montreal Gazette*, October 20, 1832.

THE OTTAWA STEAMBOAT COMPANY, hereby gives Notice, that on and after the 15th October next, the rate of FREIGHT to Bytown and Hull will be *Three shillings and nine pence per hundred weight*, and to intermediate places in proportion.

The Company further gives notice that in case the setting-in of the ice should prevent the Boats delivering goods at their destinations (as was the case last year,) such goods shall be held at the risk and subject to the order of the owners and charged as far as carried only, but the Company will forward such goods by Sleighing, if requested, as soon as the roads are formed at the expence and risk of the Owners.

Montreal, August 30, 1832

8

The Advantages of the Trent Canal

From Canadian Archives, *Upper Canada sundries*, enclosure in Jameson to civil secretary Joseph, October 1, 1836.

At a public meeting of the inhabitants of the Township of Fenelon, Verulam and neighbourhood held at Fenelon Falls on the 24th day of September 1836, for the purpose of considering what measures should be adopted by them for assisting to forward the great & important work of opening the navigation of the River Trent & chain of waters connected therewith between Rice Lake, Lake Simcoe, & Lake Huron, the following resolutions were proposed and agreed to:—That the opening of the navigation from Lake Huron down to the Bay of Quinte by way of Lake Simcoe, the River Trent and intermediate chain of waters, would be a work of the utmost importance in a national point of view, as connecting the extreme parts of Upper Canada by the best, nearest and cheapest internal communication, and thereby opening up the interior of the country, and concentrating her powers & energies.

In a military point of view it is almost essential to the proper defence of the country, as affording in time of war a safe and easy communication remote from the frontier to the most distant parts of the province. And in a mercantile point of view the benefits to the country would be innumerable:—It would divert a great part of the carrying trade of the Western States to U. Canada & thence either across to Oswego or down the St. Lawrence, from the present circuitous route through the United States. The whole line of Canal being also thro' one of the richest tracts of country, which at present is almost shut out from every market, it would be a great stimulus to agriculture and commerce throughout the internal parts of the province. It would also be the means of opening up to Canada a new and Extensive country for lumber, which would be most conveniently situated for Export either to the United States or English markets. It would also open to the country extensive and valuable Iron mines, particularly the Marmora Iron works, which are not available now for want of an outlet to market. . . .

That the bill which passed both houses of Legislature last session of Parliament for granting £16,000 to improve the navigation from Buckhorn Rapids through Chemong Lake, Pigeon Lake, and Sturgeon Lake to the head of Scugog Lake, as also from Rice Lake to Peterboro would be of the greatest benefit to an extensive back country, as affording a comparative relief until the Trent is opened, to their present distressed state from want of an outlet to Lake Ontario for their produce:—and that a respectful petition should be sent to His Excellency the Lieutenant Governor praying that he would give his assent thereto. . . .

By Order of the Meeting,
Robert Jameson, Chairman

9

Proposal for a Maine-Quebec Road

From Canadian Archives, Lower Canada sundries, 1838.

Commonwealth of Massachusetts
Executive Department
Boston, 16th June 1838

To the Earl of Durham, &c. &c. &c.

My Lord,

This letter will be delivered to you by G. W. Coffin, Esq., Land agent of this Commonwealth. He has been directed to wait upon Your Lordship, in company with the Land Agent of the State of Maine, for the purpose of calling the attention of Your Lordship to the subject of a connection of the Kennebec Road leading from Quebec, with a road projected from the head of Moose Head Lake, in the State of Maine, to the Canada line. The Legislature of this State, at their last Session, appropriated a sum of money for the construction of this road, to be applied when a road from the Canada line to the present Kennebec road should have been completed or advanced so far, as to insure its completion in a reasonable time. The portion of the road lying within her Majesty's dominions is stated to be but about eight miles in length, and when it shall be constructed it will complete the shortest and most convenient route from Quebec to the Atlantic Coast. . . .

Edward Everett, governor of Massachusetts

10

The Advantages of a Canal Across Chignecto

From Canadian Archives, Lower Canada sundries, 1838.

To Sir John Harvey, Lieutenant-Governor of New Brunswick:
The Petition of the Chamber of Commerce of Saint John,
Respectfully Sheweth:

. . . That a Canal to connect the Waters bordering the possessions of Great Britain in North America has long been an object of consideration, not only with numerous private individuals, but also with the Legislature of this Province, who have had surveys and estimates made, and have been prevented from commencing the undertaking in consequence of the large sum required for its completion, and also, we apprehend, from want of confidence in the surveys. . . .

That the work, according to a survey made by Mr *Hall*, the particulars of which he forwarded to the late celebrated Sir *Thomas Telford*, was by that Gentleman, on Mr. Hall's data, estimated to cost £155,898 sterling, but this calculation does not seem to your Petitioners an exception to the observation made above. . . . We much question, had that Gentleman been on the spot, if he would have relied on the uncertain and periodical high tide mark, as the most proper level for the range of a Canal. . . . Should a stranger observe that one part of your command is completely cut off from all water intercourse with another most extensive and important part of the Province, save by a voyage of eight hundred miles, while a Canal of fifteen or seventeen miles, through a particularly level country, would completely connect and bind them together, he would be astonished that no attempt has yet been made to cut such a Canal.

That on 16th March, 1836, the Legislature of this Province passed an Act, (at the suggestion of several persons who probably despaired of a canal being cut,) for the purpose of incorporating the "Shediac and the Saint John Rail-road Company," or, in other words, an Act to authorize the parties named, and their associates, to make a Railway from the Harbour of Shediac to the most convenient spot for a landing Harbour on the head waters of the Bay of Fundy; said Railway to be completed in six years, or the Charter to expire. And on the same date a like Law was enacted, to Incorporate the "Bay of Verte Canal Company," with a capital of only £90,000 sterling, which Charter is to expire and end if the object is not completed within ten years from its date. The Legislature of the Province of Nova Scotia, during their last Session, passed an Act authorising the Lieutenant Governor of that Province, for the time being, to Incorporate any persons who shall within ten years make such progress in cutting a Canal from the Bay of Verte to Cumberland Basin, as may satisfy the then Commander-in-Chief that the Canal will be completed within some reasonably distant period. . . .

That not only is New Brunswick in an especial degree interested in this undertaking, but that the extensive and growing trade between this Port and Quebec, makes it certain that the Canadas would join warmly in promoting what would so much advantage their commerce. That various products of the Eastern part of Nova Scotia would find a ready and advantageous market at this Port;—that fleets of small vessels would be fitted out in this Province for general trade on the shores of the Saint Lawrence, and also for the Gulf Fisheries, if such a Canal were completed. Another object of vast importance to the British Government, as well as to the trade of the North American Colonies and the West Indies, seems likely to be attained by the completion of this work. We refer to the opening of a safe and easy passage to Quebec, *several weeks earlier in the Spring* than can be reckoned upon by the present route, and wholly avoiding the great danger of encountering the ice between Newfoundland and Cape Breton, or in the Gut of Canso. We believe it is well known that a clear passage along the Northern shore of New Brunswick, and thence by Gaspé to Quebec, is generally open in the month of April, and frequently in its first week. That Prince Edward Island would be greatly benefitted by such a Canal; and that the trade of the whole Colonies would thereby be increased in times of peace, and their energies become closely united in time of war. . . .

ISAAC WOODWARD,   LAUCHLAN DONALDSON,
Secretary   *President*

Saint John, New Brunswick 18th June, 1831

11

The Ottawa-Lake Huron Ship Canal

From Canadian Archives, *Upper Canada sundries*, 1838.

At a meeting held at New Edinburgh . . . Thomas Mackay, Esqr., M.P.P., was called to the Chair, and Robert Lang, Esqr., appointed Secretary.

Mr Mackay explained the nature of the meeting as follows. A few years ago a proposal was made by influential noblemen, capitalists and merchants in England, for forming themselves into a company to open up a communication from Lake Huron to the Sea, by the Ottawa River, and upon such terms as were likely to be advantageous to this section of the country. . . .

The inhabitants bordering upon the Ottawa and its neighbourhood, sent a petition to Lord Aylmer, and one to Sir John Colborne, signed by 447 names, craving that their Excellencies would investigate into the merits of the proposal made by the London Company, and if they found it to be of such immense advantage to the country as described, That their Excellencies would recommend it to the favourable consideration of the Home Government. . . .

Among others, the following resolutions were proposed:

Resolved—That the meeting respectfully call upon their Member, Thomas McKay, Esqr. to procure for them a copy of the Report of the Surveyors who were appointed by the Government to survey and report upon the practicability of opening up a navigation from Lake Huron to Montreal by the River Ottawa. Proposed by James Stevenson Esqr. and seconded by Mr Wm. Lang,

Resolved—that the opening up of the trade of the Great Western Lakes and states to Montreal, by the short route of the Ottawa, is an event to be hailed as a precurser to the future prosperity of the Colony in general. That the terms upon which the London Company came forward in 1835 are fraught with many valuable advantages to the Colony by the circulation of such a vast sum of money in the Province, and by peopling the waste lands.

Mr Stevenson laid before the meeting a Map shewing that the distance from Lake Huron to Montreal by Lake Nippissing and the Ottawa in the proposed route, is not much above 540 miles, whereas by the present route from Lake Huron to Montreal by Lake Erie and Ontario, it is above 840 miles. Mr Stevenson also laid before the meeting a very able paper on the subject written by Charles Shirreff, Esqr. of Fitzroy Harbour, opening in a clear manner the many advantages to be derived by opening up the trade of the Western Lakes and states to Montreal. . . . Mr S. stated the advantages in a political point of view that Government would gain by the formation of such a company, in securing a strong interior population, away from the contamination of Republican principals [sic], and called upon all who had the interest of the Colony at heart, to join in petitioning His Excellency the Governor General to assist in forwarding the views of the proposed company, provided the terms they offered were in accordance with the interest of the colony. . . . Proposed by Robert Lang Esqr and seconded by Mr Fraser.

Resolved—That the view which our late Lieut. Governor, Sir F. B. Head, took of the resources of that noble River the Ottawa, in his opening speech in Parliament, is in accordance with the opinion of every one who has taken the trouble to consult the local advantages offered to commerce by improving the navigation of the Ottawa. . . .

New Edinburgh   Thomas McKay, Chairman
   July 16th 1838   Robert Lang, Secretary

12

The Montreal-Bytown Service

From *Montreal Transcript*, May 6, 1847.

The *Bytown Gazette* of the first of May observes that the river is free from ice, and yesterday the first raft left Bytown, destined for Quebec.

We learn from the same paper, that the arrangements for conveyance between Montreal and Bytown, for the present, remain the same as last year. After the middle of June, it is intended to place the *Speed*, a new handsome steamer now fitting out, to ply in connexion with the old favorite *Oldfield*, when the whole route, 120 miles, is expected to be performed during daylight; this, taking into account the various transhipments, is doing well.

This route is likely to be greatly improved shortly by the substitution of a railroad between Grenville and Carrillon, and when a similar arrangement is perfected from Lachine, it will be both expeditious and comfortable. Concerning transportation of goods, the Bytown and Ottawa forwarders contemplate doing a portion of their business via the St. Lawrence, but a sufficiency of craft will still ply via the Ottawa and Rideau canals, to enable the citizens of Bytown an opportunity of availing themselves of a daily departure from and to Montreal, and their rates will be fixed at a moderate and reasonable figure. On the Rideau canal, a couple of steamers will ply regularly during the season, for the conveyance of freight and passengers. On the waters above, two new iron steamers are being refitted with great taste, under the management of the spirited proprietors Messrs Egan & Aumond. Altogether the arrangements for the forthcoming season are of a very auspicious character, and reflect great credit on the owners and projectors of the several departments.

THE IMPROVEMENT AND CANALIZATION OF THE ST. LAWRENCE

From one point of view, the history of a considerable part of this continent is the history of the rivalry between the ports of Montreal and New York. Its climatic advantage, superior command of capital, and the political unity of New York State, reaching from the Atlantic to the lakes, has enabled New York to overcome the disadvantage of lack of a natural connection by water with the interior and to draw a great part of the trade of that region. The period under review witnessed New York first challenge, then wrest supremacy from Montreal, and lastly apparently utterly defeat the latter city, a defeat from which the next period was to see a remarkable recovery, as Montreal in its turn slowly acquired the command of capital.

Before the Erie Canal was undertaken, Montreal (together with Quebec) had command of a vast hinterland stretching westward as far as settlement went. As soon as the Erie Canal was opened, this hinterland was abruptly reduced to Upper Canada, and had the imperial and American trading laws permitted importation *via* New York, Upper Canada, too, would gladly have escaped from Montreal's control, as, indeed, after 1846, it did. The Canadian reply to the Erie Canal, a reply in which Lower Canada was too short-sighted to have much interest, was not long in coming:—the plan, first for a canal around Niagara Falls and then for the canalization of the lower river. This great project, the spinal cord of the Canadian economic system to this day, is to be associated with the name of one man, William Hamilton Merritt. From the inception of the idea of the Welland Canal to the completion of the locks between Prescott and Montreal, he was indefatigable in his efforts and it is in great part owing to him that the task was completed. It was no fault of his that a complex of causes seemed at the time to rob him and his creation of its fruits.

These documents should be read along with those of the next section, number III, it being almost impossible to dissociate the two aspects of the matter, the canals and the trading system based on the St. Lawrence.

REFERENCES: George W. Brown, "The opening of the St. Lawrence to American shipping" (*Canadian Historical Review*, March, 1926), "The St. Lawrence in the boundary settlement of 1783" (*Ibid.*, September, 1928), and "The St. Lawrence waterway in the 19th century" (*Queens Quarterly*, autumn, 1928); Donald C. Masters, "W. H. Merritt and the expansion of Canadian railways" (*Canadian Historical Review*, June, 1931); J. P. Merritt, *Biography of the Hon. W. H. Merritt, M.P.* (St. Catharines, 1875).

1

The Hinterland of the St. Lawrence

From *Montreal Gazette*, June 3, 1816.

London, March 16

It is gratifying to observe the growing increase of the exports from this country to British North America. In 1814 they

161

amounted in value to 4,070,987. sterling, exclusive of the freight in British ships. The accounts for the last year are not yet made up. We are satisfied that if this trade is properly encouraged, it will afford constant employment, not only to our shipping interest, but also to our manufacturers who will find in the new countries to the west of the Ohio, Mississippi &c. an increasing demand for their woolens, linens, &c. The rapid increase of the white population in those countries almost exceeds belief; and the difficulties of supply, across the high lands, from the United States, or up those great rivers from New Orleans, afford us such advantage of supply by the St. Lawrence, that it will be attributable to our own neglect and folly, if we do not reap the benefits which the possession of the Canadas, and the water communication with the great Lakes give us. At a trifling expense, and in a very short period, the communication with the Lakes from Montreal might be so improved, as to enable the traders to avoid all the portages; and in time of war, to relieve them from passing by a long line of the enemy's frontier. We wish to direct the attention of our manufacturers and ship owners to British North America; as we are convinced, from the advantages before alluded to, and the exclusion of the Americans from the fisheries on the coasts of these provinces, the most lasting benefits are to be derived; while the possession of them will add to the naval and military power of the Empire.

2

Inception of the Plan for the Welland Canal

From *Montreal Gazette*, September 23, 1818.

CANALS.—It must be highly gratifying to every one who has at heart the prosperity of the Canadas to hear it is in contemplation to connect the waters of Lake Ontario with those of Lake Erie, by cutting a Canal from the head of the Twelve Mile Creek to the Cheppawa River. The ground has been surveyed and the level taken; it is now ascertained that it will neither be difficult nor expensive to accomplish this grand and most useful work. Through this Canal when finished will pass what now must be disembarked at Queenston and transported over a carrying place of three leagues to Cheppawa at a vast expense, to avoid the Falls of Niagara.

The two greatest and almost the only obstructions in the navigation from the Lakes to Montreal, are the La Chine and Niagara carrying places; were these removed by means of Canals, the trade of all the settlements on each side of the Lakes and River would glide into this port; nor would there be any reason to fear that the great American Canal now making[1] could divert it to New-York.

3

The Right to Navigate the St. Lawrence:—The American View

From *Montreal Gazette*, February 14, 1823.

On the subject of the navigation of the St. Lawrence in international politics, see George W. Brown, "The opening of the St. Lawrence to American shipping" (*Canadian Historical Review*, March, 1926).

In introducing the Resolution, which was adopted by the House of Representatives on the 23d inst. relative to the British restrictions on our trade with Canada, Mr. Stearling said, . . .

"A very advantageous and profitable traffic had for a long time been prosecuted by the inhabitants living on the northern and north-eastern borders of the United States, with the British Provinces of Upper and Lower Canada. This traffic, on the part of the United States consisted principally of bulky articles, which found their way to market down the River St. Lawrence.

"The free navigation of that river is all essential to the continuance and prosperity of this commerce.—Upon it also depends, to a great extent, the value of those extensive tracts of land, which border upon this river, and the immense bodies of water which discharge themselves into it. An extensive population had seated itself upon the shores of these rivers and lakes, looking to Montreal and Quebec as their natural and proper market, and to the river St. Lawrence as the great highway which nature has opened to them, for the conveyance of their produce to a place of profitable sale. Many of their products are of so bulky a nature as forbids their being transported to any other market.

"They believed, and still believe, that their right to the navigation of this river was secured to them both by treaty and natural law. . . ."—American paper.

Is this to be tolerated, or is it to be resisted by all the means in our power?

---

[1]The Erie Canal, completed in 1825.

4

First Suggestion of the Rivalry of New York and Montreal for the Trade of Upper Canada

From *Montreal Gazette*, March 22, 1822.

Mr. BROWN:—

I noticed last week . . . a memorial of the inhabitants of several of the western counties of New-York to the Legislature, praying for an Act to authorise the making another Canal from Great Sodus Bay on Lake Ontario to the Seneca Lake, with a view of uniting the waters of the Susquehannah with those of our noble river the St. Lawrence. Among the various representations in this memorial which have arrested my particular attention, is the following. . . .

"That it would open to the Erie Canal and city of New-York the immense commerce of the extensive coasts of Lake Ontario and its navigable streams, not merely from our own shores, but also from those of Upper Canada, experience having abundantly proved that Montreal and Quebec cannot compete with the commercial capital of this State, provided means of easy access to it be furnished in manner now proposed. The fluctuating and forbidding course of the Canadian markets, the capricious regulations of the Colonial trade, and the hazards attending the navigation of the St. Lawrence from rapid currents, rocky coasts, and a rigorous wintry climate, are all calculated to drive business from that quarter to New-York."

5

An Association for the Improvement of the St. Lawrence

From *Quebec Mercury*, December, 1824.

To the Editor of the *Quebec Mercury*—
Sir—As it may be thought necessary that some idea of the views and intentions of the gentlemen who organized the St. Lawrence Association should be given to the public, permit me to trespass on your useful paper. . . .

The objects of the Association will extend generally to inquiry into the most feasible methods of improving the navigation of the river St. Lawrence, throughout its whole extent, in connection with steam machinery, railways, canals, deepening channels, or other methods that may be suggested in the course of research— The improvement of the navigation of the Ottawa, as well as of all the other smaller rivers and streams that empty themselves into the St. Lawrence, will also claim the attention of the Association. . . .

The views, therefore of the Association will not certainly be confined to the mere inquiry of improvement in the method of ascending the rapids between Lachine and Johnstown; this, however, is a subject of primary importance and claims immediate attention. . . .

It appears upon inquiry that produce, upon the contemplated improvements, can with facility be brought from Niagara to Quebec, in the short space of 60 hours—A vessel may, with a fair wind, cross Lake Ontario in 24 hours; a boat from Kingston can descend the river to Montreal in 20; and a steamboat to Quebec, in 16, making in all the 60 hours.

These contemplated improvements could be carried into effect by the 1st of July next, and it only remains for the discerning inhabitants of the two Provinces to yield their support with zeal in promoting a measure of such unprecedented advantage to the whole country; for it will appear evident, that in the article of flour alone, with the protecting duty in our favour, no country can enter into competition with us in supplying the West India Islands, and sister provinces of Nova Scotia, New Brunswick, &c. . . .

James George

Quebec, 27th Nov. 1824

6

The Welland Canal:—Completion to St. Catharines

From *Farmers' Journal* (St. Catharines), quoted in *Montreal Gazette*, June 5, 1828.

WELLAND CANAL.—DEPARTURE OF THE FIRST VESSEL. —Saturday last was a proud day for St. Catharines; and indeed, for Upper Canada. A scene was witnessed within its borders, that will long be held in remembrance by the active friends and steady supporters of the splendid plans of internal improvement now in progress in this section of the colony—the free and uninterrupted passage of the first loaded vessel, that ever floated on the waters of the Welland Canal, from this village (where she was built) to lake Ontario, a distance of five miles of artificial Steam Boat Navigation, constructed up the valley of the 12 mile creek, directly into the interior of the country. A scene which was at once, so grand, so novel and interesting, as to call forth the spontaneous acclamations of every liberal and patriotic spectator assembled on the joyous occasion.

It was a matter of sincere regret to many, that the projector of this great work, (Wm. Hamilton Merrit, Esq.) was not present—being now in London endeavouring to procure the necessary means for its completion to Lake Erie; and there can be little doubt but his efforts will be crowned with success.

7

"Natural Law" and the American Claim to Navigate the St. Lawrence

From *New York American*, quoted in *Montreal Gazette*, June 29, 1829.

It is now about five years ago, that, in this paper, the doctrine was broached, for the first time publicly, we believe, of the right of the United States, to the free navigation of the St. Lawrence, from its source to its outlet, and of a correlative right of deposit on one of its banks at the head of ship navigation. This doctrine, reposing as it does, upon natural justice and common interest, was enforced by reference to the proceedings of the Congress of Verona, where this right, as regarded the Rhine and other European rivers flowing through the territories of different sovereigns, was distinctly recognized, to which recognition England was by her minister (Lord Clancarty, we believe) a party. . . . .

8

Buffalo, the Welland Canal, and the West

From *Buffalo Republican*, quoted in *Montreal Gazette*, July 27, 1829.

Until the increasingly protective nature of American fiscal policy rendered it impossible, British manufacturers supplied a large share of the needs of the western states; before 1825, they were brought in by the St. Lawrence, after that date by New York.

There are several houses at Niagara, Upper Canada, extensively engaged in importing woollens and cottons from Liverpool. So reasonably are British manufactures obtained there, that a great many of the dealers in the vicinity, and in the western part of Upper Canada, purchase their stocks at Niagara.

The old House of G. & T. Weed, at this place, dealers in hardware and ironmongery, were the first who imported goods direct from England west of Albany, which was several years since. The wants of the West, have now become of great magnitude: the amount of the produce, minerals furs and peltries of the west, has augmented within a few years to a great sum. This trade centres to this place.—Every thing within from 50 to 100 miles of the southern shore of Lake Erie,—from the northern parts of Indiana,—from Illinois,—from Michigan, and the vast unexplored regions south of Lake Superior, will arrive at this end of Lake Erie.

Buffalo and Black Rock, Waterloo and Chippewa, will, in process of time, be the marts for the produce of the West. The mouth of the Grand River, in Upper Canada, is out of the question as furnishing a rival town for trade. It is very true, that in some seasons the port to be constructed at the mouth of that river would be open a few days earlier than Buffalo. There might be a vessel load of produce collected at the southern ports of Lake Erie and sent to that place; it would be too early for the Montreal market, and there would be presented no choice of distant markets, as at Buffalo or its vicinity. This then, must be the place where merchants of ample capital will deal in foreign goods directly. The goods would generally arrive in forty days from Liverpool. The rent of stores is not one fifth as much as in New York: the Buffalo importer could therefore afford to sell on as favourable terms as those in New York, as his expenses would every way be less. The Western merchant, with his cargoes of produce, &c. could exchange them entire for merchandize and salt, and in ten days return to his home with his goods; while his expenses would be greatly lessened, and his goods would all be paid for. . . .

The Welland Canal will do more business through the Chippewa and by the Niagara River than by the Grand River. The slack water navigation of the Niagara, & the construction of a harbour at Waterloo, would early bring the Welland Canal into profitable operation. We have believed that a ship canal between Lakes Ontario and Erie, would be more remarkable for its novelty than its utility. A lateral boat canal is to be made to Niagara.

When that is done, and Niagara becomes, what present facts indicate, an importing town, then will be *there* established a mart, which will draw business and capital, and will render it superior to any town on Lake Ontario. It is not very likely that ships will load at any of our western ports, destined for a particular port on the lower Lake, because from the operation of the British Corn Laws, it might be imprudent to place flour and ashes under the key of the British warehouse keepers—in other words our own markets, for home consumption or for exportation, would be the best. If then there is a good market at Niagara or the Twelve Mile Creek, and another, equally as good, at Buffalo, the intercourse between the lakes by ships will be far less than by boats, which by their construction carry nearly as much as the ordinary loads of schooners, injuring the Canal much less, and proceed with greater speed.

9

The Western States and the Welland Canal

From *Farmers' Journal* (St. Catharines), quoted in *Montreal Gazette*, August 20, 1829.

Governor of Indiana to W. H. Merritt, agent of the Welland Canal Company

Let me assure you that we in this country view the Welland Canal as an indispensable facility to an uninterrupted outlet to the ocean. . . . The Indiana Canal[1] . . . must become a powerful aid to the profits of the Welland Canal: for it certainly will be laid on the nearest route for the Gulf of Mexico to the Lakes. . . .

10

Opening of the Welland Canal

From *Buffalo Republican*, December 3, 1829.

To the surprise of the citizens of Buffalo and Black Rock, the Lake Schooners *Ann & Jane*, of York, U.C. and *R. H. Boughton* of Youngstown, arrived in our harbour on Wednesday last, having on board the enterprising projector of the Welland Canal, William

---

[1]Between the Rivers Wabash and Maumee.

Hamilton Merritt, with a company of gentlemen, ... The British vessel led the van. The locks were passed on the 30th of November, just five years from the commencement of the important work. The question is not, whether this work will increase or diminish the receipts of the Erie Canal,—we trust that we possess too much national pride, to complain of the success of even a rival work, begun by our neighbours before ours was completed. Its progress to its termination is now flattering, and the news we now communicate, that of the passage of vessels, from Lake to Lake, surmounting the declivity which causes the fall of the Niagara, must be cheering indeed to the stockholders, and gratifying to the inhabitants of Upper Canada.

11

First Cargo through the Welland Canal

From *York Courier*, quoted in *Montreal Gazette*, July 15, 1830.

Major Ives, of Burford, has passed down the Grand River and through the Welland Canal, with 1600 barrels of flour, pork and whiskey, on four arks.[1] This is the first transit of produce through the Welland.

12

How the Welland Canal Draws the Produce of the West

From *Kingston Patriot*, quoted in *Montreal Gazette*, August 16, 1830.

We are informed by a gentleman who has just visited the Welland Canal, that from a rough calculation, he supposes 300,000 staves have already been brought through it. This is a new article of exportation from Lake Erie and must have been new in centuries to come but for the Canal. It is painful, however, to reflect that the Americans are nearly, if not quite, the sole carriers of Lumber and Staves from the head of the Lake to Quebec and Montreal. Somebody must be off their guard to allow this. The cause should be immediately sought for, and a remedy applied. We hope those immediately interested, will bestire themselves and take proper steps to abate so vile a nuisance. We understand the quantity of White Oak on the shores of Lake Erie, and in the Michigan

---

[1]An ark was a flat-bottomed craft used in shallow rivers.

Territory, is prodigiously great, the whole of which, is now open to a market; but in the name of common sense, let us not throw away the bread which a kind providence has put into our mouths.

13
The Colonial System and American Produce
From *Montreal Gazette*, September 30, 1830.

Sir.—A tour through Canada has drawn my attention to a subject deeply connected with the prosperity of the Province. . . . The free navigation of the St. Lawrence must lead to (I might say command) a commerce equal to the Mississippi. The subject is not understood, and deeply will those who succeed us lament our blindness to the great advantages which that river ought to produce,—but without urging more at present, I will propose for consideration, in order to have an abundant and regular supply of Wheat, Flour, Corn, and Provisions at Montreal and Quebec, that all such as were brought in boats or vessels belonging to His Majesty's subjects, from Port Dalhousie, Niagara, York, Port Hope and Kingston should be looked upon as the produce of the Province; that all wheat, Corn and Live Stock brought into the Lower Province by land or by Lake Champlain should be also so regarded: that all Wheat exported from Montreal and Quebec to the United Kingdom be considered as Colonial: and that all Flour, Provisions, Meal, &c, exported from Montreal and Quebec to the British West Indies be taken as the produce of the Canadas.

The supply of the West Indies can only be retained by an abundant supply at Quebec and Montreal, on as good terms as they could obtain them elsewhere, The St. Lawrence can furnish such supply. This may be done at the same time, and preserve to the Canadian farmer considerable advantage over the American agriculturists, viz, the expense of transhipment. A further and most important advantage would arise from an abundant supply at Montreal and Quebec, as a regular trade might be thereby secured, not only of the British West Indies, but of the United Kingdom, thus affording the farmer a regular market for his produce. I understand that above sixty thousand barrels of Flour were shipped this year from New York alone to England—the proposed measure of opening the St. Lawrence would have secured that immense trade to Canada, and I repeat that only by making

Quebec and Montreal a great granary, we can retain the West India Trade and such uniform prices to farmers. . . .

Free Trade

14

W. H. Merritt Opens the Campaign for the St. Lawrence Ship-Canals

From *Montreal Gazette*, March 29, 1831, reprint of circular on improvement of the navigation of the River St. Lawrence addressed to members of the legislature of Upper Canada.

Sir,—The improvement of the River St. Lawrence is now under the consideration of your Honourable Body, and a more important measure, for the future welfare and prosperity of the Canadas, cannot engage your attention.

Debarred, as we are, from the benefits of a sea-port town or commercial city, by the unnatural and unjust division of Upper and Lower, Canada, this Province can never increase in population and wealth, in proportion to her acknowledged natural advantages, until we have a free and uninterrupted access to the ocean.

A diversity of opinion appears to exist as to the best mode of effecting that object. By some it is contended, that the Rideau Canal, (now on the eve of completion,) will remedy every inconvenience. Others assert, that a boat navigation between Prescott and Montreal, from the cheapness of its construction, would be preferable, and answer all the purposes required. On this subject I beg to offer the following remarks.

Lake Ontario is already connected with the Hudson River, by a canal 208 miles in length, with 574 feet lockage, and 4 feet depth of water. The Rideau Canal is 264 miles long, has over 500 feet lockage, with five feet water. By the projected St. Lawrence route, there will be only 120 miles of artificial navigation, containing less than 200 feet lockage; or, in fact, a canal of $37\frac{1}{2}$ miles in length will connect Lake Ontario with the ocean.

You will perceive, by reference to the actual rates of transportation between given points, that the price is always in a ratio, to the extent of water, and the burden of the vessel or craft employed. For instance: the price of conveying a ton of merchandise from Liverpool to Montreal, a distance of 3,000 miles, is 12s. 6d. to 15s. from Quebec to Montreal, 180 miles, 6s. 3d. to 7s. 6d.; on the Erie Canal, for 100 miles, 22s. 6d. up, and 15s. down; and so on, in proportion as the navigation contracts or becomes smaller, will the charges increase. From Montreal to Prescott, 120 miles, £4 per ton up, and 26s down is paid. Hence it follows, from the distances and rates above set forth, that a Canal along the St. Lawrence, of the largest dimensions proposed, would be the shortest, best and cheapest medium of conveyance.

The principal objection urged against a ship Canal is, first, the inability of this Province, with her present debt, to complete it. This debt, (about £100,000,) was incurred, principally, for Bank stock, and in aid of the Burlington and Welland Canals. The former has been in use three years; it now pays the interest on its cost, and is rapidly reducing the principal. After as many years use of the Welland, the same result will follow. Therefore, the Province cannot, with propriety, be said to have a debt at all. This, however, is unimportant, in regard to the subject under consideration.

By the late surveys, the expense of executing the most difficult part of this work, (from Prescott to Cornwall,) is estimated at £173,643. Suppose the distance from Coteau to Point Clair, and from Lachine to Montreal, in Lower Canada, to cost an equal sum, making a total of £347,296; or, as improvements of this description *always* exceed the estimates, we will double it, and admit that the outlay for the whole line may amount to £750,000, or $3,000,000; the following calculations will show, that the quantity of merchandise and produce now transported on the St. Lawrence, by charging the same tolls as on the Erie Canal, would soon pay the whole expense of constructing the work.

According to the Report of Messrs, Whiting & Crawford, upwards of 300,000 barrels passed down, and 8,000 tons of merchandise up, the St. Lawrence, during the season of 1830—

On which has been paid for transit, the sum of	£69,500	
Breakage, damage and risk	£4,000	
Insurance on down freight, 3d. per bbl. (left out of their calculation)	3,750	
Making the total expense of transit and risk		£77,250

On 120 miles of the Erie Canal—

Toll on one barrel of flour is 18 cents—on 300,000 bbls	£13,500	
Transportation, 11 cents, do	8,250	
Toll on 8,000 tons of merchandise, at 3 cents per ton per mile	7,200	
Transit, do. at 1½ cents do	3,600	
Making the toll, £20,700. Transit, £11,850		
Total		£32,550

A barrel of flour is conveyed from Buffalo to Albany, a distance of 366 miles, for 4s. 4¼d. or 87½ cents, (toll 54, transit 33½;) and merchandise at the rate of 3 cents per ton mile toll, and 1½ do. transit which is rather more than was paid last year.

The toll on lumber passed down the St. Lawrence in 1829, at the same rate as now charged on the Erie Canal for 120 miles, viz: on pipe staves 40s. per M. puncheon do. 10s. hard timber 90s. per 100 feet, pine do. 30s. do. would amount to £13,137.

The result of the above calculation is as follows:—

Toll on produce and merchandise	£20,700
Do. lumber	13,137
Total	£33,837

Besides what may be derived from the hydraulic situations. The saving to the country, after paying the toll and transit, from the prices now charged—

On produce and merchandize	£44,700
Do. Lumber	14,750
Delay, insurance or risk	5,000
Total	£64,450

The interest on the cost of the Canal, (£750,000 at 5 per cent.) is.......£37,500

Exceeding the toll on merchandise, produce and lumber, £3,663

Take this from the total amount of *saving* (£64,450,) and it leaves a surplus in favour of the Province,

annually of........£60,787

As Durham boats can now pass down the St. Lawrence without the aid of locks or towing-paths, it has been asserted by some, that no tolls would be paid on downward freight. The above calculations show a different result. They are made from the actual prices now paid for transportation between Prescott and Montreal, and an equal distance on the Erie Canal—the truth of which can be ascertained by referring to any Merchant in Upper Canada, (who has paid a bill of freight on the St. Lawrence,) or to any forwarder on the Erie Canal. The difference, after allowing a sufficient toll to pay for the construction of the Canal, shows the actual saving which would accrue to the Province on a boat Canal only. When compared with a ship Canal, the result would be still more favourable.

By taking another view of the subject, and the one upon which every statesman should found his calculations and opinions, in a new and growing country like ours, on the supposition that the commerce of this Province should double within the next four years, (as we find, by Messrs. Whiting & Crawford's Report, it has in the last,) our tolls would then amount to £67,674; and by thus continuing to increase, would effect an incalculable saving to the country.

It may be said, that no allowance is made for the trade which will be diverted to the Rideau. By giving to it the whole of the toll on the 8,000 tons of goods now sent up, it only amounts to £7200. You may safely make double that allowance, and still have abundance left for the St. Lawrence route.

Connect this distance with a Canal of suitable dimensions, thus making in effect, a sea coast of our inland lake shores, and no other route can successfully compete with you. The merchants of Ohio, and in all the other American States bordering on our waters above, will become their own importers; their produce will pass this channel, and an extent of business will be carried on through it, in a few years, far beyond the expectation of the most sanguine at the present day.

Two methods suggest themselves for effecting this improvement. The first is, for this Province to undertake it alone, lend her credit to obtain the money, and become sole proprietor, on the same principle adopted by the state of New York in constructing the Erie Canal.

Secondly, to incorporate a Company, with a capital of £750,000: let individuals subscribe one-third of the stock, Lower Canada one-third and this Province the other; or, in case the Lower Province declines, let this Province take the remaining two-thirds at once; appropriate £100,000 per annum, and finish the most important sections first, the tolls on which would pay the interest on the amount expended, from year to year, as the work progressed; and in four years, if prosecuted with vigour, we should be enabled to ship our produce to any port on the Atlantic.

In either case, as we are at present situated, it will be necessary to obtain an Act from the Legislature of Lower Canada, permitting us to cut the Canal from the Province line to any part of the St. Lawrence that may be found most advantageous. One most serious and almost insurmountable objection to a small

Canal is the necessity it creates for the trans-shipment of property. This amounts, already:—

On the 300,000 bbls, now sent down at 3d. per bbl. to.............	£3750
On merchandise, (say on half,).................................	1875
Total...	£5625

And in a few years will increase to an annual tax of £25,000 on the commerce of the country.

It is a reproach upon the intelligence and enterprise of the country that this improvement was not commenced long since; it should not be delayed another year. If the present House cannot comprehend the superiority of a ship navigation, or do not feel satisfied that the present population of the western country demands it, there should be no hesitation in appropriating £50,000 for a boat Canal. The tolls will pay the interest, and redeem the principal, without ever being felt.

On the contrary, if the present state and future prospects of our country, now that the Ohio Canal is nearly completed, and the navigation around the Falls of Niagara is accomplished, (which open a water communication to the valley of the Ohio River) should induce you to undertake the ship Canal, a quantity of produce would be conveyed to the ocean through our northern ports, the first year after it was opened far beyond the anticipation of the most sanguine; and you would be rendering a lasting service, not only to the Province, but to the western world, which will entitle you to the grateful remembrance of future ages.

I have the honor to be, Sir, your obedient servant,

Wm. Hamilton Merritt

St. Catherines, Feb. 15, 1831

15

Commencement of Work on the Long Sault Canal

From *Cornwall Observer*, quoted in *Montreal Gazette*, September 9, 1834.

St. Lawrence Canal.—On the 2d. September inst., Mr. Hervey, contractor for section No. 1, on the Long Sault, commenced excavating with about one hundred and fifty men. After the roll was called in the morning at five o'clock and receiving their tools, they mustered, gave three hearty cheers and proceeded with the greatest spirit and enthusiasm to the commencement of the im-

mense work which Mr. H. has undertaken. After the commencement of the labors of the day, a great number of laborers offered
their services, who will be added to the number already employed,
and will probably in a few days increase the number to five or
six hundred. It was a matter of surprise and admiration to spectators, who were numerous and respectable, to observe the great
regularity, industry and system, which immediately took place
under the direction of Mr. Hervey and his assistants. It is not a
little astonishing to observe the Long Sault, which was but yesterday an obscure country settlement, now assuming all the activity,
bustle and business of a city or large market town.

16

Inland Waterways and the Progress of Montreal

From *Montreal Gazette*, May 7, 1835.

Of all cities in BRITISH NORTH AMERICA QUEBEC
is the most important in its position, its strength, and its direct
influence upon the maintenance of that connection which now
happily exists between the Parent State and the Colony. MONT-
REAL is content with a position less warlike, though more beneficial in its nature. She is at the head of the river navigation of
Canada, and has all the ports of the world open to her ships;
while, from other local advantages, she has become the emporium
in which has centred the trade of the whole of UPPER CANADA,
and of a great portion of the States of NEW YORK, PENNSYL-
VANIA and OHIO, which border upon Lakes *Ontario* and *Erie*;
she forms the nucleus of that extensive and valuable commerce
arising from the lumber brought down the noble *Ottawa*; and it
may be safely said, that her imports go far to supply the wants
and necessities of the majority of the inhabitants of our own
Province. Within the last years, since the completion of the
Lachine, Grenville, Welland and Rideau Canals, the introduction
of towboats upon the *St. Lawrence*, the establishment of Montreal
as a free and independent port, and the erection of substantial
and extensive wharves, her trade has steadily augmented, and
bids fair, if properly encouraged, to become still more valuable.
The small schooners, that a few short years ago frequented our

apology for a port, have been, as it were, converted into large and goodly merchantmen, yielding in elegance and convenience to but few of the shipping of Europe. And were the spirit and enterprise which ought to actuate the community, fairly aroused to a full sense of what inevitably awaits them, if they will but avail themselves of the advantages that offer, Montreal would not yield in commercial rank to any of the ports of America.

One of the greatest drawbacks to the increase of the trade of Montreal is the shallowness of the *Lake St. Peter* during the summer season and the consequent impediments which it offers to the progress of vessels of large burthen. This frequently obliges the shipping to remain in Quebec, and transmit their freight by steam-boats and barges to the port of original destination.

17

Upper Canadians Consider Importation *viâ* New York

From *Upper Canada Courier*, December 24, 1835.

At a meeting of the Principal Merchants of the City of Toronto . . . for the purpose of taking into consideration the propriety of promoting the importation of British Goods, through the United States; . . .THE HONORABLE WILLIAM ALLAN was called to the CHAIR, when it was:—Resolved.—That this meeting has much satisfaction in returning its best thanks to the Honorable Chairman, and the Members of the Committee of the Board of Trade, for the intention they have evinced for the interest of the Commerce of Upper Canada on the subject of the importation of Goods through the United States, from Europe and agree with them in the opinion that the subject which has induced them to convene this meeting is one of the greatest importance, and which they would recommend to the favorable attention of others through out the Province.

Resolved.—That considering the subject as one inviting very general and extensive consideration as applying to all classes of the community—The Chairman of this meeting be requested to call a General Meeting of the Inhabitants of the District . . . for the purpose of a full expression of public sentiment on this important subject. . . .

12

18

The St. Lawrence the "Unnatural Highway" for Upper Canada

From Correspondent of *Kingston Chronicle*, quoted in *Montreal Gazette*, January 26, 1836.

Mr. Editor,—The proposed improvement of making New York the sea port of Upper Canada, and receiving British goods by that channel, instead of by the St. Lawrence, has, I perceive, attracted the especial notice, of some of the good people of Montreal. The Editor of the *Morning Courier* has devoted considerable attention to the subject, which he conceives would seriously affect the interests of that city. The Editor may be perfectly correct in presuming that the commercial interests of Montreal would, to a certain extent, suffer from the arrangement in question, but he is not quite correct in supposing that this circumstance forms any just and tenable objection to the measure, or that anything like injustice would be done to Lower Canada. This Province has suffered greatly from the present cramped and unfavourable condition of its trade. We have been subjected to serious disabilities, have contributed largely in establishing the commercial character of Montreal and now that we find it to be our interest to withdraw that support and direct our trade through a better channel, surely our friends of the sister Province cannot pretend to complain of *injustice*. If we have long been deprived of the natural profits of our commercial transactions and enriched the merchants of Montreal by impoverishing ourselves, it furnishes no argument that we should continue to do so. The adoption of the proposed improvement would doubtless affect Montreal, inasmuch as many of the principal houses in that city, which are now dependent upon us for support, would be transplanted to the principal towns in this Province. And would not this be *just?* Is it not naturally due to this Province that those who receive the chief benefit of its trade should reside here, and should feel some interest in, and contribute to the prosperity of the country? . . .

But the *Courier* is not the only journal that has been awakened by the meeting in Toronto. I find the editor of the *Irish Advocate* requesting the particular attention of his Upper Canada readers to a communication in his paper signed G.P. which he regards *"as conveying the most cogent and convincing reasoning against the proposed measure."* After more fully reading the letter referred to, we cannot feel that the *reasoning* employed is so very conclusive. . . . The main positions assumed are that the communication proposed would *"create a too intimate alliance with the States to prevent an assimilation of interest and feeling,* that *Upper Canada in the course of time would merge in that vast republic"* and that *"The St. Lawrence is nature's highway to the ocean for both Provinces."*

The first of these assertions cannot be regarded as intitled to much weight by any persons acquainted with the true state of public feeling in Upper Canada. . . . The effect dreaded by G.P. would never be produced by the improvement in question. Upper Canada stands eternally clear of any such imputation. Her fame is spotless, her loyalty is pure. . . . If it were true that the devoted loyalty of this Province was a subject for doubt, no better course could be adopted by the Mother Country than to concede the privilege desired, and thus free our commerce from the shackles which now depress, cramp and curtail its operations.

The opinion that "the St. Lawrence is nature's highway to the ocean" for this Province, cannot be maintained. As far as we are concerned this *"Highway"* is exceedingly unnatural, and is replete with danger and difficulty. If it is the natural and most advantageous channel for our trade our friends of the sister Province need entertain no fears but that they will secure the entire trade. But of this they evidently have little hopes.

19

The St. Lawrence *versus* New York:—Comparative Costs:— The Annexation of Montreal

From *Toronto Recorder*, quoted in *Montreal Gazette*, February 2, 1836.

Sir.—

The advantages in favour of the New York route are assumed by its supporters to be—gaining a port in a friendly country— a quicker and a cheaper mode of transit for goods—less risk by fire, &c.—a saving of interest on the merchants' capital invested, in consequence of goods remaining a shorter period at the intermediate ports and from a more frequent supply, less capital being requisite—and lastly, the advantages to Upper Canada and the

West India Islands, by the greater facility afforded, for the conveyance of the produce of the former Colonies at all seasons to the latter ones, &c. . . .

On the first point, I maintain, that we possess now all the advantages to be gained by having a port in a "friendly country", without one of the disadvantages that must accrue from adopting the proposed arrangements. Our merchants' orders, letters, and invoices are forwarded to and from England by that route, a season when our own ports are closed: the New York packets are open to such persons as wish to avail themselves of the accommodation in proceeding to and from Europe—and we are only debarred, and wisely debarred too—from passing our merchandize in the same way.

With regard to the second point urged, "a quicker and cheaper mode of transit"—let us examine the data upon which it is founded, and I think it will be apparent to every unprejudiced mind, that the present route via Montreal, has many advantages over the one proposed. I admit that the New York packet ships make, *generally*, quicker passages than our merchant ships, and indeed than other carrying ships trading to this Continent: but their rates of freight are also much higher, and their profits upon passengers render the proprietors more independent of freights than the owners of other ships. . . . From the first of May to the first November, there are quicker passages made by the Quebec and Montreal carrying ships, than by vessels of a similar class in the New York trade, while the expense of freight is in all cases fifty per cent less, and frequently indeed not more than one-eighth of the American rates.

Dead weight and heavy goods, are constantly shipped from England for Montreal, as low as two shillings and sixpence, and never exceeding ten shillings per ton. On the other hand the rates to New York are frequently as high as thirty and seldom less than twenty shillings per ton with a proportionate difference for light freight or measurement goods; while the difference of insurance (so much dwelt upon by some of the supporters of the proposed measure,) in vessels of a similar class, seldom exceeds one quarter per cent in favour of New York—when a greater difference exists it arises solely from the character of the vessel, or her commander. . . . Suppose that the New York vessel gains a week in her passage on the Montreal ship, it will take eleven days for the goods to reach Toronto by way of Oswego—at the cost of 81 cents per 100 lbs. nett, or of £4. 10. 6d. currency per ton, with a certainty of three and a probability of five transhipments on the route, to which add commission to the New York agent, brokerage, Custom house entries on import and re-export, &c. say three per cent, and insurance to Toronto, one per cent. We have upon a supposed annual importation of ten thousand tons of goods, worth five hundred thousand pounds, Cy— a total charge from New York to Toronto, all in round numbers, £65,250, or about thirteen per cent. On which sum, supposing the whole carrying trade from Oswego to Toronto to be British bottoms, £25,250, goes to swell the profits of the Erie canal, and the American Commission merchants. Not one shilling of which sum ever returns directly or indirectly into the pockets of our agriculturalists or merchants here.

On the other hand, I shall suppose the Montreal ships arriving seven days later than the New Yorker—It has been proved last season that the goods from Montreal can be delivered at Toronto in five days by way of the Rideau Canal, at an expense of two pounds ten shillings per ton with a certainty of two, and probably of only one transhipment. We also save two and a half per cent in commissions, brokerage, &c.; the forwarders at Montreal upon receipt of the duplicate invoices from the merchants here, passing the entries, paying the duties, &c. at a trifling cost, under one half per cent, the cost of insurance being the same as by the New York route, say one per cent, thus saving the Provincial merchants on freight in transit £20,230, and in commissions &c. £12,500 or about six and a half per cent on the supposed importations. While the remaining £32,500 are every shilling returned to the Province, again to circulate among our farmers, traders and mechanics: it being well known that the most extensive forwarders are large purchasers of produce and always glad to take the produce from the retail country store keepers and others, in payment of their forwarding accounts. So much on the score of expedition and economy. . . .

But for a port of entry, and for the means of collecting the full amount of our own revenue, why not in mild but firm and respectful language, address our most Gracious Sovereign and the Imperial Parliament of Great Britain, for the annexation of Montreal to this Province.

Are we pusillanimously to beg from the courtesies of a friendly state, (and that state too upon the verge of a war which must be essentially maritime,) that accommodation which as an integral part of the Great British Empire, we should claim as a right from the Supreme Government? I for one answer NO. Let us be but firm and unanimous, and the Imperial Parliament must do us justice—for the granting us a port of entry in the St. Lawrence, will be but an act of justice. The time is most opportune for pressing the question. A powerful and wealthy body of our countrymen in the sister Province call aloud for the junction, and if we press the subject home it must be granted. This, sir, I take to be the most open—the most honorable—and the most manly way of obtaining our just rights—*the collection and disbursement of our own revenue*—by this means our real value to the Parent State will be ascertained, our internal improvements now in progress, be completed with our own resources—and these resources still further developed. . . .

MERCATOR

20

Advantages to Montreal of the Welland Canal

From *Montreal Gazette*, December 15, 1836.

Next in importance to the question of the Union of the provinces of CANADA, or the annexation of MONTREAL to the Upper Province, which is proposed in lieu of the former more decided measure, we regard the proposal for effecting a change in the WELLAND Canal as demanding the attention of the Lower Canadians.

This Province has much more direct interest in the success of that undertaking, than the mere stock held by our merchants, or the quasi-loan of £25,000 which our Legislature granted at the close of the Session of 1825. . . . The interest of Lower Canada is to see the work completed in a solid, substantial and effectual manner, to enable it to afford every facility not only to the existing trade of the Lakes, but to that large increase which must naturally arise from the extensive emigrations into ILLINOIS, INDIANA, OHIO, MICHIGAN, and other of the Western States. The AMERICAN government are aware of the advantages we enjoy in this key to the trade of the "far west", and they are anxious to divert to themselves the profits arising to Upper Canada by the inland transportation. The Canal Commissioners and their Engineers throughout the state of New York, make numerous allusions, in their reports to the value of the WELLAND Canal. . . .

Judge Wright of NEW YORK, one of the most able Engineers of that State, in his report to the WELLAND Canal Committee, dated the 3d October, 1833, points out most forcibly the advantages which the *St. Lawrence* has over the *Hudson* or the *Mississippi*, for forwarding the produce of the immense regions lying to the eastward of the ROCKY MOUNTAINS, and northward of the line 37°—a tract of country capable of supporting a population of fifty millions, and within which will be found before twenty years are past, not less than ten or twelve millions. The contest in reality will exist only between NEW YORK and MONTREAL. Produce can be conveyed as cheaply from the upper end of *Lake Ontario* to the summit of our canal navigation at PRESCOTT, as to OSWEGO, while from PRESCOTT to MONTREAL our facilities are certainly more encouraging than between OSWEGO and NEW YORK, through the OSWEGO and ERIE Canals and the *Hudson* river. . . .

There cannot be a doubt therefore, that the completion of the WELLAND Canal is a most desirable object for the CANADAS. But whether a work, which has so important a bearing upon the prosperity of the Provinces, should be confided to the care of a private company, or be the property of the Government solely, has become the subject of discussion in the Legislature of UPPER CANADA.

21

The Canalization of the St. Lawrence as the Key to the Trade of the Continent

From Canadian Archives, *Upper Canada sundries*, 1839.

This document nicely illustrates the intimate connection between politics and the economic situation. Hostility on the part of the French to English commerce and all its works and apathy on the part of the inefficient government of Upper Canada had allowed the prize of the western trade to slip through Canadian fingers.

William Hamilton Merritt to Sir George Arthur

St. Catharines Feby 16th 1839

. . . Another evil arising from our defective system is the want of operation and design on the part of the several Legislatures in the construction of such public works on the main Line of our Water Communications, as require to be constructed on the same dimensions—The Lachine Canal in Lower Canada has only four feet depth of water—The Rideau Canal constructed by the Home Government has five feet and the Welland Canal, the work of a private company aided by the Legislature of Upper Canada, has eight feet water—Never a vessel freighted with produce from Lake Michigan may pass through the Welland Canal to within 130 miles of our natural Sea-Port, but up to the present moment has been unable to pass through either of the former Canals—I have already addressed your Excellency on the subject of the Rideau Canal shewing that the freights have increased instead of diminishing. . . .

From our defective system we have lost the trade of the entire Country bordering on Lake Champlain at the North, and from thence as far West as Lake Superior—lying within the boundaries of the United States—It now behooves us to regain what we have lost by the negligence, ignorance supineness and powerless situation of two divided Legislatures—as well as by the want of attention to our best interests on the part of the Home Government—and to open this communication on such a scale as will ensure the *transit* in all time to come. . . .

The St. Lawrence and Mississippi Rivers are the two natural outlets in a North and South direction, from the interior of this continent—Lake Michigan is the summit from which to Quebec, when our contemplated improvements are completed, a communication will be opened—presenting all the properties of an ocean having throughout, wide, deep, navigable waters excepting the Welland Canal of 27 miles and the St. Lawrence of 28 miles in length—with 340 and 160 feet lockages—These two outlets will be the only formidable rivals in the transit of the products of the immense country adjoining and leading to them, already containing a population of millions—It is an object worthy of the efforts of *great minds*. Nature has placed their trade and commerce within our reach—and future ages will applaud the wisdom of the Legislature who commenced the St. Lawrence Canal on a sufficient scale to insure its full and complete usefulness. . . .

William Hamilton Merritt

22

Reasons for the Loss of the Western Trade:—How the Canals will Reduce Freights

From *Journals of assembly, Upper Canada*, 1839, Appendices 36, Second report of the committee on finance, April 9.

Prior to 1812 we were in a far more prosperous situation than the adjoining portion of the U.S. the trade of which was conveyed through the Montreal outlet of the St. Lawrence to the ocean through Canadian waters and Canadian ports. The command of the trade, by giving employment to our vessels, ensured us the control of both lakes, a circumstance to which the safety of the Province, in the late American War, may be in a great measure ascribed.

The completion of the Erie and Oswego Canals diverted this trade to the Hudson and conferred the advantages we possessed on the inhabitants residing on the opposite frontier.—This instantaneous change to our disadvantage produced a corresponding depression and the necessity of regaining what we had lost became apparent.

A general desire prevailed to improve the natural facilities we were known to possess, but it was impossible to overlook the formidable barrier which the occupation and control of our only seaport, by a Legislature entertaining separate views and feelings presented.—Many abandoning all hope of inducing the Legislature of Lower Canada to open the communication, turned their attention to the outlet offered by the Port of New York, and had it not been for the restrictions imposed by the General Government of the United States on our commerce, it would ere this have reached the Ocean by this channel. . . .

The price of conveying a ton of merchandize, at present, from London to Montreal, 3200 miles, is One Pound, from Montreal to Prescott, 130 miles, £2. 10s. The charge, when the improvements are made, will average from London to Lake Erie 2 to 2. 10s., which is less than the present cost from Albany to Buffalo.

Wm Hamilton Merritt,
Chairman

23

A Comparison of the Natural Advantages of Canada and the United States

From Canadian Archives, *Upper Canada sundries.*

William Hamilton Merritt to Charles Poulett Thomson

St Catharines, 28th Novr, 1839

Sir.—

. . . Various reasons are assigned for the striking difference in the prosperity of the two countries, which to a person not conversant with our past history may appear plausible—1st   It is ascribed to their earlier settlement.   Quebec was peopled nearly as early as New York, and the settlement of this, the Niagara District, commenced before there was a house or a white man this side or west of Utica—

2nd To their natural advantages.   It is notorious that up to 1812, the entire trade of the western country as far East as Utica passed down the St. Lawrence to the Ports of Montreal and Quebec. The moment their canals were opened, our trade vanished as if by magic to the Hudson River, to which they are indebted for the great increase of their internal trade.   The only natural advantage they possess is the port of New York and even this for the competition of the Great Western Trade is overrated, as we could, were the necessary and contemplated improvements completed, pass down the St. Lawrence as early as they can through the Erie Canal below Utica.

3rd, To their increased wealth.   Ten years preceding the opening of the Erie and Champlain Canal, the wealth of the City and State of New York increased but a mere trifle.   The next ten years after those works were in operation it increased upward of two hundred millions of dollars, thus affording additional proof, derived from accurate statistical information, that to their internal improvements, created by and within themselves, is their increased wealth to be attributed.

4th To their greater population.

Before the late war, Upper and Lower Canada nearly equalled the State of New York in population.   Now theirs amounts to two millions, ours not to one.

5th. That their public works pay.

True—and the only reason why ours do not, is that they are not completed throughout. We have had no common interest—no system. The one canal is constructed on one scale, another on a different scale, so that a vessel or craft suitable for the one is unfit for the other.

The true cause, after all, of the prosperity of new countries may be found in the following quotation from the able author of "An Inquiry into the Wealth of Nations":—"Plenty of good land, and liberty to manage their own affairs their own way".

William Hamilton Merritt

24

Geographical Factors in the Control of Trade

From *Montreal Transcript*, January 25, 1845.

On Thursday evening last, a lecture on "The Trade of Canada," was delivered by W. H. Merritt, Esq., before the Mercantile Library Association of this city. . . .

The first part of Mr. Merritt's address embraced an enlarged view of the extent of the inland coast of the valley of the St. Lawrence; he explained its advantages and disadvantages, in respect to situation and climate, and proved, from various statistical tables, its rapid annual increase in population and in extent of trade.

He next proceeded to demonstrate that the trade of this great country must ultimately centre on the shores of Lake Erie, bringing within its scope several of the neighbouring States of the Union; and that on the completion of the Canals now in progress, an easy and direct communication would be established with that part of the country, particularly should the Canal be made continuous, by the Province furnishing tug boats, to tow the vessels from the debouchement of one to the entrance of another. He instituted a comparison between the length and expense of transit by the Erie Canal, leading to the Hudson, and by the Welland and St. Lawrence Canals, leading past Montreal and Quebec, and showed that the latter route, when completed as above, and freed from all unnecessary restrictions, will be the cheapest and best, and command, in consequence, the greater portion of the Lake Erie trade.

Mr. Merritt then entered on the second part of his subject,

by pointing out the conduct necessary to be pursued by the Imperial and Provincial Governments, in order to secure and retain this trade. On the one part, the policy recently commenced by the Home Government,[1] ought to be carried into full effect by the removal of all duties on the products of Canada, entering the ports of Britain; on the other, British products and manufactures ought to be admitted into Canada duty free. That these duties could be dispensed with by the Province on the opening of the Canals now in process of construction, was shown by Mr. M., from an examination of our present revenues and resources; the increase of revenue from these Canals alone, would, he argued, from the immense increase of transit, more than counterbalance the reduction of duties from the Customs now levied.

Mr. Merritt lastly adverted to the consequences which would result from such a course as he advocated. Canada would become, in effect, one entire warehousing port; the six States and Territories adjoining Lake Erie would be colonies of Great Britain, as far as regards their consumption of her manufactures, a most extensive Home Market would be opened to Canadian industry, and the bonds which unite Canada to the Mother Country being thus drawn more closely and intimately together, would render British connexion for ever secure and permanent. . . .

25

Approaching Completion of the Canals:—Will Quebec Steal Montreal's Trade?

From Canadian Economist, May 16, 1846.

A short time only can now elapse before our improved internal navigation will be completed. About July in 1847, steamers of a large size from Lake Ontario, propellers and other vessels from the Canadian shore on Lake Erie, and from Ohio, Michigan, and Illinois, of a size fit to pass through the Welland Canal, will be seen in our port. We will suppose that the commercial policy of the Province will not be of that character to prevent vessels from the United States coming here. Now, as the vessels from Lakes Ontario and Erie will be of the largest possible size, from the fact

---

[1]Of admitting flour made in Canada from American wheat into Great Britain duty free.

that the price of freight will be in proportion to the tonnage, and as the smallest of these coming through the Welland Canal will carry from 3000 to 3500 barrels of flour, the question may reasonably be asked, Will vessels with such large cargoes stop at Montreal, or will they not proceed at once to Quebec? . . . Hitherto, during the summer months, when the water on the shallow part of Lake St. Peter is only 11 feet, ships from sea have had to tranship part of their cargoes, at an enormous expense, to Montreal, below which port the small craft hitherto used on our Canals, carrying only from 500 to 1100 barrels flour, were not adapted to navigate. Very soon, however, the case will be different, and unless Lake St. Peter is deepened, the trade of the country can be cheaper done in Quebec than here.

26

The St. Lawrence Route *versus* New York:—A Comparison of Costs[1]

(i)

Ocean shipping charges

From *Canadian Economist*, June 13, 1846.

[*The American bonding system and the repeal of the corn laws*]

Our attention is recalled to the important subject of our foreign and inland carrying trade, by the recurrence of an exorbitantly high rate of foreign freights, and also by the prospect of an effectual check being ultimately established by the American bonding system. When it is recollected that the present cost of carrying a barrel of flour from Toronto to Liverpool amounts to 7s. 6d. sterling, or more than one third of its entire value, and that, late in the season, even this high rate is likely to be exceeded, the advantage of such a check being put to excessive rates must be apparent to our agricultural friends. Every shilling added to the freight of flour is so much taken from the value of their produce; and of course every shilling of reduction obtained by the facilities

---

[1]This and the following document are typical of many writings of the time. Note that all calculations are based on the unit of a barrel of flour, or its equivalent in wheat.

now afforded, of passing that produce in bond through the States, is a clear gain to them. We are well aware that, so soon as the reduction of duties in Britain takes place, the Western merchants will not be slow to avail themselves of the New-York route; but we do not apprehend any evil consequences to the colony from their doing so. The immediate result will be a decline in the rates of inland transportation, and sea-going freight, on the St. Lawrence line of navigation, and that to one extent sufficient to attract in this direction cargoes enough for a large amount of tonnage; and it will be strange indeed, if, during the three years' continuance of the 4s. duty, we do not retain the whole of the carrying trade *outwards* in its present channel. The moderating effects of the American bonding system will certainly be experienced in a reduced, though remunerating, rate of freights, and we congratulate the millers and farmers of Canada on this important point being gained.

The termination, however, of the proposed three years of protection, will bring about a new order of things. Then, and not till then, will the comparative merits of the New-York and St. Lawrence routes be fully tested, the value of our great lines of internal conveyance ascertained, and the destinies of our commercial cities fixed. In the struggle which will assuredly arise, we foresee much advantage to the staple interests of Canada. So nicely will the advantages of both routes be balanced, and so vigorous we apprehend will be the competition, that, we have good reason to anticipate such a reduction in the charge of conveying produce from the interior of Canada to England, as will go far to compensate the loss of English protection, and enable us to triumph in a competition with other foreign markets. It is true that the merchants of the Lower Province, and more especially of Montreal, have something to fear in the diversion of the carrying trade to, what may turn out to be, a better channel; but we are not among those who entertain much fear of loss on this score. We cannot join in the cry to impose a tax on the English labourer for the sake of forcing our produce by the route of the St. Lawrence; neither do we fear that our direct export trade will be lost when it ceases to be protected. . . .

[*Voyages to New York and Montreal compared*]

Spring voyage, Liverpool to Montreal and back, present charges

Insurance on hull, spars, &c., going and returning, of a ship of 520 tons valued at £15 [*per ton*], £7,800 at 3½ per cent.................................. £273	0	0	
Insurance on freight list outwards, £1000 at 1½ do... 15	0	0	
Do. do. homewards, £1000 at 1 do.... 10	0	0	
Pilotage below Quebec, upwards, 15½ feet draught... 13	0	0	
Do. do. downwards, 16½ do. ... 12	6	11	
Do. above Quebec, upwards, 15½ do. ... 8	9	0	
Do. do. downwards, 16½ do. ... 5	7	6	
Towage from Quebec to Montreal.................. 91	5	0	
Do. Montreal to Quebec.................. 52	10	0	

£480 18 5

Spring voyage from New-York to Liverpool, and back

Insurance on ship of same size, £7,800 at 40s. p. cent £156	0	0	
Do. on freight list outwards, £900 at 25s. p. cent 11	5	0	
Do. do. homewards, £550 at 17s. 6d. 7	8	9	
Pilotage, about.................................. 10	0	0	
Towage, occasional.............................. 15	0	0	

£199 13 9

Net cost of Montreal over New-York voyage.................... £281 4 8

Fall voyage, Liverpool to Montreal, and back

Insurance on ship out and home, at 6 p. cent on £7,800 £468	0	0	
Do. freight list out, £1000, 1½ per cent...... 15	0	0	
Do. do. home, £1000, 3½ per cent..... 42	0	0	
Pilotage, as before............................. 38	19	5	
Towage in full........................ £143 15 0			
Add lighterage, less allowance for towage saved thereby.................... 60 0 0			

203 15 0

£767 14 5

Fall voyage, from Liverpool to New-York and back

Insurance on ship out and home, £7,800 at 50s. p. cent £195	0	0	
Do. on freight list out, £900 at 30s. per cent.... 13	10	0	
Do. on do home, £900 at 20s. per cent... 9	0	0	
Pilotage and towage, as before..................... 25	0	0	

£242 10 0

Net cost of Montreal over New-York voyage.................... £525 4 5

It thus appears that the voyage to Montreal considerably exceeds that to New York in actual expense, especially in the fall, and we do not believe that any reduction of the balance against us can ever be made, except in the item of towage, which we are sure will be reduced, as one of the consequences of the completion of our great inland improvements.

On the other hand, it may be said that we have left out of the reckoning several drawbacks to the Montreal trade. There is first the assertion that extra men are required in the Montreal over the New-York trade. This we do not believe. Extra men may be employed; but to navigate a ship effectually across the Atlantic, to overcome the difficulties of the English channel, and encounter the storms of the Atlantic, requires as efficient a crew as to navigate the St. Lawrence and its gulf, except in the end of November and later, which part of the season we exclude from our calculation. The tonnage of ships employed in the New-York trade, it is said, is greater, and the advantage is thus secured to them. No doubt a few very large ships are found in that trade, but the average size of regular traders is not so much greater than that of our own as to exclude competition, and by sending our large barges to Quebec we can have our flour shipped in vessels as large as the largest of the New-York leviathans. Again, the loss of time in the winter is alleged as an objection to this trade; but as the loss is almost entirely a mere loss of interest on the capital invested, it can but slightly affect the calculation of the cost of carrying a barrel of flour; and we do not see what is to prevent our traders from making a winter voyage to some of the United States ports. The fact of one of our traders having made a winter voyage last season to Demerara (a much longer voyage), is a sufficient proof of what they might do if they were compelled to work at lower rates.

Having thus ascertained as nearly as possible the difference in the general expenditure of the two voyages, we shall now endeavour to distribute the extra cost on Montreal cargoes, so as to show the extent to which the freight of certain descriptions of produce is thereby affected. The first difficulty that meets us in this attempt is derived from the uncertainty, whether, after the rates of inland conveyance through Canada are reduced, any part of the saving can be laid on the outward cargoes of ships arriving from Great Britain. So long as the differential duties operate against the transmission of British goods through the States, we believe the whole or nearly the whole of the extra cost of the voyages might be laid on outward freights. We cannot, however, reason on the assumption of their permanence. We shall, therefore, apportion to the outward cargo, only a small part of the sum to be disposed of, and when the great facilities that will be secured for transporting heavy merchandize by the St. Lawrence are taken into account, we believe this part of our estimate will not be questioned, even supposing the abolition of the discriminating duties. The balance against Montreal, it has been shown, amounts on the spring voyage to £281 4s. 8d. Allow that £100 of the sum is borne by charging higher rates of freight on some of the heavier kinds of goods imported into Canada, and a balance of £181 4s. 8d. remains to be distributed over the produce exported. The ship we have selected as an example, carries like most of our traders, rather over 10½ barrels to the ton register, or 5500 barrels as her complement; or taking part wheat, a cargo of 1000 quarters of wheat and 4000 barrels of flour. Entire cargoes of flour are seldom shipped, and as our advantages in taking wheat from the interior are greater as compared with the Erie line, in proportion than in the carrying of flour, owing to the saving of double transhipment, we assign a corresponding proportion of the charge for freight, to that part of the cargo. We believe that, although we charge 2d. per bushel or 1s. 4d. per quarter more than the New York rate, we shall still have the carrying of our own wheat, and of part of the United States growth. The balance of £181 4s. 8d. referred to is thus made up:—

```
1000 quarters, at 1s. 4d......................  £ 66 13 4
4000 barrels, at 6⅞d..........................    114 11 4
                                                 ─────────
                                                 £181  4 8
```

These may be deemed the essential differences in cost, that must always render our foreign freights higher than those of New York; but we do not see any reason why our rates should exceed the essential difference of expense we have thus indicated, adding ¼ per cent. for extra cost of insurance on the produce.

With regard to the fall trade, we are at much greater disadvantage. But as this arises entirely from the enhanced rates of insurance then current, it applies only to the latest part of that season. It does not apply to any produce shipped up to the middle of October, and much of the new crop might be shipped before this time if proper exertion were used. We know that one great part of the advantage to be derived from the completion of our magnificent chain of canals—will be that a great saving of time now lost by transhipment at Kingston, will be effected. The early harvests of Ohio and our south-western districts will arrive at Montreal, and in fact our whole fall business will be transacted, at least two weeks earlier. This is a great saving at that season, and its effect will be to extend the cheap export freights of summer over a considerable part of the fall shipments to which they cannot now be applied.

We despair, however, of overcoming the disadvantage we labour under at that later period of the season to which our second estimate refers. Making the same allowance for additional outward freight, we find the balance against us, in the case supposed, to be £425 4s. 5d., which we must assign as follows:

1000 quarters of grain, at 3s.	£150
4000 brls. of flour, at 1s. 4½d	275
	£425

Adding the extra cost of insurance, the excess of the cost of conveyance over the New-York rates must be at least 4s. 6d. per quarter for wheat, and 2s. 6d. per barrel for flour. These weighty charges arising from unalterable circumstances in our climate and geographical position, can only, we apprehend, be combatted by the construction of the projected railroad to Portland.

We have pointed out. . . the great advantages which this new means of exportation would give us in the close of the season. . . .

If it should happen, however, that the Portland railroad is abandoned, what man of sense will, on that account, deny the advantage of saving 10 per cent. on the whole value of our exported surplus, by sending it through the cheapest lines of conveyance to England, wherever they may be. It is one of the first principles of our economical creed that trade should never be *forced* into any particular channels at the public cost, and from the advocacy of this principle, in whatever way its operation may affect particular localities, we shall never flinch. The general welfare of the community demands that all monopolies of this kind should cease.

(ii)

An analysis of inland freight charges to New York and to Montreal

From *Canadian Economist*, June 27, 1846.

Our enquiry into the comparative merits of Montreal and New York, as ports of shipment to Great Britain, shewed as its result a difference of 7d per barrel and 1s. 4d. per quarter, in favor of the latter port. We now come to enquire, can this be met by lower rates of inland forwarding than our competitors on the Erie and Oswego line are able to offer? Our conviction is that it can be so met. . . . But we do not wish to see the vital interest of the Province sacrificed for the purpose of retaining a trade which we cannot offer the means of carrying on. We do not wish to see the resources of our merchants, our millers, and our farmers passing into the pockets of British shipowners or even of Canadian forwarding companies,—a process we are unfortunately compelled to witness in full operation at the present moment. Our forwarders cannot find boats enough to bring down the produce; and when it gets here, we cannot find ships enough to take it away; and therefore . . . . we are now paying 3s. 6d. stg. per barrel more for freight from Toronto to Liverpool, than the charge by way of New York. . . . Because we point out to our productive classes that, what is lost by the withdrawal of English protection, will be fully compensated by the abandonment of English restriction, by cheap imports and cheap freights, . . . we are stigmatized as the supporters of "schemes" which have for their end "the ruin of the trade of Montreal". We assure our readers that we have no "schemes" in view whatever:

Rates of forwarding from Toronto to New York

Toronto to Oswego.....................................	0s. 6d.
Oswego to Troy.......................................	1s. 4½d.
Troy to New York.....................................	0s. 6d.
Per barrel of flour...................................	2s. 4½d. Cy.

Rates from Cleveland to New York

Cleveland to Buffalo...................................	0s. 9d.
Re-shipment..	0s. 1½d.
Buffalo to Troy...............................(55 cents)	2s. 9d.
Troy to New York.....................................	0s. 6d.
	Cy. 4s. 1½d.

Now when it is borne in mind, that, after deducting tolls, the whole sum left for the forwarder is only 20 cents for a distance, by canal, of 362 miles, it cannot be supposed that any further reduction from this low rate is possible. We think, then, that we are safe in assuming the above rates as the minimum. They are one-third less than the rates of the previous years, which have averaged 87½ cents from Buffalo to New York, while so lately as the fall of last year, the rate was a dollar and upwards per barrel.

In attempting to arrive at the minimum rate on our own lines, we find ourselves unable to judge altogether from past experience.

The improvements in the navigation of the St. Lawrence, now nearly complete, are of a kind that must revolutionize the whole system of forwarding. They are designed to meet that great peculiarity of our navigation, its *extraordinary variety*, comprising a continual alternation of lake, river and canal. With canals of the dimensions hitherto in use, it has been impossible to employ craft adapted for lake navigation. Transhipment at Kingston— involving much expense, loss of time, and damage to the cargoes,— has been the consequence. Of this evil we now see the end. In the fall of next year, if not in the spring, we shall have craft with cargoes of 16,000 bushels of wheat or 3000 barrels of flour, making their voyages direct from the head of Lake Ontario to Montreal. We shall also see the steam propellers in use, carrying 2500 barrels, and making the voyage from Hamilton downwards in three days, and upwards with return freight in four. Compare this with the present system, requiring the use of barges fitted to carry only 800 or 1000 barrels, the frequent delay of a month in the transit, and two distinct voyages, with the expense of relanding and separate establishments at Kingston, and is it not plain that a charge of 1s. per barrel under the new system will pay as well as a charge of 1s. 6d. per barrel under the old? Such a conclusion would seem an obvious one, looking merely at these general considerations; but we have to corroborate it, the deliberate opinion of most of those engaged in the trade. . . . We think, therefore, that we are fully warranted in assuming the minimum rate of 1s. per barrel.

The comparison will therefore stand as follows:

	Per Barrel
From Hamilton or Toronto to New York	2s. 4½d.
Do. Do. Do. to Montreal	1s. 0d.
Add extra cost of conveyance to Britain over New York rate...	0s. 7d.
	1s. 7d.
Difference in favor of Montreal Route	0s. 9½d.

From Cleveland, U.S. to New York	4s. 1½d.
Do. Do. Do. to Montreal	1s. 10½d.
Add extra cost of conveyance to Britain over New York rate...	0s. 7d.
	2s. 5½d.
Difference in favor of Montreal Route	1s. 8½d. Cy.

To these decided differences in favor of Montreal, it would only be fair to add 3d. per barrel for saving of time and of injury by double transhipment, making the balance in our favor about

1s. per barrel from Lake Ontario, and 1s. 8d. per barrel from Lake
Erie. In regard to the carrying of wheat, our advantage will be
still more remarkable. Everyone knows how injurious it is to the
quality of the grain to have it long on board of river craft, and
how desirable it is to save storage in Montreal, by loading cargoes
direct from the barge into the seagoing ship, a mode of shipment
which will be much facilitated. The expense also and loss of weight
incurred on the Erie line by double transhipment give us still more
decided advantages over that route; and we do not hesitate to
avow our conviction that the grain of Ohio, Illinois, and Michigan
will be sent by way of the St. Lawrence to Britain and the Continent, in vast quantities after the equalization of the English duties.
There is one preliminary condition, however, to which we attach
much importance. The monopoly of the carrying trade must be
put an end to by the admission of foreign competition on our inland
waters. We must be allowed to go to the cheapest market for
ships as well as for everything else.[1]

27

The "Soo" Canal in Contemplation

From *Montreal Transcript*, September 22, 1846.

SAULT ST. MARIE.—The *Buffalo Morning Express* discourses
on the practicability and advantage of constructing a canal
round the falls of St. Marie—if not by public, by private
enterprize. $200,000—not more than the cost of two good steam-
boats—it has been estimated, would defray the expense of the
construction of a canal, which would afford a passage for steamers
and vessels into Lake Superior; a trifle, when compared with the
lasting benefits that such a work would secure to trade, commerce,
and civilization.

---

[1]For documents on the repeal of the navigation laws, see section IV.

THE INITIAL STAGES OF THE RAILROAD ERA

The desirability of the new invention was canvassed in Canada even before the first line was opened in England, but the poverty of the country prevented anything but projects on paper, which were legion, until after other countries had built their roads. While at first railroads in America were designed merely to cross the portages between water-routes, it was not long before the notion of the "trunk" road was born. The two stages came close together in Canada. As soon as it had completed its effort to regain the western trade for the St. Lawrence by building the canals, the country had to turn to the new form of transport, for the United States had circumvented the St. Lawrence canals by railways from the sea to the lakes. The railroad-building of the next decade is the product of this competition.

REFERENCES: R. G. Trotter, *Canadian federation: its origins and achievement* (Toronto, 1924); O. D. Skelton, *Life and times of Sir A. T. Galt* (Toronto, 1920); W. T. Jackman, *Economics of transportation* (Toronto, 1926); H. A. Innis, *A history of the Canadian Pacific Railway* (Toronto, 1923).

1

Suitability of Canada for the New Invention, the Railroad

From *Montreal Gazette*, November 24, 1824.

We are not in possession of a sufficiently minute description of this invention [*i.e. the railroad*] to give a detail of its construction.—We understand the steam engines used are upon the same plan as those now employed in propelling boats; with the difference of having their wheels toothed instead of paddles. The rails are also toothed like racks; and on the revolution of the wheels their teeth taking in those of the rack or rail, gives the progressive motion to the machine by the rotary movement of the wheels.[1] It is also stated that both the rails and wheels, can be cast with teeth at the same expense as if plain.

Our attention has been forcibly drawn to this subject from a consideration of this country being by nature peculiarly well adapted for the construction of rail roads. Its immense extent of level surface, perhaps is not exceeded in any country in the known world; and which must obviously make the construction of such roads attainable at little expense compared with those situations where much excavation or embanking is required. The

---

[1]Some of the early experiments employed this device.

198

whole distance from Lake Superior to Quebec does not perhap exceed the difference of level admissible in a rail road. Through the whole of that extended tract of country lying between the Ottawa and St. Lawrence rivers, there is not an elevation so great as to prevent the application of this improvement. From the Township of Hull, on the former river to the River du Loup, there is a level line running in rear of the surveyed lands on the north side of these Rivers, admirably suited for a rail road, and where the construction of one would open a tract of country unrivaled in fertility of soil by any part in the two provinces.

If abundance of materials necessary for their construction contributes to the cheapness of making such roads, Canada may compare with any country in this respect. Her rich beds of iron-ore would supply all that could be required of that article for making rails or engines;—Of timber, the quantity she could supply for laying the rails upon may be said to be almost inexhaustible. If we suppose these roads once made . . . there is perhaps no place where the requisites for using them are more amply furnished than in these provinces. In every part of the country plenty of water for the engines could be found,—and as to fuel, many ages must elapse before our immense forests fail to supply it; and even when this takes place, there are in many places so sure indications of coal that no doubt can be entertained, that this country will ever be deficient of this article. In short should the application of this improvement be found practicable in Great Britain; . . . no long period will elapse, before we may expect to see it extended to Canada, where nature has done so much to facilitate its application.

2

The First Railroad in Canada

From *Journals of assembly, Lower Canada*, XXXVIII, 122, December 10, 1828.

The first railroad, here referred to, ran from Laprairie, opposite Montreal, to the Richelieu above the Chambly Rapids, a distance of fifteen miles. Merely a portage road, the first stage of the route to New York, it was not opened until 1837.

A petition of the Honorable *C. W. Grant* and others . . . was presented to the House by Mr *Viger*, setting forth:
That inasmuch as the Roads between the *Saint John's* and the River *Saint Lawrence*, are at all times so bad as to cause great delay,

inconvenience and expense in the transportation of Merchandize to and from that Port: And inasmuch as the Establishment of a Rail Road would greatly facilitate the commerce between this Province and the *United States*, and be a remedy to the inconveniences now experienced. The Petitioners therefore respectfully pray that this important subject be taken into the consideration of the House.

3

Project for a Railroad on the Niagara Portage

From *Quebec Mercury*, June 23, 1831.

The plan of a Railway, from the river Chippawa to the village of Queenston, where the navigation of Lake Ontario terminates, for the purpose of forming a communication between that Lake and Lake Erie, has been at length taken up. . . . This is now rather an after-thought, had such a railroad been set on foot, when the Welland Canal was first projected it would, ere this, have paid the proprietors, and brought back the carrying trade to the Niagara Frontier. The Welland Canal being now open, it appears to us that the rail-road will be serviceable only for local purposes, and that the transport upon it will be of too limited an extent to repay even the moderate outlay such a work will require.

4

Birth of the Great Western Railroad[1]

From *Toronto Courier*, quoted in *Montreal Gazette*, May 3, 1834.

LONDON and ONTARIO RAILROAD.—We perceive by the *True Patriot*, that the first meeting of the friends of the London and Gore Railroad was held in London on Monday the 7th instant [*i.e., April 7*]; and we rejoice to find that stock to the amount of four or five hundred shares was taken up before the meeting adjourned. A Committee to solicit subscriptions along the line of the contemplated road was appointed, and stock books placed in their

---

[1]This "London and Gore" Railroad had a continuous legal existence but did not become a material project until 1853, when its first section, under the title of the Great Western Railroad, was opened, Hamilton to London. In the next year the road was completed to Windsor.

hands, or transmitted by mail to such gentlemen of the Committee as were not at the meeting. . . .

When it is considered that every landholder within ten miles of the intended road must be greatly benefitted by its completion, and that the produce of the finest and most fertile country in America, must in a few years be of little value, unless some such improvement is effected; we are not at all surprised to hear that the farmers are coming forward to take up stock, solely under the influence of an impression that should the business on the road make no return in the way of tolls their lands would increase in value to such an extent, as fully to justify the investment of whatever capital they may possess. The sum of £100,000 is said to be amply sufficient to make an excellent wood and iron railway from London to Hamilton or Dundas, and if every farmer, whose land would be increased in value fifty per cent, by the completion of so magnificent an undertaking, was to take up two shares, which, at the most would subject him for two years to a quarterly payment of £3 2s 6d, it would be unnecessary to open a stockbook beyond the line of the intended road. Should the Company succeed in making the road from the head of the Lake to London, there can be no doubt of its being continued to the navigable waters of the Thames, or of its being one of the most profitable investments of money in this country. A single glance at Lieut. Taylor's new map, on which the intended line of the road is marked, and the extensive region bordering on Canada west of the St. Clair, will be sufficient to show that in the event of its continuance either to the navigable waters of the Thames, or to the south western extremity of Lake Huron, the Company must derive all the benefit of the extensive carrying trade and travel now going on between the eastern and western States of the Union.

5

The Railroad and the Local Market

From *Montreal Gazette*, September 10, 1835.

A notice of the present condition of the St. JOHN'S and LAPRAIRIE Railroad, cannot but prove interesting to CANADIAN readers, as well as to many in the UNITED STATES, who have expressed an anxiety to see this greatly desired improvement in full operation. . . .

Many of our Southern friends have been debarred from visiting this city and QUEBEC, by the generally impassable condition of the existing road, over which, although only eighteen miles in length, it often requires some three or four hours to accomplish a passage. By the railroad, which will be in a direct line, the distance will be reduced to fifteen miles, and the time required for the journey to one hour.

The completion of the railway cannot but produce a very important effect upon the MONTREAL market. The farmers of the distant Eastern Townships, and the habitants of the surrounding seigneuries, will find themselves in possession of a route, enabling them to transport with greater ease, and at less expense a larger quantity of their produce than they have yet been enabled to do, and experience a sensible increase in the amount of hard cash they can return with to their homes and this too in a shorter period of time, and without the destruction of, or injury to horse, cart and harness, which at present is the ordinary accompaniment of a trip upon the existing road. The settlers along the borders of *Lake Champlain*, as far up as PLATTSBURGH and Burlington, will then have it in their power, by the steamboats and railroad, to visit our markets as regularly as can now be done by any of the farmers upon our own island. . . .

6

The Northern Railway and the Western States

From *Montreal Gazette*, November 3, 1835.

The public meeting . . . for the purpose of taking into consideration the contemplated railroad between Toronto and Lake Simcoe, was held at the Court House, Toronto.[1] . . . The most casual observer, by merely taking a map of the Province in his hand and considering the relative situations of Toronto, on Lake Ontario, Mackinaw, on Lake Huron and Chicago, on Lake Michigan, will perceive, that by this contemplated railroad, a saving of quite three hundred miles in distance, and a more speedy, safe, and cheap mode of conveyance, will be afforded to the thousands of emigrants from the Northern and Eastern States, which are now pouring onwards to that immense Western country. . . .

---

[1]The road here referred to is the Northern Railway opened as far as Lake Simcoe in 1853 and completed to Collingwood on the Georgian Bay in 1855.

7

Railroads and the Racial Question

From *Montreal Gazette*, November 24, 1835.

Did we wish for any proof that the Assembly are determined, in a great measure, to oppose every public improvement, which might lead to the profitable investment of capital among us, we should find ample evidence among the proceedings of the last week. The railroads to LACHINE and the COTEAU DU LAC, and those through the Eastern Townships have all been *burked* by that patriotic body, while they have sanctioned only that which is proposed to be established along the line of the CHAUDIERE to the Province line, in connection with a contemplated route to PORTLAND. We cannot well understand upon what grounds the former plans should all receive an unfavourable report from the Committee of Private Bills. We can only suppose that they have not been notified to the public according to the strict letter of the nearly obsolete rules of the House. Upon this point we should like to be informed by some of our Quebec contemporaries, who can obtain access to the report in question. . . . We are certainly at a loss for an excuse for the House, except the one we have just urged, and yet we are loth to suppose it, seeing that the same day they entertained the Bill for the PORTLAND Railroad, which has never been advertised to our knowledge. While we are thus trammelled and retarded in the public improvements that have been contemplated, UPPER CANADA, the adjoining Provinces, and the neighbouring Republics, are advancing with giant strides.

8

Backwardness of Canada in Construction of Railroads

From *Montreal Gazette*, March 20, 1836.

While it appears impossible from an unfortunate concatenation of circumstances to obtain railroads throughout this Province, which is by nature so admirably adapted for their construction, our neighbours around us are pressing forward in the grand march of improvement, and leaving us at an immeasurable distance behind. We cannot take up a paper from the STATES, but we are startled by some dozen contemplated routes, wherein the distance and the cost appear to be deemed of trifling moment compared with the ultimate benefit to be derived by the enterprising people, who not only talk of improvements but really and effectually carry them into execution. Upper Canada is not deficient in enterprise in this branch of public amelioration, and the Lower Provinces on the seaboard, with diminished means, possess ten times greater anxiety for such works than the proud, wealthy but ignorant Province of Lower Canada.[1]

9

The Ancestor of the Intercolonial Railway

From Canadian Archives, *Lower Canada sundries*, 1836.

Captain Yule, R.E., to the Earl of Gosford

Royal Engineers' Office, Montreal,
13th July, 1836

My Lord,

. . . As soon as the country[2] is examined and the practicability of a Railway through it ascertained, I shall propose to Sir Archibald Campbell to use what remains of the money allowed for the Survey in opening a line through the forest sufficient for winter travelling, in order that depots of provisions, forage, &c may be made along the whole route, and no time lost in beginning the railway itself as soon as the snow disappears.

If the arrangements made by the post office will admit of their stations being transferred to the new route at a diminished cost and greater speed, the co-operation of that department may be confidently expected. . . .

T. Yule
Capt. R[1] Engineers

---

[1]A reference to the refusal of the French majority in the assembly either to grant public aid for public projects or to authorize private charters. This opposition to all improvement, as something English, was a prominent factor in the political disturbances of the period.
[2]Between Quebec and St. Andrew's, N.B.

10

From New York to Toronto in Thirty Hours

From *Toronto Constitution*, quoted in *Montreal Gazette*, August 30, 1836.

Already are the stage coaches giving up the contest on the Utica and Schenectady line of road, and the mails will be carried by steam on the railway after next month. The next step will be to continue the railroad to Syracuse, not far distant from Oswego, and the last to bring it to Lockport, already connected with Buffalo. Two years hence the traveller or the mail bag may be enabled by means of American capital, industry and enterprise to reach this city from New York by steamers and railroad cars in thirty hours. Every day will render Upper Canada more and more dependent on and commercially connected with New York city and State.

11

Opening of the First Railroad in the Maritime Provinces

From *Mechanic and Farmer* (Pictou, N.S.), May 20, 1840.

Last Thursday morning, intelligence reached town that the new line of Rail Road, from the Albion Mines to South Pictou was completed, and that the Locomotives, with their trains of cars, would on that day travel through the whole length of the Road. The announcement was hailed with joy by the inhabitants of the town; and as the Steamboat *Albion* made two trips to South Pictou, in the early part of the day, many persons availed themselves of the opportunity thus afforded, of witnessing an event in every way so important to the prosperity of Pictou. The Volunteer Artillery Company, in full costume, with their field-pieces, joined the party, to add sound and effect to the general expression of public feeling.

Soon after the parties had landed at the terminus of the Rail Road, the smoke of the two Locomotives was discovered rising over the adjoining forest, presenting the novel appearance of proceeding from a moving body beneath, outstripping the wind in velocity. There was a good breeze blowing at the same time, in the same direction as the trains; but their superior swiftness gave the columns of smoke the singular appearance of proceeding for some distance against the wind.   The spectators were ranged on the banks of the Rail Road; and to those who had not before seen such a sight, as well as to those that had, the passing of the trains presented a feature in the history of the British American Colonies, possessing intense interest, and which called forth from the assembled multitudes the most enthusiastic cheers, accompanied by discharges of artillery.

The event was every way an interesting and important one; and we doubt not, many of the boys who were there will, when their heads are "silver'd o'er with years," talk of the opening of the first[1] Rail Road in [British] America.

. . . We may now say, for the information of those who may be interested, that the delays heretofore experienced in loading ships with coal, need not now be apprehended, as they will henceforward be delivered from the end of the Rail Road, directly on board of all vessels drawing 18 feet of water and under. . . .

12

Montreal's Quest for a Winter Port[2]

From *Montreal Witness*, quoted in *Montreal Transcript*, August 4, 1846.

A great effort is making in this city to awaken public interest in the St. Lawrence and Atlantic Railroad, *via* Portland and we trust it will be successful.   A few of the advantages of such a railroad may be enumerated:—

1. It would render Montreal almost an Atlantic city, with the choice of exporting and importing either by the River or by a constantly accessible sea-port, as might in each particular case be deemed cheapest or most convenient.

2. It would complete a second great chain of internal communication from Chicago to the Atlantic, which would, in our opinion, successfully rival the first by way of the Erie Canal and Hudson River.   Indeed, it would be more expeditious, have less

---

[1]Local pride doubtless made the Albion Mines the first, but it was in reality the second, the first being the Laprairie and St. John's Road, referred to above.

[2]The "St. Lawrence and Atlantic" was chartered in 1845 to connect with the "Atlantic and St. Lawrence", from Portland, Me.   The line failed of completion by private means and it was not until taken over by the Grand Trunk that it was finally put through to the coast.   It by no means met the extravagant claims made for it and most of the produce of Upper Canada continued to come down and go out by water.

lockage, and, being farther north, would transport wheat and flour with considerably less risk of damage, of heating or souring. A reason which, when duly appreciated, would, we think, turn a great part of the produce, which now goes by way of New Orleans, to this northern route.

3. It would cause our markets to be much better and more regularly supplied, not only with country produce, but with fresh fish and other marine productions.

4. It would put the benefits of sea-bathing and sea air within reach of our whole population—an incalculable boon to the invalid, and scarcely less so to persons in health.

5. It would open up the country through which it passed to great comfort and prosperity.

6. It would probably prevent much annual waste of life and property, by taking away the inducement for vessels to sail too late in the season by way of the Gulf.

Finally, we would say to proprietors of real estate in Montreal, and especially those who have stores or dwelling-houses to let, that, as a mere question of pounds, shillings, and pence, they had better subscribe twenty-five per cent. of the value of their property at once to this railroad, than allow it to drop, for if the plan fail, there is every indication that there will be that amount of depreciation in the value of their property, without any thing in the shape of dividends on railroad stock to represent it; whereas, if it succeed, the value of property will be likely to rise, and probably also the value of railway shares.

DEEP-SEA SHIPPING OUT OF THE ST. LAWRENCE

Just as the valley was the hinterland of Montreal, so in some respects the whole continent was the hinterland of the ports of England. Consequently, aided by the navigation laws, British shipping monopolized the trade of the St. Lawrence. It was the inferior ships which came and it was not until the age of steam that much regularity or luxury of traffic developed. There was no class of fast-sailing packets as there was from New York. Ships were of two types, "regular traders" and "seekers", the latter resembling the "tramp" of to-day. Nine out of ten ships were in the timber trade, a sorry class of vessels, too old for anything but the roughest of loads. Their outward cargo was immigrants, bricks, salt, or ballast—mostly ballast. Until steam-tugs came into use, few ships came up to Montreal, which, until about 1830, was a distributing centre rather than a sea-port.

REFERENCE: *Canada and its provinces*, X, 589 ff.

1

Shipping Entering the Port of Quebec, 1780-1861

From H. Y. Hind, "Commerce and trade" in *Eighty years' progress*, 274.

	Vessels	Tons	Average tonnage[1]	Average Crew[1] per ship	Steamships No.	Tons	Average tonnage[1]	Average Crew[1]
1780	69	8,792	127	10.5				
1791	81	14,760	182	10				
1801	175	20,517	117	9				
1811	582	116,687	200	9.5				
1821	434	102,786	237	10.7				
1831[2]	1,026	263,160	263	13	1	363		
1841[2]	1,221	425,118	356	13.5	13	5,057	389	17
1851[2]	1,300	533,427	410	13.6	..	......	....	..
1861[2]	1,277	703,908	551	15.7	67	71,894	1,073	65

2

The Navigation Season in the St. Lawrence

From H. Y. Hind, in *Eighty years' progress*, 274.

The earliest period recorded of the dates of the opening of navigation at Quebec is the 12th April, in 1828; the latest period was the 11th May, 1847, a difference of one month.

---

[1]Averages supplied by editor.
[2]Sailing ships only.

The latest date of the closing of navigation occurred on the 21st December, 1826; the earliest was the 25th November, 1833; also a period of about one month.

With respect to the period of navigation between Montreal and Quebec, the longest duration was in 1830, when the number of days between the first arrival and the last sailing was 223 days or from April 26th to December 4th. The shortest period occurred in 1836, from May 11th to November 25th; 199 days.

3
A Typical Cargo in the West Indian Trade
From Canadian Archives *Reports*, 1882.

Reports, outwards, of vessels from Quebec, June 10 to 18, November, 1791

The Friends, for Grenada, 155 tons:
110 bbls flour, 185 quintals biscuit.
896 bus. oats in puncheons.
8,391 bbl staves.
1,115 headings.
1,087 pine boards, 15 ft.
2,000   ''   '' , 10 ft.
4,000 hoops.
44 tierces and 26 bbls salmon.

4
A "Regular Trader"
From *Montreal Gazette*, May 30, 1833.

SHIP NOTICES

FREIGHT AND PASSAGE TO LONDON.—By the fast sailing and fortunate ship the GREAT BRITAIN, Swinburne, Master, well known in the trade, as delivering her cargoes in prime order. She is a most eligible conveyance for Wheat, Flour and Ashes, and has excellent accommodations for Passengers; burthen, 323 tons, coppered and copper-fastened. Apply to the Master, on board, or to

PETER M'GILL & Co.

Montreal, May 14, 1833

14

5

The First Ship from Seaward

From *Quebec Gazette*, quoted in *Montreal Gazette*, May 5, 1836.

FIRST VESSEL—Nothing is known of the vessel below, which was announced by telegraph[1] on Saturday. The master of the schooner of the Hudson's Bay Company, which was announced at the same time, and has returned to St. Patrick's Hole, whence she sa led about the middle of last month, having wintered there, came up along the North Shore, and saw the brig beating up the South Channel, with top-gallant sails set. The report that she might be a wrecked vessel, two of which are expected up, would, from this rig, not appear likely to be the case. The Captain is perhaps also under the impression that he cannot land without a heavy penalty, nor allow any person to come on board, under the Quarantine regulations. A few dollars might by this time have solved the mystery, if a messenger had ridden down the South shore, and taken a boat to go alongside and hail her, and brought news, which may be three weeks later! But the season and the times deaden all our exertion.

6

An Average Passage

From "Recollections, travels and adventures" (London, n.d.).

I started off May 21, 1839, in a merchant vessel from London docks. I paid £4 10s. for my passage and found myself in provisions for six weeks—as the captain told us. . . . The voyage occupied eleven weeks and four days. We were allowed a gallon of water a day for all purposes and when our provisions were gone the captain could only sell us some very dark biscuit and we were reduced to a quart of water a day. When we wanted to drink a little we had to hold our noses and drink it like physic. We soaked the biscuit in salt water, then got some of the cook's grease out of his tub and fried it, and that was a great luxury for us. We lay in dead calms for weeks together. We were told when we got to the banks of Newfoundland we should get plenty

---

[1]That is, by mechanical, not electric, telegraph.

of fish, but it was so foggy we could not see the water. When we got into the river St. Lawrence it was very pleasant, and it would have been more so if we had had enough to eat and drink. As we proceeded up the river we had to cast anchor to wait for the tide. The captain then gave us the opportunity of going on shore, but there were no inhabitants so we amused ourselves by collecting mussels and crabs, so we had quite a feast. Then later we bought fish of the Canadians. . . . . Eventually the mate came to us and said: "Ladies, we are in view of Quebec". We were all up like a shot and on deck.

7

The First Trans-Atlantic Steamship

(i)

Construction and dimensions

From *Quebec Mercury*, April 30, 1831.

. . . Lady Aylmer performed the ceremony at the launching of the Halifax Company's steam ship *Royal William*. This vessel had a magnificent appearance on the stocks; the prow, stern and quarter galleries are particularly tasteful; her actual builder's measurement is 1,370 tons, but she will not carry more, we suppose, than 4 or 500, owing to the space occupied by the engine and her sharp build. She went off beautifully amid cheers and firing of cannon, and when she floated, looked a "gallant ship." Mr. Black was the constructor; she is built with the greatest fidelity and strength, the sides forming a protection to the wheels against heavy seas. We have no doubt she will prove very fast. Her cost, when ready for sea, will be about £16,000, and her proportions are as follows:—

Length of keel 146 feet; breadth of beam across 44 feet.

Length of deck 176 do.; depth of hold 17 ft. 9 in.

We witnessed these new strides to wealth with pride.   Three of the steamers on the St. Lawrence, the *John Bull*, *British America*, and *Royal William*, are not surpassed by any other vessels of the kind any where, and from the common deal seat to the elegant decorations of the cabin, and the ingenious and finished workmanship of the engines, all on board is of the manufacture of Canadian establishments. . . .

(ii)

Rigging, speed, accommodation

From *Quebec Mercury*, August 16, 1831.

The *Royal William*, Halifax steam ship, Capt. Jones, arrived on Sunday night from Montreal and is now lying at the King's wharf. She came down by the use of her engines, having left Montreal at 2 on Saturday and stopped at Sorel and Three Rivers. The engines worked very well and her average speed was estimated by some persons at ten miles an hour. When the engines are better secured and every thing in proper trim she will sail we have no doubt remarkably well.

The *Royal William* is rigged like a three masted Schooner, with three square sails on her foremast, besides large fore and aft sails. Her masts are as lofty as those of a vessel of 300 tons. Her under deck cabin is fitted up with upwards of fifty ample berths, and a large parlour. In a round house on deck is a spacious dining room. The whole of the cabin is fitted up with an elegance and taste of the best style.

It is understood she will sail on her first voyage on Tuesday week.

8

The Trans-Atlantic Passenger Line

From T. C. Keefer, "Travel and transportation", in *Eighty years' progress*, 141.

The magnificent subsidy awarded by the British Government to the Cunard line had the effect of diverting Canadian traffic with Europe from the St. Lawrence river through the ports of Boston and New York. The policy of the Imperial government which tended to build up American seaports at the expense of Canadian, left the colony no other resource than competition.[1]

---

[1]This competition took the form of subsidies, first to a Liverpool firm and then to Hugh Allan of Montreal, for the operation of a steamship service from Quebec to Great Britain. By 1867, it was estimated that the subsidy was no longer necessary (Keefer in *Eighty Years' Progress*.)

THE TELEGRAPH

Note, from the following documents, how similar has been the evolution of the Canadian telegraph system to that of other types of communication: the railroad, the motor-road, the air-mail routes, the telephone, all tend in their first stages to get their east-west connections through the already completed American systems. All-Canadian (and in the case of overseas shipping, cables, *etc.*, all-British) routes come later and often from sentimental or political motives. Local development and extension is the next stage.

1

The Mechanical Telegraph[1]

From *Quebec Gazette,* quoted in *Montreal Gazette,* February 11, 1837.

TELEGRAPHS.—There is no part of the world which offers such facilities for telegraphic communications as North America; a clear atmosphere, ridges of high lands, extending throughout in the direction of the sea coast, and visible from it, thousands of miles of country, under the same Government or speaking the same language, all these are to be met with no where else. There can be no doubt but that the project mentioned in last *Gazette* of the establishment of a line of telegraphs from Boston to New Orleans will soon be executed. We hope it will be extended from Boston to Quebec. The natural facilities in Canada, Maine, New Hampshire and Massachusetts, are greater than to the southward. Cape Diamond could communicate to the high lands of La Beauce, from which the Bald Mountains in Maine are visible. From there, the course of the Kennebec offers advantageous elevations to the sea. From Cape Elisabeth, west of Portland, a communication from headland to headland would be easy to Boston.

---

[1]The mechanical telegraph, much like the modern naval semaphore system, was used to communicate over considerable distances. Thus as early as the first decade of the century, the admiralty had a line of telegraphs from Portsmouth to London, over which a message could be sent in quite a short time. There was also a naval telegraph from Quebec down the river during the war, but this was afterwards abandoned and does not seem to have been used for commercial purposes.

2

"Magnetic Telegraph to New York"

From *Canadian Economist*, October 10, 1846.

A few years ago, no one could have dreamed that communication could be held, from one end of this vast continent to the other, by means of the electric fluid, conducted upon wires! And yet this is about being effected. Already New York, Boston, Philadelphia, Baltimore, Washington, Albany, Buffalo, and numerous other cities, communicate with each other in a few seconds; and means are now in operation to connect New Orleans, St. Louis, &c.

. . . Overtures have been made to our Board of Trade by a gentleman now in this city, skilled in the construction of magnetic telegraphs, to connect Montreal with the net work of wires already in operation, by intersecting the line of communication at Saratoga.

We understand that the necessary arrangements are nearly completed, and that our merchants will shortly be called upon to subscribe to the stock. It is expected that the whole work will be finished and in operation in *June next*. Toronto and Hamilton are already moving in this work, by connecting those cities with the line at Buffalo.—We must not be left behind. Not only is it our best policy, but it is our interest to go forward with the improving spirit around us.

3

The Best Route for the New Magnetic Telegraph

From *Canadian Economist*, December 36, 1846.

. . . The Montreal Board of Trade has, for some time, been engaged in examining the merits of various projects which have been submitted to them by parties interested in the lines to the United States, and they are now about coming to a conclusion which will warrant them in recommending a particular line to the favorable notice of their fellow-citizens. . . .

A line direct from Halifax, running entirely through British territory, was the first project which engaged their notice; but though allowed to be, on national as well as commercial grounds, the best that could be adopted, provided means could be raised to accomplish it, it was abandoned for the present, as being impracticable except as a national undertaking. The reasons which led to this conclusion must be so obvious as scarcely to require enumeration. One or two, however, may be mentioned:—first, the difficulty of crossing the Bay of Fundy; and next, the enormous expense of keeping the wire in repair through some hundreds of miles of dense, uninhabited wilderness. . . .

The next projects which engaged their attention, were, first, a line to connect with Saratoga and New York; and, secondly, a line to connect with Portland and Boston: in either case, the connection with the *West* being the same.

The merits of these respective routes depended in a great measure, on the first cost of construction, which was materially in favour of the route to Portland, provided the wire could be carried over the surveyed line of the St. Lawrence and Atlantic Railway. But here a difficulty presented itself,—that of keeping a wire in repair passing through some two hundred miles of wilderness; a difficulty which cannot apparently be obviated till the railway is completed, which cannot be in less than two years to come. This obstacle is so great that we cannot see how it is to be got over, and such was the view which the Board of Trade took of it.

Next, then, with respect to the route to Saratoga. The objections to this project are chiefly its expense, the terms of the American patentees being rather exorbitant; besides which Canada would be obliged, not only to build her own line, but to furnish a considerable share of the capital required to carry it from the frontier to Saratoga; while on the Portland line she would merely be required to furnish capital to build her own end of it. . . .

Within the last day or two, however, an entirely new plan has been submitted to the Board by a gentleman from the United States representing the contractors of the Toronto-Buffalo line. This project is to extend the line from Toronto to Montreal, through all the intermediate towns, viz. Port Hope, Cobourg, Kingston, Brockville, Cornwall, &c., &c.; and this is considered the most deserving of favour, and the most likely to be adopted. In the first place, no line would be complete, whether it came from Halifax, or Portland, or New York, to this city, unless it were afterwards carried hence to Toronto, and for this reason it appears to us that the main question for the Board and the public to determine upon is simply, *Which end shall be constructed first?*

In our opinion it does not afford room for doubt or hesitation. By building the line *first* from hence to Toronto, we get the advantage of instantaneous communication not only with the seaboard, the Western States, and Western Canada above Toronto, *but also with all the intermediate Canadian towns;* whereas by beginning at the other end first—that is, from hence to New York by way of Saratoga . . . we should entirely lose the advantage of immediately communicating with these intermediate Canadian towns, and thereby it appears to us render the undertaking less profitable as well as less useful.

4

The Progress of the Telegraph in Canada, 1847-1861

From T. C. Keefer, "Travel and transportation", in *Eighty years' progress*, 266.

The whole of the telegraphic system of Canada (except the private lines belonging to railway companies) is in the hands of one company.

The Montreal Telegraph Company was organized in 1847 and first opened between Quebec and Toronto. . . . .

	1847	1861
Capital stock	£15,000	£100,000
Length of line	540 mls	3,422 mls
No. of stations	9	150
Persons employed	35	400
Messages sent	33,000	300,000

TRADE AND INDUSTRY IN THE CANADAS, 1783-1850

INTRODUCTORY

THE economy of a young country is dominated by the extractive industries, by trade in one or two staple commodities, and by a shortage of labour and capital. Money is scarce and wages are high. No elaborate and delicate system of financing and handling the colony's trade and products has been built up. The Canadas were further characterized by complete dependence, for the greater part of the period, on one market, the mother country, and it was two months away and accessible only for half the year. During the other half they lived completely unto themselves, nothing coming in and nothing going out. It was impossible for trade to be other than precarious, a matter of high profits and unforeseen losses.

Until almost the end of the period, everything centred about the merchant, of whom some three species may be distinguished: (1) the "factors" of the English timber firms who had their local headquarters in Quebec and financed the country lumberman; (2) the importers, chiefly of Montreal. These men gave orders in England in the fall and winter, had their goods arrive in the spring, distributed them on credit of six months or a year during the summer, and the following year got in their money. The large amount of capital necessary and the uncertainties of credit easily explain the high prices of British goods and the unmitigated dislike with which the Montreal importers were viewed by the Upper Canadian. A comparison may be made between them and the British merchants of the pre-Revolutionary southern colonies; the chronic indebtedness of the planters to these merchants was a factor in producing the Revolution in such provinces as Virginia. The type has developed in every port in the world which has a hinterland of exploited country. (3) The local merchants, "general store-keepers", traders in the widest sense, selling everything, buying everything (for consignment to Montreal), acting as bankers, issuing paper "money", and so on. They customarily held their *clientele* in the hollow of their hands for they saw to it that the farmer was never out of debt.

Secondary centres of importation arose in due course, notably Kingston and later York. The channels of trade had the usual geographic determinants, the St. Lawrence and its affluents. In 1825, but for political regulation, which enabled the "natural highway" to maintain itself for another twenty years, the Erie Canal would have upset this basis, as at last it did.

References: Adam Shortt, "General economic history, 1763-1841" (*Canada and its provinces*, IV, 521); *Ibid.*, 1841-1867 (*Ibid.*, V, 261); A. R. M. Lower, *Lumbering in Canada* (forthcoming), chapter on "The Quebec merchant"; D. L. Burn, "Canada and the repeal of the corn laws" (*Cambridge Historical Journal*, II, no. 3).

THE TRADING SYSTEM BASED ON THE ST. LAWRENCE

The documents which follow indicate the course of trade from 1783 to 1850 and illustrate the general lines on which it was conducted, as described in the introduction to this section.

1

The Organization of the Trade of Upper Canada

From Canadian Archives, *Q*, CCLXXX, 347, J. G. Simcoe, *Report to the board of trade.*

This document describes the general economic factors in the domestic life of the young colony; the pressing need for some staple product, the strategic position of the local merchant, and the abuses resulting from his control of the currency through the issue of his own notes.

Navy Hall, Sept. 1, 1794

Proposition for the Establishment of a Staple Universal in respect to the Inhabitants of this Country

The great object to which the wisdom of Government ought to be applied is to furnish the Inhabitants of Upper Canada with sufficient cash, or a proper medium that shall supply those deficiencies which necessarily occur between the bartering of the product of the Earth for the manufactured goods of Great Britain, the exclusive subjects of exchange.

[Wheat, the province's staple]

The product of the Earth which forms the Staple of Upper Canada must be Wheat. The necessity of this medium is evident in every Commerce of Life; it has been of late the Subject of much investigation in this Colony in what manner it may be procured to public advantage—this investigation has arisen from the Government being desirous to purchase the supplies for the King's Troops from the Settlers, in such a manner, as to promote the general agriculture of the Colony.

It was found, or supposed, that the Merchants were the only people of sufficient responsibility to ensure the necessary supplies.

219

[Currency difficulties:—"bons"]

This opinion of the Commissaries limited the Market, a late contract now done way [*sic*], appearing still more to straiten the market, was most respectfully complained of by the House of Assembly, and represented by me to the King's Ministers. The Grievance consisted in the Universal Necessity of barter, having introduced among the Merchants the custom of their issuing their own notes as current cash; & by the direct or indirect means by which these Gentlemen obtained the supply of the Garrisons, they would receive no flour but in such quantities as they chose from their own customers & debtors, paying them for it in goods, to which they affixed the price, or, in their own Notes, payable only on the 10th of October.

Hence the Flour Merchant stipulated to the Farmer the price which he should receive for his Flour, & that which he should give for the Goods he was compelled to take in barter.

The necessity of a paper Currency, where there is not sufficient Gold or Silver is most obvious, but the American Colonies having misused such a Medium of Commerce and converted what might have been a general benefit into public injury, by an Act of Parliament at present binding on the Province of Upper Canada, no emission of this kind can be legally made.

The late appointment of an Agent for all purchases in this province which are to be made, under certain restrictions has given universal satisfaction.

The public confiding that the advantages derived from the supplying of the King's Troops will no longer be monopolized, that store supplies will be received in as small quantities as practicable, and as far as this market shall go, that Gold or Silver or its equivalent, will be paid for the price of labour. It is therefore, at this moment that with peculiar propriety I offer most respectfully for their Lordships consideration, ideas which embrace a variety of circumstances useful I trust to the Internal prosperity of this Province, & to the encreasing Power of the British Empire.

The improvement of the Navigation of the St. Lawrence is of the utmost importance to the British Empire in America. The facility or difficulty of its transport influences the relative cheapness or dearness of the Commodities which are exported or imported.

The Communication between Kingston and Montreal is carried on by means of Batteaux belonging to the Merchants, or hired of them. They receive a most extravagant price on either mode of freightage. To lessen the burden therefore would be an object of great public Utility.

It appears, therefore, that to preclude the advantages derived from the purchase of Flour for the King's Forces or Garrisons becoming a Monopoly of the Merchants, who also are Millers, Landowners, Mortgagees and retailers; to obtain a circulating Medium in Money or its value, & to reduce the Transport on the St. Lawrence may be reckoned as three distinct and important objects in which the Welfare of every individual of the province of Upper Canada is particularly concerned, on which its general prosperity depends, & with which viewed in its political Relations with Great Britain are connected the welfare and strength of the Empire beyond all powers of calculation.

It is most certainly with great doubt & hesitation that I offer to Your Lordships the means of promoting these objects.

. . . I am therefore diffident, when I state an opinion that these distinct Objects may be combined in one system of operation. . . .

It may not be improper I should state that during the late War, being in Virginia, I was so forcibly struck with the advantages derived to that Colony from the use of notes on the receipt of Tobacco as a circulating medium that I have ever since retained the strongest impression of its Utility. I have been lately informed that Brissot the French man had adopted similar ideas from the same observations.

[A currency based on flour]

It is proposed that the province of Upper Canada shall be furnished with a certain sum of money for the purposes hereafter specified.

That this sum should be replaced to Great Britain if thought expedient by the produce of a sale of part of the Lands bordering on Lake Erie—that the sum of money so to be raised should be vested in certain Trustees. That these Trustees should be the Members of the Executive, and Legislative Councils, & other of the principal Inhabitants.

That under the Superintendance of these Trustees, regulations & rules should be formed for the improvement of the manufacture of flour, the staple commodity of his Majesty's Province of Upper Canada.

That so soon as circumstances shall admit no other Flour shall be purchased by the Agent or Commissaries but such as shall be manufactured agreeably to the above mentioned regulations & rules.

That in order to facilitate the Exportation of Flour, a principal store house shall be built below the Rapids of the Town of Montreal, & other receiving Houses at the termination of the Navigation of the several Lakes and Communications. That a principal Flour Inspector shall reside at Montreal with an adequate Salary; that inferior Inspectors shall be appointed at the other Posts—that these inspectors be duly sworn after proper examination to admit or condemn any Flour that may be offered to them. That the Flour be transported across the Lakes in the King's Vessels in preference to all other Merchandize at a given price, the average of which must fall on the owner, in proportion to the distance of transport.

The Merchant Vessels are encreasing & are more than adequate to the back Carriage of the Peltries & Furs. That for every Flour Barrel received at the store, a Note be issued payable in Gold or Silver on demand at stated periods. That these Notes be made a legal tender in all Taxes.

That the Company contract on the Average price of the three or four last years, to bring up the River St. Lawrence all Government Stores in Batteaux, & constantly to keep in readiness as many Batteaux as shall be requisite for Military Services on the Communication between Kingston and Montreal, their profits arising from the back conveyance of Flour.

The result will be as formerly has been shewn, of infinite importance to the Colony, first in providing for the Consumption of its staple, secondly, in giving it a certain medium of exchange instead of the Merchants Notes, whose excess cannot be regulated, or regulate itself, whose modes of payment are not unconditional, diminishing at once the security of the Public, & contributing to private extorsion—and thirdly, by the means of possessing the back carriage. It will lessen the inconvenience of its remote situation from the Ocean, & it is probable that the proposed Company may find it their Interest to augment their Batteaux so as to lower the price of freightage on the importation from Montreal to Kingston.

In respect to the Interest of the Empire at large, it will render the victualling of the Army cheap & certain; It will gradually provide for the supply of all our West India possessions. It will render the Agriculture of the province fully competent to the utmost extension, that so necessary a Market as that of Flour, precarious in a limited view, but certain in the widest range, may be capable of embracing, & what is perhaps of very great moment for providing for all those persons who shall inhabit on the banks of the. Lakes or rivers which flow into the St. Lawrence certain means of exchanging their produce for British Goods; It cannot fail of conciliating their affections, & insensibly connecting them with the British People & Government.

The British Consuls may have instructions constantly to communicate with the Company the various means of rendering the Flour suitable to the Markets of the respective Countries in which they reside, a strict and just attention to the quality of the Commodity may ensure that Trade which the United States are now losing, not more from the failure and inferiority of the lands, than from the want of principle in the Manufacturers: and Montreal may become in a few years the seat of the most extensive and useful commerce to the Parent Country. . . .

J. G. Simcoe

2

The Merchant in the Economy of the Young Colony

From La Rochefoucault-Liancourt, *Travels in North America*, 280.

Kingston is, at present, the chief town of the middle district of Upper Canada, the most populous part of which is that situated on Queen's [*Quinte*] Bay. This district not only produces the corn requisite for its own consumption, but also exports yearly about three or four thousand bushels. This grain, which, in winter, is conveyed down the river on sledges, is bought by the merchants, who engage, on the arrival of the ships from Europe, to pay its amount in such merchandize as the sellers may require. The merchants buy this grain for government, which pays for it in ready money, according to the market price at Montreal. The agent of government causes a part to be ground into flour, which he sends to the different posts in Upper Canada, where it is wanted;

and the surplus he sends to England, probably with a view of raising the importance of the colony in the estimation of the mother-country. The price of flour in Kingston is, at present, six dollars per barrel.

The district of Kingston supplied, last year, the other parts of Canada with large quantities of pease; the culture of which, introduced but two years ago, proves very productive and successful. In the course of last year, one thousand barrels of salt pork, of two hundred and eight pounds each, were sent from Kingston to Quebec; its price was eighteen dollars per barrel. The whole trade is carried on by merchants, whose profits are the more considerable, as they fix the price of the provision, which they receive from Europe, and either sell in the vicinity, or ship for the remoter parts of Upper Canada, without the least competition, and just as they think proper. . . .

3

The Value to Canada of the American Western Trade

From Canadian Archives, Q, CCLXXXVI, 119.

This document illustrates very vividly the key position of the St. Lawrence in regard to the American west. As long as the Americans levied no tariff, the whole trade of their west, above Niagara, remained in British hands. The surrender of the posts in 1796 had made no difference. It was the Erie Canal which changed the situation.

Memorandum, Enclosure in Russell to Portland, May 18, 1799

The Trade carried on by the Province of Lower Canada through the Province of Upper Canada in the Territory of the United States about Detroit, and towards the Illinois & Mississipi forms one of the most considerable Branches of its Commerce, and may be computed to amount to about one hundred thousand pounds Province Currency annually as may be seen by the Documents No. 1 & 2 hereto annexed, which are calculated upon a very moderate average and are sufficiently accurate to shew that the preservation of this Trade, which appears also from the annexed Returns to be still encreasing, merits very serious attention.

The goods furnished for this Trade consist of British Manufacture, Wines and the produce of the West India Islands, all which according to the Table of American duties would be liable to pay from 25 to 50 Cents per Gallon on Spirits, from 20 to 56 Cents on Wines—9 Cents per pound on loaf sugar—5 Cents per pound on Coffee, 15 per Cent ad valorem on Arms, Leather and several Articles, 12½ per Cent on others; and not less than 10 per Cent on any—as may be more particularly seen by referring to the Law of Congress. Compared with this our Scale of duties is low indeed, limited at present to a very few articles, and will we presume never be extended to those of British Manufacture which greatly exceed in value all the other Articles employed in this Trade. Admitting therefore for a moment that we received from the United States, Articles to an equal amount with those we send into their Territory; and that the duties were collected on each side agreeably to the Treaty; it is evident that the balance would be very greatly against us. But this equallity in the Trade is [so] far from existing, that what we receive from the States is really almost nothing. It is notorious that no established Mercantile house in the States hath yet engaged in this Trade. The few Articles which are brought are generally brought by Adventurers who seldom appear a second time, and so far from having lost anything by the American Treaty, the Trade of this Country has visibly encreased by that Mutual and unrestrained Intercourse which has taken place between the Americans and us in consequence of this Treaty. It is demonstrated from the Returns of the Officer at Coteau du Lac that a very large augmentation has been made to the Exports of even Rum and Sugar, almost the only articles in which any competition was to be feared. The demand for Goods of all Kinds from this Province must further encrease with the progress of the American Settlements which are forming along the South side of the River St. Laurence and the Lakes. The natural, we may indeed say the only Outlet for all the produce of these Settlements is by the river St. Laurence, whose Waters are sufficient to carry the largest Rafts of lumber to the sea ports of this Province. And this lumber which is itself a valuable Article of Commerce may at the same Time be made a vehicle for transporting their Wheat, Flour and Pot Ash to a Market. This by the way of Oswego is impracticable; for besides the impossibility of going against the current in the Oswego River, no Rafts could be got through Wood Creek; and there is moreover the Land-carriage from Schenectady to Albany. That this Lumber and Surplus Produce will be exchanged here may be fairly presumed;

15

because all other things being equal, such exchange would be in the natural order of Trade. But there are in this case other Inducements; for the high Duties in the United States must necessarily make the different Articles dearer there than they will be here; and they can besides be transported at one third of the Expence from Montreal to Kingston that it would cost to bring them from Albany to Oswego; the Carriage of a Barrel of three hundred weight being in the one case usually but from three to three and a half Dollars and in the other from Nine to Ten Dollars. Could the United States enforce the collection of their Atlantic Duties on our inland Commerce with their Territory they must necessarily act as a Bounty to take the Trade from us and turn it into their own Channels, or at least we should have to pay a pound where we could collect a penny. It is therefore evidently and greatly for the advantage of these two Provinces, for Lower Canada in a greater degree than for us, that our Commercial Intercourse with the United States by way of the Lakes should be left unincumbered with Custom house Establishments & Restrictions. But it will perhaps be said that we have no security that the Government of America will allow it to remain so. This is certainly true, and it is so much for their Interest that they should not; that they can have been passive on the occasion from no other motive than the difficulty or rather the impossibility which is common to them and us of enforcing the collection of Duties under the relative Geographical Situation of the two Countries, which are separated from each other only by a chain of Lakes and Rivers of several hundred Leagues in extent, rendered by Treaty equally free to both parties. But as we should lose more than we can well calculate were they to make the experiment, it does not seem consistent with common prudence for us, by first adopting the measure to provoke them to it; and it would be great Weakness to suppose that they would not immediately retaliate.

No. 1

Note of Merchandize and Rum from Montreal which passed the Niagara portage in *1797* consigned to Merchants residing on the American side of the River at Detroit—Vizt—

1213 Barrels of Liquor averaged @ 36 Galls each is 43,668 Galls.
2611 Numbered packages of Merchandize valued by the owners

at a general Estimate when delivered there at £20
Prov. Currency each............................ £52,220
261 Barrels Salt 4 minots ea. is.....................1044 minots

These are exclusive of the goods for Michilimackinac. The quantity of goods is certainly encreased this season tho' neither this nor the Rum for this year can yet be ascertained—

R. Hamilton[1]

Queenstown 24 September 1798

No. 2

Value of Returns in Peltries from the American Territory for the year 1797.

2616 Packs of Peltries from Detroit passed the Niagara portage in that year by an account received from Robert Hamilton Esqr.

3210 were collected at Michilimackinac agreeable to an Acco't furnished by Mr Robert Dickson—

5826 Total—Which taken at the very moderate average of £15 Curr'y per pack amounts to £87,390 and it is well known that very considerable remittances have been made in Bills of Exchange and Bank Bills of the United States—

Richard Cartwright[2]

No. 3

Packs from Detroit transported over the Niagara Portage vizt.—
in the year 1796—1910
in 1797—2616
in 1798 to 24 Septr. 2704

Queenstown, 24th September 1798.

R. Hamilton

The Packs from Michilimackinac for these different years cannot be easily ascertained as many of them are sent by the Grand River.

---

[1]Hamilton was a prominent merchant of the Niagara district.
[2]A Loyalist merchant of Kingston, ancestor of the late Sir Richard Cartwright.

4

Trade in Cattle and Horses with the United States[1]

From Canadian Archives, *General Hunter's military correspondence*, II, 167.

Lieutenant-General Hunter to Anthony Merry, British minister at Washington

York, Nov[r.] 12, 1804

From the best information I have been able to obtain, the sending of cattle from Upper Canada to the United Sates for sale, is not confined to any particular district, but is general throughout the Province. For instance, an American Trader by the name of Freeman or Freeland has at various periods received cattle in payment for Debts in the Midland District, which cattle he drives to the United States to be disposed of. . . . Some of the Farmers desirous of lessening their stock and to obtain Cash, send Cattle out by Freeland to be sold. Captain Everts a very respectable Farmer residing within a few miles of Kingston, sent out very lately Twelve head by him, considering the market in the States as superior to that of Canada, both in regard of price and mode of Payment. Not long since a Drove of from Fifty to one hundred head of cattle were crossed—Niagara river for the United States. They came from the River Thames, where they had been either purchased or received in payment of Debts.

The Exportation of Horses from Lower Canada to the United States, is a Trade that has existed to a considerable extent for these twenty years past. . . .

5

Trade between Vermont and Canada during Jefferson's Embargo

From Canadian Archives, *Upper Canada sundries*.

William Armstrong to Lieutenant-Governor Gore

Quebec, 26th May, 1808

. . . Notwithstanding all the supplements & attempts to enforce the embargo or more properly the Non Intercourse Act,

---

[1]According to F. J. Turner, raising cattle and driving them eastwardly for sale in the older regions was one of the invariable stages in the frontier experience of the American people as they marched westward. The above document would tend to show that pioneer Upper Canada passed through a similar stage.

Immense quantitys of Produce come in by every fair wind from Lake Champlain, & the inhabitants of Vermont publickly declare they will not allow it to be stopped.—Of this the Government is convinced & rather chuse to wink at the infringement than run the risk of an insurrection which I really expect will take place should the embargo continue a few months longer. . . .

6

A Year's Complete Trade:—Exports and Imports for 1812

From *Journals of assembly, Lower Canada*, 1813, appendix.

Trading returns in the Canadas were not systematically kept and there is no means of securing total values. The list hereunder is given as showing the nature of the imports and exports of a typical year. Only the dutiable imports were noted, all free goods, perhaps the larger part, being unrecorded.

EXPORTS from the Port of Quebec—1812.

399 vessels cleared, containing 86,196 tons, 3950 men, twenty-one of which was built this year in Canada, containing 5898 tons.

19837 pieces oak timber,	45000 b. staves,
28670 do. pine do.	263178 bushels wheat,
90 do. walnut,	22384 do. pease,
24 do. elm,	888 do. Indian corn,
11 do. black birch,	130 do. beans,
87 do. cedar,	1098 do. oats,
20 wainscot logs,	9347 do. flaxseed,
60 log ends,	27652 barrels flour,
1845395 staves & heading,	19237 quintals biscuit,
15342 stave-ends,	2483 barrels of pork,
207631 boards and planks,	2 tierces ⎱beef,
4491 handspikes,	1693 bbls. ⎰
29702 oars,	18 kegs tongues,
3578 masts & bowsprits,	5 half-barrels and
1867 spars,	60 kegs, rounds, beef,
205200 hoops,	16 do. tripe,
136411 lathwood,	13 bbls. ⎫
640 battens,	40 firkins ⎬ hogs' lard,
131400 treenails,	371 kegs ⎭
433 drab-ends,	23 hhds. ⎱sausages,
16000 shingles,	55 kegs ⎰
2000 scantling,	9 puns. [*puncheons*]⎫
7650 wedges,	18 casks ⎬hams,
16½ tons logwood,	28 loose ⎭
2302 pipes, ⎫	734 kegs and firkins butter,
489 hogsheads, ⎬ packs	460 boxes soap,
525 qr. casks, ⎭	541 boxes candles,

217 casks ⎫
283 bbls. ⎬ oil,
13 boxes ⎭
59 barrels tar,
2 do. pitch,
29 do. turpentine,
10 puns. ⎫
1 tierce ⎬ salted hides,
18 bbls. ⎭
5 sides sole leather,
466 tierces ⎫
644 barrels ⎬ salmon,
37 half bls ⎭
763 barrels herrings,
86 boxes smoak'd do.
137 bls. pickled fish,
31 boxes ⎫
669 casks ⎬ loose pickled & dried codfish,
927 cwt. ⎭
12 firkins ⎫ cod-sounds,
5 kegs ⎭
42 hhds. ⎫
53 bls. ⎬ essen. spruce,
32 cases ⎭
24 butts ⎫
287 hhds. ⎬ ale and beer,
26 bbls. ⎭
51 doz. ⎫
2 hhds. ⎬ cider,
4 hampers ⎭
1 bag and 1 case hops,
1 pun. ⎫
2 tierces ⎪
10 bbls. ⎬ tobacco,
58 kegs ⎪
1 case ⎪
15 tierces ⎭
5 barrels bees' wax,
6 do. feathers,
130 metal stoves,
1 pun. stoves,
2 tierces tobacco,
130 bbls. ⎫ apples,
57 barrels ⎭
9613 do. pot & pearl ashes weight
35077 cwt. -0-1.

FURS AND PELTRIES
95099 beaver skins,
2735 bear,

595 marten,
884 raccoon,
7480 cat,
4789 deer,
21901 musquash,
7800 otter,
3222 fox,
335 loupserviers,
130 seal,
22 elk,
65 mink,
1063 fisher,
2543 swan,
3 wolf,
1507 wolverines,
4 casks and 3 kegs castorum,
35 bales cotton wool.

SUNDRIES IMPORTED AND EXPORTED

2 butts ⎫
2 pipes ⎬ wine,
4 hhds. ⎪
1 qr. cask ⎭
13 puns. ⎫ rum,
1 hhd. ⎭
2 hhds. 1 bbl. sugar,
2 puns. molasses,
1992 minots salt,
62 cases shot and ball,
5 bales ⎫
7 puns. ⎬ dry goods,
44 packages ⎭
2 bales, 2 baskets, kettles,
6 cases books,
42 coils cordage,
3 barrels vinegar,
1 tierce lime juice,
7777 lbs. old copper and tin,
412 lbs. old bell metal,
8 cwt. iron hoops,
4 casks 44 kegs paint,
14 casks nails,
24 shovels,
16 iron knees,
3 casks, 37 bars copper,
80 bbls. gun-powder,
2 iron chests.

[*Imports of dutiable goods*]

362 vessels entered, containing 77,100 tons—3,452 men,—2 butts, 36 pipes, 33 hhds, and 5 qr. casks of Madeira wine, containing 11,539 gallons: 105 pipes, 26 hhds and 1 qr cask, 24 cases, Port: 137 pipes, 7 hhds, 22 cases Spanish: 425 pipes, 136 hhds, 77 qr. casks, Teneriffe: 6 pipes, 63 hhds, 173 cases, French: containing 954,068 gallons. 7722 puncheons, 454 hhds, 411 cases noyeau rum, containing 853,444 gals—88 pipes brandy, 10,000 gals. 4 do. Geneva, 468 gals., 482 puncheons, and 330 hhds. Molasses, 73,805 gals. 479 hhds, Loaf Sugar, 413,335 lbs. 2176 tierces and barrels Muscovado and clayed Sugar, 849,597 lbs. 43 casks, 318 bags Coffee, 64,330 lbs. 36 casks Leaf Tobacco, 42,426 lbs. 1 do. manufactured do. 97 lbs. 12,780 packs playing cards. 120,881 bushels Salt. 1695 lbs. Hyson, 22,000 lbs. Black, 328 Bohea Teas. 17,055 lbs. Pimento.

7

The Supply of Upper Canada from Montreal

From Howison, *Sketches of Upper Canada*, 87.

The North-west Company forward a considerable quantity of stores to the Indian territories by this route,[1] and the country merchants receive annual supplies of goods from Montreal, and send down pork, flour, staves, and potash, in return.

8

Value to Great Britain of the Trade of British North America

From David Anderson, *Canada, or a view of the importance of the British American colonies* (London, 1814), 13.

The two grand motives for the acquisition and protection of colonies are: first, the increase of our merchant-shipping, for the supply of our navy with men; and, secondly, the vending of our manufactures.

With respect to the support of our shipping, the amount of the tonnage of British ships annually cleared out to foreign parts, the whale-fisheries excepted, upon an average of the last ten years, was 801,408 tons, upwards of one third of which was in the trade

---

[1]The St. Lawrence.

with our American colonies, whilst the shipping employed in the trade with China and the whole of our East Indian possessions form only about a twentieth part.

The amount of the earnings of British ships in the whole of our imports from foreign ports, upon an average, for the same period was only about £1,212,672; yet, such has been the late rapid increase of the trade of our American provinces, that, previous to the commencement of actual hostilities with the United States, two millions and a half arose from our intercourse with these valuable settlements.

As a market for British and colonial produce and manufactures they have lately afforded a demand for upwards of two millions and a half for their own consumption, besides about £3,000,000 for the supply of the United States, in defiance of her prohibitory laws. Thus, at a period when our merchants and manufacturers were suffering the greatest distress, these colonies furnished a demand for upwards of five millions sterling of British manufactures and colonial produce. From the improvement of their own trade, and, by the access they opened for our commerce through the strongest bulwark of American prohibition, they have in the short space of four years, (1806 to 1810,) added upwards of four millions to the annual demand for our manufactures, &c. whereas, the whole demand for China and our East-Indian possessions, through the East-India Company, has not amounted to more than about £1,200,000, without any probability of increase.

9

The Calamities of Peace

The conclusion of every European war has meant hard times in Canada, this country always having thrived on the business of supplying the belligerents.

(i)

Effect of the peace upon the price of grain

From *Montreal Gazette*, March 2, 1815

We already perceive the effects of the peace on the price of grain in this market—the quantity of wheat for sale yesterday and Tuesday, was very considerable, and purchases were made as low as 7s. 6d. per minot. Oats have fallen in the same proportion,

as will undoubtedly all kinds of provisions. The peace, if it produces no other advantage, has certainly been the means of ascertaining that the crop was more abundant last year than was
acknowledged by the farmers in general, and in reducing the enormous prices to which every article of expenditure had been raised
by the war.

(ii)

The West Indies as a substitute for war trade

From *Montreal Gazette*, March 30, 1815.

We are now placed in a situation different to any that we have
experienced since the year 1792; during which period a war has
prevailed in Europe, (with the exception of the short truce occasioned by the treaty of Amiens, and the lapse of time since the
late peace of Paris). That situation was favorable to these provinces, for the exportation of grain, lumber, and other productions
to Great-Britain, and they became the channel of export for considerable supplies from the United-States, during their restrictions;
and in the late war with America our provisions have been absorbed
in the country—the scene is now totally changed; peace has been
established in Europe, and is restored with America. The exportation of lumber to England will now unavoidably cease to be a
material object; that of wheat must be at a very low rate to meet
the prices of the European markets, where from their redundancy
they will have no occasion for ours; the quantity of other articles
is comparatively trifling, and the fur trade is confined to few
individuals, and not a matter of general interest.—Where are we
then to look for a consumption of our surplus produce at such
rates, as to encourage the agriculture of the country, the only
sure source of general prosperity? To the fisheries and the West-
Indies it may be answered: but how are we to come in competition
with the investments from the United States, if they are not
entirely excluded, or only permitted an intercourse according to
circumstances, subject to the payment of foreign duties, to be
imposed in the islands and our sister colonies, on their shipments
and tonnage? is a question that will naturally occur. In our trade
to Nova-Scotia, New-Brunswick, Newfoundland, &c. we have
not the same difficulties to cope with that we have to encounter
in our communications with our West-India islands. From the

proximity of the United-States, they have an advantage which we cannot remove, but we have the means in our power of lessening that advantage, by granting bounties on the exportation of our flour, lumber, provisions, &c.—such bounties here, and the foreign duties in the West-Indies on similar articles from America, would open a trade to Canada, that could not but enrich her more in a few years than the expenditure of the war has done, and free from those demoralizing effects that a state of war must unavoidably produce—£50,000 expended in this way would in my opinion be quadrupled at least in profit to the country—We should soon see mills erecting in various parts of this province, for the manufacturing into flour of that wheat which must otherwise be exported in grain, according to the practice of former years; the consequent increase of employment to thousands, from the nature of this change in favorable crops must be obvious—the forests of the Canadas, ought to afford extensive supplies of staves, boards, planks, shingles, hoops, &c. Salted provisions would also become an object of considerable importance, and many articles of provincial manufacture would find a market independent of the internal resources of the Canadas. What attractions in addition to the facilities of our water communications, particularly when improved, would be afforded for the extensive produce of the American side of Lake Ontario, the St. Lawrence and Lake Champlain, to the markets of Montreal and Quebec? the immense supplies from the United-States of cattle, during the late war, is an evident proof of what we could draw from the same source in time of peace, under proportionate encouragement—the advantages arising from the different branches of agency to this province, from this channel of export to American produce would also be considerably augmented by the sale it would occasion of British manufactures and West-India produce in return. From all the preceding considerations, added to the extensive supplies of lumber, and particularly of fish, that can be furnished by our sister-colonies, and the salted provisions from Ireland, I am convinced that under such encouraging regulations as have been alluded to, British North-America would prove fully adequate to the supply of the whole consumption of our own West-India possessions; in the staple articles of which, their imports formerly were considerable from the United-States, and on which they appeared to be in a manner dependent—the result of this contemplated increase, in our commercial intercourse, could not fail to produce mutual advantages to colonies under the same paternal government, materially benefit the shipping interest of Great-Britain, augment the national resources, and in some measure tend to reimburse the mother-country for the immense expence incurred in the preservation of the Canadas.

(iii)

How Montreal benefited from the war

From *Connecticut Courant*, quoted in *Montreal Gazette*, March 11, 1816.

The sapient restrictions upon our commerce, together with the no less sapient war for sailor's rights and Canada lands, has thrust this place [*Montreal*] forward at least thirty years beyond what would have been its regular advance in ordinary times. These measures of infatuation have built up Montreal quite as fast as they pulled down our cities. It now promises to be shortly a great emporium of wealth and commerce. There will be pouring into it a considerable part of the trade of the United States, as well as that of Upper-Canada. The traders there, and the Canadian farmers, have, instead of a fictitious, depreciated and fluctuating currency, a plenty of solid coin. They have a free trade with the British West Indies. Their taxes are small, and their imposts trifling. And no wonder that so many of the United States-men betake themselves thither to get clear of the griping hand of democracy, which taxes with a vengeance almost every thing that is eaten or worn, and whose pernicious policy has driven the specie out of the country, and left it naught but a tottering paper credit. If the two last Presidents are entitled to the honour of monuments, any where upon the globe, it surely is at Montreal.

(iv)

Post-war depression and the imperial control of colonial trade

From *Quebec Gazette*, August 9, 1821.

See introduction to section IV, page 315, for comment on this document.

The power of regulating the trade of the Colonies, which belongs to the British Parliament, is in fact a power over the fortunes, the industry, and the prosperity of every individual in the Colonies. It is a Magic Wand at whose motions our limbs may be dried up, and our prosperity vanish like a shadow.

This power belongs to Great Britain, and we would be the last to question any thing that is established by law—neither have we heretofore had any reason to complain of its exercise or its effects.

Peace, after twenty-five years war, public debts, taxes, and paper systems, has occasioned great changes in the state of trade all over the world, and particularly in every part of the British Dominions. There has been an universal derangement in the money prices of every thing, creating innumerable losses and difficulties in effecting the exchange of commodities of one country against those of another, and consequent inconveniences and distress in all.—Changes of existing laws have been effected to meet this state of things in Great Britain and Ireland. The Colonies have, however, been lost sight of altogether; or if any Legislative Acts have been made, nominally affecting them, *the change has been to their disadvantage.*

Lumber made up about one half of their exports, or in other words, they were supplied with one half of the foreign goods which they required in exchange for their lumber. An alteration has been made by the Act of the 28th May last, which must greatly diminish this trade, if not destroy it altogether. Wheat, our other agricultural produce, made up a great proportion of the remainder of our exports, or articles to be given in exchange for European goods. The state of trade to which we have alluded, and which has produced such a fall in the price of Grain, has, in consequence of the regulations in the British Parliament, excluded our agricultural produce altogether from a market. The granaries of our farmers, and the stores of our merchants, are now loaded with wheat, and no price whatever can be obtained for this article, which is of a perishable nature, and diminishing in intrinsic value daily; while a great number of the farmers, having been so imprudent as to get into debt, calculating on the usual price for their grain, are in danger of seeing their lands, their houses, their cattle, implements and furniture, altogether devoured in the Courts of Law, or sold for not one half their usual value.

If this state of things were solely the result of natural causes, or of our own acts, it would be silly and useless to petition; but, partially at least, it is owing to the operation of British Statutes.

These Statutes restrain us from trying to obtain a market, and making our purchases all over the world; they restrain foreigners from coming here to purchase or sell, should they be so inclined; they oblige us to have our goods carried solely in British ships—in short, they establish a monopoly of our trade in favour of Great Britain; they oblige us to buy and sell there, and then, by the operation of the Corn Laws, they enact, in effect, that we shall not buy or sell at all.   It is not the monopoly to which we object; we adhere to the doctrine and language of the Act of Parliament which declares that "the power of regulating the trade of the Colonies is essential to the general welfare of the British Empire". It is the partial interdiction of all the trade, by the operation of the Corn Laws, of which we complain. . . .

In the present state of the agriculturists in Great Britain, we would be loth to ask anything which could increase their burthens or diminish their profits.   We have reason to believe that the average of our surplus grain, and our exports of the last twenty years, even if the whole were to go to Great Britain, will be found not to amount to two days consumption of the people of that country; a quantity which even if it were admitted on the same footing as the produce of our fellow subjects at home, while it would be important to us, would scarcely be felt in the market there.

(v)

The commercial and agricultural distress of 1820-21

(a) From Canadian Archives, *Q*, CLVIII, 4, Petition of the merchants of Montreal.

Recent changes in the timber tariffs add greatly to the prevailing stagnation in every department of business.

(b) From *Le Canadien*, quoted in *Montreal Gazette*, August 8, 1821.

La détresse generale du pays devient de plus en plus alarmante. Les restrictions dernièrement mises sur notre commerce des bois . . . ne peuvent manquer que d'être vus d'un très mauvais oeil. . . . Le plus grande mal dont nous ayons à nous plaindre . . . c'est les lois restrictives qui empêchent l'entrée de nos graines dans le royaume. . . .

(c) From Nova Scotia Archives, *MSS. docs.*, CCXCVIII, doc. 213, February 2,
1822.

At no period since the commencement of the late war has the
province been under such severe and general distress, as at the
present time.

10

The Calamities of War:—Evil Results of War Prosperity

From Howison, *Sketches of Upper Canada*, 94.

Every war generates a feverish temporary prosperity in its insatiable demand for
supplies regardless of price. It also generates the bad habits and conditions
which make the aftermath of peace so painful.

The last war was productive of most injurious consequences
to the colony; and these have not been counterbalanced by a
single advantage, except that the militia now feel a confidence in
the efficiency of their arms, which may induce them to take the
field with boldness and alacrity, should hostilities again commence.
Before the declaration of war took place, Upper Canada was in a
state of progressive though slow improvement, and her inhabitants
prudently attempted such exertions only as were proportioned to
their means. Agriculture was pursued by all classes, and few
thought of enriching themselves by any other occupation. But
militia duty obliged them to abandon their farms, which were of
course neglected,—the lands became waste, the cattle were carried
away, and the buildings perhaps burnt by the enemy. However,
the military establishments had brought such an influx of money
into the country, that every one forgot his distresses, and thought
himself on the high road to wealth, when he found he could sell
any thing he possessed for double its real value, and have his
pockets stuffed with army-bills, as a recompense for some trifling
service done to government. At this time, the abundance of
circulating medium, and the liberality with which it was expended,
induced many people to bring large quantities of goods from
Montreal, and retail stores soon became numerous in every part
of the country. As the people continued to buy a great deal, and
to pay for a great deal, the merchants willingly allowed them unlimited credit, erroneously supposing that their customers would
always be able to discharge their debts, and that the temporary
wealth of the Province would continue. But when peace was

restored, when the troops were withdrawn, and all military operations suspended, the people soon perceived that a sad reverse
awaited them. They found that the circulation of money gradually
decreased, that they could no longer revel upon the bounty of a
profuse government, and that they began to grow poorer every
day; while the prospect of returning to their ravaged and uncultivated farms afforded but little consolation, as the spirit of industry
had been extinguished by the lavish manner in which most of
them had lived during the war. As a large portion of the live
stock which the country contained had been carried away by the
enemy, or consumed by our own troops, the farmers were obliged
to purchase cattle from the Americans, and thus the country
was still farther drained of much of the circulating specie, and in a
way too that produced no commercial advantages.

In course of time, the Montreal wholesale merchants began
to urge their correspondents in the Upper Province for remittances,
which many of the latter could not make; for, on applying to those
whom they had formerly trusted to a large amount, they found
that, with a few exceptions they were alike unable and unwilling
to discharge their debts. The country thus fell into a state of embarrassment which continues to increase; most of the merchants
have very large outstanding debts, which, if collected by means of
suits, would ruin two-thirds of the farmers in the Province; and
should the Montreal wholesale dealers have recourse to similar
measures, many of their correspondents would become insolvent
likewise. Both parties, therefore, judiciously temporize, being
satisfied that it is, at present, the most advantageous policy they
can pursue. . . . Time has in some degree ameliorated the two
first bad effects; but the merchants have been, and will be, the
means of perpetuating the last. The number of merchants that
Upper Canada contains, and the mode in which they carry on
business, are circumstances equally destructive to the interests of
the colony. Extensive credit is almost universally given to the
farmers, not one-tenth of whom have either inclination or prudence
enough to adapt their expenditure to their means; and, as they
generally pay and contract debts in an inverse ratio, their difficulties increase every year, and often at last terminate in the sale
of their property, which sometimes takes place with the consent
of the owner, but oftener in consequence of a suit. If the merchants
desisted entirely from selling on credit, it would be equally advan-

tageous for themselves and their customers. The latter might indeed be sometimes put to a little inconvenience, if they wanted to purchase any thing, and had not produce or money to pay for it at the time; but this would teach them a habit of economy, which they never can acquire while the present facility of supplying their wants exists, or as long as their absurd and monstrous vanity remains unchecked, and urges them to indulge in luxuries and finery to which their condition in life does not entitle them. Had the farmers of Upper Canada been prevented from getting into debt, and had they remained satisfied with homespun, they would now enjoy, in its fullest extent, that independence which they profess to value so highly, but the substantial part of which they have wholly lost, as there is hardly an individual among them who is not liable to have an execution served against him when it suits the interest of those to whom he is indebted.

11

The "General Store"

From *Montreal Gazette*, October 2, 1822.

FOR SALE

Pot and Pearl ASHES.
Mess, Prime, and Cargo Beef and Pork, in barrels and half barrels.
Superfine, fine & middlings, Genessee and Upper Canada Flour
Hogs Lard in barrels and kegs,
A few excellent Smoaked Hams,
Rock and Liverpool Salt, and Salt Petre
Leeward Island Rum,
Molasses and Muscovado Sugar,
Liverpool Stoved Salt in barrels,
Bottled and Draft Beer.

And in rear of the Counting House,

A few Packages of Fine and Superfine Cloths and Cassimeres, also Printed and Plain Cassimere Shawls,

By JOHN BROWN

Montreal, 11th June, 1822

12

The Depression of 1825-26

From John McGregor, *Historical and descriptive sketches of the maritime colonies* (London, 1828), 155.

The Canadian business cycle faithfully followed that of the mother country. The great panic of 1825 was severely felt in the colonies, especially in New Brunswick. While this document deals primarily with that province, it may be taken as illustrative of the panic elsewhere also.

The effects of the romantic projects of 1824 have not hitherto it is true, spent their force. The reaction has been indeed terrible to the merchants of New Brunswick. What Halifax suffered after the last American War, St. John, was now doomed to endure. The docks of London and Liverpool were at this time crowded with fine ships built by the merchants in North America, and sent to England for sale. The demand and price for such vessels having previously increased to a most unaccountable extent, the commercial men of New Brunswick were not only more extensively engaged in this trade than the merchants in other provinces were, but from the facility which they had experienced before this time in making large remittances to England, in ships and timber, they incautiously plunged themselves deeply into debt, by importing great quantities of goods of all descriptions.

The consequence was that their ships have been disposed of for less than half the prime cost; their timber was sold for less than the expense of carrying it to the United Kingdom; bills drawn by houses of long standing, and the highest respectability were returned dishonoured. The unparalleled suddenness of so unexpected a commercial calamity prevented the most cautious and experienced from guarding against the ruin which awaited them. They had all their funds locked up, either in ships already built and rigged, in ships on the stocks; or else in timber. It became necessary, at whatever loss, to finish and send to England the vessels then in progress of building, or submit to lose all the money they had laid out. In most cases it would have been well to have done so.

13

The Merchant in his True Colours

From John MacTaggart, *Three years in Canada* (London, 1829), 243.

The lumberman,[1] with all his roughness of manner, is the person who does good to the country. He brings an article to market with much risk—the only staple commodity, in fact, that is; and, consequently he is the means of bringing the greater portion of cash to Canada. What is the storekeeper but a person living on his exertions,—a person that might be dispensed with? He is the rogue, not the lumberman. His intent is to have three values for goods, which, were they not forced on the poor woodsmen, he would not take. He thus contrives to get him into what he calls his debt, although in common justice he is no such thing, and then abuses him for being so; although, to get a lumberman in debt, is the drift of the storekeeper, as there he keeps his victim, feeds, clothes, kicks, and tantalizes him into madness, making him a character far worse than he otherwise would be. Let this matter be better considered than it has been—let the saddle be put on the back of the right horse. The lumberman has a rough beard, a wild countenance, is in the habit of using uncouth language, and performing many ugly actions, certainly; but there is the sleek-shaven storekeeper, mild as a lamb, and tame as a dove, uttering delicious phrases, and, nevertheless behaving abominably. Crafty old fellows! but we see through them. The poor lumberman and shantymen are not properly represented; we have the tales of the cities respecting them and these are false. To know them, we must visit their wigwams afar in the depth of the forest, we must live with them for a time, and partake of all their joys and sorrows; we must run the rapids with them, and get well wet with spray and sweat alternately: then begin to judge of the character. But to hear it attempted to be developed over a counter by a smart looking fellow with a quill behind his ear, is all humbug and falsehood.

---

[1]The word "lumberman" at this period was used in a rather different sense from its present one. The "lumbermen" of a century ago were small *entrepreneurs*, employing perhaps only their own family, perhaps one or two men at taking out square timber. Consequently the present distinction between "lumberman" as the *entrepreneur* and "lumberjack" as the rather unkempt employee did not obtain. Both employer and employee, alike, were unkempt.

14

Canada's Balance of International Indebtedness

From *Neilson's Quebec Gazette*, quoted in *Montreal Gazette*, March 3, 1829.

In looking back over your *Gazette* for the last ten years, I observe you have given an annual *exposé* of the Imports and Exports, the difference of amount inward exceeds that outward rising £300,000: leaving the rate of exchange out of the calculation which for the last ten years may have added £50,000 annually to the cost of goods imported: but to meet that something near a like sum as premium on exchange, drawn for goods exported, has been received, but for the most part by a different class of gentlemen traders. Does this difference flow from the Treasury of Great Britain, and is there something near this sum expended by the Military and Staff in Lower and Upper Canada, outlay in wages of labour in this garrison, Isle aux Noix, St Helen's Island and the Mountain at Montreal, or on the Rideau and Welland Canals and other works in Upper Canada? Are the persons that are paid out of the Public Chest for their services, principal consumers of imported goods, and do the disbursements from the Public Chest equal or exceed the annual difference between the Imports and Exports?

15

American Wares Displace British in Upper Canada

From *Notes on America and Canada* quoted in *Montreal Gazette*, July 20, 1839.

They [*the Americans*] have a very useful mixture of woollen and cotton, called satinetts, the wool being thrown on the face; they are much used, and great quantities are sent across the lines into Canada. The fine ones are a neat article. I am surprised that the Huddersfield manufacturers have not successfully competed with them, their cassinetts are far too thin and poor to answer the purpose. Unbleached stout calicoes are manufactured and worn to a great extent in summer; they have entirely superseded the imports of such from England and the East Indies. These cottons, five years since, in like manner interfered in Canada with the direct imports from England; but at Manchester, Glasgow, and even Belfast, they now make similar goods so much better as to have left the American goods far behind, both as regards quality and cheapness. . . .

The iron tools of America have completely superseded Birmingham and Sheffield goods; the excessively bad quality of our edged tools, made like Pindar's razors, to sell and not to shave, had brought them into disuse and discredit—even in Upper Canada, States' tools are universally preferred at a great difference in price. The American axe is as different in shape as superior in manufacture; the Pennsylvanian sickle is in like manner superior both in shape and material. Scythes also are differently, as well as better made, for mowing among the stumps.

16

Upper Canadian Dislike of the Montreal Merchant

(i)

From a Niagara paper quoted in *Montreal Gazette*, July 9, 1829.

The spirit of enterprise and rivalry which seems to animate some of our Town Merchants, in the *direct* importation of Foreign Goods, bids fair to eclipse the Lower Canada Emporium, and supersede the necessity and expense of the semi-yearly trips to Montreal, hitherto imposed upon the country traders of this part of the province.

(ii)

From *Montreal Gazette*, August 17, 1829.

As something new and curious, we copy for the edification of our Mercantile friends the following very charitable and *characteristic* effusions of the *York Observer*:—

"The importation of Dry Goods from Europe, during the present season are of incalculable advantage. The Lower Canada merchants who have been devouring for years the fruits of this Province, are in a sad plight. The ruin of many of them is inevitable. They have fleeced and driven to beggary by their enormous charges, hundreds of families; and now that their day of calamity has arrived, we cannot pity them. Goods are sold at the stores of Messrs. Dougall, Gamble, &c., of York, 35 per cent cheaper than they can be obtained at Montreal. This is owing to Montreal Merchants purchasing at a credit of twelve to eighteen months in England, whilst our York merchants pay cash."

17

Trade of Upper Canada with Rochester, N.Y.

From *Montreal Gazette*, November 5, 1829.

ROCHESTER: This place is not only a large manufacturing town, but a depot for merchandise in general for the extreme Western settlements, and the Indian trade, even to the Rocky Mountains. The Upper Canadians, I am told, buy many articles here, which if they pleased they could buy better at Montreal; but possibly a trifling premium on dollars, and a *supposed* advantage in paying cash, causes it in some degree;—a small sum they may not think worth spending by their Montreal connection, besides which they can get credit from them, which they cannot from these sharp gentlemen on the American side.

18

Isolation of Upper Canada:—Annexation of Montreal

From Captain Basil Hall, *Travels in North America, in the years 1827 and 1828* (3 volumes, Edinburgh, 1830), I, 228.

Upper Canada was the first British province not on tidewater. Its inland position left it to a very considerable extent at the mercy of Lower Canada, and its natural emporium, Montreal, was beyond its control. Hence the agitation, continued until the Act of Union, for the annexation of that city.

Upper Canada, by political birthright, as well as her steady loyalty to Great Britain, is certainly entitled to be placed on equal terms with her neighbours. But until the only seaport she can possibly obtain, be included within her boundary, and her Legislature be thus vested with efficient control over the commercial resources of the colony, that Province must be virtually separated from us, and from the rest of the world. She will be even estranged from her sister colonies in that continent, and also from those of the West Indies, with all of which she is unquestionably entitled to hold as open relations as are enjoyed by any of the rest of His Majesty's possessions. But these relations it is almost a mockery to suppose she can keep up without a free access to the ocean, not as a matter of favour, but as an inherent territorial right, independent of the good-will of any other county or province. This claim is much strengthened, in the opinion of its advocates, by the fact that, although she has no seaport, two-thirds of the exports from the river St. Lawrence are the produce of Upper Canada, and as this ratio will probably go on increasing in her favour, it becomes daily more and more important for England to consider the question attentively.

The Lower Canadians are, I believe, and not unnaturally, averse to the relinquishment of Montreal; but they might well be contented with the magnificent port of Quebec; especially as there can be little doubt that any augmentation of wealth in their sister colony must be fully shared by them, and their profits from that source would, probably, very soon over-balance any loss incident to this nominal sacrifice.

The first effect of bringing the boundary of Upper Canada further down, would inevitably be the adoption of an extensive set of improvements in the navigation of the St. Lawrence; for the capital and enterprise of the great city of Montreal would then coalesce with those of the western parts of the Province, the inhabitants of which have already done so much, higher up, at the Welland Canal, and Burlington Bay. Thus measures, which are now starved by the want of a vigorous concert, would start into efficiency at once. Lower Canada would immediately feel the advantage of such improved intercourse while the resources of the Upper Province—almost boundless—would for the first time be called into full operation. The city of Montreal, which, under any possible view, must be the great point of transit, would then reap the advantages of both.

19

Increase in Trade of Montreal as its Hinterland Opens Up

From *Montreal Gazette*, February 12, 1833.

George Auldjo, chairman, Montreal committee of trade, to Nathaniel Gould, chairman, North American Colonial Association, London

Notwithstanding the irremediable disadvantage of a periodically closed navigation, the distance of Quebec from the sea, and the risk of delay and damage by ice in the gulf of the St. Lawrence, preparations for an increase of trade are making throughout the Canadas. Several large steamboats and attending barges will be added to the present establishments: large stores are building at

Montreal, and the wharfage for boats and seagoing vessels will be greatly extended next spring. These operations and the hopes of augmented commerce are partly encouraged by the rapidly increasing population and production industry of Upper Canada, and partly by the new channels of intercourse opened by the Ohio, Welland and Rideau Canals between this Province and the State of Ohio and the extensive shores of Lake Erie.

20
A New Trade with England

From *Neilson's Quebec Gazette*, quoted in *Montreal Gazette*, October 8, 1833.

The *Clifton*, Captain Bushby, which sails on Sunday for Liverpool, takes 115 barrels of pork and beef for the English market. This, we believe, is the first instance of provisions of that description being shipped from Canada. It is expected that the shipment will realize a fair profit, and lead to the introduction of a new article of export which might become of importance.

21
Ship-building and the Lumber and Coal Trades in 1833

From *Montreal Gazette*, December 19, 1833.

EXPORTS

Lumber.—Upon review of the trade of this port during the season of navigation just closed, that article appears to constitute the most important product of our exports, to meet per contra, the great and encreasing amount of our import of British manufactures and produce; consequently, the demand for timber, staves, deals, &c. continues steadily progressive, and our prospect for next year is apparently very good and cheering, notwithstanding the continual apprehension of an alteration in the duties on Foreigners. . . .

New Ships.—Fourteen square-rigged vessels, averaging 460 tons, are in progress of building, to be completed by the opening of the ensuing navigation. It is more than possible that one or two more will be laid down in the course of the winter. The largest of these are probably intended for the China trade, . . . Price per ton for the hull, £7 10s. Completely rigged and ready to load for sea, £10 10s.

IMPORTS

Coal.—The supply of this article the past season greatly exceeded that of any former year, and fully kept pace with the increasing consumption of the country. The quantity of smith's coals remaining over is great; the stock of grate coals is probably not more than will be required for the winter's demand.

22

The Business Cycle:—The Depression of 1833-37[1]

(i)

The initial stages

From *Neilson's Quebec Gazette,* quoted in *Montreal Gazette,* May 3, 1834.

The very depressed state of business in the Canadas, which has been marked by many more failures in the last twelve months than at any former period, and proportionately greater and more extended, has so far passed by without any resort to extra assistance; on the contrary, some portion of the usual resources of trade, the public expenditure, has been withheld. We trust that the improving state of things in the States will be felt in Canada. We have borne a fair share of the weight of the evil. The information received from some of the merchants who left Great Britain about the middle of March, does not create any very inviting anticipations of the trade of the ensuing season. It is admitted by nearly all, that the shipments of goods will be very limited, several of the London vessels, which easily obtained full cargoes, not having, at the latest dates, the prospect of having one half or three fourths. The emigration will also be under that of last year, but nearly limited to persons of some capital, and in that respect less burthensome to the towns of Quebec and Montreal. While the state of trade over the whole of North America has been under such a deplorable depression, that of Great Britain, has been rather more vigorously sustained than in the five or six preceding years.

---

[1]This depression continued, with very little intermission, until 1838. Hard times, along with crop failures, had much to do with the outbreak of the Rebellion —more perhaps than inflammatory speeches. The depression came into Canada by way of the United States, in which country it was accentuated, if not caused, by President Jackson's novel methods of finance.

(ii)

Analysis of causes:—Prospects of improvement

From *Montreal Gazette*, September 6, 1834.

Since our last report there has been a moderate return of activity to our Trade. The usual stagnation of the season has given way, and auction sales are now going on to a considerable extent. The dreadful scourge with which we have been visited,[1] but which happily has now entirely subsided, does not appear to have produced the same disastrous effects upon our trade, as in 1832. It broke out when the spring trade was over, and has ceased before the fall trade can be said to have commenced. From the peculiar state of the money market in New York in 1833, the stagnation was even more decided than during the present season. In one of our weekly reviews last year, namely, that for the 23d. July, we said "with the exception of West India produce every thing is dull, in fact there is nothing doing in sales, every one complains of the scarcity of money, the Banks not even discounting to retire paper." At the same period the state of affairs was certainly worse in 1834. On the 6th August, 1833 we wrote "the business transactions during the week have been but limited, smaller indeed than in the previous week". On the 14th August we characterized business transactions as "unusually small for the season." The week ending 21st August, was "fully as dull as the preceding," and it was not until the 3d. of September that we were enabled to say, "the business done in the past week, though moderate, has far exceeded that of any other during the last six weeks, and may be considered as indicating the commencement of the fall trade." We have said enough to show that the commencement of the fall trade of 1834 has not been retarded, and we think also, to prove, that the cholera has not exercised any serious influence upon the trade.

It appears to us that our prospects are by no means disheartening. Providence hath blessed the labours of our husbandmen with a most abundant return, a circumstance which must ever act favorably upon trade; and the state of the American Money market is such as to produce confidence and credit, and, we think, to preserve it, and our own importations are sufficiently

---

[1] The second outbreak of cholera, the first having occurred in 1832.

moderate to promote an improved state of our market. We think, therefore, we are fully justified in offering these cheering reflections to our commercial readers.

(iii)

Unlooked-for continuance of the depression

From *Montreal Gazette*, May 23, 1835.

COMMERCIAL DISTRESS.—The inhabitants of Toronto, we believe, never before nor since it was a city, have experienced any thing like the depression in business which this spring has produced. There are, upon every hand, day after day failures, even of persons who were formerly considered in at least comfortable circumstances. And to what can this be owing? We pretend not to know the minutiae of the matter, but should be inclined to think that a deficiency in the circulating medium, however caused, has led to the destruction of many persons possessed of property more than sufficient to cover any demand that might be made against them, but who could not raise the ready means, at the moment by which those demands could be answered.

23

First Imports of American Coal

From *Kingston Chronicle*, quoted in *Montreal Gazette*, October 16, 1834.

COAL.—It is a fact perhaps, not very generally known, that there is a cargo of coal, of very superior quality, at present for sale at the wharf of Messrs, Macpherson & Crane, in this place, under the charge of Mr. Brown. The coal is from Ohio, and was forwarded in a schooner through the Welland Canal. It is sold here for about a quarter of a dollar a bushel—and we have no doubt that upon trial, it will be found a much more pleasing and profitable article for consumption as fuel, than cord wood. We sincerely hope our new House of Assembly will take this subject into consideration, and afford every facility to the introduction of the article in question into the country, by taking off the duties, &c. In the course of a short time, the advantages that would accrue to the Welland Canal from this single article of commerce would be immense.

24

Beginnings of an Export Trade in Native Products to the United States

Heretofore, all exports to the United States had been merely British goods in transit. Canada and the contiguous American territory produced the same things and there could be little trade between them. When population increased to the south and the forest disappeared, Canada was drawn on for its typical supplies, food and wood. The following two documents, therefore, indicate the genesis of Canada's second market. See also no. 26.

(i)

From *Quebec Gazette*, quoted in *Montreal Gazette*, June 11, 1835.

United States traders have this year come into Canada, bought up wheat, flour, provisions and lumber, and paid heavy duties on their transport out of this country. We believe that the rise in the prices which warranted these experiments, was more speculative than founded upon scarcity, although scarcity to some extent exists, in the great producing countries to the West, where extensive emigration has lately turned exports *westward*, instead of eastward. The progress of emigration to the West is this year almost unprecedented. . . .

Among other speculations entered into, we learn that a miller on the Chambly lately contracted, to be exported to the State of New York, for 60,000 boards part of which has already been forwarded by the Chambly Canal,[1] now open, though not altogether completed.

(ii)

From *Kingston Herald*, quoted in *Montreal Gazette*, May 14, 1836.

A vast quantity of lumber has been prepared on the Ottawa River, for transportation by the Rideau Canal to Oswego and New York. Two gentlemen alone have *two millions* of feet ready for the American market by this route; and a new steamboat is nearly built at Smith's Falls, which is specially designed to convey this lumber to this town, from which it will be shipped in schooners for Oswego. The Kingston Stave Forwarding Company have engaged two schooners to bring their staves from the different ports on Lake Erie, by the Welland Canal, to their wharf at Garden

---

[1]The Chambly Canal provided passage past the rapids of the Richelieu.

Island: these and other schooners will take lumber from this port to Oswego, and from thence to the upper lakes.   Hence by carrying freight along their whole route, they will be able to reduce the rates, and the public will be doubly benefitted—by an increase of trade and a reduction of expense.   Thus besides the other benefits of the Rideau Canal, it is opening an entire new trade to this part of the Province, and will render the immense pine forests on the Ottawa available for supplying the demand from the States. The prosecution of this new trade becomes doubly important as it is almost certain that the British Ministry will reduce the duties on Baltic .timber next year.   Besides lumber, we are also sending grain of different kinds to Oswego, as oats, barley, pease of which two or three schooner loads have gone already, and more are to follow.

25

The System of Spring and Fall Imports[1]

From *Toronto Recorder*, quoted in *Montreal Gazette*, February 2, 1836.

... There are other reasons why the great bulk of importations should take place during the spring and summer months only. Nearly the whole of the purchasers from important merchants in Toronto and elsewhere, are the retail country storekeepers, and those persons invariably make their purchases during the summer and fall months, devoting the winter season to the disposal of their goods, and the collecting of grain and other produce, which they take to market after the navigation opens, dispose of, and again lay in their stock of goods in the summer and fall.   Again, the markets in England are more favorable for the purchase of manufactures during the winter and spring months, than at any other period of the year.   Nearly the whole of the importations of raw material into England from her vast possessions abroad and from all foreign nations, take place between May and December; and the most active period in her manufacturing districts, is invariably between October and June.   But the Americans themselves, and the New Yorkers in particular, are forced to adopt

---

[1]Until the steamship and the railroad altered conditions, ships arrived at Quebec in May or June, departed, and returned in the latter part of August. In the interval the port was very quiet.   The arrival of the spring and fall fleets was the determining factor in business activity.

the spring and fall system; and it is notorious that Rochester and Buffalo (the greatest Western emporiums of the commerce of New York) are both obliged to lay in their winter supplies, of foreign and domestic manufactures, at the same periods and in the same way as we do in this Province. . . .

Mercator

26

Migration of American Capital to Upper Canada:—Montreal's Objections

From *Montreal Gazette*, August 27, 1836.

See no. 24 of this section, page 251.

An application is to be made, during the next session of the Upper Canada Legislature, for a law to authorise foreigners to hold real estate, "under such stipulations as may be found necessary to guard against political interference, or undue speculations tending to monopoly."

If we are to judge from the high tone assumed by the *Kingston Whig*, the scheme aims at the introduction of AMERICAN capital into the lumber trade, with a view of trading with the NEW YORK market through the Oswego and ERIE canals. We should have no objection to the mere introduction of such capital, but certainly when real estate is to be acquired, we would distinctly require that allegiance to the Crown should be insisted upon ere any political or civil rights are conferred upon aliens. If AMERICANS or other foreigners comply with a regulation, which they themselves exact from British subjects settling amidst them, we should of course welcome them among us with pleasure.

We are sorry to notice in Saturday's [*Kingston*] *Chronicle* a numerous and influential list of signatures, giving notice of an intention to apply to Parliament, for an Act enabling Foreigners to hold real estate in this Province in *free* and common soccage, under *restrictions*,—that is, without taking the oath of allegiance, or becoming British subjects. It seems, the valuable Lumber Trade of Upper Canada, its inexhaustless pine forests, its Canals, &c., have excited the greedy appetite of our southern neighbors who wishing to monopolize the New York timber trade, from their capital and commercial enterprise, have hit upon this scheme for effecting their purpose. The gentlemen of Kingston are made the cat's paw—they are to hold a knife to their own throats, to ruin a lucrative trade to themselves and children, while the Yankees are to reap the harvest. How they could be so gulled as to put their names to this infamous document, is a mystery to us. . . .

It is probable, however, that the gentlemen who took round this notice for signature, represented the matter in the light that Americans entering into the Province with their money, would give an impetus to business of every kind, and consequently induced unreflecting men to append their names. That a partial benefit may be effected through the introduction of foreign capital, we do not pretend to deny, but that it will do much greater injury, by depriving us of a lucrative trade, and by inundating the land with the refuse of other countries, in the shape of Yankee lumbermen, must be self evident. . . . . . We can compare this project to nothing else but the abortive attempt made last fall to turn the carrying-trade of the Province from the Rideau to the Erie Canal. Both projects were first broached and recommended in the *Chronicle;* and both, if we mistake not, were set afloat by designing speculators in Oswego. The first was scouted from decent society a very few weeks after it obtained publicity, and such, we predict, will be the fate of this second edition of the same treason for treasonable that scheme must be, that would take the bread from out the mouths of King's subjects, to bestow it upon men, who are the King's natural enemies.[1]

If Americans or other foreigners choose to become citizens of Upper Canada, we are among those most desirous of receiving them with open arms; but for them to come here, holding no allegiance to our King, buying up our lands, engrossing our trade, sending their profits to their own country, and having nothing in common with ourselves, is what we must denounce with the utmost vigilance and perseverance. What answer would the Congress of the United States give to an application from Canadians, to enjoy the privileges of American subjects, for the purpose of monopolizing a particular and highly important branch of trade? Would not such a petition be denied all consideration? And what right then have Americans to ask from our Legislature, that which would surely be refused by their own.

---

[1]Neither project met with so easy a fate, of course. The day came when Upper Canadian trade did go by New York, and also the Americans came close to dominating the lumber industry.

If the people of Kingston wish to increase the trade of their town why not enter into this valuable lumber trade with New York themselves? Why not raise a Joint Stock Company, for the express purpose, and if money be wanting, what is easier than to apply to Parliament for Banking privileges; and should that be refused as it probably might, what can prevent them from issuing their own notes, in the same way as the Farmer's and Peoples Banks do, or as the Bank of British North America intends to do? We have been asleep too long—it is time to get up and be stirring, and not suffer the Yankees to engross our trade, while we stand and look on with our hands in our pockets. The Province wants more Banks. The State of New York contains a population of two millions, with a Banking capital of $60,000,000. The Province of Upper Canada has a population of half a million nearly, with a Banking capital of $3,000,000 only that is, in proportion to the population, one fifth of what the New Yorkers enjoy. This is the great secret—this is what makes the Yankees flourish while we comparatively decay. Our natural resources are as great as theirs and yet we are denied the privileges arising from the same credit system that has made Great Britain what she is, and daily, before our eyes, enables our neighbours to make those gigantic strides in commerce, manufactures and the arts, alike the wonder of the two hemispheres.

27

Review of Trade in Chief Commodities, 1836

From *Montreal Morning Courier*, December 31, 1836.

IRON.—In consequence of the great advance in the price of this article, the consumption during the past year has very materially diminished; and although the quantity of English Iron imported has been much smaller than last year, it has been found sufficient for the demand, with the exception of the sizes most used in ship-building which have been scarce. The stock on hand is larger than it was expected it would be, but not more than will be absorbed by the winter and spring demand. Common sizes of English Iron sold throughout the summer at £17. 10s. The article has since declined a trifle, and may now be quoted at £16. . . .

WHEAT AND FLOUR.—The almost total failure of the Wheat crop in Lower Canada in 1835, and the surplus Upper

Canada being nearly all sold there, for exportation to the United States, the transactions in wheat in this market afford very limited scope for comment.   We have received a large supply of Foreign wheat, say about 480,000 bushels,[1] and had it not been for this, Lower Canada would not only have been unable to export a barrel of Flour to the Lower Ports, but would have been forced to draw a supply for consumption from the Upper Province or United States at whatever prices might be demanded. . . .

We are happy to think that the prospects for next year are more cheering, the last crop having been proved pretty nearly an average one in quantity, and better than an average one in quality. The best Lower Canada Red Wheat is now selling in this market at 7s. 6d. per minot of about 63 @ 64 lbs.

The earliest importations of Foreign Wheat were sold by sample to arrive at 5s. 3d. to 5s. 7d. for good sound German, and Inferior Archangel brought on arrival 4s. 6d. @ 5s. per 60 lbs.   At these rates the market continued steady, until the failure of the Wheat crop in the Southern States was confirmed beyond a doubt. This was about the 20th August, when the price suddenly advanced in New York, which was followed by a corresponding rise here, about the 1st Sept.   Hamburg and mixed Dantzic then brought 6s. 3d. @ 6s. 9d., and shortly afterwards 7s. per 60 lbs. was paid for export to Lake Champlain.   Our total import of Upper Canada Wheat, it will be seen, has been a mere bagatelle—it sold early in the season at 5s. 3d. @ 5s. 6d., and further on, small lots were placed at 6s. 9d. @ 7s. per 60 lbs.

WHISKEY.—The great decrease in the consumption of all imported Spirits we have elsewhere stated to be ascribable solely to the increase of spirits of native manufactures.   This branch of trade has now attained considerable importance, and it is estimated that in Lower Canada alone 400,000 gallons of proof Spirits have been made during the past season.   This large quantity is all used in the Lower Province, and the French Canadian population are now large consumers of it.   We have no means at present of ascertaining the quantity of spirits distilled in Upper Canada, but it must be very great and daily increasing.   The price of the

---

[1]That is, of European wheat.   The year 1836 marked the last importation of European wheat into Canada.   The editor hazards the suggestion that the Lower Canadian crop failure of 1835 was not without its bearing on the political agitation of these years.

native Whiskey has this year ranged from 2s. 6d. @ 2s. 10d. per gallon. . . . When we compare this low price with the prices at which low brandy and other Foreign Spirits can be afforded, it need not be matter of surprise if the importing trade in the latter, should in a measure cease. . . .

28

Evils of the System of Barter

From Howison, *Sketches of Upper Canada*, 127.

All mercantile business throughout the Province, but particularly in the western parts, is carried on by means of barter; circulating medium being so scarce, that it cannot be obtained in exchange for almost any thing.   The causes of this deficiency are very obvious: Upper Canada receives the various commodities she requires from the United States, or from the Lower Province; and she must pay money for every thing she buys from the Americans, they having a superabundance of flour, pork, and every kind of produce which she could give in exchange.   Thus, almost all the commercial transactions that take place between Upper Canada and the United States are the means of drawing specie from the former country; and this specie, of course, never returns to the inhabitants of the Province under any form whatever.   Again, the retail merchants send all the money they receive to Montreal, to pay the debts they have contracted there; or, if they do retain any in their own hands, the country is not benefited, for they never put it into circulation.   The only channel through which a regular influx of money took place was by the sale of flour; but this is now stopped, as that article has of late brought no price in Lower Canada, and those persons in the Upper Province who used to buy it up, and speculate upon it, can no longer do so with profit or advantage to themselves.   Formerly, the farmers received cash for their wheat, because Montreal and Quebec then afforded a ready market;[1] but things are now altered, and the agriculturist rarely gets money for any kind of home-produce, in consequence of its being unsaleable abroad.

Specie becomes daily more scarce, and will continue to decrease in quantity, until a European war with America creates a market

---

[1]That is, during the War of 1812.

17

for the produce of Upper Canada.   The inhabitants are continually wishing that the Province may again become the scene of hostilities, not aware that in consequence of this the necessary influx of circulating medium would be as temporary as it formerly was, and that the return of peace would be followed by a crisis infinitely more disastrous than any that has yet occurred in the Province. The scarcity of specie is indeed a circumstance highly injurious to the interests of the colony.   The farmer is discouraged from raising grain or making agricultural improvements; mechanics and artizans cannot prosecute their labours with advantage; and the merchants are obliged to impoverish and oppress the people by exorbitant charges.

The system of barter which exists in the Province has a very injurious effect upon the character of the peasantry.   It necessarily affords many opportunities of cheating to those who are inclined; and I lament to say, that the mass of inhabitants have more or less of this propensity, which they endeavour to palliate and conceal under the term of "taking advantage", and exercise without injury to their reputations; for, in Upper Canada, a man is thought dishonest only when his knavery carries him beyond the bounds prescribed by the law.   Various kinds of deception may be practised by the parties buying and selling, when barter is the medium of exchange.   A dollar, for instance, has a specific value, and cannot possibly be made to appear worth more or less than it really is; but other exchangeable articles vary continually, as far as respects value and quality, both of which points must often be solely decided by the judgment of him who proposes to receive them in barter.   The ignorant and inexperienced are thus daily exposed to the knavery and deceit of those who think there is no harm in "taking advantage".

29

The Panic of 1847

From Forsyth and Bell's *Annual circular and prices current of timber, deals, etc. for 1847* (Quebec).

For the commercial revolution of the 1840's see section IV.   Here we have to do with a complicating factor in that revolution, frequently overlooked, that is the great English railway panic of 1847.   The railroad building boom had entailed a huge demand for Canadian timber, and this in turn had produced demand for other Canadian products, notably flour.   In 1846, the new flour-milling industry was officially despatched by Sir Robert Peel; in the next year commercial conditions did the same for timber.   In consequence, Canada was never more hopeless than in these years, and political effects were numerous.

In taking a retrospect of this most disastrous season, we have to remark that although great depression has been felt in our timber trade since the opening of the navigation, the transactions have been much more extensive than many suppose, and comparing our prices current now issuing and those of last May, there is scarcely any difference, except in Red Pine, prices having ruled low all season.   The scarcity of shipping—the high rates of freight, the continued and increasing rate of money in England with its consequent embarrassments, the stoppage of Railways, have all injuriously affected our exports generally and we wish we could say that there existed any chance of immediate improvement, but such has been the pressure at Home, that considerable time must elapse before trade resumes its former buoyancy.

Last February we wrote our Upper Canada correspondents to the following effect:—"We regret to inform you the prices of White Pine in Liverpool were far from satisfactory, and taking into consideration the prices of Bread-stuffs and the disorganized state of society in England, we are constrained to say we look to a year of much depression for all kinds of Timber and although reluctant to advise, we would enjoin on you the necessity of extreme caution. . . ."   Many of them acted on this advice and in every way lessened their transactions and those who did not have been heavy sufferers.   The heavy stock wintering over must convince every party interested that over-trading has been carried on in wood as in most other articles, and a glance at the exports will furnish convincing proof that there can be no scarcity next year if nothing is done in the woods this winter.

30

Commercial Depression and Surplus Funds:—The New York Money Market as an Outlet

From *Montreal Morning Courier*, quoted in *Quebec Gazette*, May 5, 1850.

The decline in our trade has swelled the funds in the city banks which cannot find safe investment. . . . It is worth consideration whether it would not be advantageous to open (Bank) agencies in New York, now that our export and import trade has passed to that city.[1]

---

[1]The reference is to the depression which overtook the St. Lawrence as ? result of English and American legislation of 1846 and of the panic of 1847.

31

The Pre-Reciprocity Recovery of Trade

From *Montreal Gazette*, August 5, 1851.

The real cause of firmness in our market arises from the eager and extensive transactions of the Americans for the New York markets.[1]

---

[1]It is usually assumed that it took the Reciprocity Treaty of 1854 to bring back prosperity to the St. Lawrence. That, however, as this extract indicates, was not the case and Canada was once more flourishing before that treaty came nto effect.

THE STAPLE TRADES OF THE CANADAS

Even a naturally rich new country cannot make progress unless it can market its riches. Most new countries have advanced on the basis of some staple product, the supply of which is large and the quality fairly uniform. In the period under review, numerous attempts were made to find a staple as satisfactory as, say, cotton was proving to the southern states. New Brunswick, Lower Canada, and certain districts of Upper Canada did find a reasonably satisfactory staple in wood and its products, and the new lands of the St. Lawrence plain found another, considerably less satisfactory, in wheat and flour. On these two commodities and to a much less degree, a third—potash—most of the economic structure of the Canadas was reared.

REFERENCE: W. A. Mackintosh, "Economic factors in Canadian history" (*Canadian Historical Review*, March, 1923).

(a)—THE WHEAT AND FLOUR TRADE

The difficulty with wheat and flour as a staple was that the only possible market, the mother country, was so uncertain owing to the capricious action of the corn laws that the exporter could never know whether his consignment was to be allowed in for sale or to be kept, perhaps for years, in a British warehouse until prices, under the sliding scale of duties, had risen enough to permit its entry. Secondly, there was the expensive transport down the river and across the ocean. A new chapter began with the British budget of 1843, when not only was free entry allowed but allowed also to American wheat ground into flour in Canadian mills. In 1846, with free trade in wheat in Britain, the hot-house milling industry erected upon the political favour collapsed and much distress resulted. Since that date Canadian wheat has had to look after itself. As pioneer conditions were left behind, wheat became of less importance in colonial economy but, with all its drawbacks, it had been chiefly on it that Upper Canada had been built, an experience to be repeated a century later in the case of the prairies.

REFERENCE: D. A. MacGibbon, *The Canadian grain trade* (Toronto, 1932).

1

Plan for an Export Flour Mill at Queenstown

From Canadian Archives, *Upper Canada sundries*.

R. Hamilton to Governor Hunter

Oct. 10, 1800

. . . A Bank I cannot doubt will most essentialy tend to the improvement of our County, which as I allready have had the honour to Represent to your Excellency in my Notes on the

County of Lincoln, is completely an Agricultural Country, of which wheat is the great Staple. To bring this Staple by Manufacture to its highest Value, but still more to render it as conveniently Portable as may be, is a material Consern. Our flatt Country has but few streams for the Establishment of Mills on a large Plan.—Our great River more especialy about the Falls of Niagara, offers a power for this purpose, perhaps unequaled in the World.— Some considerable Works in this way, have been erected there, But for the purpose of Manufacturing Flour for Exportation, which requires to be packed as dry as is possible, we fear this Situation will not Answer. The constant Vapour which arises from these Falls, so completely fills the Air for a considerable distance round, as must materialy affect both the wheat and the Flour.—

It has been suggested that a more eligible Situation may be found, still on the great River, a few Miles above Queenston, where a Rapid offers itself, equal in power to any thing that can be required, to the foot of which Boats of any Size may be draged, and this intierly removed from the moist influence of the Falls.— From the allmost perpendicular banks, (not less than Two hundred feet in height) this Spott is unaccessible by any Road—It has been thought that this inconvenience, apparently unsurmountable, may be obviated, and even turn'd to a good Account. The Plan suggested is, That the wheat should be collected and if found (as we beleive) necessary for the preservation of Flour for Exportation, Kiln dried, on the top of the Bank, where the clear dry Air, and Limestone Soil, would tend to keep it in the highest preservation. That these granaries should be connected with the Mills below, by stairs supported on Stone Pillars, which our Artificers assure us they could construct. That allong side of these Stairs, a Trough should be fixed, for conveying the wheat as Wanted to the Mills. That this trough should have its bottom, or lower side, constructed of Sheet Iron or Tin, perforated as a Grater, with the rough side for the wheat to Roll on. That some part of it, towards the lower end, should be of wire wrought as a Seive, permitting every particle of dust or sand to Run through. It has been strongly alledged, that Wheat properly dried, in the Kiln above, would by this means be so completely cleaned in its descent, without further Labour, as would produce a flour equal to any made. Considering this Situation as Centrical between the two immence Lakes of Ontario, & Erie; Accessible to the first by boats, and to the Water communication of the other at the Chippewa, by a land carriage of not more than Six Miles, of excellent road; Considering it also as Centrical to the County of Lincoln, as fine a Corn Country as any in the Province; Supposing as good wheat as grows, thus Manufactured as well as can be; Allowing what we have fair reason to beleive, that we should be enabled to deliver a Barrel of Flour from these Mills in Montreal, at the expence of One Dollar; I think I might be warranted in presuming, that the Amount of Business that may at some time hereafter be done in such a Situation, exceeds our present powers of Calculation.

I need hardly Suggest to your Excellencys enlarged Mind, the infinite consequence such a Mart would be of to the Staple of our Country, more especialy when Joind to the Scheme of the Bank, which being secured on the Sales in Montreal, would Willingly enable the Merchant to pay the Farmer for his wheat, in a Current Medium, which would answer all his purposes, and free him from his present discouraging Bondage on the Shopkeeper, who can pay him only in Goods, which perhaps at the time he does not want. . . .

R. Hamilton

2

Special Properties of Canadian Wheat

(i)

From *Montreal Gazette*, February 27, 1821.

Canada wheats after being on the straw during a part of our severe winters possess that valuable consistence for mixing with the new wheats in Scotland and the north of England, which come into the Bakers hands after harvest soft, and what is sometimes called not kindly, this mixture affording that increase of weight in the bread, which is the baker's profit.

(ii)

From Liverpool letter printed in *Montreal Gazette*, April 15, 1830.

The Upper Canada Wheat that has come here by the late ships is beautiful, and sales of it have been made as high as 10s. 6d. Sterling 70 lbs. which is higher by much than any other description of Wheat will bring in our Market.

3

Hardship Imposed by the Corn Laws on Canadian Wheat Growers

From *Montreal Gazette*, August 15, 1821.

Notice, we perceive, is given, that a meeting of the Merchants and others concerned in the commerce of the Canadas, will take place next Saturday in the Exchange, St. Joseph's Street, at one o'clock in the afternoon, to take into consideration the distressed state of Agriculture and Trade in these provinces at the present time, with a view to obtain relief.

It is generally known that foreign wheat is not admitted into the ports of Great Britain when it sells there at 80s. sterling a quarter, nor colonial when it falls so low as 67s. Such is now the reduced price of Wheat in England that this difference in favour of the Colonists is of none avail; they are therefore in a worse situation than foreigners, as their wheat, according to the Corn regulations, cannot be admitted, unless to be put into the warehouse, nor are they allowed to send it elsewhere; but, we trust, when this state in which they are now placed shall be fairly represented to the Parliament of Great-Britain, that some means will be adopted to afford them relief, which must be, either to allow them an unrestricted importation or to seek for a market for their wheat in some other country.

4

Exports of Wheat from the Niagara District:—Lake Transport

From Niagara newspaper, quoted in *Montreal Gazette*, May 17, 1830.

We believe more Wheat and flour has been exported from this quarter, at this early period, than ever was heretofore known. On Sunday morning last we counted eleven sail of vessels off the mouth of the River—some from the River, and many, we believe, with loads received at Burlington, and on the shore between that harbour and this. The three large Steamers have made two trips each, with full loads, so that vast quantities of Wheat and Flour must already have gone down, most of which has been paid for in cash, which must enrich the Province, and render us more independent of the merchants of Lower Canada, to whom we have been too long tributary.

5

"Souring" of Wheat on the Trans-Atlantic Voyage

From *Montreal Gazette*, February 12, 1833.

George Auldjo, chairman, Montreal committee of trade to Nathaniel Gould, chairman, North American Colonial Association, London

The wheat of last year's Canadian crop, owing to its own humidity or to some extraordinary mixture of heat and moisture in the atmosphere during the loading, was nearly all landed in bad condition, threatening on this account and by fluctuating in price, an average loss of at least one shilling and eight pence per bushel. Great part of the flour shipped during the summer heat was landed sour, and it is now supposed that not less than one hundred and fifty thousand pounds will be lost by the shipments of grain and flour from Quebec this season, of which at least one third will fall on Canadian houses.

Geo. Auldjo

6

Exports of Wheat and Flour from the St. Lawrence, 1793-1830

From *Montreal Gazette*, November 1, 1831.

Statement of the Exports of Wheat and Flour from Canada, from 1793 to 1830.

Years	Wheat and Flour = Wheat, Bushels[1]	Years	Wheat and Flour = Wheat, Bushels
1793	541,500	1803	438,052
1794	482,500	1804	270,378
1795	485,000	1805	114,966
1796	24,606	1806	151,894
1797	101,000	1807	333,753
1798	139,500	1808	399,168
1799	201,000	1809	295,849
1800	317,000	1810	233,495
1801	660,000	1811	97,553
1802	1,151,033	1812	451,303

[1]One barrel of flour is taken as the equivalent of five bushels of wheat.

| | Wheat and Flour | | Wheat and Flour |
Years	=Wheat, Bushels		=Wheat, Bushels
1813...............	2,585	1822...............	383,520
1814...............	6,086	1823...............	535,760
1815...............	9,600	1824...............	214,901
1816...............	5,675	1825...............	918,031
1817...............	335,895	1826...............	396,835
1818...............	554,506	1827...............	661,535
1819...............	98,325	1828...............	296,314
1820...............	535,893	1829...............	99,377
1821...............	431,658	1830...............	948,826

1802 to 1830 are from official returns. 1793 to 1801, are given in round numbers and are sufficiently accurate for all purposes.

7

Exports of Wheat and Flour from the St. Lawrence, 1838-1861

From H. Y. Hind, "Commerce and Trade", in *Eighty years' progress*, 291.

Year	Bushels	Year	Bushels
1838.............	296,020	1850.............	4,547,224
1839.............	249,471	1851.............	4,275,896
1840.............	1,739,119	1852.............	5,496,718
1841.............	2,313,836	1853.............	6,597,193
1842.............	1,678,102	1854.............	3,781,534
1843.............	1,193,918	1855.............	6,413,428
1844[1].............	2,350,018	1856.............	9,391,531
1845[1].............	2,507,392	1857.............	6,482,199
1846[1].............	3,312,757	1858.............	5,610,559
1847[1].............	3,883,156	1859.............	4,032,627
1848[1].............	2,248,016	1860.............	8,431,253
1849[1].............	3,645,320	1861.............	13,369,727

(b)—TIMBER AND LUMBER

Until the west found its great staple, wheat, wood was the most successful of Canadian primary products. In the eighteenth century, distance made it impossible to compete in the British market but the enormous colonial preference granted in 1808 and the following years, combined with the demands of war, set

---

[1]Note the very temporary effect of the repeal of the corn laws in 1846. It was the milling industry rather than the farmer that was hurt. Hence the urban character of the annexation movement.

the industry on its feet and from that time on it has been the chief reliance of a great part of the country. It is only since the railroad crossed the height of land that the industry has extended beyond the St. Lawrence watershed and the Maritimes, and this region (together with British Columbia) is still its chief seat.

Before 1850, the wood industry in its simplest form, square timber making, gradually extended up river as far as the southern end of Lake Huron and up all the tributaries (save those of the upper lakes), especially the Ottawa, where Lake Temiscaming was reached perhaps as early as the thirties. This trade was especially subject to the extremes of ups and downs which characterized Canadian trade generally. It was also constantly attacked for its bad social effects.

Sawn lumber was the second branch of the industry. Mills in the export trade had to ship by water and consequently never got off the main waterway until the era of railroads. In 1835, export began to the United States, first to the east and thence westerly, following settlement, and this first foreign market for a Canadian product mounted until at last it exceeded the British.

REFERENCES: A. R. M. Lower, "A sketch of the history of the Canadian lumber trade" (*Canada year book*, 1925) and *Lumbering in Canada* (forthcoming); W. A. Langton, *Early days in Upper Canada* (Toronto, 1926); John Rankin, *A history of our firm* (Liverpool, 1921); R. G. Albion, *Forests and sea power* (Cambridge, Mass., 1926).

1

New Brunswick Loyalists and the Lumber Industry

From W. O. Raymond (ed.), *The Winslow papers, A.D. 1776-1826* (St. John, N.B., 1901), 266.

Wm. Donaldson to Thos. Newland, 9th Feby., 1785

To view this town [*St. John*] in so short a time would astonish every stranger as it would to see the improvements going on in the Country. The number of Saw Mills erected are very great, and can only be imagined from the noble prospects this Country opens for Lumber, and which is not to be equalled in any of the States.

2

An Early Mill near Niagara Falls

From La Rochefoucault-Liancourt, *Travels in North America*, 222.

About a mile above the falls, two corn-mills and two saw-mills have been constructed in the large bason, formed by the river on the left . . . the logs are cut here into boards, thrown into the Chippaway creek near its mouth, and by means of a small lock conveyed into a canal, formed within the bed of the river by a double row of logs of timber, fastened together and floating on the water. The breaking of these is prevented by other large balks floating at a certain distance from each other, which form, as it were, the basis of this artificial canal.

The water retains in this canal the rapidity of the current, and conveys the logs into the lower part of the mill, where, by the same machinery which moves the saws, the logs are lifted upon the jack and cut into boards. Only two saws at a time are employed in this mill. The power of the water is almost boundless, but the present wants of the country do not require a greater number of saws. The very intelligent owner of the mill has constructed it on a plan, which admits of the addition of a greater number of courses, according as these shall be required by an increased consumption. On the same principle he has built his corn-mill, which has at present only four courses. The miller's dues for grinding, as fixed by the legislative power, amounts to a twelfth throughout all Upper Canada, and for sawing logs to a moiety of the wood sawed.

3

Rafting down the St. Lawrence Rapids

From D'Arcy Boulton, *Sketch of his majesty's Province of Upper Canada* (London, 1805), 27.

So well known are these rapids now that the grain of the upper country is taken down on rafts, or in boats, to Montreal and an accident scarcely ever happens. The lumber trade is carried on with more safety down these rapids than by those which pass Chambly from Lake Champlain. In truth this trade is of considerable importance to the country, being the cause of much money being brought into the province. Attempts have been made to establish this trade, even from the most distant parts of Lake Ontario, but we conceive the risk to be far beyond the probable advantage: for though the produce of that very fertile country is exported to the Montreal market, it is generally thought more safe to transport grain across that large lake by vessels, than by rafting.

4

Vermont Timber and Canadian Raftsmen

From Canadian Archives, *Q*, CVII, 265.

Until the construction of the Champlain Canals, northern Vermont's only outlet was by the Richelieu and the St. Lawrence. Much subtle fraud was necessary in proving the timber from the American side of the line to be Canadian and thus entitled to the preference in the British market.

Quebec, 13th May, 1808

Sir

You will of course have heard of the disposition shewn by the people of Vermont and the Northern part of New York, to resist the embargo, particularly in what regards the usual supply to our markets here of timber and lumber. In this, tho' some may be actuated by views of future profit, yet I have reason to believe that the greater number are induced to it, principally by an honourable desire to discharge their obligations to our merchants (from whom they had received large advances in money before that part of the law passed which regards them) by the only means in their power, for the money has been expended in their purposes, for which the advances are made, viz.: In paying the expence of the winter in cutting the timber. Some rafts are actually arrived. Tho' upon enquiry, I find that many subjects of the States were employed in conducting them, yet, there is no doubt that, as might be expected, and as has been always usual when it was not contrary to the laws of the States, there were many Canadians among them also. These are the people who every year are employed in cutting the wood and are generally speaking, a lawless set, over whom we have little authority or controul. I understand some of them have been stop'd and convey'd to jail, they will certainly receive no protection from this Government, nor shall I take any steps to claim them.

J. R. Craig

5

War as a Stimulant to the Timber Industry

From *Winslow papers*, 633.

Captain Hatch to Judge Edward Winslow

St. Andrews, April 23, 1809

The great demand for this article the last season and the consequent high price, induced every exertion to be directed to this object and there are now twenty Thousand Tons of squared pine timber[1] ready for market, two-thirds more than has been

---

[1]Squared timber was the first form of the industry both because of the habit of the British market and because little fixed capital was necessary for getting it out. Sawn lumber predicated the mill.

obtained in any other season prior to the last, with the Logs sufficient to employ Forty saws in the different mills within the County.[1]   Your astonishment will be less when you understand that seventeen twentieths of the male-population of this County are what is termed here "Lumbermen", and were employed in procuring this large quantity of timber.

6

The Qualities and Sizes of Canadian Oak Timber

From David Anderson, *Canada or a view of the importance of the British American colonies*, 170.

Quebec Oak consists of two kinds, which are White and Red; the white is only exported, the red not being considered merchantable.

The merchantable size is 12 inches and upwards on the side; and 20 feet long and upwards.   There is not much brought to market under 12 inches; the general size is from 13 to 16 inches square, and from 30 to 40 feet long.   In some few instances, however, a few pieces may be found to square even from 16 to 30 inches; and some sticks, perhaps, to run the length of 60 feet.

The quality of Quebec white oak is considered superior to any which we import from any other part of America, or even from Europe.   This may be proved by inspecting the prices current at those ports, wherein all the varieties of qualities we import are to be found.

Before oak can be exported from Canada, it must be inspected by a person, appointed by the government, for that purpose, and stamped as merchantable. . . .

The faults for which it is considered unmerchantable are, its being red oak [or] under 20 feet long, under 12 inches upon the side, having unsound knots, being crooked or ill squared; and its being ringed, which last is the most general and the greatest of all faults.[2]

Ringed timber is that which has begun to rot or decay in the heart.   When this disease has but just commenced, it requires a

---

[1]Charlotte County.

[2]Much good timber, which should never have been made into square timber but should have been sawn up into boards and planks, was rejected and allowed to rot for just such slight defects as the extract mentions.

good judge to discover the defect, which, in a circular manner, appears, by showing a small shade of difference in the colour.

From this variety of the quality of oak in the Quebec market, a proportionate variety of prices are produced; the unsound selling, perhaps, at 6d. per foot, and the best at 2/6d.

7

The Hamilton Company's Mills, Hawkesbury, 1817[1]

From Robert Gourlay, *Statistical account of Upper Canada* (London, 1822), 580.

This mill was among the earliest of those cutting for export: it was established about 1809, at the head of navigation on the Ottawa, as far up as a mill could at that time be placed and still export.

On an island in Ottawa river, opposite the higher parts of Hawkesbury township, are erected saw mills of the best construction, and upon a scale superior to any other in the province. They were first owned by Mr. Mears, of Hawkesbury; but are now the property of Mr. Hamilton, from Ireland; and the business seems to be carried on by him with great spirit; about fourscore people being employed in the works on the island. Nothing can be better situated than these mills, either as it respects the command of water as a moving power for machinery, or as a conductor of the log timber to the mills.

8

American Timber Thieves in New Brunswick

From *New Brunswick executive council minutes*, 1819, doc. no. 131.

New Castle 2nd July 1819

Honorable Sir.

... I have seized nearly one thousand sticks of Timber cut and fell on the Kings Reserve mostly by the American Subjects there is two men by the name of Turner and Emmery who was cuting and hauling on their own Account—unconnected with any Subject of this Country with six oxen and did even after the timber was marked persist in hauling he was marched down to the forks and kept in custody for three days and I dont know but I would

---

[1]This business, after having passed under various names, is still in existence at Hawkesbury, Ontario, as a branch of the International Paper Company.

be authorized to march him down to jaol something decisive must be done with those daring Trespassers their Christian names I have not found out. . . .

I have the Honor to be

Your most obedient Humble Servant
Richard S. Clarke

Honble. Thomas Wetmore
Attorney Gen[l.]

9

How the Timber Trade Has Served New Brunswick

From John McGregor, *Historical sketches of the maritime colonies*, 154.

The timber trade has no doubt been one, if not the principal cause of the growth of St. John. Great gains were at first realized both by it and ship-building; and although the merchants and others immediately concerned in these pursuits were nearly ruined afterwards by the extent of their undertakings and engagements; yet, it must be recollected, that each of those trades has enabled New Brunswick to pay for her foreign imports, and with the timber trade she has built St. John, Fredericton, and St. Andrew.

10

The Timber Raft

From John MacTaggart, *Three years in Canada*, I, 241.

On these rafts they have a fire for cooking, burning on a sandy hearth; and places to sleep in, formed of broad stripes of bark, resembling the half of a cylinder, the arch about four feet high and in length about eight. To these beds, or *lairs*, *trams*, or handles are attached, so that they can be moved about from *crib* to *crib*, or from crib to the shore, as circumstances render it necessary. When they are passing a *breaking up rapid*, they live ashore in these lairs, until the raft is *new withed*, and fixed on the still waters below.[1]

---

[1]When about 1830, the timber slide was devised by Ruggles Wright of Hull, it no longer became necessary to break up the cribs into their constituent timbers.

11

The "Shanty"

Ibid., 242.

As these people live in huts in the woods, which huts are houses only for a season, they are called *shanties*, and hence, *shantymen*; but there is something more attached to the name of shanty than a mere hut, in the lumberman's dictionary. Thus, so many men, oxen, so much pork, flour, and etc., compose a *shanty*. A *beehive*, with him, is not one, unless it be stocked with bees, combs, honey, and etc.

12

The Shantyman:—His Nature

Ibid., 242.

Great quantities of spurious whisky are swallowed, many battles fought, and so forth; yet these things being perfectly natural to the shantyman, he could hardly endure life without them. In the conceited towns he is held in abhorrence by the clerk and counter-jumper, who know no more of the laws of Nature, or the elements of human life than a parcel of magpies. They fancy that the wood-cutter from the wilderness should be made up of nods and smiles, starch and ruffles, like their dear affected selves, never thinking that he is a creature by himself, like the sailor, bred amid dangers and difficulties, and made somewhat roguish by the sharking rogues of the cities.

13

The Standard Arguments against the Repeal of the Differential Duties

From Upper Canada, Legislative assembly debates, February 4, 1831, reported in *Montreal Gazette*, February 17, 1831.

The battle waged about the colonial preference in timber was as fierce, if not as public, as the battle over the corn laws and lasted about the same length of time, from 1820 until 1846. It was a battle of vested interests in Great Britain, the importers of Baltic timber clamouring for abolition, the colonial interests for continuance. The duties, almost prohibitive in amount, were reduced by Peel to a moderate figure in the budgets of 1842, 1845, and 1846. They did not completely disappear until 1860.

18

On motion of Mr. Morris, the House went into Committee on certain resolutions respecting the Timber Trade.

Mr. Morris said, . . . "The Imperial Parliament are about to alter the duty on Baltic Timber. . . . Any material change affecting the Timber Trade of the Canadas will cause its utter ruin and the bankruptcy of many persons, who have embarked their fortunes with a confident belief that no sudden change would take place. . . . The expensive voyage to Canada, and the high rate of wages to labourers and seamen put it out of the power of the Canadian merchant to compete with the Baltic trade, unless some protection is afforded. . . . The importance of this trade to the Empire ought to induce His Majesty's Government to listen with caution to representations [as to the repeal of the duties] which would drive 700 ships out of a trade that employs thousands of British seamen and causes the consumption of vast quantities of the manufactures of our countrymen, and thereby give employment to foreigners. Another advantage of the trade with Canada he thought to be the means of removing vast numbers of emigrants to the Colony, who could not leave home but for the cheap passage afforded by the ships arriving at Quebec in ballast. These persons become respectable settlers and thereby relieve the nation of a most serious burthen. It had been argued that the lumber trade was an injury to the country as it diverted the farmer from agricultural pursuits, but this opinion he could by no means agree to. The thousands of persons employed in that business consume vast quantities of the flour and pork sent from the western parts of the Province, and are the means of introducing an extensive circulation of money which could not otherwise exist. . . .

14

Wood as the Major Factor in Canadian Trade

From *Montreal Gazette*, August 29, 1835.

Nearly two thirds of the whole amount of exports from Canada to Great Britain consists of lumber, amounting in 1834, to £784,457.[1]

---

[1]By 1850, wood seems to have given way to grain and flour in the value of exports.

15

Loss of Timber *en route* to Quebec

From Canadian Archives, *Correspondence of the governor-general's office*, no. 1526.

David Thompson to Sir Charles Bagot, May 23, 1842

. . . The deepening of Lake St. Peter will be attended with great advantages to the Timber Trade of Canada. At present the Timber Trade is as safe a business as most others exposed to the weather as far down as Lake St. Peter; but once there, the safety of the Rafts is doubtful, in fine weather they pass the Lake in about fifteen hours, but more frequently they are delayed several days, even to three weeks; they dare not attempt the Lake in an easterly wind, and when in the Lake and an easterly gale comes on, the Rafts are wrecked and sometimes with loss of life, when safe over the Lake they are still liable to be wrecked above Quebec, and even when close to Quebec are sometimes carried below it with a strong ebb tide. In the rocky coves of Quebec the timber receives much damage, if it lies any time, from the agitation of the water, chafing the timber against the Rocks. An old Lumber Man said to me, Sir there is Oak enough sunk in Lake St. Peter to build a wall around it. A deep channel through Lake St. Peter will enable the Ships to come up to Sorrel [*Sorel*] and its vicinity, where they can load in safety; and to which place the Rafts of Timber can also arrive in safety. . . .

David Thompson

16

The Qualities of Canadian Pine Timber

From a letter in *The Times* (London), quoted in *Canadian Economist*, June 20, 1846.

. . . Yellow Pine,[1] the description of Canada Timber which has been most abused, is the most useful timber in the world; it gives us a mast thirty feet long and ninety-six inches in diameter, cheaper by one half and as good as can be produced in any other quarter. This is the most magnificent form in which Yellow Pine comes to hand; as illustrative of its utility, I may just here mention (going to an opposite extreme) that it is the material exclusively

---

[1]The English term for white pine, *pinus strobus*.

used for lucifer matches, and this paltry article consumes deals by the thousand; and such are its properties that it can be split into boards of 30 to the inch. Between these extremes, the mast and the match, there extends a large space, in which this timber proves itself useful. It is used by engineers for patterns, it is exclusively used for sign-boards, for mouldings, for picture and looking-glass frames, for inside work in house-building, for steamers' decks, for Venetian blinds, and for various other purposes where lightness, cleanness, and mild quality are required. . . . This timber for mast-yards, topmasts, and booms, is unequalled. The Baltic produces nothing like it; it is tough, clean, durable, clear of sap, obtainable in any length required, and is more free from defects than any other timber with which I am acquainted. . . . In conclusion, allow me to say that Canada has never been in competition with the Baltic to any extent. The two trades are nearly separate and that of Canada is in that state which is peculiar to every protected trade—it is but partially developed. Nothing will show what the Canada trade is, . . . but the removal of protection. . . .

17

The Crisis of 1847-48 in the Timber Trade and its Causes[1]

From Journals of assembly, Canada, 1849, VIII, appendix P.P.P.P.

Minutes of Evidence

68. Are you aware that the trade has been in a depressed state for the last three years, and can you state the causes which appear to you to have brought about this state of depression? W. H. Dawson, Esq., of Bytown, examined:—

15th March, 1849

The year 1845 was the most prosperous to which my knowledge of the [*timber*] trade extends. The quantity of timber brought to market that season was 27,702,344 feet, and the quantity exported was 24,223,000 feet. . . . At the close of the navigation therefore, in the fall of 1845, allowing something for local consumption, the stock in hand was but little greater than in the fall of 1844. . . . The demand continued good in 1846, and if the trade had been well regulated, the presumption is that it would

---

[1]The *debâcle* in the timber trade was a prime factor in the political discontents of the time, the annexation manifesto, *etc.*

have been as profitable that year as it had been before.   In 1846, however, the quantity of square timber brought to Quebec Market was 37,300,643 feet, and the quantity exported was 24,242,689 feet.   Thus it appears that the quantity exported had actually increased, the demand had increased, and yet in the face of this the prices fell to a ruinous degree, and this simply because . . . the supply was out of all proportion to that demand. . . . In the two succeeding seasons, 1847 and 1848, although other causes entered into combination with it, the over-production of 1846 . . . still operated as the principal depressing influence.   Thus in 1847, including the quantity brought to market and the stock in hand, there was a total supply of 44,927,253 feet of square timber, to meet a demand for 19,060,880 feet, and in 1848, there was in like manner, a total supply of 39,447,776 feet to meet a demand for 17,402,360.   The other causes which have combined to depress the trade in the two latter years, resolve themselves, so far as we are concerned, into one, viz., a decreased demand.   The causes which have led to the decreased demand, we have no control over. In the first place, our own large export of 1845 and 1846 may have tended in some measure to overstock the British market; in the next place it would appear, that an enormous supply has been thrown upon the market in these latter years from the Province of New Brunswick, quite unprecedented at any former period. What influence the Baltic trade may have had I am not very clearly aware, as it does not appear that, at least of square timber, there has been any great increase of the quantity thrown upon the market from that quarter.   The greatest and most apparent cause of all, however, is to be found in the diminished consumption arising from the depressed state of commerce in general in Great Britain, and throughout the whole of Europe. . . .

18

The Timber Coves of Quebec

From Rollo Campbell, *Two lectures on Canada, delivered in the Sheriff Court Hall* (Greenock, 1857).

. . . It is here that the immense foreign business of Quebec is transacted, and the small strip so occupied, which is not over an eighth of a mile wide by one mile in length, is valuable almost beyond price.   The straitness of the place has caused business to be pushed out along the foot of the Cape westward, and one street runs up some three miles. Here wharves and stores, booms enclosing untold quantities of timber, piles of deals and boards almost defying measurement, bewilder the eye, and suggest the question of where all this wood will go, or when it will go. However, the sight of five or six hundred ships at the same moment, stowing away in their capacious insides whole rafts of immense logs, return the answer; and when it is borne in mind that from 10 to 15 hundred such cargoes are despatched every summer, the wonder as to what becomes of the wood ceases. Yet it is one of the greatest sights in America, to behold from some eminence in the neighbourhood, the acres upon acres of squared pine, oak and elm logs, which the coves present, and the spectacle immediately impresses the observer with the vast extent of the timber trade of Canada.

19

The *Entrepreneur* in the Timber Industry

From Thomas C. Keefer, *The Ottawa* (Montreal, 1854), 54.

The first step necessary for a lumberman[1] is to secure his limits, which is done by an application for a license to cut timber on Crown lands at a certain stumpage. The next is a more common but less easy one in other matters, viz.:—"raising the wind." If you have a little property, you will find a class of gentlemen known among lumbermen as the *big bourgeois*, (which is the synonym of *boss*,) who will advance you, at least to the value of your property, what are called supplies, in order that you may indulge in your propensities for speculation. Your supplier gives you provisions and clothing for your men, axes, ropes, augers, anchors and cables, and a little cash, for which he charges a sort of premium of insurance over ordinary profits. At the same time you are privileged to run into debt as much elsewhere as you can, provided always that no other person receives a prior mortgage on your timber. When your timber reaches Quebec (if you survive that stage) it is consigned to your supplier who sells it for you, for which trouble he only charges the usual commission of five per cent. Your men

---

[1]By 1850, the undifferentiated "lumberman" of a generation previous was disappearing and his place being taken by the capitalist *entrepreneur* on the one hand and the "lumberjack" on the other.

stick like leaches to the raft, until they are paid off. Your supplier then strikes the balance, which he either hands to you or
demands from you, according to the price of timber and your own
management.   If you have understood your business and attended
to it, and if white pine is "up," that is, worth about 7½d. per foot,
or if your supplier will hold on to it for you when it is "down,"
and does not sell it to himself, despite all the other drawbacks, you
may return from Quebec with a broad-cloth suit, a gold watch, new
hat and a brass mounted portmanteau.   If otherwise, as you will
find the place rather hot, you will prefer a linen wrapper, and decline
being encumbered with much baggage.   If you are fortunate
enough to have acquired experience, and a capital of £1,000 or so,
and are wise enough to make no more timber than you can get
to market without the aid of suppliers, you are on the high road to
fortune, and your success is certain.   But the rock on which many
a lumberman has split, or technically speaking, the "jam" on which
he has been "picked up," is, a rule of three estimate of his profits.
If he has been fortunate enough to clear £500 from one raft made
with borrowed money, he undertakes two or three the next year,
in the hope of doubling or trebling his profits.   He thus doubles
his liabilities, and sooner or later the supplier has him.

20

"Laissez passer les Raf'mans"

From E. Z. Massicotte and C. M. Barbeau, "Chantes populaires du Canada"
  (*Journal of American Folk-Lore*, XXXII, (123), January-March, 1919, 83).

La y ou c'qui sont, tous les rafmagne
Dedans Bytown ils sont allés.
(Chorus).
Dedans la ville ils sont allés
C'était pour ben s'habiller

Oh! c'était pour ben s'habiller
Des belles p'tites bottes dans leurs gros pieds

Et tous les cooks sont des damnés
Ils font des beignes[1]; on n'en mange pas.

---

[1]Beignes: "flap-jacks".

(Chorus).
 Beign sur la rigne
 Vous laissez passer les rafmagn
 Bagn sur la rign, bagn, bagn.
 Bardi bardagne, bardi bardan
 Laissez passer les rafmans.
 Bon bardi, bardagne, bon bardagne.

(c)—POT AND PEARL ASHES

The sole use to which the hardwood which stood on the most fertile lands could be put was to burn it and extract the pot and pearl ash from its ashes. These products were thus a by-product of clearing. A considerable export trade was done in them until the discovery of mineral equivalents and new technical processes superseded them. For the method of their manufacture see volume I, pages 448*ff.*

1

Potash as a Major Item in Canadian Trade

From *Montreal Gazette*, January 17, 1824.

Quebec, January 5

The articles of ashes, which now forms perhaps the staple of the country, exceeds in 1823 that of the year preceding, by a very large amount, viz.: 76,603 cwt. which taking for both kinds, the average price of 30s. per cwt. would give an excess in the value of the exports of 1823, above that of 1822, of £115,205; applying the same average price to the export of the article in 1823, we should have a capital employed in that branch of our trade of £327,511. It is indeed probable from the unusually high price of ashes last winter, that more than this amount has been engaged in the trade, & that £350,000 has been employed, a sum somewhat less than half the whole value of merchandise imported in the same year. This profitable part of our trade we owe in a great measure to the free admission of the article from the bordering States, which is perhaps one example of the advantages of unrestricted trade between this colony and our neighbours.

2
High Standard of Inspection in Canadian Ashes

Every staple trade seeks uniformity of product. This aim has unvariably entailed the building up of a system of inspection and grading, usually under governmental sanction and management.

(i)

From *Montreal Gazette*, March 30, 1829.

Extracts from a Circular of Messrs. Gates & Co. of Montreal.

The improvement in Montreal inspection of ashes is noticed by our English correspondents, and we have now the proud satisfaction of saying that it stands as high in foreign markets as any from this continent. The alarm that we at one time felt that American ashes, lumber, staves, &c. passing through Canada would be subject to foreign duty on being introduced into the English markets, is now completely dissipated, the object of the British Government in directing that certificates of origin should accompany shipments from Canada, appearing to be solely with a view of ascertaining for their own satisfaction the actual capabilities of their colonial possessions, and therefore the articles in question coming from the U. States to Canada by land or inland navigation exported in British bottoms, accompanied by certificates that they were imported by land or inland navigation, go into the English markets for consumption upon the same terms as if they were actually the growth and production of the Canadas.

(ii)

From *Montreal Gazette*, July 6, 1829.

By the statement which we give below, it will be seen that this important article of our exports is in an improving state; the quantity received this year, exceeding that of last year, by 1573 barrels.——This, we are inclined to think, is in no small degree owing to the amendment of the Inspection Law. By the appointment of one Chief Inspector, guarantee is held out to purchasers, that the same brand will invariably indicate the same quality, which was not formerly the case when the several Inspectors acted independently of one another. Another very pregnant source of evil, i.e., competition in obtaining business has, by the present regulations, been done away with; and a more vigilant and careful examination of every barrel is, we believe, now enforced. . . .

The increase in the quantity brought to market, is a proof that the confidence of country merchants in our brands, is increasing.

Pot and Pearl Ashes.

1829.

Stock on hand 22d April...............5508 barrels.

20th June,........Received............7433

12,941 total.

1828.

Stock on hand 12th April..............3689

20th June,————Received............7679

11,368

—Courant.   1573 over.

3

Spread of Ash Industry down the St. Lawrence

From *Neilson's Quebec Gazette*, quoted in *Montreal Gazette*, January, 1832.

Commercial

Remarks on the principal exports and imports the past season

Ashes.—The quantity shipped the past season at Montreal and Quebec, including those on board the *Margaret*, wintering at Three Rivers, exceed the export of 1830 by 3146 barrels........ More ashes have been inspected at this port the past season than heretofore, and we have observed that the Quebec brand is getting into favour in the English market, and now ranks equal with the Montreal brand, a character which is justly due to the abilities, industry, and strict integrity of our inspector:

Ashes shipped at Montreal and Quebec

	Pearls.	Pots.	Total.
1830.........................	15812	31684	47496
1831.........................	20375	30267	50642

PRICES

The following documents are given merely as illustrations. Distinguish between sterling and Halifax currency, the latter at $4.00 to the pound being the invariable way of reckoning within the colony. Lists of prices supplementing those given here will be found in W. S. Herrington, *History of the County of Lennox and Addington* (Toronto, 1913).

1

London Prices of Canadian Commodities

From *Quebec Herald*, August 3, 1789.

PRICE CURRENT

Of Quebec and American States produce in London, May 8th, 1789.

	£.	s.	d.		£.	s.	d.	
American Pot ash, from	1	11	0	to	1	12	0	per cwt.
Pearl do...........	1	16	0	.....	1	19	0	do.
Pitch,...............	0	6	0	.....	0	7	0	do.
Black rosin,..........	0	9	0	.....	0	10	0	do.
Yellow do............	0	10	0	.....	0	11	0	do.
Lint seed,.............	0	16	0	.....	2	0	0	per Qr.

SKINS.

	Sound.				Damaged or ordinary.			
	s.	d.	s.	d.	s.	d.	s.	d.
Deer, winter in hair, from	3	0 to	8	3	... 2	6	to 4	0 per skin
Summer do............	3	4...	5	6,	... 1	0	... 3	2 do.
Indian dressed.........	1	10...	3	0,	................per lb.			
Elk.................	4	0...	15	0,	................per lb.			

	s.	d.	s.	d.	s.	d.	s.	d.
Beaver parch, fine,	10	0	12	0	5	6	6	6 per lb.
Cub. do........	9	0	10	0	4	6	5	6 do.
Coat do........	7	0	 7	6	4	6	5	6 do.
Canada,........	5	0	 6	6	...3	0	4	6 do.

STAVES

	£.	s.	d.	£.	s.	d.	
American pipe, from	9	00	0	to 12	00	0	per 1200 ps.
Hogshead.......	6	00	0	 8	00	0	do.
Barrel, ...	3	10	0	 4	10	0	do.
Quebec pipe, ...	47	00	0	...48	10	0	do.
Hogshead, ...	32	00	0	....			do.
American tar, ...	0	12	0	00	13	0	per brl.

TIMBER.

	£.	s.	d.	£.	s.	d.	
American oak......	3	00	0	 3	10	0	per L.[1]
Pine timber........	1	10	0	 1	15	0	do.
Plank.............	2	8	0	 2	10	0	per L.
Turpentine	0	13	0	 0	14	0	per cwt.
Bee's wax..........	9	9	0	 9	15	0	do.
Wood, box	4	00	0	 5	00	0	per ton

INSURANCE

From London, Bristol, Liverpool, and Cork to Canada three guineas. From Do. do. do. do. to the United States two guineas. From Canada to London two guineas.

2

Prices Current of Wheat and Flour at Quebec, 1805-1831

Collected from Canadian Archives, *Q.*

Year	Month	Wheat per bushel	Flour per barrel	
1805	May	9/6 stg.	superfine	60/- stg.
			fine	55/-
			common	45/-
1808	Jan.	5/6	s.	35/-
	Feb.	5/6	s.	33/-
			f.	32/6
			c.	25/-
	March	7/6	s.	35-37/6

---

[1] L = Load, 50 cubic feet.

Year	Month	Wheat per bushel	Flour per barrel
	April	7/6	s. 37/6-40/-
	May	7/9	s. 42/6
	June	8/-	s. 45/-
	July	8/-	s. 55/-
	Aug.	7/9	s. 55/-60/-
	Sept.	7/9	s. 55/-
1809		6/-	s. 50/-
1810	June	8/6	s. 55/-
1811	Sept.	None for sale	10½ to 12 dollars
	Oct.	do.	do.
1812	June	9/6 to 10/-	s. $11½
			f. $10½
			c. $9½
1813		12/6 to 13/4	s. none
			f. $18
			c. $13 to $15
1821	Aug.	4/3 to 4/6 per *minot*	s. (kiln dried) 21/6 to 22/6
			f. 19/- to 20/6
			middlings 18/- to 19/-
1831	Average	5/4	1st quality, 13/- per 100 lbs.

3

Conditions in British Markets affecting Prices of Canadian Products

From *Montreal Gazette*, June 26, 1824.

By private letters of the latest dates from England, we learn that Lumber in the British Market bears a fair price, and that there is a prospect of its succeeding well this season, provided the number of vessels for its transport be sufficient. Pine was as high as 2s. 2d.; Oak not so good; but Staves bore a fair price. Ashes were dull sales, by the latest intelligence, and with difficulty brought the last quoted prices. This is perhaps attributable to the large quantities on hand, both here and at home, since last year. In the Grain Market, there was a more favourable prospect for this country. It was very generally believed that the Ports would be open for Colonial Grain during the summer; but while this kept buyers back, it also made holders anxious to sell, but unwilling to reduce their prices.

4

Prices of Timber at Quebec

From *Montreal Gazette*, July 7, 1831.

		s d	
Oak,	per foot........	1/4	@ 1/6
Elm,	"	7½	@ 8
Ash,	"	4½	@ ...
White Pine,	"	4	@ 4½
Red Pine,	"	7½	@ 8½

	L s	
Deals, white pine, bright, per Quebec standard hundred.....11/0		
floated, " 8/10.....9/0		
white spruce....................... 8/0......8/10		
Staves, standard, per mille.................. 30/0......31/0		
West India, white oak, do............ 10/0......31/0		
" , red oak, do........... 6/0 .....6/10		

5

Prices of Imported and Local Commodities

From *Montreal Gazette*, August 20, 1831.

European Produce, Prices Current.

	s.	d.	s.	d.
Vinegar, Bordeaux, per gal........	1	5	1	6
English, ...	1	6	0	0

East and West India Produce.

	s.	d.	s.	d.
Coffee, Jam[aica], middling, per lb...	0	10	0	11
Sugar, W. I. best, per cwt..........	41	0	0	0

Sundry British Productions.

	s.	d.	s.	d.
Coal, Newcastle, per chald[ron]......	25	0	30	0
Paint, White Lead, p. keg 28 lb.....	7	6	10	0

Iron, Pig, per ton................. £16   10 ...... £0   0

Exchange on London

Private........................ 60 days   ...... $9\frac{1}{2}$ 9
                                   90 days   ......   9 $8\frac{1}{2}$

Drafts on New York, 3 days sight, $\frac{1}{2}$ to 1 per cent.

Freight to Liverpool	s.	d.
Wheat, per bushel..............................	1	0
Ashes, per ton meas............................	40	0
Timber, do. do. do.............................	40	0
Deals, do. do. do............................	6	10

Canadian & United States Produce.

	s.	d.		s.	d.
Ashes, 1st. Pot, per cwt..............	32	3	......	32	6
Flour, Canadian Superfine...........	29	6	......	30	6
Fine................	28	0	......	28	6
Middling............	25	0	......	0	0
Grain, Wheat, U. C. per 60 lbs.......	6	4	......	6	7
L. C. per minot........	5	3	......	5	4
Hay, per ton......................	25	0	......	37	6
Provisions, Hams, per lb.............	0	7	......	0	8
Lard...................	0	$5\frac{1}{2}$	......	0	0
Butter, Salt..............	0	7	......	0	0
Cheese, ...	0	4	......	0	5
Wood, Timber, W. Oak, p. cu. ft......	1	0	......	1	3
R. Pine..............	0	6	......	0	0
W. Pine.............	0	$3\frac{1}{2}$	......	0	4
New Ships with Spars, per ton .	£8	0	......	£8	10
Whiskey, U.C. Proof, per gal.........	2	7	......	0	0

6

Prices of Tailored Clothing in Montreal

From *Montreal Gazette*, December 7, 1833.

Fall arrivals:—Metropolitan fashion

Bax & Co. *Tailors and Habit makers*, from Messrs. Stultz & Coopers, London, have the pleasure to inform their numerous

Friends, they are now receiving their WINTER STOCK of Superior West of England CLOTHS and CASSIMERES, which (for cash upon delivery) they are enabled to afford at the following extremely low prices:—

	£.	s.		£.	s.
Extra Saxony Black or Blue Dress Coats...	4	4	@	0	0
Surtout do, faced with silk, Serge.........	5	0	@	0	0
Do. do. do. do, Cassimere Trowsers...	1	14	@	0	0
Vests................................	0	15	@	0	17
Fancy Figured Silk Vests................	0	15	@	1	0

Ladies Habits and Cloaks, (some of which B. & Co. are now making in a most elegant style), Gentlemen's Great Coats and Cloaks, Liveries, &c. &c. at equally moderate prices.

Place d'Armes, Oct. 22, 1833

7

Quebec Lumber Prices for 1847

From Forsyth and Bell's *Annual circular and prices current* (Quebec), December 9, 1847.

	s.	d.		s.	d.
White pine, inferior and ordinary rafts, measured off, according to size, quality and manufacture..............	0	0	@	0	3
Do. Good and Superior......	0	3¼	@	0	5
Do. in Shipping Order.......	0	3½	@	0	5
Red Pine, in shipping order, 40 feet, average.............	0	9	@	0	9½
Do. in the raft, according to size and quality...........	0	6	@	0	9½
Oak, by the dram, (Lake) measured off.................	1	2	@	0	0
Elm, in shipping order, 38 @ 40 feet	0	7½	@	0	8½
Do. in the raft, according to average, quality and manufacture.................	0	5	@	0	8
Tamarac or Hacmatac, square...	0	5½	@	0	7½
Do. Do. flatted..........	0	4	@	0	6

	£.	s.	£.	s.	
Staves, standard, per M., fair specification.............	30	0	@ 32	10	
Do. W.O. Pun..............	11	10	@ 12	10	
Do. R.O. Pun.............	8	0	@ 9	0	
Deals, Pine, floated..........	9	0	@ 9	10	} and 2/3
Do. Bright................	10	10	@ 12	10	} for seconds
Do. Spruce, 1st quality......	6	10	@ 7	0	
Do. do. 2nd quality.......	5	0	@ 5	5	

N.B. Parties in England will bear in mind that timber sold *in the Raft* subjects the purchaser to great expense in dressing and at times heavy loss for culls—if sold in shipping order, the expense of shipping only to be added.

INDUSTRIAL GROWTH:—THE BEGINNINGS OF FACTORY INDUSTRY

The colonial system of the first empire had jealously guarded against the development of manufacturing in the colonies, that of the second, beyond imposing preference on colonial imports of British goods, was indifferent. The shelter of the protection given by distance, the difficulties of transportation, and the stimulus of favourable conditions together with local initiative, slowly developed industry. Thus in Lanark County, suitable water-power and the skill in weaving brought over by the pioneers (weavers displaced by power looms were.the first settleis) produced an industry which still constitutes the district one of the chief centres of woollen manufacturing. Again, the blacksmith shop of the original McLaughlin at Oshawa became first a shop for making waggons, then a small factory, later a large carriage factory, and lastly a motor-works.

REFERENCE: Andrew Haydon, *Pioneer sketches in the district of Bathurst* (Toronto, 1925), for the woollen industry.

1

Ship-building at Montreal

From *Montreal Gazette*, May 3, 1814.

On Sunday last was launched from the Yard of Mr. David Munn the fine Ship *Britannia*, of 650 tons; the largest vessel ever built in this port.

2

Fulling and Carding Mill in Montreal

From *Montreal Gazette*, September 30, 1816.

Under the Wind Mill Point, there is now building a floating manufactory, or in other words, a House for a Fulling and Carding Machine. This building is about 28 feet square, forming two respectable and separate apartments: the one for a family to live in, the other for business. The building is supported by two scows, or boats, solidly built, about 4 feet apart. In the interval, a large water wheel will be fixed to propel the machinery. The proprietor, early in the spring, intends anchoring in the middle of the strongest current of the St. Lawrence, where the machinery will be set in motion, and his family all lodged in comfort, on the watery expanse; thus saving the expence of purchasing a dear building lot. In the winter the building will be removed to a place of safety, where it will answer as an excellent tavern.

3
Iron Works and Hemp Manufacture in Upper Canada
From *Montreal Gazette*, November 6, 1822.

YORK, October 17

It would be difficult for us to do justice to those feelings of exultation with which we announce the compleat success of two experiments highly important to the commerce, manufacturers, and future wealth and power of this great and promising country. They are indeed feelings of exultation, of honest pride, and of brilliant hope.—We allude to the progress of the *Marmora Iron Works*, and the superior articles of Bar Iron manufactured there; and to the success of an experiment wherein a specimen of Canadian *Hemp* was tried against an English Bolt in the Navy-Yard at Kingston. . . .

The people of Canada, generally, are not sufficiently aware of the great natural advantages of their situation, and the political advantages they enjoy, or they would prize them more highly than they do, and evince more activity and spirit of enterprize. We have repeatedly endeavoured, both by public and private admonition, to rouse such a spirit as would seize upon every ground of honorable competition in all those points which affect national wealth and aggrandizement. Before that universal insurrection of the provinces of America, which led to their independence of the Crown of Great Britain, one of their most serious complaints was that *they were not allowed to work their own iron*, but were *obliged to transport it to England, there to be manufactured into the most necessary articles*, such as *axes, nails, ploughs*, &c. &c. in order that England might monopolize the benefits of every species of manufacture.

But the really free and happy Canadians of the present day are under no such restrictions. So far is it otherwise, that the government, itself, has given a large order to the proprietor of the *Marmora Iron Works*, with a view to encourage them;—and there is no question that the patronage of government may be at all times obtained for any great or useful project.

4

The Fisheries of Lower Canada and their Encouragement

From Debate of the assembly of Lower Canada, reported in *Montreal Gazette*,
January 19, 1832.

House in Committee on Mr. CHRISTIE'S motion for the encouragement of the fisheries in this Province, Mr. PROULX in the Chair.

Mr. CHRISTIE said this was a proposal merely to enquire whether it was expedient to make legislative provision for the encouragement of the Fisheries in the Province. Fisheries were in all countries, which possessed the means of prosecuting them, considered as material objects of national industry, a source of prosperity and wealth, and merited liberal encouragement, or at least were well worth the attention of every legislature.—Accordingly every maritime nation had felt their importance, and gone far to encourage and extend them; particularly on the ground of their being a nursery for seamen. . . . The fisheries on the coast that belonged to this Province and to the other British Provinces in America, were a gold mine which had yet, as regarded this Province, scarcely been explored, and would be found to contain inexhaustable treasures, if properly cherished. The Fisheries in and adjacent to the Gulph of St. Lawrence had been a great object of jealousy and envy to the United States,—they coveted its participation— and every commercial treaty and convention made with them, shewed their eager desire to avail themselves of them—Such being the case, the only difficulty he saw in the question, was what was a reasonable encouragement, and how far we might go in that respect with a due consideration of the object, and of our means. He would endeavour to detail the encouragement already given to the fisheries alluded to, by law. The encouragement given by the British Act of 6 Geo. IV. cap. 114, is, in general terms, that "any sort of craft, food, and victuals, except spirits, and any sort of clothing and implements or materials, fit and necessary for the British fisheries in America, imported into the place, at or from whence such Fishery is carried on, in British ships," shall be "*duty free.*" . . .[1]

---

[1]For details of encouragement given to maritime fisheries at this time see section VI C, page 412*ff.*

There had been cleared from the port of Quebec for the fisheries in 1828, 138 vessels, the tonnage of which was 5738. This statement had been furnished by the Custom House, but it was proper to remark that some of these vessels had cleared out more than once during the season, the number of vessels therefore appeared greater than it really was.

Allowance was therefore to be made—perhaps one half of the number would be about the truth. He could not precisely state the tonnage of the small vessels employed in the country trade of Gaspé, but from a sketch furnished by a gentleman conversant in that trade, there were about 80 vessels belonging to the district of from 35 to 70 tons register that generally made three or four trips to Quebec, besides several others and about 15 shallops of from 15 to 20 tons, that are employed in the coasting trade in fish of the district and lower parishes. The whale fishery was also carried on from Gaspé Bay, which was subject to peculiar risks and disadvantages, and yet as being the beginning or germ, as it were, of that profitable pursuit, was highly deserving of encouragement and of the attention of the House. . . . A bounty for the cherishing of this fishery, would be expedient. Upon the whole his object was the encouragement of the fisheries in the Province in general, and not merely for those of the county he represented. If the House should adopt his proposal, it was his intention to move for a Special Committee to take into consideration the most eligible means of obtaining the end desired; and it seemed to him that the following propositions would deserve the attention of such Special Committee. 1st. A premium to the Quebec Merchants for the exportation of fish, equivalent at least to the freight from Gaspé or the Gulph to Quebec. 2d. A drawback of the $2\frac{1}{2}$ per cent. on all articles necessary for the fisheries, sent from Quebec thither. 3d. Premiums or bounties to the three barges or boats at every fishing station that shall catch and cure the greatest quantity of merchantable cod-fish. 4th. A tonnage bounty to whalers and bankers, sufficient at least, in case of an unfortunate season, such as the last one, to save them from ruin. The bounties and premiums should be so arranged as to go into the pockets of those who are actually engaged in taking the fish and preparing it for market. . . .

Mr. PAPINEAU observed, that in our situation the examples of other countries ought not to be allowed any weight.

The situation was widely different. As commercial and maritime states their political relations were different from ours, and ought to have no influence on our conduct. This colony was essentially agricultural, and nothing ought to be introduced to withdraw the attention of the people from that occupation. Only a small part of the province could be engaged in maritime objects and fisheries. Countries that have a great extent of coast will naturally have a numerous maritime population, the surplus of those engaged in agriculture when carried to its height; but in this country, with a vast extent of land uncleared and uncultivated it would be wrong to withdraw the attention of the people from agriculture and direct it to fisheries; it would be absurd to encourage them by premiums and drawbacks to abandon the permanent sources of prosperity which the hand of nature had opened up. The inhabitants were suffering distress from the failure of the crops, and it would be very impolitic, to lay out expense upon a distant and very thinly peopled portion of the province. The attempt to convert Canada which had but one outlet to the sea into a maritime country, and to bring her into competition with the United States, and with the province of Nova Scotia, and New Brunswick, would be as preposterous as if Austria which possesses only two sea ports in one corner of the empire, were to aim at becoming a great maritime and mercantile power.

5

Commodities Imported which could be Produced in Canada

From *Montreal Gazette*, November 5, 1829.

Upper Canada takes a great deal of salt from here [*Rochester, N.Y.*] and with it other purchases are made. However, Canada itself is not without salt springs, but a little more intelligence, activity, and capital is required to make them valuable; a duty of 6d. Halifax currency. per bushel on salt imported from the United States, which was about to be enforced, may be the means of their being worked more successfully. Plug tobacco in small quantities is also sold to the Canadians; they buy it for something under twelve cents, or sixpence the pound. This article would long since have ceased to be purchased by Canadians, had sufficient encouragement been given for its production there as an export to the Mother Country. . . .

Iron work is another article of Canadian imports; this would immediately cease if the superb works of Marmora, in Upper Canada, were brought into full play. There, with the finest ore in the world, plenty of limestone, fuel, and water power, nothing is wanting but a capital to continue the works in full operation for three years. Such a capital as is required is perhaps too large for a single mercantile house to lay out for so long a time. A liberal advance from Government, or the union of a body of wealthy partners, or a joint-stock company, would render the works a source of wealth to the proprietors, and of inestimable benefit to the Colony. I had subsequently an opportunity of seeing these works, and was astonished as much at their capabilities if brought into full operation, as at the capital that has already been laid out to render them so. The nature of the situation and climate require a three-year's outlay of money, as the transport to markets must be made over the snow in the winter, of the wares made the proceeding season, and then they must wait the year for sales, to be paid for in produce the third year; of course such outlay is like employing three capitals, a matter of too serious a consideration to one mercantile house of even large means. . . . Some of the metal has been sent to Birmingham, where its superior qualities have been fully acknowledged, in no way inferior to the finest Swedes' iron, and in other superior.

6

The Construction of Ships' Engines at Montreal

From *Montreal Gazette*, June 16, 1831.

We noticed the intended meeting of the proprietors of the *Tow Boat Company* to consider the expediency of adding to their line two Passage Boats, to give further facilities to the travelling community to pass between this city and Quebec. . . . The first of these Boats will be laid down immediately, and it is expected will be launched and have her engine put on board this fall, so as to commence her trips at the opening of the navigation in spring. Her engine, which will be 150 horse power, will, we understand, be built by the Messrs. Ward, who have already distinguished themselves highly as the manufacturers of those on board the *Hercules*, *John Molson*, and *British America*, and whose talents have more conspicuously shone forth in preparing those for the *John Bull*, whose power (260 horse) is believed to be infinitely superior to any other Boat now known to be in existence. The second Boat will be built during the winter, and will be propelled by an engine of 100 horse power, to be imported from England in the spring. It is satisfactory to state that the importation arises from the two foundries here being unable to undertake any additional work. The Messrs. Ward are actively engaged in placing on board the *John Bull* her engines and machinery, while Messrs. Bennett & Henderson are similarly employed with the Halifax steamer, *Royal William*. When the latter has her works on board, the St. Nicholas ferry boat, *Lady Aylmer*, is expected at the foot of the *Current* for a similar purpose. The last named engineers have likewise, we believe engines to make for the steamer *William IV*. building at Gananoque, and intended for the Lake *Ontario* trade.

7

Opening of a Paper Mill at Belleville

From *Montreal Gazette*, November 1, 1831.

We are happy in being enabled to announce, among the many improvements constantly going on in Belleville, the erection of an extensive and excellent paper mill, now in full operation. We have by us samples of straw and other wrapping paper, made at this mill, and we have no hesitation in pronouncing it at least equal to any paper of the kind manufactured in America. We are given to understand, that in the course of six weeks publishers of newspapers throughout the Province can be supplied with all kinds of paper at a reasonable price, and we sincerely trust that Messrs. John M'Lenehan & Co. the proprietors of that establishment, may meet with that support and success to which their enterprise so justly entitles them.

8

York's Elaborate Engine Works

From *Montreal Gazette*, May 7, 1833.

YORK FOUNDRY and STEAM ENGINE MANUFACTORY.— There is perhaps no establishment of the kind superior, if equal to this, in the British North American Provinces.—The works comprise seven turning lathes, a boring mill, drilling machine, blowing apparatus, &c., all of which are put into operation by one ten horse power high pressure engine. There are also ten or a dozen separate apartments in which are carried on the various businesses of moulding, pattern making, blacksmithing, Copper and Tin working finishing, Plough making, wheelwrighting, &c., &c. The quantity of iron melting averages at near a ton a day, and the number of workmen employed amounts to about eighty. Messrs. Sheldon, Dutcher, & Co. the proprietors of these extensive works are now making a number of steam engines—two of fifty horse power each, for the new steamer "Cobourg" now building at the village of that name, two ditto of thirty horse power each for the John By at Kingston—one of twelve horse power for Dry Dock at Niagara, and some others, to the amount altogether of near nine thousand pounds.

9

Annual Sale of Three Rivers' Stoves

From *Montreal Gazette*, August 29, 1833.

St. MAURICE AND THREE RIVERS' IRON WARES.—The Annual Sale of STOVES &C., will take place on the premises of Mr. JOHN PORTEOUS, *Notre Dame Street*, on Thursday, the 12th day of SEPTEMBER next, at ONE o'clock, when will be sold:—

600 to 700 Double Stoves, from 2 feet to 3 feet.
500 Single Stoves, from 20 inches to 3 feet.
—Also,—
Cooking and Franklin Stoves, Potash Kettles,
—and—
A quantity of Hollow Ware.
BEGLY, KNOX & Co

10

The Introduction and Improvement of the Coal Stove

(i)
From *Montreal Gazette*, December 7, 1833.

Dr NOTT'S PATENT STOVES
For Burning Coal.
ON SALE, with the Subscribers, the above named Stoves, of various patterns adapted to fire places, or to stand in the Room.

The public attention is particularly requested to these Stoves, combining as they do so many advantages over every other kind of Stove or Grate yet introduced in Canada.

The principle upon which these Stoves are constructed, is the result of innumerable scientific experiments, and they are recommended as possessing the following advantages:—

The quantity of Fuel requisite is not over one third to one quarter of that necessary to produce the same heat in any other Stove or Grate.

They are adapted for use in houses having little or no yard room, and save the labour and inconvenience attending the use of fire wood, and burn a much cheaper material. The fire requires making up but twice a day, is left with perfect safety, and is therefore, very suitable to Nurseries.

Of their suitableness in this climate, it is only necessary to observe, that in the Northern States of America they have superseded the use of every other kind, where coal is procurable, and are now doing so in the Churches, Chapels and large Public Halls in England.

The elegant and ornamental appearance given to these Stoves is an additional consideration to their convenience and economy, as compared with the ungainly form of the Canadian Stove used in burning wood as Fuel. Apply to

Atkinson & Co.
St. Eloi Street

(ii)

From Montreal Gazette, December 19, 1833.

This article is rapidly superseding the use of wood in the dwellings of our citizens, experience having removed the prejudice that existed against it when wood-fuel was cheaper and more abundant. Now it is pretty generally admitted that coal can be burned in a Canadian stove, and answer all the purposes required, with the advantage in saving of at least 50 per cent.

11

The Manufacture of Coaches at Toronto

From Toronto Patriot, quoted in Montreal Gazette, January 8, 1835.

Manufactures too are rapidly advancing in Toronto. Could it have been believed but a short time ago, that in 1834, carriages would be built in Toronto equal to London built? No man could have supposed it yet it is the fact. Messrs. Evans, Mills & Millar have an establishment that would do credit to Long Acre, and turn out as substantial and beautiful carriages as can be manufactured anywhere, and glad are we to learn that the wealthy afford them deserved patronage. Within a few days they have delivered a splendid coach to the Lord Bishop of Quebec which we all must feel proud to say, "this is of Toronto manufacture".

12

First Cotton Mill in Canada

(i)

From *Montreal Transcript*, August 20, 1844.

We refer our readers to the advertisement of Messrs. H. Wills[1] & Co., of Chambly, respecting their establishment at Chambly[2] for the manufacture of cottons. We hail the appearance of domestic manufactures among us with great satisfaction, as they will be the means of giving employment to the dense population of our rural districts, and of keeping the money spent in such articles in the Province—a serious matter when the balance of trade is most generally against us. We copy the following article on the subject from the Gazette of yesterday:—

"We received on Saturday, with peculiar gratification, a specimen of what we believe is the very earliest essay of Canadian Manufacture of Cotton. It is the produce of the British North American Cotton Company at their mills on the Richelieu above Chambly, the erection of which has been regarded with so much interest in the province. The article is a wadding, or thick fabric of cotton, not woven but compressed, and rather felt, and will be found of the greatest use in this climate in winter, for clothing and bedding, and for other purposes in combination with woollen or other more solid fabrics. It is a very excellent article of its kind, but we trust is but a beginning; for a very little extention of the same machinery as that employed in producing it will convert it into a thread, and from heavy twist the transition, by hand or power, to the manufacture of calico, is easy. This enterprise is

---

[1]Or Willis. See next document.
[2]In its edition of August 22, 1844, the *Transcript* corrected this to "St. Athanase, opposite St. Johns". See the next document.

one which deserves all encouragement. It is a healthy and a natural one, availing itself of the physical advantages the country affords, and directing its surplus labour into a proper channel."

(ii)

From *Montreal Transcript*, September 10, 1844.

British North American Cotton Company

A. H. Willis & Co.

HAVING opened their Manufacturing Establishment at St. Athanase, on the Richelieu, opposite St. Johns, beg leave to inform the Merchants throughout the Province, and particularly those in the Wholesale Branch of Trade, that they are now prepared to execute upon the shortest notice and most reasonable terms, all Orders for WHITE and BLACK COTTON WADDING, in packages containing 30 @ 40 dozen pieces each, 12 yards in length by 36 inches wide, or 36 inches square, as may best suit purchasers.—This article is admirably adapted to the various purposes for which in this climate it may be used by Clothiers, Milliners, Families, &c.

A. H. W. & Co. being in possession of the most perfect machinery, by which the raw material is thoroughly cleansed and manufactured, with other facilities for the management of this business, they indulge the belief that the Public will appreciate the advantages of consuming a superior article manufactured in this Province, thereby avoiding the Duties, Freights, &c. of importation.

Orders left with the undersigned, will meet with prompt attention.

CHARLES SEYMOUR,
Agent B. N. A. Cotton Company,
No. 201, St. Paul Street, Montreal

August 20

13

Commencement of Textile Industries in Eastern Townships

From *Montreal Transcript*, August 27, 1844.

HOME PRODUCTIONS

By the last number of the *Sherbrooke Gazette* we learn that a number of enterprising persons are about forming themselves into a Company, with the object of establishing a Cotton Factory, and other manufactures in the Township. The amount of capital required is $25,000, which is to be raised in shares of $100 each. A Committee composed of Messrs. E. Hale, S. Brookes, H. Smith, D. Thompson, and A. T. Galt has been appointed to take the necessary steps to organize the Company, procure machinery, &c., and arrangements have been entered into with a gentleman from Massachusetts,[1] who was present at the meeting, and who proposes to invest $2,000 in the undertaking, to purchase the machinery, and to act as general Superintendent.

It is intended to erect a building this fall, 40 by 80 feet, three stories high, to be located on the site of the old Saw Mill, just below the Magog bridge—the Land Company having generously offered to give the choice of a water privilege with its use free of rent for a term of 20 years. Machinery is to be employed to drive 1000 spindles, capable of turning out 300,000 yards of cotton cloth per annum.

In addition to a Cotton Factory, there are about to be put in operation in Sherbrooke, by the gentlemen named above, some half a dozen *Knitting Machines*, for the manufacture of woollen Drawers, Shirts, Stockings, &c. Arrangements have also been made for commencing soon, the manufacture of *Sewing Silk*, from the raw material.

For the establishment of these important works, the *Sherbrooke Gazette* says the Townships are mainly indebted to the exertions of Mr. James Scott, who, assisted by Mr. J. P. Lee, late of Boston, now of Sherbrooke, and a few other gentlemen, has been unceasing in his endeavors to effect the object.

14

A Review of the State of Manufacturing in Canada

(i)

From *Canadian Economist*, August 8, 1846.

As to manufactures, we conceive that both provinces are very well adapted for the development of that species of industry; and although we have not hitherto brought any kind of manufacture,

---

[1]Many, perhaps most, Canadian industries have received their initial requirements of technical skill from the United States.

except *Ashes*, to that degree of perfection which enables us to compete with other nations in *foreign* markets, it would be wrong on that account to infer that we have made no progress whatever in manufacturing industry.

We enumerate a few of the leading arts in which we have already made some progress:

1st. Distilling and Brewing.—Montreal alone produces about 4,000,000 gallons of Whiskey annually, and as many more of Table Ale, worth, together, about £750,000; and the quantity produced in the whole Province may be judged of by these facts.

2nd. There are four Foundries in Montreal, capable of producing steam-engines of the largest dimensions, and we may say machinery generally of the first order. We are not prepared to say how many more there are throughout the province. In addition to these may be enumerated the following crafts, viz.: Cabinet-makers, Tailors, Carpenters, Tinsmiths, Blacksmiths, House-builders, Stone-cutters, Nail-makers, Brick-makers, Carriage-makers, Soap and Candle makers, and a number of other arts and crafts, which employ thousands of our population, and the demand for whose industry is every year on the increase.

But our correspondent, we presume, in putting his question respecting Manufactures, had reference more particularly to manufactures of Wool, Cotton, Silk, and such like. There is a Cotton Factory in full operation at Chambly, and another, we believe, at Sherbrooke; a Woollen Factory recently established in the Upper Province; and a Glass Factory at St. Johns,—in short nothing but apathy among the people of this colony can prevent such establishments growing and multiplying year by year. The country is admirably adapted for them, abounding as it does in water-power and a numerous half-employed population.

As to the woollen manufacture, the Lower Province has been partially devoted to it from its earliest settlement. Every *habitant*, male or female, is clad to this day more or less in the rude fabrics of their own manufacture,—the man in his "étoffe du pays," and the woman in her "jupon." Why then is this manufacture, after thirty or fifty years' duration, not in a more advanced state of excellence? The answer to the question is the same as has been given respecting agriculture,—the want of education. Had the rural population been enlightened, they would have seen long ere this that their labour should be organized and directed; that, instead of each family in a district having its *loom*, which could furnish the family only with apparel of the rudest kind, each district should have had its *factory*, where the population could have been employed, and clothed at less expense and with superior fabrics. Had this been done years ago, the factory or factories in every district of Canada would now be powerful and flourishing; and the men, women, and children, who are now wasting half their life in idleness in the rural districts, would be *skilled operatives*, earning good wages and promoting the welfare of society at large.

(ii)

Can Canada become a manufacturing country?

From *Canadian Economist*, September 12, 1846.

This is an important inquiry, and more particularly so, since the change which has taken place in the commercial policy of Great Britain. Canada is now thrown upon her own resources, and if she wishes to prosper, those resources must be developed. . . . We now propose to give some additional particulars by which it will be seen that Canada is not destitute of the means of entering extensively into manufactures, and thereby greatly enlarging the means of her prosperity. And the first point we would notice is, the great water power which Canada possesses. This is an important element in the great resources at her command; and is an abundant compensation for the loss she experiences in the absence of all coal beds within her boundaries. Mr. Logan, our provincial geologist, not yet having completed his labours, we cannot now say what untold wealth lies buried under the surface of our earth; but we do know and have experienced the great value of the surface itself, in the magnificent crops which it is yielding, and therefore we can afford to wait awhile for the more full development of our mineral wealth. We have, however, but to turn our attention to Lake Superior, where copper ore is found in great abundance, and where the first steps are now being taken to open up the beds which there have been discovered. But to return to the manu-factories—

The cotton manufactory . . . in operation at Sherbrooke has been established about one year, and turns out about 1000 yards per day.

The one at Chambly was put into operation the past year, and turns out about 800 yards per day. The fabrics from both of these manufactories, although not equal in finish to those imported, are, nevertheless, superior in point of firmness and durability, and are sold at about the same price.

There is a woollen manufactory at Sherbrooke which has been in operation a number of years; but, unfortunately, we have not been enabled to obtain any statistics regarding it for our present number.

In Cobourg, Canada West, a woollen manufactory has been put into operation this season, which, when in full employ, is calculated to work off near 5000 yards of cloth a week. About 100,000 lbs. of wool is grown in the Newcastle District annually, and this amount, doubtless, might and will be quadrupled in a few years. Indeed, there are but few parts of Canada West where wool could not be produced to a large extent; and in the Eastern Townships, of Canada East, the fine grazing lands there ought to produce, at least, 1,500,000 lbs. annually. The neighbouring state of Vermont produces about 4,000,000 lbs. annually. We have three cordage manufactories in Montreal where about 300 tons of hemp are manufactured, and the amount could be doubled in case of need.— To one of these manufactories is attached machinery for grinding and calcining Plaster of Paris for agricultural purposes, and for stucco work, where about 1000 tons per annum are disposed of.

Hemp surely can be grown in Canada West, and we hope soon to hear that the experiment which has already been made at Niagara, most successfully, in growing hemp, will be followed up in other favourable sections of the Province.[1]

There are three paper manufactories in Canada East. The most important one is at Portneuf, about forty-five miles above Quebec. It is owned by the Messrs. Miller of this City, who have expended but recently about £10,000 in enlarging the premises. They manufacture printing, writing, and wrapping paper— principally the former. They estimate that they can turn out about 600 tons of paper annually.

There is a paper manufactory at Chambly, in full operation, and another at Stanstead, both of which together turn out about the same quantity of paper as the Portneuf mills.

---

[1]Attempts to introduce the culture of hemp into Canada have been repeatedly made, the first during the French régime. See volume I of this work, also document no. 3 of this section, page 291.

There are five or six paper mills in Canada West, of whose capacities we have no certain information. We think, however, that with these data there is sufficient assurance that, in a few years, Canada will be enabled to supply her own demand, with the exception of the more costly qualities of paper.

The most extensive manufactory, however, in Canada East, are the St. Maurice iron works, in the rear of Three Rivers. The iron ore found there is not only abundant, but is of the best description. The hammered iron manufactured from it, is quite equal to the best English iron; and the stoves cast from it are considered superior to the best Scotch castings. Although we have no statistics at hand to guide us in our estimates of the amount of iron manufactured there, yet we know that many thousands of tons are annually turned out even under the very great disadvantages with which the forges and blasts are worked. The system hitherto adopted and carried out there is of the most primitive description; but since a change is about taking place of proprietors, we may naturally look for an improved method being adopted, whereby a much larger amount of manufacture will be produced at a great reduction in price. Some idea may be formed of the magnitude of these works, when we state that from 1200 to 1500 mouths are dependent upon them.

The glass manufactory, noticed as established at St. Johns, has been in operation something more than one year. It has two furnaces, and can turn out 100 half boxes of glass a day. Sand, used in the manufacture of glass, is said to be found in abundance at Beauharnois and at Vaudreuil.

LEATHER, an article of great importance, is manufactured extensively throughout the Province. There are two or three tanneries in the vicinity of Montreal, which employ, severally, a capital of from £12,000 to £15,000.

STOVES are being cast in almost all sections of the Province, and we hope to see the time when we shall supply our own demand.

NAIL FACTORIES already exist to such an extent that we do not require to import a single cut nail.

AXES are manufactured largely; if not to the full requirement of the Province, we have no doubt they might be.

AGRICULTURAL IMPLEMENTS, thus far, have but imperfectly engaged the attention of the manufacturer, although we see no reason why we should not make them as well as our neighbours.

20

MINING

Bog iron had been utilized around Three Rivers long before the English conquest. By 1836, deposits in Upper Canada had also been found and were being worked (see section I C, page 126; also section III D, page 291). The presence of copper and silver in the region of the upper lakes having been determined, much money was spent in its development, but in this period little was accomplished. There was virtually noo ther mining activity.

REFERENCE: W. J. Donald, *The Canadian iron and steel industry* (Boston, 1915).

1

A Native Supply of Salt

From *Hamilton Free Press*, quoted in *Montreal Gazette*, January 8, 1835.

We return our thanks for the sample of salt sent us last week by Messrs. Parker & Co. of this town from the manufactory at Saltfleet. The article is good and will bear comparison with the best specimens of Onondaga. It is highly gratifying to us, as it surely must be to all who have the interests of the Province at heart, to find that we can now supply ourselves with this prime necessary of civilized life, without obligation to a foreign country or even a Mother Country.

2

Discovery of Lithographic Stone in Upper Canada

From *Montreal Gazette*, quoted in *Montreal Transcript*, November 23, 1844.

Our able and indefatigable geologist, Mr. Logan, has in one of his recent surveys of the Upper Province, made a discovery which promises to be of great importance. He has found near Lake Simcoe, and explored to the extent of sixty or seventy miles, a great bed of lithographic stone, namely, that which is used in the lithographic art for taking the drawings and producing the impressions on paper. Hitherto Germany has been the sole source from which the world has been supplied with this valuable article, and the supply there is limited, and distant from any port of shipment. Specimens have been sent to London, and pronounced by competent judges to be of the finest quality.

3

The St. Maurice Forges:—Value of the Property in 1846

From *Montreal Transcript*, August 8, 1846.

The sale of the property known as the St. Maurice Forges, situated about seven miles in rear of the town of Three Rivers, took place on Tuesday. The bidding was spirited between the purchaser, Henry Stuart, Esq., Advocate, of this city, Theodore Hart, Esq., and a son of the Hon. Mr. Bell the present lessee. Mr. Hart bid up to £5,575. It was not generally expected at Three Rivers that it would realize so much. It will be necessary to adopt many improvements, and to expend a large sum of money on the property which it is understood the present proprietor is prepared to do.

4

The Copper Mines of the Upper Lakes

From Charles Robb, "Mineral resources of British North America", in *Eighty years' progress*, 322.

The attention of travellers was attracted to the rich copper ores of this region as far back as the middle of the seventeenth century; and in 1770 a company was actually formed by some enterprising Englishmen to work copper mines on the north shore of Lake Superior; but owing to the remoteness and inaccessible nature of the country, it was found impracticable to continue operations for any lengthened period. In 1845 when the excitement consequent upon the great discoveries of copper on the south shore of Lake Superior was at its height, similar mining schemes were instituted on the Canadian side, and companies were formed in Montreal, Quebec and various other Canadian cities, who with praiseworthy zeal, though questionable discretion, sent armies of explorers and miners into the field, equipped in the most extravagant style, and who certainly obtained abundance of ore, but at a cost greatly above its value. The consequence of these rash and imprudent proceedings was that most of the companies speedily abandoned their operations, after the irretrievable loss of large sums of money; and with those who have continued in the business till the present time, the debts thus incurred have proved a severe drag upon their subsequent more cautious proceedings. The Montreal Mining Company have prosecuted their works till this time, and with tolerable success, at the Bruce Mine located on the shores of Lake Huron.

5

Prospects for Copper- and Silver-mining on the North Shore of Lake Superior

From *Montreal Herald*, quoted in *Montreal Transcript*, August 27, 1846.

A correspondent furnishes the following, from Sault Ste. Marie:—

It is now ascertained, beyond a doubt, that the north shore of Lake Superior is as rich, if not richer, than the south, in copper and silver ores. The explorations that are now going on, are bringing to light some of the richest veins of these minerals, that have been found on the shores of this wonderful Lake. . . .

I have been shown some magnificent specimens both of native copper, and of the best of all ores, the gray sulphuret; and I am assured by those who have visited the mineral regions, and on whose statements I can rely, that there is "any quantity" of mineral there. I hear of four companies that have been on the ground this season, exploring and making their locations, and I am glad to learn that these companies are composed of men of wealth and influence, and engage in the business of mining, as a safe and profitable way for the investment of capital, and not like many of the American Companies, merely for purposes of specula- tion. These companies have contributed, for the first outlay of expenses, from ten to twenty thousand dollars, and they are all making preparations for going into the business in an extensive manner, though the most that can be done this season will be to secure and examine locations, and open the doors to these long concealed mines of wealth.

From what information I can gather from those that are not, as well as those that are, interested, I think they have all dis- covered rich veins of mineral, and have need now of only proper management, in order to turn their discoveries to good account. These four companies are:—'The British North American Mining Company,' on a location made by Colonel Prince, of Sandwich,

C. W., on Spar Island—the ' Quebec and Lake Superior Mining Association,' located with the two Montreal Companies at Mamainse, Michipicoten Island and St. Ignace.

The rich mineral discoveries on Lake Superior are beginning to attract the attention of English capitalists, and a few more such men as Colonel Doran, President of the 'Montreal and Lake Superior Copper Company,' will do much for their success. This gentleman came from England early in the spring, and besides his wealth, he brought with him great practical experience in the whole business of Copper mining.

Nothing shows the favourable position which the Canada Companies have taken, better than the value already placed by the public on their Stock. While many American companies' Stock, founded on very good locations, is selling at from five to ten dollars a share, twenty-five to forty dollars per share is offered here for Stock in the 'North Shore Companies,' as they are termed.

As yet all the ores from Copperdom have been taken to Boston to be smelted—this mistaken notion, I see, is soon to be corrected, by having smelting works erected either on the ground or at the most favorable point, the Sault. It is estimated that the extra expense for the next year of transportation on the bare ores, over that of the pure metal, would amount to a sum sufficient to build a smelting establishment. For this purpose a Company has been formed, called the 'Ste. Marie Falls Mining and Smelting Company,'—composed of the principal men of the Sault, together with some Eastern Capitalists, and they mean to have their works in operation early the coming season.

LABOUR AND WAGES

Wages are quoted incidentally in the documents of section I. But little organization of labour was effected in this period, what there was naturally being either in the skilled trades or in that occupation in which a large number of men were concentrated, *ie.* "longshore" work.

REFERENCE: H. A. Logan, *The history of trade union organization in Canada* (Chicago, 1928).

1

Wages of Labourers

From *A few plain directions*, 100.

Labourers are paid from four to six shillings a day, besides their provisions.

2

Wages of Agricultural Labourers and of Country Artizans

From *Quebec Mercury*, quoted in *Montreal Gazette*, June 30, 1831.

In the recent discussions which have taken place on the condition of emigrants arriving from the Mother Country, many of whom, it must be confessed, are in a state of great wretchedness, the rate of wages has been variously estimated for both Provinces. In this Province, it is, perhaps, a more difficult matter to fix a standard than in Upper Canada, because few of the inhabitants of French origin have more land than they can cultivate with the aid of their families, and, therefore, they rarely employ hired servants, except in hay time and harvest. In Upper Canada, it is much more common to hire agricultural labourers, and there the rate of wages may be more easily ascertained. We are enabled, on good authority, to state, that in the Newcastle District, in that Province, where the Hon. Peter Robinson is at present engaged in locating settlers, the following were the general prices paid during the past month:—

Carpenters, 7s. 6d. per diem. ⎱ without board.
Masons....ditto.......... ⎰

310

Labourers, by the day, 2s. 6d. to 3s. and found in board. By the month, 40s. to 60s. and boarded, and the same rate is paid to those who engage by the year.

Women servants, living in the family, earn from 15s. to 20s. per month.

It is also stated, that tailors and shoemakers find ready employment in that District; and that a brickmaker, having a little capital to commence with, would find an advantageous opening. Thus, there is encouragement in that quarter, at least, for a portion of the strangers who have arrived this year in our harbour.

3

One of the First Canadian Trade Unions

From *Montreal Gazette*, March 4, 1834.

It is hereby intimated to the Public in general, and to JOURNEYMEN CARPENTERS in particular, that in consequence of the recent conduct of JOURNEYMEN CARPENTERS and joiners in this city, and of a COMBINATION entered into by them, it has been deemed necessary to obtain the general sentiments of the Masters who have unanimously adopted the following RESOLUTIONS, viz.:—

1st. That the Trade of Carpenters and Joiners, has from the earliest date to the present day, been considered by all nations and countries as one of the most useful and ornamental.

2nd. That in order to support its respectability it is the duty of Masters to agree in the establishment of such rules and orders, as will most effectually protect it from any arbitrary impositions either by the Journeymen or others who have not its interest at heart.

3d. We view with distrust the combined exertions of those Journeymen who have lately formed themselves into a Society called "The Mechanics' Protecting Society of Montreal," who by their conduct last year most decidedly injured both their Masters and themselves, without any advantage resulting to the public, and who, by their present conduct, are bringing further discredit upon themselves and ruin upon the Trade generally.

4th. We did not last year oppose the journeymen in their demand of reduced time, with a continuance of their former summer wages, because they took advantage of the season after our general work was engaged, and it would have greatly retarded our business; we, therefore, suffered an average loss of about fifteen per cent upon all labor on contracts engaged, and of course the public suffered the same proportion in the accounts of days' work.

5th. We now, in consequence of the present combinations consider ourselves called upon to make a stand against their arbitrary and injurious conduct, and after mature and calm deliberation, have resolved that the long established custom of this place previous to last year is the best, and that it shall remain unaltered; we have, therefore, agreed that from the first of April to the first of November a day's work shall consist of eleven working hours; and from the first of November to the first of April a day's work shall be regulated by the old established custom, and we have confident reliance in the concurrence of the public, to enable us to carry these regulations into effect.

6th. We find from our comparative statements of journeymen now in employ, that the disaffection is not unanimous, nor so general as has been supposed. Out of ninety Society-men now at work there are only twenty-five who have not expressed themselves dissatisfied with the conduct of the Society, and satisfied, according to verbal agreement, to continue work until the first of April, without alteration; furthermore,. we find that we can very well dispense with any or all of those men who have left their work, until they may be willing without opposition to continue their services as formerly.

7th. This understanding of masters is not partial, upwards of thirty (which comprises nearly the whole of those who have men in their employ) having agreed to the foregoing Resolutions, and resolved by their future actions to support the respectability of the Trade. The masters pledge themselves to the public to use all diligence to give satisfaction, disclaiming any attempt at arbitrary or oppressive measures, as charged against them by the Society of Journeymen.

8th. We are further unanimous in declaring our opinion that the Society calling itself the "Mechanics' Protecting Society," is calculated to produce the worst consequences; such a body of men cannot be considered competent to what they have undertaken, neither are they likewise [likely?] to confine themselves to decent and becoming order, they are therefore dangerous to the peace and safety of good citizens. They have already attempted, by combined threats, to force peaceable men to leave their working employ; not wishing to create difficulty and dissension we have hitherto overlooked the circumstance, which we hope will not occur again.

Montreal, March 1, 1834

4

La Société du Bord:—A Longshoremen's Union

From Narcisse Rosa, *La construction des navirès à Québec et ses environs* (Quebec, 1897), 17, 19.

La Société du Bord. . . .

D'après les règlements de la société, le minimum d'ouvriers qu'elle mettait au chargement d'un navire de ce tonnage était de vingt-un.

Pour charger le dit navire onze hommes auraient suffi. . . .

Le coût du chargement ne fut que de soixante-deux cents le mille pieds, tandis qu'en employant la Société de Bord il aurait été de un dollar et dix cents.

5

Wages in the Ship-building Industry of Quebec

From *Ibid.*, 10, 14.

Les gages de l'ouvrier étaient autrefois (vers 1839) à peu près les mêmes qu'aujourd'hui; cependant il vivait avec plus d'aise que l'ouvrier de nos jours.

La moyenne du salaire des galfats et des charpentiers était de cinq à sept schellings par journée de travail; cependant elle variait avec les circonstances et la compétition que se faisaient les patrons-constructeurs. Ainsi, en 1840, ils ont gagné jusqu'à onze schellings par jour et ce maximum a diminué dans l'espace de quelques mois à trois schellings et dix-huit sous. Mais ce n'était pas là le cours régulier des gages.

En l'année 1843, les gages ont généralement été meilleurs qu'en 1842, et cette augmentation a duré jusqu'en 1848. Pendant l'hiver de 1848-49, ils ont baissé à deux schellings, tandis que de 1850 à 1854 ils ont monté jusqu'à deux et quatre dollars par jour.

6

Emigration of Labour for Ship-building from Quebec

From George Gale, *Quebec 'twixt old and new* (Quebec, 1915), 74.

Many of the laborers, when the shipping trade showed a permanent decline, left Quebec, the residents of the coves locating in the Southern States, while those of Cap Blanc, who were experts with the axe, found their way to the shipyards on the shores of the Great Lakes.

TRADING POLICY, IMPERIAL AND LOCAL, 1783-1850

INTRODUCTORY

BOTH in the mother country and the colonies most of the period was dominated by the principles of mercantilism and when that doctrine was given up in the metropolis it continued to be pursued with unabated fervour in the colonies. It was more than a mere scheme of trade; it was a complete theory of empire, providing for the appropriate participation of each unit in the life of the whole, all being bound together with the magic thread of trade. Hence its persistence, despite the destruction by the withdrawal of the original colonies in 1783 of the conditions which had given it reality.

Our period may be described as marked by the decline and fall of mercantilism, the problem being to trace the steps of the decline and to understand the consequences of the fall. To do this satisfactorily requires an acquaintance with British and colonial public opinion and with the chief statutory enactments. These matters must be studied in other works.

After the Revolution the aim of English commercial policy continued unchanged—the maintenance of a self-contained, regulated empire, with the scales loaded somewhat, but not unduly, in favour of the British merchant. That ideal under the new conditions was impracticable and mercantilism became even more a mere struggle of vested interests than it had previously been.

Two lines along which policy ran may be distinguished after 1783. In the first place, what was to be the relation of the remaining colonies to the lost? Was the letter of mercantilistic law to be applied, with its complete prohibition of trade between colonies and foreign countries? Were ships from the south side of the lakes to be kept out of the harbours on the north? Were they to be kept out of the Atlantic harbours? Logic would have said yes, but, fortunately, in the case of the inland commerce, common sense prevailed and, except for the prohibition of American vessels in the lower St. Lawrence, interference with the intercourse between the two countries was slight. Interference would have been short-sighted for it would have brought fiscal retaliation and the loss of the American western market. On the coast the case was different and there was waged a long and dreary war of orders-in-council and presidential proclamations, with the use of such weapons as tonnage duties, absolute prohibitions, free ports, "most favoured nation" clauses, and so on.

The second line has to do with the establishment of a new set of colonial preferences. The people of the British Isles had long been forced to eat no other sugar than West Indian; in this period, they were to be forced to use very little other wood than British North American. These "differential duties", acting so markedly in favour of the colonist, resulted in the attitude of the new empire towards imperial control of commercial policy (including the monopoly of colonial trade), being the reverse of that of the old; the revolted colonies had disliked control because it exploited them, those remaining loved it because it gave them valuable privileges. Thus, when the imposts at last became too onerous for the British taxpayer to bear, it was Great Britain that revolted from the old colonial system and the colonies which clamoured for its continuance. Peel's budgets of 1842-1846, especially that of 1846, may be said to have been the British Declaration of Independence, the British Revolution from the British Empire.

Peel's budgets were but the culmination of the tendencies of a generation. The old system had held almost unchanged until 1820, but, from that year on, change was rapid and under William Huskisson at the board of trade, several acts were passed which removed nearly all the restrictive provisions of the old system but did not touch the privileges of the colonies. From Huskisson to Peel and thence to the last requisite measure, the abolition of the navigation acts in 1849, is a straight line.

REFERENCES: A. T. Mahan, *Sea-power in its relations to the War of 1812* (Boston, 1905); S. E. Morison, *Maritime history of Massachusetts* (Boston, 1921); H. E. Egerton, *A short history of British colonial policy* (London, 1897, now more or less superseded); Alexander Brady, *William Huskisson and liberal reform* (Oxford Press, 1928); Gerald S. Graham, *British policy and Canada, 1774-1791: "A study in eighteenth century trade policy* (London, 1930); A. R. M. Lower, The sentimental view of empire" (*History*, January, 1927); "Three centuries of empire trade" (*Queen's Quarterly*, May, 1932).

THE COLONIAL POLICY OF GREAT BRITAIN

(a)—IMPERIAL COMMERCIAL POLICY, 1783-1846

The documents in this division are designed to give a view of the general principles of mercantilism and of their Canadian application in the period of their decline.

1

Vermont and the St. Lawrence Outlet

From Canadian Archives, *series B*, The Haldimand papers, CLXXVII (2), 681. For the "Vermont question", see W. A. Mackintosh, "Canada and Vermont; A study in historical geography" (*Canadian Historical Review*, March, 1922).

Sir:—

The under written letter is a copy of an original brought in by the loyalists; the woman refer'd to says it was given to her by Capt Ebenezer Allen and a Mr. Sawyer, two noted rebels and they requested she might deliver it to a certain person (with whom they are well acquainted) at this place.

I am, Dr. sir,
Your humble & oblig'd servant,

Geo Smyth

To Captain Mathews   Freedom, 1782
Sir:—

There is no law in Vermont to prohibit trading with the Government of Canada at this time, and as interest is the governing principle of mankind, we who compose this piece, would wish to take a share in common blessings and as we are acquainted with you, knowing that you can help yourself in helping us, would request you to give one of us the earliest intelligence, respecting that matter, viz.:

Wheather if we should be able to advance one thousand hard dollars to you, you would procure that worth of light goods at some place hereafter to be agree'd upon, at such a price as would answer to open a trade, if so, give us the notice by a letter, which you can convey to your wife. Writing names is dangerous, for knowledge of us enquire of Mrs Putman, who bears this letter.

Freedom

2

Extent of Trade Desired by Vermont

From Canadian Archives, *Q*, XXVIII, 7.

Levi Allen to Lord Dorchester

May it please your Lordship:—

The wishes of the inhabitants of Vermont to me signified, are to have your Lordship's permission to bring into the Province, free of all duties and customs, masts, spars, bowsprits, yards, oak ship plank, pine deck ditto, futtocks, knees, ship timber, and lumber of every sort, kind and quality, tar, pitch, turpentine, tallow, and all sorts of naval stores, iron, flax seed, hemp, honey, beef, pork, wheat, barley, pease, indian corn, rye, butter, cheese and all and every kind of provision, pot and pearl ashes, apples, cider and vinegar, or anything else therein not enumerated, the same being the growth and produce of Vermont.

And further, to have liberty to sell or barter the produce of Vermont aforesaid in the Province of Quebec, or any other of his Majesty's Provinces, and if need be to transport the same to Great Britain, or the British West Indies, in British bottoms, agreeably to the Navigation Act, and to bring back in return British manufactures, East or West India goods, or the produce of His Majesty's Colonies, by way of the waters of the River St. Lawrence to Vermont, (peltries of all kind only excepted) paying the same duties and customs the inhabitants of Quebec pay and no more.

Levi Allen

Quebec, 22nd November, 1786

3

First Actual Provision for the Transit Trade

From Canadian Archives, *Q*, XXVIII, 4.

Dorchester's allowance of the entry of American products marked the origin of a problem that was not disposed of until Great Britain made herself into a free-trading nation. Were these products, coming in over the inland border and going out from the St. Lawrence to the British market, to enter British ports on the same favourable fiscal terms as colonial? Until about 1825, timber was the chief item and while an attempt was made (1821) to tax American timber, in practice it proved impossible to determine the origin of any given parcel and consequently American timber enjoyed the colonial preference until its export ceased. Flour and wheat were more easily watched but owing to the vagaries of the British corn laws, the importance of these was not so great.

Lord Dorchester to Lord Sydney

Quebec, 13th June, 1787

My Lord:—

Soon after my arrival here, Mr. Levi Allen came to me, said he was commissioned by the State of Vermont to form a treaty of commerce and produced his credentials. I told him I was not authorized to form treaties, but that I was well disposed to live in friendship with all the neighbouring States, and after taking care of the King's subjects and their interests, I should in the second place pay every reasonable attention to their prosperity and convenience, desiring at the same time he would give me in writing the wishes of the people of Vermont (A)[1] that they might be duly considered.

An opinion had prevailed here, that by the King's order in Council, all things were prohibited from coming into the Province by land or inland navigation, which I conceived to be an erroneous construction of that order, the true object and meaning whereof appeared to me clearly to concern the navigation by sea, and the third and fourth articles of my instructions, relative to trade and navigation, I thought sufficient to remove any doubt; besides I could not think it possible that British ships were forbid to carry from the river Saint Lawrence, what is permitted to be imported into Great Britain by ships of the United States, from their own ports. However, notwithstanding my own conviction, I consulted the Chief Justice whose opinion of its legality being very clear and satisfactory and being also convinced of the utility of the measure I issued the order (B)[1] for opening in some degree a commercial intercourse, by Lake Champlain, and as it was suggested that under certain restrictions it might also be of advantage to permit tobacco, pot and pearl ashes to come into the Province, I recommended to the Legislative Council to pass an ordinance for that purpose (C),[1] which was done accordingly, with a clause impowering the Governor and Council to repeal the same, should they at any time judge it expedient.

The whole of these regulations form but an experiment, the effects of which we shall soon perceive on the minds of our neigh-

---

[1]The documents referred to (A, B, C) are enclosed with the original despatch. Enclosure A is the previous document.

bours and on our own trade and navigation, and this mode seems the most advisable for the present.

Dorchester

4

A Specific Example of the Vermont Trade

From Canadian Archives, Q, XXXVI (2), 466.

July, 1788

His Excellency the Rt. Honourable,
Guy Lord Dorchester, etc. etc. ;

Your Lordship having been graciously pleased to transmit to the principal officers of the navy our proposal of the 20th July 1787, in the name of Levi Allen only, for a mast contract, in consequence whereof the business is in great forwardness and on Saturday last was further pleased to give encouragement to remove such obstacles as might otherwise prevent carrying the business into execution, for which we entertain a high sense of your Lordship's beneficence to us.   In the proposal your Lordship transmitted home, we had no idea of going further than delivering the masts, spars etc, in some part of America, as had heretofore been practised, in which case there would have been no obstacle in the way, as we have the trees on our own land, and two of the present subscribers are well skilled in cutting, drawing and rafting timber.

We have before us a copy of the proposals of contract sent out to your Lordship, by which we see that the masts etc., are to be delivered into his Majesty's yards in England and the West Indies.

The want of connections in Great Britain is the main obstacle, bonds being requisite previous to making the contract for carrying the same into execution agreeable to the spirit of the contract, we have no objections to deliver the masts, etc., in England, provided we can get the contract, in which case we would immediately before the same was published purchase all the trees proper for the use of the Navy on both sides of Lake Champlain, to prevent their being destroyed, by the rapid increase of settlements and agriculture, reserving large quantities on our own land for his Majesty's Navy in future.

The business we are highly sensible is extensive, at the same time our local situation, connections and circumstances are very well adapted to carry the same into execution.

21

Nothing is wanting but the foreign connections and as a day is to be appointed in the latter end of August next, to receive proposals, not one moments time is to be lost in forwarding ours.

Ethan Allen
Levi Allen
Ira Allen

5

Regulation of the Inland Import Trade

From Canadian Archives, *Q*, CCLXXXIV, 245.

Lieutenant Governor Russell to the Duke of Portland

Upper Canada
York, July 17th, 1798

My Lord Duke,

As the Commerce between the United States and this Province is now increasing to a considerable Magnitude, and sundry articles are daily brought in from thence, which are the Produce & Manufacture of the East & West Indies as well as of Great Britain & Ireland, I judged it to be my Duty to take such measures (for collecting the Duties imposed thereon by the British Parliament—and laying others by the Legislature of this Province equal to those which had been laid on the like articles by the Legislature of Lower Canada) as can be taken consistently with the letter & Spirit of the late Treaty of Amity & Commerce between Great Britain & the United States of America.

I was influenced herein by two important considerations. The one—That, since the Lower Province had agreed to give to this Province a share of the Duties collected on Imports into Quebec and Montreal proportioned to its annual consumption of those Imports, the Merchants of Lower Canada had in my opinion a right to expect that we should enable them to come to our Markets upon equal Terms at least with those of the United States, by subjecting the latter to the Payment of the same Duties &c which the others paid below—The other was, that I might secure to the Revenue for supporting the Civil Expenditure of this Province, the Duties on that part of its Consumption, which is supplied by

Imports from the United States of such articles as are liable to duties in Lower Canada.[1]

Peter Russell

6

Anticipated Post-war Policy of England in Regard to the United States

From "A candid examination of the advantages obtained by the late war, compared with those that might have been gained by peace"—*United States Gazette*, April 26, 1815, quoted in *Montreal Gazette*, May 22, 1815.

Of the commercial views of England towards this country we as yet know but little. That she will be disposed to bestow upon us any favours, we must not expect. That she will be disposed to remember the time and circumstances, under which we declared war, and the designs which she has alleged actuated our government, we may naturally expect. She has complained of our ambitions, hostile temper, and gave as a reason for her high demands upon the Lakes, the necessity of fortifying her growing strength. It appears by the London papers that an order in council was published on the 24th December, the day the treaty was signed at Ghent, in the London Gazette, admitting certain articles, such as dry provisions and live stock of the various kinds, into the British West Indies.—But Lumber, the great article from this part of the country, was not included in the articles admitted. This seems to be a strong indication of the future policy of England; Canada and Nova Scotia to supply her colonies with lumber, if she will reserve that privilege exclusively to them. This of itself will be an immense source of wealth to Canada in supplying the lumber and to Nova Scotia in helping to carry it. This policy of the mother country is too obvious not to be seen even by the most superficial observer. While it will reward the Canadians for their persevering constancy in resisting our hostile attacks, it will serve to augment their resources, population and wealth, and make them more secure against our future hostility. Our restrictions and war have taught the British lessons, by which they will no doubt profit. Before the embargo, they considered their West India settlements as *dependant on us* for many of their necessary supplies,

---

[1]It was a prime object on the part of the more far-sighted to keep the inland trade as free as possible, since most of it consisted of exports to the western territories of the United States.

especially lumber. Before the war, they were ignorant of the strength, extent and value of the Canadas. They have seen we could not "starve" the former, and that the latter have defended themselves against our boasting armies of invasion and conquest.

7

A Drastic Remedy for Smuggling[1]

From *Montreal Gazette*, February 17, 1817.

Smuggling has arrived at such a height that parties of the 19th Light Dragoons have been stationed between Laprairie and St. Johns, to prevent it. Some time ago Mr. Forsyth passing Laprairie in the night was challenged three different times to stop, but instead of doing so he drove on with more rapidity; upon which a Dragoon fired and wounded him in the arm.

8

The Navigation Laws and Lake Shipping

From Canadian Archives, *Q*, CCCXXIV, 194.

Lieutenant Governor Maitland to Earl Bathurst

York, Upper Canada,
December 8th, 1818

My Lord,

Among those [*bills*] to which I have assented, Your Lordship will observe one, entitled "An Act to regulate the Trade by Land or Inland Navigation between this Province and the United States of America". . . . On further enquiry, I find that the clause imposing a distinct tonnage duty on vessels belonging to American Citizens entering our Ports, is not contained in any Provincial Statute heretofore passed; though a regulation was made in 1816 to the very same effect, by a Proclamation issued by the Lt. Governor in Council, under a general authority given him by a Provincial Statute of that year, to regulate the Trade between this Province and the United States of America.

---

[1]Until 1846, probably as many goods were smuggled across the border as came in by the St. Lawrence. Compare with similar practice in the first empire, in circumvention of the navigation and trade laws. There was no political significance in either case.

As to the other Provisions of the Bill, imposing duties on goods imported from the United States of America, it seems, the Legislature has long assumed and exercised the right of making Laws for the regulation of this same Trade, which laws appear not to have been disallowed in England, and to have been acted upon without question.

In truth, the restriction of the Legislative Power of this Province in matters of Trade and Duties, imposed by the 31st of the King, seems to have been overlooked by the Legislature. And with respect to the Navigation Laws, or Laws for the regulation of Plantation Trade, I find, that, either from inattention to their provisions, or from a persuasion that they did not apply to the inland Navigation of the Waters which separate this Province from the United States of America, they have been hitherto so little regarded, that Vessels of American build, and owned and navigated by subjects of the United States, have been permitted without interruption to import, and carry from port to port in this Province, in the same manner as our own shipping. It is only within these last two years that one or two seizures of American Vessels, carrying from port to port of this Province, have been made under the navigation Laws, which, after the former acquiescence, seem to have created much surprize and discontent.

I am extremely anxious that there should be no question upon points of such general importance; and seeing no good reason for imagining that the comprehensive words of the Navigation Acts, particularly the 7th & 8th William and Mary Ch. 22d and the 12 Chs. the 2nd do not extend to all His Majesty's Colonies, whatever be the nature of the Navigation leading to their ports; I have referred to Your Lordship's consideration, as bearing upon the Bill in question, the two points adverted to in this dispatch. . . .

There are, at present, eighty schooners employed in navigating Lake Erie, Vessels, capable of carrying, in the event of War, either one or two Guns of the larger Calibre; of these, not more than ten, belong to, or are navigated by Subjects of His Majesty.

P. Maitland,
Lt. Governor

9

The Commencement of the New Colonial System

From *Montreal Gazette*, January 4, 1826.

The Colonial Trade Acts of 1822 and 1825 allowed the colonies to ship their products freely where they would and not merely to Great Britain, and to import from whence they wished. Foreign ships could, on certain conditions, enter colonial ports. But foreign ships could not carry between ports in the empire.

TO-MORROW being the day appointed for the commencement of the late Colonial acts, particularly of the Geo. IV. cap. 114, it may be proper to say something with respect to them. As to the general principles of these important laws, all are agreed that they do infinite honour to the nation from whence they have sprung, and that the commercial system of which they form the basis is no less calculated for the benefit of the colonies than for the advancement of the commercial interests of the empire at large. It is to be sure a *peace system*, and one which has consequently been found fault with as of no avail, once the horrors of war break out again in Europe.—This, if true, is certainly a great blemish in any plan of national commerce; but it may be asked, has not peace its own peculiar system of commerce as well as war; and, considering the present state of the world, the new empires and states that have arisen in the cis-Atlantic hemisphere, was it possible that the old navigation laws, with their long train of monopolies and restrictions, could longer be continued with safety or profit? It is our own opinion that they could not, and that, in particular, it became indispensably necessary to establish, with regard to the Colonies, a more liberal system of trade.

Generally speaking the freedom of trade thus secured to the Colonies places them on a level with the mother country, and consequently raises them both in value and importance.

10

Another Aspect of Huskisson's Reforms:—Complaints

From *Journals of assembly, Lower Canada*, 1826, XXXV, 360.

23d. March, 1826

Your Majesty's faithful Commons most humbly represent; That the Measures adopted by Your Majesty's Ministers during the last Session of the Imperial Parliament, regarding Colonial Commerce, had raised the most sanguine expectations in the minds of the Inhabitants of this Province, that the liberal Principles then manifested would have pervaded the whole of the Enactments on Colonial Intercourse, modified only by the paramount Claims of the Interest of the Empire at large. That the Acts passed during the last Session of the Imperial Parliament regarding the Trade and general Interests of the Province, however well adapted to Colonies differently situated, are from the geographical position of this Province, highly injurious to its Trade and Prosperity. That the Acts of the Sixth *George* the Fourth, Chapters Seventy-three and One hundred and fourteen, imposing Duties and Prohibitions on Articles of Merchandise introduced into this Province by Land and by Inland Navigation from the United States, must inevitably ruin a Branch of Trade generally beneficial to this Province and to the Navigation of the Mother Country, whose Ships are employed to a considerable extent in conveying to Market those bulky Articles of Produce heretofore imported therein, under the sanction of the British Act of the Thirtieth *George* the Third, Chapter Twenty-nine, and since under various Provincial Laws. That it is in a great measure owing to the said Intercourse that the Trade of this Province has rapidly encreased, to the great benefit and advantage of the said Province, and to the benefit and advantage of the Mother Country, by the encreased employment of British and Colonial Shipping, from an amount of Nine thousand two hundred and twenty-four Tons, which were employed at the period of passing the aforesaid Act, to Two hundred and twenty-seven thousand seven hundred and seven Tons, the Amount now employed. That to permit the Importation into *Lower-Canada* by the River *Saint Lawrence*, of all bulky Commodities adapted to Exportation, such as Timber and Lumber of all kinds, Pot and Pearl Ashes, salted Provisions and other Articles the Produce of the United States, as if the same were of Canadian origin, would assure to British and Colonial Shipping an extensive and encreasing employment, to His Majesty's Subjects in this Province the benefit of those Charges which arise from the Conveyance, Sale and Transhipment of such Goods, and to British Commerce the advantage of the encreased facility afforded of making returns for British Manufactures, the consumption of which would thereby be greatly augmented. That the most injurious of the Prohibitions in the aforesaid Acts are those which regard the Importation by Land and by Inland Navigation of salted Beef and Pork, which articles are not only requisite to assort Cargoes of Canadian Flour, Fish and Lumber for *Newfoundland*, the *West India* Islands, and other Possessions of His Majesty, but are likewise at present indispensably necessary for the consumption of the Province, more particularly for the supply of Emigrants settling on new Lands, and the numerous Labourers employed in the Lumber trade and Fisheries. . . . . . . That the following Articles imported into Upper-Canada, Duty free, namely, Horses belonging to Persons travelling into or through that Province, and necessarily used in removing themselves, their Families and Baggage, Cord Wood for Fuel, and Saw Logs, may be permitted to be imported into *Lower-Canada* in like manner.

11

Canadian Version of Boston Tea Party[1]

From *Montreal Gazette*, January 14, 1830.

January Tea Sales, 1830

THE AGENTS to the Honourable EAST INDIA COMPANY in Canada, give notice, that there will be put up to PUBLIC SALE at their Warehouses in Quebec, on SATURDAY, the 9th January— a quantity of TEAS, equal to about 500 Chests; and, at Montreal, on SATURDAY, the 23d January, about 1,500 Chests.

Catalogues will be ready for delivery and Shew Chests open for inspection, at each place, from the Monday Morning until the Thursday Afternoon of the week of Sale.

The Sales to commence at Eleven o'clock in the Forenoon.

FORSYTH, RICHARDSON & Co.

Agents to the Honourable East India Company.

Montreal, Jan. 2, 1830

---

[1]The Canadian acceptance of the monopoly of the East India Company is in marked contrast to the behaviour of the Americans sixty years before. Perhaps the explanation is the ease with which it was circumvented by smuggling. See documents no's 15 and 19 of this section, pages 332 and 338.

12

Effect on Canadian Farmer of Export of American Produce as Canadian

From Debate of assembly, Upper Canada, reported in *Montreal Gazette*, December 8, 1831.

In the discussions which took place in the House, on the adoption of the address, we were much pleased to find the benefits likely to arise to the Colony from the provision of the late Colonial Trade Act, fully admitted and enforced by practical men in that body. Mr. Ketchum, one of the members for the County of York, spoke in opposition to one of Mr. Mackensie's tirades, as to the injury it would inflict upon the agriculture interests of the Colony. Mr. K. said, "he thought that the advantages of the late commercial relations were on their side; it would increase the shipping business on the Lakes, and materially assist the prosperity of the Colony, by bringing into it commodities at a much cheaper rate. It would also promote the commercial and manufacturing interests of Great Britain, from whom the Americans would obtain some of the finer articles of manufacture, and, by thus promoting the manufacturing interests of England, the agricultural interest of this Colony would be advanced, as our surplus produce would be carried to that country, and the articles which are required here would be brought back in return, and at a much cheaper rate. It was the interest of Great Britain to keep down the manufacturers of the United States, which it was the tendency of these commercial regulations to effect. It was evident that the advantages were on the side of England, from the fact that the rate of Exchange was in her favor, and from the circumstance that the British gold, which came to this Continent, generally found its way back again in less than three months."

Mr. William Chisolm, of Nelson, who sits as Member for Halton, and who is deeply interested in the agriculture and shipping of the Colony, was another advocate of free trade, as he said he believed "that the late regulations, with regard to the trade with the United States, would prove beneficial to the country. He was as anxious to promote and protect the farming interests of Upper Canada as any man in it, for he was himself a farmer; but he denied that that class of persons would be injured by the present regulations. There was, in some of the townships, an insufficiency of many articles of stock and produce, which rendered it desirable to import those articles from the United States. Before the late treaty, however, beef, pork, &c. could be brought in fresh, and, when cured in this country, were considered as Canadian produce, and consumed or exported as such. If articles of Canadian growth and manufacture should be lowered in price a little, it would benefit the labourer and the tradesman, and would not, in the end, injure the farmer, who, in consequence of the increasing influx of labouring emigrants from the old country, would get his labour performed much cheaper than he had hitherto done."

13

Inconsistencies of Imperial Trading Regulations

Extract from a petition to the house of assembly of Lower Canada from the Quebec committee of trade, December 16, 1832.

The direct trade between this Province and His Majesty's possessions in the West Indies and South America has of late years been much extended under the system of protection afforded thereto by the Imperial Parliament, by means of the several Acts passed for the regulation of the colonial trade since 1825.

That trade, consisting chiefly of an interchange of the produce of the colonies, and carried on entirely in British vessels, is eminently deserving the encouragement and protection which it has experienced.

Your Petitioners, while they fully acknowledge their sense of the parental regard of His Majesty's Government in passing these enactments, have to express their regret that they should have been partially defeated by circumstances which they humbly request permission to submit to your Honourable House:—

1st.—The unequal duties to which several articles, the produce of the West Indies, are subject on importation into this Province, and into Upper Canada.

Thus Coffee cannot be imported into this Province from the British Colonies on payment of a less duty than 7s. sterling per cwt, and 2d. currency per lb, and foreign coffee pays 5s. sterling per cwt. additional; whereas, foreign coffee imported into Upper Canada is admitted on payment of 5s. sterling per cwt. only. Muscovado sugar imported into Lower Canada from a British Possession pays 4s. 8d. currency per cwt. and if of foreign production, it pays 5s. sterling per cwt. additional.   The same article of foreign production is admitted into the Province of Upper Canada on payment of 5s. sterling per cwt. only.   Molasses from the British possessions, imported into Lower Canada, pay 7d. sterling per gallon, and 5d currency; if of foreign production, 3s. sterling per cwt. additional; whereas, in the Upper Province the duty is only 7d. sterling per gallon, and 3s. sterling per cwt.—Such being the case it cannot be a matter of surprise that the Upper Canadian should derive part of his supplies of these articles from the United States, that the shipping interest of a foreign rival state should be encouraged at the expense of the British ship-owners, and profitable employment afforded to the various classes of foreigners engaged in the transport of these articles from the port of importation in the United States to the borders of Upper Canada, and that the Lower Canadian merchants, engaged in the direct trade with the West Indies, should find a ruinous competition in foreign articles imported on payment of lower duties than similar articles from the British possessions.

2d. Another cause which tends to diminish the benefits intended to be conferred on the trade of this Province by the Colonial Trade Acts, may be found in the Comparatively high duties to which Molasses, Coffee, Muscovado Sugar and Salt are subject.

By a late Act of the Congress of the United States of America it is provided that all Teas imported from China in American vessels, after the 3d. day of March next, shall be entirely exempted from duty and your petitioners, looking to the high amount of duty leviable upon Teas imported into this Province, entertain serious apprehensions that unless the operation of the above-mentioned Act of Congress be counteracted by the reduction or abolition of duties here, an irresistible temptation will be held out for the re-introduction of the former illegal traffic with all its pernicious effects.

With a view to remedy the above evils and to the extension of the trade of the Province, your Petitioners request most respectfully to be permitted to submit to your Honourable House the advantages—

1st. Of taking off the whole of the Provincial duty on Coffee.

2d. Of taking off the whole of the Provincial duty on Molasses.

3d. Of taking off the whole of the Provincial duty on Salt, the produce of, and imported direct from the United Kingdom, or her Colonies.

4th. Of reducing the Provincial duty on Muscovado Sugar, from 4s. 8d. currency, per cwt., to 2s. 6d. currency.

5th. Of reducing the Provincial duty on Refined Sugars, from a 1d. per lb. to a ½d. per lb.

6th. Of taking off the duty on Tea.

14

Evasion of the Differential Duties on Baltic Timber

From *St. John Observer* (N.B.), quoted in *Montreal Gazette*, September 12, 1833.

This document gives some idea of the tremendous height of the "differential duties"; they were high enough to permit shipment from the Baltic and re-shipment to England. Anything that touched colonial soil became colonial and was entitled to the preference.

We have the present summer observed in the Halifax papers, the arrival at that place of about eight or nine vessels from different ports in the Baltic, with timber, which, after being landed at Halifax is to be re-shipped and carried to England, and entered as *Colonial timber*. Several vessels with similar cargoes have also arrived at Pictou.—If these circuitous voyages prove successful, the plan will doubtless be followed up more extensively hereafter, unless Parliament should, by some timely act, prevent so glaring an evasion of the Revenue law of the country.

15

The Smuggling Zone on Either Side of the Boundary

From *New York Journal of Commerce*, quoted in *Montreal Gazette*, October 29, 1833.

We learn that "frauds on the revenue" are increasing to an alarming extent on our northern frontier. The merchants from that section want but few woollens goods from our market. They say they can buy them cheaper at home. The people generally, they say, are getting indulgent to the operations which furnish them cheap goods. There is a belt along the frontier, the centre of which is the Canada line, on the Canada side of which there is a remarkable abundance and cheapness of teas and silks, and on the States side an equal abundance and cheapness of loaf sugar and broad cloths. And the people love to have it so. The belt, we are told is constantly enlarged on both sides, so that the white sugar country threatens to spread even to the Hudson River. It is a shame indeed, that in a free country, a citizen should be obliged to pay five dollars for broad cloth, which the subject of a King gets for two and a half, and use brown sugar, when but for the government he might have white at the same price.

16

Imposition of Duties on American Agricultural Produce

From *Kingston Herald*, quoted in *Montreal Gazette*, June 4, 1835.

The reference is to the imposition of colonial duties, not imperial. These could not exceed five per cent.

Among the anomalies of trade this season may be mentioned, the transportation last week of pork from Kingston to Port Hope and Niagara. In the last mentioned place the merchants were entirely destitute of the article, until they were supplied from Kingston. This state of things, when the richest farming districts of Upper Canada derive a large part of their supplies of pork and beef from the States, gives another proof of the infatuation of our Assembly when they voted to tax American produce imported into this country. Had they confined their measure to the imposition of a duty on American wheat and flour, when imported into Upper Canada for *home consumption*, the plan would have received but little opposition; for only few persons would have been unwilling to pay a little extra for those two articles, in order to protect our farmers in those things with which they do supply the country. But when the proposed duty was extended to beef, pork and mutton of which Canada does not raise half enough to supply its own wants, and was also made to include all articles which were only passing through the Province for exportation, thus giving the carrying trade entirely to the Americans, every principle of patriotism and sound policy dictated the rejection of such an absurd measure. In the Assembly's debate a great parade was got up of the few articles that are cheaper in the States than in Canada, and great use was made of the smuggling from the former to the latter; but it was convenient to pass by the numerous articles that are dearer in the States than in Canada, and also the extensive smuggling from the latter to the former. Mackenzie would have returned the duty on iron imported into Canada from the States. The Solon did not know that there are no such importations; on the contrary, great quantities of iron are smuggled into the States from Canada.

17

The Absurdity of Imperial Regulation of Colonial Trade

From Canadian Archives, *Upper Canada sundries.*

W. H. Merritt to Sir George Arthur

St. Catherines, Feb. 13th 1839

. . . The object of this is to call Your Excellency's attention to the practical operation of the Canada Trade Act. . . . This subject although of vital interest to the inhabitants both of the Mother Country, and these provinces, appears to be wholly misunderstood by the Home Government and but little understood by the Colonial Governments; or most shamefully neglected by those whose duty it is to attend to it.

In the first place, the power of regulating and imposing duties on every article grown or consumed in this province should be transferred to our Provincial Legislature.

This proposition may on the first view appear unreasonable, and so great an innovation on the present established principle, that little hope of its attainment need be entertained. . . .

It has hitherto been the policy of the Home Government to retain the power of regulating the trade of all the British Colonies and as a *general principle* it may be correct, for in many instances they are so situated as materially to affect the General Trade of the Empire. The Lords of Trade and Plantations pertinaciously adhere to this general principle without a due consideration of the *geographical position* of the different Colonies, otherwise they would admit that a measure necessary for one of those Colonies might prove nugatory or injurious to another.

The local situation of Upper & Lower Canada affords a most striking and permanent illustration in support of this position. The entire Commerce of these Two Provinces is confined to *two Ports of Entry—Quebec* . . . . . and *New York*. . . . . . The only communication to the interior by the former is the River St. Lawrence and the Lakes above—And the Champlain, Oswego and Erie Canals by the latter, the boundary of the Provinces forming one continuous line on those great lakes and rivers adjoining the State of New York as far up as Lake Erie, the Termination of the Erie Canal. This peculiar feature in our geographical situation should be most clearly and forcibly brought under the consideration of the Home Government by which they will understand that those two communications, leading so far into the interior and terminating at one common point must ever excite a *spirit of emulation and rivalry* between the inhabitants of the two Countries.

By the Canada Trade Act, 4th Wm. 4th some few articles, therein enumerated, are altogether prohibited, others are subject to a high duty, and all not enumerated, to a duty of 15 per cent ad valorem.

In reply to one of the addresses of the House of Assembly in 1837, The Lords of Trade declare "That they do not believe that by mere dint of mercantile superiority Tea can be introduced from China into Upper Canada by way of New York cheaper than by Quebec". Adhering strictly to general principles their position was correct—it could not be done by mere *mercantile superiority*, we admit, but that it *is done* and that it is caused by the provisions of an Imperial Act is a matter of *public notoriety* here. I mention this as one incident to shew the absurdity of the Imperial Parliament legislating for us on a subject which even the *Board of Trade* cannot comprehend.

I shall now proceed to shew that however expedient or necessary it may be considered to leave the regulation of duties under the control of the Imperial Parliament it is *impracticable*.

1st. From the extent of our Frontier, its proximity to the United States and the facilities thereby afforded at all points for smuggling, every article will be introduced by that means, the *expense and risque* of which is less than the duty imposed. Consequently any restriction is *inoperative*. The ad valorem duty of 15 per cent enables the Custom House Officer to admit articles at the valuation of the owner, some at a mere *nominal value*, others higher, thereby creating a constant fluctuation and uncertainty in prices, and it is equally inoperative for the purposes intended.

2^{ndly}. It is important for a correct understanding of this subject that the Home Government should feel convinced that it is the *personal Interest* of every Inhabitant in Upper Canada to direct the entire trade of the Country through the *Port of Quebec*: 1st. Great Britain furnishes the articles we consume at the cheapest rates and offers the best markets for our products—consequently if no Law or impost existed to prevent it, our *interest* would lead us to her markets. 2ndly. By transporting through the St. Lawrence every article we grow or consume, however small, it lessens the expense on other articles by encreasing the Tolls on our Canals and diminishing the Cost of Transportation, besides increasing the general revenue—whereas an opposite effect is produced upon every article introduced or exported through New York.   3rd. The only articles not furnished direct from Great Britain are a few French goods and Tea, unimportant both in quantity and value. They are now introduced and consumed *without* duty, which as before stated cannot be prevented by proscription, whereas those very articles could by a judicious arrangement be introduced at the Port of Quebec.

With those views and those feelings how absurd must it appear to the inhabitants of Upper Canada to have an Act passed by the Imperial Parliament, the effect of which is to *injure the trade of the Mother Country*, & to force the Trade from the St. Lawrence through the Ports and Waters of our Rivals, thereby conferring a greater benefit upon the commerce of the United States than they could confer by any Act of their own.

The remedy is plain and simple and in accordance with the dictates of *common sense.*

By placing the duties wholly under the control of the Legislature, they will of course be regulated and disposed of in accordance with the motives and principles by which mankind are in general governed. Their *Interest* will be, first to increase the revenue of the Province, by closely watching any change in the duties on any given article at the Port of New York. By lessening the duty on that article at the Port of Quebec and increasing it at the interior Ports from the United States we secure its introduction at a Canadian Sea-Port and through Canadian Waters, an effect which, besides securing the Revenue now lost, gives the best evidence that it will promote the interests of the British and Canadian Merchant, who will under this additional protection introduce the whole of his stock at the Port of Quebec. . . .

Wm. Hamilton Merritt

18

Importance of Free Admission of Canadian Wheat into England[1]

From Canadian Archives, *Upper Canada sundries*, 1839.

W. H. Merritt to Sir George Arthur

St. Catharines Feby. 15th 1839

May it please Your Excellency

The first year I came into the Legislature an address was sent home praying that wheat and flour the growth and product of these Colonies might be admitted into the Ports of Great Britain free from duty. It was declared by the Government to be inadmissable.

Recently.—The renewed agitation of the Corn Law question may induce the Colonial Minister to give the subject a moment's reflection. If so he will see the policy of the measure in a more extended light. Sir Henry Parnell informed me in 1828 that he obtained this boon for Ireland, and recommended our never ceasing to ask and demand it for Canada, as we were, or should be considered an integral part of the Empire. Our great distance from the Sea Coast and the consequent increase of Expense, will prevent our competing with the grower in Britain, and the certainty of remunerative prices would have the effect of increasing the value of wheat grown here, when the markets were higher in Europe than in America. The duty we would place on American wheat introduced here would give the advantages now possessed by the American farmer to the Canadian, it would increase the value of property and labour and have a tendency to restore the Country to the position it enjoyed prior to 1812. It would do more to promote Emigration than all the puerile attempts heretofore made in the Land granting department, or any other measure yet adopted. And the Government may rest assured that unless some change is effected in the situation of this Country, it will continue to be a mere thoroughfare for Emigrants to the United States. It would prove by ocular demonstration the value of our connection with Great Britain, for it should be well understood, that at this moment no article the growth or produce of these provinces is benefited by

---

[1] Free admission was obtained in 1843.

22

that connection except timber and every person who honestly thinks that that connection will improve and better the condition of the inhabitants, should use every exertion to obtain the sanction of any measure calculated to extend and perpetuate that conviction in the public mind.

Wm. Hamilton Merritt

19

Smuggling and the Imperial Regulation of Canadian Trade: —The Tea Trade and Smuggling

From Canadian Archives, *Q*, CDXIX, 172.

Lieutenant-Governor Sir George Arthur to the Marquis of Normanby

Government House,
Toronto, 10th September 1839

My Lord,

During my recent tour through the western divisions of this Province, my attention was particularly called to the nature of the commercial intercourse between it and the neighbouring States; and, more particularly, to the ruinous extent to which smuggling is carried on along the whole line of frontier.

The present temptations to prosecute this illicit traffic are such, that many persons are engaged in it whose conduct in other respects is above reproach and who claim consideration from their station in the community; indeed, smuggling is become so general as to be scarcely regarded by the people in the light of an offence. . . .

That part of the Provincial revenue which accrues from Customs' Duties, is collected in virtue of Acts of the Imperial Parliament, the Acts of the Imperial Parliament, the Acts of Lower Canada, passed for limited periods, but prolonged by the British Statute 3 Geo. 4. C. 119, under the conditions therein prescribed, and an Act of the Legislature of this Province.

The duties on imports by the Gulf of St. Lawrence, are wholly collected in Lower Canada, and divided between the two Provinces, in the proportions fixed from time to time, by arbitration; the proportion at present received by Upper Canada, being about one third of the net amount.

The other duties of customs, pertaining to this Province, are collected in it.

The trade between Upper Canada and the United States, is, at present, regulated by the Imperial Statute 3 & 4 Wm. 4 C. 59; and the returns from the several Provincial Collectors show that the legitimate commercial intercourse between the two countries is steadily increasing.

Even Muscovado sugar, I am informed, is introduced from thence in considerable quantities; being in such cases, the produce of the foreign slave colonies of Cuba, Porto Rico, &c. The importation, however, of this article, is contingent on the relative state of the sugar markets of New York and Montreal; inasmuch as if the commodity happen to be scarce and high-priced in the latter, while it is the converse in the former market, there is at once an inducement for importing it from the United States, both into Upper and Lower Canada.

The establishment of the fact that the legitimate commercial intercourse between the two Countries is steadily increasing, is the best proof that the nature of the traffic is mutually beneficial to the parties concerned in it; and, as regards the Canadian people, this view is confirmed by the consideration that a staple commodity, —namely, deal planks,—is what they mostly give in exchange for the articles they receive.

The commercial, like the geographical position of Canada is peculiar; differing from that of every other Colony in the British Empire.

Upon such an extended line of frontier as Upper Canada presents it is manifestly impracticable to prevent clandestine trade by any system of penalties or forfeiture that can be enforced. The only preventive appears to consist in the establishment of a low scale of import duties; but it is quite evident that they must be levied to a sufficient amount to meet the exigencies of the public service; since it is very questionable, whether the people of this Province would be induced, by the pressure of almost any public necessity, to add materially to their present direct taxation:—unless, probably, for the promotion of Education.

If the foregoing be a correct view of the case, as respects commodities admissible on payment of duties, I think the principles on which it rests, must apply with increased force to such articles as are declared by Imperial Statute to be contraband, when coming from the United States, but which are in common use in this country.

Among the latter, the principal to which I shall confine my present remarks is Tea, which may be purchased in any part of the United States, at prices far lower than it can be procured for in Lower Canada.

The consequence is that it is continually smuggled into the Canadian provinces at all points; generally in small quantities, but to an amount which, in the aggregate, is immense. The effect of this practice, as Your Lordship will readily conceive, is injurious to the revenue, to the fair trader, and most detrimental to the morals of the community.

The difference in the price of Tea in the New York and Montreal Markets, amounting as I understand to about 25 per cent, I am unable to account for, unless on the assumption that the *direct returns* which the Americans are enabled to make, in their own ships, for the Tea they purchase, give them the advantage as importers over the Canadian merchant.

Be the cause, however, what it may, the fact is notorious, that the Americans import Tea, and good Tea too, at a price which defies at present all competition in Canada.

The difference of price on the opposite shores of Lake Ontario is very striking.

At Rochester, Oswego, and other of the American frontier towns, Tea of the quality in general use in this Country, and sold under the name of Young Hyson, may be purchased wholesale at from 1/9d to 2/3d per lb; whereas, in Toronto, Tea of a similar description cannot be purchased wholesale at less than from 3/. to 3/6d per lb. The difference therefore, between these respective sums forms the profit produced on the smuggled article; and as the expense of transport is very trifling, the *net gain* may be computed, on the average, at 1/- per lb; and this is divided between the actual smuggler and the consignee.

The prohibition to import Tea from the United States (originating in a desire to protect the interests of the East India Company, and British Shipping) is at present no protection to English Commerce; while it produces among the Canadian people, daily visible discontent. Their revenues are not increased by its operation; and they regard it as a restriction of no use in any quarter, and very injurious to them.

If, on the contrary, Tea were admitted into this Province from the United States on payment of such moderate duty as would give fair protection to British trade, the people themselves would feel an interest in enforcing that duty; and it would prove a sensible and seasonable relief to the provincial embarrassments resulting from a deficient revenue.

Independent of these considerations, it would be difficult adequately to describe the importance in a political point of view, of destroying the smuggling trade in this Province. Under its protection, the persons engaged in it can assist very materially in spreading disaffection through the country, and are readily enabled to keep up treasonable communications with the enemies of the provincial Government, in the United States.

Furthermore, the clandestine trade in Tea induces a similar trade in numerous other articles; since the same vessels and the same individuals engage in smuggling of all kinds; whereas *if the chief inducement to the practice, which is unquestionably Tea, were removed*, the probability is, that it might be nearly, or wholly suppressed.

If,—and the impossibility is but too apparent,—we *cannot* prevent the introduction of smuggled Tea on such a line of frontier as we possess, nor afford, consequently, to the fair trader, more than a nominal protection, it should seem evident, that no better course would be pursued than to legalize the importation of an article, the present exclusion of which, serves only to confer unlawful gains on individuals, at the expense of the public revenue, and to operate against the interests of the community at large.

Formerly, the importation of Tea from the United States, was permitted under the authority of Canadian Acts. An Imperial Statute, on the close of the American war, superseded those laws; but with an effect so remarkable in promoting the growth of clandestine traffic, that in 1824, a joint Address was presented to the King, from the two Branches of the Provincial Legislature, forcibly describing the lamentable condition of the Tea trade, and soliciting an alteration in the system.

Soon afterwards the East India Company made arrangements for holding periodical sales in Lower Canada, of Teas imported by them direct from China; and they continued this practice until their monopoly was abolished, and the Free trade Teas then found their way to Canada—though as I understand, they have not been imported to the extent that might have been expected.

Meanwhile, however, the policy of Congress, led to the abolition of all those duties upon Teas imported in American ships, from
China to the United States, which had served theretofore, to maintain the price of that Article in the American markets, and had thus
also served to check its illicit introduction into Canada.

Under all these considerations, I recommend most strongly to
Her Majesty's Government, the propriety of causing such a
modification of the existing prohibitory laws applicable to Upper
Canada, as would permit the importation of Tea from the United
States, at a moderate rate of duty—say, 3d or 4d per lb and if
this measure can be permitted I hope it may be adopted *quickly*.

Geo. Arthur

(b)—THE COMMERCIAL REVOLUTION OF THE 1840'S

By the end of 1846 most of the preferential duties had been swept away. As
a result, the new Canadian flour-milling industry was ruined and, with the aid
of the British panic of 1847, profound depression created in the lumber trade.
The Americans chose this precise time to pass their bonding act, which by allowing
goods to pass without duty through American territory, transferred the trade
of the St. Lawrence to New York. Canadian ports continued to be bound by
what was left of the navigation acts and foreign vessels could not carry between
them and the ports of any other British country, with the apparent result that
freights were much higher than from American ports. No wonder that under
this succession of blows, a people who had always conceived of the empire as a
tissue of trade and trading policy now began to wonder whether it ought not
logically to disappear and that such symptoms as the Montreal annexation
manifesto appeared. After 1846, Canada for the first time had to stand on its
own feet and it was not a pleasant experience. But the country soon turned to
the obvious expedient. If it could expect no favours from the parent state, it
might be able to do something with its neighbour. Hence the beginning of the
re-orientation of Canadian trade, a process well under way before the Reciprocity
Treaty of 1854, but probably hastened by that treaty.

REFERENCES: C. D. Allin and G. M. Jones, *Annexation, preferential trade
and reciprocity* (Toronto, 1911); D. L. Burn, "Canada and the repeal of the corn
laws" (*Cambridge Historical Journal*, II(3), 252).

1

The Heart of the Old Colonial System:—Vested Interests

From *London Morning Chronicle*, quoted in *Canadian Economist*, May 16, 1846.

It is now evident that an attempt is being made to organise
a strenuous opposition to the reduction of the timber duties.
For this purpose printed circulars and letters, and copies of correspondence from provincial newspapers, are extensively circulated
with assiduity. In these papers there is not a fallacy, however

ancient or exploded, that is not revived; nor a prejudice that is not appealed to. The colonies are applauded for every thing which they have been so recently over and over again proved *not to be.* Manufacturers in Manchester, Birmingham, Sheffield, and Glasgow, are called upon, at any cost, to save the colonies, as their only permanent foreign markets. Shipowners are implored to rescue from danger the main branch of the carrying trade of the kingdom. Artisans and mechanics are persuaded that the safety and extension of the colonial system are the only means by which a "*nine or ten* hours bill" can be obtained; and finally, the humane and benevolent, who witness the sufferings to which, especially at particular periods, our labouring classes have been exposed, are appealed to, on the ground that the colonies offer the only safe asylum for our increasing surplus population.

It may be in vain that we prove that not only is our colonial trade comparatively small of itself, but that it does not progress in the same proportion as that to foreign countries. Where we are without the benefit of protection, it may be in vain that we show, from the best authority, that even our shipowners are far more indebted to the foreign than to the colonial trade for the employment of their craft;—it may be in vain that we prove that for every mechanic who finds employment in supplying the colonies with the manufactures of this country, at least four earn their bread by working for independent foreign markets;—and it may be of little use that we should produce evidence, which cannot be doubted, that even a majority of the emigrants who have left their native country in search of another home, have found it not in the colonies, but in foreign states. All this, we know, may be useless and in vain, as far as these inveterate monopolists themselves are concerned, whose main object is to secure the continuance of a system of restriction, on which they ignorantly believe their own immediate interests to be dependent. Fortunately, however, there is a large and enlightened public, who are now, above all things, anxious to form a correct opinion on these subjects, based upon unquestionable facts.

As might be expected, the parties who are now taking these active measures to raise in the public mind a prejudice against any further reduction of the timber duties dwell entirely, or mainly, on the importance of the Canada market. We would not, for a moment, wish to depreciate either the importance or the value of

our North American colonies. We seek for the *real* colonists—
that is, the people who actually live in the colonies, dependent on
their own industry—every privilege which we seek for ourselves
at home. We altogether deny our right, or the policy, of taxing
them indirectly, by imposing protecting duties upon our manufactures entering their territory for consumption. If they can
obtain their clothing or their luxuries cheaper or better from
another market, we contend they are entitled to do so. But what
say these *soi-disant* friends to the colonies here? The overture
they make amounts to a kind of compromise of the real interests
of the consumers at home and in the colonies, in order that *thus*
a small class shall be benefited. They virtually propose that the
great mass of the community in Canada shall be taxed in the form
of dear clothing, and that the large mass of consumers at home
shall be taxed in the form of dear timber and dear food, in order
that the comparatively small class engaged in the timber trade
from Canada, and in the export trade to Canada, shall advance
their own interests. These men, mostly residing at home, who call
themselves the colonial interest, have objects and motives as wide
apart from the real advantage of the large mass of the people in
the colonies as it is now generally admitted the labouring population at home have in the objects for which landlords have struggled
to maintain dear bread. Too great a distinction cannot be made
between individuals interested in colonial monopolies, of whom a
large majority have never so much as set foot in any of our colonial
territory, and the great mass of the population of the colonies.

2

A Comparison of the Old and New Colonial Systems

From *Canadian Economist*, May 2, 1846.

THE great changes now taking place in the commercial
policy of Great Britain lead us to propose the inquiry, whether we
shall derive benefit or injury from the restrictive system as it will
in future exist. Hitherto, the heavy differential duties, by means
of which our productions secured, in the English market, a decided
advantage over those of other countries, have led us to overlook
the serious loss which has resulted from the restrictions on our
import trade. We have always been accustomed to admit, with-

out hesitation, that the balance of advantages was in our favor, and that we had nothing to gain by opening the question. So far we may perhaps have been right; but a new era in legislation has arrived. The foundation on which our commercial system has been built up is now in process of removal, and as the Mother Country is about to withdraw the preference she has extended to our timber and our breadstuffs, it devolves on us to point out the injury we sustain, by being confined to her markets for our supplies, and to demand the privilege of obtaining those supplies wherever we can procure them most advantageously for ourselves. . . .

As we cannot expect any modification or postponement of the measures recently sanctioned by the British House of Commons, we feel the necessity of adapting our own commercial legislation to the altered legislation of the Mother Country; and in making this attempt, we desire that the same sound principles which govern her statesmen should also be the guide of ours. We desire that all unnecessary restrictions should be removed from our commerce, and that no one interest be protected at the expense of others. . . .

It may well be doubted whether, under the modified tariff of 1842, we derived greater profit from protection on the one hand, than we suffered loss from restriction on the other; but we do not entertain a doubt that, under the proposed tariff, the Colony will sustain a positive loss when the balance of these advantages and disadvantages is struck. For three years we are to receive a preference of 3s. per quarter for our wheat, and at the end of that period this preference is to be entirely withdrawn. Our timber is to be protected for one year to the extent of 20s. per load, and after that to the extent of 15s. per load, subject, of course, to further reduction. If we estimate the full value in money of these preferences, we shall find that it does not amount to any very great sum; but we should greatly delude ourselves if we fancied that we shall profit to the full amount of the valuation we have supposed. The experience of past years has demonstrated that the removal of duties is not followed by a fall in prices to the same extent. The increase of consumption, and the difficulty of increasing the supply, are found to sustain prices at a point considerably above that which the simple deduction of the duty from their former value would give. . . .

Let us examine, on the other hand, how our commerce is affected by discriminating duties within the Colony. These duties vary from 4 to 20 per cent., and they establish a preference in a similar ratio for British over foreign goods, amounting in the aggregate to the sum of £104,555 during the year 1845. But this sum does not represent the exact loss to the Colony which they have occasioned, and in fact affords no criterion of it. For, as they apply to every article we import, their effect has been to raise the price of a great variety of goods besides those which actually pay these duties. We go on importing from England until the price we pay her is found to exceed the price in foreign countries and the regulating duty together; and it is not till we have resorted to the foreign market that we are subjected directly to the discriminating duty, although before that we have been paying it indirectly, in the shape of an enhanced price to the English producer. Thus we suffer extensively, without being made aware of it by any result in the shape of revenue returns; and if due consideration is given to the loss thus occasioned, and also to the injurious effects, both to the producer and consumer, of the restrictions on our shipping trade, we believe it will be admitted that these losses greatly exceed any profit we derive from that small portion of the English protective duties which remains.

We think these considerations ought at least to remove all the alarm expressed by some men at the prospect of our trade being exposed to foreign competition. Let us be permitted to buy in the cheapest as well as to sell in the dearest markets we can reach; let our commerce be freed from all restraints, and we shall have nothing to fear. It is a mistake to suppose that our prosperity has been created by the Colonial system of trade. It has been created by the industry of a free, intelligent, and virtuous people employed in developing the resources of a country of great natural wealth, covered with excellent timber, possessing a rich and virgin soil, and abounding in lakes and navigable rivers communicating with the ocean. It is to these causes alone, and to the security from foreign aggression which the arms of Great Britain have given us, that we must attribute our prosperity, and to them we must trust for its continuance.

3

Commencement of the American Bonding System

From *Canadian Economist*, May 30, 1846.

Import by way of the American ports, especially New York, in order to circumvent the monopoly of Montreal was what the Upper Canadians had been desiring for many years. American duties had hitherto prevented this. See documents numbers 17, 18, 19 of section IIC, pages 177*ff*.

We observe that the United States Government has obtained the sanction of Congress to the Bonding Bill, and that it is likely to come into operation at an early date. The measure is one of great importance and utility to the trade of Canada, especially of Western Canada. It will effect a saving in the cost of many commodities imported for consumption, and it will enhance the value of our agricultural produce in the event of Sir Robert Peel's measure becoming law, by limiting the cost of transportation to England *via* the St. Lawrence, to the rate payable *via* New York, including, in the meantime, the differential duties. When it is borne in mind that the cost of sending a barrel of flour from Toronto by way of the St. Lawrence to England, last fall, reached the exorbitant rate of 12s. sterling, per barrel, the advantage of such a check being given to our forwarding charges and foreign freights is apparent. . . .

4

Free Trade and British Connection

From *Canadian Economist*, May 30, 1846.

We resume the consideration of a question which has of late frequently been mooted:—How far the adoption of Free Trade principles in Great Britain, and as a consequence in her Colonies, is compatible with the nature of the connection subsisting between them.

A few years back, but one opinion would probably have existed on this point [*the connection would have been severed*]. . . .

This important question then naturally arises: Protection in the home market being withdrawn, shall we continue to derive such important advantages from our dependency on Great Britain, as to make it probable that our present relations as parent state and colony will be of long duration?

The opponents of Free Trade unhesitatingly furnish us with a negative answer to this question. They tell us, and truly, that the only cement which binds us to the mother country is self-interest. We agree with them that those high-sounding words, "attachment to the land of our birth," or to that of "our fore-fathers," serve little other purpose than to round a period when applied to the management of state affairs; the true maxim being, *non ubi nascor, sed ubi pascor.* We are perfectly convinced with them that the hallowed recollections of the past will give way to the stern realities of the present, and the cold calculations of the future. But we are not prepared, thence, to conclude that the tie which binds us to Great Britain, is severed; and for these, amongst other reasons:

First, That our commerce will still be protected, and our coasts and territory guarded, by her fleets and armies; and this, not at our expense, but at hers; not in such a manner as to detract from, but to add to, the sum of our national wealth.

Second, That this will continue to be the country to which the tide of emigration from the British Isles will continue to flow, fertilizing and enriching the land in its progress.

Third, That through the assistance of British credit and capital we shall be enabled to construct those public works which are necessary for our commerce, entering as we are about to do into competition with our powerful and enterprizing neighbours.

5

How the Old Colonial System Favoured British Manufactures

From *Canadian Economist*, July 18, August 15, 1846.

Hitherto the amount of protection conceded to the products of Canada in the British markets has been so great as to throw into the shade the advantages which British products have enjoyed in this market,—at least such has been the prevailing opinion; but the following table, shewing at one view the discrimination which our tariff makes between British and Foreign, in some of our principal articles of import, amply proves that the inhabitants of Canada have not been lightly taxed in return for that protection:—

Articles	Foreign Duty	British Duty
Glass and Glassware.......	20%	5%
Hardware...............	12%	5%
Leather Manufactures.....	12%	5%
Manufactures, Cotton,		
Linen, Woollen.......	12%	5%
Paper Manufactures.......	12%	5%
Brandy and other spirits...	2s 3d gal.	1s 3d gal.
Wine..................	17% and 8d gal.	10% and 8d gal.

. . . As a proof that these discriminating duties impose heavy burdens on us in their operation, it may be added that the amount of duty collected under them last year was no less than £104,555 or about one fourth of the whole net revenue of the province derived through the Custom House. . . .

6

Necessity for Repeal of the Navigation Laws

From Canadian Economist, July 25, 1846.

At the present moment there is perhaps no object of equal importance to the well-being of this colony that can be sought for from the mother country, as that of bringing about a repeal of the British Navigation Laws, in as far as they affect our interests. Well may we exclaim, in the words of the memorial lately presented to Government by the Free-Trade Association, "This Colony is now labouring under the loss of protection on the one hand, and the crushing effects of the severest restrictions on the other." Protection, or preference for our products in the markets of the mother country, there is none now of any value; but all the restrictions that were imposed on us as an equivalent for those lost advantages, are left in full vigour, depressing our industry and paralysing our commercial enterprise.

Whilst a reciprocal state of things existed, we were content, although, on a review of our past circumstances, we candidly believe that England had the best of the compact. It was, in the language of Mr. Gladstone, "a mutual sharing of benefits, or rather a mutual bearing of burdens." But now the case is altered: the *benefits* are destroyed; but the *burdens* are left to oppress and gall the industry of our hard-working population. And what are the burdens? We cannot too often draw public attention to them.

First, the differential duties; but next, and by far the most important, the restrictions imposed on our commerce by the ruinous operation of the British Navigation Laws. Let us not be misconstrued. Let no timid person turn upon us here, and accuse us of disloyalty, or a desire to weaken the springs of England's naval grandeur. To such we would reply, that our love of country cannot be shaken, nor ought it to be questioned. But we have a duty to perform to ourselves, as well as our successors; and craven must be the individual among us who refuses, at this crisis, to exert himself to obtain those comprehensive reforms that our peculiar situation renders manifest and necessary. At present we shall confine ourselves to the discussion of the most important of them,—*the repeal, absolute with reference to Canada, of the British Navigation Laws!* . . . .

Let us compare the rates of freight between New York on the one hand, and Montreal on the other, and Great Britain, that have been current during the present summer; and the result will be seen to bear out what we have asserted.

Rates of Freight current at New York in the year 1846.
To Liverpool:—
Average,. . . . . 2s. 6 1/2d. per brl. 8 1/3d. per bushel.

Rates of Freight current at Montreal in the year 1846.
To Liverpool.
Average,. . . . . 5s. 1 1/2d. per brl. 9s. 3 1/2d. per qr.

————————

1s. 2 1/2d. per bushel.

What do these tables exhibit? An average loss to the Canadian producer of 2s. 7d. stg. or nearly 3s. 2d. cy. per brl. on his flour, and 5 2/3d. stg. or about 7d. cy. per bushel on his wheat, by being restricted to the employment of British vessels.

7

Imperial Government's Restrictions on Colonial Trade

From *Parliamentary papers*, 1847-48, XX (2), 913 *ff*.

W. E. Gladstone, colonial secretary to the governor-general

5 March, 1846

. . . The desire of Her Majesty's Government is, that the trade of Canada may, in all respects, approach as nearly to perfect freedom as the disposition of its inhabitants and the exigencies of the public revenue there, may permit. . . .

8

Opening of the St. Lawrence between Montreal and Quebec to Foreign Vessels

From *Montreal Transcript*, May 13, 1847.

Before the navigation laws were repealed by the act of 1849, they had been modified and in part suspended by order-in-council; this document illustrates the gradual process by which colonial trade was freed from the restrictions of the old system, once the benefits had been taken away.

The Civil Secretary conveys the gratifying intelligence of a further relaxation of the Navigation Laws. It will be recollected that the late Board of Trade, in March last, applied to Mr. Cayley, to learn whether, under the act of the Imperial Parliament suspending the Navigation Laws, foreign vessels would be permitted to ascend the St. Lawrence, and that the answer they then received from the Attorney General, to whom the question had been referred, was, in effect, that they could not. Since then, a communication has been made home on the subject, and the result has been the favourable answer published in this day's paper.

Under the law, as it has up to the present time existed, no foreign vessel could come above Quebec, between which port and Montreal, the St. Lawrence is absolutely closed against them. This policy of excluding strangers from the navigation of internal waters, is one that has at all times been claimed by independent nations, and is based on principles recognized by the law of nations. It may be doubted, however, whether these principles are altogether applicable to the present commercial age; and it is certain that their rigid enforcement in our own case would be greatly injurious to our interests. By the change which has taken place at home, a merchant has now the option of sending his flour to Great Britain by the shipping of any country it may best suit his interest to employ. When it once gets to Quebec, its national character vanishes, and it is admitted on the same terms as though it were the actual growth of a British possession. Yet, to get to Quebec, it is necessary that it should be transferred at Montreal into a British bottom. From the most extreme port in the West there is nothing to impede an American forwarding craft from coming direct to Montreal—from Quebec to Liverpool, the produce brought by the same craft can be conveyed in an American vessel; but between Montreal and Quebec, the St. Lawrence is sealed. The policy of Great Britain, to use the words of Lord Stanley's despatch on this subject, is irreconcilable with such a concession.

The effect of thus breaking the chain of commercial traffic was likely to have a most serious effect on the best interests of this country. The delay and expense of the unnecessary transhipment are sufficient to turn the balance against us, and drive the Western trade into the Erie canal, instead of bringing it through on our waters. . . .

The grounds on which these restrictions could be defended, have lost any value they once possessed by the changes which Great Britain has found herself compelled to resort to. The British ship-holder, whose interest was for a long time considered to be involved in this policy, can now have no interest in the question. If he succeed in keeping away foreign vessels from Quebec, he can only do so at the expense of the trade itself and the competition which he so dreads, will meet him with increased force at New York. In short, with a suspension of the navigation laws, the restrictions imposed on the trade by the St. Lawrence could only have the effect of ruining ourselves without benefiting any one. It is our interest to invite trade this way, and not drive it away. If our canals are ever to pay any return for the sums which have been expended on their construction, it must be by making the St. Lawrence the great highway to the ocean, and following the excellent advice preferred by the late Board of Trade.

We have little doubt in our own minds that the result of the experiment the British Government are about to make, will be so satisfactory as to induce its final permanent adoption, and that whilst it is safely left to our feelings of loyalty to keep an intrusive spirit of Yankeyism away, there will be no obstacle to our availing ourselves to the fullest extent of the enterprise and industry of that singularly enterprising and magnificently unscrupulous people!

CIVIL SECRETARY'S OFFICE,
Montreal, 10th May, 1847

SIR,—I am commanded by the Governor General to acquaint you, for the information of the Board of Trade of Montreal, that in answer to communications from His Excellency on the subject of the trade of this Port, the Governor General has received a despatch from the Secretary of State for the Colonies, stating that, in their solicitude to afford the utmost possible facility to the trade of Canada, the Lords Commissioners of the Treasury will, by the next mail, transmit to the officers of Her Majesty's Customs at Quebec, orders that, so long as the existing suspension of the Navigation Acts in respect of vessels engaged in the corn trade shall remain in force, foreign vessels are permitted to go in ballast up the St. Lawrence to Montreal, and thence to bring down corn and flour consigned to any port in the United Kingdom, on first obtaining a license for that purpose from the principal officers of Customs at Quebec.

T. C. CAMPBELL, Major
Civil Secretary

9

Reciprocity:—Free Navigation of the St. Lawrence in Return for Free Entry of Canadian Wheat

From *Parliamentary papers*, 1847-48, XX, part 2, no. 54, Memorandum of the executive council of Canada on the subject of the navigation laws, enclosed in Elgin to Grey, May 12, 1848.

Connected with this Subject of the free Navigation of the St. Lawrence West of Quebec, which the Americans are desirous to procure, is a corresponding Desire on the Part of the Canadian Farmers to avail themselves of the American Home Market, whenever it affords superior Prices to those derived from Exportation to Europe. The price of Wheat and Flour in the Eastern States intended for Home Consumption is often much higher than the Price in Canada for Exportation; when this happens to be the case it would be an immense Advantage to the Canadian Agriculturist could he export his produce for Consumption in the United States. This, however, he is prevented from doing by, a protecting Duty of a Quarter of a Dollar a Bushel upon Wheat. Efforts have been made in the United States to abolish this Duty, but the Advocates of its Abolition have been defeated by the cry for Protection on the Part of American Farmers and met also by a Difficulty as to the "most favoured Nation Clause," in Treaties with Foreign Powers, which might make a Relaxation in favour of

Canada require a like Favour to all Nations with whom such Treaties existed. It is thought, that if the free Navigation of the St. Lawrence were offered to the American Government, in return for the Abolition of the protecting Duty, the one measure to be co-existent with the other, the American Legislature, upon that Consideration, would be induced to abolish the protective Duty; while the Abolishment being a matter of reciprocal Treaty all Difficulty arising from the Arrangement as to the commercial Relations of the United States with Foreign Countries might be avoided. Thus two Objects in which Canada is deeply interested might be obtained at once through the Interest which Americans feel in one; and there is Reason to believe that this is not a mere Supposition, but that it has been the Opinion of leading Men in the United States, who are the Advocates of Free Trade Principles, and who think that popular Objections to the Admission of Canadian Wheat on the same terms that American Wheat is admitted into England would be obviated by permitting to American Vessels the free Navigation of the River St. Lawrence above Quebec.

10

Fatal Effects of the Navigation Acts on the New Canadian Canal System

From *Ibid.*, Memorandum of the executive council of Canada.

. . . During the temporary suspension of the Navigation Laws last year, twenty-two ships arrived from Bremen at the port of Montreal loaded with emigrants intended for the United States, who chose the route through Canada for its great facility and cheapness. . . . This is but one instance of many which might be expected were foreign vessels permitted to resort to Canadian ports. . . .

The American Merchants of the West are no doubt anxious to avail themselves of the Facilities afforded by the River St. Lawrence. Were their Vessels permitted to come down to Montreal and Quebec, there to meet American or Foreign Ships to take their Freight to Europe or elsewhere, it is thought that a most extensive and profitable Commerce through Canada would immediately follow. The American Vessels now confined to the Navigation of the Lakes and Upper Part of the River would then be enabled to come to a Port of Embarkation for Sea, without Transhipment of Cargo. It is confidently anticipated that a great Portion of the Importations for the North-western Portion of the United States would take place through the same Channel; and thus, instead of the Lower Ports of Canada being deserted, they would at once assume the Position, as commercial Depots, to which their Location upon the great River Outlet of Northern America seems to entitle them. The great Works of the St. Lawrence, instead of being idle and unproductive, through the Means of protective Regulations which produce no Benefit in any Quarter, would then become a Means of enriching a Country which the Expense of their Construction has now exhausted.

11

Canadian and American Wheat Prices as Factors in Reciprocity

From Annual report of the council of the Toronto board of trade for 1847, *Toronto Globe*, January 8, 1848.

The attention of your Council has been called to a subject of much importance to the agricultural and commercial interests of the Province, in consequence of the price of Wheat and Flour in the Canadian markets bordering on the North shores of Lake Erie and Ontario being invariably much lower than in the United States markets similarly situated on the South shores. The average monthly market price of these two articles in Toronto for seven months ending 30th. November last, compared with their market price in Rochester for the same period, will afford a fair criterion by which to judge the others. . . .

	Wheat per Bushel.		Flour per Barrel.	
1847	Toronto	Rochester	Toronto	Rochester
May	$0.95	$1.36	$5.25	$6.25
June	1.25	1.60	6.16	7.73
July	0.86	1.05	5.15	5.38
Aug.	0.78	1.05	4.75	5.14
Sept.	0.78	1.05	4.25	5.06
Octr.	0.83	1.24	4.37	5.38
Novr.	0.80	1.20	4.32	5.45
Average	$0.89	$1.22	$4.89	$5.77

Thus it appears the average price of Wheat and Flour between May and November last, was 33 cents or 1s. 8d. currency per bushel for wheat, and 88 cents or 4s. 5d. currency per barrel for Flour higher in Rochester market than in Toronto. If the absurd restrictions which imprudent legislation has imposed on the importation of these articles into either country were removed, the price on the North shore of the Lake would immediately rise to nearly the current rates in the markets on the South shores, and thus benefit very considerably the agricultural and commercial interests of Canada, without injuring those of the United States.

Your Council considers the present time most favourable for effecting through Her Majesty's Government a reciprocal treaty of Commerce and Navigation between the United States and this Colony, by means of which the Wheat and Flour of either country will be allowed to enter the markets of the other, free from customs duty.

12

Examples of Conditions Underlying the Annexation Movement of 1848

From Canadian Archives, *Correspondence of the governor-general's secretary,* no. 4995, enclosures.

A large milling industry grew up in the years 1843-1846 based on the free admission of Canadian flour, including flour made from American wheat, into the British market. The repeal of the corn laws put an end to this industry overnight. The letters following reflect the conditions which furnished the driving power for the Reciprocity Treaty.

(i)

Jacob Keefer to William Hamilton Merritt

Thorold, April 19th, 1848

William Hamilton Merritt Esqre.

St. Catherines,

My Dear Sir

Understanding that you are about to visit Washington for the purpose of promoting . . . the objects had in view by the Millers on the line of the Welland Canal . . . allow me to wish you a pleasant journey and great success in procuring for us the free admission of our agricultural products into the markets of the United States— *our forlorn hope.*

The condition of our trade alluded to by the millers last fall has experienced no amelioration, on the contrary every day manifests more fully the legitimate effects of legislation in which we have no voice, and about which our opinions are not enquired. For the last twenty-four years I have watched with much anxiety the progress of this magnificent Welland Canal, and in the fall of 1845, seeing things here reduced to a state of permanency and order, and before the passage of Sir R. Peel's corn Law Bill, I commenced to build the *Welland Mills* and finished them about midsummer last at a cost of eight thousand pounds—but my *mill has done nothing since it was finished,* "the glory is departed". I embarked my *all* in the enterprise, with now the almost certain prospect that *all* will be a loss, such establishments to be maintained, must work, and though the lapse of years *may* bring back the business of the country, time is so essential an element, that, so far as I am concerned, it may as well be 300 as 3 years. Other men who have had the benefit of a few years' operation of their mills, may not feel so decidedly at once the falling off in their business. Farmers who are not in debt may be able to endure this state of things for a couple of years, but it cannot continue another twelve months without producing the most disastrous consequences in every department of business. Am I wrong in desiring to promote my interest? Should my being a subject of Gt. Britain be to my disadvantage in that particular? Are not the great questions of the day discussed upon the principles of political economy? what is the profit and what the loss of certain conditions of things. Now what would my condition be if instead of passing through Canada this splendid Canal ran through the State of New York, ten miles east of this? No man in his senses doubts that the difference in that case would be wonderfully in my favor. I am really glad you are going to Washington, because if anything can be brought about for our benefit, no time should be lost in trying and when it is known that all fails, then the sooner the connection between Gt. Britain and Canada is dissolved, the better for Canada, and surely, Gt. Britain would be more magnanimous than to ask Canadians to continue her subjects to their utter ruin, with us the thing would not be of choice but of necessity. . . .

Jacob Keefer

(ii)

James R. Benson to W. H. Merritt

St. Catherines 20th April 1848

Dear Sir. . . .

I have been many years engaged in business, but at no time have I witnessed so great depression, or more gloomy prospects for the future trade of Canada than at the present time. Having invested a very considerable amount of capital in the shipping trade on our lakes I feel in common with the miller from the want of employment for our vessels—the investment is not only profitless but I am sustaining a great loss, without any hope of amendment under the existing unequal and unjust laws regulating our trade with Great Britain and the United States; if we do not obtain a removal of the restrictions upon our produce going into the latter, and an alteration of our Navigation Laws it is no difficult task to tell what the result will be.

Since the passing of Sir Robert Peel's bill allowing the produce of the United States to enter Great Britain free of duty without obtaining for us the same advantage in their market a general feeling of dissatisfaction has manifested itself among all classes connected with trade and agriculture. Its effects during the past and present season has [sic] been too plain to be misunderstood. While at Buffalo wheat finds a ready sale at 5/9 Cy per bushel, with us 3/9 could scarcely be obtained. If the former system of protection is not adopted by Great Britain or she should not obtain for us the free admission of our produce into the United States market, I am well convinced the result will be an alienation of the minds of the most loyal men in Canada from the Mother Country and a desire to become a State of the Union; it is already frequently asked if such was the case would our property become less valuable—the answer is undeniable. . . .

James R. Benson

13

Reciprocity:—The Sister Colonies Preferable to the United States

From *Montreal Gazette*, quoted in *Quebec Gazette*, April 16, 1850.

The Parent has now departed from those principles,[1] and so perhaps in the course of ages, may the children, but until they

---

[1]The principles of mercantilism, that is, the system of differential duties.

arrive at the same height, it will be wise, prudent and profitable for them to adhere to the old example rather than to the new theory. The secret, then, is a complete reciprocity among all the British American colonies. . . . It is incumbent upon us . . . to provide permanent markets in which to dispose of our surplus products, independent of the United States. . . . These markets are to be found in the sister provinces below and in the West India Colonies.

THE DEVELOPMENT OF COLONIAL MERCANTILISM

From the first, certain interests in the colony sought protection against American products, both in the markets of the mother country and at home. Wiser heads saw that it was very much to the colony's advantage to permit these to come through Canada on their way to Great Britain, giving them the most favourable terms possible. But the farmer could never forget the difference in price of identical commodities, especially wheat, on both sides of the line, and put the American's advantage down to (a), the American duty on wheat, (b), the imperial trading system, which placed no duty on wheat entering Canada and refused to allow Canadian wheat into the imperial market free. Consequently, when in 1837 and succeeding years, bad harvests came and European wheat was actually imported (duty free), Canadian farmers urged a protective tariff on farm products. They did not secure it but the agitation was kept alive, and after 1846, the hard times of the milling industry were interpreted as due to the same causes. The farmer naturally joined in the cry for free entrance into the American market and the result, after some years of effort, was the Reciprocity Treaty.

Meanwhile, shortly after the province secured self-government it began itself to experiment in tariff-making. Under the old régime, in addition to the duties imposed by the imperial government, the legislature had been free to impose small flat rates of duty for local revenue. Under the new, the imperial government at first attempted to keep control, disallowing a local bill of 1845, but after 1846 it was less easy to do so and, in 1847, the province enacted its first real fiscal measure designed not so much for revenue as for regulation of trade. In many respects it was a protective tariff and the beginnings of Canadian protection may be dated from that year.

REFERENCES: S. J. McLean, *Tariff history of Canada* (University of Toronto studies, 1895); E. Porritt, *Sixty years of protection in Canada, 1846-1907* (London, 1908); Sir Francis Hincks, *Reminiscences of his public life* (Montreal, 1884).

1

Loyalist Petition against Rival Commodities from Vermont

From Canadian Archives, *Q*, XXVII(2), 992, enclosure in Dorchester to Sydney, June 13, 1787.

Petition of Loyalists from Point au Baudet Westward to Niagara, to Lord Dorchester, New Johnstown, April 15, 1787

. . . . *4th.*, They pray for a prohibition of pot and pearl ash and lumber from the State of Vermont to prevent a door being open'd for an illicit trade from the United States, which wou'd be a detriment to the Province in general, to this settlement in particular, and only beneficial to a few interested individuals. They also pray for a bounty to be laid on the above articles, as well as on hemp, in order to stimulate their industry and encourage their internal trade.

2

An Attempt to Protect the Canadian Farmer

From Canadian Archives, *Q*, CDXXVI, 109, Report on reserved bills passed 3rd Victoria, March 2, 1840.

Chapter 1.

An Act to impose duties on certain articles imported into the Province from the United States of America.

This act authorizes the levying and collecting to the use of Her Majesty the several duties of Customs mentioned in the Schedule thereto annexed on goods, wares and merchandize imported into this Province from the United States of America.

Persons importing flour, Pork, Wheat and other grain from the United States, not intended for consumption in the Province to give the bond of some resident to double the amount of the duty on such articles with a condition that the same shall be exported within nine months. This bond to be taken by the collector and sent immediately to the Inspector General and unless proof be forwarded to the Inspector General of the fulfilment of the condition, the bond shall be forfeited and the penalty appropriated to the public uses of the Province.

Wheat, Corn or other grain so imported may be ground into flour or meal, the exportation whereof shall be taken as the exportation of the wheat &c so ground.

These duties not to be imposed on goods in transit through the Welland Canal from one American Port to another.

All monies arising from such duties, necessary charges excepted, to be paid to the Receiver General for the public uses of the Province.

This Act not to prevent actual settlers from bringing with them when they come into the Province such Horses, sheep, cattle and Hogs, as they require for individual use, free of duty, upon making oath, if required, by the Collector, that such Horses &c are not imported for sale. Nor to impose a duty on travellers with Horses, Carriages or Stock passing through the Province.

This Act was reserved for the signification of Her Majesty's pleasure.

1st. That it might be determined whether duties could in this manner be imposed by the Provincial Legislature other than those mentioned in the Table of duties set forth by the Imperial Statute 3d & 4th Wm. 4 c. 59 under the true meaning of the 56th & 57th Clauses of that Act—and

2nd. As a Bill affecting Trade and Commerce generally.

3

Protection against Foreign Agricultural Produce

From Canadian Archives, *Private secretary's office, Upper Canada, Register, 1840-41*, enclosure in no. 2787.

Copy of the resolutions passed in the agricultural meeting which was held at Richmond Hill in the home district on December 9, 1840

. . . 5.—That almost every article of agricultural produce is now selling in our markets at prices that will not reimburse the cost of production. That this, so far as relates to articles of Home Consumption, is clearly attributable to the supply rapidly exceeding the demand, and to the free admission of like productions from the United States. As respects wheat and flour our chief exports, the duty levied upon them in Great Britain, the high rates of transportation, together with the want of a circulating medium commensurate with the business of the country, are the causes now operating to the injury of the agriculturist, transferring to others those profits that have been earned by the sweat of his brow.

6.—That so long as the present regulations continue in force the producer will in vain look for remuneration. Bounteous harvests may be bestowed but not for his benefit. When grain is higher in America than in Europe, the price in Canada is just the amount of the American duty less than in the United States, while our exports are met at Quebec and the lower ports by Russian wheat bonded in England, re-exported and admissible at one shilling per quarter duty. When the crops partially fail, and an increased value ought to make some compensation to the grower for diminished quantity, our markets are glutted from the opposite shore; and when our land has yielded a plentiful harvest, the before-mentioned causes so depress its worth, that the very abundance which should gladden the heart of the Farmer and reward his toil, is thus made to contribute to his disappointment.

7.—That in the opinion of this meeting the remedial measures for the evils complained of, are neither hard to be discerned nor difficult of accomplishment. The free admission of wheat and flour of Canadian Growth into Great Britain, the declaration of the Royal assent to the Bill of last session,[1] subjecting American produce to the payment of a duty when imported into Canada for Home Consumption, and such improvement of the navigation of the St Lawrence as will prevent transhipment, in conjunction with a provincial coinage and increased Banking facilities—These or similar Amendments to our present Regulations would afford the protection sought by our agricultural interest, and tend to the promotion of our Commerce and the general prosperity of the province.

4

The First Protective Tariff of Canada, 1847

From Annual report of the council of the Toronto board of trade, in *Toronto Globe*, January 8, 1848.

Before your Council introduces its remarks on the provisions of the Consolidated Customs' Bill [*1847*], it may not be out of place to state the Provincial and Imperial legislation in relation to the commercial affairs of the country. In the Provincial Customs Bills a uniform percentage was imposed on the general imports of the country for revenue purposes only, and additional duties were levied on foreign goods under the authority of Imperial Statutes for the purpose of giving similar articles of British origin a preference in the Canadian market through the duties so imposed. The Colonists enjoyed in return the protection afforded to their produce in the markets of the Mother Country under the operation of the British Corn Laws. The first instance in which the Provincial Legislature deviated materially from the policy stated was in the Customs' Bill of 1845, when it introduced a set of discriminating duties for the purpose of favouring certain interests. This Board was unsuccessful in its application to the Legislature at that time to have the objectionable clauses expunged; and it forwarded a memorial to Her Majesty to withhold her assent, for the reasons before stated. The Bill was afterwards disallowed.

[1]See the previous document.

The repeal of the British Corn Laws has left the agricultural produce of Canada unprotected in the markets of the Mother Country; to compete there with similar products of the world: and the Provincial Legislature availed itself of the privilege last session to repeal the Imperial statutes before mentioned; and in the Customs' Bill the duty on salt is very considerably reduced, a number of articles generally used in manufactures within the Province are placed on the list of goods at one per cent. ad valorem duty, and a few others added to the list of free goods.

Your Council fully concurs in the policy of encouraging the manufactures of the Province as far as it can be done by placing the raw materials required for them on the list of free goods; or admitting them at a nominal duty; but it is opposed to Class Legislation; which introduces unequal rates of customs duties on the general imports of the Province, for the purpose of protecting particular classes of the community at the expense of others; to avoid which, it is necessary to advocate the policy of imposing as low and uniform a rate as may be thought compatible with raising a sufficient revenue to meet the exigencies of the Government— and as the ad valorem mode of rating duties is generally considered the fairest, and the specific less equitable and often resorted to in legislation for the purpose of imposing higher rates according to value than might be desirable to name under the ad valorem form; your Council would prefer to see the latter adopted in all practicable cases.

This Bill contains a list of about 138 articles under the head of Specific Duties, and five of these are subjected to ad valorem duties in addition. Again, there are five rates of ad valorem duties, varying from one to twenty per cent., those which comprise the principal imports of the Province being subject to $7\frac{1}{2}\%$, a very high rate certainly when compared with those formerly imposed on a similar class of goods. Next may be noticed the injury inflicted on the Farmer by imposing a higher rate of duty on all Machines for agricultural purposes than on the general imports of the country; thus preventing him so far as unequal and high rates of customs duties can, from introducing those improvements in his profession which science and experience are accomplishing in other countries. And accordingly a duty of $12\frac{1}{2}\%$ is imposed upon Threshing Machines, Fanning and Bark Mills, and Scythes, and 10% on all other Machines for agricultural purposes.

It is stated in the Bill that when the duties are imposed upon Goods according to the value thereof, such value shall be the invoice value of the goods at the place whence the same were imported, with the addition of Ten pounds per centum thereon; but whether the result thus obtained is to be considered as provincial currency or the currency of the country from which the goods are imported, is not explained; and will possibly lead to difficulties between importers and Collectors of customs.

If Her Majesty assent to the Bill it will come into operation on the fifth of the present month, but your Council is not aware that it has yet received this sanction, and will not regret to hear it has been disallowed.

SUBSECTION C

ECONOMIC UNION:—A COLONIAL ZOLLVEREIN

Nova Scotian Proposals for a Colonial Customs Union

From Canadian Archives, *Correspondence of the governor-general's secretary, 1847,*
Nova Scotia, no. 4619.

Sir John Harvey to the Earl of Elgin

Government House Halifax,
March 17th, 1847

My Lord:

I hasten to transmit to Your Excellency a copy of an Act to
which I have this day given my assent relating to the Trade
between the British North American possessions, and to express
my hope that the Legislature of Canada will concur with us in the
opinion that the freest commercial intercourse between the several
Colonies would be attended with common benefit, and will consequently lose no time in providing by Law for the removal of all
restrictions on inter Colonial Trade in this part of Her Majesty's
Dominions.

J. Harvey

Province of Nova Scotia

An Act in relation to the Trade
between the British North American
Possessions passed 17ᵗʰ March 1847.

Whereas it is desirable that the Trade between the British
North American Provinces of Canada, New Brunswick, Prince
Edward Island, Newfoundland, and Nova Scotia should be con-
ducted in the most free and unrestricted manner.

Be it enacted by the Lieutenant Governor Council and Assembly that whenever from time to time the importation into any
other of the British North American Provinces hereinbefore
mentioned of all articles the Growth Production or Manufacture
of this Province (excepting Spirituous Liquors) shall by law be
permitted free from duty the Governor with the advice of the
Executive Council shall forthwith cause a Proclamation to be

366

inserted in the Royal Gazette fixing a short day thereafter on which the duty on all articles (excepting Spirituous liquors) being the Growth Production or Manufacture of any such Province as aforesaid into which the importation of all articles the Growth Produce or Manufacture of this Province (excepting Spirituous Liquors) shall be so permitted free from duty shall cease and determine. And from and after the day so limited and appointed all such articles the Growth Produce or Manufacture of any such Province in such Proclamation to be named (excepting Spirituous Liquors) shall be admitted into this Province Duty free upon such proof of origin and character as may from time to time be required in and by any order of the Governor in Council.

And be it enacted that this Act shall continue and be in force until the thirty first day of March which will be in the year of our Lord one thousand eight hundred and forty eight and no longer.

SECTION V

MONETARY AND FINANCIAL PROBLEMS IN
THE CANADAS

SUBSECTION A

CURRENCY AND BANKING

One of the chief problems of a new country is to secure and retain a supply of currency. Its wants are so much larger than its production that as a rule all coin is promptly gathered up by importers to meet their overseas accounts. Bills of exchange only partially relieve the situation, for exchange is invariably against the colony. "Hard money" was nowhere scarcer than in the Canadas, the main dependence being on the shipments the imperial government made in payment of officials and troops. Consequently all sorts of devices were resorted to to meet the deficiency, the most usual being barter and the issue of private notes by the merchants, the so-called "bon" (from the first word, when in French, "bon pour . . ."). These notes, redeemable in goods at the store of issue, passed from hand to hand and became an unofficial and irresponsible paper currency. The system, profitable for the merchants, led to grave abuses. Usually as a solution a bank was advocated, but though projects were many,[1] the first bank was not established until, in 1817, the present Bank of Montreal was founded. Long after that, the money of the Canadas continued to resemble the contents of a numismatic museum, the country being the last resting place of the battered and discredited coinage of two continents. It was not until self-government and after the dollar had officially, as long since in practice, displaced the imaginary colonial pound, that some order was introduced into the monetary chaos.

Many of the general economic problems of the country are broached in the copious references to monetary subjects in the source materials of the period.

REFERENCES: Adam Shortt, "Currency and banking, 1760-1841" (*Canada and its provinces*, IV, 599); *Ibid.*, "1841-1867" (*Ibid.*, V, 261); Victor Ross, *A history of the Canadian Bank of Commerce* (Toronto, 1920); A. R. M. Lower, "Credit and the Constitutional Act" (*Canadian Historical Review*, June, 1925); *Journal of the Canadian Bankers' Association, passim.*

1

The Issue of Private Paper Money

From Canadian Archives, *Wolford Simcoe papers*, 1792, I, book 2, 323-324.

The present state of the Paper Currency of this Province is a novelty in the History of Banking and may well warrant the fears and apprehensions of persons, in the smallest degree attentive to their property.

---

[1]The first banking project in Canada was one between three Montreal and London fur-trading firms in the year 1792 for the establishment of "The Canada Banking Company". The agreement between them is reproduced in H. A. Innis, *The fur trade in Canada*, 423.

The first person that made Paper Money in this Quarter was Captain Grant of Detroit, who at the request of the people there, issued small Bills, to answer the purposes of their internal intercourse. So little was it then thought a desirable thing to issue money, that he would engage to pay his, years after date; and I have seen some of his Bills in Circulation on these terms, since I came here.

During the War with America, the Expenses of Government at these posts, made more money necessary, and the principal trading house at each Post, having just given ample Security for the Payment of their Bills in Montreal, furnished the necessary supply. Other Houses afterwards took a share in this till within these two years, it was understood that the security of responsible houses in Montreal was necessary to render any paper Money Current. Since that time every body has become *Banker*. From the King's Receiver General to the Sergeant Major of the Rangers, from the first Commercial houses to the person who retails drams, *Everybody makes Money.*

As to security that is now not thought of. In a payment the other day of twenty five pounds I received the Bills of twelve different persons; To realize this by a draft on Montreal would require an application to as many different people, some at Detroit, some of York, some the Lord knows where.

'Tis perhaps easier to point out the evil, than to find a Cure. The system adopted by the Government, of bringing up specie for the payment of their Officers and Contingent Expenses is attended with so much trouble, expense, and risk, that I apprehend it will soon be found very inconvenient. Indeed the present state of the Country, in need of Cattle, and tempted by many contraband articles, which specie only can purchase from an American Neighbor, will produce such a drain for this as will effectually prevent its stay in the Country, & will make the Business of supply a constant and a permanent one.

Were we once in the situation, to which I hope time will bring us to pay for our imports, by our Produce, I without hesitation would recommend a Bank among ourselves, either as a private or a public speculation. Managed by Government on a liberal scale, and free from the insane policy of Inducements, its uses might be of the most essential consequence, by furnishing the necessary to the beginnings of Industry, in supplying the means for the most

24

useful projects.   But while every shilling we can scrape together, must be sent below in payment of a Debt, this Bank would find no employment but in drawing Bills, and for which Capital must be lodged below to answer these.

A Bank has been established in Montreal, on perhaps as secure a basis as the country can offer.   The Managers have I believe made a proffer to supply.

[not signed]

2

"Halifax" and "New York" Currency

From La Rochefoucault-Liancourt, *Travels in North America*, 242.

The value of money in Canada should, according to law, be equal to that which it bears in Halifax, and consequently a dollar be worth five shillings.   This standard is strictly adhered to in all government accounts, but not so scrupulously observed in the course of private business.   The currency which circulates in New York, passes also, especially in that part of Canada which borders on New York.[1]

3

The Question of the Establishment of a Bank

From *Quebec Mercury*, January 5, 1807.

To the editor of the Quebec Mercury

. . . .For years past the establishment of a Bank, in this province, has engrossed the attention of some of our best informed men, in private circles, but never yet, to my knowledge, have any remarks, on such a measure been offered to the public, and, in no period nor in any country has that subject ever more merited attention than it does, at present, in this province. . . .

In all countries the circulating medium should be proportionate to the wants and useful purposes of the inhabitants; where commerce does not exist no other is required than hard money as it is wanted for few other purposes than procuring the necessaries of life, and, comparatively speaking, little will suffice; but where

---

[1]New York currency reckoned eight shillings to the dollar. Hence the old expression, a "York shilling", meaning twelve and a half cents.

commerce takes her busy stand money is its life, and must there be more easily and abundantly procured: the current coin can never be sufficient for the purposes of a commercial country or of one aiming to become such. . . . Indeed if the quantity of specie necessary for commercial purposes could be obtained trade could not be carried on largely with that alone. Different mediums of intercourse must be resorted to, of which none is so safe, so convenient, and so adapted to the purpose as the notes of a Bank, authorized and supported by the monied interest of the country. Among the many advantages resulting from a Bank, in this country, would be the assurance of punctuality in the dealings of Merchants, by enabling them to make large purchases without selling their bills at a discount. (This, it is too obvious to be mentioned, is done by borrowing of the Bank on their notes, or by getting notes of others discounted.)

In the increasing trade with the United States, our Merchants would be enabled to make their remittances in Bank notes, and thereby retain the gold and silver which are now carried out of the province, the amount of which rises annually to between sixty and seventy thousand pounds. This would, in part, remedy what is considered a serious and growing evil to the province, under the existing regulations of commerce with the States; an evil which calls for redress, as those regulations, without being for the general interest of the empire, serve only to cramp the commercial exertions of his Majesty's subjects.

The following statement, in round numbers, of our trade with the United States, which I am certain is correct, will shew the importance of the object:—

The imports from the U. States consist annually of

Teas to the amount of £15,000
India & other Goods 25,000
Pearl & Pot Ash 37,500
Leather 15,000
Pork, Butter, Cheese & Grain 7,800

Making in the aggregate a sum exceeding 100,000*l*. For the payment of these goods there are exported from the province annually, to the United States, Peltries, Salt and other goods, to the value of 37,500*l*. and the ballance, of upwards of 62,000*l*. is paid in cash. If nothing else was gained but the use of so much money to the province, could it be doubted that a Bank would be highly beneficial? But from the ready currency which Bank notes obtain in the States, we should be enabled to keep (if we desire it) the greater part of the capital of our Bank in circulation in that country, and in lieu thereof procure for ourselves the use of their money. In addition to all this is to be considered the facility with which Merchants would be enabled to transact their business, by the use of Checks, and the saving of a cashier and additional clerks in large houses. Lands also would thereby rise in value, as farmers would find a ready market for their produce.

However various may be the opinion of the good people collected together in this province, on many subjects, there could not, I must fain flatter myself, be found many dissentient voices to so salutary a measure as the establishment of a Bank. What may perhaps, at this day, be *considered* the personal interest of our great capitalists, in trade, might possibly lead them to a temporary opposition; but I trust, from the known patriotic spirit of our great commercial characters, that will not be the case.—Should I be mistaken I should not hesitate to say that their opposition would be contrary to their own *real interests*.

I am aware that it has been objected that a Bank would raise the price of produce and of the necessaries of life, beyond their *real value*, as has been said to have been the case in New York; the assertion is erroneous, one Bank or even two would not have that effect in the smallest degree. The person who should offer such an opinion, must do it with an interested view. The position is absurd, for the comparison of the State of New York with its eight Banks, doing business with an aggregate capital exceeding six millions of dollars, for the use of a population scarcely exceeding 500,000 persons; or of Massachusetts, with its twenty-two Banks, for a population of 600,000, cannot be seriously made with the establishment of a single Bank, with a moderate capital, in this province, of which the population is, to a certainty, between 2 and 3 hundred thousand souls. . . .

Dec. 1st, 1806   A. T.

4

Founding of the Bank of Montreal

From *Montreal Courant*, quoted in *Montreal Gazette*, September 24, 1817.

Montreal Bank

We learn that the last undisposed shares in the Bank were taken up on Friday last, and that a hundred shares more would have been taken had they not been previously disposed of. The holders now consider the stock much above par.

5

Opposition of the French Party to the Growing English Economic Structure

From Debates of the assembly of Lower Canada, March 5, 1831, reported in *Montreal Gazette*, March 19, 1831.

The House in Committee on the Quebec Bank Bill. . . .

Mr. Bourdages expected that the Hon. Members who supported these bank Bills would content themselves, as they did last year, to tell us that we did not understand the matter, and that they alone understood it; but it was plain to every man of common sense and reflection that the Banks had done more harm than good. On the specie question, everybody must be convinced that they were the cause of its disappearance, as well as of what was called deteriorated coin being first introduced in large quantities and then banished. They first speculated upon sending for large amounts of it, and circulated them here and there, when it was *reformé* they got hold of it again and sent it back to be passed again at a profit, speculating thus both ways, pocketing the profits and leaving the mass of the people to bear the loss. . . .

Mr. Bedard said that was the very reason why he was against Banks, because he and many more had no confidence in them. He believed the Banks had done great harm. Their only real use to the public was an Office of Discount, but they were of no use in that respect, for the Directors and stockholders absorbed all the money for discounts, and there was none left for others. If he was not mistaken, Directors and stockholders were not, in other countries, allowed to participate in the discounts. Before the Bank, young beginners got credit to go into business, and if they could not realise in time, their credit was bad; but now notes were taken, with which the merchant ran directly to the Bank to get discount. . . .

Mr. De Montenach spoke from the experience of twenty years that he had lived in this country. We had seen quantities of gold and silver of the best assay in circulation, and in large quantities up to the very times the Banks were established; now we have comparatively no specie in circulation, and when we go to the Banks to get cash, we are paid in the worst kind of specie; that was perhaps the reason why the country people, who formerly would take nothing but good silver, now even preferred notes. The practice of Directors discounting for each other had already been noticed; but it produced also the consequence that when a man of landed property, a man whose real wealth far surpassed the fictitious paper riches of these Directors, wanted to discount a miserable Bill of £100, he could not get it, whilst thousands were profusely given to people who perhaps were worth nothing. The country had not gained by the Banks, but lost. He did not, however, say it would be right, under existing circumstances, to put them down altogether; but their Charters ought to be revised with all circumspection. . . .

6
How "Hard Money" was Gathered up for Export

From *Montreal Gazette*, January 31, 1832.

WANTED IMMEDIATELY, 5,000 SOVEREIGNS and GUINEAS, for which the highest premium will be given . . . .

Horatio Gates & Co.

7
Popular Indifference to the State of the Currency

From *Montreal Gazette*, February 12, 1833.

George Auldjo, chairman, Montreal committee of trade,
to
Nathaniel Gould, chairman, North American Colonial Association,
London

. . . The subject of reforming the currency is the more difficult, because the bulk of the community express no feeling or grievance respecting it; and I am persuaded that no efficient change will take place except at the expense of the Imperial Government and in the responsibility of the Provincial Executive.

8
The Trade Balance and Exchange Rates

From *Observations on a metallic currency for Lower Canada* (Montreal, 1837), reprinted in *Montreal Gazette*, February 2, 1837.

It is, I know a common assertion, even of men of business that the trade of the Colony is too much against it to permit specie, unless debased here, to remain in the country. These good people, in the first instance, do not always distinguish between a "balance of trade" and a "balance of payments"—for it may very well be, that while the former appears against us, the latter may actually be in our favour. Some of the imports into Canada yearly are nothing more than the property of the emigrants and ought not, therefore, to be considered in the balance of trade. Again, a considerable portion of the foreign commodities are capitals loaned to individuals in that shape, and not to be repaid, probably, for years. This is quite a natural course with a wealthy country, that cannot more profitably use a part of its surplus money, towards a poorer one, but one that is not only industrious, but has the germs of riches in her soil. This portion, therefore, of the imports, ought likewise to be deducted from the balance of trade—at least from that year's foreign debt. . . .

Now, in the case of Canada, she may be importing more largely than she exports, and be running year after year in debt to England; but it does not, therefore, follow, that each year's "balance of *payments*" is against her, or that she is getting poorer. The balance of payments could not be yearly against her, and she could not be getting every year more impoverished, without coming very soon to a stand. She would speedily be in the situation of the indolent and luxurious spendthrift—her coffers exhausted—energies decayed—and credit lost. I shall shew in reference to the balance of payments not being yearly against Canada, that, consequently, there would not exist a continuous drain of the precious metals, by exhibiting the state of the exchange with England over a period of sixteen years.

It has been noted, that the par of exchange, between England and her American Colonies, was fixed at 4s. 6d. sterling for the dollar, or equal to 5s. currency, when the Spanish dollar, or piece of eight was actually worth 4s. 6d. mint price. Further that "the Spanish dollar" (the one now generally seen, and so called,) has since been reduced alike in weight and fineness, and is now, at the market price of 5s. per oz. only equivalent to 4s. 2⅛d. sterling, thereby making our real par of exchange nearly 8 per cent. premium over our present nominal par. With this explanation let us now observe the average rates of bills on England, in this market, in each year, from 1821 to 1836, both inclusive.

1821..	7¾ per cent. premium.		1829..	9½ per cent. premium.	
1822..	12	"	"	1830..	8	"	"
1823..	6¾	"	"	1831..	9½	"	"
1824..	9¾	"	"	1832..	11	"	"
1825..	8¼	"	"	1833..	10	"	"
1826..	8¾	"	"	1834..	6	"	"
1827..	10½	"	"	1835..	10	"	"
1828..	10¼	"	"	1836..	10½	"	"

About 9½ per cent. premium over our nominal par, for the whole period of sixteen years.

This would apparently shew an adverse state of trade, and a balance of payments against us; and I admit it would be a true index of the reality, were the country in possession of a sound Metallic Currency. It is, however, not a correct, though a prima facie criterion, since it is notorious that the bank rate here is usually from 1½ to 2 per cent. above the New York market, where we could, at any time, with a sound currency, purchase our bills at a cost of little over ½ per cent. instead of the 1½ or 2 per cent. paid to the Banks. Deducting, therefore, this excess of 1 or 1½ per cent. paid on our remittances abroad as a direct tax for the support of a debased local coin, from 9½ per cent., the average rate in Montreal since 1821, it would shew that our remittances would have been made, throughout the time, at about par, had the country a sound metallic medium; and will also exhibit the fact of there being an equality in our foreign dealings, at least in our payments. I think, therefore, I may affirm, that I have established the accuracy of my position, that "the balance of payments" is not, and could not be steadily against Canada, and that there need not, consequently, be any dread of a *continuous* drain of specie.

The English Government, by not exacting any seignorage on the coinage of *gold* (the sole standard of value,) has shewn its anxiety not to add to its value, by this cost, and so ought to be a lesson to us in determining, whether the real exchangeable value, or a fictitious local value should be given to coin intended to be used equally as a circulating medium at home and as a foreign remittance. If confined to one purpose alone, it performs only half its office, and, it may be, the least valuable half.

... It might be worthy of consideration, in how far it would be of service to the internal business of the country, to confine a small coin as change in our circulation by rating it above the real value, under such directions as would keep it very limited in amount and only be a legal tender for say not over five pounds.[1]

Should this course be adopted, and a coin be struck expressly for the purpose I would then suggest that the depreciation of the coin be rather in weight than in its purity as there would be the less temptation left to counterfeit it. . . . It may be thought "passing strange" that I have not as yet stated what should be done with the French crowns and half-crowns[2] for it is certain that if we want to introduce foreign coin here and to continue it any time in circulation, this could never be effected while the former remain at their present legal value. It is a rather difficult matter to arrange satisfactorily: but I would suggest as the only feasible and just method that they may be called in, and redeemed by the local government at their present value; the crowns, or such of them as are not much defaced, to be reissued at their intrinsic worth; but the half-crowns, the "bare-faced rogues", to be condemned to the crucible, and if possible, that a small provincial coin, for "change", should be minted from them.

I may just allude to the wretched state of our copper coin . . . to shew how profitable a coinage of this description of money might be made to a provincial mint, if one were established in Canada: independently of the immense service that an issue of good copper coin would be to the public, to supply the place of brass buttons and pieces of clipt copper.

9

The Crisis of 1837:—Suspension of Specie Payments

From Debate of the assembly of Upper Canada, June 24, 1837, reprinted in *Montreal Gazette*, July 4, 1837.

Report of the Committee to whom was referred that part of the Speech from the Throne, relating to the monetary state of the Province.

---

[1] As is the case with our modern subsidiary silver coinage.

[2] The reference is to the "hard money" that was poured into Canada by the French government in the years just prior to the conquest. This money was paid out for goods and services and immediately disappeared into the hoards of the inhabitants, not to reappear for many years later when security had been established under the English régime. It gradually became the common circulating medium of Lower Canada and by the time of the pamphlet from which the extract is taken had become wretchedly debased.

Mr. Merritt,—The principle of the two Bills under consideration embraces two important objects . . . .

The second object is intended to bring the credit of the Province, (by the sale of those debentures which will supply the place of specie) immediately in aid of the Banks, and enable them to extend their credit, and restore the circulating medium, to the agricultural, commercial and general business of the Province. . . .

Mr. Cameron was not aware of any great commercial distress in the Province, he was a merchant himself, and had felt latterly a good deal inconvenienced, but he considered that that arose from other causes, and he believed that our trade was at present in a very healthy state. When the banks in the United States and in Lower Canada suspended specie payment, he thought our banks should have immediately done so too. He did not know that this measure would be of much relief to the Banks, and thought that it would be far more advantageous that the Legislature should compel all the Banks to suspend specie payments at once, for some limited time. . . .

10

Copy of a "Bon" or Merchant's Paper Note[1]

6644C　　　　　　　Petit Saguenay, 15 Novembre, 1853

Ordre au Magasin pour les Travailleurs
AU COMMIS DU MAGASIN.
Delivrez au porteur des provisions, &c., du Magasin au montant de
CINQ CHELLINS COURANT
Pour gages dans mon emploi.
5S　　　　　　　　　　　　Pour W. Price,
　　　　　　　　　　　　　[*Signed*] R. W. Price
Non Pour Circulation.　5S.

---

[1]See the first document in this section, page 368.

PUBLIC FINANCE

In this period public finance is political rather than economic in nature and it is, therefore, treated briefly. Revenues came from two sources, taxation granted by the legislatures and moneys under the immediate control of the crown, such as the income from lands and forests, the revenue from duties imposed by the imperial government and miscellaneous fees, licenses, and so on. The political struggles arising out of this situation need no comment here. The jealousy between government and assemblies led to mal-administration, corruption, waste, and lack of efficiency in the prosecution of public objects. The documents also touch on the division of the customs duties between Upper and Lower Canada, a clumsy financial expedient and a constant source of friction.

REFERENCES: Durham's *Report, passim*; D. A. McArthur, "History of public finance, 1763-1840" (*Canada and its provinces*, IV, 491); *Ibid.*, "1840-1867"; (*Ibid.*, V, 165); D. G. Creighton, "The struggle for financial control in Lower Canada, 1818-1821" (*Canadian Historical Review*, June, 1931); A. R. M. Lower, "Credit and the Constitutional Act" (*Ibid.*, June, 1925).

1

The Public Revenue of Lower Canada, 1793

From Canadian Archives, *series E*, State book "B", Lower Canada.

This statement serves to show the proportion of revenue under the direct control of the crown and the amount brought in by legislative enactment.

Statement of revenue, Lower Canada, December 25, 1792-January 5, 1794.

Gross Receipts		£ 8623 –5 –0
Details:—		
Casual and Territorial Revenue	£389 –7 –8½	
Duties 14 Geo. III[1]	5692 –3 –8	
Licenses do.	754 –4 –0	
Duties by legislature[2]	1613 –6 –1	
Fines and Forfeitures	174 –3 –6½	
Fees on licences		271 –3 –0
Total taken from subject		£8894 –8 –0

The gross revenue—£8623 –5 –0—was diminished by £715 –8 –8 and £120 –3 –6, charges for collecting items 2 and 4, and by £77 –17 –8 issued on account of collection. This left a net balance in the Treasury of £7709 –15 –2.

[1]The Quebec Revenue Act, 14 Geo. III, cap. 88.
[2]The provincial, as distinct from the imperial, tariff.

2

Division of the Customs Duties between the Two Provinces

From *Journals of assembly, Lower Canada,* V, 25.

Articles of Provisional Agreement made and entered into by the undersigned Commissioners on the part of Lower Canada . . . and the Honorable Richard Cartwright, The Honorable John Munro and John M'Donell, Esquires, on the part of the Province of Upper Canada. . . .

I. That the legislature of Upper Canada will not impose any duties whatever on any goods, wares or merchandises imported or brought into Lower Canada and passing into Upper Canada but will allow and admit the legislature of Lower Canada to impose and levy such reasonable duties on such goods, wares and merchandises and such articles aforesaid as they may judge expedient for the purpose of raising a revenue within the province of Lower Canada.

II. In consideration of the Legislature of Upper Canada relinquishing the imposition of duties as aforesaid, the Legislature of Lower Canada will allow a just proportion of the duties imposed by them to be paid to Upper Canada; And in order to ascertain such proportion, a fit and proper person shall be appointed . . . to reside at Coteau du Lac as inspector, for the purpose of demanding and receiving accounts of articles subject to duties, contained in boats, canoes and carriages passing by that place. . . .

VI. That the Legislature of Upper Canada shall impose and levy upon all articles subject to duties in Lower Canada which shall be brought into Upper Canada from the United States of America without passing through Lower Canada, duties equal to those as are or shall be imposed and levied on similar articles when brought from the United States into Lower Canada: . . .[1]

IX. That the Legislature of Lower Canada will not impose any

---

[1]The sixth article was not accepted by Upper Canada for the reason that the United States at this time had not yet begun to impose duties on goods entering its territory from Canada by inland navigation. Upper Canada feared retaliation on the part of the Americans, which would injure the supply trade to the newly settling American communities south of the lakes to an extent far beyond any revenue derived from duties collected on goods coming into the province from the United States. As it was as much in the interest of the lower province to preserve this trade as in that of the upper, Lower Canada accepted the agreement with the sixth article deleted. See the section on transportation for more information as to the importance of this early transit trade.

duty upon any article passing from Upper Canada into Lower Canada. . . .
This done and concluded at Montreal, this 28th day of January, 1797.

[Signed by the commissioners for both provinces]

3
The Case for Indirect Taxation in a New Country

From Debate of the assembly of Lower Canada, January 21, 1818, reported in *Montreal Gazette*, February 4, 1818.

In a committee of the whole House on the Bill granting a duty of two and a half per cent on merchandise imported into this province, &c. . . . Mr. SPEAKER[1] rose to say, that, no subject of deliberation can more deeply interest the representatives of a people, than that in which the imposition of duties is put in question. . . .

Our situation is happy; we in fact pay fewer imposts than any other civilized people. Upon those articles which may be considered as objects of luxury, such as teas, coffee, sugar, wine, spirituous liquors, &c., we pay at most from six to ten per cent. and upon articles of manufacture, but two and a half per cent This latter duty was the present subject of consideration. . . . It is some years since the misconceived interests of trade brought into contact with the general interest of the other classes of the population, occasioned discussions which have ever since fixed the public opinion on this point. The merchants were for the establishment of direct taxes. There are perhaps circumstances under which this mode of taxation might be the best, but it was certainly erroneous to prefer such a mode to the present, by which nine-tenths of the revenues were collected in a single port of entry; to substitute for the small number of custom house officers which we employ, a host of excisemen; to prefer, to the duties, paid insensibly by the consumer and in a way entirely at his own option, a forced revenue upon every acre of soil payable at a fixed period, which necessarily must operate with unequal weight upon the rich proprietor of fertile land, and the poor proprietor of an arid and fruitless soil. Such an impost must necessarily have retarded the progress of

---
[1]Louis Joseph Papineau.

clearing the woodlands, the primary source of the prosperity of all new countries where lands are of moderate value; inasmuch as none but cleared lands were to have been liable to it.

4

Revenues and Expenditures of Lower Canada for 1828

From *Montreal Gazette*, February 5, 1829.

The net Revenue of Lower Canada, paid into the hands of the Receiver General within the year is stated at £113,149 18s. 11d.

The Estimate in Sterling of the expenses of Government for the year is £62,128, 10s. 9d. Additional Estimate, £2910, in all £65,038 10s. 9d.

The Estimate of expenses of Government for the last year remaining unpaid is £9221 9s. 9d.

The amount alleged to be at disposal of the Legislature is upwards of £120,000 currency (not including the disputed Revenue).

The various sums voted, or proposed to be voted for hospitals, Education, Chambly Canal, Light Houses, execution of certain Laws, &c., it is understood may be estimated at about £80,000 independently of the sum of thirty or forty thousand pounds long due and for which interest is paid, on the Lachine Canal.

5

Division of the Customs Duties as Illustrating the Growth of Upper Canada

From *Montreal Gazette*, November 3, 1836.

A new division of the import duties levied at Quebec, between Lower and Upper Canada, must take place during the present season.

In 1828 the proportion of one fourth or twenty-five per cent was awarded to Upper Canada; but, in 1832, the Hon. G. H. MARKLAND, who again acted on behalf of the Province, claimed thirty-three and one-third per cent, which was objected to by the Hon. T. Pothier, who acted for Lower Canada, though he was willing to allow thirty per cent. Not being able to agree upon this subject, nor upon the selection of a third Arbitrator, His Majesty appointed the Hon. WARD CHIPMAN, of NEW BRUNSWICK, as Umpire, and that gentleman, with the Hon. Mr. MARKLAND, being a majority of the Arbitrators, rendered an award on the 26th June, 1833, by which one-third or thirty-three and one-third per cent of all the duties collected at Quebec for the four years succeeding the 1st July, 1832, was awarded to UPPER CANADA.

The UPPER CANADA papers mention that the Hon. JOHN MACAULAY has been appointed by His Excellency as Arbitrator for UPPER CANADA to apportion the duties for the four years succeeding the 1st. July, 1836.

6
The Public Poverty of Upper Canada and its Alleviation

From Canadian Archives, *Upper Canada sundries*, 1839.

William Hamilton Merritt to Sir George Arthur

St. Catherines, Feb. 18, 1839

. . . In the preceding letters, I have endeavoured to draw your attention, first, to the past mismanagement of our finances and entire monetary system. . . . Your Excellency cannot be expected to devote your attention to the minute operations by which a revenue is obtained from each article. . . . In comparing the wealth and prosperity of this province with that of the adjoining country, there is one general feature which Your Excellency . . . cannot have failed to observe, viz., their immense superiority over us with respect to the value of property, products, internal revenue, the credit of the state stocks on the London market and the extent of the appropriations made on their public works, all of which afford the most striking and positive proof that some cause . . . must exist to produce this extraordinary difference. This cause I have endeavoured to trace and find that in the two old states of New York and Pennsylvania it proceeds from the creation of an internal revenue and in the new states from a revenue derived from the sales of land and its judicious application to the payment of interest on the money borrowed for the construction of their public works.

And from an attentive observation of many years, I feel equally confident that we cannot from our present prescribed boundary, obtain a similar revenue without a concentration of power in one body. The remedy is therefore to be found only in a union of the two provincial legislatures or in the more limited and partial measure of obtaining the control of a seaport.[1]

My remarks are not intended to be either personal or political. They are merely directed against our present system, under which the wisdom of *Solomon* can never make Upper Canada a prosperous country.

William Hamilton Merritt

7

Influence of the Erie Canal on Customs Revenue of Lower Canada

From *Journals of Assembly, Upper Canada*, 1839, appendices, p. 36, Second report of the committee on finance, April 9, 1839.

It appears by the returns from the Port of Quebec, the amount of revenue collected in 1820 was £95,086. 11. 0. that it increased in 1825, the year the Erie Canal was finished, to £127,854. 12. 0, since which it has fluctuated from year to year but up to 1838, in place of increasing in a progressive ratio, it has actually decreased to £115,956.

Wm Hamilton Merritt,
Chairman

8

Canadian Revenues and Their Expenditure

From Canadian Archives, *Upper Canada sundries*, 1839.

William Hamilton Merritt to Charles Poulett Thomson

St. Catherines, 28th Nov., 1839
. . . Canada has at present a revenue derived 1st from duties

---

[1]A reference to the proposal frequently made at the time, for the annexation of Montreal to Upper Canada.

on imports, amounting per annum to £226,000, 2nd Casual and Territorial Revenue
arising from lands &c............................   80,000
                                                      ———
Say for both provinces...........................   300,000
   . . . Three fourths of our revenue has been expended in Lower Canada where it has been of little or no service, but as it is hoped this evil is about to be remedied I will not enlarge on it.

William Hamilton Merritt

SECTION VI

THE ECONOMIC LIFE OF THE MARITIME
PROVINCES

INTRODUCTORY

THE lands about the entrance to the gulf have a somewhat less extreme, a moister, and perhaps less
favourable climate than the valley of the St. Lawrence, along with a less fertile soil. They constitute the
northern termination of the Appalachian region, country
characterized by low and irregular ridges, often with good
valleys between them. Arable and non-arable are, therefore,
not sharply divided as they are in the upper provinces. In
New Brunswick, the River St. John reproduces in miniature
the conditions of the St. Lawrence, having a dependent and
international hinterland. The presence of the same tree,
the white pine, gave lumbering much the same predominant
position that it had in Canada. Nova Scotia is almost an
island and the extent and indentation of its coast line turned
its life to the sea. Its position precludes a hinterland and
it has, therefore, to depend on its own resources. The best
natural market of the three provinces, New England, is from
political causes, unreliable. This unreliability and limitation
of markets, not compensated for by the absence of the
winter's isolation of the Canadas, has been a major factor
in the economy of these provinces.

REFERENCES: *Canada and its provinces*, XIII; T. C. Haliburton, *An historical
and statistical account of Nova Scotia* (2 volumes, Halifax, 1829) and *The Clock-
maker* (3 volumes, London, 1843); J. Hannay, *A history of New Brunswick* (2
volumes, St. John, 1910); W. O. Raymond, *The River St. John* (St. John, 1910);
A. B. Warburton, *History of Prince Edward Island* (St. John, 1923); John Young,
Letters of Agricola (Halifax, 1822); there is no satisfactory provincial history of
Nova Scotia, if Beamish Murdoch's, long out of print, be excepted.

COLONIZATION, SETTLEMENT, AND PUBLIC LAND POLICY

The three Atlantic provinces were settled by "layers" of population, just as were the Canadas; first came the French Acadians, then Halifax Irish, Lunenburg Germans, and Annapolis valley New Englanders before the Revolution, Yorkshire Methodists during it, Loyalists immediately after it, and the Scots during and after it. After the War of 1812 these provinces received a share of the rush across the Atlantic, the later-comers, Irish and English mostly, filling up a good part of New Brunswick. The task of disposing of the public land was essentially the same as in the St. Lawrence valley and handled in only slightly less bungling fashion; since there was not nearly so much desirable land, there were—with the notorious exception of Prince Edward Island, the lands of which were given to a handful of English absentees—fewer large "land-grabbers". And there was no complicating question of clergy reserves. The fertile areas being small, markets uncertain, and New England convenient, emigration began early and has since remained a constant and embarrassing problem of Maritime life.

REFERENCES: Chester Martin, *Lord Selkirk's work in Canada* (Oxford, 1916); William F. Ganong, "A monograph of the origins of settlements in New Brunswick (*Transactions* of the Royal Society of Canada, 1904, section 2); W. H. Siebert and F. E. Gilliam, "The Loyalists in Prince Edward Island" (*Ibid.*, 1910); A. W. H. Eaton, "The settling of Colchester County, Nova Scotia by New England Puritans and Ulster Scotsmen" (*Ibid.*, 1912); Joseph E. Howe, "Quitrents in New Brunswick" (*Report* of the Canadian Historical Association, 1928, 55); see also references to section I B, page 96.

1

Escheat of Land Grants for Non-fulfilment of Conditions

From Canadian Archives, *series Nova Scotia A*, XCVIII, 6.

A Brief account of the present Mode by which Lands in Nova Scotia are taken from Original Grantees for non-performance of the Conditions of their Grants, and regranting the same to others, together with an humbly proposed Amendment thereof.

The commissioner of Escheats upon Complaint being filed in behalf of the Crown alleging certain Breaches of the Conditions in the Grants mentioned, issues a precept under his Hand and Seal directed to the provost Marshal, returnable at a short day named, commanding him to summon twelve lawfull Freeholders of the province, to inquire upon Oath touching the performance or nonperformance of such Conditions; and the Clerk of Escheats and Forfeitures puts up an Advertisement (in Halifax only) of the time and place of taking the Inquisition—At the day appointed, the

Jurors being impannelled and Sworn—the Evidence in behalf of the Crown is laid before them, upon which they make an Inquisition under their Hands and Seals, and the Hands and Seal of the Commissioner, whereby they find and declare the Defaults of the Grantee. It has been usual for some years past, to make two parts of those inquisitions indented alike, and to publish in the Halifax Gazette the taking of them, but this Advertisement is lately disused by direction of the Commissioner—both parts of the Inquisition remain in the Commissioners Office, with the Clerk of Escheats and Forfeitures—and the Government immediately make new Grants of such Lands to other persons applying for them. . . .

R. Gibbons
Solicitor General of Nova Scotia

2

Arrival in Nova Scotia of Loyalists from South Carolina

From Canadian Archives, *Nova Scotia A*, CIII, 10.

Halifax 23^d January 1783

Sir,

. . . Five Hundred Refugees arrived in November from Charlestown, everything has been done to assist them in settling themselves in the Province, and I flatter myself they will be a great acquisition to it. . . .

J. Patterson, M.G.

3

Grants of Land to Disbanded Loyalist Regiments

From Canadian Archives, *N.S. A.*, CIII, 201.

To His Excellency John Parr Esquire
Captain General and Governor in Chief
of His Majestys Province of Nova Scotia
in America Chancellor and Vice Admiral
of the same &c. &c. &c.

The Memorial of John Small Esquire Lieutenant Colonel Commandant to the Second Battallion of His Majestys 84th Regiment (of Highlanders)

Humbly Sheweth,

That the Battalion The Memorialist has the honor to Command was the Earliest levied of all the corps form'd for the Augmentation of His Majesty's Land Forces, in 1775, on the commencement of a Recent Rebellion against the Government and constitution of Britain.

That the proposals for levying and forming this corps, from political Utility to the Royal Cause, as well as the Military Duty to be deriv'd from their Services, was so fully and favorably consider'd as to receive offers from their Sovereign for the men who shoud voluntarily Engage to serve therein to be promis'd to each man or head of a Family 200 Acres Vacant or ungranted Lands, together with 50 more in addition for every individual the family might consist of. The whole to be free of Quit Rent for twenty years. The Royal faith thus Pledg'd (and Signified by the Right Honorable Earl of Dartmouth Secretary of State for the Colonies in 1775) was sanction'd to the men individually by the hand & Seal of the Commanding Officer on their Enlisting.—Copies of these important papers having been laid before, and perus'd by your Excellency: The Memorialist now humbly Approaches you, being bound to represent that as the Battallion under his Command is now at the Eve of Reduction he will do himself the honor of minutely specifying the Officers and Men now belonging thereto who have intentions to settle in the Province you govern and of course entitled to grants of Lands therein to the end that he and they may be indulg'd with a favorable answer to the following Prayer Viz^t.

To have your Excellencys Immediate Sanction for surveying, and on the same being compleated to have a Patent for the Quantity of Land they may appear to be entitled to. In certain Tracts as yet ungranted on the Kenetcook, Minchio and Meander Rivers in the District of, and not distant from, Windsor, Adjoining to the Township of Newport, and to other Tracts already granted, according to a map and Description thereof, herewith presented.

The Benignity of His Majestys Gracious intentions, the Benevolence and Zeal of the Public Good, which mark your Excellencys Publick as well as Private Character, the just and Equitable disposition of the Honorable Council of the Province Leave no room to doubt of the Success of this Application.

The Memorialist therefore for himself and the Corps he commands as in Duty bound will ever pray &ᶜ. &ᶜ. &ᶜ.

John Small

Lᵗ Col. Comm 2ᵈ Battallion 84ᵗʰ Regiment at Halifax
Halifax Nova Scotia
October the 7ᵗʰ 1783

4

Inducements to Loyalists to Settle in Cape Breton

From Canadian Archives, *series M*, I, 87.

BY HIS EXCELLENCY JOSEPH FREDERICK WALLET DES BARRES Esqʳ. Governor of the Island of Cape Breton and Dependencies, Commanding His Majesty's Forces therein &c, &c.

A PROCLAMATION

WHEREAS I have received good Intelligence, that a number of loyal Families, desirous of continuing their Allegiance to His Majesty, and to enjoy under the protection of His Gracious Government the Blessing of the British Constitution, are at a loss where to fix themselves in a way and situation so as to secure to their Posterity the comfortable Enjoyment of the Fruits of their Industry and Labour. I have thought fit to inform them; that a large Body of Land extending several Miles into the Country, mostly covered with fine Timber on the Eastern Shore of Sydney Harbor, with a commodious and safe Anchorage for Shipping of all Sizes, comprehending valuable Beaches, and conveniences for Curing Fish, Erecting Stages, building Stores &c is laid out upon a Plan, calculated to become an opulent Fishing Town surrounded by a fine Farming Country, for the Reception and accommodation of Families who intend to carry on Navigation, Trade, Fishing and Farming, and peculiarly adapted for establishing the Whale Fishery on the largest Scale.

The Plan hereto annexed explaining the method observed in laying out the Lands will shew the peculiar advantage which Individuals will derive from it, by being enabled to accommodate themselves agreeable to their respective means and abilities, and be certain of reaping the real value of their Labours in proportion to their respective Industry and Ingenuity, let whatever be the degree of their exertions; By which means every Settler will have the Choice of as much Land, as he can undertake to cultivate, in an Eligible situation either abutting upon some Navigable Water, or upon some principal great Road, which are opening to form an easy intercourse of Commerce with all parts of the Island.

Provisions will be allowed at the same Rate, and for the same Time as has been allowed to Loyalists in Nova Scotia, to commence from the day of their arrival in this Government, when they will also have a Supply of Implements and Material for Building. Those who mean to avail themselves of these advantages, it is expected they will signify the same, as speedily as possible that they may be Received upon the Spot within the Term of one year from this Date: Every reasonable assistance to those who may stand in need thereof for their removal will be afforded.

Besides the Tract of Land before described, I have also set apart the Harbour and District around Louisbourg, as appearing to me peculiarly advantageous for the Reception and accommodation of Families who intend to follow the Fishery and principally the Whaling Business.

Dated at Sydney the 1st of September 1785

GOD SAVE THE KING

5

Evils Resulting from Large Grants of Land

From Canadian Archives, *series New Brunswick A*, XIV, 258.

Mr Stewart's memorandum

March 1802

Nothing has contributed so much to prevent the Settlement of these two Colonies, as the Mode in which the granting Land has hitherto been conducted; Immense tracts being granted to Individuals, who having nothing to pay but the Fees on the Grants, keep them in an unsettled state on Speculation. For as the Grants require but one Person to two hundred Acres, to fulfill the terms of settlement, the Grantees of these large Tracts by giving away about a Sixth or a Seventh part of them, in small Tracts to poor Families, acquire without any other expence or exertion, the number of settlers required to secure the whole Grant from confiscation for non-performance of the terms of settlement. That object being secured the rest of the Grant is kept unsettled, and cannot be had but by Purchase on terms which the Class of People who generally settle in these Countries are seldom able to Pay. In this way large Tracts of Land in both Provinces particularly in Nova Scotia is locked up in the hands of Individuals to the manifest Injury of the Publick.

It is true that many large Grants in both Provinces have been escheated for non-performance of the terms of settlement, but it is equally certain that it has happened, chiefly in Cases where the Grantees have not been resident in the Province, and it has too often happened, that these escheated Lands, instead of being parcelled out in small Tracts to actual Settlers, or kept in the hands of Government for that purpose, have been immediately regranted in whole, or in part, to Persons of Consequence in the Province, who by making a shew of complying with the terms, are by their Influence enabled to keep them in a State of very little more value to the General Prosperity of the Country, than if they had been left in the hands of the Original Grantees.

What renders this state of things so highly injurious to the public Interest, is the Consideration that above one half the extent of both Provinces is totally unfit for Cultivation, being either covered with Rocks or barren Swamps. And it may easily be conceived that it has been the best Lands that have become the Objects of these Speculations, And perhaps not much less than one-half of the granted Lands in both Provinces are held in this manner. The effect of which has been the driving away of many thousand People who, disgusted at seeing so much of the best Land and most convenient situations in the Province taken up in this manner and not to be obtained but by Purchase, have emigrated to the American states.

I know of no remedy that would so effectually correct this evil, as collecting the Quit Rent in future, which tho' it would not be felt by the bulk of Settlers, who hold only a few hundred acres more than they Cultivate, (the rate being only one farthing an Acre) would soon when it came to be regularly paid tire the great Speculators, and force them either to settle their Lands or give them up, a Circumstance that would contribute exceedingly to the Prosperity of the Provinces.

When the Instruction against granting Lands which has now been in force for some years, is recalled, it might be of great benefit, to restrict Grants in future to a much smaller Quantity, to wit, from three to five hundred Acres to one Person, and not to allow any Additional Quantity on account of Children or Servants, but leave them to apply for themselves when they are in a situation to become Settlers. The old way was to allow beside the Quantity given to the applicant in his own Name, fifty or a hundred Acres for every person in his Family, which in the end was the same as giving the whole in one Name, as it did not preclude the Children and servants from afterwards applying for themselves.

It would likewise tend to Check farther Speculations in Land, if every applicant was required to make Oath, that the application in his Name was with a real intention on his part to become an actual Settler on the Lands applied for, And that no other Person was directly or indirectly interested in the event of his application: It having been a common Practice to procure the Signatures of a number of People to applications for large Tracts, and when the same has been obtained, it has immediately for a trifling Consideration been conveyed to the Instigator of the Application, who Pays the Fees of the Grant.

But what would effectually prevent most of the abuses that have hitherto prevailed in granting Lands would be, instead of a Grant, to give only a Licence of Occupation in the first Place, which should Pledge the faith of Government to the holder thereof, that when he or his Heirs has persevered for three years in settling and improving the Lands described in the Licence, upon producing a Certificate thereof signed by the Judges, and Foremen of the Grand Jury of the County Court which shall sit next after he has compleated the said Period of Residence, he, or they shall then be entitled to His Majesty's Grant in the usual Form, which shall thereupon be issued with all convenient speed.

6
Emigration from Nova Scotia to the United States
From *Journals of the assembly, Nova Scotia*, volume 1803-1805, p. 28.

Sat., 1st December, 1805

A petition of William Sabatier, James Fraser, and others, a committee of the merchants and other inhabitants of Halifax interested in the trade to the West Indies, was presented by Mr Lyon and read, setting forth. . . .

That the Petitioners have, since that time, received answers
to their representations, which, with other circumstances, afford
the most flattering prospect of success, in excluding the citizens
of the United States from the Trade of the British West-India
Islands; but they are concerned to be obliged to state that, from
various causes, so great has been the emigration of Fishermen, and
others, from this Province to the American States, that the customary offers of the Merchants, which is all they can possibly afford,
have hitherto proved insufficient to draw them back again to this
Province, on the contrary, during the last season, even a great many
industrious families have gone to that country. This has been, in
a great measure, occasioned by the encouragement by bounties
held out by the Legislatures of those States, and, partly, by the
burthens, expences, inconveniences and depressions, to which this
Trade is peculiarly subject in time of war: and which, during this
last summer, have, in one instance, at least, increased beyond any
former precedent. . . .

7

Effect on Inhabitants of Inability to Obtain Title

From Canadian Archives, *series M.*, CXXXII, 5.

Major-General Swayne to the Earl of Bathurst

Sydney Island Cape Breton
March 1st, 1814

My Lord:—

I have the Honor to transmit herewith for Your Lordships'
Consideration, the Copy of a Petition, which has been addressed
to me, signed by the Principal Inhabitants of this Colony, in the
hopes of obtaining, if consistent with the intentions of His Majesty's
Government, the Titles of Permanent Grants, in lieu of Crown
Leases, and other undefined Titles made to them during pleasure.

The advancement of this Island in Cultivation, and Improvement, I am informed, would have been far greater than it is at
present, had the same Terms been held out to its Settlers, which
exist in the Neighbouring Colonies: It appears some hundreds
had emigrated to it, who would have remained, could they have
obtained Lands under Hereditary Titles; but the restraining Laws
induced them to remove and Settle in the United States.

The Lessees of Lands in this Island, finding they can neither dispose of, or bequeath them, with Improvements, to their families, have become careless in their Cultivation, and are not inclined to labour, but for a mere subsistence.

From the great Zeal, and Loyalty which I have observed in the Inhabitants, and Peasantry of this Country, I beg leave to recommend the Prayer of their Petition to your Lordship's Consideration under the impression, that were they permitted to hold their lands, upon the same Tenures with those of Canada, & Nova Scotia, that it would add very much to their happiness, and the Agricultural Improvement of the Colony.

H. Swayne

M. General & Pres^t. of Council

8

The Westward Flow of Population

The two documents following illustrate a phenomenon which has been of continuous occurrence on this continent: each period of hard times has uprooted men and sent them in search of better conditions. As the hard times pass, their places are taken by newcomers, as a rule immigrants from overseas. The process of creating a community very largely has to begin over again.

(i)

Emigration from New Brunswick as a result of hard times

From J. F. W. Johnston, *Notes on North America* (Edinburgh, 1851), I, 37.

What added to the apprehension of the colonists at this time [*1826 on*] was the comparatively extensive emigration which began to take place when the demand for timber became less, and, consequently, for labourers to procure it. Undisposed to continuous farm-work, the lumberer left the province—as our "navigators" wander from county to county—to seek employment in Maine or elsewhere towards the West, where their peculiar employment was to be obtained. Even the pine forests of Georgia were not too distant for their love of free adventure. Unable to shake off their encumbrances at home, many of the embarrassed owners of farms also hastened to leave them—some in the hands of their creditors, without even the form of a sale—and made for the new states of the West, under the idea that in a new sphere they would be free men again, and that probably a less degree of prudence or industry

might there secure them the competence which their own neighbourhood had denied them. No love of home, or attachment to
the paternal acres, restrained either class of men; for these Old
World feelings or notions have scarcely yet found a place among
he Anglo-Saxons of any part of North America.

(ii)

The evils of unregulated immigration in New Brunswick

From *Ships, colonies and commerce, an appeal to the Right Hon. Wm. Huskisson
. . . on the present condition of the maritime and internal interests of the
Province of New Brunswick*, by "A Colonist" (St. John, 1828).

. . . Emigration[1] as it now exists, . . . differs most widely in its
effects upon the colony. The voluntary emigrant in the majority
of cases, arrives amongst us in poverty; frequently suffering from
disease, a stranger to our labour, and ill provided to bear the
inclemency of the season: and in general, burdened with a wife and
numerous family. He is brought from his home under delusion
and thrown on our shores alike destitute of sustenance and hope.

Individual charity may afford some relief and our public
institutions . . . may extend that; but the constant influx of so
many needy beings dries up of itself the fountain of charity . . . we
are not a wealthy people and cannot afford to become the alms-
house for another portion of the nation. . . . Opposition since the
abrogation of the Act regulating vessels carrying passengers has
been materially increased owing to the very distressed hosts
brought out, until from one end of the province to the other, we
have been under the necessity of erecting provisional hospitals,
lazarettos, and pest houses for the reception of those suffering and
deluded beings, the dupes of men whose avarice has led them into
the traffic from Ireland and by whom the most seductive arts are
used to procure a cargo. . . . Hence a principle cause of the misery
and disease witnessed on their arrival in the colonies. . . .

9

Emigration from Nova Scotia and its Supposed Causes

From Montreal Gazette, August 20, 1835.

Our last HALIFAX papers put us in possession of a fact, the
existence of which we had never for a moment imagined, namely,

---

[1]No distinction was made in the early nineteenth century between the words
"immigration" and "emigration", the latter word being invariably used.

that emigration from the Province of NOVA SCOTIA to the UNITED STATES exists to a great extent.   The *Acadian Recorder* states that not less than two thousand, five hundred individuals have left for that country within the last twelve months, and that more are preparing to follow them.   One cause, and indeed the only one at present assigned for this, is the present state of the Colony, whose resources are cramped, and enterprise is paralysed. The introduction of Banks, the *Recorder* conceives, has tended to this result; acquiring an intimate acquaintance with the affairs of every individual in the community, which, by the way, is of limited extent, they, it is asserted, use the power thus acquired to the detriment and hindrance of many, who, although not rich might yet, by a judiciously applied confidence, become useful and valuable members of the community.

The Editor of the paper above named promises further information on this point, and we confess we look for it with interest and trust that the subject will be analyzed in all its bearings.   While in every other British Colony, saving always our own Province of LOWER CANADA, every additional emigrant is considered as additional wealth and strength to it, it would appear no less anomalous than painful, that local mismanagement or misgovernment in any one Colony should compel the artizan and the labourer to abandon the asylum he had found after all the perils and expense of his first emigration had been overcome.   If, therefore, there be any thing vicious in the mode of conducting the affairs of the Banks a circumstance we can scarcely imagine to exist in an intelligent community, or in any department of the Civil Administration of the Government, to force the emigrants to do so, we trust the virtue and the firmness to obtain redress of such a grievance will be found and vigorously exerted to that end.

TRADE AND INDUSTRY IN THE MARITIME PROVINCES

(a)—GENERAL ASPECTS OF TRADE

The Maritime colonies had been founded on fish as a staple. In this period they added lumber and ships and small exports of coal. These products sought overseas markets, chiefly the West Indies, New England, and for square timber and ships, the mother country. Maritime trade consisted in the export of these goods and the import of manufactures from England, food from the United States, and sugar, rum, and specie from the West Indies. The English trade was similar to that of the St. Lawrence. That with the United States was subject until 1830 to much political interference by both countries, thenceforth to fiscal action, and, as a result, was uncertain and unorganized. Frequently it was clandestine, American fishing vessels on the excuse of putting into outports for wood and water, supplying local needs in foodstuffs and other wares. As the period wore on, Canadian flour competed with American but never displaced it. Trade locally was conducted much as in the Canadas, although the distributive system cannot be seen at work as clearly.

1

Smuggling on the Coasts of New Brunswick

From *St. John Gazette and Weekly Advertiser*, November 23, 1798.

WHEREAS Complaints have been made by the fair British Merchants trading directly to Great Britain, that they are unable to form a profitable estimate of the quantity of Goods they may safely import from thence or the British Plantations, and are also deprived of the produce they have contracted to receive for any supplies by them entrusted to the Planters and Fishermen on the Coast, as it is bartered by them for articles clandestinely and illegally imported.

THIS IS TO GIVE NOTICE, That His Majesty by His Royal commission and instructions, has empowered me as Superintendent of Trade and Fisheries to put a stop to those illegal proceedings, and has furnished me with the means of preventing the same.

I do therefore caution and advise all traders and other persons that have been in this practice of illicit trade that they withhold from the same, as such attention will be shewn to the Sea Coast of these His Majesty's Colonies in future, as will prevent the like illegal practices, a continuation of which will occasion to those concerned much loss of property.

GEORGE LEONARD,

St. John, 12th October, 1798

2

The Manufacture of Refined Sugar in Halifax

From Nova Scotia Archives, *Legislative council, manuscript documents,* CCLXXXIX, 1816-1822, no. 9.

To the Honourable His Majesty's Council

The petition of John Moody, James Tidmarsh, William Bruce Almon, Temple Foster Piers, Lewis Edward Piers, and George Piers Lawson, of Halifax

humbly sheweth,

That your petitioners having some time since undertaken the establishment in Halifax of a manufactory for refining sugar, have at length completed it, and have commenced the sale of refined sugar made there; That your petitioners have had many difficulties to obviate and risks to encounter in this enterprise; It is one which they believe was but once before undertaken in this province many years since, and which was abandoned owing to a variety of causes then existing, and now unnecessary to be explained to your Honours and that for a length of time, no undertaking similar to that of your petitioners, (and from which they might have derived the benefit of experience) has been attempted—

That from the expensive nature of the undertaking in itself, your petitioners have in the formation of the establishment, necessarily been compelled to make large advances, and have incurred very heavy expenditures; The building erected by your petitioners for the purpose of this manufacture, is necessarily very large; the utensils with a very few exceptions have been imported from Great Britain, or made in this province, at great expense; and the business not being practically known in Halifax, your petitioners have been obliged to procure from abroad, Workmen who were accustomed to the management of it, and your petitioners find that their establishment to answer the demands even of a limited consumption cannot be supported without very great expenses—

But serious as have been the difficulties and expenses which your petitioners have had already, and must continue to meet, it is in the purchase of the raw material, and the advantage which (owing to the large duties payable on the importation of those materials) the refined sugar imported into the province, has in the market, over those manufactured by your petitioners, that your petitioners still more forcibly feel the pressure of their undertaking.

And your petitioners most respectfully represent, that they are encouraged to beg the assistance of your Honours, in favour of the manufacture in which they are concerned, by the consideration that it is one favorable to the most essential interests of the Country. That it is carried on alone with materials procured with the products of the province, and which therefore to the extent to which it shall operate will afford encouragement and employment to the Fisheries, Agriculture, and Navigation, of this province; and that as the accustomed importation and consumption of raw sugars in this province will not be the least impaired by the manufacture of your petitioners, the assistance which they beg of your Honours, while it will afford encouragement to an undertaking of general advantage, will have no tendency to diminish the usual trade or revenue of the province.

And your petitioners further beg leave to state that as they hope to be able to manufacture refined sugar at a price that will allow them to export that article, should their undertaking succeed thro' the encouragement which its nature leads them to hope it may receive, the usefulness of their establishment to the general interests of the Country, will thus by an increased operation, to which it is fully equal be extensively felt.

Your petitioners therefore humbly pray that your Honours will be graciously pleased to grant them a drawback of the provincial duties of such imported Sugar as shall be actually manufactured by them into refined Sugar, or otherwise afford them such assistance as your Honours in your wisdom shall see fit. . . .

Jno. Moody (*et al*)

Halifax, 18th February, 1817

3

The Advancement of the Prosperity of Nova Scotia

From *Montreal Gazette*, September 8, 1819.

The legislature of Nova Scotia, at its last Session, appointed a committee to inquire into the present state of the trade of that colony, and on the measures which are necessary to be adopted in regard to the British North American colonies generally, to encrease their prosperity, provide for their future security, and counteract the ambitious projects of the United States. . . .

We cannot undertake, in this paper, to give the voluminous documents which the report contains; but we think it our duty to inform our readers, briefly, of the objects which the Nova Scotia legislature has in view. . . .

2d, The same freedom of trade with all the world, that the United States have acquired.

3d, Laying out lands in all parts, on which settlers may be immediately and advantageously located, without wandering as they do now, in search of situations. . . . . .

7th, Prohibiting the export of the produce of the British West Indies, to or from either the domestic or foreign free ports, in the West Indies, and American vessels from entering the domestic free ports, and also their entry there from foreign ports. . . .

10th, Regulations to prevent the abuse by the Americans, of the right of fishing on the British American coast, by the late convention, limiting their entering the bays and harbours except in cases of real necessity.

4

The Mainstays of the Trade of New Brunswick

From *Ships, colonies and commerce, an appeal to the Right Hon. Wm. Huskisson.*

. . . Timber, lumber and the fisheries are the mainstays of the welfare of this colony. They are the means of its existence, and the resources for the application of its industry, which can at all times be put into beneficial and extensive operation, if the channels for transporting its products are not sealed up by the too easy admission of alien competitors into the home and colonial market. . . .

5

An Analysis of the Trade and Industry of New Brunswick in 1828

From *Montreal Gazette*, October 27, 1828.

The COMMERCE OF NEW BRUNSWICK is like our own, somewhat limited in its extent. The number of vessels which arrived at the Port of St. John during the year 1827, amounted to 1659, of which 383 were from Great Britain, 1156 from the British colonies, 115 from the United States and 5 from Foreign States. The total amount of tonnage, inwards, amounted to 195,109, of which 113,131 were from Great Britain, 66,402 from the British colonies, 14,259 from the United States and 1,317 from Foreign States. The number of men employed in this trade was 9,886. The value of the imports from Great Britain was £194,857, from the West Indies £47,398, from the North American Colonies, £133,914, from the United States £101,182; from Foreign States £1546, making a total of estimated imports of £478,897. . . .

The amount of exports to Great Britain was £186,991, to the West Indies and Africa £73,785, to the British North American Colonies £71,642, to the United States £5600, and to Foreign States £3986, making a total of exports £341,932. There were 77 vessels, of 16,323 tonnage, built during the year within the District of St. John, and 17 ships of 3774 built in Nova Scotia, for owners in St. John, making a total of 20,097 tons of new shipping. . . .

The principal articles of imports from Great Britain into the Province are provisions, liquors, groceries, hardware, and dry goods, for which in return are exported timber of various descriptions. The imports from and exports to the British Colonies, consist chiefly of rum, sugar, flour, breadstuff, provisions, live stock, fish, &c. The imports from the United States are much the same as those from the British Colonies and the return principally consists of gypsum, grindstones, and timber. The imports from other Foreign States are limited to wine, cider, &c. and returns made in rum, molasses, timber, tar, indigo, mahogany, logwood, &c. . . .

As connected with the commerce and trade of the Province, it may be proper to mention, that a Provincial Bank is established at Frederickton, and another in Charlotte County, St. Andrew's. Saving's Banks are also established at St. John's, Frederickton and St. Andrew's and a Provincial Marine Insurance Company exists in St. John's.

6

Energetic Industrial Progress in New Brunswick

From *Montreal Gazette*, September 10, 1835.

Every mail that arrives from New BRUNSWICK, furnishes tidings of some new speculation, in which the enterprising and industrious people of that Province are about to engage. It is not long since we announced, that in addition to the respectable private mercantile houses who have embarked in the whale-fishing trade, a Joint Stock concern had been formed for the same purpose, with a capital of £50,000. More recently, a Bridge Company, Water Company, and East India Company have been established, the amount of capital embarked in which is £60,000. Steamboats are building in different parts of the Province, and everything wears a prosperous look. This happy condition is, we believe, to be attributed to the great amount of American capital lately expended on timber lands, mill seats and quarries, as well as to the additional facilities rendered to commerce, by the establishment of Banks.

7

Products and Trade of Nova Scotia

From Rev. William Murray, "The progress of Nova Scotia", in *Eighty years' progress*, 690.

The chief exports to Great Britain consist of ships built in the province, and squared and sawed timbers. The West Indies is the principal market for our fish. The United States is also an important market for some kinds of our fish, also for potatoes, coal, gypsum, and freestone. The trade of Nova Scotia with Canada is rapidly increasing.

Nova Scotia imports the greater part of what she needs of textile manufactures; also hardware, cutlery, pottery, chinaware, ship-chandlery, chemicals, glassware, etc., from Great Britain.

Breadstuffs, tea, sugar, tobacco, woodware, etc., are largely imported from the United States.

(b)—THE WEST INDIAN TRADE

Of the first empire, the West Indies had been the most important component, for they supplied the mother country with tropical products. They also provided an outlet for the fish, lumber, and food of the continental colonies, which in turn bought their manufactured goods in England. This mutual dependence was the arch on which the old colonial system rested. The Revolution took out its keystone and much effort to find a substitute for it in the remaining provinces resulted. The revolted colonies were treated strictly as foreigners and kept out of West Indian ports. But Canada was too far away and Nova Scotia had neither food enough for herself nor the essential white oak for staves for rum and molasses barrels. She could and did get a good share of West Indian business in fish and lumber:—planks, boards, shingles, door and window frames, *etc.*

The attempt to give her the total supply was kept up for many years, the West Indies either living on American goods smuggled through the foreign islands or going without. One ingenious British device was the regulation by which American goods could be landed in certain Maritime ports and then allowed to proceed as British (on a British ship). The Americans retaliated by such measures as *tonnage duties* on British shipping entering American ports. By 1830, the plight of the Islands, ground between the upper and the nether mill-stone, had become so bad that the government removed the restrictions on the Americans—surrenderèd, Nova Scotians called it—and the West Indian trade had to stand on its own feet. Geography and climate saw to it that it ranked as a poor second to the American trade with these islands, as it has continued to do.

REFERENCES: See section IV.

1

The New Brunswick Loyalists Commence the West Indian Trade

From *Winslow papers*, 197.

Lieutenant-Colonel Fanning to Ward Chipman

Halifax, 27th April, 1784

. . . There is a commerce commencing from thence [*St. John*] with the West Indies. That they have actually loaded six large vessels with inch Boards, White Oak Staves, Hoop poles, and etc., for the West Indies. . . .

2

The West Indian Trade and the Stimulus of War

From *Journals of assembly, Nova Scotia*, volume 1803-1805, p. 27.

Saturday, 21st December, 1805

A petition of William Sabatier, James Fraser, and others, a Committee of the Merchants, and other inhabitants, of Halifax, interested in the trade to the West-Indies, was presented by Mr. Lyon, and read, setting forth, That the Merchants of Halifax, and others, interested in the West-India Trade, finding their business very much obstructed by means of the free trade to the Islands permitted to the citizens of the United States of America, contrary to the true principles of the Navigation Act, the real interests of the British Empire in general, and of this Province in particular, appointed the Petitioners a Committee to state their situation to

His Majesty's Ministers, which they accordingly did, in a Petition and Memorial, dated the twenty-third day of March, 1804. . . .

That the obstacles which the Petitioners have to encounter are so great, and so numerous, that, in order to complete their share of those encouragements which the Merchants of this and the neighbouring Provinces have entered into with Government, and their fellow subjects in the West-Indies, every aid will be required: but, at the same time, so encouraging are their prospects, derived from the late measures of Government, and which have, though reluctantly, been adopted in the West-India Islands, that they are induced to proceed, well knowing the immense advantages which must necessarily result to every description of persons resident in this Province, if their efforts are finally successful; and, also, dreading the inevitable consequences of a failure, which, however unfairly used, will, assuredly, in adverse hands, furnish so unfailing an argument, as will destroy the means of every future application on this interesting subject; and praying the House would take the premises into consideration, and, from its wonted zeal for the prosperity of the Province, afford the Petitioners, and their Constituents, such aid and encouragement as lies within their power to grant.

Mr. Lyon also delivered, to the House, several papers which accompanied the said petition; and, thereupon,

On motion, *ordered*, that the said petition, and papers, be refered to Mr. Lyon, Mr. Mortimer, Mr. Barss, Mr. Pool and Mr. Rutherford, who are to examine into the subject matter thereof, and report their opinion thereon to the House.

3

An American Attempt to Break the British Colonial Policy

From Report of debate, U.S. house of representatives, February 5, 1816, in *Montreal Gazette*, February 26, 1816.

Mr. King of Mass. presented for consideration the following resolution: "Resolved, That the Committee on Foreign Relations be instructed to inquire into the expediency of excluding from the ports of the U. States, all foreign vessels owned in, coming from, bound to, or touching at, any of his Britannic Majesty's possessions in the West Indies, and on the Continent of North America, from which the vessels of the United States are excluded: and of prohibiting, or increasing the duties on the importation in foreign vessels of any articles, the growth, produce, or manufacture of such possessions."

Mr. K. said, . . . When you turn your attention to that nation, you do see in operation one of the most rigid, exclusive colonial systems that ever was adopted by any nation; well digested and prepared, as to her interest, for the present state of commerce in the world. . . . Her ships from Great Britain may come to any of our ports, with full freights of dry goods—with part of the proceeds, purchase a load of lumber, stock, provisions &c. (such I mean as they choose to admit in the islands) sell it at their islands, at great profit, take in a cargo of West India produce, and carry it to any port of Europe—giving them full freights in three distinct voyages. And a portion of our lumber, and pot and pearl ashes, will, and does, by Champlain and other waters, find their way to the St. Lawrence, are bought up by the British capitalist at his own price, and sent to a most profitable market in Great Britain and the West-Indies—giving employment to their ships and great profit to their merchants.

4

Enforcement of the Colonial Trade Act against American Ships

From *Montreal Gazette*, September 23, 1826.

Every inhabitant of the Cabotian Provinces[1] will peruse with interest the following extract, taken from the LONDON COURIER of the 15th ultimo:—

"Orders have been sent out to all our Colonies in the West Indies, to put in force the Act of the 6th of the King,[2] in respect to their trade with foreign countries. By that Act the Ports of those Colonies are to be closed against the vessels of such States as do not place British shipping, trading between those Colonies and such States, upon the footing of the most favoured nation. The United States of America have declined to place our shipping upon that footing in their ports, and, in consequence, their ships will not be admitted to entry in our West India Colonies after the 21st December."

---

[1] *i.e.*, the provinces of British North America.
[2] The Colonial Trade Act, 6 Geo. IV, c. 114.

This is considered as a fortunate event for British shipping, and the countries of the north of Europe will, in common with the British North American Colonies, benefit by this interruption to American trade, as the supply of flour, provisions and timber, hitherto furnished by the United States, must now be drawn from them.

It is not for us to deprecate the extreme folly of the UNITED STATES in thus refusing to place our shipping on the footing of the most favoured nation; because we are convinced that all the advantages derivable from such a refusal, will be entirely on our own side, and because our natural partiality for our own welfare in preference to that of others forbids us to rejoice in national advantages, except those which are calculated to promote our more immediate and individual prosperity. But we admit, that we behold this event with infinite pleasure, whatever its nearer or more remote consequences may be. It is a convincing proof to us, that, in so far at least as regards the improvement of our colonial wealth and commerce, and the maintenance of our naval superiority the great bulwarks of our national glory and independence, the free trade system was founded on most erroneous and dangerous principles. Of this system, in a more general point of view, we have always expressed our approbation, and entertained a confident hope in its success, while and while only, the nations of EUROPE could be prevailed upon to cultivate the blessings of peace with each other. But when we found that it interfered with the intercourse which, from the nature of their wants and their capacity of supply, ought ever to subsist betwixt the Cabotian provinces and the West India colonies, we did not hesitate a moment in raising our voice against it; as any of our readers will find by perusing our file from the first of January last. We knew it was altogether owing to the favour shown to the UNITED STATES in their intercourse with the West India Islands, to the prejudice of the British North American provinces, that these provinces, having no adequate demand for their produce, were thrown so far back in every line of improvement; that they were so long and so cruelly treated with neglect; and isolated, in a manner, from the fostering care, and commercial prosperity of the mother country, while equally capable with the United States not only in furnishing all the necessary supplies of the West Indies, but in augmenting the political and commercial prosperity of the empire. We knew also, that until the Cabotian provinces, in carrying their supplies to the West Indian market, experienced little restraint or competition except that which by nature and right proceeded from the mother country, they should never rise in any kind of political or commercial importance whatever; and that, instead of being, as nature pointed them out to be the storehouse of our West India colonies in time of peace, and of both these colonies and the mother country, in time of war, they would become the charnel-house of all that is injurious in politics and ruinous in commerce. It is, therefore, with no small degree of satisfaction that we behold the prospect of a much better state of things.

5

Opening of West Indian Ports to American Vessels

From *Montreal Gazette*, June 10, 1830.

To the Right Hon. The Lords of the Committee of the Privy Council for Trade.

The petition of the undersigned Merchants, and others interested in the trade and prosperity of the British North American Colonies. Most Humbly Sheweth:—

That the re-admission of American ships into the British West Indies would be very injurious to the British North American Colonies, and to the general interests of British trade and navigation, and be of very little benefit to the West Indies, as your Petitioners humbly conceive.

Because,

1st. Since the last exclusion of American ships, the West Indies have been more abundantly supplied than before.

2nd. The prices of such supplies have never risen much, and are now lower than before.

3d. The exportation of such supplies from the North American Colonies to the West Indies has greatly increased.

4th. The importation of West India produce into the North Anerican Colonies has greatly increased.

5th. The exchange of produce and supplies between the West Indies and North American Colonies is greatly intercepted by the admission of American ships.

6. The West Indies sold more of their produce to the North American Colonies when American ships were excluded, than they could or did to the United States, American ships being admitted.

7th. Since the exclusion of American ships, British tonnage in the Colonial trade has greatly increased.

8th. Whatever advantage the United States offer in permitting British ships arriving there from the United Kingdom, to load and depart for the West Indies, is already enjoyed through the North American colonies.

9th. And from the efforts now making in the North American Colonies to increase their production of West India supplies, there is great reason to believe, that by adhering to the present system, the whole of those supplies may already be procured from, and shortly be produced within the British dominions.

And your Petitioners most respectfully beg leave to annex hereto, such information as they have been able to collect under each of these heads, and to submit the same to your Lordship's consideration.

Your Petitioners therefore humbly pray that American ships may not be admitted into the British West Indies.

6

An American View of the West Indian Controversy

From *Baltimore American,* quoted in *Montreal Gazette,* October 14, 1830.

As the pending negotiations in London for a renewal of our direct trade with the British West Indies, naturally excite much attention, the following suggestions may not be uninteresting. . . . The two principal interests against which the granting of this privilege would militate, are the British Provinces in North America, and the West India merchants of Great Britain. The latter form a body of merchants, equal in wealth and influence to any in the Kingdom; their weight has always been thrown in the scale against the efforts of the Colonists to obtain the trade with the United States, and has had no little influence in producing the present state of things. The West India merchant and the West India planter have few interests in common, though they both derive their profits from the same estate. Most of the estates are mortgaged to the merchants, to whom the crop or produce of the estate is shipped every year.   His profits arise from the interest of the money loaned on the estate, from the commission paid on the sale of the crop, from the freight, of it to England in his own vessel, and from the freight, commission and profit on the supplies required by the plantations. The planter, or owner of the estate, is generally allowed a yearly sum out of the crop by the mortgagee, for his living expenses; and he is to pay for the supplies, out of that portion of the produce which is not suited to the English market.   This is the molasses, the rum, and the inferior qualities of coffee, for which the only market is the United States.   If this market were opened to the planter, the merchant would be deprived of his freight and profit on the supplies.—Not only staves, flour, and corn meal, (a great part of which would in any event go from the United States,) but dry goods, negro clothing, implements of husbandry, and a great variety of other articles would be drawn from this market, which is near at hand, instead of that whence from the nature of the trade, they can be drawn but once a year.   The merchant, indeed, might send his ships to this country, but they could not compete with the smaller vessels of the American merchants, which supply the planter more frequently, more regularly, and in pro- portions better suited to his wants.   The privilege that would be given to American vessels of going from the Colonies with Colonial produce to any part of the world, Great Britain and her possessions excepted, is another cause of the opposition of the West India merchant to granting the Islands this trade, as here again he loses the freight on that portion of the crop of the estate, which not being mortgaged, it is in the power of the planter to send where he pleases.   This, to be sure is very small; yet he would be deprived of that, the long enjoyment of which has made him look upon it as a right.

These are some of the instances in which the interests of the merchant and planter clash; but as the Government has thought proper to consider the direct trade between the Colonies and the Mother Country a sufficient monopoly for the West India merchant, and as now the demand on the part of the United States to this direct trade has been withdrawn it is probable that the opposition of the West India interest at home, will have little weight with the Government in keeping the Colonies closed.

The other interest we have mentioned is that of the British Provinces which, as is well known, it has for some years past been the peculiar care of the British Government to foster and bring forward by all the means in its power; and in this wish it has been greatly aided by the refusal of the United States to accept of the Colonial Trade on the terms on which it was offered to them and to other nations, thus relieving it from the charge of injustice to the West India Colonies, since it was in pursuance of a policy (that is, the breaking off the direct intercourse) long continued by Great Britain, and a departure from which would have compromised interests of far greater importance to the country in general, than the comparatively small benefit to be derived from acceding to the wishes of the Colonies themselves.   The Government at home seized this opportunity of benefiting her favourite Provinces, and of diverting the supplies of the West India Colonies from the more natural channel of the neutral Islands, by decreasing the duties on many articles when imported through America, and extending the warehousing system to almost all those ports.   The already great increase of the trade thence to the West Indies bears ample testimony to the success of its efforts, and it only required a continuance of the present state of things for one or two years longer, to have insured to the Provinces the supply of the whole of the West Indies through their ports.   The expectation that this trade would be secured to them for a long period has induced a large outlay of capital in several places in British North America, but more particularly in Halifax, St. Johns, and St. Andrews, and this would be almost entirely sunk, if they were to be deprived of the trade which they had some right to think, from the conduct of the British Government, would be guaranteed to them.   Their claims to the consideration of the parent Government were certainly strong, and this was represented in more than one petition recently sent to England, when their fears for the trade were awakened by the great efforts that have lately been made by the United States to recover the direct intercourse.   But justice is equally due to the Colonies in the West Indies, and as the act of Congress lately passed did away with the objections to granting a direct intercourse to the United States, putting out of the question the desire that Great Britain has of conciliating this country,—it would be guilty of the injustice of making a monopoly, for the benefit of the North American Provinces, of the carrying of that part of their supplies which the Islands derive from the United States.   The trade therefore, we should think, would be opened, modified, however, in such a manner as a fair and just regard to the interest of the Provinces requires.

THE STAPLE INDUSTRIES IN MARITIME LIFE

(a)—THE FISHERIES

The documents simply introduce some of the more important aspects of industrial life in the Atlantic provinces. There will be found in volume one of this work adequate illustration of the technical aspects of fishing: here, in addition to some general descriptions, are illustrations of the battle waged for the control of their own inshore fisheries by these provinces after the surrenders of 1763 and 1783 to France and the United States.

1

Exports of Fish in 1805 and Following Years

From David Anderson, *Canada: or, A view of the importance of the British American colonies*, 339.

Estimate of Quintals of FISH EXPORTED *from the British Colonies in North America and Newfoundland, in the Years* 1805, 1806, 1807, *and* 1808.

		Quintals, or Cwt.	qrs.	lb.
1805. Dry Fish.....Cod.....................		623,908	0	0
Salmon, 17,491, of 5 lb. each =		780	3	11
Herrings, 8,178 boxes, 6 lb. each................:..... =		438	0	12
Pickled Fish...........57,441 casks, 200 lb. each............... =		102,573	0	24
Quintals, or Cwt........		727,700	0	19
1806. Dry Fish.....Cod.....................		804,819	0	0
Salmon, 17,638, of 5 lb. each =		787	1	18
Herrings, 10,388 boxes, 6 lb. each................... =		556	2	0
Pickled Fish.. ....78,738 casks, 200 lb. each............. =		140,603	2	8
Quintals, or Cwt........		946,766	1	26

1807. Dry Fish.....Cod......................	631,537	0	0
Salmon, 12,653, of 5 lb. each =	564	3	13
Herrings, 12,666 boxes, 6 lb. each.................... =	678	2	4
Pickled Fish...........73,683 casks, 200 lb. each................ =	131,576	3	4
Quintals, or Cwt........	764,357	0	21

1808. Dry Fish.....Cod......................	695,794	0	0
Salmon, 2,441, of 5 lb. each =	118	3	25
Herrings, 15,716 boxes, 6 lb. each.................... =	841	3	20
Pickled Fish...........74,942 casks, 200 lb. each................ =	133,825	0	0
Quintals, or Cwt........	830,579	3	17

2

Exclusion of Americans after the War of 1812-14

From Circular letter from lieutenant-governor of Nova Scotia to the collectors of customs and the collectors of light duties, printed in *Montreal Gazette*, July 28, 1817.

Secretary's Office, Halifax, 24th June, 1817

Rear Admiral Sir David Milne having communicated to his Excellency the Lieutenant Governor, that the American government has declined to accede to the propositions which have been made to them by His Majesty's government for the purpose of endeavouring to frame some arrangement by which the citizens of the United States of America might be permitted to a participation of the fisheries within the limits of the British Jurisdiction, I have it in command from his excellency the Lieutenant Governor to apprize you, that American fishermen are not permitted to frequent the harbours, bays or creeks, of this province, unless driven into them by acute distress; and I have to desire that you, on no account, ask or receive any light money, anchorage, or any other fees whatsoever from vessels belonging to American subjects.

Rupert D. George, Secretary

3

State Aid to the Fisheries of Nova Scotia and New Brunswick

From Debate of the assembly of Lower Canada, reported in *Montreal Gazette*, January 19, 1829.

The House in committee on Mr Christie's motion for the encouragement of the Fisheries:

Mr. Christie said

". . . By an Act passed in February last year, the legislature of Nova Scotia voted £5000 for the encouragement of the Fisheries of that Province, to be distributed in bounties, viz.: 1 shilling on every cwt. merchantable dry cod fish—5s per ton to vessels employed for 4 months in the fishing of cod, haddock, mackeral, &c. on the coasts of Nova Scotia, and Gulf of St. Lawrence,—3s 6d additional per ton, for such vessels as fish on the coasts and banks of Newfoundland, and the straits and shores of Bellisle, and Labrador—5s additional per ton, for such vessels as land their cargoes of fish within the Province of Nova Scotia. And £500 to be distributed in premiums for the greatest quantity of dried cod-fish caught, cured, and brought to market, at the harbours and fishing stations of the Province, The bounties, it appeared, were thus divided into 5 classes in Nova Scotia. With respect to the encouragement given in New Brunswick, he was not provided with the authority of a Provincial Act; but he had a private letter, by which it appeared that there, all necessaries for the fisheries were duty free, and that bounties were given of 1s 8d per cwt for all codfish brought in fit for exportation, and 20s Halifax per ton on all vessels that fished in Gulf of St. Lawrence or on the Banks of Newfoundland. . . ."

4

French and American Aggression on British Rights

From *Glasgow Free Press*, quoted in *Montreal Gazette*, July 18, 1835.

An important subject was brought before the House of Commons on Tuesday—that of the right of the French and Americans to fish on our shores within the Gulph of St. Lawrence, and along the banks of Newfoundland. Some of the most vital interests of this country are involved in this question. The Newfoundland,

Gulph of St. Lawrence, and Labrador fisheries, are fitted for inexhaustible nurseries of seamen; and yet, by our ignorance, or
remissness, or something worse, by far the better part of these
have been usurped by our French and American rivals; the first
claiming to themselves the exclusive right of fishing all along
from Cape John to Cape Ray between Newfoundland and the
continent, and employing in that trade about three hundred
vessels, of from one hundred to four hundred tons burthen, manned
by from forty to one hundred and twenty men each, and employing
a total of about twenty-five thousand seamen; while the Americans
are permitted to fish anywhere they please, within three miles of
the shore,—a stipulation they easily evade, and, like the Dutch off
Shetland, beat back our fishermen with impunity whenever they
see fit, and actually go often ashore and dry their fish, dislodging
and maltreating all who oppose their proceedings. By this means,
the Americans have established for themselves even a greater trade
there than the French,—their amount of tonnage being one hundred
and ninety-two thousand, five hundred tons, and the number of
their men employed, about thirty thousand. The value of our
own fisheries is thus enormously reduced, and, according to all
accounts, is rapidly falling into insignificance; while the fisheries
of the French and Americans, stimulated by bounties and protected by privileges, are every year extending and becoming more
remunerative. Government, through Mr Poulett Thomson, stated
on Tuesday that the Law officers of the Crown are at present
engaged in preparing an opinion on this subject, and that, until
that opinion be received, nothing can be done in providing a remedy.
But will a remedy be promptly and vigorously provided, if the Law
Officers report against the French and Americans as we feel assured
they must? Will America and France forego the advantages of
so great a trade on our merely remonstrating with them on the
violation of treaties of which they have been guilty?—and, if they
heed us not, are we prepared to vindicate our rights by force of
arms? In our opinion nothing short of war which should cancel all
past arrangements between France, the United States, and this
country, affords any hopes of our rights and interests in that
quarter being placed upon a wiser footing, and enjoying a more
vigilant defence. Whenever that shall arrive, the French and
Americans ought to be banished from the Gulf of St. Lawrence and
the coasts of Newfoundland altogether, and the rich fisheries of

those seas retained exclusively to ourselves. We have a perfect right to do that, the whole being within our own territories,—as is admitted, even by our rivals, who venture on their present practices only under cover of treaties, both the spirit and letter of which they grossly violate.

5

Disabilities of Maritimers as Fishermen

From Abraham Gesner, *New Brunswick, with notes for emigrants*, 280.

The Americans are far more successful in fishing than the inhabitants of the British Provinces, and supply their fish at a lower price than will remunerate our own people. This fact has its origin in a variety of circumstances. Their Government affords great encouragement to this branch of industry. . . . In consequence of the great advantages afforded to the citizens of the United States . . . their whole system of taking and curing fish has been rendered superior to that followed by the people of New Brunswick and Nova Scotia. They have also the advantage of obtaining provisions at a much lower rate, a greater sea-going population, and, from long experience, a better knowledge of the most productive fishing grounds. . . . Each of the crew have the share agreed upon [*of the catch*]. . . . The crews of British fishing vessels, although equally active, are most frequently hired by the month, and consequently they have less interest in the profits of the voyage. Nor is it a rare case that they become disheartened by the threats and insults heaped upon them by their more numerous rivals.

6

The Americans and the Inshore Fisheries

From Canadian Archives, *Correspondence of the governor-general's secretary*, enclosure in no. 5811, Le Marchant to Elgin.

To His Excellency Sir John Gaspard Le Marchant, Lieutenant-Governor of Nova Scotia:

May it please your Excellency:

We, Her Majesty's dutiful and loyal subjects, the Mayor and Aldermen of the City, and Representatives of the City and County of Halifax, respectfully request that Your Excellency will be pleased to transmit, by this night's mail, to the Right Honourable, the Secretary of State for the Colonies, to be laid at the foot of the Throne, a dutiful and loyal petition, unanimously adopted this day by a very large and influential meeting of our fellow Citizens, held in the Province Hall.

We also pray that the Resolutions, a copy of which is annexed, and which were passed with equal unanimity, may be also forwarded to the Right Honorable the Colonial Secretary.

This Petition, and these Resolutions, have been adopted in consequence of the alarming intelligence having been received, that negotiations are pending between the British Government and the American Minister in London, for surrendering to the citizens of the United States the right of Fishing on the Coasts and within the Bays of the British North American Colonies,[1] from which they are now excluded by the Convention of 1818.   We entreat Your Excellency, as the Queen's Representative in this Province, to convey to Her Majesty's Government a strong remonstrance against any such concession of Fishing rights as appear to be contemplated.

The immediate departure of this mail will not permit our detailing all the disastrous results to be apprehended from the concessions now required by the American Government, but we must beg that you will assure Her Majesty's Ministers that the information just received has occasioned the most intense anxiety throughout the community, it being evident that our rights, once conceded, can never be regained.

By the terms of the Convention of 1818, the United States expressly renounced any right of fishing within three marine miles from the coasts and shores of these Colonies, or of entering their bays, creeks, and harbours, except for shelter, or for food and water.

If this restriction be removed, it must be obvious to your Excellency that it will be impossible to prevent the Americans from using our fishing grounds as freely as our own fishermen.

They will be permitted to enter our Bays and Harbours, where, at all times, *unless armed vessels are present in every harbour*, they will not only fish in common with our fishermen, but they will bring with them Contraband Goods to exchange with the inhabitants for fish, to the great injury of Colonial Traders and loss to

---

[1]The basis of the negotiation of the Reciprocity Treaty of 1854.

27

the Public Revenue.   The fish obtained by this illicit traffic will
then be taken to the United States, where they will be entered as
the produce of the American fisheries, while those exported from
the Colonies in a legal manner are subject to oppressive duties.

We need not remind your Excellency that the equivalent said
to have been proposed—that of allowing our vessels to fish in the
waters of the United States—is utterly valueless, and unworthy of
a moment's consideration.

We would fain hope that the reports which have appeared in
the public Press respecting the pending negotiations between the
two Governments are without any good foundation.

We cannot imagine that Her Majesty's Government, after
having taken prompt and decided measures to enforce the true
construction of the Treaty, will ever consent to such a modification
of its terms as will render our highly valued rights a mere privilege
to be enjoyed in common with foreigners.

We therefore pray your Excellency to exert all your influence
to induce Her Majesty's Ministers to stay any further negotiations
on this vitally important question until the rights and interests
of the inhabitants of this Province are more fully enquired into and
vindicated.

Halifax, 2nd September, 1852

7

The Fisheries of New Brunswick

From M. H. Perley, "The progress of New Brunswick" in, *Eighty years' progress*, 574, 579.

The sea-coast of New Brunswick, as well in the Bay of Fundy
as within the Gulf of St. Lawrence, abounds with fish of various
descriptions; and all its rivers possess fisheries more or less valuable. . . .

THE BAY OF FUNDY.—The principal sea fisheries in the
bay are those of cod, pollock, hake, haddock, herring and mackerel.
The chief fishing grounds of these are near the entrance to the bay,
and in the vicinity of the islands of Grand Manan, Campo Bello
and the group known as West Isles, whence the fishing is pursued
along the coast eastwardly to the harbor of St. John, and sometimes much further up the bay.   The estimated annual value of
these fisheries is about £40,000 sterling.

The fishing for cod, pollock, hake and haddock, is with hook and line only. It is chiefly followed by fishermen resident on the coast and adjacent islands, in small open boats, which go out in the morning and return in the evening, except in hake fishing, which is pursued during the night. The boats generally in use are from twelve to eighteen feet in length; the twelve feet boat has one man, the eighteen feet boat usually three men. These boats have sharp or pink sterns, with one mast shipped very close to the stem, and a mainsail very broad at the foot, stretched well out with a light boom, and running up to a point at the top. They sail uncommonly well, and lie very close to the wind. Small schooners are also employed for winter fishing, and for the distant banks or fishing grounds.

The *cod* of the Bay of Fundy are large and of the finest quality, equal to any taken on the coast of North America. They bear the highest price in the United States market being always selected for the best tables. The cod fishery may be followed nearly the whole year, when the weather permits, sometimes close to the land, and at others ten or fifteen miles from it, in very deep water, according to the season, and the course of the herring or other fish upon which the cod feed at different times. When caught, the cod are usually split, salted and dried, and in that state are known as the dry cod of commerce, which is always sold by the quintal of 112 lbs. At those seasons when cod cannot be dry-cured, they are salted in pickle and packed in barrels; these are called "pickled cod".

The very best cod are taken at the close of winter, or very early in the spring, in about sixty fathoms water. These are thick, well-fed fish, often attaining the weight of 70 lbs. or 80 lbs. and sometimes more. The oil extracted from the liver of the cod is valuable, and, when refined sells at a high price for medicinal purposes. . . . . . .

The islands of Grand Manan, Campo Bello and West Isles, own and employ in the fisheries sixty-eight vessels manned by 558 men; 350 boats, manned by 900 men; besides 200 men employed in connection with the herring-weirs. The settlers along the shores of the Bay of Fundy all fish more or less in their own boats chiefly for their own use. The value of their fishing cannot be stated with any degree of precision.

The rivers which fall into the bay yield a variety of fish; but the most valuable river fishing is in the harbour of St. John, at the mouth of the St. John river, which yields annually about 40,000 salmon, 12,000 to 16,000 barrels of alewives, and about 1,000 barrels of shad. The salmon are large and fine, precisely similar to the salmon of Europe. They are worth at St. John about six-pence sterling per pound, and are sent in ice in large quantities to the United States, yielding a considerable profit and forming a valuable export. The *alewife* is a small species of shad, generally known in New Brunswick by the name of gaspereau; its length is from eight to ten inches, tolerably good when eaten fresh, early in spring, but very dry when salted. It is exported in pickle to the Southern States, where it is eaten by the slaves; in that hot climate a fatter fish will not keep. . . . The fisheries in St. John Harbor give employment to two hundred boats and five hundred men; their value is estimated at £20,000 sterling annually.

THE GULF OF ST. LAWRENCE.—The fisheries in this gulf are prosecuted only from April until the end of November, the ice preventing their being followed during the rest of the year.

The principal fishery is for cod; it commences early in June, and continues until late in November. In the early part of the season, cod are taken very near the shores; as the season advances they draw off into deep water. The best fishing grounds, or, rather those most frequented, are from Point Escuminac to Miscou, and thence along the bay of Chaleur to the Restigouche. The fishermen go out in boats from one to fifteen miles from the land, in the morning, and when at the longer distance do not return until the evening of the second day. Their boats are large but not decked; they have two fore-and-aft sails and a jib. Each boat is managed by two men, and there is frequently with them a boy. The fishermen generally build their own boats during the winter; the keel is of birch; the timbers of cedar; and the planks of pine or cedar. The boat has oars, an anchor and rope, compass and small stove for cooking; the cost is about £18 for each boat and outfit. A boat will last from six to eight years and so will the sails also, with care.

It is considered a good day's fishing at Miscou, or Shippegan, for one of these boats to take ten quintals of fish, which they frequently do. When first caught, 112 of the small fish, and thirty of the large size are reckoned to the quintal. The fishermen generally split, salt and cure their own fish; when they do not,

252 lbs. of green fish, salted and drained, are given to a curer, who returns a quintal, or 112 lbs. of merchantable dry fish.

The Bay of Chaleur cod are more prized in the markets of the Mediterranean, and will at all times sell there more readily, and at higher prices than any other. They are beautifully white, and being very dry, can better withstand the effects of a hot climate and a long voyage than a more moist fish. The peculiarity of their being smaller than cod caught elsewhere, is also of great importance as regards the South American market, for which they are packed in tubs of a peculiar shape called "drums", and into which they are closely pressed by means of a powerful screw.

(b)—SHIPPING AND SHIP-BUILDING

Ship-building was at first based on the fisheries, the "banks" producing one type of craft, the inshore fisheries another. After 1783, the attempt to transfer the West Indian trade to Nova Scotia extended the industry but did not change the type of ship, the "bankers" being used for winter voyages southward. But the enormous demand for ships during the Napoleonic wars revolutionized it and created an export business in ships of every type. With ups and downs following the general course of trade, the industry remained of great importance until iron and steel hulls brought about its collapse.

After 1815, there was a temporary recession but as the timber trade grew under the pressure of British preference, ship-building increased also—there was naturally an intimate relationship between the two. New Brunswick was the chief beneficiary, its ship-wrights developing a very cheap class of ships, built mainly out of local wood and as a rule rating on the lowest "letter" at Lloyd's, or Al for four years (as contrasted with British built ships, Al for 12 years). These ships were fitted with rigging and hardware sent from England, loaded with timber, and sent to England for sale. It was a business subject to great fluctuations and one which earned the dislike of everyone in England who knew a good ship from a bad one. Probably owing in part to criticism, New Brunswick ships gradually improved and by the close of the period, much of the prejudice against them was no longer sound.

Nova Scotian ships, while cheap, never earned as bad a reputation as those of New Brunswick, possibly because they were rather for home consumption than for export. Later on they were built for what would now be called "tramp" purposes (ownership remaining in Nova Scotia but the vessel rarely seeing her home port), and in this pursuit, the province produced a class of designers and seamen who have come down as legendary and gigantic figures, among them Donald Mackay, the originator of the famous "clipper" ship, the last blaze of glory of sail before its capitulation to steam.

References: *Canada and its provinces,* XIII; William Wood, *All afloat* (Chronicles of Canada, Toronto, 1914); F. W. Wallace, *In the wake of the wind-ships* (Toronto, 1927) and *Wooden ships and iron men* (London, n.d.); Archibald MacMechan, *There go the ships* (Toronto, 1928) and *Samuel Cunard* (Toronto, 1929).

1

Effects of the Peace of 1815 on the Shipping of New Brunswick

From *Ships, colonies and commerce, an appeal to the Right Hon. Wm. Huskisson....*
by "A Colonist".

. . . The effects of the peace of 1814 and 1815 began not to
display themselves upon our navigation until the year 1816,
when the great number of vessels discharged from the service of
government was thrown into the carrying trade, wherever a freight
could be found. This occurrence, as might be expected, reduced
the value of vessels generally, and our plantation built ones
suffered with the rest, and in a most severe degree; but at that
period they were here confined to fewer hands than the present,
and to those better able to bear the losses, and therefore they were
less generally felt; whilst the countervailing action operated for a
time in keeping up a profitable business in the country which sprang,
too, from the same cause that so materially depreciated the price
of our shipping, viz., the vast influx of British vessels thrown out
of government service, in quest of cargoes, which raised the prices
of our staple articles, timber and lumber, so far above their usual
rates, that what was lost on the one hand was by the merchants
made up on the other. . . .

2

The Ship-building "Boom" in New Brunswick

Extract from St. John letter in *Montreal Gazette*, May 14, 1825.

St. John's, April 7, 1825

Our Governor, Sir H. Douglas, is able and zealous, he is cordi-
ally supported by the country in his plans for promoting its advancement, and we are I think, on the full tide of prosperity. For
the population of the province, its revenue and commerce are
astonishing. Our population is about 75,000 souls. The last year's
revenue near £45,000 currency, the imports upwards of £500,000
sterling, and the exports full as much, including upwards of 16,000
tons of new shipping, built principally for sale, or for merchants in
England, and to be fairly considered as exported manufactures:—
the value of the new shipping may be reckoned at £10 sterling
per ton.

3
Revival of Ship-building:—Disastrous Effects of the "Boom" of 1825

From *Ships, colonies and commerce.*

. . . In the years 1821 and 1822 ship-building began to revive here after a suspension of several years, during which natural decay and other destructive elements had so reduced the old stock that we opened the business with the fairest prospects of success, which were amply realized. We were the more ready at this period to enter into the speculation from the great difficulty we experienced in making remittances for the goods imported from Great Britain, bills of exchange being at the high rate of fifteen to seventeen and a half and even twenty per cent premium and the usual want of specie to buy them. . . . We therefore adopted the above means of remitting our agent for the goods shipped to us. At that time a vessel could be built in the harbour of St John for £4/5s to £5/15s (for the hull and spars) per ton, payable in the following manner— one-third in money, one-third in British manufactures, and one-third in West India and American produce, all of which save the first, bore a considerable advance, so that when the vessel was completely fitted, nine pounds currency per ton would pay for her. The materials and rigging being received from Great Britain, were paid for by the sale of the vessel there, which bringing in that market what they cost here, left us a fair profit by paying for our goods without the sacrifice of the premium demanded for British exchange and giving a bonus in the freight of the cargo. Such an advantageous mode of remittance soon brought many into the speculation, which the home prices for our commodities seemed to warrant, and a consequent rise followed here until £7/10s and up to £10 per ton, according to the quality, was given for hulls and spars. This naturally drew on a rise in ship-timber and the wages of carpenters got to a most extravagant height, from five shillings to ten shillings, twelve and sixpence and fifteen shillings per day, whilst a very material advance in the fastenings took place in Britain. Payments made here became payable in money alone, and sailors' wages followed in the trend of advance.

Such was the excited state of business here when others, no less overstrained in England, began to affect those engaged; Money became scarce, and our agents being straightened, forced

our property into market to meet their own engagements—the
necessity of selling which, as usual, reduced the price of the article
offered; and our shipping, which had much increased, being under
the controul of those pinched agents in Britain, first received the
shock and sunk even below the sadly depressed state in which we
find it at the present moment. . . .

4

Tonnage of Nova Scotian Shipping in 1828

From *Montreal Gazette*, March 1, 1830.

In that year [*1828*]
In her trade with Great Britain she [*Nova Scotia*]

had employed	27,162 tons.
The West Indies	27,714 tons.
The United States	16,058 tons.
Brazil, first permitted in 1826	1,549 tons.
Foreign Europe, opened at the same time	1,638 tons.
Coasting tonnage	58,924 tons.
Total	132,045 tons.

5

The Character of New Brunswick-built Ships

From Abraham Gesner, *New Brunswick, with notes for emigrants*, 303.

Ship-building has been followed with much spirit, and still
forms an important branch of industry in New Brunswick. An
opinion has prevailed in Great Britain, and not without just
foundation, that the ships built in the Province are imperfectly
constructed and insufficiently fastened. Ships are frequently built
by contract for from £4 to £7 per ton: the result has been that
many of them have not been faithfully and substantially put
together, and the discovery of their imperfections has injured the
reputations of all the vessels of the Colony. Since 1840, a successful effort has been made to improve the ship-building, and the
vessels now built by the merchants under proper inspection are
equal, if not superior, to any ever launched. The abundance and
good quality of the wood give New Brunswick an advantage in
the building of ships and other vessels.[1]

[1] A doubtful statement: the lack of good white oak was always a handicap
to Maritime ships. Even American white oak was not reputed as good in lasting
qualities and strength as British.

6

Ship-building as Injurious to the Best Interests of New Brunswick

From *Parliamentary papers*, session 1847-48, XX (1), 64-65, Examination of John McGregor before the committee of the house of commons on the navigation acts.

Question 660.   Do you think that ships could be built in the Baltic at a cheaper rate than that?[1]—No, not cheaper than those ships were sold at; but I should be exceedingly unjust if I did not explain the circumstances as regards those ships.   Those ships were sold under particular circumstances, at actually less money than the rigging and materials cost.   I must state this, because having repeatedly been before Committees of the House of Commons, and having had, perhaps, as much knowledge of the British North American provinces as any man, I have always regretted to see the extent to which ship-building was carried in the North American provinces, as diverting labour from agriculture; and I have known ships in the years 1826, 1827, and 1828, that were built in New Brunswick, not one of which could have cost less than 5£, or 6£ a ton, most of them having cost 8£., 9£. and 10£. a ton; I have known ships built in Canada during those years which cost from 7£. to 13£. a ton; and I have known those ships sold in the London Docks and Liverpool for less than the cost of their very materials, which were taken up on credit; and not only that, but I found that under the expectation of great profit, farmers in the province of New Brunswick and in the neighbouring provinces, the Canadas, and of Prince Edward Island, and who were prospering on their land, were led to embark in the building of ships; and these farms along the River St. John's, and in other places upon which they had prospered, were afterwards sold under an execution at the sheriff's sales.   I was at one time holding the office of high sheriff in one of those colonies, and I have sold such lands to pay for the foreclosure of mortgages; and frequently they were sold for the payment of the rigging and other materials, which had been bought in this country.   I must in justice state those circumstances, I do say, that those ships would never have been built except under those peculiar and imprudent circumstances.

---

[1]That is, than in New Brunswick.

661. Sir H. Douglas. That was the panic of 1826 and 1827?—
Yes, during 1826 and 1827; it continued during 1828 and 1829.
The different farms in New Brunswick and other colonies which I
allude to, were principally sold before I returned to this country.

7

Ships Built in New Brunswick, 1825-1860

From M. H. Perley, in *Eighty years' progress*, 598.

Year	No. of vessels	Tons.	Year	No. of vessels	Tons.
1825	120	28,893	1843	64	14,550
1826	130	31,620	1844	87	24,543
1827	99	21,806	1845	92	28,972
1828	71	15,656	1846	124	40,383
1829	64	8,450	1847	115	53,373
1830	52	9,242	1848	86	22,793
1831	61	8,571	1849	119	39,280
1832	70	14,081	1850	86	30,356
1833	97	17,834	1851	99	49,595
1834	92	24,140	1852	118	58,399
1835	97	25,796	1853	122	71,428
1836	100	29,643	1854	135	99,426
1837	99	27,288	1855	95	54,561
1838	122	29,167	1856	129	79,907
1839	164	45,864	1857	148	71,989
1840	168	64,104	1858	75	26,263
1841	119	47,140	1859	93	38,330
1842	87	22,840	1860	100	41,003

(c)—COAL-MINING

Although the coal mines of Cape Breton had been known from an early
period but little use had been made of them. Within the quarter century after
the Peace of Paris, what were destined to be the two principal markets of the
more mature industry—the St. Lawrence and New England—had apparently been
opened in a small way (volume I of this work, pp. 211, 213), but only the most
primitive methods and the most meagre of results obtained until, in 1826, as a
consequence of a grant made by George IV to his brother, the Duke of York, all
the mineral rights of the province, both island and peninsula, found their way
into the possession of the General Mining Association. This company, having
command of capital, sent out good technical men and, under their guidance,
Nova Scotian coal-mining forged rapidly ahead. The company finally incurred
odium as a monopoly and, gradually pared of its original rights, at last merged

into still-existing institutions.   Markets throughout the period were precarious: in the St. Lawrence, Nova Scotian coal had to compete with English, brought out in the timber ships as ballast, and in New England, having to meet the uncertainties of the American tariff.   At first, these handicaps were added to by the careless way in which the coal was prepared.   It was in connection with the Pictou mines that the first railway in Nova Scotia was built (see document 11, page 205).

Of the other minerals of the Maritimes, gypsum, used as fertilizer, was the chief in this period.   Its market was also in the United States.   In addition, rough grindstones were quarried and exported.   The mining of gold and of iron did not commence until about 1860.

1
The General Mining Association
From Abraham Gesner, *New Brunswick, with notes for emigrants*, 344.

Of the British North American Colonies, New Brunswick was the first to undertake an examination of her mineral resources. Since the commencement of that survey, similar ones have been instituted in Newfoundland and Canada... Nova Scotia would have engaged in such a work long ago, were not her mines and minerals sealed up by a close monopoly which withholds from the inhabitants any participation in the mineral wealth of the country.

2
State of Mining in New Brunswick about 1840
From *Ibid.*, 304.

Mining scarcely forms any part of Provincial labour, . . . New Brunswick contains great mineral wealth; coal and iron are abundant; besides these, manganese, copper, lead and other ores have been discovered, and limestone, gypsum, and freestone, of the best kinds, occur in certain districts; yet the home consumption and exportation of those objects are extremely limited. . . . Small quantities of coal are raised annually on the borders of Grand Lake for the supply of Fredericton, and small cargoes are sometimes sent down to St. John. . . . The iron and coal employed in foundries are imported from Great Britain.

3
Production of Coal in Nova Scotia:—The Coal Trade
From Charles Robb, in *Eighty years' progress*, 350.

The coal-fields of Nova Scotia have long been known to be of vast extent and value, and have been worked more or less since the first settlement of the colony by the British; when the imperial government, in making their grants of land, reserved for the crown all mineral rights, and subsequently leased them to a company of capitalists styled the General Mining Association, by whom the coal has been for the most part mined and exported. The most important are the Albion mines in the county of Pictou, in the northern part of the province, where two seams of excellent coal occur, of the enormous aggregate thickness of thirty-seven and thirty-two feet respectively; although of this total thickness only about twenty-four and twelve feet can be said to be good coal. The *main seam* has been very extensively worked, and its outcrop has been traced for several miles; but it is remarkable that it retains its character as a seam of good coal only for a very limited distance on either side of the main shaft. The coal hitherto exported has been obtained almost exclusively from the upper part of this seam, the workings being from twelve to nine feet deep, and the lowest shaft sunk to a depth of about 400 feet. . . . The quantity of coal raised at these mines in 1851 was about sixty thousand chaldrons, and subsequently this yield has been still further increased. It is chiefly exported to the United States, and is admirably adapted and extensively used in making gas, as well as for general purposes. These mines afford employment to a population of 2,000 and their produce is conveyed by a railway worked by locomotives to the harbor of South Pictou, a distance of six miles.

The following is an extract of returns of coal raised, sold and exported at Pictou in the year ending 31st December, 1858:

	Large coal	Slack coal
Total quantity raised and sold in tons...	100,607½	14,344½
Of this there was—		
Sold for home consumption.........	9,212½	4,519½
Exported to the United States......	89,217	6,396
Exported to the neighboring colonies	2,178	3,419

Next in importance to the Pictou coal mines are those of Sydney, at the north-eastern extremity of Cape Breton. Here the productive coal measures cover an area of 250 square miles and the aggregate thickness of the coal seams amounts to thirty-seven feet, of which, however, only twenty feet are of good quality, or workable thickness. The mines are worked here, as in the preceding instance, by the General Mining association who raise annually from the Sydney main seam 80,000 tons of coal, which is conveyed by railway to the bar at North Sydney for shipment. About 30,000 tons are annually consumed in Nova Scotia, the remainder being exported to the United States. The quantity of coal annually raised in the county of Cape Breton, and almost entirely at Sydney, is stated in the census of 1851, at 53,000 chaldrons.

TYPICAL MONETARY AND BANKING PROBLEMS

The documents given are drawn from Nova Scotia, for which province there is a vast range of original material available. The problems of the other two provinces were virtually the same:—the primary difficulty of securing a supply of the precious metals, the attempts to overcome this by overrating one or other of the coins which came in in the way of trade (chiefly the Spanish dollar and the doubloon, which found their way up from the West Indies, as they did to all the Atlantic seaboard, thereby making the dollar our monetary unit), by creating an irredeemable paper currency (Nova Scotia had a well-managed issue of "Province Notes" during the whole period) or by establishing banks, and lastly, the task of devising some simpler medium than the cumbrous arithmetical fiction, "Halifax currency". This latter is reflected in the unsuccessful struggle instituted by the imperial treasury to introduce the sterling standard and in the later adoption of the dollar.

Banks came late, the first one being the "Halifax Banking Company", a remote ancestor of the present Bank of Commerce. The Bank of Nova Scotia, the first chartered bank, began in 1832. Not long after that date, the more extreme manifestations of *malaise* in currency disappeared.

REFERENCES: See section V, page 368 *ff*.

1

Hard Times and Soft Money

From Nova Scotia Archives, *Legislative council manuscript documents*, CCLXXXIX, 1816-1822, no. 48, *ca*. January, 1818.

In a country such as Nova Scotia where capital was small and coin scarce, hard times always brought about great monetary stringency: these periods invariably witnessed demands for the issue of irredeemable paper.

To the Earl of Dalhousie, lieutenant-governor of Nova Scotia, etc. the memorial of the magistrates and inhabitants of King's County

Respectfully Sheweth—

That your memorialists hailed with thankful joy the happy restoration of peace to our conflicting nation, anticipating from it, in common with mankind, an amelioration of circumstances, notwithstanding it would deprive this Colony of particular advantages, resulting from a state of warfare: Aware that the great transition from a long and universal war, to an entire cessation of hostilities must necessarily excite embarrassment, your Memorialists were prepared to participate in difficulties, which they hoped would have a temporary existence and lead to a favourable termination;

but they view with anxiety and alarm a prospect of continual perplexity, involving consequences of serious magnitude, threatening the improvement of agriculture, creating a spirit of emigration from this province, producing poverty, distress, and failure among the farmers, forcing the adventurers wandering through the country to seek employment elsewhere; weakening the resources of our nation in the event of war, and finally making those our enemies, whom when our friends we were unable to support. That your Memorialists have investigated the cause of these evils, and attribute them exclusively to the want of a circulating medium, which has been almost exhausted in the country by a stoppage of the usual supplies connected with the war; and by the afflictive dispensations, of Providence, for the two preceding seasons, whereby the expectation of the agriculturists has been frustrated and their exertions rendered abortive. That such calamities have plunged them into unavoidable debt, from which nothing but the timely interference of the Legislature can possibly extricate them.

That there are many whose labours have been conspicuously beneficial to the country; who contemplate a removal elsewhere; if a succedaneum be not furnished to avert the pressure of the times.

That your memorialists having duly considered the nature, extent and probable consequences of the existing difficulties, foresee no alleviation unless a paper currency be established upon such a system as your wisdom and prudence shall judge best calculated to relieve our exigencies and ensure the welfare of the Province.

That from the want of such a medium the law-wrecked property of industrious men is sacrificed at public sale: The numerous and needy strangers who are flocking to the country, and who might be usefully engaged in making roads, clearing woodlands and aiding agriculture pass unemployed to the United States, because money cannot be realized sufficient to satisfy their limited demands.

That your Memorialists therefore most earnestly pray that your Excellency; and the Honourable the Council take into consideration this serious distress of the Province, and recommend to the House of Representatives, who have been duly memorialed, to adopt whatever measures may be found most expedient to relieve our necessity, and which may be compatible with the interests of the Province: and your Memorialists as in duty bound will ever pray &, &, &,

> Elisha Dewolf
> Chairman of a Committee
> met to investigate the present
> Distress'g State of the County

2

Dire Consequences of the Overrating of the Doubloon

From *Acadian Recorder*, October 21, 1820.

The doubloon had been rated at £3/12/0 sterling or sixteen dollars. With the dollar at 4/2 sterling, the doubloon should have gone only for about £3/5/0 sterling. Hence the dollars disappeared.

Messrs. HOLLAND & CO.

Gentlemen,

An old fellow has been writing in your paper about printed fifteen pences and said a great deal more about them than I pretend to understand; but he has not stated above half the grievances the public suffer from this trash of paper that is passing from hand to hand. This morning I went to the green market to buy a bunch of carrots, one of turnips, a squash, and two cabbages, and I carried with me a province note for 20s.—after I had made my bargain I offered my note in payment. First, one said he could not change it; another shook his head and shrugged his shoulders, uttering with a foreign accent "me no small money, will keep my cabbage till you pay them;" a third who had the squash, began to fumble in his waistcoat pocket, and emptied out of it, coppers, ragged bits of paper and one solitary seven-pence-half-penny in silver; "my squash, sir if I change the note is 6d. but only 3d. if you give me coppers—change the note, said I, and the d—l take it; for I am tormented." Well, gentlemen, he began to count the 19s. 6d. of change that should come to me; and after consuming full 10 minutes, and spreading the stall all over with the vilest dregs of our currency, he at length looked up and said "I believe it is all right". I began to take it up; and for the information of others, and probably for the benefit of posterity, I shall faithfully set down what I received in this trifling transaction:—

1st.	George Legget and Wm. Lawson's note each 5s.	£0	10	0
2d.	H. H. Cogswell's team boat note for	0	1	0
3d.	Adam Esson and John A. Barry, each for 1s. 3d.	0	2	6
4th.	Wm. Smith, for three 7½d. in his notes	0	1	10½
5th.	In silver	0	0	7½
6th.	In coppers	0	3	6
		£0	19	6

I had thus 8 paper notes, 1 silver piece, and 84 coppers—in all 93 separate things before I could get vegetables for my family's dinner—For God's sake, gentlemen, let us get back our

DOLLARS;

and send these plaguy doubloons to the Yankees, although we should sell them at a loss. What is the reason that we have now no dollars? I shall briefly tell you, and I defy any man to contradict it. Whenever a dollar, I mean a silver one, is in any one's possession, he keeps it till it brings him from 5s. 4d. to 5s. 6d. in real value, either by selling it to another, or paying it away himself in trafficking at that rate. Flour can be regularly purchased out of the American vessels at 5 or 5½ dollars per barrel, payable in silver, whereas they ask 5½ to 5¾ payable in doubloons. A Spanish dollar can never therefore appear in change at 5s. when it is worth 6 or 7 per cent. more to any merchant. If I could pay them away at 5s. 4d. or 5s. 6d. I believe I should be tempted to put my hand into my chest and break upon 1500 that have lain there without seeing the light for the last 3 years; and save myself from this pest of small notes that are now down to 7½d. or ere long I suppose will be printed for 3½d. or, peradventure, for a single copper.

Our currency is now like a Scotch haggis, made up of contradictions, of things good and bad, oatmeal, onions, hog's lard, butter, crumbs of bread, salt, pepper, garlic, leeks, parsley, &c, &c.

I tell you the "Haggis will burst, and scald many who are little expecting it."

I am, gentlemen, your constant reader,

PETER DAVIDSON

Halifax, Oct. 10

28

3

The First Bank in Nova Scotia

From *The Novascotian*, September 7, 1825.

The co-partnership was a device to circumvent the assembly's refusal of a charter to a banking institution which would not make its notes "responsible in specie".

BANK

The Subscribers respectfully acquaint the public that they have entered into copartnership for the establishment of a Bank, under the firm name of

"The Halifax Banking Company".

They have appropriated a large capital exclusively to this object, and have opened their Bank for Business, in the new stone building owned by Mr Collins. The Company are fully sensible that the success of the institution must depend upon the friendly support which it may receive from the community, and earnestly solicit the public patronage in its behalf

Henry Cogswell, President
William Pryor, Vice President
Enos Collins
James Tobin
Samuel Cunard
John Clark
Joseph Allison
Martin Gayblack.

Halifax, August 31, 1825

4

Collection of Duties in British Sterling

From Colonial office records, *series 217*, CXLVIII, 119.

Memorial of the chamber of commerce of Halifax to the lords commissioners of his majesty's treasury

. . . The imports into this province from the mother country are to a very large amount, whilst the exports in return are of comparatively trifling value, consisting chiefly of timber, lumber, fish, oil, etc., the deficiency is supplied either by specie or bills of exchange, which are procured by the exportation of our staple commodity, fish, to the British colonies and islands in the West Indies or to foreign countries, and when the returns are made in specie, the gold and silver are universally of foreign coinage. Having thus no means of exchanging our products for British coins, the supply of these must and does depend altogether on the expenditure of His Majesty's military department in this province, and as no other moneys are received by the Commissariat for bills of exchange, the small and limited amount of these coins in circulation is eagerly bought up for the purpose of purchasing bills by those who are obliged to make remittances to England. . . .As there can therefore be no materially increased circulation of these coins in the province until we acquire some products to give in exchange for the goods of the parent country, the price of this money will be so much enhanced by the demand for it, should the order of the Commissioners be carried into effect[1] as to increase the duties on goods far beyond the amount contemplated by the act. . . .

Dollars have hitherto been rated in almost all countries to which we trade, at 4/6 sterling, and the demand for them is now such in the United States that they bear a premium upon even this value of $2\frac{1}{2}\%$, and consequently very few of them remain with us. Doubloons and the parts thereof, being the most common specie returned for our exports to foreign countries, bear the same relative value in these as in this province, where they are current at sixteen dollars each, being equivalent to £3/12/0 stg. and are received and paid as such by the provincial government, which also issues notes that have been in great credit for many years; a note of twenty shillings being considered equal to eighteen shillings sterling, but which at present, when tendered for duties at the Custom House, are refused in payment, and although these duties are finally payable into the provincial treasury, yet the province is thus obliged virtually to discredit its own paper. . . .

It appears to your memorialists that foreseeing the difficulty of establishing a scale of equal duties from the various values placed on gold and silver, it [the Imperial Parliament] has regulated this matter fully by fixing the value of silver at 5/6 stg. per ounce, . . . when any general duties have been made applicable to the colonies, at which rate the officers of H. M. Customs at this port have for many years received the King's duties when paid in foreign silver coin. . . .

Halifax, Nova Scotia, 1st May, 1828.

[1]Requiring the payment of imperial duties in sterling money.

5

Attempt to Regulate the Private Issue of Irredeemable Paper

From *Nova Scotia Royal Gazette*, March 27, 1833.

Resolutions of the committee on currency of the legislature of Nova Scotia, 1833

. . . 4. Resolved that it is inconsistent with the public safety to permit any notes, whether of banks or of individuals, to pass as currency unless convertible on demand into specie at the will of the bearer.

5. That the passing of such notes not convertible into specie be prohibited from and immediately after the passing of this bill, which is proposed to be introduced on that subject.

6. That it be recommended to the house to prohibit by a bill to be passed, the issue of any notes designed to constitute a circulating medium unless the same be issued by the present or some other chartered bank, or the Halifax Banking Company, or some partnership composed of not less than seven members; and unless such partnership hereafter to be formed, shall by public advertisement, published five months previous to any such issue, have declared their intention to issue such notes. . . .

Charles R. Fairbanks, Chairman

March 21, 1823

6

A Proposal for the Introduction of the Sterling Standard

From *Nova Scotia assembly*, session of 1839, Report of the committee on currency.

The following document represents the high-water mark of the effort to reform the old haphazard state of the currency by the introduction of the sterling standard. It also shows how impossible it was to get along without a second standard, that of the doubloon and the dollar, coming up from the West Indies, and the report compromises by proposing to allow the two sets of coins as legal tender at fixed ratings, thus adopting bi-metallic principles.

1. That the money of account in this province, contemporaneously with the other North American colonies, should cease to be the old Halifax currency and that British sterling should be substituted in its stead.

2. That the sovereign should be established as a legal tender at its full value of twenty shillings sterling.

3. That doubloons of not less weight than 416 grains each, containing not less than 360 grains of pure gold, of the fineness of twenty carats and three grains, should be established as legal tender at sixty four shillings sterling.

4. That dollars of not less weight than 415 grains each, containing not less than 372 grains of pure silver, should be established as a legal tender, at 4s 2d stg. each, being the value set upon them by the Treasury minute promulgated in the West Indies.

5. That our Treasury Notes should be received in payment of duties, and be paid out as heretofore, at 16s. stg.

6. That all subsisting contracts, debts, salaries, etc., should be reduced to and paid in sterling by deducting one fifth from their present amount in currency. . . .
Committee Room, 4 March, 1839

7

The Evolution of Halifax Currency

From *Report upon currency submitted to the committee of trade and manufactures and approved by them at their meeting, 1st March, 1839* (Halifax, 1839).

. . . The accounts in these five provinces are kept in what is called the old Halifax currency, being a mode of accounting introduced at an early time in colonial history, and which, however justifiable then, is now admitted to be a perfect fiction and at variance with all the well-known principles and laws of a sound currency. In the New England colonies, previous to the American Revolution, the old Spanish dollar was the only species of coin then in circulation. Its value in England at that time, compared with the standard price of British silver or bullion, was equal to 4s 6d stg.

The colonies being attached, it is presumed, to the mode of accounting in pounds, shillings and pence which prevailed in the mother country, and having no coin or money representing British sterling as their money of account, they seem to have agreed unanimously to create a currency of their own, by adding one ninth to the nominal value of the dollar, so as to make 4s 6d stg. equal to 6s. currency—four dollars, 18s. stg. equal to 20s. or £1 currency,—and a system thus based on the circumstances or expediency of the age has been persevered in by us up to this time, altho' these circumstances have long ago been varied, and the expediency has been completely changed.[1]

. . . At the time of its introduction [*Halifax currency*] one ninth was the par of exchange between the mother country and the colonies but this is no longer the true par, for this ninth and the premium on the bills forms the real par. . . .

8

Bimetallism without Argument

From *Report upon currency* (Halifax, 1839).

. . . The committee deem it superogatory to enter here into an enquiry between the comparative merits of a standard of silver coin and gold. It is a question of too complex a character to be entered upon here and besides, even if treated upon, it would, in their opinion, be of no practical value, as the government in the late system introduced into the West Indies, have adopted both standards at the same time. . . .

---

[1]The origin of Halifax currency is not quite so simple as this statement would make it appear. Before the Revolution a dollar had very different ratings in different colonies and at different periods in the same colony. Thus in the 1760's it was rated at eight shillings in New York and at six shillings in Massachusetts, but there are records of the five shilling rating being used in Nova Scotia as early as 1756. Halifax currency was probably a local variant of New England money of account. See Horace A. Fleming, "Halifax currency" (*Journal of the Canadian Bankers' Association*, XXX, 1922-23, 92-93).

THE ISLAND OF CAPE BRETON:—ITS RESOURCES AND INDUSTRIES

From Colonial office records, *series 217*, CXXXIV, 1816, 289-312.

A sketch of memorandums on the local and natural advantages of the Island of Cape Breton

. . . There are two rivers within these lakes[1] the Shennacadia and the Bennacadia which take their rise in the eastern range of mountains which surround the lake and abound with salmon in such a degree as passes almost belief. About four leagues to the southward of the Great Entrance is the Little Entrance, these two channels bound the island of Boularderie. This entrance is barred having only 9 feet water at low tide but when over this bar, depth of water for any vessel. Near this entrance at Point Iconia are remarkable fine veins of coal and within the lakes are all the species of gypsum in immense abundance. From hence to the north headland of Spanish Bay is three leagues.

[Trade]

In the government of Cape Breton there are existing 217 registered vessels all built in the island and measuring 7510 tons and employ 713 seamen. Until the war of 1793 all the vessels in the island were employed in the fishery. The markets became then precarious and the supplies exorbitant induced the owners to become coal carriers which they have in a great measure continued to the present time making a freight to Halifax and Newfoundland of seldom less than 20/ a Chaldron. The building of vessels is generally done during the winter. The construction of the vessels built in the Island and their sailing are esteemed preferable to any in America they will not compleat at Hull for less than four Pounds a Ton. The timbers used in building are yellow birch, black birch, maple and black spruce, of all which the Island affords an inexhaustible supply. The whole Island is surrounded with fishing banks, and often great voyages are made in the bays and within the headlands of rivers. A vessel with four hands in general kills

[1]The Bras d'Or Lakes.

about 400 Quintals of dry fish in the season.   These are cured by
the wife and children of the owner.   The merchant receives them
about the last week in September at a price, too generally fixt by
himself.   This alludes only to cod fish—The herring & mackarel
fishery continue only about 14 days.   The first takes place in May
the other in August, both kinds are extremely plenty, some years
they fail.   The *Salmon fishery*, which might be pursued to any
extent, has not been attempted to any degree so as to draw a fair
conclusion of its importance.   The finest eels in the world and any
quantity may be taken the rivers & lakes abound with them.
Oil has not yet become an important article in trade the best is
made from the liver of the dog-fish.   This fish comes upon the
coast in the Month of September in great numbers.—Seal Oil might
also be obtained to any amount in the month of March some years
all the Bays round the Island are filled [*with them*] but the catching
them is attended with much danger and many vessels and lives
have been lost, by the fields of ice dividing when the men are employed in killing this animal.   *Coal* is the great article of exportation from 7 to 8000 Tons are annually shipped to Halifax in Nova
Scotia and Newfoundland they are put on Shipboard at 18/ a
Chaldron and the average price at Halifax 37/6 and at Newfoundland 45/.

[*Minerals*]

Plaister of Paris is in immence quantities and a few loads have
been carried to the United States where it is found to be a most
excellent manure for the Southern Wheat Lands.

Black Cattle, and fresh Butter are becoming Articles of considerable exportation chiefly to St. Johns' Newfoundland.   Lumber
has not yet been procured sufficient for the Islands internal Consumption.   There are as fine timber of the best kinds as any in
North America and might be made an object of great national
importance.   Every where in the Island, there are fine streams of
water for saw-mills. . . .

Gypsum is in the greatest abundance.   The Blocks are sufficiently large to be cut in any form that can be moved, it is poris[1]
but not transparent there are two kinds soft and hard.   The hard
is of the alabaster kind—some are variagated—but mostly a pure
white.   They make a strong effervescents with acids.

---

[1]"Poris": porous.

Stones—free stone—fire stone—and a good whet stone with many other classes of the Aronata Limestone abounds every where in the Island.

Slate—a very fine blue Slate lately discovered near the sea shore to the northward of Cape Fumée, in very large slabs.

Black Lead, its quality and class not yet ascertained.

Iron ores, of several degrees. The Bog and Mountain ores are in great abundance a small quantity of bog ore was fluxed and produced fine iron in the ratio of 63 to 100, it lays[1] in its natural state surrounded by a strata of red ochre.

Coal, extends almost the whole breadth of the Island, commencing on the western shore of Caw Bay about 16 miles East of Sydney River—running in nearly a S.W. course to the Western shore of the Island at Maboo.   The strata[1] runs from 4 ft. 8 in. to 6 feet and dips to the N.E. in a proportion of one foot in eight or nine.   The Mines at present in working lay on the N.W. shore of Prince William Henry Sound about 8 Miles North of Sydney Town, they have not been yet worked on a level deeper than low water Mark.   The pits are from 10 to 14 fathoms deep the thickness of the seam or strata increases with the dip a small degree.   The coal is of a remarkable fine quality.

[Timber]

The Island affords a large quantity of all the growths peculiar to the North America soil and climate.   Oak: Red and White—it does not grow to such a size as the English nor is it so hard—is very tall and very straight.   Beech is preferable to the European, grows to a large size straight, clean and of a fine grain.   Birch: White, Yellow & Black.   The *White* is a soft useless wood, except for some articles of turnery wares.   The *Yellow* is a very tough strong grained wood, used very much in ship-building.   The *Black* is a very hard wood, takes a fine polish not inferior to mahogany and in articles of furniture which require a thickness of 1½ Inch or upwards is in every respect preferable.   But less it is apt to warp.   It is much in estimation for keels and plank for vessels.   It is yet doubtful whether the *Black Birch* is a distinct wood or the aged *Yellow*.[2]   The Author has never been able to discover a *young*

---

[1]The author's grammar is not all it should be.

[2]There are only the two species of birch in Cape Breton, the white and the yellow.   Black birch is a popular name for the yellow, *betula lutea*.

black birch.   Yet the grain of the wood is different from the yellow— it branches differently in growth, and has a different bark.

Maple: the *Rock*, the *Soft* and the *Curled.* From the sap of the Rock Maple[1] the Indians make excellent sugar, and when purified and granulated is not much inferior to the Muscovado. The Indians form it into large cakes of about from 8 to 10 lbs each and they are not very clean in their operations. When made by the farmers it is very beautiful. Taking the juice does not destroy the tree, but every year the sap improves in richness and lessens in quantity. They begin to tap the trees the last week in March; a tree of 16 or 18 inches diameter will the first year run 7 or 8 gallons, a good deal depends on the soil.

Elm: very fine, large and in great quantities the best grows on interval Lands.

Ash: the *Swamp* and *Mountain*, the last is good for nothing the other nearly of a quality with the European—not quite so hard.

Horn-beam: is found only on the Barrens of La Indian Bay and appears to be of a more hard and firm texture than the English.

Poplar: in great quantities the same as the English.

Hackmatack[2] alias Tackmahack: is an ornamental tree of a very quick growth, no use have yet been [*made*] of it, except planting for ornament.

Dog-Wood: more properly a Shrub, in some parts of the United States they esteem the bark equal to the Peruvian—the Author made some experiments and found the bark very astringet [*astringent*] but not absorbent—yet it destroys the sharpness of acids.

Wild Cherry: Where-ever hard wood is cut down and burnt on the land the wild cherry springs up the next year and covers the whole surface unless the Land is croped [*cropped*] the same year it is cleared. This happens in places where not a cherry tree is found within 20 miles. The *Elder* in general Accompanies the wild cherry.

Hemlock: grows to a very large size—is used for wharf logs only of which it makes the best of all other timber. It remains under water impenetrable to rot or worms. The bark has been

---

[1]Rock Maple: that is the ordinary hard or sugar maple.

[2]Hackmatack, that is, tamarac, or larch. It was later used in ship-building, especially its roots, the curved portions of which made excellent "compass" timber, for knees, futtocks, *etc.*

tried and found a very good substitute for the oak bark in tanning: this wood is difficult to be consumed by fire.[1]

Pine: Red, Yellow[2] and White—of the first two there are great plenty all over the Island, and of equal quality and size with any in North America—the *White* is found only in a few places in the Bras D'Or Lakes, particularly on the Rivers Dennée and Mat-a-Wat-Cook where there are some very fine and large.

Spruce: Black, Red and *White* in inexhaustible quantities—the Essence of Spruce is made from the young black tree.   It grows to a very large size—tall and straight and is much used for masts to schooners & small vessel's yards and top masts, the red and white are used only for fencing poles—the young buds of the red make the finest yellow dye in the world.

Candle Berry Tree or Shrub: its soil is moist Swampy Land—grows in great abundance.

Larch[3] and other firs in great quantities all over the Island—the Larch is much esteemed in planking small boats & vessels—and makes the best fencing poles, being straight long and not liable to decay so much as the other firs.

The Oak and Elm are top-rooted all the others Stool.   There cannot be any doubt but that the timber of Cape Breton might be appropriated to many valuable purposes and form a very profitable and extensive commerce—every-where affords fine and suitable streams for saw-mills and the various species of timber procured in any form, dimension and quantity.[4]

[*Soil and climate*]

The Soil in every part of the Island except towards the sea-shore and the mountains towards Cape North and some few spruce barrens is extremely rich and fertile and capable of yielding on cultivation all the species of Grain, corn, seeds, roots and vegetables in high perfection.   Hemp & flax grow very luxuriant. *Indian Corn* to great perfection.   Potatoes in particular are produced in astonishing crops.   30 for one is a common produce.

---

[1]Did the author confuse the hemlock with the tamarac? the description here given would better fit the tamarac.

[2]Yellow pine: probably a reference to the northern "pitch pine" of the Atlantic coast.   Not a merchantable timber.

[3]The tamarac: see above.   This seems to be a description of the white cedar, not elsewhere mentioned.

[4]Cape Breton later became the scene of a considerable timber industry.

A Gentleman farmer once came to the author to make oath to the produce of his crop of potatoes and had actually written out an affidavit stating that the produce was *one thousand bushels* from *ten* planted—he was not permitted to make the affidavit for on consideration and inspection of the ground planted it was found that the space could not contain 1000 Bushels if packed close on the surface. The crop was very great perhaps from 50 to 60 for one.—It was new ground of a light soil.

Weather. The Climate is remarkably healthy and salubrious, notwithstanding the changes in weather are very rapid and severe. Sydney River which is one mile wide near the town has frequently been crossed on the ice by persons who had 16 hours before crossed it in a boat.

Snow is sometimes 5 feet deep upon a level, and no travelling but on snow shoes.

Fogs are never known at Sydney nor further to the northward than the Island of Scatterie. *May* is the most unpleasant month in the Year. June July and August are Seldom too hot for labour. September, October and November are delightful months a clear, serene sky and pure air, prevail, sometimes, to January.

Aurora Borealis is very beautiful in this Island especially after a dry summer, it shoots with the most rapid and vivid rays.

Thunder: is very seldom heard.

PART TWO

INTRODUCTION

PART II of this volume is intended to show the trends of movements traced in the first volume of *Canadian economic documents* (covering the period from 1497 to 1783) and in the first section of this volume by Professor A. R. M. Lower (covering the period from 1783 to 1850). Documents dealing with the period prior to 1850 have been primarily concerned with economic growth as based on water-transportation. In the first volume the fishing industry and the fur-trade were stressed as basic economic activities and the documents were presented to suggest the relationship of subsidiary economic development. Professor Lower in the first part of this volume has shown the importance of lumber as the staple which followed fur in the St. Lawrence, and which was added to fish in the Maritimes. The middle of the nineteenth century serves as a rough dividing line to mark the beginnings of steam navigation and the railways. Transport by land became supplemental to transport by water. The following section is concerned, therefore, with the coming of industrialism based on steam and with the transition from an economy based on wood and water to an economy based on iron and steam and to a large extent on wheat as a staple export.

The material has been arranged to illustrate the outstanding economic developments in the St. Lawrence drainage basin, the Atlantic drainage basin (the Maritimes), the Hudson Bay drainage basin, and the Pacific Coast drainage basin, with particular emphasis on the effects of mechanized transport and its drive toward unity. The dominance of water-transport, the shift to water-and-land-transport and the effects of iron and steam on basic staples and on secondary industries are emphasized throughout. The task of choosing documents to illustrate these changes has been difficult. The wealth of printed material available in the publications of the various governments concerned has defied selection. It was found necessary to abandon the earlier arrangement of documents and to include copious extracts chiefly from official sources with reference to a general suggestion of their relationships to broad underlying factors. This problem has also necessitated ending the volume at 1885 rather than at 1914 as planned earlier.

The inadequacy of work in the field precludes a definitive economic history and it is hoped that references to important sources and to various monographs may serve to stimulate further interest in the general subject and to facilitate later research. The essential unity of economic history has been stressed at the risk of suggesting conclusions which will need modification as the result of further work. The material has been chosen to stress the evolutionary and technological points of view and to provide a background for the interpretation of phenomena which have been recorded quantitatively, for example, in succeeding censuses and *Canada yearbooks* and in *Statistical contributions to Canadian economic history* (Toronto, 1931). The work is supplementary to the constitutional documents in W. P. M. Kennedy, *Statutes, treaties and documents of the Canadian constitution 1713-1929* (Toronto, 1930); and to economic studies of Great Britain, such as J. H. Clapham, *An economic history of modern Britain I, 1820-1850; II, 1850-1886* (Cambridge, 1926-1932) and C. R. Fay, *Great Britain from Adam Smith to the present day* (London, 1928). It is scarcely necessary to point out the limitations of work based chiefly on official documents but it should be noted that governmental bodies commanded the services of a fairly competent body of trained servants, many of them interested throughout a life-time in the economic problems of the period, and of the ablest business men, especially on royal commissions and special committees.[1] An attempt has been made to supplement their observations by references to the work of numerous authorities but, in the

---

[1]See S. M. Wickett, "Study of political economy at Canadian universities", appendix to the *Report* of the Ontario bureau of industries, 1897; Rev. W. Hincks, two articles on the place of economics (*Canadian Journal of Industry, Science and Art,* 1861, VI, 20 *ff.*; XI, 96 *ff.*); A. Ashley, *William James Ashley* (London, 1932), chapter vi. Lest the documents appear to over-emphasize the place of the state in Canadian economic development, the reader is referred to the very great importance attached to the preservation of records by private interprises and to the publication of histories of private undertakings described in volume I (p. viii) of this work. Such studies would emphasize the continuity and toughness of Canadian economic growth and offset the tendency of government documents to emphasize elements of disturbance and difficulty.

main, economic knowledge was generally confined to these groups.

Part II represents an attempt to develop the economic history of the period of Confederation in line with the important work of Professor Trotter and earlier studies of the fur-trade and the fishing industry,[1] and to rewrite the introductory sections of *A history of the Canadian Pacific Railway.* (London, 1923). In point of arrangement it is an introduction to the amphibian stage of Canadian economic history in which an economy based on wood and water was in part supplemented and in part displaced by iron and coal and by land-transport.[2]

I am indebted to a large number of individuals in the preparation of this section but mention should be made of Mr. R. H. Fleming, Mr. R. E. English, Professor E. S. Moore, and Mr. S. A. Saunders who have read critically various chapters. I owe a debt of gratitude to Mr. W. S. Wallace, the librarian of the University of Toronto, and to his staff for extending privileges beyond all reasonable limits. I must also thank the University of Toronto for assistance at various stages and I cannot refrain from mentioning the editorial work of Miss Alison Ewart and the interest of Mr. R. J. Hamilton and his committee in making this venture possible. My uncle, Mr. George Henry, has kindly permitted the extensive use of a manuscript written by him on settlement in western Canada. His Honour Judge F. W. Howay of New Westminster and Mr. W. Adams of Lillooet have been generous with information on details of development in the Cariboo. If a formal dedication of this section were in order it would be due pre-eminently to the memory of my grandparents who lived and worked through this period on farms in western Ontario.

H.A.I.

---

[1]"An introduction to the economic history of the Maritimes including Newfoundland and New England" (Canadian Historical Association *report*, 1931).
[2]See also H. A. Innis, *Problems of staple production* (Toronto, 1933).

THE ST. LAWRENCE DRAINAGE BASIN

SUBSECTION A

TRANSPORT AND COMMUNICATION[1]

(a)—OCEAN NAVIGATION[2]

1

The St. Lawrence Canals

COMPLETION of these canals in the forties paved the way for the improvement of the waterways below Montreal. They included the Lachine (9 miles) and the Beauharnois, Cornwall, and Williamsburg Canals (33 miles) with a total of 26 locks of dimensions 200 feet by 45 feet and a depth of 9 feet on the sills. In a total of 168 miles from Montreal to Lake Ontario they extended over 116 miles and involved an ascent of 225 feet above tide water.

The route included stretches of broad lake and strong currents on which towpaths for sailing vessels were impossible.[3] Consequently a subsidy was granted by the government to a line of steam tugs between Montreal and Prescott in 1849 "to leave each end of the line at stated intervals of time, and to tow vessels and barges at certain fixed rates, according to the size and tonnage of vessels". In 1849, 3 tugs were employed; in 1850, 2; and in 1851, 4. The

---

[1]*Canada, an encyclopedia of the country* (Toronto, 1898), II, 73-247, III, 285-365; *Eighty years' progress of British North America* (Toronto, 1863), 99-267; General report of Sir Hector L. Langevin, 1867-1882, *Sessional papers*, 10, 1883; also *S.p.* (*i.e., Sessional papers, Canada*), 19, 1901; Reports of the department of railways and canals, *S.p.*; Reports of the select standing committee on railways, canals and telegraphs, appendices to the *Journals of the house of commons; Sessional papers, Ontario; Sessional papers, Quebec.*

[2]See *Reports of the department of marine and fisheries; Reports of the Montreal board of trade* and especially *Semi-centennial report of the Montreal board of trade* (Montreal, 1893); Le Baron Quinette de Rochemont et H. Vetillart, *Les ports maritimes de l'Amérique du Nord sur l'Atlantique: Les ports canadiens* (Paris, 1898); N. C. Taylor, "The economic development of Canada's merchant marine" (M.A. thesis, University of Toronto).

[3]*S.p.*, 3, 1863.

subsidy was withdrawn in 1852 with unsatisfactory results and, in 1853, 6 tugs were employed to cover the whole river between Montreal and Kingston.   An agreement[1] was made with Messrs Calvin and Breck to maintain 6 tugs for 3 years (1855 to 1857).   After 1857 at least 9 were employed. Other efforts to improve navigation on this section included the blasting of rocks in the rapids.   In 1854, following the success of Maillefert in blasting rocks under water without drilling in Hell-Gate on the Hudson, work was carried out in the Coteau Rapids.

2

The St. Lawrence Ship Channel

Completion of the St. Lawrence Canals necessitated improvement of the ship channel and in November, 1852, the ship channel in Lake St. Peter was completed to 15 fe

---

[1]"That they shall and will upon the opening of the Navigation of each and every year during the term of this agreement, place and continue steamboats (to be used for the purpose of towing) . . . on the following routes respectively, namely:

One steamboat between Lachine and and the Beauharnois Canal [*19 miles*].

One steamboat between the Beauharnois Canal and Cornwall [*40 miles*].

Two steamboats between Dickinson's Landing and Prescott [*41 miles*].

Two steamboats between Prescott and Kingston [*61 miles*].

The boat placed on the route between Lachine and Beauharnois Canals shall make two trips daily, that is to say, two trips from Lachine to Beauharnois Canal and back to Lachine.

The boat placed on the route between the Beauharnois Canal and Cornwall shall make one trip daily, that is to say, one trip daily from the head of the Beauharnois Canal to the lower end of the Cornwall Canal and back to the Beauharnois Canal.

The two boats placed on the route between Dickinson's Landing and Prescott shall each make a daily trip over the whole, starting from opposite ends of the said route.

The two boats placed on the route between Prescott and Kingston shall also make a daily trip each over the route in opposite directions. . . .

That they shall and will during the continuance of this agreement so manage and conduct the said boats, that vessels shall be towed from Lachine to Kingston within four days, and from Kingston to Lachine within three days, unless such vessels or vessel shall be detained for an unusual or unreasonable time in passing through the Canals or some or one of them. . . .

And it is further agreed by and between the said parties that the rates per mile which may be charged for the towage of all such vessels as pass through the Canals on either of them, shall not exceed the sum specified in the Schedule here unto annexed and signed by the parties to these presents for towage upwards, and shall not exceed one-third of such rates for towage downwards."

The schedule is attached to the end of the document.   Boats drawing 2 feet of water with 12 feet beam were charged 10d. per mile—a minimum, and drawing 9 feet water, 26 feet beam, 4s. 8d. per mile.   An annual subsidy of $12,000 to this firm is mentioned in the *Report of the commission of public works for 1866*.

at low water.   In the spring of 1853 "several vessels made their appearance at our wharves, of larger tonnage than were ever employed before in the trade of this city."   The *Sarah Mary*, of 1,000 tons, the *Bannockburn* and *Water Lilly*, each of 800 tons, and later the *Sarah Sands*, 1,200 tons, came up to Montreal during the season.[1]   Sailing vessels of 700 to 900 tons and steam propellors of 1,750 to 2,000 tons and 300 feet in length could be employed on the route.   On November 20, 1853, John Young, chairman of the harbour commissioners of Montreal, wrote that "the opening of the St. Lawrence canals was followed by an expansion of the trade with the country lying west of us, and a great reduction in the rates of freight both upwards and downwards."[2]

In 1868 Hugh Allan urged the deepening of the channel to 23 feet and its widening to 500 feet.   He pointed out that experience had shown that "a steamship propelled by her own power, and going at full speed requires to have two feet, or more, in addition to the water she draws.   It seems as if she pushed the water away faster than it returns to her."   With newly-built vessels of 350 feet "if by any accident, one of them was to turn across the channel, the entire navigation would be interrupted, and as such an occurrence is by no means improbable, the channel should be widened to a

---

[1]Routes, distances, and rates of passage.   From Quebec to Montreal, 180 miles, by steamers, every day at 5 o'clock, through in 14 hours:

	Steerage		Cabin	
	Stg.	Cy.	Stg.	Cy.
By the Royal Mail Packets	3s 0d	3s 9d	14s	17s 6d
By Tait's Line	3s 0d	3s 9d	10s	12s 6d

See an account of a trip from Montreal to Quebec and to Rivière du Loup on a river boat in S. P. Day, *English America* (London, 1864), I, 229-30.

[2]*Journals of the legislative assembly*, XIII, 1854-5, app. G.G.   The general increase of traffic had interesting results in difficulties with regard to labour.   Hugh Allan as president of the Montreal board of trade stated in a petition dated June 12, 1851:

"That during the present season the evils resulting from the absence of such a Police force, have been increased in consequence of the number of vessels which have arrived in port, and the consequent demand for labor.

That the labourers now dictate to the trade, in what manner the vessels shall be discharged and loaded, and during what hours the work shall be continued, and if any attempt is made to act otherwise than is insisted on by them, the most riotous and lawless proceedings are immediately adopted and the lives of persons connected with the vessels endangered.

That on several occasions of late the captains and crews of American vessels have been grossly maltreated, in addition to having been compelled to pay for work in the expensive manner insisted on by the labourers."   They made it impossible to use horses (*Journals of the legislative assembly*, XIII, 1854-5, app. G.G.).

breadth of 500 feet."[1]   The invention of a new system of
dredging[2] facilitated the rapid improvement of the channel

---

[1]*S.p.*, 28, 1869.
[2]"The importance of this system [*of dredging*], as well as its bearing upon
future operations, is such as to call for a description of its advantages. While
the fact, that a greater amount of work has been done, and a greater result
produced in less time and at less cost, by the Harbour Commissioners under
Captain Bell's system and superintendence, than in any other dredging operations
in the world, makes it a subject of the highest interest to the profession, as well
as to corporations and other public bodies or departments, requiring a large
amount of dredging to be done.
    Under the old system, the dredge was moved to its work by two chains laid
out forward, in the direction of the channel to be excavated. In giving a head
a ditch was cut, the width of the buckets, and of a depth proportioned to the
hardness of material, as far as the length of the chain would permit: the buckets
were then lifted, and the dredge dropped back to the place of beginning, when
the process was repeated by cutting a similar and parallel trench, until the
proposed width of channel was attained. Between these parallel trenches, a
ridge from one to two feet in width was left, it being impossible to cut these
trenches without leaving a ridge to sustain the tumbler, which otherwise, would
have carried the buckets out of cutting into water, and brought them up empty.
After the channel had thus been 'groved,' or 'fluted,' by the 'trench-cutting'
system, the removal of the intermediate ridges was commenced. To steady the
buckets upon the narrow space, guys were employed, and in working ahead to
feed the buckets, the direction of these guys was necessarily altered, whereby the
dredge immediately lost her hold of the bottom.
    The bucket frame was then lifted, the vessel again steadied on another
ridge, and after all, the bottom instead of being uniform in depth, was left like
the teeth of a saw. When it is remembered that these operations were carried on
in a wide Lake, exposed to wind and sea, with a current of about one mile per
hour, the great loss of time in raising and lowering the buckets, in 'dropping
back,' 'guying out,' and 'steadying' over the ridges, the cost of fuel, wages
and provisions during this loss of time (the cost of these items for each dredge,
with her tender, being about £30 per diem,) and the utter impossibility of doing
anything like true work, under such circumstances, will be appreciated; nor can
we resist the conclusion, that under such a system, with any appropriation
which Parliament would sanction, failure was inevitable, where a channel ten
miles in length, and three hundred feet in width, with sixteen feet at low water,
was attempted. . . . The system employed by Captain Bell, on assuming the
charge of operations in the lake, is that known as 'radius cutting' as distinguished
from the ordinary or trench cutting method. The dredge is moored on chains
leading from the bow and stern in the direction of the channel, and also by four
chains at right angles to the channel, are out from each quarter of the vessel.
In this position she may be compared to a turtle chained by the head, tail, and
the four feet, and floating over the channel to be cut. Instead of cutting a
continuous trench, by hauling a head on the tow chain, the buckets take a feed
of two or three feet, after which this chain remains taught and the dredge is
breasted over by means of the side chain, broadside on, from one side of the
channel to the other, the buckets crossing the whole width of a channel of 150
feet and leaving the bottom true and even. When the opposite side of the channel
is reached she is heaved forward for another feed, and recrosses the channel in
the same manner, cutting from right to left and left to right alternately. Her
bucket frame sweeping across the channel acts as a huge plain with revolving
cutters; thus from the very nature of the system, there is a good guarantee that
when she has once gone over the ground, no obstruction can have been left
behind, above the level to which the buckets were lowered. The four side winches
are worked by the engines. The adaptation of the old Board of Works dredges to
this mode of working is due to Captain Bell, and to this arrangement chiefly, I

and by the end of the season 1878 a depth of 22 feet was completed.[1]

High rates of towage between Montreal and Quebec were gradually forcing the sailing vessels out and even the steamers were in many cases forced to pay $100.00 to $120.00 to each of 2 or 3 tugs required to tow them against the current. By 1875 the chain tug had reduced the cost of towage by $100.00.[2]

Deepening of the ship channel and completion of the trunk railways strengthened the position of Montreal and of the iron steamship. Ocean steamers increased from 40 with a tonnage of 51,298 in 1860 to 117 with a tonnage of 117,965 in 1869 and ocean-sailing vessels from 222 with a tonnage of 26,174 to 440 with a tonnage of 141,898 in the same period. In 1877[3] it was reported that of 513 sea-going vessels at Montreal, 276 of 297,884 tons were of iron, and 237 of 78,795 tons of wood. In 1879 the harbour master reported

---

attribute the great advance made in dredging. I am not aware of any similarly efficient gleaning in use elsewhere. In the 'trench cutting' method it is necessary to heave ahead on the tow chain in order to feed the buckets while the latter are cutting. This strain is avoided in the 'radius cutting' plan, where the tow chain is only wound up when the dredge has crossed the channel, and remains of the same length while the buckets are cutting again, the irregularity of the working of the buckets when removing the ridges in the trench cutting system, was productive of greater wear and tear on the machinery than occur in the improved method, where they are constantly in full work" (*Journals of the legislative assembly*, XIII, 1854-5, app. G.G.).

[1]1850—11 feet
1851—13 feet
1852—15 feet 2 inches
1855—16 feet 6 inches
1857—18 feet
1865—20 feet
1878—22 feet 6 inches
1882—25 feet

"Prior to 1870, very little dredging was required, but in 1873, dredging operations were begun in a systematic manner with an initial expenditure of $40,000. As years rolled by, and the country became more thickly populated, as manufacturing grew and commercial routes began to establish themselves, the need for deeper harbours and improved channels claimed public attention. In 1885, the department owned and operated 13 dredges and 1 stone lifter, and one dredging contract was awarded; the total expenditure on dredging for that year being $113,000" (*S.p.*, 19, 1911).

[2]*S.p.*, 5, 1875. Steamboats operating between Montreal and Quebec also weakened the position of sailing vessels. See J. G. Kohl, *Travels in Canada* (London, 1861), I, 123 ff. At Berthier, an important export centre for grain, hay, and livestock in 1881, sailing vessels, schooners, and scows of 125 to 200 tons called throughout the season, and steamboats provided daily communication with Sorel, and 3 times a week with Montreal (*S.p.*, 6, 1881). See C. Després, *Histoire de la famille et de la seigneurie de Saint-Ours* (Montreal, 1917).

[3]*S.p.*, 1, 1878.

a total of 612 sea-going vessels of 506,969 tons; 321 of 405,442 tons were iron, and 291 of 101,527 tons were wood; 289 vessels of 378,353 tons were propelled by steam and 323 of 128,616 tons by sail.[1] . The port warden gave a total of 384 ships (221 steamships) of 444,574 tons, or an average of 1,158 tons. "This shows that the carrying trade of the port is gradually being diverted from ships of moderate tonnage to ships of large carrying capacity."[2] "The deepening of the channel of the river between this city and Quebec [*1878*] has resulted in attracting a class of ships to this port of a much larger size than formerly, and many of them were able to load full cargoes, thus saving a large amount of money for lighterage to Quebec."[3] Steam tonnage increased from 68 per cent. in 1878 to 84 per cent. in 1881.[4] In 1883, in a total of 335 ships, 264 were steamers of 450,518 tons or an average of 1,707 tons and 71 sailing ships of 39,223 tons or an average of 552 tons.[5]

---

[1]*S.p.*, 9, 1880, app. no. 8.

[2]*S.p.*, 9, 1880, app. no. 44.

[3]*S.p.*, 3, 1879. The results were shown in part in complaints as to port accommodation. As early as 1864 the trade in wood, timber, and lumber was handled with difficulty at Lachine Canal (*S.p.*, 5, 1865). In 1871 goods were left lying on the wharf 6 or 8 days after the ship had left. Importers abused the privilege which allowed them 5 days' grace in removing the goods. The regular traders, making 3 voyages a year, and the transients required a large space of top wharfage to land their cargoes (*S.p.*, 5, 1872). The Lachine Canal with its milling and manufacturing interests, its transfers of freight from ocean to inland craft, its elevators, warehouses, and wharves and its steamboats and ferries was seriously crowded for space (*S.p.*, 2, 1873). "The trade of the port has greatly increased in the last six years, and . . . the vessels that now visit the port are much larger than those that came to the port some years ago, consequently of greater draft of water. To find suitable berths at all times on arrival for these large class of vessels which are generally of great length and heavy draught of water, is a very difficult task" (*S.p.*, 8, 1873). On August 28, 1873, there were 84 sea-going vessels and 236 inland vessels in port, the largest number arriving in summer rather than in the spring and autumn (*S.p.*, 4, 1874). Delays and losses to shipping were inevitable (*S.p.*, 6, 1877). "It had to accommodate the trade of the river St. Lawrence, both for export and otherwise, also the lumber trade of the Ottawa river, for both its Quebec and American markets." The demand for labour also created problems. In 1877 difficulties were noted as a result of "incompetent and inexperienced men working in the harbour as stevedores and others equally incompetent as liners" (*S.p.*, 1, 1878). In May, 1881, ship-labourers protested against low wages and in June held meetings and processions and made threats of violence and intimidation. On July 7 "a hand-to-hand contest" between the labourers and the police was followed by the use of fire-arms (*S.p.*, 5, 1882). "Lighting was commenced on 11th June, 1880. . . . The system is worthy of note as being the first known example of lighting an extensive line of wharves by electricity" (*S.p.*, 11, 1880-1).

[4]*S.p.*, 5, 1882.

[5]*S.p.*, 7, 1884, app. no. 30.

With steel-built ships, compound condensing engines and various mechanical improvements, to which at present no limit can be placed, the cost of sailing a ship across the Atlantic is being yearly lessened. The expenditure of coal on board steamships is being rapidly reduced, and the size of the ships increased, so that a 5,000-ton vessel can be navigated now at very little more cost than was entailed by a 2,000-ton ship ten years ago. Freight at 25s. a ton in 1880 pays better than freight at 50s. a ton did in 1870. This is brought about by enlarged ships, a smaller expenditure of coal, and a larger space on board for freight. The ships now building, though larger than those running, will run at less cost and carry very much more freight, and although freights for some time past have been and still are very low, it is an open secret that freights pay far better than passengers.[1]

Montreal steadily improved its position at the expense of Quebec. Decline of the trade in square timber, the increasing importance of agriculture[2] in Ontario, and the development of steamships were factors responsible for rapid growth.[3]

3

The Gulf of St. Lawrence

(i)

Lighthouses[4]

Improvement of the St. Lawrence ship channel and of the St. Lawrence Canals was accompanied by the develop-

---

[1] *S.p.*, 12, 1881.

[2] "Recapitulation of Produce carried from Canada by the Steamers in about 7 months. ["*Montreal Ocean Steamship Company*" *from Liverpool to Quebec and from Quebec to Liverpool 1861.*]

7,666 Barrels Pot and Pearl Ashes.	24,780 Kegs Butter.
41,681 Barrels Flour.	292 Boxes and hhds. Bacon.
789,150 Bushels Grain.	

3,319 Barrels bulk of other articles, besides those above mentioned, not reduced to barrel bulk.

Making a total bulk transported (exclusive of certain articles not reduced) nearly equal to 237,665 barrels Flour" (*S.p.*, 1, 1862).

[3] Vessels were able to make practically the same number of voyages in a season to Montreal as to Quebec and a smaller number of inland craft was necessary to bring traffic from the interior to Montreal than to Quebec. The high tide and wide tidal beaches of Quebec were a guarantee of control over the square timber trade (*Journals of the legislative assembly*, XIII, 1854-5, app. G.G.).

[4] See William Smith, "On the lighthouse system of Canada" (*Canadian economics*, Montreal, 1885), 17-39.

ment of facilities for navigation below Quebec. In his *Sketch of Canada, its industrial conditions and resources* (Paris, 1855), J. C. Taché stated that 7 lighthouses had been built in the Gulf of St. Lawrence, 2 on Anticosti Island in the gulf, and 5 in the river—Point des Monts, Green Island, Red Island, the Pillars, and Little Island of Briquet, the 2 latter with revolving lights and the last with a 36-pounder fired every half hour in foggy weather; and that 4 new lighthouses, 2 in the Straits of Belle Isle, one on Anticosti, and one at Point Gaspé were under construction to be equipped with Fresnel's lanterns. A floating light in St. Roch traverse completed the list. After Confederation and the establishment of the department of marine and fisheries, facilities were rapidly extended and by 1872 there had been built 93 lighthouses, 4 lightships, and 10 steam fog alarms.[1] The rate of expansion is shown in the following table.

Provinces of Ontario, Quebec, New Brunswick,[2]
Prince Edward Island, and British Columbia

	Light Stations	Lights Shewn	Fog Whistles	Automatic Fog-horns
1868	198	227	2	..
1869	219	233	2	..
1870	240	278	4	..
1871	264	297	8	..
1872	280	314	13	..
1873	316	363	17	..
1874	342	384	18	..
1875	377	444	22	..
1876	407	488	24	..
1877	416	509	25	2

Increase in the number of lighthouses was accompanied by increased efficiency. The discovery of petroleum in Ontario and the general discovery in 1868 that mineral oils could be used more effectively than other oils revolutionized the development of lighthouses and became significant to expansion in Canada. Messrs F. A. Fitzgerald and Company of the Union Petroleum Works, London, Ontario, agreed to supply 46,500 gallons of oil ("non-explosive at a vapor test

---

[1]*S.p.*, 8, 1873.
[2]*S.p.*, 1, 1878.

of 105°F., must burn brilliantly without smoking until entirely consumed and not crust the wick, must be free from all deleterious substances and remain fluid at 10°F.") at an average cost of 19$\frac{4}{10}$ cents, "the lowest rate at which oil was ever purchased by the Government".[1]   The importance of the low rate to Canada became evident in her position as a country with an enormous "extent of sea-coast, lake and river shores to be lighted up". Emphasis was essentially on the problem of maintaining a brilliant, efficient, and regular light. In addition to about 20 "very superior costly lighthouses, having stone towers, and nearly all having very expensive dioptric apparatus [*invented in 1862*], the bulk of the lighthouses are mostly of a cheap but substantial description, made of wood, with iron lanterns, and fitted up with catoptric apparatus." It was estimated that "a good and powerful sea light, on the catoptric principle" could be "fitteg up complete with modern frame tower, oil shed, dwellind house, iron lantern, and large circular burner lamps, and powerful 20-inch diameter reflectors for about $8,000". With cheap construction, management, and supplies it became possible to expand rapidly the number of lighthouses, to introduce more efficient lamps (no. 1 circular burner lamps), and to build up an efficient system for navigation on the St. Lawrence.[2]

(ii)

Telegraphic communication

The effectiveness of the lighthouses was dependent in part on the linking up of a telegraph system. Inventions of the telegraph and of the Morse code were followed by rapid construction of telegraph lines. A line was extended from Quebec to Father Point in 1859. Following the valuable report of the commission in 1876,[3] the superintendent of the telegraph and signal service stated on November 30, 1880, that:

---

[1]*S.p.*, 5, 1872.
[2]*S.p.*, 8, 1873.
[3]Report of the select committee appointed to enquire into the possibility of establishing a submarine telegraph system and into the advantages and necessity of such a system of telegraphy in the waters of the river and gulf of St. Lawrence and the waters joining the approaches to the gulf, *J.h.c.*, 1876, app. 9.

Submarine electric cables have been successfully laid between the Island of Anticosti, and the coast of Gaspé, between the Bird Rock and the Magdalen Islands, and between Cape Breton and the Magdalen Islands, all of which are in perfect working order. Land lines have also been constructed about two-thirds of the distance between English Bay and Fox River, Anticosti, and throughout the Magdalen Islands.[1]

In the following year he reported the completion of land lines on the Island of Anticosti (214 miles) and on the Magdalen Islands (84 miles),[2] and the completion of land lines on the north shore between Bay St. Paul and Chicoutimi (92 miles), and between Murray Bay and Mille Vaches (84 miles). By the end of 1882 the latter line had been extended to Betsiamits (Bersimis), and by the end of 1883, cable and land lines had been completed to 235 miles below Murray Bay.[3] The line reached the Moisie River in 1885.[4]

The St. Lawrence system during the same period was linked up with Halifax. The report[5] of November 30, 1880, stated that a land line had been constructed between Canso and Halifax (208 miles) and a year later a line was completed from North Sydney *via* Baddeck to Meat Cove (126 miles) to link up with the Magdalen Islands system.[6] In August, 1881, reports of observations were received by telegraph from Anticosti and Bird Rocks: "Those from Anticosti have been forwarded with great regularity and have proved of the utmost service."[7]

(iii)

Meteorological service

A telegraph system provided a base for the development of a meteorological service and the efficiency of lighthouses was enhanced by the development of facilities for forecasting weather and the establishment of systems of storm signals. In 1871 a grant of $5,000 was devoted to establishing meteorological stations at lighthouses. "It was considered that the

---

[1] *S.p.*, 6, 1881.
[2] *S.p.*, 7, 1882.
[3] *S.p.*, 9, 1884.
[4] *S.p.*, 12, 1886.
[5] *S.p.*, 6, 1881.
[6] See *Atlas of Canada*, 1915, 31-2.
[7] *S.p.*, 5, 1882.

lighthouses, being for the most part near the highways of commerce, and in exposed positions, were suited locally for furnishing data for the study of atmospheric movements." "Register books suitable for recording the direction and force of the wind, the temperature, the rainfall and the state of the weather were supplied to 37 lighthouses" (13 with no instruments, 13 with rain gauges, and 11 with thermometers—including screen and portable thermometer shed—and rain gauges). The *First report of the meteorological office*, by G. T. Kingston, presented in January, 1872, outlined objectives including "the collection of trustworthy meteorological statistics", the determination over a series of years for every locality of average frequencies, average periodic variations, "average nonperiodic variability" and the average mutual dependence of the several elements and phenomena, and "to prognosticate coming weather". For these objects a central meteorological office with a normal observatory, a few chief stations with observations "sufficiently frequent and continuous and prolonged . . . , several observing and reporting telegraph stations . . . , several receiving and publishing telegraph stations" and "a large number of ordinary stations" were required.[1]   In 1873, 12 stations were reporting 3 times a day to Toronto and information was despatched to Washington from whence notice of anticipated storms was given to the director at Toronto.[2]   Beginning in 1876, "probabilities for the next 24 hours" were made out at Toronto at 10 a.m. daily and supplied to telegraph companies for publication in the evening editions of newspapers in Ontario and Quebec. On October 1, 1877, probabilities for the station concerned were sent to 75 principal places daily and copies posted in post and telegraph offices.[3]   By 1877 there were 10 chief stations, 14 reporting by telegraph, 4 reserve, 39 cautionary storm signal stations, and upwards of 100 ordinary stations. New stations improved the accuracy of predictions and in that year included remote districts such as Inverness, Skeena River, McLeod Lake, and Stewart's

---

[1] *S.p.*, 5, 1872, app. 13; R. F. Stupart, "Meteorology in Canada" (*Journal of the Royal Astronomical Society of Canada*, 1912).
[2] *S.p.*, 4, 1874.
[3] *S.p.*, 1, 1878.

Lake in British Columbia. In the winter of 1880-81 reports were received by telegraph from Edmonton, Humboldt, and Livingston.[1]   A system of storm signals was worked out and adopted for the lake regions in 1881 and extended in 1882 to "all stations in Quebec and the Maritime Provinces . . . by which the direction and force of an approaching storm is indicated at all stations".[2]   It was hoped that this completion of the telegraph system in the linking up of the lighthouses and the expansion of a meteorological service would warrant a reduction in insurance rates.[3]

(iv)

Other aids to shipping below Quebec

The use of tug-boats

The overwhelming importance of sailing vessels during the early years of the period led to the development of methods of overcoming the difficulties of sailing in the narrower portions of the rivers. Steam began as auxiliary to sail. On August 24, 1855, F. Baby and F. Lemieux contracted to supply 2 first-class, iron screw steamers, of not less than 300 horse-power each "to run between Quebec and Anticosti for the purpose of towing and aiding vessels coming up or going down the River St. Lawrence". The contract ran for 10 years and involved an annual bonus of £11,300, a loan of £19,000—to build the vessels—,and fixed rates of towage.[4]

---

[1]*S.p.*, 5, 1882, app. 28.
[2]*S.p.*, 7, 1883.
[3]*S.p.*, 6, 1881: "An effort should be made to reduce rates of premium of ocean marine insurance in accordance with lessened risks secured by the Port Warden's service, and the electro-signal and telegraphic system in the Gulf and River St. Lawrence."
[4]"One shilling and two-pence currency per foot for each mile from Pillar light and above the same; one shilling currency per foot, for each mile from Kamouraska and below Pillar light; eleven pence currency per foot, for each mile from Brandy Pots, and below Kamouraska; and for the remainder of the distance, namely, from the Brandy Pots to Anticosti, ten pence currency per foot for each mile, the distance to be computed by the following divisions, namely, a vessel taken up between Brandy Pots and Bic, to pay from Bic, between Bic and Metis, to pay from Metis, between Metis and Cap Chat, from Cap Chat, and between Cap Chat, and Anticosti, from Anticosti; and the same rate of towage, in the same proportion downwards from Quebec, all fractions of a foot to be charged as a foot and the deepest draft to be taken."

Postal subsidies

The development of ocean steamship traffic[1] on the St. Lawrence was accompanied by numerous difficulties and disasters. On August 13, 1852, a Liverpool firm, the Canadian Steam Navigation Company, contracted to run a line of screw steamers twice a month to Quebec in summer and once a month to Portland in winter in return for a subsidy of £1,238 currency per trip, or £24,000 annually. The ships were required to average not over 14 days outwards and 13 days homeward and to be of 1,200 tons burden, and 300 horse-power. In 1853 the ship *Genova* (700 tons and 160 horse-power) averaged 20 days out and 15 home, the *Lady Eglinton* (600 tons and 160 horse-power) 14 days out and 12 home, the *Sarah Sands* (1,200 tons and 150 horse-power) 22 days out and 18 home. In 1854 the *Cleopatra* reached Quebec in 43 days (April 11 to May 24), the *Ottawa* (910 tons and 200 horse-power) failed to reach Quebec, and the *Charity* (1,007 tons and 400 horse-power) took 27 days (May 10 to June 17). Freights were required by the agreement not to exceed 60s. per ton but 80s. were asked. Passenger charges were: first-class cabin, 20 guineas; second-class, 13 guineas; third-class, 7 guineas.[2] The contract was cancelled and a new arrangement, dated September, 1855, made with Messrs Allan of the Montreal Ocean Steamship Company for similar service in return for £25,000 annual subsidy. The average outward passage in 1856 was 12 days and 3 hours; and in 1857, 11 days and one hour; homeward in 1856, 11 days and 6 hours; and in 1857, 10 days and 15 hours. The number of passengers carried increased from 4,321 in 1856 to 6,685 in 1857.[3]

As a result of the depression the government increased the subsidy to £55,000 per year in return for a weekly service

---

[1]See William Smith, *The history of the post office in British North America, 1639-1870* (Cambridge, 1920), chapters xvii-xviii; also James Croil, *Steam navigation and its relation to the commerce of Canada and the United States* (Toronto, 1898); H. Fry, *The history of North Atlantic steam navigation with some account of early ships and ship owners* (London, 1896); J. Young, *The origin of the ocean mail steamers between Liverpool and the St. Lawrence* (Montreal, 1877); W. Smith, "Canadian ocean steamships and their early difficulties" (*Queen's Quarterly*, 1914-15, 244-254); Sir J. M. LeMoine, *Quebec past and present* (Quebec, 1876), chapter ix; F. C. Bowen, *History of the Canadian Pacific line* (London, n.d.).

[2]*Journals of the legislative assembly*, XIII, 1854-5, app. 0.

[3]*Journals of the legislative assembly*, XVI, 1858, app. 19.

leaving Liverpool and Quebec every Wednesday in summer
and every Saturday in winter for Portland in a contract dated
October 12, 1857, and effective on May 1, 1859.   The line
included 8 steamships, 300 feet in length, of 1,800 to 2,500
tons burden with a speed of from 8 to 13 miles an hour.   They
averaged 9½ miles an hour—the average passage westward
being 11 days 5 hours; the fastest passage by the *Hungarian*,
9 days 14 hours—eastward, 10 days 10 hours; the fastest
passage by the *Anglo-Saxon*, 9 days 5 hours.   The passengers
in 1861 totalled 12,279 (3,875 eastward and 8,404 westward).
Unfortunate difficulties in loss of steamers led to a revision
of the contract in 1860 and the payment of £104,000 subsidy.
A new contract in 1864 called for stricter observance of
regulations with the result that the St. Lawrence became
definitely established as a postal route with regular connections to Great Britain.[1]

Shipping regulations

In spite of the improvement of the St. Lawrence for
passenger and postal steamships, the serious losses of freight
ships were a handicap to its development.   Losses were
particularly high in 1872 and an agitation for improved
regulations followed.   Henry Fry, in a paper read before
the dominion board of trade at Ottawa in January, 1873,
wrote:

> When I state that during the season of 1872 no less than 62
> large sailing ships and nine iron steam ships, all engaged in
> the lumber and grain trades between the St. Lawrence and
> Great Britain, have been totally lost; that the value of these
> vessels, their cargoes and freights amounts to over four
> millions of dollars, and above all, that over 250 valuable lives
> have been sacrificed, I have said enough to prove that the
> subject is one demanding the careful attention of this Board
> and of the Government of the Dominion. . . . It is somewhat
> remarkable that of the 62 sailing ships only 13 were wrecked

---

[1]See "Memorandum of agreement entered into between the Postmaster
General and Mr. Brydges on behalf of the Grand Trunk railway Company"
Ottawa, March 23, 1869, *S.p.*, 34, 1869, and agreement dated February 1, 1873,
with Hugh Allan for weekly service from April 1, 1873, to April. 1, 1878, the
subsidy to be reduced from $218,000 to $126,533.33 (*S.p.*, 16, 1873).   The
vessels included the *Austrian, Hibernian, Moravian, Peruvian, Nestorian, Prus-
sian, Polynesian, Sarmatian, Scandinavian, Nova Scotian,* and *Circassian.*

on their outward voyage, no less than 49 being homeward-bound; . . . Of the 49 sailing ships, 42 were laden with wood, six with grain and flour, and one with fish . . . but a close acquaintance with the North American trade for the past thirty years has convinced me that *fully three-fourths of all the losses of wood-laden ships in the North Atlantic in the fall of the year, may be traced directly or indirectly to the practice of carrying deck-loads*, and the facts I have been able to collect with reference to recent losses confirm me in this opinion. Most of the Quebec ships that reached Great Britain last fall were those which either wisely took no deck-loads, or lost their deck-loads, either in part or the whole, by throwing them overboard when the ship began to leak, or allowing them to be washed overboard; whilst of the 42 wrecked ships, so far as I have been able to ascertain the facts, *only one left the St. Lawrence without a deck-load*, and 35 were abandoned in the Atlantic waterlogged. The harrowing details of these wrecks conclusively show how much deck-loads contributed to the loss, and the various ways in which they bring about the destruction of ships and their crews. Most of the ships engaged in this trade are necessarily second-class ships, many of them having seen their best days, and some of them not too well found. They are, too, peculiarly unfitted for deck-loads, from the fact that most old ships are weak in their upper works from decayed iron fastenings, and defective frames and beam arms. As soon, therefore, as a ship begins to roll in a heavy sea, she strains and leaks, and the deck-load causes her water ways to open; if the pumps are good, *and the crew can stand at them*, she may possibly escape; but far more frequently when the pumps are most needed, they are least available; a sea breaks on board, the deck-load gets adrift, the sailors get their limbs broken, or they are killed by loose logs in trying to get them overboard; or the pumps are broken off at the deck by loose timber washed about, and thus rendered useless; the ship becomes waterlogged, provisions and fresh water are destroyed, and the unhappy crew take to the rigging or the tops, there, also! to freeze or perish, amid the horrors of starvation, cold and delirium. . . . It is plain enough, that if the value of Canadian wheat or Canadian lumber is regulated by its value in the markets of Great Britain, where they have to compete with the products of other countries, then whatever is paid in increased cost of insurance or freight must come out of the pockets of the producer; and thus every Canadian farmer and every Canadian lumberer is interested in the question. Our fall premiums of insurance do in fact kill a great deal of our fall business, or render it unprofitable. . . .

Regulations enacted by the imperial parliament had proved

30

inadequate. An act (5 and 6 Vic. c. 17) which prohibited, for one year, the carriage of deck-loads of timber between British North American ports and the United Kingdom after September 1 and before May 1, was renewed (8 and 9 Vic. c. 45), repealed (8 and 9 Vic. c. 84), re-enacted (8 and 9 Vic. c. 93), and continued (16 and 17 Vic. c. 107) until July 29, 1862. These acts were interpreted as giving permission to take a duplicate of every spar in the rough, ostensibly as a spare. A full-rigged ship carried 42 rough spars of varied dimensions, a barque 36 spars, and a brig 26.

> The deck cargoes of spars usually carried by vessels in the winter time, amounted to a pretty heavy deck-load, and of a very dangerous description, as the spars were generally rough and wet out of the ponds, very heavy and very long, and in the event of the vessel getting on her beam ends, they were generally more dangerous than deals, as in a very short time they would tear to pieces the rigging and top work on deck.

Shippers from ports on the Bay of Fundy, after the differential duties between British and colonial timber and deals had been repealed in 1861, and all vessels placed on an equal footing in Great Britain, found it advantageous to avoid the deck-load law by proceeding to Eastport, Maine, and securing a clearance for the United Kingdom. As a result of these difficulties and the losses in 1872 an act was passed prohibiting the carriage of timber on deck from Canada to Europe between October 1 and March 16 "and no other cargo higher than three feet above the deck during that period". Spar-decked vessels were not allowed to carry deck-cargo except two spare spars between November 15 and March 16. The act became effective on October 1, 1873.[1]

The handling of grain and other products with the increasing use of steamships to Montreal was subject to similar regulations. In 1863 the port of Montreal passed a by-law requiring vessels to bag a proportion of cargo according to tonnage. Steam vessels carrying 50,000 to 80,000 bushels of grain and loading in a couple of days "which does not allow time for it to settle" were alleged to be subject to

---

[1]Statements and evidence in relation to a bill entitled "An act respecting Deck Loads", *S.p.*, 4, 1873.

serious losses through shifting of cargo. Lloyd's regulations were applied to the port of Montreal and required "that no vessel over 400 tons register can be loaded entirely with grain in bulk and all vessels over that tonnage may take two-thirds of cargo in bulk and one-third in bags."[1]   In spite of objections these regulations were enforced and it was claimed that from 1873 to 1880 "we have had no missing ships or ships lost from overloading or shifting of cargo from this port."[2]   The rule applied to lining stated "that any vessel intending to load grain (without distinction) must be first lined".   Complaints arose, especially from vessels accustomed to loading at ports on the Black Sea, as to the small cargoes. These open-deck vessels required 50 to 70 tons of coal on the Mediterranean voyage and 250 to 270 tons on the Atlantic voyage.   With easy access to shelter at Constantinople, Malta, and Gibraltar, restrictions as to loading and storage were unnecessary.   Moreover, the loading of grain by manual labour from baskets gave time for the cargo to settle. Finally, vessels had deeper draught in the fresh water of the St. Lawrence.[3]   In 1875 complaints were made regarding cargoes of glass from Antwerp being insufficiently dunnaged following the practice of chartering vessels at a lump sum for the voyage.[4]   By 1878 general improvement in the condition of cargoes was noted and "less damage done to ships from grounding, collision, contact with ice and other causes."[5]

Regulation of Crews—Officers

In 1871 a new system was inaugurated making it compulsory on masters and men of certain vessels to be provided with certificates of competency or service before they could clear their vessels.

---

[1]*S.p.*, 4, 1873. Regulations with particular relation to a coastal and inland navigation were introduced at about the same date. The chairman of the board of steamboat inspection reported (1871) in favour of the inspection of steamboats annually, the application of standard gauge and test pumps to test the strength of boilers, the use of standard size boiler plates, the adoption of uniform signals, the use of "Low Water Alarm Indicators", and the introduction of various regulations designed to prevent accidents (*S.p.*, 5, 1872).

[2]*S.p.*, 11, 1880-1.

[3]*S.p.*, 4, 1873.

[4]*S.p.*, 5, 1876.

[5]*S.p.*, 3, 1879.

No master or mate can now obtain in Canada a certificate either of competency or service until he has produced evidence of his sobriety, a most important element in our examinations for either description of certificates, as there was reason to believe in former years that many of our marine disasters were caused by the too free use of intoxicating liquors.

Men—Problem of Crimping

Crimping apparently developed at Quebec because of the ship-building industry. Lack of an adequate supply of local seamen in face of the demand for men to man the new ships in addition to the ships calling at Quebec was regarded as the cause of its development.[1] Mr. H. Fry, Lloyd's agent at Quebec, wrote to *The Times* (London):

> The crimping system has now reached such a pitch that the force of law is completely set at defiance, the life of a British ship master in a British port is no longer safe, and piracy stalks abroad unchecked, in the midst of a British population, and under the very walls of a British fortress. Night after night ships in the harbor are boarded by crimps well armed with revolvers, the crews carried off, the masters and officers threatened with instant death if they resist, and the owner's property plundered. And for this state of things the authorities here either cannot or will not find a remedy. . . . During the whole of this season we have paid £10 to £12 sterling per month for sailors; the majority of ships lose the whole or a portion of their crews, and the dead loss to British ship owners engaged in this trade will not be less than £100,000 sterling for the present season alone.[2]

In the third annual report of the department of marine and fisheries, in the year ending June 30, 1870, it was stated that there were 1,433 desertions, principally from ships registered in the United Kingdom. An amalgamation of the offices of the shipping-master and the chief of police proved of value in making possible the building up of an adequate force. An act (31 Vic. c. 32) substituted punishment by imprisonment for punishment by fines since the remunerative profits had rendered fines of little value as a deterrent. It was proposed that to protect the sailors by founding a sailor's home,[3] and detailed provisions should be established by the chief of the

---

[1]W. H. G. Kingston, *Western wanderings* (London, 1856), I, 87-8.
[2]*Journals of the legislative assembly*, 1857, app. 37.
[3]*S.p.*, 5, 1871.

Quebec River police for registering seamen and boarding houses.[1] These measures proved effective. In 1880, however, a marked rise in wages, following a large increase in shipping and scarcity of sailors, was held responsible for a new outbreak of desertions. A vigorous search in the crimping dens and boarding houses and later, in the Plains of Abraham and the neighbouring country, proved successful in capturing numerous deserters and in facilitating the prosecution and conviction of crimps.[2] A decision of the court in October, 1880, favoured the position of the crimps and in the following season numerous desertions were reported. Deserters were captured, taken before the judge, ordered to be put on board their ships, "and the very next day, in nine cases out of ten, these men again deserted their ship." In some cases men were captured and recaptured three times. Wages were high because of desertions—£8 per month and even £10 per month.[3] A change in the wording of the act from "going on board without the permission and consent of the master, or the person in charge" to "without the permission and against the will" was stated in the report on the Quebec River police force dated December 31, 1886, as responsible for a marked increase in crimping.[4] As late as 1891 the police complained that ship-masters, because of the scarcity of men, paid a bonus of $5.00 to $25.00 (blood money) per man to crimps. "It is said that two ship captains comparing notes found out that they had actually bought up each other's seamen."[5]

Assistance to local traffic

Improvement of through traffic on the St. Lawrence stimulated the local coasting trade but handicaps were numerous. The height of the tides and the dangers from storms increased the expense of construction of wharves below Quebec and seriously limited their numbers. Schooners

---

[1]S.p., 1, 1878. See also S.p., 5, 1872.
[2]S.p., 11, 1880-1.
[3]S.p., 5, 1882. In New Brunswick stringent regulations were regarded as the cause of a rise in wages from $45.00 to $80.00. Crimping "to a considerable extent" was prevalent but general indifference kept wages down.
[4]S.p., 5a, 1888, app. 37.
[5]S.p., 10, 1892, app. 9.

from 50 to 85 tons drawing from 10 to 12 feet frequented the ports on the gulf and carried grain, potatoes, butter, and cordwood westward. In 1878 a steamer ran tri-weekly between Quebec and Montmagny and, although drawing only 5 feet of water, could only enter at half tide.[1] Batteaux were used to carry lumber to vessels anchored in deep water.

(b)—INLAND NAVIGATION[2]

The application of steam to inland navigation above the St. Lawrence Canals and especially on the upper lakes, had effects, similar to the application of steam to ocean navigation, in the rapid expansion of trade. The increasing size of steam vessels on the upper lakes rendered the Welland Canal increasingly obsolete and favoured the development of traffic to New York by the Erie Canal and later by rail. In turn deepening of the Welland Canal and assistance of the Welland Railway made the St. Lawrence Canals an increasingly serious handicap to the utilization of the St. Lawrence route as a competitor for western grain.[3]

The end of the period witnessed the marked development of traffic by ocean steamship from Montreal, the marked improvement of traffic from the western states to Buffalo and to Oswego, and an increasingly serious block in the St. Lawrence Canals.[4] Improvement of the steamship on the lakes accentuated the character of the handicap. "The St. Lawrence canals were designed for side-wheel steamers; the

---

[1]*S.p.*, 7, 1878; *S.p.*, 8, 1879. See also B. Demers, *La paroisse de St. Romuald d'Etchemin* (Quebec, 1906).

[2]See J. Williamson, *The inland seas of North America and the natural and industrial productions of Canada* (Kingston, 1854); J. C. Mills, *Our inland seas* (Chicago, 1910); *History of the Great Lakes* (Chicago, 1899), 2 vols.; G. A. Cuthbertson, *Freshwater* (Toronto, 1931), chapters xi-xii; J. G. Kohl, *Travels in Canada*, II, 1-3, 112-128; J. E. Middleton and F. Landon, *The Province of Ontario (1615-1927)* (Toronto, 1927), 674-714; Reports of the commission of public works, *S.p.*

[3]"With reference especially to grain, the great article of transport, being both bulky in its nature, and low in value in the Districts surrounding the great Lakes where it is produced, cheapness of Transport is peculiarly important, and is becoming yearly more so, as the regions of production get more and more remote from the place of consumption" (Report of the commissioner of public works for the year 1859, *S.p.*, 11, 1860).

[4]Passenger traffic was less subject to these restrictions.

From Montreal to Western Canada.—Daily, by the Royal Mail Line steamer, at 9 o'clock, A.M., or railroad to Lachine, at 12 o'clock.

Welland Canal for sail vessels and screw steamers."[1]

1
The St. Lawrence Waterway *versus* the Erie Canal

The problem of the St. Lawrence waterways cannot be adequately understood from isolated studies of the various sections.   The St. Lawrence route[2] was a unit competing for

	Distance Miles	Deck Fare		Cabin Fare	
		Stg.	Cy.	Stg.	Cy.
From Montreal to Cornwall.....	78	5s	6s 3d	11s	13s 9d
Prescott.................	127	6s	7s 6d	14s	17s 6d
Brockville..............	139				
Kingston...............	189	8s	10s 0d	20s	25s 0d
Cobourg................	295	12s	15s 0d	28s	35s 0d
Port Hope..............	298				
Bond Head.............	313	14s	17s 6d	34s	42s 6d
Darlington.............	317				
Whitby.................	337				
Toronto................	367	16s	20s 0d	36s	45s 0d
Hamilton...............	410				
Detroit................	596	24s	30s 0d	56s	$14
Chicago...............	874	32s	40s 0d	80s	$20

"Passengers by this line tranship at Kingston to the lake steamers, and at Toronto for Buffalo" (J. S. Hogan, *Canada*, Montreal, 1855, 97).   "Regarding the vessels that frequent the harbor [*Coteau Landing*], they are as follows: the Richelieu and Ontario Navigation Company's through line of steamers from Montreal to Hamilton, calling daily on their way up and down.   Two market boats from Cornwall to Montreal, calling twice a week on their way down and up.   The steamer Alexandria from Trenton to Montreal, once a week, on her way down and up.   The steamer C. Anderson, plying between Valleyfield and Coteau Landing as a ferry boat, twice a day" (*S.p.*, 6, 1881).

[1]*Eighty years' progress*, 181-2: "A vessel with twenty-six feet beam may proceed to sea, from any of the upper lakes, by the route of the Welland and St. Lawrence Canals, but she cannot enter Lake Champlain with more than twenty-three feet or pass down the Ottawa route with more than eighteen feet beam.   She may carry ten feet draft into Lake Ontario but must lighten to nine in descending the St. Lawrence."

[2]W. H. Merritt as a protagonist of the Welland Canal reported as chairman of a committee on trade and commerce in favour of

(1) Removal of all duties on the productions of British possessions in America imported by the St. Lawrence;

(2) reciprocity to be extended to manufactured products, registration of Canadian and United States built vessels, shipping and coasting trade;

(3) that the imperial government cancel the bounty on steamers between Liverpool and Boston and grant an equivalent bounty to the St. Lawrence;

(4) removal of all duties on cheap, heavy, and bulky articles by the St. Lawrence;

(5) deepening of channel between Lakes St. Francis and St. Louis and granting of aid to building of tidal locks at Quebec;

(6) construction of St. Lawrence and Champlain Canal "with locks of the same dimensions as Sault Ste. Marie";

(7) extension of a credit to the importers, so as to admit of a reduction in the number of inland ports of entry (*Journals of the legislative assembly*, XIII, 1854-5, app. D.D.D.D.).

western traffic with the New York route. Geographically the Welland Canal and the St. Lawrence ship channel could be improved most easily and these improvements served as increasingly powerful factors in the improvement of the central section of the St. Lawrence Canals. The improvement of the central section made it possible to reap the advantages of the earlier improvements of the Welland Canal and of the St. Lawrence ship channel. It explained in part the rapid development of traffic after 1850 and after 1900 and, in turn, the slow growth of traffic after 1860.

As early as 1851 the report of the chief commissioner of public works, following an investigation of the previous year, attributed the diversion of trade by the Erie Canal to New York to the high price of ocean freight from Quebec to Liverpool and to the substantial postal subsidy of £350,000 paid by the governments of Great Britain and the United States which had the effect of forcing "an equal amount of tonnage in packet ships (which were displaced by those steamers) into the emigrant trade, thereby reducing return freights to ballast prices". Emigration at Quebec increased from 20,000 in 1844 to 90,000 in 1847 but declined to 32,292 in 1850, and at New York increased from 80,000 in 1847 to 331,276 in 1851. A select committee appointed with power to inquire into the past and present course of trade between the lakes and the seaboard and between the different Atlantic ports in

---

In a report in 1858 he argued that although reciprocity had removed the handicaps of the corn laws (Imperial Act, 9 and 10 Vic. c. 22, 1846) which provided for the admission of American products on the same basis as Canadian products to the markets of Great Britain but not for the admission of Canadian products to the markets of the United States, and thereby reduced the value of Canadian products 20 per cent. below American products, it was still interpreted against the importation of "flour and breadstuffs ground in Canada, from grain grown in the United States". Moreover, for goods imported *ad valorem*, value was interpreted (16 Vic. c. 85, 1853) as "fair market value in the principal markets of the country whence the same were exported directly to this province" and not as (12 Vic. c. 1, 1849) "the actual cash value" in the principal markets "where the same were purchased". The trade between Halifax and Canada was transferred by the change to New York. The report asked that the consumer should be charged "no greater duty via the St. Lawrence than by New York and that the St. Lawrence canals be immediately deepened, to admit vessels of the same draught of water as those which pass through the Welland canal" (*Journals of the legislative assembly*, XVI, 1858, app. 2). See G. W. Brown, "The St. Lawrence waterway as a factor in international trade and politics" (Abstract of University of Chicago thesis, humanistic series, 1924-26, 179-185), and "The opening of the St. Lawrence to American shipping" (*Canadian Historical Review*, VII, 1926, 4-13).

America and Great Britain, of which W. H. Merritt was chairman, in the report dated July 27, 1858,[1] stated that "the proportion of the lake trade diverted to New York is as six and one-half million tons to about half a million forwarded to Quebec", or, according to another statement, "as 85 to 15 in favor of New York".

In 1863 the importance of the influence of New York was recognized as a factor in the difficulties of the St. Lawrence.

> Notwithstanding the noble efforts which have since been made by Canada to regain a fair share of this trade, by the construction of canals of more than double the tonnage capacity of the Erie Canal, and by the formation of a more direct and cheaper channel of inland navigation, still, such has been the commanding influence of that great commercial metropolis [New York] in drawing trade to itself and in keeping down the price of ocean transport, that these efforts, though not fruitless, have not been so successful as at first anticipated.[2]

A year later the cause of the supremacy of New York was more clearly stated.

> The greatest drawback to the success of this [St. Lawrence] route, as a competitor for European trade, is the high rates of ocean freight from Montreal and Quebec, when compared with those from New York. The latter city being the great commercial emporium of the Northern States, controls the bulk of the import trade; consequently, freights rule lower at that port than any other on this part of the continent, because vessels arriving out with cargo can afford to carry produce to Europe cheaper than those trading to Quebec or Montreal, which, in great part, have to make the voyage here in ballast. Besides, as the staple exports of Canada are bulky, whilst the tonnage of her imports is comparatively small, it is evident that we cannot hope to compete for European freights, except by carrying so much cheaper on our line of internal communication, as to compensate for the disadvantage of the ocean voyage.[3]

The effects were outlined in detail by ship-building interests in 1881.

---

[1] *Journals of the legislative assembly*, XVI, 1858, app. 2.

[2] S.p., 3, 1863.

[3] S.p., 4, 1864 and S.p., 54, 1871. It was pointed out further that successful competition with New York involved the employment of sailing ships of 1,000 tons and steamers of 3,000 tons. These vessels could be employed to Montreal only with improvement of navigation (S.p., 28, 1869).

And it should be especially observed that during those weeks in particular, towards the close of the season of navigation, when our inland shipping should be the most actively and profitably employed in transporting the natural products of the Great West to the seaboard, as is the case with our American rivals, scarcity of ocean tonnage at Montreal becomes the most likely. The owners of such ocean ships as may happen to be there then, dictate their own terms for rates of freight, which is usually six or seven cents per bushel higher than rates simultaneously from New York to Europe, on a route considerably longer. . . [1] Thereupon the Canadian inland vessel owner is compelled to accept any rates of freight from Chicago or Milwaukee to Montreal that may be offered, though, as has happened not unfrequently, considerably less than that obtained at the same time between those ports and New York. Presently the shipper rejects the Montreal route altogether on account of the uncertainty of getting ocean tonnage to carry his grain to Europe. He prefers one or other of the rival American routes.

Thereupon business for Canadian propellers and sailing vessels in the grain trade dwindles away, and the season of navigation closes in a most unsatisfactory manner. Being the direct opposite of that on the Buffalo and Erie Canal routes. . . .

The grounds are readily stated for the disfavor with which the port of Montreal, as compared with New York, is regarded by the owner and captains of ocean shipping. Montreal is situated hundreds of miles away inland from the Atlantic,—navigation of the Gulf of St. Lawrence, particularly during the fall months, is undesirably hazardous, the result being high rates of insurance[2] on hulls and cargoes.

---

[1]Rates on 60 pounds from Montreal to Liverpool during September, October, and November, 1879, were higher than rates from New York to Liverpool by $2\frac{1}{2}$ to 5 cents in September, $1\frac{1}{2}$ to $8\frac{1}{2}$ cents in October, and 5 to $6\frac{1}{2}$ cents in November. In 1871-2 they varied from equality in September to 4 and 5 cents in October and 5 to 9 cents in November (*S.p.*, 6, 1881). An average of the yearly average rates from 1862-1870 to 1871-1879 for 480 pounds increased from 5s. 7d. to 5s. 11d. for sailing craft and declined from 6s. 6d. to 6s. 3d. for steamships. "It would appear therefore that . . . all the advantages of larger vessels have not yet accrued to Montreal exporters. There can be no doubt, however, that the greater tonnage of the vessels employed in the regular grain-carrying trade of the River St. Lawrence (especially of steamships) in later years, has given facilities for vastly more rapid transportation of larger cargoes." The average difference in price between Chicago and Liverpool was 33 cents and reduction in canal tolls, harbour dues, costs of pilotage, and towage was urged as a means of favouring the Canadian route.

[2]   Ocean Rates of Insurance

'Statement of rate of Insurance on grain in first-class Sailing Vessels and first-class Iron Steamers from Montreal to Liverpool, in September, October and November

A rapid river must be ascended entailing heavy pilot fees,[1] and in the case of a sailing vessel, costly towing (more than half the produce exported from New York is carried in sailing

	Sailing Vessels	Steam Vessels
September 1st to 15th	Per cent. 2	Per cent. 1
" 16th to 30th	do $2\frac{1}{2}$	do $1\frac{1}{4}$
October 1st to 15th	do 3	do $1\frac{1}{2}$
do 16th to 31st	do 4	do 2
November 1st to 5th	do $4\frac{1}{2}$	do $2\frac{1}{2}$
do 6th to 10th	do $5\frac{1}{2}$	do $2\frac{3}{4}$
do 11th to 15th	do $6\frac{1}{2}$	do 3

Rates of Marine Insurance

At Montreal, before the 1st of September, risks have been taken this year on grain in A1 steam tonnage at $\frac{3}{8}$ths per cent., and at $\frac{1}{2}$ to $\frac{3}{4}$ths per cent. by iron clippers and steamers in the regular trade. There is a rule—not exactly an iron-clad one,—by which there is a rise in rates of $\frac{1}{8}$th per cent. on and after 1st September, and further similar advances on 15th September, 1st October and 15th October respectively. Each addition of $\frac{1}{8}$th per cent. is equal to $1 on every 1,000 bushels of wheat so insured; the increase of $\frac{1}{2}$ per cent. within the six weeks would, therefore, be equal to $4 on every 1,000 bushels of wheat, and would add more than $7,000 to the cost of the quantity (about 1,785,000 bushels) shipped from Montreal from 1st September to 20th October, in the present year. It is said, that the ratio of advance on and after 15th October depends upon the weather; this therefore, involves a special arrangement . . ." (*S.p.*, 6, 1881).

[1]   Rates of Pilotage

Port of Montreal

"The pilotage charges to a 600-ton sailing vessel, drawing 18 feet water,when towed, are as follows:—

Father Point to Quebec, 161 miles, $3.60 per foot	$64.80
Quebec to Father Point,—$3.15 per foot	56.70
	$121.50
Quebec to Montreal, 150 miles, $2 per foot	$36.00
Montreal to Quebec, same rate	36.00
	72.00
	$193.50

It should be stated that, from 10th to 19th of November, the rates from Father Point or Bic to Quebec and return, are $4.60 and $4.15 per foot draft respectively. The pilotage of a vessel of 18 feet draft, towards the close of the season, would therefore be $229.50. . . .

How the Towage Business is Worked

The towing-service in the River and Gulf of St. Lawrence has been characterized as inefficient—, it being alleged that there are steamers of one kind and another engaged in it, that were not originally intended for that sort of work, and which, as might be expected, are poorly adapted for it. The tariff rates charged, too, are exorbitantly high, the mode of exacting them is arbitrary and irregular, often oppressive—it seeming to be the settled belief of tow-boat organizations, that the commerce of Canada's Great Water-Highway *must* afford them revenue. . . .

The vessels which suffer most are those which come into the St. Lawrence trade for the first time; and their experience is often so hard and cheerless that they never return. The greatest perplexity and annoyance experienced by owners of tonnage in Europe are believed to arise mainly from the uncertainty of towage expenses; and there can hardly be a doubt that this keeps away many a ship from Montreal, giving color to the exaggerated reports which have gained credence respecting exorbitant charges of every kind to which all vessels are subjected. . . ." (*S.p.*, 6, 1881).

vessels,) must be employed. In the harbor itself heavy dues on vessels and cargoes are imposed. The port is only open half the year, and there is usually a scarcity of westerly freight to assist in meeting the expenses of the round trip.

Throughout the period from 1850 to 1885 the position of the Welland and of the St. Lawrence Canals was steadily weakened. A "Petition of . . . ship-owners, manufacturers, merchants, ship-builders, master mariners and others interested in the trade, inland shipping and commerce of Canada", dated St. Catharines, March 23, 1880,[1] stressed the general trend of navigation which had been accentuated during the depression of the decade from 1870 to 1880.

> That for a term of years extending from 1874 to the present time the competition of rival routes by rail and especially the great water route by Buffalo, the Erie Canal and Hudson River, to the port of New York, has been unprecedently keen and persistent, and so successful as to leave for transport by our route merely a small fraction of the entire amount of produce moved forward.
>
> That coincidently, rates of freight to Kingston and Montreal were forced so low in order to get business at all, as to leave little or no margin of profit, and frequently to entail positive loss on the season's business to the Canadian vessel owner.
>
> The commercial value of Canadian Inland shipping afloat has been decimated, and it has been impossible to make provision from its surplus earnings to replace with new ones, vessels that have become worn-out and worthless. No increase of Canadian inland tonnage is taking place, and, in a word, our vessel property bears more the character of a liability than of a valuable asset such as it once was.
>
> That the advantages for competition against ourselves conferred upon the water route to New York by the low tolls (boats and numerous articles are toll free) on the Erie Canal, the large size of the upper lake craft employed for transportation on that route, the assistance afforded by a plentiful supply of westerly-bound freight and the cheapness of ocean rates of freight from New York to Europe, render the outlook gloomy for extensive or profitable business on our water route to Montreal unless some substantial relief is afforded from the burdens resting upon it.
>
> That the falling off in the amount of traffic carried on and tolls collected on the Welland and St. Lawrence Canals, and

---

[1] *S.p.*, 6, 1881. An importer at St. Catharines stated in 1880 that he had abandoned the Montreal-Portland route in favour of the New York route because of "freights insurance and dispatch".

the deserted and desolate appearance presented by those costly highways of commerce, so conspicuous the last and several previous years, must be expected to continue unless some liberal policy shall be adopted pointing to a better state of affairs.

Meanwhile the present large staff of Canal employés will be maintained as hitherto in comparative idleness, although capable, without being overworked, of forwarding quadruple the tonnage offering to pass the locks.

On more than one occasion, last fall, for twenty-four consecutive hours lock-tenders were not required to turn a gate winch. At the same time the resources of the Erie Canal were taxed to their utmost to move produce forward. . . .

"The superiority of a natural route" in "the cheap and rapid transport of the heavy and bulky articles of agricultural produce"[1] declined rapidly. In 1855 rates on a barrel of flour from Cleveland to Boston were 5s., to New York 4s., to Portland 3s. 6d., and to Quebec 2s. From Toronto to Quebec rates were 1s. 6d. and from Toronto to New York, 2s. 6d.[2] From 1865 to 1869 the average rate of freight per bushel of wheat between Chicago and New York *via* Buffalo declined from 26¾ cents to 23 cents and *via* Oswego from 27½ cents to 23¼ cents. The average rate per bushel by propellor from Chicago to Montreal was 13 cents in 1868 and the time 10 or 11 days shorter than to New York—8 to 10 days in contrast with 20 to 22 days.[3] To the close of 1869 wheat was carried at 6 to 7½ cents from Chicago to Montreal less than to New York. The reduction of the Erie Canal tolls by one-half (3½ cents) in 1870 still left the Montreal rates 3½ to 5 cents less. Freight and charges on wheat were about 20 per cent. less to Montreal than to New York.[4] In 1880, however, the cost of moving a bushel of wheat from Chicago to New York was estimated at $5\frac{7}{10}$ cents and from Chicago to Montreal at $10\frac{35}{100}$ cents.

As a result of the intensity of competition:

The Current of traffic, say, of grain for Great Britain, appears to flow increasingly eastward without regard (1) to distance, and preferring the longest route; (2) this preference being against the cheaper mode of transport by the Welland Canal

[1] *S.p.*, 6, 1876.
[2] J. C. Taché, *Sketch of Canada*.
[3] *S.p.*, 54, 1871.
[4] *S.p.*, 47, 1875.

and River St. Lawrence; and (3) a fair inference is, . . . that railway transport is now much less expensive than it was twenty or thirty years ago.   To enable carriers by water, therefore, to maintain a fair relative position, every impediment must be removed, and every item of expense reduced.[1]

2

The Welland Canal

"The Welland Canal must be considered as that link which is indispensable to the complete development of the St. Lawrence navigation.   Our great object should be to seek the control, as much as possible, of the Western traffic and take it to tide water."   A canal around Niagara Falls was the key to traffic developed in the western states and in western Canada tributary to the upper lakes, for the St. Lawrence route.[2]   Prior to 1850 this canal (28 miles) had been built to a depth of 8 feet 6 inches on the sills and had 27 locks of 150 feet by 26 feet to overcome a height of 330 feet.   Although deepened to 10 feet in 1853 its narrow locks were responsible for the situation in which "whilst the St. Lawrence canals can pass vessels [*800 tons*] of double the tonnage capacity of those [*400 tons*] which can get through the Welland canal, yet, their draught being one foot less, the same vessel which can pass through the latter canal, cannot, without being lightened, pass through the St. Lawrence canals."[3]

The effect of completion of the canal was shown in the growth of traffic.   Total tonnage increased from 820,000 in 1849 to 2,500,000 in 1869.   On the other hand, its proportion

---

[1] *S.p.*, 6, 1881.   These items were enumerated to include wharfage at Montreal, canal tolls on bread-stuffs and provisions, low rates on tonnage, reduction of pilotage, and of charges for transfer, storage, and loading of grain, and marine insurance.   In 1882 the Erie Canal tolls were abolished with the result that Welland and St. Lawrence tolls were reduced by one-half in 1884 on wheat and certain food products for Montreal and ports east of Montreal.   In 1885 tolls were further reduced to 2 cents per ton (*S.p.*, 10a, 1891).

[2] See W. Kingsford, *The Canadian canals* (Toronto, 1865); T. C. Keefer, *The canals of Canada* (Montreal, 1894); B. Cumberland, *A century of sail and steam on the Niagara River* (Toronto, 1913); E. M. Hodder, *The harbours and ports of Lake Ontario* (Toronto, 1857); J. P. Merritt, *Biography of the Hon. W. H. Merritt, M.P.* (St. Catharines, 1875); and D. C. Masters, "W. H. Merritt and the expansion of Canadian railways" (*Canadian Historical Review*, XII, 1931, 168-173).

[3] *S.p.*, 3, 1862.

of total traffic—for example, of western wheat and flour moved to tide water by New York and the St. Lawrence routes—fluctuated from 7.3 per cent. in 1856 to 15.4 in 1857, to 12.01 in 1858, 16.08 in 1859, 7.16 in 1860, 8.26 in 1861, and 11.4 in 1862.[1] An attempt to regain control of traffic had been made in an order-in-council dated May 28, 1860 (effective May 19, 1860), abolishing tolls on the St. Lawrence Canals and refunding 90 per cent. of the tolls paid on the Welland Canal to vessels entering the St. Lawrence Canals "or reported inwards at any Canadian port or on the River St. Lawrence; and vice versa—vessels coming up through the St. Lawrence canals or hailing from any Canadian port and passing upwards through the Welland Canal",[2] with the result that tonnage increased "by 7½ per cent. in 1861 over 1860 and in 1862 by 15 per cent. over 1861".[3] But in view of "the greatly increased production of cereals in the Western States . . . we have not obtained so large a traffic since the removal of the tolls as we obtained prior to the adoption of that policy."[4] Tolls were reimposed in full in 1863 and traffic on the Welland Canal declined 8.26 per cent. and on the St. Lawrence 7.19 per cent. In spite of improvements in facilities for trans-shipping grain at Kingston and Montreal and of other advantages, the proportion of traffic continued to decline. W. P. Howland, the minister of finance, wrote on May 12, 1862:

> I am persuaded that the chief cause of that failure lies in the absence of sufficient competition among forwarders engaged in the St. Lawrence trade, in the financial relations between shippers engaged in the western trade and the capitalists of New York; and finally and chiefly in the lower rates of ocean freights from New York to Europe, occasioned by the greater competition at that Port than is to be found at Quebec or Montreal.[5]

---

[1] *S.p.*, 2, 1863. The decline was attributed in part to inefficiency since it took generally 2 days to pass a 400-ton vessel because of the monopoly of towage which had been assumed by "about fifteen individuals who employ, upon the whole, about one hundred and fifty teams" (*S.p.*, 4, 1861).

[2] *S.p.*, 3, 1863.

[3] Goods imported by the St. Lawrence increased from $13,548,665 in 1860 to $17,249,055 in 1861 and exports from $14,037,403 in 1860 to $22,524,735 in 1861. Goods in transit from the western states by the St. Lawrence totalled $3,505,511 in 1861 (*S.p.*, 2, 1862).

[4] *S.p.*, 3, 1864.

[5] *S.p.*, 2, 1863.

The canal commission of 1871, of which Hugh Allan was chairman, presented an elaborate survey of the problem.[1] It emphasized the rapid growth of trade on the Great Lakes. The gross value of trade on the lakes had increased according to estimates from $65,000,000 in 1841 to $300,000,000 in 1851 and to $700,000,000 in 1871. Tonnage increased from 212,000 (74,000 steam and 138,000 sailing vessels) in 1851 to 450,000 tons (80,000 Canadian)in 1862 and to 547,267 in 1866. In 1869 Buffalo alone had 131 steam vessels, 127 sail, and a total tonnage of 91,328. Chicago[2] increased in population from 30,000 in 1850 to 110,000 in 1860 and to 299,000 in 1870; Milwaukee from 20,000 in 1850 to 72,000 in 1870; and Cleveland from 17,000 in 1850 to 92,000 in 1870. The grain-growing states (Ohio, Michigan, Indiana, Illinois, Missouri, Iowa, Wisconsin, Minnesota, Kansas) increased in population from 3,000,000 in 1840 to 12,000,000 in 1870 and in their aggregate production as follows:

---

[1]*S.p.*, 54, 1871. Hogan estimated forest exports from the lakes basin in 1851 by the Hudson and St. Lawrence routes at £1,000,000 and agricultural exports at £6,000,000 and total imports at £18,000,000 (J. S. Hogan, *Canada*, 23).

	Ships inwards		Ships outwards		Tonnage through provincial canals exclusive of Rideau
	No.	Tonnage	No.	Tonnage	Totals Tons
1851	1,647	593,255	1,704	637,447	3,390,635
1852	1,461	541,144	1,524	574,126	3,724,761
1853	1,798	622,579	1,821	658,853	3,944,383
1854	1,890	705,342	2,018	781,755	3,799,927
1855	1,168	419,553	1,219	451,241	4,072,656
1856	1,494	550,573	1,532	573,648	4,680,349
1857	2,047	748,425	1,848	731,367	4,162,902
1858	1,657	613,618	1,662	632,046	4,203,353
1859	1,715	641,662	1,618	640,571	3,807,089
1860	1,992	831,434	1,923	821,791	4,898,389
1861		1,087,128		1,059,667	

[2]Exports of grain from Chicago increased as follows:

1852	5,873,141
1853	6,412,181
1854	12,932,320
1855	16,633,700
1856	21,583,221
1860	31,256,697

See W. Pross, *The Toronto and Georgian Bay ship canal* (Chicago, 1864).

		1850	1860	1869
Wheat	Bush.	43,842,038	89,293,603	166,100,000
Corn	"	222,208,502	392,289,631	556,050,000
Oats	"	42,328,731	62,748,901	146,200,000
Rye	"	739,567	3,997,001	4,802,000
Barley	"	831,517	4,865,761	8,755,000
Swine	No.	8,536,182	11,039,332	19,100,000

Ontario increased in population from 952,000 in 1851 to 1,396,091 in 1861 and in production of wheat from 12,000,000 bushels in 1851 to 25,000,000 bushels in 1861. Lake craft increased from 4,875 with a tonnage of 523,991 in 1862 to 5,866 with a tonnage of 721,324 in 1869.

To explain the relative decline of traffic on the St. Lawrence route the commission stressed the changed character of lake vessels. As early as 1855 engineers had declared that the screw steamer had "fully established its superiority".[1] The Sault Ste. Marie Canal[2] had been built to 12 feet in 1855 and the channel of the Lake St. Clair flats had been dredged to 300 feet width and 13 feet low water or 14 feet ordinary lake level, and vessels measuring respectively 234 feet length and 34 feet beam and 265 feet length and 34 feet beam, of 1,500 to 1,600 tons, were successfully employed.

> Then again as the line of navigation is extended, so the long voyage demands larger tonnage. As an approximate rule for the size of a vessel for any particular route, it has been observed that any vessel to be properly adapted to its business should have one ton of measurement for every mile of her voyage; and as examples, in illustration of the rule, it may be remarked that the vessels plying between Chicago and Buffalo, 916 miles, now range between 600 and 1,500 tons, while many persons, of considerable experience in the trade, are of opinion that a medium size of about 1,000 tons is best suited for this route.

As early as 1854, 37 propellors of a total tonnage of 20,181 tons were unable to descend to Lake Ontario. In 1860 one-third to one-fourth of the vessels in the grain trade could not pass the canal and nearly three-fourths of the propellors were

---

[1] *Journals of the legislative assembly*, XIII, 1854-5, app. G.G.G.
[2] See O. Fowle, *Sault Ste. Marie and its great waterway* (New York, 1925), chapter xxxii.

31

too large. These numbers increased to 70 of 50,101 tons in
1864 and 122 of 114,192 tons in 1874[1]. In 1869 Buffalo
owned 11 screw steamers of about 1,100 tons and 4 over
1,400 tons (largest 1,470), 20 between 800 and 1,000, 19
between 600 and 800, and of a total of 58 only 4 were
within the capacity of the canal. Between 1860 and 1866
the tonnage of paddle steamers declined from 69,150 to
41,870 and of propellors increased from 61,550 to 75,287.
Moreover, a great number of large barges varying from 200
to 1,000 tons were being employed, "some of them with
motor power within themselves; but the majority have masts
and sails and are towed through the Lake by powerful tugs
with from three to five in a row." In 1866, 234 tugs of a total
tonnage of 23,678 were enumerated. In 1871 the Oswego
board of trade reported that three-fourths of the tonnage of
the upper lakes could not pass the Welland Canal. The commission stated in its report:

> Experience proves that the largest class of vessels, especially
> steam, now plying on the lakes, carry property at the cheapest
> rates. The larger class of vessels, both sail and steam, carrying
> from 20 to 35,000 bushels of grain, are increasing year by year,
> and must entirely obtain, according as the artificial channels
> of communication are improved. A very general opinion
> prevails that steam, that is the screw vessel, must prevail in
> the end over sail on the lakes, for it has all the advantages in
> respect to rates of Insurance, expedition, safety and competi-
> tion with railways, all important elements in the transportation
> of the bulky produce of the West.

The increase in number and in size of propellors strengthened
the position of the Buffalo-New York route.

> The tendency in shipbuilding for the last quarter of a
> century on the Upper Lakes has been to construct larger
> vessels every way, whether propelled by steam or sails; while
> the screw is superseding the paddle everywhere on the lakes
> as well as on the ocean, the relative number and tonnage of
> screw steamers is gradually increasing upon the sailing craft. . . .[2]
> The superior economy[3] of the larger vessel is sufficiently
> established by the present cost of transport on the great

---

[1] *S.p.*, 47, 1875.

[2] *S.p.*, 54, 1871.

[3] "At the same rates a vessel carrying 60,000 bushels of corn makes a profit
of $740 on the round trip from Chicago to Buffalo and return, where a vessel
carrying 21,000 bushels gains but $83.30, the rates in this case being 2 cents per

channels of trade between Chicago and Buffalo, and Chicago and Oswego. On the former route, where all classes of vessels from 600 to 1,500 tons are in use, the average charge on a bushel of wheat, in 1869, for the whole year, struck from the weekly· quotations, was 5.65 cents, while on the latter route, where the size of the vessels is limited to 500 tons, the average cost for the same year taken in the same way was 11.13 cents, or a difference of 5.48 cents for only 143 miles extra distance. Making a fair allowance for this extra distance, and the time and tolls on the Welland Canal, there is still a difference due to the different kind of vessel of about four cents a bushel . . . the cost of carrying a bushel of wheat from Kingston to Montreal.

Attempts to solve the problem by the construction of the Welland Railway completed on October 8, 1858, were inadequate. In 1860 it carried down grain to the extent of 81,243 tons of through freight to American ports and 4,761 tons to Canadian ports.

The Railway conveyed 1485 tons of through freight, which it received at Port Colborne from 24 vessels, lightened to 10 feet draft of water, so as to pass through the Canal. It received the cargos and parts of cargos of 230 vessels at Port Colborne, 150 of which were of such dimensions as admitted of their passing through the Canal.

The canal carried down a total of 766,288 tons of which 404,463 tons were grain (278,334 wheat, 136,129 corn).

Of the total movement of freight between these lakes (1,040,197 tons) the grain trade is about one-half, of which it is to be observed that the railway has conveyed seventeen per cent . . . while its proportion of the entire traffic is nine and one-third per cent.[1]

The report of the commissioner of public works for the year 1861 stated that the St. Lawrence Canals in that year had increased their business 100 per cent. on grain, 20 per cent.

bushel for corn and $1.00 per ton for coal (carried on the return trip), giving to each vessel the same proportionate return cargo. Calling the rate 4 cents per bushel for corn and $1.00 per ton for coal, the smaller vessel would gain $743.50 where the large one would show $2,540 on the profit side of the ledger" (*S.p.*, 6, 1881). In 1876 it was estimated that 27,000 vessels passed annually through the Detroit channel "20,000 of which carry masts from 80 to 160 feet in height". The total freight carried was estimated at 9,000,000 tons (*S.p.*, 6, 1877). Regular steamer lines on the lake included 3 steamers from Lake Huron to Lake Superior, 4 steamers between Collingwood and Chicago, 3 steamers from Collingwood to Sault Ste. Marie (*S.p.*, 6, 1881).

[1]*S.p.*, 4, 1860.

on flour, and 8 per cent. on other freight and that the number of vessels passing through the Welland Canal increased by 13¼ per cent.   By 1871 it was reported that: "During the three months ended on the 30th June, 1871, 133 vessels carrying 78,425 tons of grain transshipped the whole or a part of their cargo."   Of these, 40 trans-shipped their entire cargoes amounting to 24,037 tons and the remainder sent partial shipments totalling 11,975 tons enabling them to pass the canal.   Of the total 78,425 tons, 36,012 were carried by rail from Port Colborne to Port Dalhousie, and 42,413 by canal.[1]   During the 1871 season the railway carried nearly 3,000,000 bushels, making a total with the canal of over 24½ million bushels.   The downward movement for the season totalled 867,085 tons in 1870 and 962,565 tons in 1871, made up as follows:[2]

		1870	1871
Wheat	bushels	12,838,749	12,828,005
Corn	"	3,280,320	8,389,658
Oats	"	Not given	309,008
Lumber	ft. B. M.	46,812,600	54,994,491
Timber	cub. feet	2,489,900	3,421,439

The difficulties of the railway were numerous.   With one elevator at Port Colborne vessels requiring to reduce their cargoes from 19,000 to 24,000 bushels of wheat with 12 feet draught to 14,000 to 18,500 bushels with 10 feet draught, and vessels forced to trans-ship their entire cargoes because of their inability to pass through the locks, were detained "for a considerable time.   This detention frequently occasions more loss to the owners than the railway charges for carrying the quantity lighted will amount to."[3]   In 1882 the *I.C. Gault* of Toledo with 43,000 bushels unloaded 15,000 bushels to be taken down by railway but found the very moderate railway rates too heavy for profitable business.[4]

The canal was deepened to 12 feet in 1883 and to 14 feet in 1887.   In 1883 "several large propellors, steam barges

---

[1] *S.p.*, 6, 1872.
[2] *S.p.*, 6, 1873.   In 1875 "vessels and all classes of staple products" passing through the canal decreased in quantity.   The depression was particularly serious to traffic in reducing the American demand for sawn lumber (*S.p.*, 3, 1876, and *S.p.*, 4, 1877).
[3] *S.p.*, 6, 1872.
[4] *S.p.*, 8, 1883.

and schooners . . . passed through the canal for the first time carrying from 40,000 to 60,000 bushels of grain."[1] At about the same date, however, vessels of 16 feet draught were admitted to Buffalo.

Kingston as a trans-shipping point offered a valuable index as to the handling of grain brought down the Welland Canal for Montreal since rates were on a basis of equality with Oswego from Chicago.[2] Receipts of corn and wheat increased from 1,480,959 bushels (58 cargoes of 839,948 bushels in British vessels and 46 cargoes of 641,011 in American vessels) in 1858 to over 6,000,000 bushels in 1870 (the largest proportion in American vessels). A large forwarding company gave receipts from the United States in 1870 as 3,020,862 bushels (79 cargoes and 1,127,987 bushels British and 111 cargoes and 1,892,875 bushels American). In 1871 the trans-shipment of grain "assumed very large proportions".[3] In 1876: "It is stated to be more profitable for sail vessels loaded with grain to tranship their cargoes at Kingston, than to proceed with it to Montreal."[4] The difficulties incidental to the St. Lawrence Canals became particularly serious after the deepening of the Welland Canal in 1883.

Receipts of flour and wheat at Montreal (reduced to bushels of grain) increased from 2,786,315 in 1845, to 2,799,372 in 1855, to 6,558,754 in 1865, and to 12,333,458 in 1869, and shipments increased from 495,440 in 1855 to 3,972,943 in 1865 and 11,425,667 in 1869. "While there has been a steady increase in the quantity of grain passed through the Welland Canal, bound for United States ports, during a period of five years [*1880-4*], the quantity passed through the Welland and St. Lawrence Canals, bound to Montreal, was less in 1884 than during any previous year of the five."[5] The quantities of grain and flour (reduced to

---

[1] *S.p.*, 10, 1884.

[2] Rates to Oswego were often ½ per cent. less as vessels were more certain of despatch and return freights.

[3] *S.p.*, 6, 1872.

[4] *S.p.*, 6, 1876. At Coteau Landing in 1880 over 200,000 bushels were shipped in barges carrying from 10,000 to 15,000 bushels.

[5] *S.p.*, 6, 1881. Grain vessels from American ports through Port Colborne to Kingston or Montreal totalled in 1879: September, 132; October, 53; November, 9; in contrast with vessels arriving at Buffalo (chiefly grain): September, 659; October, 716; November, 355. American vessels averaged about 3 times the tonnage of Canadian vessels.

bushels) exported from New York, Philadelphia, Boston, and Baltimore, were in 1878, 157,491,000 bushels, and in 1879, 194,984,000 bushels. The same exported from Montreal in 1878 were 16,051,622 bushels (7.12 per cent.); and in 1879, 18,338,973 bushels (6.80 per cent.). The number of bushels shipped from Montreal (not including flour reduced to bushels) totalled 20,419,885 in 1880; 13,114,138 in 1881;[1] 8,293,830 in 1882; 9,781,001 in 1883;[2] 7,421,152 in 1884.[3] 294,353 barrels of flour were shipped in 1883 and 446,480 in 1884.

In the decade ending 1881 it was pointed out that movement of goods by the Welland Canal in the first 6 years had increased but in the last 4 years had declined at an average of 14.40 per cent. for each year, while the movement eastward on the two trunk railways of New York State increased 62.36 per cent. in 1870 "bounding upward year by year until in 1879 the augmentation was over 300 per cent."[4] The decline on westbound traffic was serious for the canals. Freight through the canals from Montreal to ports west of Port Colborne declined from 37,190 tons in 1881 to 9,425 tons in 1884 (iron and salt declined from 30,682 tons in 1881 to 3,242 tons in 1884).[5]

(c)—RAILWAYS

1

Through Lines

The construction of through lines as a device for supplementing the canals in their struggle to attract western traffic in part accentuated the problem it was expected to solve. The share of traffic was not proportionately increased and was divided between the railways and canals. Fixed capital was increased and in turn overhead costs in the face of a relative decline in traffic. Even Canadian railways intensified

---

[1]*S.p.*, 7, 1883.
[2]*S.p.*, 7, 1884.
[3]*S.p.*, 9, 1885. In 1873-4 exports of grain from Montreal totalled 20,745,105 bushels (13,370,559 Canadian and 7,374,546 American) (*S.p.*, 4, 1875).
[4]*S.p.*, 6, 1881.
[5]*S.p.*, 4, 1885.

the struggle between New York and the St. Lawrence by favouring the New York route. The Grand Trunk Railway[1] was designed in Canada, however, to supplement the canals and as a means of recovering traffic which was being taken to New York by American railways "with rapid and uninterrupted" transportation. Allan McNab, chairman of the standing committee on railways and telegraph lines, in the first report dated July 21, 1851 stated:

> After a full consideration of the subject, Your Committee have come to the conclusion that the interests of the Province will be best consulted by the construction of a grand Trunk Line of Railway, extending from Quebec to Windsor on the River Detroit, and connecting with any line which may be constructed between Halifax and Quebec. This great line is considered by the people of Canada as a Provincial undertaking, and should be taken up as such, . . . as it will in the opinion of Your Committee, in conjunction with our magnificent chain of Water Communication, secure for Canada a large portion of the Trade and Commerce of Western America. The magnitude of the proposed line of Railway and the consequent expense of construction is such that its completion will be postponed for an indefinite period, if left to private enterprise, even though assisted by Government under the provisions of the Guarantee Act.[2] Your Committee are therefore glad to learn that the Government are prepared to act promptly and efficiently in the matter, and to pledge the

---

[1] See D. A. MacGibbon, *Railway rates and the Canadian railway commission* (Boston, 1917); Gustavus Myers, *History of Canadian wealth* (Chicago, 1914), I, chapters x, xi; L. H. Jenks, *The migration of British capital to 1875* (New York, 1927), chapter vii; M. Pennington, *Railways and other ways* (Toronto, 1896); W. H. Breithaupt, "Outline of the history of the Grand Trunk Railway of Canada" (Railway and Locomotive Historical Society *bulletin*, no. 23, 37-74); O. D. Skelton, *The railway builders* (Toronto, 1916); S. J. McLean, "The early railway history of Canada" (*Canadian Magazine*, XII, 411-426); *Poor's manual of railroads* (New York, 1867—); William McNab, "Historical narrative of the inception and development of the Grand Trunk Railway of Canada" (Manuscript copy in University of Toronto library); R. Ayre, "When the railway came to Canada" (*Queen's Quarterly*, May, 1932, 274-290); M. L. Bladen, "Railways in Canada to 1885" (*Contributions to Canadian Economics*, V); S. J. McLean, "Some phases of early Canadian railway development" (*Proceedings* of the Canadian Political Science Association, 1932).

[2] The Guarantee Act (12 Vic. c. 29) was regarded as too liberal and as involving possible serious drains on the credit of the province. The committee recommended limitations of the act to the main trunk line and a continuation of the privilege to the Great Western, the St. Lawrence and Atlantic, and the Northern Railways. It also recommended more rigid control over the incorporation of railroad companies by the legislature. See an act to incorporate the Grand Trunk Railway of Canada, November 10, 1852 (16 Vic. c. 37).

credit and resources of the Province in aid of the construction of the line.[1]

The Grand Trunk Railway was described as supplying

> a means of intercommunication through the valley of the St. Lawrence during the whole of the year, an advantage, which, owing to the river being frozen over for at least six months annually, had previously been enjoyed only during the summer. Even during the season, when the navigation is open, the means of transport, by water, are imperfect. Seagoing vessels, of 700 to 800 tons burden, could proceed safely as far as Lake Ontario; but the limited dimensions of the Welland Canal made it necessary that the produce from Lakes Erie, Huron, Michigan, and Superior should be conveyed to Lake Ontario in smaller vessels, not exceeding 300 tons burden. The Grand Trunk Railway was intended to obviate the necessity for this transhipment of cargo.[2]

Through lines of railway were built to handle western traffic and to avoid the difficulties and distance of the canals. Between Chicago and Buffalo the railways were about 500 miles and the waterways 1,000 miles in length. The Great Western Railway Company completed a line from Hamilton to Windsor (January 27, 1854) and London to Sarnia (December 27, 1858), Hamilton to Niagara River (November 10, 1853), and to Toronto (December 3, 1855).[3] The first

---

[1] *Journals of the legislative assembly*, X, 1858, app. U.U.: "Unless Canada could combine with her unrivalled navigation a railroad system connected therewith, and mutually sustaining each other, the whole of her large outlay must for ever remain unproductive."

[2] Arthur Helps, *Life and labours of Mr. Brassey* (London, 1872), 183-4; also J. G. Kohl, *Travels in Canada*, II, 343 *ff*.

[3] "From Hamilton to the Western States, by the Great Western Railroad— *The new short route to the West.*—Trains leave Hamilton daily for Detroit connecting at that city with the Michigan Central Railroad for Chicago.

	Distance Miles	Emigrant Train		First Class Train	
		Stg.	Cy.	Stg.	Cy.
To Dundas	6	0s 6d	0s 7½d	1s 0d	1s 3d
Flamboro'	9	"		"	
Paris	20	2s 0d	2s 6d	3s 8d	4s 6d
Woodstock	48	3s 0d	3s 9d	5s 0d	6s 3d
Ingersoll	47	3s 6d	4s 4½d	7s 0d	8s 9d
London	76	4s 9d	6s 0d	9s 0d	13s 3d
Eckford	96	6s 0d	7s 6d	14s 0d	17s 6d
Chatham	140	7s 0d	8s 9d	"	"
Windsor / Detroit, Michigan	}186	8s 0d	10s 0d	20s 0d	25s 0d
Chicago, Illinois	465	16s 0d	20s 0d	44s 0d	55s 0d"

(From J. S. Hogan, *Canada*).

locomotive crossed the suspension bridge on March 8, 1855. An additional through line was completed between Goderich and Fort Erie (June 28, 1858). Shorter lines accentuated the competition. The Canada Southern was completed from Fort Erie to Amherstburg (229 miles) on November 15, 1873, and in the same year the Great Western shortened its line by a branch from Glencoe to Fort Erie. The Northern Railway was completed from Toronto to Collingwood (94 miles) on January 2, 1855, to offset by Georgian Bay the effects of competition from Buffalo and New York. Finally, the Grand Trunk Railway was completed from Toronto to Montreal (October 27, 1856) to overcome the difficulties of the St. Lawrence Canals. With this line direct communication was available to Portland over lines which had been built at an earlier date (July 16, 1853). Connections were also available to New York and Boston. On November 27, 1854, the line was completed from Richmond to Point Lévis opposite Quebec and in 1860 to Rivière du Loup. The Grand Trunk strengthened its position by a line in western Ontario from Toronto to Sarnia (November 21, 1859). Almost a month later, on December 16, the Victoria bridge which was started on July 21, 1854, was completed. "Not many days after, trains laden entirely with bales of cotton from Louisiana, and others with flour from Chicago and pork from Cincinnati were passed through the iron tube, two miles in length, on their route to England."[1] With the completion of through connections to Montreal and the seaboard,

---

[1] J. Croil, *Dundas* (Montreal, 1861), 302. On the other hand, the road was still in bad shape—large numbers of rails were broken in the winter of 1860 and the grades and curves east of Toronto were such that an engine hauling 20 cars from the west was forced to drop 5 at Toronto. See Watkins, Recommendations for improvement dated London, December 2, 1861, *Journals of the legislative assembly*, 1862, app. 9; also O. D. Skelton, *Life and times of Sir A. T. Galt* (Toronto, 1920), chapters iii and iv; J. M. and E. Trout, *The railways of Canada for 1870-1* (Toronto, 1871). See a glowing account in Prospectus The Grand Trunk Railway Company of Canada, Statements, reports and accounts of the Grand Trunk Railway of Canada, *Journals of the legislative assembly*, 1857, app. 6; *Report of the special committee . . . Grand Trunk Railway Company* (Toronto, 1851); H. A. Lovett, *Canada and the Grand Trunk* (n.p., 1924); T. S. Brown, *A history of the Grand Trunk Railway* (Quebec, 1864); C. Legge, *A glance at Victoria bridge and the men who built it;* A. T. Galt, *Canada, 1849 to 1859* (Quebec, 1860); Sir Francis Hincks, *Reminiscences of his public life* (Montreal, 1884), chapters x, xxi.

Outline of arrangement of trains on Grand Trunk Railway of Canada for winter of 1859-60 after completion of the Victoria bridge:

numerous lines were built, partly with a view to attracting through traffic and partly to develop local traffic. Lines were extended from Hamilton to Guelph, and to ports on Lake Huron—Southampton in 1873 and Kincardine in 1874; and to share Toronto's advantages on the short cut to Georgian Bay—to Barrie in 1878, to Midland in 1876, and to Collingwood in 1879. Traffic on Lake Erie was tapped with a road to Port Dover in 1876. Toronto strengthened its control on Georgian Bay with a line to Owen Sound in 1873. The opening up of the Georgian Bay and Lake Superior districts, especially after the construction and completion of the Canadian Pacific Railway to Port Arthur and Fort William, was responsible for a rapid expansion of traffic.[1] The metropolitan areas of Toronto and Hamilton[2] took advantage of the difficulties of the Welland Canal and of their position on Lake Ontario.

The Grand Trunk route gradually strengthened its position. On February 8, 1880, the railway obtained direct connections with Chicago. Running rights were granted between different lines and the amalgamation of the Grand Trunk Railway and the Great Western Railway on August 12, 1882, and, in turn, with the Midland Railway on January 1, 1884, facilitated the growth of a uniform policy. The introduction of standard railway time in 1883 facilitated the task of building up schedules.

Effectiveness of the railways was improved through the introduction of new technique and through closer co-operation. On July 22, 1871, the Grand Trunk was connected with the harbour of Montreal—"one of the most important

---

Going West			Going East		
Leave Portland	9 A.M.		Leave Chicago	5 P.M.	
do Quebec	1 P.M.		do Detroit	7 A.M.	
do Richmond Junc-			do Toronto	5 P.M.	
tion	5 P.M.		do Montreal	8 A.M.	
do Montreal	9 P.M.		do Richmond Junc-		
do Toronto	11 A.M.		tion	11 A.M.	
do Detroit	8 P.M.		Arrive Quebec	3.30 P.M.	
Arrive Chicago	10 A.M. 2nd day.		do Portland	8 P.M.	

Between Quebec and Chicago as above, 45 hours.
    do   Portland and Chicago as above, 49 hours (*S.p.*, 8, 1860).
    [1]See W. Roland, *Algoma west* (Toronto, 1887); *Northwestern Ontario* (Toronto, 1879); F. Yeigh, *The Rainy River district* (Toronto, 1892).
    [2]The position of Hamilton had been strengthened by the Burlington channel and the Desjardins Canal to Dundas.

events in the trade of Canada".[1] Increasing efficiency followed the replacement of iron rails by steel rails after 1870, and the change from wide to narrow guage[2] (5 feet 6 inches to 4 feet 8½ inches) from 1872-4. Moving the track and adjusting the rolling stock on the other hand involved heavy initial expenses. Wood became increasingly scarce, rising from $8.00 to $18.00 a cord in 1871-2 with the result that coal was used to an increasing extent after that date.

The railway system was rounded out by the construction of elevators and suitable machinery for unloading, storing, and re-shipping. The advantages of these facilities in financing the movement of wheat on the basis of bills of lading and warehouse receipts were fully appreciated. The Grand Trunk report stated about 1859:

> As regards the Traffic from the West, we have long been made aware of the fact, that if the same monetary facilities were not afforded Western Shippers of Produce to the New York and Boston Markets, or intermediate Ports, such as Buffalo or Oswego, as were granted them at present by parallel lines, we could never expect these Shipments via Canada, and therefore it is with much satisfaction that I am able to state that arrangements are in course of completion for making advances on shipments to Toronto, Kingston, Montreal, Quebec, or Portland, on depositing at the place of shipment the bills of lading with accredited Agents. The importance of this arrangement cannot be over estimated, as we are now at every point well qualified to compete successfully with these parallel lines for

---

[1] "The cars of the Grand Trunk removed from the wharves from the 24th of July to the 15th December, about 32,000 tons of goods, while the ordinary carters during the same period, had more to do than they could perform, and in the absence of the rails, it is a question how those extra goods could have been removed before being overtaken by the close of navigation. The rails since then have been extended as far as the Richelieu Pier, but it is intended to continue them down next Spring as far as the ground is graded on Molson's Wharf, and also put in a number of sidings, so that the same complaints as were made last year of the wharves being crowded will not exist, and further, if the Commissioners decide on connecting the Molson's Wharf, the Ferry Wharf, and the Hochelaga Wharf, the railways can have a common terminus" (S.p., 5, 1872). Connections between the railway and the harbour were improved throughout the period.

[2] See G. Laidlaw, *Reports and letters on light narrow-gauge railways* (Toronto, 1868). The introduction of air-brakes contributed to the reduction of the large numbers of harrowing accidents of the period. "Having disposed of the general details, I proceed to call the attention of the Department to the necessity of emigrant trains being provided (as other passenger trains are) with Miller couplings, whereby the danger from re-crossing from one car to another, would, in a great measure, be avoided. The emigrants cannot, and indeed will not, be kept still, and the opening of nearly two feet between the cars is attended with very great danger" (Carleton Place, December 31, 1881, S.p., 11, 1882).

this Western Traffic, and under similar arrangements, we shall be able to transport from other districts of the Mississippi, their produce for manufacture in the New England States, and also that for export to Europe.[1]

The effectiveness of the trunk railways in competing for western traffic in spite of numerous improvements was not striking. John Rose, commissioner of public works, in his report, dated February 9, 1860, gave the following returns of freight carried eastward by them in 1859:

The Welland Railway carried (chiefly grain)...		14,713 Tons
The Great Western do. do:—		
Through freight to Suspension Bridge	22,700	
do. to Toronto 8,717 and		
Buffalo 2,984..................	11,701	34,401 do.
The Northern Railway to Toronto through....		24,897 Tons
The Grand Trunk:		
Through and local to Montreal.....	55,763	
Of which was carried by Northern R.R. and delivered to Grand Trunk at Toronto, already entered above	12,778	42,985 do.
Grand Trunk, brought to and passing Montreal not included in the foregoing........................		23,913 Tons
Buffalo and Lake Huron Railway, to Buffalo; Foreign, 4500 tons and Local, 51,800.................		56,300 do.
Total Tonnage of Freight eastward carried by Rail...............................		197,209 do.

And yet the arrivals of Grain at the two ports of Buffalo and Oswego alone, have during the last 5 years, averaged 1,313,277 barrels of flour and 27,527,088 bushels of grain, while the average shipments from Canadian Ports Seaward have been but 205,821 barrels and 672,625 bushels.

Even from Toronto, of shipments of 63,627 barrels of flour, 805,224 bushels of wheat and 167,364 bushels of barley, only 19,715 barrels of flour and 21,691 bushels of wheat (2 per cent.) went to Montreal and Quebec, the remainder going to Oswego and American ports. "The entire shipments by sea from Canada 1859 were only 140,235 bbls. flour, 58,029 bus. wheat, 439,328 bus. other grain."[2]

---

[1]See T. B. Veblen, "The price of wheat since 1867" (*Journal of Political Economy*, I, 67 *ff.*).
[2]*S.p.*, 11, 1860.

Instead of becoming supplementary to the canals the railways were becoming competitive. The report of 1871 of the canal commission stated: "The Grand Trunk railway has proved a very important competitor for the trade of the St. Lawrence. Flour appears to have found its way very largely by rail but the corn and wheat and bulky products go by canal." Tonnage passing through the Welland Canal between American ports suggested that the railways were also competing for bulky products. Vegetable food increased .08 per cent. in 1870, 13.46 in 1871, and decreased 6.62 in 1872, and heavy goods increased 1.20 in 1870, 5.32 in 1871, and decreased 18.88 in 1872. It was concluded that:

> The quantity carried by the railways has increased at a greater ratio than the quantities carried by canal. This greater ratio of increase may be, and doubtless is, in some measures due to the increased local trade taken at way stations, but it is also largely and mainly due to the increasing share the railways have obtained of the through business.[1]

"Flour, animal food, and such other kinds of freight as either require to be conveyed speedily to market or the value of which will bear higher transport rates, are now frequently carried by rail."[2]

Not only was competition with canals becoming more effective but also with marginal through routes by rail and water. The low rates of grain freights on the western lakes following cut-throat competition from the trunk-line railways, especially "the shorter and more southern lines",[3] eliminated the small class of vessels and the relatively inefficient routes. For example, Collingwood as the terminus of the Northern Railway, became the terminus also of a tri-weekly line of steamers to ports on Lake Michigan and a weekly line to

---

[1]S.p., 4, 1873. The decline in tonnage in the inland trade between Canada and the United States was attributed to the development of traffic on through lines crossing the boundary (S.p., 5, 1874).

[2]S.p., 6, 1873. "The extraordinary growth and development of railways, the constantly improving nature of their construction and equipment, and the fact that they are available all the year around, while the waterways of Canada are closed during three or four months of every year, are of course altogether in their favour, while their great comparative speed must secure them the preference on the part of passengers, and for the conveyance of goods whose value is high in proportion to their weight. Even the bulkier and less valuable goods, under some circumstances, choose the railway channel" (S.p., 11, 1885).

[3]S.p., 6, 1877.

Green Bay, and the development of traffic for trans-shipment to Toronto was rapid. A memorial of the mayor and corporation of the Town of Collingwood dated December 15, 1862, reported that trade at Collingwood in 1861 "assumed the gigantic proportions of over two and a half millions of dollars" and protested against the reduction of Collingwood to the position of an outport of Toronto.[1] In 1870 it was described as a town of 2,000 or 3,000 people with steam saw-mills and huge rafts of lumber "and a grain elevator which lifts out of steam barges the corn from Chicago, weighs it, and pours it into railway freight waggons to be hurried down to Toronto, and there turned into bread or whiskey, without a hand touching it in all its transportations or transformation."[2] In 1878 it was reported that: "Vessels drawing 11 feet of water can enter this port. But the increase in the draft of vessels in the Lake Superior trade makes this depth insufficient—14 feet being the depth now required."[3] Similarly Goderich was the terminus of the Buffalo and Lake Huron Railway Company. This company "erected a grain elevator and extension freight sheds."

> They further engaged a line of propellors to run between Chicago and Goderich, and made the necessary arrangements for transporting southwards, by railway, the grain and other freights, thus brought to the port. . . . Within the past few years, the line of propellors above referred to have been discontinued, and that portion of the American trade which for a time passed through Goderich for the east, now finds its way by Sarnia or other channels.[4]

Even in most advantageous circumstances Canadian through lines suffered with the weakness of the St. Lawrence route because of its inability to attract the highly remunerative inbound traffic. Successful competition for bulky raw materials with low freight rates was handicapped by the effectiveness of New York and American roads in attracting manufactured products.

---

[1] *S.p.*, 40, 1863.
[2] G. M. Grant, *Ocean to ocean* (Toronto, 1873), 12-13.
[3] *S.p.*, 8, 1879.
[4] *S.p.*, 49, 1870. At Trenton only boats of 7 feet draught could approach the elevators and of 10 feet the saw-mills (*S.p.*, 6, 1877).

2

Local Lines

The weakness of the competitive position of the canals and railways in attracting through traffic was offset in part by the development of local traffic.[1] Through lines developed traffic in the immediate vicinity and provided bases for the growth of feeders to outlying territory. Losses sustained on through traffic strengthened the policy of developing local traffic. The abrogation of the Reciprocity Treaty in 1866 and the consequent decline of through traffic were powerful incentives to the construction of feeders. Moreover, the ambitions of numerous ports, which had flourished with the dominance of transport by water, to take advantage of the possibilities of transport by rail, and of inland centres, anxious to link up with new territory and the waterways, were realized in the construction of feeders through the assistance of municipal loan funds. Unfortunately the railway was destined to dominate over water-transport[2] in the handling of traffic. For example, Port Stanley was regarded in 1853 "as one of the most important ports in the western part of the province".[3] The completion

---

[1]"The past year [*1885*] has been very severe on all classes of railway property, caused by the severe competition entered into by some of the railway managers on lines leading to and from Chicago and other western points. One of the chief causes that has brought about the ruinous competition has been owing to the numerous fast freight lines established upon the same roads, the agents of the same company cutting rates against each other.

Grain has been carried from Chicago to New York for 10 cents per 100 pounds, a distance of 983 miles, the emigrant rate from Philadelphia and New York to Chicago and intermediate points being $1, and from New York to Hamilton first-class passengers have been carried at $4.40, a distance of 487 miles.

Although the through traffic has been carried at a serious loss, the local rates have been well sustained at paying rates.

Owing to the heavy losses sustained by carrying through freight, railway Managers have been compelled to cut down the wages of the employees, although the volume of traffic shows an increase.

At a late meeting of the pool managers of the through lines, rates have been established on a paying basis, the roads already showing an increase, in the mileage earnings.

All railway supplies, including coals, have ruled exceedingly low during the year. . . . " (*S.p.*, 10, 1886).

[2]The railways displaced navigation on small rivers—the line from Fort Erie to Stratford destroying navigation on the Grand River and from Port Hope to Lindsay crippling navigation through the Lindsay lock.

[3]*S.p.*, 49, 1870. In 1868 imports over the line included 510 tons of iron, 2,196 tons of coal, 21,009 barrels of salt, 1,080 tons of sundries, and exports: 196,250 bushels of peas, 80,935 bushels of wheat, 143,173 bushels of barley. In 1877, 35,000 tons of coal were imported and 4,000,000 bushels of grain exported (*S.p.*, 8, 1879).

of a railway to London (24 miles) in October, 1856, to handle "the rapidly increasing trade of this district" proved unsuccessful and "the bulk of the exports were carried by the Great Western Railway so that the Port Stanley line now acts merely as an outlet for the overflow of traffic of the Main Trunk line."

Various feeders served to support through lines in western Ontario. In 1858 a road was completed from London to St. Mary's and in 1875 from London to Wingham. A line from Brantford to Tillsonburg was completed in 1878. The metropolitan area of Toronto and Hamilton was supported by various lines. Railroads were built from Toronto to Coboconk in 1872, to Jackson's Point in 1877, to St. Thomas in 1879, and to Perth in 1884. Partly as an attempt to link up lines converging on Lake Ontario, and possibly reflecting the effects of the deepening of the Welland Canal, a road was built from Port Dover to Wiarton in 1882. Ports along the north shore attempted to maintain control of their respective hinterlands. Cobourg supported a line to Peterborough which was completed in 1854 and later extended to the Marmora Iron Mines. Port Hope, which had been at an early date the outlet for an extensive wheat-growing area, was guaranteed control over the interior by the construction of the Port Hope and Lindsay Railway (43 miles) completed December 30, 1857. This line was extended to Beaverton in January, 1871, and to Midland in 1875. Lines were built from Whitby to Port Perry and to Lindsay in 1877, from Belleville to Peterborough in 1879, from Kingston to Renfrew, and from Napanee to Tamworth and Tweed in 1884.

In Quebec the large centres along the St. Lawrence developed railroads to their respective hinterlands. A branch from near Arthabaska to opposite Three Rivers was completed in 1865, a line from Quebec to Sherbrooke in 1881, and from Montreal to Sorel in 1882. Numerous short lines radiated from Montreal and extended throughout the territory between Montreal and Sherbrooke. To gain control of prospective traffic from the west, Quebec City supported the north shore road to Montreal, completed in 1879 to join with the road to Hull, completed in 1877.[1]

The results of the expansion of railroads were shown more clearly in statistics of general growth and improvement. In 1860, 16 railway companies[2] operated 1,880 miles in the Province of Canada and 227 miles in the United States. These railways had 384 locomotives (Grand Trunk Railway, 217). Wood was used as fuel and the rails were of iron. Employees totalled 6,606. In a mileage of 1,974, costing with equipment $97,179,641, the government had given assistance of $20,246,247. Earnings on 2,030 miles in 1860 totalled $6,722,666 and expenses $5,675,511. Passengers carried totalled 1,825,755 and freight 1,459,446 tons. The average speed of express trains was 24.3 miles. In 1875-6, 37 railways operated 5,157 miles (228 miles in the United States). Except for 79 miles of double track in the Great Western, all were single track, and 2,373 miles were laid with steel and 2,758 miles with iron. Equipment included 1,000 locomotives, 773 passenger cars, and 13,647 box-freight and cattle cars. Total paid-up capital was $333,886,047 of which $60,283,026 were contributed by the dominion. Freight carried totalled 6,331,757 tons and passengers 5,544,814. Earnings were $19,358,084 and cost of operations $15,802,721. The through lines joined up the principal cities with American lines and followed closely the River St. Lawrence—the exceptions being lines to Ottawa and to Pembroke. In 1883-4[3] receipts had increased to

---

[1]This line provided a 10-hour service between Quebec and Ottawa (*S.p.*, 4, 1879). See Reports of the commissioners of the Quebec, Montreal, Ottawa, and Occidental Railway, *S.p.*, *Que.*

[2]*S.p.*, 10, 1896.

[3]"The securities of all the railways have been very much enhanced in value since my last report, and the Great Western Railway Company, owing to the increased traffic and rates of freight combined, with the low price of all railway supplies, both raw and manufactured, and the very low price of steam coal (during the first two years) for locomotive running, have enabled the Directors to meet all their engagements, including the interest on the bonded debt and preference stock of the railway, in addition to providing for the past due interest upon their preference stock, also providing for a small dividend upon the ordinary stock of the Company, a desirable state of affairs that they have not been able to accomplish for years past" . . . December, 1880 (*S.p.*, 12, 1880-1). At an earlier date (1868) the Great Western had found it necessary to ask for relief from a loan of £583,000 obtained from the government in 1860 and totalling with interest £220,000. It was urged that after paying dividends of 6 per cent. from 1854 to 1858 they were forced, as a result of competition from the Grand

$33,422,204. Mileage had increased to 7,530. Consolidation of connecting lines improved the efficiency of the railroads and provided a basis for expansion to new territory.[1]

> This strong desire on the part of the leading railway interests for absorption, consolidation and extension, has probably done more than anything else, during the past few years, towards increasing the railway mileage throughout the country, and thus developing the resources of remote districts, which would otherwise have remained isolated from railways and their civilizing influences.

3

Communications[2]

Construction of railways, especially between the important cities, was accompanied by a parallel growth of the telegraph[3] and by a marked expansion of postal facilities. By the end of the period postal facilities had been unified throughout Canada. They constituted an index of increasing efficiency in promoting the dissemination of information, of increasing business activity, and of general improvement in education. In 1860 it was noted that the railways permitted punctual and regular delivery of mails:

> ... and the regular delivery secured at all the principal points, by a description of conveyance but little influenced by the variations of weather or of the seasons, as a matter of course greatly facilitate the observance of punctuality in the transport

Trunk built at a distance of 20 miles between Toronto and Guelph, to lower the rate to 3 per cent. in 1859, to zero in the 3 following years and an average of 2 per cent. in the 9 years preceding 1867. Incidentally the plea was disallowed (*S.p.*, 7, 1869).

[1]*S.p.*, 11, 1885. On the problem of rates see *Journals of the house of commons*, 1883; also *S.p.*, 8a, 1888, app. 1. Through traffic was carried at low competitive rates.

[2]See Reports of the postmaster-general, *S.p.*; also J. R. Robertson, *Landmarks of Toronto*, series 6 (Toronto, 1914), 49-99; E. P. Prentice, "History of Canadian telegraphy" (*Canada, an encyclopedia*, VI, 530-536); W. White, "The postal service of Canada" (*ibid.*, 516-527); W. Smith, *The history of the post office in British North America, 1639-1870.*

[3]The Montreal Telegraph Company under Sir Hugh Allan expanded rapidly and in 1875 had in operation 20,000 miles of wire, 1,400 offices, and 2,000 employees. In 1874 about 2,000,000 messages were transmitted. In 1881 the company amalgamated with the Great North Western Telegraph Company and at that date had 20,479 miles of wire, 1,507 offices, 2,625 instruments, and employed 2,337 persons. Lines extended from Sackville, N.B., to Detroit, from Portland to Montreal, and Montreal to Oswego, from Toronto to Buffalo "and to the most northerly boundaries of Ontario".

of the Mails over the country Post Routes, and lead to a comparative regularity in Mail Service generally, not attainable in former years.[1]

The services on the upper lakes were improved with railway connections and in 1865:

Two trips instead of one are now being performed by the Mail steamboats between Collingwood and Sault Ste. Marie, during navigation, and additional trips between the Sault and Fort William, Lake Superior; the whole equivalent to 20,700 miles of additional service per season. A winter service has also been established between Fort William and the nearest United States Post Office at the head of Lake Superior.[2]

In 1870 mail travel was extended up the Ottawa to Lake Temiscaming and Lake Nipissing.[3]

The post office became more efficient partly as a result of improved urban transport.[4] In 1860:

The experiment of placing Street Letter Boxes in our cities for the reception of letters, has been commenced at Toronto, and with very encouraging results as to the extent to which the number of letters posted in these boxes would appear to demonstrate their usefulness. These Pillar Boxes are visited, at least twice each day, at suitable hours, by Post Office Messengers, in order to convey the letters deposited in them to the Post Office.

In 1866 the system was extended to Montreal.[5] In 1871, following the example of the United States, post-cards were introduced.

These post cards will be sold at one cent each, and may be posted for any address within the Dominion—and will be conveyed to destination, and be delivered in like manner with letters—the one cent covering the cost both of the card and of postage. They may be used for any communication, which can advantageously be written and sent by such a medium.[6]

Free delivery by letter-carriers was begun at Montreal on October 1, 1874, at Toronto on March 1, 1875, at Quebec on April 1, 1875, at Ottawa on May 1, 1875, at Hamilton on May 1, 1875, at St. John, N.B., on June 1, 1875, at Halifax

[1] *S.p.*, 6, 1860.
[2] *S.p.*, 2, 1866; also D. McKellar, "History of the post office and early mail service" (Thunder Bay Historical Society *annual report*, 1912-13).
[3] *S.p.*, 2, 1871.
[4] *S.p.*, 6, 1860.
[5] *S.p.*, 2, 1866.
[6] *S.p.*, 2, 1871.

on July 1, 1875,[1] at London on April 24, 1876. "Since its establishment the number of letters and papers delivered by carriers has more than doubled."[2]

> Large numbers of letters and papers which, under the old system would have either remained in the Post Office for several days, until called for, or have failed in delivery altogether, are now promptly delivered at their addresses . . . the facilities for the interchange of local correspondence notably increased, a great amount of travel to and from the Post Office has been saved to the public, errors in delivery arising from the similarity of names much diminished, and the delivery service generally essentially improved.[3]

The system was made more efficient by the enactment of legislation in 1875 adopting "the principle of compulsory prepayment in respect to all letters, newspapers[4] and other mailable matter passing by post within the Dominion, and [reducing] the charges on newspapers, periodicals and miscellaneous articles".[5]

Registered letters also increased in importance and reached a total of 1,100,000 in 1871. The steady increase caused "great pressure on the points where correspondence centres in the course of conveyance such as the travelling post offices, the city post offices and principal country distributing offices". In 1873 in Ontario and Quebec registered letters increased 16 per cent.[6]

---

[1]*S.p.*, 3, 1875.
[2]*S.p.*, 3, 1877.
[3]*S.p.*, 4, 1876.
[4]The rise of the newspaper was closely dependent on expansion of postal facilities, improved educational facilities, and the growth of advertising. Paper mills were a partial index of development. The Don Valley Paper Mills were established prior to 1850. To these the Provincial Paper Mills were added at Georgetown in 1853 (enlarged 1858), the mills of Angus Logan and Company on Magog River about 1859, and the Riordon Mills at St. Catharines in 1863 and at Meritton in 1867. The number of paper mills totalled 10 (5 in each province) in 1851, 8 in 1861, 19 in 1871 (12 in Ontario), and 36 in 1881. In the latter year capital employed totalled $237,950; employees, 1,520; value of raw material, $1,409,429; value of finished product, $2,446,693. Wood was relatively unimportant as a source of raw material. The first soda pulp mill was installed at Windsor Mills in 1864 and was followed by the introduction of wood pulp at Meritton in 1869. In 1881 5 pulp mills employed a capital of $92,000, and 68 men and produced finished products valued at $63,300. The first sulphite mill was built in 1886. See *Canada an encyclopedia*, V, 117 *ff.*; also N. Reich, *The pulp and paper industry in Canada* (McGill University economic studies, 1926, no. 7).
[5]*S.p.*, 4, 1876.
[6]*S.p.*, 2, 1871; *S.p.*, 5, 1873. In 1868 Canada had 3,638 offices handling 18,100,000 letters and in 1872, 4,135 offices handling 30,600,000 letters and cards and 24,400,000 newspapers.

Ocean mails were speeded up with the construction of railroads, and in 1860 with the completion of the Grand Trunk to Rivière du Loup, arrangements were concluded with the American government for handling closed mails between Liverpool and Cork and Detroit and Chicago.[1] European connections were further improved with the reduction of the letter-rate between Canada and the United Kingdom to 5 cents in 1876 and the exchange of closed mails with Germany in the same year.[2]   With Canadian membership in the general postal union, letter-postage to Europe was made uniform at 5 cents per half ounce[3] after July 1, 1878.

[1]*S.p.*, 16, 1861.   On August 12, 1863, the Grand Trunk arranged to undertake one daily mail service each way between Toronto and Quebec, Toronto and Sarnia, and St. Mary's and London, Quebec and Rivière du Loup, and Richmond to the boundary line at $60.00 per mile per year (*S.p.*, 1, 1864).

[2]*S.p.*, 4, 1876.

[3]*S.p.*, 4, 1879.

LUMBER[1]

1

The Decline of the Timber Trade and the Growth of the Lumber Industry

Export trade had concentrated on lumber—"the peculiarly characteristic industry of Canada"—during the preceding period chiefly because of the accessibility of pine forests to the St. Lawrence and its tributaries and of the ease with which soft woods could be floated to Quebec. Timber, in a sense, supplied its own methods of conveyance to Quebec, and with its support to ship-building, to the British market. Revolution in transport had far-reaching effects on the industry and on the trade. The decline of wooden ship-building was responsible for increase in costs of transport to old markets and for decline in costs of transport to new and more distant markets to which the wooden vessel was forced by the iron steamship. New markets in South American countries and the expansion of the home market and of the American market following the con-

---

[1]See G. H. Perry, *The staple trade of Canada* (Ottawa, 1862); W. Quinn, *Rapport sur le commerce des bois* (Quebec, 1861); A. R. M. Lower, "The timber trade in Canada" (Doctorate thesis, Harvard University); J. E. Defebaugh, *History of the lumber industry of America* (Chicago, 1906), I; *Handbook of Canada* (Toronto, 1897), 297-305; J. E. Middleton and F. Landon, *The Province of Ontario, 1615-1927*, **484-504**; T. W. Poole, *A sketch of the early settlement and subsequent progress of the Town of Peterborough and of each township in the County of Peterborough* (Peterborough, 1867); *History of the County of Peterborough, Ontario* (Toronto, 1884); Reports of the commissioner of crown lands, *S.p., Ont.* and *Que.* See also names of licensees of timber limits, for example, February 19, 1877, *S.p., Ont.*, 45, 1877; also *S.p., Que.*, 18, 1876. Annual production of timber after 1867 in Quebec, *S.p., Que.*, 4, 1882-3; Forestry report, *S.p., Ont.*, 4, 1885; First annual report by J. B. Charleson—respecting lumber operations in the woods in 1887-8, *S.p., Que.*, 114, 1889. On July 17, 1868, a 12-inch limit was fixed on pine logs. See Regulations from July 1, 1867, to date fixing and determining the minimum diameter of the trees which license holders may cut upon crown lands, *S.p., Que.*, 78, 1904; Statement showing number of acres of crown lands alienated by sales and free grants July 1, 1867, to June 30, 1912 and comparative statement of the amounts collected each year since 1867—timber dues, ground rent, timber limits, sales, *etc.*, *S.p., Que.*, 5, 1913; Forestry notes in connection with stumpage dues in Quebec, *S.p., Que.*, 5, 1917; Report of the select committee on culling timber, *J. h. c.*, VIII, 1874, app. 1; *Canada Lumberman and Woodworker* (Toronto, 1880—); A. R. M. Lower, "The trade in square timber" (*Contributions to Canadian Economics*, VI).

struction of railways created demands for sawn lumber. Decline of American home supplies, rapid growth of population in the eastern states, and the Reciprocity Treaty were followed by an increase in exports of planks and boards to the United States from $1,866,712 in 1854 to $5,043,367 in 1867. Increasing inaccessibility of the larger timber hastened the decline of the trade in square timber to Great Britain and contributed to the increasing importance of sawn lumber obtained from smaller trees. In 1867 total exports of forest products ·to the United States were $6,831,252 and to Great Britain, $6,889,783. The rise in importance of the steamship and of Montreal as a shipping port, and the construction of railroads, improved the market for sawn lumber, especially deals in Great Britain, and hastened the development of the lumber industry in Canada as contrasted with the decline of the timber trade. Canals, railways, and the introduction of steam hastened the expansion of the industry from the Ottawa valley and the north shore of Lake Ontario to Muskoka and Georgian Bay and to the tributaries of the lower St. Lawrence. Spruce became increasingly important in supplementing pine. The industrial revolution and its effects on the lumber industry were of first importance in weakening the supremacy of the St. Lawrence and its dependence on timber and wooden ships.

> The products of the forest are second only to those of agriculture in importance, and are at least their equal in value. The exports in 1853 amounted to £2,355,255, to which may be added the value of the ships built at Quebec, being £620,187. Of the timber, £1,682,125 was exported to Great Britain, £11,000 to the British Colonies, and £652,544 to the United States. The white and red pine, oak and elm, form the most important items in this amount. The export of pot and pearl ashes[1] was £157,000, and of furs and skins £32,000. The timber exported, however, forms a very small proportion of the forest-wealth, as the home consumption, for domestic purposes, for building, and for the construction of wharves, railways, fences, etc., is valued at considerably more than £2,000,000, and this would give the total value of the produce of the forest in 1853 at about £4,532,000. . . .
>
> In sawed lumber the increase has been very great, as appears by a comparison of the quantities exported during the

---

[1]Potash was an important by-product of settlement, especially in the clearing of the forest.

last three years. Of this the year 1851 produced 120,175,560 feet, and 1853, 218,480,000 feet, and added to eight millions for the broken item of planks and deal ends, and 38,740,168 cubic feet of squared timber, the total would be 727,188,010 feet of board measure, which is equal to 61,265,667 cubic feet of timber.[1]

2

The Ottawa Valley

(i)

Facilities for transport

The Ottawa valley and the north shore of Lake Ontario[2] continued to be of first importance. Improved facilities for transport lowered the cost of moving supplies to the areas producing lumber and encouraged expansion of the industry. On the Ottawa, St. Anne Lock with 5 feet of water gave access to small steamers as far as Carillon, and a broad gauge railway between the latter point and Grenville[3] was completed in 1854 to connect with steamers to Ottawa. Above the Chaudière Falls, small steamers proceeded to Chats Falls to connect by *the Aboriginal railroad* with steamers above the falls to Portage-du-Fort: "Route from Montreal to Bytown,[4] by steamer, daily, 129 miles; Bytown to Aylmer, by land, 9 miles; Aylmer to Sand Point, by steamer, 45 miles; Sand Point to Castleford, by steamer, 8 miles; Castleford to Portage-du-Fort, 9 miles; Portage-du Fort to Pembroke, by land and water, 33 miles". Railway lines from the St.

---

[1] J. S. Hogan, |Canada, an essay, 19, 46-7, 96. For a description of lumber operations on the Ottawa, see J. Fraser, *Shanty, forest and river life in the backwoods of Canada* (Montreal, 1883), *passim;* also J. M. Mitchell, *Ottawa County its resources and capabilities* (Ottawa, 1882); J. G. Kohl, *Travels in Canada,* I, 139 *ff.;* H. B. Small, *The resources of the Ottawa district* (Ottawa, 1872); J. L. Gourlay, *History of the Ottawa valley* (1896); *Lumber trade of the Ottawa valley* (Ottawa, 1872); *Picturesque Canada,* I, 163-239; G. Thompson, *Up to date* (n.p., 1895); A. H. D. Ross, *Ottawa past and present* (Toronto, 1927); Greenough, *Canadian folk life and folk lore* (New York, 1897).

[2] See Adam Shortt, "Down the St. Lawrence on a timber raft" (*Queen's Quarterly,* July, 1902); W. A. Langton, *Early days in Upper Canada* (Toronto, 1926); W. A. Foster, *Canada first* (Toronto, 1890), 172-3; G. Thompson, *Up to date, passim.*

[3] R. R. Brown, "The Carillon and Grenville Railway" (Railway and Locomotive Historical Society *bulletin,* no. 23, 29-32).

[4] Report—on improvement of Ottawa River navigation, *J.h.c.,* 1869, app. 9.

Lawrence were completed from Prescott to Ottawa[1] in 1854 and from Brockville to Almonte with a branch to Perth in 1859 and to Sand Point in 1867. This line reached Pembroke in 1869 and Ottawa from Carleton Place in 1870. Sand Point, Renfrew, and Pembroke were linked up in 1882.

Lower cost of transportation of supplies hastened the exhaustion of the larger trees and the decline of the trade in square timber and stimulated the sawn lumber industry: It gave access to new and wider markets. In 1855 the Ottawa sent about 25,000,000 cubic feet of timber, 850,000 deals and planks, and quantities of staves and other lumber to Europe. "The square timber trade reached its height in 1877, and owing chiefly to the disappearance of the supply of timber fit for squaring, has declined steadily since that date."[2]

> In 1861 waney pine was made for the first time, this wood being left with a wane of from three to six inches on the corners, so avoiding the excessive waste of wood resulting from hewing the timber exactly square. Previous to this, the timber was square and of large average, beautifully hewn by the lumbermen in the woods; but board (waney) pine, that is, short logs of large girth, were sent down the drives with the other timber, and soon found their way into the market. Being cut from the lower part of the tree accounted for the waney character of the logs, but the quality of the timber was excellent. It gradually almost altogether supplanted square pine.[3]

In 1861, 15,731,000 cubic feet of square timber and 6,735,000 cubic feet of waney were exported. Saw-logs were less wasteful than waney timber and involved less danger from fire[4] and by 1873 "the very large trade of the Ottawa valley

---

[1]See Walter Shanly, *Report on the location, surveys and estimates of the Bytown and Prescott Railroad* (Bytown, 1851) for a description of the possibilities of the road in the export of sawn lumber to the United States.

[2]Report of H. R. Macmillan, *S.p.*, 25, 1912. In 1851 Quebec reached its peak in the largest quantity of timber for shipment—the Hon. John Egan alone having 31 rafts of 75,000 to 100,000 cubic feet each. Another estimate gives 20,032,520 cubic feet in 1864 as the peak of white pine.

[3]*S.p.*, 19, 1911.

[4]"In making square pine, the waste of timber is generally estimated at one-fourth of the whole, and the best part of the tree, too, that part which in sawlogs gives the splendid broad deals, for which Canada is famous. As it is not every tree that is sound enough for square timber, many a pine is cut down and left to rot. There may be something wrong about the heart or in the length, that would not have prevented it from being turned into saw logs, but won't do for square timber, and so it is condemned. Chips made in squaring trees considerably

is now nearly equally divided between the square timber and sawn-log interests."[1] In 1870 the Hull slide handled 213,143 saw-logs and the Gatineau booms, 496,099 saw-logs; and in 1871 the Chaudière slide handled 353,488 pieces of square timber. In 1880 it was stated that "a few years ago, from 200,000 to 300,000 saw logs constituted the arrivals of that class of timber at this city, in a season; now there are between one and two millions of pieces annually passing through the Deschenes Lake, and the Gatineau River also shows a very heavy increase in this branch of the lumber trade."[2]

(ii)

Problems of water-supply

The problems of water-supply, contributed to the difficulties of the trade in square timber. In 1872 it was stated:

> The clearances effected by settlers and a more extensive system of drainage than existed in past years, have done much to cause extremes in high and low water; this, taken in connection with the fact that the operations of the lumbermen are gradually being extended into the interior, leaves it uncertain whether one or more seasons will be consumed in taking timber and saw logs to their destination.[3]

In 1881 "the lower limits have been pretty much stripped of the bulk of the most valuable timber, supplies have largely to be drawn from the remote forests at the head waters of the Temiscamingue and Kippawa regions."[4] Clearing of the land caused the water to drain off earlier in the spring and more rapid changes in the level of the water, while the increasing distances from which the logs were brought meant

increase the danger of fire. In summer they get very dry and inflammable, and the way in which they are disposed in straight lines, thirty, forty, and fifty feet long, like trains of gun-powder, appears well calculated for spreading the flames through the dead pine leaves, dry branches and moss" (*S.p.*, 9, 1878).

[1]*S.p.*, 2, 1874. Lumber interests found it increasingly difficult to engage in the trade in square timber and in the saw-log industry and rapidly shifted toward the latter, finding it more profitable to take out trees suitable for square timber as saw-logs.

[2]*S.p.*, 6, 1881.

[3]*S.p.*, 6, 1873.

[4]*S.p.*, 7, 1882. See A. Buies, *L'Outaouais supérieur* (Quebec, 1889); C. C. Fair, *The Lake Temiscamingue district* (Toronto, 1893); *The Ottawa region* (Quebec, 1908); A. Pelland, *Le Temiscamingue* (Quebec, 1910); I. Caron, *Le Temiscamingue l'Abitibi* (Quebec, 1912).

that larger numbers of logs arrived at low water. As early as the sixties the last of the square timber was not down until the middle of September. The spring freshets became less important. In 1879[1] low water retarded the progress of the rafts of square timber on the way to Quebec, and accentuated the dullness of the market, with the result that large rafts were laid up *en route* to be taken down the following season. In 1881 an unusual drought "hung up" thousands of pieces.[2] These tendencies were especially serious for the Quebec timber trade, but in that year even the mills at Ottawa "only ran for half the usual time".

Meanwhile the increase in the production of saw-logs and the rise of the saw-mill industry created new demands for power. "The manufacture of lumber had of late years assumed such proportions at the Chaudière Falls that the dams and works hitherto used to bring the water to the mills there were found insufficient, and on every occurrence of lower water than usual, the operations of the mills were more or less retarded."[3] As a result of unusually low water early in the season of 1868 a dam was built with crib work in the lowest part of the channel leading to the falls, and higher

[1] *S.p.*, 11, 1880.

[2] *S.p.*, 9, 1884. In 1889: "The clearances effected by lumbermen on berths in the Ottawa valley, that have been worked on for a number of years and the opening up of large tracts of country for settlement, have tended to an earlier breaking up of the ice and a more rapid melting of the snow in spring, and, as a consequence, the freshets bring the streams to flood height about the time of the opening of navigation, to be soon followed by a low water pitch, modified only to a limited extent by the reserve waters held in check by the lumbermen through the erection of reservoir dams on the upper reaches of the tributaries" (*S.p.*, 18, 1890).

Driving operations late in the season became tedious and expensive with low water. The railroad became increasingly important with the increasing importance of the saw-mill and the decline of square timber. In 1887 the Canadian Pacific and the Canada Atlantic Railways were reported as formidable competitors of the Ottawa Canals.

	Carried by railways from Ottawa and Hull		Carried by Ottawa Canals	
	1886	1887	1886	1887
Sawn lumber, feet, B.M.	89,923,430	100,369,429	357,132,600	335,094,000
Shingles, M	633	90	6,072	6,732

(*S.p.*, 16a, 1888).

The difficulties were overcome in part by the railroad. "In 1883 came another change in the mode of conveying the timber to market, for in this year a raft of timber was shipped by rail from Mackey's station on the Canadian Pacific Railway and another lot from North Bay on the same line; this timber was thus conveyed to Papineauville, 40 miles below Ottawa, and there rafted and taken to Quebec by the old methods" (*S.p.*, 19, 1911).

[3] *S.p.*, 2, 1870.

parts of the channel were excavated. In addition, stop logs were added on a shallow part of the channel to be taken out in high-water seasons. The Ottawa was brought more directly under the control of the lumber industry.

(iii)

Breakdown of the trade in square timber

The depression of the seventies[1] accentuated the problems of the trade and hastened the breakdown of the organization which had centred on the production and export of square timber.

> In the face of a glutted market we persist in overproduction . . . with a few exceptions, the lumbermen of Canada, as a rule cannot stop their production of timber; they can scarcely curtail it. . . . At every step they must feel their dependence on the will and caprice of others, from the obtaining of timber berths to work upon, the hiring of men, the supplying of provisions, the sending men, stores, and horses hundreds of miles away, into the wilderness, down to the cutting, squaring, hauling, driving, booming, rafting, culling, leading and shipping; and this is why I use the unpalatable expression that they cannot be considered as free agents. Their relations with the advancers of money,[2] the banks, the brokers, the pur-

---

[1]The lumber market in both England and the United States was dull as a result of the depression. Canadian lumber was forced to compete to an increasing extent with the lumber from Michigan and Wisconsin.

[2]"The year's expenditure from the time the first tree has been cut in the fall, until the whole raft has been passed over into the hands of the buyer at Quebec, foots up a heavy sum, all gone in hard cash. There is no business that I know of in which there are so many and such large demands upon the purse as that of the lumber merchant. No wonder, then, he is anxious about the state of the market, which perhaps is the most uncertain and fluctuating of any in the world. A European war, a depression in stocks, a rise or fall in Turkish or Egyptian bonds, a score or more of causes, may so operate as to make or mar a fortune for the lumberman. [*The American Civil War created a depression through its effects on the English market.*] And such is the nature of the business that these gentlemen are not satisfied, like ordinary mortals, with a fair and reasonable profit; no, they expect a bonanza with every recurring season. A few thousands will not do; they look for tens and scores of thousands to stand at the foot of the balance sheet to their credit when the year's business is wound up. And very often, if they cannot get the price they want, they will let their timber lie over for another year, and, if their means can hold out, for yet another, if the market is not to their liking. I have known cases in which the merchants have held on for five years, in the hope that the market would rise to the standard of their lofty expectations. When, finally, they do sell it is often either an avalanche of ruin, or a reflux of enormous profit. The lumbering business is something like Indian life, either a feast or a famine, or, like gold mining, a million or nothing" (J. Fraser, *Shanty, forest and river life in the backwoods of Quebec*, 347-8). On fluctuations in prices see, *Statistical contributions to Canadian economic history* (Toronto, 1931), II; also J. C. Taché, *Sketch of Canada.*

chasers in England, are of such a complicated nature, that it is difficult for them to realize, at any time, what their financial position is; they know they are dependent upon others, they have been so from the beginning, and they continue so, until at last, after long years of harrassing, desperate work, with both body and mind worn out, they find themselves poorer than when they began.

The vested interests gradually lost control:

Between the consumers and the Canadian lumberman stand a few men, the importers of square timber. It is their steam mills that cut up our big square sticks into bits; their interest is directly opposed to our sending timber reduced by us to such dimensions as would suit the consumers, and they oppose strenuously the introduction of our two-inch deals, inch planks, narrow deals, etc. . . . For several years past, some of our most enterprising manufacturers have been sending some cargoes of worked timber to South America, Australia, etc., but we still send the great bulk of our production unmanufactured to England.[1]

(iv)

Saw-mills

The lumber industry was stimulated by cheap water-power, decline in the size of trees, and the increasing market in Canada and the United States for sawn lumber.[2] During the early period, rafts of pine logs were taken from the Gatineau and other limits to be converted into deals at Montmorency near Quebec. In 1862 Mr. G. B. Hall had 6 extensive saw-mills and a pail factory run by power obtained from Montmorency Falls.[3] Mills grew up nearer

[1]H. G. Joly, Report on forestry and forests of Canada, S.p., 9, 1878.

[2]"At one of the leading mills, great baulks of pine were neatly hauled up from the river near the Chaudière Falls, and almost solely by the water power judiciously applied from the Falls they were placed in position on the great saw benches, the process being watched and directed by a foreman so situated that his range of vision took in all that was going on; and I was informed after seeing the sawing done, and the great mass of timber moved by machinery, apparently as easily as a skilled nurse turns over a tiny infant, that a great tree can be converted into joists cut to a given thickness and length at an average of eight minutes per log. Of course there is much refuse from these logs, and men and lads have to be tolerably active in clearing this away in order to prevent impediments and delays. The larger refuse is rapidly converted into water pails by very ingenious machinery. Such as is not available for pails is used by a neighbouring match manufactory, which works up the scraps, except the bark and what adheres to it and the saw dust" (S.p., 12, 1887).

[3]S. L. Spedon, Rambles among the blue-noses (Montreal, 1863), 17. One mill at Montmorency had from 80 to 120 saws and produced from 10,000 to 20,000 tons of sawn lumber per year.

the source of the logs and the Chaudière Falls, with its abundant power and its position at the head of navigation for boats and barges designed to handle lumber, became an important centre. Hamilton's at Hawkesbury and Gilmour and Company at Chelsea rafted deals down to Quebec to be shipped "either wet as floated deals or after being landed and piled as dry floated deals", a practice which disappeared with the emergence of Montreal as an ocean port for steamships and with the growth of the American market. Montreal had the advantage of being nearer the mills that produced pine lumber and deals, and the freight by barge or rail was much less than to Quebec.

The rise of the mills at Ottawa for the production of lumber and deals, particularly following the Reciprocity Treaty, is suggested in the following list.[1]

Bronson and Weston (1853) 175,000 logs and 35,000,000 feet, A. H. Baldwin (1853) 125,000 logs and 25,000,000 feet, J. R. Booth (1858) 28,000,000 ft., Perley and Pattee (1857) 150,000 logs, 35,000,000 ft. and 500,000 ft. of square timber, Levi Young (1854) 20,000,000 ft., E. B. Eddy 40,000,000 ft., Wright Batson and Currier steam mill 20,000,000 ft., Gilmour and Co. 35,000,000 ft., McLaren and Co. 16,000,000 ft.

	1871		
Bronson & Weston	65,000,000 ft.	BM.	
J. R. Booth	70,000,000	"	"
E. B. Eddy & Co	69,000,000	"	"
Perley & Pattee	70,000,000	"	"
Hurdman & Co	56,000,000	"	"
Grier & Co	35,000,000	"	"
Total	365,000,000	"	"

In 1873 McLachlan's Mills at Arnprior produced about 20,000,000 feet annually and Caldwell's Steam Mill at Gillies and McClaren's Water Mills produced about 25,000,000 feet annually. In 1874 the Ottawa district had 24 mills with 100 gang saws and 6 circular saws and a total capacity of 400,000,000 feet.

---

[1]*S.p.*, 65, 1890; H. B. Small, *The resources of the Ottawa district* (Ottawa, 1872); also A. H. D. Ross, *Ottawa past and present*, 156 *ff.*

(v)

Export trade in lumber

The effects of the increasing importance of lumber-mills were shown in the trade from Montreal to South America. Sailing vessels were being forced into longer and less profitable voyages and the opening of the Argentine created a new market for lumber. In 1872, 66 vessels of 30,685 tons cleared for the River Plate carrying 23,721,753 feet of lumber, and 6 vessels of 4,523 tons for Callao carrying 3,115,628 feet.[1] In 1873, 72 vessels of 39,008 tons cleared for River Plate carrying 32,251,758 feet, and "part of Windmill wharf, part of Victoria Pier, part of Commissioners Wharf and the whole of the Hochelaga Wharf was occupied by parties engaged in that business."[2] In 1874 the effects of the depression were evident in a decline in exports of lumber[3] to South America. By 1878 this trade recovered and 20 vessels of 11,013 tons carried 8,680,000 feet in contrast with 10 vessels of 4,387 tons carrying 3,400,000 feet in 1876.[4] A slight decline to 20 vessels of 10,868 tons carrying 8,663,563 feet followed in 1879.[5] The 1873 level was nearly reached in 1884 with an increase of 20 per cent. over the 1883 level to 24,386,378 feet. Sawn lumber exported chiefly to South America increased from 31,457,265 feet in 1884 to 32,162,109 feet in 1885.

Not only were the new countries in South America the purchasers of sawn lumber but also England was gradually being forced to purchase larger quantities of deals. In 1876 lumber merchants of Quebec and Ottawa were reported as turning their attention to Montreal and beginning "to find that it is in every respect convenient and suitable for them to carry on their business".[6] Quebec merchants found it more profitable to ship deals from Montreal than from their own port. Shipments of deals from Montreal to Great Britain increased from 7,991 (St. Petersburg standards) in 1881 to

---

[1]*S.p.*, 8, 1873. The lumber was brought down in barges and piled on the wharves to be dried before shipment, with the result that pressure on wharf accommodation was evident at an early date.

[2]*S.p.*, 4, 1874.

[3]*S.p.*, 5, 1875; *S.p.*, 5, 1876; and *S.p.*, 5, 1877.

[4]*S.p.*, 3, 1879.

[5]*S.p.*, 9, 1880.

[6]*S.p.*, 5, 1877.

22,407 in 1882, to 23,094 in 1883, to 23,367 in 1884, and to 39,393 in 1885. The American market contributed to the expansion of the lumber industry, and in 1872 it was reported that the Chambly Canal[1] was taxed to nearly its full extent "when large quantities of timber passed through it for the American markets. . . . American canal boats and barges . . . come in with cargoes of coal, sugar, molasses, etc. and take return freights of sawed lumber."[2] In 1871 it was estimated that 45 steamers and 251 barges employing about 2,000 men and representing a capital of $1,250,000 were engaged in taking 260,000,000 feet of lumber down the Ottawa.

Exports to the new countries of South America and to the United States to meet the demands for the finished product (sawn lumber) coincided with the shift in the character of exports to old countries, such as Great Britain, from the raw material (square timber) to the semi-manufactured product (deals) and the change in both cases registered the increasing importance of saw-mills, the decline of large trees, the shift from Quebec to Montreal, and the movement of industry toward the supply of raw material.

(vi)

Fluctuations and changes in the industry

Machine industry had numerous repercussions. The lumber industry was subject to numerous fluctuations and these fluctuations reacted in turn on a range[3] of subsidiary

[1]This canal, with 9 locks 118 feet by 23 feet, and 7 feet depth, and the St. Ours lock gave access to Lake Champlain.

[2]*S.p.*, 6, 1873.

[3]"In common with the larger portion of the Ottawa valley, the district is totally unfit for cultivation. The few settlers who farm the land depend entirely upon the lumber business for their bare subsistence. Not only does it afford a ready and high market for the scanty produce of their farms—consisting almost solely of oats and hay (for not one in ten ever has a bushel to sell in a year) . . . but both men and horses obtain steady employment during the winter in the shanties. With all the available resources which they can possibly command, the great majority of them are a poor, hard-working, hand-to-mouth class of people" (J. Fraser, *Shanty, forest and river life in the backwoods of Quebec, 18*). Carleton, Hastings, Lanark, Haliburton, and Renfrew Counties were particularly affected. Hay was also sold from Dundas County. See a reference to a large farm of 500 acres which produced about 1¼ tons per acre of hay valued at $10.00 (J. Croil, *Dundas*, 194-6). In 1871 an extensive sale of timber limits in Muskoka district gave rise to a demand for hay and oats in that area. Lumbering which centred at Parry Sound, at Gore Bay on Manitoulin Island (cedar ties,

industries. The areas of production were changing as it became necessary to move to more distant limits; the quality of the product changed as larger trees were cut out; technique of production and of transport of this bulky commodity were causes of change; the shifting of population to new centres and the rise of industrialism occasioned changes in the areas of demand; and in its dependence on the construction industry it was subject to violent swings in the business cycle. In 1863 it was estimated that the industry in the Ottawa valley employed 15,000 axemen, and 10,000 in other manufacturing establishments, involving an outlay of wages (at the rate of $26.00 a month) of £1,250,000 sterling. The square timber and the saw-log industries consumed in each division 12,000 barrels of pork, 100 tons of sundries, 6,000 tons of hay, 275,000 bushels of oats.[1] In addition, nearly 25,000 men were engaged in manning the fleet of about 800 ships to carry the timber from Quebec to Europe and from other points to the United States. Rapid expansion of the industry was followed by a rise in the prices of agricultural

---

telegraph poles, pavement blocks), and at Spanish River, Thessalon River, and Blind River created a demand for hay and oats from the country tributary to Owen Sound. The serious effects of the depression on the lumber industry of the Ottawa valley in the seventies led to the settlement of the land. "Many of those who in years past looked only for employment, have through lack of it taken up land for themselves, and have settled in various parts of the counties of Ottawa, Pontiac, Renfrew and some have located in the Muskoka district" (*S.p.*, 9, 1879). In 1875 a "large influx of artisans and labourers from the United States" was noted (*S.p.*, 8, 1876). In 1873-4 and 1874-5 extensive lumber operations were accompanied by a large importation of salt pork (*S.p.*, 2, 1876). See H.N.B,, *Manitoulin* (London, 1895).

[1]S. P. Day, *English America*, II, 287-9. In 1870 it was estimated that the Ottawa River produced 250,000,000 feet board measure for the American market and 50,000,000 feet board measure and 18,000,000 cubic feet of square timber for the English market. To produce the lumber for the American market required 5,000 logging men, 2,000 teams, 9,000 sleighs, 2,500 tons of hay, 3,500 barrels of pork, 4,000 barrels of flour, 23,000 pounds of tea, 14,500 pounds of soap, 400,000 pounds of iron chain, and 2,000 men for sawing and shipping (Charles Marshall, *The Canadian dominion*, London, 1871, chapter iv). To get out 150,000 logs or 30,000,000 feet of lumber required 450 men getting out logs, 300 men piling and forwarding, 300 teamsters: and provisions—825 barrels of pork, 900 barrels of flour, 925 bushels of beans, 33,000 bushels of oats, 300 tons of hay, 3,750 gallons of syrup, 7,500 pounds of tea, 1,875 pounds of soap, 1,000 grindstones, 6,000 pounds of tobacco, 900 axes, 60 cross-cut saws, 225 sleighs, 3,750 pounds of rope, 1,500 boom chains, 45 boats, 900 pairs of blankets—costing $54,367. Subsidiary industries expanded to the export basis. It was claimed that, whereas saws were formerly imported from the United States, after 1879 Canadian manufacturers captured the home market and began to export to the woods of Michigan and Wisconsin. Factories producing saws, axes, and knives had an expanding market.

33

produce in the more immediate vicinity and by growth of settlement. On the other hand, the effects of depression were widespread. The depression which began in 1874 was felt with great severity in the Ottawa valley.[1]   Settlement which had been brought into existence in order to support the lumber industry was left stranded with its disappearance.[2]

The decline in the importance of the drive to Quebec with the emergence of the saw-mill displaced the French-Canadian and the skilled timberman and led to the employment of settlers in the vicinity of the mill. A change in the men brought a change of administration. "The old bullying, brute force principle of governing is now about entirely done away with." The skill of cutting, squaring, and driving timber became less important. The cross-cut saw and relatively unskilled labour became increasingly important with the growth of the saw-log industry. Shanty government changed with the appointment of a manager who had "full oversight and charge of all the foremen and men, and is directly responsible to the proprietors for the general running of the concern".[3]

3

The North Shore of Lake Ontario

In other localities than the Ottawa valley similar trends were in evidence. The relatively smaller rivers along the north shore of Lake Ontario favoured the early growth of saw-mills. Lack of water-power hastened the development of steam mills.[4]   Railroads became increasingly important

---

[1]*S.p.*, 8, 1876; *S.p.*, 9, 1878; and *S.p.*, 7, 1878.

[2]See A. R. M. Lower, "The assault on the Laurentian barrier 1850-1870" (*Canadian Historical Review*, X, 1929, 294-307); *Trent watershed survey* (Toronto, 1913).

[3]J. Fraser, *Shanty, forest and river life in the backwoods of Quebec*, 18-38. See also Ralph Connor, *The man from Glengarry* (Toronto, 1901).

[4]The relation of construction of railroads to lumbering on the financial side was emphasized as detrimental to lumbering. It was estimated that returns from fees for cutting timber at ½d. per foot for square timber and 5d. each for logs totalled about $20,000 in 1860. Other returns are suggested in the increase from revenue from the Ottawa trade from $100,998 in 1851 to $219,533 in 1861. Export duties on saw-logs totalled $37,912 in 1869-70. "It will be said that, without the large sums of money derived from the cutting of timber on our Crown Lands, the building of railways could not have been encouraged as it

as a means of importing supplies and of exporting the finished product. With the railroad it became possible for the steam mill[1] to move nearer the timber limits.[2] Railways were built from Lake Ontario to the lumber areas—the line from Whitby to Port Perry in 1877 and from Lindsay to Haliburton in 1878. In the seventies Fenelon Falls had 2 water saw-mills, one producing 8,000,000 to 9,000,000 feet of lumber; Lindsay, on the Scugog River, a saw-mill producing 2,000,000 feet; Port Perry, several mills. In 1874 there were 13 mills north of Kingston, Brockville, and Prescott with a capacity of 106,000,000 feet and 57 mills north of Lake Ontario with a capacity of 285,000,000 feet. In 1885 there were 6 saw-mills on the Otonabee River above Peterborough and, in addition, about 200,000 logs representing about 200,000,000 feet of lumber went down to Rathbun Company at Deseronto, Gilmour and Company at Trenton,[3] Fowles at Hastings,

---

has been. Nothing can contribute to the prosperity of a new country more than a railway carefully located so as to satisfy some great public necessity, without calling for sacrifices beyond the forces of the country; but, while looking forward to the benefit to be derived from it, the cost must not be forgotten. We have been sacrificing our forests for the sake of our railways.

So far as mere power is concerned, it seldom happens that a Government can control any trade, as completely as our Provincial Governments can control the timber trade, without laying itself open to the charge of undue interference with business. In this case, the Governments themselves are parties to the trade, since they are the owners, and the sellers of the standing timber" (*S.p.*, 9, 1878).

[1] The complaints and investigating committees which followed the dumping of great quantities of sawdust and refuse in the rivers and the consequent hindrance to navigation provided an additional stimulus to the introduction of steam mills. See Report of the commission appointed to enquire into the condition of navigable streams, *S.p.*, 29, 1873; *S.p.*, 12, 1887; and *S.p.*, 65, 1890. According to the latest report it was estimated that 12,500 cubic yards of sawdust were deposited in the Ottawa River by the Chaudière Mills annually in addition to slabs broken up into refuse by "hogging" machines. See Report . . . extent and effect upon the Ottawa River of the deposit therein of sawdust and other refuse, *Journals of the senate*, 1888, app. 2.

[2] For example, in the early eighties a mill was built at Clyde Forks near Ottawa, and lumber, produced at the rate of about 60,000 feet daily, was shipped over a switch on the railway.

[3] In 1873 Gilmour and Company's Mill was described as "one of the finest steam mills probably in the Dominion" with 14,000,000 feet annually. This mill had 5 gates or gangs of saws, double and single edging and splitting and cutting saws, lath machine, and planing machine, employed over 100 men and had a capacity of 100,000 to 110,000 feet every 24 hours (1863). Another steam saw-mill of Mr. Sandford Baker of Trenton had 4 gangs (slabber, stock gang, Yankee gang, and single) in all 75 upright saws, a butting table, edging machine, and lath mill. In 12 hours its capacity was 340 18-inch logs, or 60,000 feet, and 20,000 lath. It employed from 60 to 70 hands and cut from April 20 to November 20 about 10,000,000 feet (*S.p.*, 65, 1890). In 1881 Harwood had 2 large saw-mills.

and Ulyott at Harwood.   Square timber and saw-logs were
produced in these districts and exports of sawn lumber to
the American market became increasingly important.[1]   The
railroads from Toronto and Hamilton to Collingwood and
Meaford (1872), Allandale and Gravenhurst (1875), and
Barrie and Midland (1876) were promoted largely in relation
to lumbering.   The construction boom in the fifties and the
growth of the larger cities, especially in the early eighties,
were responsible for a marked increase in local demand.
New steam mills came into existence and at Belle Ewart on
Lake Simcoe steam mills produced about 40,000,000 feet
annually in the early seventies.   North Simcoe had 49 mills
with a capacity of 182,000,000 feet of which 140,000,000 feet
were sent to Toronto.   Following the opening of the Muskoka
district in 1871, 2 steam saw-mills were built on the Muskoka
River and 4 water mills.   In 1874 Georgian Bay had 7 mills
producing for American and Canadian markets.   In addition
to mills supplying the local market, the American market,
and other export markets, from territory on Georgian Bay[2]
tributary to the Lake Ontario and St. Lawrence routes,
Essex, Norfolk, and Elgin Counties became exporters of logs
to the United States.[3]

[1]*S.p.*, 6, 1877.   In 1864 about 5,000,000 cubic feet of square white pine and
500,000 cubic feet of oak and elm were rafted to Quebec from Trenton. About
140,000 logs from the Trent and 40,000 from the Moira and Salmon Rivers were
sawn up for the American market.   Schooners took lumber to Oswego and other
ports and brought back salt, plaster, lime, *etc.*   By the nineties decline was in
evidence in the district.   Writing at Peterborough on November 30, 1892,
regarding the Trent Valley Canal the engineer stated that: "Owing to the
immense country drained, and the country becoming cleared, and the lumbermen's dams (which formerly checked the flow) becoming abandoned, there is a
liability, till some provision is made to counteract it, of the heavy spring freshets
damaging the several structures along the route" (*S.p.*, 9, 1893; also River Trent
and Newcastle navigation and canal works, *J.h.c.*, 1879, app. 3).

Ontario production 1868-1877

Public lands	Saw logs	Square and waney lumber	Total
Pieces............	22,200,816	1,678,831	
Ft. board measure..	3,328,196,600	cu. ft. 87,620,135	
			Bd. ft. 3,838,612,882
Private lands			cu. ft. 119,250,420
Pieces............	3,436,991	559,952	
Ft. board measure..	510,416,282	cu. ft. 31,630,285	

(*S.p.*, *Ont.*, 62, 1879).

[2]J. C. Hamilton, *The Georgian Bay* (Toronto, 1893).

[3]See J. Charlton, *A brief statement of objections to the policy of imposing export
duties upon saw-logs* (Lynedoch, 1869), suggesting the effects of the export duty
of August 15, 1866, repealed December, 1867, and of the export duty of April,

4
The Lower St. Lawrence

The development of the lumber industry in the lower St. Lawrence with its larger tributaries and abundant supplies of spruce was also dependent on water and on steam mills but to a lesser extent on railroads. The first saw-mill on the St. Maurice River, built in 1846 by Messrs Baptiste at the head of the Grais Rapids, had an annual capacity of about 10,000,000 feet. The completion and successful operation of booms and slides in 1853 were responsible for an immediate expansion of lumber operations. Lumber roads were cut, a steamboat was put in operation between Grand Piles and La Tuque, and an American firm erected "a steam sawmill on a very extensive scale". In 1867[1] an additional saw-mill was built on Ile Bellerive. A fourth saw-mill built by Messrs Stoddart and Company, producing about 20,000,000 feet annually was added about 1872.[2] As early as 1873 lumber "has become so valuable, the inferior kinds are much more extensively manufactured"[3] and "complaints arose that the cutting of this lumber was responsible for the formation of more frequent jams." On the Batiscan River, batteaux, carrying 80 to 100 cords of firewood, proceeded as far as St. Genevieve. 5 miles above, Mr. Price's saw-mill, of an annual capacity of 8,000,000 to 10,000,000 feet, sent its lumber down a long shoot or "dahl" of 3 miles in length to be loaded into barges.[4] At St. Thomas Montmagny[5] the same firm loaded from their extensive saw-mills about 10 vessels of deals annually for Great Britain. They were also the owners of the large lumber establishment at the mouth of the Chicoutimi on the Saguenay.[6] The total

1868. An embargo was imposed in 1851 through the payment of double duties on logs cut for export. This was removed with reciprocity but re-imposed as stated above. The export duties on oak logs and stave bolts were abolished in 1875.

[1]*S.p.*, 8, 1893.
[2]*S.p.*, 29, 1873.
[3]*S.p.*, 2, 1874.
[4]*S.p.*, 29, 1873.
[5]*S.p.*, 8, 1879.
[6]The Chicoutimi Mill with from 80 to 120 saws turned out from 10,000 to 20,000 tons of sawn lumber annually.

Lake St. John district

	1861	1871	1881
Wheat, bushels	11,912	136,099	154,389

pine shipped from Ontario and Quebec in 1874 was 1,434,-000,000 feet board measure.

5

Secondary Industries

(i)

Tanning extract

Soft-wood products for export of minor importance included tanning extract made from hemlock bark. In 1868, 10,000 acres of hemlock land were stripped and 23,000 barrels of extract exported. In 1876, 29,000 barrels and 43,000 cords of bark were exported—five-sixths being produced in the Eestern Townships.[1]

(ii)

Manufactured products

Construction of railways, expansion of agriculture, increased population, and the growth of towns, were factors responsible for an increase in the home market. Secondary stages of production became more important. By-product industries developed in relation to the large mills producing for export. E. B. Eddy at Ottawa had an annual production about 1870 of 600,000 pails, 45,000 wash-tubs, 72,000 zinc

Oats, bushels	39,361	117,249	211,216
Potatoes, bushels	101,382	156,996	287,238
Butter, pounds	61,771	148,106	393,127
Population	10,478	17,493	32,490

In the seventies large quantities of birchwood and huckleberries were sent to Quebec.

As early as 1886 settlement came in conflict with lumbering as shown in the following extract regarding dams at Petite Décharge. "The dams were built for assisting the lumber trade at a time when settlers around the lake were but few in number and farming was of little importance; but of late years there has been a very large influx of settlers into that region, and the question now arises, which is of the most importance to the country, the lumber traffic which exists and does not add anything to the development of the country, or the welfare and prosperity of people who have made their homes around the lake, and by whose exertions and labour the country must become of importance" (*S.p.*, 7, 1888). See A: Buies, *Le Saguenay et le bassin du lac Saint Jean* (Quebec, 1896) and *Le Saguenay et la vallée du lac St. Jean* (Quebec, 1880).

[1]Bark was also exported from Bruce and Simcoe Counties. See Report of the select committee on the best means of protecting hemlock bark from destruction, *J.h.c.*, 1867-8, app. 10. In 1876 increased exports of extract of hemlock bark—"a comparatively new industry"—to Great Britain were reported (*S.p.* 2, 1876).

wash-boards, 270,000 gross of matches, besides the output of a sash, door, and blind factory. The growth of industries and trade stimulated the demand for packing cases, box-shooks, and oak staves—the trade in oil, flour, and salt created a demand for staves and slack and tight barrels. The growth of agriculture was responsible for the expansion of the local lumber industry and for the rapid spread of the small steam mill. The hard woods were particularly adapted to the new and varied demands and since the export trade in hard woods was limited through the high costs of transport,[1] cheap supplies were available for local demands. Large hard-wood trees[2] occupied the best agricultural areas and exploitation

---

[1]"The railway to Montreal has turned the forests along its line into gold" (G.T.R.) (*Transactions* of the Canadian Institute, series I, III, 46). Oak was used for barrel staves, ties, and ship-building—logs being exported from western Ontario to Tonawanda—ash for bent stuff (tools), elm for barrel-heads, waggon-hubs, and cheese-boxes, hickory for axe and hammer-handles, walnut for furniture—although the supply disappeared rapidly—chestnut for charcoal-burning for export to iron smelters in the United States, especially from Essex County (also from Sharbot Lake). The building industry, carriage factories, plants manufacturing agricultural implements and furniture, and the railroads were the chief consumers. See J. Squair, *The Townships of Darlington and Clarke* (Toronto, 1927), 2-12, for a description of the importance of wood as fuel and as raw material for industries. Cutting hard wood for the Montreal market and soft wood for domestic use as well as for railways and steamers was mentioned by Croil as an important part of the farmer's work in winter in Dundas County in 1860. The sale of wood to the railways was an important occupation for farmers and served to reduce the cost of clearing. At Ailsa Craig in 1868 "the railroad alone keeps many teams in active employ, procuring wood, of which there are immense piles around the station. A large business is also being done in getting out square timber for shipment" (*History of the County of Middlesex*, Toronto, 1889, 591). Consumption of wood on the railways declined rapidly after 1875. See *Fifth annual report* of the Waterloo Historical Society (Kitchener, 1917).

Steam Boat "May Flower"
Toronto July 20, 1855

Received from G. M. Jarvis

16½ cords hard wood 4.50 per cord $108.37
9¾ cords soft wood 3.50 per cord . . . .
R. Sinclair

On the problem of cordwood in relation to railroads and to urban demands, see G. Laidlaw, *Reports and letters on light narrow guage railways* (Toronto, 1868). Hard wood was taken down the river on cedar floats. Sugar maple was rapidly being cut off and maple sugar supplemented by cane sugar. Croil refers to the manufacture of 4,000 pounds annually by a farmer near Williamsburgh and to a decline to 300 and 400 pounds. See M. F. Goddard, Manufactures of maple syrup and sugar in Canada in the past and present time, *S.p.*, *Que.*, 5, 1908.

[2]"Where beech, maple, hickory, butternut, and chesnut grow, we find a good soil of yellow or hazel loam; where elm, white ash, white oak, butternut, and red oak grow, the soil is strong; where white pine, hemlock-pine, birch and spruce grow, the soil is sandy; cedar swamps, though often composed of good soil, are not desirable, unless easy to drain, black ash, soft maple, or plane swamps, are mostly on a clay or marl, and if well-drained make lasting meadows; where there are small poplar and small white birch, the soil is poor, being light loam on white clay" (*Journals of the legislative assembly*, 1850, app. TT.).

was rapid. The railroad opened the market for square timber, chiefly oak and elm, but the supply was rapidly exhausted.

Steam engines partly as a result of the higher cost, roughly $100.00 per horse-power, were used to an increasing extent in the production of finished products. With abundant supplies of raw material these industries[1] were widely scattered. In 1864 Cobourg[2] had a sash, door, and blind factory with 2 planers, 2 circular saws, moulding and bevelling machines, one saw-mill, and 4 cabinet factories. In the same year Port Hope was shown with a planing mill, door, sash, and blind factory with 2 circular saws; Newcastle with a planing mill and a chair factory; Galt[3] in 1857 with a stave and shingle factory, a chair and furniture factory, a pail factory, a last factory, 2 planing mills, and a sash and door factory, and in 1879, with 2 chair factories, 4 sash factories, and a stave and shingle factory. At about the same date[4] a lumber dealer in Guelph shipped 96 car-loads of shingles and 800,000 lath, and handled from 5,000,000 to 6,000,000 feet of pine lumber. At Hamilton medium grades of furniture[5] were produced for consumption in surrounding towns. The Upper Canada Furniture Company was located at Bowmanville. It was reported that in 29 establishments concerned with the manufacture of wooden products, of which 12 had started after 1879, employment had increased between that date and 1885, 68 per cent.

---

[1]Cabinet and furniture.

	1871		1881	
	Number	Value of product	Number	Value of product
Ontario	536	$2,306,076	625	$3,013,259
Quebec	218	859,491	397	1,736,392
Sash door and blinds.				
Ontario	156	1,546,898	281	3,982,117
Quebec	41	1,174,949	35	303,335

[2]*Gazetteer and general business directory for the united Counties of Northumberland and Durham for 1865-6* (Woodstock, 1865).

[3]James Young, *Reminiscences of the early history of Galt* (Toronto, 1879).

[4]*Guelph Herald*, May 22, 1878.

[5]The national policy was held responsible for starting 13 out of 43 plants in 1885. Employees increased nearly 61 per cent. and average wages from $348.83 to $370.73. Improved plant and marketing increased the production per employee (*S.p.*, 37, 1885).

(iii)

Small steam mills

The lumber industry in the agricultural and settled areas was confined during the early stages to the rivers for power, and for supplies of raw material. As settlement increased the demand for lumber increased, more supplies of logs were available from cleared land, and, as a result, the small steam mill increased rapidly. The imperfect statistics of the census of 1851 give 158 steam and 1,473 water-power mills producing 772,612,770 feet of lumber and 4,590,000 planks (Upper Canada, 1,567 saw-mills; Lower Canada 1,065).[1] In 1859 Croil gives 26 saw-mills with 43 saws and a capacity of 2,500 feet per day, and involving a capital of $1,000 to $1,500 for each saw in the County of Dundas. Of a total of 42 factories worked by power, 31 used water-power, probably including most of the saw-mills. Steam saw-mills could be placed in the most suitable location, could be operated chiefly through burning the refuse, and were independent of seasonal changes involving fluctuation in water-supply.

Steam power made rapid headway in the secondary stages of the operation and in the growth of the hard-wood industry. Croil describes—

the steam stave-cutting machine in Matilda [*as cutting*] 10,000 staves per day, or from 60 to 70 per minute, while working. It is driven by a steam engine of 25 horse-power, which is worked by consuming the refuse shavings alone for fuel, and gives employment to ten hands. Ash and elm are the materials from which the staves are manufactured. These are brought to the mill in blocks split out of large trees, and sawed in stave length, worth about $3 per cord. The blocks are soaked in boiling water until softened, sliced off 5/8 of an inch, in thickness, by a ponderous knife, and are then shaped and finished by machinery and sent to Montreal to be made into flour, salt

---

[1]   1860-1.

	Total mills	Steam	Water	Annual produce value
Ontario	1151	305	689	$3,969,464
Quebec	797	20	628	3,482,871

Saw-mills	1870-1		1880-1	
	Number	Value of product	Number	Value of product
Ontario	1837	$12,733,741	1761	$16,629,075
Quebec	1708	9,548,810	1729	10,542,649

and plaster barrels. Staves cut by circular saw are a trifle more valuable than those cut by the steam soaking process, and are made at the rate of from seven to eight per minute. White-oak staves were produced in Elgin County for Quebec and for the West Indies.

(iv)

Carriage factories

The overwhelming importance of transportation led to the development of factories[1] producing carriages, waggons, wheels, and hubs. Depreciation in these manufactured products was rapid. A report of the president of the carriage builders' guild of London stated of timber-yards visited at London, Chatham, Ottawa, Aylmer, Hull, and New Edinburgh that "only at Aylmer did I see hard and tough timber suitable for carriage building purposes."[2]

(v)

Manufacture of organs

Specialization was evident in the hard-wood industry at an early date partly as a result of its limitations for water-transport and of the character of local demands. In 1865 the Bell firm started operations at Guelph and by 1878 employed 115 men and turned out 1,230 organs annually.[3] In that year trade was carried on to all parts of the dominion and, at about the same time, a large Australian trade had been built up. The national policy was alleged to have been responsible for a marked improvement in the industry and by 1885 it was claimed that the trade had been captured

---

[1]Carriage-making.

	Number	1871 Value of product	Number	1881 Value of product
Ontario............	1421	$3,078,841	1690	$4,319,197
Quebec............	841	1,257,736	969	1,410,526
Cooperage.				
Ontario............	669	1,281,868	640	1,282,876
Quebec............	472	320,989	267	251,137

In 1857 Galt had a waggon factory and carriage shop. In 1859 Dundas County had 4 carriage factories turning out annually 38 buggies at $90.00 each, 70 cutters at $70.00, and 30 sleighs at $24.00.

[2]S.p., 12, 1887.

[3]Guelph Herald, May 22, 1878.

from Americans and that 70 per cent. of trade in Ontario and 50 per cent. of trade in Quebec was in Canadian hands.[1] In 1885 the Guelph plant employed over 200 hands with a pay-roll of $75,000 per year and turned out 15 instruments a day. Organs were exported to Great Britain, Germany, Russia, and Australia. "Maple wood, so largely used in the manufacture of organs, is abundant in the neighbourhood, and the manager of the factory told me it was due chiefly to this fact that Guelph was now manufacturing organs and exporting them."[2]

6

The Decline of the Lumber Industry and the Rise of Agriculture

The lumber industry bridged the gap between relatively isolated communities and the growth of large centres dependent on railroads, in providing capital in return from exports, in providing a demand for agricultural products, and in providing a cheap, raw material for construction and other industries. It provided the framework around which was built up the later and more permanent industrial structure.

Throughout the period its supremacy as a product for export declined and by 1861 agricultural products[3] had definitely surpassed it.

	1859	1860	1861
Export of agricultural products	$7,339,798	14,259,225	18,244,631
Export of forest products	9,663,962	11,012,253	9,572,645

In 1863:

> the remarkable increase in the grain trade of Montreal is seriously affecting the shipments of lumber at Quebec. Fully one-half of the vessels which formerly took in cargoes of lumber at Quebec now go to Montreal for grain. This withdrawal of 400 or 500 large sea going vessels is diminishing the industry of the port of Quebec while Montreal is becoming the great seat of foreign commerce.

---

[1]*S.p.*, 37, 1885. In 23 industries producing musical instruments, 11 of which had started after 1879, employment increased by 331 per cent. from that date to 1884 and wages from $417.64 to $467.20.

[2]*S.p.*, 10, 1886.

[3]*Eighty years' progress*, 64-74, 284-289. Another estimate gives $12,572,759 "more than half of the whole trade of the province for the year" for 1859.

The change coincided with the difficulties of the St. Lawrence route and the rise of the iron steamship and the railroad. The new demands for lumber were closely related to the spread of industrialism in Canada, the United States, and other countries. The decline of lumber in contrast with the rise of agricultural products precipitated the problem of the St. Lawrence.

AGRICULTURE[1]

1

Effects of Improved Transportation

The effects of the development of railways and of improved facilities for water-transport were of profound importance to agriculture which became "the staple and stable wealth of the province". "On the prosperity of the farmer may be said to depend the prosperity of all classes." The difficulty of attracting through traffic for the railroads, and the blow sustained by the St. Lawrence with the decline of lumbering and ship-building necessitated increased attention to the expansion of agriculture and the possibilities of increasing agricultural exports. The effects of the iron steamship and of the railway were conspicuous in the growth of

---

[1]See especially Report of the Ontario agricultural commission (Toronto, 1881); Reports of the commission of agriculture and arts, *S.p., Ont.;* Annual reports of the bureau of industries beginning *S.p., Ont.,* 3, 1882-3; Reports of the minister of agriculture, *S.p.;* Census statistics, 1850-1881; Reports of the commissioner of agriculture and public works, *S.p., Que.;* Reports of the commissioner of crown lands, *S.p., Que.;* Reports of standing committees on immigration and colonization, *J.h.c.;* Report of select committee on agricultural interests, *J.h.c.,* VIII, 1874, app. 2; X, 1876, app. 7; Report . . . into the operation of the tariff on the agricultural interests of the dominion, *J.h.c.,* 1882, app. 2; Report . . . to obtain information as to the agricultural interests of Canada, *J.h.c.,* 1884, app. 6 (recommending the establishment of an experimental farm); Report of the commissioner of agriculture on the products, manufactures, *etc.,* of Ontario exhibited at the international exhibition, Philadelphia, 1876, *S.p., Ont.,* 33, 1877; Preliminary report of the agricultural commission, *S.p., Que.,* 81, 1888; *Journal of agriculture* (Quebec, 1879); *Journals and transactions of the board of agriculture of Upper Canada 1855;* Reports of various associations—fruit growers, dairymen, *etc.,* in both provinces; *Farmers' advocate;* W. L. Smith, *The pioneers of old Ontario* (Toronto, 1923); J. C. Geike (ed.), *Life in the woods* (Boston, 1865); E. S. Dunlop, *Our forest home* (Montreal, 1902); N. Robertson, *The history of the County of Bruce* (Toronto, 1906); *The Province of Ontario (1615-1927)* (Toronto, n.d.), 459-484; *Canadian economics,* 75-93, 99-113. Also histories of counties: T. S. Shenston, *The Oxford gazetteer* (Hamilton, 1852); *History of the County of Middlesex* (Toronto, 1889); *History of the County of Brant* (Toronto, 1883); *Frontenac, Lennox, and Addington* (Kingston, 1856); J. T. Coleman, *History of the early settlement of Bowmanville and vicinity* (Bowmanville, 1875); *Directory of the County of Hastings 1861;* Mrs. C. M. Day, *History of the Eastern Townships* (Montreal, 1869); R. Sellar, *The history of the County of Huntingdon and of the seigniory of Chateaugay and Beauharnois* (Huntingdon, 1888); J. Squair, *The Townships of Darlington and Clarke;* A. J. Madill, *History of agricultural education in Ontario* (Toronto, 1930); J. C. Bracq, *The evolution of French Canada* (New York, 1924); A. Gérin-Lajoie, *Jean Rivard* (Montreal, 1913); F. M. F. Ossaye, *Les veillées canadiennes; traité*

exports of wheat after 1850. Opening of new areas by the railroads was followed by increased demands for labour and capital. These demands stimulated immigration and industry, *e.g.*, agricultural implements. Concentration on the production of wheat in pioneer areas weakened the position of relatively self-sufficient agriculture and hastened the growth of industry and the rise of towns. Marketing of agricultural products in Great Britain released agricultural labour for emigration. Steamships reduced the costs of transport for agricultural products, and of labour. With the disappearance of the best lands, the drain of new areas on the livestock of older settled areas declined, with the result that animal products were available for export. The steamship, the demands of the United States during the Civil War, and the difficulties which followed the continued cropping of wheat hastened the expansion of export trade in these products. The opening of new lumber areas, as has been seen, was followed by the development of agriculture, chiefly in the production of oats, hay, and horses.

élémentaire d'agriculture a l'usage des habitants Franco-Canadiens (Quebec, 1852); L. A. Wood, *A history of farmers' movements in Canada* (Toronto, 1924); *History of Toronto and County of York* (Toronto, 1885), 2 vols.; *Handbook of Canada*, 330 *ff.*; E. L. Marsh, *A history of the County of Grey* (Owen Sound, 1932); D. Boyle, *The Township of Scarboro 1796-1896* (Toronto, 1896); W. Riddell, *Historical sketch of the Township of Hamilton* (Cobourg, 1897); W. Johnston, *The pioneers of Blanshard* (Toronto, 1899); A. Jodoin, *Histoire de Longueuil* (Montreal, 1889), chapter xxii; A. F. Hunter, *A history of Simcoe County* (Barrie, 1909); W. S. Herrington, *History of the County of Lennox and Addington* (Toronto, 1913); F. Neal, *The Township of Sandwich* (Windsor, 1909); L. S. Channell, *History of Compton County* (Cookshire, 1896); A. H. Ross, *Reminiscences of North Sydenham* (Owen Sound, 1924); J. F. Pringle, *Lunenburgh or the old eastern district* (Cornwall, 1890); J. D. Reville, *History of the County of Brant* (Brantford, 1920); J. S. Carter, *The story of Dundas* (Iroquois, 1905); T. W. H. Leavitt, *History of Leeds and Grenville*; W. Kirkconnell, *Victoria County centennial history* (Lindsay, 1921); E. M. Taylor, *History of Brome County* (Montreal, 1908); C. Thomas, *History of the Counties of Argenteuil, Que. and Prescott, Ont.* (Montreal, 1896); *Histoire de la paroisse de Champlain* (Three Rivers, 1915); E. A. Wright, *Pioneer days in Nichol* (1924); W. R. Wood, *Past years in Pickering* (Toronto, 1911); J. A. Cornell, *Pioneers of Beverly* (Dundas, 1889); F. L. Desaulniers, *Notes historiques sur la paroisse de Saint-Guillaume d'Upton* (Montreal, 1905); H. Magnan, *Monographies paroissiales* (Quebec, 1913); C. A. Gauvreau, *L'isle verte* (Lévis, 1889); E. L. Lacroix, *Histoire de la paroisse de Saint Adéle* (1927). See also publications of local historical societies (*Canadian Historical Review*, XII, December, 1931, 357-363); H. B. Small, *The products and manufactures of the new dominion* (Ottawa, 1868), 17-37; Goldwin Smith, *Canada and the Canadian question* (Toronto, 1891), especially 303-7. County histories owe much to a prize contest of the board of agriculture in 1859; for example, Croil on Dundas County.

2

Upper Canada

(i)

Settlement

Largely as a result of the construction of railroads, land under cultivation increased rapidly in the first decade and in Upper Canada increased 35¾ per cent. to 1861 above 3,702,788 acres in 1852 and in Lower Canada 29¾ per cent. above 3,605,167 acres in 1852. The Clergy Reserves Act (18 Vic. c. 2) and the Seigniorial Tenures Act (18 Vic. c. 3) passed[1] in 1854 paved the way for increased settlement. The Counties of Huron, Perth, Grey, York, Ontario, and Simcoe were chiefly responsible for Upper Canada's rapid expansion. As a result, the commissioner of crown lands in his report for 1862 noted a decline of 252,471 acres, or 38½ per cent., in the quantity of land sold from the previous year, for which the Civil War and its effects on trade and immigration and the deficient harvest of 1862 were not regarded as adequate explanations.

> Another cause may be mentioned, which in an official view, is more important than either of these, because its influence is not accidental or temporary. It is the fact that the best lands of the Crown, in both sections of the Province have already been sold. The quantity of really good land now open for sale, is, notwithstanding recent surveys, less than formerly, and is rapidly diminishing.[2]

---

[1]See W. P. M. Kennedy (ed.), *Statutes, treaties and documents of the Canadian constitution 1713-1929* (Toronto, 1913), 516-532.

[2]"The Clergy, School and Crown lands of the Western Peninsula, the most desirable, both as to quality and situation, of all the public lands of the Province are mostly sold, the few lots that remain are generally of inferior quality. The new townships between the Ottawa and Lake Huron contain much good land, but they are separated from the settled townships on the St. Lawrence and North Shore of Lake Ontario, by a rocky, barren tract which varies in width from ten to twenty miles, and presents a serious obstruction to the influx of settlers. Moreover, the good land in these new townships is composed of small tracts, here and there, separated from each other by rocky ridges, swamps, and lakes which render difficult the construction of roads, and interrupt the continuity of settlement. These unfavourable circumstances have induced the better class of settlers in Upper Canada to seek, at the hands of private owners, for lands of a better quality and more desirable location, though the price and terms of sale are more onerous than for the lands of the Crown" (*S.p.*, 5, 1863).

The disappearance of good land and the fixed price of land (crown lands $1.25 per acre, school lands $1.50, and clergy lands $2.50—5 years and 10 per cent. paid up on first instalment) accentuated the problem of ownership. Day reported that in the Counties of Lambton, Middlesex, Oxford, and Wentworth, nearly 1,300,000 acres were held, of which about 8,000 acres were under cultivation. In Wentworth County 40 to 50 farmers owned over 10,000 acres each and 100 to 200 over 500 each. Middlesex and Oxford had the largest number of small holders.[1] "One of the great banes of Canadian farmers consists in the occupancy of too much land." Ruinous speculation and poor cultivation were caused by rivalry for the possession of land. In some counties non-resident capitalists held nearly one-half of the granted lands and settlement was discouraged. By the end of the period land was distributed more evenly[2] although not before various systems of tenancy made their appearance. Croil stated that the great majority of farmers in Dundas were their own landlords but short leases from year to year and seldom more than 5 years, generally at about $1.50 an acre, were not unknown. "A different method of letting land, has during the last few years become somewhat prevalent, that is the *shares* system."[3]

[1] S. P. Day, *English America*, II, 192-3.
[2] *Ibid.*, 141-2.

Upper Canada	1851-2	1860-1	1870-1	1880-1
Occupiers of land	99,906	131,983	172,258	206,989
10 acres and under	9,746	4,424	19,954	36,221
10 to 20	2,671	2,675 ⎫	38,882	41,497
20 to 50	19,143	26,630 ⎭		
50 to 100	47,427	64,891	71,884	75,282
100 to 200	3,404	5,027	33,984	42,476
Lower Canada				
Occupiers of land	95,813	105,671	118,086	137,863
10 acres and under	14,477	6,822	10,510	19,150
10 to 20	2,702	3,186 ⎫	22,379	24,567
20 to 50	17,522	20,074 ⎭		
50 to 100	37,893	44,041	44,410	47,686
100 to 200	18,629	24,739	30,891	34,723

[3] "Firstly the tenant finds all his own implements, stock, and seed, performs all the work of the farm, and yields the landlord *one-third share* of the gross produce of the land, including hay and straw. Secondly, the tenant finds his own implements and stock, and one-half of the seed sown each year, and yields to the landlord *one-half share* of the gross produce. In this case the landlord usually bears half the expense of threshing all the grain. Thirdly, the landlord finds all the implements, working horses, and seed, and receives *two-thirds* of the gross produce. The *second* method is most commonly adopted" (J. Croil, *Dundas*, 206).

(ii)

Roads

Increase in settlement was accompanied by gradual improvement of the roads. The railroad displaced the stage coach and reduced the importance of the trunk roads. Roads[1] converging on new railway centres were improved slowly. Mileage of established post roads increased from 7,595 in 1851 to 14,202 in 1860. Dependence on the winter season for the hauling of grain gradually became less pronounced with the construction and improvement of roads. Following the disposal of better grades of land and the opening of new lumber districts, the government undertook the construction of colonization roads. In Upper Canada roads were built "where bodies of people arriving from Europe are to be located in small settlements".[2]   The Ottawa

---

[1]Galt stated that the government spent about £15,000 per year in opening up the leading county roads. Road companies were formed to construct and maintain macadamized, plank, and gravel roads. The municipalities financed the minor roads. "Every male inhabitant of any township, over 21 years of age and under 60, is required to perform two days of statute labor, on the roads and highways in such township, and every party assessed for real or personal property in proportion to the value of such property, thus under £50. two days' labor are required; under £100, 3 days; £150, four days; £200, five days; £300, six days, and so on, adding one day for each £100, until it reaches £1000, and for every £200 above that sum, one additional day." See S. P. Day, *English America*, II, 322-3; J. Croil, *Dundas*, 73. On the general bad state of roads and the unsatisfactory character of statute labour see numerous accounts but especially, J. C. Geikie (ed.), *Life in the woods*, chapters ii, xvii. The relative scarcity of railroad facilities and the long hauls of wheat and other products over bad roads stimulated the hotel trade. The toll roads were generally unsatisfactory. "There is no stronger instance of the patience and law abiding disposition of the people than in their toleration of so great an imposition as most of the toll roads of Upper Canada." Surveys were regarded as a handicap to the development of roads because of their insistence on straight lines. For a valuable account of roads and road policy see *Eighty years' progress*, 98 *ff.* See *Manual of instructions for the information of Ontario land surveyors* (n.p., n.d.); H. L. Seymour "Colonization and settlement schemes" (*Eleventh annual report* of the Association of Dominion Land Surveyors, Ottawa, 1918, 62-90); T. Adams, *Rural planning and development* (Ottawa, 1917). For a valuable account of toll roads at the end of the period see *S.p.*, *Ont.*, 42, 1888 and *S.p.*, 13, 1889.

[2]See *Eighty years' progress*, 303 *ff.*

Day gives the following estimate of lands made available (about 1863):

Canada West

In the Ottawa and Huron Country	600,000 acres
Continuation of Lennox, Frontenac, Addington, and Nipissing district	660,000
Continuations of Hastings and Peterborough, Victoria, Simcoe, and a portion of Nipissing	1,170,000
District of Algoma	200,000
Fort William (Lake Superior)	64,000
Total disposable	2,694,000

34

and Opeongo road (171 miles) from the Ottawa River to
Lake Huron was joined to Lake Ontario by the Addington
road (61 miles), the Hastings road (68 miles), the Bobcaygeon
road (40 miles), the Frontenac and Madawaska road abutting
on the Madawaska road and "branching off from the Mississippi road, with which it forms a junction, running parallel
with that of Addington", the Muskoka road, from the head
of navigation on Lake Couchiching, and the Sault Ste. Marie
road from Sault Ste. Marie to Goulais Bay.

To facilitate the colonization of lands opened by these
roads which were built with public funds:[1]

> The Government has authorised free grants of land, not ex-
> ceeding one hundred acres, and obtainable upon the annexed
> easy conditions, viz., that the settler be eighteen years of age;
> that within one month he take possession of the land allotted
> to him; that in the course of four years he put into a state of
> cultivation twelve acres of the said land; and, finally that he
> erect a log-house, twenty feet by eighteen feet, and reside on
> the "cot" until these conditions be fulfilled.

By 1858 the opening of 52 miles on the Ottawa and
Opeongo road had been followed by the settlement of 132
families or 515 individuals; of 45 miles summer and 30 miles
winter road on the Hastings road, by 126 families or 529
individuals; of 17 miles summer and 39 miles winter road
on the Addington road, by 44 families or 170 individuals: a
total of 332 location tickets and 1,218 people, "almost
wholly the descendants of old settlers or persons who have
been some years resident in the province".[2]   The Free

Canada East

Counties North of the Ottawa...........................	1,093,000 acres
Do. North of the St. Lawrence......................	1,378,000
Do. South of the St. Lawrence......................	1,544,000
Total disposable................................	4,015,000

(S. P. Day, *English America*, II, 321-2).

[1] In addition to free grants, land was fixed at 70 cents per acre cash or $1.00
credit and large proprietors were able to purchase townships of 50,000 acres at
2s. sterling per acre.   Grants were also given to the extent of 50 acres free with
50 acres purchase (E. L. Marsh, *A history of the County of Grey*).

[2] Free grants were generally seized and squatted on by farmers' sons and
others.   "The emigrant is virtually excluded from all share in the benefits intended to be conferred on him by the Province" (*S.p.*, 3, 1867-8).   See *Journals
of the legislative assembly*, XV, 1857, app. 54.   Additional road included 5 miles
Bobcaygeon, 18 Frontenac and Madawaska, and 14 Elzevir and Kalader, total
of 137 miles summer and 83 winter roads.   From 1853 to 1860, 481 miles of
colonization roads had been built in Upper Canada and 1,458 miles in Lower
Canada.   The government of Canada spent $2,316,027 on roads from 1841 to

Grant Act of 1868 and the opening of the Muskoka district[1] with the sale of timber limits were followed by settlement in that area.

3

Lower Canada

(i)

Settlement

In Lower Canada similar problems prevailed but the task was "to provide principally for the establishment of the redundant population of the old parishes" rather than for the immigrant.[2]   In 1850 it was held that "in Lower Canada the new land is covered with timber; the greater part of the trees being from two to three feet in diameter—the larger the timber the better the soil—and therefore the choice of land is generally directed by the growth of timber on it." By 1865 complaints regarding new lands opened for settlement referred to the difficulty of finding large trees on land which had been cut over for timber—an indication that the best lands had been taken.[3]   "The settler of our times hardly finds wood enough on his land to serve for the erection of his farm buildings.   Moreover, the lands easy of access are taken up, and the man who seeks a settlement must now plunge far into the forests of the back country."   The ownership of vast tracts of land by individuals and com-

---

1867.   On colonization roads built in Upper Canada after Confederation see *S.p.*, *Ont.*, 24, 1885.   Nationalities tended to isolate themselves in new settlements. In Simcoe County, 5 townships were Protestant from the north of Ireland, 4 were Irish Roman Catholic, one Highland, one Isle of Islay (S. P. Day, *English America*, II, 80-1; J. G. Kohl, *Travels in Canada*, II, 36 *ff.*).

[1]On the free grant lands in the Muskoka region see Charles Marshall, *The Canadian dominion*, chapter v; also T. McMurray, *The free grant lands of Canada, from practical experience of bush farming in the free grant districts of Muskoka and Parry Sound* (Bracebridge, 1871); A. Kirkwood and J. J. Murphy, *The undeveloped lands in northern and western Ontario* (Toronto, 1878); also Public Lands Act of 1860 and Free Grants and Homestead Act of 1868; and the *Report of the Ontario agricultural commission, 1881*, app. R1, S1.

Persons located under Free Grants and Homestead Acts up to
January 1, 1878.   8,000
Number of acres granted.   1,092,970
Number of patents in free grant townships 1872-1877.   2,958
Or at 15 acres cleared per patent. . . . .   44,370 acres
(*S.p.*, 30, 1878).

[2]On attempts to introduce Belgian immigrants see P. J. Verhist, *Les Belges au Canada* (Turnhout, 1872).

[3]*S.p.*, 6, 1865.

panies proved a hindrance to settlement in Lower Canada as in Upper Canada.[1]

(ii)

Roads

As early as 1851 roads were regarded as the key to the settlement of the Eastern Townships and the report of a committee on the subject recommended a tax on all unoccupied and uncultivated lands of non-resident proprietors of 1½d. per acre and on all occupied lands benefited by the construction of roads a tax varying from 1d. to ½d.[2] "Such amelioration would operate as a check to the emigration of the colonists who every year leave Canada to take refuge in the neighbouring states."

By the end of the first decade colonization roads were built as in Upper Canada. The Elgin road was extended from St. Jean to Port Joli and the provincial line, and roads from Matane to Cap Chat, Buckland to Metapedia, the Rivière du Loup to Lake Témiscouata, and Métis to Restigouche opened up country to settlers. In 1862 sales[3] were

---

[1]Journals of the legislative assembly, XV, 1857, app. 47.

[2]Journals of the legislative assembly, X, 1851, app. U. See S. Drapeau, Études sur les développements de la colonisation du bas Canada depuis dix ans (1851 à 1861) (Quebec, 1863); also G. Vattier, Esquisse historique de la colonisation de la province de Québec (1608-1925) (Paris, 1928), passim; also T. De Montigny, La colonisation (Montreal, 1896) and Au nord (Saint Jérome, 1883); C. E. Mailhot, Les bois-francs (Arthabaska, 1914); A. J. D. Michaud, Le Bic (Quebec, 1925-6).

[3]S.p., 5, 1863; S. P. Day, English America, II, 321-2. Crown lands sold at 50 cents an acre and clergy lands less than $1.00.

SCHEDULE of Lands Surveyed and subdivided into Farm Lots, from 1851 to 1860, inclusive

Year	Lower Canada	Upper Canada
	Acres	Acres
1851	130400	266856
1852	544700	423275½
1853	355250	1034906
1854	220950	311326
1855	471916	179830
1856	280420	560955½
1857	210000	290690¾
1858	214608	307559¼
1859	366495	717046
1860	328639	403349
Total Acres	3123378	4495794
		(S.p., 3, 1861).

more than double the sales of Upper Canada as a result of the discovery of copper and minerals in the Eastern Townships, improvement of roads, and success in forcing large numbers of squatters to purchase their lands. These activities were apparently inadequate and in 1865 the inspector of agencies reported:

> The commercial class, though far less numerous, has, in many instances, been favored, even to the detriment of the colonization of our waste lands. I do not by any means assert that this favoritism has produced no great results for the country; on the contrary, all have benefited largely by the grants made for the improvement of our communications by water and by railway; but, commerce cannot but gain by the encouragement afforded to agriculture, and the two interests, far from being mutually antagonistic, form but one; hence, in order to multiply commercial transactions, it is important that agriculture should receive its full share of the favors of Government, that our great forests should be pierced by roads, so that our population instead of flying to foreign countries, may become attached to the soil and redouble our strength.[1]

---

[1] *S.p.*, 6, 1865; also *S.p.*, 4, 1863; also *Journals of the legislative assembly*, XV, 1857, app. 47. Lack of roads was apparently only one cause of the lack of colonization. "One circumstance there is, however, which, in many cases, proves an obstacle, to the progress of settling and clearing new lands, deterring many from attempting this work in the townships. In the old parishes the subdivision of property is a habit so prevalent, and so deeply rooted, that children inheriting from their parents the most trifling bit of paternal estate, persist in their attachment to their home in their native parish, either ignorant of the advantages they would find in the township, or afraid of encountering, in the toil of clearing, difficulties too great to be surmounted. Accordingly, they settle on their paltry portion of their family property, and remain till a time comes when, the whole being overburthened with mortgages, they are driven to give it up to their creditors; then, and then only, they bend their steps towards the forest, oppressed by debt and totally destitute of the means of carrying on the first labor of clearing. Then they lose heart, and their next inevitable step is to emigrate to the United States, the natural consequence of their blindness and obstinacy". (*S.p.*, 3, 1867-8.) See also *S.p.*, 9, 1874, and F. Gerbie, *Le Canada et l'émigration française* (Quebec, 1884). The French had worked out an effective weapon for colonization in the type of buildings [*1877*]: "The first peculiarity one notices about the farms in this northern country is the close proximity of the house and barn, in most cases the two buildings touching at some point,—an arrangement doubtless prompted by the deep snows and severe cold of this latitude. The typical Canadian dwellinghouse is also presently met with on entering the Dominion,— a low, modest structure of hewn spruce logs, with a steep roof (containing two or more dormer windows) that ends in a smart curve, a hint taken from the Chinese pagoda. Even in the more costly brick or stone houses in the towns and vicinity this style is adhered to. It is so universal that one wonders if the reason of it also be not in the climate, the outward curve of the roof shooting the sliding snow farther away from the dwelling. It affords a wide projection, in many cases covering a veranda, and in all cases protecting the doors and windows without interfering with the light. In the better class of clapboarded houses

4

Labour

The opening up of new land, the demands of the lumber industry, of the construction of railroads, and of new industries contributed to the scarcity of labour. Wheat production with primitive equipment created a heavy demand for labour especially in the harvest season. The family farm and relative self-sufficiency were the result. Croil wrote in 1859:

> The greater part of the labor of the farm in Canada, is performed by the farmer himself, his sons and his daughters: the former managing all the out of door operations, and the latter, the dairy and domestic departments. Herein lies the secret of the farmer's success. Whatever qualifications a farmer should have mental or physical, all are agreed upon this point, that a good wife is indispensable. . . . The demand for labor is therefore limited, and the supply is generally equal to the demand . . . . Laborers are chiefly immigrants—Irish, German, and a few Scotch; they seldom continue at service longer than four years, and if during that time they are industrious and economical, they will have laid by enough to stock a small farm; remaining as tenants for a few years, they meantime look for a desirable bush lot that they may call their own. . . . The usual rate of wages for laborers is from $12 to $14 per month for the summer; $10 to $12 for the year round; $7 to $10 for the winter. Daily laborers in summer receive from 50 cents to $1, in winter 50 cents, and expert cradlers earn $1.25 per day—all boarded.[1]

Married men with their families could be hired at $8.00 per month the year round—the wages paid in produce.[2]

---

the finish beneath the projecting eaves is also a sweeping curve, opposing and bracing that of the roof. A two-story country house, or a Mansard roof, I do not remember to have seen in Canada; but in places they have become so enamored of the white of the snow that they even whitewash the roofs of their buildings, giving a cluster of them the impression, at a distance, of an encampment of great tents" (John Burroughs, *Locusts and wild honey*, Boston, 1901, 191).

[1] J. Croil, *Dundas*, 211.

[2] "In *the first place*, the family must be supplied from the farm in such a way that nothing may be bought which the farm can produce; the home-market will always be the best, and unbought supplies are always the best tasted. *Next*, as far as possible, something corresponding with the truck system in the payment of wages must be adopted. A system, however, which, instead of being unfair (as in too many districts in England), may be made perfectly fair. Straw, grain, anything a workman may require, should be given in preference to cash. Where the rate of wages is so good as it is in Canada, it is well-known that this is the only way the generality of farmers can afford to employ labourers. Instead, however, of any agreement that wheat should be taken at 8s. a bushel, when

The growth of the livestock industries in the older settled areas and the movement of families from settled districts to the newly-opened districts, especially after 1860, increased the demand for labour. The "letter of instructions", issued to emigrant agents abroad dated Quebec, April, 1862, stated that: "Skilled agricultural labourers can always find ready employment, and female domestic servants are always sure of good wages and certain employment." Periods of good crops were favourable to employment. The immigration agent at Kingston in 1867 wrote:

> The demand for farm laborers during the past season has been very great, I having received applications for upwards of one thousand laborers, and the wages offered were from $1 to $1.50 a day, and board, for those who knew anything about farming, the crops being unusually heavy and laborers very scarce; and I have no doubt but the demand will be fully as great, if not greater, the next season. The prices of all kinds of grain being so high, farmers will endeavor to put in as much as possible; therefore I am of opinion that ploughmen will be much needed in the spring of the year, and in harvest laborers of all kinds will be much required.[1]

Seasonal unemployment was partly offset by the demand for labour in winter in the lumber camps and on farms, in such tasks as teaming, cutting roads, sawing firewood, piling lumber, cattle-tending, and threshing. On the whole, "farm labour for hire is in Canada only a transient avocation, there being in this country no large body of men who

---

it is only worth 5s. in the market (a custom, I believe, still prevalent in the North of Devon), everything is taken at the market price. A man with a family to maintain would not be ready 'to hire' for twelve months and to give up the whole of his time, and attend to horses and live stock on the Sunday, unless he was paid perhaps at the rate of £1 5s. sterling per week all the year round. But if the farmer can give him half an acre of land, can keep a cow for him in summer and winter, can provide him with fuel (no trifle in Canada when fuel has to be bought, but not felt by the farmer who reserves a bush for the purpose), and find him a house to live in rent free, he would consider himself well paid if he had 15s. per week. So, again, the farmer with an ample store of provisions—as pork, potatoes, &c., can afford to find meals for his extra men during the busy time of harvest, and by so doing he has to pay nearly a third less cash for wages. Besides this gain in cash, he gains the additional advantage of securing a well-fed workman, in the place of one who may have denied himself requisite food, in order to indulge in liquor" (Mrs. Edward Copleston, *Canada, why we live in it and why we like it*, London, 1861, 114-6). On the self-sufficiency of farms in meat, chiefly pork, fruit, milk, and bread, see J. S. Hogan, *Canada*, 30-1.
[1] *S.p.*, 3, 1867-8.

expect to devote their lives to working for wages, as every healthy and sober man can easily become a landholder."[1]

5

Immigration

The various governments attempted to meet the demands for labour by encouragement of immigration. Encouragement became more necessary with the access to poorer grades of land, the depression of the seventies, and competition of newly-opened areas in other countries. With the disappearance of the best lands, the native population moved to new areas, or migrated to the United States or to urban centres, whereas immigrant labour in part filled in the gaps, and in part moved also to new areas. In 1871 it was stated that there was "a general disposition on the part of youth to abandon farming and overcrowd the learned professions and commercial avocations."[2]

(i)

Steamship rates

The supply[3] of unskilled agricultural labour depended on competition for labour in Great Britain by other competing new countries, on the cost of immigration, and on the agricultural revolution in Great Britain. The steamship became an important factor in the movement of population.[4]

---

[1]Report of Mr. A. Spencer Jones, delegate from English Labourers' Union, *S.p.*, 8, 1876.

[2]*S.p.*, 2a, 1872. "What we term educated labor, is very much at a discount here; such is the excellent education given to our young men, that the surplus of those who do not care about farming pursuits study either for the Bar, Medicine or Commerce; and, having local connections, generally supplant any foreign competitor.

I would therefore strongly advise the educated class of the middle ranks in England to think well before emigrating to this country, unless they have some certain prospect of a good start" (*S.p.*, 3, 1867-8).

[3]See W. A. Carrothers, *Emigration from the British Isles, with special reference to the development of the overseas dominions* (London, 1929); F. H. Hitchins, *The colonial land and emigration commission (1840-1848)* (Philadelphia, 1931); *The Province of Quebec and European immigration* (Quebec, 1870); also *S.p., Que.*, 13, 1869.

[4]C. R. Fay, *Youth and power* (London, 1931), chapter vi, especially references to N. W. Senior, *Industrial efficiency and social economy* (New York, 1928).

In 1855 the cost of a steerage passage to Quebec[1] in sailing vessels was from Liverpool, £4 to £5; from Cork, £3.15 to £4.5; from Limerick, Galway, and Londonderry, £3.5 to £4; from Dublin, £2. 15 to £3.10; and from Glasgow, £3.10 to £4.10. Steamships were not responsible for a decline in direct cost since in 1873 steamship passage[2] was £6. 6s. in contrast with 4 guineas or £4.10 for sailing vessels, but other considerations gave the steamship a predominant position.

> The average time of the mail steamships from Liverpool to Quebec in 1873 was 11 days, and from Londonderry to Quebec 10 days.[3]   The average time of sailing vessels from the United Kingdom was 45 days, being more than four times greater than that of the steamships.   In the case of a mechanic or laboring man earning wages, the saving of his time is of much more value than the difference of the fare, to say nothing of the superior comfort and better meals provided by the steamships, together with greater immunity from sickness.[4]

> Besides making a very great saving of time, a steam vessel brings a cargo of emigrants to port in a far better condition of health than a sailing vessel, and thereby lessens the danger of epidemics, as well for the emigrants as for the country which receives them.   This important result is illustrated by the fact that the sickly passengers landed at Grosse Isle Quarantine Station, are almost invariably taken from sailing vessels, especially after long voyages.

The results were inevitable.

> The employment of Steamships in conveying emigrants from the United Kingdom to North America, has greatly increased within the past few years.   In 1863 the proportion of those who took passage in steamships to Canada, was only 45.85 per cent.; in 1865, it rose to 73.50 per cent.; in 1867 it further increased to 93.16 per cent.; and in 1869 it still further rose to 94.99 per cent.   In 1870 it was 90.51 per cent.

In 1873, 34,860 came by steamship and 2,041 by sailing vessel and in 1875 all immigrants came by steamship.

(ii)

Government subsidies

These changes were partly a result of government subsidies.   An arrangement between the government and the

---

[1]See J. S. Hogan, *Canada*, 68.
[2]*S.p.*, 2a, 1879.
[3]*S.p.*, 9, 1874; also *S.p.*, 9, 1879.
[4]*S.p.*, 64, 1871.

Montreal Ocean Steamship Company in 1872 reduced the passage of adult immigrants from £6.6 to £4.15 and established a preference for steamships.[1]   In 1873:

> A system of passenger warrants was inaugurated under which approved immigrants have been enabled to obtain their passages at £4. 15s., instead of £6. 6s.; and a certain class of families of farm labourers and female domestic servants, at £2. 5s. sterling.   The rates quoted are for what are termed "ocean adults", as by a condition made by a combination of the North Atlantic Steamship Companies, all children over the age of eight years are counted as adults.   Reductions of price are only made for children under eight years.   In addition to aid in the ocean passage to Canada, immigrants settling in the Provinces of Quebec and Ontario[2] have had their railway fares, or other cost of inland transport, paid to their points of destination.   And immigrants for New Brunswick, landed at Halifax, have been carried free over the Government Railways in Nova Scotia.   Meals and lodgings and medical attendance have been provided both by the Dominion and Provincial Governments to all immigrants who stood in need of such assistance.   And the Government of Ontario has given a *bonus* of $6 per adult to settlers in that Province after three months residence.[3]

On May 7, 1874, the North Atlantic conference broke up and rates dropped from the fixed price of £6.6 to about £3 with the result that the agreement to pay £4.15 was in abeyance.[4]   The conference was reconstituted in June, 1875, and a fixed rate of £5.5 established and the passenger warrant arrangement with the Allan, Dominion, Temperleys, and Anchor lines was accordingly re-established.[5]   As a result of the depression the £2.5 passage rate for agricultural labour was abolished in 1877 as was also the Ontario bonus of $6.00 per head to agricultural labourers.[6]

---

[1] *S.p.*, 26, 1873.

[2] The province paid two-thirds and the dominion one-third of the cost of transportation.   The arrangement was withdrawn in 1882 (*S.p.*, 14, 1883). On assumption of control of immigration by the dominion see *S.p., Ont.*, 7, 1874, and annual reports, *S.p.*, 60, 1875-6 following.

[3] *S.p.*, 9, 1874.

[4] *S.p.*, 40, 1875.

[5] *S.p.*, 8, 1876.

[6] *S.p.*, 9, 1878.

(iii)

Competition from other countries

The granting of assisted passages was largely the result of competition from other areas.[1] In 1872: "It is certain that advances to enable immigrants to pay for their outfit and passage money are largely made by societies in the United States, by the governments of several of the British colonies and by Brazil."[2]

> The very active exertions made by the Australian Colonies, particularly New Zealand, and the very large expenditure of money made by them in granting free passages, caused very large drafts to be made upon the class of emigrants who would otherwise have come to Canada. The number who sailed for those colonies in 1874 was 53,958.

Canadian wooden ships became important in the transfer of emigrants to Australia. "Iowa, Nebraska, Kansas, Missouri and Pennsylvania are making great efforts to attract emigrants" (1872).[3] Canadian emigration agents were actively engaged in "combatting great ignorance displayed about Canada, and most absurd ideas entertained about the so-called severity of the winter".

(iv)

Effect of conditions in Great Britain on emigration

Business conditions in Great Britain had important effects on movements in emigration, and the revival of trade in Great Britain in 1870 and 1871 was regarded as the cause of a decline in emigration to Canada.[4] In 1875 when depression in Canada was responsible for a decline in demand:

> It must also be borne in mind that besides the competition of other colonies, wages have risen considerably in England during the last two or three years, that in many villages there are several cottages standing empty, that in some parts so far from there being a surplus there is a scarcity of labourers

---

[1] S.p., 2a, 1872. The policy of colonization roads and grants of free land was also regarded as a part of the policy of assistance necessitated by competition from other colonies (S.p., 4, 1862).

[2] S.p., 40, 1875; also S.p., 8, 1876; and S.p., 9, 1878.

[3] S.p., 26, 1873.

[4] S.p., 2a, 1872.

on the land, so that suitable emigrants being now so much more difficult to obtain they are the more valuable when obtained.[1]

Improved transportation by steamship had far-reaching effects on British agriculture by developing competition in agricultural products from new countries. The able dominion agent at Liverpool, John Dyke, wrote[2] on December 31, 1878:

> British agriculturists of all grades, indeed, are in a gloomy mood. A good harvest was experienced this year, but the ruinously low rates which rule for all kinds of cereals, in consequence of the immense importations from abroad, have left the corn-growing farmer nothing wherewith to retrieve his position. Grass and root crops have been exceptionally good; but the grazing farmer, in face of the continuous stream of live stock from Canada and the United States, has had to submit to a reduction of 10s. sterling to 15s. sterling per cwt. for his cattle. This means a reduction of something like a penny to three-halfpence per pound; and, it is more than probable, represents nearly if not quite the producer's margin of profit. The middle men, in fact, are pocketing the profit, since the purchaser so far at least, has received little if any benefit, though it must be borne in mind that a reduction of one penny to three half pence per pound to the consumer would increase the demand by at least 10 per cent. It is only this year in fact that the meat-producing farmer here has begun to feel the shoe pinch severely. Whilst he could get 80s. sterling per cwt. for his best beeves he had something to depend upon; but at 70s. sterling it is stated that he has nothing, and that it may not improbably carry him to the wrong side of his ledger. If prices remain as low as at present, and in the face of the vast importations now being made, there is not much chance for an increase; the British farmer must find that meat raising, one of his last remaining sources of revenue has disappeared, as wheat and oat raising have already done. With this state of affairs it is clear that not only is the farmer unable to improve the position of his labourers, but he has himself only a very slender margin left, which appears to be steadily and not slowly growing less. . . .

---

[1]*S.p.*, 8, 1876. "The decrease in the emigration from England may be attributed to the increased activity in nearly all branches of manufactures, giving employment to the masses, so that very few laborers or mechanics were out of employment, or required assistance, as is seen by the decreased numbers sent out by the various charitable and emigration societies. The number assisted by these societies in 1870, was 9,787 souls, against 4,445 in 1871" (*S.p.*, 2a, 1872).

[2]*S.p.*, 9, 1879.

The partial failure of the crops in Great Britain, and the low prices obtainable there for all kinds of farm produce, on account of the large supplies received from Canada and the United States, affected the British tenant farmer to such an extent that they are unable to pay present rents, and many of the most enterprising of them are looking out for fresh fields wherein to invest their capital and labour.[1] More than the usual number of British farmers with means arrived this season, some of whom proceeded to Manitoba and the North-West, whilst others purchased farms in the Provinces of Quebec and Ontario.

6

Agricultural Machinery

Marked rise in the price of wheat in the decade from 1850 to 1860, opening of new land, gradual clearing and levelling of the old land, especially in the removal and rotting of hard-wood stumps,[2] construction of railroads, expansion of industry, and consequent scarcity of labour provided an incentive to the rapid adaptation of agricultural machinery invented in the United States. William McDougall, in his report on agricultural methods[3] in the United States, dated Toronto, December, 1853, stated that:

During the last two or three years, manufactories of farmers tools and implements have been established in all the principal

---

[1]The revolution in English agriculture hastened a readjustment of population. Imports of cheese and butter increased from £3,119,323 in 1859 to £14,188,746 in 1879 with the result that the English dairy industry became increasingly dependent on the sale of fresh milk to the large centres of population. "It is estimated that something like one million gallons of milk are consumed every day by the population of Great Britain, representing an annual money value of something like forty to fifty millions of dollars, and this is rather more than one third of the whole estimated produce. The demand will of course increase every year, not only from the growing population, but also from the more extended use of milk, as an article of diet" (*S.p.*, 10, 1880).

[2]Stumping machines were being improved especially to handle pine and more resistant species. For a description of the screw type of stumping machine see J. C. Geikie (ed.), *Life in the woods*, 400.

[3]See J. Squair, *The Townships of Darlington and Clarke*, 481 ff.; J. E. Boyle, *Chicago wheat prices for eighty-one years* (Ithaca, 1922); *Journals of the legislative assembly*, XIII, 1854-5, app. 1. 1. Wm. McDougall, the author of the statement, reported in favour of granting patents to American inventors for short periods to encourage the introduction of American inventions. See P. W. Bidwell and J. I. Falconer, *History of agriculture in the northern United States, 1620-1860* (Washington, 1925), chapter xxiii; also W. T. Hutchinson, *Cyrus Hall McCormick* (New York, 1930). Canada became in part a dumping ground for American machinery. Provincial exhibitions served a useful purpose in introducing new implements from the United States. See Charles Marshall, *The Canadian dominion*, chapter vi, especially 74 ff.

towns and cities in Upper Canada. So great is the demand for improved machinery that even American manufacturers have set up branch establishments in Canada, with very profitable results.

The various improvements included the plough[1] of which Croil wrote about 1860: "We have an endless variety, economy in weight and price seems to be the chief aim of the makers . . . but there is much room for improvement as to shape, none of the country-made ploughs can turn a furrow so well as the Scotch plough." The plough clevis was an original Canadian invention of about 1850.

> The ploughing is invariably done with two horses harnessed abreast and driven by reins, and from one acre to one acre and a half, according to the quality of the soil, is considered a day's work. On a heavy soil you are likely to find four acres and a half will have occupied a week (when loss of time is allowed for).[2]

After ploughing, the American or Share's harrow was used to cultivate the soil. "This is a most effective implement, almost equilateral and triangular. Two horses can readily draw it, and its numerous inverted teeth, or coulters, slice every furrow into four; and after thrice harrowing with this instrument, we made the best seed-bed we ever saw on a farm." Croil described "the 40 tooth diamond Scotch harrow, covering nine feet" as "fast superseding all others on cleared land". "Cultivators between drills of corn and potatoes are commonly used and recently a larger size of implement covering 5 feet, and working to a depth of 8 inches, has been introduced to good advantage upon summer fallow." "Wooden rollers are used to some extent, but they are very perishable, and cast iron ones too dear." Machines for drilling in grain or broadcasting were generally scarce.

More rapid progress in the development of machinery was evident in harvesting implements.[3]   H. A. Massey

---

[1]At the Paris exhibition in 1855 a plough made by Bingham of Norwich was favourably commended as "very fine and light in its build; the handles are longer than ordinary which makes the plow much more easy to manage" (*Eighty years' progress*, 41).

[2]Mrs. Edward Copleston, *Canada, why we live in it and why we like it*, 105.

[3]Vehicles and farm implements 1871.

	Light carriages	Vehicles for transport	Ploughs harrows culti-vators	Reapers Mowers	Horse rakes	Thresh-ing mills	Fanning mills
Ontario	206,243	299,367	289,362	36,874	46,246	13,805	120,732
Quebec	240,018	404,966	206,663	5,149	10,401	15,476	37,262

began the manufacture of mowers and reapers in 1852, combined mowers and reapers in 1856, and a self-rake reaper in 1863. A reaper required about 5 men to bind, carry, and stack the grain. Croil reports 10 reaping machines and 200 threshing machines in Dundas County in 1859. Reapers and mowing machines sold for £20 to £25 currency. "These are not essentials, yet those who possess them maintain they last for ten years and save their prime cost in two."

Threshing machines used in Dundas County were chiefly made by Paige and Johnston, Montreal, and cost $200.00 cash. The first portable threshing machine was introduced about 1835. By 1860 the mills were described as compact, durable, and effective, "with separator and fanning mill combined, and will thresh and clean from 60 to 100 bushels of wheat and from 150 to 250 bushels of oats per day." Machines were hired in many cases, the owner furnishing 4 horses and the farmer 4 horses. 10 to 15 men were employed. The owner was paid in proportion to the number of bushels threshed. This method required a large granary to store the grain and had the disadvantage of mixing the grain- and weed-seeds of neighbouring farms. A small—2 horse-power threshing machine, requiring only a small number of men and costing about £35 sterling worked by a tread-mill and threshing from 100 to 150 bushels of oats per day, was in use as a method of avoiding these inconveniences.[1] Fanning mills were produced locally and sold for about $25.00.

> The American horse-rake is a most useful, ingenious and economical machine, as patented in Canada West; it is made almost entirely of wood—consisting of a frame some twelve feet in width, mounted on wheels, with shafts; to this frame are attached twenty-four teeth, three feet or so in length, made of the hardest and toughest ash, strung upon an iron rod, so as to rise over any obstruction, and fall again immediately. The driver stands on the platform, and by the aid of a lever, on which he merely plants his foot and leans his weight, he raises the teeth off the ground, and they immediately drop the hay or grain, whenever he does so. About eight acres can be gone over with this rake in about half a day. After this,

---

[1] For prices of agricultural implements in 1851 see J. C. Taché, *Sketch of Canada*.

the land is so clean, that when the hay waggon has left the field no litter is visible anywhere.

This machine alone saves the labour of three or four hands in haying time, and does about as much work in one hour as they would in two, with no labour to the man who directs it; and it is quite light work for the horse that draws it. This really useful implement so little known to fame, and, for some unaccountable reason, so kept out of the market (although all who have tried it prefer it to any other), is made, and mounted on well tired wheels, with shafts complete, for £4 sterling.[1]

Additional implements included lumber waggons costing about $70.00 and sleighs about $25.00. Circular saws driven by horse-power and costing $40.00 and with 4 or 5 men cutting 30 cords a day are "much used". It was estimated that farms using agricultural implements varied in different counties from 20 to 90 per cent. by the end of the period.

7

Farm Improvements

Increasing use of machinery in the older districts was accompanied by general improvements in farming equipment.[2]   Mrs. Copleston estimated for a pioneer settlement

---

[1]Mrs. Edward Copleston, *Canada, why we live in it and why we like it*, 116-7.

[2]The extent of drainage was a valuable indication of the increasing value of land and the increasing importance of capital.   Underdraining was recognized as a valuable means of overcoming the difficulties of wet springs and of drought but it was little practised.   Tile-making machines were available at about $300.00 and tile was produced at Yorkville for sale at 1½-inch tile for $4.50 per thousand, 2-inch, $5.00, 3-inch, $10.00—each tile 13 inches long.   Mr. McDougall reported the use of Scragg's Tile Machines imported from England to Geneva, New York, in 1848.   The machine cost £50 and produced 3,000 2-inch tiles per day.   The cost of tile was reduced from $20.00 and $25.00 to $9.00 per thousand. These tile could be laid down at a cost of 30 to 38 cents a rod whereas a stone drain cost about 54 cents a rod.   Stone drains covered with about 3 feet of earth and strips of hemlock boards nailed together in triangular shape were used; ". . . but the best substitute for tiles, is common cedar rails; three or four of these laid in the bottom, blinded well with cedar bark or chips, make an excellent drain, and very durable, although the expense is little less than that of tiles, it has this advantage, that every farmer can find the materials on his own farm, without paying out the money" (J. Croil, *Dundas*, 208-10).   Labour was too dear to permit extensive underdraining.   Drainage made slight progress prior to 1885 although the Drainage Act had important effects.   Production of tile had increased materially by the end of the period and 3-inch tile were sold at $12.00 a thousand.   The tile and brick industry expanded slowly.   In 1881 a brick machine, manufactured in Woodstock, produced 12,000 bricks in 10 hours or about 750,000 bricks annually at $5.00 to $8.00 per thousand.   See *S.p., Ont.*, 29, 1881; and *S.p.*, 102, 1884; also Report of the drainage commission, *S.p.*, 32, 1893; *S.p., Que.*, 2, 1887; Drainage Act, *Ont. statutes*, 41 Vic. c. 9, 1878.

a stove[1] and cooking utensils at £6 currency or £5 sterling, furniture £1.10s.; and sundries, £1 currency or a total of £7.2s. 2 horses cost from £35 to £50; plough and harness, £6; waggon, £15; cows, £4 to £6; sheep, 10s. to 25s.—the outfit for a farm of 40 acres costing about £100.[2]   Croil in Dundas County estimated the cost of a well-furnished house of brick or stone, 36 feet by 26 feet, with kitchen 24 feet by 18 feet, a storey and a half in height, with cellar, at $1,600. A barn 16 feet high and 36 feet wide cost $4.00 per foot in length, and a cedar fence $1.00 per rod.   Bricks cost $4.00 per thousand; stone,$1.50 per cord; lime, 15 cents per bushel. Day commented on the churches, brick and frame school-houses, and on the villages and roads of the Counties of York, Ontario, and Peel.   In 1880 farms in Ontario, varying in size from 100 to 300 acres, required £2.10s. to £3 capital per acre.   "The houses of the better class of farmers are comfortable brick houses of the Swiss villa type."   Log houses were giving way to improved buildings.

8

Wheat

The opening of new territory, increase in immigration, and spread in the use of machinery were factors contributing to the increase in agricultural production and particularly in wheat as a frontier product.[3]   High prices for wheat especially in the fifties accelerated expansion in production. In 1856[4] exports of wheat increased nearly 46 per cent. over 1855 and estimated production increased from 16,155,956 bushels in 1851 to 26,555,684 bushels in 1856.   Barley and

---

[1]On the effects of the introduction of the stove see N. Robertson, *The history of the County of Bruce*, 72-3.

[2]Estimates for provisions for 12 months for a man, wife, and 3 children, seed, and necessaries for a settlement made up by the government totalled £47 sterling.   See *Eighty years' progress*, 304-5.

[3]See D. A. MacGibbon, *The grain trade of Canada* (Toronto, 1932) and "The future of the Canadian export trade in wheat" (*Contributions to Canadian Economics*, V). Kincardine exported by the end of the decade 1860-1870 "about a quarter of a million bushels of grain, besides large quantities of other farm produce".   Goderich, on the other hand, declined as a wheat-buying centre as small villages grew up in the interior following construction of the railway (*S.p.*, 49, 1870).

[4]*Journals of the legislative assembly*, XV, 1857, app. 54.

35

rye increased in exports from 56,534 bushels in 1855 to 989,447 bushels in 1856; Indian corn from 831 bushels in 1853, to 57,636 in 1854, 73,066 in 1855, and 164,495 in 1856; oats from 370,275 bushels in 1855 to 1,296,677 bushels in 1856. Along the north shore of Lake Ontario, the Counties of York, Ontario, and Peel produced in 1860 as much wheat as Lower Canada in 1831 and nearly 1,000,000 more bushels than Lower Canada in 1860. Whitby with its open harbour was regarded as "the best wheat market in the province".

The railroads lowered cost of production and cost of marketing in the less accessible areas. In Simcoe County:

> It was no advantage to the farmer on the north side of Lake Simcoe to have his wheat conveyed to the opposite shore by water when it would then be forty miles distant from a market, while the expense and difficulty of transit absorbed most of his profits. But there were other disadvantages. To the Toronto price of every pound of tea consumed by the farmer of Simcoe, had to be added the price and profits of carriage; while from the price of every bushel of wheat that the farmer sold had to be deducted the cost of transit.[1]

Increasing attention to the production of wheat, on the other hand, brought serious problems. Upper Canada tended to follow the general trends of Lower Canada.[2] Loss

---

[1]S. P. Day, *English America*, II, 141-2. In Dundas County "the value of lands in the rear has thereby increased ten fold, precious time has been saved, and wear and tear proportionably diminished."

[2]In Upper Canada production of wheat increased to 24,620,425 bushels in 1861 or 103 per cent. over 1852; other grains increased to 38,122,340 bushels or 115 per cent. Lower Canada in the same period increased 16 per cent. for wheat and nearly 100 per cent. for other grain. Both areas produced 27,183,539 bushels of wheat and 61,657,043 bushels of other grains representing an increase of 79 per cent. for wheat and 106⅓ per cent. for other grains over 1852. Wheat acreage for Lower Canada increased from 798,275 in 1851 (15¼ bushels per acre) to 1,386,366 acres in 1861 (18 bushels per acre). See S. P. Day, *English America*, II, 277-8, 284-7, 311-2. Production of wheat in Upper Canada in 1860 averaged 43 bushels per head in contrast with 23 bushels per head in Lower Canada. "The cultivation of wheat is rapidly diminishing in Lower Canada which is becoming more of a grazing country." "Upper Canada raises most wheat, most Indian corn, and most peas, Lower Canada most barley, most oats and most potatoes" . . . (J. C. Taché, *Sketch of Canada*).

J. C. Taché as chairman of the special committee on the state of agriculture in Lower Canada in 1850 stated: "Independently of all other defects, there are three capital vices in the system generally followed in Lower Canada: one relates to manure, another to the rotation of crops, and the third to the raising of cattle. These three evils arise from the same cause. . . . The primitive soil, which was in itself endowed with an extraordinary fertility, which yielded abundant harvests without the use of manure, or rather with the manure deposited on it for centuries, rendered the work of man useless, or rather of less utility in this respect. The virgin state of the soil and its durability, admitted of the same crops being raised

from midge, Hessian fly, and rust extended back to an early date and the census of 1851 estimated losses of wheat in Frontenac, Lennox and Addington, Hastings, and Prince Edward Counties to be about 400,000 bushels.[1]   Lincoln, Welland, and Haldimand also suffered severely.[2]   In 1862 a serious drought from early spring until nearly the end of June combined with the appearance of the grain aphis ("simultaneously in almost every part of the province, about the middle of July, multiplied with extraordinary rapidity till before the end of the harvest every standing stalk of grain was thickly studded with hundreds of the insects, which absorbed the nutriment of the plant, and consequently prevented the proper filling and maturing of the grain") caused serious losses.[3]

> The cultivation of Fall wheat, formerly the grand staple crop of Upper Canada, continues to be a precarious industry in the front townships, owing to the depredations of the Wheat midge, and the danger of being winter killed from the want of sufficient covering of snow.   Our farmers, therefore, besides the cultivation of Spring wheat, which has largely taken the place of the fall sorts, are learning more and more to turn their attention to the production of other articles of a marketable character.[4]

---

on the land for several years.   Wheat being the most profitable grain, nothing but wheat was sown, and all the land was sown with it; what was barely sufficient for the stock of cattle kept, being only just what was necessary, and the manure furnished by them not being taken into consideration.   Thus our soil went on getting poorer until having lost all its strength it ceased to produce wheat, or produced only a sickly grain without sufficient strength to resist accidents. The evil arose so suddenly, and was so little expected by the agricultural class, who enjoyed, without anxiety, the blessings of the present, that many persons were utterly discouraged, and resigned themselves, with all the apathy of despair, to an evil which they thought it beyond their power to put an end to.   It may be useful to remark here, that abundant harvests had given a great number a taste for luxury, which is the cause of a large portion of our population being deeply in debt at the present day" (*Journals of the legislative assembly*, IX, 1850, app. T. T.).

[1]*Journals of the legislative assembly*, XV, 1857, app. no. 54; H. Y. Hind, "Essay on the insects and diseases injurious to the wheat crops" (*Journal and transactions of the board of agriculture of Upper Canada*, II, 1858); *Eighty years' progress*, 53 ff.   In 1851 the wheat midge was held responsible for a decline in yield from 22 to 6 bushels in some counties.

[2]These counties averaged in yield 26 to 35 bushels of wheat, 40 to 45 bushels of oats per acre.   In 1861, 188,095 acres produced 3,469,000 bushels of wheat.

[3]*S.p.*, 4, 1863.

[4]*S.p.*, 3, 1867-8.   On the subject of exhaustion of the soil from continued wheat-cropping and the necessity of resorting to other methods of farming, see *S.p.*, 29, 1872, and *S.p.*, 9, 1879.   "An average of forty bushels or only sixteen

Spring wheat was of first importance in 1861 but declined rapidly to a position of equality with winter wheat in 1871 and was largely replaced by the latter in 1881.[1]

9

Other Products

In spite of the importance of wheat as a product for export, difficulties of production and improved transport led to the development of other products. The relatively self-sufficient type of agriculture provided a base for the expansion of trade in numerous commodities. In Dundas County at the end of the decade from 1850 to 1860, on farms of 100 acres probably 50 to 60 acres were cleared of which two-thirds were in pasture and the remainder in tillage. Croil[2] refers to a Glengarry 100-acre lot with 28 acres of stumps used for pasturage and the remainder for the following rotation:

1st.	6 acres	Oats ploughed from sod.
2nd.	6 "	Wheat, with a half dressing of manure ploughed fall and spring.
3rd.	6 "	Barley, sowed after the wheat with one ploughing.
4th.	6 "	Oats, sowed in early spring, upon the fall furrow.
5th.	6 "	Peas, land ploughed in fall, harrowed in spring, and the seed *ploughed* in.
6th.	6 "	Potatoes and corn, land fully manured in the fall.
7th.	6 "	Wheat, sowed in spring upon fall furrow.
8th.	6 "	Barley, half dunged and seeded to grass.
8th.	24 "	Grass, cut three years and pastured one.

This rotation provided for the sowing of 24 bushels of wheat

---

bushels per acre is Canada's experience. We did not stop at sixteen bushels, first, because we could easily increase the productive area; secondly because grain is less expensive to produce; thirdly, because it is a lazy system of farming, and thus most acceptable to the majority; fourthly, because the product has always been in demand" (*Canadian economics*, 79). In the vicinity of Cobourg the average yield of wheat from 1841 to 1867 was 19 bushels per acre. From 1878 to 1880 the yield fell to 12 and 13 bushels. "The farms on the whole line in the old settled townships from Montreal to Hamilton are (to use the words of the president of the agricultural association of Western Canada in 1850) what is termed worn out" (H. B. Small, *The products and manufactures of the new dominion*, 17). The general decline was attributed in part to the cutting off of the forests and consequent winter killing.

[1]Johnston described the destruction of the wheat midge in 1863-4 as responsible for the displacement of spring by fall wheat.

[2]See J. Croil, *Dundas*, 198-9.

on 12 acres bringing a return of 240 bushels; of 3 bushels per acre of oats on 12 acres and a return of 360 bushels; of 2¼ bushels of barley on 12 acres and return of 35 to 50 bushels per acre; of 3 bushels of peas on 3 acres, and returns of 20 to 25 bushels per acre; and of 6 acres of corn and potatoes.

> The whole of the hay and straw, oats, peas, corn and potatoes, are consumed on the premises, which secures me a large pile of manure, my wheat straw is all used for bedding, and I am thus enabled to manure 12 acres each year. I keep ten cows, four horses and a few sheep, I sell yearly about 140 bushels wheat, 360 of barley, and $100 worth of pork. My expenses are merely nominal.[1]

In the more remote areas and in new settlements the self-sufficient type of farming was even more in evidence. Mrs. Copleston suggested the following arrangements for a new farm near Orillia: 15 acres of spring wheat to yield 320 bushels; 15 acres of Canadian peas, 420 bushels; 6 acres of oats, 240 bushels; 2 acres of barley, 94 bushels; and 2 acres of potatoes, 240 bushels. Livestock included 3 cows, several pigs, 20 sheep, poultry, turkeys, chickens, and ducks. Pigs were regarded as of special importance for the consumption of grain and for the sale of meat. With a cow to supply 7 pounds of butter per week, hens for a supply of eggs, and chickens and ducks and turkeys for sale and consumption in the autumn and winter, the farm was largely self-supporting. Orchards and gardens supplied the house with fruit and vegetables.

---

[1] "In summer time, we live upon bacon, beef, and pork hams, nicely cured and smoked, and fried with eggs, supplemented with cheese, bread, and butter, all home made, and of the best. In October, we kill a beast. The blacksmith takes a quarter, the shoemaker another, the tailor or the carpenter a third, and ourselves the remaining one. In December, we kill a second, cut it up, freeze it, and pack it away in barrels with straw, where it will keep till the first of April. The hides go to the tanner, who takes one half of each, and gives me the other when tanned; the shoemaker comes to the house once a year and makes out of it boots and shoes for young and old. The tallow is rendered and made into candles, and all the refuse scraps at 'killing time' are boiled up with lye, and converted into barrels of soap. And then the women folk spin the wool and weave the stockings, sew the quilts and counterpanes, and make the feather-beds, so that come what may, we are always sure of a living. When a son or daughter is to be married, I sell a span of horses and a cow or two, give them a decent outfit and am none the poorer, as there are always young ones coming on to take their places." See also a description of a frontier farm near Lake St. Clair in J. C. Geikie (ed.) ,*Life in the woods.*

They [poultry] will do for themselves until the frost and snow set in, then a general wholesale slaughter ensues, as their keep in winter would be too expensive. All superfluous ducks, geese, and fowls share the same fate at this period, and are either marketed or kept for home consumption. The severe winter cold is here turned to an economical account, as all this vast amount of poultry would be wasted but for the plan adopted of exposing it, and all kinds of meat and fish to the frost, or burying it in snow, which is by many preferred. All can be preserved in this manner in excellent condition for three months, and even as seasons vary, for four.

10

Livestock Industry

(i)

Sheep-raising

Demands of the lumber industry, growth of towns, demands of newly-settled areas and advantages of the Reciprocity Treaty, especially during the Civil War, in opening a market in the United States were factors contributing to the increasing importance of agricultural products other than wheat. In the frontier areas sheep occupied a position of first importance in the production of wool and meat for clothing and food.

A ready sale for sheep is always found in the home-market, especially for lambs during the summer months; and many a lamb is then sold for about the same money as the wool on his back would be worth in the ensuing spring. They thrive well, although they consume little else than the pea straw (which they doat upon, and which other cattle care little about), during winter, and live upon the pastures during summer, so that they are the most profitable of any kind of stock; their wool certainly pays for their keep, and the continued addition to the flock from lambs every spring, more than replaces any that may have been required for market or consumption.[1]

Emphasis was primarily on the production of wool to support a domestic industry with the result that the opening of

---

[1]Mrs. E. Copleston, *Canada, why we live in it and why we like it*, **112-3**. Sheep were difficult to raise because of the dog nuisance (*S.p., Ont.,* **1, 1869**).

the livestock market in Great Britain which followed the improvement of the steamship brought serious problems. It was suggested that the practice of selling ram lambs in the autumn to the United States instead of keeping them as stock should be stopped and the crosses should be made with Oxford and Shropshire Downs and Scotch Cheviots with the Canadian long-woolled Leicesters, Shropshires, and Cotswolds. Difficulties in the British market,[1] decline in the price of wool, increasing importance of dairying and disappearance of the frontier contributed to the decline of sheep-raising.

(ii)

Horses

Oxen were also important as part of a frontier economy and the cattle industry became a base for the growth of livestock[2] and of dairy products. The increasing importance of horses contributed to the decline of oxen[3] and to greater dependence on cattle as a supply of meat and dairy products. By the end of the period the market for horses had expanded rapidly. In addition to the lumber districts, horses were sold for use in the rapidly expanding American iron and steel industry, especially after the Civil War, and in American cities for use on street-railways. Canadian horses fed on hay and oats were regarded as stronger boned than corn-fed American horses, and Carleton County and the Seaforth district exported horses to Pennsylvania where they were finished to be sold to Boston and New York.

---

[1]"The great objection of first class butchers here to looking into a pen of Canadian sheep is that there is no wether mutton, which is essential to them if they conduct a first-class trade. A pen equally divided half wethers and half guinners would realize from a penny to two pence per pound more than a pen of mixed ewes and guinners" (S.p., 10, 1880).

[2]See N. A. Drummond, "Marketing of Canadian live stock" (M.A. thesis, University of Toronto); also H. J. E. Abbott, "Marketing of live stock in Canada" (M.A. thesis, University of Toronto).

[3]Number of oxen

	Ontario	Quebec
1871	47,941	48,348
1881	23,263	49,237

Horses were particularly important as a result of the improvement of roads and the rise of teaming. See Report of the special investigation on horse breeding in Ontario, S.p., Ont., 65, 1907.

Moreover, sections such as Essex County were beginning to supply the newly-opened markets of Manitoba and the north-west.[1]

(iii)

Improvements in cattle-breeding

Improved agricultural technique, and rise of towns were factors contributing to the growth of the cattle industry. In 1857 Rollo Campbell in *Two lectures on Canada* (Greenock, 1857) stated that "the chief cities in Upper Canada are largely dependent upon the Western States for their supply of beef and mutton." As a result of these demands and improvement of transport by rail, increasing attention was given to agricultural technique. The government assumed an active interest in dissemination of information, encouragement of fairs[2] and of agricultural societies, and improvement of breeds. In 1854-5 it was stated that:

> The large importations of Short-horn Cattle and of Leicester Sheep evince an advanced state of agriculture in the vicinity of their purchasers. We do not find these breeds without at the same time seeing an abundance of food upon which they are to subsist. Nor is either to be seen where the farmer does not possess large intelligence and a taste for fine animal forms.[3]

By 1863 farming had improved to the extent that:

> At the present day our most distinguished cattle breeders go to the United States and carry off the highest prizes on the American continent from their rivals. This result is immense, and must be followed by important consequences; for no one can for a moment doubt but that the agricultural produce of a country must always be in proportion to the proportion of its cattle and material. . . . It has been well said that agriculture and cattle are one, and the last ten years have added another confirmation of this principle.

"The number of livestock returned for 1861, exceed that for 1852 by considerably over a million, and amount to 3,525,060, inclusive of colts and fillies."

---

[1]*S.p.*, 12, 1880-1; *S.p.*, 11, 1882.

[2]See a list of entries of livestock at the provincial exhibition, Toronto, 1862 (S. P. Day, *English America*, II, 16-17). See also *Eighty years' progress*, chapters ii, iii.

[3]*S.p.*, 4, 1863. On the other hand, for comments on the slow improvement of breeds of cattle, sheep, horses, and pigs, see J. Croil, *Dundas*, 204-5. The Berkshire pig had made some progress.

(iv)

Export of cattle

The Civil War stimulated demand and in 1865 a marked increase in exports was reported—increase of cattle, $1,000,-000; horses, $2,500,000; sheep, $500,000: about equal to the total increase of flour and wheat of $4,000,000.[1] Improvement of the railway and of steamship navigation on the St. Lawrence to Montreal led to the opening of the British market. Cattle which formerly were sold "across the Suspension Bridge to Buffalo, whence they were distributed over the Eastern states to be fed for home consumption" were sent by Canadian shippers to England.[2] Writing from London, on January 1, 1877, the Canadian government agent referred to "the trade begun in Glasgow three years ago, when a firm of salesmen in that city imported as an experiment a few head of fat cattle."[3] Mr. George Roddick of Liverpool wrote on December 31, 1879: "I have disposed of large numbers of cattle since I commenced the business in 1875 in the Liverpool, Manchester, and London markets."[4] The St. Lawrence route was found to possess decided advantages and whereas it had failed to command its share of western wheat, it was conspicuously successful in handling livestock.

> The superior advantages of the St. Lawrence route for the shipment of live stock, which were plainly evident from the fact of a considerable portion of the voyage being performed in comparatively calm waters and through a channel where the extreme heat of the warm months is tempered by the cool breezes of the River and Gulf of St. Lawrence, checking to a great extent the always heavy losses of the beginning of each voyage, are now confirmed by the result of experience. The losses of animals on board the Allan and Dominion Lines of Steamships have been on the whole considerably smaller than those by other routes.[5]

---

[1] *S.p.*, 3, 1867-8.
[2] *S.p.*, 11, 1882.
[3] *S.p.*, 8, 1877.
[4] *S.p.*, 10, 1880.
[5] *Ibid*.

(v)

Problems of shipping cattle

Improved methods of handling reduced losses and increased the value of the animals. In 1878 complaints were made that some spar-decked ocean steamships had fitted up stalls on the upper deck "in a very slight and flimsy manner, fastened to the deck by cut nails". Some had even erected sheds for the sheep above the cattle-stalls and carried cattle-feed on top of the sheds.[1] Danger from fire, the difficulty of working sails in case the engines were closed down, and the necessity of throwing livestock overboard in case of storm because of the top-heavy condition of the vessel were factors increasing losses. In 1879 one steamer alone had 186 sheep washed overboard. Sheep and swine crowded at the rate of 10 per bullock's space of 2 feet 9 inches were subject to losses.

The difficulties were increased by lack of railway and port facilities. Following long journeys before reaching Montreal and exposure to "long fasts, scarcity of water, heat and fatigue, most of the animals died on the river". A Montreal by-law prohibiting the railway from moving cars to and from the wharf during the day, and lack of accommodation, necessitated running the cattle directly to the wharf:

> And there it was no unusual occurrence for the poor animals to remain twenty-four hours in crowded cars without food or water, exposed to a broiling sun by day and a hot suffocating air at night, and in an exhausted condition, from want of rest and food, placed in the close between-decks of a ship in dock. No wonder many died before the steamer reached the sea, and no wonder under such treatment at the start, instead of gaining weight as they should do at sea, they lost weight and value. Every one experienced in feeding animals, knows how rapidly fat stock will lose flesh from exposure, and how long it takes them to recover from a "back-set". . . .
> The majority of the private yards and sheds into which the stock were often crowded, and through which the Inspectors were compelled to walk ankle-deep in filth, should be condemned as unfit to receive stock for exportation.[2]

---

[1]*S.p.*, 3, 1879; *S.p.*, 11, 1880-1.
[2]*S.p.*, 10, 1880.

Ocean steamships gradually improved and competition kept down rates. In 1879 several lines (the Allan, Dominion, Beaver, London, Donaldson, and outside lines) "converted a large number of their passenger and freight steamers into cattle carrying boats". "Rates ruled in some cases about double that paid to steamers from Boston." In 1880 the ships formed a "ring", engaged most of the regular line ships "as high as £6 per head" and endeavoured to corner the supply of cattle, but steamers were fitted up to carry 800 head and sent out in ballast from Liverpool to defeat the ring. Rates from Boston of £2.10s. per head proved an effective check. Large numbers of Canadian cattle were sent to Boston and Portland.[1] Insurance rates were lowered. For all losses in shipment the ratios were about 8 per 1,000 on cattle, 5 per 1,000 on horses and mules, and 24 per 1,000 on sheep.[2] As a result of these favourable statistics John Dyke, Liverpool agent, wrote that he was enabled

> to induce Underwriters at Lloyds for the first time to issue a policy on live stock coming from the St. Lawrence, in April last [1878], at what was then considered the low premium of five guineas per cwt. to include all risks. The result was so satisfactory that the premium was further reduced to 2½ guineas during the summer months; . . . The marked advantage of being able to secure our shippers from loss, and to afford them thereby increased banking facilities, has no doubt contributed in a material degree to the immense development of the trade during the year just concluded.[3]

By 1884 deaths on the ocean passage were under one per cent.

(vi)

Marketing

Marketing conditions were also improved.[4] In 1879 about one-half of Canadian stall-fed cattle were reported as suitable for the best class of trade. Competition with Irish, Scottish, German, and other grass-fed cattle was avoided by

---

[1]*S.p.*, 12, 1881; *S.p.*, 11, 1882.
[2]In 1879 losses were reported: 1 per cent. cattle, 2½ per cent. sheep, 4½ per cent. swine (*S.p.*, 10, 1880).
[3]*S.p.*, 9, 1879.
[4]The embargo on American cattle (1878) was of considerable assistance to the Canadian trade.

shipping between February and August.[1] In 1880 store
cattle were "eagerly snapped up by British feeders at prices
ranging from £12 to £18 sterling per head."[2] The value
per head had increased from $24.00 to $65.00 through improved breeding and less shrinkage which followed reduction
in cost of transport and improved transit.

(vii)

The hog industry

The hog industry expanded slowly and provided the
coarser product of mess pork suitable for local consumption
and the demands of the lumber industry. Wheat and cattle
tended to restrict the production of hogs. Dairying militated
against sheep-raising and probably favoured the raising of
hogs. Pea-fed bacon occupied an important position in the
export market but production was handicapped as a result
of the pea weevil. Corn as a stable base to hog-raising
increased slowly and by the end of the period was generally
restricted to the Counties of Essex and Kent—the districts
around London, St. Thomas, and Chatham. Costs of production were high[3] and the total product was shared with
the distilleries.[4] The large plants producing for the English
market were forced to import a better class of hogs from the
United States. The Davies Packing Plant, which had been
rebuilt at a cost of $40,000 in Toronto in 1883, handled 50,000
hogs in a season.[5]

(viii)

Expansion of the livestock trade

As a result of these improvements trade expanded
rapidly—in 1877, 7,000 to 8,000 cattle, three-fourths of which

---

[1]S.p., 10, 1880.
[2]S.p., 12, 1881. Complaints referred to the uneven character of Canadian
shipments. Increased trade on the other hand was followed by improved breeding. See Evidence on the export cattle trade of Canada, S.p., 7b, 1891.
[3]Corn was harvested and husked chiefly by hand and stored in corn cribs.
Elm bark was used to tie the shocks.
[4]The distillery at Walkerville exported about 2,200 head of cattle annually.
[5]The plant at Aylmer was of the smaller type.

were American; in 1878, 690 horses and mules, 18,655 cattle, 41,250 sheep, and 2,027 swine, including a very large proportion of American cattle (two-thirds) bought by Canadian shippers or shipped by American dealers; in 1879, 24,682 Canadian cattle, 79,085 sheep, 4,745 swine from Montreal, which, in addition to shipments of Canadian cattle by Boston, gave a total of 25,009 cattle, 80,332 sheep, and 5,385 swine valued at $3,197,406; in 1881, 45,535 cattle and 62,404 sheep; in 1882, 35,378 cattle and 75,905 sheep; in 1883, 55,625 cattle and 114,352 sheep; and in 1884, 61,843 cattle and 67,197 sheep.[1] In 10 years exports increased to 90,664 cattle valued at $5,912,890 (1884).

11

The Dairy Industry

(i)

Butter

Increase in the size of towns also created a demand for dairy products. Durham cattle had developed as the basis of the livestock trade and in turn supported the dairy industry. Even at the end of the period Ontario had very few Holsteins. The production of butter emerged in response to local demand but as a product of domestic economy it varied greatly in quality and was unsatisfactory for the export trade. As late as 1875 imports were substantial.

---

[1] *S.p.*, 12, 1881; *S.p.*, 14, 1883; *S.p.*, 14, 1884. Montreal shipped in 1882, 28,491 cattle, 64,590 sheep; in 1883, 50,345 cattle, 102,347 sheep; in 1884, 56,643 cattle and 63,143 sheep (*S.p.*, 9, 1885). Expansion of the trade in fresh meat following the discovery of methods of refrigeration was apparently checked by the growth of the livestock trade, and increase in shipments of meat from Australia and other countries. The first successful shipment of frozen meat from Australia in 1879-80 brought that area into competition with North America. Competition for labour was followed by competition in the products of that labour. In 1877 Canada and the United States sent over, according to one estimate, about 1,500,000 pounds weekly (*S.p.*, 8, 1877). The immigration agent at Nottingham wrote on December 31, 1877, that the prejudice against Canadian fresh meat had entirely passed away. "At the outset the poorer classes were the only purchasers; but the consumption is no longer confined to any one class. It is eaten by high and low; by rich and poor. There is but one opinion about it, and that is, that it is quite equal in every respect to the best classes of Scotch and English meat" (*S.p.*, 9, 1878).

"The large increase in the importation is due as far as can be ascertained, to the scarcity and high price of butter during the greater part of the year, and the consequent substitution of lard for culinary and other domestic purposes."[1] The public analyst reported in Quebec in 1879 that tub-butter 5 months old was "badly prepared and contained too much water. . . . The most of them *even among those that had been best prepared* had a rancid taste", a result of returning empty tubs, the wood of which had become deteriorated, to the farmers in the spring. With butter selling at 20 cents in the spring and hog's lard at 10 cents per pound, the temptation on the part of grocers and farmers to wash old salt butter to render it white and to add hog's lard was too great.[2] Of 49 samples of butter examined by the public

---

[1] *S.p.*, 2, 1876.

[2] *S.p.*, 3, 1880. Country merchants regarded the purchase of farmers' butter as unsatisfactory but probably made a profit from the book system. Cash transactions were regarded as means of improving the product. Western Ontario produced notoriously bad butter and the general lack of attention to production especially as regards cleanliness and the lack of uniformity seriously restricted the development of foreign trade. The Eastern Townships were more successful. Creameries were small in number. The difficulties of production of domestic butter in its lack of uniformity and general unsatisfactory methods of manufacture were overcome in part by adoption of the Fairlamb system by which only cream was shipped to the factory and the costs of hauling and handling milk avoided—the range of haulage being increased from 6 to 20 miles. A report in 1881 emphasized the difficulties of domestic production. "Three varieties of butter are offered for sale on the markets of my division—spring butter, summer butter and autumn butter.

Spring butter is the white butter produced before the cows have been put out to grass, while they are still fed upon hay. This butter is to be found until the 1st of June. In June and July the butter assumes a yellow color, which is owing to the chlorophyll contained in the herbage of the pasture. Autumn butter (August, September, October,) is also of a yellow color. Winter and spring butter should not be salted down for use during the same year, still less for use during the ensuing year. . . .

Butter is made in two different ways . . . by churn and by hand.

Butter made by hand is always bad; that made by churn is alone to be recommended. The churn should be entirely of wood, either pine or fir; the latter wood is to be preferred. The tub should be made without ears, and fitted with a tightly-closing cover. If the tubs have ears, the butter contained in them passes for Canadian butter on the English market, a reputation of which the Americans are careful to avail themselves. Before the butter is put into new fir tubs, care should be taken to scald out the latter with an infusion of raspberry bush twigs. The same tubs should never be used twice; those that have already been used are utilised as vessels for the making of soap, or for keeping it for use. One of the principal precautions to be observed in the making of good butter is to entirely remove the butter-milk full of caseine, and this can only be done effectively by powerful compression.

Compression may be effected in two different manners. It is done by hand, with the assistance of a rolling-pin, on a marble or birch table. Compression may also be applied by aid of a machine, and this method is infinitely superior. Machines are now sold at Montreal for the purpose, which cost only $12" (*S.p.*, 3, 1882). See also *S.p.*, *Que.*, 2b, 1890.

analyst in 1872, 23 were adulterated. Lack of attention, the keeping of "too few cows to produce cream in sufficient quantities to churn whilst in a fit condition", the use of ordinary Canadian salt instead of specially-prepared factory salt, and store packing by which no attempt was made to separate qualities or colours were held responsible for difficulties of the export trade. Tub-butter with acidity of 6° (with long and careless handling of 26.4°) could not compete in the British market with oleomargarine produced in "large and well-appointed factories".[1]

By the end of the period the factory system with more uniform and satisfactory production had made its appearance. The introduction of the centrifugal cream separator[2] in 1882 was responsible for rapid expansion. In Quebec, the smaller French cattle and relatively inadequate system of farming which precluded the development of an export trade in cattle, nevertheless provided an important base in the quantity and richness of the milk for an expansion of the dairy industry. In the decade from 1871 to 1881 the number of creameries increased from 22 to 111. The butter industry for Ontario and Quebec expanded as follows:[3]

	1871	1881	1891
Number of creameries	No creameries in census	46	170
Capital invested	....	$97,027	$540,598
Persons employed	....	151	425
Wages paid....	....	$30,043	$106,303
Value of raw material.....	....	$263,483	$595,421
Value of product	....	$341,478	$913,391
Home-made butter.......	75,000,000 lb.	102,000,000 lb.	111,000,000 lb.

---

[1]*S.p.*, 5b, 1891; and *S.p.*, 6d, 1891.

[2]See M. E. Bouchette, "Les débuts d'une industrie et notre classe bourgeoise" (Royal Society of Canada, *mémoires*, series 3, *vi*, section 1, 1912, 143-157); also S. M. Barre, Report on the manufacture of butter in the principal dairy farming countries of Europe followed by a treatise on the teaching of dairying and notes on dairy farming in Canada, *S.p.*, *Que.*, 2, 1880-1; J. C. Chapais, The past, the present and the future of the dairy industry in the Province of Quebec, *S.p.*, *Que.*, 5, 1909.

[3]*S.p.*, 8h, 1894.

(ii)

Cheese

In contrast to butter the production of cheese was closely dependent on the factory and the growth of export trade was rapid. Indeed, the difficulties of the trade in butter were accentuated by the rapid increase in the production of cheese.[1] Moreover, cheese was more easily adapted to the early handicaps of steam navigation.[2] According to Croil (about 1863): "Dairy farming is not extensively practised in the County of Dundas. We have but one farmer who devotes exclusive attention to this branch of agriculture."[3] This farmer kept on 300 acres, 56 cows and made annually 230 cheese averaging 60 pounds each, "which he sells for ten cents per pound, raises 13 calves, and fattens 6 pigs, both chiefly fed upon whey". The increasing importance of cattle-raising and the improvement of roads in Upper Canada were factors contributing to the development of the cheese industry. Roads[4] permitting a daily haul of milk over a wide range of tributary territory were essential to the establishment of factories. Introduction of the co-operative factory paved the way for rapid expansion. In western Ontario Mr. Harvey Farrington, formerly from New York, started the first factory in Oxford County in 1864 and in eastern Ontario Mr. Ketchum Graham of Belleville started his factory, "Front of Sidney", in 1865. In Quebec Mr. James Burnett started a factory at Dunham in 1864. Mr. Adam Brown arranged for the shipment of the first lot of Canadian cheese to Great Britain.[5] The report of the

---

[1]Exports of butter declined from $3,058,069 in 1880 to $340,131 in 1890, in contrast to cheese, which increased from $3,893,365 in 1880 to $9,372,212 in 1890. Exports of butter in 1894 were still below the Confederation level. The relative position of butter and cheese is suggested in the following table:

	1871	1881	1891
Average butter per milch cow	58½ lbs.	65½ lbs.	62½ lbs.
Average cheese per milch cow	17¾ "	40½ "	62 "

[2]Report of J. P. Sheldon, professor of agriculture at the Wilts and Hants Agricultural College, *S.p.*, 12, 1881; also J. P. Sheldon, "British and Canadian agriculture" (*Canadian economics*, 113-117); Report of the Dairymen's Associations, *S.p.*, *Ont.*, and *S.p.*, *Que.*
[3]J. Croil, *Dundas*, 202.
[4]See a description of the effect of good roads on the size of factories (*S.p.*, *Que.*, 3, 1897).
[5]*S.p.* 15a, 1907-8; *S.p.*, 15a, 1909.

Montreal board of trade for 1868 stated that:

> The repeal of the treaty [*Reciprocity Treaty*] has stimulated the erection of cheese factories, which are shutting out the products of foreign dairies from the Canadian market and enabling the dairymen of Canada to compete successfully with their American neighbours in sending supplies to the British market. . . . Up to the close of 1865 there were only ten in operation in Upper Canada and two in Lower Canada. At the close of 1866 there were 60 in Canada West and 12 in Canada East using in the aggregate the milk of 21,600 cows, and producing about 6,480,000 lbs. of cheese; there are now [*1868*] 180 factories in Ontario, with an annual productive capacity of 12,000,000 lbs., worth (at 9 to 10 cents per pound) from $1,080,000 to $1,200,000, and in the province of Quebec, 17 factories with a capacity equal to 1,530,000 lbs., valued from $137,700 to $150,000.[1]

The report of the board of agriculture of Upper Canada for 1866 estimated 100 factories

> using daily the milk of from one hundred to five hundred cows each. The cheese produced is, generally speaking, of good quality and commands a ready sale at remunerative prices. . . . Formerly there were very large quantities of this article imported for domestic use. Now, this home demand is to a great extent supplied from our own factories, and considerable quantities are exported to England and the United States as well, where it has met with a very favorable reception. This is a most important and salutary change in our agricultural practice. By devoting an increased breadth of land to pasturage under the dairy system, instead of keeping the larger proportion under the plough our soil will gradually recover its former fertility.[2]

The growth of the cheese industry is indicated in the following table:

	1871	1881[3]	1891
Number of cheese factories.......	353	709	1,565
Capital invested..	$400,754	$1,021,435	$2,586,659
Persons employed.	998	2,003	3,013
Wages paid......	$120,026	$382,615	$753,067
Value of raw material.......	$1,249,904	$4,264,798	$6,804,611
Value of product..	$1,601,738	$5,464,454	$9,784,288
Home-made cheese	5,000,000 lb.	3,000,000 lb.	6,000,000 lb.
			[increase chiefly in Quebec]

[1]*S.p.*, 8h, 1894 and *S.p.*, 3, 1867-8.
[2]*S.p.*, 3, 1867-8.
[3]In Quebec the number of cheese factories increased in the decade from 1870 to 1880 from 25 to over 200 (*S.p.*, *Que.*, 1880).

36

Like the number of cheese factories the capital invested more than doubled in the ten years between 1881 and 1891, but the number of persons employed increased only 50 per cent. Their average wages, however, increased from $190 to $250 and their average product from $2,730 to $3,260, showing at the same time a growth of skill and of remuneration.[1]

"The factory system and weekly fairs, the improvement of the cows by judicious crossing thereby developing a class of animals with a large flow of milk with curd-producing qualities", and improved technique[2] were factors responsible for the growth.

(iii)

Milk

Increased population in the towns led to an increase in the consumption of fresh milk. As in the case of butter the product was not satisfactory. In 1872 regarding a sample

---

[1]*S.p.*, 8h, 1894.

[2]Mr. Ballantyne's factory at Tavistock: "The milk received daily, at the time of my visit, was about 17,000 lb. from nearly 1000 cows, but this was in the latter part of September. Mr. Ballantyne contracts with his patrons to make the cheese for them at 1 1/3c. per lb., and the cheese I saw there was of very good quality, well made and carefully cured; the temperature of the curing-room is kept about 80° for spring cheese, and 75° for summer, and at 65° for rich autumn cheese. The quantity of salt used is 2 to 2¾ lb. per 1000 lbs. of milk; the smallest quantity is used when the curd is driest. . . .

Formerly there was great difficulty and uncertainty in making autumn cheese in Ontario; it was liable to be puffy and porous; and, as the whey was not always got well out of it, the flavour was frequently, unpleasant. This difficulty has been completely overcome by "ripening" the milk before adding the rennet to it. The summer's milk kept through the night is not so deadly cold as the autumn's, and so is in a more natural condition; its warmth has brought it into that state which produces the best cheese . . . that is, it has ripened somewhat, because warmth as well as time is necessary to the ripening of anything. The best cheese cannot be made from fresh, warm milk; because, though it is of course warm enough, and has never been cold, it has not the required age, and so is unripe. Hence he prefers that one-half of the milk he makes cheese from should be twelve hours old, and this being ripe enough in itself, ripens the fresh morning's milk when the two are mixed together. In summer the ripening of the evening's milk is enough for the purpose, but in the colder weather of autumn it is not, so the morning's and evening's milk are warmed up together to a temperature of 90° or so, and allowed to stand several hours before the rennet is mixed with them for coagulation, and this is done because the autumn's evening milk has been too cold to admit of enough, if any, ripening. As the mass of milk stands at the temperature named, it ripens, and the difficulty previously so common disappears, the autumn cheese having all the warmth and mellowness of character of the summer cheese, it is not so liable to be injured by the excessive heat of the summer climate; this autumn cheese, in fact, take it for all in all, is probably the best of the season, whereas it was formerly, in many cases, the worst" (*S.p.*, 12, 1881).

of milk supplied to the Toronto general hospital the public analyst reported: "From the above results, I conclude that the milk is diluted with from 15 to 20 per cent of water, a grave matter in such an important item of the diet of the sick".[1] In 1879 the public analyst reported that, of 66 samples of milk, 33 were adulterated, 7 by skimming and 26 by watering.[2] The percentage of skim milk was largest in April, and the percentage of watered milk increased from March to June.   In the Kingston district in 1888 the analyst reported

> that the milk supplied by cows in large cities is often unwholesome on account of the unhealthy condition of the animals. The bad health of cows kept in the mephitic atmosphere of large cities is aggravated by the tendency of their owners to unduly promote the secretion of the milky fluid by means of a particular diet, and it is not to be wondered at that it is thus rendered watery and insufficiently nourishing.   In children it produces inanition and *cholera infantum*, and prepares the way for phthisis, that fatal ending of all physical debasement.[3]

12

Change in Agricultural Technique

By the end of the period the livestock industry and the dairy industry began to concentrate[4] in specialized areas. Professor Sheldon reported in 1880 that dairying was restricted to certain areas, such as the Belleville[5] district and the Ingersoll[6] and Stratford districts, partly because of the scarcity of water for livestock and partly because of the difficulty of introducing satisfactory rotations.   The trade in cattle was largely limited to the district west of Belleville and particularly to Wellington and Simcoe Counties and the districts near London, St. Thomas, and Goderich.

---

[1] *S.p.*, 3, 1878 and *S.p.*, 6, 1879.

[2] *S.p.*, 3, 1880.

[3] *S.p.*, 16c, 1888.   See also Report of the milk commission, *S.p.*, *Ont.*, 55, 1910.

[4] In Lanark County it was held that the cheese industry was responsible for the killing off of calves and the deterioration of stock.   Specialized districts were probably complementary, the calves of the dairy industry being sold to the cattle breeders.

[5] Leeds and Grenville, Perth, Norfolk, and Huron were among the important counties.

[6] The energy of Mr. Edwin Caswell contributed to the success of this district.

Cattle were generally 3 and 4 years old and grain-fed, or winter-fed and summer-grazed. Middlesex County[1] exported a large number of grass-fed cattle. The better grades of cattle were exported to Great Britain and the poorer grades were exported, along with flour and other products, to the Maritimes.

Expansion of the livestock and dairy industries produced a marked change in agricultural technique. It was necessary to grow very large crops of forage for use in winter, especially clover and timothy and abundant crops of swedes and mangels.

> The demand arising in the Old Country for beef, and the improved means of transportation over the sea, have provided a new and profitable opening towards which the energies of the farmers are being directed. The raising of stock suitable to the English market is now a leading and profitable branch in this part of the Dominion, and it is encouraging to the cultivation of root and green crops, of clover, timothy and other forage crops, of green corn, etc., for soiling.

Ontario became increasingly interested in the production of root crops and Wellington County was said to have raised more turnips and sold more beef than any other county. Whereas in 1850 the deficiency in root crops, especially turnips, was the occasion for general comment, in 1880 "every homestead has a large cellar in which to store roots."[2] Canadian cattle were regarded as superior to American corn-fed cattle, as a result of being fed on roots and straw. Nevertheless, the decline in the production of peas as a result of the pea weevil was followed by the importation of American corn.

Root crops provided a hoe crop which helped to clean the land of weeds and solved the problem of exhaustion of the soil and continued wheat-cropping by providing a wider rotation, and, in supporting the livestock industry, a means of fertilizing the soil. The rise of dairying checked the exhaustion of the soil which followed the sale of grain by feeding the grain to livestock and providing manure to build up the

---

[1] *S.p.*, 12, 1881. Ailsa Craig in one year exported from a radius of 6 miles 4,101 head of cattle and 5,994 head of sheep.

[2] *Journals of the legislative assembly*, XIII, 1854-5, app. I. I. See *S.p., Que.,* 2, 1886. On the problems of the sugar beet industry see *S.p., Que.,* 2, 1883; *S.p., Ont.,* 48, 1890; *S.p.,* 48, 1901; *S.p.,* 63, 1902; *S.p.,* 5a, 1903.

soil. Stock was improved,[1] the quality of the milk was improved, cows were cared for during the winter, and labour otherwise unemployed was given employment. Farming buildings "are said to have been much improved within the last few years" but in spite of a few warm and well-ventilated stables, proper feeding and housing were seriously neglected and large numbers of cattle suffered during the winter. The snake-rail fence was extended. "The farms are generally divided into good-sized fields by wooden fences."[2] "Lately a barbed fencing wire has been introduced."[3]

As a result of new markets, agriculture became increasingly diversified by the development of numerous minor products. The Civil War, by cutting off a supply of cotton and other products from the south, was responsible for a rapid expansion in the production of flax[4] and tobacco.

[1]The practice of dehorning was introduced from Illinois in 1888. See *S.p., Ont.*, 2, 1893.

[2]*S.p.*, 12, 1881; S. P. Day, *English America*, II, 77.

[3]*S.p.*, 12, 1881. The stump fence became more important with the clearing of coniferous areas and the improvement of the stumping machine. Splitting rails was an important occupation.

[4]   Flax Production

	1852	1862
Upper Canada	59,680 pounds	1˙225,937 pounds
Lower Canada	145,755 pounds	976,495 pounds

(S. P. Day, *English America*, II, 78).

The increase continued in 1863 and 1864 and in the latter year the western part of Upper Canada had increased in acreage to about 10,000 acres. Upper Canada had 40 scutching mills and 2 linen manufactures and later at Doon (1881) a plant was built to manufacture twine ropes and cordage (*S.p.*, 6, 1865). In 1865 Riga flax seed was imported by the government and supplied to farmers. The acreage in 1866 increased from 10 to 15 per cent. and Canada had about 100 scutching mills and 3 linen mills in operation. Both flax and seed were in demand for manufacturing or for export to the United States (*S.p.*, 3, 1867-8). Unfortunately, the end of the war and the heavy demands of the industry for labour were responsible for a marked decline in Upper Canada. In Lower Canada flax continued as an important item in domestic economy, "every farmer working up into linen the raw material with his own loom" and the decline was less conspicuous. Montreal consumed locally about 80,000 to 85,000 bushels of flax seed (*S.p.*, 42, 1867-8).

"Messrs. Lymans, Clare and Company, have a large factory on the Canal for grinding paints, plasters, and for manufacturing linseed oil. They employ 35 men at a rate of $1.50 to $2 per day for skilful men and $5.50 to $7 per week for unskilled.

To show the growth of Montreal manufactures, I need simply state that these mills produced in 1865, about 50,000 gallons of oil, in 1866 about 90,000 gallons, and from 900 to 1,000 tons linseed cake. In fact, we now successfully compete with the Hull manufacturers of raw and boiled linseed oils" (*S.p.*, 3, 1867).

The oil cake produced from a good crop in 1878 was sent chiefly to Great Britain. The Civil War was also responsible for an increase in the growth of tobacco especially in Lower Canada in 1864 (*S.p.*, 6, 1865).

Refrigerated steamships opened a market for poultry products in Great Britain. The Canadian government agent wrote on January 1, 1877, from London: "Large quantities of Canadian turkeys have reached Leadenhall Market this winter, equalling in freshness those received from France or bred in this country and excelling them in quality."[1] Eggs and poultry were being collected by country merchants to be sold in New York and other American cities. The production of fruit began to support an export trade. It was produced chiefly for local consumption—in Upper Canada "the plum, apple, strawberry, raspberry" and in Lower Canada, especially in the vicinity of Montreal, "the apples from thence are considered superior to any other". The Niagara peninsula had developed as the chief producing area and peaches were sent from Grimsby to Toronto. Oakville became an important strawberry centre, although strawberries were sent from the extreme western areas of Ontario to Detroit. Plums were grown in the region of the Bay of Quinte. Apples were grown over much wider areas. The small peeling machine and the drying of apples over stoves and on strings were very slowly replaced by the establishment of evaporators in the production of dried apples. Tillsonburg, for example, had a plant with a capacity of 25,000 bushels per season.[2] South Oxford was an important section. Early apples were sent to Chicago from Essex County and by 1877 steamship navigation had been responsible for the growth of the apple trade in Great Britain. The agent for Nottingham district suggested in that year that the trade could be expanded by packing in boxes rather than in barrels.[3] By 1880 fruit was being exported from Hastings, Lambton, and Lincoln Counties. Barley was exported in large quantities; notably from the region of the Bay of Quinte and from Dundas County to the United States—3,691,608 bushels in 1868 and 5,295,131 in 1869.[4] Napanee exported large quantities about 1880. Exports

---

[1] S.p., 8, 1877.
[2] S.p., 12, 1881.
[3] S.p., 9, 1878.
[4] S.p., 54, 1871. 2 steam elevators at Trenton handling up to 10,000 bushels of grain per day in 1875 for export to Oswego or Cleveland were probably chiefly concerned with barley.

increased rapidly in the reciprocity period and reached a peak of 7,175,379 bushels in 1886.

By the end of the period "the disposition manifested by wheat growers to depend less on that single and not always certain crop" was evident in many directions.[1] A serious failure of cereals in 1883 accentuated the tendency to depend on the trade in cattle.[2] The marked change in technique throughout the period had varied effects for the farmers.

> There are three causes at work which place these farms in the market:—1st. Many farmers have so run down naturally good land that they find it no longer profitable to farm it in the old way, and are either ignorant how to bring it into heart again, or have not capital enough to enable them to do so, and must therefore sell. 2nd. Many find the 200-acre farm too small to keep a large family together. 3rd. Many farmers, having made money and liking town life, prefer to sell their farms and go into business.[3]

Farmers, having exhausted their land with wheat, along with others stranded by the decline of the trade in lumber, were prepared to move to new areas. Those who had succeeded in working out a new technique of agriculture had prepared a diverse base from which new demands could be met. The opening of the west provided new territory for the first and new markets for the products of the second.

---

[1]*S.p.*, 14, 1884. The harvest of 1874 was "generally very good and the price of coarse grains offset the low price of wheat" (*S.p.*, 40, 1875). In 1879 there was a "good demand for all kinds of produce with increasing prices" (*S.p.*, 10, 1880). In that year a large crop of cereals and "a good demand for farm labourers" were reported. Diversification of agriculture provided a more elastic base with which changes in world conditions could be met more effectively. In 1881 bad crops in Britain and on the continent and improved local trade were responsible for a very successful year. In 1882 larger crops in Britain and on the continent, and an increased supply from India were responsible for a decline in the price of bread-stuffs but the increased yield and the success of "heavy crops including, cereals and roots . . . the yield being one of the largest ever produced in Canada" served to offset the effects of the decline (*S.p.*, 14, 1883).

[2]*S.p.*, 14, 1884.

[3]The problem of defrauding farmers became serious at a later date. See Report of select committee to consider the fraudulent obtaining of promissory notes from farmers for seeds, agricultural implements, lightning rods, etc., *J.h.c.*, 1888, app. 4; Report of bureau of industries, *S.p., Ont.*, 80, 1890.

13

Summary

Upper Canada

	1851	1861	1871	1881
Land occupied.......	9,828,655	13,354,896	16,162,676	19,259,909
Land improved.......	3,705,523	6,051,609	8,833,626	11,294,109
Horses..............	201,670	377,681	489,001	590,298
Cattle..............	744,264	1,015,278	1,403,174	1,702,167
Sheep..............	967,168	1,170,225	1,514,914	1,359,178
Swine..............	571,496	776,001	874,664	700,922
Wheat, bushels.......	12,682,550	24,620,425[1]	14,233,389	27,406,091
Oats, bushels........	11,395,467	21,220,874	22,138,958	40,209,929
Farmers............	86,224	132,064	228,708	304,630

Lower Canada

	1851	1861	1871	1881
Land occupied.......	8,113,408	10,375,418	11,025,786	12,625,877
Land improved.......	3,605,167	4,804,235	5,703,944	6,410,264
Horses..............	184,620	248,505	253,377	273,852
Cattle..............	591,652	816,972	783,462	1,030,333
Sheep..............	647,465	682,829	1,007,800	889,833
Swine..............	257,794	286,400	371,452	329,199
Wheat bushels........	3,073,943	2,654,354[2]	2,057,076	2,019,004
Oats bushels.........	8,977,380	17,551,296	15,116,262	19,990,205
Farmers............	78,264	105,784	160,641	201,963

	1861	1871	1881
[1]Fall wheat...................	7,537,651	6,341,400	20,193,067
Spring wheat................	17,082,774	7,891,989	7,213,024

	1881
[2]Fall wheat...	65,630
Spring wheat..	2,588,724

FISHING

Improvement of transportation widened the market for fish caught in the lakes. According to Day:

For several years fishing has been carried on during October and November by companies of experienced fishermen, and from ten to fifteen hundred barrels of salted herring and trout are brought into Goderich harbour every year. There is likewise constant summer and fall fishing of trout and white-fish—which is very delicious—carried on daily off Goderich harbour, so that each season from one thousand to twelve hundred barrelsful are procured. A considerable portion of these are sold fresh in the town and neighbouring villages, at from one to four cents a pound. The remainder are cured and barrelled for exportation. Winter fishing is also prosecuted as long as practicable, when large hauls are usually taken, and the fine fresh fish become hawked all over the country as far as London and Woodstock.[1]

Fishing in Georgian Bay expanded rapidly following construction of railroads. In certain areas the fishery declined as a result of rapid exploitation. By the end of the period fishermen at Windsor in the Detroit River complained that their numbers had declined from 100 to 30 as a result of the use of pound nets on Lake St. Clair.

---

[1]S. P. Day, *English America*, II, 296. Southampton became an important port. See *White fish of the Great Lakes: Sea fisheries of eastern Canada* (Ottawa, 1912), 13-24; also *S.p.*, 10c, 1893.

SUBSECTION E
MINING[1]

The construction of railroads, the expansion of agriculture and industry, and the growth of towns were followed by the development of mining, particularly of non-metallic minerals. Clay[2] for the manufacture of bricks and tile became increasingly important in areas with rich deposits and near the centres of population, for example in Toronto. Public buildings in municipal, provincial, and federal centres created a demand for stone.[3] Cement works were in operation at Napanee.[4] Plaster was obtained from gypsum near Paris. Industries based on these minerals were generally local and scattered over wide areas partly as a result of high costs of transportation. In the main the mineral development associated with the early construction of railroads and with agriculture was limited to later geological formations capable of producing such minerals as oil, salt, and gypsum. The more accessible minerals were subject to the earliest and rapidest exploitation.

1
Petroleum
In exploiting petroleum[5] surface wells were replaced by

---

[1]See E. S. Moore, *Canada's mineral resources* (Toronto, 1929), *passim*; W. H. Merritt, "The economic minerals of Canada" (*Canadian economics*, 153-159); Reports of the commissioner of crown lands, *S.p., Ont.*; also *S.p., Que.*; Annual reports of the bureau of industries, *S.p., Ont.*; Reports of the commissioner of colonization and mines, *S.p., Que.*; Reports on the mines of the Province of Quebec, *S.p., Que.*; *Canadian Mining Review*, 1879; *Report of the royal commission on the mineral resources of Ontario and measures for their development* (Toronto, 1890); A. B. Willmott, *Mineral wealth of Canada* (Toronto, 1897); H. B. Small, *The products and manufactures of the new dominion*, 60-109; "Report on the mining industries of Canada" (*Transactions* of the Royal Canadian Institute, series III, V, 240-251); *The Province of Ontario, 1615-1927* (Toronto, n.d.), I, 504-526; W. Roland, *Algoma west* (Toronto, 1887); *Eighty years' progress*, 308-372.

[2]Lime was manufactured on a small scale chiefly to meet local demands.

[3]The parliament buildings at Ottawa, and the McMaster building with dependence on stone from Credit Forks, were among new buildings responsible for quarry activity. See R. Snider, "A tale of a vanished fleet" (*Toronto Star Weekly*, September 24, 1927), for a valuable account of the work of the stone-hookers which collected stone along the lake front for Toronto buildings.

[4]A. C. Tagge, *The cement industry in Canada* (Montreal, 1924).

[5]See R. Bell, "The petroleum field of Ontario" (Royal Society of Canada *proceedings and transactions*, V, 1887, section 4, 101-113); *Report of the royal commission on the mineral resources of Ontario*, 156 *ff.*; Victor Ross, *Petroleum in Canada* (Toronto, 1917).

570

drilled wells. Drilling became more efficient with the dis-placement of cribbing[1] by augers, and with the change from cables to poles. (Spliced ash poles were found to be more efficient in going through rocks.) Flowing wells became pumping[2] wells and, with cheaper drilling and larger numbers of small wells, the "jerker" system, by which one engine pumped several wells, flourished (about 1863). The relative decline of Oil Springs and the rise of Petrolia (after 1865) led to the migration of refineries from out-lying points such as Hamilton, London, and Ingersoll to the source of supply. Pipe lines and the introduction of extensive storage systems (about 1867) by digging large underground tanks, holding about 8,000 barrels, in the stiff clay, to reduce costs and to avoid dangers from fires, hastened the concentration of refining. Improved methods of refining in the shift from

---

[1]"The operation of boring is as follows. In the first place, an opening of from four to five feet is made to the rock. When the rock is reached, a hole two or three inches in diameter is drilled to the extent of twelve feet. Then an iron pipe is introduced, being driven in a similar manner to pile driving. An iron bar, of three hundred pounds weight, nearly as large in diameter as the pipe, is passed down, attached to which are steel cutters. The drill and bar are suspended to a strong pole by means of a rope, when the men place their feet in a kind of stirrup, and by pressing the same, and quickly removing the pressure, the drill becomes lifted a few inches. This process is continued until the oil is reached. It often happens that the wells 'cave in,' or that the tools drop in the wells; disasters which add to the labour of the well sinkers. When sufficient rock has been pounded, the workmen clear out the aperture. This is accom-plished by the instrumentality of what is termed a sand-pump, which consists of an iron tube having a valve opening inwards at the bottom. Shells, coals, and other deposits, are by this means brought to the surface, so that the oil may be suffered to flow freely.

The average charge for boring in rock is two dollars per foot; and for drilling it is one dollar per foot for the first hundred feet; for the second hundred feet, two and a half dollars per foot; for the third hundred feet, three and a half dollars per foot; and so on in proportion to the depth. Below three hundred feet a steam engine becomes indispensable. The work is necessarily tedious, and but from four to six feet can be accomplished in a day" (S. P. Day, *English America*, II, 174-182).

[2]"The method of pumping is somewhat ingenious. A long and pliable tree acts as the lever, having its thick end firmly fixed to a stump of another tree in the vicinity, while a post planted in the ground acts as the fulcrum. Between the fulcrum and the thin end of the lever the pump shaft is attached, the whole being kept in motion by one man, who stands on a 'pedal', which at one side is attached to a small end of the lever by a rope, and at the other is fixed in a frame on the ground, so as to admit of the necessary motion. The pump is put in operation by the man keeping his foot steady on the lower part of the 'pedal', while he exerts all his force on the other part. This is necessarily a tedious process, producing but from forty to fifty barrels of oil daily. When a well stands for a short time it will take hours to discharge all the water therein col-lected. . . . The flowing wells occasionally run dry but are in some instances restored by clearing out the bore, or penetrating some few feet deeper" (*ibid.*).

the sulphuric acid[1] to the lead process, about 1870, and to the redistillation process (1885) were accompanied by an expansion in the manufacture of by-products—wax, candles, axle-grease, wool-oil, benzine, paraffin, tar, and coke. The emergence of a combine in 1869 to set domestic and export prices and the development of subsidiary industries producing engines, boilers, chemicals, and other supplies brought the industry to a complex stage. Railways facilitated the expansion of local demand for illuminating oils. Candles were displaced by lamps. The increasing importance of industries increased the market for by-products such as lubricating oils. The mushroom growth of towns such as Wyoming with their houses, refineries, stores, hotels, and facilities for oil storage reached a state of stagnation and eventually declined.

Operations in the petroleum fields were begun by W. M. Williams of Hamilton in 1857. In 1859 surface wells were dug at Oil Springs and were followed by rock-drilled wells. On January 16, 1862, the first flowing well was struck in the flats of Black Creek valley at a depth of 200 feet and by September, 25 flowing wells and 200 wells worked by pumps were in operation. One well alone produced 2,000 40-gallon barrels.

> The clear stream of oil rushes out bright and white, shining in the sunlight, but assumes a greenish tinge and thickness after laying for some time in vats—a necessary process, in order to disengage the gas contained therein, and to obviate the possibility of dangerous explosion. In this condition forty gallons are sold for 100 cents., or 4s. English, as "crude oil" or petroleum; and is extensively employed for lubricating

---

[1]"Whenever possible of accomplishment the oil is refined at the numerous establishments erected for the purpose in the locality of the wells. The process necessitates great waste, as products otherwise of considerable mercantile value, although not used for lighting purposes, are indiscriminately suffered to become lost. Most of the refineries are small, containing merely one or two stills, an agitator, a cooling tank, and perhaps two settling vats [*turning out about 40 barrels a week*]. The *modus operandi* of refining is extremely simple. The crude oil is passed through a retort, to separate the benzoli, the burning oil, and the creosote, from which is distilled a transparent liquid, having a blue tinge. This is afterwards 'washed' with sulphuric acid to improve the smell and whiten the oil, the acid being next absorbed or destroyed by an admixture of caustic potash. The liquid is then passed into settling vats, and after standing a certain time is ready for barrelling." The oil was deodorized with letharge and sulphur. Sulphuric acid was made from crude brimstone imported from Italy or from iron pyrites from Lennoxville, Quebec. Later a large refining plant had a capacity of 120,000 gallons of refined oil per week from 200,000 gallons of crude oil.

machinery on the Canadian railways. . . . To shippers the price of the oil is about 50 cents, or 2/- the barrel, but the cost of barrels, freight, railway carriage, shipment, and brokers' charges will bring the price up to 35/- or 40/- before the oil reaches the wholesale dealer in Europe. Hence the refined oil that on the spot is sold for 1/- the gallon would here in England be charged from 3/- to 4/- to the consumer. On the railways the Canadian native oil is mixed with sperm[1] oil so as to intensify the light of the hand-lamps; while in every house the glass globe-lamp[2] in which this oil is burnt is as common as a candlestick with us.

Oil was teamed from the Enniskillen district and loaded on ships along the St. Clair River and about 1870[3] the district produced about 5,000 barrels per week which sold at $1.60 a barrel, Germany being the principal export market. The railways, however, were of first importance in the oil trade.

The quantity of petroleum produced increased from 2,772,224 gallons in 1868-9 to 9,221,088 in 1869-70 and 14,602,087 in 1872-3, but declined to 6,752,282 gallons in 1873-4, and to 4,838,215 gallons in 1875-6. Export increased from 758,060 gallons in 1868-9 to 5,274,098 gallons in 1869-70 and 9,635,998 gallons in 1872-3, but declined to 1,065,287 gallons in 1873-4 and 47,246 gallons in 1875-6. Quantities entered for consumption increased steadily from 2,081,461 gallons in 1868-9 to 5,202,175 gallons in 1874-5, and declined to 4,550,187 gallons in 1875-6. Decline in the quantity produced and in exports after 1873-4 was the result of marked increase in production in the United States and consequent fall in prices. Imports from the United States increased rapidly in 1878 as a result of further decline in prices, and a

---

[1]On the effects of petroleum on whaling see W. S. Tower, *A history of the American whale fishery* (Philadelphia, 1907), chapter vi. In the early sixties whale oil to the extent of $28,000 was produced in the Gaspé area. Whalers from New Bedford and New London left in July, arrived at Marble Island in September, remained frozen in over the winter, began operations in June cruising to Rowe's Welcome about the end of July and returning home with blubber and whalebone in early September. An average catch of the whales brought $40,000 and during the 11 years preceding 1874 about 50 voyages brought returns of $1,371,000 or $27,240 per voyage.

[2]For a description of the St. Lawrence Glassworks at Montreal and their technique of producing lamp chimneys, see H. B. Small, *The products and manufactures of the new dominion*, 143-6.

[3]Charles Marshall, *The Canadian Dominion* (London, 1871), chapter viii; see also Charles Robb, *The Dominion of Canada* (Toronto, 1869), 347.

reduction in the duty from 15 to 6 cents per gallon.   Coal-oil had become a necessity and dependence on American production inevitable.

2

Salt

The oil boom was responsible for the search for oil near Goderich and the discovery of salt in 1866.   Other wells of about 1,000 feet depth were opened at Clinton in 1867 and at Seaforth in 1869.   The technique of pumping was similar to that of oil.   Brine was pumped into wooden vats and from these run into kettles.   The latter were rapidly displaced by cheaper, large, shallow, quadrangular, iron pans varying in size up to 100 feet by 10 feet and over.   Increasing cost of wood for fuel and decline in the price of salt were followed by the introduction of coal from the United States and of coal-tar from Petrolia.   Wooden vats with steam pipes were introduced into flour mills, in order that the exhaust steam might be used to dry salt.   High costs of transport by land gave the wells located near the lake shore an advantage, especially in the sale of salt to packing industries in Chicago and Milwaukee.   As in the case of oil, the domestic market was subject to competition from other countries, especially from England and the United States.[1]   Coarse salt was sold to a limited extent for fertilizing, and specialized plants were adapted to the production of table and dairy salt.   Defective technique in part restricted domestic demands and checked expansion.   Depression in the seventies[2] and "over-pro-

---

[1]See *Ontario agricultural commission report* (Toronto, 1881), app. M. Complaints were numerous against the flooding of the market by English salt brought over as ballast in timber ships.   On the other hand, it was held that salt dried with wood fires was unsatisfactory and the William Davies Company refused to use it.   The dairy interests were satisfied on the whole.   See Report of select committee . . . to enquire into the salt interests of Canada, *J.h.c.*, X, 1876, app. 2; also J. Lionel Smith, "Observations on the history and statistics of the trade and manufacture of Canadian salt" (*Report of the geological survey of Canada*, 1874-5, 267-300); L. H. Cole, *Report on the salt deposits of Canada and the salt industry* (Ottawa, 1915).

[2]   Salt industry in Canada

	1874		1873
Value of plant......	$163,715	Salt manufactured..	451,576 barrels
Value of works.....	408,123		(280 lbs.)
		Value..............	$436,217
Capital invested....	624,000	Land salt..........	3,040 tons
Wages for season....	89,524	Value..............	$8,360

duction" were followed by a decline and by serious problems for Kincardine and Goderich. Finally, an association[1] was organized to fix prices in 1880 but was abandoned on March 29, 1885.

3
Gypsum

The low cost of mining gypsum ($4.50 per ton) by the use of drifts in the river banks of the Grand River in the district between Caledonia and Cayuga and at Paris led to its use as fertilizer within a radius of about 100 miles by 1880 and later over a wider range. Nova Scotian plaster controlled the market in Ontario until at least 1890.

4
Phosphate

The domestic demand for minerals in a relatively non-industrialized country was limited, with the result that mining development was closely related to improved transportation to foreign markets. Railways built to the north of Lake Ontario to meet the demands of the lumber industry laid bare the diverse mineral resources of the area. The Kingston and Pembroke Railway and the railway to Marmora were particularly important.

Apatite was mined as early as 1872 at various locations, but the development of lumber exports from Montreal hastened further expansion in providing lower costs of transport by taking this mineral as ballast. With relatively slight requirements of labour and capital the mineral was raised and sent to market. On the Watt Location: "With very little outside help . . . two young men succeeded in

	1873		1873
Fine salt	438,076 bbls.	Cooperage	8,400 bolts
Coarse salt	13,500 bbls.	Value	$ 25,200
Sold in Canada	226,576 bbls.	(The cooperage industry of the
Sold in U.S.	225,000 bbls.	locality also supplied flour-mills
Wood consumed	50,635 cords.	though with lighter barrels.)
Cost	$143,096		

[1]See J. W. Jenks, "The Michigan salt association" (*Political Science Quarterly*, III, 1888, 78-98); also W. Z. Ripley, *Trusts, pools and corporations* (Boston, 1905), 1-21.

mining and raising upwards of two hundred and twenty-five tons of a very pure apatite, which they sold to Mr. Schultze for export to Germany, at the rate of $10.50 per ton, at the mine." The latter was reported as having "mined, raised and bought, in North Burgess, upwards of 960 tons [*2,240 pounds*], of which he has shipped 600 to Germany". From Alex Cowan's location no. 7 over 800 tons averaging 85 per cent. had been mined in the year ending April, 1871, and shipped to the Brockville Superphosphate[1] Works, "whence it is exported as superphosphate both to the United States and Europe". At Cowan's location no. 19, 549 tons had been raised prior to the autumn of 1871 at the rate of about 3 tons a day.[2] Kingston exported about 5,000 tons in 1882.[3] Production in these areas was limited. "The only reason for not going deeper is the cost, it is more economical to go to another place."

By the end of the decade the industry had developed on the Lievre River near Buckingham in the Ottawa district. Improved transport was responsible for a marked increase in production.

> The greater part of teaming and hauling the phosphate from the mine to the river is done in winter,[4] as the roads are then best adapted for hauling large and heavy loads, and the snow roads may always be calculated on from early in December, and frequently earlier, to about the 10th of April. During that period any quantity of material can be drawn to the river bank and piled there ready for shipment. This plan is now adopted by all the mines in operation, and where they formerly paid from $1.50 and $1.65 per ton for teaming to the railway, the same quantity is carried during summer by water for from 30 to 50 cents.
>
> "Little Rapids" is obviated by the phosphate being loaded on flat-bottomed scows, which, drawing very little water, easily pass the rapids, being towed to the head of them by a small steamer, and being taken in tow by another waiting at the foot of the rapids after the scows have floated over, much in the same way as cribs of timber are sent over the slides here or over the various rapids between here and Quebec. . . . The C.P.R. has erected bins at the landing in which the ore is

---

[1]The Smith Falls Superphosphate Works began operations about 1881.
[2]*S.p.*, 31, 1872.
[3]*S.p.*, 14, 1883.
[4]In the winter of 1881-2, 250 teams were employed daily (*S.p.*, 11, 1882). See R. C. Adams, "The phosphate industry of Canada" (*Canadian economics*, 189-193); also R. A. F. Penrose, "Apatites of Canada" (*Report of the royal commission the mineral resources of Ontario*, 436-443).

deposited before being placed on the cars, and steam cranes at convenient points, by means of which phosphate can be transhipped in the summer season direct from the flat boats in which it is floated down to the cars. . . . In the early days of phosphate mining in this vicinity small operators were beset by countless difficulties, which materially retarded the development of this industry. But within the last few years it has been stimulated by the investment of foreign capital and the organization of powerful companies, composed of men of practical business ability, intelligence and means. The introduction of steam power and improved machinery, economy in the business management of the mines, and the necessity of shipping only a high grade of purity, have now placed these works on a sound and permanent basis.

The old unbusiness-like system of mining, which characterized the first attempts in this district, has now been abandoned. At that time, instead of cutting in the hillside, and developing the veins of phosphate, operations were commenced at the very top, taking out such material as was easily accessible, and as soon as it became at all difficult to manage the opening was abandoned, and another made. Water accumulated, and the quarry of small dimensions became a pond. Adits and drifts or hillside openings are easily drained and kept dry. Capital and energy are evidencing the practicable results attainable thereby. From fifteen to twenty tons of rock are often displaced at a single blast, and a blast will sometimes produce five or six tons of pure phosphate. In addition to the yield of pure phosphate in large masses, frequently large quantities of rich phosphate are mixed with mica, pyrozene, or pyrites, and if shipped in that state the value of the whole would be materially deteriorated. To get rid of this, what is known as "cobbing" is made use of. This consists of the separation by hammers of the phosphate itself from the matrix accompanying it—an easy operation, owing to the softness of the phosphate as compared with the intrusive materials—in a hut or "cobbing" house. On one side of the building, through or around which solid tables or stands are located, are empty tram-cars or waggons, into which the refuse is thrown as broken off by hand, whilst the phosphate thus cleaned is thrown into another receptacle on the other side. Boys and old men are employed at this work, which no machinery has yet been found adapted to perform, and they earn from 50 to 75 cents per day, being paid mostly by piece work. . . . The actual cost of a ton of phosphate[1] from the

---

[1] "The method of mining this mineral is very simple and cheap, the common derrick and horse-whin being so far the only machinery used outside of the shovel, pick and drill. The cost of mining and transportation is reported to be about $8.00 per ton, and the phosphate sells readily in Montreal for from $17.00 to $20.00 per ton (12 c. ft. of the mineral making a ton of 2,240 lbs.)" (*S.p.*, 14, 1883).

Ottawa district delivered alongside the ship in Montreal is from $6.00 to $7.00. This is putting it at its highest figure. The cost of floating the mineral from the mines to Buckingham in scows ranges from 30 to 50 cents per ton. The railway freight thence to Montreal may be set down at $1.00, although cheaper special rates may be bargained for. The ocean freight varies from 75 cents to $1.50 per ton, according as freights are offering, and there have been instances where vessels were glad to carry it as ballast, without charge. With a ready market in Liverpool[1] at from $25.00 to $28.00 per ton, the above shows a large margin for profit, and accounts for the dividends of 25 to 30 per cent. declared by some of the larger existing mining companies.[2]

Exports from Montreal increased from 7,500 tons in 1880 to 15,556 tons in 1882, 17,160 tons in 1883,[3] and 20,461 tons in 1884. The development of phosphate-mining led to the discovery of mica. A small number of mines were operated and the product sold for use in stoves.

5

Iron

The increased demands of the iron and steel industry of the United States during the periods of constructing railroads and of the Civil War, and lower costs of transportation, were factors contributing to the revival of iron-mining.[4] The St. Lawrence Canals had exposed the mines to severe competition but temporary difficulties from that source were offset by the opening of new markets. Iron-ore was exported from the Counties of Leeds, Frontenac, and Lanark, chiefly to Cleveland. In 1870 and 1871 about 14,520 tons were shipped from the Chaffey Iron Mine and the Yankee or Mathews Mine. The former employed, in 1871, 12 men to

---

[1] In 1881 Liverpool quotations for Canadian phosphate were $25.50 (S.p., 11, 1882).

[2] S.p., 10, 1886.

[3] S.p., 9, 1885, app. 27. The total of 17,160 tons in 1883 was valued at $327,667, and 13,197 tons were shipped to Great Britain, 2,080 tons to the United States, and 1,469 tons to Germany (S.p., 11, 1882; and S.p., 14, 1883). The British farmer was becoming interested in Canadian deposits as "the great guano beds of Peru and Chili are approaching exhaustion" (S.p., 5, 1889).

[4] Ontario department of mines, 1924, *Ontario iron ore committee report*; also J. H. Bartlett, *The manufacture, consumption and production of iron, steel and coal in the Dominion of Canada* (Montreal, 1885).

raise about 3,500 tons. "At the mine it is worth $2.25 per ton, and delivered at Cleveland it brings from $6.00 to $6.50 per ton. The cost of carriage to Kingston—a distance of 44 miles—is 75 cents per ton." In the latter mine "during the year 1871, fifteen men were steadily employed and upwards of 4,000 tons of ore mined and raised, 3,300 tons of which were sold." The Dalhousie Iron Mine raised from April 1 to November 6 about 2,500 tons.

> From this opening there has been extracted very close upon 10,000 tons of ore. About twenty-five men are employed, including one mining-captain and one blacksmith. The ore is drawn to Perth by waggons in summer, at the rate of $1.70 per ton, and in winter by sleighs, at $1.00 per ton of 2,240 lbs. From Perth it is carried by railroad to Brockville, and shipped thence to Cleveland, Ohio. The cost of the ore, laid down in Cleveland, is $5.00 per ton.[1]

In 1881, 19,000 tons and in 1882, 40,922 tons were forwarded from Kingston, chiefly from the Townships of Palmerston and Levant—the Bethlehem Iron Company's mine in Levant Township producing 50 tons per day. "The present working capacity of the Mississippi Iron Mine, in Palmerston Township, is 100 tons (magnetic) ore per day—depth of shaft, 173 ft.; width of vein, 60 ft.; length now open 300 ft.; and it is the intention to nearly double the output of ore at this mine."[2] Mines were also in operation in Madoc and Marmora[3] Townships.

6

Quartz Gold

The development of iron- and phosphate-mining in the district north of Lake Ontario was followed by the discovery of quartz gold, especially in Hastings County. Quartz-mining was limited to operations on a small scale and was conducted under serious handicaps, chiefly as a result of the difficulties of extraction. At the Cooke or Williams Mine a shaft of over 60 feet was sunk. The ore was placed in an

---

[1]*S.p.*, 31, 1872.
[2]*S.p.*, 14, 1883.
[3]See W. J. A. Donald, *History of the Canadian iron and steel industry* (Boston, 1915), chapter iii.

open kiln holding 40 tons and calcined in 4 days—one clean-up of 107 tons of ore giving $1,035.   On the other hand, a mill with a battery of 5 circular, rotating stamp-heads worked by a 15-horse-power engine which had been bought from a mine in Barrie Township gave a yield of about $10.00 a ton from ore which had not been calcined.   In 1871 an attempt to use a patented mill, called the J. W. Forbes Automatic Steam Quartz Crusher, was unsuccessful.   In 1871-2 the old stamps were used and 15 stamps and a revolving cylinder-furnace added—all of which were run by a 50-horse-power engine. "The quartz is crushed in the batteries with water and the pulverized ore passed over a set of blanket troughs previous to its treatment in amalgamating pans of the Wheeler pattern."[1]   In spite of the gradual improvement of technique the deposits of high-grade ore were relatively small and the Deloro Mine alone continued to be important.

7

Copper

Limited industrial development necessitated exports of metallic ores to more highly industrialized countries because of both lack of demand and lack of technique.   Generally mining was confined to locations within a comparatively short distance of the water-routes, because of the high cost of moving heavy ores and of transporting heavy machinery for producing refined ores, and the lack of information available as to the relatively inaccessible, mineral-bearing formations. Exploration and development of the rich mineral-bearing Pre-Cambrian area were limited to the accessible portions along the north shores of Lake Huron and Lake Superior and to the relatively valuable minerals and the richly concentrated ore bodies, as in the case of silver and copper.   The development of mining was limited to the relatively small deposits of high-grade ore and to the more valuable minerals.

The development of copper-mining was particularly dependent on transportation because of the problems of extraction.   Smelting at the mines proved unsuccessful.

---

[1]*S.p.*, 31, 1872.

Copper had been prospected and mined in the Lake Superior region over a long period. Opening of the canals and reports of geologists in Michigan led to the formation of the Montreal Mining Company in 1845, and to the discovery of copper at Bruce Mines and Copper Bay in 1847. De Rottermund wrote in 1855:[1]

> At the period of my arrival a new apparatus for washing the ore was in course of construction. It is an American invention; by it the ore is first reduced to powder as fine and as uniform as possible; this powder is then placed upon sieves of different numbers, which have a continual horizontal motion with a slight concussion. By means of this "rocker" the copper ore is separated from the ordinary stone, the action of the machine being based upon the well known principle—that all matters being reduced to the same volume, if they are of different weights, and are equally exposed to the same action of displacement, range themselves in the order of their respective weights.[2]

The Bruce Mines were closed down but the Wellington Mines on the same vein started operations with the construction of smelting works. These were burned down, and by 1864 the Canada West Mining Company had bought the property from the Montreal Mining Company and was employing 400 men. ◦ "The copper ore is crushed by powerful machinery, and then put into 'puddling troughs', and washed by water, and 'dressed' up, so that when shipped —as it is direct from there to Swansea, England—it contains about 20 per cent. of copper, and is worth about $80 per ton."[3]

> The number of British and foreign steamers and "sail vessels" to and from the Port of Bruce Mines last year [*1863*], was 116; since then a line of first-class vessels, owned by Cunningham Sons, of Liverpool, have been put on the route between Liverpool and "Bruce Mines", calling with freight at various places, as they go up to the mines, and on arrival there are loaded with copper ore direct for England.

In 1863, 4,532 tons of copper-ore at a value of $270,791, were exported and a dividend of $60,000 declared. Later, apparently, ore was sent to the United States, but a duty of

---

[1]Bruce Mines at this date had about 100 houses, wharves, blacksmith's shop, and mining buildings.
[2]*Journals of the legislative assembly*, XIV, 1856, app. 37.
[3]*S.p.*, 37, 1865.

5 cents per pound, higher costs of mining, and difficulties with regard to labour led to a cessation of activities.[1] In eastern Canada the Acton Mine in Bagot County began operations in January, 1862, the Harvey Hill Mine in Leeds County, and the Ascot Mine near Sherbrooke at earlier dates, all of which exported quantities of ore to England.

> The great drawbacks to the successful and profitable operation of mining in the Province are the scarcity and consequently exorbitant cost of labour; the charges incidental to transportation, which twice exceed those in England; and having to send the ore to Wales for the purpose of being smelted. A few smelting works have been tried in the neighbourhood of Lake Superior, but they did not answer. It was found necessary to amalgamate the ore with metal of a similar description so as to render it marketable; and, besides, its production cost less by shipping it to Wales than if it had been manufactured in the Province.[2]

8

Silver

In the search for copper, silver was discovered on Silver Islet about 1868 by the Montreal Mining Company. After being sold to a New York syndicate, operations were begun in the autumn of 1870.[3] In spite of tremendous difficulties with the water, $100,000 worth of silver-ore was sent out by the end of November. In 1875 J. C. Hamilton wrote:

> A busy place is this Silver Islet, with crushing mills, storehouses, and clap-board dwellings, all owned by a great American Company, and under charge of the able and ingenious manager, Captain Frue. Fifty stamps are being worked, and from 100 to 150 tons of ore crushed per day. The yield is reported by the Company to be in value from $36,000 to $40,000 per month, the whole cost of getting out, crushing and washing the ore by Captain Frue's process amounting to only $2.25

---

[1]Development at Bruce Mines was encouraged through the establishment of a free port area. Imports at Sault Ste. Marie increased from $54,421 in 1860 to $92,704 in 1861. Mining costs were lowered by the remission of duty on machinery, tools, and supplies; and consumers' goods were reduced in price. On the other hand, it was claimed that clothing remained practically unchanged in price while tea was reduced 20 per cent., gin 30 to 40 per cent., and wine 20 per cent. Sugar remained unchanged (*S.p.*, 2, 1862; *S.p.*, 37, 1865).

[2]S. P. Day, *English America*, II, 291-3.

[3]See R. A. Haste, "The lost mine of Silver Islet" (Thunder Bay Historical Society, 18th and 19th *annual reports*, 36-43); A. Blue, *The story of Silver Islet* (Ontario bureau of mines, VI, 1896).

per ton, while eight ounces of silver are, on an average, extracted from that quantity of rock of low grade.[1] The mine was closed in 1884,[2] nearly $3,000,000 of silver having been extracted.

9

Gold

Geological formations were not favourable to placer gold[3] but successful operations were carried out on the Chaudière River in 1863 and were followed by a gold-rush in 1864.

When in October 1863 I visited the Gilbert River for the first time, I found upon the lots 18, 19 and 20, from 100 to 120 gold miners, divided into companies of from four to ten. Their workings consisted of a series of open excavations ten or fifteen feet deep, and of dimensions varying according to the number of workers. These open pits were sunk side by side, without method or regularity. While it is certain that large quantities of gold were extracted from these excavations, it is equally certain that a great quantity has been lost and left behind. The walls, often of considerable thickness, which separated the different pits, constitute in themselves a considerable volume of alluvion as yet untouched; and if we add to this the gold which was certainly lost by imperfect washings, it is safe to suppose, that a regular and methodic re-working of the deposit, including both the portions of undisturbed gravel and the refuse of the previous washings would be profitable to whoever would undertake the operation.[4]

---

[1] J. C. Hamilton, *The prairie province* (Toronto, 1876), 3-4.
[2] By this date the shaft had been sunk to 1,300 feet.
[3] H. White, *The gold regions of Canada* (Toronto, 1867).
[4] *S.p.*, 6, 1865. The Reciprocity Company built a wooden flume, 1,800 feet by 4 feet by 3 feet deep, supported by trestles to take the water from the channel higher up and to bring it down to wash the dirt. The dam built to hold the water for the flume was washed out in July, 1865, and after an expenditure in building and repairs of $12,000 to $15,000 the company removed about $2,500 in gold by open cutting in the bed of the stream (*S.p.*, 3, 1866).

"I must here call attention to a fact which is not without importance for the future of gold mining in Lower Canada, namely, the subterranean working of the alluvions during the winter season. This was attempted in the winter of 1864-65 by about thirty miners divided into companies of from four to six. By the aid of pits and galleries they were able to carry on their search for gold throughout the winter, and to extract and wash a large quantity of gravel, in which the gold was so abundant as to richly repay their energy and perseverance. Among others was a mass of gold weighing a little over a pound. When I visited the

It was estimated that nearly $3,000,000 worth of gold was recovered in this area by 1885.

10

Asbestos[1]

By the end of the period through lines of railway had penetrated richer mineral-bearing formations and mining had taken root in the country's growth. Asbestos was first worked in Quebec in 1878 following its discovery in 1877 during the construction of the Quebec Central Railway. In 1885 Thetford employed nearly 250 men and the 4 companies, King Brothers, The Boston Company, Johnston's Company, and Ward Brothers, produced about 1,100 tons annually. 3 companies at Black Lake—Lionai's, Hopper's, and Frechette's—employed about 100 men and produced about 60 tons monthly. These companies operated only in summer, although Jeffery's Mine at Danville worked also in winter and produced about 15 tons. The price of asbestos in 1885 was:—no. 1, $75.00 to $80.00; no. 2, $50.00; and no. 3, $10.00 —"the latter being largely used for paper stock".[2]

Gilbert in May last, these subterranean workings were still going on, and I was able to examine them. The pits, fifteen in number, and all on lot 18, were opened on the left bank, at distances of from fifty to one hundred feet from the stream, and sunk to the bed-rock, a depth of from twenty to twenty-five feet. They were connected by galleries, one of which, draining the whole of the works, carried the waters into a pit, from whence they were raised by pumps and carried into the river. The auriferous materials were washed in rockers, generally at the bottom of each pit. Some gold was found in the gravel which covered the slates and sandstones, but the greater part was extracted from the fissures in these rocks. The same was true in most of the rich workings on this river, and particularly on lots 19 and 20, where, of two layers of gravel, separated by a stratum of bluish or yellowish clay, only the lower one was auriferous. The bed-rock, formed of interstratified clay-slates and sandstones, is sometimes broken up to the depth of five or six feet, and it is in its joints and between its laminae, where the gravel has penetrated and often become indurated, that the gold has been found in the greatest abundance and in the largest masses. It is impossible to form an estimate, even approximate, of the quantities of gold extracted from the Gilbert and its banks during the last three years, the interests of opposite parties having led some to depreciate and others to exaggerate the amount" (M. A. Michel, Report on the gold region of Lower Canada, S.p., 3, 1866).

[1] F. A. Stilgenbauer, "Economic geography of Canadian asbestos" (*Bulletin* of the Geographical Society of Philadelphia, XXIII, 13 ff.); also M. M. Mendels, *The asbestos industry of Canada* (McGill University economic studies, no. 14); F. Cirkel, *Chrysotile-asbestos* (Ottawa, 1910); J. G. Ross, *Chrysotile asbestos in Canada* (Ottawa, 1931).

[2] S.p., 8, 1886.

11
Nickel

Even more important was the discovery of copper and nickel[1] at Sudbury along the main line of the Canadian Pacific Railway. The rich mineral-bearing Pre-Cambrian area was at last unlocked and the road begun which ended in Cobalt, Porcupine, Kirkland Lake, and Noranda.

12
The Geological Survey

Throughout the period organizations were gradually built up in relation to the collection, compilation, and distribution of information on geological formations. The formation of the geological survey in 1843 and the publication of its reports and of the *Report of the progress of the geological survey, 1843-1863*, were pre-requisites to the development of prospecting and mining. Officers of the geological survey were required to make a geographical map of the country before laying down their geological observations and the telegraph facilitated determination of the longitude of principal points. With the addition of information provided in the admiralty charts of Admiral Bayfield, valuable maps were published.[2] The select committee[3] appointed to report upon the best means of making public the valuable information already obtained by the geological survey, and completing it at an early period upon a uniform system, under the chairmanship of John Langton, reported (on March 29, 1855) that "the public should provide general information for all; the individuals who are to turn it to their private profit, must supply the rest", and advised "the republication of not less than 20,000 copies of the revised reports", and the publication of annual reports to the same extent in future. They recommended the gratuitous distribution of copies to

[1]*Report of the royal Ontario nickel commission, 1917*; A. P. Coleman, *The nickel industry with special reference to the Sudbury region* (Ontario department of mines, mines branch, Ottawa, 1913); *The Sudbury nickel field* (Ontario bureau of mines, XIV, pt. 3, 1905).

[2]See S. P. Day, *English America*, I, 196. See *Reports of the geological survey of Canada*, index volumes, 1863-84, 1884-1906, 1905-16.

[3]*Journals of the legislative assembly*, XIII, 1854-5, app. L.

governments, educational institutions, and societies. They also recommended the establishment of the "museum and library upon an efficient footing" and the enlargement of the staff to include topographical surveyors and geologists. They suggested "requiring all railway companies to furnish plans and sections of their surveys".

In spite of the effectiveness of the work of the geological survey, limited resources, the vast extent of country to be covered, and the limited character of the work necessitated the formation of provincial organizations. By the end of the period the provinces were becoming more directly interested in detailed surveys of their mineral resources, the formation of museums, the collection of statistics, and the establishment of more effective educational institutions.[1]

13

Development of the Mining Industry

The character of mining development was an index of the economic growth of the St. Lawrence drainage basin. In a period dominated by the expansion of railways in agricultural areas and by lumbering, the possibilities of metallic minerals were relatively slight. Labour and skill as well as capital were attracted elsewhere. It was significant, however, that by the end of the period more than half the capital employed in the industry came from the United States and that more Canadian capital was employed than English capital. Moreover, in the period from 1881 to 1887, exports of minerals to the United States totalled $18,567,710 and to other countries $4,828,313. *The report of the royal commission on the mineral resources of Ontario* (Toronto, 1890) urged the removal of duties on mining machinery—hoisting works and stamp mills—and supplies and the adoption of measures leading to easier access to American markets. American markets, American capital, and American management were in demand. Railways were expected to encourage

---

[1]See *Report of the royal commission on the mineral resources of Ontario*, section VI. See annual reports of the inspector of mines, *S.p., Ont.*; Bureau of mines report, *S.p., Ont.* (first report, *S.p.*, 88, 1892); Reports of the minister of lands and mines, *S.p., Ont.*

rapid development not only by giving access to markets but also by providing cheaper supplies of coal with the disappearance of the supply of wood.

In spite of these handicaps, valuable experience had been gained during the period. The shift from wood to metals was pronounced in spite of the limitations of mining, of primitive technique, of relatively slight deposits, and of competition from other areas. Skilled miners from Cornwall and Wales came into the country; steam had been adapted to mining demands; mining machinery was made on a small scale; and subsidiary industries had grown up. The "boom" character of mining accentuated diversification of industry. Mining laws were gradually improved and brought into line with American experience. Royalties and reserves were abolished in 1869 and strong attempts were made to improve the position of the prospector.[1] Finally, the mining and metallurgical industries[2] had advanced to support rapid strides in Canadian industry. Lower costs of iron and steel were basic to the expansion of the mining industry. Canada had made substantial progress in mining. Her next advance was based on metallurgy. The railroad, cheap supplies of coal and hydro-electric power, and the penetration of the Pre-Cambrian area were essential to expansion.

---

[1]See *Report of the royal commission on the mineral resources of Ontario*, section IV.

[2]" It could have had no existence without the raw materials of ore and fuel; it could have had no beginning without labour; it could have made no progress without the support of capital; but without the aid of invention the industry would be still in puling infancy. In every step and stage of the business from raising the ore out of the earth to the finishing touch upon the manufactured metal, the ingenuity of man is found overcoming the forces of nature, lightening labour, cheapening production, improving the qualities of the material itself, finding out new areas for it in the arts and adapting it in a thousand ways to the wants of an advancing civilization. Mining of any kind would have been difficult and costly and deep mining would have been all but impossible, but for the service of the air compressors, the drills, the explosives and the hoisting apparatus now employed at every well equipped mine, while means of cheap and rapid transit of ores and methods of treating them in preparation for the smelting furnace have made properties workable and valuable which otherwise might have remained unused and idle to the end of time" (*ibid.*, 354).

INDUSTRY[1]

Improved navigation and the railway hastened the expansion of agriculture, the rise of the sawn-lumber industry, and the development of mining. The demands of an increased population for manufactured products were met by an increase in imports[2] and an increase in industry. Concentration

[1]*The Cambridge history of the British Empire*, VI, 608 *ff*.; H. B. Small, *The products and manufactures of the new dominion*; J. Young, *Reminiscences of the early history of Galt* (Toronto, 1880); C. A. Burrows, *The annals of the Town of Guelph (1827-1877)* (Guelph, 1877); J. R. Robertson, *Landmarks of Toronto*, I-VI; J. E. Middleton, *The municipality of Toronto* (Toronto, 1923), I, 501-515; W. H. Pearson, *Recollections and records of Toronto of old* (Toronto, 1914); G. M. Adam, *Toronto old and new* (Toronto, 1898); *The handbook of Toronto* (Toronto, 1858); *History of Toronto and County of York*, 2 vols.; C. C. Taylor, *Toronto "called back" from 1886 to 1850* (Toronto, 1886); J. Timperlake, *Illustrated Toronto past and present* (Toronto, 1877); J. R. Connon, *Elora* (Elora, 1930); W. A. Craick, *Port Hope historical sketches* (Port Hope, 1901); L. Brown, *A history of Simcoe (1829-1929)* (Simcoe, 1929); E. E. Cinq-Mars, *Hull, son origin, ses progrès, son avenir* (Hull, 1908); A. C. Després, *Histoire de Sorel* (Montreal, 1926); J. E. Bellemare, *Histoire de Nicolet 1669-1924* (Arthabaska, 1924); T. E. Kaiser, *Historic sketches of Oshawa* (Oshawa, 1921); F. E. Page, *The story of Smithville* (Welland, 1923); J. H. Thompson, *Jubilee history of Thorold Township and town* (Thorold, 1897-8); H. Têtu, *Resumé historique de l'industrie et du commerce de Québec* (Quebec, 1899); A. Bremner, *City of London* (London, 1897); A. Gravel, *Histoire du lac Mégantic* (Sherbrooke, 1931); E. J. Auclair, *Histoire de Coaticook* (Sherbrooke, 1925); R. P. Leduc, *Beauharnois,—Paroisse Saint Clement* (Ottawa, 1920); J. U. Forget et E. J. Auclair, *Histoire de Saint Jacques d'Embrun Russell, Ontario* (Ottawa, 1910); A. Sandham, *Ville-Marie or sketches of Montreal past and present* (Montreal, 1870); J. C. St. Amant, *L'avenir townships de Durham et de Wickham . . . du comté de Drummond* (Arthabaskaville, 1896); R. Tanghe, *Géographie humaine de Montréal* (Montreal, 1928); W. H. Atherton, *Montreal* (Montreal, 1914), chapter xxxvi; F. W. Terrill, *A chronology of Montreal* (Montreal, 1893); W. D. Lighthall, *Montreal after 250 years* (Montreal, 1892); A. L. de Burmath, *Histoire populaire de Montréal* (Montreal, 1890); Lamothe and others, *Histoire de la corporation de la cité de Montréal* (Montreal, 1903); Annual reports of the bureau of industries, beginning *S.p.*, Ont., 3, 1882-3; *The Province of Ontario*, 633-658; Report of select committee . . . manufacturing interests, *J.h.c.*, VIII, 1874, app. 2. For valuable sketches of various industries, see *Picturesque Canada* (Toronto, 1882); *Reports* of the Montreal board of trade, and of the Toronto board of trade, especially *Reports of the president and treasurer of the Toronto board of trade for the year 1883 . . . to which is added an appendix containing tables of imports and exports of the port of Toronto for the years 1844 to 1883 inclusive* (Toronto, 1884); *Hamilton, the Birmingham of Canada* (Hamilton, 1892); *Canadian Manufacturer* (Toronto, 1880); *Canadian Textile Journal* (Gardenvale, 1883).

[2]"Articles which are imported in the largest quantities, with the total value of importation of each kind of article, for 1853:

Raw Sugar	£264,919 cy.
Tea	390,105
Manufactured Tobacco	106,794
Cotton	1,315,635
Iron Manufactures	648,720

on products for export, made possible by improved transport, hastened the decline of domestic industry and the rise of the factory system and the growth of towns. Wood gradually gave way to iron.[1] Demands for labour stressed the importance of capital and machinery.

It could not reasonably be expected that Canada, where it is so difficult to procure labor, to turn to advantage the great number of natural productions which the soil itself contains, on account of the comparative scarceness both of capital and workmen, should contribute any extensive collection of articles, for the most part belonging to those classes of manufactures which require a low rate of labor, and a large consumption, and which are adapted to an advanced stage of society.[2]

1

Ship-building

The demands of the transport industries were of first importance. The rise of iron steamships and of the port of Montreal, the emergence of wheat and sawn lumber, and the decline of square timber were factors responsible for the difficulties of the wooden ship-building industry, especially at Quebec.[3] Improvement of the St. Lawrence ship

---

Linen	133,414
Woollen Goods	254,255
Bar and Sheet Iron	310,805
Railway Iron	343,593
Books	103,245"

[1]"That this being essentially a wooden country there are few opportunities of seeing or hearing anything about the detailed processes of manufacture" of iron (J. H. Bartlett, *The manufacture, consumption and production of iron, steel and coal in the Dominion of Canada*).

[2]J. C. Taché, *Sketch of Canada.* See also a list of prices of machinery and of manufactured products (*ibid.*). "One leading feature of these establishments is that machinery is made to do what in the old country is accomplished by human hand" (S. P. Day, *English America*, I, 179).

[3]For the trade in timber, barques of 600 to 700 tons were employed to carry 750 to 960 tons of timber, making a return voyage to England in 8 or 12 weeks. In 1859, 970 vessels of 510,814 tons and 17,046 men entered Quebec and 1,051 vessels of 539,135 tons and 17,834 men cleared. To all ports of the province 17,413 vessels entered and 16,499 cleared. On the difficulties of wooden ship-building at Quebec see Third and fourth reports of the select committee appointed to inquire into the general conditions of the building of merchant vessels in the Dominion of Canada and as to the means of promoting its development, *J.h.c.*, 1867-8, app. 2. See F. W. Wallace, *In the wake of the wind ships* (Toronto, 1927), part II, and *Wooden ships and iron men* (Toronto, n.d.), *passim*, and *Record of Canadian shipping* (Toronto, 1929); also S. P. Day, *English America*, I, 32-3. In 1876 it was stated that wooden ships were being forced out of long voyages and were returning to compete in the already unremunerative coasting trade.

channel, deepening of canals, and completion of railways of the portage type—the Welland Railway and the Northern Railway—stimulated ship-building,[1] but the completion of through lines, the weakening of the St. Lawrence route, and the increasing importance of large vessels[2] contributed to its decline. The diverse industries built up around wooden ship-building suffered in turn. From 1845 to 1862 the Canada Marine Works[3] built 94 vessels chiefly for navigation on lake and river—high speed, large carrying-capacity, and light draught. With recovery from the depression of 1857, trade increased and the steamboat industry improved after 1861. Such improvement was destined to be of short duration. Following the abrogation of the Reciprocity Treaty, complaints were made in 1868 that Canadian vessels were subject to unfair discrimination as contrasted with American vessels. Canadian vessels were barred from the coasting trade of the United States and from the use of American canals and were subject to the payment of the war tax on shipping and of custom-house fees on entering and clearing American ports. American vessels were given privileges similar to Canadian vessels on Canadian canals, were allowed to enter and clear custom-houses without payment of fees, and were able to procure British registry free in Ontario and Quebec and for a low charge of $1.50 to $4.00 in New Brunswick and Nova Scotia.[4] As a result of a petition on the part of "shipowning, forwarding and ship-building interests" for a more equitable arrangement, a bill was passed (33 Vic. c. 14, 1870) prohibiting foreign vessels from carrying "goods or passengers between any ports or places in the Dominion" without permission by order-in-council which would declare the coasting trade open to countries willing

---

[1]See G. A. Cuthbertson, *Freshwater*, chapter xii; also *Canada, an encyclopedia of the country*, III, 285-365. Construction of railways provided minor demands, for example, the *Beaver* and the *Muskrat* were built for the use of the contractors of the Victoria bridge (S. P. Day, *English America*, I, 187-9).

[2]Decline in the trade in timber in the small ports also affected the ship-building industry—the small ship-building yards, for example, at Trenton at which the Gilmours built a schooner of 115 feet keel, 26 feet beam, and 9 feet 6 inches depth of hold, of 385 tons in 1864.

[3]These works covered 15 acres and included a foundry, boiler, and finishing shop. A condensing steam engine was used to operate the plant as well as a saw and planing mill. The plant included 2 basins 500 feet by 100 feet. In 1858 the *Colon*, a screw propeller for Cuba, was built in these yards.

[4]*S.p.*, 37, 1870.

to enter into reciprocal arrangements.[1] The decline continued throughout the depression of the seventies in spite of
this measure and further complaints were made in a petition
of ship-owners, ship-builders, steamboat-owners, and other
citizens of Quebec and Lévis (signed by Ross and Company
and 119 others) against the admission of American-built
vessels to British registry.

> There are now a great number of steamers and other
> vessels of United States build which have been admitted to
> registry in Canada, which have not contributed one cent to
> the Revenue of the country, while Canadian built vessels,
> more particularly steamers have been obliged to pay duties
> on nearly every thing entering into their construction, as iron,
> brass, copper, boiler plate, rivets, tools, cutlery, crockery,
> lamps and a hundred other things required in their construc-
> tion and equipment. . . .
>
> That several hundred of those American-built vessels now
> owned in Canada are, by the laws of the United States, for-
> ever excluded from returning thence or of being employed in
> any of their waters, and have now to a great extent, by recent
> improvements in machinery, become a dead loss to their
> owners and the country.[2]

But the problems of ship-building, as the ship-builders of
Welland County pointed out in 1881, were linked with the
problem of water-competition by the St. Lawrence.[3] The
decline was offset in part by the opening up of new routes
to the north in the latter part of the period. The construction of railroads, the grain trade, and the development of
mining and lumbering on Lake Superior and in the north
stimulated ship-building at terminal points such as Collingwood and Owen Sound.

2

Construction of Railways and Subsidiary Industries

The relative decline of ship-building and its subsidiary
industries was offset by the construction of railroads and

---

[1] *S.p.*, 11, 1870.
[2] *S.p.*, 40, 1879.
[3] American vessels in 1870 paid tolls of $18,937 as contrasted with Canadian
vessels which paid $11,828. American vessels were much larger in 1870—2,884
of 765,543 tons in contrast with Canadian vessels, 3,856 of 591,574 tons. In
1870, 878 American vessels and 1,119 Canadian vessels went through the Welland
Canal but the tonnage of American vessels was more than double the Canadian
(*S.p.*, 54, 1871).

its subsidiary industries. The equipment and experience
of England and the United States supported industrial
growth in Canada. "The greater part of the rolling stock
for the Grand Trunk railway of Canada had to be constructed at Birkenhead." But English manufacturers
were

> obliged to adopt the American system of locomotives. These
> American engines were all constructed with "bogies". It is
> well known that "the bogie" carriage yields to every irregu-
> larity in the railroad, whether it be horizontal or lateral, where-
> as, in an ordinary English locomotive, the leading wheels
> would soon be worn out from the violent oscillation and vibra-
> tion arising from the traffic on the rough railroads which exist
> in America.

Morticing and planing machines were not made in England
but were supplied by American manufacturers to the work-
shops of the "Canada works". The short season and
scarcity of labour placed a premium on the use of machinery.
Mr. Rowan one of the 4 agents in charge of divisions during
construction wrote:

> Towards the last, in consequence of the extreme cost of
> labour, we employed steam excavators, not because they were
> cheaper than men, but because they supplied the want of
> labour, and enabled us to get on faster. A steam excavator
> is found to be profitable only in very hard material, such as
> hard pan, in which a very large force is required to excavate.
> In lighter materials such as sand or gravel, it is more expensive
> to use than men at five or six shillings a day. We used them
> notwithstanding, even in filling ballast, and I undertook a
> large quantity of ballasting myself in that way.
>   This scarcity of labour gave rise to great difficulty in the
> execution of the railway works on the Grand Trunk Line.
> Wages were very high. A man who received five shillings in
> England per diem, would receive seven shillings and sixpence
> in Canada. This difference in the rate of wages was caused
> not only by the scarcity of labour, but by the circumstance
> that, in Canada, out-of-door work is impossible for four months
> in the year.[1]

The building of Victoria bridge involved the development
of engineering technique. Stone piers were specially de-

---

[1]Arthur Helps, *Life and labours of Mr. Brassey*, 190 *ff.*; also J. H. Hodges,
Construction of the great Victoria bridge in Canada (London, 1860). Wages for
constructing railroads in eastern Ontario in the early eighties were $1.50 per day
of 10 hours not including board at $3.00 per week (*S.p.*, 14, 1883).

signed to support the bridge and resist pressure from the ice in spring. Floating dams were employed for building the piers and a large steam traveller transported the stone. "Over 70,000 tons of stone were twice moved by this machine." The materials included 2,713,095 cubic feet of masonry, 2,280,000 cubic feet of timber for temporary works, 9,044 tons of iron, 1,540,000 rivets, and the work employed 6 steamboats, 75 barges, 3,040 men, 144 horses, and 4 loco-motives.[1] The works developed in connection with the bridge at Point Charles became a basis for the Grand Trunk work-shops. The Toronto Locomotive Works turned out the first locomotive in 1853 but large numbers were imported from Great Britain. New machine-shops were completed at Stratford and a new car-shop at Brantford in 1871. In 1881 the Kingston Locomotive Works[2] employed about 350 men.

3

The Iron Industry

The immediate demands of the railway stimulated the iron industry. In 1860 Messrs Gzowski and Macpherson built a large rolling mill at Toronto to reroll iron rails and in 1864 the Great Western Railway opened a rolling mill at Hamilton. These mills, in addition to that of the Steel Iron and Railway Works Company at Toronto, were forced to close down as a result of the shift from iron to steel rails in 1872-3. Special demands for charcoal iron supported small smelting plants engaged chiefly in the production of car-wheels and axles. The Radnor forges, a descendant of the industry at Three Rivers which had grown up over a long period in relation to bog-iron, were engaged in the pro-duction of charcoal pig-iron after 1860 for the manufacture of car-wheels, wrought iron, scythes, and nail rod-iron. Resources of Yamaska bog-iron supported an industry from 1869-1880. The Grantham Iron Works were opened in 1880-1. It was estimated that 8,000 to 10,000 tons of iron were used yearly for car-wheels. In 1878 the Hamilton

[1]Arthur Helps, *Life and labours of Mr. Brassey*, 202-211.
[2]See "The Canadian Locomotive Company Limited" (*Queen's Quarterly*, April, 1903, 455-464).

38

Iron Forging Company engaged in the production of car-axles, and in 1879 the Ontario Rolling Mill Company, also at Hamilton, began operations in the manufacture of bar-iron, nail-plate, fish-plate, and nails. The increasing cost of wood for the production of charcoal, the exhaustion of high-grade bog-ores, and lower costs of production in other countries weakened the position of the domestic iron industry. The demands of the railways were chiefly responsible for building up an industry dependent on the imports of iron from other countries. By the end of the period foundries producing car-wheels were in operation at St. Thomas, Montreal, Lachine, and Hamilton.

The construction of railroads, followed by growth of population and expansion of agriculture, hastened the development of iron manufactures. Lower costs of producing iron in the United States and Great Britain and lower costs of transportation of pig-iron contributed to the growth of foundries. Industries engaged in the manufacture of farming equipment, stoves, edge tools, farming implements and utensils expanded rapidly. The foundry, the plant supplying iron work to railways,[1] and the blacksmith shop provided a base for the development of the iron industries.

(i)

The north shore of Lake Ontario

The wood and iron industries tended to develop over wide areas but as iron became increasingly important, access to cheap supplies of coal and to water-transport became determining factors in the location of the industry. Along the north shore of Lake Ontario and the St. Lawrence, in 1860, Dundas County[2] had one foundry (which cast 65 tons of metal annually, turned out 400 ploughs at $8.00 each, and

---

[1]Firms engaged in supplying iron work for bridges, turntables, and stations became engaged in other work after completion of the road. The firm of McKittrick Brothers of Orangeville, for example, shifted their work to the production of reapers, mowers, sulky rakes, and plows. Construction of railroads apparently favoured the production of dynamite and giant powder and in 1877 a marked increase in imports of sulphuric acid was reported (S.p., 2, 1879).

[2]Croil describes a fanning mill factory at Williamsburgh with an 8-horse-power engine employing 6 hands and turning out 250 mills per annum at $24.00 each. The mills were sent chiefly to Montreal, Ottawa, and Glengarry.

75 stoves at $20.00); Newcastle one foundry and machine-shop with 20-horse-power engine and employing 40 to 50 men (in 1864, 3 carriage and waggon factories and one pitch fork factory); Trenton, a foundry with machine-shop and engine-house. The foundry developed as a centre for the manufacture of special products. In Cobourg (1864) the Ontario Foundry produced reaping machines, steam engines, and mill-gearing. In the same locality an engine and mill works employed 20 to 30 hands. The firm of A. S. Whiting Company of Oshawa developed an export trade in agricultural tools (scythes, hoes, forks) in Europe after 1870.[1]

(ii)

Western Ontario

In western Ontario, foundries and blacksmiths were widely scattered and served also as a basis for the development of an economy based on wood and iron. In 1857 Galt, for example, had 3 foundries. At a later date Owen Sound also had 3 foundries, and Chippewa had one of the largest foundries in Canada. A blacksmith shop in Mount Forest in 1855 expanded its production to 160 vehicles and a large number of plows by 1878. The founder of Cossitt's Agricultural Works came to Guelph from the United States in 1859 and, beginning with fanning mills (200 per year), his products included in 1878, lawn-mowers (1,000 per year), plows (100 per week), and turnip-sowers (200 per week). The Raymond Sewing Machine was founded by Charles Raymond of Massachusetts. The firm in 1878 employed 160 men and manufactured about 28,000 machines, chiefly for the home market but also for Mexico, South America, Australia, New Zealand, Spain, Portugal, Germany, Great Britain, and Denmark. The Guelph Sewing Machine Company was concerned chiefly with Ontario. The Guelph Carriage Goods Company exported Armstrong carriage-springs to Great Britain. Crowe's Iron Works were established in the same city (1869) to supply castings for the Raymond Sewing Machine and added castings for knitting machines, axle-boxes, crestings, fencings, and "the lighter class of iron work". The firm

---

[1] *S.p.*, 9, 1878.

employed 30 men. "The sand used is chiefly obtained in the United States—from Albany,—while the iron is mostly Summerlee, (Scotch pig) mixed more or less with American." The Harriston Agricultural Works produced in 1878,

> separators, horse powers, sawing machines, hand and horse power straw cutters, land rollers, fanning mills, grain crushers, cultivators, gang and other plows, wrought iron and steel scufflers, horse hay rakes, stump machines, and other implements, and besides this long list the Works have other specialties, the leading one being school desks, of different patterns and styles—light, graceful and above all, comfortable.

W. H. Mills of Guelph had by 1878 been forced to limit his activities to stoves, tinware, plows, and castings to order, and employed 20 men. "He furnishes a large amount of tinware to peddlers." Inglis and Hunter manufactured Corliss engines from 15-horse-power up, which were sold from Sarnia to Quebec, "in the latter province a very good business is held both in engines and mill machinery". Tolton Brothers[1] patented an invention for pea-harvesters and manufactured this product.

(iii)

Agricultural implements

Agricultural expansion in western Ontario, development of protection, migration of skill from the United States, and advantages of protection with an inland location favoured the growth of industries in the towns of the peninsula. On the other hand, the increasing importance of iron, steel, and coal, with a tendency toward production on a large scale and the amalgamation of large plants, favoured the concentration of industry where it had the geographic advantage of cheap transportation by water. The Massey firm[2] at Newcastle produced the first mowing machine in Canada in 1852. Later a reaper was added and in 1855 a combined hand-rake, reaper, and mower was produced. The first self-rake reaper appeared in 1863—the Ithaca steel rake— the first automatic dump-horse rake in 1869, and the Massey harvester in 1878. In 1879 the financial demands of the

---

[1]*Guelph Herald*, May 22, 1878.
[2]*Massey-Harris, An historical sketch 1847-1920* (Toronto, 1920).

industry, and the demands for cheap transport and labour made it advisable for the firm to move to Toronto. The plant was rapidly enlarged and in 1883 employed between 300 and 350 men. The experience of the Harris firm was concerned generally with lighter forms of equipment. In 1857 at Beamsville this firm began the manufacture of revolving hay-rakes. After 1860 mowers, hand-rake reapers, root-cutters, clover-threshers, corn-shellers, and plows were added. In 1872 the firm moved to Brantford. The self-rake reaper was improved and in 1879 a distributing branch was established in Winnipeg. In 1884 the first self-binder made by the Harris firm was used in western Canada. By the end of the period the industries related to the demands of agricultural communities had reached maturity and were in a position to support the expansion of western Canada. The enormous demands of wheat for labour had been met in a large part by mechanical invention.

(iv)

Rolling mills[1]

The development of rolling mills with heavy demands for power was particularly dependent on cheap transport for coal and iron. Water-power and cheap coal were important factors at an early date but water-power became less important. Again immediate demands of the railway and, in addition, expansion of the building industry and the growth of towns were responsible for increased production of nails and spikes. Prior to 1851 Canada employed exclusively English-wrought nails but shortly afterwards Montreal, with cheap water-power on the Lachine Canal and cheap supplies of coal, began the manufacture of cut-shingle nails and later expanded to the production of board and larger-cut nails. Sheets and hoops were imported and nails cut from these. In 1857 puddling and rolling mills were introduced and imports of sheets declined. The Victoria Iron Works imported an average of about 4,000 tons of

---

[1]See W. J. Donald, *The Canadian iron and steel industry*; also S. P. Day, *English America*, I, 180-185, especially for a description of the puddling furnace employed to take out sulphur.

nail-plate yearly. In 1860 this firm[1] produced about
2,000 tons of nail-plate from scrap iron, but inadequate
supplies of that material necessitated reliance on the close-
grained pig-metal brought chiefly from Glengarnock, Collness,
and Blair Brand and on iron-ore imported from Fort Henry
and Lake Champlain Mines. Coal consumed by the rolling
mills totalled 6,000 tons in 1861 and was brought from the
Albion Mines in New York. The blast furnaces used
Pictou coals which were free from sulphur. In 1866 Montreal
reported the iron and nail works as "about the most important of all our manufacturing interests" and employing
"the largest amount of men's labor".

> There are three Rolling Mills and Nail works, which at
> present give employment to skilled workmen—say 420—at
> wages from $2 to $5 per day; and apprentices and laborers
> 164, from 80 cents to $1.20 per day. . . .
> The fact is, that the manufacture of not only nails, but
> also of tools of all descriptions for agricultural purposes, must
> every year increase largely. At present our manufactures of
> axes, scythes, and other necessary agricultural implements,
> surpass the English; and, with a fair amount of capital placed
> in our trade, three times the amount of labor might be fully
> employed.
> There are several manufactories of saws and edge tools,
> such as axes, chisels, augers, &c., &c. These give employment
> to rather over 200 men; but the greatest proportion of the
> skilled labor comes from the United States, the workmen there
> being more accustomed to the peculiar tempering of the steel
> required for our cold climate. . . . [2]

By 1883 there were 4 rolling mills in Montreal which
depended in part on English sheet-iron for spikes, nails, horse-
shoes, tack brads, springs, bolts and nuts, and on Swedes
charcoal tack-strips for butt-welded iron-pipe. The Montreal
Rolling Mills Company was operated by steam power, the
Pillow Hersey and Company rolling mill by steam, and the
bolt factory by water-power, the Peck, Benny and Company
by water-power, and the Metropolitan Rolling Mills by
steam.

Hamilton was dependent on cheap supplies of coal for
the growth of its rolling mills—"the principal ones being

---

[1] In 1862 this firm employed 120 hands—the rolling mill turning out 12 tons
of nail-plates per day.
[2] *S.p.*, 3, 1867.

the Hamilton Tool Company, who have commenced to construct iron railway and road bridges, and T. Cowie & Co., who have constructed works specially for the purpose of manufacturing cast iron pipes of large dimensions, and which has given an impetus to the labour market here."[1] Again in 1879:

> There have been many new industries and manufactories opened up in this district . . . this is particularly the case with the establishment of the rolling mills here for the purposes of manufacturing iron; also the nail works in connection with the same establishment. The Britannia Co., from Meriden, Connecticut, have also erected a factory here for the purpose of manufacturing plated ware, being a new industry in Canada; the Forge Company have enlarged their shops to double their former capacity, and are now running night and day to keep pace with their orders.[2]

In 1885 "another rolling mill has been started for the manufacturing of bar and rod iron."[3]

(v)

Effect of imports and tariffs on the industry

The demands for iron products during the period stimulated the growth of iron industries but even more conspicuously the growth of imports in iron products. Improvement of the St. Lawrence contributed to the increasing importance of Great Britain as a source of iron supplies.[4]

---

[1]*S.p.*, 8, 1877.
[2]*S.p.*, 10, 1880.
[3]*S.p.*, 10, 1886.
[4]

	Imports of pig-iron (tons)				Imports of puddled bars (cwts.)			
	Ontario		Quebec		Ontario		Quebec	
	Great Britain	United States	Great Britain	United States	Great Britain	United States	Great Britain	United States
1875	281	17,870	23,160	1,772	......	......	......	......
1876	991	7,058	19,850	......	......	......	......	......
1877	2,872	5,291	23,061	8	......	......	38,863	161
1878	3,486	3,633	19,599	......	641	123	26,422	28
1879	1,237	1,830	12,059	2	......	11	4,720	237
1880	3,959	2,814	14,891	1	221	......	195,220	23
1881	8,587	8,058	23,072	78	......	14	177,652	......
1882	18,444 (5,851 charcoal pig)	8,097	27,545	......	......	6	203,882	......

As a result of these heavy demands it is difficult to determine the effects of the tariff on the growth of the industry.[1] The establishment of a branch of the Singer Manufacturing Company in Montreal was regarded as a result of higher duties. Of 45 foundries in 1884, 12 were started after 1879 (the national policy); employment had increased 83 per cent., and average wages from $386.36 in 1878 to $407.94 in 1884. Production had increased "in a greater ratio than the number of hands". Of 57 agricultural implement works in 1884, 18 were established after 1879, the number of hands increased 87 per cent., and average wages from $390.51 to $395.86. The relatively slight increase in wages was accounted for by the increasing importance of machinery. Miscellaneous iron manufactures increased from 43 to 64, the number of men employed by 107 per cent., and average wages from $355.86 to $407.31. Manufactures of machinery

1883	29,375	7,641	31,707	1,478	......	2,123	256,510	....
1884	16,436	6,167	21,810	855	......	869	248,956	10

	Imports of bars and rods (cwts.)				Imports of steel rails (tons)			
	Ontario		Quebec		Ontario		Quebec	
	Great Britain	United States	Great Britain	United States	Great Britain	United States	Great Britain	United States
1877	125,563	68,770	332,523	3,847	1,489	139	25,514	771
1878	124,361	72,868	265,259	2,657	693	52	19,915	687
1879	137,926	45,730	282,957	2,831	2,023	673	18,473	19
1880	112,573	5,835	304,391	2,844	3,544	....	68,101	2
1881	181,500	5,748	298,906	3,365	8,602	....	65,783	2
1882	334,543	6,732	418,807	5,694	18,784	915	44,005	200
1883	340,512	8,075	295,682	1,656	11,788	2,646	48,283	10
1884	217,573	7,840	353,468	2,944	2,956	6,061	24,981	...

[1]See W. J. Donald, *The Canadian iron and steel industry, passim*, for a general argument that the tariff was ineffective. The value of total imports (dollars) for Canada in the period were as follows (chiefly from Great Britain):

	Iron	Steel	Rails	Castings and forgings	Cutlery	Hardware	Machinery engines	Total iron and steel	Per capita consumption of iron and steel
1868	2,763,009	341,098	523,648	256,460	14,024	2,457,403	529,723	6,885,365	2.04
1869	2,687,105	384,539	743,516	552,927	206,669	2,019,110	791,914	7,385,780	2.17
1870	3,043,884	361,139	917,283	381,036	297,088	2,193,342	557,095	7,750,867	2.25
1871	4,211,513	506,895	1,325,021	407,955	349,362	2,934,108	3,791	10,808,645	3.01
1872	6,494,043	624,926	3,005,529	409,535	456,785	3,601,577	1,320,694	15,913,179	4.55
1873	9,214,182	754,319	6,891,861	725,512	476,393	4,398,051	2,974,702	25,435,020	7.01
1874	5,367,829	679,863	4,326,695	1,580,776	853,412	4,799,190	3,092,622	20,700,387	5.77
1875	5,473,803	575,032	5,287,861	524,852	604,267	5,101,994	1,431,389	18,999,198	5.15
1876	3,507,929	384,105	3,897,770	307,569	445,798	3,535,946	886,000	12,965,117	3.46
1877	3,781,818	431,474	1,048,368	302,833	524,090	3,128,839	947,151	11,082,321	2.89
1878	2,937,650	393,073	1,403,821	546,811	560,512	2,777,768	778,671	9,398,306	2.40
1879	2,478,674	347,992	1,049,881	415,695	511,875	2,206,486	951,692	7,962,295	2.00
1880	3,384,876	654,874	2,345,231	444,975	734,859	1,382,087	1,181,758	10,128,660	2.49
1881	4,028,343	797,687	3,172,829	508,478	917,669	1,664,608	1,866,241	12,955,855	2.98
1882	5,377,302	900,931	3,790,281	656,140	1,317,793	1,721,100	3,735,941	17,499,488	4.05
1883	5,821,490	1,253,394	4,248,073	881,303	1,420,660	1,854,358	4,600,996	20,080,274	4.56
1884	4,605,703	547,273	3,173,202	800,860	1,050,985	2,150,670	2,462,034	14,790,727	3.32

increased from 53 to 63, employment[1] 76 per cent., and average wages from $360.91 to $376.18. Canadians were said to have gained control of general lines of production of machinery from the United States and some firms had developed an export trade.[2] Skilled labour gradually improved the position of industries producing equipment for other industries such as engines and machines.

Increase in the imports of iron products stimulated the development of industries. Industries which had grown up in relation to lumber and to water-power became increasingly dependent on iron and coal. Water-power and wood as a source of steam power were gradually supplemented and displaced by coal. Large supplies of raw material were available as a result of the expansion of agriculture; larger markets, domestic and external, were provided with improved transport; and specialized agriculture contributed to the decline of domestic industries and to the rise of the factory. Widening of the market for the home manufacturer as a result of improved transport was accompanied by increasing competition from the more efficient foreign manufacturer for similar reasons. Industry was, therefore, closely linked to the production of staple raw materials in which competition was necessarily weak. Increased population provided a strong demand for consumers' goods and for industries such as flour-milling, distilling, textiles, tanning, and the manufacture of boots and shoes.

4

Flour-milling

According to the census of 1851 there were 1,153 grist mills in Canada (692 in Ontario) of which 45 were steam power. 10 years later Quebec had 344 water-mills of a total reporting of 356, and Ontario 382 of a total of 442. With relatively small requirements of power and of capital[3] mills tended to follow settlement. Increase in the pro-

---

[1] In 1881, 17,950 males and $16,014,186 of capital equipment were employed to produce work valued at $20,665,364.

[2] For a criticism of Blackeby's report see *Monetary Times*, 1884-5, 1057-8.

[3] Croil estimated that a first-class grist mill of stone or brick with fluem complete would cost from $3,500 to $4,000 per run of stones capable of grinding 6 bushels of wheat per hour each.

duction of wheat and in the size of towns led to the growth of larger mills and to the introduction of steam[1] as a supplementary source of power. The first grist mill in Newcastle built in 1845 had 4 run of stone and a second built in 1853 had 3 run. Port Hope had 2 mills of 4 run each, built about 1854. Trenton had a steam grist mill and 3 grist mills run by water, one of which had 3 runs of stone and a capacity of 100 barrels a day, and Cobourg had 2 grist mills in 1864. Croil refers to 8 flour-mills and 19 runs of stone in Dundas County in 1859. Day noted the existence of numerous flour-mills in the united counties "of an imposing character, among the largest of which are the Victoria Steam Mills at Brampton, and those at Meadowvale and Streetsville".[2]

(i)

Western Ontario

Expansion of the railroad and of the production of wheat in western Ontario were followed by the growth of flour-mills in that area.[3] Skill migrated from the United States. For example, about 1860 Mr. Goldie moved from New York State, where he had been connected with the trade in flour and lumber, to Guelph and erected a mill with a capacity of 150 barrels per day. In 1878 the mill had been increased to 6 run of stone and a capacity of 300 barrels and had its own cooper shops. "Three double chests of bolts are performing their duties. Middlings purifiers, coolers, grain cleaning machinery, packing apparatus—all the component parts of a first class mill. . . ."[4] The Elora Mills had 6 run of

---

[1]Clearing of the forest was held responsible for the decline of streams and the increasing difficulties of small mills. These mills became more important as grist mills. Tillsonburg, for example, had a corn, oatmeal, and pea-splitting mill.

[2]S. P. Day, *English America*, II, 74.

[3]See a discussion of the important influence of raw material on the location of the flour-milling industry, in C. B. Kuhlman, *The development of the flour milling industry in the United States* (Boston and New York, 1929). The railroad and the steam engine favoured concentration of the industry at points strategic with regard to transportation rather than power as in the case of the early mills dominated by water-power.

[4]"The motive power of all this machinery is a handsome engine. This is an apparently perfect piece of machinery, and it moves, with irresistible power and matchless regularity, with scarcely a sound or vibration to indicate the motion. It is provided with improved valves, after the Putnam style. The cylinder is 22 inches calibre and 4 feet stroke, and makes, ordinarily, 50 strokes

stone 4 feet 4 inches in diameter and a capacity of 200 barrels of flour a day.

(ii)

Montreal

Exports of wheat from Ontario through Montreal, abundance of water-power on the Lachine Canal, and the growing importance of the Maritime markets were factors strengthening the position of Montreal mills. Day[1] refers to 3 "immense" mills, the Royal, the City, and the Canal Mills. The warehouse had a frontage of 160 feet, a width of 75 feet, and was 100 feet in height, and the milling department was 65 feet square and 70 feet in height (8 storeys).

These mills contain forty-four grain bins, having a depth of from twenty-four to twenty-six feet, while the capacity of the warehouse exceeds two hundred thousand bushels. The grinding capacity of the mills is reckoned at eight runs a stone; there are four millstones, and every two make what is called "a run". Five hundred barrels of wheat can be ground daily with ease. The most remarkable feature about these mills is the introduction of "elevators", by means of which a wonderful economy of human labour is realised. The elevators are worked by water-power and remove grain from

to the minute. The motion of the engine is regulated by Wilson's patent governor, the peculiarity of which consists in its rapid motion, being provided with light balls, and the quickness with which it acts. The main engine shaft is 9 inches in diameter and the line shaft which drives the machinery is 5½ inches in diameter. On the former is the fly wheel, a monstrous affair, 17 feet 6 inches in diameter, and 32 inch face. It was cast in two segments, and weighs 8 tons. The belt which encircles the fly wheel and drives the main shaft is 80 feet long, formed of double leather, is 30 inches wide, and costs $6 per foot. . . .
There are two boilers, each 14 feet long and 64 inches in diameter, and each one containing 170 three inch tubes. The arrangement of furnaces is most complete, and the smoke is carried off by a stack 66 feet high, and 2 feet 6 inches in diameter. When both boilers are in operation 60 lbs. of steam is found sufficient for the work, and when, in case of repairs, only one boiler is used, 75 lbs. is found necessary. The boilers are supplied with water by means of a Goldie & McCulloch automatic steam pump, to which is attached a water safety valve, which latter announces the fact of any error having been committed in turning taps or other manipulation of the automatic feeder. The cold water is passed through a Goldie & McCulloch new heater, where it is heated, by the action of the exhaust steam, up to 200 degrees Fahrenheit, and is then ejected into the boilers. A condenser has also been introduced which increases the power of the engine about 2½ runs of stone. In connection with the condenser is an atmospheric valve, by means of which the change from high to low pressure can be made at will.
Besides the engine, the mill is supplied with water power—turbine wheels—which can be used a great portion of the year" (*Guelph Herald*, May 22, 1878).
[1]S. P. Day, *English America*, I, 185-6.

vessels to the bins. . . . While grain was being taken from a barge in the Canal up into the warehouse and weighed, it was transhipped into another vessel lying alongside. By means of elevators a barge could be loaded or unloaded in an hour; a process that would otherwise occupy an entire day, even with the assistance of a large number of hands. There is a "barrel elevator" in the mills for the purpose of raising barrels from one story to another. Even the very barrels are filled and weighed by means of machinery. The complicated and varied work of the Royal Mills is accomplished by the aid of twenty men and boys—an economisation of labour truly wonderful. . . .

In 1864[1] there were 2 flour-mills capable of grinding 460 barrels of flour per day with storage capacity of 105,000 bushels of grain and 6,000 barrels of flour at Côte St. Paul Lock; 2 mills with a capacity of 310 barrels of flour daily, and storage for 114,000 bushels of grain, and 5,500 barrels of flour at St. Gabriel Lock; and 3 mills with a capacity of 1,250 barrels, and 4 elevators with storage for 540,000 bushels of grain and 34,000 barrels of flour at basin no. 2.

(iii)

Changes in the industry, 1871-1881

The number of flour and grist mills and production changed as follows in the decade from 1871 to 1881:

	Number of establishments		Capital		Employees		Salaries and wages	
	1871	1881	1871	1881	1871	1881	1871	1881
Quebec	810	790	$3,461,723	$3,697,060	1,506	1,791	$280,266	$509,799
Ontario	951	1,034	5,797,853	8,922,249	2,759	3,561	833,959	1,215,411

	Raw materials used		Value of products	
	1871	1881	1871	1881
Quebec.............	$8,152,797	$7,309,208	$9,897,714	$8,861,752
Ontario.............	22,615,814	25,075,047	27,115,796	29,859,118

(iv)

Exports

The manufacture of flour was stimulated by improved transport to foreign markets and by the increasing importance of the domestic market[2] especially in the Maritimes.

---

[1]*S.p.*, 5, 1865.
[2]In 1885 there were 19 confectionery and biscuit establishments. 2 had been started after 1879. The number of hands increased after that date by 55 per cent. and average wages from $273.00 to $278.71.

Exports increased from 306,339 barrels in 1871 to 439,728 barrels in 1881.[1] Shipments to the Maritimes increased rapidly following the establishment of through connections to Portland,[2] completion of the Intercolonial, and improvement of facilities for navigation on the St. Lawrence River. Abrogation of the Reciprocity Treaty and Confederation contributed to the expansion of trade. Total shipments increased from 139,581 barrels in 1864-5 to 542,412 barrels in 1869. In 1874 flour was sent in large quantities, dealers such as W. Lukes of Newmarket reporting a large increase. As a result of the depression 463,586 barrels were sent in 1876. Regarding the Goldie Mill at Guelph it was stated in the *Guelph Herald* of May 22, 1878, that:

> At one time Mr. Goldie exported fully nine-tenths of all the flour he manufactured. Considerable quantities are still shipped to England and to Glasgow, but we believe we are right in saying that Ontario and the Maritime Provinces now consume the greater portion. The business is so wide-reaching in its extent that Mr. Goldie is necessitated to be away from home a considerable portion of his time, but he leaves able assistants in charge.

In 1881 Halifax imported 133,675 barrels by rail and 43,675 by water and in 1882, 142,266 by rail and 62,279 by water. Summerside, P.E.I., imported between 60,000 and 65,000 barrels. In the early eighties it was estimated that Ontario sent about 2,500,000 barrels of food-stuffs and Quebec about 650,000 barrels to the Maritimes.

5

Brewing and Distilling Industries

Cheap supplies of grain and increasing population led to the growth of the brewing and distilling industries. By Confederation the brewing industry had spread to various centres. "Formerly Kingston stood unrivalled in the pro-

---

[1]See *The flour and grist milling industry in Canada, 1921* (Ottawa, 1923).

[2]Total shipments of flour *via* Portland from Canada to Nova Scotia and New Brunswick increased as follows:—

1865	58,233 barrels (Nova Scotia alone)
1866	157,859 "
1867	228,345 "
1868	328,204 "
1869	293,754 "

(*S.p.*, 6, 1881).

duction of a first class ale; but with a continually increasing English population in the west, the demand for a superior article became so great that brewing has been largely entered into in all the cities of the Dominion, the places whose ales are most noted being Kingston, Toronto, Montreal, Quebec, Hamilton, London and Prescott."[1]   In Montreal in 1866: "The brewing trade . . . has rapidly developed itself during the past few years and all our local establishments are in full work.   They employ over 500 men, at wages ranging from $1.25 to $2.50 per diem."[2]   In addition, the smaller towns had their own breweries, for example, Trenton, Galt, and, at a later date, Tillsonburg.   At Cobourg the Victoria Brewery, established in 1862 and run by steam, produced about 2,000 barrels annually.   In 1878 Guelph had a brewery which purchased $12,000 to $18,000 worth of barley, $4,000 to $6,000 worth of hops, chiefly Canadian, and employed 20 people and distributed ale through an agency at Hamilton to   Toronto,   and   to   the   adjoining   towns—Kincardine, Southampton, Goderich.   The number of breweries in Upper Canada increased from 49 in 1851 to 69 in 1861 and in Lower Canada declined from 13 to 7 in the same period.

The number of pounds of malt manufactured increased from 32,968,738 in 1868-9 to 51,876,385 in 1875-6.[3]   Production declined during the depression but reached a new peak of 59,040,565 pounds in 1879-80 and increased to 85,512,222 pounds in 1882-3.   It declined to 55,447,616 pounds in 1883-4.   Exports increased from 6,524,850 pounds in 1868-9 to 10,193,631 pounds in 1872-3 but declined to 4,677,960 pounds in 1874-5.   From that point they increased to 19,151,181 pounds in 1877-8, 37,077,709 pounds in 1879-80, and 45,882,486 pounds in 1882-3.   The large quantities available for home consumption were used chiefly in the manufacture of malt-liquor.   In 1883-4, of 40,533,102 pounds, 3½ millions were used by distillers and the remainder used to produce 13,098,700 gallons of malt-liquor.

The production of spirits was relatively limited.   Concentration of industry was rapid.   The number of distilleries

---

[1]See H. B. Small, *The products and manufactures of the new dominion*, 137-8.
[2]*S.p.*, 3, 1867.
[3]See Reports of the commissioner of inland revenue, *S.p.*   These statistics are for Canada as a whole but Ontario and Quebec were of outstanding importance.

in Upper Canada declined from 100 producing 1,174,595 gallons of whisky in 1851 to 49 in 1861 and in Lower Canada from 7 producing 303,600 gallons of whisky to 3. The firm of Gooderham and Worts[1] enlarged its plant at Toronto in 1859. In 1864 the Ontario Distillery at Cobourg employed 35 hands, used about 10,000 bushels of grain per month, and had 3 steam engines. Small distilleries were in operation, such as those at Leith and Galt. Indian corn became increasingly important as raw material and was responsible for the expansion of the distillery at Walkerville. In 1881-2, 6 distilleries in Ontario and one in Manitoba produced 4,028,847 gallons of spirits from 70,402,810 pounds of grain (77 per cent. Indian corn, 4½ to 5 per cent. malt, 15 per cent. rye, and the remainder wheat, oats, and grain). It was estimated that consumption per head[2] increased 10½ per cent. from 1850 to 1860 and declined 30 per cent. to 1870. Total consumption declined during the depression. Exports declined from a high point of 2,432,047 gallons in 1871-2 to a nominal amount in 1883-4. Total production declined from 5,619,507 gallons in 1874-5 to 4,028,847 in 1881-2.

6

The Woollen Industry

The textile industries illustrated the effects of improved transportation in lower costs of raw material and in increasing emphasis on export staples. Sheep-raising, especially in relation to the production of wool, was a frontier industry.[3] Wheat and livestock weakened the position of sheep-raising and woollen mills became increasingly dependent on imports of wool. Domestic industries in relation to wool declined with the growth of woollen mills and with the expansion of the cotton industry. Improved transportation emphasized the trend toward specialization throughout the new countries of the world with the result that Canadian

---

[1]See a valuable history—E. B. Shuttleworth, *The windmill and its times* (Toronto, 1924). In 1884 this company was feeding 400 cattle in its sheds.

[2]See N. S. Garland, *Banks, bankers and banking in Canada* (Ottawa, 1890), 291.

[3]See C. W. Wright, *Wool growing and the tariff* (Harvard economic studies, V); also E. O. G. Shann, *An economic history of Australia* (Cambridge, 1930).

agriculture specialized in wheat and livestock and imported
raw materials for the clothing industries.

At the beginning of the period the carding and fulling
processes were carried out in mills and the spinning, and
occasionally the weaving, by farmers' families.[1] In the
united counties (York, Ontario, and Peel) 38,000 yards of
fulled cloth were produced in 1861, 126,000 yards of flannel,
and 1,200 yards of linen (less than a yard per inhabitant).
In 1848 Upper Canada had 239 fulling mills and 65 woollen
mills; Dundas County had 4 carding mills in 1859. According to the census of 1861 the number of fulling and carding
mills in Upper Canada had declined to 62 handling 442,560
pounds of wool. The number of woollen mills increased to
82 producing 1,079,159 yards of cloth. At the same date
Lower Canada had 88 fulling and carding mills handling
183,310 pounds of wool and 45 woollen mills handling
284,295 yards of cloth. The number of carding and fulling
mills increased rapidly to 1871 and declined rapidly to 1881.
Small woollen mills were scattered through the province, for
example, at Owen Sound, Thornbury (70 hands), Galt,
Newcastle, and Port Hope (a custom carding mill and, in
addition, a woollen mill which purchased 40,000 pounds of
wool annually). Day reported that Messrs Barber Brothers
at Streetsville (later Toronto, failing 1884) had the largest
mills and employed about 50 people. They turned out
satinettes, jeans, and tweeds. Another large mill known as
the Ontario Woollen Mills was established at Cobourg in 1849.
By 1860 it had 45 looms and produced about 700 yards of
tweed per day. It consumed about 200,000 pounds of wool
annually, employed 100 hands, and was driven by 2 engines
of 30-horse-power each.[2] In 1864 this mill began the use
of dyes. The Rosamond Woollen Company started operations at Almonte in 1857 and rapidly expanded its production.

The industry received a direct stimulus from the abrogation of the Reciprocity Treaty.

> Another and most important element of our prosperity is the
> extensive erection of woollen factories. There is little doubt
> that the impulse to these is mainly owing to the high protective

---

[1] S. P. Day, *English America*, II, 75-6.
[2] Another report dated 1862 states that this mill had 2,000 spindles and
employed 90 hands.

duty imposed by the American Legislature on Canadian wool in its raw state. The home market for this article is large, and will remain so for many years, and cannot fail to furnish a large increase of employment, both on the farm and in the factory, thus producing labour for the operative and the agricultural workman.[1]

The success of the industry was also attributed to the character of the domestic raw material, the demand for few patterns, and relations with wholesalers which checked price-cutting. In 1878 the Elora Woollen Mills had

among its other appointments four looms, one jack of 200 spindles, cards, including one custom roll card, and all the necessary dying, fulling and other apparatus. Its ordinary consumption of wool is about 15,000 lbs. per annum in the custom department and from 35,000 to 40,000 in merchant work. This latter is made up into yarns, tweeds, blankets, flannels, etc. . . .

The Mount Forest Mills at about the same date had 5

looms, two broad and three narrow; one custom and three merchant roll cards, and all necessary dying, fulling, scouring and other apparatus required to make the mill complete. Both steam and water power is used; the building is heated by steam, and all the appointments are modern. The product of the mills are tweeds, blankets, flannel, full cloth and yarns, and the consumption of wool may be fairly estimated at about fourteen tons weight per year. All of this wool comes from this vicinity and last year, although not in operation a full year by any means, the firm received more than twenty-four thousand pounds of wool in exchange for manufactured articles. The goods made, too, are for a local market.

The largest woollen mill in Canada in 1880 had been started by Andrew Paton who first began to manufacture tweeds at Galt in 1858 but moved to Sherbrooke in 1866. The Paton Woollen Mills

are very large. The washing and cleaning machine disposes of 4,000 lbs. of Canadian wool per 10 hours, or from 2,000 to 4,000 lbs. of fine wool. Saw the dyeing vats, the burr-picking machine, 20 sets of carding machines, 24 spinning mules, each having 336 spindles; 135 looms producing last week 711 pieces of cloth, each 25 yards long; the hydraulic press, the patterns, and the machine shop. The work employs from 500 to 550 hands. It is the largest in the Dominion, and the machinery is of the latest and most approved invention.[2]

---

[1] *S.p.*, 3, 1867-8. On the textile industry see, *Canada, an encyclopedia of the country*, V, 485 *ff*.
[2] *S.p.*, 12, 1881.

Knitting mills were started at Belleville in 1855 but the founder moved to Paris in 1867 to form the Penman and Adams Knitting Mills Company. The Ancaster Knitting Company was started in 1858. The Guelph Knitting Mills in 1878 employed 120 people and used 250 pounds of wool per day of which two-thirds was of domestic production. This firm sold its products—underwear, hose, scarfs, cardigan jackets, *etc.*—exclusively through the wholesale trade, chiefly in the Canadian market.

By the end of the period the dominance of medium wools produced by the prevailing Cotswold and Leicester breeds forced mills to import long wool. Careless production and decline in price of medium wools which were sold chiefly in the United States market, contributed to the decline in sheep-raising. The coarsest and roughest tweeds were made from the local product. High-class goods depended on imports.

In 1874 it was claimed that woollen manufactures were moving to the United States but by the end of the period, with the support of the national policy and the widening of the domestic market, the industry had apparently adjusted itself to new sources of supply of raw materials. The report on the effects of the national policy stated that, of a total of 54 woollen factories, 19 had been started since 1879 and that employees had increased 91 per cent. Wages increased from an average of $239.86 in 1878 to $244.18 in 1884. In the knitting industry 10 out of 20 firms were started after 1879, employment increased 185 per cent., and average wages from $220.13 in 1878 to $227.82 in 1884.

7

The Cotton Industry

The rise of the cotton industry paralleled the changes in the woollen industry throughout the period. Hogan wrote in 1855: "In cotton fabrics Canada has made but little progress but in woollen goods and mixed fabrics she is a large producer." The difficulties of the cotton industry were in contrast with those of the woollen industry and suggested the problems of establishing industries for which the raw material

was imported. Mills at Sherbrooke and at Thorold[1] suc-
cumbed after numerous difficulties. A cotton factory established at Montreal on St. Gabriel Lock in 1853 employed
70 people and produced about 300 yards of denims and ticks,
6,000 yards of wadding, and 1,200 pounds of batting per day,
but eventually closed down. Recovery from the depression
of the seventies, improved transportation, and the national
policy brought a rapid expansion in the latter part of the
period. At Hamilton it was reported in 1878 that:

> The demand for cotton operatives has been largely in excess
> of the supply, and in some instances this class of hands has
> been imported from the mills in New England by our mill
> owners owing to the increased capacity of the mills, and the
> demand for this class of goods. Several of the mills have had
> great difficulty in supplying the orders, their stock being sold
> out and orders given ahead.[2]

In 1879: "The Dundas and the Lybster Cotton Mills Companies have both increased their capacity, and the mills
are running to their fullest capacity in order to supply the
demand made upon them and to keep up with their contracts."[3] In 1881 the Ontario Mill Company at Hamilton
and the Hespeler Manufacturing Company at Hespeler completed mills which employed 600 hands[4] and in 1882 a mill
was opened at Kingston to employ 200 operators. It was
claimed in 1885 that 13 out of 17 cotton mills had been
started after 1878, that employment increased 210 per cent.,
and average wages rose from $202.79 to $210.28. In 61
establishments manufacturing clothing, of which 24 were
started after 1879, employment increased 90 per cent.
between that date and 1884.

8

The Boot and Shoe Industry

As in the case of the woollen industry the boot and shoe
industry was based on domestic supplies of raw material but
was more fortunate in having available larger supplies as the

[1]John H. Thompson, *History of Thorold* (Thorold, 1897-8).
[2]*S.p.*, 9, 1879.
[3]*S.p.*, 10, 1880.
[4]*S.p.*, 11, 1882.

livestock industry developed. Supplies of hides and skins were accompanied by cheap supplies of hemlock bark for tanning purposes. The tanning industry was widely scattered. In 1861 Lower Canada reported 184 tanneries chiefly in the Eastern Townships employing 395 hands and turning out annual products valued at $646,699 and Upper Canada, 264 plants with 855 hands turning out annual products valued at $1,409,429. The leather industry supported an important saddle and harness industry and a boot and shoe industry.

The introduction of machinery was followed by an early expansion of the boot and shoe industry. The Singer Sewing Machine was introduced in 1847 by the Montreal firm of Brown and Childs and the McKay Machine for sewing soles by Scholes and Ames, also of Montreal, about 1860. An increase in the duty from 12½ to 25 per cent. in 1859 excluded American shoes and stimulated Canadian production especially of medium and coarse grades.

> By 1860 the prices of staple lines had fallen to lower figures than those which prevailed when the goods were imported, and to-day Canada is said to be the cheapest market in the world for medium and coarse grades of boots and shoes. Our manufacturers are building up a large export trade; the products of Canadian factories now find their way into Newfoundland, South America, Great Britain and the West Indies.

In 1866 the boot and shoe business in Montreal was referred to as "one of the most important in the province" employing from 3,000 to 4,000 men and women.

> During the past year (*1866*) the demand for labor in the different factories has been unusually great, and very high wages have been paid to all skilled hands. This is not a branch of industry to attract British or European emigrants, as the manufacture by machinery of boots and shoes is comparatively new, but our American friends would find plenty of excellent openings for skilled workmen. The value of boots and shoes manufactured in Montreal, is rather over $2,500,000 per annum.[1]

As a result of the national policy it was claimed that Canada made rapid strides in the production of finer lines of goods. In 1882 Montreal was estimated to have had 30 boot and

---

[1] *S.p.*, 3, 1867.

shoe factories employing 3,500 people and producing 4,500,000 pairs (total for Canada, 6,750,000 pairs) valued at $5,400,000. Of a total of 60 factories in 1884, it was alleged that 20 started after 1878, that employment increased 62 per cent., and that average wages increased from $265.42 to $275.66.[1]

9

The Sugar Industry

The relative decline of self-sufficiency was evident in the rise of the sugar industry and the decline in the importance of maple sugar.[2] A sugar refinery involving a capital investment of £50,000 and working capital of the same amount was started at Montreal by Messrs Redpath and Company in January, 1855. In 1862 it produced about seven-eighths of the white sugar produced in Canada and consumed about 7,000 tons annually of raw sugar. Animal charcoal was produced on the premises. "The great difficulty experienced consists in the extremely limited market that the country affords for refined sugar. For this reason the manufacture of the commodity is discontinued during two or three months every year." In 1866, 2 refineries in Montreal employed over 400 persons.

In spite of competition[3] and with assistance from the

---

[1]S.p., 37, 1885.
[2]Production of maple sugar (pounds)

	Ontario	Quebec
1851	2,212,850	6,057,532
1861	6,970,612	7,324,147
1871	6,277,442	10,497,418
1881	4,160,706	15,687,835

[3]In 1874 imports of sugar equal to or above no. 9 Dutch standard totalled 85,452,194 lbs valued at $4,292,706 (5¼ cts. per lb.) . . . 26,839,495 lbs. nearly 5 cts. per lb. from Great Britain, 29,164,957 lbs. at 5.65 cts per lb. from the United States, and 29,447,742 lbs. at 4.46 cts. per lb. from the West Indies. Sugars below no. 9 Dutch standard totalled 16,469,485 lbs. at 3.73 cts. per lb. of which Brazil supplied 10,133,145 lbs. at 3.55 cts. per lb. Imports of no. 9 Dutch standard from Great Britain increased by 11,444,123 lbs. or over 50 per cent. from 1872 to 1875 but from the United States by 17,663,107 lbs. in 1873 over 1872 and 2,792,113 lbs. in 1874 over 1873 and 5,420,401 lbs. less in 1875 than 1874. Total imports declined 2,834,461 lbs. in 1875 but imports of sugar below no. 9 Dutch standard increased 2,429,668 lbs. Direct imports, all grades, increased from the West Indies 5,280,982 lbs. Imports of low grades, on the other hand, declined rapidly from 14,146,798 lbs. in 1876 to 493,530 lbs. in 1877 and 1,108,065 lbs. in 1878. Imports of sugar of high grades over no. 13 increased about 10,000,000 lbs. in 1877 over 1876 and 8,000,000 lbs. in 1878 over 1877 in about equal ratio from the United States and Great Britain while medium

tariff, the industry persisted. Raw sugar imported from the West Indies, Brazil, Java, and other areas employed 21,636 tons of shipping in 1882, 18,960 tons in 1883, and 34,707 tons in 1884. In addition the Intercolonial brought sugar from Halifax and St. John to the extent of 14,300 tons in one of the later years of the period.

10
The Tobacco Industry

As in the case of sugar and cotton, the tobacco industry was largely dependent on imports of raw material. Consumption per capita increased from 1.804 pounds in 1861 to 1.985 pounds in 1871 or 10 per cent., but in spite of this increase the industry leaned heavily on protection. In 1866 Montreal[1] plants employed 75 skilled hands and about 250 women and children but "since the close of the American war this branch of business decreased." An increase in the tariff in 1870 was followed by a marked increase in the consumption of Canadian-made tobacco but by very wide fluctuations—645,119 pounds in 1873-4, a low point, and 10,018,373 pounds in 1881-2. As a result of an increase in the duty and the stocking of warehouses before the duty came into effect, imports of cigars declined 261,487 pounds in 1874-5—of which German cigars "of a very common cheap description" declined 228,701 pounds. Cigars of Canadian manufacture increased 73,328 pounds. German cigars continued to decline in quantity in 1877-8 and in price from $1.00 per pound in 1876 to 50 cents in 1878. Imports from

---

qualities (no. 9 to no. 13) declined about 11,500,000 lbs. in 1877 and over 9,000,000 lbs. in 1878. These imports declined from the United States and increased from Great Britain. Imports of all grades from the West Indies declined. The new duty in 1878 raised the *ad valorem* rates on the higher duties from 25 per cent. to 35 per cent. but "on the net cost of sugar imported from the place of growth and production direct on the net price per pound without the addition of packages, etc. as before and hence it is not really much more than five per cent. increase." The new duty was applied to drawbacks on refined sugars granted by the United States and other countries and consequently favoured Great Britain. It was also expected to increase direct trade with the West Indies and in turn increase the market for fish, lumber, and other products (*S.p.*, 155, 1879).

[1]See a description of the plant of McDonald Brothers and Company in Montreal in H. B. Small, *The products and manufactures of the new dominion*, 146-7. Cigar factories were scattered—a plant at Guelph in 1878 employed 25 to 30 persons making 25,000 to 30,000 cigars per week.

the United States, "the value of which is about three times that of the German manufacture", on the other hand, increased in 1877 and 1878 although prices declined from 2.67 cents in 1876 to 2.14 cents in 1878. As a result of the national policy 6 of 21 plants were started between 1879 and 1884 and employment increased 81 per cent., but average wages declined from $201.54 to $198.38. The consumption of Canadian leaf increased rapidly after 1880-1.

11

Transportation and Water-power

The development of specialized industries following the increasing importance of iron accentuated the importance of cheap water-transport and ample supplies of power. The limited possibilities of water-power[1] hastened dependence on supplies of coal. The railroads contributed to the concentration of industry and the growth of large centres toward the end of Lake Ontario. On the other hand, in such towns as Galt, Guelph, Brantford, and Berlin (now Kitchener) the advantages of the power sites[2] of the Grand River valley were strengthened by the support of coal brought by the railroads. For example, Brantford by the end of the period had plants engaged in the manufacture of engines and boilers, portable saw-mills, grist mill machinery, agricultural implements, stoves, ploughs, cotton, and other manufactured products. The importance to the iron industries of coal and cheap water-transport tended to favour

---

[1]Of 42 plants in Dundas County in 1859, 31 used water-power. In 1890 the Province of Ontario had the following number of stationary engines and boilers:

	Engines	Boilers
79 villages................................	438	469
59 towns..................................	834	896
8 cities...................................	583	583
288 townships............................	1,485	1,504
	3,340	3,452

This number included saw-mills, 651; planing mills, 173; shingle mills, 85; sash and door manufactories, 50; hoop and stave factories, 46; furniture factories, 96; cheese factories, 289; flour and grist mills, 234; foundries, 112; driving machinery, 111; not specified, 264; machine shops, 90; tanneries 62; textile, 80; brick and tile, 60; (*Ont. S.p.*, 45, 1891).

[2]See *Sixth annual report* of the Waterloo Historical Society (Kitchener, 1918), 20 *ff*.

localities which had cheap, accessible supplies of coal as in the case of ports on Lake Erie (Port Stanley for London) and on Lake Ontario (Hamilton and Toronto) and on the St. Lawrence (Montreal). The existence of abundant supplies of water-power, coal, and cheap water-transport strengthened the position of Montreal as an industrial centre. The Lachine Canal provided water-transport and about 4,000,000 horse-power.[1]

12

Imports of Coal

Imports of coal were a valuable index of the shift in industry to steam power.

	Imports of coal[2] tons	Sales of coal from Nova Scotia to Quebec
1868	356,836	......
1869	389,485	......
1870	394,052	......
1871	366,073	......
1872	484,826	......
1873	574,308	187,059
1874	804,827	162,269
1875	652,435	189,754
1876	793,880	117,303
1877	979,692	95,118
1878	896,446	83,710
1879	911,174	154,118 (50 cents duty)
1880	982,743	239,091
1881	1,166,196	268,628
1882	1,284,417	383,031
1883	1,683,951	410,605
1884	2,010,936	396,782

[1]After 1855 industrial development along the banks of the Lachine was rapid. In 1864 plants at the Lachine Canal included at Côte St. Paul Lock an axe factory, a shovel factory, a scythe factory, an auger factory, a door and sleigh-bell factory, a saw-mill and cooperage plant; at St. Gabriel Lock, 2 foundries and finishing shops, a machine shop, bolt and nut factory, nail factory, agricultural implement factory, saw factory, axe factory, 3 saw-mills, a dry dock, a rubber factory, 2 furniture factories, a cordage factory, plaster mill, and 2 door and sash factories; and at basin no. 2, 3 nail and spike factories, 2 rolling mills, one machine shop, a dry dock, 2 graving docks, a saw-mill, an oil, drug, and plaster mill, a tanning and glove factory (*S.p.*, 5, 1865). It was estimated that capital investments in industries in Montreal increased from $800,000 in 1860 to $11,000,000 in 1870.

[2]Toronto harbour receipts of coal
1873.........188,735
1874.........128,334
1875.........150,016 also a considerable importation by rail particu-
1876.........152,319 larly before navigation opened.
1877.........174,417—48,000 tons discharged at Don channel docks.

13

Summary of Industrial Progress, 1871-1881

	1871 Number	1871 Value of product	1881 Number	1881 Value of product
Agricultural implements				
Ontario..	173	$2,291,989	141	$3,928,411
Quebec..	65	$382,533	82	$390,456
Boots and shoes				
Ontario..	1965	$5,025,455	2042	$ 5,045,582
Quebec..	1429	$9,074,187	1516	$10,754,314
Brick and tile				
Ontario..	309	$577,904	400	$971,158
Quebec..	69	$293,233	78	$387,924
Carding and fulling				
Ontario..	158	$ 539,857	72	$253,196
Quebec..	323	$1,206,915	239	$290,426
Flour and grist				
Ontario..	951	$27,115,796	1034	$29,859,118
Quebec..	810	$ 9,897,714	290	$ 8,861,752
Foundries				
Ontario..	258	$4,631,850	342	$5,749,467
Quebec..	111	$1,607,464	128	$1,693,249
Saddle and harness				
Ontario..	676	$1,645,398	836	$2,033,785
Quebec..	235	$ 572,508	304	$686,652
Tanneries				
Ontario..	426	$3,420,218	316	$3,555,198
Quebec..	420	$4,397,999	419	$9,686,248
Tailors and clothing				
Ontario..	942	$5,425,464	1121	$8,012,756
Quebec..	359	$2,665,699	553	$5,263,938
Tin sheet and iron works				
Ontario..	440	$1,327,276	670	$2,178,629
Quebec..	261	$ 824,379	420	$ 902,587
Wool cloth				
Ontario..	233	$4,589,119	993	$6,077,444
Quebec..	23	$ 691,978	170	$1,531,899
Meat curing				
Ontario..	105	$3,193,122	94	$2,763,685
Quebec..	39	$ 429,716	70	$ 950,182

	Employees	Value of product	Employees	Value of product
Total industries (including lumber and wood-working indusdries, see p. 502)				
Ontario....87,281		$114,706,709	85,673	$104,662,258
Quebec.. 66,714		$ 77,205,182	118,308	$157,989,870

14

The Growth of Towns

The relative growth of towns was a further index of the shift of industry to strategic geographic centres such as London, Hamilton, Toronto, and Montreal.

	1851	1861	1871	1881
Toronto	30,775	44,821	56,092	86,415
Hamilton	14,121	19,096	26,716	35,961
Kingston	11,585	13,473	12,407	14,091
Bytown (City of Ottawa)	7,760	14,669	21,545	27,412
London	7,035	11,555	15,826	19,746
Belleville	4,569	6,277	7,305	9,516
Brantford	3,877	6,251	8,107	9,616
Montreal	57,715	90,323'	107,225	140,747
Quebec	42,052	59,990	59,699	62,446
Three Rivers	4,936	6,058	7,570	8,670

Expansion of towns stimulated the construction industries.[1] As has been shown, the lumber industry became increasingly important in meeting domestic demands. For example, in 1885[2] in Hamilton "more buildings having been erected during the year than in any previous one", lumber was imported over the Northern and North Western Railways from Georgian Bay and northern territory in larger quantities.

---

[1]Toronto increased rapidly in the building mania of 1854-5 when the Grand Trunk and other roads were under construction. Plank sidewalks, in some places flags, were said to be in good condition in 1860 in contrast with Quebec and Montreal. Toronto, on the other hand, was more poorly lighted with very inferior gas, and lamps few and far apart (S. P. Day, *English America*, II, 4). Gas was first introduced in Toronto in 1841, Montreal in 1840, Halifax in 1843, Quebec in 1849, Kingston in 1850, Hamilton in 1851, Brockville in 1853. Coal-oil became a competitor with the expansion of petroleum. The carburetted water gas process was introduced in Toronto in 1880 and gas stoves and gas heaters increased rapidly after that date. (*The Consumers' Gas Company*, Toronto, 1923). The street railway depending on horses was begun in Toronto and Montreal in 1861. Improved navigation was followed by rapid expansion in Montreal in the fifties (S. P. Day, *English America*, I, 160-164, 15-17). Roads in Montreal and Quebec were in very poor condition. In Quebec wooden houses and crowded population made fires extremely dangerous.

[2]*S.p.*, 10, 1886.

LABOUR[1]

1

The Decline of the Apprentice System

Concentration of industry in the larger towns and the shift from water-power to steam-power and from wood to iron was followed by the decline of the individualistic handi-craftsman and the rise of the labour problem. The jack-of all-trades[2] was gradually supplanted by specialized trades and these in turn were replaced by machines and the "labouring" class. At the end of the period "the apprentice system is almost a thing of the past. The factory system, the introduction of machinery and the division of labour have nearly put an end to it." In 1851 the adult male population in trades and professions was 228,567 for Canada West, of which 86,224,[3] or three-eighths, were farmers and 185,462 for Canada East, of which 78,264, or three-sevenths, were farmers. Labourers of every description totalled 81,764 in Canada West and 68,924 in Canada East. In Canada West:[4]

---

[1]See J. E. Middleton, *The municipality of Toronto,* chapter viii; *Canada, an encyclopedia,* VI, 251-266; R. H. Coats, "The labor movement in Canada" (*Canada and its provinces,* IX, 277 *ff.*); Annual reports of the bureau of industries, *S.p., Ont.*; Reports of the commissioner of agriculture and public works, *S.p., Que.*

[2]"Dis be man of omnibus vocation. Sometime he make de pig-pen; sometime he drive nail in shingle on de house; den he cut me hare, shave me berd, make me shoe, and den he make de music for de dance" (S. P. Day, *English America,* I, 239).

[3]Not including 12,417 occupiers of less than 10 acres.

[4]*Second report of the secretary of the board of registration and statistics on the census of Canada for 1851-2.* Toronto had a monopoly of 7 axe-makers and 5 brush-makers.

1861 (occupations with over 1000 people)

	Canada East	Canada West
Boot and shoe makers	4,916	6,270
Blacksmiths	3,460	5,431
Butchers	....	1,055
Boat and boat men	2,816	6,270
Carpenters	7,291	9,866
Carters	2,999	....
Clerks	4,717	4,262
Coopers	....	1,798
Grocers	....	1,010

The trades and occupations occupying the greatest numbers, are, Carpenters and Joiners, 8,122—about 1/28 of the whole; Blacksmiths, 4,235, 1/54; Tailors, 2,662; Merchants and Shopkeepers, 2,794; Clerks, 3,100; Coopers, 1,935; Millers, 1,083; Weavers, 1,738; Inn-keepers, 2,026; Waggon and Carriage Makers, 1,409; Cabinet Makers, 1,030; Masons and Bricklayers, 1,718. Among the Professions we find, of Clergymen, 963; Medical Men, 382; Lawyers and Notaries, 321; Engineers, 373; and of Teachers there are 2,120.

In Canada East:

Carpenters and Joiners are 6,580, or as in Canada West, about 1/28 of the whole; Shoe makers, 3,069; Blacksmiths, 2,840; Tailors, only 671; Merchants and Storekeepers, 2,785; Clerks, 2,222; Coopers, 473; Millers, 667. Of Weavers there are only 166 returned, the Habitans for the most part weaving everything for their own use, and furnishing much for the market. Of Inn-keepers and Tavern Keepers 443 only are returned, and no doubt, correctly. Of Cabinet Makers, 311; Masons and Bricklayers, 1,022. Among the Professions there are, of Clergymen, 620; Medical Men, 410; Lawyers and Notaries, 811; Engineers, 225; and of Teachers there are 1,136.

2

Wages

Demands on the part of the railroads, the lumber trade, and construction industries, and of agriculture, following the high prices for wheat, were followed by a marked increase in wages. Hogan, writing in 1855, stated that:

Labourers	44,984	96,543
Inn-keepers	....	1,568
Lumbermen	3,815	4,114
Masons	1,099	1,650
Merchants	1,165	....
Millers	....	1,816
Painters	....	1,118
Servants, female	12,003	13,778
Servants, male	5,931	3,783
Shop-keepers	2,407	3,661
Tailoresses	1,526	....
Tailors	....	2,739
Teachers, female	1,995	1,119
" male	....	2,956
Traders	1,312	....
Saddlers and harness-makers	....	1,152
Waggon and cart-makers	....	1,509
Weavers	....	1,110

The rate of wages . . . during the past year [1854] has in many instances been more than doubled. The average rates of wages for Lower Canada have been 6s. per day for bakers, butchers, brickmakers, cabinet makers, and most other trades; stone cutters received 7s., and bricklayers and stone masons 7s. 6d. Agents from Upper Canada, and the Western States, guaranteed steady employment for unskilled labour[1] at 6s. 3d., and bricklayers and stone masons from 10s. to 12s. 6d. a day; farm labourers from 10 to 18 dollars per month.[2]

3

Fluctuations in the Demand for Labour

The depression of 1857, *l'année terrible*, brought a sharp decline.

Agricultural demands predominated in the fifties and it was not until the effects of the Civil War, the abrogation of the Reciprocity Treaty, and Confederation were evident in the increasing importance of industry that demands became pronounced for industrial labour. In Montreal in 1866:

Nearly all the branches of the manufacturing interest offer very lucrative employment for the skilled laborer, and even hard working un-educated men can earn good wages. There are two dangers attending all working men; the first is, that at certain periods of the year the demand for labour is far in excess of the supply; and secondly, money earned comparatively easily is spent quickly, in a manner that generates bad habits.[3]

---

[1]For work on the Grand Trunk "A large number of Lower Canadians were brought up in organized gangs, each having an Englishman or an American as their leader. These gangers received a guinea a week for each man they brought. The French Canadians, however, except for very light work, were almost useless. They had not physical strength for anything like heavy work.

They could ballast, but they could not excavate. They could not even ballast as the English navvy does, continuously working at "filling" for the whole day. The only way in which they could be worked was by allowing them to fill the wagons, and then ride out with the ballast train to the place where the ballast was tipped, giving them an opportunity of resting. Then the empty wagons went back again to be filled; and so, alternately resting during the work, in that way, they did very much more. They could work fast for ten minutes and they were "done". This was not through idleness, but physical weakness. They are small men, and they are a class who are not well fed. They live entirely on vegetable food, and they scarcely ever taste meat.

These men, however, though their powers of work were but feeble, proved to be of great use, inasmuch as their coming prevented the stalwart men from leaving" (A. Helps, *Life and labours of Thomas Brassey*, 196-7).

[2]J. S. Hogan, *Canada*, 66.

[3]*S.p.*, 3, 1867-8.

Wages for various types of skilled labour at Confederation varied from $5.00 to $8.00 per week for compositors, $1.00 per day for labour in soap and candle factories, and $8.00 to $9.00 per week for first-class furriers, $5.00 to $7.00 for second-class, and $3.00 to $5.00 for skilled women workers. In 1871 projected public works, such as the enlargement of canals and construction of the Canadian Pacific and other railways, created additional demands for labour.[1] Depression beginning in 1873 in the United States was followed by a return of immigrants to the United Kingdom and "caused the entry into the Dominion of large numbers of the mechanic class"[2] and in 1874-5 "great distress no doubt exists in the large towns but from minute enquiry in Toronto and Ottawa, I am satisfied that very few, if any of the sufferers are or have been agricultural labourers."[3] Recovery from the depression brought demands for labour.   At Hamilton in 1880:

> The general business of the district shows a large increase in all branches of trade, both of exports and imports; the wholesale merchants have been prompt in their payments, and liabilities have been greatly reduced, whilst the country merchants have met their payments more satisfactorily than for some time past, and the retailers have been fairly prosperous, doing a larger and more satisfactory business.   Failures have been fewer, confidence with traders has been restored, and new houses have been established in the various branches of business.[4]

The following year it was reported:

> The past year has been the most eventful in the history of Canada, in the development of the manufacturing industries; all branches of trade have been fully employed, the shops, factories and mills being taxed to their fullest capacity, a large number of them having been compelled to run overtime to keep their engagements, and large orders had to be refused owing to the manufacturers not being in a position to avail themselves of their several new factories; new mills have been erected during the year and new industries established, and those previously in existence have had to enlarge their works and increase their plant so as to be in a position to meet the continual and growing demand made upon them.

[1]*S.p.*, 2a, 1872.
[2]*S.p.*, 40, 1875.
[3]Report of Mr. A. Spencer Jones, delegate from English Labourers' Union, *S.p.*, 8, 1876.
[4]*S.p.*, 12, 1880-1.

Railways have also participated in the general prosperity of the country, their rolling-stock being taxed to its utmost capacity to meet the demands made upon them for transportation, which has caused an increased activity in all the mechanical shops not only for repairs, but also for the construction of new plant; in addition, large orders have been given to the different rolling-stock construction companies to meet the requirements of the different railways.[1]

A recession followed in 1883 and 1884:

The bad crops of the past two years, over-production, the diminished purchasing power of the industrial classes from this cause, the locking up of capital by investments in non-productive enterprises, over-production in certain industries, depression in the lumber trade, and the revolution which the substitution of steamers for sailing craft has brought about in the carrying trade of the world, are among the leading causes variously assigned for the troubles which have clustered around the year 1884.[2]

In 1885 flour-mills were fairly active, "running altogether on Canadian wheat". Textile fabric mills "started on full time to meet the growing demand for all classes of domestic goods". The foundries were "on full time, with a larger output than any previous year".

The "Report of A. H. Blackeby on the state of the manufacturing industries of Ontario and Quebec",[3] intended to stress the beneficent effects of the national policy, claimed that a large number of industries were developed between 1878 and 1885, including

. . . iron bridge building, sugar-refining, cotton-printing, rice-hulling, and the manufacture of cutlery, emery wheels, pins, clocks, haircloth, enamelled oilcloths, jute, felt goods, organ reeds, writing papers, silver tableware, organ and piano keyboards, Britannia metal work, cashmere and other dress goods, glucose, steel, and many lines of textiles, in both cotton and wool.

While one or two plants had closed down, for example the bolt works at the Humber River, other plants were opened—"the rubber works and sugar and syrup refinery at Toronto; Rasconi Woollen and Cotton Manufacturing Co. at Acton Vale, wincey mill at Brantford, paper and pulp mill at Sorel,

---

[1]*S.p.*, 11, 1882.
[2]*S.p.*, 37, 1885.
[3]*S.p.*, 37, 1885.

and the Taylor Manufacturing Co. at Montreal". A window-glass factory was started at Napanee in 1881.

The rate of growth was suggested in·describing various industries. In 26 establishments producing paper, of which 12 were started after 1878, employment increased 122 per cent. In 33 establishments manufacturing metal, of which 15 were started after 1878, employment increased 81 per cent. and wages from \$313.53 to \$333.22 in 1884. In 65 factories producing miscellaneous products, of which 33 were started after 1879, employment increased by 213 per cent. In 25 factories producing leather, brushes and brooms, and rope, of which 7 were started after 1879, employment increased by 157 per cent.

The increase in the total number of hands in the factories visited amounts to, as nearly as possible, 100 per cent. The wages have increased 106 per cent.; or, putting it in another way, the wages averaged in 1878, \$293.33, and in 1884, \$304.53, an increase of \$11.20 per hand. The increase in the value of products was 126 per cent., and the capital invested increased by 85 per cent. . . .

4

General Changes in Employment

The general changes in employment throughout the period are roughly indicated in the following table.

The ratios of occupation to 1,000 of population—

Upper Canada	1851	1861	1871	1881
agricultural class	91.0	96.2	141.1	158.4
commercial class	9.7	10.6	17.9	23.3
domestic class	18.9	15.3	16.5	17.3
industrial class	47.2	43.3	57.9	67.7
professional class	7.1	6.7	10.3	12.1
not classified	84.8	71.2	42.1	49.1
Lower Canada				
agricultural class	88.1	97.2	134.8	148.6
commercial class	9.9	17.0	21.4	25.3
domestic class	19.2	17.8	17.7	17.9
industrial class	29.4	40.0	55.1	60.1
professional class	5.3	6.4	12.6	13.5
not classified	76.1	45.8	44.3	53.4

5
Evils of the New Industrialism

Although it was stated in the *Report of the royal commission on the relations of labor and capital*, that

> the testimony taken sustains a belief that wages in Canada are generally higher than at any previous time, while hours of labor have been somewhat reduced [*and*] at the same time, the necessaries and ordinary comforts are lower in price than ever before, so that the material condition of the working people who exercise reasonable prudence and economy, has been greatly bettered, especially during the past ten years,[1]

and that machinery[2] had been chiefly responsible for this reduction of living costs, nevertheless the factory system brought numerous and serious problems.

A "Report of the commissioners appointed to enquire into the working of mills and factories of the dominion and the labour employed therein"[3] dated Toronto, January 18, 1882, brought out the more significant results.

> The employment of children and young persons in mills and factories is extensive, and largely on the increase, the supply being unequal to the demand, particularly in some localities, which may partially explain why those of such tender years are engaged. . . .
>
> We are sorry to report that in very many instances the children, having no education whatever, could not tell their ages; this applies more particularly to those from twelve years downwards . . . some being found as young as eight and nine years. . . .
>
> It must be borne in mind that the children invariably work as many hours as adults, and if not compelled, are requested to work overtime when circumstances so demand, which has not been unusual of late in most lines of manufactures. The appearance and condition of the children in the after part of the day, such as may be witnessed in the months of July and August, was anything but inviting or desirable. . . . They have to be at the mills or factories at 6.30 a.m., necessitating their being up at from 5.30 to 6 o'clock for their morning

---

[1] For statistics as to rates of wages, see *Report of the royal commission on the relations of labor and capital in Canada* (Ottawa, 1889), 134 *ff*.

[2] Machinery "has another advantage . . . that of doing the hard part of the work, and if it takes no more space than one person and does four times as much work, it will save 75 per cent of the room required and so cause cheaper production." Machinery was exempted from duty in 1871 (34 Vic. c. 10) and imports increased rapidly to 1873.

[3] *S.p.*, 42, 1882.

meal, some having to walk a distance of half a mile or more
to their work. This undeniably is too heavy a strain on children
of tender years, and is utterly condemned by all except those
who are being directly benefitted by such labor, and which
they attempt to justify on the grounds,—

1st. That the labor is light.

2nd. That it is not practicable for those more advanced in
years.

3rd. That their competitors in the trade use this kind of labor.

4th. As there is no law or restriction on the question, some use
it, and others who might be more liberally inclined have to
follow.—

Kind of Labor Children are employed at.—Non-attendance of Factory-Children at School

We find, in some trades where piece-work is done and
where children are employed, that they are not engaged by
the firm or managers of the shop or factory, but by the hands
who take such piece work to do, who arrange with the children
as to the value of the labor, and who are solely interested in
procuring the cheapest labor possible, irrespective of any other
consideration as to the interests or condition of the labor
employed. As to the attendance at school of children under
fourteen years employed in factories, there is no attempt to
attend school at all, from the fact that the regulations under
which they work would not allow it. We have observed with
regret a serious lack of education in very many of the adult
factory hands. In some parts of the country a large proportion are to be found who can neither read or write, and employers are seriously inconvenienced by this lack of education
in those applying for work, necessitating the importation of
educated labor when our own people should be trained for
these positions. . . .

Dangerous machinery.—Hoists.—Accidents.—Indifference on the part of Employers

Dangerous machinery which is not protected, is quite
common in most of our mills and factories. Gearing, fly-
wheels, pulleys, belts and steam engines are in many cases
entirely unprotected, and many accidents have resulted from
this cause, the only matter for surprise being that they are
not more numerous. In connection with this we deem it our
duty to call attention to the faulty construction and dangerous
manner in which hoists and elevators are operated in mills,
factories and warehouses. . . .

Bad Ventilation

4th. Very often, on entering a mill or factory, our senses
have been convincingly informed of imperfect ventilation and

drainage of closets, the only ventilation in many instances being a door opening directly into the factory. The above facts in relation to the imperfect sanitary arrangements of some factories cannot be too harshly commented on, and show a callous indifference on the part of the employer toward the physical and moral interests of those under his charge.

Meat-curing Factories

There is much room for improvement, in the matter of cleanliness in meat-curing, meat-canning, fruit and vegetable-canning, bakeries and confectionery establishments. Instances have come under our notice which were nauseating in the extreme, and a prompt and careful supervision and frequent inspection are imperatively demanded for some of these places.

The *Report of the royal commission on the relations of labor and capital in Canada*[1] emphasized similar trends:

In acquiring the industries at one bound [*after national policy*] we have also become possessed just as quickly, of the evils which accompany the factory system . . . to obtain a very large percentage of work with the smallest possible outlay of wages appears to be the one fixed and dominant idea. . . . To arrive at the greatest results for the smallest expenditure the mills and factories are filled with women and children, to the practical exclusion of adult males. The reason for this is obvious. Females and children[2] may be counted upon to

---

[1]See also John Davidson, *The bargain theory of wages* (New York, 1898), chapter viii.

[2]The evils were similar to those reported in 1882. "The darkest pages in the testimony which follows are those recording the beating and imprisonment of children employed in factories . . . the lash and the dungeon are accompaniments of manufacturing industry in Canada." "At one place in Ontario children certainly less than eleven years of age, were employed around dangerous machinery. Some of them worked from six o'clock in the morning till six in the evening, with less than a hour for dinner, others worked from seven in the evening till six in the morning. At Montreal boys were employed all night in the glass works. In the cotton factories the ordinary hours of labor were from 6.30 a.m. till noon; and from 12.45 till 6.15 p.m. . . . this for five days in the week." In a cigar plant in Montreal "it is very clearly proved that . . . apprentices were imprisoned in a "black hole" for hours at a time. . . . Occasionally this Oriental despot would himself be the executioner of his own decrees and did upon one occasion, personally chastise, in a flagrantly indecent manner a girl eighteen years of age. And for all this the law provides no remedy—nay incredible as it may appear, law, in the person of the recorder of Montreal, expressly authorized the punishment inflicted. This gentleman, on being examined, stated that he had authorized employers to chastise their operatives at their discretion, so long as no permanent injury was inflicted, and this evidence was given in the year of our lord one thousand eight hundred and eighty-eight." "Sweating" was a further result, "young girls who work sixty hours a week for 80 cents". (See J. T. Scott, *The conditions of female labour in Ontario*, Toronto, 1892; also Report on sweating system in Canada, *S.p.*, 61, 1896.)

work for small wages, to submit to petty and exasperating
exactions, and to work uncomplainingly for long hours. . . .
So long as one employer is permitted to fill up his factory with
this cheap labor, without any restrictions, the others are compelled to do likewise.

Other evils were evident in the "congested industrial centres".
"In all large cities rents have risen very materially." "It
is undeniable that workmen are badly lodged in houses
badly built, unhealthy, and rented at exorbitant prices."
Municipal taxes were shifted to the poor class of tenants.
Landlords were given preference over other debtors. Long
hours of labour were prevalent, longshoremen working from
30 to 40 hours at a stretch. The truck system was in evidence
in various forms, especially in mining and lumbering. Employees were subjected to fines. Wages were in a weak legal
position. "The law protects, only very feebly, wages; that
is to say payment is assured when it is so only by laws of an
application as slow as costly." Legislation became inadequate, especially in the case of the Apprenticeship Acts
and the Factory Acts of Ontario and Quebec,[1] the act to
assure, in certain cases, compensation to workmen (*Ontario
consolidated statutes*, c. 141), and the Masters and Servants
Act of Quebec. Accidents were numerous as a result of
unguarded machinery, particularly on railroads, and of unskilled labour operating engines and boilers. Unemployment
was in the offing. "The labour market of Canada is already
overstocked." Monetary assistance to immigrants ceased
after April 27, 1888. Labour organizations had grown up in
relation to the crafts and offered little resistance to the evils
of the new industrialism.[2]

---

[1]Ontario legislation included the Apprentice Statute, 1852, Apprentices
and Minors Act, 1871, Mechanics Lien Act, 1873, Railway Accidents Act, 1881,
Employers Liability (threshing machines), 1874, Factories Act, 1884. The
Quebec Factories Act, 1885 was closely modelled on that of Ontario.

[2]See H. A. Logan, *The history of trade-union organization in Canada* (Chicago, 1928), chapters i, ii.

POPULATION[1]

1

Growth of Population

The growth of population was an index of the far-reaching developments of the period.

Total population

	Upper Canada	Lower Canada
1851	952,004	890,261
1861	1,396,091	1,111,566
1871	1,620,581	1,191,516
1881	1,926,922	1,359,027

2

The Birth-rate

The rapid increase in Upper Canada was in part a result of immigration but, in spite of the inaccuracies of the census, it is generally agreed that the birth-rate in both Upper and Lower Canada[2] was high. An analysis of the census of 1851 shows the trend of the period.

In Upper Canada which had received the larger number of immigrants the males exceeded the females by 46,130 or nearly 5 per cent. while in Lower Canada the males exceeded by 9,773 or a little over 1 per cent. The high proportion of young population was also strikingly evident. In Upper Canada there were 37,732 under one year of age or nearly 1/25 of the population and about the same number over one

---

[1]See Census volumes; also R. R. Kuczynski, *Birth registration and birth statistics in Canada* (Washington, 1930), especially bibliography. For a searching criticism of census statistics see J. Langton, "The census of 1861" (*Transactions* of the Canadian Institute, series II, X, 1-19).

[2]See J. Davidson, "The growth of the French Canadian race in America" (*Annals* of the American Academy of Political and Social Science, September, 1896, 1-23). This author gives the rate of increase per cent. per decade

1851-61	30.6
1861-71	23.0
1871-81	25.38
1881-91	21.64

See also A. R. M. Lower, "The growth of the French population in Canada" (Canadian Political Science Association *proceedings*, II, 1930, 35-47).

and under two years while in Lower Canada each group formed about 1/22 of the total. The number of births in 1851 in Upper Canada was 32,681 from 162,143 women between 16 and 50 years of age and in Lower Canada[1] 36,739 from 124,910 women. For Canada ten children were born in 1851 to every 43 women living in 1852 between those ages.. . . In 42,000 families [*in Great Britain with no children*] there were not half the same amount without children; instead of 12,000 [*out of 42,000 as in Great Britain*] there were only 4,760; instead of 8,500 having only one [*as in Great Britain*], there were 7,000. In Canada having two, there were 6,610 [*in Great Britain, 7,300*]; having three, 5,600 [*in Great Britain, 5,600*]; having four 6,440 [*in Great Britain, 4,000*]; having five, 5,880; having six, 2,520; having eight, 1,680, and so on—numerous families being more predominant in Canada than Great Britain. It is quite easy to account for this, for servants being more difficult to be procured in Canada than in Great Britain, young men are obliged to marry earlier in life, and they are better able to do so; and another way of accounting for it is, that Emigrants, when transplanted, increase faster in this climate than if they had remained at home, and moreover, Emigrants always number an excess of healthy people at a reproductive age, the old people seldom coming with them, and the average Immigration to British North America has been about 41,200 per annum for the last 10 years, by far the larger number of which have come to the Canadas.

3
Infant-mortality and the Death-rate

A high rate of infant-mortality offset in part the effects of the high birth-rate.

During the infantile ages up to five years, the mortality in the Lower Province is in a much greater ratio, in fact nearly cent. per cent.; but it must be remembered that the Births in Lower Canada are one-eighth more numerous than in Upper Canada. . . . Epidemic Diseases, such as Small Pox, Meazles, Scarlet Fever, and other Fevers, Hooping Cough, Croup and Cholera &c., are much more fatal in Lower Canada than in Upper Canada, . . . the Deaths in the latter, under this head, being only 1,783, whilst in the Lower Province they were 3,098. Pleurisy also is more destructive, as is Consumption, though not to a great degree. . . .

---

[1]Second report of the secretary of the board of registration and statistics, on the census of the Canadas for 1851-52, *Journals of the legislative assembly*, XIII, 1854-5, app. C.

The death-rate was generally high.[1] Epidemics[2] were responsible for heavy loss of life. Smallpox was a menace throughout the period.

4

Immigration

On the other hand, population, especially in Upper Canada, was reinforced by immigration and by the arrival of large numbers of younger people, especially in the fifties.[3] With the disappearance of the best land in Upper Canada, the United States became a more effective competitor. According to Day, large numbers of immigrants arriving at Quebec prior to 1860 passed on to the western and southern states—a total

[1]

	Males	Females	Total
The Births in 1851 in Upper Canada, were..	16,916	15,765	32,681
The Deaths in Upper Canada, were......	4,107	3,668	7,775

Being nearly one-fourth the number of Births.

	Males	Females	Total
In Lower Canada the Births were........	18,926	18,113	36,739
The Deaths were.......................	6,112	5,562	11,674

Not quite one-third the number of Births.

[2]The fourth epidemic of cholera in Canada took place in 1851 and was responsible during a period from August 25 to October 2 for 206 deaths in Quebec city. In the fifth epidemic of 1854, 3,486 deaths occurred (*S.p.*, 3, 1867-8).

"The first working season at the Victoria Bridge was a period of difficulty, trouble and disaster. The agents of the contractors had no experience of the climate. There were numerous strikes among the workmen. The cholera committed dreadful ravages in the neighbourhood. In one case, out of a gang of two hundred men, sixty were sick at one time, many of whom ultimately died. After the harvest, towards September, the cholera at length disappeared; labour became more plentiful; and the work in consequence proceeded more satisfactorily" (A. Helps, *Life and labours of Mr. Brassey*, 204). See regarding an epidemic of smallpox at Hungerford, *S.p.*, *Ont.*, 25, 1885. There was also an epidemic in Quebec in 1885-6. See J. J. Heagerty, *Four centuries of medical history in Canada*, (Toronto, 1928), *passim*. See also Report . . . . . on the subject of hygiene and public health, *J.h.c.*, 1873, app. 8; Reports of the provincial board of health 1882, *S.p.*, *Ont.*

[3] Immigration by sea

Country	1851	1852	1853	1854	1855	1856	1857	1858	1859	1860
England....	9677	9276	9585	18175	6754	10353	15471	6441	4846	6481
Ireland.....	22381	15983	14417	16165	4106	1688	2016	1153	417	376
Scotland ...	7042	5477	4745	6446	4859	2794	3218	1424	793	979
Germany ⎫ Norway ⎭ .	870	7256	7456	11537 ⎱ ⎰	3597 1267	4537 2806	4961 6407	922 2656	966 1756	533 1781
Lower Provinces....	1106	1182	496	857	691	261	24	214	....	.....
Total......	41076	39176	36699	53183	21274	22439	32097	12810	8778	10150

The decline following 1858 was in part a result of bad harvests in 1857 and 1858. "To Emigration the Province is principally indebted for its progress; and in no way can the material wealth of the country be so rapidly increased, and its burdens of taxation so easily diminished, as by the introduction of industrious and frugal emigrants from the British Isles and Europe" (*S.p.*, 3, 1861).

of 6,000 had left from 1859 to 1861. The Civil War checked this trend. Indeed, large numbers of Canadians returned and, according to Day, large numbers of young Americans ("skidaddlers") came to Canada to escape conscription.[1] After the war immigration resumed its normal course, and in 1866 it was estimated that two-thirds of the British arrivals at Quebec proceeded to the United States.[2] During the depression of the seventies immigration from Great Britain suffered a decided check.[3] With recovery the rise of the livestock trade attracted the attention of British farmers and the expansion of industry attracted skilled labour.

5

Emigration

Increase in immigration was offset by an increase in emigration.

Canadians in the United States increased as follows:

1850	147,711
1860	249,970
1870	493,464
1880	717,157
1890	980,938

and emigration has been variously estimated[4] as follows:

1850-60	102,000	135,000
1860-70	243,000	305,000
1870-80	224,000	325,000
1880-90	264,000	410,000

According to Wickett, the heaviest drain was in evidence from 1875 to 1885. The immigration of a large number of

[1] S. P. Day, *English America*, I, 257-8; II, 318.

[2] *S.p.*, 3, 1867-8.

[3] *S.p.*, 8, 1876 and *S.p.*, 9, 1878.

[4] See G. E. Jackson, "Emigration of Canadians to the United States" (*Annals* of the American Academy, May, 1923, 24-34); S. M. Wickett, "Canadians in the United States" (*Ibid*, January, 1913, 83-98); also *Political Science Quarterly*, XXI, 190-205; R. Wilson, "Migration movements in Canada, 1868-1925" (*Canadian Historical Review*, XIII, June, 1932); W. MacDonald, "The French Canadians in New England" (*Quarterly Journal of Economics*, April, 1898, 245-279); E. Hamon, *Les Canadiens-Français de la Nouvelle Angleterre* (Quebec, 1891); also Second report of the select committee appointed to examine into the causes of the emigration movement, *Journals of the legislative assembly, Quebec*, 1893, app. I, and Report of Rev. P. E. Gendreau, special agent, of his visit to French Canadians in the United States, *S.p.*, 9, 1874.

young and vigorous male immigrants was essential to the expansion of Upper Canada in the fifties. Disappearance of the better lands, the attractions of the western states, and a high birth-rate contributed to the growth of towns and to emigration. Both Upper and Lower Canada lost large numbers of young and vigorous native Canadians. Population poured out to the United States and to the newly-opened western Canada.

CREDIT AND MONEY

1

Financing of Canals and Railroads

The shift from wood to iron which accompanied the construction of canals and railroads and the concentration of industry involved dependence on capital from Great Britain.[1] Expansion of technology and of capital equipment was accompanied by extension of credit. Organization designed to support credit for construction of canals involved union of the provinces. Failure to attract traffic necessitated the addition of railroads and the encouragement of private enterprise as a further basis of credit. Finally Confederation emerged as a solution to the problem.

> The Government of this country has had under its exclusive control the improvement of the navigation nearly since the commencement of the works while private companies have built our railway lines, those other great channels for traffic, which assist so materially in the development of the country. These two systems have become co-operative, uniting as the separate parts of one machine, to accomplish the carrying trade of the country. . . .
>
> In undertaking the construction of a railway system passing through Canada, which should connect the great lakes with the ocean, the province did not propose to effect this entirely through its own resources; the Legislature only sought to offer such inducements to capitalists as might cause their attention to be directed to Canada, believing that such works as railways, the success of which is almost wholly dependent upon attention to details, were better under private management than under that of the Government.[2]

The ordinary inducements to private enterprise involved assistance under the act of 1849 in the form of "6 per cent. guarantee by the province on one half the cost of all railways of 75 miles in extent". In 1852 further assistance was provided especially in the establishment of a municipal loan

---

[1] See L. H. Jenks, *The migration of British capital to 1875* (New York, 1927), chapter viii.

[2] *S.p.*, 8, 1867-8.

fund (16 Vic. c. 22).[1] Construction of a through line involved the dilemma of building a road at low initial cost[2] and losing through-traffic in competition with better roads, and building a road with heavy initial cost and a consequent heavy burden of overhead costs. As a result of the difficulties following the Crimean War and the "consequent rise in the value of money",[3] the government was forced to come to the assistance of the Grand Trunk Railway by enacting legislation in 1856 and 1857 giving the private capital of the company priority over the provincial lien of £3,111,500. In 1858 the direct debt of Canada[4] was $24,430,975 "which has been created almost wholly for the great canals[5] and other works of national improvement".

[1] The fund was limited to £1,500,000 in 1854 (18 Vic. c. 13) and loans stopped in 1859 (22 Vic. c. 15).

[2] "In America, a railway is like a river, and is regarded as the natural channel of civilization. Extended into a thinly populated district, it is the pioneer of civilization; it precedes population; and is laid down, even before common roads are thought of. As the expectation of traffic is, in many instances, but small, the cost of construction must be kept down as much as possible. With this object in view, timber is universally substituted for the more costly materials made use of in this country. Tressel bridges take the place of stone viaducts, and, in places in which in this country you would see a solid embankment, in America a light structure is often substituted" (A. Helps, *Life and labours of Mr. Brassey*, 198-9).

[3] See Memorial of the Grand Trunk Railway Company of Canada, *Journals of the legislative assembly*, 1857, app. 6.

[4] See *Canada and its provinces*, V, 165 *ff*.

Expenditure December 31, 1858

Welland and St. Lawrence Canals	$14,155,206.35
Other canals	2,766,146.40
Harbours and light houses	2,817,057.92
Roads and bridges, and	1,610,267.34
Miscellaneous	1,326,346.21
	$22,675,024.22
Works transferred to consolidated funds as unproductive	$1,982,039
Sinking fund for imperial loan	3,752,843
	$5,734,982
Direct public debt including deficits 1857 and 1858	$24,430,975
Minus amount on consolidated fund	621,726
	$23,809,248
Surplus	$4,600,658

[5] Total funds expended by the board of works on canals and improvement of waterways

1852 and 1853	$1,959,239
1854 and 1855	3,217,306
1856	1,629,124
1857	1,365,640
1858	1,042,656
1859	844,769
1860	1,452,224
Total	$11,510,958

The indirect debt of the province in 1859 included:

Railways...............................	$20,295,098.47
Municipal loan fund[1]....................	9,057,792.00
Sundries...............................	1,169,684.85
	$30,522,575.32

On account of railroads...................	$20,295,098.47
Of which, the advance to the Great Western Railroad can alone be regarded as secure..	2,810,500.00
Leaving.............................	$17,484,598.47

for which the province may have ultimately to provide—meantime advancing the interest.

In the decade from 1850 to 1860, 2,093 miles[2] were constructed "while the present charge to the province connected with those railways which have received public aid is £4,161,150 or £249,669 per annum". By 1861 the province had outstanding debentures of nearly $66,000,000.[3] According to Galt, the debt of Canada was £9,677,672 or, after deducting the sinking fund for the redemption of the imperial

----

[1]Upper Canada, $7,294,792; Lower Canada, $1,763,000. The municipal loan fund was used largely to build railroads with the support of municipal credit and reached a total of $12,015,800 assumed by the government. Municipalities under other powers granted $3,000,000. Port Hope, for example, subscribed £130,000 and Cobourg £100,000.

[2]Grand Trunk, 1,112 miles; Great Western, 357; Northern, 95; Buffalo and Lake Huron, 159; minor lines, 370. To 1860 these lines had been assisted—Grand Trunk total 853 miles, $15,172,931; Great Western 228 miles, $2,810,500; Northern 96 miles, $2,311,666; total $20,295,097.

1851		91 miles in operation
In 1852 there were opened		98 miles
1853	do	212 do
1854	do	330 do
1855	do	236 do
1856	do	435 do
1857	do	70 do
1858	do	140 do
1859	do	251 do
1860	do	29 do

Total now open for traffic 1,892 miles (S.p., 3, 1861). See T. C. Keefer, *Philosophy of railroads* (Montreal, 1850). In 1860 a loan of £583,000 was made to the Great Western and in 1861, as a result of a threatened strike and a difficult winter, $120,000 to the Grand Trunk (S.p., 11, 1861).

[3]*Report of the select standing committee on public accounts* (1862). In 1860 provision was made for the conversion of the public debt which included £9,677,672 chargeable on consolidated revenue fund with annual interest of £546,345 and, £1,983,338 on various other funds with annual interest, £119,000 (S.p., 1, 1860).

"The whole direct and indirect debt of Canada, as shown by the Public Accounts of the Province, may be, therefore, classed:—

guaranteed loan, £8,884,672,[1] of which payment on public works were:

Imperial Guaranteed Loan	£ 1,500,000
Sterling Debentures, payable in London	7,702,925
Currency and Sterling, payable in Canada	2,458,085
Total	£11,661,010

The total charge for interest being	£ 665,345
To pay up, in full, the Sinking Fund for the Imperial Guaranteed Loan, about	700,000
To reimburse the Consolidated Revenue Fund for advances made in 1859, on account of Redemption of Debt	400,000
To redeem so much of the Feudal Tenure Fund	250,000
For Public Buildings at Ottawa	200,000
For redemption of remainder of 6 per cent., Currency Debt, both direct and indirect, about	1,250,000
	£2,800,000

The charges now borne by the Revenue on the foregoing items, are as follows:—

Interest and Sinking Fund, Imperial Loan	£ 90,000
Six per cent. Interest on £2,100,000	126,000
Total per annum	£ 216,000

By the issue of 5 per cent. Consols or Bonds, the annual charge will be reduced to,—

For interest	£ 140,000
For Sinking Fund, half per cent	14,000
	£ 154,000

Making a reduction of charge upon the Revenue of Canada, of £62,000 per annum, while at the same time the existing Imperial Sinking Fund will by this operation be increased to £1,500,000, thus practically extinguishing so much of the present debt (*S.p.*, 1, 1860; see also S. P. Day, *English America*, I, 65 *ff*.).

[1]STATEMENT of the Public Debt from the year 1851 to 1860

Year	Direct	Indirect	Total
	$	$	$
1850, Existing Debt			18,782,565
1851	17,807,847	2,673,625	20,481,472
1852	18,664,773	3,690,640	22,355,413
1853	18,485,161	11,437,591	29,922,752
1854	17,415,797	21,436,036	38,851,833
1855	17,242,546	28,612,671	45,855,217
1856	18,813,214	29,944,404	48,757,619
1857	21,470,256	30,864,655	52,334,911
1858	24,430,975	30,461,429	54,892,405
1859	25,535,031	28,607,013	54,142,044

The legislation prior to 1852, has produced a debt of		$27,974,900.49	
From 1852 to 1854	$16,298,040.06		
Less redeemed	2,554,736.05	13,743,304.01	
From 1854 to 1858	$15,337,906.26		
Less redeemed	4,080,658.90	11,257,247.36	
From 1858 to 1859	$4,269,186.63		
Issued as shewn in 1860	$27,264,011.77		
do Cons. M. L. Fund, L.C.	71,500.00	27,335,511.77	
Less—redeemed 1858-9	$3,102,594.03	$31,604,698.40	
do 1860	15,885,086.42		
do India Gov'-ment Stock.	7,300,000.00	26,287,680.45	5,317,017.95
Present debt			$58,292,469.81

Canals, lighthouses, and other works connected
with the development of the navigation of the
St. Lawrence, represent.................... £3,962,900
Railway advances.......................... 4,161,150
Roads and bridges, and improvement of rivers.   738,350
                                            _____
                                            £8,862,400

2

Tariffs

Increased expenditures on improved transportation and
navigation on the part of the government involved increased
revenues. Direct taxation was regarded as impossible[1] and
duties on imports were the essential bases of revenues. In
a reasoned statement Galt suggested that the tariff on imports was designed to raise revenue to pay interest on British
capital invested in improved facilities for transport and that
improvement in transportation eliminated the protectionist
character of the tariff.[2]

The argument was supported and enlarged by manufacturers who claimed that improvement in transportation
exposed them to more effective foreign competition. The
depression had serious effects on the home market by checking
the demands of industries which had arisen during the period
of prosperity in response to the stimulus of heavy capital
imports and by increasing the possibilities of dumping from
older industrial countries. Manufacturers complained that

---

[1]*S.p.*, 4, 1862. "The *Quebec Chronicle*, then the ministerial organ, in
dilating upon the financial position of the Province, boldly averred that the time
was not far distant when resort must be had to other sources of revenue than the
customs duty upon imports and the sale of Crown lands. But direct taxation
in any form is as repulsive to the Canadian as to the American mind. Although
such a contingency is not improbable, and for many reasons would be desirable,
it must be a strong government who would peril their existence by having recourse
to such an alternative."

[2]*S.p.*, 23, 1862. He argued that the burden of customs duties although
increasing per capita from $1.60 in 1851 to $1.70 in 1860 was offset by lower
charges accompanying improved transportation (*S.p.*, 3, 1861). See also H. A.
Innis, "Transportation as a factor in Canadian economic history" (*Proceedings*
of the Canadian Political Science Association, III, 166-184); O. D. Skelton, *The
life and times of Sir Alexander Tilloch Galt*, chapter x and *passim*; also E. Porritt,
Sixty years of protection in Canada (London, 1908), chapters iii-viii; J. M. Du-
hamel, "L'orientation de notre politique, douanière sous l'union" (*Etudes Écono-
miques*, Montreal, 1931, 205); C. K. Ganong, "The Canadian reaction to American
tariff policy" (Doctorate thesis, University of Wisconsin). In 1865 total cost
of roads and equipment was $121,543,189 (*S.p.*, 10, 1866).

they were in danger of losing the industrial progress made during the period of expansion. They argued that a definite attempt should be made to maintain and advance the industrial growth of the country from the standpoint of labour, of agriculture, and of finance as well as that of industry.

The report[1] of the special committee on emigration in 1857 suggested as a cause of decline in immigration:

> the want of employment for a large portion of the population during our long winters, arising from the absence of manufactures.
>
> Your Committee consider it to be of the highest importance to the prosperity of the country that reciprocity in duties as well as in Free Trade should exist between this Province and the United States, that the same duties should be charged upon every article imported from the United States, as charged upon the same article when sent from any port of Canada; that, in short, the tariff should be so modified as to ensure to the manufacturer such protection as other Governments have accorded, and still accord, in those countries where his condition, in other respects, analagous to what it would be here, is thought to require such encouragement.

Goods which might be manufactured in Canada included the following imports of 1856:

Articles	£
Iron and Ironware	648,853
Porcelain and Earthenware	71,024
Glass and Glassware	76,706
Combs and Brushes	13,077
Hats and Caps	62,038
Boots and Shoes	93,690
Paper	18,053
Soap	34,439
	1,014,883

and in addition

Bar Iron,	Sheet Iron,
Wheels and Axles of Locomotives,	Chains,
	Hoop Iron,
Connecting Rods,	Cranks,
Boiler Plate,	Iron Machinery of all kinds. . . .

---

[1] *Journals of the legislative assembly*, XV, 1857, app. 47.

When a country has no coinage of its own, and the amount in circulation must depend on the result of commercial transactions in the export of its productions to foreign countries, it is very important that the amount of its imports should be so regulated as to establish a balance in its favor, in order that the amount of coin in circulation may increase in proportion to the wants of an increasing population.

At a later date it was stated that the legislation[1] in 1858 had brought into existence over 1,000 tanneries and increased the manufacture of paper, wool, wooden ware, and agricultural implements. Consequently they were spared "the necessity of sending out of the Province at least two millions of dollars in cash per annum".

By manufacturing these articles we not only cause an immensely increased employment for our own population that are not fit for other sorts of labour, but we retain in the Province the money for the use of the farming and other interests, thus not only increasing our supply of capital in the Province, but reducing the rate of interest at which it can be borrowed. (Cheers.) Free-traders will say, you pay more for the articles you manufacture than if you imported them. Now I deny that this is the case. Every article, I believe

---

[1] A petition of manufacturers dated April 14, 1858, advocated the adoption of the following guiding points:

"1. All raw material upon which there is but a small amount of labour expended prior to its importation, and leaving the larger proportion of labour to be performed in Canada, it is considered should be admitted free, or at a duty not to exceed 2½ per cent.

2. Articles entering largely into consumption in this country, and which Canada cannot produce, such as Tea, Coffee, raw Sugar, Molasses, &c., should not be charged with a high rate of duty, but should be admitted free, or at the lowest possible rate consistent with the requirements of the Revenue.

3. Merchandise in the Dry Goods, Hardware and Crockery Trades, being articles of luxury or for use, and not likely for some time to be manufactured in this country, and of which some are used to form parts of the goods and wares manufactured in Canada, should be chargeable with a medium rate of duty of about 15 per cent. as at present, or not to exceed 20 per cent., but at the rate of about 10 per cent. below what may be charged on articles coming directly into competition with our own manufactured products.

4. All manufactures in Wood, Iron, Tin, Brass, Copper, Leather, India Rubber, &c., competing with our industrial products, as more fully specified in the proposed list of articles and duties, now submitted and adopted, should be charged a duty of about 25 per cent., excepting—

Books, Drawings, &c., which should be charged with a duty of 10 to 15 per cent.

Cottons and Woollens, Cordage, Lines, and Twines, with a duty of 20 per cent.

Clothing and Wearing Apparel, with a duty of 30 per cent."

See I. Buchanan, *Relations of the industry of Canada with that of the mother country and the United States* (Montreal, 1864); also W. Weir, *Sixty years in Canada* (Montreal, 1903), chapters xi *ff*.

without exception, that we now manufacture is furnished to the people at a lower price than it was sold for before 1858. But even supposing that we did pay a higher price by the amount of the customs duty, this would not be injuring the people. It would only be making them pay the tax indirectly, instead of directly. It is obvious that the great fact of our being in debt compels us to collect the money either in one way or the other. The only policy for northern countries in America is to limit their purchases of foreign labour to the greatest extent, for neither the Northern States nor Canada can produce exports to pay for even the very smallest imports, which the natural "go-a-headitiveness" of our people makes possible. . . . To the extent, however that our imports are over our exports we pay for the balance with the Province's life blood, for although there may not be an open removal of the specie on which all bank circulation and monetary confidence is built, there is the loss of the equivalent. . . .

The policy of developing manufactures was expected to increase employment and to provide a market for products of the Canadian farm which would enable the farmer to avoid the dangers of dependence on the staple wheat for export.

And what I wish for Upper Canada is a system of rotation of crops, to render which possible it is essential for us to have an oppidanic or manufacturing population to eat the vegetables and other perishable or bulky productions of the Canadian farmer. . . .

"A nation that manufactures for itself, as well as grows food for itself, produces two values and two markets instead of one."

It was proposed to build up a home market for the white wheat of the Canadian farmer rather than to export it to the superior market of the United States. "The great American economist Carey" was quoted at length and with hearty approval.

In 1847 duties on practically all imported manufactures except heavy iron products were raised to 10 per cent. and 2 years later to $12\frac{1}{2}$ per cent. The objections of the home government "to the assumption by the local Legislatures of the office of imposing differential duties on goods imported into the respective colonies" were disregarded. "You will, therefore, exercise all the legitimate influence of your office to prevent the introduction into the Legislature of the colony under your government of any law by which duties may be imposed on goods in reference to their place of production or to the place from which they may be exported."[1] Protests of Sheffield manufacturers against duties on English goods and of American manufacturers against violation of the Reciprocity Treaty were in vain. In 1856 duties were increased to 15, in 1858, to 20 per cent. on important manufactured articles and to 15 per cent. on non-enumerated articles, and in 1859 to over 20 per cent. on a few items and to 20 per cent. on most products.

The results were shown in the following table:

Year ending December 31	Duty	Rate per cent.	Income	Expenditure
1851	$2,955,727	13-1/3	$3,882,321	$3,050,449
1852	2,956,633	14-1/2	3,976,706	3,059,081
1853	4,119,131	13	5,282,637	3,478,726
1854	4,900,769	12	6,088,110	4,171,941
1855	3,527,098	10	4,870,166	4,779,522
1856	4,510,128	10-1/3	5,989,543	5,143,624
1857	3,927,208	10	5,352,794	5,692,942
1858	3,368,157	11-1/2	4,929,709	6,433,274[2]
1859	4,456,326	13-1/4	6,248,679	6,099,570
1860	4,756,724	14	7,047,930	7,536,179

---

[1]Copy of a circular despatch from the Right Honourable Lord J. Russell to the governors of her majesty's colonies, 12 July, 1855, *Trade reports relating to Canada 1847-1891.*

[2]The indirect costs of improved transportation and settlement were evident in the management of crown lands and customs revenues. Explorations and surveys of new townships totalled £69,000 in 3 years and the establishment of inland ports of entry at central points along the newly-opened lines of railway involved heavy charges without compensating returns.

The government was required to advance funds on debentures issued by local municipalities to the extent of $159,096 in 1857 and $368,503 in 1858. Heavy outlay was also the result of: the transfer of ordnance lands to the province, $162,351; legislation, $684,442; administration of justice, $711,890; railroads, $1,061,756; navigation, $217,555. Revenue from other sources declined along with revenue from customs.

Revenues in 1858

Public works	$400,727.17
Territorial	415,372.68
Post office	295,395.76
Other revenues, of consolidated fund	867,878.77
Receipts from other sources	247,441.67

Day noted that the public offices were imperfectly organized and that extravagance was constantly in evidence. He cited the case of Dunville in which it cost $1,973 to collect customs totalling $1,942. "A statesman in the European signification of the term, Canada cannot boast of." It was stated in

3

Financial Difficulties of the Government

The disturbances created by the enormous imports of capital which were essential to the improvement of transportation—shown in the expansion of industry directly dependent on the construction of railroads and indirectly on the growth of agriculture—created serious financial difficulties for the government. Imports of capital and the construction of railroads stimulated industry and agriculture, and increased imports and revenues. Labour[1] and capital were applied to new areas and their efficiency increased by improved technique. On the other hand, the Crimean War and consequent scarcity of capital, the slow rate of returns on investment in railroads, completion of major portions of line,

a report: "That he [the minister of finance] regrets to have to state that the result of their [Worthington and Brunel] inspection thus far, shews that many of the officers employed in that branch of the Public Service are inefficient, and not properly qualified for their duties; that many others, regardless of the laws and regulations of the Department, have, for a length of time, been in the practice of allowing dutiable goods to go into consumption without payment of duties, and in several cases the duties collected have been retained and appropriated to their own use.

That the Reports shew that, in many cases, a larger number of officers are employed than is deemed necessary, and that in others, officers are stationed at places where the risk of smuggling or the business transacted is not of sufficient importance to warrant the expense incurred" (Copy of a report of a committee of the honorable the executive council approved—24th October 1862). See John Langton, Early days in Upper Canada, letters from the backwoods of Upper Canada and the audit office of the Province of Canada (Toronto, 1926); R. M. Dawson, The civil service of Canada (Oxford, 1929).

[1]The amount of capital brought in by immigrants was difficult to estimate. In 1864 it was stated that immigrants brought in capital to the extent of $255,000. "The following table will show, for the purpose of comparison, the value of cash and effects reported as brought into the Dominion by settlers since the year 1875, the date at which this record was commenced—

Years	Value
1875	$1,344,573
1876	686,205
1877	632,269
1878	1,202,563
1879	1,152,612
1880	1,295,565
1881	4,188,925
1882	3,171,501
1883	2,784,881
1884	4,814,872
1885	4,143,866
1886	3,455,576

(S.p., 12, 1887).

decline in industries directly concerned, and bad harvests in 1857 and 1858 were factors responsible for a decline in imports and a decline in revenue. The rise in prices, which went with the rapid construction of railroads and large imports of capital, were accompanied by high prices for wheat; and restriction of funds and consequent fall in prices were accompanied by a decline in the price of wheat.[1] Heavy fixed charges and governmental guarantees were accompanied by a decline of revenue. The indirect debt of the province of over $30,000,000 incurred prior to 1855 became "an absolute charge".

> Thus the increased charges required to meet these demands, have arisen when the country was least prepared for them, and no doubt has caused a feeling of dissatisfaction with present legislation, which, if justifiable at all, really appertains to the acts of former Parliaments. . . .

These difficulties were accentuated by the effects of the wide fluctuations, and decline in imports was reflected directly in customs, and fluctuations in exports had a direct effect on other sources of revenue and an indirect effect on imports and on revenue.

	Imports	Exports
1851	$21,434,791	$12,964,721
1852	20,286,493	15,307,607
1853	31,981,436	23,801,303
1854	40,529,325	23,019,190
1855	36,086,169	28,188,461
1856	43,584,387	32,047,017[2]
1857	39,430,598	27,006,624
1858	29,078,527	23,472,609
1859	33,555,161	24,766,981
1860	34,441,621	34,631,890
1861	43,054,836[3]	36,614,195[4]

---

[1] Wheat declined from a high point of $1.36 in 1856 to 85 cents in 1858. See *Statistical contributions to Canadian economic history*, II, 59. For a valuable discussion see *Ibid.*, 47 ff.; also Adam Shortt, "Railroad construction and national prosperity" (Royal Society of Canada transactions, section ii, series 3, volume VIII, 1914, 295-308); J. Viner, *Canada's balance of international indebtedness, 1910-13* (Cambridge, 1924); W. L. Thorp, *Business annals* (New York, 1926), chapter xii.

[2] In spite of increased agricultural exports low prices brought an increase in this item of only £485,469.

[3] $34,717,248 plus 12½ per cent. to cover goods not reported.

[4] $3,304,675 of coin and bullion. Exports of corn increased to $1,087,277 from $528,630 and of wheat to $4,260,380 from $2,308,627.

1862	48,600,633	33,596,125[1]
1863	45,964,493[2]	41,831,532[3]
1864	23,882,216	13,883,508
1865	44,620,469	42,481,151
1866	53,802,319	56,328,380
1867	59,048,987	48,486,143

A diminished demand for our staple products has produced a corresponding check upon the purchasing power of our people, and a corresponding loss to the principal sources of our revenue. These tendencies have been widened and strengthened by the derangement in the currency of our neighbors, creating, as it has done, irregularity and uncertainty in the various branches of industry and commerce, and bringing certain of them within very narrow compass. So long as these disturbing influences exist, we cannot anticipate an increase of our revenues to the extent which, under more auspicious circumstances, we might confidently expect.[4]

Imports of dutiable goods in 1861 totalled $25,094.748 and duties increased slightly to $4,768,192 as a result of increases in brandy, tea, green coffee, linens, woollens, hosiery, fancy goods, earthenware, and glassware, and in spite of a decline in revenue from railroad iron from $31,852 in 1860 to $5,893 in 1861 which followed the lack of development of railroads and the establishment of mills for rolling railroad bar and other iron, and of a decline in revenue from sugar of $129,000 (imports increased from 31,712,252 pounds in 1860 to 40,425,483 pounds in 1861 but the duty was reduced according to the sliding scale of 1859). The deficit totalled $1,476,869. In the following year dutiable goods declined to $23,971,370 and duties to $4,652,748, as a result of the Civil War. Total revenue was $7,375,050[5] and the deficit was $5,200,000. In 1863 dutiable goods again declined to $22,938,270, but total revenue increased to $7,662,490

---

[1]The bad harvest of 1862 brought a decline of exports of wheat of $2,119,519 and of flour of $770,581.

[2]From Great Britain, $20,177,572 (a decline of $1,001,340), from United States, $23,109,362 (a decline of $2,063,795); trade with Great Britain averaged about £2,250,000 sterling imports and £4,000,000 exports at the end of the fifties (See *Tables of the trade and navigation of the Province of Canada*).

[3]Timber and lumber increased $4,000,000; ships built and exported at Quebec increased from $988,428 in 1862 to $2,287,901 in 1863.

[4]*S.p.*, 10, 1863.

[5]In addition to customs, revenue in 1862 included post office, public works, investments, and special revenues, $3,131,900 and excise, $402,404.

giving a deficit of $981,991. Attempts to avoid borrowing[1] and to balance the budget by taxation met with partial success as is suggested in the following table.

	Customs	Total receipts	Interest on debt	Total payments
1864	6,142,792	15,653,484	3,818,576	15,087,280
1865	5,660,740	11,722,027	3,664,447	12,890,311
1866	7,328,146	12,672,880	3,590,706	12,418,105

The debt of the province increased from $18,782,565 in 1850 to $54,142,044 in 1859 and to $77,020,082 in 1866. In the latter year "the government found itself unable to raise more than half of a moderate loan even when offering 8 per cent. interest. The financial agents in Britain frankly stated to the Finance minister that the result was due to the disastrous effect on Canadian credit of the experience of British investors."

The problem of the upper province was fundamentally that of transportation. Private enterprise and the railroads, especially the Grand Trunk, were interested in the possibility of increased traffic to meet the deficits. The government, with increased deficits, largely due to the decline in customs revenue and largely the result of railways and canals, was anxious to increase imports and, in turn, revenue and to increase traffic on the waterways and railways and, in turn, revenue from public works and earnings on the railways. Both railways and government were interested in developing traffic on the St. Lawrence from the standpoint of earnings and revenue. Efforts had failed to attract traffic from the western states and alternatives were necessary. The policy of direct taxation could not be adapted to the problem of increased traffic on the railways and the St. Lawrence in the face of increasingly effective competition from American channels.

The alternative involved the development of a fiscal system designed to encourage traffic on the St. Lawrence route. The application of tariffs, and especially of the *ad*

---

[1] ". . . The borrowing process has unfortunately been employed too generally and too long, encouraging unnecessary expenditure, and relieving the community from the burdens which it should be made to bear as the consequence of its own acts. . . .

Instead of taxing our credit, and so transferring burdens from ourselves to posterity, it is desirable that we should now tax our available resources to an extent indicated by the deficiency . . ." (*S.p.*, 10, 1863).

valorem duties in 1859, and the reduction of canal tolls were among the devices intended to increase traffic by the St. Lawrence. This policy contributed to the problems of the Reciprocity Treaty which led to its abrogation[1] in 1866. Moreover, it became a powerful stimulus in the movement toward Confederation. The Grand Trunk,[2] the Canadian government, and imperial interests were vitally concerned with the improvement of trade between the Maritimes and Canada.

Confederation

Confederation and construction of the Intercolonial Railway temporarily solved the problem of the difficulties

---

[1]The difficulties of the Reciprocity Treaty were in direct relation to the difficulties of transportation by the St. Lawrence route. Deficits on transportation necessitated dependence on higher tariffs. For important studies, see C. C. Tansill, *The Canadian Reciprocity Treaty of 1854* (Baltimore, 1922); F. C. Haynes, *The Reciprocity Treaty with Canada of 1854-66* (American Economic Association, 1892); C. D. Allin and G. M. Jones, *Annexation, preferential trade and reciprocity* (Toronto, n.d.); Hatch, Report on reciprocity, *Executive documents, house of representatives*, 1859-60; F. W. Taylor, Report on reciprocity, *Executive documents*, no. 9, 1859-60; C. Robinson, *A history of two reciprocity treaties* (New Haven, 1903), 21-82, especially bibliography; J. L. Laughlin and H. P. Willis, *Reciprocity* (New York, 1903), chapter ii; A. Désy, "Le Canada économique sous l'union et le traité de réciprocité de 1854" (*Revue trimestrielle canadienne*, August, 1915); H. Keenleyside, *Canada and the United States* (New York, 1929).

Trade with the United States increased rapidly especially as a result of the period of expansion in Canada. Total trade with the United States in 1861 nearly trebled that of 1851. Imports from the United States in 1861 totalled $21,069,388. For trade statistics before reciprocity, see I. D. Andrews, *Report on trade and commerce of British North American colonies 1851*.

| Commodities | 1861 | |
Exports	Total Exports	United States
	Dollars	Dollars
Wheat, flour, and corn	14,560,111	5,566,582
Other agricultural products	3,684,520	2,137,554
Timber and lumber	8,693,638	2,065,870
Animals	1,397,034	1,396,994
Manufactures, minerals, *etc*	6,381,945	2,219,427
Totals	34,717,248	14,386,427

The high duties imposed by the United States as a protective measure as well as a means of raising revenue to meet the heavy war debts were regarded as important factors leading to the abrogation of reciprocity. See John McLennan, "A sketch of Canadian finance" (*Canadian economics*, 269-277).

[2]See a valuable account of the activities of Sir E. Watkin of the Grand Trunk in R. G. Trotter, *Canadian federation* (London, 1924), especially chapter xiv, and part II, *passim*, and "British finance and Confederation" (Canadian Historical Association *report*, 1927, 89-96); H. A. Innis, *A history of the Canadian Pacific Railway* (London, 1923), 70 *ff*.; E. W. Watkin, *Canada and the states* (London, 1887).

after 1867. The debt of Upper and Lower Canada to the extent of $62,500,000 was assumed by the federal government and provision was made on the basis of an imperial guarantee for the construction of the Intercolonial Railway to extend the line of the Grand Trunk to Halifax.[1] Imports of capital and continued construction of railways accentuated the recovery which became conspicuous after Confederation.

4

Provincial and Municipal Finance

The Provinces of Ontario and Quebec were given annual subsidies under the British North America Act and control over their own resources.[2] The relative importance of these sources is shown in a survey[3] showing total receipts of Ontario from 1867-1899 of $103,815,404, including $47,624,136 received from the dominion government and $34,740,200 from territorial revenue. Total receipts in

---

[1]See W. P. M. Kennedy (ed.), *Statutes, treaties and documents of the Canadian constitution*, 535 ff. The political effects of agricultural expansion and construction of railways were shown in increased population and problems of representation and the difficulties which precipitated a deadlock. The growth of Toronto led to the struggle against domination by Montreal. See F. H. Underhill, "Some aspects of Upper Canadian radical opinions in the decade before Confederation" (Canadian Historical Association *report*, 1927, 46-61). For a general account of the constitutional problems, see W. P. M. Kennedy, *Constitution of Canada* (Oxford, 1928) and C. Martin, *Empire and commonwealth* (Oxford, 1929). "For the revival of this project we are no doubt indebted to the exigencies of the Grand Trunk Company, aided by the re-establishment of the *entente cordiale* between the colonies and the colonial office, consequent upon the visit of H.R.H. the Prince of Wales, by the subsequent Civil war in the United States and especially by the Trent affair. The Grand Trunk at it's wits end to raise more money, and seeing the capitalization of a postal subsidy yet remote, sought to revive the intercolonial project in order to transfer to it as much of the unproductive sections east of Montreal as possible—no doubt at a bargain—and therefore the influential owners of this road brought about another colonial conference" (*Eighty years' progress*, 243-4). See also T. C. Keefer, *Free trade, protection and reciprocity* (Ottawa, 1876).

[2]See A. W. Boos, *The financial arrangements between the province and the dominion* (Toronto, 1930); also W. P. M. Kennedy and D. C. Wells, *Law of the taxing power in Canada* (Toronto, 1931); John Davidson, "The financial relations of the Dominion of Canada and the provinces" (*Economic Journal*, 1905, 164-185); A. Lessard, *Le subside fédéral: Étude d'histoire politique relative au réajustement de la subvention fédérale aux provinces* (Quebec, 1906); W. Lavigne, "L'orientation des dépenses publiques depuis la Confédération" (*Annals* of the American Academy, May 1923); *Canada, an encyclopedia of the country*, I, 285 ff.; also V, 301 ff.

[3]Report of the royal commission on the financial position of the Province of Ontario, *S.p., Ont.*, 50, 1901. Also a detailed statement of receipts and disbursements 1867-1890, *S.p., Que.*, 3, 1891. Details of provincial debt from 1867 to 1911 are given in *S.p., Que.*, 58, 1911.

Quebec from 1867 to 1883 were $36,477,411 of which dominion subsidies formed a substantial part.[1]

Railways gradually assumed a less important position in relation to provincial and municipal finance. From Confederation to 1875 Ontario paid $154,388 on railways and in the period from 1870 to 1880, $1,685,409. Quebec paid $15,627,229 (Quebec, Montreal, Ottawa and Occidental, $13,117,730—later sold to C.P.R.) on the same item between 1867 and 1883.[2] Ontario municipalities under the municipal loan fund had borrowed to the extent of $7,300,000 by 1871 ($5,867,400 for railways and $1,432,600 for local improvements) on which, on January 1, 1871, the principal unpaid was $6,612,092 and interest in arrears $5,007,491.[3] In returns on railway assistance in Ontario in 1877, municipal bonuses totalled $6,385,980; orders-in-council, $1,939,000— under 39 Vic. c. 22, 1876, $481,000; railway subsidy fund, $114,069; and municipal loan fund, $556,292.[4] Quebec had a gross debt at the end of the period of $18,871,593 and carried interest charges totalling $923,042. Ontario had practically a clean sheet.[5] The rapid growth of towns, improvement of roads, and expansion of facilities involved a demand for capital which was met by the development of municipalities.[6] In Ontario municipalities had a bonded

---

[1]*S.p.*, *Que.*, 84, 1883-4.
[2]*Ibid.*
[3]*S.p.*, *Ont.*, 8, 1871.
[4]See Report of and by Ontario municipalities to railways 1867-1875, *S.p.*, *Ont.*, 1875-6; also *S.p.*, *Ont.*, 42, 1885.
[5]See J. R. Perry, *Public debts in Canada* (University of Toronto studies, history and economics, I, *passim*).
[6]The basis of municipal government was an act passed in 1849. "The inhabitants of every county, city, town, and township are constituted corporations, their organization proceeding wholly upon the elective principle; and provision is made for the erection of new municipalities, as the circumstances of the country require, by their separation from those already existing. A complete system is created for regulating the elections, and for defining the duties of the municipalities, and of their officers. Their powers may be generally stated to embrace everything of a local nature, including . . . the opening and maintenance of highways; the erection of schoolhouses, and the support of common and grammar schools; the provision of accommodation for the administration of justice, gaols, &c., and the collection of rates for their support, as well as for the payment of petty jurymen; granting shop and tavern licenses; regulating and prohibiting the sale of spirituous liquors; providing for the support of the poor; preventing the obstruction of streams; effecting drainage, both in the cities and country; inspection of weights and measures, enforcing the due observance of the Sabbath, and protection of public morals; establishing and regulating ferries, harbours, markets, &c.; abating nuisances; making regulations

debt of $28,663,771 and a floating debt of $3,920,390 in 1885—
Toronto alone having a general city debt of $7,107,470 and
a local improvement debt of $1,112,792. In 1894,[1] muni-
cipal debts totalled $49,118,818 of which cities had
$33,562,793, including roads and bridges, $4,759,360; municipal water-works, $7,642,530; schools, $2,187,861; sewers,
$3,566,871; and local improvement debt, $3,911,269.

5

Development of Corporations

Industrial development accompanied the growth of
towns, with the result that firms required fresh supplies of
capital to expand their operations. The corporation[2] began

for, and taking precautions against fires; establishing gas and water works;
making police regulations; levying rates upon all real and personal property,
including incomes for all purposes; and, for certain objects, borrowing money;
together with a great number of minor matters essential for the good government of a community" (A. T. Galt, *Canada 1849 to 1859*; also Report of select
committee to inquire into the working of the Municipal and Road Act for 1855,
Journals of the legislative assembly, XV, 1857, app. 30). See also Reports of the
commission on municipal institutions, *S.p., Ont.*, 42, 1888; and *S.p., Ont.*, 13,
1889; Report of the Ontario assessment commission, *S.p., Ont.*, 44, 1901; *S.p.*,
48, 1902; also municipal statistics in sessional papers. For valuable surveys of
municipal problems see S. M. Wickett (ed.), *Municipal government in Canada*
(University of Toronto studies, history and economics, 1907); also J. M. McEvoy,
The Ontario township (Toronto, 1889); A. H. Sinclair, *Municipal monopolies and
their management* (Toronto, 1891); S. Vineberg, *Provincial and local taxation in
Canada* (New York, 1912).
    [1]See a detailed list, *S.p., Ont.*, 68, 1896.
    [2]For lists of companies incorporated see *S.p., Ont.*, 16, 1874 (especially
under 27-28 Vic. c. 23) and particularly *S.p., Ont.*, 95, 1892, and names of companies incorporated in Quebec under 31 Vic. c. 25, *S.p., Que.*, 15, 1875, *S.p.,
Que.*, 6, 1913, 176. The reports of the secretary and registrar of the provinces
and reports of the secretary of state for the dominion give annual lists. In
Ontario and Quebec companies were incorporated as follows: 1868, 19; 1871, 24;
1875, 57; 1877, 38; 1881, 119; 1883, 114; 1886, 90.

Quebec		
Year	Number	Capital
1868	14	$1,605,000
1869	4	185,500
1870	9	1,168,433
1871	14	1,711,000
1872	14	2,575,000
1873	20	2,758,000
1874	27	3,685,000
1875	24	1,329,000
1876	10	675,000
1877	6	560,000
1878	4	443,000
1879	9	218,000

to displace individual ownership and partnership. Corporations were organized in connection with street-railways, gas-works, and water-works.[1] Lumbering, mining, the cheese industry, the iron industry, and the industrial growth of the St. Lawrence generally involved the support of larger supplies of capital. By the end of the period stock exchanges[2] were in operation in Toronto (1852) and Montreal (1875).

6

Life Insurance

The increase in permanent equipment, which accompanied the construction of canals and railways and the growth of towns, was followed by the development of organizations for the mobilization of capital. Insurance companies and loans and savings companies were organized in relation to domestic capital and to foreign capital. The Canada Life was organized in 1847. It drew on the experience of the banks, which had acted as agents of British fire insurance companies and which carried in some cases a small amount of life insurance. Investments were made in bank stocks and mortgages. The company expanded rapidly in the period prior to 1857 and in 1856 took over the Gore and District Savings Bank. The depression was weathered in spite of failure of towns to meet interest on debentures, decline in the value of mortgages, difficulties of the subsidiary bank, and an investigation by a parliamentary committee in 1862. With the return of prosperity in 1865 business in force increased from $4,013,000 in 1865 to $13,430,000 in 1875. Investments in real estate were gradually reduced and municipal and provincial securities increased. New companies were organized—the Mutual Life in 1870, the Sun

1880	14	2,002,533
1881	15	1,112,000
1882	21	2,838,333
1883	28	5,177,255
1884	18	582,833
1885	18	1,355,000

[1]See L. G. Denis, *Water-works of Canada* (Ottawa, 1912); L. G. Denis, *Water-works and sewerage systems of Canada* (Ottawa, 1916); also M. E. Richardson, "Development of street railways in Canada" (*Canadian Magazine*, 1902).

[2]Stocks dealt on the exchange were chiefly banks, loan companies, telegraph, gas, insurance, cotton.

Life[1] and Confederation Life in 1871, and the London Life in 1874. Withdrawal of the Mutual Life of New York because of its refusal to comply with the large deposit requirements of dominion legislation in 1871 gave room for Canadian companies. Life insurance reflected sharply the effects of depression and prosperity. Decline in the amount of new insurance began in 1872 and continued to 1879. Recovery followed in 1880. New insurance increased and decline from lapses and surrenders fell off rapidly in 1881.

> These circumstances are gratifying indications of the increasing appreciation by the people of the advantages of life insurance, and of their growing ability to avail themselves of and to maintain these advantages, and also of the continued prosperity of the commercial and other interests of the country.[2]

The North American Life began operations in 1881. Business in force in Canadian companies increased from $26,870,224 in 1877 to $101,772,080 in 1887, in British companies from $19,349,204 to $28,173,585, and in American companies from $39,468,475 to $61,734,187. As epidemics became less serious and as experience was gained with Canadian mortality tables, the effectiveness of the companies was steadily improved. The creation of an insurance department for the dominion in 1875 and for Ontario in 1878 and the passing of a general insurance act in 1886 were important as means of eliminating irregularities in the business.

7

Loans and Savings Companies

Loans and savings companies developed rapidly as devices for mobilizing capital in building and real estate, which accompanied the growth of towns. Terminating societies were replaced with permanent societies and, with the ability of the latter to receive deposits, an organization was built up for the mobilization of domestic capital. The Canada Permanent[3] began in 1855 and the Huron and Erie

---

[1]See G. H. Harris, *The president's book* (Montreal, 1928); also *Report of the royal commission on life insurance* (Ottawa, 1907), *S.p.*, 123a, 1906.

[2]*S.p.*, 12, 1883.

[3]See a valuable account in *The story of the Canada Permanent Mortgage Corporation, 1855-1925* (Toronto, 1925).

Mortgage Corporation in 1864. An act providing for the establishment of permanent societies (22 Vic. c. 45) was passed in 1859 as a recognition of the growth and extent of operations. In 1865 moneys held by permanent building societies totalled $3,233,985.[1] In 1874 power was given to issue debentures with the result that a new channel for the flow of British capital to Canada was completed. In 1883, 85 loan companies and building societies had a total paid-up capital of $30,899,446 of which 70 paid dividends on a capital of $27,596,511. In addition, these companies had $13,954,460 of Canadian deposits and $29,620,470 on debentures ($22,792,904 from Great Britain). Loans totalled $74,126,165 of which $68,380,000 were on land in Quebec, Ontario, and Manitoba. The rate of interest declined from 12 per cent. in 1863 to 7 per cent. in 1884.

8

Fire Insurance

The growth of organizations for the mobilization of capital which accompanied the growth of towns and the shift of industry to large centres proved a valuable asset but it accentuated the losses which followed in the smaller centres and which were registered in the number of bankruptcies and the difficulties of small industries.[2] The shifting of population, and, in turn, of commercial organization and of industry, to large centres involved heavy strains in depreciation of equipment through obsolescence. The losses were borne in part by the small centres and in part by the insurance companies. The history of towns and villages was a history of fires[3] destroying the principal industry and of migration of the loser with the assistance of insurance to the larger centres. The dominance of wood in outlying centres was undermined in part by its susceptibility to fires. Fire was a solvent loosening the control of wood and hastening concentration on large centres which were becoming increasingly dependent on iron. The importance of credit

---

[1]*S.p.*, 10, 1860. See *Loan corporations statements, Ontario*; also *Monetary Times*; W. A. Douglass, "Ontario loan and savings companies" (*Canadian economics*, 265-8).

[2]See the lists of bankruptcies in *Monetary Times*.

[3]See records of fires in *Monetary Times*.

relationships with Great Britain and the extensive character
of the burden necessitated dependence chiefly on British
insurance companies. Banks acted as agents for English,
Scottish, and American companies.[1] Canadian companies
were forced, in the face of heavy losses, to amalgamate with
foreign companies and independent growth was slow. British
companies lost throughout the period. In the fire at St.
John, New Brunswick, in 1877 they lost nearly $5,000,000
and after a slow recovery suffered another set-back from the
fire at Quebec on June 8, 1881. Property to the extent of
$3,000,000 was destroyed and losses of the insurance com-
panies totalled $800,736 ($362,502 to the Quebec Fire Insurance Company). A very hot, dry summer, numerous
fires in the agricultural districts of western Ontario, and
numerous sporadic fires occasioned the statement: "It is to
be hoped that such a year may not come again for a long
time."[2] It was not until 1887 that an adverse balance of
the British companies was reversed and a favourable balance
of $341,938 shown.[3] Fire insurance strengthened the position
of credit from Great Britain.

The rapidity of growth of large centres and the cheapness
of lumber were factors responsible for the dominance of
wooden buildings and the disasters from fires. "Where wood
enters so largely into the construction, not only of sheds and
outbuildings, but also of dwelling houses, as it does in Toronto,
and where the water supply as a protection against fire is
so exceedingly deficient, insurance offices are necessarily
very much in requisition."[4] Dependence on candles and
later on oil-lamps and the slow development of water-works
and of equipment for fighting fire increased fire hazards[5]
and placed a heavy burden on fire insurance companies.

---

[1]See *S.p.*, 10, 1866; also Report of the inspector of insurance 1879, *S.p.*,
Ont., 21, 1880 and later years; also fire insurance companies operating under
Ontario charters 1881-7, *S.p.*, *Ont.*, 38, 1889; also reports of inspector of insurance
(Quebec) after 1883. The dominion department of insurance was organized in
1875. On effects of this legislation, see S. Thompson, *Reminiscences of a Canadian
pioneer* (Toronto, 1894), 325 *ff.*
[2]*S.p.*, 12, 1883.
[3]*S.p.*, 9a, 1888.
[4]Mrs. G. M. Barrett, *The hand-book of Toronto* (London, 1858), 95-6.
[5]"In a metropolis like Quebec, densely populated in some parts, and containing numerous old wooden fabrics that a spark is sufficient to ignite, an efficient
fire brigade would appear indispensable. But there is no such institution. I
much doubt whether there be even a fire-engine. Of this, however, I am certain,

9

Banks and Banking

Financial institutions concerned with the investment of long-term securities and the introduction of capital paralleled the growth of the larger centres. Older institutions, concerned with the shift of industry from towns dependent on water-transport to towns dependent on rail-transport, and with the full sweep of the changes which followed the introduction of steam and iron, felt the full impact and with disastrous results. Banking institutions were subject to strains even severer than those imposed on fire insurance. Expansion of agriculture, the shift of industry, the growth of towns, the period of intense activity in construction of railroads in the fifties involving an importation of over $100,000,000 ($60,000,000 spent by private interests), and the period of depression which followed in 1857 were among the factors seriously affecting the position of the banks.[1] Finally the heavy government debt left its stamp on the history of Canadian banking.

---

that to the police is entrusted the duty of extinguishing fires, a feat they seldom succeed in effecting. The entire organization—nearly composed of *habitans*—for the wide and numerous districts into which the city is divided, does not exceed thirty or at most forty men. These are generally scattered in pairs about those localities considered most in need of their presence. Certainly they are the most stupid and stultified looking mortals of their class that it has been my ill fortune to have encountered in any country through which I have travelled. They are far from being a preventive force; and as to interfering in street quarrels, which, by the way, are of frequent occurrence, they consider it the wisest policy to avoid them.

Those districts laid bare by the awful calamities to which I have referred were not long in becoming re-populated. But, unfortunately, most of the newly-erected dwellings are likewise of wood, plastered over, and therefore equally liable to destruction as the others. It seems unaccountable that with a municipal bye-law prohibiting the further erection of wooden structures, the same should be suffered without opposition or even remonstrance on the part of the civic authorities" (S. P. Day, *English America*, I, 26-8). See W. O. McRobie, *Fighting the flames or twenty-seven years in the Montreal fire brigade* (Montreal, 1881).

[1] "The large expenditure upon our railroads and public works, and the great influx of foreign capital between 1852 and 1856 induced extravagant speculations, and excessive prices to be given for wild lands; schemes for new villages and towns were set afloat in every direction; meanwhile transactions were carried to an extent far beyond the wants of the country, and bank accommodation was pressed to its utmost limit. Then came a revulsion. The large expenditures on railroads and the foreign supplies were cut off or greatly diminished. The land speculations had absorbed the means of many a farmer and diverted them from the proper cultivation of his farm. Then followed two years of bad crops, and on the back of all, the commercial crisis in the United States which extended to Europe and seriously aggravated the general depression under which the province was labouring" (*Journals of the legislative assembly*, 1859, app. 67).

Demands for increased banking facilities were met at the beginning of the period by "an act to establish freedom of banking" (13-14 Vic. c. 21) in 1850. Of 6 banks incorporated under the act, 2 survived from 1856 to 1858, and 3 became chartered banks of which one had its charter repealed in 1863, a second was merged with the Imperial Bank in 1875, and the third continued as Molson's Bank. The Bank of British North America was in a position to take advantage of the act. The difficulty of obtaining foreign capital through private banks weighted the balance heavily in favour of chartered banks.[1] 12 banks were incorporated from 1855 to 1857 and £6,326,666 currency added to the authorized banking capital. 5 of these banks had disappeared by 1863. 12 charters were issued between 1858 and 1866 but only 7 survived and these with extensions granted by parliament. Free banking was repealed in 1866. The final blow to banking organization came with the failure of the 2 largest banks, the Bank of Upper Canada in 1866 and the Commercial Bank in 1867. The difficulties of these banks as a result of dependence on land and railroads were accentuated by the problems of the government. The provincial note act (29-30 Vic. c. 10) of 1866 involved the issue of $8,000,000 of provincial notes to be distributed to the extent of $3,000,000 in exchange for provincial debentures to be taken by banks which surrendered their power of issue and of $5,000,000 with a basis of protection up to 20 per cent. by specie and the remainder by provincial debentures. Over that amount specie was to be kept to the extent of 25 per cent. The weakness of the financial structure and the difficulties of the government combined to introduce this inflationary device. Of more immediate significance the act was held responsible for a sharp crisis.[2] The banks

---

[1] "English capitalists would recognize the large chartered banks, because these banks had been known for many years as a safe means of investing capital—capitalists had confidence in them but they would not have confidence in private banks established under a new banking system" (See Francis Hincks, cited in R. M. Breckenridge, *The Canadian banking system 1817-1890*, Toronto, 1894, 118); also Sir Francis Hincks, *Reminiscences of his public life* (Montreal, 1884), 72-4; *Canada and its provinces*, V, 261-291.

[2] See Report of the select committee of the honorable the senate upon the causes of the recent financial crisis in the Province of Ontario, *Journals of the senate*, I, 1867-8, app. 1. Depression in the lumber trade and the dry goods industry could not be held responsible for the difficulties of the period, and it

refused to give up their powers of issue, with the exception of the Bank of Montreal, and in 1868 the dominion took over provincial notes to the extent of $8,000,000 (31 Vic. c. 46).

The new banking structure

Conditions which in some sense destroyed the old banking structure were responsible also for the growth of the new banking structure. Increased production and increased trade placed increasing emphasis on institutions concerned with short-term credit. The Bank of Toronto developed in relation to the activities of the Millers' Association (1854). Senator McMaster with capital acquired in the rapidly expanding wholesale business became active in the development of the Bank of Commerce (1867). The Dominion Bank (1871) and the Imperial Bank (1873-1875) developed as offshoots from the Bank of Commerce. The Bank of Hamilton began operations in 1872. With its roots in new soil the financial structure of Toronto gradually emerged as independent from Montreal.[1] The new area developed chiefly in relation to the demands of agricultural expansion and primarily in relation to wheat. The violent fluctuations of the lumber industry tended to eliminate banks confined to that industry as in the depression of the seventies. The new structure expanded rapidly with the disappearance of the old. The effects of these changes were shown in banking legislation. In 1859, in 1861, in 1870, and

was concluded: "That under the provisions of the provincial note act of 1866 the Bank of Montreal having withdrawn its own notes from circulation and substituted for them the notes of the province it was no longer interested, in common with the other kindred institutions in maintaining unimpaired the credit of all; and that the effect of that act was to place the interests of the Bank of Montreal the most powerful monied institution in Canada and the fiscal agent of the government in antagonism to those of the other banks." See also First report of committee on banking and currency, *J.h.c.*, II, 1869, app. 1.

[1]For a description of the struggle as carried out by McMaster against E. H. King of the Bank of Montreal, see Victor Ross, *History of the Canadian Bank of Commerce* (Toronto, 1922), II, chapters i, ii; and R. M. Breckenridge, *The Canadian banking system 1817-1890, passim*. Montreal was not subject to the strains of Upper Canada. Molson's Bank representing brewing, distilling, and transport interests was formed as a result of withdrawal from the Bank of Montreal and incorporated in 1855 (B. K. Sandwell, "The Molson Family" (Royal Society of Canada *transactions*, XXII, series 3, section II, 1928, 203 ff.). The Merchants' Bank was formed under Sir Hugh Allan's direction in 1861. French Canadians had also made substantial progress in the development of their own banks.

42

in 1871 legislation provided for the extension of activities of the banks in handling commodities. The banking legislation of 1870 and 1871 (33 Vic. c. 2 and 34 Vic. c. 5) provided for revisions every 10 years, for dependence on large banks,[1] and for joint control over the note issue by the banks and the government. Scarcity of money emphasized the importance of a strongly guaranteed note issue and the difficulties of the government continued to emphasize the importance of a dominion note issue. The legislation of 1871 (34 Vic. c. 5) provided that banks should be allowed to issue notes up to the amount of unimpaired, paid-up capital against one-half cash reserves and never less than one-third dominion notes. Banks were not allowed to issue notes under $4.00 (under $5.00 in 1881). In 1880 (43 Vic. c. 22) notes were made a first charge on assets and double liability was introduced. 3 years later (46 Vic. c. 20) the minimum reserves of dominion notes were raised from one-third to forty per cent. and penalties were imposed for excess of circulation. Bank notes in circulation totalled $29,692,803 in 1885.

Further protection to banking facilities was provided in the establishment of a post office savings bank.[2] Deposits in these banks increased from $2,926,000 in 1875 to $3,946,000 in 1880 and $13,245,000 in 1884.

Rapid expansion from 1867 to 1873 followed by the severe and prolonged depression of the seventies materially reduced the capital of the banks but their solvency was, at least in part, a tribute to the provisions of the first general banking act of Canada in 1871 and to the development of banking in relation to new conditions. Recovery of the banks paralleled the expansion of the early eighties. The gradual emergence of large centres and the relative development of industry in relation to the staples of lumber and wheat strengthened the position of the larger banks. On the other hand, large numbers of small private banks con-

---

[1]Evidence presented to the committee on banking and currency in 1859 was practically unanimously in favour of large banks (*Journals of the legislative assembly*, XVII, 1859, app. 67).

[2]J. C. Stewart, "The post office savings bank system of Canada" (*Canadian economics*, 243 *ff.*); R. Gill, "Post office savings banks" (*Journal* of Canadian Bankers' Association, IV, 361-395).

tinued to flourish in small centres and to bridge the gap which preceded the growth of the large branch banks. The establishment of large banks[1] in centres of increasing importance and the increasing difficulties of small banks hastened amalgamations and the development of branch banks. The Canadian Bank of Commerce absorbed the Gore Bank in 1870. The Niagara District Bank provided valuable branches for the Imperial Bank in their amalgamation in 1875. Banking was moulded to an increasing extent to the new industrial structure. As in the case of fiscal policy it reflected the effects of improved transportation and of the burden of public debt.

10

Currency

Expansion of agriculture, industry, and trade created demands for efficient means of exchange.[2] The Free Banking Act of 1850 permitted authorized banks to issue notes up to the face equivalent of provincial securities

---

[1] See O. D. Skelton, *The Dominion Bank* (Toronto, 1922); *Fiftieth anniversary of the Royal Bank of Canada* (Montreal, 1919); *Canadian Bank of Commerce, 1867-1907* (Toronto, 1907); *Eastern Townships bank, 1859-1912*; *Imperial Bank of Canada* (Toronto, 1900); *The centenary of the Bank of Montreal, 1817-1917* (Montreal, 1917); C. A. Curtis, "Statistics of banking" (*Statistical contributions to Canadian economic history*, I); Reports of the select committee on banking and currency, *J.h.c.*, appendices; *Canada, an encyclopedia of the country*, I, 452 ff.; B. H. Beckhart, *The banking system of Canada* (New York, 1929); J. F. Johnson, *The Canadian banking system* (Washington, 1910); E. L. Stewart Patterson, *Banking principles and practice* (New York, 1917) and *Domestic and foreign exchange* (New York, 1918); W. A. Atherton, *Montreal* (Montreal, 1914), II, 535-553; J. E. Middleton, *The municipality of Toronto*, I, 471-501 and *The Province of Ontario*, I, 658-674; H. M. P. Eckardt, "Canadian Banking" (*Annals* of the American Academy, January, 1913, 158-170); *Canadian economics*, 225 ff.; A. W. Flux, "Canadian banks and the financial crisis" (*Yale Review*, XVII, 1908-9); *Journal* of the Canadian Bankers' Association; G. Hague, "The late Mr. E. H. King" (*Journal* of the Canadian Bankers' Association, IV, 20-29). "In its banking operations the private bank of Howitt & Kerr does not differ materially from the chartered banks. It buys and sells exchange, loans money, discounts paper, receives deposits—in short, performs all the functions of any other bank. It also has a saving's bank department, in which interest at six per cent. per annum is paid upon deposits. The firm are also interested in insurance matters, being agents for the Royal of England, the British and Mercantile and the British American Fire Companies, and also for the Life Association of Scotland, all first-class, staunch companies, for which they will be pleased to write up desirable risks at all times. Some real estate business is also done. . . . (*Guelph Herald*, 1878).

[2] See R. Chalmers, *A history of currency in the British colonies* (London, 1893), 175-206.

deposited by the banks.   Canadian banks also had the right
to issue coins.[1]   The demands for cash with increasing trade
following the construction of railways and canals, and
attempts to attract traffic from the United States, which
culminated in the Reciprocity Treaty, and to develop trade
with the Maritime Provinces, were accompanied by a movement toward general uniformity of currency between Canada,
the United States, and the Maritime Provinces.

As early as 1850:

> The Committee of Council concur in the opinion expressed by
> Sir Edmund Head, that it is extremely desirable that there
> should be an uniform currency throughout British North
> America, especially as there is a prospect of an extensive
> inter-colonial trade between the said Provinces, and likewise
> a common system of postage.   The Committee of Council
> entertain no doubt that it would tend much to facilitate the
> growing commercial intercourse between all the Provinces,
> and the neighbouring states of the American Union, if the
> currency were assimilated as much as possible to that of the
> United States.[2]

In 1853 an act (16 Vic. c. 158) was passed permitting the
use of dollars and cents as optional to pounds, shillings, and
pence and providing for the issue of token money in terms
of 20 cents, 10 cents, 5 cents, and 1 cent.   Following the
Reciprocity Treaty more energetic measures were taken in
1855 to secure "the legal adoption of a decimal currency
and coinage of like denominations and value as that of the
United States",[3] and in 1857 the arrangement providing
for the optional issue of dollars and pounds was abandoned
and dollars and cents became compulsory.   On December 10
Canadian coins were first issued.[4]

Provincial notes were added as has been shown in 1866
and later taken over by the government.   The coinage of

---

[1]R. W. McLachlan, "The copper currency of the Canadian banks 1837-
1857" (Royal Society of Canada *transactions*, IX, series 2, section II, 1903, 217 *ff.*).
    [2]*Journals of the legislative assembly*, X, 1851, app. Y. Y.
    [3]*Journals of the legislative assembly*, XIII, 1854-5, app. J.J.   The arguments
advanced were greater accuracy, less labour in calculation, ease of comparison
with the United States currency, advantages in book-keeping and accounting,
and facilitating "the education of the people".   See Report on the decimal system
of measures, weights and coins, *Journals of senate*, 1870, app. 2.
    [4]$150,000 . . . . 20 cents species
        125,000 10   "   "
         75,000 5   "   "
        100,000 1   "   "

the provinces in Confederation was assimilated in 1871 (34 Vic. c. 4). In 1870 dominion notes to the extent of $9,000,000 were issued against a security of 80 per cent. debentures and 20 per cent. specie (above $9,000,000, 100 per cent. specie) (33 Vic. c. 10). In 1872,35 per cent. specie was required for issues above $9,000,000 (35 Vic. c. 7, 1872). The limit was raised to $12,000,000 in 1875 (38 Vic. c. 5) requiring 50 per cent. specie and 100 per cent. above the limit. In 1880 the limit became $20,000,000 secured by 15 per cent. specie, 10 per cent. dominion securities guaranteed by the United Kingdom, and 75 per cent. dominion securities. In 1885 dominion notes outstanding totalled $17,791,000 and were secured by $3,188,000 of gold.

11
Weights and Measures

Trade was facilitated further by the adoption of more efficient and accurate weights and measures for commodities. The ton of 2,240 pounds, cwt. of 112 pounds, and half cwt. of 56 pounds, was reduced to the ton of 2,000 pounds and its subdivisions in 1855. Provision was made for inspection of weights and measures in 1874,[1] but in 1877 complaints were made that "many traders and manufacturers do sell uninspected weights and measures, and it has been found that many so sold are inaccurate and purchasers of them are put to much trouble and expense in consequence."[2]

12
Adulteration of Commodities

Attempts were made to check adulteration of commodities. Condiments were reported to be adulterated to

---

[1]The imperial gallon was adopted as a fifth larger than the wine measure because of the tendency "to determine quantities of fluids by weight rather than by measure", e.g. petroleum and spirits. It was more satisfactory, holding "exactly ten pounds avoirdupois of standard water", was one-eighth of an imperial bushel, and was used generally throughout the empire (S.p., 2, 1875).

[2]S.p., 3, 1878. In Brant County near Paris a miller was reported as losing $1,260 in 1876 "from an excess in a barrel weight . . . the weights on his platform scales were, in nearly every case deficient. . . . The condition of platform scales in the county, particularly those in use in merchants' shops, and also such as were presented by farmers, was bad almost beyond belief, and required a great deal of labour before they were made to work correctly" (S.p., 6, 1879).

a very considerable extent[1] (ground cloves, ginger, mustard, pepper, coffee, and tea).   In 1879 sugars were reported with excess of glucose and of moisture—chiefly as a result of mixing with cane sugar, corn-stalk sugar, starch sugar, maize sugar, and other sugars.[2] Tests for determining adulteration were gradually worked out and procedure outlined for prosecution of the offenders.

The growth of towns brought numerous problems in adulteration.   Before inspection of gas was provided for by legislation: .

> There were incessant contentions between buyers and sellers, as there were no means then of determining the actual value of the article sold or the accuracy of its measurement.   The law has since established rules for ascertaining the actual illuminating power of gas and its purity; and the Government has procured costly instruments for discovering any defects in the gas distributed.   The illuminating power of the gas has been much improved and raised—in some localities from 20 to 50 per cent.—and its purity secured by penalties against manufacturers in all cases of deficiency.

Inspection of gas was regarded as "of great advantage to all".[3]

13
Changes in Marketing Structure

Increasing efficiency of the monetary system, standardization of commodities, improvement of transportation, and concentration of industry in the larger centres led to marked changes in marketing structure.   During the early years of the period numerous ports along Lake Ontario and the St. Lawrence served to support the general store of the adjacent

---

[1] Spices were adulterated in nearly all cases, cloves and allspice with wheat and flour, ginger with cornmeal and cayenne pepper.   3 of 4 samples of pepper were adulterated with mixed flour, and 4 out of 8 of coffee had chicory, roasted wheat, peas, and beans.

[2] *S.p.*, 3, 1880.   "Patent medicines" were particularly subject to abuse. "No more pernicious class of goods is to be met with on the markets, buoying up by false representations the failing strength of the really afflicted, exciting fears and anticipations of evil in the minds of the hale though weak minded, and robbing the poor of his hard earned savings, while in very many cases they inflict untold evils on the constitution of their ready victims" (*S.p.*, ¡5, 1886; also S. P. Day, *English America*, II, chapter x).

[3] *S.p.*, 5, 1886; also *S.p.*, 6, 1879.   The removal of impurities was important in safeguarding the health of those living in rooms where gas was burned, and in preserving many classes of goods in shops which otherwise seriously deteriorated. Impurities of frequent occurrence were sulphur and ammonia in Montreal and ammonia and sulphuretted hydrogen in Toronto (*S.p.*, 3, 1880).

hinterland. Goods were imported and exported[1] through these stores. For example, Croil states that Dundas County in 1859 had 72 stores, handling $240,225: 30 in Williamsburg Township handling $112,500, 24 in Matilda handling $57,600, 11 in Winchester handling $56,250, and 7 in Mountain handling $13,875.

Nine shopkeepers in Williamsburgh sell for $7,500 each. Five sell for $4,500, six for $2,250, five for $1,050, and five for $750 each. In Matilda, four sell for $4,875 each, seven for $3,000, six for $1,800 and seven for $900 each. In Mountain, one sells for $6,000, four for $1,500, and two for $937½ each.

Traders sell at an average advance of 25 per cent. for cash, upon invoice prices, so that the farmers of the county paid the sum of $320,300 for store goods. The number of families in the county was about 3,000, shewing an average annual expenditure by each family for merchandize of $106.76.

---

[1]   Produce exported from Dundas County—1859

		$ cents
5,677 barrels	Flour at $6.00	34,062.00
37,000 bushels	Wheat at $1.10	40,700.00
18,474 "	Oats at 35 cents	6,465.90
32,238 "	Barley at 60 cents	19,342.80
2,000 "	Peas at 60 cents	1,200.00
535 barrels	Potash at $30.00	16,050.00
180,000 pounds	Butter at 15 cents	27,000.00
4,327 "	Poultry at 5 "	216.35
2,700 "	Lard at 8 "	216.00
65,000 dozen	Eggs at 10 "	6,500.00
13,500 pounds	Wool (washed) at 30 cents	4,050.00
25,650 "	Hides (dry and green) at 8 cents	2,052.00
22,000 "	Pork, beef, ham, bacon, at 7 cents	1,540.00
10 tons	Bran and shorts at $13.00	130.00
578 head	Cattle at $20.00	11,560.00
150 "	Horses at $100.00	15,100.00
2,583 "	Sheep and pigs at $3.00	7,749.00
9,000 cords	Firewood at $1.50 to $1.75	14,500.00
1,633,000 pieces	Cut staves at $5.25 per 100	8,573.00
250,000 "	Sawed staves at $5.50 per 100	1,375.00
750,000 "	Racked hoops at $3.50 per 100	2,625.00
100,000 "	Shaved hoops at $9.00 per 100	900.00
580,000 "	Sawed pine lumber at $8.00	4,640.00
128,000 "	Squared timber at $35.00	4,480.00
20,000 pieces	Hickory hand-spikes at 6 cents	1,200.00
30,000 feet	Oak steamboat buckets at $19.00	570.00
200 pieces	" " paddle arms at $1.00	200.00
100 "	" " tenders at $1.50	150.00
	Shingles and lath	45.00
200	Fanning mills at $24.00	4,800.00
8	Buggies at $90.00	720.00
80	Ploughs at $8.00	640.00
4	Sleighs at $32.00	128.00

Total exports from the country $239,480.05

Along the lake front, Trenton, for example, had 10 dry-goods stores, 3 drug stores, 2 harness shops, grocery stores and provision stores, and Newcastle 6 general stores and 4 grocery stores as well as a wholesale and retail druggist. The area was largely dependent on Montreal wholesale houses.

The growth of agricultural population in western Canada which accompanied construction of the railroad was followed by a marked increase in the number of general stores and by the rise of wholesale houses[1] in the large adjacent centres and particularly in Hamilton and Toronto. The railroad shifted the trade to Toronto at the expense of Hamilton. As an illustration of the rapidity of development, John MacDonald[2] began as a retailer in Toronto in 1849, started in the jobbing trade in 1852, and became exclusively engaged in the wholesale trade in 1853. His success was apparently based on direct purchases from manufacturers rather than from exporters.

The introduction of the bonding system in 1852 reduced overhead costs by admitting goods in bond through United States ports. Competition from Montreal, especially following the construction of railroads, led to the rapid increase in importance of the commercial traveller[3] and to the decline in importance of the visits of the general merchant to the large centres.

Changes in retail organization

The growth of large centres was followed by marked changes in retail organization. Increasing use of cash, the

---

[1] Wholesale houses became important as distributors for domestic products as well as imports. The Elora Brush Company, a small industry with 30 hands, for example, distributed its products through Ontario and Quebec by 1878 with the assistance of wholesale houses. Expansion continued to the Maritimes and in spite of complaints that railroad rates hampered local development, industries producing goods "small in bulk" were developing an export trade.

[2] Hugh Johnston, *A merchant prince: Life of Hon. Senator John Macdonald* (Toronto, 1893).

[3] J. Hedley, *Canada and her commerce* (Montreal, 1894). The Dominion Commercial Travellers' Association was formed as a result of a withdrawal from the Commercial Travellers' Association of Canada by the Montreal group in 1875. The change was an indication of increasing competition between the two areas. Mr. Taylor of Taylor and Stevenson claimed to have been the first commercial traveller in 1850. In 1886 Toronto had 2,300 travellers with the result that a large trunk trade had grown up. See C. C. Taylor, *Toronto called back*.

ability to depend on wholesale houses for cheap supplies of goods, the growth of newspapers and of advertising, improved urban transportation, and the demands of the newly-created labouring class for cheap, uniform goods were factors contributing to the success of departmental stores. The general store of the country districts was adapted to new demands. Timothy Eaton,[1] with training in general stores in Ireland and at Kirkton and St. Mary's in Canada, moved to Toronto in 1868. His first advertisement—"We propose to sell our goods for cash only, in selling goods to have only one price"—suggested the basis of the new revolution in retailing. The number of clerks in Eaton's increased from 4 in 1871 to 48 in 1881. The transfer system and the development of controlled departments were adopted in 1878, the first contract for a daily advertisement was made in 1879, and the first catalogue issued in 1884.

Imported goods were financed chiefly by long-term credits especially from English and Scottish houses. The wholesaler extended credit in turn to the general store-keeper and the latter to the farmer in terms of book accounts. These long-term credits were regarded as partly responsible for the difficulties of the depression of the seventies. Expansion of credit and improvement in marketing organization which accompanied the growth of towns were facilitated by increasing attention to protection from fires and by expansion of fire insurance. The introduction of a branch of the credit agency, R. G. Dun and Company in 1855, had similar effects. Imports became less important with the rise of manufactures and the elaborate import organization with its foreign buyers lost ground.[2]

By the end of the period a financial organization had grown up particularly in relation to the metropolitan area of Toronto and to the economic growth of Upper Canada. Capital from its import trade was supplemented by foreign capital and poured into industry.

---

[1]See G. G. Nasmith, *Timothy Eaton* (Toronto, 1923).

[2]See a list of goods formerly imported but manufactured in Toronto in 1886 (C. C. Taylor, *Toronto called back*, 247-9). See N. S. B. Gras, *An introduction to economic history* (New York, 1922).

SECTION II

THE MARITIME PROVINCES[1]

SUBSECTION A

TRANSPORT AND COMMUNICATION

Improvement of navigation on the St. Lawrence, construction of railroads, and the expansion of agriculture, especially in Ontario, and in turn the growth of towns and development of industry, financial institutions, and marketing organization were factors of profound significance to the Maritime Provinces. As has been shown, the enormous increase in fixed capital in Ontario and Quebec became a powerful force in the movement for Confederation and in the provision for a more extensive base for expansion of credit necessary to complete the Intercolonial Railway.

The effects of steam navigation and transport were even more disturbing for the Maritime Provinces than for United Canada. The industries of the Maritime Provinces

[1]See "The Maritime Provinces" (*Cambridge history of the British Empire*, Cambridge, 1930, VI, 659 *ff.*); T. F. Knight, *Nova Scotia and her resources* (Halifax, 1862); P. S. Hamilton, *Nova Scotia* (London, 1858); J. V. Ellis, *New Brunswick* (Saint John, 1860); Duncan Campbell, *Nova Scotia* (Montreal, 1873) and *The Maritime Provinces* (Boston, 1875); A. Monro, *New Brunswick with a brief outline of Nova Scotia and Prince Edward Island* (Halifax, 1855); C. H. Lugrin, *Province of New Brunswick, its resources, advantages and progress* (1886); A. W. H. Eaton, *The history of Kings County* (Salem, 1910); W. A. Calnek, *History of the County of Annapolis* (Toronto, 1897); J. W. Regan, *Sketches and traditions of the Northwest Arm* (Halifax, 1908); W. Lawson, *History of the Townships of Dartmouth, Preston and Lawrencetown* (Halifax, 1893); J. L. MacDougall, *History of Inverness County, Nova Scotia* (1922); W. F. Ganong, "A monograph of the origins of settlement in the Province of New Brunswick" (Royal Society of Canada *transactions*, X, series 2, section II, 1904, especially 94 *ff.*); *The Maritime Provinces since Confederation* (Ottawa, 1926); R. H. Whitbeck, "A geographical study of Nova Scotia" (*Bulletin* of the American Geographical Society, June, 1914, 413-9); Beckles Willson, *Nova Scotia* (London, 1912); S. A. Saunders, *Economic welfare of the Maritime Provinces* (Wolfville, 1932); *Eighty years' progress*, 542 *ff.*; A. Gesner, *New Brunswick* (London, 1847); H. B. Small, *The products and manufactures of the new dominion*. See also census statistics of provinces and of the dominion, and *Canada and its provinces*, XIII and XIV. The appendices of the *Journals of the assembly* are of first importance prior to 1867 on all subjects. After that date material on the fisheries, railroads, and post office is found in the *Dominion sessional papers*. See also D. R. Jack, "Acadian magazines" (Royal Society of Canada *transactions*, IX, series 2, section II, 1903, 173 *ff.*); R. R. McLeod, *Markland or Nova Scotia* (n.p., 1903); W. M. Whitelaw, *Maritime union and Canadian federation* (New York, 1933).

were dominated by water-transportation and were based on the important staples of lumbering and fishing. Intro- duction of the railroad and steamship was closely linked to the geographic background of these industries in relation to water-transport. The railroad and the steamship became competitors with sailing ships and destroyed the wooden ship-building industry.

The impact of the ocean steamship on the Maritimes was direct and did not involve the long struggle to improve the St. Lawrence route to Montreal. Indeed, the experience of the Maritimes became an important factor in the growth of ocean steamship navigation. Through Samuel Cunard[1] steamship navigation on the Atlantic had its roots in the maritime activity of the Maritime Provinces. Halifax was linked to the expansion of trade between the United States and Europe which accompanied the steamship. The trans- Atlantic steamship was a powerful factor leading to concen- tration of economic activity on ports with large harbours. Halifax and St. John received a powerful stimulus as metro- politan centres. Internal transportation dominated by steam and rail began to converge in more determined fashion on these ports.

1

Nova Scotia

The first sod in the construction of railways[2] was turned at Richmond near Halifax on June 13, 1854, and a road[3] was completed to Truro (61 miles) on December 15, 1858, to Windsor (32 miles) on June 3, 1858, and to Pictou (52 miles) on May 31, 1867, "making in all 145 miles of railway from Halifax to the waters of Pictou Harbor on the Gulf of St. Lawrence in the East, and Windsor on the Basin of Minas, connecting with the Bay of Fundy in the West".[4]

---

[1]See F. L. Babcock, *Spanning the Atlantic* (New York, 1931).

[2]R. R. Brown, "The Nova Scotia Railway 1854-1872" (Railway and Loco- motive Historical Society *bulletin*, no. 23, 33-36). See *Reports* of the board of railway commissioners and other reports on railways, *Journals and proceedings of the house of assembly of Nova Scotia.*

[3]About 1860, 2 trains a day each way ran between Halifax, Windsor, and Truro. The speed was about 20 miles per hour and fare first class, 3 cents a mile, second class, 2 cents a mile. The railway supplemented the roads and during the early period "parties in charge of teams were allowed to travel free". The horse and waggon traffic declined following the charge of regular fares (*S.p.*, 2, 1870).

[4]*S.p.*, 8, 1869.

The line was extended to Annapolis on the west (December 18, 1869) and to Mulgrave on the Strait of Canso on the east in 1881. In 1870 a tri-weekly steamship service was changed to a daily service between Halifax, Annapolis, and Yarmouth. A tri-weekly steamship service from St. John to Digby and to Windsor gave an alternative route between Halifax and St. John.[1] A schooner was subsidized to the extent of $400.00 to maintain communication between Pictou and the Magdalen Islands. A southern entrance was given to Bras d'Or Lake by completion of St. Peter's Canal in 1869.

The railways displaced earlier trunk roads and stage lines and, in turn, created demands for new roads. Numerous roads were built, chiefly by legislative grants. Telegraph lines extended from Halifax along the railway lines and beyond to the more important centres[2] of the province. Submarine cables were laid across Pugwash Harbour, the Strait of Canso, and Lennox Passage. A cable was laid from New Brunswick to Prince Edward Island in 1851, Pictou to Sydney in 1852, and Cape Breton to Newfoundland in 1856. Messages were sent at 12 cents for 10 words not exceeding 80 miles and 24 cents for 10 words up to 160 miles. In 1860 the post office department[3] had 72 central offices and 344 branch offices with a uniform postage of 5 cents for letters of one-half ounce. The first Atlantic cable was completed on July 27, 1866.[4]

---

[1]*S.p.*, 2, 1871. A steamer connected St. John and Yarmouth in competition with Halifax. In 1893 "in New Brunswick there are only five steamboat services, two of them on the St. John River; two in Passamaquoddy Bay (one extending to Grand Manan); and the fifth in the Bay of Fundy. The connections between various ports in Nova Scotia, and other points by means of steamships is much more extensive. There are three services to Boston, two connected with Halifax, and one with Yarmouth. Between Halifax and Newfoundland there are four services, three to St. John's, and the fourth to the west coast. Weekly trips are made between Pictou and the Magdalen Islands; and trips of varying frequency are made through the Bras D'Or Lakes" (*S.p.*, 12, 1894).

[2]"In proportion to extent and population, the province of Nova Scotia has a greater extent of telegraph wire, a greater number of offices, and the tariff is lower, than in any other country in the world" (*Eighty years' progress*, 701).

[3]See reports of postmaster-general and reports of supervisors of main post roads, *Journals of the house of assembly of Nova Scotia*; W. Smith, "The early post office in Nova Scotia 1755-1867" (*Collections* of the Nova Scotia Historical Society, XIX, 53-73).

[4]See W. J. Brown, "Canada and the Atlantic cables" (*Canada, an encyclopedia of the country*, VI, 536-544). The first cable was completed from North Sydney to Placentia in 1872, Hearts Content, Newfoundland, to Valentia in 1873, Halifax to Ballenskillings in 1875, Canso to Penzance in 1881 (F. W. Chesson, *The Atlantic cables*, London, 1875).

2
New Brunswick

Prior to the construction of railways, the St. John River and its tributaries, and other rivers were the chief routes to the interior. In 1855 it was reported that "steamers can this fall run safely between Woodstock and Grand Falls, seventy miles, some feet under one third freshet, and from Fredericton to Woodstock sixty-four miles, below a quarter freshet."[1] And in 1856: "The improvements made in the navigation during the past four years have enabled tow-boats to increase their loads by from ten to twenty-five barrels, and shortened the time of trips between Fredericton and Woodstock two days, and from that to Grand Falls over a day." At the same time (1855) steamboats were placed on the St. John above Grand Falls.[2] Spedon wrote about 1860 that 6 small steamers were employed daily between St. John and Fredericton and that about 6,000 people passed up and down the river. In 1870:

> Steamers propelled by stern wheels, and drawing from two to three feet of water, run to Woodstock, sixty-five miles above Fredericton, for about ten weeks in the spring and twelve weeks in the autumn. Above Woodstock the same steamers can run to Tobique Village, a further distance of fifty miles, for about eight weeks in the spring and about ten in the autumn. Irregular trips are made to the Grand Falls, twenty-four miles above Tobique, whenever the state of the river permits. During the summer, when, in consequence of the lowness of the water, the steamers are withdrawn, freight is taken up the river in flat boats, which carry from 110 to 120 barrels bulk each, and are drawn by two or more horses. Above the Grand Falls, flat boats are the only vessels now in use. At one time, about the years 1846 and 1847, a small steamer ran between the Grand Falls and the mouth of the St. Francis River, a distance of about seventy-five miles.[3]

The railroad became a direct competitor with this important route. Lines[4] were built from St. Andrews north to Wood-

---

[1]S.p., 4, 1872.
[2]T. Albert, *Histoire du Madawaska* (Quebec, 1920).
[3]S.p., 8, 1869.
[4]See T. C. L. Ketchem, *A short history of Carleton County, New Brunswick* (Woodstock, n.d.); and W. T. Baird, *Seventy years of New Brunswick life* (St. John, 1890); *Account of the Saint Andrews and Quebec Railway* (St. John, 1869); W. F. Ganong, "The St. Andrews and Quebec Railway" (*Acadiensis*, III, 163-169).

stock (completed in September, 1868); and from St. John to Fredericton (1870), to Woodstock (1873), and to Edmunston (1878). St. John was connected directly with St. Stephen in 1880. In New Brunswick, as in Nova Scotia, railroads[1] were built to connect important water-routes and were responsible for serious inroads on shipping and wooden ship-building. A railway was completed from St. John, on the Bay of Fundy, to Shediac[2] on the north shore (108 miles), in 1860. Branches were built between Havelock and Elgin (1885), Salisbury and Albert (1877), and Kent Junction and Richibucto (1883). In 1860 New Brunswick had in addition 60 lines of great roads totalling 2,200 miles, chiefly built by the government, many of which were displaced by the railroads. The post office[3] department had 50 post offices and an equal number of way offices with routes totalling 3,000 miles. A uniform rate of 5 cents on letters and free postage for newspapers prevailed. At about the same date New Brunswick had 700 miles of telegraph line, the most important being from St. John to Woodstock and from Sackville to Calais.

3

Prince Edward Island[4]

Prior to the construction of railroads, transportation as in the other Maritime Provinces was largely restricted to the waterways. On the Hillsborough River, large vessels were able to go 8 miles, and smaller vessels, 18 miles, above Charlottetown. A steamer ran up the river to Mount Stewart bridge, a point of importance as a ship-building centre, twice a week to pick up at various wharves, passengers and freight, especially for the city market. A second

---

[1]Reports of the railway commissioners of New Brunswick, *Journals of the assembly, New Brunswick.*

[2]J. C. Webster, *A history of Shediac* (n.p., 1928). An agreement dated January 12, 1864, provided for the operation of a steamer between Shediac and Campbellton and intermediate ports.

[3]See Reports of the post office department, *Journals of the assembly, New Brunswick.*

[4]See Duncan Campbell, *History of Prince Edward Island* (Charlottetown, 1875), 202 *ff.*; also Reports of the department of agriculture, and of the commission of crown and public lands, *Journals of the assembly, P.E.I.*; *Prince Edward Island, information regarding its climate, soil and resources* (Ottawa, 1888).

steamer ran at short intervals between Charlottetown and Southport.[1] With the completion of the railway small steamers ran between Charlottetown, Orwell, and Crapaud three times a week.

By 1875 a narrow-gauge railway was completed as follows:[2]

Main line—Cascumpec to Georgetown.........	146.2 miles
Western extension—Tignish to Alberton.......	13.3 "
Eastern extension—Mount Stewart to Souris...	39.0 "
Total length.............................	198.5

Completion of the railway on the island and on the mainland necessitated the improvement of connections. In summer, products from the eastern end of the island were exported from Souris, the eastern railway terminus and an important fishing depot. Completion of railways from Halifax and St. John to tap the trade of the Gulf of St. Lawrence was followed by the establishment of connections with Charlottetown. In the centre of the island, Charlottetown and Summerside were connected with the railway on the mainland at Point du Chêne (Shediac), New Brunswick, and Pictou, Nova Scotia, by steamers. In February, 1864, the Prince Edward Island Navigation Company contracted to run steamers twice a week between Charlottetown and Pictou in return for a subsidy of $1,600 paid by each of the two governments of Nova Scotia and Prince Edward Island. This contract was assumed on Confederation by the dominion and an additional subsidy of $1,400 was paid for an extension of the route from Pictou to Port Hawkesbury.[3] Steam packets ran to Halifax and Boston once a week. The New Brunswick government paid a subsidy of $1,500 for the connection at Shediac.

Winter presented the main problem.

A great drawback to the progress of Prince Edward Island is the stagnation of trade arising from its almost complete isolation in winter. The navigation generally closes about the middle of December and does not re-open until the end of April. During that time there are no means of transit to and from

---

[1] G. B. Bagster, *The progress and prospects of Prince Edward Island* (Charlottetown, 1861), 46-7.
[2] *S.p.*, 6, 1876.
[3] *S.p.*, 5, 1871.

the main land, except by crossing on the ice. The mails are carried with tolerable regularity, but passengers can cross only with great labor, and being subjected to exposure to fatigue and danger. Freight cannot be carried at all. The present winter crossing is from Cape Traverse, Prince Edward Island, to Cape Tormentine, N.B. The distance across at this place is 8½ miles in a direct line, but in general a much greater distance is travelled, owing to the constant drift of the ice floes and the divergences which are enforced in the choice of the best route. The passage occupies from three to eight hours, according to the state of the weather and the condition of the ice. The trip from Charlottetown involves, besides the crossing of the straits, 30 miles of stage travel on the island and 40 miles between Cape Tormentine and the Intercolonial Railway Station at Amherst, N.S.[1]

In 1874 a contract was made for the conveyance of mails between Georgetown and Pictou by the steamship *Albert* between December and May,[2] but it was not until the winter of 1876-7 that connections were made regularly by the steamer *Northern Light*.[3] Later attempts to improve communications included the building of a branch from County Line to Cape Traverse (13 miles), completed on January 22, 1885, to connect with the mainland at Cape Tormentine[4] (9 miles). The time of former routes from

---

[1]*S.p.*, 7, 1875. "The working of the winter crossing has been undertaken by men who professionally take up the work as the means of livelihood. The boat used is of a peculiar structure sheeted with tin, with a keel and two side runners, the bow has a flattened point, while the stern has the ordinary square form. The crew consists generally of from 6 to 8 men. When the ice is good the boat is pushed over it, but when there is open water the boat is launched. Should the open space exceed the extent which it is considered prudent to face or when a gale unexpectedly springs up, the passage is not attempted and the boat returns whence it came.

In ordinary weather the boat is propelled through open water spaces, until the floe is reached, it is then once more hauled on the ice, and the passage continued on runners. The passengers on any one trip may be set down as under 12. The men who are passengers, are held to assist in propelling the boat across the ice but in order to prevent accidents, they are fastened to the side of the boat by straps. The females retain their seats, as those who pass over the ice are frequently immersed in water to the depth of one and two feet. These rules are observed on the trips of the ordinary Ferry, but a private boat with a special crew can be obtained by any one who will pay the expense" (*S.p.*, 6, 1880).

[2]*S.p.*, 57, 1875.

[3]*S.p.*, 7, 1878. Her trips were not without difficulty as she was held in the ice from February 4 to March 21, 1882, but nevertheless made 61 round trips in the season (*S.p.*, 7, 1883). See Report—steam communication between Prince Edward Island and the mainland in summer and winter, *J.h.c.*, XVII, 1883, app. 3.

[4]*S.p.*, 13, 1886.

Shediac to Summerside and Pictou to Charlottetown (4 hours) was shortened accordingly.

4
External Connections

Construction of railways in the Maritime Provinces was accompanied by improvement of connections with the continent. Communication was established between Portland and Halifax by the Grand Trunk line of steamers. During the open season, a line of vessels ran from Quebec to Pictou, the S.S. *Lady Head* making 14 trips in 1862. After Confederation, the dominion government subsidized the Quebec and Gulf-Ports Steamship Company to the extent of $750.00 for each round trip from Quebec to Pictou touching at Father Point, Gaspé, Percé, Miramichi, and Shediac, and, if necessary, Charlottetown.[1] An additional subsidy of $50.00 to $100.00 was paid for a call once a fortnight at Dalhousie and points along Chaleur Bay to encourage the trade in fresh salmon to Quebec. In 1874 the Gulf Port line called fortnightly at Charlottetown from Montreal and Quebec.[2] Improved steamship connections were accompanied by improved rail connections. A most important improvement was made with the completion of a line between Truro and Amherst on November 9, 1872, to connect with a line from Amherst to Painsec Junction (41 miles) completed the preceding year. Railway communications were established as a result between Bangor, Maine, and the boundary line and from the boundary, *viâ* Woodstock and Fredericton, and St. John,[3] "uniting the Nova Scotia System of Railways with the Railways of New Brunswick and the United States, and giving a continuous line of Railway mail communication from Halifax to Montreal and Ottawa, and the other Cities of Quebec and Ontario".[4] This arrangement, in conjunction with the contract providing for a fortnightly service from Queenstown to Halifax beginning July 6, 1868, provided an all-year communication *viâ* Halifax between Great Britain

[1] *S.p.*, 5, 1871.
[2] *S.p.*, 7, 1875.
[3] *S.p.*, 2, 1872.
[4] *S.p.*, 5, 1873, and *S.p.*, 13, 1893.

and the St. Lawrence.[1] In 1876 with completion of the Intercolonial Railway a weekly service was provided during the winter season.

The Intercolonial completed connections by rail on Canadian soil[2] between the Maritimes and the St. Lawrence. It was extended from Rivière du Loup to St. Flavie (84 miles) on November 2, 1874, from Moncton to Campbellton (155 miles) on November 8, 1875, and from Campbellton to St. Flavie (105 miles) on June 12, 1876 (mail service July 3).[3] "This completed a continuous railway of the gauge of 4 ft. 8½ inches between the western limits of Canada on Lake Huron and the Detroit River and Halifax and St. John on the Atlantic Ocean." After completion of the line, weekly mail steamers from Liverpool *viâ* Londonderry landed and embarked mails at Rimouski and accelerated communication to Canada, the Maritimes, and the western states. In winter, mails for Canada and the western states were landed at Halifax instead of at Portland.[4] The completion of the bridge across the St. John River on October 1, 1885, finally shortened effectively connections between Halifax and the interior.[5]

---

[1]*S.p.*, 34, 1869. This contract with Mr. Inman terminated June 30, 1871, and was followed by a new one with Sir Hugh Allan dated July 1, 1871, on the same terms at a subsidy of £16,250 per year, the imperial post office paying one-half. Post office facilities were steadily improved. The parcel post system was extended to parcels between Canada and New Brunswick and Nova Scotia at a uniform rate of 25 cents per pound and in April, 1865, the money order system was extended to New Brunswick and included all the Maritime Provinces and Newfoundland. The Uniform Currency Act of 1871 facilitated the development of trade (*S.p.*, 2, 1866; *S.p.*, 2, 1872). In November, 1872, rates to Newfoundland were reduced from 12½ cents to 6 cents per half ounce.

[2]A road had been built following the Témiscouata portage from Rivière du Loup in 1861-2 and a second road following the Matapedia portage from St. Flavie to Restigouche (110 miles) was completed in 1868 (*S.p.*, 3, 1862). See F. M. Victorin, "Le portage du Témiscouata" (Royal Society of Canada *mémoires*, XII, series 3, section 1, 1918, 55-93); also J. D. Michaud, *Notes historiques sur la vallée de la Matapedia* (Valbrillant, 1922).

[3]*S.p.*, 6, 1877; and *S.p.*, 4, 1876; also *The route of the Intercolonial Railway in a national, commercial and economical point of view* (1867); Sandford Fleming, *The Intercolonial, an historical sketch 1832-76* (Montreal, 1876); D. R. Cowan, "A history of the Intercolonial and Prince Edward Island Railway of Canada" (M.A. thesis, University of Toronto); *Canada, an encyclopedia*, III, 298 *ff*.

[4]*S.p.*, 3, 1877. Passenger and freight traffic by ocean steamers increased steadily and large quantities of merchandise were forwarded to the upper provinces (*S.p.*, 8, 1879; *S.p.*, 3, 1879). This traffic was especially heavy in 1883-4 (*S.p.*, 13, 1886). See *The Maritime Provinces since Confederation*, chapter iv.

[5]*S.p.*, 130, 1882.

TRADE AND SHIPPING

The effects of iron and steam on the wood and water economy of the Maritime Provinces were directer and severer than on the similar economy of Canada. Wheat and other agricultural products provided an escape for Upper Canada while in the Maritimes no direct outlet was available. At the end of the first decade the railroad and the steamship had not yet had sufficient time to affect seriously Maritime economy; and fishing, lumbering, and ship-building, and transportation by water were dominant.

1
Exports

Exports from New Brunswick in 1861 totalled £947,091 sterling, including $3,077,039 to Great Britain, $59,879 to P.E.I., $843,141 to the United States (including 17 deal-laden vessels cleared to Eastport from St. John to evade the deck-load law), and $87,050 to Cuba and Porto Rico, and not including lumber shipped from the British side of the St. Croix and cleared from the American side, and ships valued at £334,000. Exports included; sawn lumber, 316,657,750 feet or total produce of the forest, $3,437,910; produce of the mines, $332,970; fisheries, $269,259; new ships, $1,651,200.

2
Shipping and Ship-building

Ships built in New Brunswick in 1861 totalled 40,523 tons as compared with 33,187 tons in Canada, 23,664 tons in Nova Scotia, 9,000 tons in P.E.I. Ships registered in New Brunswick totalled 813 vessels of 158,240 tons (137,873 tons at St. John, 11,029 tons at St. Andrews, 9,338 tons at Miramichi) or ships valued at £700,000 sterling owned by the province. Tonnage entered totalled 727,318 in 3,518 vessels (27,684 men) and cleared 774,092 in 3,342 vessels (26,834 men), of which 386,951 tons were for the United

Kingdom (195,122 tons British, a large number from Yarmouth clearing from St. John, and 191,829 foreign—107,939 tons from the United States). The Norwegians monopolized the vessels from the ports on the north shore to the United Kingdom (121 of 41,435 tons). Of the British vessels, 1,954 arrived with cargoes (705 in ballast) and of the foreign, 460 in cargo (399 in ballast) while of the British, 1,904 cleared with cargoes (851 in ballast), and of the foreign, 820 in cargo (37 in ballast). Of total tonnage entered—727,138 tons— St. John claimed 435,661; St. Andrews, 56,888; Richibucto, 37,316 (chiefly foreign); Newcastle, 34,723; Chatham and Shediac, over 32,000 tons each; Dalhousie, 20,000; St. George, 14,772; Hillsborough, 14,170; Bathurst, 12,990; Buctouche, 9,642. Nationalities of vessels entering were 119 Norwegian, 728 American, 141 United Kingdom, 2,419 colonial.

In 1858 imports in Nova Scotia totalled £1,615,118 and exports £1,264,298 of which £529,731 came from the United Kingdom and £61,762 were sent to the United Kingdom and £583,675 came from the United States and £408,645 were sent to the United States. The Reciprocity Treaty stimulated trade with the latter country. In 1858, 89 vessels of 47,045 tons (3,534 men) cleared for Great Britain and 2,355 of 264,941 tons (15,552 men) cleared for the United States, 342 of 44,671 tons (2,497 men) for the West Indies (carrying chiefly fish), and 2,461 of 201,999 tons (14,049 men) for the other British North American colonies. Shipping was confined chiefly to ports on the Atlantic coast which were free of ice; especially Halifax, 384 vessels of 23,956 tons valued at £240,657; Yarmouth, 125 of 35,300 tons valued at £284,265; Arichat, 251; and Lunenburg, 220, chiefly fishing vessels. East (from Halifax to Guysboro) ports owned 460 vessels of 26,508 tons valued at £265,472 and west ports (from Yarmouth to Chester), 640 of 61,980 tons valued at £499,064 (Barrington, 88; Ragged Islands, 23; Shelburne, 13). On the shore of the gulf, Pictou, as the centre of the coal trade, was the chief shipping port, the ice being a serious limiting factor. Rapid growth in the Bay of Fundy led to the development of 11 outports with 249 vessels of 21,159 tons valued at £155,912 between Yarmouth and Annapolis, and 312 vessels of 38,772 tons valued at

£213,955 in the Basin of Minas. Hantsport owned 49,050 tons; Windsor, 30,000; the Parrsboro shore, 67 vessels of 29,815 tons; Maitland, 33 of 26,310 tons; Londonderry and Walton owned about £25,000 of shipping. Cumberland Basin exported a few small vessels, coal, and some agricultural produce in 1872. In 1861, 6,323 vessels of 696,763 tons (41,804 men) entered Nova Scotian ports and 6,089 vessels of 695,582 tons (41,520 men) cleared. Abundance of timber near the coast and numerous convenient harbours and rivers were factors stimulating the ship-building of Nova Scotia. The average number of ships constructed from 1853 to 1861 was 200 of 32,132 tons. "The greater number of vessels constructed are of the smaller class, adapted to the coasting trade of the province, the sister colonies and the neighboring states."[1]

Ship-building[2] reached its peak in 1874. The depression of the seventies accentuated the effects of competition from iron steamships. Lumber, as a basic source of traffic for wooden ships, was subject to marked fluctuations. St. George, for example, in 1876 reported "a falling off of lumber vessels going to the United States". The report on industry in 1885 stated:

---

[1]An "Enquiry into wrecks and rewards for saving life" reported that the defective state of coasting vessels was responsible for numerous disasters (*S.p.*, 5, 1872), and similar information was brought out in the investigation on deckloads. In 1873 an act was passed adopting the Imperial Merchant Shipping Act to supersede the Inland Canadian Act. The fourth part of the act provided for the establishment of rules and regulations for inspection and classification of Canadian ships. Up to that date surveyors of British Lloyd's generally inspected vessels built in Quebec and Prince Edward Island, and vessels over 150 tons built in Nova Scotia and New Brunswick were inspected by officers of the French "Bureau Veritas". The act planned a system of "national classification of the shipping of Canada . . . which would command as much weight and confidence as any existing classification, not only amongst ship-builders and ship-owners of this country, but also amongst the under-writers of the United Kingdom and other countries visited by Canadian shipping". It also included provisions as to measurement and registration, as to small vessels without decks or vessels with decks not exceeding 10 tons, and as to methods of financing ships under construction (*S.p.*, 4, 1874). See F. W. Wallace, *Record of Canadian shipping; Wooden ships and iron men; In the wake of the wind ships*; also F. H. Patterson, *A history of Tatamagouche, Nova Scotia* (Halifax, 1917); E. Crowell, *A history of Barrington Township and vicinity, 1604-1870*, 334-405; G. S. Brown, *Yarmouth, Nova Scotia* (Boston, 1888), 352 *ff.*; J. R. Campbell, *A history of the County of Yarmouth* (Saint John, N.B., 1876), 193 *ff.*; J. M. Lawson, *Yarmouth past and present* (Yarmouth, 1902); W. Smith, *An alphabetical list of all the shipping registered at St. John, N.B. on 1st January, 1867* (Saint John, n.d.).

[2]See F. W. Wallace, *Wooden ships and iron men*.

In ship's work there is an undoubted drop so far as St. John, Portland and Quaco, N.B., are concerned, the revolution in the shipping interest caused by the introduction of cheap iron steamers and cheap iron ships, having paralyzed the building of wooden ships—an industry in which for many long years St. John stood proudly pre-eminent.[1]

In Nova Scotia it was stated that "trade used to be done by hundreds of coasters carrying goods between its various ports and P.E. Island, United States, Newfoundland, etc. Nine tenths of this is now done by railways and a few steamers."[2] In Prince Edward Island "the trade of the Island has hitherto been mainly carried on by small craft running into the numerous harbors along the coast."[3] In 1877 the superintendent of the Prince Edward Island Railway reported "the gradual withdrawal of business from the old water channels of communication to the railway".[4] Few localities[5] were without railways by the end of the period and freight carried by railroad in 1880 totalled 37,208 tons.

---

[1]*S.p.*, 37, 1885.
[2]*Monetary Times*, 1884-5, 239.
[3]*S.p.*, 6, 1877.
[4]*S.p.*, 7, 1878.
[5]For example, Orwell and Pinette (*S.p.*, 7, 1870).

SUBSECTION C

LUMBER

1

Saw-mills

The serious effects of the depression in the lumber industry, the exhaustion of more accessible supplies of lumber, and, in consequence, the concentration of the industry on the large rivers, and the effects of the railway and steamship on lumber traffic were factors of serious consequence to the ship-building industry. The decline of wooden ship-building was accompanied by a shift in the lumber industry[1] which followed trends similar to those of the St. Lawrence drainage basin. The increasing scarcity of pine and square timber was followed by the rise of the saw-mill and increasing dependence on spruce deals and lumber. In New Brunswick large saw-mills were established at the mouths of large rivers—the St. John and the Miramichi, and later the Restigouche—and were dependent on steam. The large rivers tapped the forested areas of the interior and sailing vessels could load the finished product for foreign markets. In 1851 there were 584 mills in New Brunswick employing 4,302 men. In 1861 "water power is still used very extensively; but the number of mills worked by steam is becoming large, especially at and near the various sea-ports."[2] The size of New Brunswick mills contrast sharply with those of Nova Scotia.

New Bruns-wick	Saw-mills	Em-ployees	Yearly wages	Value of raw material	Value of finished product
1871	565	6,293	$1,400,562	$3,747,963	$6,575,759
1881	478	6,440	$1,243,628	$4,355,735	$6,532,826

[1]See reports of the crown land office, *Journals of the assembly, New Brunswick*, and *Journals of the assembly, Nova Scotia*; John Rankin, *A history of our firm* (Liverpool, 1921); B. E. Fernow, *Forest conditions of Nova Scotia* (Ottawa, 1912); C. H. Jones, "The lumber industry in New Brunswick and Nova Scotia" (M.A. thesis, University of Toronto, 1930).
[2]*Eighty years' progress*, 599.

Nova Scotia	Saw-mills	Em-ployees	Yearly wages	Value of raw material	Value of finished product
1871	1,144	2,710	$330,417	$755,167	$1,397,937
1881	1,190	3,970	$549,480	$1,446,858	$3,094,137

The larger number of Nova Scotian mills was in part a result of greater diversity of resources. At about 1860 Queens County produced over one-half the pine boards of Nova Scotia; Pictou produced hewn timber; Halifax, staves; and Cumberland, deals. Lunenberg and Digby Counties also produced lumber. In New Brunswick, Restigouche, Northumberland, and Victoria were important lumbering counties.

2

The Depression of the Seventies

In the fifties[1] New Brunswick exported an average value of lumber of about $2,400,000 annually which employed over 300,000 tons of shipping. In 1861 exports of lumber from New Brunswick totalled $2,920,000 and from Nova Scotia, $1,098,888. The depression in England following the Civil War caused a depression in the market for lumber and for ships. The depression of the seventies was even more serious.

> The lumber trade has been passing through a longer critical period than almost any other. The glutting of the English markets, upon which our spruce deal manufacturers have largely depended, by our own manufacturers as well as by the manufacturers of other lumber-producing countries, and the *under-consumption* to which the world's business troubles have given rise, have brought down upon the lumber-producing countries unpleasant results. Depression in this industry means depression in every branch of labor to the sustainment of which it contributes, and for a year or two this condition of things has prevailed.

3

The Importance of the Railroad

Partly as a result of concentration at the large lumber-producing centres of New Brunswick, and partly as a cause of this concentration, small ship-building and lumbering

---

[1] In 1853 Rankin Gilmour and Company had 130 square-rigged vessels at St. John. Deals were floated down by this company from Nashwaak and loaded for the English market.

centres especially on the shore of the gulf (for example the ship-building centre on the Phillip River and the saw-mill centres up the Tidnish[1] River) declined.   The growth of settlement and exhaustion of timber accentuated the decline. "The timber trade of this place [*Pugwash Harbour*] has much decreased of late years, the stock of timber in the neighbourhood being nearly exhausted, but the settlements in this neighbourhood are increasing." The difficulties of lumbering and ship-building in this district and in the smaller rivers such as the Richibucto[2] hastened concentration on the large rivers, notably the Miramichi.   In 1877 over 50 vessels arrived to take in cargo at Newcastle mills[3] and the trade of the port was reported as increasing rapidly every year.   In 1883 the port of Miramichi exported 137,000,000 feet of lumber chiefly obtained from the north.

At these points of concentration the railroad became increasingly effective. The report on traffic of the Intercolonial for 1882 stated: "The traffic in lumber has increased and it is now frequently carried longer distances by railway than in former years."[4]   And in 1883:

It will be observed that there is a very large increase in the quantity of lumber, grain and flour carried. It is worthy of remark, that the quantity of lumber carried has doubled since the year 1879-80, that the quantity of flour is almost double what it was in that year, and that the quantity of grain is more than three times as much as was carried in 1879-80.[5]

---

[1]*S.p.*, 6, 1873.

[2]See a petition dated February 11, 1884, stating that 4 saw-mills in the neighbourhood of St. Louis producing about 15,000,000 feet as well as 2 grist mills and extensive fisheries would gain materially with the construction of a railway (*S.p.*, 21, 1884).

[3]*S.p.*, 1, 1878. "Owing to the size and depth of the Miramichi, ships can load along its banks anywhere for miles, and, consequently, detached villages have sprung up, wanting many of the advantages which would be gained from having one large town" (*Eighty years' progress*, 631).   The geographic character of the river restricted water power mills and necessitated the use of steam power.

[4]*S.p.*, 8, 1883. Fluctuations in lumber became increasingly serious as an item of railway traffic.   In 1879 local freight suffered severely (*S.p.*, 6, 1880).   A rise in price in 1879-80 was followed by a revival of the industry (*S.p.*, 5, 1880-1). Lumber as material for construction was particularly subject to the effects of the business cycle.

[5]*S.p.*, 10, 1884.

	1877-78	1876-77
Barrels of flour, no.	637,778	254,710
Bushels of grain, no.	331,170	292,852
Head of livestock	46,498	37,414
Lumber, in feet	56,606,547	58,096,475
All other goods, tons	375,025	311,756

Increase in the handling of lumber was accompanied by an
increase in traffic in flour, grain, and livestock.   The railroad
and steamship to the north shore overcame the difficulties
of ice on the gulf and provided for the movement of lumber
and lumber products to Halifax.   Large exports of bark,
wood, and lumber were "annually sent for shipment to
Europe *via* steamships from Halifax".   Messrs Miller sent
over the Intercolonial Railway about 2,200 car-loads in one
season[1] and in 1883 shipped 9,000 barrels of hemlock bark
extract valued at $117,000.

4

Exports

Deals were exported from the ports on the gulf and from
eastern Nova Scotia to Great Britain.   For the shore of
the Bay of Fundy, the United States, the West Indies, and
South America became increasingly important markets.[2]
Increase of settlement on the St. John River and its tributaries, tendency toward decline of lumber resources, the forcing of wooden ships off the Atlantic routes to the longer
routes to the south, and the increasing importance of demands
from southern areas were factors favouring the growth of
trade along new lines.   The decline of better grades of lumber
in this area contributed to the same movement.

In 1872 it was reported that:

> The trade between ports in the Lower Provinces of Canada
> and the West Indies is rapidly increasing; in fact the shook
> and lumber supply to those islands is mainly procured from
> these Provinces.   The description of lumber manufactured in
> the United States being very valuable, is almost entirely for
> other markets, as the quality required in the West Indies,

---

[1]*S.p.*, 21, 1884; *S.p.*, 14, 1884.

[2]The European market continued to be important especially in conjunction
with ship-building.   In 1876 at Bear River "vessels now building are of a large
class; our exports being now principally deals to Europe, consequently our vessels
require all the depth of water in the river to get out" (*S.p.*, 5, 1877).   The variety
of demands and markets stimulated the lumber industry.   In 1871, 3,000,000
feet of lumber chiefly pine and spruce, obtained about 30 miles up the river, were
exported from Sissiboo.   Maitland was the "centre of a large district where
ship-building is carried on" (*S.p.*, 4, 1872).   At Cape Spencer vessels loaded
with timber, "sawn by mills near the entrance from logs brought down the
streams", and at Quaco Head, and in some of the creeks, many ships were built in
1871 (*S.p.*, 6, 1873).   The depression had serious effects for territory dependent
on the United States market as well as on ship-building.

although merchantable, is not No. 1; the boards being chiefly what is called shippers, and the poorer kinds of lumber stock are worked up into shooks. The material for the manufacture of such boards and shooks is more readily obtained in the Provinces, and the cost of manufacture much cheaper, for shooks are frequently sold at St. John, N.B., to merchants in Portland and Boston for re-shipment from those ports. These Provinces have, therefore, enjoyed the monopoly of exporting lumber to the West Indies. . . .[1]

From Meteghan Harbour lumber was shipped in large quantities "to the West India Islands and the United States, and regular packets run, during the summer season, to Boston and St. John".[2]

5

Secondary Industries[3]

Expansion of the local market in addition to the demands of other markets, growth of the lumber industry (particularly with the production of·deals) and the introduction of steam engines, supported the development of industries producing

---

[1]This trade employed chiefly "small barques, brigs or brigantines, and schooners, having a depth of hold of ten feet and upwards, so as to stow three tiers of hogsheads of molasses on the return passage. These vessels are entirely different from coasters, being of deep and comparatively narrow model, with requisite dimensions for carrying dead weight or under deck cargoes".

As a result of the increase in trade: "For some years past the practice has been adopted of carrying very heavy deck loads from St. John and other ports in the Lower Provinces. During the winter months the deck loads of lumber, or wet sugar-box shooks, which were carried to the West Indies from ports in New Brunswick and Nova Scotia, were frequently piled several feet above the rail, and it became very dangerous for men to walk on them, and extremely difficult to manage the vessels, more particularly if they became iced, as they generally do in our severe winter weather, and in consequence many vessels have been lost and many lives sacrificed." The piled-up deck-loads were "more trying upon the vessel than even a full cargo of dead weight, for the heavy deck-load destroys the trim of the vessel and interferes with her proper handling, the crew being deprived of the protection of bulwarks, &c.: then, when stormy weather is experienced, the excessive weight on deck makes the vessel tender, opens her waterways, seams and stanchions, strains the topsides or throws the vessel on her beam ends, when she is apt to become waterlogged, as the water running along the bilge while the vessel is hove down cannot be reached by the pumps, (there being no bilge pumps in this class of vessel), thus the overloading is the primary cause of many disasters. . . ." A bill was consequently passed prohibiting "a cargo higher than four feet six inches above the deck on single decked vessels from Canada to the West Indies . . . between the 15 of November and the 16 of March" (*S.p.*, 4, 1873). See also H. B. Small, *The products and manufactures of the new dominion*, 47-8.

[2]*S.p.*, 6, 1873.

[3]The effects of the growth of towns were shown in the construction of wooden, clapboarded (shingled sides and roof) frame houses.

semi-finished and finished products. In St. John County in 1881, William Davidson's mills included one double-gang water mill and one 40-horse-power steam mill which, employing about 100 men the year around, produced 9,000,000 deals and in addition lath, pickets, shingles, clapboards, and scantling. St. Martins Manufacturing Company in the same year had one steam saw-mill of 60 horse-power employing 20 men for ship-building purposes but a new mill of 80 horse-power was built to employ 60 men producing "broom handles, cloth boards, hard wood squares, spool wood bobbins and turned work of every description for English markets". A mill with 100 horse-power to employ 40 hands was built at Henry's Lake on the St. Martins and Upham Railway to manufacture similar goods. Still another mill employing 15 men cut 3,500,000 deals annually and in addition laths, palings, and shingles.[1] At Hampton village in King's County a factory was engaged in producing zinc wash-boards. "They sold 700 dozen last year and the demand increasing has completely replaced not only the American but the Upper Provinces' articles altogether. They also turn out friction matches largely, shooks for onion boxes for Bermuda (have shipped several cargoes), and lumber for our trunk factories."

Small wood-working establishments, sash and door factories, and planing mills thrived in a local market. The report of 1885 stated that:

> Those interested in the door, sash and blind factories are covering the home market well, because the National Policy enables them to do so; and then, success at home is enabling them to put forth vigorous efforts to compete for the trade of outside territory, Rhodes, Curry & Co., of Amherst; Brookfield, of Halifax; Risteen & Co., of Fredericton, and three or four in St. John and elsewhere furnishing notable examples. . . .[2]

---

[1] *S.p.*, 11, 1882.
[2] *S.p.*, 37, 1885. Small cooperage plants and box-making plants were closely linked to the fishing industry and later to the apple industry.

AGRICULTURE[1]

The importance of water-transportation and its emphasis on the handling of staple raw materials in the lumbering, fishing, and mining industries drained off the energy available for less fortunately located industries such as agriculture.

Another very efficient cause why so small a quantity of land is under tillage is the universal tendency of the people to lumbering and shipbuilding. As the forests of New Brunswick afford an unlimited supply of timber for those purposes, and for transportation to foreign markets in various forms of manufacture or preparation, these branches of industry have been largely entered upon to the neglect and exclusion of agriculture. The cultivation of the soil has therefore occupied only a secondary consideration. In the manufacture of lumber thousands of the people are engaged, and a large amount of capital is invested. . . .

Distracted as the attention of settlers has been with a speedy realization of wealth presented by lumbering operations, the hardiest of the population have forsaken the ease and immunity from labour which they might enjoy on their farms during the most inclement season of the year, and, leaving the quiet of home, have spent the winter campaigning in the forests; while in the spring, when they should be clearing and preparing their land, they are engaged in floating their timber down the rivers, to the neglect of farming operations. It is impossible for any settler to combine two interests so widely different as farming and lumbering. If he applies his mind to one of these pursuits, it must be to the detriment of the other. As the lumbering business is precarious in its nature—depending upon the state of the British markets,— some seasons abundantly remunerate the toil of the lumberman, and thus encouraged, he obtains larger supplies, and prepares for more extensive operations in the lumber woods; but one unsuccessful season arising either from a depression of the lumber trade, or from his inability to get his timber

---

[1]See A. B. Balcom, "Agriculture in Nova Scotia since 1870" (*Dalhousie Review*, VIII, 29-43); H. Trueman, *Early agriculture in the Atlantic provinces* (Moncton, 1907); Major-General Laurie, "The agricultural resources of Nova Scotia" (*Canadian economics*, 93-98); J. D. Rankin, *A history of the County of Antigonish, Nova Scotia* (Toronto, 1929), 3-52. Also *Annual reports of the board of agriculture . . . of New Brunswick;* and later reports of the secretary for agriculture, *Journals of the assembly, New Brunswick;* and reports on agriculture, *Journals of the assembly, Nova Scotia.*

and logs to market on account of the early breaking up of winter, or from the lowness of the water in spring, will not only seriously embarrass him, but may even sweep away the rewards of all his toils.[1]

Similarly in Nova Scotia, fishermen and ship-builders were also farmers to the detriment of agriculture.

The agriculture of Nova Scotia is in a transition state. It is to be found in all the stages of advancement—from the rude attempts of the half-lumberer half-farmer to the productive

---

[1]A. L. Spedon, *Rambles among the blue-noses*, 80 *ff*. Spedon remarked regarding the Miramichi country: "It appears singular to me that so large a quantity of cereal produce is annually imported to these parts.".

The following report was made in 1865 on counties on the shore of the gulf:

Counties	Popu- lation	Total no. of acres of land	No. of acres occu- pied Culti- vated	Not culti- vated	Value of farm pro- duce, domes- tic manufac- tures, etc.	Value of produce of fisheries
Restigouche	4,874	1,426,560	14,628	63,318	$190,544.00	$11,885.00
Gloucester	15,076	1,037,440	35,355	147,389	299,835.00	85,783.00
Northumberland	18,801	2,980,000	40,800	223,571	490,408.00	37,893.00
Kent	15,854	1,026,400	55,186	164,732	497,230.00	51,635.00

(*S.p.*, 18, 1867-8).

See also J. F. W. Johnson, *Report on the agricultural capabilities of . . . New Brunswick* (Fredericton, 1850).

In 1859 the Province of New Brunswick imported 226,649 barrels of flour valued at $1,031,241; 21,518 barrels of corn meal valued at $79,958; 67,152 bushels of wheat valued at $82,430; 303,205 pounds of butter and cheese valued at $50,361; animals to the value of $96,000; cured meats valued at $153,600; or a total of $1,493,590 of agricultural produce ($1,700,333 in 1861). Of total exports from Canada to Nova Scotia of $1,030,939 in 1861, agricultural produce was $605,076. Exports of flour to New Brunswick fluctuated as follows:

1857	153,315 barrels
1858	226,649
1859	205,356
1860	198,323
1861	210,676

These conditions continued to the period of the war as is shown in the following statement: "One of the things that has tended to depreciate agriculture has been our great lumber interests. Our people have been lumbermen, and agriculture is simply a side issue with them. Conditions of the lumber industry have changed. The business of the small operator is being absorbed by the large operator and the small man does not have the opportunity that he had a few years ago." An indication of the change was evident in the replacement of oats by potatoes. "We are producing today scarcely enough of anything in the agricultural line, outside of potatoes and hay. We are exporting large quantities of potatoes and large quantities of hay but we are not raising enough agricultural produce for our own consumption, much less for export. . . . I think we are producing about 75 per cent. . . . We are importing a large percentage of our bacon and hams. We imported last year quite a quantity of butter. . . . We are importing large quantities of beef" (Evidence of Mr. J. B. Daggett, secretary for agriculture, *Royal commission on the natural resources, trade, and legislation of certain portions of his majesty's dominions: Minutes of evidence taken in the Maritime Provinces of Canada* (London, 1915).

results of more formal and scientific husbandry. The deficiency then in agricultural products may be ascribed, in a great measure, to the want of a more advanced and intellectual system of culture, and the injudicious impoverishment of the soil; another great evil is, that as a general thing, too much land is brought under half tillage.[1]

1

The Development of Agriculture

Nevertheless the immediate demands of the staple industries were responsible for the development of agriculture in the more favourably located areas and along lines closely related to the staples. Agriculture in the Maritimes had not escaped the dominance of the lumber industry as in the St. Lawrence basin. The lumber industry created a demand for horses, hay, oats, and food-stuffs. The fishing industry in the Maritimes and Newfoundland and shipbuilding and mining created demands for meat products. Apples and cattle were sent from Nova Scotia to St. John, New Brunswick, and to Newfoundland. Potatoes were sent to various centres in the Maritimes as well as to the United States. Agriculture was influenced by the immediate demands of the staple industries and by the geographic background particularly as to soil and climate. Moreover, competition from products of newly-opened areas in Upper Canada and in the western states was a powerful factor limiting the possibilities of commodities, such as wheat, capable of being carried over long distances. Potatoes and root crops were in a strategic position because of perishability, large bulk, and low food value. Agricultural products, like non-metallic minerals, were limited to non-resistant formations which had broken down to provide soil, and to areas near the sea which provided cheap transport. The district surrounding the Bay of Fundy, and Prince Edward Island were of first importance.

---

[1]A. L. Spedon, *Rambles among the blue-noses*, 139.

2

Settlement

Improved transportation and navigation increased the extent of land under cultivation.   In Nova Scotia[1] improved land increased from about 1,000,000 acres in 1851 to nearly 2,000,000 acres in 1881.   In New Brunswick[2] large quantities of land were held for purposes of speculation, and in 1861 it was estimated that of a total of 17,000,000 acres, 12,000,000 were available for cultivation, of which one-half had been granted and about 700,000 acres cleared and cultivated.

	Land acres improved	Land acres occupied
1871		
Nova Scotia.................	1,627,091	5,031,217
New Brunswick..............	1,171,157	3,827,731
1881		
Nova Scotia.................	1,880,644	5,396,382
New Brunswick..............	1,253,299	3,809,621
Prince Edward Island........	596,731	1,126,653

3

Population

With even less advantageous possibilities of agricultural expansion than Upper Canada, the Maritimes were unable to increase their population by immigration.   The attraction of the discoveries of gold in British Columbia and Australia, and of new land in the western states, and, in turn, competition of agricultural products from new areas weakened the position of the Maritimes and population increased slowly.

---

[1] In 1861 improved land totalled 1,027,792 acres, land granted 5,748,893 acres, and total area 11,767,173 acres.   Crown lands were sold at 45 cents an acre.

[2] Public lands were sold at auction for an upset price of 60 cents per acre with 25 per cent. discount for cash.   A settler was allowed to pay for his land with labour on the roads and was required to pay the full amount of his purchase by labour within 5 years and to clear and cultivate not less than 5 acres (A. L. Spedon, *Rambles among the blue-noses*, 84).   Later settlers were required to pay $20.00 for 100 acres—the money to be spent on roads and bridges, or to "perform work on the roads to the value of $10 a year for a period of three years".   In addition, he was required to build a house of at least 16 by 20 feet and clear and cultivate 10 acres within 3 years (*S.p.*, 80, 1870).

Population

	1851	1861	1871	1881
New Brunswick.....	193,800	252,047	285,524	321,233
Nova Scotia........	276,117	330,857	387,800	440,572
Prince Edward Island............	62,678	80,857	94,021	108,891

Of the total population the number engaged in agriculture and other occupations was as follows:

Occupations

	New Brunswick		Nova Scotia		P.E.I.
	1871	1881	1871	1881	1881
Agricultural class	40,394	54,590	49,769	63,684	20,530
Commercial class	2,081	8,170	13,531	15,103	2,183
Domestic class..	5,358	5,198	6,755	7,832	2,040
Industrial class..	18,683	19,437	34,547	39,956	6,388
Professional class	2,858	3,776	4,151	4,844	1,034

4

Character of Agriculture

The character of agriculture was suggested in the *Reports of the tenant farmer's delegates on the Dominion of Canada as a field for settlement:*[1]

The soils I have spoken of as possessing certain remarkable features and properties are the "dyke" and the "intervale" lands.[2]   Both Nova Scotia and New Brunswick are celebrated for the former, while the latter are a peculiarity of New Brunswick, in the valley of the noble river St. John. The dyke lands of both Provinces are found bordering on the inlets of the Bay of Fundy.   Those I saw in Nova Scotia are in the neighbourhood of Kentville and Amherst; in New Brunswick I saw them at Dorchester and Sackville.   As the name suggests, they are dyked in from the sea, from which they have been from time to time reclaimed.   In many cases

[1]*S.p.*, 12, 1881.
[2]In 1861 dyked land in Nova Scotia was valued at $62.06 per acre, salt marsh, $26.04; cultivated intervale, $27.45; cultivated upland, $15.58.   The agricultural counties in Nova Scotia in order of importance were Pictou, Colchester, Cumberland, Kings, Annapolis, Inverness, Sydney, Hants (in almost inverse ratio to fishing); and in New Brunswick the agricultural counties, chiefly up the St. John River valley, were Kings, Queens, Sunbury, York, and Carleton. The upper counties expanded rapidly with improved transportation.   The New Brunswick and Nova Scotia Land Company owned substantial acreage in York County.

marsh grass is cut from saline swamps which have not yet been dyked, and over which the high tides for which the Bay of Fundy is noted, still during certain seasons, continue to flow. The grass is made into hay in the best way possible under the circumstances—on the ridges of higher land, on platforms, etc.—and is stacked on a framework which is raised several feet above the land, supported on piles; and it is a curious sight to see the water flowing under the stacks and in and about the piles when the tide is at its height. In one case I counted, near the town of Annapolis, upwards of 140 of these stacks, each of them containing a ton or so of hay. They are put up in this manner hurriedly, and are fetched into the farmyards, in winter, as they are wanted, to use along with ordinary hay, with straw and with roots, to which they are found to form a tolerable though coarse addition. But the dyke-lands proper are so fenced in from the water by a strong bank of earth thrown up some six or eight feet high, with a broad and substantial base, that the land within them is firm and solid, of excellent quality, and covered with a thick sward of coarse though vigorous and nutritive grass. The fertility of these reclaimed soils is unusually high; they are never manured, but cut on the average upwards of two tons of hay to the acre—a yield which has been sustained for many years, and shows no signs of running out.

The land, however, under this system of farming is found to become weedy in the course of time, and it becomes expedient to plough up portions of it in rotation, at intervals of ten or twelve years, taking one crop of wheat or oats, with which new grass seeds are sown, to form the new sward which is desired. This once ploughing is found to kill the weeds for the time being, and they do not again become very troublesome for some years; and when at length they do, the land is simply ploughed up again in the way described.

These bottom-lands are valuable acquisitions to the upland farms adjoining, most of which have more or less of them attached; and they do much towards maintaining the fertility of the uplands, obviating the necessity of using purchased fertilizers on them. These dyke-lands are in much request on this account, and they are worth from $50 to $150 an acre, in a country where ordinary upland farms are not worth as many shillings an acre. The portions of these dyke-lands owned by different men are marked out for identity's sake, but are not fenced off from the rest. Each man cuts off the hay from his portion, and takes it home, sometimes several miles, and the aftermath is eaten in common by the stock of all the owners combined, commencing on the 1st of September. A few days before this date a committee of assessors is appointed to place a value on each man's portion of the land,

and to decide on the number and kind of animals he shall send for pasturage. So it follows that we see very large tracts of land, on which hundreds of cattle roam about and feed at will. The extent of these dyke-lands is said to be about 65,000 acres, and there is still a large area to be reclaimed. . . . The expense of dyking fresh marshes has ranged from eight dollars to twenty dollars per acre, and it is worthy of note that the system of constructing dykes and *aboideaux* adopted by the first French settlers is the one still employed. The system of cultivation is very simple, and consists of surface draining by cutting ditches 22 yards apart, 3 feet wide at the top, 2 feet 9 inches deep, and sloping to 1 foot wide at the bottom; about three years afterwards the land is ploughed in ridges of 6 to 8 feet wide, sown, with oats, and seeded down with timothy and clovers. It then yields large crops of grass of a coarse description, and it would seem to me that careful draining, generous cultivation, and discriminating manuring would increase the quantity, or at all events improve the quality of the grass. . . .

The "intervale lands" of New Brunswick are, as the name suggests, found in the valley . . . [*and*] receive a periodical manuring in the deposit which is laid on them each spring by the freshets of the rivers. They are, in fact, flooded more or less for several weeks in the spring of the year, and the deposit left by the receding waters is of a character to add fertility to an already rich soil and at the same time, to add to its depth. An inch or two of rich alluvial mud deposited on these lands each year is gradually raising them above the influence of the freshets; and they are to-day among the most valuable soils in the Province.

The effects of improved transportation were evident by the end of the period in the widening of the market and the emergence of specialization which followed competition from other areas. The grazing area (for example, the Counties of Kings, Annapolis, Cumberland, Colchester, and Hants) exported hay in large quantities over the Intercolonial through Halifax to the West Indies ($10.00 loose and $13.00 pressed per ton).[1] Agriculture, which had been dominated by the demands of the lumber industry, and which suffered from exhaustion of the soil with continuous cropping, and from the application to upland farms of agricultural technique suitable to dyked land, recovered as in Upper Canada

---

[1] *S.p.*, 12, 1881.

through the introduction of mixed farming. In a report[1]
from Elmville, St. Patrick, in 1884 it was stated that:

> The farmers in this district are improving their farms very
> much; in the way of manures they now use barn manure
> composite of seaweed and peat with pommace and plaster.
> Some years ago their whole attention was lumbering. They
> hauled the hay from their farms to the woods, which was a
> great loss to the farms. It made poor farms, also poor stock.

5

Livestock Trade

The livestock trade of the Maritimes followed the trade
of Upper Canada. In 1879 butchers in St. John bought
cattle and sheep for export to England and shipped them
via Quebec because of lack of steamship connections at St.
John. Following this experiment large farmers, especially
in Westmoreland County with its abundance of hay, bought
stock to be wintered and fattened during the winter of 1879-
80 for the English market. Halifax displaced Portland as a
winter port for the shipment of cattle from Montreal, and
the development of handling facilities encouraged the Maritime trade.[2]

Cattle and sheep brought by rail and shipped at Halifax from
December 29, 1879, to May 11, 1880

	Cattle	Sheep
From the upper provinces..............	3,625	3,195
From Nova Scotia and New Brunswick..	1,253	99
Total........................	4,878	3,294

In 1880 the Sackville district alone exported 600 cattle to
Great Britain. In addition to the export of cattle[3] to
England large numbers of sheep were exported to the United
States. In 1879 it was estimated that Carleton County ex-
ported $50,000 of sheep and sheep-skins and that the St. John
and Maine Railway alone carried about 12,000 head (11,000

---

[1] *S.p.*, 8, 1885.
[2] In 1878-9, 47,584 head of livestock were carried over the Intercolonial
(*S.p.*, 6, 1880; *S.p.*, 5, 1881; and *S.p.*, 5, 1880-1).
[3] In 1882 a policy of slaughter and compensation was introduced to handle
the disease of the Pictou cattle. It was not discovered until 1905 that the disease
was caused by ragwort (*S.p.*, 16, 1906).

in 1880) from the eastern counties and Prince Edward Island, chiefly to Boston. In 1880 Carleton County exported sheep, sheep-skins, cattle, horses, hay, and cereals to the extent of $100,000. Refrigeration stimulated the livestock trade and the Amherst Meat Company exported large quantities of meat in refrigerator-cars by rail to Halifax and to Europe. In 1881 Nova Scotia with 300,000 cattle and 400,000 sheep sold 63,000 cattle and 151,000 sheep.

6

The Dairy Industry

The dairy industry developed chiefly in response to local demands. A cheese factory was opened at Sussex, New Brunswick, as early as 1867. In 1881 Nova Scotia had 24 cheese factories[1] (Pictou County, 4; Cape Breton, one; Hants, one; Colchester, 2; Kings County, 5; Annapolis, 8; and Yarmouth, one). The production of butter[2] in Nova Scotia was estimated to have increased from 3,500,000 pounds in 1851 to 7,500,000 pounds in 1881.

7

Other Products

Root crops became more important and turnips produced in Nova Scotia were estimated to have increased from 300,000 bushels in 1851 to 1,000,000 bushels in 1881, hay from 300,000 tons to 600,000 tons.

The apple industry of the Annapolis valley followed improvement of connections with Halifax and Great Britain and

---

[1] S.p., 12, 1881. The character of operations is suggested in a description of a factory at Bridgetown. The plant manufactured about 15 cheeses per day of 18 to 20 pounds weight, or 1,250 cheeses (27 tons) in a season from May 10 to October 10 and using the milk from about 300 cows. It was run by a joint stock company of farmers who sent in their milk and after paying expenses received profits of about 1 cent per pound of milk. Drivers of 5 teams and 2 hands in the factory constituted the labour force. The cheese was sold in local markets at St. John, Halifax, and Yarmouth at about 12 cents per pound. The whey was used to feed 35 head of swine. "No finer beef is produced in America than that of Kings county and the praise of Annapolis cheese bids fair to be as widespread as that of Gloucester, Cheshire or Dunlop cheese." The census gives 13 cheese factories in N.S. and 4 in N.B. in 1881.

[2] The butter industry suffered from problems similar to those enumerated in Upper Canada. The dairy commissioner reported in 1892 that the "old fashioned dash churn, involving more arduous labour, has given place to the revolving or swing churn" (S.p., 7g, 1892).

beginnings of the export trade were in evidence before the end of the period.[1] The potato industry flourished with increasing demands from the United States, and the potato beetle and the American tariff had appeared as menaces.[2]

1871	Acres	Bushels
Nova Scotia	52,588	5,560,975
New Brunswick	47,689	6,562,355
1881		
Prince Edward Island	39,083	6,042,191
Nova Scotia	60,192	7,378,387
New Brunswick	51,362	6,961,016

Wheat as a pioneer crop was exposed to the difficulties which prevailed in the St. Lawrence drainage basin, but in addition, it felt most sharply the effects of competition from the opening west. Production declined rapidly in the sixties as a result of the weevil. The introduction in 1878 of new varieties of seed—Fife, Black Sea, and Lost Nation—from Ontario was partly responsible for an increase in acreage and production[3] in 1879 but the recovery was destined to be of a short duration.

8

Prince Edward Island

Prince Edward Island was less favourably located from the standpoint of lumbering, mining, and fishing, and more

---

[1] See C. C. Colby, "An analysis of the apple industry of the Annapolis Cornwallis valley" (*Economic Geography*, I, 173-197, 337-355); F. G. J. Comeau, *The introduction and development of the apple industry in the Province of Nova Scotia* (Halifax, 1923).

[2] The potato beetle was reported in 1876 as having reached the Ottawa valley and the more northerly latitudes. In 1878 its eastward progress was again noted as well as its disastrous effects on the quality and quantity of the potato crop (*S.p.*, 8, 1877; and *S.p.*, 9, 1879). In 1882 it became a serious menace in the vicinity of Harvey, New Brunswick, and in 1883 at South Tilley settlement, Victoria County. The remedy, however, was speedily adopted. In 1877 the public analyst reported regarding Paris green that "a large demand" had "sprung up for it of late years as a 'specific poison' for the destruction of the potato destroyer, the Colorado beetle and its larva, the potato bugs" (*S.p.*, 3, 1878). In 1883 a report in New Brunswick stated: "One application of Paris green will make complete annihilation of the marauders. It is quite cheap, and easily applied. Put on at the rate of two pounds to an acre, mixed up in plaster, one pound to the bushel, one acre may be successfully cleared for five shillings" (*S.p.*, 14, 1884).

[3] "As a result of the increased supply of home grown wheat, and the general excellence of the harvest of 1879, several new and extensive flour mills have been erected, and sundry repairs have been made in others, and the grist mills, as a rule, have been busier than they had been for years past" (*S.p.*, 10, 1880).

favourably located by virtue of soil and climate from the standpoint of agriculture. Improved transportation brought agriculture in closer relationship to the demands of the mainland, and, as in the other provinces, of foreign markets. The importance and character of agriculture are shown in an estimate of traffic in 1870 for the Prince Edward Island Railway. Of a total of 300,000 tons as an estimated weight of the agricultural products,[1] the areas tapped by the railway would yield 125,000 tons, and of total exports of 60,000 tons, the railway would carry 25,000 tons, and in addition 12,500 tons from areas not directly served by the railway, and lumber and fish, 2,500 tons. With return freights of 10,000 tons the railroad would carry 50,000 tons to the principal ports, especially to Charlottetown and Georgetown.

Prince Edward Island[2] was especially effective in the growing of potatoes (250 bushels per acre in contrast with New Brunswick's 226 bushels) and turnips (over 500 bushels per acre to New Brunswick's 456 bushels). Potatoes were also exported in large quantities. In 1876 "considerable trade has recently been carried on in the shipment of potatoes in bulk from Prince Edward Island, and from ports in this Province to the United States, and in three cases within the present month vessels have put in here [Halifax] with their cargoes shifted, seriously ·endangering their safety."[3] Decline in the price of potatoes to 15 and 20 cents a bushel in 1880, in part a result of an American tariff of 15 cents a

---

[1]The principal farm stock and products were

No. of horses	25,329
" " cattle	62,984
" " sheep	147,364
" " pigs	52,514
Bushels of wheat	269,392
" " buckwheat	75,109
" " barley	176,441
" " oats	3,128,576
" " potatoes	3,375,726
" " turnips	395,358
" " Indian corn	2,411
Pounds of flax	27,282
" " butter	981,939
" " cheese	155,524
Tons of hay	68,349

(S.p., 7, 1875).

[2]C. B. Bagster, The progress and prospects of Prince Edward Island (Charlottetown, 1861), 121-2.

[3]S.p., 5, 1877.

bushel, was followed by a substantial reduction of a "once large export trade".[1]

The trend of agricultural production was illustrated in part in railway traffic. In 1876 the railroad reported: "The heaviest tonnage was oats, which is always a large crop on the island."[2] An abundant harvest in 1877 was responsible for increased traffic in oats, potatoes, flour, and livestock. But an abundant harvest in 1878 with low prices occasioned a decline in oats from 628,792 bushels in 1877 to 571,420 bushels in 1878, and in potatoes from 174,911 bushels to 60,302 bushels.[3] An abundant harvest of wheat in 1880 caused a decline in the imports of flour.[4]

As in the other provinces continuous cropping exhausted the land. Concentration on staple crops impoverished the soil of lime. Apparently the relative scarcity of hay as contrasted with Nova Scotia and New Brunswick checked the growth of the livestock and dairy industries and it was not until the introduction of Indian corn in the nineties that dairying obtained an important foothold. Farmers were consequently forced to rely on fertilizer rather than on mixed farming as a means of escape in the eighties. The railroad facilitated the exploitation and distribution of mussel mud. This was found in thick beds in the bays and river mouths and became important as a fertilizer. In 1880 increases in traffic in this item were reported:

> This singular deposit is obtained, as a rule, below low-water mark, and in winter when the water is a solid mass of ice. Holes are cut through the ice until the mud is reached, and a powerful and ingenious horse-power scoop is used to fetch up the mud and dump it in the sleighs. It is then taken to shore and laid in heaps until it is wanted.[5]

---

[1]Attempts to develop starch factories met with difficulty. The report of 1885 noted regarding the factories of the island. "First, there is the depression in the cotton trade in England and Canada; secondly, Germany and Holland, both of which countries are rivals of the Island in the English market, have yielded an immense potato crop; and thirdly, the Western States have produced a heavy crop of corn. These three causes—powerful they unquestionably are—have contributed in no inconsiderable degree to lower the price of starch in the Island market, and to depress the industry" (S.p., 37, 1885).

[2]S.p., 6, 1877. [3]S.p., 8, 1879. [4]S.p., 5, 1880-1.

[5]S.p., 12, 1881. 20 to 30 sleigh loads were used per acre, and in 1879 it was estimated that 200,000 loads were raised. "During the season of winter the cumbrous digging machines, worked by horse power, and each attended by two or three men, cover the oyster creeks like a scattered encampment" (Ernest Kemp, Report on Canadian oyster fisheries and oyster culture, S.p., 11a, 1899; also Report of royal commission on shellfish, 1922).

FISHING[1]

1

Nova Scotian Fishery

At the beginning of the period the fishing industry was largely dominated by the staple cod. Improved transportation and wider markets hastened the development of other species of fish. Nova Scotia with its extensive coast line and numerous ports and its proximity to the outlying banks occupied a pre-eminent position.

Nova Scotian fishery

	Vessels	Men	Boats	Men	Cod qx.	Herring (barrels)	Mackerel (barrels)
1851	812	....	5,161	.....	196,434	53,200	100,047
1861	900	....	8,816	.....	396,425	194,170	66,108
1871	722	5,573	7,940	11,855	380,308	135,266	69,647
1881	755	6,854	13,214	17,782	587,203	140,831	120,242

Counties along the Atlantic coast were of first importance and in 1861 Halifax ranked first and was followed in turn by Guysborough, Richmond, Lunenburg, Shelburne, and Yarmouth. Fishing vessels proceeded to the Labrador coast and brought back green fish to be dried for foreign markets, especially for the West Indies.

---

[1]This section includes the fisheries of the Gulf of St. Lawrence under the jurisdiction of Quebec. See reports on fisheries, *Journals of the assembly, N.B.*; *Journals of the assembly, Nova Scotia*; E. T. D. Chambers, *The fisheries of the Province of Quebec*, part I, *Historical introduction* (Quebec, 1913); J. E. Roy, *In and around Tadousac* (Lévis, 1881); J. C. Langelier, *Esquisse sur la Gaspésie* (Quebec, 1884); A. Pelland, *La Gaspésie* (Quebec, 1914); J. M. Clarke, *The heart of Gaspé* (New York, 1913); J. M. Clarke, *Sketches of Gaspé* (Albany, 1908); A. Bernard, *La Gaspésie au soleil* (Montreal, 1925); P. Hubert, *Les îles de la Madeleine* (Rimouski, 1926); J. Schmitt, *Monographie de l'île d'Anticosti* (Paris, 1904); V. A. Huard, *Labrador and Anticosti* (Montreal, 1897); G. Guay, *Lettres sur l'île d'Anticosti* (Montreal, 1902); M. J. U. Gregory, *En racontant, récits de voyages en Floride, au Labrador et sur le fleuve Saint-Laurent* (Quebec, 1886); Sir J. Le Moine, *The chronicles of the St. Lawrence* (Montreal, 1878); F. de Saint Maurice, *De Tribord à Bibord* (Montreal, 1877); *Promenades dans le golfe Saint Laurent* (Quebec, 1879), *En route sept jours dans les provinces maritimes* (Quebec, 1888); *Report of the royal commission investigating the fisheries of the Maritime Provinces and the Magdalen Islands* (Ottawa, 1928).

Fortin[1] estimated that over 100 schooners chiefly from Nova Scotia and the United States were engaged in the cod-fishery at Bradore Bay and Blanc Sablon along the north shore in addition to a large number of others which took in their cargoes on the Mingan shoal, at Natashquan, Good Hope, and Salmon Bay. This fishery began about June 20 and extended for about 6 weeks. "The quantity of cod taken by all the vessels fishing on the Canadian coast may be computed at 90,000 quintals, whilst that taken by our fishermen does not amount to more than 20,000 quintals, of which 15,000 quintals at least, are destined for the markets of South America and the Mediterranean." Expansion of the fishery from Gaspé to the Labrador shore and settlement in that area apparently contributed to the increasing reliance of Nova Scotian fishermen on the banks. Halifax was the centre of the fishery on the banks, with about 200 vessels averaging 110 tons and the Lunenburg fleet[2] began operations on the grand banks in 1865. The boat fishery, carried on within relatively short distance from the shore, was prosecuted along the Atlantic coast of Nova Scotia, at Grand Manan, Campo Bello, and West Isle in the Bay of Fundy and at Gaspé, Miscou, and the vicinity of Chaleur Bay in the Gulf of St. Lawrence. This fishery was reported on the decline as a result of the increasing importance of the fishery on the banks.

2

Gaspé

The Gaspé region with its limited agricultural develop-ment and its established trade with the Mediterranean was under the control of large firms. These firms had establish-ments at Gaspé and Paspebiac and at Arichat, Cheticamp, and Ingonish in Cape Breton involving an outlay of capital of £150,000, employing 3,500 fishermen, and owning 16 vessels "of three or four hundred tons engaged in carrying

---

[1]See especially Annual report of Pierre Fortin—1865, *S.p.*, 36, 1866.
[2]The first schooner to go on the banks with dories and trawls went in 1871. Expansion was rapid following the discovery of the under-running method of trawl fishing.

their fish to foreign markets".[1] At Paspebiac and other stations large firms, such as Robins and Le Boutilliers from the Jersey Islands, imported alone upwards of 16,000 barrels of flour and 3,000 barrels of pork annually in addition to large quantities of other agricultural produce.[2] These firms had "a direct trade with the Mediterranean Ports, Brazil, England, the United States, the West Indies, Newfoundland, Halifax, Prince Edward Island, Quebec and Montreal".[3]

New establishments were begun about 1855 at the king's posts along the north shore. An abundance of *lançon* which served as food and bait helped to prolong the fishery throughout the season. In 1855 about 20 batteaux of 2 men each sailed from Chaleur Bay to Seven Islands. Expansion along the north shore warranted the establishment of a mail service by schooner in 1872 between Gaspé Basin and the Island of Anticosti, Mingan, Eskimo Point, Natashquan, and other points. A winter service was established between Bersimis and points lower down.[4]

---

[1]C. B. Bagster, *The progress and prospects of Prince Edward Island*, p. xxxv. On the Bay of Chaleur and Gaspé fishermen cured their own fish but to some extent also sold to firms at the rate of 252 pounds of green fish for 112 pounds of dry.

[2]*S.p.*, 43, 1872; also *S.p.*, 5, 1877; and A. C. Saunders, *Jersey in the 18th and 19th centuries . . . containing an historical record of commercial enterprise* (Jersey, 1930). An attempt to develop the trade of Gaspé basin by the establishment of a free port was not successful. Claims of merchants at Gaspé, Percé, New Carlisle, and Paspebiac that the removal of customs duties was followed by advantages to the fishermen were denied.

Flour, grain, pork, cattle, lumber and the chief articles of consumption as well as fishing supplies, twine, cod lines, seines, and ship-building materials entered free prior to the establishment of a free port. The rise in the price of cotton and of woollen and linen following the American Civil War offset the advantages of a free port. Sugar, molasses, and tea and whisky were cheaper. "The chief advantage has gone to the principal merchants." The regulation requiring vessels to report first at Gaspé was the cause of numerous complaints. Vessels built at Paspebiac by Robins and Company were obliged to import juniper for timber heads and planking of top sides from Caraquet *viâ* Gaspé, and sugar from Halifax for Paspebiac followed the same route. Merchants of the Magdalen Islands preferred to pay duty rather than import *viâ* Gaspé. Sawn lumber sold from New Brunswick to the north shore of Chaleur Bay could not be exported on that basis.

[3]In 1878 a large number of sea-going vessels were reported at Gaspé as "carrying cargoes of dry codfish to the Brazil, Mediterranean and West India ports" (*S.p.*, 3, 1879).

[4]*S.p.*, 5, 1873. In 1855 about 2,000 barrels of herring were caught along the coast from Blanc Sablon to Salmon Bay (*S.p.*, 25, 1856). See N. Comeau, *Life and sport on the north shore of the lower St. Lawrence and Gulf* (Quebec, 1923), 336 *ff.*; E. Rochette, *Notes sur la côte nord du bas Saint Laurent* (Quebec, 1926); R. Nettle, *The salmon fisheries of the St. Lawrence and its tributaries* (Montreal, 1857).

The control of the "Jersey houses" which commanded large capital checked competition from small capitalists, and became responsible for the evils of the truck system.

That those monopolists practically control the price of fish, which they regulate by an understanding among themselves; that the fishermen, who are generally improvident, are usually fitted out by these houses, who also make advances (in goods) to the fishermen during the winter on account of the succeeding season's fishing, and thereby obtain entire control over them and their property, and generally take care so to determine the price of the fish on the one hand, and of the supplies on the other, as to give them (the merchants) the whole season's catch for what it costs the fisherman to live through the year.[1]

By the end of the period improved transportation had paved the way for the first inroads on monopoly. The completion of the Intercolonial was followed by the establishment of a line of steamers between Campbellton and Gaspé Basin. The steamer *City of St. John* made 4 trips a week and the steamer the *Beaver* one a week, with the result that the port of Carleton reported a marked falling off of sailing vessels.[2] Later the opening of a branch line to Dalhousie led to the displacement of Campbellton.[3]

3

West Indian and South American Trade

As in the lumber industry sailing vessels were crowded into the West Indian and South American trade. By the end of the period steam navigation began to displace sailing vessels even on this route. Treaty arrangements were eventually made with the West Indies leading to the development of trade and improved navigation. Proposals,[4]

---

[1] *S.p.*, 37, 1865.
[2] *S.p.*, 6, 1881.
[3] *S.p.*, 13, 1886. In 1893 a report from Bridgetown, Barbadoes, stated "that with regard to fishstuffs from Gaspe, what in former years used to be sent by sailing vessels appear this year thus far to have come forward by steamers, each of the recent steamers having brought several hundred packages of the article—both dry and pickled; no doubt this mode of conveyance has been found to be more certain and expeditious, and thus to better answer the requirements of this market."
[4] *Journals of the legislative assembly*, XIV, 1856, app. 25.

after the abolition of the corn laws and the repeal of the navigation acts, to increase trade between Canada and the British West Indies by reduction of duties were negatived by the imperial government as it was feared that further arrangements would encourage development along the lines of the Reciprocity Treaty which was a deviation "from the rule which forms the fundamental principle of their recent commercial policy".[1] In 1866[2] "the report of the commissioners from British North America, appointed to enquire into the trade of the West Indies, Mexico and Brazil" advised early completion of the Intercolonial Railway, a weekly line of steamers between Montreal and Halifax, semi-monthly communication between Halifax and St. Thomas touching at Portland until the completion of the Intercolonial Railway, improved communication *via* American ports, and reciprocal treaties involving reduction of duties on American produce. With the arrangement of a new tariff after Confederation, 35 firms, merchants, and importers of Halifax petitioned for the reduction of rates on raw sugar from duties of "$3, 2.60, 2.25, 1.90, 1.68 and 1.37 per 100 lbs. according to quality ranging from choice grocery to melado" to "a uniform rate of one dollar per 100 lbs. and 20 per cent. *ad valorem*" on all grades of sugar imported. They asked also for a reduction of the duty on rum.

> Under a fair Tariff cargoes of West India produce will, as usual, be returned for shipments of fish, lumber, &c. Our coals, gypsum, &c., will be shipped in exchange for the flour, barley, pease, &c., of Ontario and Quebec, making cargoes both ways—either by Gulf of St. Lawrence or *via* Grand Trunk Railroad, by which means a reciprocal trade can be sustained.
>
> The charges, commissions, freight, &c., now being paid to merchants of New York, and to foreign vessels and railroads, would be retained among ourselves, thus benefiting the whole people of the Dominion.

A more specific petition was presented by Charles Robin and Company and 29 others in 1883 asking that an agreement should be arranged with Brazil by which the duties on raw

---

[1]Whitehall, June 26, 1855, (*Trade reports relating to Canada, 1847-1891*).
[2]*S.p.*, 43, 1866.

sugar be reduced and that in compensation Brazil should be asked to reduce her high duties on dry cod-fish.[1]

Steam navigation became important only at the end of the period with an agreement between Canada and the West Indies and Brazil and "the first steamer the *Comte d'Eu* arrived from Rio de Janeiro at Halifax on the 31st December last, bringing mails from Rio de Janeiro, Bahia, Pernambuco, Para, and St. Thomas, West Indies; and the first direct mails by this line for Brazil left Halifax on the 11th January, 1882."[2]

The decline of wooden ship-building coincided with the increase in production of beet sugar[3] in Europe and the decline in the price of cane sugar from the West Indies. As a result the important market for cod in the West Indies suffered a severe blow.

4

Fisheries other than Cod

(i)

Mackerel and herring

Development of rapid transportation and the evolution of refrigeration had profound effects on the inshore fishery and the growth in importance of species of fish other than dried cod. Mackerel[4] fluctuated widely. Herring was also

---

[1] *S.p.*, 98, 1883.

[2] *S.p.*, 4, 1882. It was reported in 1888 that Halifax had 60 to 70 sailing vessels in the trade but that steamers and telegraphic communications had revolutionized conditions. Violent fluctuations in the West Indian market were checked by a more adequate knowledge of available supplies.

[3] The discovery of the diffusion process in 1860 was followed by marked increase in the production of beet sugar. See G. Martineau, "The statistical aspect of the sugar question" (*Journals* of the Royal Statistical Society, June, 1899, 296 *ff.*).

[4] In the Gulf of St. Lawrence large numbers of vessels engaged in the herring fishery at Bay de Plaisance on the Magdalen Islands. For about 2 or 3 weeks after May 10 the fishing was at its height. "The herring fishing is carried on by means of nets or seines, the latter, which are most generally employed by foreign fishermen, are sometimes a hundred fathoms in length by ten fathoms in depth. With fishing implements of this great magnitude, they sometimes take most extraordinary quantities of fish, and I have been informed by persons worthy of belief that they have seen as many fish as would fill two thousand barrels at one haul of the net." In 1855, 50,000 barrels of herring were taken at Magdalen Islands. "Our fishermen, who do not possess the capital necessary to carry on the fishing on such an extensive scale, make use of nets which they

subject to wide fluctuations but tended to expand in relation
to favourable territory such as the Bay of Fundy.[1]

	Mackerel (barrels)		Herring (barrels)	
	N.S.	N.B.	N.S.	N.B.
1851	100,047	.....	53,200	......
1861	66,108	.....	194,170	......
1871	69,647	2,421	135,266	181,792
1881	120,242	25,272	140,831	263,832

New markets were made available for the fresh product and
the road was opened for the spread of industrialism in
methods of production.

(ii)

Salmon

The establishment of regular steamers between St. John
and Boston led to an expansion of exports of fresh salmon
packed in ice. The extension of the railway to Shediac
tapped the rich salmon areas of the north shore and especially
of the Miramichi and largely converted the pickled salmon
industry into a fresh salmon industry. In 1877 a report on
the Intercolonial Railway stated that: "The trade in salmon
is already large, and what are called 'freezers' are being
erected by private enterprise at many stations on the line,
which enables fresh fish to be placed in all the cities of Canada
and the United States, weekly, throughout the year."[2]

---

set in the Bay and visit each morning for the purpose of removing the fish which
may have been taken during the night" (*S.p.*, 25, 1856). The Americans also
dominated the mackerel-fishery in the Gulf of St. Lawrence. It was estimated
that 500 vessels passed through the Strait of Canso to fish for mackerel but a
failure of the fishery in 1876 reduced the number to 65. Americans were able to
fish in British waters under the Reciprocity Treaty from 1854 to 1866 and, under
the Treaty of Washington of 1870, the Halifax award of 1877 gave an indemnity
to Canada of $5,500,000 which was invested and the interest spent in bounties
and support of the fisheries. See Hon. Wallace Graham, "The fisheries of
North America and the United States fishermen" (*Collections* of the Nova Scotia
Historical Society, XIV, 1-39); *Proceedings of the Halifax commission, 1877;*
C. Lindsey, "The Atlantic fisheries of Canada and the treaty of 1871" (*Canada,
an encyclopedia*, XI, 119-131); H. L. Keenleyside, *Canada and the United States*
(New York, 1929), chapter vii; Sir Robert Falconer, *The United States as a neigh-
bour* (Cambridge, 1925), chapter iii.
    [1]On the production of smoked pickerel and frozen herring in the Bay of
Fundy, see *S.p.*, 5, 1877.
    [2]*S.p.*, 7, 1878. See also M. H. Perley, *Reports on the sea and river fisheries of
New Brunswick* (Fredericton, 1852).

The first shipment of fresh salmon to Great Britain was made in 1879.[1]

(iii)

Sea bass and sturgeon

The effect on the more easily exploited species was disastrous. The sea-bass fishery and the sturgeon fishery on the St. John River were rapidly exhausted. In spite of regulations the catch of sturgeon declined.[2] "In 1880, the catch of this fish reached 602,500 lbs.; in 1881 it fell to 453,450 lbs.; in 1882, only 284,350 were taken; in 1883, 125,280 lbs.; in 1884, 42,450 lbs.; while the catch of 1885 yielded only 26,240 and in 1886 it had dwindled down to 16,264 pounds, a decrease of 97 per cent. in seven years".

(iv)

Oysters

The oyster beds of Prince Edward Island and other parts of the gulf suffered from the effects of digging for mussel mud, but over-fishing which followed higher prices and improved transportation became inevitable. Consequently production of oysters in Prince Edward Island increased from 7,905 barrels in 1876 to the peak of production in the history of the fishery, 57,042 barrels in 1882, declining to 28,204 barrels in 1885.[3]

(v)

Lobster

The lobster-canning industry in the Maritime Provinces followed decline on the Maine and Massachusetts coasts and

---

[1]*S.p.*, 5, 1895. In 1887 the Intercolonial reported that "the traffic in fresh fish to the Upper Provinces has largely increased" (*S.p.*, 8, 1888). In 1889, however, "though the transport of fish, both fresh and salted, shows an increase over that of last year, it is not considered that it has developed to the extent that might have been looked for from the steps taken for its encouragement in the provision of special refrigerator cars and special fast trains, and the concession of low rates" (*S.p.*, 19, 1890).

[2]*S.p.*, 21, 1905.

[3]See J. Stafford, *Conservation of the oyster*; J. A. Matheson, *Oyster fisheries of Prince Edward Island, sea fisheries of Canada* (Ottawa, 1912), 25 *ff.* and 83 *ff.*; Ernest Kemp, Report on Canadian oyster fisheries and oyster culture, *S.p.*, 11a, 1899; also *S.p.*, 39, 1915, 303-306; *Dominion shell fishery commission 1912-13* (Ottawa, 1913); W. A. Found, The oyster fishery on the Atlantic coast, *S.p.*, 22, 1911.

depended on American organization and technique. The total number increased from 44 in 1872 to about 200 in 1880 of which two-fifths of the valuation was controlled by United States firms.[1] Production expanded rapidly from 61,100 cans in 1869 to 10,244,329 cans in 1879 and to its highest point, 17,490,523 cans in 1881. By the end of the period Prince Edward Island, for example, had over 80 canneries costing $2,000 to $3,000 each with an output of $7,000 to $9,000. Each cannery was open for about 4 months and employed on an average 14 fishermen, 10 men, and 15 women.[2] Improvement of steamship connection was followed by the growth of the trade in live lobsters from Yarmouth to Boston beginning about 1878.

(vi)

Other species of fish

The importance of other species of fish was relatively slight. For example, St. John had 125 boats employing 250 men to take 10,000 barrels of alewives valued at $45,000; 50 boats and 100 men to take shad[3] valued at $12,500; and

---

[1]R. H. Williams, *Historical account of the lobster canning industry* (Ottawa, 1930). For a critical review of statistics see *The lobster industry* (Amherst, 1929). See also Report of the Canadian lobster commission 1898, *S.p.*, 11c, 1899.

1881

	Canned lobsters	Fresh lobsters
Nova Scotia	$734,353	$1,400
New Brunswick	813,157	....
Prince Edward Island	1,262,573	....

[2]The effects were shown in the complaints of London buyers who noted "a very serious falling off in quality, some of the goods being absolutely unmerchantable. This arises, we are informed, partly through the multitude of small people preserving lobsters on the coast not understanding their business, and also, partly owing to the fact that last season, for six weeks after the packing season had closed, these small men continued to preserve; we consider the trade has been seriously damaged in consequence. We have never received so many inferior goods as we have this last season. Unless the Canadian Government enforces the law more strictly in regard to closing the canning season at the date legally fixed, we believe that this trade will in a few years become extinct, as there will be no demand. We must say that we think the canned lobster business has degenerated more than any other commodity from Canada with which we are acquainted; and it is very desirable that a considerable improvement should be made in the packing of this article. We would suggest that it should never be preserved without a paper lining in the can, and that nothing but the whole lobster should be packed, no broken pieces, or at any rate not any larger proportion than 10 per cent" (*S.p.*, 2e, 1893). See also Report of the Canadian lobster commission 1898, *S.p.*, 11e, 1899; Report of Commander W. Wakeham—on the lobster industry of the Maritime Provinces and the Province of Quebec, *S.p.*, 22a, 1910; and *Dominion shell fishery commission, 1912-1913* (Ottawa, 1913).

[3]Beginning in June shad were taken in large numbers in Cumberland and Minas basins (*Shad commission, 1908-10*).

45

125 boats and 250 men to take 10,000 hauls of salmon valued at $155,000. Salmon-fishing, lobster-fishing, and smelt-fishing were reported as very profitable at Chatham.

In addition to the derangement of economic life which accompanied the displacement of the sailing vessel by the steamship and the railroad, the fishing industry was subjected to far-reaching changes which included the serious difficulties of their staple product, dried cod,[1] and the shift to the production of other species. The Maritimes were exposed in the fishing industry and in other industries to the revolutions which accompanied the spread of industrialism in the Atlantic basin.

---

[1]The peak of dried cod production (823,484 cwt.) in Nova Scotia came in 1886 and was in part a result of the Fisheries Act of 1868, of the work of the protective fleet in keeping American vessels from Canadian waters, (1870-2), of the lack of employment in other industries during the depression of the seventies, and of the bounties originating in 1882. Decline after 1886 followed the displacement of sailing vessels and the development of inshore fishing with small boats with less reliance on cod, the restriction of markets by tariffs, rise of the fresh fish industry, the demands of new industries for labour, the development of agriculture which weakened domestic demand for dried cod by supplying meat substitutes, and for molasses by supplying butter, and competition from other countries in the foreign market. See R. F. Grant, "The cod fishing in Nova Scotia since Confederation" (M. A. thesis, University of Toronto, 1933).

MINING

1

Coal

The impact of industrialism was shown directly in the expansion of coal-mining. Construction of railways and development of steamship navigation created new demands for coal. The rise of coal-mining[1] coincided roughly with the decline of wooden ship-building. The breaking of the monopoly of the General Mining Association in 1856, and the market provided by the industrialism of the United States, especially during the period of the Reciprocity Treaty and the Civil War,[2] were responsible for an increase in exports from 103,322 tons in 1855 to the highest point of 465,194 tons in 1865. Local consumption increased from 310,352 tons in 1873 to 701,869 tons in 1884. In 1869, 35,630 tons of coal were shipped from Acadian mines to Pictou;[3] in 1871, 75,798 tons; and in 1872, 85,127 tons.

---

[1]See R. Drummond, *Minerals and mining in Nova Scotia* (Stellarton, 1918); R. Brown, *The coal fields and coal trade of the Island of Cape Breton* (London, 1871); also R. Brown, *History of the Island of Cape Breton* (London, 1869), especially 452-464; Duncan Campbell, *Nova Scotia* (Halifax, 1873), 484 *ff.*; A. Heatherington, *Mining industries of Nova Scotia* (London, 1874); H. How, *Mineralogy of Nova Scotia* (Halifax, 1869); *Canadian economics*, 161-189; L. W. Bailey, *Mines and minerals of New Brunswick, 1864*; R. G. Haliburton, *The coal trade of the new dominion* (Halifax, 1868); and appendices to the *Journals and proceedings of the house of assembly of Nova Scotia* and of the *Journals of assembly, New Brunswick* for annual reports on mines.

[2]See E. Forsey, *Economic and social aspects of the Nova Scotia coal industry* (McGill University economic studies), no. 5, 18 *ff.*

[3]The Pictou fields had 6 strata: first 33 feet, second 25 feet, third 11 feet, fourth 5 feet, fifth 2 feet, sixth 2 feet. Spedon described the Albion Mines as "the most important coal fields". Situated about 2 miles from New Glasgow near East River "the company had three pits entering the mines, and the coal is brought to the surface by machinery driven by steam. The lower pit is about 450 feet in perpendicular depth. Part of this section is worked beneath the basis of the river, from which water can immediately be obtained should fire occur in the mine. The Dalhousie pit is the latest opened; its depth is about 400 feet. This section is the most extensively worked at present and can be entered also on foot by a dark winding passage over a quarter of a mile in length. The passage had formerly been a side pit from which the coal had been taken by horses. At length we came to the basis of the perpendicular pit, from which a main tunnel runs parallel with the seam of coal that is being worked. The length of this tunnel or passage is 3,000 yards, with a dip of 45° N., having a fall

Small quantities were "run east for home consumption", 1,294 tons in 1869 and 3,189 tons in 1871; and "run west for home consumption", 4,730 tons in 1869 and 12,578 tons in 1871.   In 1871, 4,759 tons were sent to Halifax for shipment in winter.   In 1872 shipments other than to Pictou totalled 35,976 tons.   Total shipments increased from 41,654 tons in 1869 to 65,226 tons in 1870, to 96,315 tons in 1871, and to 121,103 tons in 1872.   The coal traffic in the United States tended to decline with the imposition of a high duty ($1.25 in 1867 and 75 cents in 1871) in spite of low water-rates which permitted the sale of coal at $2.50 a ton at Boston and $3.00 at New York.

Shipments of coal over the Intercolonial from the Pictou

---

of one foot to every three, this being the position of the coal strata. A railway is laid the entire length of this passage, from which minor branches diverge, leading into sections called *bores* where the miners are at work. The roof is supported by wooden pillars, and partitions of coal left for the purpose. In extracting the coal, the miner has recourse to blasting. The explosion on account of the porous material around only produces a short blunted sound. Each person has fastened to his cap a small inextinguishable lamp which keeps dangling about with the motion of his head. From each of the "bores" the coal cars are taken by horses to the trunk railroad whence they are drawn up the grade to the bottom of the pit or cageway by a cable chain winding upon a cylinder driven by an engine under ground. The empty cars return down the grade by gravitation with furious rapidity, but are regulated by the cable which is also attached to them. The filled cars separately and in turn are placed upon the cages—two frame boxes which are drawn up and let down alternately through the pit by means of a cable winding upon a revolving windlass at the top, also driven by an engine.

The average number of persons employed in connection with the Albion Mines is 600; and a community of over 2,000 is supported from the labor arising from them. About sixty horses are kept under ground drawing the coal-cars to the different stations on the main-track. The foremen or overseers are called *caffars*. Accidents occur occasionally in the mines from foul air, the railway, &c. Every morning before the workmen enter the pit the condition of the air therein is ascertained by a person appointed for the purpose. Mining operations, &c. on the whole are conducted on a very regular and economical system. As each car reaches the top of the pit it is placed upon a wheel-cage, which very ingeniously empties it into other and larger cars under the side of the platform; during the process of which, the larger and smaller coal are separated. The coal is then either taken to the immediate coal-yard, or to the 'Loading Ground' at a distance of six miles, on the East River; whence it is shipped to different ports. During the month of September last, it being the busy season, the amount of coal raised per day from the Albion Mines averaged 900 tons. The number of vessels coaled at the loading ground during that month was 250" (A. L. Spedon, *Rambles among the blue-noses*, 186-195). The Albion Mines had a bad record for fires and loss of life (*S.p.*, 12, 1881; also R. Drummond, *Minerals and mining, Nova Scotia*, 34 *ff.*). See also E. Gilpin, "Coal mining in Pictou County" (Royal Society of Canada, *transactions* ser. 4, II, 1896, 167-181); also G. Patterson, *A history of the County of Pictou* (Montreal, 1877), chapter xviii. On the growth of the organization of labour in coal-mining, see H. A. Logan, *History of trade union organization in Canada* (Chicago, 1928); also on the truck system in the coal-mines of Cape Breton, J. Davidson, *The bargain theory of wages* (New York, 1898), chapter viii.

and Spring Hill[1] Mines (Joggins) to Halifax increased with the development of a port for ocean steamers. Improvement of the Richmond wharves "for coaling vessels of the largest size" was followed by an increase in shipments of coal from 28,326 tons in 1880-1 to 36,836 tons in 1881-2.[2] Low rates also stimulated the movement of coal to the upper provinces by rail, and shipments to Quebec and Chaudière increased from 21,000 tons in 1880-81 to 44,400 tons in 1881-2 and to 51,000 tons in 1882-3.[3]

The rise of industrialism in the St. Lawrence drainage basin and the growth of steam navigation to Montreal[4] which followed the improvement of the St. Lawrence ship channel were factors of first importance to the expansion of the Cape Breton mining area. In 1868 experiments were made in Montreal following a miners' strike in Pennsylvania in using coal from the Gowrie Mine in Cow Bay, Cape Breton. The improvement of a break-water to facilitate the loading of vessels[5] and lower costs facilitated the expansion of trade. In 1873 the harbour-master of Montreal referring to this increasing branch of business stated: "The steamers carrying coals from the Lower Provinces are increasing in size and numbers; some of them were granted special berths, with permission to dump their coals upon the wharves, so as to give them every facility of making as many voyages as possible."[6] The coal trade which flourished through

---

[1] A branch railway was completed from Springhill to Parrsboro in 1876.

[2] S.p., 5, 1880-1; S.p., 5, 1881; S.p., 7, 1882; and S.p., 8, 1883. See statistics of production of coal of Nova Scotian mines in 1884 (Monetary Times, 1883-4, 832, 1171).

[3] S.p., 10, 1884.

[4] Coal as the chief commodity for export was excluded from the Ontario market by the shallow character of the St. Lawrence Canals. "Direct trade between Ontario and the lower ports has no actual existence, and cannot be developed whilst the canal communications above Montreal are so imperfect. . . . The growth of intercolonial trade depends on cheap transit, since the merchandise passing between the Maritime Provinces and Ontario must be of a bulky character requiring large vessels and rapid despatch to be really profitable. When a propeller can go direct with a cargo of coal or other produce of the Eastern Provinces, to Kingston and Toronto, and there get a return freight of flour, barley and other Western produce, intercolonial trade will have entered on a new era" (S.p., 6, 1881).

[5] S.p., 2, 1870.

[6] S.p., 8, 1873. Coal-mining was well established by 1860. 15 new mines were opened in 1858, 19 licences taken out in 1860, and in the same year 319,420 tons of coal raised (59,121 for home consumption, 72,881 to British-American colonies, and 187,506 to the United States). As early as 1862, 66 vessels coaled at Sydney although these mines at that date produced chiefly for domestic consumption.

the return of timber ships from England to Quebec with coal in ballast was displaced by Cape Breton.[1] In 1874, 3 lines of steamers were engaged in the trade of the Maritime Provinces, the Quebec Gulf Port line, the Montreal and Acadian line, and the Mitchell line. The coaling station at Sydney served as a support[2] to the development of ocean steamship navigation to Montreal. "In 1877 a large number of our cargo steamers call at Sydney, C.B. to coal on their homeward voyage."[3] After 1878 shipments increased rapidly.[4]

	Old Mines North Sydney	International Sydney	Cape Breton Pier, Sydney	Totals
1878.....	106,366 tons	14,348 tons	7,347 tons	128,061
1879.....	108,259 "	21,523 "	17,269 "	147,041
1880.....	115,307 "	58,897 "	13,614 "	205,818

In 1882 North Sydney sent 150,000 tons to Canada and in 4 years its exports had increased 144 per cent. (118 per cent. in the St. Lawrence, 26 per cent. in bunkers).[5] Exports to the Province of Quebec increased after the imposition of a duty on American coal (50 cents in 1879, 60 cents in 1880) from 154,118 tons in 1879 to 493,917 tons in 1885.

2

Iron

The iron industry like the coal industry was closely related to the immediate demands of industrialism. At the latter end of the period they were interlocked. Abundant supplies of wood supported the uncertain production of charcoal-iron at Woodstock, New Brunswick, and the success of the Acadia Iron Works at Londonderry which produced about 45,000 tons of pig-iron between 1853 and 1874. The demands of the railroads and of industry led to the establishment of the Coldbrook Rolling Mill in 1873

---

[1]Small vessels brought the coal from Quebec to Montreal and also from the United States (*S.p.*, 8, 1873, and *S.p.*, 6, 1881).

[2]*S.p.*, 1, 1878.

[3]See Report of the select committee on the state of the coal trade and for the promoting of inter-provincial trade, *J.h.c.*, XI, 1877, app. 4.

[4]*S.p.*, 5, 1882.

[5]*S.p.*, 7, 1883.

and the Portland Rolling Mill near St. John, and of the Halifax Iron Works for the production of nails, spikes, bar-iron, ships knees, forgings, and car-axles. The importance of coal to the growth of the iron and steel industry was of basic importance in the establishment of plants at New Glasgow. The Steel Company of Canada, which succeeded the Acadia Iron Works, was shipping in 1877 "pig and merchant bar iron, as well as car wheels. . . in considerable quantities to all parts of Canada".[1] Its success was not conspicuous, however, contrasted with the Nova Scotia Forge Company and the Nova Scotia Steel Company, which, with the advantages of proximity to the Pictou coal-fields and to water-transportation, engaged in the production of car-axles, ships knees, steamship and mill shafts, and, after completion of the steel plant in 1883, of steel plates and bar-spring and machinery steel. By the end of the period production of iron-ore had reached 54,000 tons annually and specialized products had become important.[2]

3

Gypsum

Mining of non-metallic minerals was closely dependent on water-transportation. Coal was dependent in its early stages of development on its accessibility to water-transport as also was gypsum. The latter could be carried from Windsor to New York at $2.25 per ton. In the sixties about 25 ports were engaged in exporting gypsum and by the end of the period exports totalled over 50,000 tons. Mines at Windsor and Hillsborough were of first importance. The existence of the non-resistant formations[3] near the seaboard, the ease of exploiting large deposits of non-metallic ores, cheap transportation by water, and the increasing demands of industrialism in the United States were factors contributing to the emphasis on such commodities as coal and gypsum.

---

[1]*S.p.*, 7, 1878.
[2]See W. J. Donald, *The Canadian iron and steel industry*; J. H. Bartlett, *The manufacture, consumption and production of iron, steel, and coal in the Dominion of Canada* (Montreal, 1885).
[3]Douglas Johnson, *New England-Acadia shoreline* (New York, 1925).

4

Gold

The resistant formations which tended to be located at greater distance from the shore line, and which involved higher costs of exploration and exploitation were developed chiefly in relation to the precious metals.[1] But even with gold, placer-mining was of first importance and quartz-mining was developed in its early stages at points near the sea. The discovery of gold provided a short but powerful stimulus to economic activity. Moreover, quartz-mining with its difficulties provided an experimental background[2] which was

---

[1]Other mineral developments were of slight importance—for example, a manganese mine employed 20 hands at St. Martin in 1882. Grindstones were exported in considerable quantities from Shediac and Gloucester County.

[2]"As soon as the intelligence of a new gold-discovery is received at 'head quarters,' a deputy gold commissioner and surveyor are sent to inspect, or rather, '*prospect*' the grounds, which, if bearing an auriferous character, are immediately laid off into lots, or areas.

Area No. 1 is 150 feet along a '*leade*,' by 250 feet across; No. 2, is 200 feet by 300; No. 3 is 300 feet by 500; No. 4 is 450 feet by 500, &c.

These areas are leased to any person or persons who become subject to the conditions of the act relating to the gold-fields. The rents per annum of these lots: for No. 1, $40; No. 2, $80; No. 3, $160; and for No. 4, $240; one quarter of the whole sum to be paid down, the remainder in three equal instalments, each of which to be paid at the end of every four months. As one man is incapable of operating alone working companies are generally formed, each person being an equal sharer in the expenditures and profits. The first thing that is generally done is to '*prospect*.' This simply means, to investigate the grounds for a good '*leade*,' or the indication of a lot bearing an auriferous character, which privilege is allowed on any of the areas not taken up.

Having procured a '*claim*', they erect a house, furnish it, and provide themselves with such other articles as are essentially indispensable, including a general assortment of mining and cooking utensils, &c. One of the party is appointed house-manager, and the others begin mining operations. A ditch is then cut across the lot through the surface soil, by which means the quartz veins are discovered. On the *leade* that assumes the most prolific appearance they commence sinking a shaft or pit.

When gold was first discovered in Nova Scotia the inexperienced began mining on the top of the leade at the surface of the ground, extracting the quartz in ditch-like form; but at present the shafting and undermining system is universally established. A shaft or pit, averaging from ten to twelve feet square at the mouth, is sunk through the solid rock to the depth of from thirty to sixty feet, the quartz being carefully separated from the other material,— all of which are brought to the top by means of a windlass. During this dangerous and laborious process, mining operations are frequently impeded by water dropping from the porous surface deposits, or filtering through the crevices of the rocks, &c. During the night, and the Sabbath also, when mining operations are suspended, a considerable quantity of water accumulates in the pits. Subsequently an hour or two are frequently spent in pumping it out, either by hand or horse power. When the shaft has attained its intended depth, the process of tunnelling along the '*leade*' then commences. By this subterraneous system the miner is enabled to perform more with less labour and expense as none of the refuse material re-

invaluable to the later development of mining in Canada. In 1861 a rush[1] followed the discovery of placer gold at Ovens. Vessels arrived with men and supplies from Halifax and American ports. In the same year discoveries of quartz gold[2] were made at Sherbrooke on Goldmouth. In June and July, 1862, 3 small steamers plying between Halifax and Sherbrooke brought in 5,000 people. 4 large crushing mills were established and over 15,000 miners employed. As a result of this and other developments, the production of

---

quires to be taken out. He allows it to accumulate beneath his feet; and it thus supplies the place of a scaffold in enabling him to prosecute his work upwards. For several weeks or perhaps months after a mine was discovered, extracting the gold was performed by beating the quartz to a powder with a hammer, then washing the material with water mixed with mercury so as to extract and amalgamate the gold. But now that three or four quartz mills are erected at each of the principal gold-fields, the miner is thus enabled without any inconvenience, to have his quartz crushed whenever he pleases. The quartz mill or 'crusher' as it is frequently termed, is generally driven by a steam-engine of from ten to fifteen horse-power, and is placed within a large building erected for the purpose. The 'crusher' is comprised of two or more stamp batteries, each of which consists of a large metal box, containing from three to six long iron stampers, weighing from six to eight hundred pounds each. By a revolving axle, having projecting pins and suspended at some height above the batteries, these stampers are lifted up alternately by these catch-pins, which, in the act of revolving, allow them to slip off, and they fall by their own weight upon the quartz, when it has entered through a hopper into the box, into which a continual stream of water is running from a pipe and thus carrying off all the pulverized ingredients from the battery, through a screened aperture in the opposite side of the box—thence passing over galvanized plates, into large iron vessels containing from fifty to eighty pounds of quicksilver. These contain smaller vessels, which are kept in circular motion, and in these also are revolving cylinders. The whole apparatus is termed the 'amalgamators' which have a resemblance to the prophet Ezekiel's vision of a wheel within a wheel. Each battery has a set of these amalgamators. By this process the gold is separated from the powdery liquid by the attractive affinity of the mercury. The amalgam is then put into a retort, and the quicksilver is driven off, leaving the pure gold in a congealed mass. It not unfrequently happens that those amalgamators become insufficient to perform the work satisfactorily; but this arises chiefly from the ingredients of other metals with which the quartz is impregnated, in counteracting the attraction of the gold and mercury. The amount of quartz crushed by one mill per day is from four to twelve tons; the amount depending chiefly upon the size and power of the crushers. The average cost per ton paid for crushing is $6. The amount of gold extracted from each ton depends upon the quality of the quartz; the average quantity may be estimated at four ounces; each ounce having an equivalent in value of about $18½ or $19. . . .

From the great demand for domestic articles and sawn timber at the mines, merchants and mill proprietors were enabled to realize immense profits during the heat and hurry of the new discoveries; but the golden season to this class was only a short though profitable one" (Spedon, *Rambles among the blue-noses*, 170 ff.).

[1]See M. B. DesBrisay, *History of the County of Lunenberg* (Toronto, 1895), 137-8, for a valuable diary.

[2]For details on gold-mining see the invaluable work, W. Malcolm, *Gold fields of Nova Scotia* (Ottawa, 1929).

gold in the province increased from 7,275 ounces in 1862 to 27,583 ounces in 1866, and declined to 9,140 ounces in 1874. It was estimated that frcm 1862 to 1885, 389,219 ounces were extracted. At the latter date "the almost total discontinuance of work by companies and the introduction of the system of working the mines by tribute", "tributors" were reported.[1] In 1879 the inflow of American capital brought a return of company operation. The difficulties which had accompanied over-expansion, careless planning, and "picking the eyes out of the mine" or "selecting all the rich material to secure a few high yields" were overcome by the development of more scientific mining. The number of ounces recovered reached 22,203 in 1885.

---

[1]D. Campbell, *Nova Scotia*, 496-8; also E. Gilpin, "Results of past experience in gold mining in Nova Scotia" (*Canadian economics*, 181-188).

INDUSTRY[1]

1

Effect of Improved Transportation

The revolution in transport which involved the decline of wooden sailing ships and the introduction of the railroad and the iron steamship had profound effects on industry. Decline in ship-building was accompanied by a decline in numerous subsidiary industries. The Maritimes felt the effects of improved transportation more seriously than the upper provinces chiefly because their basic industries of shipping and ship-building felt the impact more directly. Not only did improved transportation in the railway and steamship injure the shipping industry and the numerous subsidiary industries, but it brought surviving industries into competition with older established industries in the upper provinces. The effects were felt at a later date and consequently with greater severity. The report for 1885 stated that the disastrous fire in St. John on June 20, 1877, the decline in ship-building, and the national policy had serious effects on the industries in that locality. In the City and County of St. John:

> Prior to that time [*June 20, 1877*] industries of various kinds had been struggling into life. A small cotton warp factory was being cautiously worked; shoe factories were cropping up; rolling mills, foundries, machine shops, rope-walks, and what not, were fighting hard for position in the busy life of the place; but the fight with the competition from the United States, superadded to the ordinary competition from Dominion communities, was too much for them. . . .
> The total number of persons employed all over the city and county of St. John[2] at the various industries, with the exceptions already noted, was 8,555 in 1878, and 8,562 in 1884. The total weekly wages paid to the operatives in the respective years amounted to $63,749.16 in 1878 and $61,980.00 in 1884.

---

[1]See *The Maritimes since Confederation* (Ottawa, 1926), chapter iii.
[2]See D. R. Jack, *History of the City and County of St. John* (St. John, 1883), chapter xi.

715

On the other hand, the railroad contributed directly and indirectly to the survival of old industries which could be adapted to new demands and to the establishment of new industries. The development of coal-mining and of the iron and steel industry was in part the result of construction of railroads. At Moncton the government work-shops employed from 400 to 600 men in constructing railway-cars.[1] Within 10 years its population increased from that of "a squalid village" to 7,000 in 1882.[2] "Every manufacturing establishment is working full time and can't supply the demand." 50 to 80 new houses were built annually, employing "over 200 carpenters, besides masons, painters, bricklayers, etc." The difficulties of St. John paralleled the prosperity of Moncton. Machine-shops in connection with the railway and the steamship repair-shops, employing large numbers of men, were located at Halifax and Dartmouth.

Indirectly improved ocean navigation and transportation by railroad brought cheaper raw materials and cheaper finished products to compete with existing industries. Transportation by water favoured the import and export of raw materials in bulk, and transportation by land the importation of manufactured products. As in agriculture so in industry, the Maritime Provinces were forced to specialize on commodities in which they had geographic and other advantages.

2

The Sugar Industry

Efficient and regular transportation with the West Indies was followed by the growth of the sugar industry. At Moncton a plant with a daily capacity of 250 barrels of refined sugar began operations in December, 1880, and within 6 months was responsible for the development of over 7,700 tons of traffic in raw and refined sugar and 3,000 tons of coal.[3] This plant, including a barrel factory, employed about 200 men and consumed 20 tons of coal per day.[4] The

[1]*S.p.*, 11, 1882.
[2]*S.p.*, 14, 1883.
[3]*S.p.*, 7, 1882.
[4]*S.p.*, 11, 1882.

Halifax refinery with a capacity of 600 barrels began operations in May, 1881, and in 2 months exported 1,500 tons over the Intercolonial Railway. This refinery, from its position, necessarily receives its supply of raw sugar by water, and no doubt, a considerable portion of its output finds its destination in the same way, without passing over the railway. The largest portion of the coal used, however, has hitherto passed over the Intercolonial.[1] By 1885 Halifax had 2 additional refineries.[2] On the other hand, Maritime refineries were exposed to competition in the sugar markets of the world. Decline in the price of sugar which had serious effects on the market for dried fish also had serious effects on the refining industry.

3

The Cotton Industry

The railroad[3] stimulated the construction of cotton factories but it also brought these factories into competition with imported goods. The new mill at Moncton (1881) was built at a cost of $35,000, nearly two-thirds of the machinery being imported from England and the United States. It was expected to employ 300 hands. In the same year a new cotton mill of 30,000 spindles was erected at Milltown. About 400 people were employed in construction and as many were expected to be employed when the mill was in operation.[4] Unfortunately the report on the effects of the national policy in 1885 was forced to state:

> This industry has for some time been in rather an unhealthy condition. The decline is due to a number of causes. First, to the failure of certain important crops for a couple of years, and to the depression in the lumber trade; secondly, to the miscalculation of manufacturers as to the consuming powers of the world's cotton centres in a time of short crops and

---

[1] *S.p.*, 7, 1882.
[2] *S.p.*, 37, 1885. Recovery was in evidence in 1886-7, and shipments on the Intercolonial totalled, from Halifax, 88,996 barrels; and from Moncton, 56,992 barrels.
[3] In 1882 the chief superintendent of the Intercolonial reported that: "A number of manufacturing establishments have been erected near the railway, the principal being glass-works and steel works at New Glasgow, and cotton factories at Windsor, Halifax, Moncton and St. John. All these works are connected with the railway by sidings" (*S.p.*, 8, 1883).
[4] *S.p.*, 11, 1882.

general business depression; thirdly, to the large sameness in
the cotton product of the Dominion, and the shortsightedness
of usually shrewd men, in overlooking the variety requirements when taking advantage of the stimulating influence of
the tariff; fourthly, to the too great dependence placed upon
special centres to distribute the manufactured goods, and the
inadequate efforts to secure more extended markets; fifthly,
to the high price ruling for raw cotton, due to the shortness
of the cotton crop of the past year or so, and the brisk demand
for raw cotton by producers who, blind to a state of facts with
which they should be familiar, kept glutting the market and
burning their fingers; and lastly, to the depression in trade
generally all over the world.[1]

4

Other Industries

Industries closely linked to the demands of population,
to sources of raw material peculiar to the Maritimes, and
to the demands of the basic industries were in the strongest
position to survive. The tanning industry and the woollen
industry were supported by the livestock industry. Foundries were in evidence at such centres as Amherst, Truro,
Pictou, Yarmouth, and Halifax and were engaged in the
production of steam engines, saw and grist mills, stoves,
ploughs, ship-castings. A brass foundry at Halifax was
engaged in the manufacture of steam and gas fittings.
The Starr Manufacturing Company established a reputation in the manufacture of skates. A cordage plant operated
successfully at Dartmouth in relation to the demand of
shipping. Halifax exported quantities of ice to the West
Indies. The increasing importance of coal[2] hastened the

---

[1]S.p., 37, 1885.
[2]Sales of coal in the Maritime Provinces.

1873	310,352
1874	335,754
1875	342,239
1876	374,456
1877	405,777
1878	438,829
1879	407,742
1880	497,497
1881	555,252
1882	662,665
1883	687,155
1884	701,869
1885	646,096

shift from water to steam power. On the other hand, insufficient capital, deficiency in management, and heavy municipal taxes were held responsible in part for the difficulties of Maritime industry.

5

Trade between Canada and the Maritimes

Completion of the Intercolonial and development of ocean steamship traffic to Montreal stimulated trade between Canada and the Maritimes. Before the Intercolonial had been completed it was stated that:

> The through business between Quebec, Montreal and the west and the Lower Provinces, along the line of the Intercolonial Railway, has largely exceeded expectations and is steadily increasing. This trade, it is now clear, is to be a steadily growing one, not only in provisions, but in general merchandise, which used to be so largely purchased in the United States. This trade is now, by the aid of the railways, being largely diverted to Canadian markets.[1]

In the report on manufactures in 1874 it was noted that Edward Gurney, stove-dealer at Toronto, sent "considerable of our goods"; William Muir, wholesale clothier of Montreal, out of a total trade of $120,000 to $150,000, estimated that "not less than one-third of my own trade is with Nova Scotia and New Brunswick"; while William Chaplin of St. Catharines sent probably $18,000 to $20,000 of agricultural implements to the Maritime Provinces. In 1876 Frost and Wood sent about $12,000 of implements by boat to Pictou. Cossitts Agricultural Works at Guelph manufactured fanning mills, lawn-mowers, plows, and turnip-sowers chiefly for Ontario but with improved transportation large quantities were exported to the Maritimes. In 1882 the Waterous Engine Works of Brantford sold in New Brunswick and Nova Scotia 25 portable steam engines and 4 grist mills. Knitted goods were exported from Guelph first to St. John. "The people of Halifax were so sore about Confederation that they would not look at our goods although they were cheap." Clothing establishments and

---

[1] *S.p.*, 7, 1878.

boot and shoe industries in Moncton employed 220 hands in 1881, but in 1885 it was stated that:

The clothing trade is affected injuriously by the general depression, and to a very considerable extent. The purchasing power of their usual markets is curtailed, and Ontario and Quebec dealers are forced to throw upon a tardy market competitive goods at low prices.

The boot and shoe business in New Brunswick and Nova Scotia is not so flourishing as in some former years. The general depression has retarded its progress, and over-production, which gives rise to keener competition, has cut into prices.[1]

---

[1]*S.p.*, 37, 1885. See G. J. Marr, "The effect of Confederation on the trade of the Maritime Provinces" (M. A. thesis, University of Toronto, 1918), in which it is argued that the national policy had serious effects. In 1861 New Brunswick imports of £1,238,133 sterling included boots and shoes, $101,967; haberdashery, $1,271,180; hardware, $153,912; coffee, 112,219 pounds; tea, 653,288 pounds; molasses, 880,945 gallons; sugar, 2,548,620 pounds; spirits, 263,417 gallons. In the total imports were included $1,712,282 from the United Kingdom, $296,570 from Nova Scotia (partly English imports *viâ* Halifax and Windsor), and $3,014,736 from the United States. Of these imports a relatively small quantity was secured from Canada. Exports to Canada increased from $317,148 in 1858 to $478,130 in 1861 (in the latter year Nova Scotia supplying $280,495 and Newfoundland $119,233), and imports from Canada increased from $960,428 to $1,030,939. In 1861 exports from the Maritimes were 1.15 per cent. of total exports and imports were 2.84 per cent. of total imports (*S.p.*, 14, 1863; also S. P. Day, *English America*, I, 318-9). In the seventies it was estimated that Ontario and Quebec exported about $10,000,000 of goods to the Maritimes and imported about $2,000,000, chiefly coal, fish, and gypsum. In 1882 exports to the Maritimes were over $20,000,000. An estimate for 1884, however, gives $11,440,000 (flour $2,750,000; boots, shoes, rubber, $2,000,000; textiles, $4,000,000), and imports from Maritimes, $4,271,332 (sugar $1,695,722). See Report . . . interprovincial trade, *J.h.c.*, XVII, 1883, app. 4; Appendices of the *Journals and proceedings of the house of assembly of Nova Scotia*; and of the *Journals of the assembly, New Brunswick*, for statistics on trade and reports on trade and manufactures; J. C. Hemmeon "The British North American provinces before Confederation—trade and tariffs" (*Facts and factors in economic history*, Cambridge, 1932, 328-338).

CREDIT AND MONEY

1

Financing of Railroads

In the Maritimes as in Upper Canada, construction of railways linking up the waterways, involved reliance on government support. By 1858 New Brunswick had a total debt of £864,364 currency (£706,800 funded debt and 157,564 floating debt) which had been chiefly incurred in construction of railways. In 1860 Nova Scotia had a debt of $4,901,305 also chiefly a result of expenditures on railways. To June 30, 1867, Nova Scotia had spent[1] on railways, $6,292,028 (145 miles); New Brunswick, $4,761,979 (341 miles); and Prince Edward Island (1874), $3,235,550, and the debts assumed by the federal government totalled for Nova Scotia, $9,188,756; New Brunswick, $7,000,000; Prince Edward Island, $4,927,060. The problem of revenue was not a driving force[2] toward Confederation as in the united

[1]*S.p.*, 8, 1869.

[2]See *Province of Nova Scotia: A submission of its claims with respect to Maritime disabilities within Confederation as presented to the royal commission* (Halifax, n.d., July 21, 1926), 1-13. See also a protest against Confederation by A. W. McLelan on behalf of Nova Scotia (*S.p.*, 9, 1869) stating that Nova Scotia imported "more dutiable goods per head . . . than any other province", averaging $39.50 in 1866-7 as contrasted with $20.00 in Canada. A comparison of the income available for the purchase of goods from exports in 5 principal industries was as follows:

"Branches of Industry	Value in Canada Pop. 2,507,647	Per Head	Value in N.S. Pop. 330,857	Per Head
Agriculture	$14,259,225	$5.66	$786,526	$2.37
Mines	558,306	.22	658,257	1.98
Sea	833,646	.33	3,094,449	9.35
Forest	11,012,363	4.36	767,136	2.31
Shipbuilding, 1863	3,000,000	1.19	2,000,000	6.06
		11.76		22.07

You may safely assume as a rule, that our people, mainly engaged in Fishing, Mining and Shipbuilding, will import more largely than yours, differing so much in geographical position, occupation and habits. As Confederation gives Free Trade with Canada in manufactured goods, part of our wants will be supplied there, but in many cases at as high a cost to the consumer as if imported elsewhere under a ten per cent. tariff, the only benefit being to the Canadian Manu-

provinces.   In 1858 New Brunswick received in import duties
£168,726 and in railway impost, £24,634. While Nova
Scotia's expenditure increased from $423,742 in 1851 to
$852,133 in 1860, revenue increased from $433,120 to
$870,055. A relatively low tariff[1] of 10 per cent. in Nova
Scotia and of 12½ per cent. in New Brunswick with an extensive trade was in the main adequate.

In addition to shouldering the debt, largely a result of
railroads, the dominion became responsible for recurring
deficits which were chiefly the result of competition from
water-transport. Since the railways were essentially competitors with the waterways and were dependent on an
economy built up in relation to the waterways, their completion involved, in the first place, depreciation through
obsolescence of water-transport and, in the second place,
low returns and deficits in competition with water-transport.
The Maritime Provinces were directly involved in the first
result and the Canadian government in the second. The
Prince Edward Island Railway reported that "these vessels
have carried at very low rates and therefore railway transport
has had to be fixed at low rates."[2]   The necessity of building

facturer."   The tariff and taxes were increased to Nova Scotia.   While released
from the payment of interest on $8,000,000, a total of $126,213, Nova Scotia was
obliged to pay a higher tariff, new taxes, and to stand a reduction of her average
sum for local services of over $200,000.   Moreover, the act allowed Canada
$62,500,000 or $24.92 per head; New Brunswick, $7,000,000 or $27.77 per head;
and Nova Scotia, $8,000,000 or $24.17 per head.   On the basis of income from
customs and excise Canada should only have been allowed $59,200,000 in 1866
as contrasted with $8,000,000 allowed to Nova Scotia, and allowing for the in-
crease in tariff to Nova Scotia after Confederation only $50,000,000 should be
given to Canada, or if $62,500,000 to Canada then $10,000,000 to Nova Scotia.
Moreover, it was claimed that against the total of $62,500,000 Canada had but
$58,153,122 assets, of which over $30,000,000 yielded no return and the remainder
about three-fourths per cent.   Nova Scotia had assets in lighthouses, harbours,
piers, and roads and bridges equivalent to Canada in relation to population.
"That is, we have public property . . . representing our debt equal by population to
all of yours yielding a return, leaving our railways and some other public property
in your hands without an equivalent."   Railways and public buildings increased
the public debt from $678,835 to nearly $9,000,000.   "In assuming eight millions
of this debt you have, as we claim, taken our railways and many other public
works without giving a return."   While the railroads had not paid interest, the
opening of the line to Pictou tapped trade to Canada and the coal-fields, the
Windsor and Annapolis opened new territory, and the Halifax to Truro line
constituted part of the Intercolonial.   In the main these contentions were
conceded in the arrangement which gave "Better terms" (*S.p.*, 9, 1869).
    [1]S. J. McLean, *The tariff history of Canada* (Toronto, 1895), 7-8; also
E. Porritt, *Sixty years of protection in Canada 1846-1907* (London, 1908).
    [2]*S.p.*, 6, 1877.

stretches of line with substantial roadbed to handle through traffic between important centres in the Maritime Provinces precluded the possibility of gradual construction and necessitated the immediate expenditure of large sums which were available chiefly by governmental support. The basic dependence of the Maritimes on transportation by water delayed the development of railroads and necessitated dependence on governmental finance. In Prince Edward Island a long stretch of line was forced to depend on the slow growth of agricultural resources, and in 1884 Collingwood Schreiber reported that:

> During the greater part of the year the business is very small, the regular trains run very light. It is only during the autumn months while the movement of grain continues that any considerable amount of traffic offers itself. For about six weeks the rolling stock, almost idle for the rest of the year is taxed to its uttermost capacity.[1]

It is difficult to say whether the sections of line built by New Brunswick and Nova Scotia, which were merged in the Intercolonial Railway, would have been more successful than the Prince Edward Island Railway. The Intercolonial fulfilled the voice of the prophets and continued to register deficits.

2

After Confederation

After Confederation the Maritime Provinces received subsidies in lieu of former receipts from the tariff and provincial finance became subject to the problems of a rigid financial structure. The effects of the straight jacket[2] were shown in the difficulties of the provinces and in their attempts to secure better terms.[3] These difficulties were

---

[1]See D. R. Cowan, "A history of the Intercolonial and Prince Edward Island Railways of Canada." The minister of railways stated in 1910: "It is not fair to expect . . . that the revenue account of the Prince Edward Island railway will ever balance. . . . Parliament must be prepared to run the railway for the accommodation of the people and to take out of the Consolidated Revenue fund whatever deficit there may be."

[2]See J. A. Maxwell, "A financial history of Nova Scotia" (Doctorate thesis, Harvard University).

[3]See *Report of the royal commission on Maritime claims* (Ottawa, 1926); A. W. Boos, *The financial arrangements between the provinces and the dominion* and *The Maritime Provinces since Confederation*, chapter vii; also on P.E.I., *S.p.*, 56, 1897.

accentuated by the depression of the seventies and its effects on the lumber industry and on shipping and by the revolution in Maritime life which accompanied the decline of wooden sailing vessels in the face of competition from railroads and iron steamships. Increase in the tariff[1] created further complaints by providing protection to Canadian industries in the Maritime market and by raising the price of raw materials for Maritime industry. In some measure it enabled Canada to shift the burden of railway deficits in the Maritimes to Maritime shoulders. Attempts to guard Maritime interests by appointing finance ministers from that area were of slight avail.[2] The compromise tariff[3] of

---

[1]Confederation, the tariff, and competition with improved transport by rail and water were blamed in turn. The committee on trade and manufactures reported in 1870: "That your committee has had nothing brought to their notice in connection with the interests usually under the consideration of similar committees appointed previous to the passage of the British North America Act; and your committee cannot avoid expressing their regret that the important interests in relation to the trade commerce and industry of the country has been withdrawn from their consideration by the provisions of the said act" (*Journal of assembly, Nova Scotia*, 1870, app. 31).

[2]See George E. Foster, "Sketch of Canadian financial history" (*Canada, an encyclopedia of the country*, V, 301 *ff.*).

[3]A strong petition dated Halifax, January 15, 1868, asked that corn, corn meal, and rye flour should be admitted duty free partly on account of "very great distress . . . owing to the partial failure of the fisheries in certain localities and a total failure of both fisheries and crops in some districts" (*S.p.*, 86, 1867-8). On March 18, 1868, merchants of St. John petitioned that "the tariff now in force is in many respects, very unacceptable to the people of New Brunswick and injurious to various branches of Provincial industry." Admitting the necessity of providing a revenue they suggested a specific duty on wines "including champagne and other sparkling wines in wood and bottle" of 25 cents a gallon and 20 per cent. *ad valorem*, that wine and spirits in ordinary wine bottles pay only on the contents, say 5 bottles to the gallon, that beer and porter pay 10 cents a gallon, brandy, $1.00 per gallon proof, that alcohol pay an excise duty of 70 cents per gallon, that the import duty on spirits "be regulated with regard to strength, that is when under proof by Syke's hydrometer", that all packages including bottles be free of duty, that the duty on dried fruits be raised from 15 to 25 per cent. *ad valorem*, and that oranges and lemons be charged 15 per cent. *ad valorem*, that 2½ per cent. *ad valorem* be charged on all iron except rail and boiler plate, and that all anchors, chains, and cordage be charged the same duty, and that printed books with the exception of bibles be charged five per cent. Increased revenue from these sources should be used to offset declines from recommended reductions. They asked that grain, bread-stuffs, bran, and horse-feed be admitted free of duty, that printing paper and printing materials be admitted free, that newspaper postage be abolished, that the duty on molasses be 2 cents per gallon and 10 per cent. *ad valorem*, that all raw materials for manufactures be admitted free, that "drawbacks on exportation should apply not only to articles exported in original packages and condition, but also to the products of manufactures from goods on which duty has been paid", that original invoices be returned to importers and not at the custom house, that "the practice of sending every tenth package to warehouse for examination" be abolished, that duties should "be paid on the net amount of invoices, that is, upon the actual first

15 per cent. which prevailed from 1867 to 1874 was followed by a tariff of 17½ per cent. from 1874-78 and, after the completion of the Intercolonial, by a tariff of 20 per cent. under the national policy.[1]

In spite of readjustments which gave an additional debt of $1,807,720, or a total of $8,807,720 of debt, from New Brunswick to the dominion, the provincial debt in 1895 totalled $2,912,986, represented in part by $2,759,000 of provincial debentures of which $2,003,000 had been incurred for the construction of railways. In Nova Scotia $2,343,059 of debt were added to the dominion, making a total of $11,531,615. In spite of this adjustment, gross debt increased to $1,137,818 in 1885 chiefly for the construction of roads, railroads, and bridges.[2] The weakness of municipal government placed heavier loads on the provincial governments.[3]

3

Local Debt

The steamship[4] hastened concentration on strategically located ports and determined the terminus of railway lines built to act as feeders. Improved transportation consequently facilitated the growth of metropolitan centres and particularly of St. John and Halifax. Population in those centres increased as follows.

	1861	1871	1881
Halifax	25,026	29,582	36,100
St. John	27,312	41,325	41,353

cost of the goods and not upon the face of the invoice", that pitch-pine plank for purposes of ship-building be admitted free of duty, that canvas of all kinds, linen and cotton, duck and sail cloth be subject to a duty of 2½ per cent., that "felt of all kinds whether for hats, boots, steam packing for machinery or otherwise" and hat plushes, shoe threads, machine threads, silk twist, and sewing silks be subject to a duty of 5 per cent., and that the policy of admitting articles used in ship-building and other manufactures duty free be consistently followed (*S.p.*, 86, 1867-8).

[1]See S. J. McLean, *The tariff history of Canada*, 10 *ff.*

[2]See J. R. Perry, *Public debts in Canada* (University of Toronto studies, history and economics, I), 50 *ff.*; also financial statistics of the provincial governments in Canada, dominion bureau of statistics.

[3]See W. Murray, *Local government in the Maritime Provinces* (University of Toronto studies, II), 27 *ff.*.

[4]The demand for larger vessels was indicated in such problems as related to the unloading of ballast. Harbour masters were forced to introduce and enforce regulations prohibiting the dumping of ballast. Halifax harbour was particularly endangered (*S.p.*, 4, 1874).

The demands for capital which followed the growth of larger centres were shown in part in the growth of local debt. Incorporation was an indication of the necessity of borrowing. In Nova Scotia, Pictou and Dartmouth were incorporated in 1873, Truro and New Glasgow in 1875, Windsor in 1878, Parrsboro in 1884, Lunenburg, Sydney, and North Sydney in 1885, and Kentville in 1888; and in New Brunswick, Woodstock in 1856, Portland and St. Stephen in 1871, Moncton and Milltown in 1873, Bathurst in 1885, Maysville in 1886, and Campbellton in 1888. The net debt of St. John increased from $654,367 in 1868 to $1,258,303 in 1880 and to $2,733,702 in 1890—chiefly incurred in the construction of water-works, sewage system, street improvements, and wharves. The net debt of Halifax increased from $937,300 in 1868 to $1,699,401 in 1885. Charlottetown had a debt of $111,806 in 1888.

4

Capital and Credit

The financial institutions of the Maritimes were strongly entrenched prior to the beginning of the period and capital had accumulated from profits in the staple industries and in ship-building. Institutions for the handling of long-term securities occupied a position of relatively slight importance. Corporations[1] were less conspicuous than in Canada as a result of small-scale industry. Banking had developed over a long period in relation to the peculiar demands of Maritime industries. Merchants had developed facilities for trade and credit over a wide area. In the lumber industry[2] credit was supplied through firms established in Great Britain; in the fishing industry Jersey firms supplied credit in the Gaspé area; and in other industries banks and merchants occupied an important position. Mining developed in relation to capital from Great Britain, the United States, and from local sources.

---

[1]See reports of the provincial secretary, *Journals of the house of assembly of New Brunswick and Nova Scotia.*
[2]See John Rankin, *A history of our firm* (Liverpool, 1921).

5

Banks and Banking

The decline of ship-building during the depression of the seventies placed a severe strain on financial institutions. Local capital invested in ships and ship-building vanished.[1] Nova Scotia's financial history had not been marred by the failure of a bank prior to 1873 but the difficulties of the lumber industry in that year involved the failure of the Bank of Liverpool and the Bank of Acadia. Failure of the fishing industry in Prince Edward Island in 1877, 1879, and 1882 accentuated the difficulties created by the ship-building industry and the depression and led to the failure of the Bank of Prince Edward Island in 1881 and the absorption of the Union Bank of Prince Edward Island by the Bank of Nova Scotia in 1883.[2] "Indeed so severe was the depression and so considerable the losses that the operations of the banks of these provinces, taken in the aggregate, produced a net return for the ten years ending with 1886, of only about four per cent. per annum on the total capital employed."[3]

The difficulties of the weaker banks in the outlying centres dependent on ship-building paved the way for increasing control of the stronger banks in the metropolitan

[1]As early as 1870 New Brunswick sold about one-half of her tonnage annually on the English market and placed the remainder in the carrying trade on the owner's account and at about the same date Nova Scotia sent about 40 per cent. abroad for sale. The effects of decline were obvious. "I can recollect visiting a locality in which I was informed that the recent loss of a ship had forced the sale of their farms on ten well-to-do men who had been bitten by the prevailing mania and had mortgaged their farms to build a ship which was lost on the first voyage" (*Canadian economics*, 94-5).
[2]*S.p.*, 8, 1883.
[3]*History of the Bank of Nova Scotia, 1832-1900* (n.p., n.d.), 44 ff. See also R. M. Breckenridge, *The Canadian banking system, 1817-90* (Toronto, 1894), 159 ff.; Victor Ross, *A history of the Canadian Bank of Commerce*, I, chapters ii-iii; *J.h.c.*, 1869, app. I; also on savings banks in the Maritimes, T. D. Tims, "Dominion government savings banks" (*Canadian economics*, 259 ff.).

Dun Wiman and Company's list of failures for Canada

	Number	Liabilities
1873	994	12,334,191
1874	966	7,696,765
1875	1968	28,843,967
1876	1728	25,517,991
1877	1890	25,510,147
1878	1615	23,152,262
1879	634	11,648,697

centres dependent on steam navigation. Moreover, banking legislation brought the financial institutions of the Maritimes into line with those of the united provinces. The severity of the blow sustained by the economic upheaval of the Maritime Provinces left the field open for penetration by the banks of the upper provinces or necessitated the migration of the stronger banks to the St. Lawrence basin. The difficulties of industry and agriculture which followed improved transportation to the St. Lawrence, and increasing competition from Canadian products, were accentuated by the problem of securing adequate supplies of capital.

6

Currency

Money was also made uniform with Canada and facilitated the growth of trade. In 1859 Nova Scotia[1] enacted legislation making dollars and cents optional and, in 1860, compulsory. At Confederation it was provided that 73 cents of Canadian currency should be made the equivalent of 75 cents of Nova Scotian currency. New Brunswick made dollars and cents optional in 1852 and compulsory in 1860. Both provinces issued subsidiary coinage in the latter year. The dominion system of currency was not adopted in Prince Edward Island until 1881. Improvement in transportation hastened the penetration of a money economy but it was not until a later date that the evils of the truck system at the coal-mines of Cape Breton, and in the fishing industry at Gaspé,[2] were forced to yield to the full effects of direct contact with the outside world.

---

[1]H. A. Fleming, "Halifax currency" (*Collections* of the Nova Scotia Historical Society, XX, 111-137); R. W. McLachlan, "Annals of the Nova Scotia currency" (Royal Society of Canada *transactions*, X, section II, 1892); also P. N. Breton, *Illustrated history of coins and tokens relating to Canada* (Montreal, 1914) showing variety of coins issued by private firms for both the Maritimes and Canada.

[2]"The fishermen were irritated at the treatment received from certain of the agents and clerks of the merchants, who had annoyed them and members of their families by alleged arrogance and discourtesy. The investigation showed also that The Truck System was in operation between merchants and fishermen by virtue of which fish were exchanged for provisions and other goods. This system, it was pointed out by Mr. DuBreuil, is disastrous to the fishermen, if they make a poor catch, the latter being unable to deal with other business places on account of their previous indebtedness to the local merchant. The fishermen, on account of their inability to read, are often charged extortionate prices, and Mr. DuBreuil reports the case of one man who was repeatedly charged for articles which he never obtained. The merchants sold their goods on credit

The effects of the disaster which overtook the economic life of the Maritimes were mitigated in part by insurance companies but in the main the blow was direct and heavy.[1] Financial institutions from Canada began to establish branches and agencies in the important Maritime centres.[2]

to the fishermen, and sometimes a period of a whole year elapsed before a final settlement was made, as the supplies bought during the winter were only paid for after the fishing season opened. The Companies had an arrangement among themselves by which the prices to be paid for fish were fixed, and the existence of such a combination, in Mr. DuBreuil's opinion, proved to be one of the causes of the tumult. Discontent was also caused by the unsatisfactory method of weighing the fish, old-fashioned devices being in use" (*S.p.*, 36, 1911).

[1] It has been estimated that about 30,000 people, at least one-half of which were native stock, emigrated from the Maritimes in the decade 1861 to 1871, 40,000 native stock from 1871 to 1881, and 91,000 native stock from 1881 to 1891 (*The Maritimes since Confederation*).

[2] For a description of financial integration at Yarmouth, an important shipping centre, see J. M. Lawson, *Yarmouth past and present*; J. R. Campbell, *A history of the County of Yarmouth, Nova Scotia*; G. S. Brown, *Yarmouth, Nova Scotia*.

SECTION III

WESTERN CANADA[1] (HUDSON BAY DRAINAGE BASIN)

SUBSECTION A

TRANSPORT AND COMMUNICATION

Upper Canada or Ontario had begun to shift from the production of wheat to the production of other types of agricultural commodities by the end of the period, but not before wheat had left its stamp on the economic structure of the country. Railroads, steamships, industry, finance, and marketing organization had grown up in relation to the agricultural demands of the province. The elaborate machinery which had been built up served as a base for the development of the production of wheat in western Canada. The organization which characterized an economy closely moulded to the demands of the production of wheat in Ontario was extended to support its demands in western Canada. This extension contributed to the rapidity of western expansion[2] but in so far as it involved the production of wheat under new geographic conditions, modifications were slow and

[1]For general works see F. H. Schofield, *The story of Manitoba*, 3 vols. (Winnipeg, 1913); John Blue, *Alberta past and present* (Chicago, 1924); *A handbook to Winnipeg and the Province of Manitoba* (Winnipeg, 1909); L. Thwaite, *Alberta, an account of its wealth and progress* (Chicago, 1912); N. F. Black, *History of Saskatchewan and the old northwest* (Regina, 1913); L. Gilbert, *La Saskatchewan, essai de monographie provinciale canadienne* (Paris, n.d.); M. McWilliams, *Manitoba milestones* (Toronto, 1928); H. J. Boam, *The Prairie Provinces of Canada* (London, 1914); E. J. Chambers, *The unexploited west* (Ottawa, 1914), especially bibliography; G. M. Adam, *The Canadian northwest*; H. A. Innis, *Fur trade in Canada* (New Haven, 1930), chapter v; C. R. Tuttle, *Our northland* (Toronto, 1885); J. Macoun, *Manitoba and the great northwest* (Guelph, 1882); G. Bryce, *Manitoba* (London, 1882); W. H. Williams, *Manitoba and the northwest* (Toronto, 1882); A. C. Garrioch, *First furrows* (Winnipeg, 1923); N. F. Davin, *The great Canadian northwest* (Ottawa, 1891); "The story of the press" (Canadian Northwest Historical Society *publications*, I, no. IV, pt. I, Battleford, 1928); J. W. Dafoe, *Clifford Sifton in relation to his times* (Toronto, 1931); *Agriculture, climate and population of the Prairie Provinces of Canada, a statistical atlas showing past development and present conditions* (Ottawa, 1931); E. D. Fagan, "Economic factors in the migration and present location of the wheat belt in the United States" (Summaries of theses, 1926, Harvard University, 1930, 117-125); C. E. Koeppe, *The Canadian climate* (Bloomington, 1931), chapter vi.
[2]See D. A. MacGibbon, *The grain trade of Canada* (Toronto, 1932), pt. I.

hampered expansion. American experience in similar geographic areas to the south contributed to the solution of
new problems.[1] In spite of their importance, Canadian and
American techniques were adapted to the earlier economic
structure built up under the fur trade. The latter had been
responsible for the organization of transport along the
important rivers to the north, for the development of agriculture[2] at various depots, especially at Red River, and for
the growth of numerous activities. The importance, for
example, of Winnipeg and the position of the Canadian
boundary was shown in the location of the Canadian Pacific
Railway along the southern route.

In the period prior to 1885 the economic development
of western Canada was largely dominated by construction
of railroads. The difficulties of constructing railroads in the
face of water-competition in the St. Lawrence drainage basin,
as shown in deficits of the government and of the railroads,
were partially overcome by Confederation and widening of
the credit structure and expansion of railroad territory and
markets to the Maritimes, and partially by extension of
Confederation to western Canada and British Columbia and,
in turn, further widening of the credit structure and expansion of railroad territory and markets to the west. Construction of railways by means of private enterprise and
governmental support continued in western Canada.[3] The
national policy and the Canadian Pacific Railway agreement
were designed to attract a flow of capital essential to the
opening up of the west.

1

Steam Navigation and Railways

Steam navigation and railways were fundamental to the
opening up of western Canada. The displacement of steamboats by railroads on the Mississippi led to the migration
of boats and skill to the Red River and the Saskatchewan.

---

[1]See H. A. Innis, "Industrialism and settlement in Western Canada"
(*Proceedings* of the International Geographical Congress, Cambridge, 1928).

[2]See A. H. R. Buller, *Essays on wheat* (New York, 1919), chapter i; also
Canada, an encyclopedia, I, 53 *ff*.

[3]See H. A. Innis, *A history of the Canadian Pacific Railway*.

The beginning of steamboat navigation[1] on the Red River heralded the coming of industrialism to the west. In July, 1875, the Hudson's Bay Company's steamer *Northcote* successfully made her first trip to Edmonton. In 1882 2 steamers[2] ran between Emerson and Winnipeg, 2 steamers between Winnipeg and Fort Ellice (Fort Pelly in high water), one mixed passenger and freight steamer and 8 freight steamers and 17 barges on Lake Winnipeg to Grand Rapids, 5 steamers (total capacity 1,000 tons) on the Saskatchewan River to Edmonton.[3] On January 8, 1879, the railway was completed from St. Paul *via* Emerson to Winnipeg.

Rapid construction of the Canadian Pacific to the west and to the east brought territory to the north and to the south in more direct relationship to the railway.[4] Winnipeg and Brandon were connected by postal-car service on January

---

[1]Moorhead, Minnesota. "The *International* is of the scow-built, light water kind used on these waters, where, in the dry season, the bottom often lies at twenty or thirty inches from the surface—scow-built, with round nose, propelled when floating by a horizontal wheel at the rear; and when stuck on the stones or mud, pulled off by a cable, one end of which is attached to a tree on the bank, the other to a capstan turned by the "Nigger" engine. . . . She is in length 140 feet; breadth about one-third of length; three decked—the lowest for freight, engine, deck passengers, cattle, etc.; the second, with cabin, state-rooms and covered promenade; the third has the wheel-house and open deck. . . . The crew of thirty or more . . . worked the craft and the scows, which sometimes ran on in the more rapid current, but were more generally lashed to our side. We started with one such, laden with bags and barrels, over 50 tons, for Garry, but at Grand Forks exchanged these for two barges, laden each with 50 tons of rails for the Canada Pacific" (J. C. Hamilton, *The prairie province*, Toronto, 1876, 17-18). For various descriptions of travel see G. Stewart, *Canada under the administration of the Earl of Dufferin* (Toronto, 1878); S. Fleming, *England and Canada* (London, 1884); W. F. Rae, *Newfoundland to Manitoba* (London, 1881); J. E. Ritchie, *Pictures of Canadian life* (London, 1886); A. B. Routhier, *De Québec à Victoria* (Quebec, 1893); B. McEvoy, *From the Great Lakes to the wide west* (Toronto, 1902); M. Roberts, *The western Avernus* (Westminster, 1890); John Palliser, *Journals, detailed reports, and observations relative to the exploration . . . 1857-8-9, 1860* (London, 1859-63).

[2]"During 1879 and the season of 'highwater' *one* steamer plied to Fort Ellice, and *three* to Portage de la Prairie. These steamers draw light, 14 to 15 inches, and are capable of carrying from 150 to 250 tons of freight, then requiring a depth of water in the river of from 3 to 4 feet. The amount of freight each carries is regulated by the height of water in the river, and they usually tow from 2 to 4 barges carrying about 300 tons of freight. The navigation of the Assiniboine usually begins in the first week in May, and, for the want of water, closes early in September. . . . During the season of 1880 *four* steamers plied on the Assiniboine, *two* of which draw when loaded 4 to 4½ feet, the other two drawing less. . . . 3800 passengers were conveyed by these steamers, freight being generally towed in barges to permit the passage through the rapids" (*S.p.*, 6, 1881). See also W. J. Carter, "Reminiscences regarding the west" (MSS. in the University of Toronto library).

[3]*S.p.*, 3, 1883.

[4]See H. A. Innis, *A history of the Canadian Pacific Railway*, 134 *ff*. In addition, the Northern Pacific had a branch from Winnipeg to the boundary and

2, 1882,[1] and mail service was provided to Calgary on
October 1, 1883.[2] In November, 1884, the time between
Winnipeg and Montreal was reduced to 66 hours.[3] Trails[4]
were gradually displaced by railroads. Increase of settlement necessitated the building of roads in relation to the
survey system.

from Morris to Brandon. The Canadian Pacific lines from Brandon to the
Souris coal-fields and its connections covered southern Manitoba effectively by
1893 (*S.p.*, 12, 1892). The Calgary Edmonton line completed in 1891 displaced
finally the old stage route from Winnipeg. Portage la Prairie, Brandon, and
Qu'Appelle as points of departure were displaced and stages were run from
Qu'Appelle to Prince Albert, Swift Current to Fort Saskatchewan, and Calgary
to Edmonton. In 1893 a railway was completed from Calgary to Macleod.
New stage routes followed from new rail heads, from Prince Albert to Cumberland
House, from Pakan to Lac la Biche (*S.p.*, 1894), Edmonton to Shaftsbury, and
Fort Chipewyan to Fort Simpson (1897) (*S.p.*, 12, 1898), and to the Mackenzie
River district in general (1901) (*S.p.*, 24, 1906).

[1]*S.p.*, 4, 1882.

[2]See a detailed list of improved schedules, *S.p.*, 5, 1884.

[3]*S.p.*, 7, 1886. "The first through train left Montreal on Monday, June 28,
and arrived at Port Moody, the Pacific terminus of the road on July 4" (*S.p.*, 10,
1887). Sir Edward Watkins in his trip over the main line, leaving Montreal on
September 15, 1886, outlined the main features of the road. The line had steel
rails of about 56 pounds to the yard, and about 2,640 ties per mile. For 60 to 70
miles from Callander the road was ballasted with sand, was without fencing, and
had chiefly timber bridges. North Bay was a divisional point. Beyond Sudbury
numerous large trestles had been built and the schedule running time was 24 miles
per hour. From Chapleau to Heron Bay the time was reduced to 20 miles.
From Heron Bay to Port Arthur several large streams were crossed with timber
trestles or iron bridges and masonry. "The line through this district is winding,
having many sharp curves and steep grades. There are several short tunnels, all
of them through rock, and not lined. The schedule time for trains on this
portion of the line is 16 miles per hour." Nipigon River was crossed with a
steel-trussed bridge. The running time from that point to Port Arthur was 24
miles. The line to Port Arthur was in many places inadequately ballasted. On
the government section to Winnipeg, 57-pound steel rails had been laid and
the line was well ballasted. At Winnipeg machine shops, round-houses, and
yards were a part of the equipment. West of Winnipeg, little ballast was used
other than material provided from the ditches, but the schedule was 24 miles
an hour. At Portage la Prairie a line was built north-west to the fertile belt, and
at Drummond a 3-feet gauge line was built to the Lethbridge mines. The
average running time to the foothills was about 22 miles an hour (Sir E. W.
Watkins, *Canada and the states*, London, 1887, 41 ff.).

[4]Methods of crossing rivers are described in the following extract. A cable
was "so arranged that, on the bows of the ferry boat being turned up-stream by
a wheel whenever a trip across is necessary, the force of the water is sufficient by
itself to carry the boat over to the other side. . . . On the Bow River, the charges
for crossing—are somewhat high.

Single vehicle, 1 horse..............	100 cents—4s.	English money
Double " 2 horses..............	150 " —6s.	"
Horse and rider....................	50 " —2s.	"
Horse, mule, or cow................	25 " —1s.	"
Sheep, hog, calf, or colt.............	25 " —1s.	"

For all articles over one cwt., not conveyed in a vehicle, 15 cents for every
cwt. For every person, except team-drivers, 25 cents. These charges are
doubled after sunset" (W. H. Barneby, *Life and labour in the far, far west*,
London, 1884, 268-9).

2

Communications

Post office facilities kept pace and went beyond the territory occupied by the railways.[1] In 1871 Manitoba and the North-west Territories had 21 post offices with a regular weekly or semi-weekly service and, in 1872, 27 offices handled 80,000 letters and cards. Closed bags were exchanged between Fort Garry and Windsor and a tri-weekly stage route was arranged in 1872 (daily in 1875) between St. Cloud (the railway terminus) and Fort Garry (427 miles) giving a 10-day service from Ottawa to Fort Garry. A money-order system was added in the same year.[2] In 1877 the system was extended to Edmonton. With completion of the railway to Winnipeg:

> A speedy and direct communication has been had with all parts of the United States, and through the United States with all parts of the Dominion. Two mails daily are now received and despatched at Winnipeg, the time occupied in the transit of a letter either to or from
>
> Windsor (Ont.) being................. 2½ days[3]
> Toronto   "   3   "
> Ottawa   "   .... 3½   "
> Montreal   "   .... 3½   "

The dominion telegraph[4] preceded the railway. After linking up at Fort Garry with the American system in 1871 it was extended north-west to Battleford in 1876 and to Edmonton in 1879. Additional telegraph lines were built to accompany the railroad.

---

[1]Attempts continually to improve the postal service involved heavy expenditures in wages and equipment (*S.p.*, 3, 1883).

[2]*S.p.*, 3, 1874; *S.p.*, 3, 1875; *S.p.*, 6, 1878; *S.p.*, 3, 1883.

[3]See *S.p.*, 4, 1879. "[*Winnipeg, 1877*]. The ice did move the next day and on the 27th [*April*] at the sound of the steamboat whistle, I ran to the window. As if by one impulse, every door on the main street opened, and the inmates poured forth, men putting on their coats, women their bonnets, while holding the kicking, struggling bareheaded babies they had snatched up in their haste to reach the landing as soon as the boat; boys of all sizes, ages, and description, gentle and simple, rich and poor, mustered as though by magic. In five minutes the streets and banks of the river were black with people rushing to meet the steamer, and the shout that greeted her at the wharf was loud and genuine. It was the last time her arrival caused such excitement, as before another season the railway was running to St. Boniface, and freight and passengers could get to Winnipeg all through the winter" (Mary Fitzgibbon, *A trip to Manitoba*, London, 1880, 69-70).

[4]"The dominion telegraph" (Canadian Northwest Historical Society *publications*, I, VI).

AGRICULTURE

1

System of Survey

The development of transport hastened the elaboration of machinery designed to facilitate rapid settlement. This machinery[1] included railways, the Mounted Police,[2] the post office department, and the dominion lands service. The lands service was forced to keep ahead "of the settlement of the country in the way of surveys and facilities for acquiring land".

The system of survey adopted by order-in-council of April 25, 1871, was based on the system in the United States with important modifications. For example, "instead of the allowance made in the area of every section for roads, whose position would afterwards be fixed by need and authority, there was provided by the Canadian system, and laid off in the field, a road allowance all round the exterior of every section."[3]

> It remains to say a few words on the system of survey which has been adopted through the whole of the North-West region, and which makes it easy to describe the country with accuracy, and to define any particular locality. A first principal meridian was taken a little to the west of the 97th meridian, at about 12 miles to the west of the city of Winnipeg, the southern foundation of the survey being of course the 49th parallel, the boundary line between Canada and the United States. The whole of this district is surveyed out into blocks six miles square. On going westward these blocks are spoken

---

[1]*S.p.*, 25, 1911.

[2]See S. B. Steele, *Forty years in Canada* (Toronto, 1915); A. L. Haydon, *The riders of the plains* (London, 1910); R. Burton Deane, *Mounted police life in Canada* (Toronto, 1916).

[3]*S.p.*, 12, 1884. "After due consideration it was deemed advisable to follow in the main the method of survey into square townships, sections and quarter-sections, which obtained in the adjoining Territories of the United States; in which the condition of natural surface, climate, and mode of settlement, were to a very great degree similar." See R. G. Riddell, "The influence of United States precedent upon dominion land policy" (M.A. thesis, University of Toronto, 1931).

of as "ranges", and on going north, as "townships", and in their enumeration on the maps, the latitude of the townships is marked by Arabic numerals, the longitude of the ranges being in Roman numerals. From the one principal meridian to the next principal meridian is 33 ranges. The only difficulty arises from the narrowing of the degrees of longitude as you progress northward, necessitating a correction[1] in the western ranges of each principal meridian. Each of these ranges or townships is six miles square consisting therefore of 36 square miles. Beginning from the south-eastern corner of this block, each square mile is numbered, sections 11 and 29 in each township being set apart for the endowment and the maintenance of the schools of the township; sections 8 and 26[2] being allotted to the Hudson Bay Company in respect of their charter rights; within the range of 24 miles on each side of the main line of any branch of the Canadian Pacific Railway the odd-numbered sections have been granted to the railway, the even-numbered sections being reserved for free-grant homesteads and their attached pre-emptions. Each of these sections of one mile square, or 640 acres, is again sub-divided into its four quarter sections of 160 acres each, and every settler has a right to take up as a homestead any block of 160 acres that he may find unoccupied, for which he will have to pay only a small registration fee, and he may occupy for pre-emption the adjoining or any other section of 160 acres, for which he will have to pay at the rate of $2\frac{1}{2}$ dollars per acre at the end of three years from the date of his entry. It will be seen, therefore, that it is within the power of a settler to obtain a farm of 320 acres upon payment of somewhere about £80, the payment of almost the whole of this sum being, as I said, postponed for three years. . . .[3]

Following the adoption of the system the surveys were carried out energetically.[4]

The surveys of Dominion lands were, at the outset, divided into two classes, the first consisting of those by which the outline boundaries of blocks containing four townships

---

[1]Correction lines for meridians were made at 12 miles from the border and at intervals of 24 miles to the north.

[2]South half and north-west quarter of section 26 and north-east quarter of section 26 in townships numbered 5 and its multiple—or one-twentieth of the total area.

[3]A. S. Hill, *Autumn wanderings in the northwest* (London, 1885), 41-3.

[4]"A manual of survey, setting forth the system in detail, and containing standing instructions for the guidance of surveyors of Dominion Lands, consisting of 32 pages, together with maps illustrating the instructions, and containing also forms of the contract to be entered into by Deputy Surveyors, was compiled and published.

A supply of Transit Theodolites of a class required for the use of surveyors who might be employed on the block surveys, and which were not attainable here, was ordered from Troughton & Sims, in London, England" (*S.p.*, 22, 1872).

were surveyed, and termed Block Surveys. The second, named Subdivision Surveys, followed the first, dividing up the land within the outlines of each block into sections and quarter sections, laying off the road allowances and filling in the topographical details. The lines established by the Block Surveys thus formed a frame for the subdivisional ones governing them and limiting their accumulation of error. . . .[1] In 1880 an intermediate survey (township outline survey) was made between these surveys. The block survey was increased in size to include 16 townships—24 miles to a side—the township-outline surveyor cut the block into 16 townships and the subdividing surveyor laid off the 36 sections and quarter-sections as before. In 1881 the road[2] allowance was reduced to 66 feet and 3 east and west roads across a township were eliminated, thus saving the cost of survey and adding about 4,000,000 acres to the cultivable territory in the north-west. The rapidity[3] of the work following the establishment of the survey system was shown in the report for 1883. In that year 1,221 townships, or 27 million acres, were subdivided into sections and quarter-sections and the boundaries of 360 townships were surveyed. The townships included 1,059 along the line of the railway, including its land belt and extending beyond to a depth of about 50 miles from the line, and 162 chiefly near advancing settlements at Prince Albert and Edmonton.

2

Regulations Regarding Lands and Homesteads

Homestead regulations were adopted and improved as a result of experience with settlement. The policy was necessarily related to the policy of the United States since Canada was forced to compete for settlers. Land regulations were

---

[1]S.p., 12, 1884. For a short history of surveys, see S.p., 13, 1892.
[2]See Reports of the minister of public works, *Journals of the legislative assembly, Manitoba.*
[3]The technique of surveying was improved steadily—for example, the survey chain was replaced by the continuous steel band as a measure. "Blocks of twelve miles square, including four townships each, with iron bar boundaries at the several angles, the number and range of the townships being stamped thereon, and with the section and quarter section corners marked on all the outlines, it will be understood is one of the features in carrying out the system of survey adopted, and is effected in all cases preliminary to the subdivision of townships into sections and quarter sections" (S.p., 22, 1871). 7 contracts covered the block survey of Manitoba.

47

adopted on March 1, 1871, allowing anyone over 21 years to enter for 160 acres. After paying $10.00 and living on the land for 5 years (3 years after April 25, 1871) he was entitled to ownership.[1] In 1874, the age limit was lowered to 18. Entrants were required to be British subjects in 1871 and British subjects before securing a patent in 1872. The lands taken up increased from 400,424 acres in 1877 to 682,591 acres in 1878, of which 280,022 were taken as free grants, 256,791 acres as pre-emptions or forest-tree claims, and 145,778 acres purchased by cash, scrip, or location of warrants.[2] In 1879 an attempt to tighten regulations was made in requiring 6 months' residence each year.[3]

3

Speculation in Lands

The liberal conditions of the Dominion Lands Act and of the regulations of December 23, 1881, and the pouring in of capital which accompanied rapid construction of the railway contributed to the boom of 1881 and 1882. The boom of the fifties in Upper Canada following the construction of the railroad was paralleled in the eighties and in the nineteen hundreds in western Canada. "Speculation in lands was assisted largely by banks and loan companies, who brought a very large amount of capital into the country in 1881 and 1882."[4] Homesteaders hastened to obtain titles in order to sell, or to mortgage their lands and make second entries, or purchases of other land. The professional homestead-jumper or "suitcase homesteader" became a menace and steps were taken to check his activities.

Owing to the industry with which these "jumpers" plied their calling, and the extent to which the choice lands were being taken up by speculative squatters and spurious home-

---

[1]Dominion Lands Act, 1872. See J. R. Maxwell, "Land policy of the federal government", chapter iii.

[2]*S.p.*, 7, 1879.

[3]Regulations included breaking 15 acres and the erection of a house at least 18 feet by 16 feet.

[4]*S.p.*, 8, 1886. In 1882, 7,483 entries were made of which nearly half had been cancelled by 1900. Periods of boom characterized the history of numerous towns in the west. See W. J. Carter, "Reminiscences regarding the west" (MSS. in the University of Toronto library); J. B. Bickersteth, *Land of open doors* (Toronto, n.d.), 110-4; *Canada, an encyclopedia*, I, 484.

steaders, hired for the occasion, to the manifest injury of the
bona fide settler, one tier of sections on each side of the line
of the Canadian Pacific Railway [*the one-mile belt*] and the
residue of the even numbered sections between the southern
limit of the Railway Company's 48 mile belt and the International Boundary, were in 1882 temporarily withdrawn from
homestead and pre-emption.[1]

This section was re-opened on January 1, 1884. Moreover
the Amended Land Act of 1883 inaugurated a system of
inspection of homesteads. The pre-emption system developed
in the Lands Act of 1874 which permitted a homesteader
to enter a pre-emption on a second 160 acres by which he
was entitled to purchase at $1.00 an acre on obtaining his
patent (later $2.50 an acre or 50 cents an acre for 5 years),
was held in part responsible for the evils of the boom in
appealing to the acquisitiveness of the settler and was
abolished in 1885 by the act of 1883. It did not finally
disappear until 1889 when it was made possible for a settler
to acquire an additional quarter-section, but the payment
for the section and the fulfilment of the settlement duties
were made to run concurrently.

The effects of the boom were serious:

> In almost every locality one meets numerous homesteads, once
> under a fair state of cultivation, but now deserted; the land
> that was once tilled being weed-grown and less easily cultivated
> than the virgin prairie; the buildings fast decaying. Many
> settlers who have suffered from this wild speculation would
> never have either mortgaged or sold their first homesteads
> had the privilege of second entry not been open to them. At
> present, the privilege is used to enable persons who have
> earned patents to acquire additional lands in the vicinity of
> the first homestead. It is seldom an actual advantage to
> them to increase their holdings, having insufficient capital to
> properly cultivate even 160 acres; but the acquisitive tendency
> is too strong to be resisted.[2]

In 1886 the government was still faced with the problem of
refusing patents to those who had made "a perfunctory
compliance with, which in reality is an absolute evasion of,

---

[1] *S.p.*, 12, 1884.
[2] *S.p.*, 8, 1886 and *S.p.*, 14, 1888. The period of inflation in 1882 and the
enormous sales of land especially in the Birtle country came to a sudden end.
Homestead and pre-emption lands taken up declined about 200,000 acres each
in 1883.

the provisions of the law".[1] However, cancellations in that
year declined materially as a result of the following considerations:

> (First), to a more faithful discharge of their duties by home-
> steaders; (second), to the more lenient course which the
> Board, at your suggestion, has adopted in dealing with settlers
> who were reported to be in default in the performance of their
> homestead duties; and (third), to the fact that the speculative
> entries made in 1881 and 1882, which added largely to the
> number of the cancellations in former years, were disposed of
> before this year.[2]

4

Immigration

The development of facilities to encourage settlement
was followed by the migration[3] of settlers. The occupation
of the more accessible land in Ontario by 1861, the fluctuations and decline of the lumber trade, the increasing density
of population in certain areas, the decline of wheat-farming,
and the migration of wheat-farmers to new areas, and the
attractions of new territory suggested by the railroads, were
responsible for the movement of population to the west.
As early as 1871[4] it was estimated that 1,500 souls "made
up principally of farmers", had migrated to Manitoba
("some twenty families at most from Quebec and the Maritime provinces; the remainder came from Ontario, principally
from the Huron peninsula . . . from the most densely peopled
counties").

---

[1]*S.p.*, 8, 1886.

[2]*S.p.*, 7, 1887.

[3]See J. T. Culliton, *Assisted emigration and land settlement with special
reference to western Canada* (McGill University economic studies, no. 9); S. O.
Johnson, *A history of emigration from the United Kingdom to North America,
1763-1912* (London, 1913); W. G. Smith, *A study in Canadian immigration*
(Toronto, 1920); G. Pelletier, "Le partage de l'immigration Canadienne depuis
1900" (*Revue trimestrielle canadienne*, 1917), and Royal Society of Canada *mémoires*,
XII, series 3, section I, 1918, 33-41; W. A. Carrothers, *Emigration from the British
Isles* (London, 1929); *Report of the Saskatchewan royal commission on immigration
and settlement* (Regina, 1930); *Pioneer settlement* (New York, 1932).

[4]*S.p.*, 2a, 1872. "This Province [*Ontario in 1877*] supplied more immigrants
than all the others put together, and this immigration may be divided into two
distinct classes; that of the farmers, a good number of whom were in easy circumstances; and that of the labourers; among the latter class there were some mechanics, of this latter class a good number went away again, not having found
work enough, but I cannot state precisely how many" (*S.p.*, 9, 1878).

Most of the new arrivals at once proceeded westward, and there are now more than one hundred families settled at Poplar Point, at High Bluff, and Portage la Prairie and at White Mud River. In those localities they have found a more fertile soil, a better wooded country, a population more homogeneous as respects language and religious belief. . . . Some fifteen families have settled at Winnipeg, and about as many more are dispersed at Pointe de Chêne, Rivière aux Ilets de Bois, and along Red River between Pembina and Fort Garry. . . . The general tendency is towards the west, and there can be no doubt but that future emigration will be directed towards that point. At White Mud River, where there were barely twenty families last spring, there are now seventy-five, and in three months there will be over two hundred. The most remote settlements are only some ten miles from the frontier of the Province, and new settlers will very soon pass beyond that line. The attraction which induces new settlers to proceed westward will be still further increased by the fact that two steamers will run during the summer on Lakes Manitoba and Winnipeg, and on the Saskatchewan. . . .

The difficulties of the lumber trade during the depression of the seventies in the Ottawa district led to an increase of emigration:

The majority of those who left here for Manitoba took a large amount of means with them, the proceeds of their farms which they sold before leaving. Many took cattle, horses, stock of every description, together with farm implements, such as reapers, mowers, threshing mills, fanning mills, etc., etc. A large number of young men, farmer's sons, were amongst those who left, their fathers having previously gone to make selections of the land for their new homes. My impression is that for years to come large numbers will annually go from here to the North-West, and the vacancy thus created will afford room for newly arrived immigrants to fill their place.[1]

The prospect of completion of the railway, the good crop of 1877, and the absence of grasshoppers for 2 years were also factors responsible for a marked increase in settlement in 1878[2] (estimated at 12,000 and with a larger proportion in possession of sufficient means for settlement).

---

[1]*S.p.*, 9, 1879. "The exodus from this district [*Ottawa*] to Manitoba during the year has been very great owing to the great commercial depression; many farmers sold their properties and would have gone to the United States if it had not been for the favourable accounts which reached them from friends already settled in Manitoba" (*S.p.*, 10, 1880).

[2]*S.p.*, 7, 1879. In 1875 the plague of grasshoppers practically wiped out the crops (*S.p.*, 8, 1876). See also J. C. Hamilton, *The prairie province*, 157-8, 161.

(i)

Competition for immigration

Improvement of transportation offset competition from the western states. Grant described the activities of land agents and railway directors at St. Paul in attempting to divert emigrants from western Canada in 1870. Even in Winnipeg "pothouse politicians" attempted to turn back new-comers.[1]

In 1880 complaints were made against the energetic efforts of Mr. Drake, land commissioner of the St. Paul and Sioux City Railroad, "to capture English and Canadian capitalists and farmers". Settlers established in Dakota, Minnesota, Iowa, and other western states became valuable propagandists for other immigrants by writing and advising their former neighbours and friends of the advantages of the new country.[2]

> The railway stations swarm with runners for railway and land companies, passenger trains are boarded by them, large quantities of printed matter are distributed, and all sorts of inducements are held out to the newcomer to make his home on the lands of the companies represented. . . .These people are in the habit of flying the British flag in front of their offices, thereby attracting the attention of Old Country people passing through the city. In addition to this, they keep in their offices the leading English political, agricultural, and general newspapers, and are doing everything possible to create the impression that their place is the English head-quarters for this region. Their runners make it a practice to meet our people on the trains or at the station, and, while abusing Manitoba and the North-West, they set forth in glowing terms the attractions offered by the country they represent.

In the United Kingdom, as in Ontario and the United States, the spread of education, the growth of newspapers, and the development of advertising contributed to the mobility of population. As has been shown, the ocean steamship had become of basic importance to immigration.[3] During the early part of the period competition for immigration was intense for British settlers. American land, railway,

---

[1] G. M. Grant, *Ocean to ocean* (Toronto, 1873), 85.
[2] *S.p.*, 12, 1881.
[3] *S.p.*, 11, 1882.

and steamship companies were effective competitors with the dominion in the United Kingdom. Australia and South Africa were assisting emigrants. According to A. T. Galt,[1] the Canadian high commissioner, Queensland offered free passages to agricultural labourers and domestic servants, and families were taken out at £4 for males and £2 for females, and half those rates for children between one and 12. New South Wales assisted passage rates were £5 and £2 for domestic servants; New Zealand gave free passage to domestic servants. "Each emigrant sent to Australia costs the government . . .£10 sterling."

(ii)
Foreign immigrants

Attempts were made to attract foreign immigrants as well as English-speaking immigrants. Mennonites were granted 8 townships about 40 miles west of West Lynne for settlement by an order-in-council of March 3, 1873.[2] Each 160 acres were surveyed 4 rods wide to provide for the arrangement of the community in a village. An Icelandic settlement was established on the west shore of Lake Winnipeg at Gimli in 1875.[3]

(iii)
Growth of immigration

By the end of the period Canada began to attract wider attention. The visit of the tenant farmer delegates to Canada in 1879 and 1880 and the publication of their re-

---

[1] *S.p.*, 14, 1883.

[2] "1. Entire exemption from military service;
2. A free grant of lands in Manitoba;
3. The privilege of religious schools of their own;
4. The privilege of affirming instead of making oaths in courts;
5. The passenger warrants, from Hamburg to Fort Garry, for the sum of $30 per adult, $15 for children under eight years, and $3 for infants under one year;
6. These prices not to be changed during the years 1874, 1875 and 1876, and if changed afterwards, not to exceed $40 up to the year 1882;
7. The emigrants to be provided with provisions during their journey between Liverpool and Collingwood" (*S.p.*, 9, 1874). See a description of this settlement in W. H. Barneby, *Life and labour in the far, far west*, 358-367.

[3] *S.p,.* 8, 1876.

ports,[1] Canadian displays at the fisheries exhibition, the visit of the British Association to Montreal in 1884, the colonial and Indian exhibition of 1886 were indications of the effectiveness with which improved transportation contributed to the mobility of population.[2] The total population of Manitoba increased from 25,228 in 1871 to 62,260 in 1881 and 152,506 in 1891.

(iv)

Settlers from Ontario

The large proportion of settlers from Ontario accentuated reliance on agricultural technique matured in that area.

But numbers of the Ontario farmers seem to be so wedded to wheat-raising, that rather than go extensively into stock-raising and fattening, and the growth of various rotation crops, more after the English and Scotch models, they prefer to sell out and go to Manitoba and the North-West, a territory which is *par excellence* a wheat country, and which must soon become, perhaps, the greatest granary in the world. They are the more inclined in this direction because they can sell their Ontario farms at $40 to $100 an acre, and can buy virgin soil in the North-West at $1 to $10. By an exchange of this nature they can easily establish their children in separate farms, a thing but few of them could hope to do in Ontario, where land is comparatively high.[3]

---

[1] *Canada in 1880* (Ottawa, 1881).

[2] *S.p.*, 4, 1888.

[3] *S.p.*, 12, 1881. In 1889 the Winnipeg immigration agent reported: "The numbers arriving from Ontario were as usual very large, and the amount of live-stock and effects brought in surprisingly great. This is, to a certain extent, I believe, the result of visits made by our settlers, who, through favourable excursion rates afforded by the different lines of railway (which will eventually add materially to their traffic account) were enabled to re-visit the homes they had left behind and speak for and in the interests of our great Province" (*S.p.*, 6, 1890). In 1895: "The large harvest this year has necessitated the importation of labourers from Ontario, some six thousand men being brought in by the Canadian Pacific Railway Company. It is known that many of these will remain here, and in any case the sight of the wheat fields and the accounts of their vast yield which will be carried back to the older province cannot but have a good effect next year. The excursionists who visited us speak highly of the country, and a large proportion have announced their intention of locating here permanently" (*S.p.*, 13, 1896). Lord Brassey stated that: "He was told, and he believes the statement is correct, that of those who have settled in Manitoba one-third had never before touched farming—they were quite raw hands. They began as pioneers in circumstances of great difficulty, with no experience or skill. One could not look for a great measure of success from such men for some time. Another third had tried agriculture elsewhere, and failed at it. They had not, perhaps, on the whole, had bad returns from the prairie soil, but their former failure was probably in a great measure due to want of personal skill,

The following account[1] of the experience of one settler from Ontario may be regarded as typical:

In the spring of 1878 an excursion—the first of its kind for the North-west—was organized by Robert Patterson, a newspaper man of Paris, Ontario. He was editor and proprietor of the "Paris Transcript". He secured running rights over the American railroads, and conducted several excursions from Ontario after that. Five young men from the same neighbourhood, the writer included, made up their minds to take the advice of Horace Greeley to go west and grow up with the country. We went through Detroit, on to Chicago, Milwaukee, St. Paul and Minneapolis. It took us ten days to get to the end of the railway, a place called Fisher's Landing in Minnesota.[2] Our fare was thirty dollars a single ticket. ... At Fisher's Landing we took the boat on the Red River

and that want of personal skill was often still evidenced. The remaining third were men who came to the country with skill, experience, and abundant energy, and there were no failures with them. Such men—and younger sons from Ontario, settlers from the United States, and some Scotchmen and Englishmen were among them—have succeeded and are bound to succeed. . . . The best settlers in Manitoba are undoubtedly the sons of Ontario farmers" (*S.p.*, 13, 1895).

[1]From George Henry, "Reminiscences" (MSS. in University of Toronto library). See also *Letters from a young emigrant in Manitoba* (London, 1883) for a description of farming near Beaconsfield during the period of the boom. See also H. Grange, *An English farmer in Canada* (London, 1904); W. M. Elkington, *Five years in Canada* (London, 1895); E. B. Mitchell, *In western Canada before the War* (London, 1915).

[2]Immigrants travelling by the most direct and cheapest route went from Detroit to Grand Haven by train, steamer to Milwaukee, railway to Prairie du Chien, steamer to McGregor, and railway to St. Paul. Canadians were able to sell their horses and vehicles at St. Paul in order to pay for the remainder of the passage and to diminish the cost of the last stage of transport. A bonded line of transport between St. Paul and Pembina in 1871 necessitated through shipment and increased costs, 60 agricultural families being obliged to spend $8,000. "The following is a statement of importations thus made in bond from Ontario to Manitoba:

	no.	value
Horses	194	$19,508
Horned cattle	49	2,132
Sheep	60	450
Vehicles	98	6,058
Other property		32,299"

The bonding system stimulated imports of livestock from Minnesota and adjoining states as seen in the following table for 1871:

	no.	value
Horses	30	$3,330
Horned cattle	737	35,500
Sheep	178	480

The cost of passage and freight from Georgetown to Fort Garry by steamer was $12.00 for each passenger, $10.00 for each horse or head of horned cattle, and $1.50 for each hundred weight of merchandise or other goods (*S.p.*, 2a, 1872). The Dawson route was not a success in competition with the route through American territory.

for Emmerson on the boundary in Manitoba. There were several boats running on the Red River. They ran from Fargo in North Dakota to Winnipeg. They were what was called stern-wheelers and they burned wood . . . We rested up in Emmerson for a day or two and then we struck west. I had a friend in Ayr, Ontario, who had been on a trip to the old country and in going over on the boat came in contact with a stone mason by trade who had been all through'the Northwest building stone forts for the Hudson Bay Company. They got to talking about the west. My friend asked him where in his opinion would be the best part of the country to settle in. He said by all means to go to the Pembina Mountain district. So in talking over the matter with my friend in Ayr, he advised me to go to that part of the country, and we did. . . . Of course each man of us took from Ontario as much provisions as would do us for two weeks, but we took an extra fifty pounds of flour to make flap-jacks. To make a flap-jack, when it gets done on one side, you flip it up in the air and down it comes on the other. We had also two well-cooked hams brought from home and they tasted fine as long as they lasted. We could get our provisions from the Hudson Bay store. The flour we got cost twelve dollars per cwt. Food as a rule was high, as for instance, rattlesnake pork by the barrel was thirty dollars. . . . We travelled about sixty miles and then we came to the homestead of a settler who had located there the year before, and who had been on the Government Survey that year. We employed him as a land guide. He knew the country and we travelled for miles and selected the kind of land we wanted [*near Manitou*]. . . . The land we selected was a nice rolling prairie with a depth of about six inches to two feet of a dark loam, where it was shallow. Below that was a crumbly shale. That was the kind of land we wanted, but it was not the kind of land that stood the heaviest cropping. It dried out too soon and in the spring when the surface of the land was dry, the high winds would leave the seed bare, and we sometimes had to resow the land. That was when we did all our sowing by hand as we had no seed drills in those days. Of course we wanted the clear prairie. It looked the easiest to work and it was, but the land on which the scrub grew was by far the strongest as it would contain the moisture longest, but it was a great deal harder to break up for man and beast. We broke a lot of scrub land—all kinds of willows, young poplars and oak. It requires a lot of chopping and grubbing. We used a four horse team, big heavy horses, and a twenty inch scrub breaking plough. . . . The land was surveyed in our district in 1875. I am told they could survey as much as thirty miles of it in a day through clear prairie. . . . It was not hard to choose our land as it was all about alike. It seemed to run for about five miles rolling and about two miles wide. Being first on the spot, we had the first choice and we took the best. No better water could be had anywhere. Just outside of that lay of land you could not drink the water it was so bad with alkali.[1] We settled just eighteen miles north of the international boundary line, one hundred miles southwest of Winnipeg. The Deloraine branch of the C.P.R. was built through there seven years after we went there. . . . Of course we then began our tramp back to Emmerson to the land office to make our entry. Then we went over the boundary line to get our oxen from a big rancher there. We bought two yoke of oxen—one yoke cost $165 and the other $175. They were better suited for our work than horses.[2] They could do a lot of work if you gave them plenty of time to feed on the grass. We also got our wagons and harness from the same man. Both wagons cost $80 and the harness cost $15 each set. . . . They [H.B.C.] had one of their trading posts at a place on the west side of the Red River called West Lynne. The provisions we used all came from there until some fellow from Winnipeg came up and started a store about forty miles from us. We could get anything and everything at the Hudson Bay store. We loaded up our stove and all our household utensils and off we went to our new home. . . . We got there after a few days and then began to get out logs for a shack.

---

[1]Complaints of poor water were common in the district. The lack of water in various localities was an additional handicap. In 1893 in the German settlements of Langenburg, Beresina, Neudorf, and Neu Kronan and other parts of Assiniboia, farming was seriously hampered. The territorial assembly employed well-boring machines (S.p., 13, 1894).

[2]According to Hamilton, horses were sold at $300.00 to $400.00 a span and oxen, $120.00 to $180.00 per yoke. Ox teams could be hired at $2.00 a day and the cost of breaking was $5.00 per acre (J. C. Hamilton, The prairie province, 254-5). About 1884 Barneby suggested £300 to £400 for 160 acres homestead and 160 acres pre-empted.

"Yoke of oxen (say) at Qu'Appelle	£50
Waggon	16
Plough	5
Farm tools (say)	20
One year's supply of food for self and wife (and this is a low estimate)	60
Lumber for house and stable, for building a four-roomed house	60
Two cows (say)	30
Journey out for two (say)	40
Extra cash for seed, etc., and contingencies	
Homestead fee, 160 acres	2
160 acres pre-emption land @ $2½ per acre	80

£363"

(W. H. Barneby, Life and labour in the far, far west, 252). Prices declined after the boom of 1881-2. Hamilton quoted cows, $30.00 to $60.00; sheep, $6.00; half grown pigs, $5.00. "$1,000 is the very least that an emigrant should attempt to settle with on a quarter section."

We got one built sixteen by twenty, with two nicely carved
beds made out of green poplar. They were made large enough,
as we were not particular as to how we lay down in them.
When we moved into our new house, the mosquitoes[1] were
getting something awful. . . . Then our oxen took a notion in
their heads that they would go on a visit back home, something over one hundred miles. All hands were out night and
day hunting those oxen. Had we known they would go right
home; we could have found them in half the time. But when
we got them home, we made them work for lost time. We
started right in and began breaking up the prairie, and getting
out logs for houses and stables as there was plenty of oak and
poplar close by. The flies were getting worse for man and
beast. We had to keep smudges going night and day. . . .
The rainy season in that country is in the month of June
and we always started to do our breaking in that month.
If we got the rain it was easy ploughing for the oxen. When
the ground was moist we could usually break an acre of
prairie a day. In those days we always ploughed lightly about
two and one half or three inches deep. Then the ground
would be fine and mellow in the spring. Nowadays the
tendency is to plough or break six inches or more and then sow
on top of that. . . . In Emmerson there were a number of
agencies for implements mostly from the United States. The
John Deere Company made the best breaking ploughs. We
used a fourteen-inch breaker which cost $26.00. Those farm
machinery men had agents out all over the country where it
was settled selling ploughs, mowers, binders and all kinds of
machinery.[2] Most of them travelled on foot at that time.
Their commission in some cases was 100%. . . . A great many
of the incoming settlers from Ontario would bring their horses
and cows, pigs and hens with them to have a car-load of
settler's effects. They could only get as far as Emmerson by
rail and then had to draw their effects from there by team to
their homesteads. . . . The weather began to get wet. We
never saw any rain like it in Ontario. The roof of our shack
was thin sods and might have kept out a small shower. It

---

[1]These pests were the source of constant complaint on the part of settlers
and contributed to the livestock problem.

[2]W. H. Barneby, *Life and labour in the far, far west*, 340.

"Cutter and binder: $350 at 3 yrs. purchase, 7% interest; worked with
    either a pair of good horses, or 3 small ones; binds with cord, and will
    cut and bind 15 to 20 acres a day.

Waggon: $90, 1 yr's credit at 7% interest; or, $85 for cash.

Plough, Breaker, and Backsetter: $24, 1 yr's credit at 7%.

Stubble Plough: $18, 1 yr's credit at 7%.

Sulky Plough: $90 to $100, for cash.

Horse Rake: $35 to $40.

Mowers: $80, $90, to $100.

Threshing Machine (12 h.p.): $1200 to $1400."

rained three days outside and after it quit, then it rained four days inside, but we were happy and did not mind getting wet. . . . One or two of the boys went out on construction work[1] east of Winnipeg on the C.P.R. for the summer. Wages in construction work varied considerably. Men in rock work where they were handling dynamite or glycerine east of Winnipeg got $4 to $5 a day. From Emmerson to Winnipeg, sixty miles, it was mostly loose earth and they would get from $2 to $2.50. . . . The rest of us were breaking and getting our logs. We built our first shack close to the old Missouri trail, which came up from that state through Minnesota, the Dakotas, across the boundary, right through Manitoba and on to the Rocky Mountains. Incoming settlers were always calling in to inquire the way to such and such a section and where we came from, and we were glad to know where they came from. There were not very many Americans coming in when we came. They came in when Alberta and Saskatchewan were opened up. . . . It was customary in those days for nine out of every ten prairie wagons to have the old-fashioned two or five gallon jug filled with the very best. Lawyers, doctors, ministers and professional men of all classes, too, carried that kind of goods with them. . . . We had to go out perhaps forty miles to our nearest post office to get our mail once a week. We used to take turns at it. . . . We got ten acres of prairie broken[2] for each of us and in about six weeks it was quite rotted enough, so we set to work to backset it, which is going deeper and subsoiling ready for wheat the following spring. I went about fifty miles east where they had crops and worked in the harvest to secure seed for my ten acres. We paid $1 a bushel for our seed wheat and in supplying settlers located west of us with their seed wheat we would get $1.25 or perhaps $1.50 for an extra good sample. . . . [3]

---

[1]According to Hamilton, wages ranged from $1.70 a day to $2.00 a day but living was expensive, common board and lodging $5.00 a week. Agricultural labour in 1883 was paid 75 cents to $1.00 a day and general wages, $1.50 a day. Board and lodging was $6.00 a week and washing, $1.00. "Two of us have cleared one hundred and sixty dollars per month all summer, burning lime and selling it at 45c. per bushel; another has averaged $5.00 per day with his team, sometimes teaming to the new penitentiary, and sometimes working on the railroad. The fourth works at his trade, waggon making, in Winnipeg for $60 per month, steady employment" (J. C. Hamilton, *The prairie province*, 55-6, 112).

[2]In breaking, the top soil was turned over 2 inches deep and 12 broad in June and July. Backsetting or ploughing up the under soil to the top began about August and seeding in the following April or May. Ploughing in the spring generally began in the latter part of April and harvesting in the middle of August. The yield varied from 30 bushels per acre for wheat, 40 bushels for barley, and 57 bushels for oats as an average for Manitoba. Potatoes were planted late in May by ploughing the seed in furrows. The yield varied from 250 to 400 bushels. Hay was cut between the middle of July and the middle of August. These yields given by Barneby are probably high.

[3]Oats were quoted by Hamilton as $1.00 per bushel; wheat, $1.50 to $1.75; barley, $1.50 to $2.00; and potatoes, 75 cents in 1875 and higher in 1876.

After that, I went back home for the winter and worked in the bush, as there was nothing doing out on the prairie, and then went back west in the following Spring. We still had to go back through the States but we had all rail this time. We came through to St. Vincent in Minnesota right on the boundary. We always sowed our wheat as soon as there was enough loose soil to cover the seed. . . . In the autumn we commenced to put up our houses. There was some very nice building timber in our district, and some very good oak. The oak we used for the foundation of our buildings, as it would last longer. We would select a spot to build a house on, then go to work and dig out the cellar and get our oak logs squared. The corners were all dovetailed as all of us were handy with an axe. One of the boys was a very good carpenter, and had all the necessary tools. After the foundation was laid, our poplar logs were used, and there were a lot of very fine ones. Some would run as long as thirty feet and they were hewed on both sides. Then the doors and windows were cut out. The doors were six and one half feet high, and the windows had the usual six lights in each half-glass ten by twelve inches. The front door was always cut out on the south side of the house, with two windows on each side of the door facing the south, and one window in each end of the house upstairs. . . . Some built a lean-to for a kitchen if the family was larger, and it gave them more room. The ordinary size of the houses was twenty feet wide by twenty-six or thirty feet long. Very few were larger than that, and some were sixteen feet wide by twenty or twenty-four feet long. Then the rafters were poplar, as straight as could be got, and they were squared on all sides. Our window frames and glass came from West Lynne, but our carpenter made the doors and frames. . . . The roofs on the houses were given considerable pitch to keep out the rain. We could not afford shingles, so we cut the long grass in the coulees or ravines. One of our crew was an expert hand at putting on that kind of shingle. He had the experience in the old country. We made small sheaves using the full length of the grass which would be about three feet, then put a band around them, then a rope twisted out of the grass. The rope was lashed around the rafter and secured through the band on the shingle, and you could not tear them off. It could rain a month and not leak a drop—it was completely waterproof. . . .[1] The second year we had more of a crop to take off and it was very good too. One of our neighbours sent to Ontario for a threshing machine and we were all right for getting our crop threshed. The threshing machines in our part of the country were all brought up from Ontario and they

---

[1] The sod shack with poles and a dirt roof was more typical.

varied in price. A separator would cost about $500 and a horse power $300. That would be Ontario prices. Then there was transportation which would make it $150 more. . . . In December the horse power broke down. There were one or two farmers still to get threshed out and they had to wait about six weeks before repairs came from Ontario. Then when we started up again, the thermometer was ranging around forty and forty-five degrees below zero and every man of us was flying about with bags tied around our heads. . . . The first crop of wheat we threshed yielded thirty-two bushels to the acre. We cut it with the old-fashioned cradle—pretty hard work too. We just had the ten acres of wheat the first year. After that the average yield would be from twenty-five to thirty bushels for wheat. The oats would run from sixty to eighty bushels per acre. But on a measured acre of oats I have threshed one hundred and ten bushels. Then some years they would run twenty up to seventy-five bushels. . . . That was the first year we had binders.[1] The first binder we used was a wooden one and the price was $350. It tied with wire and was made in Brantford by the Osbourn Company. They made a good job of tying the sheaf. The wire was wound on spools and cost eleven cents a pound. The farmer who cut my crop with the wire binder charged me $1.50 per acre for cutting and he furnished everything. . . . I had eight stacks of grain—wheat and oats—and the snow was drifted in around the stacks about six feet deep. It had all to be shoveled out before we could get the separator in to the stacks and a place cleared for the horse power. The next thing was to get the straw away from the carriers. We could not take it away with a team as the snow was too deep, so the boss said to me,

"What's to be done with the straw?"

"Just one thing," I said, and that is that I will have to stand at the end of the carriers and touch a match to it and let it burn. . . . So we did and there was a pile of red hot wire about the size of a house. We were all very glad when it was done. . . . Then we had to haul our grain to Emmerson, our nearest market, something over one hundred miles. It used to take us about eight days to make the round trip, and sometimes we would get caught in a blizzard and have to wait over until the weather cleared up. The buyers were very keen to get our grain and prices were $1 to $1.25 per bushel for wheat. . . . For four or five years we had to draw our grain

---

[1]As early as 1883 Portage la Prairie distributed the following agricultural implements: "Self Binders, 283; mowers, 207; harrows, 128; seeders, 162; wagons, 123; sulky ploughs, 228; other ploughs, 200", of which 60 per cent. were of Canadian manufacture. In 1885 10 self-binding grain elevators were sent to Edmonton from Calgary at $360.00 f.o.b. Calgary plus $70.00 to Edmonton, or $430.00.

to Emmerson until we got the railroad. Those years we had
very good crops, but always in the winter and sometimes
toward Spring the roads were so slippery for our oxen we had
to get them sharp shod to get a better footing for them. Then
something came which nobody was looking for in the shape
of frosts which stayed with us far too long. For a number of
years our wheat was frozen so as to be useless. I have had
my wheat frozen when it was in blossom and had to cut three
or four swathes around the field and set fire to it. In the
middle of the day you could hear it cracking for miles. No
one would buy frozen wheat. It would not make flour or
bread. Black looking stuff it was, but we had to eat it. . . .
We had an elevator built in our nearest town by the Ogilvie
Milling Company. They bought the better grades of frozen
wheat and all kinds of grain. They would pay fifteen cents
a bushel for wheat and eleven cents a bushel for oats. I have
seen farmers come from as far west as Turtle Mountain with
wheat which they could not sell or give away. What could
they do with it? It was no use to take it back home with
them because they had too much on hand. They just untied
the bags and dumped it out on the road, and they were not
able to pay for their night's lodgings. . . . Then a great many
farmers lost a lot of grain if it was a wet fall through not being
able to stack their grain in proper condition. . . . Then gradually the farmers began to have their wheat ground ploughed
in the fall and to seed it in earlier in the Spring, and conditions
were a lot better. There was less frozen grain. If a farmer
got his grain frozen, it was considered to be his own fault.
We were almost sure to have a fair crop if we got rain in June.
If it did not come then there was a poor chance. The best
crop in our district[1] was in 1887 and we only had two good
rains in June. Our wheat that year yielded forty bushels per
acre. Of course there were some farmers who said they had
sixty-five per acre but I never saw it. . . . There was another
pest which did a great amount of destruction. The gopher

---

[1]The large crop created a demand for labour and the small increase in land
taken up in that year was attributed to the following causes: "In the first place,
intending settlers arriving in the North-West during the past year have been
to a greater extent than formerly impressed with the desirability of acquiring
some experience of the modes of agriculture suitable to the country, and have not
been in such a hurry to select and enter homesteads on their own account as those
arriving in previous years. In the second place, the extraordinary grain crop,
of which there was almost an assured prospect from the beginning of the season,
made it necessary for the farmers to increase the number of their employees, very
largely, and the consequence was that new arrivals were in great demand, and
the scale of pay offered them was quite tempting. In this way was absorbed a
very much larger proportion than usual of the immigration of the season, and a
smaller proportion than usual entered homesteads on their own account" (*S.p.*, 14,
1888). The limited labour market and high wages suggested that labour was at
a premium in comparison with land.

was a most annoying little animal for its size. They were more destructive in dry warm weather. They would have four or five families in a season. . . . They were so bad the municipalities gave a bounty for every tail produced. . . . The government took the matter in hand and issued so much strichnine to each half section to poison them. That was all right providing every farmer put the poison out on his own land, but some of them made a very poor attempt at it. I always found the best and most effective way to get them out of the way was to go at them in the Spring. We used to take the stone boat and get two barrels of water, go around to their holes and pour down a pail or two of water. They would soon come to the top blowing like a porpoise and we would knock them on the head. We could not get them all as they would come running over from our neighbours. . . . The winters were long and bitterly cold and they had to draw their wood a long way. We had to take the wood from wherever we could get it. At that time the government would give or sell to settlers twenty acres of timber for building purposes or firewood. There was a fine quarter section, one hundred and sixty acres, about 8 miles from our district, and eight farmers clubbed together and bought this hundred and sixty acres. It was all poplar, nice big stuff, and some oak. We bought it for $1.00 per acre. . . .[1] We were still getting more land broken up and under cultivation and adding more stock. I traded two yoke of oxen with their harness for the first team of horses[2] we had. . . . a sorrel team with their

---

[1] "This quantity—a cord—would last him for two fires for a fortnight. Wood is worth $5 (£1) per cord delivered; undelivered it is half that price. The government reserves woodlands, which it sells to the farmers in lots of twenty acres at $100 the lot. It will also give them permission to cut for firewood at 25c. (1/-) per cord, or rails for fencing at $5 per 1,000. There are thus two plans open, viz., to buy from an owner of woodland, or to employ a man to cut wood; which latter costs 75c. per cord for cutting, in addition to the Government charge of 25c., or 1c. per rail (*i.e.*, $10 per 1,000) in addition to the Government charge of $5.00."

[2] In 1878 "the importation of cattle was not quite as large as last year, consequently they fetched a higher price; but larger importations of horses from Ontario and Quebec have taken place. Older settlers who had a sufficient quantity of broken land sold their working cattle to new arrivals and bought horses" (*S.p.*, 9, 1879). "When Trotter & Trotter began business, there was almost as much trading in oxen as in horses. That was the case with every livery stableman who bought and sold, as well as hired out drivers and teams. It is a curious aspect of what was really a big trade in trail and plough power, that nobody advertised himself as an ox-trader. The ox was the infantry, the foot soldier of a campaign against the emptiness of the plains. Everybody used him, nobody praised him though he was patient under affliction, constant in toil and frugal in his diet. . . . On the plains collars and chain traces superseded the yoke, and in the wagon a strap around each neck carried the neck yoke and the front of the tongue and steered the vehicle. As a characteristic of prairie evolution a friend tells me that forty years ago between Whitewood and Broadview, where he settled, not a team of horses was owned; and that the oxen he bought cost

harness. I got them from a Frenchman. They were a good
team and well matched. Of course they came up from Ontario.
The Frenchman was more used to oxen than to horses. We
kept those horses till they died. They were worth about $350
when we got them. Any pigs in the country at that time
came from the east, and chickens were all brought in by the
incoming settlers. They would bring from one to three or
four cows. We got two brood sows and two good milch cows
brought out with us. But prices were very poor for grain or
cattle. Hogs were selling for 2½c. a pound live weight.
Cattle were about 3c. live weight, eggs were 5c. a dozen and
butter 7c. a pound. . . . I remember one year we had a fairly
good crop of wheat and it graded No. 2 Northern. All I
could get for it was 35c. a bushel. Our wheat in those days
was the soft variety and it got so bad with smut that in
threshing and cleaning it the smut balls would break. It
made the wheat black and gave it a very strong smell.[1] The

him $130, which he would have known was more than they were worth had he
been aware that cattle grow a ring on each horn every year after their second.
One grieves to say that in places where oxen were marketed the device was not
unknown of filing down the horn so that the price might be exalted. The horned-
team phase of agriculture was bound to pass with the growth of settlement and
the abundant production of oats, without which it is a folly to attempt to keep
horses working steadily on the land." Farming capital of Ontario built up in
relation to production of wheat was constantly drawn upon. Improved breeds
of horses following the importation of thoroughbred Clydesdales in Ontario
provided a reserve for the western states and western Canada. Around Stratford,
for instance, owing to the heavy nature of the land, the horses were the biggest
and best of any in the province, and showed more effectively the effects of high-
class importations. "Much of the rich land in Iowa was broken by Ontario-bred
horses. I found splendid fire brigade horses in St. Paul that were brought in
from Ontario. . . . The period of importing horses to Iowa from Ontario gave
place to a time when they were exported from Iowa to Western Canada . . . a sort
of advance guard of the Iowa farmers who flocked to our prairies during the first
decade of this century. We brought horses to Manitoba and the West from that
state during several years. At Grundy Centre, I bought excellent animals at
an average cost of $62.50 each" (Beecham Trotter, *A horseman and the west*,
Toronto, 1925, 237 ff.; also W. Johnston, *History of the County of Perth*, Stratford, 1903, 162-3).

[1]"The 'bunt' smut has been a very serious pest for many years past and
has been more prevalent than usual during 1891. The wheat grown by many
farmers which would otherwise have realized the best prices has, from this cause,
been much depreciated in value, and in some instances become quite unsaleable.
The total annual loss to the farming community in the North-West from smut is
immense, and would be difficult to estimate" (*S.p.*, 7f, 1892). An outbreak of
smut in 1905, along with the increase in weeds, was reported as the cause of much
loss to the grain-growers (*S.p.*, 15, 1906-7). "The character of the season is a
most important factor in determining the value of the wheat crop. The year
1904 was comparatively unfavourable, while the present year has been favourable.
That portion of the crop (probably about two-thirds of the whole) marketed
before December 1, 1905 is largely No. 1 Northern. It is also worthy of comment
that the number of ears of wheat graded rejected this year on account of weed
seeds is more than double that of 1904. The total number classed as 'rejected'
for smut has also more than doubled" (*S.p.*, 16, 1906).

buyers, when they were looking at the wheat, would put a handful to their noses the first thing and—"Pouf! Smutty!" Then we had to treat our wheat before we sowed it in the spring with bluestone or formaldehyde or formalin, which was a very effective way of checking the smut. . . . The head of a large milling company, paid a visit to our section one year and advised the farmers to give up growing soft wheat. If they would do so, he would supply them with a hard wheat called Scotch Fife,[1] and he would guarantee them ten to twenty cents more per bushel. We gradually got into the hard wheat, but we failed to find any difference in the price. . . . The first year we had the railroad in our section, the Ogilvy Company built an elevator of forty thousand bushels capacity and it was filled several times during that season. There was considerable frozen wheat that year. The flour from that wheat was to feed the fishermen down by the sea.

5

Advantages of Agriculture in Western Canada

The attraction of new land contributed to the difficulties of developing a technique suitable to settled agriculture. In 1870 Grant[2] stated that, in addition to free land to the extent of 160 acres, one-third of which was sufficient to raise "beets, potatoes or wheat", the farmer had several advantages.

He does not need to use manure, for so worthless is it considered that the Legislature has had to pass a law prohibiting people from throwing it into the rivers. He has not to buy guano, nor to make compost heaps. The land, if it has any fault, is naturally too rich. Hay is so abundant that when threshing the grain at one end of the yard, they burn the straw at the other end to get rid of it. He does not need to clear the land of trees, stumps or rocks—for there are none. Very little fencing is required, for he can enclose all his arable land at once with one fence, and pasture is common and illimitable. There is a good market all over Manitoba for stock or produce of any kind, and if a settler is discontented he can sell his stock and implements for their full value to new comers.

---

[1] The railways carried this seed wheat free of charge. Wheat was sown with 1½ to 2 bushels per acre.

[2] G. M. Grant, *Ocean to ocean*, 82-3.

6
Problems of Agriculture in Western Canada

The boom accentuated the problems. Barneby travelled extensively over the west in 1883 and noted the effects of the speculation of 1881 and 1882.

So much land is being held unoccupied and uncultivated that settlers do not feel inclined to come and buy at a price to pay another man's profit; when, within a few miles (namely, over the United States border in Dakota) they can procure equally good land on reasonable and indeed liberal terms. Not only does this evil system of locking up the lands prevent immigration, but it also disheartens the settlers already established. In proportion as population ebbs away from them, so also the civilisation they had expected, in the shape of education for their children, and church services for themselves, ceases to be possible. Looking at it from a practical point of view, it does not answer to erect a school or church in a thinly-populated district; they may indeed be built, but even supposing funds to be forthcoming to keep them going, the long distances would preclude a regular and constant attendance, and thus the success would be, at the best, but partial. . . . Many of the farms are not as well cultivated now as they were formerly, for, during the "boom" of 1881-2, numbers of the original settlers sold their land to speculators, and these latter, unable to re-sell them on account of the reaction in prices, have also failed (whether from want of knowledge, cash, or will, I cannot say) to cultivate their purchases; the result being that many farms are at present out of cultivation.[1]

Moreover, settlers were encouraged to become speculators. With very little capital they attempted to sell their homesteads after securing a patent and after taking the "cream" of the soil with three years' cropping. With the second or third years wild buckwheat and lambsquarter became serious menaces. The raising of livestock to provide manure was impossible because of lack of cash, expense of buildings for long winters, as well as expense of feeding[2] during the same period.

---

[1]Barneby noted "the half-profit system; a plan which is much in vogue"
[2]Hay cut at the rate of 2 to 3 tons per acre sold fresh at $3.00 to $5.00 and in the spring $5.00 to $10.00 per ton. "As regards the crops; wheat, oats, barley, and potatoes grow most luxuriantly upon the land when first broken and for from one to four years afterwards according to the depth of soil. Potatoes, especially, do exceedingly well; I hardly saw a bad crop in all southern Manitoba. Those named are the staple crops of the country, and I particularly noticed that

Between Deloraine and Wakopa, and between Cartwright and Manitoba City, near Pembina crossing, complaints were constant that, after 5 years, fertility declined
and weeds[1] became a serious menace. "As far as the
section of the country between Deloraine and Wakopa is
concerned the land is being ruined by small men with small
means and there is too little of the real farming element
about." With capital at 12 per cent., holdings of even 320
acres were worked with difficulty. "Owing to their small
means, the present race of settlers find it more feasible, as
well as more immediately profitable, to crop as much as
they can; and, accordingly, each year they break and backset a portion of their 160 or 320 acres, thus gradually diminishing their grass land." The profits made by settlers[2]
during the boom was an additional incentive "to sell at a
profit after the first few years and to move on elsewhere in
order to repeat the process". By 1883 free lands in southern
Manitoba had been taken up and Qu'Appelle and Moosejaw
were regarded as the most promising districts. The best
wheat-fields were stated to be in the district between Battleford and Prince Albert in the north and Qu'Appelle and
Brandon in the south—200 miles long by 100 miles broad.

7

Export of Wheat

In spite of the difficulties of agriculture, western Canada
was slowly developing a base for the export of increasing

---

we nowhere came on any clover. Cattle thrive well on the grasses; but as to
sheep, I saw so few of them, and hear so many conflicting opinions on the subject,
that I was led to assume that they cannot do well." Livestock was scarce. "In
the whole course of our drive from Brandon to Manitoba City we did not see
100 sheep and not more than perhaps 200 head of cattle." See a description of
a cattle farm near Winnipeg in 1882 in W. H. Barneby, *Life and labour in the
far, far west*, 382-3.

[1] "Among the most noticeable weeds are those known as 'tumbling mustard',
'hare's ear mustard', and tall 'ragweed', which in the vicinity of Fort Qu'Appelle,
N.W.T., are reported spreading to an alarming extent. The Russian thistle or
tumbling weed is reported to have gained a foothold in southern Manitoba, and
in the Prince Albert district, N.W.T." (*S.p.*, 8, 1896).

[2] See, for example, the case of Mr. Harmer near Manitoba City, who
started about 1878 with $90.00. After acquiring a homestead and pre-emption
he sold the whole in the boom for $12,000 with which he bought an improved
farm of 160 acres for $4,000 and a grazing farm for $5,000 (W. H. Barneby, *Life
and labour in the far, far west*, 335-7). Scrip was on sale in large quantities and
accentuated the effects of speculation (*ibid.*, 323-6).

quantities of surplus wheat.[1] The local demands of a
steadily increasing population were met and with improved
transportation exports developed. Wheat had peculiar
qualities facilitating the development of an export trade and
as a food-stuff it supported settlement[2] in a direct and
cumulative fashion. Low costs of production made it a
powerful direct and indirect stimulus to the growth of
settlement. By 1877:

> Besides the ordinary exports of furs and wheat, the house of
> Gerry & Co., of Winnipeg, have exported wheat to Europe.
> The exports of this year were greater than those of last year;
> but exportation of the produce of this Province cannot
> be carried out effectually until the means of transport are
> greater and more advantageous. The interval between the
> appearance of grain in our market and the close of navigation
> is too short to admit of exportation on a large scale.[3]

The first shipment of grain from Winnipeg to Toronto was
made in 1876 and totalled 412 sacks (857⅛ bushels). It
consisted of seed grain consigned to Steele Brothers and
purchased at 85 cents a bushel plus 26 cents per cotton sack
and 35 cents a bushel freight (Winnipeg to Duluth, 24 cents,
Duluth to Sarnia, 5 cents). The first wheat was shipped
from the big plain in the autumn of 1881. Freight charges
to Cornwall—its point of destination—were $1.12 a hundred-
weight.[4] The first grain elevator was completed at Port
Arthur in 1883 and the railway linked with shipping on the
Great Lakes.[5] "In 1884 England[6] imported nearly 5,000,000
bushels of our wheat—a very satisfactory showing—two

---

[1]On production of wheat see D. A. MacGibbon, *The grain trade of Canada;*
W. W. Swanson and P. C. Armstrong, *Wheat* (Toronto, 1930); A. H. R. Buller,
Essays on wheat (New York, 1919); H. S. Patton, *Grain growers cooperation in
western Canada* (Cambridge, 1928); W. A. Mackintosh, *Agricultural cooperation
in western Canada* (Kingston, 1924); J. Mavor, "Report to the board of trade on
the north-west of Canada" (*Command papers*, 2628, 1904); J. Mavor, "Agricultural development in the northwest of Canada 1905 until 1909" (*Proceedings*
of the British Association for the Advancement of Science, 1909, 209-230). See
Reports of the department of agriculture, *Journals of the legislative assembly,
Manitoba*, especially 1881, app. B. On the importance of development of technique in flour-milling, see C. B. Kuhlmann, *The development of the flour-milling
industry in the United States* (Boston, 1929).
  [2]Winnipeg had steam flour-mills as early as 1876.
  [3]*S.p.*, 9, 1878.
  [4]Beecham Trotter, *Horseman and the west*, 209.
  [5]J. McCannel, "Shipping on Lake Superior" (Thunder Bay Historical
Society, 1926-27 and 1927-28, 11-20).
  [6]*S.p.*, 10, 1886.

years, only, after our first surplus for exportation; but a year later the Canadian Pacific Railway carried wheat from the Northwest to Liverpool for 25c. to 30c. per bushel." "American roads, having no direct communication with the seaboard, cannot hope to compete against this."[1] Higher prices were an effective weapon in competition for immigrants with Dakota and Minnesota. In 1885 samples of wheat were sent to representative millers in the British Isles and the superiority of Manitoba no. 1 hard wheat for milling purposes was established and made generally known. At Brandon[2] prices ranged from 35 cents to 71 cents, and by the end of the year 682,300 bushels had been sold. Implement men and lumber dealers stated that fully 75 per cent. of their obligations had been met.

---

[1]*S.p.*, 8, 1885.

[2]"The Brandon wheat market for the past three months [*October to December, 1885*] was well worthy of notice. It was a most interesting sight to see the farmers' teams, heavily laden with grain, coming into town from every direction and crowding on the avenue leading to the four large elevators, which were taxed to their utmost capacity to receive and ship the grain as fast as the farmers brought it in, it being by no means an unusual sight to see over 100 teams at once upon the street waiting to be unloaded, and no person unacquainted with the rapid growth of this country would believe that Brandon represented a town only four and a half years old, and that the crop now being marketed was only the fourth since the prairie was first disturbed by the plough of the white man" (*S.p.*, 10, 1886).

INDUSTRY

1

Construction of the Railway

The introduction of the railway was directly and indirectly responsible for the growth of industry. The immediate effects of the construction of the railroad were shown in the growth of important subsidiary industries, the development of traffic, and the establishment of nuclei for the rapid expansion of economic activities.

The organization essential to rapid construction of the railroad was worked out in relation to labour and material, and was largely dependent on American experience. Surveyors were employed to locate the route, and labour to clear the right of way, build the grade, and lay the track. Steel was mobilized and located at depots, and lumber and ties were provided for the road-bed. The line was

raised about four feet above the level of the prairie so as to keep it out of the snow in the winter. In constructing this bank the first thing done is, for a width on each side of the line of about twenty yards, to cut the turf, and to lay it as the foundation of the "dump" which is to carry the line. This having been done, ploughs set to work, and the earth beneath the turf is ploughed up to the depth of ten or twelve inches. There is then brought to bear upon this what is called a scraper—a big shovel drawn by a pair of horses. The driver puts his horses at right angles to the dump, and, digging the nose of the scraper into soft ploughed-up soil, fills it, and, as his horses cross the dump, he turns it over. Crossing to the other side and turning his horses, he repeats the same proceeding and it is wonderful how quickly, with the two span of horses and two scrapers crossing one another, the dump rises to the required height. When this is done, there is of course a considerable amount of levelling to be gone through; but the quantity of spade-labour is, by this mode of making a railway, reduced to a minimum.[1]

---

[1] A. S. Hill, *Autumn wanderings in the northwest*, 72-3. See also W. Vaughan, *Sir William Van Horne* (Toronto, 1926).

The grading was let out in sub-contracts,
the head contractor always keeping one gang of his own men
ready to finish any work that seems likely not to be completed in time for the "ironing", and when it is reported that
such an event is likely to happen, this head contractor's
gang goes to the front and finishes up the unfinished work,
and of course charges it against the sub-contractor.
Sidings were laid at intervals from 6 to 10 miles, and construction trains proceeded from these bases. Each train
carried forward materials for construction for one mile of
track, and as many as 4 trains were on a siding.

The construction train, containing ties, metals and fish-joint
plates sufficient for some two or three hundred yards of line,
is brought up to the rear of these cars [*three boarding cars*][1]
and immediately the contents are turned off to the right and
left of the line. As this is done, light wagons, drawn each by a
span of horses or mules, pick up as many of these ties and
rails as they can carry,[2] and bear them forward and deposit them
by the side of the line to the front of the boarding cars, dropping them as nearly as can be calculated at the points at
which they will be required for the laying of the line. As the
ties are dropped they are picked up and laid in their places,
two men standing by with marked rods and putting them in
at distances of two feet apart from centre to centre. When a
sufficient number of these are laid, five or six other men carry
one of the rails[3] and lay it down upon the adjusted ties, and,
as this is placed, it is fixed to the ties by large spikes; a striker
standing by with a heavy hammer drives the spike down as it
is stuck in by a person to whom this work is assigned. The
rail is then fixed to the line of which it forms the prolongation

---

[1]Barneby gives 13 cars:—no. 1, truck; no. 2, boarding car; no. 3, cooking car;
nos. 4-9, boarding cars; no. 10, blacksmith's shop; nos. 11-12, store cars; and no.
13, contractor's car.

[2]30 sleepers per team, or 15 to each rail.

[3]Hand-cars brought the rails, pins, and fish-plates to the end of the completed line after they had been thrown off the flat cars and reloaded (12 men to a
rail). "These hand-trucks are each drawn by two horses, one on either side of
the rails, at the top of the embankment. On reaching the farther end of the
last two newly-laid rails, six men on either side of the truck each seize a rail
between them and throw it down in exact position; a couple of others gauge these
two rails, in order to see that they are correct; four men following with spikes
place one at each of the four ends of the rails; four others screw in the two
fish-plates; and another four follow with crowbars, to raise the sleepers whilst
the spikes are being hammered in. All work in order, and opposite to each
other on each separate rail. After these come more men with hammers and
spikes to make the rail secure; but the truck containing the rails, etc., passes on
over these two newly-laid ones before this is done. All the men must keep in
their places and move on ahead, otherwise they will be caught up by those
behind them."

by a fish-joint plate, and as each pair is laid the trolley passes
on with other rails, spikes and plates; and these again are laid
in exact continuity. The load of the construction train that
has brought up this material being exhausted, the engine
pushes on the boarding cars to the end of the rails so laid, and
then returns and carries back its construction train to the
nearest siding, probably some five or six miles in the rear,
whence another construction train is brought up, and the
"ironing" proceeds in the same manner.

About 300 men were employed in laying track. "They
boarded and slept in rough-and-ready pullmans, having
mostly three decks of bunks." Langdon and Shepard,
"experienced railroad builders of St. Paul", had 5,000 men
and 1,700 teams at work during one season when a record
of 6½ miles of track in a day was established. Telegraph
poles were brought in and the bark removed before they
were put in place preparatory to stringing the wires. Holes
were dug,[1] the poles set in and wires strung to establish "free
communication between the end of steel and headquarters"
in Winnipeg.

Construction involved the importation of large numbers
of labourers and provided wages for settlers during periods
of inactivity on homesteads. On the government section
from Port Arthur to Winnipeg:

> Our men came from nearly all parts of the world—Russia,
> Sweden, Germany, Holland, Iceland, Ireland, Great Britain,
> and the Dominion. There were also many Scotch and French
> half-breeds, as well as full-blooded Indians among them, the
> contractors finding that associating the various nationalities
> in camp was more conducive to peace and obedience than when
> a large number of fellow-countrymen formed a gang.[2]

In 1890:

> It was estimated as many as 40,000 persons connected with
> the building of the railway, in one capacity or another, went
> into the North-West during the period of construction, and it
> is undoubted that very large numbers continued to go for-
> ward with the progress of the railway work, after it passed the

---

[1]"Post-hole excavation was my allotted modicum in a work that was to
make Canada famous. The foreman gave me a seven-foot crowbar, and as long
a spoon for scooping up the soil, the crow-bar broke. I was to dig five-foot holes
with these romantic aids to Canadian history, for two dollars a day and board"
(Beecham Trotter, *A horseman and the west*, 100). Branch telegraph lines were
also built, for example, from Dunmore to Lethbridge and Fort Macleod and
from Moosejaw to Wood Mountain (*S.p.*, 12, 1886).
[2]Mary Fitzgibbon, *A trip to Manitoba*, 155.

western boundary of Alberta and entered the Province of British Columbia.[1]

2
Growth of Cities

Cities grew up like mushrooms with the approach of the railroad. Rapid fall in prices stimulated settlement and the growth of distributing agencies. The crown timber agent reported at Edmonton on October 31, 1884, that: "The prices of all necessaries, although still high, have fallen fully 50 per cent. since the railway was built as far as Calgary; and the famine prices we had to pay within the last two years will never occur again."[2] At Winnipeg the cost of a keg of nails declined from $25.00 to $3.50 after the railway was completed. Medicine Hat became a city of from 100 to 150 houses or tents. Barneby, writing in 1884, stated:

> Medicine Hat already contains several hotels, e.g., the Saskatchewan, the Brunswick, the Lansdowne (in honour of the new Governor-General), the American, the Canadian Pacific Railroad, and the Commercial. Some of these, indeed, are only tents; but they bear the name of hotel over their doors, though they make up perhaps at the outside only half-a-dozen cribs. There are also a number of stores, six billiard-rooms or halls, a post-office, and one or two restaurants; also
> "A Parlour"
> "For Ice Creams" "For Cold Drinks"

Brandon, Regina, Calgary,[3] and other points became cities over night. The dominion government immigration agent wrote at Brandon on December 31, 1882:

> Although only eighteen months since it was an unbroken prairie, it is now a large business centre with a population of over 4000. It has all the conveniences of an old town. It has three fine churches, a splendid two-storey brick veneered schoolhouse, sixteen hotels, two banks, two banking brokers. It also has stores, blacksmith shops, harness and shoemakers'

---

[1]*S.p.*, 64, 1890.

[2]*S.p.*, 13, 1884. On the difficulties of travel and the high cost of transport in the plains area in the pre-railway period, see J. C. Hamilton, *The prairie province*, 45-6; M. McNaughton, *Overland to Cariboo;* Earl of Southesk, *Saskatchewan and the Rocky Mountains* (Toronto, 1875); W. F. Butler, *The great lone land* (London, 1873); G. M. Grant, *Ocean to ocean;* S. B. Steele, *Forty years in Canada* (Toronto, 1918); W. F. Milton and W. B. Cheadle, *The northwest passage by land* (London, 1901); D. M. Gordon, *Mountain and prairie* (Montreal, 1886); C. Horetzky, *Canada on the Pacific* (Montreal, 1874); J. M. Macoun, *Autobiography* (Ottawa, 1922).

[3]See W. H. Barneby, *Life and labour in the far, far west*, 270-3.

shops, one saw mill, two planing mills, one grist mill capable of grinding seventy-five barrels of flour daily, and furnished by farmers in the district. There are also two grain elevators capable of storing 50,000 bushels of grain, and another of greater capacity is to be erected next summer. It has also ten miles of streets, well graded and gravelled, eighteen miles of plank sidewalks, a well organized fire brigade and steam engine, and four large water tanks, nearly completed.[1]

3
The Coal Industry

Construction of the railroad and the growth of towns created demands for wood and coal. Fort Macleod had used coal prior to the coming of the railway.[2] As early as 1884, following the completion of the railway, the Saskatchewan Coal Company at Medicine Hat sold coal in Winnipeg at $7.50 per ton and forced the price of cordwood down from $8.00 and $10.00 to $3.50 and $5.00.[3] The completion of the line from Dunmore to Lethbridge in the autumn of 1885 brought a decline in prices at Winnipeg to $9.00 per ton for hard coal and $7.00 for soft coal.[4]

4
The Lumber Industry

Rapid growth of settlements and of towns led to increased demands for building material. Timber regulations were designed to encourage the production of cheap timber for settlement. In 1874 a charge of $1.00 per acre was placed on woodland for the use of settlers. Settlers were able to obtain timber under free and paid permits. In 1872 provision was made for the leasing of timber berths for 21 years in return for a ground rent plus 5 per cent. of the monthly sales account, but in 1876, 1879, and 1881, temporary one-year leases and the payment of stumpage dues were adopted as a general basis of leasing. The license covered 50 square

---

[1] *S.p.*, 14, 1883. See also Beecham Trotter, *A horseman and the west.*
[2] A. S. Hill, *Autumn wanderings in the northwest*, 165.
[3] *S.p.*, 13, 1884.
[4] *S.p.*, 8, 1886. See a description of the relation of the demands of the railway to the opening of the Lethbridge mines (O. D. Skelton, *Life and times of Sir Alexander Tilloch Galt*, chapter xviii).

miles[1] in 1881. In 1886 competition was required in the grant of all berths.

The demands of towns such as Winnipeg led to the growth of the industry on a large scale. In 1872 a saw-mill was started in Winnipeg and the lumber was cut from logs brought from the Roseau and Red Lake Rivers.[2] The great bulk of lumber floated down the Red River from Moorehead, to which point it had been shipped by American lumbermen, was gradually displaced by lumber produced on the ground. In 1875 Winnipeg had 3 saw-mills and 2 sash and planing factories, the largest mill with a daily capacity of 50,000 feet. In winter operators got out 5,000,000 feet of logs of which about one-fifth came from south-east Manitoba and the remainder from American limits in Minnesota at a cost of $12.00 per thousand feet. One mill had 2 circular saws driven by a 50-horse-power Waterous engine and in 1875 cut 3,340,000 feet. With this saw-mill, a sash, shingle and picket factory was driven by a 50-horse-power Minneapolis engine, the whole employing nearly 100 men at from $1.50 to $3.00 per day and incurring running expenses of about $1,500 weekly.[3] In 1882 the first horizontal band saw-mill for sawing slabs was introduced in the west.

The completion of the railway in 1878 was followed by the improvement of marketing facilities for American and Ontario lumber and by a marked decline in price.[4] In 1880 3 saw-mills were erected at Winnipeg and 3 on the east shore of Lake Winnipeg. In 1883 mills on Lake Winnipeg produced 12,400,706 feet. Barges were employed on Lake Winnipeg[5] to transport the lumber to market. In 1880 lumber-mills costing $75,000 to $100,000 were in operation at Rat Portage. These mills were able to draw on the pine forests of northern Minnesota and to compete with the railway in the western market.[6] As a result of competition prices declined from $31.00 per M feet BM in 1883 to $16.00

---

[1] Reduced to 25 square miles in 1906.
[2] J. H. O'Donnell, *Manitoba as I saw it from 1869 to date* (Toronto, 1909), 107-8.
[3] J. C. Hamilton, *The prairie province*, 140-1.
[4] *S.p.*, 9, 1879.
[5] *S.p.*, 12, 1881 and *S.p.*, 3, 1883.
[6] *S.p.*, 8, 1886.

in 1886.[1] In the latter year Canadian lumbermen produced 21,773,069 BM and imported 1,451,515 BM from the United States.

In 1884 the Edmonton district produced 1,087,872 feet and Prince Albert 643,725 feet. Lumber sold at Prince Albert and Battleford for $30.00 to $48.00 per thousand. The total production of the north-west in that year was 28,687,814 feet of lumber, 652,500 shingles, and 892,400 lath.[2]

5

The Ranching Industry

Increasing population created a demand for food-stuffs especially meat products and provisions, in addition to wheat. Domestic livestock production was supplemented by imports[3] and by the expansion of the ranching industry[4] in strategic geographic areas, such as the southern foothills of Alberta. The industry was limited to territory which provided abundant shelter "of the hills, and woods and coulees" to enable cattle and horses to winter out. Excellent territory included the area north from the boundary to High River and east from the Rocky Mountains, about 50 miles. It was estimated optimistically that this area of about 4,000 square miles would carry, at the rate of 10 acres per head, 256,000 head and yield about 50,000 head.

The success of the livestock trade developed from Montreal in the late seventies, and the prospect of immediate competition of the railway were factors responsible for the development of the industry. Supplies were hauled from Fort Benton on the Missouri by bull-teams to Fort Macleod and Calgary.[5] The industry proved of more immediate importance as a support to the development of the west than as a basis of export.

---

[1] *S.p.*, 7, 1887.
[2] *S.p.*, 13, 1884.
[3] In 1874 and 1875 imports of meat and butter in Manitoba and British Columbia increased rapidly (*S.p.*, 2, 1876). For the year ending June 30, 1875, imports at Winnipeg totalled $1,243,309 of which the United States, chiefly Minnesota, supplied $781,323 and Great Britain, $457,449.
[4] See C. M. MacInnes, *In the shadow of the rockies*, chapters ix-xiv.
[5] J. R. Craig, *Ranching with lords and commons* (Toronto, 1903), 83-100.

I have, after my fourth year's more full and practical acquaintance with the subject, come to the conclusion that for many years the increasing number of the Indians who, under treaty, have to be fed with beef, the crowds of immigrants and of men engaged upon the railway works, and the Mounted Police, coupled with the necessary retention of the females of the herds for breeding and filling up the land, will keep in the Northwest for many years to come all the cattle that can be reared there, and will allow of no surplus for export to Europe.[1]

The extremely important supply of labour[2] was dependent on American technique and experience. "There is always something to learn in handling cattle on the range." To the "care and industry" of the cowboy "the rancher must look in no small degree for the success of his results". His duties[3] included getting weak cows out of mire-holes in early spring, attending the round-up arranged by the association,[4] "cutting out" the cows and calves, roping and branding the calves, cutting and curing hay on the rich hay bottoms, and, in case of ice forming on the snow in winter, making the hay available to the cattle, and finally in the autumn,

---

[1]A. S. Hill, *Autumn wanderings in the northwest*, 394-9.

[2]"Mrs. Brown had had a hard life since her girlhood and, though a comparatively young woman, looked far older than her years, worn out with ceaseless work. Like the great majority of Canadian women, she was extraordinarily quick and capable, and, as I told her, would have concocted a cake and put it in the oven, and perhaps baked it, before I had collected the materials to make mine. But the demon of work had got her in its clutches, as it seems to get so many Canadian women, and she *could* not rest or take things easily. She had been for four years on a ranch—completely bare of crops, as it was a cattle-range—and she said that the great expanse got on her nerves, and she hated it, save when in the spring the ground was starred with myriads of tiny flowers. Her husband and the other men were off with the cattle during the greater part of the day, and she told me that without her children she thought that she would have gone mad. In summer the heat was great, and the mosquitoes were so bad that she hardly ever left the house, but lived behind the wire screens which were in front of all the doors and windows; and she often watched her husband riding off, looking as if he and his horse were in a mist, so dense was the cloud of these pestilent little insects" (E. C. Sykes, *A home-help in Canada*, London, 1912, 121-2).

[3]G. S. Hill, *Autumn wanderings in the northwest*, 407-13.

[4]Districts were marked off by natural boundaries such as rivers or mountain ranges. Ranchers within the district formed associations. The Willow Creek district was about 80 miles by 60 miles. Ranches varied in size. Colonel de Winton's ranch was 6 miles by 5 miles (W. H. Barneby, *Life and labour in the far, far west*, 278). Regulations in 1882 provided for rental of 100,000 acres at one cent per acre for 21 years, the lessee being required to stock the ground with one head of cattle or horses to every 10 acres leased. In 1886 the rental was raised to 2 cents per acre and the government reserved the right to cancel the lease on a 2 years' notice if the land was required for settlement. Competition in the sale of leaseholds was required in 1887.

making a second round-up and taking the finished animals to market.

6

The Fishing Industry

Other resources drawn on to meet the increasing demand for meat products included the fish of northern lakes. The Icelandic settlement at Gimli became engaged at an early date in the handling of fish for the Winnipeg market. A successful winter fishery near Grindstone Point in 1878 was sufficient to meet the local demands of the colony, the demands of farmers who exchanged flour for fish, and the demands of Winnipeg where fish was "sold at high prices".[1] The settlers worked in various parts of the province during the summer and returned to the fishery in winter. Writing on December 31, 1879, the Icelandic agent stated that 6,000 frozen white fish had been sold in Winnipeg. The Icelanders combined cutting cordwood, freighting, and barge-building with fishing.

---

[1] *S.p.*, 9, 1879.

CREDIT AND MONEY

The influx of capital on a large scale such as was necessary for the construction of railroads involved substantial support to private enterprise by the federal government[1] in terms of money and land. Confederation was extended as a wider base for security of capital borrowings.

The Province of Manitoba[2] according to the terms of federation shifted a debt of $472,090 to the dominion. This debt was increased as a result of readjustments to $3,775,600 in 1895. The provincial debt increased from $108,151 in 1882 to $1,497,620 in 1886 and to $4,656,920 in 1894 of which $2,626,523 were paid for construction of railways. The rapid growth of towns and the demand for capital expenditures, especially for streets and water-works, necessitated incorporation and the growth of debt. Winnipeg was incorporated in 1873, and in 1895 had debentures outstanding of $2,464,683. The debt of Brandon increased from $73,986 in 1882 to $528,053 in 1895. Calgary, Prince Albert, Regina, Edmonton, and other centres registered in turn their demands for capital.

Channels which had grown up for the mobilization and distribution of capital in the St. Lawrence drainage basin in response particularly to the demands of an agricultural population were rapidly extended to meet the new demands of the west. For example, Augustus Nanton[3] arrived in Winnipeg in 1883 for the purpose of opening business for the North of Scotland Canadian Mortgage Company through

---

[1] See H. A. Innis, *A history of the Canadian Pacific Railway.*

[2] See Report of the delegates of the Manitoban legislature appointed to press upon the federal government a favourable consideration of the claims of the province, *Journal of the legislative assembly, Manitoba*, 1885, app.; also J. R. Perry, *Public debts in Canada* (University of Toronto studies, history and economics, I), 53-4, 85-7; A. C. Ewart, *The municipal history of Manitoba*, and S. M. Wickett, *Municipal government in the Northwest Territories* (University of Toronto studies, history and economics, II), 133 *ff.* For later studies of problems of municipal finance, see R. M. Haig, *The exemption of improvements from taxation in Canada and the United States* (New York, 1910); A. Stalker, *Taxation of land values in western Canada* (McGill university publications, series VI, 4, 1918); A. B. Clark, *An outline of provincial and municipal taxation in British Columbia, Alberta, Saskatchewan, and Manitoba* (Winnipeg, 1920).

[3] See R. G. Macbeth, *Sir Augustus Nanton* (Toronto, 1931).

the firm of Osler and Hammond of Toronto. The financial institutions of Ontario extended operations to the west. The Dominion Government Savings Bank established a branch at Winnipeg in 1872 and the Union Bank[1] established a branch in 1877. The Canada Life Insurance Company opened an office in Winnipeg in 1879. Distributing organizations increased rapidly. Merchants formerly engaged in the fur trade extended their activities, for example J. H. Ashdown.[2] Mercantile houses from Ontario and Quebec established branches. Senator James Turner of the firm of James Turner and Company, wholesale merchants in Hamilton, visited Fort Garry in 1867 and the firm built the first brick building in Winnipeg in 1872.[3] It was estimated in 1884 that 75 houses were engaged in the wholesale and jobbing trade of Winnipeg, involving sales totalling $14,220,068 and that retail sales totalled $5,809,600. Organizations which had been built up in relation to the demands of agriculture in Ontario served as a base for the expansion of western Canada.

---

[1]See H. S. Seaman, *Manitoba* (Winnipeg, 1920).
[2]J. C. Hamilton, *The prairie province*, 37-42.
[3]See *Hamilton, the Birmingham of Canada* (Hamilton, 1892) for numerous references to expansion to the west.

SECTION IV

BRITISH COLUMBIA[1]

SUBSECTION A

TRANSPORT AND COMMUNICATION[2]

In British Columbia, as in the remainder of Canada, water-transportation dominated early economic development. Transport by land became supplementary to transport by water. The character of the rivers in the Rocky Mountain region and the distance from Europe restricted early development to commodities of slight bulk and high value, such as furs and placer gold.

The economic development of the northern part of the Pacific coast drainage basin was influenced at the beginning

---

[1]For general description, see C. Phillips-Wooley, *The trottings of a tenderfoot* (London, 1884), especially chapter iii and *A sportsman's eden* (London, 1888); M. St. John, *The sea of mountains* (London, 1877); D. G. F. Macdonald, *British Columbia and Vancouver Island* (London, 1862); J. D. Pemberton, *Vancouver Island and British Columbia* (London, 1860); C. Forbes, *Vancouver Island* (Victoria, 1862); J. Emmerson, *British Columbia and Vancouver Island* (Durham, 1865); W. C. Hazlitt, *British Columbia and Vancouver Island* (London, 1858); H. S. Palmer, *Williams Lake and Cariboo* (New Westminster, 1863); R. M. Ballantyne, *Handbook to the new goldfields* (Edinburgh, 1858); K. Cornwallis, *The new eldorado or British Columbia* (London, 1858); A. A. Harvey, *Statistical account of British Columbia* (Ottawa, 1867); W. Moberly, *The rocks and rivers of British Columbia* (London, 1885). See also for general reference, H. H. Bancroft, *History of British Columbia* (New York, 1887); A. Begg, *History of British Columbia* (Toronto, 1894); F. W. Howay and E. O. S. Scholefield, *British Columbia* (Montreal, n.d.), 4 vols.; H. J. Boam, *British Columbia, its history, people, commerce and resources* (London, 1912); *Canada and its provinces*, XXII; A. Métin, *La Colombie Britannique, étude sur la colonisation au Canada* (Paris, 1908); R. H. Coats and R. E. Gosnell, *Sir James Douglas* (Toronto, 1910); W. N. Sage, *Sir James Douglas* (Toronto, 1930); *Papers relative to the affairs of British Columbia* (1859-1862); *Copies or extracts of correspondence relative to the discovery of gold in the Fraser River district* (London, 1858); F. W. Howay, *British Columbia* (Toronto, 1928); W. J. Trimble, *The mining advance into the inland empire* (Madison, 1914); *Picturesque Canada* (Toronto, 1882), II, 867-880; *Publications of the archives of British Columbia* (Victoria); *Guide to the Province of British Columbia* (Victoria, 1877); A. C. Anderson, *Dominion of the west* (Victoria, 1872); G. M. Sproat, *British Columbia*; R. E. Gosnell, *Yearbook of British Columbia* (Victoria, 1897); *Sessional papers, British Columbia; Journals of the legislative assembly.*

[2]For a very valuable account, see E. O. S. Scholefield and F. W. Howay, *British Columbia* (Chicago, 1914), II, chapters v ff.

771

of the last half of the nineteenth century by important developments in the preceding decade. In the first place, as a result of the pressure of settlement on the Columbia, and of the Oregon Treaty in 1846, the Hudson's Bay Company had reorganized its transport system by establishing a new depot at Victoria on Vancouver Island, and by developing a transport route up the Fraser to Yale and Hope, and north to New Caledonia. The southern political boundary of the present Province of British Columbia had been established prior to the middle of the century and the transport organization adapted to the new political unit. In the second place, the California gold-rush of 1849 had led to the inrush of settlement, not only to California, but to more northern areas. The technique of mining placer gold had been matured and prospectors moved along the rivers of the Rocky Mountains to the north. In the first decade of the second half of the century they reached the Fraser River.

1

The Lower Fraser River

The system of transport elaborated under the fur trade in relation to the Fraser River served as a base for the development of gold-mining in the same region. Moreover, steam navigation on the ocean and the river supported a rapid development of mining following the discovery of gold. Steam and iron accentuated the rapidity of development. The Panama railroad was completed in 1855 and the first transcontinental in the United States in 1869. Steamers from San Francisco rushed to Victoria carrying double complements. Finally provided with necessaries at Victoria, miners proceeded by steamer,[1] sailing vessel, canoe, and boat to the mouth of the Fraser River.[2] Steamers were brought

---

[1]"Too frail to bear an ocean passage it was necessary to construct an enormous skow or lighter for each steamer. The lighter was decked over and fitted with pumps, like a caisson. It was then sunk under the steamer in shoal water, built up at bow and stern, so as to completely cover her hull, and pumped out, a mast being steeped through the deck and bottom of the steamer on to the lighter's kelson. The whole was then taken in tow by an ocean steamship" (R. C. Mayne, *British Columbia and Vancouver Island*, 47-8).

[2]The entrance to the Fraser River was very difficult and insurance rates were as high to New Westminster as to Columbia.

from the Sacramento River and remodelled for navigation across the strait. Steamers of 18 to 20 feet draught transferred their cargoes at Langley, at first to boats, rafts, and canoes, and later to stern-wheel American steamboats. The latter were

> propelled by a large wheel protruding beyond the stern, the rudders—for there are generally two or three—being placed between it and the vessel's stern. They are admirably adapted to pass between snags and close to bluffs, where a side wheel would be knocked away, and are affixed to flat-bottomed vessels drawing no more than eighteen to twenty inches of water.[1]

Going upstream these boats were subject to risks from overcharged boilers, and downstream from snags created by large trees floating heavy end downstream and pointing upstream, impaling the steamboat.

> A supply of tarred blankets is always kept handy for service, and if a hole is stove in the steamer's bottom, the captain coolly runs her ashore on the nearest convenient shoal, jams as many blankets into the crevice as seems necessary, nails down a few boards over them, and continues on his journey composedly.[2]

To make up for deficiency of depth, the steamboats were of great length and beam.

> Their bows are of the shape termed "shovel-nosed", and from this point they run away aft quite straight; very much resembling a section of a rifle-cartridge in fact. The propelling medium is a huge wheel at the stern, from eighteen to twenty-four feet in diameter, extending across the entire width of

---

[1] R. C. Mayne, *British Columbia and Vancouver Island*, 90-2.

[2] "The prodigal indifference of American Steamboat men in regard to human life was characteristically exemplified in a conversation in which I took part. The enquiry was put to a Yankee as to the safety of a certain steamer. 'She may do well for passengers, but I wouldn't trust treasure in her', was the unfeeling but candid reply" (R. C. Mayne, *British Columbia and Vancouver Island*, 233). . . . "The captain was a wary old pilot, who knew every inch of the river, every tree to tie up to, and every snag and rock in our course, and who, from long familiarity with danger, seemed to regard his arduous duties as lightly as the driver of a 'one hoss shay'. His was no easy time of it either, for in bad parts of the river he had to take the wheel himself for hours at a stretch. The mate was a burly ruffian, who exercised a strong arm and voice over the deckhands, mostly made up of Indians, and who seemed to have less to do (except in the way of talking and swearing) than any other member of the crew. The engineer was apparently a runaway fireman from a man-of-war, who had been promoted to his present position, *faute de mieux*; whilst his subordinates, who replenished continually the insatiable furnace, were, I should think, the veriest and hardest-working slaves in existence. The high-toned and elegant bar-keeper in snowy shirt sleeves, and of gentlemanly mien, was on board of course."

the boat.   This wheel is not immersed to a greater depth than that of the paddles (about eighteen inches), and is connected with the cylinders by means of cranks and connecting-rods. The boilers are well for'ard, close in the bows, and the furnaces are on a level with main deck and quite open, to enable them to get all the draught caused by the motion of the vessel.   The steam is conducted from the boilers to the cylinders in the engine-room (which is the farthest thing astern on the main deck) by long pipes, which make the place fearfully hot in summer-time.   The rest of the space on this level is occupied by freight, and by Indians, Chinamen, and niggers, whom the free and independent American citizen refuses to have in his company on the upper or passenger deck.

Above the rectagonal part of the hull (the shovel-nosed bow being retained as an open space) is the saloon deck, generally fitted up in very good style, and being much the same as the similar part of an ordinary steamer.   Sometimes yet another deck is added to this, while surmounting everything is the pilot house, placed at the for'ard extremity of the upper deck; the wheel working the rudders (of which there are four parallel to each other) by means of chains running in grooves along the hurricane-deck.[1]

From Emory's Bar at the head of steamboat navigation, goods were taken in long, wooden canoes[2] to Yale and from there up the Fraser.

2

The Upper Tributaries of the Fraser (Cariboo District)

Penetration to the upper Fraser was made by the Harrison River and Lillooet route following the completion of a trail in 1859 and of a road in 1861.   The trail from Yale to Lytton was pushed steadily forward and in 1863 extended to Soda Creek where connections were made with a steamer to Quesnel and a trail to William's Creek in the Cariboo district.   The road from Yale to Clinton rapidly displaced

---

[1]R. B. Johnson, *Very far west indeed* (London, 1872), 56-7.

[2]"They carried about four tons apiece.   They were nearly fifty feet in length, with a beam of six feet, and each one burned and chiselled out of a single cedar-tree!   They had been strengthened for their present use by strong ribs and braces, and were fitted up for eight oars, with a twenty-foot oar at the stern for steering: a rudder would not have had enough power in that tremendous stream, and the eddies and whirlpools caused by it.   In the bow of each was a strong stanchion to fix the tow-rope to; and a man was stationed in the bows to watch the run of the current and to look after hidden rocks, helping to steer, moreover, when necessity occurred, with a paddle" (R. B. Johnson, *Very far west indeed*, 125 *ff.*).

the Harrison-Lillooet route, especially after 1864.[1]   In 1865 a road was completed to Barkerville.

Road-building was facilitated by the work of miners during the closed seasons:

> There are three grades of men employed; choppers, who are the pioneers, cut down the trees in the line of the road, and fill up ravines with crib-work built of logs, or build log bridges over the streams; graders, who follow the choppers, with pick and shovel, grub out the stumps of the trees, and dig away or fill up the soil; and the blasters, who are a special class, generally Cornish or Welshmen, who assault the rocks, where they are in the way, with drill and sledge hammer, and quickly demolish them afterwards with gunpowder.[2]

Along the trails and roads, goods were transported to the mines.   On foot men packed about 80 pounds on their backs.   Mules[3] carried 300 pounds, 150 on each side; camels proved unsuccessful.   "Packing was a better business than mining."   In 1860, 2,723 mules were packed for the interior from Yale.   In 1870 the Hon. Hector Langevin reported regarding the Cariboo road:

> The mode of conveyance is, for passengers, by stages drawn by four or six horses, and for merchandise, by packed trains of two, three or four great waggons drawn by ten or twelve mules, or by sixteen or eighteen oxen.   There are packed trains composed exclusively of mules, each of which carries a certain weight, the goods or merchandise being strongly bound on the back of the animal.   The packed trains travel at a foot's pace, some few miles a day, and at four or five o'clock in the evening, the muleteers stop on the road, and unharness

---

[1] See E. O. S. Scholefield, "The Yale Cariboo wagon road" (*British Columbia magazine*, January-February, 1911); W. Moberly, *History of the Cariboo wagon road* (Vancouver, 1908); F. W. Howay, *The work of the Royal Engineers in British Columbia 1858 to 1863* (Victoria, 1910); also on the Harrison-Lillooet route, R. C. Mayne, *British Columbia and Vancouver Island*, 50.

[2] R. B. Johnson, *Very far west indeed*, 175.

[3] See R. B. Johnson, *Very far west indeed*, 69-70, 110, 189.   "You make up your goods into three packs, one goes on each side of the pack-saddle and one between them, on top.   The weight of the side-packs must be equal; that is the first important point.   The packs are attached to the saddle by a slight cord, and then comes the most important thing in the whole affair.   This is the synch or belly-band, to one end of which is spliced a long rope, and at the other end is a hook, through which the rope, after passing over the packs, is rove, a series of bights almost like the game of 'cat's cradle' surrounds all the packs, 'fore and aft', and then by putting your knee against the horse and hauling on the last end, everything jambs itself tight, and a single hitch of the end to the synch makes everything secure" (W. S. Green, *Among the Selkirk glaciers*, 178).   For a full description of packing, see J. A. Lees and W. J. Clutterbuck, *B.C. 1887, a ramble in British Columbia* (London, 1888), 229-232.

their beasts, the harness being left where the animal halts; the cattle are turned out to graze till morning, and the muleteers, who are either whites, Indians or Chinese, camp on the side of the road near a stream, which they never neglect to select for the purpose. . . . I was informed that there were on the Cariboo road, about 20 ox-trains, of 16 head of cattle each, 25 to 30 horse or mule trains, of 10 head of cattle each, and at least 400 horses or mules without vehicles, all engaged in conveying goods and merchandise.[1]

Improvement of the roads was followed by the organization of stages and expresses. The Wells Fargo Express, Ballou's Fraser River Express, Jeffray's Express, and Freeman's Express were engaged in handling mail and transporting gold.[2] Accommodation along the road was the subject of general complaint. Milton and Cheadle wrote that it

was everywhere miserable enough, but after leaving Clinton it became abominable. The only bed was the floor[3] of the "wayside-houses", which occur every ten miles or so, and are named the "Fiftieth", or "Hundredth Mile House" according to the nearest mile-post. Our solitary blankets formed poor padding against the inequalities of the rough-hewn boards, and equally ineffectual to keep out the cold draughts which whistled under the ill-fitting door of the hut. A wayside house on the road to the mines is merely a rough log hut of a single room; at one end a large open chimney and at the side a bar counter, behind which are shelves with rows of bottles containing the vilest of alcoholic drinks.[4]

"Our quarters at Cushion's Hotel were vile. A blanket spread over the floor of the loft was one bedroom, but the swarms of lice which infested the place rendered sleep almost impossible." At Clinton,[5] the junction of the 2 routes there were "three respectable hotels, a saw-mill, a butcher's shop, two blacksmiths and farriers, a store of a miscellaneous description, stables, barns, brickyard, and several shanties, among which you observe the *Celestial's sanctum*, with an announcement over the door that he has the courage to undertake the 'lively' operation of washing a Cariboo shirt".

---

[1] *S.p.*, 10, 1872.
[2] R. C. Mayne, *British Columbia and Vancouver Island*, 71.
[3] ". . . all the reply I could get was that, 'he reckoned any man that 'ud raise a growl on such an occashin was darned small pertaters; I might spread out on the side-walk, or turn in with an Injin, if I was a mind to, but his charge to a white man for nightly accomodashin was fifty cents, and niggers rigidly excluded!'" (R. B. Johnson, *Very far west indeed*, 39-40).
[4] Milton and Cheadle, *The northwest passage by land* (London, 1901), 352-4.
[5] G. M. Grant, *Ocean to ocean*, 344-6.

British Columbia as a result of the gold-rush was in possession of roads to the interior, from Harrison to Lillooet, from Yale to Barkerville, from Hope to Similkameen, and from Hope to Skagit Flat, and trails to Wild Horse Creek in the Kootenay, to Big Bend on the Columbia, to Omineca, and to Cassiar. The interior had been prospected and explored by the gold-miner. Along the coast systems of transportation had developed. The *Sir James Douglas*, a steamer of 153 tons, 110 feet keel, 18 feet 8 inches beam ran between Victoria, Nanaimo, and Comox, and the Hudson's Bay Company's steamer *Otter* ran to the Skeena River. A steamboat had even penetrated to Lake Tatla to serve the Omineca district. The River Nass had been ascended for 25 miles by a steamer in 1855 and an alternative route to Omineca was provided by steamers ascending the Skeena.

3

The Canadian Pacific Railway

Construction of the railway was a stimulus to economic development in British Columbia as it had been in western Canada. It was built on the foundation laid down in relation to steam navigation, mining, and lumbering. These industries had grown up primarily in relation to transportation by water. The railroad provided new demands in its construction and operation and in the new markets opened by it. Sir Edward Watkin described the road through the mountains as having ruling grades of 116 feet to the mile. "The rails are of steel, 70 lbs. to the yard, and the locomotives, of the 'Consolidation' pattern, with eight driving wheels are able . . . to take a train of 12 loaded cars." The grade at Kicking Horse Pass was an exception, "with two or three miles . . . of 4½ feet per hundred, say 1 to 22½. There are several catch sidings on this grade, running upwards on the slopes of the mountains for trains or cars to be turned into, in the event of a break loose or run away, and a man is always in attendance at the switches leading to these sidings." For this grade 2 engines were required for the standard load. Large timber-bridges crossed the creeks and valleys. The difficulty of hauling heavy dining cars was overcome by establishing small inns at Field, Glacier House, and North Bend. Losses from avalanches necessitated the expenditure of about $900,000 to build over 4 miles of snow-sheds.[1]

From Donald to Revelstoke or across the Selkirk range (39 miles) the speed of the train was limited to 11 miles per hour. For the trip from Montreal to Port Moody (2,894 miles) the regular schedule was completed in 139 hours or 20¾ miles per hour. Shortly after the completion of the C.P.R. a line was completed (August, 1886) from Esquimault to Nanaimo (75 miles) to improve the market for coal. This line had steel rails 50 to 54 pounds per yard and timber-bridges and trestles built from about 1,000,000 cubic feet of timber. The steepest grade ran 80 feet per mile towards Nanaimo and 79 feet per mile toward Esquimault.[2]

> Pioneer railways are not like works at home. The lines are single, with crossing places every five, ten, or twenty miles; ballast is not always used, the lines on prairies being laid for long stretches on the earth formation; rivers, chasms, canons and cataracts are crossed by timber trestle bridges. . . .
> Begun as pioneer works, they undergo, as traffic progresses, many improvements. Ballast is laid down. Iron or steel bridges are substituted for timber. The gorges spanned by trestles are, one by one, filled up, by the use of the steam digger to fill, and the ballast plough to push out, the stuff from the flat bottomed wagons on each side and through the interstices of, the trestles. Sometimes the timber is left in; sometimes it is drawn out and used elsewhere. . . . Whenever there are gorges and valleys to pass in a timbered country, the facility they give of getting "through" is enormous. The Canadian Pacific would not be open now, but for this facility.[3]

---

[1]"The sheds are constructed as follows:—On the high side of the mountain slope a timber crib filled with stones is constructed. Along the entire length of the shed, and on the opposite side of the track, a timber trestle is erected, strong timber beams are laid from the top of the cribwork to the top of the trestle, 4 feet apart and at an angle representing the slope of the mountain, as nearly as possible. These are covered over with 4-inch planking, and the beams are strutted on either side from the trestle and from the crib. The covering is placed at such a height as to give 21 feet headway from the under side of the beam to the centre of the track. The longest of these sheds is 3,700 feet, and is near the Glacier Hotel." Trestles and snow-sheds required elaborate devices for protection against fire. The trestle bridges were each manned by a watchman and the snow-sheds were continually inspected—a special section gang of 10 or 12 men and a boss was stationed at 5-mile intervals (Edward Watkin, *Canada and the states*, 47-48; also W. S. Green, *Among the Selkirk glaciers*, 56, 61-2, 91-3).

[2]W. S. Green, *Among the Selkirk glaciers*, 69.

[3]Edward Watkin, *Canada and the states*, 54.

4

Communications

Following admission of British Columbia to Confederation the colonial postal system[1] was taken over by the dominion. In 1871 arrangements were made to carry mail in closed bags between Windsor and Victoria by San Francisco on the payment of a transit rate. Mail was carried, through California, Oregon, and Washington by rail and stage to Olympia, and weekly by steamer to Victoria, or fortnightly by steamer between San Francisco and Victoria.[2] In 1872 the dominion government had 38 offices in British Columbia which handled 160,000 letters and cards and 150,000 newspapers. By 1872 telegraph lines connected Swinomish, Washington, with Matsqui, Hope, Yale, Lytton, Quesnel, and Barkerville. A branch connected Matsqui with New Westminster, and Burrard Inlet. Telegraph and cables ran between Victoria, Saanich, and Swinomish.[3] In 1884 a cable was laid between Clover Bay, V.I., and Dungeness, Washington, to connect with Seattle and Cape Flattery.[4]

---

[1]See A. S. Deaville, *The colonial postal systems and postage stamps of Vancouver Island and British Columbia, 1859-1871* (Victoria, 1928); "The colonial postal systems of Vancouver Island and British Columbia 1849-1871" (*Third annual report and proceedings* of the British Columbia Historical Association, 45-54); *Guide to the Province of British Columbia for 1877-8* (Victoria, 1877), 160 *ff*.
[2]*S.p.*, 2, 1872.
[3]*S.p.*, 5, 1872; *S.p.*, 2, 1874.
[4]*S.p.*, 12, 1886.

THE GOLD-MINING INDUSTRY[1]

The development of gold-mining on the Fraser and its tributaries was closely dependent on the geological background of placer-mining in general and of the Fraser River in particular. Gold is washed down by the swift waters of the Cordilleran region from areas in which it exists in relatively large nuggets, in fine particles referred to as flour gold. This light, fine gold is carried considerable distance down the rivers and deposited on bars.[2]

1

Methods of Mining on the Lower Fraser

On the Lower Fraser River,[3] operations began with prospecting and with relatively simple methods of mining. In 1858 mining centred about the district between Yale and Hope and was confined to the bars and the use of rockers.

---

[1]See E. O. S. Scholefield and F. W. Howay, *British Columbia*, II, chapter v *ff.* for an excellent account; also W. J. Trimble, "The mining advance into the inland empire" (*Bulletin* of the University of Wisconsin, no. 638, history series, III, no. 2, 137-392, Madison, 1914, especially chapters ii-iv, and chapter vi *ff*, and bibliography); also A. G. Morice, *The history of the northern interior of British Columbia (1660-1880)* (London, 1906), chapters xix *ff.*

[2]"Bars are formed simply by a deposit of heaps of detritus at various bends of a river flowing through accumulations of irrupted rock, and between mountains whose sides have been broken down by former great convulsions. The rushing river tears away mass after mass of this rock and gravel, and, carrying on a natural combination of the 'sluicing' and 'crushing' processes, deposits the gold, with its ever-accompanying black metallic sand and a certain quantity of common earth, at intervals along its banks, carrying most of the lighter sand, &c., out to its mouth, there to form sandbanks and flats. It will be easily understood, therefore, that these bars are formed at every place where there is or has been anything to catch the drift as it comes down. But what is somewhat curious is the very different value of the deposit at various bars, or even parts of the same bar, some being very rich, others very poor, even when they are close together; and this happens not in the vertical section, which would be to some extent intelligible, but at an equal distance under the surface. One part of a bar may 'give out', while another part will be worth working 20 feet deeper. Thus all bars are formed in the same way, even although the rivers which deposited them have long since ceased to flow, or been diverted into other channels, causing what are termed 'dry diggings'. . . . Very rich bars are often covered with sand, mud, &c., for, in some instances several hundred feet" (R. C. Mayne, *British Columbia and Vancouver Island*, 66).

[3]See F. W. Howay, *The early history of the Fraser River mines.*

The following year activity shifted to the district above Lytton and the bars were deserted for the dry diggings which involved larger supplies of capital. These large-scale operations were evident in the increasing importance of the sluice box and of hydraulic methods.

The first task of the miner attracted to a new gold country or district, by the report of its wealth, is "prospecting". For this purpose every miner, however light his equipment may otherwise be, carries with him a "pan" and a small quantity of quicksilver; the latter to be used only where the gold is very fine. Very little experience enables a miner to detect that "colour" of the earth which indicates the presence of the metallic sand in which gold is found. Wherever, as he travels through the new country, he sees this, he stops at once to wash a pan of dirt, and thus test its value. Although many diggings are found away from the bank of a stream, the river-sides are the places where gold is generally first looked for and worked. . . . The spots first searched are generally those upon the bank of a river where the deposit consists of a thick, stiff mud or clay, with stones. In some cases this is covered with sand, so that the surface has to be removed before the "pay dust" is revealed. All these workings on river-banks are called "bars", and are usually named after the prospector, or from some incident connected with their discovery.

When the prospector comes to dirt which looks as if it would pay, he unslings his pan from his back, and proceeds to test it. This he effects by filling his pan with the earth, then squatting on the edge of the stream, he takes it by the rim, dipping it in the water, and giving it a kind of rotary motion stirring and kneading the contents occasionally until the whole is completely moistened. The larger stones are then thrown out, the edge of the pan canted upwards, and a continual flow of water made to pass through it until, the lighter portion of its contents being washed away, nothing but a few pebbles and specks of black metallic sand are left, among which the gold, if there is any, will be found. The rotary movement, by which the heavier pebbles and bits of gold are kept in the centre of the pan, and the lighter earth allowed to pass over its edge, requires considerable practice, and an unskilful prospector will perhaps pass by a place as not being worth working that an experienced hand will recognise as very rich. The specific gravity of the black sand being nearly equal to that of gold, while wet they cannot be at once separated, and the nuggets, if any, being taken out, the pan is laid in the sun or by a fire to dry. When dry the lighter particles of sand are blown away; or if the gold is very fine it is amalgamated with quicksilver. The miners know by practice how much gold in a pan will constitute a rich digging, and they usually express the value of the earth as "5", "10", or "15" cent dirt, meaning that each pan so washed will yield so much in money. Panning, it may be remarked, never gives the full value of the dirt, as may be imagined from the roughness of the process. If the gold should be in flakes, a good deal is likely to be lost in the process, as it will not then sink readily to the bottom of the pan, and is more likely to be washed away with the sand. In panning, as well as, indeed, in all the other primitive processes of washing gold, the superior specific gravity of this metal over others, except platinum, is the basis of operations; all depending upon its settling at the bottom of whatever vessel may chance to be used.

The "pan" is hardly ever used except for prospecting, so that the "rocker" or "cradle" may be described as the most primitive appliance used in gold-washing. In the winter of 1859, when I first went up the Fraser, the rocker was the general machine—the use of sluices not having then begun. It was used in California as early as 1848, being formed rudely of logs, or the trunk of a tree. And yet, ungainly as they were, they commanded, before saw-mills were established in the country, enormous prices.

The rocker,[1] then, consists of a box $3\frac{1}{2}$ to 4 feet long, about 2 feet wide, and $1\frac{1}{2}$ deep. The top and one end of this box are open, and at the lower end the sides slope gradually until they reach the bottom. At its head is attached a closely-jointed box with a sheet-iron bottom, pierced with holes sufficiently large to allow pebbles to pass through. This machine is provided with rockers like a child's cradle, while within, cleets are placed to arrest the gold in its passage. One of the miners then, the cradle being placed by the water's edge, feeds it with earth, while another rocks and supplies it with water. The dirt to be washed is thrown into the upper iron box, and a continual stream of water being poured in, it is disintegrated, the gold and pebbles passing down to the bottom, where the water is allowed to carry the stones away, and the cleets arrest the precious metal.

---

[1]In the Cariboo country the "long tom" was used extensively. The dirt was "emptied into a long box, called the dump-box or 'long tom', having a false bottom of parallel bars, with narrow spaces between them, raised a few inches above the true bottom, across which several cross-pieces are placed. A stream of water, brought in a series of troughs called 'flumes', sometimes for a considerable distance, pours into the dump-box at one end, and runs out by another series of troughs at the other. As the dirt is emptied in, a man armed with a large many-pronged fork stirs it up continually, and removes the larger stones. The smaller particles and the clay are carried down the stream, while the gold, from its greater weight, falls through the spaces between the parallel bars of the false bottom, and is arrested by the transverse ones or 'riffle' of the true one" (Milton and Cheadle, *The northwest passage by land*, 365).

When the gold is very fine I have seen a piece of cloth laid along the bottom box, covered with quicksilver to arrest the gold. When a party of miners work with rockers, they divide the labour of rocking, carrying water, if necessary, and digging equally among themselves. The rocker is the only apparatus that can be at all successfully worked singlehanded; and rough as it appears and really is, I have seen men make 30 to 50 dollars a day with it, while far greater sums have been known to be realized by it. In these remarks I have assumed that my readers generally are aware that quicksilver arrests whatever gold passes over it, and, forming an amalgam with it, retains it until it is retorted from it. In washing gold, quicksilver has to be used always, except where mineral is found very large and coarse. Even then the earth is generally made to pass over some quicksilver before it escapes altogether, in order to preserve the finer particles. I may here mention that in a "sluice" of ordinary size 40 or 50 lbs. of quicksilver[1] are used daily; in a rocker 8 or 10 lbs. Of course the same quicksilver can be used over and over again when the gold has been retorted from it.

The next important method is "sluicing". This is by far the most commonly used both in British Columbia and California, employing, I suppose, one-half the mining population of both countries.

Sluicing is, moreover, an operation which can be carried on on any scale, from two or three men upon a river bar, to a rich company washing away an entire hill by the "Hydraulic" process. Whatever may be the scale of operations, however, "sluicing" is necessarily connected with a system of "flumes", or wooden aqueducts of greater or less extent, either running along the back of a river-bar, and supplying the sluices at it, or cobwebbing and intersecting the whole country as in California. I have seen flumes on the Shady Creek Canal there, conveying an enormous stream of water across a deep ravine at the height of 100 to 200 feet.

"Sluice-boxes" are of various sizes, but generally from 2 to 3 feet long, by about the same width. These are fitted closely together at the ends, so as to form a continuous strongly-built trough of the required length, from 15 to 20 to several thousand feet, their make and strength depending entirely upon the work they have to do. I will here describe sluicing upon a moderate scale, as I found it in practice at Hill's Bar upon the Fraser during my visit there in 1858.

This bar was taken up in claims early in 1858, its size being then about 1½ mile, although it has since been much extended, the richness of the soil proving, I believe, greater as it is ascended. In this place, then, a flume was put up,

---

[1] Quicksilver was brought from California.

carrying the water from a stream which descended the mountain at its southern end along the whole length of the bar, and behind those claims which were being worked. From this flume each miner led a sluice down towards the river; his sluice being placed at such an angle that the water would run through it with sufficient force to carry the earth, but not, of course, the gold with it. Its strength, indeed, is so regulated as to allow time for the riffles and quicksilver to catch the gold as it passes. The supply of water from the flume to each sluice is regulated by a gate in the side of the flume, which is raised for so much per inch. The price paid for water of course varies greatly with the cost of timber, engineering difficulties of making the flume, &c. It is ordinarily established by the miners, who meet and agree to pay to any individual or company who may undertake the work a certain rateable rental for the water. Their construction, indeed, is one of the most profitable of colonial speculations. The flume I am now speaking of cost 7000 or 8000 dollars, and each miner paid a dollar an inch for water daily. Since that time it has become much cheaper, and the usual price is about 25 cents (1s.) an inch, the width of the gate being 1 foot. The sluice-boxes here were very slight, about inch-plank, as the dirt which had to pass through them was not large. In the bottom of each box was a grating, made of strips of plank nailed crosswise to each other, but not attached to the box like the riffles. In the interstices of these gratings quicksilver is spread to catch the fine gold, the coarse being caught by the grating itself. The sluice is placed on tressels or legs, so as to raise it to the height convenient for shovelling the earth in; the water is then let on, and several men feed the sluice with earth from either side, while one or two with iron rakes stir it up or pull out any large stones which might break the gratings.

. . . I will take the opportunity of describing the most common appliances for raising water from a river for the use of a sluice on its banks. The machinery used is known as the "flutter-wheel", and the traveller in a mining country will see them erected in every conceivable manner and place. It is the same in principle and very similar in appearance to our common "undershot-wheel", consisting of a large wheel 20 to 30 feet in diameter, turned by the force of the current. The paddles are fitted with buckets made to fill themselves with water as they pass under the wheel, which they empty as they turn over into a trough placed convenient for the purpose and leading to the sluice. In a river with a rapid current, like the Fraser, they can be made to supply almost any quantity of water. . . .

As the miners in California began to gain experience in

gold-seeking, they found that at a certain distance beneath the surface of the earth a layer of rock existed, on which the gold, by its superior specific gravity, had gradually settled. Experience soon taught the miner to discard the upper earth, which was comparatively valueless, and to seek for gold in the cracks or "pockets" of this bed-rock, or in the layer of earth or clay covering it. The depth of this rock is very various; sometimes it crops out at the surface, while at other times it is found 150 to 200 feet down. Where it is very deep, recourse must be had to regular shaft-sinking and tunnelling, as in a coal or copper mine; but when the rock is only 20 or 30 feet beneath the surface, tunnelling on a very small scale, known as "Koyote-ing", from its fancied resemblance to the burrowing of the small wild-dog common to British Columbia and California, is adopted. These little tunnels are made to save the expense of shovelling off the 20 or 30 feet of earth that cover the "pay-dirt" on the bed-rock, and their extraordinary number gives a very strange appearance to those parts of the country which have been thoroughly "Koyote-ed". I have seen a hill completely honeycombed with these burrows, carried through and through it, and interlacing in every possible direction. . . .

The Koyote tunnels are only made sufficiently high for the workman to sit upright in them. They are generally carried through somewhat stiffish clay, and are propped and supported by wooden posts, but, as may be imagined in the case of such small apertures extending for so great a length as some of them do, they are very unsafe. Not unfrequently they "cave in" without the slightest warning. Sometimes, too, the earth settles down upon the bedrock so slowly and silently that the poor victims are buried alive unknown to their companions without.

The danger of this work and its inefficiency for extracting the gold, much of which was lost in these dark holes, gave rise, as the agency of water became more appreciated, to "ground-sluicing". This consists in directing a heavy stream of water upon the bank which is to be removed, and, with the aid of pick and shovel, washing the natural surface away and bringing the "pay-streak" next the bed-rock into view. . . .[1]

Hydraulic mining is entitled to some consideration. Bars that pay but a small return to the hand on the ordinary principle of working, will yield handsomely when operated upon by the hydraulic method. Inseparably connected with this is a system of flumes or sluice-boxes, generally 14 inches in length by about 3 feet in width. These are fastened together at the ends, and form a long and strongly built trough, extended as far as may be necessary—sometimes

[1] R. C. Mayne, *British Columbia and Vancouver Island*, 426-437.

thousands of feet. It is lined with thick wooden blocks, partly to resist the friction occasioned by the passage of the debris, and also to allow room for quicksilver in the interstices for attracting and detaining the gold. Sometimes the quicksilver is placed in riffles, fixed transversely upon each other. This massive and continuous line of boxes is constructed near the bank about to be attacked. It is obvious that to bring down millions of tons of earth with the ordinary appliances of manual labour would be a tedious and profitless task. Another flume is therefore prepared for the purpose of bringing water from a level so much higher than the side of the hill to be reduced as to secure for the stream thus diverted a force powerful enough to do execution upon the masses of earth that are to be washed down. Attached to this latter flume is a common hose, consisting of a double ply of canvas or gutta percha. Through the iron mouth of the hose, the volume of water, conducted in the manner described from a convenient elevation, is directed against the bank, as when the jet of the fireman plays upon a burning house. The skilful operator aims at eating into the lower strata of the hill a considerable way till the upper portion can no longer be supported. A signal is given as the moment of the threatened crash approaches that miners in dangerous proximity may betake themselves to a safe distance. After the huge masses of earth have fallen, the men return and shovel it into the sluice-boxes through which a volume of water passes that removes the dirt and precipitates the gold into the riffles. The expense attending this ingenious arrangement is often enormous in consequence of the long way water may have to be conveyed. Unproductive ground, too, may be fixed upon for bed-rock fluming. But when mining parties are so fortunate as to select the proper spot, the operation can hardly fail to be remunerative. One or two of these "water-batteries" brought to bear upon a hill side can effect more than could be done by 100 men with picks and shovels.[1]

2

Methods of Mining on the Upper Fraser

Placer-mining in the narrow creeks of the Upper Fraser differed materially from bar-mining, and operations on the dry diggings above the Fraser. The larger particles or nuggets sink to the bottom of the creek or river immediately and in the process of time rest on bed-rock, whereas the fine flour gold is washed down to the bars. The miner

---

[1]M. Macfie, *Vancouver Island and British Columbia*, 270-272.

working upstream comes in contact with the bars nearest the river's mouth and mining begins generally on a small scale with more primitive equipment and on an individualistic or partnership basis. On the Fraser, bar-mining was confined chiefly to the section between Yale and Lytton. Once gold has been discovered on the bars, however, the prospector continues his search upstream for the tributaries with the larger particles and nuggets. "Gold was first discovered on the sand-bars of the lower Fraser in the state of the finest dust. The old miners of California traced it up the river, and followed it as it became of coarser and coarser grain 400 miles along the Fraser, and then up the small affluents from Cariboo."[1] After he has succeeded in isolating the more promising tributaries, it is generally necessary to conduct operations on a relatively large scale in order to mine the larger particles which are found on bed-rock. Mountains, forests, and high costs of transport were handicaps to prospecting and the long and severe winter from October to June restricted mining operations. The character of the deposits contributed to high, but also to very uncertain, returns.[2] After the location, staking, and registering of a claim[3] it was necessary to sink a shaft to bed-rock. The pay channel was found in narrow strips and was located by tunnelling across the bed of the creek. Upright timbers and cross beams were necessary to support the roof. While British Columbia had advantages over California in the abundance of water, the problem of pumping out water by a water-wheel and chain pump was serious.[4]

---

[1]Milton and Cheadle, *The northwest passage by land*, 359.

[2]*Ibid.*, 360-1; *Cheadle's journal of trip across Canada* (Ottawa, 1931), 230 ff.

[3]The technique of placer-mining was matured by Americans but organization depended in part on the experience of Victoria and New South Wales and later of New Zealand. The gold commissioner became a basic feature in administration in British Columbia and the organization of which he became the centre provided a steadiness in the development of placer-mining which ensured rapid and methodical exploitation. (See Gold Fields Act of 1859 and Gold Fields Act of 1864.) "Many mining men came to British Columbia from California, where parts of Spanish mining laws were still in force; and beyond question, the laws of Spain have been indirectly a factor in moulding the mining laws of Canada" (J. M. Clark, "Mining legislation in Canada", *Annals* of the American Academy, January, 1913, 151-7). See also *Canada, an encyclopedia*, III, 404 ff.; and *Guide to the Province of British Columbia for 1877-8* (Victoria, 1877), 197 ff.

[4]See a valuable description of difficulties with water and of the uncertainty of mining in R. B. Johnson, *Very far west indeed*, 121-2, 186-7.

The returns varied widely. On William's Creek two distinct leads produced gold heavily alloyed with silver, and relatively pure gold. Nuggets from Lightning Creek and William's Creek were battered and water-worn. At Lowhee larger nuggets were found with little evidence of being water-worn.[1] The highest assays of Cariboo gold were obtained from Davis Creek, 718 fine valued at $18.97.64c. per ounce; and the lowest from William's Creek, 810 fine valued at $16.74.42c. per ounce. The average of Cariboo dust was 854 fine valued at $17.65.37c.[2] The shafts of Cameron Claim varied in yield from 40 to 112 ounces and the output of 3 shafts ranged from £2,000 to £5,000 per week. The yield of gold from various claims on William's Creek was estimated roughly as follows: Cameron and Aurora, $1,000,000 each; Dillar, Black Jack, Barker, Ericson, Caledonia, and Canadian, $500,000 each; Wake up Jack, Saw Mill, Moffat, and Ruby, $300,000 each. A length of 2 miles and a width of 150 feet on William's Creek produced about $25,000,000. In 1863 the Burns Tunnel Claim washed up 1,044 ounces, or $25,000, in one day, and in 1875 the Van Winkle Company on Lightning Creek produced 1,500 ounces in 6 days.[3] In 3 weeks in August, 1870, the "South Wales" Mine at Van Winkle produced 800 ounces; the "Forest Rose" Mine on William's Creek, 448 ounces in 2 weeks; and the Ballarat Mine, 167 ounces in the same length of time.

3

Total Production of Gold

In 1861 it was estimated that 5,000 men were engaged in gold-mining of which 1,500 were employed in the Cariboo country. The returns of these men were estimated as follows:[4]

---

[1]Milton and Cheadle, *The northwest passage by land*, 360.

[2]R. C. Mayne, *British Columbia and Vancouver Island*, 445.

[3]M. McNaughton, *Overland to Cariboo*, 153-4; *S.p.*, 10, 1872; H. J. Moberly, *When fur was king* (London, 1929), chapter xxiii; F. W. Howay, "The overland journey of the argonauts of 1862" (Royal Socity of Canada *transactions*, XIII, series 3, section II, 1919, 37-55); M. S. Wade, *Overlanders of '62* (Victoria, 1931).

[4]R. C. Mayne, *British Columbia and Vancouver Island*, 442-444.

79 miners known to have taken out of Cariboo...	$926,680
400 with claims producing from $1,000 to $2,000 (average)...............................	600,000
1,021 earning wages $7.00 per day lowest and many $10.00 to $16.00, working 107 days...	764,729
Total yield from Cariboo................	$2,291,409
1,500 miners in other areas, 180 days at $10.00 (Thompson River, Fraser River below Fort George, Bridge River, Similkameen, Rock Creek)...............................	$2,700,000
2,000 miners, 180 days at $5.00..............	1,800,000
	$4,500,000
	$6,791,409

In 1870 the yield of gold was estimated as follows

Cariboo...................................	$1,047,245
Lillooet...................................	15,000
Columbia, *etc*.............................	161,000
Yale and Lytton...........................	110,000

Total production increased from $750,000 in 1858, to $3,913,563 in 1863, and declined with fluctuations to $1,336,956 in 1870 and $1,786,648 in 1876. The total yield from 1858 to 1876 was estimated at $39,953,618.

4

Decline of Gold-mining

The mining boom was of short duration in the "attic of North America", chiefly because of the high costs of transportation. The pick of the claims were alone able to withstand the costs of transport and large numbers of miners were forced to return. Moreover, high costs of operation were added to high costs of transport in the Cariboo district. "As a gold mining country for the poor man, Cariboo therefore soon began to decline. . . . By the close of the sixties the entire mining population of Cariboo had fallen off to about 2,500 and the annual yield was only a tittle of what it had been in previous years."[1] With mines in the Cariboo

[1]Baillie-Grohman, *Sport and life in the hunting gounds of western America and British Columbia* (London, 1900), 381. Miners began to move north to the Cassiar, to Omineca, and the Peace River, and eventually to Yukon and the Klondike. Flour gold was washed on the North Saskatchewan and in 1884 miners averaged from $4.00 to $10.00 a day (*S.p.*, 13, 1884). In 1894 at Morinville, settlers in spare time with a shovel, pick, wheelbarrow, a few planks, and a little quicksilver took out about $20,000 of gold ($15.00 an ounce) some averaging $5.00 a day (*S.p.*, 13, 1895).

running "to a depth of 100 to 150 feet under the ground" and with galleries running off the shaft "each of which is more than 200 feet long", the poor man was not able to operate the gravels of the Cariboo and with the working out of the richest bars on the Fraser River only the Chinese could afford to earn from $1.00 to $5.00 a day.

SUBSIDIARY INDUSTRIES

"The history of British Columbia is brief. Gold made and gold unmade it."[1] Such a statement under-estimates the importance of the contributions of gold. In the area which became known as British Columbia, placer-mining was responsible for rapid economic development in which emphasis was placed in the beginning on individualistic[2] lines of growth and later on larger capitalistic types of under-taking. Gold is a commodity which is responsible for im-mediate response in economic activity and for tremendous efforts in moving commodities toward the mining area. Its exploitation is rapid, and depreciation of equipment essential to its exploitation in terms of agriculture, industry, and trans-port follows immediately. The effects on the community concerned are such as characterize an economic cyclone.

On June 27, 1858, the *Republic* brought 800 passengers, on July 1, the *Sierra Nevada* brought 1,900, and on July 8 the *Orizaba* and the *Cortez* brought 2,800. Between March and June over 20,000 people arrived at Victoria. "A large town of tents sprang up on the harbour side." Timber and planks were imported in large quantities from American mills on Puget Sound for building purposes.[3] Sawn timber cost £20 per 1,000 feet. Town lots of 60 feet by 120 feet increased from £10 to £300 and £600 in a month. Rents of small lots of 20 feet by 60 feet varied from £50 to £100 per month.[4]

---

[1]Baillie-Grohman, *Sport and life in the hunting grounds of western America and British Columbia*, 316.

[2]Individualism is suggested in the following extract: "Waal, I've been my own boss (master) for the last thirteen years, and I reckon I never intend to work for no other man again. Thar ain't a trader on the creek but what'll give old Jake jawbone (credit) fur his regular hash and whiskey; and I allus pays some-time. I'll bet the Pacific Oshin to a cup o' cold water I strike it before the season's run out" (R. B. Johnson, *Very far west indeed*, 118).

[3]R. C. Mayne, *British Columbia and Vancouver Island*, 46-7.

[4]M. Macfie, *Vancouver Island and British Columbia*, 64-5; and R. C. Mayne, *British Columbia and Vancouver Island*, 44-7. The following extract is suggestive as to the speculative aspects: "My resolution got a little shaken on the following day by an excellent offer I received from a member of the legal profession, with whom I had struck up a casual acquaintance, and who advised me strongly not to go to the mines. 'A miner', said he, 'is but the means of conveying money into other people's pockets: he is simply our agent, though he wouldn't acknow-

Flour increased in price to £6 per barrel. The marked increase in population after the rush to the bars on the Fraser River was followed by a marked decline. Large numbers arriving in the summer of 1858 found the Fraser at high water, and the bars and benches flooded. In September, 1859, Victoria had declined in population to 1,500. Business in Victoria was stagnant and was faced with competition from overland traffic in provisions and bread-stuffs from the United States. With the close of 1860 news arrived of fresh discoveries in Cariboo.[1]

The requirements of operations on a large scale in the Cariboo country carried on at long distances from the mouth of the main river necessitated ample provision for transport. With the establishment of transport lines to the centre of mining operations, the community became engaged to an increasing extent in the production of industrial materials, especially of lumber, and of agricultural products.

Gold provided the base for the later economic developments of the province. Subsidiary industries became staple industries. Heavy and immediate demands for goods from established centres to the south were responsible for a marked expansion of shipping, for a heavy inbound cargo, and a strong stimulus to the growth of industries capable of supplying an outbound cargo. Local industries, which developed in relation to the demands of placer-mining, were subjected to severe strains with the decline of placer-mining, and survived in part with the growth of demands incidental to new staple industries or as new staple industries themselves.

1

Agriculture

The high costs of transportation and high prices were important stimuli to the development of local industries

---

ledge that position. I can name to you a hundred miners who have made fortunes, and lost or spent them, for perhaps two who had been able to stick to them. We townspeople have nothing to do but sit on our beam-ends, and wait for these hard-working, deluded creatures to come and pour wealth into our laps!"'
(R. B. Johnson, *Very far west indeed*, 47-8).

[1]M. Macfie, *Vancouver Island and British Columbia*, 73-4. See F. W. Howay, *British Columbia*, chapters xvii, xix, xx; also H. A. Innis, *A history of the Canadian Pacific Railway*, 3-21.

adapted to the geographical background. The demands of large numbers of men engaged in the industry favoured the development of production of food-stuffs and especially of agriculture.[1] The experience of the Hudson's Bay Company in the development of agricultural technique was especially important in the more northerly posts. In addition, the agricultural development of the Columbia River valley provided a base for expansion to the north. Herds of cattle and sheep were brought in from Oregon.[2]

The difficulties of agricultural development were numer-ous. The large trees of the British Columbian forests had to be felled and disposed of, chiefly by burning, and the extensive network of interlaced roots had to be cut through.[3] In the drier areas of the interior these problems were less serious and combined farms and ranches developed rapidly.

A farm at Pavillon begun in 1859 had in its second crop (1860) large numbers of garden vegetables and excellent crops of oats, barley, turnips, and potatoes, the latter yielding 375 bushels to the acre. Oats and barley were sold "in the sheaf for the mule trains passing to and from the mines". Cattle ran through the winter without shelter or feed.[4] In the same locality in 1863 a large farm of 1,860 acres had 175 acres under cultivation, chiefly in barley and oats but in-

---

[1]See R. C. L. Brown, *British Columbia* (New Westminster, 1863); *Canada, an encyclopedia*, V, 68 *ff.*

[2]For reference to a herd of 500 cattle, see R. B. Johnson, *Very far west indeed*, 96.

[3]R. C. Mayne, *British Columbia and Vancouver Island*, 88, 139, 392-3. Land could be taken up as follows: 160 acres on payment of 8s. registration fee and pre-emption at low rates decided by the government. Agriculture continued to labour against difficulties, "owing to the fact that other industries, mining, lumbering, and fishing often present better opportunities for money making than farming does. We lose them because the attractions of other industries draw them away. . . . From our experience, where we have kept carefully the time and the expense of material and provisions, we find that it costs from 150 dollars to 250 dollars an acre to put rough land into a good state of cultivation. . . . The requirements of the local market are so great that it will require years to overtake. In beef alone British Columbia imported $4,000,000 in 1914 representing at least 60,000 head for slaughter. . . . Our importations of sheep last year from Washington were 29,000 head. . . . Hog raising had been getting on pretty well until the high prices on the prairies. When wheat gets very high on the prairie people sell their hogs" (*Dominions royal commission on natural resources: Central and western provinces of Canada*, 1916. Cd. 8458-8459). See L. A. Wrinch, "Land policy of the colony of Vancouver Island 1849-1866" (M.A. thesis, University of British Columbia, 1932).

[4]R. C. Mayne, *British Columbia and Vancouver Island*, 385.

cluding 15 acres of potatoes, 2 acres of cabbage, an acre of turnips, an acre of onions, corn, beans, parsnips, and carrots. Barley was sold at $6.00 a bushel, cabbage at 25 cents a pound. The exceptionally high yield brought large profits, though these were in part offset by high wages and the necessity in many cases for irrigation. Dairying flourished along with agriculture. In 1863 a farmer drove 30 dairy cows into Cariboo "and netted £15 a day for four months. In eighteen months from his arrival in the colony he realized £4000." "Two years ago [*1861*] a man bought a cow for which he paid $140; that summer he made $350 by the sale of her milk and butter."[1] Hogs were "an immensely profitable investment in the colony, bacon being a staple commodity at the mines".

Prices in Victoria were lower than on the mainland, but still adequate to the development of certain lines of agriculture. With accessibility by water-routes, wheat and flour from California and Oregon checked development in the growth of cereals. The production of dairy products, of poultry products, and of garden vegetables flourished. In 1883 Barneby described the farms as "all small, and badly worked, and are only in patches here and there, for there is so much lumber (*i.e.*, wood and timber) about that it is impossible to get one of any size." Wages were said to double the wages in eastern Canada.

Flour-mills and distilleries

With the development of agriculture[2] in the interior, small flour-mills sprang into existence and in 1870 flour-mills were in operation at: New Westminster, a grist mill, 30 barrels per day; Hope, Yale, and Lytton, 5 flour-mills, 2 at 23 barrels per day and the remainder 10 barrels per day each; Lillooet, one flour-mill, 60 barrels per day, and one, 120 sacks in 12 hours; one at Dog Creek, 2,000 pounds of wheat per day; Soda Creek, one flour-mill (water-power), 40 barrels per day; Cariboo, one flour-mill (20-horse-power), 50

---

[1] M. Macfie, *Vancouver Island and British Columbia*, 292-5, 196-7.
[2] In 1870 agricultural imports totalled $225,193 of which flour and wheat were $83,643 (*S.p.*, 10, 1872).

barrels of flour per day. Breweries and distilleries were located at points on the coast with cheaper supplies of grain. Victoria at an early date had 5 breweries producing porter, light ale, and lager beer. In 1870 it had 4 breweries and 2 distilleries and New Westminster had one distillery producing 300 to 400 gallons per month.

Agriculture and its related industries were restricted by the slow growth of population, decline of placer-mining, and decline in importance of labour[1] with the evolution of capitalistic methods. The population[2] of British Columbia increased from 36,247 in 1871 to 49,459 in 1881 and 98,173 in 1891. Immigration was difficult and in spite of the steamship, voyages[3] from England took 118 days and second-class passenger fare was £30.

2

The Ranching Industry

The difficulties of agriculture favoured the development of ranching. The Kamloops district developed as an area suitable to the raising of livestock and to the marketing of products, especially to the Cariboo district.

Stock-raising is the principal industry of the country, agriculture being subsidiary to it. The way in which it has been conducted in the past by men of small means has been to enter for a homestead of 160 acres, under the Provincial rules, at $1 per acre, situated on the bank of a stream, so that it could be easily irrigated, and in the vicinity, if possible, of a natural hay meadow. A few head of cattle has been the start of most of the present well-to-do stock-men. Sufficient of land would be cultivated to supply the necessities of life, and enough wild hay be put up to guard against a severe winter or heavy snow fall, when stock would be unable to graze. Cattle were branded and allowed to roam on the ranges, which are large areas of the public domain, with some natural boundary, such as a high range of wooded hills, or ravines, &c. In the fall they were rounded up by the owners and the calves branded. In this way, by the natural increase in their herds, most of the

---

[1] The number of miners employed declined from a high point of 4,400 in 1864 to 2,282 in 1876 and total production of gold from a high point of $4,246,266 in 1862-3 to $1,786,648 in 1876. For references regarding 5,000 destitute unemployed, see R. B. Johnson, *Very far west indeed*.

[2] See *Reports of the registrar of births, deaths, and marriages 1872*.

[3] R. C. Mayne, *British Columbia and Vancouver Island*, 356-8.

ranchers have become comparatively wealthy. After the first fall of snow in the hills, usually in November, cattle descend to the lower or winter ranges, and if necessary are fed. At times it has been difficult to procure fodder, and the want of this provision has been the cause, on some occasions in the past, of considerable loss. For several winters past the animals have been able to graze on account of the mildness of the weather. At some of the ranches stacks of hay, of three different seasons' cut, were seen side by side, not having been required. The profits from this business in the past have been large.[1]

3
The Fishing Industry

In contrast with agriculture, development of the fishing industry was based on ample resources but expansion on a large scale was dependent on improved facilities for transport to a large market. The perishable character of the commodity restricted trade in fresh fish, and demand for smoked and salted salmon was limited. Early development was dependent on the transport organization of the Hudson's Bay Company. Activity in relation to the local demands of population supported an expansion of the industry. In 1862 the Alberni Mills exported 370 barrels of salt fish and 193 barrels of fish-oil, and in 1863, 470 barrels of salt fish and 239 barrels of fish-oil. According to Langevin, a Captain Stamp "for the first time exports salmon in tin boxes" in 1870. In 1876 the province exported 486,336 pounds of canned salmon valued at $70,636 and fishing stations were in operation on the Fraser and the Skeena Rivers. In 1883, 13 canneries were operating on the Fraser, 5 on the Skeena, 2 on the Nass, and one on Rivers Inlet. The number of cases packed fluctuated widely, increasing from 9,847 in 1876 to 113,601 in 1878, declining to 61,093 in 1879, rising to 225,061 in 1882, and falling off to 108,517 in 1885. The total value of British Columbian fish products was estimated at $1,078,038 in the latter year.[2]

The whale fishery developed rapidly following the success of an invention by Captain Roys of an explosive ball which

---

[1]*S.p.*, 7, 1887.
[2]See J. Z. Joncas, "The fisheries of Canada" (*Canadian economics*, 41-75).

"on penetrating the massive monster explodes". With the first success in 1868 whaling expanded rapidly, and in 1870 3 whaling companies killed 32 whales yielding 25,800 gallons of oil worth 50 cents per gallon. The plant included one vessel with boats and 2 stations with boats and employed 49 hands and a capital of $20,000. The dog-fish industry was even more important and 50,000 gallons of oil were produced, valued at 40 cents per gallon.[1]

4

The Lumber Industry

The demand for lumber,[2] following the rapid growth of Victoria and centres on the mainland and the more extensive prosecution of mining in the interior, was met as in the case of agriculture by local production adapted to the geographical background.

The demand for lumber in the manufacture of buildings, flumes, and sluice boxes became important on the Fraser and in the Cariboo. In 1870 saw-mills in the interior included 3 saw-mills with 183,000 feet daily capacity at New Westminster; 2 saw-mills cutting 7,000 feet per day at Yale and Lytton; one mill 12,000 feet, one mill 5,000 feet, and one mill 2,000 feet per day, at Lillooet and Clinton; one water-power saw-mill, 2,500 feet at Quesnel; one 20 horse-power steam mill, 20,000 feet at William's Creek; and one steam mill, 20,000 feet at Lightning Creek. On the coast, cheap transportation by water and rapidly increasing demands hastened the development of large-scale enterprises. A wide market for the finished product, ease of transport for the raw material, and the technique of American manufacture hastened the growth of large mills.

Export of lumber

The growth in exports of lumber and coal was dependent on the search for a balanced cargo on the part of vessels bringing in large quantities of goods for a mining community.

---

[1] *S.p.*, 10, 1872.
[2] See H. N. Whitford and R. D. Craig, *Forests of British Columbia* (Ottawa, 1918); *Final report of the royal commission of inquiry on timber and forestry, 1909-10* (Victoria, 1910); M. A. Grainger, *Woodsmen of the west* (London, 1908).

In 1861, 84 vessels of 43,675 tons left San Francisco for British Columbia and Vancouver Island—a decline of 32 vessels and 19,323 tons from 1860.   In the same year (1861) 46 vessels of 29,597 tons left Victoria for San Francisco of which 15 steamers were in ballast, a decline of 11 vessels and 14,921 tons from 1860.

	Vessels	Tonnage	Exports
Soke	2	576	$6,500
Nanaimo	15	4252	34,124
Victoria	14	6533	8,381

As a result of available shipping and enormous resources the export trade in lumber increased rapidly.   Merchants, engaged in the export of timber from Puget Sound to foreign ports, began operations at Alberni and Barclay Sound in 1861. In 1863, 1,000,000 feet were conveyed to Victoria in a steamer which made 5 trips, and 2 schooners, one of which made 8 trips.   The advantages of the location, by which vessels avoided the long and difficult journey in and out of the Straits of Juan del Fuca and Admiralty Inlet, favoured a rapid growth of direct trade.   "Another consideration which carries much weight with the skipper is that there are no opportunities for men to desert at Alberni."[1]   Absence of port charges and an abundance of white pine favoured the establishment of mills at that point.   The mills contained 2 gang saws with a capacity of 18,000 feet of plank daily and employed 70 white men.   Exports of sawn lumber from these mills increased from 7,490,000 feet in 1862 to 11,273,000 in 1863 and destinations included "Callao, Honolulu, Sydney, London, Coquimbo, Adelaide, Victoria, Shanghai, Lima, Melbourne, Hongkong, Otago, Valparaiso, Manilla, Italy".[2] In addition to sawn lumber 990 spars were exported in 1862 and 1,300 in 1863, chiefly to the government dockyards of France, Spain, and Sardinia.   Mills in the gulf and strait were more directly concerned with the local market.   In 1863 Victoria consumed 2,766,000 feet of which the Alberni Mills supplied 1,000,000 feet, the Cowichan Mill 1,666,000 feet, and the Soke Mill 100,000 feet.   In the decade ending

---

[1]R. C. Mayne, *British Columbia and Vancouver Island*, 228-9.   Labour was in demand in the lumber industry, wages totalling £1 per day in 1870 and 25 to 45 gold dollars a month in 1876.

[2]M. Macfie, *Vancouver Island and British Columbia*, 134-5.

1870 it was estimated that about 60,000,000 feet of lumber were exported.

By 1870 Burrard Inlet had become the centre of the lumber trade.

The timber which is cut in the district lying between Lillooet and the Gulf of Georgia, reaches Messrs Moodie and Co's mills at Burrard Inlet by means of an immense dry slide half-a-mile in length, which gives passage to the enormous saw-logs. Leaving behind them a long trail of smoke, they plunge into the air some thirty feet and are then retained in powerful and perfectly secure booms. I have myself seen several logs from sixty to eighty feet long, and six feet in diameter, in Messrs Moodie, Dietz and Nelson's booms at Burrard Inlet. From that place—that is from the mills belonging to those gentlemen and to the company called the "Hastings Mill Company"—there were this year exported from twenty to thirty-five million feet of timber, which must have furnished lading for thirty ships of 1,000 tons. It is a fact that an order for 750,000 feet of timber was this year received from Valparaiso at Burrard Inlet, it having been found impossible to fill the order at American Sound, where wood of the required dimensions could not be found. . . .

The lumbering trade of British Columbia is carried on entirely on salt water. The logs are drawn through the woods by oxen, and are rolled into the water on ways constructed for the purpose, and are sawn in the mills situated at the water's edge, whence they are shipped direct.[1]

In 1876, 15 saw-mills were in operation in the province, chiefly in the vicinity of New Westminster, of which 3 mills[2] were engaged in producing cargoes for export.

5

The Shipping Industry

Vessels[3] trading to British Columbia in 1870 included 8 coasting steamers of 1,182 tons and 83 men; 3 inland (Fraser River) steamers, 452 tons and 22 men; a steamer running to San Francisco; a steamer to Puget Sound; and 2 steamers to Portland; 7 ships from England, 3,868 tons and 115 men, carrying lumber; 6 ships from San Francisco, 1,320

---

[1] *S.p.*, 10, 1872.
[2] In 1876 Moody, Nelson and Company at Burrard Inlet loaded 23 ships with 14,095,412 feet of lumber and 1,000,000 feet of spars, and the Hastings saw-mill loaded 27 vessels of 18,276 tons.
[3] *S.p.*, 10, 1872.

tons and 60 men, chiefly lumber; 21 ships to Australia, China, and South America, 10,894 tons and 279 men; 3 ships to Honolulu, 793 tons and 24 men; and 28 coasting schooners. Of the total of 17 steamers 9 had been built in Victoria, and of the 28 schooners 18 were built in Victoria. In 1876, 524 vessels of 320,199 tons entered and 493 vessels of 290,736 tons cleared. Total imports were valued at $1,047,166 and exports at $2,750,787.

6

The Coal-mining Industry

The accessibility of coal-mines to water-transportation and the development of shipping following the rush to the gold-mines were accompanied by the expansion of the coal-mining industry[1] in addition to the lumbering industry. As in the Maritimes coal-mines became an important support to the development of steam navigation and to industry.[2] In 1852 the first shipment of 1,840 tons was made from Nanaimo to San Francisco. Early in the sixties Nanaimo coal was sold at $12.00 to $15.00 per ton in San Francisco in competition with other coal and was sold at the mines at 25s. and 28s. In 1864 a locomotive was introduced and, to solve the shipping problem, the Vancouver Island Coal Mining and Land Company purchased 2 vessels of 600 tons each to supply the San Francisco market.[3] In 1869, 200 men were employed to mine 40,883 tons, of which 19,700 tons were exported. In the following year the mine exported about 30,000 tons and coal was sold at the pit's mouth at about $6.00 per ton. In 1885 Sir Edward Watkin described the mine at Nanaimo as operating with a shaft 600 feet deep with "heading and workings" 400 or 500 yards under the sea. "The coal is hard and of good quality making a good gas coal." With one shaft in operation the mine produced

---

[1] See *Annual reports of the minister of mines being an account of the mining operations for gold, coal and silver* (1874).

[2] Industry developed to a slight extent. In 1870 Victoria had one iron foundry, 2 sash factories, a gas works, a soap factory, and 2 tanneries. See a list of industries in 1896 in *The year book of British Columbia* (Victoria, 1897), 432. According to the census of 1881, capital employed in industry totalled $2,952,835; wages paid, $929,213; employees, 2,871.

[3] R. C. Mayne, *British Columbia and Vancouver Island*, 380-1.

434 tons in one day. "The coal comes to the surface in two 'boxes' at a time, each containing about 35 cwt." The mine was equipped with standard-gauge railway locomotives and copper-bottomed cars for loading directly into the hold of vessels. About 350 men were employed, white men as miners and Chinese as labourers and all working by piece work.[1] 4 or 5 miles from Nanaimo the West Wellington Coal Mines owned by Messrs Dunsmuir and Sons produced 17,000 tons in August 1886.

We went down the shaft of No. 5 pit, which was 240 feet deep, and found the seam was very thick, from 10 to 11 feet, but not very solid black coal, having apparently been crushed. The mines are all connected with wharves on the coast at Departure Bay by a three-feet gauge railway; the lines around the mines were all in fair order. The line is worked by small locomotives, six wheels coupled and no truck, of the Baldwin Locomotive Company's manufacture, the load handled by them being 15 cars, each containing 3½ tons. The grade down to the port is very steep, and the heaviest work for the engines is in taking the empties back again.

The coal is mined by white miners,[2] who employ each of them a Chinese labourer; they employ gunpowder for blasting purposes, chiefly Curtis and Harvey's make, and use naked lights of oil. The miners are found in all tools except their auger drills, which they all use and which cost some $30 each. Each miner has an allowance of one ton of coal per month for his own use. There was a little drip at the foot of the shaft as we went down, but otherwise the mine was quite dry. The mode of unloading cars at the wharf was rather primitive but at the same time simple and ingenious. When a car has been weighed it is run forward by five Chinamen to the end of the wharf, the front end of the car being hinged at the top, with a catch opened by a lever, a short piece of track sufficiently long for the car to stand upon is built projecting beyond the wharf and over the hold of the vessel, this piece of track is laid on a framework which is hinged to the wharf in front so as to tip up from behind, to it is attached a long

---

[1] Sir E. W. Watkin, *Canada and the states*.
[2] See Report on miners' strike at Nanaimo, *S.p.*, *B.C.*, 1878; Report of the select standing committee on mines, *Journals of the legislative assembly, British Columbia*, 1888; *Reports of inspector of coal mines;* Cheng Tien-Fang, *Oriental immigration in Canada* (Shanghai, 1931); P. H. Clement, *Chinese coolie immigration to the British Empire* (London, 1923); P. H. Clement, "Canada and the Chinese" (*Annals* of the American Academy, January, 1913, 99-130). See reports on Chinese immigration, *Journals of the legislative assembly, British Columbia*, 1879, 1884, 1885, 1888 (especially on employment of oriental labour in the mines); *S.p.*, 1886, on Chinese Regulation Act, 1884.

51

wooden pole as a lever, round the end of which is a rope, made fast to the wharf by a belaying pin; as soon as the car is on the tipping track, the lever on the front end of the car is knocked up so as to allow the coal to fall out, and the end of the long wooden pole is allowed to rise slowly by the rope being loosened, the coal then shoots out of the car. When empty the Chinamen weigh down the pole and bring the track, with the car on it, back to its former position, making the rope fast to the belaying pin, and the car is run back to make way for another. We were told that in this way five Chinese have put 1,000 tons of coal on board a vessel in a working day.

Production of coal increased from 14,600 tons in 1861 to 32,819 tons in 1865 and after declining in 1866, recovered to 44,005 tons in 1868. It declined to 29,843 tons in 1870 but increased to 140,087 tons in 1876. In 1884 production totalled 394,070 tons, of which 87,388 were used for local consumption and 291,546 tons were exported to San Francisco.

MONEY AND CREDIT

1

Currency and Prices

Large quantities of money brought in by the gold rush, the discovery of fresh supplies of gold, the urgent demands for goods, and difficulties of transportation were factors responsible for high prices. Each miner carried a small chamois leather bag of gold-dust which was the circulation medium. "The requisite amount is weighed out for each payment." Milton and Cheadle complained that beef cost 50 cents a pound, "a drink of anything except water was half a dollar, nor could the smallest article even a box of matches be bought for less than a quarter."[1] At William's Creek a bottle of stout cost $1.25. Flour cost from 50 cents to $1.50 a pound. At Quesnel bacon was 80 cents a pound; beans, 80 cents a pound; and a meal of beans and bacon, $2.50. Potatoes sold at $90.00 for a 100 pounds; nails, $1.00 a pound; frozen milk, $1.00 a pound; eggs, $8.00 a dozen; India rubber boots, $50.00 a pair; champagne, $16.00 a bottle; wages, $10.00 a day.[2]

> The first piano to reach Barkerville was carried on men's backs from Quesnelle Mouth, a distance of sixty miles, and from that point the freight cost one dollar per pound. The billiard tables cost thousands of dollars; mirrors and large stoves from five to seven hundred dollars each.

Prices fluctuated continually.

> Not only do they rise and fall with summer and winter, but any delays on the route, the non-arrival of a pack-train when it is expected, or the influx of 100 or 200 men will always run the prices up for a few days at least. The whole tendency however, is doubtless towards cheapening the supplies as the communications become more complete and less liable to

---

[1]Milton and Cheadle, *The northwest passage by land*, 364-6.
[2]M. McNaughton, *Overland to Cariboo*, 110, 157-8. Meals of bacon, beans, bread, salt, butter, tea or coffee costing 50 cents on the Lower Fraser, cost $1.00 and $1.50 up the river. See I. M. L. Bescoby, "Some aspects of society in Cariboo from its discovery until 1871." (M. A. thesis, University of British Columbia, 1932, chapter iii).

interruption from bad roads,[1] &c. . . . . In 1858-59 bacon was selling at "Bigbar", 100 miles below Cariboo, at $1.50 (6s.) per pound and flour at 75 cts. (3s.)[2]

Freight rates fluctuated with competition, ranging from £10 per ton from Victoria to Yale in 1860 to £3 in 1861. Packing rates varied from 8 to 10 cents per pound for 25 miles.

Coins and larger denominations were gradually introduced. G. M. Grant wrote in 1870:

There is no copper currency and the smallest is what is called a "bit"; the ten cent and the English sixpence, although of different values, being alike called "bits", and given to children or put in church-door plates (there are no beggars) as cents or coppers are in all other countries. This absence of small coins has much to do with the general cost of living and the indifference to small profits characteristic of all classes here. The merest trifle costs "a bit", and though there are 25 and 50 cent pieces in currency, yet, if anything is worth more than a bit, with a lofty indifference to the intermediate coins the price is generally made a dollar. Emigrants on landing and men with fixed incomes are the chief sufferers from this state of things; for as mechanics, labourers and servants are paid accordingly they like it and speak with intensest scorn of the unfortunates who would divide "a bit" because they perhaps think it too much to give for a paper of pins or an apple. "John" who comes across the Pacific to make money and then return to the flowery land doesn't heed their scorn; and so, most of it was reserved before Confederation for Canny

---

[1]Prices of goods at the Cariboo Mines

	1861	1871
A shovel	$14.00	$1.50
A pick	14.00	3.00
A pound of flour	2.50	0.20
A pound of bacon	2.50	0.60
A pound of white sugar	2.50	0.35
A pair of gum boots	40.00	9.00
A bottle of brandy	14.00	2.00
A bottle of Champagne	14.00	8.00
A pair of boots, half long to knee, Cariboo made	36.00	20.00
A pair of blankets (four points) Hudson's Bay Company	35.00	16.00
Freight per pound	0.90	0.11
One meal	2.50	1.00
One ordinary cooking stove	350.00	100.00
One sheet iron stove with six lengths of pipe	100.00	25.00
Daily wages of a carpenter	16.00	7.00
foreman	16.00	6.00
workman	12.00	5.00
Chinaman		3.50

(*S.p.*, 10, 1872).

[2]R. C. Mayne, *British Columbia and Vancouver Island*, 400-3.

Canadians who received the flattering appellation of North American Chinamen.[1]

As late as 1883:

No coin less than a five-penny-bit is taken or given in change. Some time ago the Canadian Government tried to reduce the small change to less than this sum; but the townspeople of Victoria expostulated; and on finding that no notice was taken of the complaint they collected all the coins of less value than a piece of ten cents (viz., 5d.), packed them up in sacks, and sent them back to Canada, with the settlers' compliments.[2]

2

Banks and Banking

Banks[3] developed with the express business and were in demand as deposit institutions and for the handling of gold-dust and bars. MacDonald's Bank and a branch of the Bank of British North America were established at Victoria in 1859. The firm of Stewart Meldrum and Company was largely responsible for the establishment under royal charter of the Bank of British Columbia[4] in 1862. R. Gillespie, Jr., vice-chairman of the new bank, represented Gillespie, Moffat and Company of Montreal and re-established the relations of that firm with British Columbia which had been broken after the amalgamation of the North West Company in 1821. These banks became channels for the inflow of capital, and the export of gold, and organizations for the financing of increasing trade. Branches were established in the interior. Bank notes gradually increased in importance with the demand for a more satisfactory medium of exchange than gold.[5] Competition from the Bank of British Columbia contributed to the failure of MacDonald's Bank[6] in 1864 and in turn the decline of placer-mining was responsible for the period of difficulty of the Bank of British Columbia from

[1]G. M. Grant, *Ocean to ocean*, 344-5. The description applies in the main to Dawson City at the present day. In 1926 no coin less than 25 cents was accepted.
[2]W. H. Barneby, *Life and labour in the far, far west*, 118.
[3]See E. O. S. Scholefield and F. W. Howay, *British Columbia*, I, chapter xxi.
[4]Victor Ross, *A history of the Canadian Bank of Commerce*, I, chapter v.
[5]See R. L. Reid, *The assay office and the proposed mint at New Westminster* (Victoria, 1926).
[6]R. L. Reid, "The first bank in western Canada" (*Canadian Historical Review*, VII, 294-301).

1866 to 1868. Recovery followed the shift to other lines of economic development and the emergence of industries. The Bank of British Columbia was brought under Canadian jurisdiction in 1885. Wholesale and distributing firms supplemented the position of the banks. These firms were in some sense an extension of the organization built up in relation to placer-mining in California.

3

Capital—Private and Public

The intensely speculative character of a community dependent on placer-mining tended to check the investment of funds on a long-term basis. Corporations[1] supported coal-mining and lumbering partly in relation to domestic capital but generally in relation to foreign capital. The growth of towns was followed by growth of municipal debt especially after completion of the Canadian Pacific Railway. Vancouver's net debt in 1887 totalled $191,000; New Westminster in 1890, $286,420; Victoria in 1895, $1,824,000.[2]

Capital on long terms, because of the immediate and heavy demands, was obtained largely by governmental support although determined efforts were made to pay for expenditures for roads, bridges, and other items from current receipts. The essentially short-run character of placer-mining necessitated immediate measures to secure revenue to pay for capital which depreciated through obsolescence with marked rapidity. On the mainland, a head-tax, an *ad valorem* duty of 10 per cent., mining licenses, land sales, and a tonnage tax (1859) on goods leaving New Westminster were utilized as sources of revenue. Of a total revenue of £53,326 in 1860, £30,416 were obtained from customs and £11,075 from land. In 1860 tolls[3] were introduced on sections of the road, and bridges were built by contractors in return for the privilege of charging tolls. With these devices

---

[1]For a survey of capital investments in 1896, see *The year book of British Columbia*, 436 ff.

[2]See J. R. Perry, *Public debts in Canada* (University of Toronto studies, history and economics, I), 87-8.

[3]Between Yale and Lytton a charge of £2 per ton was estimated to yield about £5,300 (5,000 mules, 300 pounds each; 400 tons, boats; 750 tons carried by Indians). The revenue of Yale district in 1860 totalled:

the Cariboo road was built at a cost of $1,250,000, involving a bonded indebtedness in 1863 of only £112,750. The decline of placer-mining was responsible for a marked increase of the debt to $1,002,983 in 1866. Interest and sinking fund became serious burdens to current revenue. Vancouver Island depended chiefly on land sales and land taxes but was forced to abandon a free trade policy in 1865. Net debt totalled $293,698 in 1866. Pressure of debt[1] was a powerful influence in the movement toward union between the island and the mainland which was accomplished in 1866, and in the movement toward Confederation in 1871. The union began with a total debt of $1,296,681 but the effects of the continued decline in placer-mining made deficits inevitable. Confederation brought direct relief with the assumption by the dominion of a debt of $1,666,200 and indirect relief with promises of railroads and public works. Further debts shouldered by the dominion gave a total of $2,029,392 in 1895.

4

After Confederation

In spite of this assistance difficulties continued after Confederation. The depression checked industries which had emerged from the subsidiary stage, particularly lumbering, and the decline of placer-mining continued. From 1872 to 1875 a deficit of $581,691 was accumulated and served

	£	s	d
Mining licences	267	0	0
Mining receipts (general)	201	6	2
Tolls and ferries	238	17	5
Sales of lands	272	0	0
Fines and fees	96	14	0
Spirit licences	320	0	0
Tracking licences	141	0	0
	1536	17	7

(R. C. Mayne, *British Columbia and Vancouver Island*, 403-4). The cost added by tolls from New Westminster to Barkerville totalled $53.00 a ton which, in addition to freight charges of 15 to 18 cents a pound, raised prices appreciably. See F. W. Howay, *British Columbia*, 141-2.

[1]See valuable articles by F. W. Howay, "British Columbia's entry into Confederation" (Canadian Historical Association *report*, 1927, 67-73), and W. N. Sage, "The critical period of British Columbia history, 1866-1871" (*Pacific Historical Review*, December, 1932, 424-443).

to accentuate disputes with the dominion. The gross debt of the province totalled $800,258 in 1885. Construction and completion of the Canadian Pacific Railway finally brought union with Canada directly and indirectly in the practical fulfilment of the terms of union.

SECTION V

CONFEDERATION AND CREDIT

Confederation, as has been shown, involved the assumption of debts accumulated on the part of the provinces chiefly as a result of the construction of railways and improvement of navigation, and served in turn as a further basis for the increase of debt on the part of the provinces and for continued improvement of transportation. In 1867, the Province of Canada was relieved by Confederation to the extent of $62,500,000; Nova Scotia, $8,000,000; New Brunswick, $7,000,000. In 1885 new provinces and additional payments[1] brought the debt assumed by the dominion on the part of the provinces to $106,311,392. In addition, new indebtedness to the extent of $90,260,393 was added from Confederation to 1885 and $57,000,000 were paid out of receipts, chiefly for: canals, $28,543,078; railways, $92,575,599; light-houses and navigation, $8,433,100; and government buildings,[2] $12,432,825. Moreover, the provinces continued to expend substantial sums on transportation. Confederation became in itself a base for expansion of credit, and in relieving the provinces of debt provided new possibilities for expansion of debt. In 1885 total debt was $264,703,607; total assets, $68,295,915; and net debt, $196,407,692.

An increase in interest charges,[3] from $4,860,757 in 1867-68 to $9,806,977 in 1885; in subsidies to the provinces from $2,753,966 to $3,959,326; in sinking fund from $355,266 in 1868-9 to $1,403,863 in 1885; and in total expenditures from $13,486,092 in 1867-8 to $34,107,706 in 1884-5 necessi-

---

[1] See George Johnson, *Canada* (Ottawa, 1886), 67 *ff.*; J. R. Perry, *Public debts in Canada*, part I (University of Toronto studies, history and economics, I); N. S. Garland, *Banks, bankers and banking in Canada* (Ottawa, 1890), 206 *ff.*

[2] "The need for increased accommodation in the matter of suitable buildings in which to transact public business has been severely felt. Prior to 1882 there were few Public Buildings outside of the principal cities; but since that time a large number of the smaller cities and towns have been supplied with suitable Post Offices, Customs Houses and other buildings, to the very great advantage of the public service and to the increased accommodation of the general public having business with the Government Offices" (*S.p.*, 11, 1887).

[3] Interest rate declined from 5.40 per cent. in 1868 to 3.80 per cent. in 1885.

tated increased revenue. Total receipts increased from
$13,687,928 in 1867-8 to $32,797,001 in 1884-5. A surplus
was available from 1867-8[1] to 1875-6 reaching the high point
of $3,712,479 in 1871-2, but was followed by substantial
deficits ranging from $1,128,146 in 1877-8 to $1,937,999 in
1878-9 in the period from 1875-6 to 1879-80. Large and
increasing surpluses were available from 1880-1 to 1882-3
but were followed by a sharp decline in 1884-5 and by heavy
deficits in 1884-5 and 1885-6 ($5,834,571 in the latter year).

Receipts from customs and excise were basic items. The
latter increased from $3,002,588 in 1867-8 to $5,594,903 in
1873-4 and, after fluctuations in the depression, to $6,449,101
in 1884-5. Customs increased from $8,578,380 in 1867-8 to
$15,351,011 in 1874-5, declined to a low point of $12,546,987
in 1876-7, increased rapidly from $14,071,343 in 1879-80 to
$23,009,582 in 1882-3, and declined slightly to the end of the
period. Receipts from customs were closely linked to trade,[2]
especially to imports, and were subject to cyclical and other
fluctuations. Imports (entered for consumption) increased
from $71,985,306 in 1867-8 to $127,514,594 in 1872-3,
declined to $71,872,349 in 1879-80, rose to $123,137,019 in

---

[1] K. W. Taylor, "Statistics of foreign trade", and H. Michell, "Statistics of
prices" (*Statistical contributions to Canadian economic history*, II).

[2] The total liabilities of all the three provinces in July, 1867, were:—
Funded debt, including Trust

Fund................	$86,488,486.89	
Liabilities to provinces......	2,573,292.92	
Miscellaneous.............	458,092.38	
Banking Accounts.........	3,526,179.54	
	$93,046,051.73	
Less Sinking Funds and other		
Investments..........	$5,785,782.30	
Debts due by Provinces.....	10,045,533.63	
Cash and Banking Accounts	1,486,094.43	$17,317,410.36

Net debt...$75,728,641.37
The gross receipts of the Dominion, exclusive of those on account
  of the Province of Canada and the several Provinces, were..$16,830,060.73
Less Loans....................................... 2,994,600.66

Ordinary revenues of Dominion......................... 13,835,460.07

The gross Expenditure of the Dominion was................ $13,704,170.53
Less redemptions...................................... 337,679.98

$13,366,490.55
Whereof on account of Public Works chargeable to Capital.... 587,783.32

$12,778,707.23

1882-3, and declined to \$102,710,019 in 1884-5. Exports increased from \$57,567,888 in 1867-8 to \$89,789,922 in 1872-3, declined with marked fluctuations to \$71,491,255 in 1878-9, rose to \$102,137,203 in 1881-2, and declined to \$89,238,361 in 1884-5.

Subsidies of Ontario and Quebec............	\$2,156,125.60
Add 1 year's interest on Trust Funds........	177,162.64
	\$2,333,288.24
Less interest on excess of debt, say \$11,000,000	550,000.00
Payable annually........................	\$1,783,288.24
Actually paid...........................	1,588,784.20

Excess payable beyond actual payments..................   \$194,504.04

Ordinary expenditure of Dominion......................   \$12,973,211.27
Surplus...   862,248.80

    \$13,835,460.07

    (S.p., 4, 1869).

July 1, 1870, the total liabilities were:—
Funded Debt, including Trust Fund........	\$107,395,637.78
Liabilities to Provinces..................	6,224,159.32
Miscellaneous..........................	131,801.44
Banking Accounts......................	2,242,108.22

    \$115,993,706.76

Less Sinking Funds, &c.....	\$13,241,266.17	
Debts due by Provinces.....	17,193,583.67	
Miscellaneous.............	11,119.41	
Cash and Banking Accounts.	7,337,995.06	
		\$37,783,964.31

Net Debt...   \$78,209,742.45
The increase of the net debt during the three years has, therefore, been \$2,481,101.08 whilst the total expenditure on capital account for Public Works, Intercolonial Railway, and the acquisition of the North West Territory, has been \$4,759,335.79, leaving an amount of capital expenditure of \$2,278,234.71, which has been met out of income.

But if we examine the interest payable on the debt, the result would be still more favourable.
Interest payable on gross debt, July, 1867..................   \$4,851,710.70
Interest on Investments and other available Assets..........   699,890.77

Net Interest..   4,151,819.93
Interest payable on Gross Debt, July, 1870...   \$5,155,597.39
Interest on Investments, &c...............   1,001,452.21

Net Interest..   \$4,154,145.18
so that whilst the net debt has increased \$2,481,101.08, the net interest has only increased \$2,325.25, at which annual cost we have been able to expend on Public Works and other capital accounts \$4,759,335.79.

John Langton,
Auditor
(S.p., 1, 1871).
Public Accounts of the Dominion of Canada, for the Fiscal Year ended 30th June, 1870.   Board of Audit, January 31, 1871

Confederation brought an amalgamation of trading statistics, and fluctuations varied with the economic activity of separate regions. In 1868-9 increase in exports was evident in minerals, forest products, animal products, ships built at Quebec, and decrease in fish and agricultural products. In 1869-70 a general increase was shown:

Increase in 1869-70 over 1868-69

Products of the mine[1].....................	19 per cent.
do fisheries[2]....................	11 "
do forest[3].....................	6 "
Animals and products of[4]..................	38 "
Agricultural products[5].....................	12 "
Manufactures[6]............................	21 "

This comparative statement, embracing all the transactions since Confederation exhibits a very satisfactory result.

The receipts of Consolidated Fund have been,

In 1867-8..............................	$13,687,928.49
1868-9..............................	14,379,174.52
1869-70..............................	15,512,225.65
	$43,579,328.66

The expenditure in 1867-8..................	$13,486,092.96
1868-9.................	14,038,084.00
1869-70................	14,345,509.58
	$41,869,686.54

Leaving a surplus income of Consolidated Fund of........... $1,709,642.12

But in the expenditure of the three years there have been included payments towards the Sinking Fund, which is so much reduction of the capital of our debt

1867-8.............	$355,266.66		
1868-9.............	426,806.66		
1869-70.............	126,533.33	....	$908,606.65

so that during the three years there has been a surplus income available for the reduction of the debt, or for other expenditure on capital account of............................... 2,618,248.77

[1]Oil increased from 690,553 gallons in 1868-9 to 4,748,557 gallons in 1870. Copper, iron-ore, and coal declined—home consumption offset decline in exports of the latter from Nova Scotia.

[2]Smoked salmon, preserved and spiced fish, salted dry and wet fish increased but fish-oil declined from 271,762 gallons to 87,043 gallons.

[3]Forest products declined with the exception of

	1868-9	1869-70
Planks and boards...................	Value $6,690,956	$8,256,599
Saw logs (dutiable)...................	" 53,092	158,252

[4]Regulations providing for the slaughtering of hogs in bond favoured the growth of the pork-packing industry and led to an increase from $869,746 in 1868-9 to $1,553,323 in 1869-70.

[5]Wheat increased 2,800,000 bushels to 3,700,000 bushels and coarse grains increased by 3,800,000 bushels. Hops increased from 411,842 pounds to 1,194,379 pounds.

[6]Industries were primarily concerned with the home market but excluding flour-mills and lumber-mills and the chief industries producing for export, manufactured products were exported to the extent of $1,500,000.

Exports were as follows:

	1869-70	1870-71
Produce of the mine............	$2,487,038	$3,221,461
do fisheries..........	3,608,549	3,994,275
do forest..........	20,940,434	22,352,211
Animals and their products......	12,138,161	12,582,925
Agricultural products..........	13,676,619	9,853,146
Manufactures................	2,133,659	2,201,331

Marked increase in exports in the 2 following years was chiefly a result of the lumber industry. Increase in exports in 1873 over 1872 was as follows:

	Increase
Produce of the mine[1]........................	$2,534,554
do fisheries......................	430,769
do forest......................	4,901,434
Animals and their products..................	1,826,404
Agricultural products......................	1,616,778
Manufactures[2]............................	532,367

In the 9 years from July 1, 1868, to June 30, 1876, of total exports of $686,424,704, Great Britain[3] received $311,371,498

[1]Gold increased to $1,035,254, silver from $1,087,839 to $1,379,380, oil from 7,897,054 gallons valued at $1,341,099 to 9,355,325 gallons valued at $1,819,183.

[2]Exports of manufactures in 1872-3 totalled $2,921,802. Ships were an important item and in 1869-70 Quebec alone built and sold abroad ships valued at $725,080. The extent of the industry is suggested in the following table:

		1869-70				1870-1	
	Built		Average	Registered		Built	
	No.	Tons	tonnage	No.	Tons	No.	Tons	Average
Ontario........	45	4,525	100	60	6,186	55	7,777	141
Quebec........	55	19,383	350	109	25,452	80	20,664	258
Nova Scotia....| 141	33,659	240	227	44,643	146	44,307	303
New Brunswick.| 88	35,599	400	99	34,571	108	33,353	308
Total......| 329	93,166		495	110,852	389	106,101	

(S.p., 3, 1871). In 1872-3 ship-building remained stationary in Ontario, although the average size increased from 141 to 187 tons; Quebec declined; Nova Scotia increased to 188 vessels and New Brunswick declined in numbers to 93 but increased in average tonnage to 393. The tendency of vessels to increase in tonnage continued in the following year. A total addition of 2 vessels brought a total tonnage of 26,315.

[3]Shipping was closely related to British trade. The aggregate of tonnage inwards and outwards employed in shipping increased from 10,461,044 tons in 1868-9 to 11,415,870 tons in 1869-70. In 1871-2 shipping was distributed as follows:

			"Ships Inwards		Ships Outwards	
			No.	Tons	No.	Tons
With Cargo	British..............		5,158	1,514,004	7,712	2,099,148
	Foreign.............		1,033	442,752	1,687	688,024
In Ballast	British..............		3,056	674,286	214	68,225
	Foreign.............		1,111	358,751	285	101,514

Showing an aggregate of 3,613,152 tons of British Shipping against 1,130,776

and the United States, $308,807,541. Of a total average value of $76,269,411, Great Britain received $34,596,833 or 45.3 per cent., and the United States, $34,311,949 or 44.9 per cent. In the same period imports totalled $874,552,315, of which $457,151,517 were from Great Britain and $341,928,755 from the United States. The total average value per year was $97,172,479 (Great Britain, $50,714,613 or 52.27 per cent.; the United States, $37,992,084 or 39.10 per cent.). Of the total excess[1] of imports of $188,127,611 Great Britain was

tons of Foreign, employed in the Import and Export carrying Trade of Canada *seaward* during the last Fiscal Year (1871-2). The vessels entering and clearing in ballast represent a tonnage of 1,202,776 of which 742,511 were British, and 460,265 Foreign" (*S.p.*, 3, 1873).

[1]Exports from Confederation to 1872-3 (6 years) increased 55.95 per cent. and imports, 77.13 per cent. The average yearly excess of the value of imports over exports for the period was $19,334,094. Excess of imports over exports had fluctuated from $28,790,864 in 1872, to $38,221,359 in 1873, to $38,861,654 in 1874, to $45,183,304 in 1875, and to $12,243,911 in 1876. In 1873 and 1874 imports exceeded exports by about $38,000,000 but the excess was regarded as due "in a great degree to the construction and extension of railways and canals, and other public and profitable undertakings, which enhance the value of property and lay the foundation of increased public and private revenue". Imports from Great Britain increased from $35,764,470 in 1868-9 to $38,595,433 in 1869-70 or about 8 per cent. In the same year imports increased 23½ per cent. from the West Indies and to a smaller extent from France, Newfoundland, and Prince Edward Island. Increase in total trade of over $4,300,000 to the United States was attributed to exports as imports had declined.

Trade with the United States

	1868-9	1869-70		
Imports	$25,477,975	$24,728,166	Decrease	$749,809
Exports	27,846,461	32,984,652	Increase	5,138,191

Abrogation of the Reciprocity Treaty had been followed by increase in trade but whereas under reciprocity, the United States were the larger exporters, after reciprocity imports to Canada declined and exports to the United States increased.

Imports from Great Britain increased from $38,595,433 in 1869-70 to $49,168,170 in 1870-71 (about 27 per cent.) and from the United States from $24,728,166 to $29,022,387 (about 17 per cent.). Exports to Great Britain declined from $24,950,925 in 1869-70 to $24,173,224 in 1870-71 and to the United States from $32,984,652 to $30,975,642. In 1870-71 exports to the British West Indies and British Guiana increased over the preceding year by $538,671 and imports from the Spanish West Indies declined from $2,423,421 in 1869-70 to $2,018,930 in 1870-71. Exports to Cuba increased from $1,280,268 to $1,498,854. In 1871-2, imports from Great Britain were 59 per cent. of total imports and from the United States, 32.62 per cent. while exports to Great Britain were 47 per cent. of the total exports and from the United States, 35 per cent. Increase in imports took place from France, Germany, and the British West Indies; from Germany, 62½ per cent. over the previous year, 1870-1. Imports from the Spanish West Indies declined as a result of the war in Cuba. Trade with Newfoundland and Prince Edward Island was also important and trade between Canada and other British countries totalled $94,681,398. Trade with Great Britain increased 20.5 per cent. in 1873 over 1872 and with the United States, 24.9 per cent. Total trade with Great Britain was $107,266,624 in 1872-3 and with the United States $89,808,204, or a total for the 2 countries of $197,074,828, or 90.73 per cent. of the whole of Canada's trade. In 1873-4 exports to Great

responsible for $145,780,019 or 77.4 per cent. and the United States for $33,121,214 or 17.61 per cent. Receipts from customs were directly dependent on imports of dutiable goods and on the rate of duties. In 1868-9 dutiable goods declined $2,586,354, largely a result of the following items:[1]

				Value
Woollens—imported in 1868-9—less than in 1867-8				$944,779
Manufactures of leather	"	"	"	160,702
Linen........	"	"	"	87,208
Leather.......	"	"	"	87,612
Sole and upper leather	"	"	"	86,208
Small wares...	"	"	"	80,773
Paper and paper hangings	"	"	"	33,026
Silks, velvets, &c.	"	"	"	32,230
Unenumerated articles.....................				74,218
				$1,586,756

Representing duties to the amount of $244,910.15.

Duties[2] increased 25½ per cent. from 1869-70 to 1870-1 and 10.15 per cent. from 1870-1 to 1871-2 and contributed with increased trade to an increase in receipts from customs. The

Britain increased $10,000,000 and imports of free goods from Great Britain, $4,000,000. Increased trade with the United States was attributed entirely to imports, exports having declined slightly. Trade with the West Indies declined but with South America increased. Imports of molasses in 1874 totalled 4,793,519 gallons at about 17½ cents per gallon, the United States supplying 1,764,734 gallons at 15.4 cents per gallon (chiefly the by-product of sugar refineries and consequently of poor quality and cheaper); the British West Indies, 1,138,791 gallons at 19.8 cents; and the foreign West Indies, 1,657,196 gallons at 19.1 cents. In 1877 imports of molasses from the United States were greatly reduced and in 1878 "somewhat increased". Improved quality in the latter year apparently accounted for the higher price. Imports from the British West Indies remained stationary, from the Spanish West Indies declined nearly one-half, and from British Guiana "a large increase". In the main, prices, as in the case of sugar, declined. The decline in total trade of $21,805,983 from 1875 to 1876 was the result of a decline in imports from Great Britain. In 1875-6 imports from Great Britain totalled $40,734,260 and exports to Great Britain, $42,740,050; and imports from the United States were $46,070,033 and exports, $29,916,876. The "unfavourable" balance with the United States was the result of imports of raw material for manufacture—coal, grain, flour, etc., chiefly free goods which totalled $24,730,371. Free goods from Great Britain totalled $8,348,778.

[1] S.p., 1, 1870. Tea declined 914,025 pounds, $202,458 value, and $26,934 duty. Spirits declined 34 per cent. and manufactured tobacco 27 per cent.; sugar declined 375,844 pounds, $238,375 and (increase) $58,549 duty; and wine declined 75,219 gallons, $161,859 value, $17,134 duty. The general decline was in part a result of increased importations in the Maritimes in 1867 to avoid the higher Canadian tariff (S.p., 5, 1874).

[2] S.p., 3, 1873. See J. C. Langelier, Revision of the Canadian tariff (Montreal, 1872).

increase was chiefly a result of expansion in Ontario and
registered in part the importance of increasing trade with the
United States.

Increase in percentages of customs paid by provinces

	1871 over 1870	1872 over 1871
Ontario.	37.98	15.98 per cent.
Quebec.	22.69	03.77 " "
Nova Scotia.	17.41	00.74 " "
New Brunswick.	19.43	05.14 " "

On the other hand, Quebec continued to indicate the importance of the St. Lawrence.

Percentage of customs paid by provinces

	1871	1872	1873
Ontario[1].	28.20	29.64	33.01 per cent.
Quebec.	50.26	47.34	45.15 " "
Nova Scotia.	11.32	10.25	9.56 " "
New Brunswick.	10.22	09.78	9.57 " "
Manitoba.	.....	00.36	0.38 " "
British Columbia.	.....	02.63	2.33 " "

Receipts from customs increased to a high point in 1875,
a result in part of the increase of 2½ per cent. on non-
enumerated goods which came into effect in May, 1874, and
"had its effect upon the whole home consumption of the
fiscal year 1875, before the general depression in trade had
reached its full development". The effects of the depression
were shown strikingly in a marked decline of total imports of
about $30,000,000 and of receipts from customs in 1875-6. In
a total decline of $18,000,000 of dutiable goods, $16,000,000
"is in the classes of goods subject to the duty of 17½ per cent.
I find a large proportion of this decline is traceable to the
import of cotton goods." Over-production of cotton goods
in the United States in 1873 and 1874 and "a heavy and
continuous fall in prices" in both England and the United
States were in part responsible. A marked increase in
domestic production with the establishment of cotton mills
in Quebec contributed to the decline in imports. Imports
of woollen goods also declined $4,000,000 for similar reasons
and the "constantly increasing manufacturing facilities of
Canada will continue to operate in the direction of diminished
importations". Imports of sole and upper leather were
valued at $127,967 and exports at $956,379. Imports of

---

[1]*S.p.*, 5, 1874.

leather and leather manufactures totalled $1,111,685 and exports, $1,105,981. In 1876-7 cotton and cotton goods declined 5 to 7½ per cent., "including brown ducks and cotton flannels from the United States". Linens and woollens declined 7½ to 10 per cent. and silks from 10 to 15 per cent. In 1878 imports of cotton totalled about $8,000,000.

Fall in prices of imported commodities, and decline in purchasing power as a result of the decline in exports—especially with the effects of the depression on the lumber industry and the effects of the steamship on wooden ship-building— contributed to the problem of deficits.

It is a well-known fact, that from the 1st July, 1873, to the present date [*December 31, 1875*], the tendency of nearly all manufactured articles, constituting the usual imports of Canada, has been continuously downward in value, and if the average decline during the year be rated at 10 per cent., which will hardly be considered by any careful observer an extravagant estimate, the result will show that without such decline the value for duty would have been $7,666,000 more, and a proportionate additional revenue would have been realized, amounting to $1,277,600.[1]

The marked decline of customs' duties in 1877-8 compared with the years from 1872 to 1875 "may be largely accounted for by the continuous shrinkage in the market values of the large classes of imports subject, under the present tariff, to *ad valorem* duties."[2] The average reduction in the value of

---

[1] *S.p.*, 2, 1876.

[2] *S.p.*, 2, 1879. Imports and prices of tea illustrated the general trend. "Comparing the trade in teas in 1872, with 1874 and 1875 it will be observed that there was a decrease in green tea from Great Britain, in 1874 of 328,192 lbs., and in 1875 of 911,051 lbs. and an increase in black tea of 157,469 lbs. and 901,685 lbs.

From the United States, there was a decrease in 1874 of 1,009,570 lbs. in green tea and of 141,854 lbs. in black. In 1875, there was an increase in green tea from the same country of 77,455 lbs., and in black of 250,170 lbs., over the imports of 1872.

From China and Japan direct the quantity entered for consumption in 1874 exceeded that of 1872, in green tea 2,182,409 lbs. and in black 44,168 lbs. In 1875 there was still an excess over 1872, in green of 718,682 lbs., and in black of 53,950 lbs."

In 1877 it was stated that the demand for good mediums and lower grades had increased and for higher grades correspondingly diminished, "probably resulting from the hard times".

"*Tea, Green.*—The total quantity of Green Tea entered for consumption in 1876 was 8,942,507 lbs.; in 1877, 7,539,502 lbs., and in 1878, 6,035,140 lbs., the price steadily declining; ranging at 30½c., 26⅜ c., and 23½c. per lb., each year.

Tea, Black.—Entered in 1876, 5,615,344 lbs.; in 1877, 5,943,155, and in 1878, 4,984,091 lbs.; the cost of this article was nearly uniform during 1876 and 1877, averaging a shade under 27c. per lb., but in 1878 there appears a shrinkage of 3c., the price being a small fraction under 24c. per lb."

52

goods during the period was probably 15 rather than 10 per cent. In the United States extreme depression in prices was the rule. The iron and hardware trades suffered particularly. In 1877 it was stated that prices of hardware from the United States had fallen 12½ per cent.; English heavy hardware, 7½ per cent.; and heavy shelf goods, 5 per cent. Iron from Great Britain declined materially in price; bar, rod, hoop, and nail sheets, 20s. to 25s. per ton; galvanized iron, 35s. to 40s. per ton; tin plates, 3s. to 3s. 9d. per box; Canada plates, 1s. 6d. to 2s. per box. Other products which declined in price included stationery from the United States— paper, 10 and other stationery, 10 to 25 per cent. Drugs and chemicals as dutiable goods declined only slightly but free goods, "caustic soda" and "sal soda" declined 15 per cent.

The effects of decline in prices were shown in severe competition from foreign goods. Industries established to meet the demands of the domestic market were exposed to increased competition as a result of lower costs of transportation, of lower prices of foreign commodities, and of relatively lower duties. A report of a select committee of the house of commons in 1874 complained that Canada was used as a slaughter market for American manufactures.

> During the past year the fall of values caused by over-production and the financial crises in the United States, have caused large importations into Canada of United States manufactured goods, at prices alleged to be from fifteen to twenty per cent. under prime cost, greatly to the detriment of the Canadian manufacturer. . . . This disturbing element in the manufacturing industry of the Dominion arising out of our geographical position and out of the trade policy of our neighbours, should induce even those who may regard free trade as a covert principle, in the abstract, to recognize the necessity for a modification of that principle as a measure of self-protection, and your committee respectfully recommend the enactment of such laws as will regulate if it cannot altogether prevent, the evil complained of. 2nd. The almost uniform testimony before your committee was to the effect that an increased protection to manufactures will not necessarily increase the cost of the manufactured article to the consumer, and, in the opinion of your Committee the witnesses have made out a very strong case in support of this view. It appears to be well established that the cost of manufacturing decreases as the quantity of goods manufactured, decreases.[1]

---

[1] *J.h.c.*, VIII, 1874, app. 3. 2 years later, on the other hand, a select com-

Severe competition from American firms was noted in the following industries—paper, furniture, carriages, tanning and leather belting, felt hats, varnish and paint, flour, pianos and organs, glass, and scales. The development of the metal industries and especially of the iron and steel industry during the Civil War was followed by severe competition in agricultural implements, shelf hardware, machinery and tools, sewing machines, safes, bolts, nuts and screws, tin, copper, brass and silver plate, and stoves. Canadian foundries were forced to close. German competition was noted in cigars and English competition in textiles, especially in shoddy.

As a result of these difficulties the national policy came into existence. The compromise of about 15 per cent. between the low tariff with specific duties of 12½ per cent. in the Maritimes and the high-tariff, *ad valorem* duties of the upper provinces was accompanied by a period of pros-

mittee argued generally in favour of free trade. It was claimed that depression in the shipping industry followed the decline of shipping in long voyages and the competition of vessels released from these voyages in the coasting trade. Lumbering declined by 50 per cent. below 1872 and 1873 because of depression in the construction industry in the United States and the competition of Michigan and Wisconsin lumber protected by a tariff in the New England and New York markets. Decline in lumbering was followed by a decline in subordinate industries, especially agriculture. The mercantile classes suffered particularly, returns showing insolvencies in this industry totalling $16,235,479 out of a grand total of $26,933,707. This was regarded in part as a result of long and easy credits to the wholesale trade. The excess of imports over exports was stated as indicating inflation. The foreign mercantile debt was estimated at $75,000,000. Ship-building increased as follows:

1868	87,203
1869	96,439
1870	93,166
1871	106,101
1872	114,065
1873	140,370
1874	174,404
1875	188,098

The iron industry was depressed by the decline of construction of railways in the United States and the unhealthy stimulus given by a highly protective tariff and, as in other industries, goods were dumped in Canada. The boot and shoe industry had a large number of failures, the agricultural industry was prosperous, woollen manufacturers complained of competition from English shoddy. "The Committee believe that under no circumstances can it be favourable to the material progress of the country that fiscal barriers should be placed in the way of receiving from other countries those commodities which their soil, climate, and present forms of industry make it to our interest to import rather than produce" (Report of the select committee on the causes of the present depression of the manufacturing, mining, commercial, shipping, lumber and fishing interests, *J.h.c.*, X, 1876, app. 3).

perity. Increased interprovincial trade and general prosperity coinciding with the Franco-German War were factors responsible for surpluses. The deficits which accompanied the depression brought a slight rise in the tariff to 17½ per cent. in 1874. The difficulties of the manufacturer incidental to the depression and the dumping of American goods coincided with the exigencies of the government in the heavy commitments for the improvement of waterways and the construction of railways—the Intercolonial and the Canadian Pacific.[1] The national policy brought higher tariffs designed to check dumping, to increase revenue, and to hasten the importation of capital essential to the prosecution of railroads. It was adopted two years after completion of the Intercolonial and in the year the railroad reached Winnipeg. The average rate of 20.45 per cent. from 1874-8 was increased under the national policy to 26.11 per cent. in 1880 and 26.40 per cent. in 1882 (25.32 in 1883).

Moreover, it was designed to increase trade with Great Britain and to stimulate traffic on the St. Lawrence. It was expected to affect about $15,000,000 to $18,000,000 of miscellaneous imports totalling $25,000,000, formerly imported free from the United States. The duties applied to cheaper kinds of cottons, bleached and unbleached, jeans, denims, and kindred goods which could be largely manufactured in Canadian factories. Imports of higher classes of cottons totalled about $5,000,000 ($4,000,000 from Great Britain) and the increase of 2½ per cent. *ad valorem* had little protective character as Canadian mills were not designed for their production. Woollen imports totalled $8,500,000, of which Great Britain supplied about $7,000,000. The higher classes totalled about $5,000,000 and on these duties were increased from 17½ to 20 per cent. Silks, satins, and velvets were imported from Great Britain to the extent of about $1,500,000 and small wares of various descriptions of

---

[1]The Conservative government returned in September, 1878, was forced to raise $2,000,000 to meet existing deficiencies and the following sums to meet later maturing debts in England: 1880, $6,665,813; 1881, $1,321,300; 1882, $2,641,626; 1883, $1,639,580; 1884, $1,305,240; 1885, $32,467,665. Moreover, they were liable for $16,000,000 for public works (Lachine and Welland Canals, $5,500,000; C.P.R., Lake Superior to Red River, $6,000,000; French River to Pembroke, $2,500,000).

about $4,000,000. Duties on these products were advanced 2½ per cent. Iron was admitted at 5 per cent. and in 1878 of total imports of $2,400,000, $1,800,000 worth were obtained from Great Britain. An increase to 10, 12½, 15, and 17½ per cent. under the national policy was expected to stimulate Canadian industry and to reduce American imports. Imports of manufactures of iron totalled $3,300,000 of which $2,437,000 came from the United States, chiefly castings and coarse types of hardware. Cutlery and high-grade manufactures, totalling $861,500, came from England. The national policy increased duties to a large extent on American products and to a less extent on British products. The tariff was definitely responsible, however, for a tendency toward monopoly control of the market. In some industries the market was overstocked with goods as a result of the limited knowledge "manufacturers had of the wants of the Canadian public".

> Up to 1879 Canadian markets had been very largely supplied from foreign sources, and it was, therefore, to some extent, a groping in the dark with home manufacturers as to how much of any particular article could find a market in the Dominion. The difficulty consisted in the fact that they could not possibly know enough of the consuming powers of the Dominion to produce just as much and no more than the people required. That knowledge had to be gained by experience. At this time of writing, producers have learned, in most branches of manufactures, just what is called for by the consuming public, and just how much of any particular class of goods can be profitably disposed of. In consequence of this better perception of the true state of affairs, changes have been and are continually being made in the class of goods produced, and it is now a question of but a very short time when, having a thorough knowledge of the requirements of our people, manufacturers in Canada will be prepared to supply, through the labor of our own mechanics and operatives, all the demands of the market, at a profit alike to themselves and the districts in which they are located.[1]

Recovery accompanied the demand in Great Britain for dairy products, bread-stuffs, and livestock which became evident in 1880. Exports to Great Britain increased in 1880-1. The United States purchased larger quantities of barley, lumber, and horses. In 1880-1 exports totalled

[1]Report of A. H. Blackeby on the state of the manufacturing industries of Ontario and Quebec, S.p., 37, 1885.

$89,290,823 and for the first time passed the former peak of $89,789,922 in 1873. After increasing from $131,000,000 in 1868 to $218,000,000 in 1873 and declining to $172,000,000 in 1878, total trade reached a new peak of $230,000,000 in 1883. By the end of the period the iron steamship and the railway had become predominant. The strain imposed by their introduction was registered in part in the national debt, and the possibilities of withstanding the strain were registered in the increased external trade.

Acton Vale, II 623
Adelaide, II, 798
Adelaide Township, II, 86
Advertisements, I, 494-5; II, 665, 742
Africa, I, 226-7, 504-5; II, 402, 743
Agriculture, I,6,8, 54-61, 64,85, 119-123, 145, 187-202, 235-248, 275-287, 295-300, 347, 352-372, 417, 434-45, 572-3; II, 22-3, 35, 40-9, 59-61, 66-8, 101-2, 219, 223, 233, 238-9, 257-8, 261-4, 274, 294, 302-3, 310, 329-30, 353, 355, 362-4, 390, 426, 432, 440-2, 445, 523, 525-68, 641, 643, 655, 685-96, 721, 735-59; products, barley, I, 277-80, 282; II, 65, 252, 319, 481, 492, 495, 545, 548-9, 566, 663, 695, 701, 709, 749, 756, 793-4, 821; beans, II, 513; corn, I, 276-7, 280-1, 314-5, 325, 362-5, 502-3, 542; II, 230, 319, 481-5, 493-4, 546-9, 556, 564, 607, 644, 647, 686, 695-6, 724; flax, I, 434-5, 463, 526, 561; II, 230, 565; fruit, I, 296, 353; II, 62, 566; apples, I, 60; II, 230, 319, 566, 684, 687, 693; hay, I, 193-4, 241-8, 358-61, 366, 443, 549-50, 572; II, 287, 455, 512-3, 526, 543-4, 549, 551, 564, 686-7, 690-6, 756; hemp, I, 178, 367, 369-72, 534, 561; II, 24, 59, 64, 291, 304, 319, 360, 481; oats, I, 279, 322, 362, 365, 438-9, 524, 532; II, 50, 65, 230, 232, 252, 481, 484, 512-3, 518, 526, 543, 546-9, 551, 568, 607, 663, 686-7, 690, 695-6, 749, 751, 754, 756, 793; peas, I, 277-282, 297, 314-5, 322, 325, 329, 340-1, 438-9, 506, 521-3, 526, 532; II, 224, 229, 252, 319, 495, 546-50, 564, 663, 701; potatoes, I, 438-9, 549, 572; II, 403, 444, 470, 518, 535, 542, 546-9, 686-7, 694-6, 756, 793, 803; starch, II, 696; rye, I, 115, 276, 279-80, 282; II, 319, 481, 546, 607, 724; wheat, I, 119-125, 196, 219, 226, 235-40, 242, 275-6, 279-282, 291-2, 296-9, 313-4, 350, 356, 358, 361-70, 405, 411, 417, 422-3, 426-9, 434-9, 443, 448, 502-3, 506-9, 511-6, 520-9, 542, 561, 569, 573; II, 11, 20, 36, 45-6, 50-1, 59-60, 63, 67, 103, 133, 170, 188, 193-7, 219, 223, 225, 229, 232-6, 251, 255-6, 261-6, 284-7, 319, 333, 337, 345, 350, 353-8, 360-2, 447, 465, 475-9, 481-5, 491-3, 495-6, 517, 526, 534, 541, 545-9, 553, 556, 567-8, 564, 589, 597, 602-3, 607-8, 620, 623, 641, 644-7, 657-8, 663, 686-7, 690, 694-5, 730, 740, 744, 749-59, 766, 793-4, 812; root crops, II,
564, 693, 695, 793; tobacco, I, 363, 367-9, 577; II, 59, 64, 565; vegetables, I, 277, 295, 435-6; II, 794; livestock, I, 173, 191-2, 196-8, 208, 229-30, 235-7, 278-9, 283, 296, 300, 357-61, 365, 370, 396, 438-9, 443, 467,514,550, 572; II, 47, 62, 118, 323, 361, 369, 402, 455, 526, 545, 549-57, 564, 607-8, 681-2, 686, 692-6; cattle, I, 124-8, 132, 134, 141, 145, 188, 191, 196, 208, 221, 229-30, 235, 238, 240, 242-5, 352-3, 357-9, 407, 438-9, 443, 467, 480-3, 503, 514; II, 228, 234-8, 441, 549-56, 563-8, 607, 692-5, 741, 745-8, 754, 757, 766, 776, 793-6; horses, I, 300, 324, 355-9, 438, 443, 467-8, 478, 480-3, 486-9; II, 228, 328, 361, 512-3, 526, 543-5, 549-53, 568, 618, 663, 687, 693-5, 741, 745-8, 753-4, 766-76, 821; oxen, II, 271, 273, 551, 747-8, 752-4, 775; pigs, I, 476, 481-2; II, 549-52, 555, 568, 663, 747-8, 754, 793-4, 812; sheep, I, 299, 324, 358, 438, 463, 467, 481-2, 578; II, 549-57, 564, 568, 607, 610, 663, 692-5, 745, 747, 757, 793; wool, I, 507; II, 549-51, 640, 645, 663; implements, I, 438, 443-5, 448, 507, 513, 539; II, 59, 60, 244, 291, 305, 364, 519, 526, 541-5, 593-600, 615-7, 640, 663, 718-9, 731, 741, 746-51, 759, 792-4, 812-3; equipment, buildings, II, 545, 565, 748-50; dykes, I, 54, 57-60, 64-6, 187-9, 192-5; II, 689-91; fences, II, 565, 755; soil, II, 31, 519, 531, 747; fertilizer, I, 436-7, 445; II, 574-5, 578, 692, 696, 755; drainage, II, 544; clearing, I, 195-6; II, 44-5, 541; pests, I, 119, 280, 282, 298, 365, 367; II, 547-8, 694, 741, 752-7; Great Britain, II, 540-1, 567
Ailsa Craig, II, 519, 564
Albany, I, 472, 477-8, 486, 491, 573; II, 12, 97, 106, 167, 173, 185, 214, 225-6, 596
Alberni, II, 796, 798
Albert (N.B.), I, 670
Alberton (P.E.I.), I, 671
Algoma district, II, 529
Alicante, I, 79
Allan, Hugh, II, 212, 453, 463-4, 480, 498, 657, 671
Allan, Hon. W., II, 177
Allandale, II, 516
Allard, I, 521
Allen, Mr., I, 522
Allen, Captain Ebenezer, II, 318

Allen, Levi, II, 320-1
Allin, Ignace, I, 493
Almonte, II, 505, 608
Amherst, Lord, I, 264
Amherst, I, 247; II, 673, 684, 689, 693, 718
Amherstburg, II, 64, 489
Amiot, Gabriel, I, 393
Amiot, Jean Baptiste, I, 303
Ancaster, II, 610
Anjou, I, 282
Annapolis basin, I, 186, 197, 240, 244; II, 387, 668, 676, 689-1, 693, 722
Annapolis Royal, I, 56-61, 63, 65, 69, 132, 155, 173, 185, 187, 215, 219, 236-40
Annexation, II, 266, 276, 342
Anticosti Island, I, 73, 251; II, 458, 460, 462, 699
Antwerp, II, 467
Arbuthnot, Lieutenant-Governor, I, 182
Archimegan Island, I, 63
Argentine, II, 511
Arichat, II, 676
Arkansas, II, 40
Arnprior, II, 510
Arthabaska, II, 496
Ascot Township, II, 85
Ashdown, J. H., II, 770
Assiniboia, II, 747
Assiniboine River, II, 732
Assomption, Rivière de l', I, 397, 481
Australia, II, 509, 522, 539, 557, 595, 688, 743, 800
Austria, II, 294
Aviero (Portugal), I, 10
Aylmer, Lord, II, 84, 109, 158
Aylmer (Ont.), II, 556
Aylmer (P.Q.), II, 23, 504, 522
Ayr (Ont.), II, 746
Azores, I, 226-7

Baby, F, II, 462
Baddeck, II, 460
Bagot County, II, 582
Bahia, II, 702
Baker, Sandford, II, 515
Baldwin, A. H., II, 510
Baleine, I, 68, 73, 83, 111
Ballantyne, Mr., II, 562
Baltic, I, 206, 575; II, 252, 273-4, 276-7, 332, 425
Baltimore, II, 214, 486
Bangor (Me.), II, 673
Banking, II, 261, 263, 368-78, 397, 402-3, 431, 435, 655-9, 726-8, 770, 805-6; Free Bank Act, II, 656, 659; Bank of Acadia, II, 727; Bank of British Columbia, II, 805-6; Bank

of British North America, II, 255, 656, 805; Canada Banking Company, II, 368; Bank of Commerce, II, 430, 657, 659; Commercial Bank, II, 656; Gore and District Savings Bank, II, 651, 659; Halifax Banking Company, II, 430, 434, 436; Bank of Hamilton, II, 657; Imperial Bank, II, 656-7; Bank of Liverpool, II, 727; MacDonald's Bank, II, 805; Merchants' Bank, II, 657; Molson's Bank, II, 656-7; Bank of Montreal, II, 368, 372, 657; Bank of Nova Scotia, II, 430, 727; Postal Savings Bank, II, 658; Bank of Prince Edward Island, II, 727; Bank of Toronto, II, 657; Union Bank (P.E.I.), II, 727; Bank of Upper Canada, II, 120, 656
Baptiste, Messrs, II, 517
Barbadoes, II, 700
Barber, Captain, II, 145
Barber Bros., II, 608
Barcelona, I, 508, 529
Barclay Sound, II, 798
Barkerville, II, 775, 777, 779, 803, 807
Barrie, II, 490, 516
Barrie Township, II, 580
Barrington, II, 676
Barrington Township, I, 243
Barry, John A., II, 433
Barsalot, I, 301
Barss, Mr., II, 405
Basques, I, 17, 51, 144, 251
Basset, Captain Guion, I, 322
Bathurst, Lord, II, 81-2, 90-1
Bathurst (N.B.), II, 676, 726
Bathurst district, II, 86
Batiscan, I, 480; II, 517
Battleford, II, 734, 757, 766
Bayfield, Admiral, II, 585
Bayonne, I, 4, 47, 78-9, 96, 101, 107-8, 116, 427
Beamsville, II, 597
Bear River (N.S.), I, 186, 204; II, 682
Beauce, I, 61
Beauport, Abbey of, I, 4
Beaupré, Canton de, I, 297
Beaverton, II, 496
Bedard, Mr., II, 373
Bedford Basin, I, 241
Begon, M., I, 307, 406, 417, 428
Belfast, I, 506, 534; II, 116, 243
Bell, Captain, II, 454
Bell Company, II, 522
Belle Ewart, II, 516
Belle Isle, I, 1, 5, 73, 317; II, 414, 458
Belleville, II, 113, 296, 496, 560, 563, 610, 618
Bennacadia River, II, 439

Bennett and Henderson, II, 296
Beresina, II, 747
Bermuda, II, 684
Bersimis, II, 460, 699
Berthier, I, 483, 491; II, 107, 455
Beverly Township, II, 33
Bic, II, 462, 475
Big Bend, II, 777
Bigelow, Messrs, II, 145
Bigot, Monsieur, I, 139
Bird Rock, II, 460
Birkenhead, II, 592
Birmingham, II, 244, 295, 343
Birtle, II, 739
Biscay, I, 9, 79
Black, Mr., II, 211
Black Lake, II, 584
Black Rock, II, 167-8
Black Sea, II, 467
Blanc Sablon, II, 698-9
Bleigh, Samuel, I, 209
Blind River, II, 513
Bobcaygeon, II, 530
Boiscler, Sieur, I, 364, 398
Bonaventure Island, I, 47, 74, 167
Bond Head, II, 471
Bonfield, J., I, 521
Bonnaventure, Monsieur de, I, 65, 121
Bonnechère, II, 22
Booth, J. R., II, 510
Boroughbridge (Eng.), I, 197
Boston, I, 56, 111, 127, 131, 133, 136,
  139, 163, 168, 173, 177, 181-2, 200,
  211, 213, 215, 217-8, 220, 222, 472,
  477-8, 484, 496-8, 501, 526; II, 151,
  212-5, 301, 309, 471, 477, 486, 489,
  491, 551, 555, 557, 671, 683, 692, 703,
  705, 708
Bouchard, François, I, 381
Boucher, M., I, 317
Boucherville, I, 411, 482
Bourdeaux, I, 18-19, 79, 101, 116, 143,
  321, 367, 382, 427
Bourdon, Madame, I, 293
Boutheyller, Peter, I, 519
Bowmanville, II, 520
Bow River, II, 733
Bradore Bay, II, 698
Brampton, II, 602
Brandon, II, 732-3, 757, 759, 763, 769
Brandy Pots, II, 462
Brantford, II, 31, 120, 593, 597, 615,
  618, 623, 719, 751
Bras d'Or, Lake, I, 117; II, 439, 443,
  668
Brazil, I, 61; II, 425, 539, 614, 699,
  701-2
Brehat, Island of, I, 4
Bremen, II, 354
Brest (Belle Isle), I, 5

Brest (France), I, 86, 389
Brewing, I, 324; II, 302, 605-6, 795
Briconnet, I, 356
Bridgetown (N.S.), II, 693
Briquet, II, 458
Brissot, II, 221
Bristol, I, 10, 459, 497, 499, 507-8;
  II, 116, 284
Britannia Company, II, 599
British Guiana, II, 814-5
Brittany, I, 5, 115, 146
Broadview, II, 753
Brockville, II, 144, 147-8, 215, 471,
  505, 515, 576, 579, 618
Brookes, S., II, 301
Brookfield Company, II, 684
Brouage, I, 14
Brougham, Lord, II, 112
Brown, Mr., II, 250
Brown, Adam, II, 560
Brown and Gilmore, I, 468, 494-5
Bruce County, II, 9, 518
Buckingham (P.Q.), II, 576, 578
Buckland, II, 532
Buctouche, II, 676
Buffalo, II, 39, 136, 166-8, 173, 185,
  195, 205, 214-5, 253, 358, 470-1, 474,
  476-7, 480-3, 485, 488-9, 491-2, 498,
  553
Buildings, I, 275-6, 278, 285-6, 297;
  II, 44, 46, 533-4, 654-5; equipment,
  crockery, II, 639-40, 645; lamps, II,
  573; stoves, II, 377, 453, 465; II,
  230, 297-8, 305, 545, 718-9, 804
Burford, II, 169
Burlington, II, 202, 264, 490
Burlington Bay, II, 246
Burnett, James, II, 560
Burrard Inlet, II, 779, 799
Burwell, Colonel, II, 26
Bushby, Captain, II, 247
Business conditions, II, 238-9, 241,
  248-50, 276-7, 377-8, 395, 422-3, 426,
  621-4, 680, 727, 738-9, 741, 747, 755
Buteux, Father, I, 280
By, Lieutenant-Colonel, II, 153

Cabot, John, I, 4
Cadiz, I, 79, 497, 499, 501
Calais, I, 427
Caldwell, II, 510
Caledonia, II, 575
Calgary, II, 733, 751, 763, 766, 769
California, II, 772, 784-5, 787, 806
Callander, II, 733
Callao, II, 511, 798
Cameron, Mr., II, 378
Campbell, Sir Archibald, II, 204
Campbell, Governor, Lord Wm., I, 176
Campbellton, II, 670, 674, 700, 726

Campo Bello, II, 418-9, 698
Canada Company (New France), I, 220
Canals, II, 451-7, 470-86, 493-4, 507, 578, 590-1, 634-5, 646-7, 651, 809, 820; tolls, II, 336, 474-9; Beauharnois, II, 451-2; Burlington, II, 172; Chambly, II, 186, 251, 382, 512; Desjardins, II, 490; Erie, II, 39, 106, 133, 161-4, 169, 171-4, 181, 183, 186, 197, 206, 218, 224, 253-4, 335, 352, 384, 470-4, 476-8; Lachine, II, 176, 184, 382, 451-2, 456, 470, 597,603-4, 611,616; Rideau, II,22, 29, 103, 148, 150, 153, 160, 171, 174, 176, 181, 184, 243, 247, 251-2, 254; St. Anne, II, 504; St. Peters, II, 668; Welland, II, 29, 39, 120, 161-9, 172, 176, 183-4, 187-8, 200, 243, 246-7, 250-1, 356-7, 361, 470-2, 476-86, 490, 493, 496, 591; Williamsburg, II, 451; Bay of Verte Canal, II, 157; Ship channel, 66, 453-7, 472; see Transportation
Caneuil, Pierre, I, 111
Canso, I, 2, 51, 57, 62, 66-7, 71, 73, 83, 112, 125-7, 129-132, 141, 144, 153-163, 167, 187, 214, 218, 221-4, 239-40, 247-8, 253; II, 157, 460
Canso, Strait of, II, 668, 703
Cap Blanc, II, 314
Cap Chat, I, 74; II, 462, 532
Cap de Tourmente, I, 285, 400
Cape Breton, I, 2, 17, 50-1, 54, 68-9, 71, 73-149, 152-3, 160-4, 167, 188, 213, 216, 218, 220-5, 235, 238, 319, 407, 411, 417, 421-3, 428; II, 11-13, 157, 390-1, 394, 428, 430, 439-4, 460, 668, 693, 698, 708-10, 728
Cape Cod, I, 243
Cape Diamond, II, 213
Cape Doré, I, 237, 246
Cape Finisterre, I, 222
Cape Flattery, II, 779
Cape John, II, 415
Cape Ray, II, 415
Cape Rouge, I, 480, 492
Cape Sable, I, 52, 62, 66-7, 118, 177, 187, 243-4
Cape St. Marie, I, 214
Cape Spencer (N.B.), II, 682
Capital, II, 643-4, 651-5, 806-7; interest rate, 653, 809
Caraquet, I, 74; II, 699
Carey, economist, II, 641
Carignan-Salières, Regiment, I, 354
Carignant and Ogiez, I, 519
Carillon, I, 386; II, 10, 160, 504
Carleton, Sir Guy, I, 182-3
Carleton (N.B.), II, 700
Carleton County (N.B.), II, 689, 692-3

Carleton County (Ont.), II, 512
Carleton Place, II, 505
Carnoyer, Sieur, I, 111
Carolina, I, 168, 178
Cartier, Jacques, I, 5, 251
Cartwright, Sir Richard, II, 227, 380
Cartwright (Man.), II, 757
Casco-Bay, I, 497, 499, 500-1
Cascumpec, II, 671
Cassiar, II, 777, 789
Castleford, II, 504
Caswell, Edwin, II, 563
Catalogne, I, 378
Cataraqui, II, 10-11
Cayenne, I, 319
Cayley, II, 351
Cayuga, II, 575
Chabot, M., I, 471
Chalet, Sieur, I, 412
Chaleur, Bay of, I, 73-4, 165, 167, 223-4, 447, 471; II, 420-1, 698-9
Chambly, I, 387, 398, 458, 515, 524, 575; II, 199, 268, 299, 304
Chamfour, I, 392
Champigny, Sieur de, I, 298
Champigny, I, 492
Champlain, Lake, I, 458, 477, 491, 575; II, 150-1, 170, 184, 229, 234, 256, 268, 320-1, 335, 406, 471, 512, 598
Champlain River, I, 480
Chapleau, II, 733
Chaplin, William, II, 719
Charles River, I, 480
Charlestown (South Carolina), I, 501; II, 388
Charlevoix, I, 378
Charlotte County, II, 270, 402
Charlottetown, I, 216; II, 670-1, 673, 695, 726
Chateaugay, II, 105
Chatham (N.B.), II, 676, 706
Chatham (Ont.), II, 27, 42, 88, 488, 522, 556
Chats Falls, II, 504
Chaudière (Que.), II, 709
Chaudière Falls, II, 504-10, 515
Chaudière River (P.Q.), II, 34, 80, 203, 583
Chedabouctou, I, 56, 62
Chefdostel, Thomas, I, 14-15
Chelsea, II, 510
Chemong Lake, II, 155
Chesnaye, Sieur de la Aubert, I, 312, 333
Chester, I, 207, 242; II, 676
Cheticamp, II, 698
Chevry, Monsieur de, I, 49
Chibouctou, I, 55, 62-3, 242
Chicago, II, 202, 206, 471, 474, 477, 480-5, 488-90, 494-5, 501, 566, 574, 745

Chicot (St. Cuthbert), I, 483
Chicoutimi, II, 460, 517
Chignecto, I, 55-6, 58, 65, 124, 126; II, 152, 155, 237-8
Chile, II, 578
China, I, 424-6; II, 232, 247, 331, 335, 341-2, 800, 817
Chipman, Hon. Ward, II, 383
Chippewa, II, 29, 138, 162, 167, 200, 263, 267, 595
Chisolm, William, II, 329
Christie, Mr., II, 292, 414
Cincinnati, II, 489
Citrus fruits, II, 724
Civil service, II, 129-30, 642-3
Civil War, II, 508, 526-7, 550-1, 553, 565, 578, 621, 632, 645, 648, 680, 699, 707, 819
Clancarty, Lord, II, 166
Clare, I, 186
Clarke, General, II, 72
Cleveland, II, 195-6, 477, 480, 566, 578-9
Climate, I, xxix-xxx, 279, 285-6, 296, 353, 363-4, 367-70, 412-3; II, 445
Clinton (B.C.), II, 774, 776, 797
Clinton (Ont.), II, 574
Clover Bay, II, 779
Clyde Forks, II, 515
Cobalt, II, 585
Cobequid, I, 214, 235, 240, 245-6
Coboconk, II, 496
Cobourg, II, 122, 144, 215, 304, 471, 496, 520, 548, 595, 602, 606-8, 636
Cochrane, John, I, 545
Codfish Bay, I, 73
Coffee, I, 503-4, 535, 558; II, 225, 231, 286, 330-1, 381, 410, 640, 645, 662, 720
Coffin, G. W., II, 155
Cogswell, H. H., II, 433
Colborne, Sir John, II, 158
Colchester County, II, 689, 691, 693
Collingwood, II, 202, 483, 489-90, 493-4, 499, 516, 591, 743
Collins, Mr., I, 203-4
Collins, Mr., II, 18
Collins, Mr., II, 434
Colonial system, II, 316, 326, 343, 346, 403, 406; colonial trade acts, II, 326-31, 334-5, 406; corn laws, II, 261, 264, 266, 273, 319, 337, 356-7, 363-4, 472, 701; navigation acts, II, 317-20, 319-20, 324-5, 342, 349-54, 358, 404, 701; mercantile policy, I, xxxiii, 2, 178-9, 212, 227, 568; II, 231, 235-7, 315-8, 358
Columbia River, II, 772, 789, 793
Combes, Captain, I, 212
Combines, I, 572, 575

Communications, II, 498-501, 779; cables, II, 668; telegraph, II, 109, 210, 213, 216, 459-62, 498, 668, 670, 702, 734, 762, 779; Great North Western Telegraph Company, II, 498;Montreal Telegraph Company, II, 216, 498; see Postal facilities
Comox, II, 777
Company of Acadia, I, 49, 56, 65
Company of New France, I, 329
Company of the Habitans, I, 329
Company of West Indies, I, 329, 332, 335, 341, 391-2, 403, 425-7
Compton, II, 35
Connecticut, I, 177-8, 187, 243
Conomo, Point, I, 246
Constantinople, II, 467
Conway, I, 186
Coote, Daniel, II, 52
Copper Bay, II, 581
Coquimbo, II, 798
Corbin, David, I, 386
Corbin, Joseph, I, 389
Cork, I, 499, 500; II, 116, 284, 501, 537
Cornwall, II, 29, 143, 145, 172, 215, 451-2, 471, 587, 758
Cornwallis, General, I, 241
Cornwallis, I, 196, 206, 239, 244
Costebelle, Sieur de, I, 98
Coteau, II, 172, 203, 225, 380, 471, 485
Cotton, Sieur, I, 392
Couchiching, Lake, II, 530
Courcelles, Sieur de, I, 338
Cow Bay, II, 441, 709
Cowes, I, 514
Cowichan, II, 798
T. Cowie and Company, II, 599
Coyon, Ebenezer, I, 448
Cramahe Township, II, 73
Crapaud (P.E.I.), II, 671
Credit, I, 431, 501, 521; II, 238-40, 242, 278-9, 634-65; R. G. Dun and Company, II, 665
Credit Forks, II, 570
Crown Point, I, 486, 491
Cuba, II, 339, 590, 675, 814
Cugnet, Sieur, I, 418
Cumberland, I, 185, 193, 197, 246; II, 155, 673, 680, 689, 691, 705
Cumberland House, II, 733
Cunard, Samuel, II, 434, 667
Cunningham Sons, II, 581
Currie, J. S., II, 88
Cuyler, Abraham, II, 12

Dairying, II, 319, 371, 441, 564, 574, 794; butter, II, 457, 470, 518, 541, 549, 557-60, 663, 686, 693, 695, 766, 794; cheese, II, 541, 549, 560-3, 615, 686, 693, 695; milk, II, 541, 562-3,

565; creameries, II, 558-9; in Great Britain, II, 541
Dakota, II, 742, 746, 749, 755, 759
Dalhousie, Earl of, II, 82
Dalhousie (N.B.), II, 673, 676, 700
Danube, II, 7
Danville (P.Q.), II, 584
Darlington, II, 471
Dartmouth, Earl of, II, 389
Dartmouth (N.S.), I, 186, 242; II, 716, 718, 726
Dauphin, Port, I, 138
Davidson, Mr., I, 228
Davidson, William, II, 684
Davies, William, II, 556
Dawson City, II, 805
Dee, Richard, I, 471
Deerfield, I, 477
Delaunay, I, 301
Deloraine, II, 747, 757
Deloro, II, 580
Demerara, II, 192
Demers, Dr., II, 107
De Meulles, I, 42, 55
De Montenach, Mr., II, 373
Denis, Sieur, I, 334
Denmark, II, 595
Dennée River, II, 443
Departure Bay, II, 801
De Pensens, M., I, 119
De Pensier, II, 22
De Rottermund, II, 581
Deschenes Lake, II, 506
Deseronto, II, 515
Desfoix, Augustine, I, 493
Detroit, I, 289, 473-4, 521; II, 137, 224, 226-7, 369, 471, 488, 490, 498, 501, 566, 745
Dick, John, I, 169-71
Dickinson's Landing, II, 145, 452
Dickson, Robert, II, 227
Dieppe, I, 321, 427
Digby, II, 668, 680
Dise, Sieur, I, 400
Distilling, I, 208-10, 464-5; II, 302, 556, 606-7, 795; liquors, I, 165, 173, 330, 336, 338, 340, 342-3, 430; II, 225, 366-7, 381, 724; brandy, I, 97-8, 131-2, 135, 224-5, 240, 287, 297, 418-9, 424, 561, 565; II, 231, 349; whisky, II, 65-6, 256-7, 273, 287, 302
Dobie, I, 524
Donald (B.C.), II, 778
Donaldson, II, 555
Doon, II, 565
Doran, Colonel, II, 309
Dorchester, II, 319, 689
Dorvillier, I, 484
Doucet, Jean, I, 219

Dougall, Gamble, II, 244
Douglas, Sir H., II, 423, 426
Doyon, Nicolas, I, 303
Dresden, II, 42
Drugs, I, 533-4
Drummond, Sir Gordon, II, 81
Drummond, II, 733
Drummond and Tordau, I, 515
Drummondville, II, 34
Dublin, I, 470; II, 537
Dublin Township, I, 243
Duchambon, M., I, 120
Dufferin County, II, 9
Duga, Joseph, I, 112
Duggan, Jeremiah, I, 523
Dumas, Alexander, I, 452
Dumfriesshire, II, 101
Du Monts, Sieur, I, 61, 277
Dundas, II, 92, 120, 146, 201, 488, 490, 611
Dundas County, II, 512, 519-20, 522, 528, 543, 546, 548, 594, 602, 608, 615, 663
Dungeness (Wash.), II, 779
Dunham, II, 560
Dunkirk, I, 79, 321
Dunmore, II, 764
Dunville, II, 642
Durham, II, 34
Durnford, Colonel, II, 153
Durocher, Mr., I, 522-3
Dutch, I, 292; II, 20
Duvivier, Sieur, I, 110-3

Eastern district, II, 87
Eastern Townships, II, 9, 32-3, 47, 85, 88, 94, 108, 118, 202, 558
East India Company, II, 232, 328, 340-1
East Indies, I, 135, 147, 502; II, 232, 243
Eastport (Maine), II, 466, 675
Eaton, Timothy, II, 665
Eckford, II, 488
Economics, II, 448
Eddy, E. B., II, 510, 518
Edenton (North Carolina), I, 499
Edinburgh, I, 470
Edmonstone, William, II, 153
Edmonton, II, 462, 732-4, 737, 751, 763, 766, 769
Edmunston, II, 670
Edward VI, I, 6
Egan and Aumond, II, 160
Elgin, Lord, II, 124
Elgin (N.B.), II, 670
Elgin County, II, 516, 522
Alexander Ellice and Company, II, 136
Elora, II, 602, 609, 664
Elzevir, II, 530

Emerson, II, 732, 746-52
Emory's Bar, II, 774
English Bay, II, 460
Enniskillen, II, 573
Eskimo Point, II, 699
Esquimalt, II, 778
Essex, II, 516, 519, 552, 556, 566
Esson, Adam, II, 434
Estang, I, 74
Evans, Mills and Millar, II, 299
Everts, Captain, II, 228
Exeter, I, 160, 459
Exhibitions, provincial, II, 541, 542, 552, 744

Fairs, I, 312, 424
Falmouth, I, 490
Falmouth Township, I, 245
Family Compact, II, 127
Faneuil, Peter, I, 476
Farmer, Mr., II, 118
Farries, Hugh, I, 438
Farrington, Harvey, II, 560
Father Point, II, 459, 475, 673
Fauconnet, I, 339
Felton, W. B., II, 81-5
Fenelon Falls, II, 154, 515
Fenelon Township, II, 118, 154
Ferguson, John, I, 451
Field (B.C.), 778
Fillis, John, I, 209
Finance, II, 217-8; corporations, II, 28-9, 650-1, 726; stock exchange, II, 651; bankruptcy, I, 521, 551-6
Finlay, Hugh, I, 486
Fisheries, cod, French fishery, I, 1-10, 14-54, 73-99, 123; II, 415; English fishery, I, 153-167; 178, 181, 208-9, 219-22, 225-30, 236-7, 240, 243-8, 269, 286, 319, 322, 325-9, 340-1, 353, 393, 407, 417, 423, 428, 471, 506, 514, 571, 576; II, 230, 233-4, 328, 390, 398, 401-3, 412,-21, 435, 439-40, 447-9, 465, 569, 640, 645, 662, 675-6, 681, 684-9, 697-706, 717, 720-1, 724, 727-8, 768, 796-7, 812-3; alewives, I, 58-9; II, 420, 705; capelin, I, 80; eels, I, 263, 287, 316, 327-8, 353-4, 366; haddock, II, 414, 418-9; hake, II, 418-9; herring, I, 34, 40-2, 67, 73, 80, 153, 165, 264, 534; II, 230, 412-3, 418-9, 440, 697, 699, 702-3; lobsters, I, 173; II, 704-6; mackerel, I, 40-2, 67-80, 153, 209; II, 414, 418, 440, 697, 702-3; oysters, II, 696, 704; porpoise, I, 236, 249, 253, 255, 263, 286; salmon, I, 167, 239, 322-3, 506; II, 230, 412-3, 420, 440, 673, 703-6, 796, 812; sardine, I, 238; seabass, I, 740; seal, I, 67, 249, 253-5, 286, 374,

428, 522; II, 440; shad, II, 420, 705; smelt, II, 706; sturgeon, I, 374; II, 19, 704; walrus, I, 249, 253-4, 257-8, 262-5; whale, I, 9, 249-53; II, 293, 390-1, 403, 573, 796-7; supplies, I, 11, 17, 22, 24-31, 39-40, 69, 71, 82-3, 87, 90-2, 100-140, 162, 536-7
Fisher's Landing, II, 745
Fitzroy Harbour, II, 159
Flamboro, II, 488
Florida, I, 61
Foodstuffs, I, 107-115, 549-50; II, 44, 62, 140, 169;meat products, II, 63-4, 557, 686, 693; beef, II, 230, 240, 247, 328, 330, 333; pork, II, 224, 230-1, 240, 247, 257, 273-4, 328, 330, 333, 361, 371, 457, 489, 513, 535, 549, 699, 746; refrigeration, II, 693, 704; packing industry, II, 617, 627; William Davies Company, II, 574; game, moose, I, 330, 335-8, 344, 428; partridges, I, 114, 443; pigeons, I, 354; flour, I, 125, 129-30, 134-7, 139-41, 297-8, 319, 322, 328-9, 340-1, 361, 363, 367, 404-5, 417, 420-1, 423, 428, 503, 506, 514-6, 539-40, 542, 549, 551, 563; II, 139, 172, 188-9, 193-6, 220-5, 230-1, 234, 240, 251, 255-8, 261-6, 273-4, 284-7, 319, 328, 333, 337, 342, 347, 350-6, 361-3, 398, 402, 407, 410, 433, 457, 472, 479, 484-6, 489, 492-3, 513, 519, 521, 553, 564, 645-7, 663, 686, 694, 696, 699, 701, 709, 720, 746, 752, 758, 764, 768, 792-5, 803-4, 812, 815, 819; mills, II, 262, 268, 356-60, 574-5, 601-5, 615, 617, 622; Ogilvie Milling Company, II, 752, 755; grist mills, I, 57, 448; II, 21, 601-3; bread, I, 313, 329, 362, 365, 367, 540-1, 577; biscuit, II, 604; adulteration, II, 627, 661-2
Forest industries, lumbering, I, 58, 116-8, 125-8, 132, 134, 177, 180, 206-8, 219, 225-8, 235-7, 243, 304-7, 319, 322-8, 341, 372-3, 378-91, 417, 454-62, 502-3, 506, 520, 529-30; II, 5, 7, 20-3, 41, 52, 217, 225, 229, 233-7, 241-2, 247, 251-4, 258-9, 266-80, 284-8, 319, 321-4, 327-8, 332, 338-9, 342-5, 360, 386, 395, 398, 401-7, 422-4, 428, 434, 443, 447, 456-7, 464-6, 470, 480, 484, 494, 589, 618, 645, 647, 657-8, 663, 675-687, 691-2, 699-701, 721, 724-7, 740-1, 759, 791, 797-8, 812-3, 817, 819, 821; masts, II, 321; square timber, II, 267-71, 277, 503-9; slides, II, 272; rafts, II, 268-9, 272, 275, 279-80; Rankin Gilmour and Company, II, 510, 515, 590, 680; sawn lumber, I, 455-7; II, 267,

269, 271, 511-2, 517, 682-4; shingles, II, 683-4; sawmills, I, 57, 387, 448, 454; II, 20-1, 42, 267-8, 270-1, 507-10, 514-7, 521, 615-6, 679-81, 684, 764-5, 776, 797-9; Bronson and Weston, II, 510; Hamilton, II, 510; Perley and Pattee, II, 510; Rathbun Company, II, 515; axes, II, 244, 291, 305, 513; saws, II, 513; box shooks, II, 682-4; cabinets, II, 520; charcoal, II, 519, 593-4; cooperage, II, 522, 684; fuel, I, 175, 286, 297, 314, 360, 390, 401, 412, 479; II, 298, 519, 589, 634, 640, 653, 753, 764; furniture, II, 520, 545, 615-6; Upper Canada Furniture Company, II, 520; matches, II, 276, 509, 519, 684; organs, II, 522-3, 819; pails, II, 509, 518, 520; potash, I, 448-53, 464-5, 503, 506, 508, 561, 576; II, 22, 33, 139, 225, 230-1, 240, 261, 280-5, 287, 302, 319-20, 327, 360, 371, 406, 457, 503, 663; sash door and blinds, II, 519-20, 684; staves, I, 307, 323-4, 387, 448, 458-62, 465, 502, 506, 523, 530, 538, 575-8; II, 42, 229, 231, 234, 247, 281, 284-6, 289, 403-4, 410, 505, 517-22, 663, 680; Kingston Stave Forwarding Company, II, 251; tar, I, 373, 379, 382-5; washboards, II, 684; *trees*, ash, I, 306, 383, 418; II, 286, 442, 519, 521; beech, I, 451, 574; II, 441, 519; birch, I, 306, 451, 574; II, 229, 439, 441, 519; cedar, I, 305, 456; II, 229, 519, 544; chestnut, II, 519; elm, I, 306, 388, 451, 547, 574; II, 229, 270, 286, 288, 442-3, 503, 516, 519-21; fir, I, 455-6; hemlock, II, 442, 518, 612, 682; hickory, II, 519; maple, I, 305-6, 355, 380, 451, 574; II, 439, 442, 519, 523; oak, I, 305, 382-4, 386, 388, 451, 454-6, 459, 465, 529, 547, 574; II, 169, 229, 270-1, 275, 278, 284-8, 319, 403-4, 425, 441, 443, 503, 516-20, 522, 750, 753; pine, I, 304, 378-9, 382-3, 455, 529, 547, 574; II, 44, 229, 259, 269, 275-9, 284-9, 319, 386, 443, 503, 516, 519, 619, 682, 798; spruce, I, 304; II, 286, 289, 439, 443, 503, 517, 519, 679-80; tamarac, II, 243, 288; walnut, I, 304, 379, 529; II, 229, 519; regulations, II, 112, 278, 502, 514-5; inspection, II, 280-1; fires, I, 384-5, 390, 426
Forillon, I, 73
Forsyth, Mr., II, 324
Fort Benton, II, 766
Fort Chipewyan, II, 733
Fort Edward, I, 477, 491
Fort Ellice, II, 732

Fort Erie, I, 473; II, 48, 54, 137-8, 489, 495
Fort Frontenac, I, 289, 400, 414
Fort Garry, II, 732, 734, 741, 743, 745, 770
Fort George, II, 146
Fort Henry, II, 598
Fortier and Orillat, I, 519
Fort Pelly, II, 732
Fort Saskatchewan, II, 733
Fort Schlosser, II, 137
Fort Simpson, II, 733
Fort William, II, 490, 499, 529
Fort William Augustus, I, 473-4
Fourchet, I, 76-7
Fowles, II, 515
Fox River, II, 460
Francheville, Sieur Poulin de, I, 375
Franciscans, II, 16
Franck, Justin, I, 546
Franklin, Mr., I, 204
Franks, John, I, 438, 439, 531, 547-8
Fraser, Mr., I, 524
Fraser, Mr., II, 159
Fraser, James, II, 404
Fredericton, II, 53, 272, 402, 429, 669-70, 673, 684
Fresnel, II, 458
Frobisher, Martin, I, 11
Frontenac County, II, 529-30, 547, 578
Frue, Captain, II, 582
Fry, Henry, II, 464, 468
Fundy, Bay of, I, 1, 8, 54, 63, 67, 124, 187, 192, 213-5, 218, 221, 234, 237-9, 244-5; II, 152, 157, 215, 418-9, 466, 667, 676, 682, 687, 689-90, 698, 703
Fur trade, I, xxxi-iii, 56, 58, 60, 65, 125-6, 141, 163-4, 218-21, 224-7, 236-8, 240, 243, 269-73, 286-9, 319, 326, 329-30, 335, 337, 342-3, 347, 349, 352, 363, 401, 403, 412, 417-421, 426-31, 473-4, 503-7, 520-1, 530-1, 541-2, 546-7, 551-2, 559, 560-5, 569, 571, 576; II, 4, 7, 20, 133, 222, 227, 230, 233, 245, 283, 319, 371, 447-8, 503, 731, 758, 770-2; beaver, I, xxxi, 269-71, 286-7, 329, 333, 335, 337-40, 342-3, 392, 403, 502, 505-6, 538, 542, 570; II, 283, 803-4; hats, I, 339, 342, 391-2, 464, 510, 538, 570
Fyall, I, 497, 501

Gaboury, I, 83
Gage, Mr., I, 472
Galt, A. T., II, 88, 301, 636, 638, 743
Galt, John, II, 88
Galt, II, 520, 595, 606-8, 615
Galway, II, 537
Galwey, D., I, 469
Garafraxa Township, II, 41

Garden Island, II, 251-2
Gaspé, I, 74, 110, 129, 166-7, 423, 447, 471, 498, 500; II, 157, 293, 408, 460, 573, 673, 698-700, 726, 728
Gatineau, II, 506, 509
Genesee, II, 17
Geneva (N.Y.), II, 544
George, Lake, I, 477, 491
Georges Cove, I, 166
Georgetown (N.S.), II, 745
Georgetown (Ont.), II, 500
Georgetown (P.E.I.), II, 671-2, 695
Georgia, I, 190; II, 395
Georgian Bay, II, 202, 490, 503, 516, 569, 618
Germany, I, 190, 502-3; II, 306, 501, 523, 573, 576, 578, 595, 614-5, 696, 814, 819
Gerrard, Samuel, II, 153
Gervais, I, 521
Gibraltar, II, 467
Giffard, Sieur, I, 281
Gilbert River, II, 583
Gill, Captain, I, 522
Gillespie Moffat and Company, II, 805
Gillies, II, 510
Gimli, II, 743, 768
Ginseng, I, 390, 417, 424-6
Glacier House, II, 778
Gladstone, II, 349
Glasgow, I, 459. 498, 500-1, 508, 534; II, 243, 343, 537, 553, 605
Glass, II, 302, 305, 349, 403, 467, 624, 639, 645, 717, 819
Glencarnock, II, 598
Glencoe, II, 489
Glengarry, II, 9, 25, 143, 548, 594
Glengarry Fencible Regiment, II, 24
Gloucester Company, II, 686, 712
Glue, I, 373-4
Goat Island (N.S.), I, 237
Goderich, II, 9, 31-2, 88, 92, 94, 489, 494, 545, 563, 569, 574-5, 606
Goldie, Mr., II, 602, 605
Goldie and McCulloch, II, 603
Goldmouth River, II, 713
Gooderham and Worts, II, 607
Good Hope, II, 698
Gore Bay, II, 512
Gore district, II, 92, 146
Gosford, Lord, II, 81
Goulais Bay, II, 530
Goulburn Township, II, 22
Gourlay, II, 38
Gourville, Sieur, I, 112
Grades, Sieur, I, 367
Graham, Felix, II, 136
Graham, Ketchum, II, 560
Graisse, Rivière à la, I, 386
Grand Falls (N.B.), II, 669

Grand Forks, II, 732
Grand Grave, I, 166
Grand Haven, II, 745
Grand Lake (N.B.), II, 429
Grand Manan, II, 418-9, 688, 698
Grand Piles, II, 517
Grand Portage, II, 138
Grand Rapids (Man.), II, 732
Grand River, II, 29, 31, 167, 169, 495
Grandville, I, 96, 146
Grant, Captain, II, 369
Grant, Mr., I, 191
Grant, Hon. C. W., II, 199
Grant, John, I, 521
Granville (N.S.), I, 197, 244
Gravenhurst, II, 516
Gray, Ralph, I, 449, 468
Green Bay, II, 494
Green Island, II, 458
Greenock, II, 496, 500; II, 116
Gregory, Rt. Hon. William, I, 469
Grenada, I, 320, 500-2; II, 209
Grenville, II, 160, 176, 504
Grenville County, II, 563
Grey County, II, 9, 527
Grier and Company, II, 510
Grimsby, II, 566
Grosse Isle, II, 109, 537
Guadaloupe, I, 320, 391
Guelph, II, 30, 32, 92, 94, 114, 146, 490, 498, 520, 522-3, 595-6, 602, 605-6, 610, 614-5, 719
Guernsey, I, 226, 499
Guigue, Louis, I, 345
Guinée, I, 147
Gunn, William, I, 470
Gurney, Edward, II, 719
Guysboro, II, 676, 697
Gzowski and Macpherson, II, 593

Hakluyt, Richard, I, 9
Haldimand, General, II, 136
Haldimand County, II, 547
Haldimand Township, II, 73
Hale, E., II, 301
Haliburton, II, 512, 515
Halifax, I, 152, 167, 169, 172-5, 185, 196, 202, 213-4, 225, 230, 234, 238-43, 247, 496-8, 515; II, 214-5, 241, 296, 332, 370, 387-8, 391, 397, 404, 411, 416, 439-40, 460, 472, 487, 499, 538, 605, 614, 618, 648, 667-8, 671, 673-4, 676, 680, 682, 684, 691-3, 697-702, 709, 711, 713, 716-20, 722-6
Halifax award, II, 703
Halifax Company, II, 211
Hall, Mr., II, 156
Hall, G. B., II, 509
Hallowell (village), II, 29
Halton County, II, 329

Hamburg, II, 743
Hamilton, Robert, II, 227
Hamilton, II, 32, 113, 120, 143, 146, 196, 200-1, 214, 471, 488, 490, 495-6, 499, 516, 520, 548, 571-2, 593-4, 598, 606, 611, 616, 618, 622, 664, 770
Hamilton Township, II, 73
Hammond, Lieutenant-Governor Sir Andrew, I, 182
Hampton (N.B.), II, 684
Hancock, Mr., I, 177
Hanna, James, I, 438, 470
Hants County, II, 689, 691, 693
Hantsport, II, 677
Harris, II, 597
Harrison, Mr., I, 524
Harrison (B.C.), II, 777
Hart, Theodore, II, 307
Hartsfield (U.S.), II, 477
Harvey (N.B.), II, 694
Harwood, II, 515-6
Hastings, II, 512, 515, 529-30, 547, 566, 579
Havana, I, 328
Havelock (N.B.), II, 670
Havre, I, 147
Hawke, A. B., II, 85
Hawkesbury (N.S.), II, 671
Hawkesbury (Ont.), II, 271, 510
Head, Sir Edmund, II, 660
Head, Sir F. B., II, 159
Hearts Content, II, 668
Hebert, I, 279, 281
Henry's Lake, II, 684
Herling and Son, II, 138
Heron Bay, II, 733
Hervey, Mr., II, 175-6
Hespeler, II, 611
High River, II, 766
Hillsborough (N.B.), II, 676, 711
Hillsborough River, II, 670
Hips, George, I, 470
Hocquart, Sieur, I, 108, 361, 398, 413
Holland, I, 101, 426, 502-3; II, 696
Home district, II, 86-7, 148
Honeywell, Rice, II, 22
Honfleur, I, 14, 47, 321, 427
Hongkong, II, 798
Honolulu, II, 798, 800
Hope, II, 772, 777, 779-80, 794
Hope Township, II, 73
Hopson, General, I, 175, 242
Horton, I, 239, 245
Hotels, I, 315-6; II, 49-50
Howe, General, I, 181
Howland, W. P., II, 479
Huckleberries, II, 518
Huddersfield, II, 243
Hudson Bay, I, 289, 319, 347; II, 150, 573

Hudson River, I, 273; II, 171, 183-7 206, 333, 452, 476, 480
Hudson's Bay Company, II, 210, 732, 736, 746-7, 772, 777, 793, 796, 804
Hull (Eng.), I, 459; II, 565
Hull (Que.), II, 21, 22, 153, 272, 440, 497, 506-7, 522
Hull Township, II, 199
Humber River, II, 623
Humboldt, II, 462
Hungerford, II, 631
Hunter and Bayley, I, 519
Hupe, I, 392
Hurdman and Company, II, 510
Huron County, II, 527, 563
Huskisson, William, II, 316

Ice, II, 152, 718
Iceland, I, 6; II, 768
Illinois, II, 37, 40, 103, 167, 182, 188, 197, 224
Immigration, see Population
India, II, 567
Indiana, II, 167-8, 182
Indians, I, 191, 220, 223, 235, 269-273, 295, 304, 311-2, 400, 412, 425, 429, 431; Hurons, II, 295; Iroquois, I, 295, 304, 334; II, 10-11
Industry, I, 206-10, 448, 462-6; II, 290-305, 549-50, 588-618, 625; engines, II, 295-7, 302, 520-1, 615, 669, 718-9; waterous engine works, II, 719, 765; steam, II, 602, 619
Ingersoll, II, 488, 563, 571
Inglis and Hunter, II, 596
Ingonish, II, 698
Inman, II, 674
Inslow (N.S.), I, 177, 246
Insurance, fire, I, 517; II, 653-4, 665; Quebec Fire Insurance Company, II, 654; fires, I, 394-5, 478-9, 517, 521, 547-8; II, 618, 653-5; life, II, 651-2; Canada Life, II, 651, 770; Confederation Life, II, 651-2; London Life, II, 652; Mutual Life, II, 651; Mutual Life of New York, II, 652; North American Life, II, 652; Sun Life, II, 651-2; marine, I, 517-8, 521; II, 402, 462, 465, 474-5, 482, 553, 729, 772; Bureau Veritas, II, 677; Lloyd's, II, 422, 467-8, 555, 677
Inverness County, II, 689
Inverness Township, II, 103
Iowa, II, 539, 742, 754
Ireland, I, 6, 177, 179, 201, 210, 222, 226, 494, 502-3; II, 19, 104, 115-6, 127, 234, 236, 271, 322, 337, 396, 531, 665
Ireland (P.Q.), II, 34
Iron, see Mining industries

Iroquois (Ont.), II, 145
Islay, Isle of, II, 531
Isle Bizard, I, 483
Isle de la Pais, I, 386
Isle Jesus, I, 482
Isle of Man, I, 222
Isle Plate, I, 73
Italy, I, 16, 78, 129, 146-7, 502-3; II, 572, 798
Ives, Major, II, 169

Jackson, Andrew, II, 248
Jackson's Point, II, 496
Jacobs, Samuel, I, 519, 531
Jacques Cartier, I, 480
Jamaica, I, 187, 220, 502, 543; II, 119, 286
Japan, II, 7, 817
Jarvis, G. M., II, 519
Java, II, 614
Jay's Treaty, II, 225-6
Jersey Island, I, 167, 226; II, 699, 726
Jesuits, I, 279
Joggins, II, 709
Johnson and Purss, I, 453
Johnston, II, 165
Jones, Mr., II, 73
Jones, Captain, II, 212
Jordan, Jacob, I, 453
Joseph, John, II, 85
Junkins, John, I, 212

Kalader, II, 530
Kamloops, II, 795
Kamouraska, I, 263; II, 462
Kansas, II, 539
Kay, Mr., I, 524
Kempt, Sir James, II, 83
Kenetcook River, II, 389
Kent (Eng.), I, 446
Kent County (N.B.), II, 686
Kent County (Ont.), II, 555
Kent Junction, II, 670
Kentville, II, 689, 726
Ketchum, Mr., II, 329
Kettles, I, 377, 419, 448, 453, 465, 507, 513, 539; II, 230, 297
Kincardine, II, 490, 545, 575, 606
Kindness, Nicholas, I, 209
King, Mr., II, 152
King, E. H., II, 657
Kings County (N.B.), II, 684, 689
Kings County (N.S.), II, 689, 691, 693
Kingsey, II, 34
King's posts, II, 699
Kingston, G. T., II, 461
Kingston, II, 15, 17, 20, 27, 62-3, 97-8, 110, 113, 120, 122, 126, 138, 141-4, 146, 149, 165, 170, 193, 196, 215, 218, 221-8, 254-5, 291, 297, 333, 452, 471,
476, 479, 483, 485, 491, 496, 515, 535, 563, 575-6, 579, 605-6, 611, 618, 709
Kippawa, II, 506
Kirkland Lake, II, 585
Kirkton (Ont.), II, 665
Kitchener, II, 615
Klondike, II, 789

Labaye, II, 34
Labour, I, 18-20, 28-41, 63-4, 77-8, 84-96, 156-7, 160, 175, 239, 281-3, 294-5, 300-3, 351-2, 360, 362, 370, 373, 393-4, 402, 466-72; II, 47, 49, 59, 100-8, 110, 114, 119, 269, 273, 278-80, 310-4, 395-6, 453, 456, 468-9, 589, 592, 598, 600-3, 619-28, 636, 708, 749, 752, 762-3, 773-4, 788-9, 794-5, 798, 803-4; accident prevention, II, 626, 628; apprenticeship, I, 303, 468-9; II, 619; child, II, 625-7; Chinese, II, 790, 801-2; crimping, II, 468-9; guilds, I, 300-2; indentures, I, 302, 466-7; II, 47; legislation, II, 628; occupations, II, 619-20, 624, 689; agriculture, II, 534-41, 619, carpenters, II, 310-1, 313; clock-maker, I, 470; longshoremen, II, 310, 313; lumbering, II, 513-4, 520; ranching, II, 766; tailoring, I, 469-70; sanitation, II, 626-7; slavery, I, 466; statute labour, II, 48, 54-5; sweating, II, 627; trade unions, II, 311-3; truck system, II, 628, 700, 708, 728-9; unemployment, II, 628; wages, II, 310-3, 378, 534-5, 620-4, 628
Labrador, I, xxxi, 73-4, 255-6, 569; II, 414-5, 697-8
La Brosse, Madame, I, 473
Lachigan, I, 482
La Chine, I, 482; II, 139, 142-3, 160, 163, 165, 203, 594
Lac la Biche, II, 733
La Heve, I, 60, 62-3, 67, 73, 177, 207, 214, 239, 242
Lambton County, II, 528, 566
La Mire, I, 115-6
La Motte, Captain, I, 334
Lanark County, II, 290, 512, 563, 578
Lanaudière, Charles de, I, 447-8
Land, I, 202-5; II, 14, 37, 47-8, 68-87, 127-9, 387-395, 527-33, 539, 568, 686-9, 732-40, 746, 755, 793, 806-7; clergy reserves, II, 33, 54-5, 68-70, 77, 85, 90-1, 128, 131, 527; crown lands, II, 55-6, 68-70, 77, 85, 87-91, 94, 638, 642; Huron tract, II, 31-2, 88, 94, 114; Indian lands, II, 86; quit rent, I, 180, 183, 205, 232-3, 447, 559; II, 389, 392; seigniorial

tenure, I, 67-8, 272, 339, 351, 356-7, 446, 527, 559; II, 68-9, 77-8, 80, 527, 637; settlement, II, 9, 19, 27, 43, 48, 97-9, 527-33, 686-8; surveys, II, 529, 642, 735-7; British American Land Company, II, 39, 88, 93-4, 301; Canada Company, II, 9, 30-2, 37, 40, 54, 87-94, 113, 122; New Brunswick and Nova Scotia Land Company, II, 689
Lang, Robert, II, 158-9
Lang, William, II, 158
Langdon and Shephard, II, 762
Langenburg, II, 747
Langley (B.C.), II, 773
Langton, John, II, 585
La Prairie, II, 199, 201, 206, 324
Larcher, Sieur, I, 138
La Roche, I, 14-15
La Rochelle, I, 4-5, 18-19, 47, 50, 66, 100-1, 116, 318-9, 321, 325-6, 328, 382, 425-7, 500
Lascorret, I, 111
Latham, Mr., I, 434
La Tuque, II, 517
Lawrence, Governor, I, 176, 231, 241-2
Lawrence Town, I, 242
Lawson, William, II, 433
Leather, II, 225, 330, 349, 371, 640, 815-9; saddle and harness, II, 617; boots and shoes, II, 611-3, 617, 639, 720, 819; Scholes and Ames, II, 612; Brown and Childs, II, 612; shoemaking, I, 301, 470; tanning, I, 225, 290-310, 324, 464; II, 549, 612, 615-7, 640, 718, 800, 819; trunks, I, 664
Le Boutilliers, II, 699
Ledster, Mr., I, 523
Lee, J. P., II, 301
Leeds County, II, 563, 578, 582
Leeds Township, II, 103, 105
Lees, Mr., I, 522
Leeward Islands, I, 502
Legendre, François, I, 148
Legge, Governor, I, 176
Legget, George, II, 433
Leghorn, I, 79
Le Havre, I, 15, 79, 102, 321, 427
Le Havre (P.E I.), I, 119
Leith, I, 459, 497; II, 607
Lemieux, F., II, 462
Lennox and Addington, II, 529-30, 547
Lennox Passage, II, 668
Lennoxville, II, 35, 572
Le Normant, I, 112
Les Escoumains River, I, 251
Lethbridge, II, 733, 762, 764
Levant, I, 49, 51, 141
Levant Township, II, 579
Lévis, II, 591

Lievre River, II, 576
Lighting, II, 456
Lightning Creek, II, 788, 797
Lillooet, II, 777, 789, 794, 797, 799
Lima, II, 798
Limerick, II, 116, 537
Lincoln County, II, 262-3, 547, 566
Lindsay, II, 495-6, 515
Lisbon, I, 79, 497-8
Litigation, I, 556-7
Liverpool, I, 127, 207, 243, 459, 508; II, 63, 96-8, 116, 144, 153, 166-7, 171, 189, 191, 195, 212, 241, 247, 259, 284, 287, 350, 352, 426, 457, 463-4, 471-4, 501, 537, 553-5, 578, 581, 674, 743, 749
Livingston, II, 462
Lloyd, William, I, 213
Loans and savings companies, II, 651-3; Canada Permanent, II, 652; Huron and Erie, II, 653
Lochaber, II, 23
Lockport, II, 205
Logan, II, 303, 306
London (Eng.), I, 173, 448, 456, 450, 561, 470-1, 485, 490-1, 496-502, 507, 510-2, 521, 533, 538, 552-3, 557, 560, 569; II, 19, 94, 114, 158-9, 166, 185, 209-10, 213, 241, 248, 283-4, 287, 299, 306, 368, 383, 409, 417, 426, 522, 553, 798
London (Ont.), II, 146, 200-1, 458, 488, 496, 500-1, 522, 559, 563, 571, 606, 616, 618
London district, II, 86-7, 91-2
London Township, II, 26
Londonderry, I, 210; II, 537, 674
Londonderry (N.S.), II, 677, 710
Long Island, I, 243-4
Lorambec, I, 111
Lorette, I, 492-3
Loudon, Lord, I, 576
Louisbourg, I, 2, 68, 71, 73-6, 81-4, 102, 110-4, 117-8, 121-2, 125-6, 130-153, 174-5, 212-3, 216, 224-5, 238, 240, 367, 423, 496, 499-502; II, 391
Louisiana, II, 489
Lowhee, II, 788
Lukes, W., II, 605
Lumber, see Forest industries
Lunenburg, I, 175, 190, 225, 242; II, 387, 676, 680, 697-8, 726
Lymans Clare and Company, II, 565
Lyon, Mr., II, 404-5
Lytton (B.C.), II, 774, 779-80, 787, 789, 794, 797, 806

Mabou, II, 441
Macaulay, Hon. John, II, 383
McCord, John, I, 470

Macdonald, John, II, 664
McDonald Brothers and Company, II, 614
McDonnell, Mr., II, 25
McDonnell, Mr., II, 121
McDonnell, John, II, 380
McDougall, William, II, 541, 544
McGregor, II, 745
Mackay, Donald, II, 422
Mackay, Thomas, II, 158
Mackenzie, W. L., II, 127, 329, 334
Mackenzie River, II, 733
Mackinaw, II, 202
McKittrick Bros., II, 594
McLaren and Company, II, 510
McLaughlin, II, 290
McLellan, Captain, I, 212
McLenehan and Company, II, 296
Macleod, II, 733, 762, 764, 766
McLeod Lake, II, 461
McMaster, Senator, II, 657
McNabb, Sir A., II, 130, 487
McNutt, Mr., I, 246
Macpherson and Crane, II, 250
Madawaska, II, 22, 530
Madeira, I, 500
Madoc Township, II, 126, 579
Magdalen Islands, I, 51, 257-262; II, 460, 668, 699, 702
Magdelaine River, I, 74
Magog River, II, 301, 500
Mahingan, I, 73
Maillefert, II, 452
Maine, II, 155, 213, 395, 704
Maitland, II, 677, 682
Maitland River, II, 31, 92
Mal Bay, I, 563
Mal Bay (Gaspé), I, 166
Malbecq, I, 119, 123
Malcolm, Daniel, I, 532
Malta, II, 467
Manchester, II, 243, 343, 553
Manilla, II, 798
Manitoba City, II, 757
Manitoulin Islands, II, 512
Mann, Captain, II, 18
Marblehead, I, 243
Marketing, agricultural, I, 311, 316, 413-4, 479, 515, 549-51; merchandise, general store, II, 217, 238, 240, 242, 252, 662-5; department store, II, 665; retailing, I, 311-2, 401-4, 526; II, 664-5; wholesaling, I, 311-2, 404-6, 408-11; II, 657, 664, 770, 806, 819; commercial travellers, II, 664
Markland, Hon. G. H., II, 382-3
Marlboro Township, II, 22
Marseilles, I, 51, 79, 81, 144, 147
Martinique, I, 86, 103, 111-3, 133, 140, 147, 320, 391

Masquinonge River, I, 447, 483, 492
Massachusetts, I, 131, 178, 241; II, 21, 213, 372, 405, 438, 704
Massey, H. A., II, 542, 596
Matane, I, 73-4; II, 532
Mat-a-wat-cook River, II, 443
Matilda Township, II, 521, 663
Matsqui, II, 779
Mauger, Joshua, I, 209
Maumee River, II, 168
Mawbray and Company, I, 513
Mayflower compact, II, 34
Mayot, Mr., I, 523
Maysville, II, 726
Meadowvale, II, 602
Meaford, II, 516
Meander River, II, 389
Mears, Mr., II, 271
Meat Cove, II, 460
Medicine Hat, II, 763-4
Mediterranean, I, 129; II, 421, 698-9
Melbourne, II, 798
Meloizes, Sieur des, I, 378
Memphramagog Lake, II, 34
Menadou, I, 83
Meneilly, Mr., II, 144
Mercantile policy, see Colonial system
Mercure, Jean, I, 493
Meriden (Conn.), II, 599
Meritton, II, 500
Merlen, Peter, I, 209
Merritt, W. H., II, 161, 166, 168, 187-8, 378, 471, 473
Metapedia, II, 532
Meteghan, II, 683
Meteorology, II, 460-2
Métis, II, 462, 532
Mexico, I, xxx, 168; II, 595, 701
Michel, M., I, 369
Michigan, II, 37, 39, 130, 150, 167, 169, 182, 198, 197, 508, 513, 581, 819
Michilimackinac, I, 364, 473-4, 521, 546; II, 227
Michipicoten Island, II, 309
Middlesex County, II, 528, 563
Midland, II, 490, 496, 516
Midland district, II, 113, 228
Miller, Messrs, II, 304
Mille Vaches, II, 460
Mills, Captain, II, 64
Mills, Major John E., II, 124
Mills, Peter, I, 469
Mills, W. H., II, 596
Milltown, II, 717, 726
Milne, Sir David, II, 413
Milwaukee, II, 474, 480, 574, 745
Minas, I, 56-9, 63-5, 124-6, 173-4, 189, 214, 219, 235-6, 239; II, 667, 677, 705
Minchio River, II, 389

Mingan, II, 698-9

Mining industries, II, 306-9, 570, 587, 675, 687, 707-14, 721, 726, 812-3; asbestos, II, 584; cement, II, 570; clay, II, 570; brick, I, 115, 127-8, 132, 206; II, 544-5, 615, 617; tile, I, 378; II, 544; coal, I, 56, 69, 107, 116, 148, 180, 211-3, 216, 221, 224-5, 235, 237, 322, 534; II, 206, 248, 250, 286, 297-8, 398, 403, 428-30, 439-41, 449, 457, 467, 483, 491, 495, 497, 512, 574, 587, 594, 596-8, 601, 615-6, 676, 701, 707-11, 716, 718, 720, 722, 728, 733, 764, 778, 797, 800-2, 812, 815; Albion Mines, II, 205, 206, 429, 598, 707-8; General Mining Association, II, 428-30, 707; copper, II, 230, 303, 306-8, 535, 580-2, 812; British North American Mining Company, II, 308; Bruce Mines, II, 308, 581-2; Canada West Mining Company, II, 581; Montreal and Lake Superior Copper Company, II, 309; Montreal Mining Company, II, 308, 581-2; Quebec and Lake Superior Mining Association, II, 309; St. Marie Falls Mining and Smelting Company, II, 309; Wellington Mines, II, 581; brass, II, 718; gold, II, 579-80, 583-4, 688, 712-4, 771-2, 780-92, 813; stamp mills, II, 580; Reciprocity Company, II, 583; grindstones, I, 227; II, 402, 428, 513, 712; gypsum, I, 56; II, 402-3, 428, 440, 570, 575, 710-1, 720; iron, I, 131, 226-7, 323, 342-3, 373, 378, 419, 452-3, 463-5, 502, 517, 537, 576; II, 126, 244, 255, 286, 291, 295, 297, 305-7, 334, 422, 428-9, 441, 447-9, 486, 491, 495, 497, 551, 578-9, 588-9, 593-601, 615, 617, 619, 623, 634, 639-41, 645, 651, 653, 655, 710-1, 715-7, 724, 800, 812, 818-9, 821; car wheels, II, 593-4; hardware, II, 349, 403, 600, 640; nails, I, 323-4, 375, 513, 533, 538; II, 230, 291, 305, 593-4, 597-9, 616, 711, 763, 803; rails, II, 491, 497, 600, 732; skates, II, 718; foundries, II, 296, 302; Crowes Iron Works, II, 595; rolling mills, II, 597-9, 616; Forge Company, II, 599; Grantham Iron Works, II, 593; Hamilton Iron Forging Company, II, 594; Hamilton Tool Company, II, 599; Marmora Iron Works, II, 155, 291, 295, 496, 579; Metropolitan Rolling Mills, II, 598; Montreal Rolling Mills Company, II, 598; Ontario Rolling Mill Company, II, 594; Peck Benny and Company, II, 598; Pillow, Hersey and Company, II, 598; Radnor Forges, II, 593; St. Maurice Forges, II, 374-8, 452-3, 464-5; Steel, Iron and Railway Works Company, II, 593; Victoria Iron Works, II, 597; lead, I, 311, 348, 419; lime, II, 570; mica, II, 578; nickel, II, 585; petroleum, II, 458-9, 570-4, 618, 812-3; Union Petroleum Works, II, 458; phosphate, II, 575-8; salt, I, 7, 10, 14, 17-8, 226, 327-8, 419, 504, 508, 520-1, 524-5, 536, 538, 540, 542; II, 227, 230-1, 240, 294, 306, 331, 364, 371, 486, 495, 516, 519, 521, 574-5; silver, II, 306, 308, 582-3, 813; stone, II, 306, 570; geological survey, II, 585-6

Minnesota, II, 742, 745, 759, 765-6

Miquelon, I, 223-4

Miramichi, I, 73; II, 673, 675, 679, 681, 686, 703

Miscou, II, 420, 698

Mississippi (Ont.), II, 530

Mississippi River, I, 472, 475; II, 162, 170, 183-4, 224, 492, 731

Missouri, II, 539

Moira River, II, 516

Moisie River, II, 460

Molasses, I, 503-4, 522, 531-2, 535-6, 542, 558; II, 230-1, 240, 331, 402-3, 410, 512, 683, 699, 720, 724, 815; see Sugar

Moncton, II, 674, 716-7, 720, 726

Mondelette, Mr., I, 524

Money, II, 633, 368-78, 430-8, 640-1, 644, 659-61, 674, 721, 728-9, 804-5; barter, II, 220, 257-8; currency, I, 200, 272, 415-6, 541-5; II, 220-2, 235, 238-9, 257-8; Halifax currency, II, 430, 437-8; coinage, I, 521; II, 377; dollars, II, 430-3, 435-7; doubloons, II, 430-3, 435-7; note issue, II, 656-8, 661; specie, II, 374-6, 398, 434-5; see Credit and prices

Montague, Lord Charles, I, 187

Montmagny, II, 470

Montmorency Falls, II, 509

Montreal, I, 273, 280, 295, 299-301, 304-5, 310-2, 315, 349, 361-2, 365-6, 369, 373, 375, 385-6, 392-8, 404, 406, 410, 425-8, 438, 450, 453, 464, 472, 477, 480-1, 484-493, 507, 509, 513-7, 521, 524, 550, 562, 567, 573, 577-8; II, 11, 15, 17, 20-1, 25, 34, 36, 40-1, 54, 64, 88, 97, 99, 104-7, 110-4, 121-3, 131-3, 138-149, 153, 158-199, 202, 206-9, 212-8, 221-3, 226, 231, 234-5, 238-9, 243-8, 253, 257, 263, 268, 281-2, 287, 290, 295, 302, 305, 307, 322, 328, 339-42, 347, 350-4, 368-70, 376,

384, 451-5, 457, 466-7, 470-9, 483-6,
489-92, 496-9, 503-4, 510-2, 519, 523,
548, 553-4, 557-8, 565-6, 576-8, 589,
594, 597-600, 603, 606, 611-4, 616,
618, 621, 624, 627, 648, 651, 657, 662,
673, 692, 699, 701, 709-10, 719,
733-4, 743, 766, 778
Montreuil, I, 356
Moore, Stephen, I, 476
Moore and Finlay, I, 534, 536
Moorhead (Minn.), II, 732, 765
Moosejaw, II, 757, 762
Morains, I, 138
Morel, Sieur, I, 111
Morin, Samuel, I, 530, 539
Morinville, II, 789
Morris, Mr., II, 17
Morris (Man.), II, 733
Morrison, Mr., I, 524
Mortimer, Mr., II, 405
Mothe d'Aulne, I, 62
Mountain Township, II, 663
Mount Forest, II, 595, 609
Mount Stewart (P.E.I.), II, 671
Mouschkodabouit, I, 239
Muir, William, II, 719
Mulgrave, II, 668
Munn, David, II, 290
Munro, Hon. John, II, 380
Murdock, Mr. Chief Secretary, II,
121
Murray, General, I, 467, 572
Murray, Sir George, II, 83
Murray, John, I, 470
Murray Bay, II, 460
Muskoka, II, 503, 512-3, 516, 530-1
Musquash Cove, I, 247

Nanaimo, II, 777-8, 798, 800-1
Nantes, I, 79, 107, 116, 321
Nanton, Augustus, II, 769
Napanee, II, 120, 496, 566, 620, 624
Naples, I, 79
Nashwaak, II, 680
Nass River, II, 777, 796
Natashquan, II, 698-9
National policy, *see* Public finance
Nebraska, II, 539
Nelson (Ont.), II, 329
Nepean Township, II, 22
Neudorf, II, 747
Neu Kronan, II, 747
Newark, II, 54
New Bedford, II, 573
New Carlisle (N.B.), II, 699
Newcastle (Eng.), I, 173, 459; II, 286
Newcastle (N.B.), II, 676, 681
Newcastle (Ont.), II, 520, 595, 602,
608, 664

Newcastle district, II, 86-7, 103, 117
120-1, 304, 310
New Edinburgh, II, 158, 522
New England, I, 2, 52-6, 60, 63-5, 71,
76, 79, 83, 100, 106, 107, 111-2,
126-141, 144, 152-168, 172-5, 177-9,
187-90, 201, 215, 218, 220-2, 225,
231, 236-7, 242-4, 247, 253, 264-5,
339, 374-5, 393, 571, 577; II, 3, 34-5,
386-7, 398, 428, 438, 819
Newfoundland, I, xxxi, 1, 4-7, 9, 10,
16-8, 49-51, 73, 89, 132, 158, 162,
165, 167, 217-8, 225, 248, 318, 499;
II, 50, 157, 210, 233, 328, 366, 412,
414, 428, 439-40, 612, 668, 674, 678,
687, 699, 814
New Glasgow, II, 707-8, 711, 717, 726
New Hampshire, I, 131; II, 213
New Jersey, I, 178
New London, I, 498; II, 573
Newmarket, II, 605
New Orleans, II, 162, 207, 213-4
New Port, I, 186, 245; II, 389
New South Wales, II, 92, 743, 787
Newspapers, I, 433, 484, 490-1, 494-5;
II, 28, 51, 110, 117, 119, 145, 159,
178, 197, 213, 300-1, 397, 461, 506,
665, 742
New Westminster, II, 776, 779, 794-5,
797, 799, 806-7
New York, I, 109, 130-3, 136, 155,
183-6, 211, 217, 464, 472, 478, 484-7,
490-1, 496-502, 526, 539, 573; II, 37,
97, 105-6, 113-5, 126-7, 133, 144,
150-3, 161-7, 170, 174-86, 189-96,
199, 205, 208, 212-6, 249, 251-6,
259-60, 269, 334-6, 339-42, 347,
350-2, 357, 370, 372, 376, 383, 438,
472-9, 482, 486-9, 491, 494-5, 551,
560, 566, 701, 708, 711, 819
New Zealand, II, 539, 595, 743, 787
Niagara, I, 289, 399-400, 412, 414, 429,
471, 473-4; II, 9, 11, 26-7, 48, 59,
63, 121, 135-6, 144, 161-9, 170, 175,
200, 224-8, 262, 264, 297, 304, 478,
488-9, 492
Nicolet River, II, 80
Niganiche, I, 73, 77, 81, 89, 110, 223
Nipigon, II, 733
Nipissing, II, 159, 499, 529
Noranda, II, 585
Norfolk County, II, 24, 516, 563
Normandy, I, 277
North, Lord, I, 187
North Bay, II, 507, 733
North Carolina, I, 497-8, 501
Northumberland County, II, 680, 686
North West Company, II, 231, 805
Norway, I, 206, 456-7, 574; II, 676
Norwich (Ont.), II, 542

Oakes, Captain, I, 211
Oakes, Forrest, I, 546
Oakville, II, 566
Ogden, Mr., II, 17
Ohio, I, 475; II, 130, 138, 150, 161,
    174-6, 182, 188, 193, 197, 247, 250
Oil Springs, II, 571-2
Olympia, II, 779
Omineca, II, 777, 789
Onslow, I, 210
Ontario County, II, 527, 545-6, 608
Orangeville, II, 594
Oregon Treaty, II, 772
Orleans, Island of, I, 330, 572
Orwell (P.E.I.), II, 671, 678
Oshawa, II, 290, 595
Osler and Hammond, II, 770
Oswego, II, 105, 144, 146, 154, 181,
    183, 185, 195, 205, 225-6, 251-4, 335,
    340, 470, 477, 482-3, 485, 491-2, 498,
    516, 566
Otago, II, 798
Otonabee River, II, 515
Ottawa, I, 273, 287; II, 9, 21-2, 41, 80,
    106, 115, 122, 132, 143, 150, 153,
    158-60, 164, 176, 199, 227, 251-2,
    267, 271, 279, 456, 471, 497-9, 503-14,
    522, 529-30, 570, 576-8, 594, 618,
    622, 637, 673, 694, 734, 741
Otter Creek, II, 29
Oudiette, Nicolas, I, 337, 339
Ovens (N.S.), II, 713
Owen Sound, II, 41, 490, 513, 591, 595,
    608
Oxford County, II, 528, 560, 566

Pabo, I, 423
Pacaud, S., I, 415
Pakan, II, 733
Palmerston Township, II, 579
Paper, I, 495; II, 296, 304-5, 349, 500,
    623-4, 639-40, 724, 815, 818-9; Don
    Valley Paper Mills, II, 500; Inter-
    national Paper Company, II, 271;
    Provincial Paper Mills, II, 500;
    Riordon Mills, II, 500; Windsor
    Mills, II, 500; printing, I, 468, 494-
    5; playing cards, II, 231
Papineau, Louis Joseph, II, 77, 293,
    381
Papineauville, II, 507
Para, II, 702
Paris, I, 50-1, 99, 147, 279, 331, 408,
    410; II, 488, 542
Paris (Ont.), II, 570, 575, 610, 661, 745
Parker and Company, II, 306
Parkhurst, Anthonie, I, 9-10
Parnell, Sir Henry, II, 337
Parrsboro, II, 677, 709, 726
Parry Sound, II, 512

Paspebiac, I, 167; II, 698-9
Passamaquoddy, I, 185-7
Paterson, Governor, I, 184
Paton, Andrew, II, 609
Patterson, Robert, II, 745
Patterson and Grant, I, 519
Patu, Sieur, I, 339
Pavillon, II, 793
Peace River, II, 789
Peel, Sir Robert, II, 258, 273, 316, 347,
    357-8
Peel County, II, 545-6, 608
Pelissier, Christopher, I, 453
Pembina, II, 741, 745
Pembroke, II, 497, 504-5, 575, 820
Pennsylvania, I, 178; II, 176, 244, 383,
    539, 551, 709
Penobscot, I, 186, 235
Penryn, I, 498
Pentagouet, I, 63, 65
Penzance, II, 668
Pepin, I, 357
Percée, I, 8, 41, 47-51, 54, 74, 153, 166-
    7, 339; II, 673, 699
Percy Township, II, 73
Perkins, Captain, I, 212
Pernambuco, II, 702
Perrot, Isle, I, 386
Perth, II, 496, 505, 579
Perth County, II, 527, 563
Perthshire, II, 25, 101, 105
Peru, II, 578
Peterborough, II, 122, 155, 496, 515,
    529
Peter McGill and Company, II, 209
Petit Dégrat, I, 68, 77, 112, 130
Petite Rivière, I, 239
Petit Nord, I, 49-50
Petrolia, II, 571, 574
Philadelphia, I, 136, 170, 212, 496-501,
    573; II, 214, 486, 495
Phillip River, II, 681
Phillips, Governor, I, 155, 157
Pictou, I, 126; II, 205, 332, 428-30,
    598, 667-8, 671-3, 676, 680, 689,
    692-3, 707-8, 711, 718-9, 722, 726
Pigeon Lake, II, 155
Pigignuit, I, 214
Pinette (P.E.I.), II, 678
Piscataqua, I, 500-1
Pitt, William, II, 3
Placentia, II, 668
Plaisance, I, 49, 52, 69, 73-5, 85, 88,
    97-8, 133, 147, 319, 329
Plate River, II, 511
Plattsburgh, II, 202
Plymouth, I, 459, 498
Plymouth (N.E.), I, 177, 243
Pointe aux Trembles, I, 493
Pointe Claire, I, 386; II, 143, 172

Point Escuminac, II, 420
Point Lévis, II, 489
Point St. Charles, II, 124, 593
Police, II, 469, 735, 767
Pontiac, II, 513
Pool, Mr., II, 405
Poole, I, 459
Poplar Point, II, 741
Population, I, 58, 62-3, 68, 75-6, 85,
  291-5, 349-52, 433-4; II, 169, 171,
  480-1, 629-33, 686-9, 729, 744, 795;
  birth-rate, II, 629-31; death-rate,
  II, 631; immigration, I, 5, 168-173,
  176-8; II, 536-41, 248, 251, 337,
  395-7, 472, 536-41, 628-33, 639, 643,
  740-4; urbanization, II, 763-4; epi-
  demics, I, 84, 86, 276, 349-52, 434,
  468; II, 109, 249, 630-1; poverty,
  I, 314, 362, 365, 472, 516; races, I,
  169, 174-5, 178, 187, 242-3, 292; II,
  102, 104, 108-9, 123-4, 387, 531,
  534, 743; census, II, 629; medicine,
  II, 107, 662
Porcupine, II, 585
Portage-du-Fort, II, 23, 504
Portage la Prairie, II, 732-3, 741,
  751
Port Arthur, II, 490, 733, 758, 762
Port Burwell, II, 29
Port Colborne, II, 483-6
Port Dalhousie, II, 170, 484
Port Daniel, I, 74
Port Dauphin, I, 68, 103, 223
Port Dover, II, 29, 490, 496
Porte, Sieur Gilles de la, I, 141
Porteous, John, II, 297
Port Hope, II, 63, 122, 144, 170, 215,
  333, 471, 495-6, 520, 602, 608, 636
Port Joli, II, 532
Port La Joye, I, 103, 119, 122, 247
Portland, Duke of, II, 75
Portland (Me.), II, 194, 203, 206,
  213, 215, 463-4, 476-7, 489-91, 555,
  605, 673-4, 683, 692, 701
Portland (N.B.), II, 678, 726
Portland (Ore.), II, 799
Port Latour, I, 62
Port Moody, II, 733, 778
Port Mouton, I, 168
Portneuf, II, 304
Porto Rico, II, 339, 675
Port Perry, II, 496, 515
Port Rossignol, I, 55
Port Rosway, I, 185-6
Port Saint Pierre (P.E.I.), I, 119, 123
Port Senior, I, 177, 243
Portsmouth, I, 514-5; II, 213
Port Stanley, II, 146, 495-6, 616
Port Talbot, II, 146
Port Toulouse, I, 68, 76

Portugal, I, 5, 7, 9-10, 16, 51, 78, 161,
  221, 247, 292, 502-3; II, 595
Postal facilities, I, 217-8, 484-94; II,
  463-4, 471-2, 498-501, 642, 666, 668,
  670, 674, 699, 732-4, 779
Pothier, Hon. T., II, 382
Poulin, Sieur, I, 375
Poutrincourt, I, 61-2
Powder, I, 311, 343
Pownall, John, II, 11
Prairie de la Magdalaine, I, 398
Prairie du Chien, II, 745
Prairie, Rivière de la, I, 397, 482
Prendergast, Mr., II, 126
Prenties, Mr., I, 467
Prescott, II, 22, 29, 141-6, 161, 171-3,
  183, 185, 451-2, 471, 505, 515, 606
Price, William, II, 150, 378, 517
Price and Morland, I, 510, 523
Prices, I, 105, 114, 138, 140, 173, 182,
  213, 306-7, 312-5, 323-7, 339-40,
  358-9, 363, 402-3, 408, 412-6, 429,
  481, 515-6, 540-2; II, 48-50, 62-5,
  113, 247, 256-7, 259, 263-4, 269, 271,
  282-9, 340, 355-6, 644, 763, 803-4;
  see Money and credit
Prince, Colonel, II, 308
Prince Albert, II, 733, 737, 757, 766, 769
Prince Edward County, II, 547
Prince Edward Island, I, 2, 74, 100-3,
  117-123, 145, 149, 171, 184, 216-7,
  224, 227, 232, 247; II, 157, 366, 387,
  426, 675-8, 687-9, 692-6, 699, 704-5,
  721-3, 728, 814
Prince William Henry Sound, II, 441
Prospect Harbour, I, 214
Provence, I, 143, 147
Providence, I, 211
Prussia, I, 455
Public finance, I, 147-9, 227-34, 241,
  329-45, 416, 426-30, 557-72; II, 379-
  385, 634-50, 721-6, 769-70, 806-22;
  tariffs, I, 147-8, 323-4, 336-7, 340-3,
  419, 427-30, 557-60, 565, 569, 572;
  II, 63, 224-6, 237, 247, 250-2, 261,
  273-4, 290-4, 316, 319, 322-5, 330-50,
  353-4, 360-7, 379-84, 406, 471-2,
  599-600, 612-4, 625, 638-43, 646-7,
  668, 695, 699-702, 710, 721-5, 806-7,
  810, 815-21; national policy, II, 520,
  522, 610-3, 615, 623-4, 684, 715, 717,
  720, 731, 818-21; taxes, I, 68; II, 48,
  78-9; fees, I, 566; poll tax, II, 111,
  806; tithes, I, 329, 331, 368; public
  debts, II, 809-12; municipal loan
  fund, II, 634-7, 642, 649; provincial
  subsidies, II, 648-9; bounties, I,
  229-31, 241, 292-4, 455-6, 458-62,
  575-6; II, 293, 414; fraud, I, 228-9;
  lottery, I, 567

Public utilities, II, 618, 651, 654, 662, 769, 800
Pugwash Harbour, II, 668, 681
Pultney, Mr., II, 17
Puslinch Township, II, 33
Pyke, Captain, I, 212
Pyrenees, I, 375

Quaco (N.B.), II, 678, 682
Qu'Appelle, II, 733, 747, 757
Quebec, I, 56, 65, 71, 102, 111, 113, 114, 213, 224, 239, 263, 273-9, 282, 299, 304-5, 310-1, 315, 317, 319, 324-6, 332-3, 337, 339-41, 349-50, 353, 361-2, 365-8, 375, 386-7, 391-9, 404-6, 409-14, 421-6, 430, 433, 435, 449-53, 458, 461, 468, 470, 472, 478-81, 485-495, 508, 511-6, 521, 523, 525, 528-30, 547-50, 553, 559, 562, 573-5, 577-8; II, 12, 13, 16, 20, 23, 25, 32, 34, 54, 81, 97, 99, 104-17, 122, 136, 140-2, 150, 155-9, 161-5, 169-71 176-7, 180, 184, 186-9, 191-2, 199-204, 208-213, 216-7, 224, 229, 234, 246, 248, 252, 257, 265, 270-1, 274-84, 286, 288, 293, 295, 299, 307, 314, 319, 322, 328, 334-6, 351-4, 362, 382-4, 453, 455-9, 462-4, 468-9, 472-7, 479, 487, 490-2, 496-502, 507-14, 516, 522-3, 537, 558-9, 561, 576, 589, 591, 596, 606, 618, 631-2, 645, 654, 673, 677, 692, 699, 709, 719
Queens County (N.B.), II, 689
Queens County (N.S.), II, 680
Queensland, II, 743
Queenston, II, 29, 120, 162, 200
Queenstown (Ire.), II, 261-2, 673
Quesnel, II, 774, 779, 797, 803
Quienchien, I, 386, 484
Quinte, Bay of, II, 9, 11, 29, 52, 143, 146, 154, 223, 566

Ragged Islands, II, 676
Raimundus, I, 4
Ramezay, M. de, I, 382
Ramsheer, I, 247
Raquette, Rivière à la, I, 386
Rastell, I, 5
Rat Portage, II, 765
Raudot, Sieur, I, 300, 307, 327
Raux, Isle aux, I, 401
Raymond, Monsieur de, I, 145
Raymond, Charles, II, 595
Razily, Sieur de, I, 62
Reciprocity Treaty, II, 260, 342, 356, 360, 417, 472, 495, 503, 510, 550, 560, 590, 605, 608, 621, 642, 647, 660, 676, 701, 703, 707, 814
Red Island, II, 458
Red Lake River, II, 765

Red River, II, 731-2, 741, 745-6, 747
Regina, II, 763, 769
Renard, Rivière au, I, 74
Renault, I, 111-2
Renfrew, II, 496, 512
Repentigny, Monsieur de, I, 284
Repentigny, I, 481
Restigouche River, I, 167; II, 80, 420, 532, 674, 679-80, 686
Revelstoke, II, 778
Rhine, II, 166
Rhode Island, I, 136, 178
Rhodes, Curry and Company, II, 684
Ricard, Sieur, I, 405
Rice Lake, I, 154-5
Richardière, M. de la, I, 400-1
Richelieu, Fort, I, 334
Richelieu River, I, 273; II, 67, 150, 199, 251, 268, 299-300
Richibucto, II, 670, 676, 681
Richmond (N.S.), II, 667, 697
Richmond (P.Q.), II, 489-90, 501
Richmond Hill, II, 148
Riga, I, 456-7
Rimouski, II, 674
Rio de Janiero, II, 702
Risteen and Company, II, 684
Riverin, I, 339
Rivers Inlet, II, 796
Rivière aux Ilets de Bois, II, 741
Rivière du Loup, I, 483, 490; II, 199, 453, 489, 501, 532, 674
Roberval, I, 5
Robins and Company, II, 699-700
Robinson, Hon. Peter, II, 129, 310
Rochefort, I, 69, 86, 101, 350, 372, 382, 401, 415
Rochester, II, 38-9, 122, 245, 253, 294, 355-6
Rogers, Mr., II, 73
Ronde, Sieur de la, I, 127
Rose, John, II, 492
Roseau River, II, 765
Ross and Company, II, 591
Rouen, I, 5, 408, 427
Rouillard, I, 356
Rouville, Sieur, I, 378
Rowan, Mr., II, 592
Rowley, John, I, 519
Rozee and Company, I, 333
Rubber, II, 616, 623, 640
Rum, I, 130-7, 140, 144, 156, 200, 207, 209, 226-8, 230, 418-421, 464, 503-4, 520, 524-8, 531-2, 536, 542, 558-60, 562, 565, 577; II, 225-1, 230-1, 240, 398, 402-3, 410, 701; see Sugar
Rundle, Captain, I, 212
Russia, II, 64, 362, 523
Rut, John, I, 6
Rutherford, Mr., II, 405

Saanich, II, 779
Sabatier, William, II, 404
Sable Island, I, 14, 78, 248
Sable River (Ont.), II, 31
Sackett's Harbour, II, 97, 106, 146
Sackville, I, 246; II, 498, 670, 689, 692
Saguenay, I, 269, 273, 563; II, 80, 150, 517
St. Andrews (N.B.), II, 204, 272, 402, 411, 669, 675-6
St. Ange, I, 492
St. Anne, I, 334, 480, 484
St. Anns, I, 247, 484
St. Ann's, I, 447
St. Augustin (Que.), I, 303, 492-3
St. Boniface, II, 734
St. Catharines, II, 165, 476, 500, 719
St. Charles, I, 528
St. Clair, Lake, II, 481, 569
St. Cloud, II, 734
St. Croix, I, 61, 63, 185; II, 52, 675
St. Denis, I, 490
St. Domingue, I, 86, 133, 140, 142, 147
St. Esprit, I, 68, 76-7
St. Eustache, I, 133
St. Fay, I, 443
St. Flavie, II, 674
St. Foix, I, 438, 492
St. Francis, I, 490; II, 108
St. Francis Lake, II, 143, 471
St. Francis River (N.B.), II, 669
St. Francis River (Que.), II, 34-5, 80
St. Frederic, Fort, I, 365, 369, 429
St. Geneviève, II, 517
St. George (N.B.), II, 676-7
St. Giles, II, 108
St. Helen's Island, II, 243
St. Ignace, II, 309
St. Jean, Jean Gatin, I, 393
St. Jean, I, 334, 532
St. Jean de Lutz, I, 78-96, 107-8
St. John (N.B.), II, 53-4, 157-8, 241, 267, 272, 401-2, 404, 411, 418, 420, 424, 429, 499, 614, 654, 667-8, 670-1, 673-6, 678-80, 682-4, 689, 692-3, 704-5, 711, 715, 719, 724-6
St. John County, II, 684
St. John, Lake, II, 517-8
St. John River, I, 57, 63, 65, 185-7, 203, 207, 214, 235, 238-9, 247, 547; II, 386, 420, 426, 668-9
St. John's (Nfld.), I, 5-6; II, 440
St. Johns (P.Q.), I, 443, 477; II, 105, 150-1, 199, 201, 206, 300, 302, 305, 324
St. Johns (P.E.I.), I, 126, 132
St. Kitts, I, 500
St. Lawrence Association, II, 164
St. Louis (N.B.), II, 681
St. Louis (St. Dominique), I, 142
St. Louis (U.S.), II, 214

St. Louis, Fort, I, 334
St. Louis, Lake, II, 471
St. Malo, I, 79, 96, 102, 106-7, 136, 140, 146-7, 326
St. Margarets Bay, I, 242
St. Martin, Dumas, I, 453
St. Martin, I, 133
St. Martin (P.Q.), I, 483
St. Martins (N.B.), II, 684, 712
St. Mary's (Ont.), II, 496, 501, 665
St. Mary's Bay, I, 186, 244
St. Mary's River (C.B.), II, 13
St. Maurice River, I, 273; II, 80, 517
St. Ours, I, 438, 525
St. Ovide, I, 83, 105-6
St. Patrick, II, 692
St. Paul, II, 732, 742, 745, 754, 762
St. Paul, Baye, I, 263, 380-1; II, 460
St. Paul's Island, II, 117
St. Pierre (C. B.), I, 117; II, 13
St. Pierre Island, I, 74, 223-5
St. Pierre, Lac, I, 358; II, 177, 189, 275, 452
St. Stephen, II, 52, 670, 726
St. Therese, Fort, I, 334
St. Thomas (Ont.), II, 146, 496, 556, 563, 594
St. Thomas (West Indies), II, 701-2
St. Thomas Montmagny, II, 517
St. Vincent (Minn.), II, 750
Salem, I, 498-9
Salisbury (N.B.), II, 670
Salmon Bay, II, 698-9
Salmon River, II, 516
Salter, Malachy, I, 209
Saltfleet, II, 306
Sampson, William, I, 519
Sand Point, II, 504-5
Sandwich, II, 146, 308
San Francisco, II, 772, 779, 798-9, 800, 802
Saratoga, II, 214-6
Sardinia, II, 798
Sarnia, II, 488-9, 494, 501, 596
Saskatchewan River, II, 731-2, 741, 789
Saugeen River, II, 67
Saul, Mr., I, 191-2
Sault aux Récollets, I, 387, 482
Sault Ste. Marie, II, 137, 197, 471, 481, 483, 499, 530, 582
Sault St. Louis, I, 387, 482
Scatary, I, 68, 77, 81, 83, 111; II, 444
Schenectady, II, 205, 225
Schermann and Molineux, I, 507
Schultze, Mr., II, 576
Scotland, I, 201; II, 88, 96, 104, 116, 127, 263, 534
Scott, James, II, 301
Scott, William, I, 531

Scugog, II, 155, 515
Seaforth, II, 551, 574
Seattle, II, 779
Seneca Lake, II, 164
Sept Isles, I, 562; II, 699
Seville, I, 79
Shaftsbury, II, 733
Shanghai, II, 798
Sharbot Lake, II, 519
Shediac (N.B.), II, 670-3, 676, 703, 712
Sheffield, Lord, II, 3
Sheffield, II, 244, 343, 642
Shelburne, Lord, II, 3
Shelburne, I, 186-7; II, 676, 697
Sheldon Dutcher and Company, II, 297
Shennacadia River, II, 439
Sherbrooke, Sir John, II, 82
Sherbrooke (N.S.), II, 713
Sherbrooke (Que.), II, 85, 301-4, 496,
    582, 609, 611
Ship-building and shipping, I, 372, 377,
    380-91, 417, 496-502; II, 208, 229,
    241, 247, 272, 287, 290, 313-4, 319,
    329, 331, 398, 401-3, 422-7, 439,
    442-3, 502-3, 525, 589-91, 645, 667,
    670, 675-9, 682-7, 699, 702, 707, 715,
    721, 724-7, 798-800, 813-4, 817, 819;
    Canada Marine Works, II, 590;
    Merchant Shipping Act, II, 677;
    regulations, II, 464-8
Shippegan, II, 420
Shipton, II, 34-5
Shirreff, Charles, II, 159
Shrewsbury, II, 118
Shubenacadie River, I, 246
Sicily, I, 61
Sills, Samuel, I, 535
Simcoe, Governor, II, 18, 19, 23
Simcoe Company, II, 518, 527, 529,
    531, 546, 563
Simcoe, Lake, II, 9, 39, 57, 154, 202,
    306, 516, 546
Similkameen, II, 777, 789
Simmonds, II, 23
Simpson, II, 34
Sisaboo, I, 207; II, 682
Skagit flat, II, 777
Skeena River, II, 461, 777, 796
Skenesborough, I, 477-8, 489, 491
Skinner, Robert, I, 467
Smith, Adam, II, 187
Smith, H., II, 301
Smith, William, II, 433
Smith's Falls, II, 251, 576
Soap, II, 513, 549, 639, 800
Soda Creek, II, 774, 794
Soke (B.C.), II, 798
Solomons, Levi, I, 551
Sorel, I, 484, 490, 515; II, 11, 34, 118,
    212, 275, 455, 496, 623

Soubras, M., I, 98
Souris (Man.), II, 733
Souris (P.E.I.), II, 671
South America, II, 330, 421, 502, 509,
    511, 595, 612, 682, 698, 700, 800, 815
Southampton, I, 459; II, 490, 606
Southport (P.E.I.), II, 671
Spain, I, 9, 16, 49, 51, 78, 101, 141, 143,
    146-7, 154, 161, 221, 247, 426, 502-3,
    512; II, 595, 787, 798
Spanish Bay, I, 116, 211, 213; II, 439
Spanish River, II, 513
Speculation, I, 203; II, 27-8, 87-8, 93,
    391-3, 424, 688, 738-9, 755, 757, 791
Spices, II, 661-2
Springhill, II, 709
Spurrier, John, I, 169
Standfield, Joseph, I, 489
Stanley, Mr., II, 84, 116, 352
Stanstead, II, 34-5, 304
Staples, I, xxxii-iii, 1-2; II, 217, 219,
    261, 266, 280, 447-9
Steamboats, II, 27, 135, 140-1, 144-6,
    165-6, 246-7, 251, 264, 403, 669,
    731-2, 734, 741, 745-6, 773-4;
    inspection, II, 467; Ottawa Steam-
    boat Company, II, 155
Steamships, II, 453-7, 463-6, 470,
    473-5, 480-3, 525-6, 536-7, 540, 554-5,
    566, 667-8, 673-8, 682, 700-1, 706-7,
    715, 724-5, 742, 772, 822; Allan Line,
    II, 457, 463, 537-8, 553, 555;
    Anchor Line, II, 538; Beaver Line,
    II, 555; Canada Steam Navigation
    Company, II, 463; Cunard Com-
    pany, II, 212; Dominion Line, II,
    538, 553, 555; Grand Trunk, II, 673;
    London Line, II, 555; Mitchell Line,
    II, 710; Montreal and Acadian Line,
    II, 710; Prince Edward Island
    Navigation Company, II, 671; Que-
    bec Gulf Ports Steamship Company,
    II, 673, 710; Richelieu and Ontario
    Navigation Company, II, 471; Royal
    Mail, II, 453, 470; Tait's Line, II,
    453; Temperley's, II, 538; North
    Atlantic Conference, II, 538; screw
    steamers, II, 481-3
Stedman, Mr., II, 135-6
Stephenson, Dr., II, 107
Stevenson, James, II, 158-9
Stewart, James, I, 450-1
Stewart Meldrum and Company, II,
    805
Stewart's Lake (B.C.), II, 461
Stoddart and Company, II, 517
Stratford, II, 495, 563, 593, 754
Streetsville, II, 602, 608
Stuart, Mr., I, 524, 526
Stuart, Henry, II, 307

Sturgeon Lake, II, 155
Subercase, M., I, 220
Sudbury, II, 585, 733
Sugar, I, 207-9, 226, 319-20, 322-5, 340, 343, 421, 503-4, 509, 513, 531-8, 551, 558, 574; II, 225, 230-1, 240, 286, 316, 330-3, 339, 381, 398-403, 512, 582, 588, 613-4, 623, 640, 662, 683, 699, 701, 716-7, 720, 804, 814; beet, II, 564, 702; maple, II, 61, 442, 519, 613; syrup, II, 513; Redpath and Company, II, 613
Sulphuric acid, II, 572, 594
Summerside (P.E.I.), II, 605, 673
Sunbury County, II, 689
Susquehannah River, II, 164
Sussex (N.B.), II, 693
Sutherlandshire, II, 105
Swansea, II, 581-2
Sweden, I, 376
Swift Current, II, 733
Swinburne, Captain, II, 209
Swinomish (Wash.), II, 779
Sydenham, Lord, see Thomson, Mr. Poulett
Sydenham River, II, 42
Sydney (Aust.), II, 798
Sydney (C. B.), II, 390, 430, 441, 444, 460, 668, 689, 709-10, 726
Syracuse, II, 205

Taché, J. C., II, 458
Tadoussac, I, 63, 251, 273, 284, 335, 337-8, 344-5, 559, 562
Talbot, Colonel, II, 23-4, 26, 91
Talon, M., I, 322, 324, 338
Tamworth, II, 496
Tartary, I, 424-5
Tatamagouche, I, 214, 239-40, 247
Tavistock, II, 562
Taylor, Lieutenant, II, 201
Taylor, Henry, I, 533
Taylor Manufacturing Company, II, 624
Tea, I, 504, 513, 533, 536, 539; II, 231, 328, 331-2, 335-6, 340-2, 371, 381, 403, 513, 546, 582, 588, 640, 645, 662, 699, 720, 815, 817
Telfer, Mr., II, 42
Telford, Sir Thomas, II, 156
Temiscaming, Lake, II, 267, 499, 506
Témiscouata, II, 532, 674
Textiles, I, 131-2, 135, 164, 220-1, 226, 240, 312, 324, 342-3, 360, 373, 418-9, 463, 465, 502-3, 510, 513, 526, 533-9, 558, 577; II, 240, 243-4, 299-303, 332-3, 349, 403; calico, II, 213; cotton, I, 340; II, 261, 299-304, 489, 588, 610-1, 696, 699, 715-8, 816-7, 820; British North American Cotton

Company, II, 299-300; linen, I, 208, 210, 450, 465, 495, 502-3, 571, 577; II, 589, 815, 817; satinets, II, 243; silks, II, 820;woollens, II, 290, 301-4, 589, 607-10, 617, 699, 718, 815-20; clothing, II, 287-8, 639-40, 645, 719-20; knitting mills, II, 301, 610; Penman and Adams, II, 610; Rasconi Woollen and Cotton Manufacturing Company, II, 623; Rosamond Woollen Company, II, 608; Guelph Sewing Machine Company, II, 595; Raymond Sewing Machine, II, 595; Singer Sewing Machine Company, II, 600, 612
Thames River (Ont.), II, 26, 27, 67, 201, 228
Thessalon, II, 513
Thetford, II, 584
Thompson, D., II, 301
Thompson and Gridley, I, 259, 264
Thomson, John, I, 486, 489
Thomson, Mr. Poulett, II, 415
Thornbury, II, 608
Thorold, II, 611
Three Rivers (Que.), I, 263, 273, 280, 282 304-5,312, 315, 349, 353, 365, 368, 375, 395, 397, 404, 453-4, 463-5, 478, 488-9, 490, 521, 529, 550; II, 108, 140, 212, 282, 297, 305-7, 496, 593, 618
Three Rivers (P.E.I.), I, 103
Tichbourne, Mr., I, 467
Tidnish River, II, 681
Tignish, II, 671
Tillsonburg, II, 602, 606
Tobacco, I, 156, 330, 336, 338, 340, 343, 509, 532, 534, 538, 546, 565; II, 221, 230-1, 294, 320, 403, 513, 588, 614-5, 815; cigars, II, 614, 819; see Agriculture
Tobique, II, 669
Tobogue, I, 243
Todd, Mr., II, 52
Todd and McGill, II, 136
Toledo, II, 484
Tonawanda, II, 519
Torbay, I, 514
Tormentine, Cape, II, 672
Toronto, II, 17-18, 27, 36, 38-9, 53-7, 109, 114, 117, 120-2, 132, 141-6, 168, 170, 177, 181, 205, 214-8, 244, 250, 252, 296-9, 340, 347, 355-6, 369, 461, 471, 476, 488-501, 516, 546, 556, 563, 566, 593, 597, 606-8, 616-8, 622-3, 648-51, 654, 657, 662-5, 709, 719, 734, 758, 770
Tracadie (N.B.), I, 73
Tracadie (P.E.I.), I, 103, 119, 123
Tracy, Monsieur de, I, 338

Trade, I, 98-9, 105-6, 141-3, 146, 218-21, 401-26, 496-517; II, 217-260, 264-6, 274-7, 280-2, 315, 375, 398-412, 644-7, 675-8, 686, 708-9, 719-21, 810-4, 820-1; grain, II, 464-7, 470-5, 478-86; bonding system, II, 189-90, 342, 347, 664; bills of exchange, I, 518-20; II, 281, 437-8; bills of lading, II, 491; embargo, I, 222; free ports, II, 699; Free Trade Association, II, 349; Non-Intercourse Act, II, 229; smuggling, I, 223-5, 335-6, 339, 341, 430; II, 324, 328, 332-4, 338-9, 341, 404, 418; merchandise, I, 532-9, 560; II, 229-31, 244

Transportation, I, 114-5, 213-7, 308-11, 317-25, 347, 394-401, 472-84; II, 28-9, 36, 39-42, 46-9, 54, 96-7, 106, 115, 133-212, 217-60, 221, 262-5, 268, 275, 290, 447-501, 504-7, 730-4, 771-8; water, I, 146-7, 152, 163-4, 474-5; II, 115, 169, 173; sack ships, I, 157-9, 162; sailing vessels, II, 453-6, 462-4, 473-5, 480; piracy, I, 86, 141-2; privateers, I, 223; deck-load, II, 465-6, 675, 677, 683; wrecks, II, 464; ports, II, 451, 456, 466-7, 474-6, 491; lighthouses, II, 457-62; pilotage, I, 318-9, 400-1; II, 474-5, 478; towage, II, 451-2, 455, 462, 474-5, 479; Tow Boat Company, II, 295; Calvin and Breck, II, 452; dredging, II, 454-5; boats, I, 399, 474, 481; batteaux, II, 221-2; Durham boat, II, 135, 138, 173; York boat, II, 135; canoes, I, 306-10, 413, 473, 478, 481, 489; II, 135, 774; forwarding, II, 147-8, 153, 195; Harrison Lillooet route, II, 774-5; Dawson route, II, 745; land, snow-shoes, I, 359; roads, I, 214-7, 231-2, 247, 314, 360, 364, 394-8, 472, 476-9; II, 54-8, 92, 120, 529-33, 539, 551, 559-60, 618, 668-70, 688, 725, 733, 737, 775-7, 806; Cariboo road, II, 775-6; Craig's road, II, 34, 103; Elgin road, II, 532; Kennebec road, II, 155; Opeongo road, II, 530; Talbot road, II, 46, 54; ferries, I, 479-80; II, 733; streets, I, 310; II, 618; street railway, II, 651; stage, II, 144-5, 205, 733, 776; expresses, II, 776; mules, II, 775, 793, 806; carriages, II, 290, 298-9, 519, 522; Guelph Carriage Goods Company, II, 595; railways, II, 29, 37, 123, 133, 135, 198, 258-9, 267, 428-30, 486-98, 504-5, 507, 514-5, 519, 525-9, 534, 546, 575, 589-93, 615, 623, 634-8, 642-9, 651, 655-6, 667-75, 678, 681-2, 695-6, 706-10, 715-6, 721-5, 732-4, 741, 749, 755, 760-4, 766, 777-8, 820, 822; Atlantic and St. Lawrence, II, 206; Buffalo and Lake Huron Railway, II, 492, 494, 636; Canada Atlantic, II, 507; Canada Southern, II, 489; Canadian Pacific, II, 490, 507, 576, 585, 622, 649, 731-2, 736, 739, 744, 749, 759, 777-8, 806, 808, 820; City of Toronto and Lake Huron Railroad Company, II, 123; Grand Trunk, II, 133, 206, 487-93, 497-8, 501, 592, 618, 621, 635-6, 646-8, 701; Great Western, II, 200, 487-8, 490, 492, 496-7, 593, 636; Intercolonial, II, 614, 647-8, 666, 674, 681-2, 691-2, 701-4, 708, 717-9, 722-5, 820; Michigan Central, II, 488; Midland, II, 490; New York Central, II, 133; Northern, II, 202, 487, 489, 492-3, 590, 636; Northern Pacific, II, 732; Panama Railway, II, 772; Port Hope and Lindsay Railway, II, 496; Quebec Central, II, 584; Q.M.O. and O., II, 649; St. Lawrence and Atlantic, II, 206, 215, 481; Shediac and St. John Railway, II, 157; Welland Railway, II, 470, 483-4, 492, 590; Victoria bridge, II, 489, 590-3, 631, 680, 694; guages, II, 491; locomotives, II, 592; Kingston Locomotive Works, II, 593; Toronto Locomotive Works, II, 593; air brakes, II, 491; freight, II, 350, 477-8, 483, 485, 492-8; passenger, II, 453, 463, 470-1, 488

Traverse, Cape, II, 672
Tremblay, I, 381
Trent affair, II, 648
Trenton, II, 471, 494, 515-6, 566, 590, 595, 602, 606, 663
Trent River, II, 120, 150, 154-5, 516
Trotter and Trotter, II, 753
Troy, II, 195
Truro, I, 177, 210, 246; II, 667, 673, 718, 722, 726
Turner, F. J., II, 5, 228
Turner, Senator J., II, 770
Tusket Islands, I, 244
Tweed, II, 496
Twelve Mile Creek, II, 162, 166, 168

Ulyott, II, 516
United Empire Loyalists, I, 168, 179-187, 204-5, 434, 468; II, 4, 7, 9-12, 22, 59, 74, 76, 96, 387-91, 404
Upham (N.B.), II, 684
Utica, II, 97, 186, 205
Utrecht, Treaty of, I, 1-2, 8, 54, 71-2, 153, 160, 218, 347

Valentia (Ire.), II, 668
Vallée, Dr., II, 107
Vallerant, I, 521, 524
Valleyfield, II, 471
Valparaiso, II, 798-9
Vancouver (B.C.), II, 806
Van Diemen's Land, II, 912
Vatteville, I, 14
Vaudreuil, Sieur, I, 327
Vaudreuil, II, 305
Verchier, Nerrain, I, 523
Vermont, II, 14, 150-1, 229, 268-9, 304, 318-20, 360
Verona, Congress of, II, 166
Verte, Bay, I, 124-6, 139, 235, 239-40
Verulam Township, II, 118, 154
Vessels, I, 496-502; II, 25, 137, 140 (*Accomodation*), 144, 146, 153, 160, 168, 205, 209,211-2 (*Royal William*), 247, 282, 290, 295-7, 453, 463-4, 471, 484, 519, 590, 672-3, 700, 702, 732, 777, 791
Viana, I, 10
Victoria (Aust.), II, 787, 798
Victoria (B.C.), II, 772, 779, 791-2, 794-5, 797-8, 800, 804-6
Victoria County (N.B.), II, 680, 694
Victoria County (Ont.), II, 529
Viger, Mr., II, 199
Villebon, I, 52-3
Virginia, I, 134, 155, 178, 500; II, 64, 217, 221

Wabash River, II, 168
Wakopa, II, 757
Wales, II, 104, 587
Walkerville, II, 556, 607
Walsingham, Commodore, I, 514
Walton (N.S.), II, 677
War, I, 67, 69, 234; Crimean, II, 635, 643
Ward, Messrs, II, 295-6
Warwick Township, II, 86
Washington, II, 214, 356-7; Treaty of 1870, II, 703
Waterloo, II, 92, 120, 167
Weed, G. and T., II, 167
Weights and measures, I, 99, 314, 401, 407-8; II, 661; decimal system, II, 660-1
Welland County, II, 547, 591
Wellington County, II, 563-4
Wendover, II, 34
Wentworth County, II, 528
Werden, I., I, 535
Western district, II, 87, 91, 110, 113-5, 146
West Indies, I, 66-7, 71, 79-80, 98-9, 111-2, 117, 130-1, 133, 135, 141-4, 154, 167, 180, 182, 200, 209, 218,
222, 226-7, 289, 291, 319-325, 328-9, 339-40, 347, 352, 360, 405, 411, 415, 417, 419, 421-2, 427, 485, 494, 498, 503-6, 514, 535, 542, 562; II, 11, 42, 61, 66, 157, 170-1, 180, 209, 223-4, 233-5, 245, 249, 286, 316, 319-23, 328-31, 359, 394, 398, 401-411, 422-4, 430, 434-8, 522, 614-5, 682-3, 691, 697-702, 716, 718, 814-5
West Isles, II, 418-9, 698
West Lynne, II, 743, 747, 750
Westminster (Ont.), II, 26
Westmoreland County, I, 193; II, 692
Whitby, II, 471, 496, 515, 546
Whitby Township, II, 66
Whitehaven, I, 459
White Mud River, II, 741
Whitewood, II, 753
A. S. Whiting Company, II, 595
Whiting and Crawford, II, 172, 174
Whitney, Captain Joseph, II, 144
Wiarton, II, 496
Wild Horse Creek, II, 777
Williams, S., II, 66
Williams, W. M., II, 572
Williamsburg, II, 519, 594, 663
William's Creek, II, 774, 788, 797, 803
Willow Creek, II, 767
Wilmot, Governor, I, 176
Wilmot Township, II, 92
Wilson, Robert, I, 197
Winchester Township, II, 663
Windsor (N.S.), I, 214, 238-9; II, 389, 667-8, 677, 711, 717, 722, 726
Windsor (Ont.), II, 200, 487-8, 569, 734, 779
Wines, I, 97-8, 508, 531-2, 535-9, 558, 560, 565
Wingham, II, 496
Winnipeg, II, 597, 731-4, 741-2, 747, 749, 757-8, 762-770, 820
Wisconsin, II, 508, 513, 819
Wood Creek, II, 225
Wood Mountain, II, 762
Woodstock (N.B.), II, 669-670, 673, 710, 726
Woodstock (Ont.), II, 488, 544, 569
Wooster, Hezekiah Calvin, II, 52
Wright, Judge, II, 183
Wright, John, I, 435-6
Wright, Ruggles, II, 272
Wright Batson and Currier, II, 510
Wyoming (Ont.), II, 572

Yale, II, 772, 774-5, 777, 779-80, 787, 789, 794, 797, 804, 806
Yamaska River, II, 34, 593
Yarmouth (Eng.), I, 459
Yarmouth (N.S.), I, 244; II, 24, 668, 676, 693, 697, 705

York, Duke of, II, 428
York, I, 197
York County (N.B.), II, 689
York County (Ont.), II, 329, 527, 545-6, 608
Yorkshire, I, 177; II, 103, 387

Yorkville, II, 544
Young, Mr., II, 42
Young, John, II, 453
Young, Levi, II, 510
Youngstown, II, 168
Yukon River, II, 789

Lightning Source UK Ltd.
Milton Keynes UK
UKHW040246230722
406167UK00010BA/2